ADVANCED ACCOUNTANCY

ADVANCED ACCOUNTANCY

M.E. Thukaram Rao
Head, Department of Commerce
Sri Sathya Sai Institute of Higher Learning
Whitefield Campus, Bangalore

NEW AGE

NEW AGE INTERNATIONAL (P) LIMITED, PUBLISHERS
New Delhi • Bangalore • Chennai • Cochin • Guwahati • Hyderabad
Jalandhar • Kolkata • Lucknow • Mumbai • Ranchi

NEW AGE INTERNATIONAL (P) LIMITED, PUBLISHERS
4835/24, Ansari Road, Daryaganj,
New Delhi - 110 002
Visit us at : www.newagepublishers.com

Offices at :
Bangalore, Chennai, Cochin, Guwahati, Hyderabad, Jalandhar,
Kolkata, Lucknow, Mumbai and Ranchi

Rs. 350.00

ISBN : 81-224-1603-9

Published by New Age International (P) Ltd.,
4835/24, Ansari Road, Daryaganj, New Delhi-110 002 and
typesetter Subham Graphics, Delhi
printed in India at Mehra Offset, New Delhi.

Preface

I have great pleasure in placing into the hands of esteemed readers this book on ADVANCED ACCOUNTING-VOLUME 1. Although several books are available on the subject, the need for a comprehensive volume covering all the important aspects of financial accounting has been felt for a long time. My long experience in teaching and the knowledge, I have acquired over there years have made it possible for me to satisfy this need.

The book is written in a simple and lucid style. At the end of each chapter a few theoretical questions and exercises are given to test the understanding ability of students.

This book serves the needs of students preparing for the examinations of B.Com, B.B.M., B.B.A., M.Com, C.S., C.A., I.C.W.A and M.B.A. and other technical courses on management.

I am thankful to Saumya Gupta for bringing out this book so elegantly. I shall appreciate comments and suggestions from readers for the improvement of the book.

M.E. THUKARAM RAO

Contents

1
CHAPTER
Accounting Theory

NEED FOR ACCOUNTING

Business is one of the sources of earning income. Whenever a business is started, it requires investment of certain amount which is called as capital. With this amount of capital the businessman may deal either with trading business or manufacturing business. In a trading business, he will buy goods at a lesser price and sells the same to others at a higher price. In case of manufacturing business, he has to buy raw materials and incur other expenses in the form of wages and salaries, rent, power, insurance, tax, transport, postal and telephone expenses and so on, in the course of production and distribution of goods. In a small sized business the transactions are simple and less in number. But in a large sized business the transactions are numerous. These business transactions enable the businessman to know the result of his business which can be profit or loss for a given period of time. In order to know the result of his business, a businessman has to remember all the transactions of his business. However, owing to lack of memory it is not possible for anybody to remember all the transactions over a period of time. This has given rise to maintenance of a set of accounting books in which business transactions are chronologically recorded. The systematic recording of business transactions enable the businessman to account for every transaction without missing any item. Such a system of maintenance of a set of accounting books to record business transactions is known as book keeping system.

ORIGIN OF BOOK KEEPING

The practice of record keeping existed ages before the formal recording of history. Barbarians began to keep records by scratching them on rocks. From there crude forms of picture writing, the process of rudimentary bookkeeping began. The Italians were the leading bookkeepers and record makers for centuries. As early as 813 A.D., Bookkeepers were recognised in Italy and from these men came many of the fundamentals of the modern double entry bookkeeping.

In 1911, a Florentine banker devised the first complete bookkeeping system as distinguished from the simple devices previously used. It had all the rudiments of a set of books including a rough plan of cross entries. The first known system of complete double entry was discovered in Genoa in 1340.

The first text book on bookkeeping was written in 1414 by Pacioli, a monk of the order of St. Francis at Venice. Many present day methods were described by this old world mathematician and the ideas he expressed have lived to the present day. Pacioli's treatise is based on the premise that where one wishes to conduct his business properly, he must first have sufficient cash or credit. Secondly, he must be a good bookkeeper. Thirdly, he must possess a proper book keeping system.

The years following Pacioli's treatise were marked by the refinement of the double entry bookkeeping system and by the use of the position of the accountant in the commercial world. Publications were released and some accountants association were formed, but it was not until the 19th century that accounting really became a profession.

It was not until the dawn of the 20th Century that the invention and perfection of the business machines of today took the business of record keeping from the "Shadow of the Pen". A new conception of accounting valuation began to take form and the bookkeeper really became on Accountant. The keeping of books was no longer restricted to the preparation of financial statement. Because of the ease with which facts could be recorded, accumulated and analysed, the accountant began to devote his time to the interpretation of "booked" facts and as a result, became a member of management's team.

MEANING AND DEFINITION OF BOOK KEEPING

The art of recording business transactions in a systematic manner is termed as bookkeeping. It is the name given to a system which is concerned with recording and summarising business transactions accurately so as to know the true state of affairs of a business.

Definition of Book Keeping. R.N. Carter in his book on Advanced Accounting defines book keeping as the Science and art of correctly recording in books of accounts all those business transactions that result in the transfer of money or money's worth". This definition reveals the following features of book keeping.

(*a*) **It is a Science.** Book Keeping is a science as it represents systematised knowledge. It is based upon a set of well defined principles which are followed throughout so that the reason for recording a transaction in a particular manner can be explained fully.

(*b*) **It is an Art.** Book keeping is an art as it deals with a system in which human skills and ability is involved in recording the business transaction according to principles of book keeping.

(*c*) **Money Consideration.** This implies recording of all transactions which can be expressed in terms of money.

Kohler in his "Dictionary for Accountants" defined book keeping as "the process of analysing, classifying, and recording transactions in accordance with preconcieved plan". This definition brings forth the following three aspects of accounting.

(*a*) **Analysis.** It refers to identifying various expenses incurred during a period of time.

(*b*) **Classification.** It refers to grouping of like items of expenses into a common group.

(c) **Recording.** It refers to entering transactions in the basic books and later on posting them into another set of book known as ledger.

B.G. Vickery in his book 'Principles and Practice of Book Keeping' defines book keeping as "the art of recording pecuniary or business transactions in a regular and systematic manner". This definition emphasises the recording of monetary transactions of the business on day-to-day basis and in a systmeatic manner, i.e., according to the set rules and regulations of book keeping.

Scope of Book Keeping

Book Keeping is concerned with two important steps involved in the procedure of accounting. They are : (i) recording of all business transactions in a book known as Journal and (ii) posting all recorded transactions into another book known as a ledger. Subsequently, the various accounts in the ledger are balanced to know the net effect of all transactions. In brief, the subject matter of book keeping includes preparation and maintenance of all records up to the stage of preparation of a statement known as Trial Balance.

DEFINITION OF ACCOUNTING

The American Accounting Association defines accounting as "the process of identifying, measuring, and communicating economic information to permit informed judgements and decisions by users of the information". This definition highlights the following aspects :

(*a*) **Identifying the Business Transactions.** Identification of transactions are useful for proper recording of them in books of accounting without missing any of the transactions.

(*b*) **Measurement of Business Performance.** Measurement or evaluation of business performance is necessary to know the progress of business.

(*c*) **Communication of Information.** Communication of information relates to reporting the results of business to all those interested in the business. This enables them to judge the efficiency of the business and to take suitable decisions to improve the business.

According to the American Institute of Certified Public Accountants Terminology committee ; "Accounting is the art of recording, classifying and summarising in a significant manner and in terms of money transactions and events which are in part atleast of a financial character and interpreting the results thereof.

This definition exmphasises the following aspects :

(*a*) It is an art

(*b*) It involves recording transactions in a set of books

(*c*) Classifying which refers to grouping of transactions according to their similarities.

(*d*) Summarising the transactions facilitate easy understanding of results by management of the business and others interested in the business. This step involves preparation of two important statements known as (i) Trading and Profit and Loss Account and (ii) Balance Sheet.

(*e*) Accounting is concerned with transactions capable of expressing in terms of money value. All business transactions of different nature are expressed in respect of money. Thus all assets such as land and building, plant and machinery, stock of goods etc., when expressed in terms of money can give total value of business. The value of a business can be compared with the value of another business.

(*f*) Only transactions of financial characters are recorded in the books of accounts. For example, the good health of a general manager is very essential for the success of a business. But this transaction is not recorded in accounting books. Similarly, cooperation of employees, good working environment etc., are essential for the success of a business. But they are not recorded as they are not of a financial character.

(*g*) Interpreting the results helps in evaluating and in making a rational judgement about the performance of business. For example, an Accountant will estimate the advertising required for increasing the sales. Subsequently, he will judge whether the advertisement expesnes yielded the desired sales. This will help him to decide whether the same amount of advertising expense result in the desired sawles for the forth-coming years.

OBJECTIVES OF BOOK KEEPING

The objectives of book keeping can be summarised under the following headings :-

(A) ***Main Objectives :***

The main objectives of book keeping are as follows :-

(*a*) To know the result of the business over a period of time. The result of a business may be profit or loss.

(*b*) To know the financial position of business at a point of time. This can be known by presenting all assets and liabilities in the form of a statement known as a Balance Sheet.

(*c*) To maintain all records for a given period to serve as permanent reference in future.

(*d*) To know the amount which a business owes to others for having bought goods on credit basis.

(*e*) To know the amount due to business by others on account of goods sold on credit basis.

(*f*) To meet provisions of various laws as in the case of Joint Stock Comapnies which have to prepare accounts according to the Provisions of Companies Act 1956.

(B) ***Other Objectives :***

These include :

(*a*) To improve the business on the basis of past performance.

(*b*) To know the composition of capital in terms of size, the causes for change in capital structure and whether maximum use of the same is made.

(*c*) To exercise control over expenses thereby to increase profitability of the business.

(*d*) To know the position of cash so that in case of need further amount can be arranged.

(*e*) To meet the requirements of tax and legal authorities.

ADVANTAGES OF BOOK KEEPING

Accounting information is useful to the following categories of persons :

(A) ***To the Management of a Business :-***

(*a*) In evaluating various alternative proposals so as to take maximum benefit from the best alternative.

(*b*) In deciding matters such as elimination of an unprofitable activity, department or product, replacement of fixed assets, expansion of business etc.

(*c*) Planning the various activities and planning of revenues and expenses and arranging for finance in case of need.

(*d*) Comparing various year's account to know the progress or deterioration of the business and take actions to improve the business.

(*e*) Accounting information helps in providing evidence in a court of law in case of legal action taken by others.

(*f*) Accounting information helps in assessing the income tax, sales tax and property tax of the business.

(*g*) Accounting information consitututes one of the basis for borrowing loans from external source.

(*h*) It helps to detect errors and frauds that have taken place in the business.

(B) ***To the Investors :***

Accounting provides information regarding :-

(*a*) Types of property owned by the business.

(*b*) Sources and amount of earnings made or losses incurred by the business.

(*c*) Particulars such as stock position, debts owed, debts due etc.

(*d*) Whether rate of earnings is high or low.

(C) ***To the Employees :*** It provides information to employees so as to claim fair wages, bonus, and other welfare facilities.

(D) ***To the Government :***

(*a*) Accounting information helps Government to extend subsidies and incentives and other exemptions to certain types of business.

(*b*) The industrial progress can be known by the Government of the country. It can formulate industrial policies for further growth and development of industries.

(*c*) It enables the Government to assess the income from the industrial sector.

(*d*) It helps in amending various laws or enacting laws governing the functioning of business enterprises.

(*e*) It helps the Government in deciding price control, wage fixation, excise duties, sales tax etc.

(E) ***To the Consumers :*** Customers are not overcharged as selling price is fixed on the total expenses incurred by adding a reasonable rate of profit.

(F) ***To the Prospective Investors :*** It helps the propsective investors in choosing the right type of investment depending upon the profit earning capacity of the business entreprises and the profit earned during past few years.

(G) ***To the Creditors and Suppliers :*** Creditors can decide the solvency position of the business through the accounting information. Similarly, suppliers can also decide whether goods can be sold in future on credit basis.

SYSTEM OF BOOK KEEPING

Book keeping can be prepared and maintained under two systems. They are known as (*a*) Single Entry System ; and (*b*) Double Entry System.

(*a*) **Single Entry System :** Kohler in his book Dictionary for Accountants has defined single entry system as a system of book keeping in which as a rule only records of cash and personal accounts are maintained, it is always incomplete double entry varying with circumtances. This system is adopted by small business enterprises for the sake of their convenience. Under this system only personal accounts of debtors and creditors and a cash book is maintained. This system ignores the two-fold aspect of each transaction. As only one aspect of the transaction is recorded under this system, it is called a Single entry system. So this system is considered as incomplete and unsatisfactory accounting system. Accurate information of the operations of the business is also lacking under this system.

(*b*) **Double Entry System :** This system of accounting is based upon exchange value of money or money's worth. As such we find two aspects in every business transaction viz., the receiving aspect and the giving aspect. Under this system, every transaction is recorded twice, one on the debit side, *i.e.*, the receiving and the other on the credit side, *i.e.*, giving aspect. For example, when a businessman buys goods worth Rs. 10000, he exchanges money for goods. Similarly, when he hires the services of a manager, he gives the money for having derived the service. Thus every transaction has two aspects. One receiving of benefit and another giving the benefit and both these aspects are recorded under this system of book keeping. The features of double entry system can be summarised under the following points :

(*a*) It records the two aspects of a transaction.
(*b*) It records both personal and impersonal aspects of a transaction.
(*c*) While one aspect is debited, its corresponding aspect is credited.
(*d*) Because debit and credit aspects of all transactions are recorded, the total of debit and credit columns are always equal. This ensures the arithmatical accuracy of accounts.

ADVANTAGES OF DOUBLE ENTRY SYSTEM OF BOOK KEEPING

(*a*) It records all the transactions considering both the aspects of the transactions. Hence it gives the complete information about the business.
(*b*) By recording both the debit and credit aspects it ensures the mathematical accuracy or correct preparation of accounts.
(*c*) It enables to prevent misappropriation and frauds involved in recording the transactions.
(*d*) By recording all types of transactions it reveals the correct result of the business for a year.
(*e*) By recording all assets, liabilities and capital it reveals the true financial position of the business.
(*f*) The accounting system satisfies external parties including government, tax authorities etc.

DISADVANTAGES

(*a*) It involves maintenance of many books and ledgers which are very expensive.
(*b*) It involves more of clerical labour.

DIFFERENCES BETWEEN BOOK KEEPING AND ACCOUNTING

Very often the terms Book Keeping and Accounting are used interchangeably. However these two concepts are not identical. They differ from each other in the following aspects.

Book Keeping	*Accounting*
1. In book keeping, financial transactions are recorded in a set of books.	1. In accounting the errors are detected and they are rectified through adjustment.
2. It is the first stage of maintaining accounts and as such it cannot give any conclusions about the performance of business.	2. It is second stage which gives useful information to draw conclusions about the performance of business.
3. Book keeping does not show the result and financial position of the business.	3. Accounting shows the results and financial position of the business.
4. Book keeping is undertaken by clerks whose responsibility is less.	4. The accounting is undertaken by accountant whose responsibility, is more.
5. It is concerned with posting the entries in the ledgers.	5. It is concerned with checking whether posting is accurately done.
6. It is concerned with totalling of Journal and ledgers and to find out balances in all the accounts.	6. It is concerned with preparation of a Trial Balance with the help of balances of ledger accounts.
7. Book keeping does not require special knowledge and ability.	7. Accounting requires special knowledge and ability.

BRANCHES OF ACCOUNTING

There are three branches of accounting. They are :

(1) **Financial Accounting.** Financial accounting refers to a branch of accounting which deals with financial transactions of a business. It is mainly concerned with preparation of two important statements, viz.,

(*a*) *Income statement or profit and loss account.*

(*b*) *Positional statement or Balance Sheet.* This information serves the needs of all those who are not directly associated with the management of business. Thus financial accounts are concerned with external reporting as it provides information to external authorities. In this book the entire study relates to financial accounting. However financial accounting suffers from certain limitations. These limitations are as follows :

(*a*) It provides only past data.
(*b*) It reveals only over all result of the business.
(*c*) It is static in nature.
(*d*) There is a possibility of manipulation of financial account.
(*e*) It fails to exercise control over resources of the business.
(*f*) It fails to provide adequate data for managerial decision making.
(*g*) It fails to provide adequate data for price fixation.
(*h*) It does not use any technique to reduce expenses which is responsible for decrease in profit.

To overcome there disadvantages the other branches of accounting was evolved.

(2) **Cost Accounting.** Kohler in his Dictionary for Accountants defines cost accounting as that "branch of accounting dealing with the classification, recording, allocation, summarisation and reporting of amount and prospective costs". An analysis of this definition reveals the following aspects of cost accounting.

(*a*) Classification which refers to grouping of like items of costs into a common group.
(*b*) Recording, which refers to posting of cost transactions into various ledgers maintained under cost accounting system.
(*c*) Allocation, which refers to allotment of costs to various products or departments.
(*d*) Summarisation which refers to condensing cost information for quick interpretation and for taking prompt action for improving the inefficiencies.
(*e*) Reporting, which refers to furnishing of cost data on a regular basis so as to meet the requirements of management.

(3). **Management Accounting.** The terminology published by the Institute of Cost and Management accounting, London, defineds management accounting as "the application of professional knowledge and skill in the preparation and presentation of accounting information in such a way as to assist management in the formulation of policies and in the planning and control of the operation of the undertaking. It is a branch of accounting which furnishes useful data in carrying out the various management functions such as planning, decision making and controlling the activities of a business enterprise.

ACCOUNTING CONCEPTS AND CONVENTIONS

Before accounting concepts and conventions are discussed, it will be appropriate to know the meaning of the term "accounting principle". In olden days when size of the business was small and less complicated, the accounting information was felt only by the proprietor of a business. In modern days, with the growth of the business organisations, the transactions have become more in number. Unless these transactions are recorded according to a definite principle by all the business enterprises it is difficult to maintain uniformity in accounting system. Such uniformity is also necessary because many parties such as investors, creditors, employees, government and general public are interested to know the affairs of the business. If every business follows its own accounting practices, the final accounts may not be understandable to all such parties. So there is a scope for misinterpreting the position of the business by all persons interested in the business. Hence there is a need to follow a uniform accounting principles from the stage of recording the transactions up to the stage of preparing final accounts.

Definition of Accounting Principle

The terminology committee of American Institute of Certified Public Accounts defines the term principles as a general law or rule adopted or preferred as a guide to action, a settled ground or business of conduct or practice.

In the words of A.W. Johnson accounting principles are the assumptions and rules of accounting, the methods and procedures of accounting and the application of these rules, methods and procedures to the actual practice of accounting.

Accounting principles are accepted by all if they possess the following characteristics :

(*a*) ***Objectivity.*** It must be based on facts and impartial attitude ought to have been adopted by it. If it is so, the principle is said to possess objectivity.
(*b*) ***Application.*** If the application of the principle is possible, it is regarded as a good principle. In case theoretically principle is sound but its application is difficult, then the principle has no value.

(*c*) ***Use.*** The principle should be such by whose "use" utility of accounting record is increased. Suppose a principle has objectivity and it is applicable also but there is no use of this principle in accountancy record then the principle is useless.

(*d*) ***Simplicity.*** The principles should be simple and easily understood by all.

Accounting principles are divided into two classes. This is shown in the following chart :

Accounting Principles

- Accounting Concepts
  - Business entity concept
  - Money measurement concept
  - Going concern concept
  - Dual aspect concept
  - Historical record concept
  - Cost concept
  - Accounting period concept
  - Matching concept
- Accounting conventions or Doctrine of Accounts
  - Doctrine of Consistency
  - Doctrine of Disclosure
  - Doctrine of Conservation
  - Doctrine of Materiability

ACCOUNTING CONCEPTS

The term concept refers to assumptions and conditions on which accounting system is based. It denotes the propositions on which principles are formulated. The principles are formulated on the basis of economic and political environment of the business. There is no exhaustive list of accounting concepts. However, the following are considered as the important accounting concepts.

1. Business Entity Concept. The business enterprise is treated as a separate organisation which is quite distinct from the owner of the business. It implies that the business transactions must be kept completely separate from the private affairs of the proprietor. This enables the proprietor to ascertain the true picture of the business.

2. Money Measurement Concept. While preparing accounts in a business, only those transactions which are capable of expressing in terms of money alone are recorded. Other transactions which are not capable of measuring in terms of money consideration are outside the purview of accouting. For example, efficient leadership is essential for the success of the business. But leadership ability cannot be expressed in terms of money. Hence leadership aspect is ignored in accounting. Another important aspect of this accounting concept is that the transactions are recorded only at their original value of money. Subsequent change in the value of money or the purchasing power of the money is ignored. This is based on the assumption that the value of money remains always stable and does not fluctuate from time to time. However, this assumption does not hold good today. Recording of transactions at its original value is justified as it facilitates the addition of all assets of the business to know the total value of assets as on a given period of time.

3. Going Concern Concept. While maintaining accounts it is presumed that the business enterprise will continue to exist for an indefinite period of time. This assumption helps in two respects. Firstly, it facilitates classification of expenditure into capital expenditure and revenue expenditure. While capital expenditure benefits the business for a longer duration, revenue expenditure relates to short duration. If this classification is not made, all expenditure is treated at revenue expenditure which is not proper while preparing accounts. Secondly, because of this assumption, fixed assets are shown at its original cost, less its depreciation.

4. Dual Aspect Concept or Equation Concept. Under this concept, each and every transaction is split up into two aspects. One aspect relates to receiving the benefit and other aspect relates to giving the benefit. For example, when a machinery is bought by the business it receives the machinery with the help of which it can produce goods or services. For having bought the machinery, the business has to pay cash to the supplier of machinery. Thus every business transaction involves two fold aspects and both these aspects are recorded without exception whatsoever. This concept is based on the maxim that for every action there is always an equal and opposite reaction. According to this concept assets of a business will be equal to liabilities and capital. Expressed in the form of an equation,

Assets = Liabilities + Capital

or Capital = Assets – Liabilities.

5. Historical Record Concept or Realisation Concept. According to this concept the sale proceeds of goods or services are realised only when the buyer is legally bound to pay for the delivery of goods or rendering of service. This concept is based on historical events of business transactions and therefore it is also known as historical record concept. To take on example suppose a businessman receives an order on 1st January, 2004 and supplies goods on 10th January and he receives payment on 15th January. In this transaction, the revenue from sale of goods is recorded on 10th January but neither at 1st January nor on 15th January.

6. Cost Concept. According to this concept all transactions are recorded in the books of accounts at the cost price or purchase price. For example, if a building is bought for Rs. 75000 which is actually worth Rs. 100000 then the cost price of Rs. 75000 will only be entered in the books of accounts.

7. Accounting Period Concept. Although it is assumed that the business will exist for a longer duration it is necessary to maintain accounts with reference to a convenient period so that results are ascertained and financial position presented for that period. Usually accounts are prepared for a period of one year which may be a calendar year or a financial year.

8. Matching Concept. One of the objectives of every business organisation is to know its results as on a given period of time. In order to know the profit or loss of the business the costs incurred during a given period is matched against the revenue earned during that period. This helps to know the profit or loss of the business during a period of time. If the revenue exceeds the cost it represents the profit. On the other hand, if the costs exceed the revenue, it represents the loss.

ACOUNTING CONVENTIONS OR DOCTRINE OF ACCOUNTS

Accounting convention refers to the customs and traditions followed by Accountants as guidelines while preparing accounting statement. They are followed so as to make accounting information more meaningful and clear. The important accounting conventions are as follows :

1. Doctrine of Consistency. This doctrine implies that the basis followed in different accounting period should be same. In other words, methods adopted in one accounting year should not be changed in another year. If a change becomes necessary, the change and its effect should be mentioned clearly.

2. Doctrine of Disclosure. According to this doctrine all significant information about the business should be disclosed. The accounting statement should be scrupulously honest. This doctrine implies that the accounting records and statements conform to generally accepted accounting principle.

3. Doctrine of Conservation. According to this doctrine the accounting information should not show a better position than what it actually is. Further the accounting information must include all reasons responsible for a reduction in profit or to incur losses. Such transactions relate to provision for doubtful debts, provision for discount on debtors etc. On the other hand the prospective profits should be ignored as it is uncertain to earn such profit.

4. Doctrine of Materiability. According to this doctrine, only transactions which are more important to the business are recorded. Trivial transactions which do not affect the result of the business drastically should be ignored as the cost of ascertaining such insignificant expenses is more than such a trivial expense incurred.

BASIS OF ACCOUNTING

There are two bases for accounting of business transactions. They are as follows :

(*a*) **Accrual Basis or Mercantile System of Accounting.** It is a system of classifying and summarising transactions into assets, liabilities, capital, cost and resources and recording there of. A transaction is recognised when either a liability or asset is created or impaired. Whether payment is made or received is immaterial in accrued basis accounting. The following are the essential features of accrual basis :

(*i*) Revenue is recognised as it is earned.

(*ii*) Costs are matched either against revenues so recognised or against the relevant time period to determine periodic income.

(*iii*) Costs which are not charged to income are carried forward and are kept under continuous review. Any cost that appears to have lost its utility or its power to generate future revenue is written off as a loss.

(*b*) **Cash Basis of Accounting.** It is a basis of accounting by which a transaction is recognised only if cash is received or paid.

However, accrual basis of accounting is the only generally accepted accounting method for business organisations which are supposed to operate for a long period. Cash basis of accounting is suitable for such business organisations which operate for a short term duration.

ACCOUNTING EQUATION

Accounting equation may be defined as an accounting formula expressing equivalence of the two expressions of assets and liabilities. Expressed in the form of an equation,

Assets = Capital + Liabilities or
Capital = Assets – Liabilities or
Liabilities = Assets – Capital.

The idea behind expressing accounting equation is that business is considered quite different from its proprietor. Whenever a proprietor provides the capital to a business he has a claim over it. It follows from the above statement that whenever an asset comes into business an equal claim arises. The accounting equation has two aspects or two sides, viz., left hand side to record any increase or decrease in the value of asset and right hand side to record any change in the value of liabilities.

Because of two-fold aspect of every business transaction, the following changes in the value of assets and liabilities will take place.

(*a*) Increase in the value of one asset will increase the value of a liability
(*b*) Increase in the value of one asset will reduce the value of other asset.
(*c*) Decrease in the value of one asset will decrease the value of a liability.
(*d*) Decrease in the value of one liability will increase the value of another liability.

The accounting equation as mentioned earlier remains unchanged. The only change that takes place is in the totals on the "Left Side" and "Right Side" of the equation.

Relationship of Accountancy with Other Disciplines

The need for and importance of accounting is felt by all the organisations—whether trading or non-trading. The relationship of accounting with various disciplines are explained below :

(*a*) **Accounting and Business.** Business organisations are run with an object of earning profit. They deal with various persons and other organisations. Unless all the business transactions are properly recorded it is not possible to know the true result of the business. Similarly, unless all assets and liabilities are properly recorded it will not be possible to prepare the financial position of the business. The importance of accounting is so much felt in large sized business, wherein accounting is considered as a separate function of the business. Hence a separate department by name accounting department is created which is incharge of the chief Accountant.

(*b*) **Accounting and Government.** Government which is considered as the biggest form of organisation also makes use of accounting discipline. Budgeting which is one of the important aspect of accounting is prepared by every state and central government. Every government is interested in knowing the total revenue and total expenditure and the balance amount available in the government treasury. In case of deficit balance, the government can raise funds through issue of bonds, bills, etc., for financing projects of national importance. In case of surplus funds it can divert to other key sectors where it lacks adequate funds. The importance of accounting is so much felt by the government that in modern days a new branch of accounting called as government accounting is involved and adopted by most of the government.

(*c*) **Accounting and Medical Science.** Medical science also heavily relies upon accounting information. Hospitals and clinics will maintain accounting books in order to know the rates to be charged to patients. They record all the expenses incurred and revenue received for a given period to know whether hospitals and clinic is run with profit or otherwise.

(*d*) **Accounting and Research.** Research organisations also will maintain a set of accounting books to know the research expenses in conducting various experiments. They evaluate the success of the research activities by knowing the corresponding benefit derived by the production and sale of new products.

(*e*) **Accounting and Education.** The promoters of education and educational institutions also will maintain a detailed accounts of various expenses incurred under different heads such as library, laboratory, sports and cultural activities, salaries payable etc. They also record the fees and donations received from students so as to know maintenance cost of educational institutions.

ROLE OF ACCOUNTANT IN SOCIETY

The accountancy profession is considered to be one of the noblest profession and is held in high esteem in public eyes. By making use of science and out of accountancy an accountant will enable public to know the exact position of a business. The profession of accountancy also enables the management to discharge its functions efficiently based upon the information provided by Accountant. The Accountant also serves the society by virtue of his education, training, analytical mind and experience. A modern Accountant can render useful service not only in the field of taxation, costing, management accounting and company legislation, but also in allied areas such as finance, budgeting, economic aspects.

The various services rendered by an accountant are summarised below

1. Maintenance of Books of Accounts. By maintaining the books of accounts, it is possible to know the result of the business and its financial position.

In the process of maintaining the books of accounts, an Accountant renders the following services :

(*a*) Helps management in planning, decision-making and controlling.
(*b*) Facilitate comparative study to know the efficiency or otherwise of the business.
(*c*) In calculating the tax liability of the business
(*d*) To furnish evidence in court in terms of conflict.
(*e*) To ascertain purchase price of business when it is sold to outsiders.
(*f*) To deal on behalf of an insolvent business.

2. To Conduct Statutory Audit. Auditing the accounts of a Joint Stock Company is compulsory. A Chartered Accountant serves as an auditor to verify the correctness of accounts of a Joint Stock Company.

3. To Conduct Internal Audit. Internal audit is conducted to know whether there is any leakage of revenue or misappropriation of property of the business.

4. Taxation. An Accountant can represent the business or person before tax authorities and settle the tax liability as per the Income Tax Act.

5. Management Accounting. A management Accountant assists management in performing various functions by way of collecting, analysing, interpreting and presenting all accounting information which is useful to the management.

6. Financial Service. These includes :

(*a*) Investment
(*b*) Insurance
(*c*) Business expansion, mergers, acquisitions etc.
(*d*) Investigation, which includes :

(*i*) Make or buy decision
(*ii*) Detecting fraud
(*iii*) Valuation of Shares
(*iv*) Achieve greater efficiency on management
(*v*) Pension and provident fund scheme
(*vi*) Use of mechanical equipments.

7. Management Consultancy Service

This includes :

(*i*) Management information service
(*ii*) Expenditure control and evaluation
(*iii*) M.B.O.
(*iv*) Management of working capital and its best possible use
(*v*) Advising management about O & M studies for effective delegation and planning of work.
(*vi*) Formulating long term plan and setting up objectives of the business
(*vii*) Assist management in conducting feasibility study of new projects
(*viii*) Advise management on the benefits of mechanised accounting system
(*ix*) Use of statistical techniques for business forecasting.

8. Other Services

This includes :

(*a*) Registering share transfers and new issues
(*b*) Company formation
(*c*) Liquidation
(*d*) Arbitration.

QUESTIONS

1. Define Book keeping.
2. Define accounting.
3. What do you mean by single entry system of book keeping ?
4. What do you mean by double entry system of Book keeping ?
5. Define accounting principle.
6. List out the four characteristics of accounting principle.
7. What do you mean by accounting concept ?
8. What do you mean by accounting convention ?
9. Define accounting equation.

SHORT ANSWER QUESTIONS

1. Explain the need for accounting.
2. State the objectives of book keeping.
3. State the advantages of book keeping.
4. State the differences between book keeping and accounting.
5. Explain the various accounting concepts.
6. Explain the various accounting conventions.
7. Examine the relationship of accounting with various other disciplines.
8. Explain the role of Accountant in a society.

2
CHAPTER
JOURNAL

THE ACCOUNTING CYCLE OR ACCOUNTING PROCEDURE

In the process of preparing accounts of any organisation, five important steps are involved. These steps are as follows :

1. **Recording in Memorandum Book or Waste Book.** First of all, the various transactions are recorded in a book which is known as a memorandum book or waste book. This book serves as a statistical book to know the number of transactions recorded in a crude form. This type of book is maintained by small traders such as petty shopkeepers.
2. **Recording in the Journal.** From the memorandum book the transactions are recorded into another book known as a Journal. In this book transactions are recorded more systematically by following principles of double entry system of book keeping. This facilitates chronological recording of all transactions without ignoring any transaction.
3. **Recording in the Ledger.** The third step involved in accounting system is to post all the entries from the journal into another book known as ledger. This book shows the balance in each account for a given period and facilitates in further processing of accounts.
4. **Preparation of Trial Balance.** All the balances which are shown by the various accounts in the ledger are then transferred to a statement known as Trial Balance. The preparation of a trial balance also ensures the arithmatical accuracy of the accounts prepared in various ledgers.
5. **Preparation of Final Accounts.** The last step involved in the preparation of accounts is to prepare the final accounts. The final accounts consists of the trading and profit and loss account and a balance sheet. The trading account reveals the gross profit or gross loss of the business, whereas the profit and loss account reveals the net profit or net loss of the business. The balance sheet discloses the financial position of the business.

After the accounting period for which accounting record is closed, again journal, ledger, trial balance, and final accounts are prepared. Thus, the cyclic movement of the transactions through the books of accounting is a continuous process. It goes on for the whole period of business in yearly cycle. This cyclic movement is briefly called the accounting cycle.

CLASSIFICATION OF ACCOUNTS

There are two basis of classification of accounts, viz., *(i)* Traditional or English System and *(ii)* Modern or American System.

1. Traditional or English System of Classification of Accounts :

Under this system accounts are broadly classified into two types, viz., *(i)* Personal account and *(ii)* Impersonal account.

(A) **Personal Account.** Personal accounts are accounts of persons with whom the business deals. Personal accounts may take the following forms :

(a) Natural personal accounts such as Ashok's a/c, Vivek's account, Naveen's a/c, Sunil's a/c etc.

(b) Artificial persons or body of personal accounts such as State Bank of Mysore a/c, M.C.C. Publications a/c, Associate Traders a/c. etc.

(c) Representative personal accounts representing outstanding expenses, prepaid income a/c. Examples : Salary outstanding a/c, prepaid insurance a/c, interest received in advance a/c.

(B) Impersonal Account. Impersonal account is classified into two types : viz., *(a)* Real account and *(b)* Nominal account.

(a) *Real Account :* Accounts of Assets and possessions or things owned by business are called real accounts. Real accounts are again classified into two types viz., *(i)* Tangible asset a/c and *(ii)* Intangible asset a/c.

(i) *Tangible Asset a/c :* Tangible asset a/c is an a/c relating to things which can be touched, felt, measured, purchased, sold etc. Examples are Land a/c, Building a/c, Stock a/c etc.

(ii) *Intangible Asset a/c* represent such things which cannot be touched, but can be measured in terms of money. Examples are goodwill a/c, trade mark a/c, patent a/c.

(b) *Nominal Account :* Accounts in which expenses, losses, income or gain of business are recorded are known as nominal accounts. Examples of nominal accounts are wages a/c, discount received a/c, interest paid a/c.

Problem 1

Classify the following accounts :

1. Buildings a/c
2. Royalty a/c
3. Loan a/c
4. Murthy's a/c
5. Garden English School a/c
6. Avinash a/c
7. Vasavi Trading a/c
8. Goodwill a/c

Solution

1. Building a/c—Real a/c
2. Royalty a/c—Nominal a/c
3. Loan a/c—Personal a/c
4. Murthy's a/c—Personal a/c
5. Garden English School a/c—Personal a/c
6. Avinash a/c—Personal a/c
7. Vasavi Trading a/c—Personal a/c
8. Goodwill a/c—Real a/c.

Rules of Debit and Credit under English System

1. **Personal Account :**
   Debit the Receiver
   Credit the Giver
2. **Real Account :**
   Debit what comes in
   Credit what goes out.
3. **Nominal Account :**
   Debit all expenses and losses
   Credit all incomes and gains.

Problem 2

Examine the following transactions and determine the two accounts affected according to the double entry book keeping.

(*a*)	Bought goods for cash	Rs. 2000
(*b*)	Sold goods for cash	Rs. 1000
(*c*)	Received cash from Kulkarni	Rs. 500
(*d*)	Received interest on loan	Rs. 180
(*e*)	Paid salary to Manager	Rs. 5000
(*f*)	Paid rent	Rs. 1500
(*g*)	Purchased goods from Desai & Co.	Rs. 1500
(*h*)	Goods sold on credit to Lalit	Rs. 1000
(*i*)	Purchased motor car equipment from Mumbai Motor Agency and paid	Rs. 8900
(*j*)	Purchased machinery from India Tools Limited	Rs. 7000
(*k*)	Withdrew cash for household expenses	Rs. 300
(*l*)	Introduced further Rs. 50000 into business in cash.	

Solution

The two account involved in the transactions are :

(*a*) Purchases a/c and cash a/c
(*b*) Sales a/c and cash a/c
(*c*) Kulkarni's a/c and cash a/c
(*d*) Interest a/c and cash a/c
(*e*) Salary a/c and cash a/c
(*f*) Rent a/c and cash a/c
(*g*) Purchases a/c and Desai & Co. a/c
(*h*) Sales a/c and Lalit's a/c
(*i*) Motor car equipment a/c and cash a/c
(*j*) Machinery a/c and India Tools Ltd. a/c
(*k*) Drawings a/c and cash a/c
(*l*) Capital a/c and cash a/c.

Problem 3

State, giving reasons, the accounts you would debit and credit for each of the following transactions :

1. Mr. Rao commenced business with a capital Rs. 1,00,000
2. Bought machinery Rs. 30000
3. Bought goods for cash from Ram Manohar Rs. 5000
4. Sold goods for cash to Harish Rs. 4000
5. Purchased goods from Jailal on credit Rs. 22000
6. Opened an account with Canara Bank and Deposited cash Rs. 20000
7. Credit sales to Hari Rs. 1700
8. Bought office furniture from Modern Furniture Ltd., Rs. 3050
9. Sold a spare part of Motor car and inverted proceeds in business Rs. 3500
10. Paid cartage to Deluxe Roadlines Rs. 700
11. Paid trade expenses Rs. 200
12. Paid advertisement expenses to Anil agencies Rs. 200
13. Received interest from Anil Rs. 500
14. Deposited cash into Bank Rs. 1000
15. Paid Rent Rs.1500

Solution

S.No	*Account involved*	*Nature of A/c*	*Debit and credit*	*Rule for Dr & Cr*
1.	Cash a/c	Real a/c	Debit	Debit what comes in
	Capital a/c	Personal a/c	Credit	Credit what goes out
2.	Machinery a/c	Real a/c	Debit	Debit what come in
	Cash a/c	Real a/c	Credit	Credit what goes out
3.	Purchases a/c	Nominal a/c	Debit	Debit expenses
	Cash a/c	Real a/c	Credit	Credit what goes out
4.	Cash a/c	Real a/c	Debit	Debit what come in
	Sales a/c	Nominal a/c	Credit	Credit income
5.	Purchases a/c	Nominal a/c	Debit	Debit expenses
	Jaslal's a/c	Personal a/c	Credit	Credit the giver
6.	Bank a/c	Personal a/c	Debit	Debit the receiver
	Cash a/c	Real a/c	Credit	Credit what goes out
7.	Hari's a/c	Personal a/c	Debit	Debit the receiver
	Sales a/c	Nominal a/c	Credit	Credit income
8.	Furniture a/c	Real a/c	Debit	Debit what come in
	Cash a/c	Real a/c	Credit	Credit what goes out
9.	Cash a/c	Real a/c	Debit	Debit what come in
	Capital a/c	Personal a/c	Credit	Credit the giver
10.	Cartage a/c	Nominal a/c	Debit	Debit expenses
	Cash a/c	Real a/c	Credit	Credit what goes out
11.	Trade expenses a/c	Nominal a/c	Debit	Debit expenses
	Cash a/c	Real a/c	Credit	Credit what goes out
12.	Advertisement a/c	Nominal a/c	Debit	Debit expenses
	Cash a/c	Real a/c	Credit	Credit what goes out
13.	Cash a/c	Real a/c	Debit	Debit what come in
	Interest a/c	Nominal a/c	Credit	Credit income
14.	Bank a/c	personal a/c	Debit	Debit the receiver
	Cash a/c	Real a/c	Credit	Credit what goes out
15.	Rent a/c	Nominal a/c	Debit	Debit expenses
	Cash a/c	Real a/c	Credit	Credit what goes out

MODERN OR AMERICAN SYSTEM OF CLASSIFICATION OF ACCOUNTS

Under American system accounts are classified into the following types

(*i*) Assets :- It refers to the property owned or possessed by the businessman. Assets can be of the following types

(*a*) Fixed assets :- Such assets are used for carrying on the business but not for immediate sale. Some examples of fixed assets are land and building, macheinery, furniture etc.

(*b*) Currents assets :- These are the assets which are capable of converting into cash immediately without much difficulty, usually within a period of one year.

These are the assets which are used in the business in the normal course of running the business. Current assets change from period to period. Hence they are also called as fluctuating assets. Examples of current assets are stock of materials, Debtors, cash, bills receivable etc.

(c) *Tangible Assets* : These are the assets which can be touched and felt. Examples of tangible assets are stock of materials, vehicles, building etc.

(*d*) *Intangible Assets* : These assets cannot be touched and felt but they have money value to the business. Examples of intangible assets are goodwill, trade mark, patent rights.

(*e*) *Wasting Asset* : These assets exhaust as they are continuously used. Mineral ores such as iron ore, quarries etc., are common examples of wasting asset.

(*f*) *Liquid Asset* : These are a type of current assets which are in the form of cash or readily convertible into cash. Examples of liquid assets are cash, bills receivables etc.

(*g*) *Fictitious Assets* : These refer to worthless assets. They cover expenses and losses which are shown for the sake of meeting legal requirements or for technical purpose. Examples of such assets are preliminary expenses, advertisement expenses etc.

2. Liability. It refers to the amount due by the business to others. Liabilities may be of the following types :

(*a*) *Current Liabilities* : They represent short term liabilities which are to be paid within a period of one year.

(*b*) *Fixed Liabilities* : They represent long term liabilities payable after a long period of time.

3. Capital. Capital generally refers to the amount or resources invested by the owner in the business. In accounting language it is taken to mean excess of assets over liabilities.

Capital = Assets – Liabilities.

4. Revenue and Profit. Revenue and profit is taken to mean income earned by a business during a given period of time. These two items constitute the liability of the business as profit is given to businessman as a reward for the risk taken by the proprietor.

5. Expenses and Losses. The cost incurred during the course of running the business is known as expense. The excess of expense over income constitute loss.

Rules of Debit and Credit under American System

The rules of debit and credit under American system is based on Accounting equation. The rules are as follows :

1. **Asset :**
   Debit increase in asset
   Credit decrease in asset.
2. **Liabilities :**
   Debit decrease in liability
   Credit increase in liability.
3. **Capital :**
   Debit decrease in capital
   Credit increase in capital.
4. **Income and Gain :**
   Debit decrease in income and gain
   Credit increase in income and gain.
5. **Expenses and Losses :**
   Debit increase in expenses and losses
   Credit decrease in expenses and losses.

It is to be noted that expenses and losses and income and gain are not the components of accounting equation. Their effect is shown through capital account. The rules given for them is only for an easier understanding.

Problem 4

Identify the debit and credit aspects of the following transactions under American system giving reasons for the same.

1.	Mr. Soumya Gupta started business with a capital	Rs. 5,00,000
2.	He purchased machinery on credit from Ram	Rs. 40,000
3.	He purchases goods for cash	Rs. 1,00,000
4.	He sold goods to Satish for	Rs. 50,000
5.	He paid rent for the month	Rs. 5,000
6.	He received commission	Rs. 10,000
7.	He received cash from Satish	Rs. 20,000
8.	He withdrew for personal use	Rs. 5,000
9.	He purchased goods from Ratan	Rs. 40,000
10.	He returned goods to Ratan	Rs. 6,000

Solution

S. No.	*Aspects*	*Debit or Credit*	*Reason*
1.	Cash	Debit	Increase in asset
	Capital	Credit	Increase in capital
2.	Machinery	Debit	Increase in asset
	Ram	Credit	Increase in liability
3.	Goods (Tangible asset)	Debit	Increase in asset
	Cash	Credit	Decrease in asset
4.	Satish	Debit	Increase in asset
	Goods (Tangible asset)	Credit	Decrease in asset

(*Contd.*)

S. No.	Aspects	Debit or Credit	Reason
5.	Rent	Debit	Increase in expense
	Cash	Credit	Decrease in asset
6.	Cash	Debit	Increase in asset
	Commission	Credit	Increase in income
7.	Cash	Debit	Increase in asset
	Satish	Credit	Increase in liability
8.	Capital (Drawings)	Debit	Decrease in capital
	Cash	Credit	Decrease in asset
9.	Goods (Asset)	Debit	Increase in asset
	Ratan	Credit	Increase in liability
10.	Ratan	Debit	Decrease in liability
	Goods (Asset)	Credit	Decrease in asset.

Journal. Journal is a tabular record in which business transactions are analysed in terms of debits and credits and recorded in a chronological order prior to being transferred to the ledger accounts. Because transactions are initially recorded in the journal, it is also referred to as the book original entry or book of prime entry.

Journalising. The process of recording transactions in the journal is called journalising. Before a transaction is recorded in the journal the accounts involved and the debit and credit aspects are to be decided. Journalising includes an analysis and an actual recording.

Journal Entry. The record of the transaction in the journal is called a journal entry.

Narration : The statement written to explain a transaction is called narration.

Simple and Compound Journal Entry : If a journal contains only one debit and one credit it is called a simple journal entry.

A journal entry which includes more than one debit or more than one credit is called compound journal entry. A compound journal entry is a combination of two or more simple journal entries.

Procedure for Recording Transactions in the Journal :

The procedure for recording transactions in the journal are as follows :-

1. **The Date.** The year, month and date of transaction are written in the date column. The year is recorded at the top of the date column of each journal page. The month is written in the first line of the date column. Neither the month nor the year is repeated on the page unless the month or year changes. The date of each transaction is recorded in the journal.
2. **Particulars.** The title of the account to be debited is listed at the left of the particulars column and traditionally recorded first. The abbreviation "Dr" is written after the name of the account debited. The title of the account to be credited is listed on the line below the account debited and is indented, *i.e.*, placed about an inch to the right of the date column. The abbreviation "To" is to be written before the name of the account credited. The narration is written below the account credited. The narration should be as brief as possible consistent with disclosure of all the information necessary to understand the transaction being recorded.

3. **Amount.** The debit amount is recorded in the debit column opposite the title of the account debited. The credit amount is recorded in the credit column opposite the title of the account credited.
4. **Writing Folio Number.** The ledger folio refers to page number of the ledger account to which debits and credits are transferred from the journal. This column is not used at the time transactions are recorded in the journal. When the debits and credits are later transferred to ledger accounts the page number of the ledger account is listed in this column to provide a convenient cross reference with the ledger.

A specimen form of a journal is shown below :

Journal

Date	*Particulars*	*Ledger Folio*	*Debit Rs.*	*Credit Rs.*

Problem 5

Srinivas started his business with the following assets and liabilities.

Cash in Hand	15,000
Goods in Hand	25,000
Furniture	6,000
Buildings	20,000
Due by A. Raman	6,000
Due to Kameshwaran	8,000
Due to Mohan	12,000

2004 January

1. Purchased goods from Mohan subject to trade discount of 5%	10,000
3. Sold goods to Murthy subject to a trade discount of 2%	5,000
5. Received from A. Raman	5,800
Discount allowed	200
10. Received from Murthy in full settlement of account	4,500
15. Paid Kameshwaran in full settlement of account	7,750
20. Paid Mohan	10,000
Discount allowed	500

Journalise the above transactions :

Solution

Journal Entries

Date	Particulars		LF	Dr.	Cr.
2004	Cash a/c	Dr.		15,000	
Jan 1,	Goods a/c	Dr.		25,000	
	Furniture a/c	Dr.		6,000	
	Buildings a/c	Dr.		20,000	
	Debtor's a/c (Raman)	Dr.		6,000	
	To creditors a/c				
	(Kameshwaran and Mohan)				20,000
	To Capital				52,000
	(Being commencement of business with above assets and liabilities and the difference between these credited to capital a/c.				
1.	Purchases a/c	Dr		9,500	
	To Mohan's a/c				9,500
	(Being goods purchased at a trade discount of 5%)				
3.	Murthy's a/c	Dr.		4,900	
	To Sales a/c				4,900
	(Being credit sales to Murthy at a trade discount of 2%)				
5.	Cash a/c	Dr.		5,800	
	Discount a/c	Dr.		200	
	To A. Raman's a/c				6,000
	(Being cash received from A. Raman and discount allowed)				
10.	Cash a/c	Dr.		4,500	
	Discount a/c	Dr.		400	
	To Murthy's a/c				4900
	(Being cash received in full settlement of a/c)				
15.	Kameshwaran a/c	Dr.		8,000	
	To Cash a/c				7,750
	To Discount a/c				250
	(Amount paid to Kameshwaran in full settlement)				
20.	Mohan a/c	Dr.		10,500	
	To Cash				10,000
	To Discount				500
	(Being payment made on account)				

Problem 6

Show how the following transactions appear in the Journals of Ram and Rahim.

1. Ram bought goods from Rahim Rs. 1,000.
2. Rahim bought goods for cash Rs. 8,000 from Ram.
3. Rahim received from Ram Rs. 5,000 and allowed him discount Rs. 250.
4. Ram sold goods to Rahim Rs. 7,000
5. Rahim supplied goods worth Rs. 2500 for Ram's domestic use.
6. Ram received Rs. 5,000 from Rahim for repairing the private car of Rahim.

Solution

(In the books of Ram)
Journal Entires

Date	*Particulars*		*LF*	*Debit*	*Credit*
1.	Purchases a/c	Dr.		1,000	
	To Rahim's a/c				1,000
	(Being goods purchased from Rahim)				
2.	Cash a/c	Dr.		8,000	
	To Sales a/c				8,000
	(Being cash sales to Rahim)				
3.	Rahim's a/c	Dr.		5,250	
	To Cash				5,000
	To Discount				250
	(Being payment made and discount received)				
4.	Rahim's a/c	Dr.		7,000	
	To Sales a/c				7,000
	(Being goods sold)				
5.	Drawings a/c	Dr.		2,500	
	To Rahim's a/c				2,500
	(Being goods bought from him for domestic use)				
6.	Repairs a/c	Dr.		5,000	
	To Cash				5,000
	(Being repair charged of car paid to Ram)				

In the books of Rahim

Date	*Particulars*		*LF*	*Debit*	*Credit*
1.	Ram's a/c	Dr.		1,000	
	To Sales a/c				1,000
	(Being credit sale of goods)				
2.	Purchases a/c	Dr.		8,000	
	To Cash a/c				8,000
	(Being cash purchase of goods)				

Date	Particulars	LF	Debit	Credit
3.	Cash a/c Dr. Discount a/c To Ram's a/c (Being cash received from Ram and discount allowed to him)		5,000 250	 5,250
4.	Purchases a/c Dr. To Ram's a/c (Being credit purchases from Ram)		7,000	 7,000
5.	Ram's a/c Dr. To Sales a/c (Being goods sold to Ram)		2,500	 2,500
6.	Repairs a/c Dr. To Cash a/c (Being repair charges of car paid to Ram)		5,000	 5,000

Problem 7

Show how the following transactions would appear in the journal of John and Joseph.
2004 Jan.

1. John bought goods from Joseph Rs. 1,000
2. Joseph bought goods from John for cash Rs. 1,500
3. Joseph received from John Rs. 780 and allowed him discount Rs. 20
8. John made cash sales of Rs. 700 to Joseph.
15. Joseph supplied goods worth Rs. 300 for John's domestic use.
19. John supplied to Joseph machinery worth Rs. 2,000 in exchange for furniture worth Rs. 1,000, goods of Rs. 800 and cash of Rs. 200
22. Joseph charged John commission of Rs. 50
25. Joseph received a cheque for Rs. 1,000 from John in full settlement of Rs. 1,050
27. John's cheque was paid into the Bank.
31. John advanced a loan of Rs. 2,000 to Joseph.

Solution

In the Books of John
Journal Entires

Date	Particulars	LF	Debit	Credit
2004 Jan 1,	Purchases a/c Dr. To Joseph's a/c (Being goods purchased from Joseph on credit)		1,000	 1,000
2.	Cash a/c Dr. To Sales a/c (Being goods sold for cash)		1,500	 1,500

Date	Particulars		LF	Debit	Credit
3.	Joseph's a/c	Dr.		800	
	To Cash a/c				780
	To Discount received A/c				20
	(Being cash paid to Joseph and discount received from him)				
8.	Cash a/c	Dr.		700	
	To Sales a/c				700
	(Being goods sold for cash)				
15.	Drawings a/c	Dr.		300	
	To Joseph's a/c				300
	(Being goods received from Joseph on credit for domestic use)				
19.	Furniture a/c	Dr.		1,000	
	Purchases a/c	Dr.		800	
	Cash a/c	Dr.		200	
	To Machinery a/c				2,000
	(Being machinery exchanged for furniture, goods and cash)				
22.	Commission a/c	Dr.		50	
	To Joseph's a/c				50
	(Being commission due to Joseph)				
25.	Joseph's a/c	Dr.		1,050	
	To Bank a/c				1,000
	To Discount received a/c				50
	(Being the cheque issued to Joseph and discount received from him)				
31.	Joseph's Loan a/c	Dr.		2,000	
	To Cash a/c				2,000
	(Being loan advanced to Joseph)				

Note :

The transactions of 27th January, 2004 will not affect John ; so no entry will be passed for that transactions in John's books

In the Books of Joseph
Journal Entires

Date	Particulars		LF	Debit	Credit
2004 Jan 1,	John's a/c	Dr.		1,000	
	To Sales a/c				1,000
	(Being goods sold to John on credit)				
2,	Purchases a/c	Dr.		1,500	
	To Cash a/c				1,500
	(Being goods purchased for cash)				

Date	Particulars		LF	Debit	Credit
3.	Cash a/c	Dr.		780	
	Discount allowed a/c	Dr.		20	
	To John's a/c				800
	(Being cash received from John and discount allowed to him)				
8.	Purchases a/c	Dr.		700	
	To Cash a/c				700
	(Being goods purchased for cash)				
15.	John's a/c	Dr.		300	
	To Sales a/c				300
	(Being goods sold to John on credit)				
19.	Machinery a/c	Dr.		2,000	
	To Furniture a/c				1,000
	To Sales a/c				800
	To Cash a/c				200
	(Being furniture, goods and cash exchanged for machinery purchase)				
22.	John's a/c	Dr.		50	
	To Commission a/c				50
	(Being commission charged to John)				
25.	Cash a/c	Dr.		1,000	
	Discount allowed a/c	Dr.		50	
	To John's a/c				1,050
	(Being cheque received from John and discount allowed to him)				
27.	Bank a/c	Dr.		1,000	
	To Cash a/c				1,000
	(Being John's cheque deposited into bank)				
31.	Cash a/c	Dr.		2,000	
	To John's loan a/c				2,000
	(Being loan received from John)				

Problem 8

Write transactions for the following journal entires :-

Date	Particulars		LF	Debit	Credit
1.	Cash a/c	Dr.		5,000	
	To Capital a/c				5,000
2.	Cash a/c	Dr.		2,000	
	To Mrs. Manohar's a/c				2,000
3.	Interest on Loan a/c	Dr.		200	
	To Cash a/c				200

Date	Particulars		LF	Debit	Credit
4.	Prepaid Rent a/c To Cash a/c	Dr.		80	80
5.	Cash a/c To Rent a/c	Dr.		30	30
6.	Mrs. Manohar's loan a/c Interest on loan a/c To Cash a/c	Dr. Dr.		2,000 100	2100
7.	Office equipment a/c To Cash a/c	Dr.		1,500	1,500
8.	Sen's a/c To Commission a/c	Dr.		30	30
9.	Drawings a/c To Cash a/c	Dr.		50	50
10.	Loss by Theft a/c To office equipment a/c	Dr.		3,000	3,000
11.	Cash a/c To Ashok's a/c	Dr.		500	500

Solution

1. Invested in the business an amount of	Rs. 5,000
2. Received loan from Mrs. Manohar	Rs. 2,000
3. Paid interest on loan for	Rs. 200
4. Paid advance rent to landlord for	Rs. 80
5. Received rent from sub-tenant	
6. Repaid Mrs. Manohar's loan with interest	Rs. 500
7. Paid cash for office equipment	Rs. 1,500
8. Commission due from Sen	Rs. 30
9. Cash withdrawn for personal use	Rs. 50
10. Office equipment stolen	Rs. 3,000
11. Ashok paid us on account	Rs. 500

Problem 9

Write transactions for the following entires :

Date	Particulars		LF	Debit	Credit
1.	Cash a/c Stock a/c To Capital a/c	Dr. Dr.		40,000 10,000	50,000
2.	Machinery a/c To Cash a/c To Loan a/c	Dr.		2,000	500 1,500
3.	Srinivas a/c To Purchase returns a/c	Dr.		50	50

Date	Particulars		LF	Debit	Credit
4.	Cash a/c	Dr.		1,000	
	To Sridhar's a/c				1,000
5.	Bank a/c	Dr.		1,000	
	To Cash a/c				1,000
6.	Drawings a/c	Dr.		50	
	To Purchases a/c				50
7.	Sridhar's a/c	Dr.		1,000	
	To Bank a/c				1,000
8.	Cash a/c	Dr.		980	
	Discount allowed			20	
	To Arun's a/c				1,000
9.	Cash a/c	Dr.		500	
	To Capital a/c				500
10.	Mahesh's a/c	Dr.		100	
	M.O. Commission a/c	Dr.		4	
	To Cash a/c				104
11.	Harish's a/c	Dr.		100	
	To Sales a/c				100
12.	Purchase a/c	Dr.		1,000	
	To Ravindra's a/c				1,000
13.	Sales Returns a/c	Dr.		30	
	To Cash a/c				30
14.	Investment a/c	Dr.		1,000	
	To Cash a/c				1,000
15.	Cash a/c	Dr.		1,000	
	To Investment a/c				1,000

Solution

1. Started business with cash for Rs. 40,000 and goods for Rs. 10,000
2. Purchased machinery for Rs. 2,000 giving Rs. 500 in cash and the balance through a loan.
3. Returned damaged goods to Srinivas for Rs. 50
4. Received cheque from Sridhar for Rs. 1,000
5. Deposited cheque into bank for Rs. 1,000
6. Goods drawn for use at home for Rs. 50
7. Cheque deposited into bank for collection was returned disohonoured for Rs. 1,000
8. Received cash from Arun in full settlement of his account for Rs. 1,000
9. Introduced further capital for Rs. 500
10. Sent money order to Mukesh for Rs. 100
    M.O. commission paid Rs. 4.

11. Harish bought goods from us for Rs. 100, or sold goods to Harish for Rs. 100
12. Purchased goods from Ravindra for Rs. 1,000
13. Received goods returned and paid value in cash for Rs. 30
14. Purchased securities worth for Rs. 1,000
15. Securities sold for Rs. 1,000

Problem 10

Complete the following Journal Entires :

1. Cash a/c Dr.
   To ___________
   (Being cash introduced to start the business)
2. ___________ Dr.
   To Sales a/c
   (Being cash sales)
3. Purchases a/c Dr.
   To ___________
   (Being credit purchases from Naryan)
4. ___________ Dr.
   To Purchase Return's a/c
   (Being goods returned to Nagaraj)
5. ___________ Dr.
   To Nirupam's a/c
   (Being goods returned by Nirupam)
6. ___________ Dr.
   To Capital a/c
   (Being additional capital paid into bank)
7. ___________ Dr.
   To Cash a/c
   (Being commission given to Nitin)
8. ___________ Dr.
   ___________ Dr.
   To Harish a/c
   (Being cheque received for Rs. 955 in full settlement of the account for Rs. 1,000)
9. ___________ Dr.
   To Bank a/c
   (Being income tax and house rent paid)
10. Bank a/c Dr.
    To ___________
    (Being Harish's cheque sent to bank)
11 ___________ Dr.
   To Bank a/c
   (Being cheque issued to repair the plant)

Solutions

Journal Entries

Date	*Particulars*	*LF*	*Debit*	*Credit*
1.	Cash a/c Dr. To Capital a/c (Being cash brought in to start the business)			
2.	Cash a/c Dr. To Sales a/c (Being cash sales)			
3.	Purchases a/c Dr. To Narayan's a/c (Being credit purchases from Narayan)			
4.	Nagaraj's a/c Dr. To Purchase Returns a/c (Being goods returned to Nagaraj)			
5.	Sales Returns a/c Dr. To Nirupam's a/c (Being goods returned by Nirupam)			
6.	Bank a/c Dr. To Capital a/c (Being additional capital paid into bank)			
7.	Commission a/c Dr. To Cash a/c (Being commission given to Nitin)			
8.	Cash a/c Dr. Discount a/c Dr. To Harish a/c (Being cash received in full settlement of the account)			
9.	Drawings a/c Dr. To Bank a/c (Being income tax and house-rent paid)			
10.	Bank a/c Dr. To Cash a/c (Being Harish's cheque sent to bank)			
11.	Repairs a/c Dr. To Bank a/c (Being cheque issued for repairs to plant)			

QUESTIONS

Simple Questions :

1. What do you mean by accounting cycle ?
2. What is journal ?

3. What do you mean by journal entry ?
4. What do you mean by journalising ?
5. What is narration ?
6. What do you mean by simple journal entry ?
7. What do you mean by compound journal entry ?
8. State the steps involved in accounting cycle.

EXERCISE 1

Pass Journal Entries in the books of Sachin :

(*a*) Sachin started business with cash Rs. 5,00,000
(*b*) He bought goods from Dravid on credit Rs. 50,000
(*c*) He opened a current a/c in a bank and deposited Rs. 1,50,000 therein.
(*d*) Sold goods to Joshi Rs. 20,000
(*e*) Returned damaged goods to Dravid Rs. 1,000
(*f*) Received goods returned by Joshi for Rs. 500
(*g*) He received a cheque from Joshi for Rs. 19,000 in full settlement of his account.
(*h*) Joshi's cheque was paid into the bank.
(*i*) Paid college fees of the proprietor's daughter Rs. 5,000
(*j*) Drew from bank Rs. 10,000
(*k*) Drew from bank for household expenses Rs. 10,000
(*l*) Sold goods to Kanitkar Rs. 10,000
(*m*) Kanitkar directly paid into the bank a/c Rs. 10,000
(*n*) Met travelling expenses Rs. 10,000

EXERCISE 2

Gangadhara commenced business as a merchant on 1st April, 2004. The following are the transactions for the month of April

1. Started business with cash Rs. 10,000, building Rs. 60,000 ; bank loan of Rs. 5,000
2. Bought furniture for cash Rs. 2,000 from Grace & Co., goods Rs. 4,000 and paid carriage Rs. 100
4. Cash sales Rs. 1,000 and credit sales to Ganesh Rs. 500
6. Bought goods from Ganesh for cash Rs. 2,000 Sold goods to Ganapathy for Rs. 6,000 paid rent of Rs. 200
9. Commission received from Dhanpal for Rs. 200 withdrew, cash for personal use of Rs. 1,000
12. Ganapathy sent an order of goods worth Rs. 3,000 .
18. Appointed Goynam as Salesman on monthly salary of Rs. 4,000
24. Supplied goods to Ganapathy as per order received on April 12, and paid Rs. 30 as freight on them.
26. Selected a building for the shop at a monthly rent of Rs. 1,500. Returned goods to Ganesh Rs. 1,000 and furniture to Grace & Co. Rs. 1,000
27. Ganapathy returned defective goods Rs. 1,000 Gajanana resigned and his salary Rs. 1,200 was paid.
29. Sent for domestic use furniture worth Rs. 500 and goods worth Rs. 500
30. Bought a motor van for the business for Rs. 1,00,000 and paid from the personal account.

EXERCISE 3

Write transactions for the following journal entries :-

1.	Cash a/c To Mrs. Nayak's Loan a/c	Dr.	20,000	 20,000
2.	Syndicate Bank a/c To Cash a/c	Dr.	10,000	 10,000
3.	Vikram's a/c To Cash a/c	Dr.	1,000	 1,000
4.	Saurav's Loan a/c To Cash a/c	Dr.	8,000	 8,000
5.	Furniture a/c To Cash a/c	Dr.	800	 800
6.	Cash a/c To Vikram's a/c	Dr.	1,000	 1,000
7.	Prabhakar's a/c To Sales a/c	Dr.	6,000	 6,000
8.	Bank a/c To Prabhakar's a/c	Dr.	6,000	 6,000
9.	Drawings a/c To Cash a/c	Dr.	300	 300
10.	Vehicles a/c To Cash a/c	Dr.	1,000	 1,000
11.	Travelling expenses a/c To Cash a/c	Dr.	100	 100
12.	Prepaid Insurance a/c To Cash a/c	Dr.	500	 500
13.	Charity a/c To Cash a/c	Dr.	1,000	 1,000
14.	Bank a/c To Bank loan a/c	Dr.	1,000	 1,000
15.	Bank a/c To Interest on Bank deposit a/c	Dr.	20	 20

EXERCISE 4

Complete the following journal entries

1. Cash a/c Dr.
   To ____________
   (Being capital introduced)

2. ____________ a/c Dr.
   To Cash a/c
   (For purchase of plant and machinery from Mohan for cash)

3. ____________ a/c Dr.
   To Outstanding salary a/c
   (For outstanding salary adjusted)

4. ____________ a/c Dr.
   To Sales a/c
   (Being cash sales to Mohan)

5. ____________ a/c Dr.
   To Commission a/c
   (Commission received from Sohan)

6. Stock a/c Dr.
   To ____________ a/c
   (Being the transfer of closing stock)

7. ____________ a/c Dr.
   To Goods a/c
   (Being goods used by the trader for private use)

8. Kalidas a/c Dr.
   To ____________ a/c
   (Returned goods to Kalidas)

9. Wages a/c Dr.
   To ____________ a/c
   (Paid wages by cheque)

10. Prepaid Insurance a/c Dr.
    To ____________ a/c
    (For adjustment of insurance prepaid)

EXERCISE 5

Correct the incorrect entries in terms of the narration :

1.	Purchases a/c To Cash a/c (Being office furniture purchased for cash)	Dr.	5,000	5,000
2.	Drawings a/c To Bank a/c (Being the cash withdrawn from office for personal use)	Dr.	1,000	1,000
3.	Purchases a/c To Cash a/c (Being the goods bought from Raman)	Dr.	500	500
4.	Drawings a/c To Bank a/c (Being the amount withdrawn from bank for office use)	Dr.	200	200

5.	Cash a/c Dr. To Bharath's a/c (Being the cash received from Bharath on account of commission)	500	500
6.	Govind's a/c Dr. To Cash a/c (Being the cash paid to Govind on account of his salary)	800	800
7.	Cheque a/c Dr. To Chandran a/c (Being the cheque received from Chandran account)	500	500
8.	Machinery a/c Dr. To Cheque a/c (Being the cheque issued for machinery repair)	250	250
9.	Cash a/c Dr. To Murali's a/c (Being the additional capital introduced by the proprietor Murali)	2,000	2,000
10.	Income Tax a/c Dr. To Cash a/c (Being the income tax paid)	500	500
11.	Bank Charges a/c Dr. To Cash a/c (Being the amount charged by bank as bank charges)	100	100
12.	Cash a/c Dr. To Interest a/c (Being the interest due from Ramesh)	50	50

3
CHAPTER
LEDGER

ACCOUNT

An account is a summarised record of all transactions relating to a person, property, or a class of income or expenditure. Accounts are of three types, viz (*a*) Personal account (*b*) Real account and (*c*) Nominal account.

LEDGER

The ledger is the principal book of accounts where similar transactions relating to a particular person or thing are recorded. It is a set of accounts. It contains personal, real or nominal accounts with which business deals with. A ledger enables to knows cumulative effect of entries for each individual account and also for the entire business.

Need for ledger

Journal records all the transaction in a chronological order as they occur. As the Journal contains numerous transactions it is not possible to ascertain the net effect of transactions on each individual asset, liability, owners equity, revenue and expens account. For example, there may be 100 or more transactions affecting cash spread throughout the journal. So to ascertain net change in cash all these effects are to be brought together in the cash account. This is accomplished through ledger. The focus of the ledger is on the individual accounts of the business. In this manner we can show for each account the cumulative effect of all the transactions which affect that account. A specimen form of ledger account is shown below.

Dr **Name of the Account** **Cr**

Date	*Particulars*	*JF*	*Amount*	*Date*	*Particulars*	*JF*	*Amount*

Differences between Journal and ledger :-

The main points of differences between a journal and a ledger are as follows :

1. Journal is the book of prime entry while ledger is the book of final entry. This is because all transactions are entered first in the Journal and then are transferred to the appropriate accounts in the ledger.
2. Journal records transactions in a chronological order while ledger records transactions in an analytical order i,e, the components of each transaction that effect individual asset, liability, owner's equity, revenue and expense account are grouped together.
3. The unit of organisation for the Journal is the transaction, whereas the unit of organisation for the ledger is the account.
4. The process of recording transactions in the journal is called "Journalising", while the process of recording transactions in the ledger is called "posting".

SUB-DIVISION of a Ledger

A ledger is a group of accounts. Hence on the basis of accounts, ledger may be sub-divided into three categories :

1. **Debtors ledger or customers ledger or Sales ledger :** It is a section of the ledger containing accounts of trade debtors, i.e, persons to whom goods are sold on credit.
2. **Creditors ledger or Supplies ledger or Bought ledger :** It is a section of ledger containing accounts of the trade creditors i,e, persons from whom goods are purchased on credit.
3. **Impersonal ledger or General ledger :** It contains all the accounts that are not recorded in the cash book, the creditors ledger and the debtors ledger. To be more specific it contains all other personal accounts (excluding those of trade debtors and trade creditors), accounts of asset, expenses, revenues and similar accounts.

Posting

The process of transferring the debit and credit items from the journal to their appropriate ledger accounts is known as posting. Each amount listed in the debt column of the Journal is posted by entering it on the debit side of an account in the ledger and each amount listed in the credit column of the Journal is posted to the credit side of a ledger account. The following procedure is commonly used in posting process.

(*a*) Locate in the Journal the account named in the debit portion of the Journal entry.
(*b*) Enter the date of the transaction in the ledger account.
(*c*) Enter the name of the account to be debited in the particular column. The world "To" is prefixed to the debit entries and the word "By" is written before the credit entries.
(*d*) Enter in the debit column of the ledger account the amount of the debit as shown in the journal.
(*e*) Enter in the folio column of the ledger account the number of the journal page from which the entry is posted.

The recording of the debit in the ledger account is now complete. Repeat the steps mentioned above for the credit portion of the journal entry.

Balancing of an Account

The difference between the sum of the debits of an account and the sum of its credits at any particular time is the balance of an account". The balance of an account is always known by the side which is greater. The process of ascertaining the difference is known as "balancing of an account".

If the sum of the items on the debit side of an account exceeds those on the credit side, then the difference is called "debit balance". If the sum of credits in an account exceeds the sum of the debits, the resulting balance is known as "credit balance".

Balancing Figure

Balancing figure is one which makes two sides of an account equal. If the totals of two sides of an account are unequal the difference is inserted on the side having the lesser total to make the two sides equal. The figure so inserted is known as the "balancing figure". The normal balances that one customarily expects to find in different categories of accounts are as follows :

Type of a/c	*Normal balance*
Asset	Debit balance
Liability	Credit balance
Capital	Credit balance
Revenue	Credit balance
Expenses	Debit balance
Owner's drawings	Debit balance

Problem 1

Rama, a businessman, entered into the following transactions with Krishna on the following dates. Draft the ledger account of Krishna and balance the same.

January 2004,

1.	Opening debt of Krishna to Rama	Rs. 100
3.	Sold goods to Krishna subject to 10% trade discount	Rs. 1000
8.	Krishna returned goods	Rs. 100
9.	Sold goods to Krishna and received a bill accepted by him	Rs. 200
10.	Krishna became insolvent and Rama realised from his assets	Rs. 850

Solution

In the books of RAMA
KRISHNA'S A/C

Date	*Particulars*	*Amt.*	*Date*	*Particulars*	*Amt.*
2004				2004	
Jan 1.	To Balance b/d	100	Jan 8.	By sales returns	100
3.	To Sales a/c (1000-100)	900	10.	By cash	850
				By P & C a/c —loss amounts not realisable	250
9.	To Bills Receivable	200			
		1200			1200

Problem 2

Record the following transactions in the personal account of Mr. Srinivas

2004 Jan.

1.	Debit balance of Srinivas a/c	Rs. 1000
2.	Sold goods on credit to Srinivas	Rs. 5400

6. Received from Srinivas Rs. 6300
   Allowed him discount Rs. 100
10. Srinivas bought goods an credit Rs. 1500
15. Received cash from Srinivas Rs. 1450
    Allowed him discount Rs. 50
20. Purchased goods on credit from Srinivas Rs. 1040
25. Paid cash to Srinivas Rs. 500
28. Returned goods to Srinivas Rs. 140
31. Paid cash to Srinivas in full settlement of his account Rs. 390

Solution

Srinivas A/c

Date	*Particulars*	*Amt.*	*Date*	*Particulars*	*Amt.*
2004			2004		
Jan 1.	To Balance b/d	1000	Jan.6.	By cash a/c	6300
2.	To Sales a/c	5400	6.	By discount a/c	100
10.	To Sales a/c	1500	15.	By cash a/c	1450
25.	To cash a/c	500	15.	By discount a/c	50
28.	To Purchases Returns a/c	140	20.	By purchases a/c	1040
31.	To Cash a/c	390			
	To Discount (Balancing figure)	10			
		8940			8940

Problem 3

From the following particulars, prepare the personal a/c of St. Thomas Trading Company : October 2004,

1. Credit balance b/d Rs. 25000
5. Bought goods from St Thomas Trading Company Rs. 6500
10. Returned goods to them Rs. 1600
14. Sold goods for Rs 7500 to them.
15. Received goods returned by St. Thomas Trading Company Rs. 450
30. Paid to St. Thomas Trading company Rs. 22600
    Discount allowed by them Rs. 250

Solution

St. Thomas Trading Co.

Date	*Particulars*	*Amt.*	*Date*	*Particulars*	*Amt.*
2004			2004		
Oct 10.	To purchase Returns a/c	1600	Oct 1.	By Balance b/d	25000
			5.	By purchases a/c	6500
12.	To Sales a/c	7500	15.	By Sales Returns a/c	450
30.	To Cash a/c	22600			
	To discount	250			
		31950			31950

Problem 4

From the following information, prepare (*i*) Satish a/c in the ledger of Chaitanya and (*ii*) Chaitanya a/c in the ledger of Satish.

2004 June,

1.	Amount due from Chaitanya to Satish	Rs. 4500
8.	Satish sold goods to Chaitanya	Rs. 6000
14.	Chaitanya sold machinery to Satish	Rs. 7500
19.	Chaitanya received machinery returned by Satish	Rs. 1500
20.	Satish received goods returned by Chaitanya	Rs. 250
25.	Satish received a cheque from Chaitanya Rs 1000 and allowed a discount of	Rs. 100
29.	Commission due from Chaitanya Rs 1060 interest changed by Satish	Rs. 60
30.	Received goods returned by Chaitanya and issued a cheque for Rs 200 to Chaitanya for the goods returned	

Solution

In the Ledger of Satish
Chaitanya A/c

Date	*Particulars*	*Amt.*	*Date*	*Particulars*	*Amt.*
2004			2004		
June 1.	To Balance b/d	4500	June 14,	By Machinery a/c	7500
8.	To Sales a/c	6000	20	By Sales Returns a/c	250
19.	To Machinery a/c	1500	26	By Cash a/c	1000
29.	To Commission a/c	1060		Discount a/c	100
	To Interest a/c	60	30	Balance a/c	4270
		13120			13120

In the Ledger of Chaitanyna
Satish A/c

Date	*Particulars*	*Amt.*	*Date*	*Particulars*	*Amt.*
2004					
June 14.	To Machinery a/c	7500	June 1.	By Balance c/d	4500
20.	To Purchases Returns a/c	250	8.	By Purchases a/c	6000
			19.	By Machinery a/c	1500
26.	To Bank a/c	1000	29.	By Commission a/c	1060
	Discount a/c	100		By Interest a/c	60
30.	To Balance c/d	4270			
		13120			13120

Problem 5

Journalise the following transactions, post them into ledger and prepare the Trial Balance.

2004 Jan,

1.	Commenced business with cash	Rs. 80000
6.	Paid into bank	Rs. 40000
13.	Bought goods for cash Rs 6000 and through cheque	Rs. 7000
18.	Cash Sales	Rs. 8000
22.	Cash purchases	Rs. 5000
29.	Paid rent	Rs. 2000

Solution

Journal Entries

Date	*Particulars*	*LF*	*Debit*	*Credit*
2004. Jan 1.	Cash a/c Dr		80000	
	To Capital a/c			80000
	(Being cash introduced into the business)			
6.	Bank a/c Dr		40000	
	To Cash a/c			40000
	(Being cash deposited into the bank)			
13.	Purchases a/c Dr		13000	
	To Cash a/c			6000
	To Bank a/c			7000
	(Being goods purchased for cash and paid by cheque			
18.	Cash a/c Dr		8000	
	To Sales a/c			8000
	(Being cash sales)			
22.	Purchases a/c Dr		5000	
	To Cash a/c			5000
	(Being goods purchased)			
29.	Rent a/c Dr		2000	
	To Cash a/c			2000
	(Being rent paid)			

Ledger Accounts

Cash A/c

To capital a/c	80000	By Bank a/c	40000
To Sales a/c	8000	By purchases a/c	6000
		By purchases a/c	5000
		By Rent a/c	2000
		By Balance c/d	35000
	88000		88000

Capital A/c

To Balance cld	80000	By cash a/c	80000

Bank A/c

To cash a/c	40000	By purchases a/c	7000
		By Balance c/d	33000
	40000		40000

Purchases A/c

To Cash a/c	6000	By Balance c/d	18000
To Bank a/c	7000		
To Cash a/c	5000		
	18000		18000

Sales A/c

To Balance c/d	2000	By Balance a/c	8000

Rent A/c

To cash a/c	2000	By Balance c/d	2000

Trial Balance

	Dr	Cr
Cash a/c	35000	
Capital a/c		80000
Bank a/c	33000	
Purchases a/c	18000	
Sales a/c		8000
Rent	2000	
	88,000	88,000

Problem 6

Journalise the following transactions, carry out the posting in the ledger, and prepare a trial balance.

2004 July,

1. Commenced business with cash Rs. 10000, goods Rs 5000, plant and machinery Rs. 5000
2. Deposited in the bank Rs. 6000
5. Purchased raw materials for Rs 2000 and furniture for Rs. 250
7. Paid wages Rs. 250
9. Sold goods to A for Rs 5000 at 12% trade discount.
12. Sold goods to B of Rs. 500
13. B returned goods worth Rs. 100
15. Purchased goods for Rs 2800 and paid by cheque

17. Purchased goods from C for Rs 3500 and sold the same to D for Rs 4000 immediately
19. Furniture purchased for Rs 900 for private use and paid by cheque
24. Bought goods paid by cheque Rs. 1000
26. Sold goods to E for Rs. 2800
28. Paid electricity charges Rs 280, paid water bill Rs 60 by cheque
30. Paid salary Rs. 500 and rent Rs. 200

Solution

Journal Entries

Date	*Particulars*		*LF*	*Debit*	*Credit*
2004.					
July 1.	Cash a/c	Dr		10000	
	Goods a/c	Dr		5000	
	Plant and Machinery a/c	Dr		5000	
	To capital a/c	Dr			20000
	(Being assets brought units business as capital)				
2.	Bank a/c	Dr		6000	
	To cash a/c				6000
	(Being cash deposited into bank)				
5.	Purchases a/c	Dr		2000	
	Furniture a/c	Dr		250	
	To cash a/c				2250
	(Being materials and furniture purchased)				
7.	Wages a/c	Dr		250	
	To cash a/c				250
	(Being wages paid)				
9.	A's a/c	Dr		4400	
	To Sales a/c				4400
	(Being goods sold to A on credit)				
	Note : Trade discount should not be entered in accounts				
12.	B's a/c	Dr		500	
	To Sales a/c				500
	(Being goods sold to B on credit)				
13.	Sales returns a/c	Dr		100	
	To B's a/c				100
	(Being goods returned by B)				
15.	Purchases a/c	Dr		2800	
	To Bank a/c				2800
	(Being goods purchased and paid by cheque)				

Date	Particulars		LF	Debit	Credit
17.	Purchases a/c	Dr		3500	
	To C's a/c				3500
	(Being purchases on credit)				
17.	D's a/c	Dr		4000	
	To Sales a/c				4000
	(Being goods sold to D on Credit)				
19.	Drawings a/c	Dr		900	
	To Bank a/c				900
	(Being furniture purchased for private use paid from office a/c)				
24.	Purchases a/c	Dr		1000	
	To Bank a/c				1000
	(Being purchases paid by cheque)				
26.	E's a/c	Dr		2800	
	To sales a/c				2800
	(Being goods sold an credit to E)				
28.	Electricity charges a/c	Dr		280	
	Water bill a/c	Dr		60	
	To Bank a/c				340
	(Being expenses paid by cheque)				
30.	Salary a/c	Dr		500	
	Rent a/c	Dr		200	
	To cash a/c				700
	(Being expenses paid in cash)				

Capital

To Balance c/d	20000	By cash a/c	10000
		By goods a/c	5000
		By plant and machinery a/c	5000
	20000		20000

Cash A/c

To Sales a/c	10000	By Bank a/c	6000
		By purchases a/c	2000
		By furniture a/c	250
		By wages a/c	250
		By salary a/c	500
		By rent a/c	200
		By balance c/d	800
	10000		10000

Drawings A/c

To Bank a/c	900	By Balance c/d	900

Purchases A/c

To cash a/c	2000	By Balance c/d	9300
To Bank a/c	2800		
To C's a/c	3500		
To Bank a/c	1000		
	9300		9300

Sales A/c

To Balance c/d	11700	By A's a/c	4400
		By B's a/c	500
		By D's a/c	4000
		By E's a/c	2800
	11700		11700

Goods A/c

To capital a/c	5000	By Balance c/d	5000

Sales Returns A/c

To D's a/c	100	By Balance a/c	100

Plant and Machinery A/c

To capital a/c	5000	By Balance c/d	5000

Furniture A/c

To Cash a/c	250	By Balance c/d	250

Wages A/c

To Cash a/c	250	By Balance c/d	250

A's A/c

To Sales a/c	4400	By Balance c/d	4400

B's A/c

To Sales a/c	500	By Sales Returns a/c	100
		By Balance c/d	400
	500		500

C's A/c

To Balance c/d	3500	By purchases a/c	3500

D's A/c

To Sales a/c	4000	By Balance c/d	4000

E's A/c

To Sales a/c	2800	By Balance c/d	2800

Electricity Bill A/c

To Bank a/c	280	By Balance c/d	280

Water bill A/c

To Bank a/c	60	By Balance c/d	60

Salary A/c

To cash a/c	500	By Balance c/d	500

Rent A/c

To cash a/c	200	By Balance c/d	200

Trial Balance

	Dr	Cr
Capital		20000
Cash	800	
Bank	960	
Drawings	900	
Purchases	9300	
Sales		11,700
Sales Returns	100	
Goods	5000	
Plant & machinery	5000	
Furniture	250	
Wages	250	
A	4400	
B	400	
C		3500
D	4000	
E	2800	
Electricity charges	280	
Water bill	60	
Salary	500	
Rent	200	
	35200	35200

QUESTIONS

1. What is an account ?
2. What is a ledger ?
3. State the differences between the journal and ledger.
4. What is meant by debtors ledger.

5. What is meant by creditors ledger
6. What do you mean by general ledger.
7. What is meant by "posting".
8. State the meaning of balancing figure.

EXERCISE 1

Record the following transaction in the personal accounts of Mr. Brown and balance the account at the end of each month

2004 Jan

1.	Solid goods to Brown	Rs. 62250
6.	Received from Brown	Rs. 60225
	Allowed him discount	Rs. 2025
20.	Brown bought goods worth	Rs. 80000
23.	Received from Brown cash on account	Rs. 30000

2004 Feb,

1.	Balance from last month	Rs. 50000
15.	Purchased goods from Brown	Rs. 85000
23.	Received from Brown	Rs. 49020
	Allowed him discount	Rs. 980
24.	Sold goods to Brown	Rs. 155500
25.	Paid to Brown	Rs. 84000
	Discount allowed by him	Rs. 1000

Answer : For the year 2004, Jan. 31st, the balancing figure is Rs. 50,000 and on 28th February, the balancing figure is 1,55,000.

EXERCISE 2

From the following transaction prepare Anand's ledger account in the books Bhaskar

2004 March

1.	Due from Anand	Rs. 4000
10.	Sold goods worth	Rs. 2000
16.	Received cheque for Rs. 4000 and allowed a discount of	Rs. 100
22.	Purchased furniture from Anand	Rs. 600
25.	Anand returned goods	Rs. 100
30.	Received commission from Anand	Rs. 125

Answer : Balancing figure is Rs. 1200

EXERCISE 3

Journalise the following transactions, post them into ledger and balance the same 2004 Jan

1.	Rao commenced business with cash	Rs. 10000
5.	Bought goods for cash from Raghu for	Rs. 2000
6.	Returned damaged goods to Raghu	Rs. 200
8.	Purchased machine from M/s HMT	Rs. 25000

10. Paid for wages for installation of machine Rs. 1200
15. Purchased goods for Rs. 8000 from Suresh, paid cash Rs. 2000 and gave acceptance on a bill for the balance.
16. Paid salary to manager Ram Rs. 1000

EXERCISE 4

Prepare Anjan's a/c in the ledger of Bhairav and Bhairav's account in the ledger of Anjan from the following transaction between them.

2004 Jan,

1. Opening debit of Bhairav to Anjan Rs. 500
5. Anjan sold goods to Bhairav Rs. 2000
10. Bhairav returned goods to Anjan Rs. 100
12. Anjan received cash from Bhairav Rs. 700 and allowed Bhairav discount Rs. 50
15. Bhairav sold goods to Anjan on account Rs. 1000
20. Anjan returned goods to Bhairav Rs. 70
24. Bhairav paid cash to Anjan Rs. 300
31. Anjan received cash from Bhairav in full settlement Rs. 400

Answer : Total of Anjan a/c Rs. 2570.
Total of Bhairav a/c Rs. 2570.

EXERCISE 5

Journalise the following transactions. Prepare ledger accounts and a Trial balance.

(*a*) T started business with Rs. 50000
(*b*) Deposited in the bank Rs. 40000
(*c*) Purchased goods from A for Rs. 20000 for which issued a cheque for Rs. 12000
(*d*) Sold goods to B for Rs. 18000 for which received cash Rs. 5000 and a cheque for Rs. 7000. The cheque was deposited in the bank.
(*e*) Expenses incurred Rs. 300
(*f*) Goods remained unsold Rs. 3000

Answer : Total of Trial balance Rs 76000

EXERCISE 6

Journalese the following transaction. Prepare ledger accounts and a trial balance.

(*a*) 'S' started business with cash Rs. 15000
(*b*) Purchased goods from A on credit for Rs. 10000
(*c*) Sold good to 'B' on credit Rs. 7000
(*d*) 'N' took goods worth Rs. 1000 for his personal use.
(*e*) Paid office expenses Rs. 800
(*f*) Paid Rs. 6000 to A an account.
(*g*) Received from B Rs. 2000 an account.
(*h*) Goods remained unsold Rs. 1000

Answer : Total of trial balance Rs. 26000

4

CHAPTER

Subsidiary Books

INTRODUCTION

The traditional method of book-keeping envisages that all transactions be initially recorded in a Journal and then posted individually to the appropriate account in the ledger. However applying such detailed procedures to a large number of transactions is impractical for two major reasons. First, recording all transactions in a single journal would seriously curtail the number of transactions that could be processed in a day simply because only one person at a time could make entries. Secondly transactions recorded in the Journal must be posted individually to the ledger and this results in a great deal of labour.

Practical System or English System of Book Keeping

In order to overcome the limitations of the Journal, a separate subsidiary book is maintained to record a particular type of transaction. After recording the transactions in the subsidiary book concerned they are posted into the ledger accounts. This system of maintaining subsidiary books is known as practical system or English system of book keeping.

Advantages of Subsidiary Books

1. Passing Journal entries for every single transaction is avoided. This saves time and energy.
2. Subsidiary books are divided according to the transactions like purchases, sales, purchase return, sales return etc. The periodical totals of these transactions can easily be ascertained.
3. Transactions of similar nature are available in one book. Therefore, it is easy to locate any entry for verification and corrections of errors.
4. Two entries to be made in a Journal, one to be debited and the other to be credited is avoided. Only one entry is made.
5. Detection and rectification of errors become easy and the system itself is a simplified one.
6. The maintenance of accounts become easy and comfortable as the work can be distributed to different persons to maintain different subsidiary books.

Sub-division of Journal or Various Subsidiary Books

The various subsidiary books maintained by a business are as follows :

1. Purchase book
2. Purchase returns book
3. Sales book
4. Sales returns book
5. Cash book
6. Bills receivable book
7. Bills payable book
8. Journal proper

Invoice

An invoice is a statement which contains details of goods, their quantity, price, total value, discount, advance received, packing charges etc. It is prepared by the seller and sent to the buyer. From the point of view of the seller it is known as "outward invoice" and from buyer's point of view, it is known as "Inward invoice".

1. Purchase Book. Purchase book is known by various other names such as purchase day book, purchase Journal, Bought day book, Inward invoice book. This book is used to record only credit purchases of goods meant for selling at a profit. Credit purchases of any fixed assets or stationery items on credit should not be entered in this book. This items should be taken to Journal proper. The ruling of a purchase book is given below :

Purchase book

Date	*Particulars*	*LF*	*Invoice No.*	*Amount*

1. **Date :** The date of the transaction is entered in this column.
2. **Particulars :** The names of the vendor from whom the goods have been purchased is recorded in this column.
3. **Ledger folio :** This records the page number of the ledger where account of the supplier is found.
4. **Invoice Number :** Invoice received from suppliers against purchases are numbered serially and these numbers are entered in this column against the name of the concerned supplier.
5. **Amount :** Net amount of the invoice is shown here.

Posting From The Purchase Book

For posting entries from the purchase book, separate account should be opened in the name of each of the suppliers (creditors) and also a purchase account. Individual entries appearing in the purchase book should be posted each day to the credit of creditors account in the subsidiary ledger for accounts payable and at the end of the month total of the purchase journal shall be posted as a debit to purchases account.

Problem 1

Enter the following transactions in the purchase book of Arun Kumar :

2004 May

May 1. Bought from Mr 'A' 10 boxes of Nirma soap @ Rs 150 per box @ discount of 20%.

8. Purchased from Mr. 'B' 5 boxes of Vim detergent powder Rs 60 per box, for cash.

10. Received from Mr. 'C' 120 pieces of sandalwood soap @ Rs 8 per piece, less discount 20%.

15. Purchased furniture from Mr. 'D' Rs 5548.

18. Received invoice from Mr. 'E' for 15 cases of "Wash bar" @ Rs 180 per box. 12 cases of washing powder Rs 60 per cake.
Forwarding charges Rs 20 less 25% discount.

30. Purchased office stationery from Mr. 'A' Rs 180.

Solution

Purchase Book of Arun Kumar

Date	*Particulars*		*LF*	*Amount*
2004				
May 1.	Mr. 'A'			
	10 boxes of Nirma soap			
	@ Rs 150	1500		
	Less : 20% Trade discount	300		
				1200
10.	Mr. 'C'			
	120 pieces of sandalwood			
	soap @ Rs 8	960		
	Less 20% trade discount	192		
				768
28.	Mr 'E'			
	15 cases of Wash bar			
	@ Rs 180	2700		
	12 cases of washing			
	powder @ Rs 60	720		
		3420		
	Less : Trade discount			
	@ 20%	855		
		2565		
	Add : Forwarding			
	charges	20		2585
				4553

Purchases A/c

To Sundries	4553	By Balance c/d	4553

A's a/c

To Balance c/d	1200	By purchases a/c	1200

C's a/c

To Balance a/d	768	By purchases a/c	768

E's a/c

To Balance c/d	2585	By purchases a/c	2585

2. Purchase Returns Book. This book is also called a Purchase Returns Journal or Return Outward Book. When the buyer returns the goods purchased to the seller, that transactions is called purchase returns. Goods are returned to the seller due to many reason, such as poor quality, supply of more goods then indented etc. At times the purchaser may claim allowance from the seller for shortage, breakage or damage of goods in transit. These allowances are recorded in the purchase return book. Entries are made in this book based on DEBIT NOTE sent to the supplier. A debit note is prepared by the purchaser regarding the details of the goods returned or allowance claimed in duplicate. The original is sent to the supplier and the entries are made from the duplicate copy. It is called debit note because the purchaser is informing the supplier that his account is debited on account of the goods returned or allowances claimed.

A specimen of purchase returns book is shown below :

Purchase Return Book

Date	*Particulars*	*LF*	*Debit Note No.*	*Amount*

Posting from Purchase Returns Book

Posting from purchases returns book is made in two stages. First the personal account of suppliers to whom goods are returned or from whom allowance is claimed are individually debited in the ledger. Secondly at the end of the period the total of purchase returns book is credited to the purchase returns a/c in the general ledger.

Problem 2

Record the following transactions in the purchase returns book of Giridhar.
2004

Jan 1.	Returned to Amarnath goods worth	Rs. 6000
5.	Returned cutting machine to Bharath	Rs. 8750
10.	Sent back goods to Swaminanthan	Rs. 455
15.	Claimed allowance from Hariharan	Rs. 65
30.	Allowance claimed from Eshwar is admitted and received a cheque for	Rs. 143.

Solution

Purchase Return Book

Date	*Particulars*	*LF*	*Debit Note No.*	*Amount*
1-1-2004	Amarnath	—	—	6000
10-1-2004	Swaminathan	—	—	455
15-1-2004	Hariharan	—	—	65
				6520

Note :

1. Transaction of January 5 relates to an asset. Hence it is not entered in purchase return book.
2. Transaction of January 30 is a cash transaction. Supplier paid the claim by a cheque. Hence, it is not recorded in purchase return book.

Purchase Returns A/c

To Balance c/d	6520	By Sundries	6520

Amaranth A/c

To purchase returns a/c	6000	By Balance c/d	6000

Swaminathan's A/c

To purchase returns a/c	455	By Balance c/d	455

Hariharan's A/c

To purchase returns a/c	65	By Balance c/d	65

3. **Sales book.** Sales book or sales journal is a book of original entry designed to record sale of goods on credit. No other transaction should be recorded in the sales book. For example, sale of goods for cash should be recorded in the cash book. Similarly sale of an asset not a part of the stock-in-trade is to be recorded in the cash book or journal proper depending on whether the sale was made for cash or on credit.

Whenever goods are sold on credit few copies of a sales invoice is prepared. The information listed on a sales invoice usually includes the date of sale, customer's name, amount of sale, the serial number of the invoice and the credit terms. A copy of the sales invoice provides the authority and the information to record the transaction in the sales book.

A specimen of sales book is given below :

Sales Book

Date	*Particulars*	*Invoice No.*	*LF*	*Amount*

Posting from sales book

For posting the sales book entries, separate accounts are opened in the name of each of the customers and also a sales account. Each transaction should be posted individually to the debit of the customer's account in the subsidiary ledger and at the end of the month the amount column of the sales journal is to be added and the total posted to the credit of the sales account in the general ledger.

Problem 3

Write up the sales book of prasad from the following information.

2004 Aug

Aug 6. Sold to Raj Kumar goods worth Rs 4000 at a discount of 10%.

14. Sent goods to Ramesh, goods of the value of Rs. 6000, Packing charges Rs 100.
18. Shankar bought one Motor car for Rs 65000
22. Mohan bought goods Rs 4000 at a discount of 20% and paid cash.

Solution

Sales Book

Date	Particulars		LF	Outward Invoice	Amount
2004					
Aug 6.	Raj Kumar	4000			
	Less : Trade discount	400			
					3600
14.	Ramesh	6000			
	Add; Paching charges	100			
					6100
					9700

Note :

1. Transaction of August 18, relates to an asset (Motor car). Hence it is not entered in the sales book
2. Transaction of August 22, is a cash transaction. Therefore it is not entered in the sales book.

Sales A/c

To Balance c/d	9700	By sundries	9700

Raj Kumar A/c

To Sales a/c	3600	By Balance c/d	3600

Ramesh A/c

To sales a/c	6100	By Balance c/d	6100

4. Sales Returns Book : This book is also known as Returns inward book. Entry in this book is make only for return of goods which are sold on credit basis. Returns of goods sold on cash should not be entered in this book because cash is normally paid for such returns. While taking back the goods returned the seller prepares a credit note in duplicate sending the original to the buyer who returned the goods. The duplicate copy is retained with him. Entries are made in the sales returns book based on the information contained in the credit note. It is called credit note because the seller informs the buyer that buyers account is credited for having returned the goods. This is also applicable to the allowances granted to the buyer.

Posting from Sales Returns Book into the ledger

Posting from sales returns book into the ledger involves two steps. First the personal accounts of customers are to be individually credited in the subsidiary ledger with the value of goods returned or allowance made. Secondly, monthly total of the Sales Returns Book is to be debited to Sales Returns Account in the general ledger.

Problem 4

Write the sales returns book from the following :

2004,

July 10.	Prabhu returned goods	Rs. 6500
18.	Allowance claimed by Murthy	Rs. 9500 accepted
26.	Received a debit note from Narayan for	Rs. 600
30.	Received the goods returned by Anand and paid	Rs. 1600 in full settlement

Solution

Sales Returns Book

Date	*Particulars*	*LF*	*Credit Note*	*Amount*
2004 July 10	Prabhu		—	6500
18	Murthy		—	9500
				16000

Note

1. **Transaction of July 26 :** Receiving a debit note is not a transaction. Sales returns book is written on the basis of credit note.
2. **Transaction of July 30 :** It is a cash transaction. It is not to be entered in sales returns book.

Sales Returns A/c

To sundrie	16000	By Balance c/d	16000

Prabhu's A/c

To Balance c/d	6500	By Sales Returns a/c	6500

Murthy's A/c

To Balance c/d	9500	By Sales returns a/c	9500

Problem 5

Enter the following transactions in suitable subsidiary books and post them into ledger.

2004 Jan,

1.	Bought goods from Mamatha less 10%	Rs. 10000
5.	Sold goods to Savitha	Rs. 5000
7.	Govinda purchased goods from us	Rs. 3000
10.	Suma bought goods from us	Rs. 800
12.	Goods returned to Mamatha	Rs. 100
18.	Allowance granted to Suma	Rs. 50
20.	Sandhya sold goods to us	Rs. 2000

Solution

Purchase Book

Date	*Particulars*		*Invoice No.*	*Amount*
2004 Jan 1.	Mamatha :			
	Goods	10000		
	Less : Discount	1000		9000
20.	Sandhya : Goods			2000
				11000

Purchases A/c

To Sundries	11000	By Balance c/d	11000

Mamatha's A/c

To Balance c/d	9000	By purchases a/c	9000

Sandhya's A/c

To Balance c/d	2000	By purchases a/c	2000

Purchases Returns Book

Date	*Particulars*	*Debit Note*	*Amount*
2004 Jan 12.	Mamatha	—	100

Mamatha's A/c

To purchases returns a/c	100	By Balance c/d	100

Purchase Returns A/c

To Balance c/d	100	By Mamatha's a/c	100

Sales Book

Date	Particulars	Invoice No.	Amount
2004, Jan 5.	Savitha — goods	—	5000
7.	Govinda — goods	—	3000
10.	Suma — goods	—	800
			8800

Sales A/c

To Balance c/d	8800	By Sundries a/c	8800

Savitha A/c

To sales a/c	5000	By Balance c/d	5000

Govinda's A/c

To sales a/c	3000	By Balance c/d	3000

Suma's A/c

To sales a/c	800	By Balance c/d	800

Sales Returns Book

Date	Particulars	Credit Note	Amount
2004 Jan 18.	Suma	–	50

Sales Returns A/c

To Suma	100	By Balance c/d	100

Suma's A/c

To Balance c/d	100	By sales returns a/c	100

5. Bill Receivable Book. Sometimes the seller sells the goods on credit for the amount to be paid by the buyer, the seller draws a bill, sending it to the buyer for his acceptance. The purchaser signs the bill. This means that he accepts the liability of repaying the amount after a stipulated period. After the buyer (Debtor) signs the bill it comes back to the seller. This bill is a Bills Receivable for the seller. All transactions relating to Bills Receivable are entered in this book. At the end of an accounting period, the amount remaining in the Bill Receivable book will be taken to the debit side of the trial balance and also to the asset side of the balance.

6. Bill Payable Book. Sometimes the buyers buy goods an credit. The seller draws a bill which is duly accepted by the buyer and sends it to the seller (creditor). This bill is Bills Payable to the buyer He has to pay the amount after a stipulated period. The bill will be in the possession of the seller. But the buyer has to pay the amount. When the amount is paid the bills payable comes back to the acceptor (i.e, buyer or debtor). All transactions relating to the bills accepted for having purchased goods on credit will be entered in this book. The balance remaining in this book is a credit Balance which is taken to the liabilities side of the Balance Sheet.

7. Journal proper. For a small business concern Journal proper is the only book of original entry. The use of Journal proper is much restricted. Those transactions which cannot be entered in any other subsidiary books only are recorded in this book. The following types of transactions are entered in Journal proper.

(*a*) Opening entries
(*b*) Closing entries
(c) Adjusting entries
(*d*) Transfer entries
(*e*) Rectifying entries
(*f*) Credit purchases and credit sales of things that are not meant for selling at a profit
(*g*) Entries regarding dishonour of bills
(*h*) Goods taken by the proprietor for his personal use
(*i*) Loss of goods by theft, smuggling, fire etc

8. **Cash book :** This subsidiary book is discussed in detail in the next chapter.

QUESTIONS

Simple Questions

1. State the limitations of recording transactions in the Journal.
2. What do you mean by Practical system or English system of book keeping,
3. List out the various subsidiary books.
4. State the advantages of subsidiary books.
5. What do you mean by purchase book ?
6. What is a purchase returns book ?
7. What is a debit note ?
8. What do you mean by credit note ?
9. What is meant by sales book.
10. What is a sales return book ?
11. What is bills receivable book ?
12. What is a bills payable book ?
13. What is a Journal proper ?

EXERCISE 1

X, a businessman, enters into the following transactions in the month of January 2004. You are required to record them in the subsidiary books and post them into ledger.

2004 Jan,

2.	Sold goods to Y subject to a trade discount of 10%	Rs. 3000
4.	Received a debit note from Y in respect of an overcharge in the bill	Rs. 200
6.	Y returned damaged goods	Rs. 100
10.	Sold goods to P	Rs. 600

Answer : Total of sales book Rs. 3300
Total of returns inwards book Rs. 300.

EXERCISE 2

Enter the following transactions in the purchase book and sales book of Mr. Nanda.

2004 Feb,

1. Purchased goods from Sonal for Rs. 6000 at a discount of Rs. 200.
3. Purchased furniture an credit from Das bros. for Rs. 10000.
5. Sold goods on credit to Keshav Rs. 6000.
7. Sold goods for cash to Chandra Rs. 8600.
10. Sold goods to Tina Traders for Rs. 4500, less discount Rs. 300.
15. Withdrew from bank Rs. 2500
19. Bilwara Traders supplied goods to Nanda worth Rs. 3600 on credit.
25. Purchased stationary for Rs. 600.

Answers : Total of purchases book 9400.
Total of sales book Rs. 10200.

EXERCISE 3

From the following transactions, prepare necessary subsidiary books and prepare purchases a/c. sales a/c, purchase returns a/c and sales returns a/c.

2004 Nov,

1. Purchased 20 carpets from Madanlal at Rs. 800 each.
5. Mr. Champalal sold 15 special carpets to us @ Rs. 1300 each.
9. Purchased from Mr. Kesarilal 10 carpets @ Rs. 1000 each.
13. Sold 10 carpets to Mr. Chandanlal at Rs. 1000 each.
16. Returned 2 carpets to Mr. Champalal .
25. Sold to Miss Fatima 8 special carpets at Rs. 1200 each.
28. Chandanlal returned 2 carpets to us.

Answers : Total of purchases book Rs. 45500.
Total of sales book Rs. 21400.
Total of purchases returns book Rs. 2600.
Total of sales returns book Rs. 2200.

EXERCISE 4

Enter the following transactions in the proper subsidiary books and post the same in the ledger.

2004 March,

1.	Purchased goods from Shankar traders	Rs. 10000
2.	Sold goods to Mr 'R'	Rs. 9000
3.	Sold goods to Mr. 'G'	Rs. 6000
4.	Bought goods from Lucky traders	Rs. 8000
6.	Received goods returned from Mrs 'G'	Rs. 2000
10.	Mr. 'R' returned us goods	Rs. 500
16.	Returned goods to Lucky traders	Rs. 1000

20.	Mr 'X' returned goods	Rs. 200
21.	Bought goods from Mr. 'A'	Rs. 6500
22.	Bought goods from 'S'	Rs. 4800
27.	Sold goods to Mr. 'H'	Rs. 4800
28.	Returned goods to Mr. 'A'	Rs. 700
30.	Mr. 'H' returned goods	Rs. 500

Answers : Total of purchases book Rs. 2930
Total of sales book Rs. 1980
Total of purchase returns book Rs. 1700
Total of sales returns book Rs. 3200

5

CHAPTER

Cash Book

1. NATURE AND OBJECTIVES

As the name implies the cash book is a book in which receipts and payments of cash are recorded. It is one of the important books of accounts as it enables the businessman to record all cash transactions both cash receipts and payments and in knowing the cash balance on hand. The cash balance on hand represents the difference between total cash received and payments made.

Among many transactions which occur in a business, cash transactions occur in a large number. All such cash transactions are recorded in the cash book. A cash book is one of the subsidiary book. It can be sub-divided into several subsidiary books as in the case of a Journal. A cash book can be sub-divided into : (*a*) cash book for recording payment to creditors, (*b*) a cash book for recording collection from debtors, (*c*) a cash book for recording remittance from the branches, (*d*) a petty cash book for recording petty cash payment and so on. In this respect the cash book is regarded as a book of prime entry or book or original entry. A cash book resembles to the book of prime entry in the following respects :

(*a*) All the cash transactions are primarily recorded as is done in the case of other primary books.

(*b*) Ledger accounts are prepared with the help of cash book as are done with the help of other primary books.

(*c*) Narrations are also given at the foot of each entry as it is done in case of a Journal. But in practice it is ignored.

(*d*) Cash book is regularly maintained as in the case of other primary books.

A cash book is also treated as a principal book or a book of final entry when it serves as the cash account in which case the balances are directly recorded in the trial balance. In this respect it resembles to that of a ledger or a book of final entry. A cash book has the following similarities with that of book of final entry.

(*a*) The proforma, i.e., specimen, of a ledger account is used in writing the cash book.

(*b*) The left hand side is used as debit side and the right hand side is used as credit side.

(*c*) Cash book is also balanced like a ledger account.

(*d*) Cash book is also a ledger account. In the ledger no separate cash account is maintained.

A cash book has the features of both the journal and ledger. Hence it is also called as "Journalised ledger".

Objectives of Cash book :

Cash book serves three important purposes. They are as follows :

(*a*) To know the total cash received and total cash paid during a given period of time.
(*b*) To know the cash balance for a given period of time.
(*c*) To know whether cash balance on hand and at Bank are correct.

Method of Maintaining a Cash Book : Cash book can be maintained in the form of a ledger account or in the form of a Journal. If it is maintained in the form of ledger account it takes the 'T' form, account having a debit side and credit side. A proforma of this type is given below :

Dr Cash Account Cr

Date	*Particulars*	*LF*	*Amount*	*Date*	*Particulars*	*LF*	*Amount*
1	2	3	4	1	2	3	4

As can be seen from the above ruling the cash account has two sides, viz. (*a*) debit side and (*b*) credit side. All cash receipts are entered on the debit side. It is so called because when a businessman receives money, he becomes a debtor to the person who pay him. This side is therefore prefixed as "To" before the name of the account is written up. All cash payments are recorded on the credit side. It is so called because when the businessman pays money to others he is credited by them with the amounts he pays them. Therefore, this side is always prefixed as "By".

A cash account as per the above proforma shows four columns on each side of the cash account. The date column on the debit side in meant for recording the date of cash receipt. The particulars column is used for recording the name of the person from whom money is received. Sometimes, the name of an asset is written under this column instead of writing the name of the person. The ledger folio column is used for writing the page of the ledger. In the amount column, the cash received is recorded.

Similarly on the credit side the various aspects of cash transactions such as date of payment, person to whom cash is paid, the ledger folio number and amount paid, is recorded. But the current trend in maintaining a cash book is in the form of a Journal. Accordingly we have two types of Journals, viz. cash receipt journal and cash payment Journal. The maintenance of cash book in the form of a Journal facilitates division of labour and helps in internal checking of these transactions.

Cash Receipt Journal : This journal records all cash received by the businessman from different sources. Some of the important sources of cash are cash from sales, cash on borrowings, cash collected from customers, interest received in cash etc. A proforma of such Journal is shown :

Cash Receipt Journal

Date	Particulars	LF	Amount
1	2	4	5
(Narration 3)			

(a) Column 1 is meant for recording the date of cash receipt.
(b) Column 2 is meant for recording the name of the person from whom cash is received or source of cash receipt.
(c) Column 3 is used for writing brief explanation about the source of cash receipt.
(d) Column 4 is meant for recording page number of the ledger on which the amount of that transaction is posted.
(e) Column 5 is meant for recording the amount of cash received.

Cash Payment Journal : This Journal records all cash payment made on several accounts. For example, payment for purchase of goods, payment of expenses such as rent, wages, salaries, electricity etc. Payment to creditors from whom goods were bought on credit basis, payment for the purchase of assets like plant, furniture, repayment of loans etc. This book is maintained as a separate book to record all payments of cash. The proforma of this book is shown below :

Cash Payment Journal

Date	Particulars	LF	Amount
1	2	4	5
	(Narration 3)		

(a) Column 1 is meant for recording the date of cash payment.
(b) Column 2 is meant for recording the name of the person to whom cash is paid or reason for cash payment.
(c) Column 3 is meant for writing brief explanation for having paid cash.
(d) Column 4 is meant for recording page number of the ledger on which the amount of that transaction is posted.
(e) Column 5 is meant for recording the amount of cash paid.

2. TYPES OF CASH BOOK

The cash book can be of four types. They are : (1) Simple or single cash book (2) Two column cash book or cash book with cash and discount column. (3) Three column cash book or cash book with discount, cash and bank column and (4) Cash book with bank and discount column.

3. SIMPLE OR SINGLE CASH BOOK

This book is used to record all receipts and payments of cash. It contains the cash column on either side of the cash book apart from other columns. It is normally maintained by small business concerns. A simple cash book can be maintained either in the form of an account or in the form of a journal. The proforma of a single cash book is already given under the sub-topic of method of maintaining a cash book.

Balancing the Single Column Cash Book : After posting all the cash entries in the cash account the businessman can know the balance of cash on hand. The process of ascertaining and recording the balance on hand is known as balancing the cash book. This involves the following procedures :

(*a*) Total the amount column an either side of cash account and find out the difference. It is to be noted that the amount column on the debit side is always heavier than the credit side. It can never be less because a trader cannot spend more than what he has. However if the businessman borrows any loans to meet expenses, the sum borrowed will have to be first recorded on the debit side before he can record any payment from it on the credit side. There is also the possibilty of having a nil balance in cash account. Then happens when the businessman pays all the amount he has.

(*b*) The difference in the amount, being the excess of debit column amount over credit column amount is then placed on credit side which has less amount. The two sides on further totalling will show the same amount.

Problem 1

Enter the following in Sri Shanbhog's cash book and show the balance.

1.	1-10-2000	Balance of cash Rs. 1,500
2.	8-10-2000	Purchased goods for cash from X for Rs. 320.
3.	15-10-2000	Sold goods Rs. 480 to Y
4.	20-10-2000	Received commission of Rs. 65.
		Paid commission of Rs. 55.
5.	28-10-2000	Paid Shantharam on account Rs. 715.
6.	31-10-2000	Paid salary to office clerk, Rs. 100 and office rent, Rs. 60.

Solution

Cash Book

Date	*Particulars*	*LF*	*Amt.*	*Date*	*Particulars*	*LF*	*Amt.*
1-10-2000	To Balance b/d		1,500	8-10-00	By Purchases a/c		320
20-10-2000	To Commission a/c		63	20-10-00	By Commission a/c		55
				28-10-00	By Shantaram a/c		715
				31-10-00	By Office salary a/c		100
					By Office rent		60
					By Balance b/d		315
			1,565				1,565
1-11-70	To Balance b/d		315				

Problem 2

Enter the following transactions in a single cash book.

1995 Jan,		Rs.
1.	Cash in hand	1,200
5.	Received from Ram	300
7.	Paid rent	30
8.	Sold goods for cash	300
10.	Paid Shyam	700
27.	Purchased furniture	200
28.	Paid salaries	100
31.	Rent due not yet paid for January	30

Solution

Single Cash Book

Date	*Particulars*	*LF*	*Amt.*	*Date*	*Particulars*	*LF*	*Amt.*
1-1-95	To Balance b/d		1,200	7-1-95	By Rent a/c		30
5-1-95	To Ram's a/c		300	10-1-95	By Shyam's a/c		700
8-1-95	To Sales a/c		300	27-1-95	By Furniture a/c		200
				28-1-95	By Salaries a/c		100
				31-1-95	By Balance b/d		770
			1,800				1,800
1-2-95	To Balance b/d		770				

Problem 3

Shri Arvind commenced business with Rs 10,000 in cash on 1-1-2005. His cash receipts and payments for the month of January are as follows :

2005 Jan,		
2.	Purchased goods for cash	Rs. 5,000
5.	Sold goods for cash	Rs. 2,000
7.	Paid office expenses	Rs. 200
10.	Purchased goods for cash	Rs. 2,000
12.	Postage	Rs. 25
15.	Gave cash to Ramesh	Rs. 3,000
17.	Received cash from Mahesh	Rs. 200
20.	Sold goods for cash	Rs. 1,000
21.	Purchased goods for cash	Rs. 900
25.	Purchased furniture for cash	Rs. 560
31.	Paid wages	Rs. 300
31.	Paid salaries	Rs. 500
31.	Paid rent	Rs. 100

Solution

Cash Book

Date	Particulars	LF	Amt.	Date	Particulars	LF	Amt.
1-1-95	To Capital a/c		10,000	2-1-95	By Purchase a/c		5,000
5-1-95	To Sales a/c		2,000	7-1-95	By Office expenses a/c		200
17-1-95	To Mahesh a/c		200	10-1-95	By Purchases a/c		2000
20-1-95	To Sales a/c		1,000	12-1-95	By Postage a/c		25
				15-1-95	By Ramesh a/c		3,000
				22-1-95	By Purchases a/c		900
				25-1-95	By Furniture a/c		560
				31-1-95	By Wages a/c		300
				31-1-95	By Salaries a/c		500
				31-1-95	By Rent a/c		100
				31-1-95	By Balance b/d		615
			13,200				13,200
Feb 1, 95	To Balance b/d		615				

4. CASH BOOK WITH CASH AND DISCOUNT COLUMNS

In this book an additional column is provided to record cash discount in addition to cash column on either side of the cash account. On the debit side the discount allowed column is provided and on the credit side discount received column is provided. This book is also called as two column cash book.

Cash Discount : Cash discount is an inducement given to a credit customer in order to encourage him to pay the debt promptly or within a certain time limit, the amount of cash discount is deducted from the amount due to the businessman. It may be represented as 4% for cash or 2% within a month. The former means that if a customer pays promptly 4% deduction is allowed. The latter means that if he pays within a month from the date of transaction, 2% deduction will be allowed. The cash discount is also known as "sale discount" from the seller's point of view and purchases discount form the purchaser's point of view. A separate column is provided on the cash book or cash receipt journal when the amount is received from a customer who has availed the cash discount, the actual amount (amount due minus discount) is recorded in cash column and discount allowed is recorded in the discount column. Similarly actual cash paid is entered in the cash column and discount received under discount column on the credit side. Discount allowed being a loss is debited and discount received being a gain is credited. A proforma of such cash book is shown below :

Cash Book with Cash and Discount Column

Date	Particulars	LF	Discount	Cash	Date	Particulars	LF	Discount	Cash

Balancing of Two Column Cash Book : The discount columns of this book are not balanced. They are merely totalled. The discount column on the receipt side shows the total discount allowed to customers. This amount is debited to the discount account. The discount column on the payment side shows the total discount received. This amount is credited to discount. However the cash columns are balanced as explained under simple cash book.

Problem 4

Gokulnath commenced business on 1st April 2004 with Rs. 2,000 as capital. He had the following cash transactions in the month of April. Prepare a cash book.

2004 April,

1.	Purchased furniture and paid cash	Rs. 250
2.	Purchased goods	Rs. 300
4.	Sold goods for cash	Rs. 150
5.	Purchased goods	Rs. 200
5.	Paid cash to Rama	Rs. 560
5.	He allowed discount	Rs. 10
6.	Received cash from Krishna	Rs. 600
	Allowed discount	Rs. 20
7.	Paid for petty expenses	Rs. 15
8.	Cash purchases	Rs. 150
9.	Cash sales	Rs. 200
11.	Received from Mohan	Rs. 600
13.	Paid for typewriter	Rs. 800
15.	Paid for telephone	Rs. 200
30.	Paid Anand	Rs. 400
	Discount allowed	Rs. 8

Solution

Cash Book with Cash and Discount Column

Date	*Particulars*	*LF*	*Discount*	*Cash*	*Date*	*Particulars*	*LF*	*Discount*	*Cash*
April 1.	To Capital a/c			2000	April 1.	By Furniture a/c			250
4.	To Sales a/c			150	2.	By Purchases a/c			300
6.	To Krishna		20	600	5.	By Purchases a/c			200
9.	To Sales a/c			200	5.	By Ramesh a/c		10	560
11.	To Mohan's a/c			600	7.	By Petty expense a/c			15
					8.	By Purchases a/c			150
					13.	By Typewriter a/c			800
					15.	By Telephone a/c			200
					30.	By Anand's a/c		8	400
					30.	By Balance a/c			675
			20	3,550				18	3,550
May 1.	To Balance b/d			675					

Problem 5

Enter the following transactions of Prakash in a Double Column Cash Book
2004 July,

1.	Balance of cash in hand	Rs. 1,600
2.	Paid to Mohan	Rs. 780
	Discount allowed	Rs. 20
3.	Cash sales	Rs. 400
4.	Sale of old newspaper	Rs. 20
5.	Paid for duplicator	Rs. 1,000
6.	Withdrawn from Bank	Rs. 400
7.	Received from Anand (in full settlement of his debt of Rs. 600)	Rs. 570
8.	Sale of old furniture	Rs. 300
9.	Received from Raghu	Rs. 400
	Discount allowed	Rs. 15
10.	Paid wages	Rs. 500
11.	Received from Raja against debt personally written off	Rs. 150

Solution

Cash Book with Cash and Discount Columns

Date	*Particulars*	*LF*	*Discount*	*Cash*	*Date*	*Particulars*	*LF*	*Discount*	*Cash*
July 1.	To Balance b/d			1,600	July 2.	By Mohan's a/c		20	780
3.	To Sales a/c			400	5.	By Duplicators a/c			1,000
4.	To Sales a/c			20	10.	By Wages			500
6.	To Bank a/c			400	11.	By Balance b/d			1,560
7.	To Anand		30	570					
8.	To Furniture			300					
9.	Ram		15	400					
11.	Bad debts recovered a/c			150					
			45	3,840				20	3,840

Problem 6

Rakesh commenced business on 1-1-05 with Rs. 15,000 cash. Prepare two column cash book taking into consideration the following :

2005 Jan,

3.	Paid cash to Suresh	Rs. 800
	Allowed discount	Rs. 10
5.	Received from Mohan	Rs. 900
	allowed him discount	Rs. 15
7.	Purchased goods for cash	Rs. 6,000
10.	Sold goods for cash	Rs. 4,000
12.	Purchased goods for cash	Rs. 3,000
15.	Sold goods for cash	Rs. 2,000

17. Amount of Rs. 600 was payable to Suresh which has been paid after deducting 2% discount.
20. Goods Purchased for cash Rs. 4,410
25. Deposited in bank Rs. 500
28. Received from Dinesh Rs. 2,000
    Allowed him discount Rs. 30
29. Paid Rs. 340 to Mahesh in full settlement of his account of Rs. 400
29. Withdrew for personal use Rs. 150
30. Purchased goods for cash Rs. 9,600
31. Purchased goods from Dinesh for cash Rs. 588
31. Sold goods to Mohan for cash Rs. 2,850

Solution

Cash Book

Date	*Particulars*	*LF*	*Dis-count*	*Amt.*	*Date*	*Particulars*	*LF*	*Dis-count*	*Amt.*
Jan 1.	To Capital a/c			15,000	Jan 3.	By Suresh		10	800
5.	To Mohan's a/c		15	900	7.	By Purchases			6,000
10.	To Sales a/c			4,000	12.	By Purchases			3,000
15.	To Sales a/c			2,000	17.	By Suresh *1		12	588
28.	To Dinesh a/c		30	2,000	20.	By Purchases a/c			4,400
31.	To Sales a/c			2,850	25.	By Bank a/c			500
					29.	By Mahesh*2		60	340
					29.	By Drawings			150
					30.	By Purchases a/c			9,600
					31.	By Purchases a/c			588
					31.	By Balance c/d			774
			45	26,750				82	26,750
Feb 1.	To Balance b/d			774					

Working Note – 1

1. $\frac{600 \times 2}{100} = 12 \; (600 - 12 = 588)$
2. (400 – 340 = Rs. 60)

5. THREE COLUMN CASH BOOK OR CASH BOOK WITH CASH BANK AND DISCOUNT COLUMNS

This book contains three columns to record discount, cash and bank on either side of the cash book. It is to be noted that discount account is a nominal account, cash account is a real account and Bank account is a personal account. This book is more important to a businessman who deals with cash and bank transactions. Sometimes a businessman deals simultaneously with cash and bank transactions As both cash and bank columns exist side by side, it is possible to record and trace transactions without delay. Some examples of transactions affecting both cash and bank accounts simultaneously are cash deposits, cash withdrawn, cheques issued, cheques deposited, etc.

Most of the medium and large sized business enterprises make use of a bank by opening an account with it for facilitating cash receipts and cash payments. Especially large sums of money is usually paid by cheques. Similarly, surplus cash which is not required for regular dealings in the business is also deposited with the bank for ensuring its safety. The type of account opened by the businessman with a bank is commonly the current account. The amount is deposited with the help of pay-in-slips and cash is withdrawn by means of cheques. Cash payments are also made by issuing cheques to the supplies of goods. So a bank column is inserted in the cash book of a businessman.

Contra Entry : If the same entry appears on both debit and credit side then the entry is referred to as contra entry. In the ledger folio column the letter 'C' is written against such contra entry.

A specimen of a three column cash book is given below :

Three Column Cash Book

Date	*Particulars*	*LF*	*Dis-count*	*Cash*	*Bank*	*Date*	*Particulars*	*LF*	*Dis-count*	*Cash*	*Bank*

Guidelines for preparing a three column cash book :

1. **Cheque or Bank draft received on some account which is not deposited into the bank on same day.** It is to be treated as cash and recorded in the cash column on the debit side.
2. **Cheque, Bankdraft or cash received on some account and is deposited into the same date.** It is to be entered in the bank column on the debit side.
3. **Cheque, Bankdraft or cash deposited into bank by others.** It has to be recorded in the bank column on the debit side.
4. **Cheque, Bankdraft or cash deposited into the bank by the businessman.** Such transaction appears on both sides of the cash book. Hence it is a contra entry. Under the cash column on the credit side an entry is to be made as "By Bank account". Under the bank column on the debit side an entry is made as "To Cash account".
5. **Payment made by cheque.** Record it under the bank column on the credit side.
6. **Cheques drawn for business use.** It is a contra entry. Record it on the debit side under cash column as "To Bank a/c" to indicate withdrawal from the bank Record on the credit side under Bank Column as "By cash account" to record the payment made by the bank.
7. **Cheques drawn for personal use.** It is to be recorded on the credit side under bank column as "By Drawings".
8. **Bank charges debited by the bank.** It is to be recorded on the credit side under bank column as "Bank charges a/c".

9. **Income earned from Bank.** It is to be recorded on the debit side under bank column as "Interest a/c".
10. **Cheque endorsed to others.** It is to be recorded on the debit side under cash column as " To concerned parties account".
    When it is endorsed it is to be recorded on the credit side under cash column.
11. **Dishonours of the cheque issued to others.** It is to be recorded on the debit side under bank column to cancel the payment made to the party.
12. **Dishonours of the cheque issued by others.** It is to be recorded on the credit side under the bank column as "By concerned person's a/c".

6. BALANCING THE THREE COLUMN CASH BOOK

As in the case of two column cash book the discount columns are totalled but not balanced. The cash columns are balanced exactly in the same manner as indicated in the single column cash book. The process is similar for balancing the bank column also. However it is possible that the bank may allow the businessman to withdraw more than the amount deposited i.e., to have an overdraft. In such a case, the total of the bank column on the credit side is bigger than the one on the debit side. The difference is written on the debit side as "To balance c/d". Then the totals are written on the two sides opposite one another. The balance is then entered on the credit side as "By balance b/d". The usual case is that payments into the bank will exceed the withdrawals or payments out of the bank. Then the bank columns are balanced just like the cash column.

Problem 7

Enter the following transactions in the cash book with discount cash and bank columns and show the balance.

1-1-2001 Cash in hand Rs. 250 and at Bank Rs. 10,650.
1-1-2001 Sold goods for cash and banked the proceeds Rs. 5,700.
2-1-2001 Received a cheque from Govind for Rs. 775 in full settlement of his account for Rs. 790.
3-1-2001 Sent Govind's cheque to bank for collection.
6-1-2001 Bought goods and paid by cheque Rs. 5,000.
10-1-2001 Paid rent for the month of November by cheque Rs. 500.
15-1-2001 Received a cheque for commission earned from Mr. Kalidas of Dharwar and sent the same to bank for collection Rs. 600.
20-1-2001 Bought postage stamp Rs. 50.

Solution

Cash Book with Cash Bank and Discount Column

Date	Particulars	LF	Discount	Cash	Bank	Date	Particulars	LF	Discount	Cash	Bank
1-1-01	To Balance b/d			250	10,650	3-1-01	By Bank			775	
1-1-01	To Sales a/c				5,700	6-1-01	By Purchases				5,000
2-1-01	To Govind's a/c		15	775		10-1-01	By Rent a/c				500
15-1-01	To Commission a/c				600	20-1-01	By Postage a/c			50	
						31-1-01	By Balance c/d			200	11,450
			15	1,025	16,950					1,025	16,950
1-2-01	To Balance b/d			200	11,450						

Problem 8

Prepare a three column cash book of the following.

2002 Jan,

1.	Commenced business with cash	Rs. 10,000
2.	Paid into bank	Rs. 8,000
7.	Purchased goods by cheque	Rs. 3,000
8.	Paid Rent	Rs. 150
12.	Purchased furniture and paid by cheque	Rs. 180
15.	Cash sales	Rs. 650
16.	Issued Gopal a cheque for	Rs. 970
	Discount received	Rs. 25
18.	Received a cheque from Narayan	Rs. 1,500
	Discount allowed to him	Rs. 30
21.	Paid into bank	Rs. 1,500
25.	Paid Wages	Rs. 60
28.	Drew for office use	Rs. 400
30.	Received from Gopu	Rs. 100
31.	Withdrew for personal use by cheque	Rs. 150

Solution

Cash Bank with Cash Bank and Discount Columns

Date	*Particulars*	*LF*	*Dis-count*	*Cash*	*Bank*	*Date*	*Particulars*	*LF*	*Dis-count*	*Cash*	*Bank*
2002						2002					
Jan 1.	To Capital a/c			10,000		Jan 2.	By Bank	C		8,000	
2.	To Cash	C			8,000	7.	By Purchases a/c				3,000
15.	To Sales a/c			650		8.	By Rent a/c			150	
18.	To Naryan a/c		30	1,500		12.	By Furniture a/c				180
21.	To Cash a/c	C			1,500	16	By Gopal a/c		25		970
28.	To Bank a/c	C		400		21	By Bank a/c	C		1,500	
30.	To Gopu's a/c			100		25	By Wages			60	
						28	By Cash a/c	C			400
						31	By Drawing a/c				150
						31	By Balance c/d			2,940	4,800
			30	12,650	9,500				25	12,650	9,500
Feb 1.	To Balance b/d			2,940	4,800						

Problem 9

Prepare a three column cash book of Sri Chandran from the following.

2002 Jan,

1.	Cash received from sale of building	Rs. 6,000
2.	Paid into bank of opening an account	Rs. 5,600
3.	Paid Albert by cheque	Rs. 2,470
	Discount allowed by him	Rs. 20
4.	Paid wages	Rs. 150
8.	Received from Balan cheque	Rs. 980
	Allowed him discount	Rs. 20

10.	Paid into bank Balan cheque	Rs. 980
15.	Paid for stationery in cash	Rs. 50
18.	Bought goods for cash	Rs. 120
20.	Paid Madhavan by cheque	Rs. 370
	Discount allowed by him	Rs. 10
21.	Drew from bank	Rs. 150
23.	Drew from bank for private expenses	Rs. 200
24.	Received for cash sales	Rs. 170
25.	Received from Raman	Rs. 1,800
	Allowed him Discount	Rs. 40
27.	Paid into bank	Rs. 2,000

Solution

Cash book with Discount, Cash and Bank Columns

Date	*Particulars*	*LF*	*Dis-count*	*Cash*	*Bank*	*Date*	*Particulars*	*LF*	*Dis-count*	*Cash*	*Bank*
2002						2002					
Jan, 1.	To Buildings a/c			6,000		Jan 2.	By Bank	C		5,600	
2.	To Cash a/c	C			5,600	3.	By Albert		20		2,470
8.	To Balance a/c		20	980		4.	By wages			150	
10.	To Cash a/c	C			980	10.	By Bank	C		980	
21.	To Bank a/c	C		150		15.	By Stationary			50	
24.	To 24 Sales			170		18.	By Purchases			120	
25.	To Raman		40	1,800		20.	By Madhavan		10		370
27.	To Cash	C				21.	By Cash	C			150
					2,000	23.	By Drawings				200
						27.	By Bank	C		2,000	
						31.	By Balance c/d			200	5,390
			60	9,100	8,580				30	9,100	8,580
Feb 1	To Balance b/d			200	5,390						

Problem 10

The Cash book of Gopal Krishna is accidentally burnt. It is known that on 1st Jan 2005, there was Rs. 100 cash on hand and Rs. 4,000 in Bank.

The Counterfoil of the Receipt Book Shows.

		Rs.	Discount
Jan 2.	Thomas & sons	2,000	5
4.	Krishna & Co.	1,000	10
5.	Menon & Co.	600	3

The counter foil of the cheque book shows

		Rs.	Discount
Jan 2.	Petty expenses	30	
	Rally & Bros	1,500	8
6.	Office Cash	400	
7.	Wilson & Co.	1,600	8

The receipt account file shows receipts given by the following :

		Rs.	Discount
Jan 3.	Sitaram Mills	500	3
5.	Addison & Co.	140	2

The Bank paying-in-Book contains memorandum of accounts passed with bank

		Rs.	Discount
Jan 3.	Cash	200	
4.	Cheque	2,000	

Write up a new cash book incorporating the above data and show the amount of cash in hand and at bank on Jan 7, 2005.

Solution

New Cash Book of Gopal Krishna

Date	Particulars	LF	Discount	Cash	Bank	Date	Particulars	LF	Discount	Cash	Bank
2005						2005					
Jan 1.	To Balance b/d			100	4,000	Jan 2	By Petty expenses				30
2.	To Thomas & Sons		5	2,000			By Rally & Bros		8		1,500
3.	To Cash	C			200	3	By Sitaram Mills		3	500	
4.	To Krishna & Co.		10	1,000			By Bank	C		200	
5.	To Menon & Co.		3	600		5	By Addison & Co.		2	140	
	To Cash	C			2,000	6	By Office cash	C			400
	To Bank	C		400		7	By Wilson & Co.		8		1,600
							By Balance c/d			3,260	2,670
			18	4,100	6,200				21	4,100	6,200

Problem 11

Enter the following transactions in cash book with discount and bank columns. Cheques are first treated as cash receipts.

2005 Jan,

1.	Chandrashekar commenced business with cash	Rs. 20,000
3.	He paid into Bank account	Rs. 19,000
4.	He received cheque from Kirti & Co. on account	Rs. 600
7.	He pays in bank Kirti & Co's cheque	Rs. 600
10.	He pays Rattan & Co. by cheque Rs. 330 and is allowed discount	Rs. 20
12.	Tripathi & Co. pays into his bank a/c	Rs. 475
15.	He receives cheque from Warshi for Rs. 450 & allows him discount	Rs. 35
20.	He receives cash Rs. 75 and cheque Rs 100 for cash sale.	
25.	He pays into Bank including cheques received on 15th and 20th	Rs. 1,000
27.	He pays by cheque for cash purchase	Rs. 275
30.	He pays sundry expenses in cash	Rs. 50
30.	He pays John & Co. in cash Rs. 375 and is allowed discount	Rs. 35
31.	He pays office rent by cheque	Rs. 200
31.	He draws a cheque for personal use	Rs. 250
31.	He pays staff salaries by cheque	Rs. 300
31.	He draws a cheque for office use	Rs. 400
31.	He pays cash for stationery	Rs. 25
31.	He purchases goods for cash	Rs. 125
31.	He gives cheque to Ramcharan for Cash purchases of furniture for office	Rs. 1,575

31. He receives cheque for commission from Raghu & Co and immediately pays the same into bank Rs. 500
31. Receives cheque from kesari & Co Rs. 450

Solution

Cash Book with Cash Discount and Bank Columns

Date	Particulars	LF	Discount	Cash	Bank	Date	Particulars	LF	Discount	Cash	Bank
1995						1995					
Jan 1.	To Capital a/c			20,000		Jan 3.	By Bank a/c	C		19,000	
3.	To Cash a/c	C			19,000	7.	By Bank a/c	C		600	
4.	To Kirti & Co. a/c			600		10.	By Ratan & Co.		20		330
7.	To Cash a/c	C			600	25.	By Bank a/c	C		1,000	
12.	To Tripathi & Co. a/c				475	27.	By Purchases a/c				275
15.	To Warshi a/c		35	450		30.	By Sundry expenses a/c			50	
20.	To Sales a/c			175		31.	By John & Co.		35	375	
25.	To Cash a/c	C			1,000	31.	By Rent a/c				200
31.	To Bank a/c	C		400		31.	By Drawings a/c				250
31.	To Commission a/c				500	31.	By Salaries a/c				300
31.	To Kesari & Co.			450		31.	By Cash	C			400
						31.	By Stationery a/c			25	
						31.	By Purchases a/c			125	
						31.	By Commission a/c				300
						31.	By Furniture a/c				1,575
						31.	By Balance c/d			900	1,794
			35	22,075	21,575				55	22,075	21,575

Problem 12

Suresh started business as a coal merchant on 1st October, 2004. He put into the business Rs. 5,500 cash which he put in to the Bank . His other transactions were

Oct 1. Drew cheque for office use Rs. 250
4. Purchased account books and stationery Rs. 50
6. Sold for cash 5 cwt of coal @ Rs. 20 year cwt
8. Paid wages Rs. 25
12. Paid by cheque to Narasimhan the amount due less 5% cash discount
16. Norwood paid his account by cheque less $2\frac{1}{2}$% cash discount.
17. Paid rent out of cash Rs. 100
31. Paid salaries out of Bank Rs. 150
31. Drew for Domestic use cheque Rs. 200

Write up a three column cash book incorporating the above transactions.

Solution

Cash Book with Discount Cash and Bank Columns

Date	Particulars	LF	Discount	Cash	Bank	Date	Particulars	LF	Discount	Cash	Bank
2004						2004					
Oct 1.	To Capital a/c				5,500	Oct 1.	By Cash a/c	C			250
1.	To Bank a/c	C		250		4.	By Stationery a/c			50	
6.	To Sales a/c			100		8.	By Wages a/c			25	
16.	To Norwood a/c		8		312	12.	By Narshimhan's a/c		125	2,375	
						17.	By Rent a/c			100	
						31.	By Salaries a/c				150
						31.	By Drawing				200
						31.	By Balance c/d			175	2,337
			8	350	5,312				125	350	5,312

Problem 13

Enter the following transactions into a three column cash book and balance the same.

2005		Rs.
Jan 1.	Cash in hand	3,000
2.	Cash at Bank	10,000
3.	Sold goods for cash	10,000
4.	Deposited into Bank	8,000
5.	Received from Nandalal	4,000
	Allowed him discount	100
6.	Paid house rent by cheque	1,000
7.	Paid to Shyamlal	5,000
	Received Discount	50
9.	With drawn from bank for office use	5,000
10.	Received a cheque of Rs. 407 from Mohan in full settlement of his account of	500
11.	Cash sales deposited into Bank	2,500
12.	Cash Sales	1,000
13.	Paid Mr. Agarwal by cheque against his claim of Rs. 2,000 at a discount of 5%	
14.	Paid travelling expenses	700
15.	Drawn cheque for personal use	1,000

Solution

Cash Book with Discount Cash and Bank Columns

Date	Particulars	LF	Discount	Cash	Bank	Date	Particulars	LF	Discount	Cash	Bank
2005						2005					
Jan 1.	To Balance b/d			3,000		Jan 4.	By Bank a/c	C		8,000	
2.	To Balance b/d				10,000	6.	By House rent a/c				1,000
3.	To Sales a/c			10,000		7.	By Shyamlal a/c		50	5,000	
4.	To Cash a/c	C			8,000	9.	By Cash a/c	C			5,000

Date	Particulars	LF	Discount	Cash	Bank	Date	Particulars	LF	Discount	Cash	Bank
5.	To Nandalal's a/c		100	4,000		13.	By Agarwala a/c		100		1,900
9.	To Bank a/c	C		5,000		14.	By Travelling expenses			700	
10.	To Mohan's a/c		30		470	15.	By Drawings				1,000
11.	To Sales				2,500	31.	By Balance c/d			9,300	12,070
12.	To Sales			1,000							
			130	23,000	20,970				150	23,000	20,970

Problem 14

Enter the following transactions in a cash book with cash discount and bank columns and balance the same.

2005 Jan,

1. Balance of cash in hand Rs. 400 and at Bank Rs. 2,000
3. Paid Ramlal by cheque Rs. 950 in full settlement of his account for Rs. 1000
5. Purchased goods for cash Rs. 100
5. Purchased goods and paid by cheque Rs. 300
7. Withdrew cash from Bank for office use Rs. 300
8. Paid wages Rs. 200
10. Paid Modi by cheque Rs. 150
15. Rajeev purchased goods from us for cash Rs. 1,000
18. Received cheque from Murthy Rs. 320 in full settlement of his account for Rs. 350
22. Paid Rs. 1,000 into the bank.
25. Paid Gulam Rs. 175 in full settlement of his account Rs. 180
31. Drew cheque for period use Rs. 50

Solution

Cash Book with Discount and Bank Columns

Date	Particulars	LF	Discount	Cash	Bank	Date	Particulars	LF	Discount	Cash	Bank
2005						2005					
Jan 1.	To Balance b/d			400	2,000	Jan 3.	By Ramlal a/c		50		950
7.	To Bank	C		300		5.	By Purchases a/c				300
15.	To Sales			1,000		7.	By Cash a/c	C			300
18.	To Murthy's a/c		30	320		8.	By Wages a/c			200	
22.	To Cash				1,000	10.	By Modi's a/c				150
						22.	By Bank a/c	C		1,000	
						25.	By Gulam's a/c		5	175	
						31.	By Drawings				50
						31.	By Balance c/d			545	1,250
			30	2,020	3,000				55	2,020	3,000

6. CASH BOOK WITH BANK AND DISCOUNT COLUMNS

This type of cash book is maintained by large sized business organisations which deposit all the cash into the bank and all payments are made by cheque. Even petty cash expenses are paid by cheques to the petty cashier. This type of cash book contains columns for Bank and discount an either side of the cash account i.e., debit and credit sides. The proforma of such type of cash book is shown below.

Cash Book with Bank and Discount Columns.

Date	*Particulars*	*Discount*	*Bank*	*Date*	*Particulars*	*Discount*	*Bank*

Problem 15

Arun Kumar of Bangalore deposits all his daily receipts in a bank and makes all payments through bank. Following transactions took place in April 2004. Prepare cash book with bank and discount columns.

2004 April,

1.	Debit balance of bank	Rs. 8,000
5.	Received Rs. 2,000 from Mohan in full settlement of the amount of	Rs. 2,050
7.	Paid Rs. 2500 to Suresh, he allowed discount of	Rs. 25
10.	Purchased goods	Rs. 4,950
15.	Paid Rs. 200 for wages and Rs. 700 for salaries.	
20.	Received Rs. 1000 from Mohan	
25.	Purchased furniture for	Rs. 500
27.	Received Rs. 300 from Dinesh and allowed him discount	Rs. 15
28.	Received Rs. 900 from Mr. 'X' and allowed him discount	Rs. 10
29.	Paid Rs. 3,000 to Mr. 'B' by cheque.	

Solution

Cash Book With Bank and Discount Columns

Date	*Particulars*	*Discount*	*Bank*	*Date*	*Particulars*	*Discount*	*Bank*
2004				2004			
April 1.	To Balance b/d		8,000	April 7.	By Suresh	25	2,500
5.	To Mohan's a/c	50	2,000	10.	By Purchases		4,950
20.	To Mohan's a/c		1,000	15.	By Wages a/c		200
27.	To Dinesh	15	300	15.	By Salaries		700
28.	To Mr. 'X'	10	900	25.	By Furniture a/c		500
				29.	By B's a/c		3,000
				30.	By Balance a/c		350
		25	12,200			25	12,200

Problem 16

Enter the following transactions in a cash book with discount and bank columns assuming that all receipts are banked immediately and all payments are made by cheque and post them into ledger.

2005 March,

1.	Capital paid into bank	Rs. 10,000
2.	Bought goods for cash	Rs. 2,000
4.	Sold goods for cash	Rs. 1,500
6.	Purchased office furniture	Rs. 500
6.	Received commission	Rs. 50
10.	Received a cheque from Sastri for Rs. 490 in full settlement of his account for	Rs. 500
12.	Gave Chand & Co. a cheque for Rs. 500 in full settlement of their account for	Rs. 520
15.	Drew for personal use	Rs. 500
17.	Sold goods to Johnson for Rs. 800 and received a cheque for the same	
20.	Drew a cheque for petty cash	Rs. 100
22.	Made cash purchases	Rs. 300
25.	Paid office rent	Rs. 200
28.	Mohan paid us Rs. 195 in full settlement of his account for	Rs. 200
31.	Paid office salaries	Rs. 300

Solution

Cash Book with Bank and Discount Columns

Date	*Particulars*	*Discount*	*Cash*	*Date*	*Particulars*	*Discount*	*Cash*
2005				2005			
Mar 1.	To Cash a/c		10,000	Mar, 2.	By Purchases a/c		2,000
4.	To Sales a/c		1,500	6.	By Furniture a/c		500
6.	To Commission a/c		50	12.	By Chand & Co.	20	500
10.	To Sastri's a/c	10	490	15.	By Drawings a/c		500
17.	To Sales		800	20.	By Petty expenses		100
28.	To Mohan's	5	195	22.	By Purchases a/c		300
				25.	By Rent a/c		200
				31.	By Salaries a/c		300
				31.	By Balance b/d		8,635
		15	13,035			20	13,035

7. PETTY CASH BOOK

A petty cash book is used to record all cash payments of smaller denominations. Examples of such payments are printing and stationery, postage and telegrams, carriage and cartage, travelling expenses etc. All transactions of this type if recorded in the cash book amounts to overloading it. To reduce the burden of the chief cashier, petty cashier is appointed and he is given a small amount of cash say Rs. 200 or 500 which is quite sufficient to meet expenses of above nature for a given period of time, say, a month. The petty cashier incurs the petty expenses and makes the entry in the petty cash book. The payment of such expenses is supported by vouchers or receipts at the end of the period, say a month. The petty cashier submits the accounts to the chief cashier. After examining the accounts of the petty cashier, the chief cashier will again pay him the actual amount spent by him. Thus it will he seen that the petty cashier will have the same amount of cash balance which he had on the first day of the previous month.

Types of Petty Cash Book :

Petty cash book can be maintained under two types, viz (1) Simple petty cash book and (2) Analytical petty cash book with impress system.

Simple petty Cash book :-

This type of petty cash book resemble to a simple cash book discussed earlier with one difference. Instead of providing separate columns for date and particulars on both debit and credit side, a single column is provided from date and particulars. In other words this type of petty cash book will not have two sides and therefore it does not resemble to an account. However a column is provided on the left extreme of the page to record the petty expenses amount received by the petty cashier from the chief cashier. One distinct feature of this book is all expenses are recorded in the particulars column. This book is closed at the end of a given period to know the balance. The balance is then carried forward to the next month and transactions for that month is subsquently recorded.

Problem 17

Prepare a simple petty cash book in the books of Saranath from the following particulars for January 2005.

1.	Balance with the petty cashier	Rs. 50
1.	Received a cheque of Rs. 450 from the chief cashier.	
3.	Paid for stationery	Rs. 75
8.	Paid for refreshments	Rs. 35
12.	Paid for newspaper	Rs. 35
13.	Paid for carriage and cartage	Rs. 50
14.	Paid for postage	Rs. 40
19.	Paid conveyance to a clerk	Rs. 15
31.	Paid for telegram	Rs. 80

Solution

Simple Petty Cash Book

Amount Received	*Cash Book folio*	*Date*	*Particulars*	*Voucher No.*	*LF*	*Amount*
50.00		Jan 1.	To Balance b/d			
450.00		1.	To Bank a/c			
		3.	To Printing & stationery a/c			75.00
		8.	To Sundry expenses a/c			35.00
		12.	To Sundry expenses a/c			35.00
		13.	To Carriage & cartage a/c			50.00
		14.	To Postage a/c			40.00
		19.	To Conveyance a/c			15.00
		31.	To Telegram a/c			80.00
		31.	To Balance c/d			170.00
500.00						500.00

8. ANALYTICAL PETTY CASH BOOK WITH IMPREST SYSTEM

This is a modified type of simple petty cash book. It consists of two sides as in the case of any other type of cash book, i.e., debit and credit sides. The debit side is used to record the imprest or petty cash received by the petty cashier from the chief cashier at the beginning of the month. The credit side is used to record various petty expenses. These petty expenses are analysed into various columns to indicate the nature of petty expenses. Hence this type of petty cash book is also known as analytical petty cash book. In other words a separate column is provided for each item of petty expenses. So this type of petty cash book is also known as columnar petty cash book. Whenever any petty expense is incurred it is first recorded in the total payment column. Subsequently they are recorded under the relevant expense column. This facilities the total amount of petty expenses of different types incurred every month by adding up the relevant columns. It also facilities posting of periodical total of each column to the ledger instead of posting individual expenses . It is also possible to know the total petty expenses of all types incurred for a given period of time. This system is also known as imprest system of petty cash book. Under this system the chief cashier hands over a certain amount of cash to the petty cashier for a specific period, say, a month. At the end of the month, the petty cashier will submit the account to the chief cashier, who will inturn hand over the exact amount spent by the petty cashier in the preceding month. Thus the petty cashier will have the same balance of cash as he had in the previous month to start with. This balance of amount which remains same throughout the commencement of every month is known as imprest amount and the type of cash book using this principle is called as imprest system of cash book.

Problem 18

Write up the following transactions in the analytical petty cash book and balance the same.

2000 Jan,

1.	Advanced to petty cash by cheque	Rs. 600
4.	Paid cartage	Rs. 50
6.	Purchased postage stamps	Rs. 30
10.	Spent for telegrams	Rs. 20
15.	Wicks for lamps purchased	Rs. 30
16.	Paid packing charges	Rs. 20
20.	Paid advertisement charges	Rs. 60
30.	Paid for letter paper	Rs. 30
30.	Bought oil for lamps	Rs. 60

***See Solution on next page**

Solution. 18

Analytical Petty Cash

Amount Received	Cash book folio	Date	Particulars	Voucher Number	Total of payment	Analysis of Payments: Carriage	Postage stamps	Telegram	Lamps	Packing	Advt.	letter paper
600	–	1-1-2000	To Bank	–	–	–						
		4-1-2000	By Carriage	1	50	50	–					
		6-1-2000	By Postage stamps	2	30		30					
		10-1-2000	By Telegrams	3	20			20				
		15-1-2000	By Wicks for lamps	4	30				30			
		18-1-2000	By Packing	5	20					20		
		20-1-2000	By Advertisement	6	60						60	
		30-1-2000	By Letter paper	7	30							30
		30-1-2000	By Oil for lamps	8	60				60			
					300	50	30	20	90	20	60	30
		31-1-2000	By Balance c/d		300							
600					600							
		1-2-70	To Balance b/d		300							

Problem 19

Rule a petty cash book with four analysis columns for postage and stationary, travelling expenses, carriage and office expenses and enter up the following transactions. The book is kept on imprest system, the amount being Rs. 750 only

2004, Jan		Rs.
4.	Petty cash in hand	30
	Received cash to make up the imprest	720
	Paid bus fare	10
	Bought stamps	50
5.	Paid railway fare	250
	Telegram charges paid	50
	Bought short-hand note book for office	10
6.	Paid carriage on small parcels	20
8.	Paid for repairs to typewriter	80
	Paid cart hire	100
9.	Paid office cleaner	50

* **See solution on page 84**

Problem 20

Mr. Ramaswamy maintains a columnar petty cash book on the imprest system. The imprest amount is Rs. 500. From the following information show how his petty cash book appear for the week ended 12th Sept. 2004

		Rs.
7-9-2004.	Balance in hand	134.90
	Received cash reimbursement to make up the imprest	365.10
	Postage	12.30
	Stationery	32.10
	Entertainment	5.40
8-9-2004.	Travelling and conveyance	12.60
	Miscellaneous expenses	1.10
	Entertainment	7.20
9-9-04.	Repairs	156.70
10-9-04.	Postage	17.40
	Entertainment	12.70
	Travelling	38.40
11-9-04.	Stationery	67.30
	Entertainment	4.10
12-9-04.	Miscellaneous expenses	1.20
	Postage	5.10
	Repairs	48.30

***See Solution on page 85**

Solution. 19

Analysical Petty Cash Book

Amount Received	*Cash Book Folio*	*Date*	*Particulars*	*Voucher No.*	*Total payment*	*Analysis of Payments*			
						Postage & Stationary	*Carriage expenses*	*Traveling expenses*	*Office expenses*
		2004							
30		Jan 4	To Balance b/d						
720			To Cash received						
			By Bus fare a/c	1	110	—		10	
			To Stamps a/c	2	50	50			
		5	To Railway fare a/c	3	250	—		250	
			To Telegram a/c	4	50	50			
			To Short hand note book a/c	5	10	10		—	
		6	To Carriage on parcels a/c	6	20	—	20	—	
		8	To Repairs to typewriter a/c	7	80	—	—	—	80
			To Cart hire a/c	8	—	—	100	—	
		9	To Office cleaners a/c	9	50	—	—	—	50
					620	110	120	260	130
			To Balance c/d		. 130				
750					750				

Solution. 20

Petty Cash Book

Amount Received	*Date*	*Particulars*	*Total*	*Postage*	*Stationary*	*Entertainment*	*Travelling & Conveyance*	*House allowance*	*Repairs*
134.90	7-9-94	To Balance b/d							
365.10		To Cash a/c							
		By Postage a/c	12.30	12.30					
		By Stationary a/c	32.10		32.10				
		By Entertainment	5.40			5.40			
	8-9-94	By Travelling & Conveyance	12.60				12.60		
		By Miscellaneous expenses	1.10					1.10	
	9-9-94	By Repairs a/c	156.70						156.70
	10-9-94	By Postage	17.40	17.40					
		By Entertainment	12.70			12.70			
		By Travelling expenses	38.40				38.40		
	11-9-94	By Stationary	67.30		67.30				
		By Entertainment	4.10			4.10			
	12-9-94	By Miscellaneous expenses	1.20					1.20	
		By Postage	5.10	5.10					
		By Repairs	48.30						48.30
			421.90	34.80	99.40	29.40	51.00	2.30	205.00
		By Balance c/d	78.10						
500.00			500.00						

Problem 21

On 1-1-05 a sum of Rs. 500 was advanced to the petty cashier who renders accounts weekly. Transactions for a fortnight are as follows. Prepare Petty Cash Book.

2-1-05	Paid printing & stationary	Rs. 100
2-1-05	Paid postage	Rs. 10
5-1-05	Paid Cartage	Rs. 200
6-1-05	Paid ledger account (A)	Rs. 180
9-1-05	Printing and stationary	Rs. 150
10-1-05	Travelling	Rs. 50
11-1-05	Postal charges	Rs. 60
12-1-05	Cooly Cartage	Rs. 40
13-1-05	Printing & stationery	Rs. 20
14-1-05	Postage	Rs. 20
14-1-05	Conveyance	Rs. 40

***See Solution on page 87**

POSTING OF CASH BOOK

The entries from the cash book are posted into the concerned ledger accounts. When an entry is posted from the cash book to the ledger book account the number of the page of the cash book is written in the Folio column against the amount in the ledger. At the same time the page of the ledger on which the entry has been posted is entered in the ledger folio column against the entry in the cash book.

Posting the entries from Cash receipt journal or debit items in the Cash Book :

The transactions from the cash receipt journal or from the debit side of cash book are posted daily to the credit side of the respective accounts. For example, if interest is received cash account is debited and interest account is credited. Similarly if cash is received from Govind, cash account is debited and Govind's account is credited. If cash is received on account of cash sales, cash account will be debited and sales account is credited. In other words all accounts which are recorded in the cash receipt Journal or the debit items of the cash book are credited to their respective accounts.

Solution. 21

Petty Cash Book

Amount Received	Date	Particulars	Total	Printing & Stationary	Travelling & Conveyance	Postage & Telegram	Cooly & Cartage	Miscellaneous
500.00	1-1-05	To Cash						
	2-1-05	By printing & stationary	100	100				
	2-1-05	By Postage	10			10		
	5-1-05	By Cartage	200				200	
	6-1-05	By Ledger A/cs (A)	180					180
			490	100		10	200	180
	7-1-05	By Balance c/d	10					
500.00			500					
10.00	8-1-05	To Balance b/d						
490.00		To Cash						
	9-1-05	By printing & stationary	150	150				
	10-1-05	By Travelling	50		50			
	11-1-05	By postage charges	60			60		
	13-1-05	By Cooly & cartage	40				40	
	13-1-05	By Printing & stationary	20	20				
	14-1-05	By Postage	20			20		
	14-1-05	By Conveyance	40		40			
			380	170	90	80	40	
	14-1-05	By Balance c/d	120					
500.00			500					

Problem 22

Enter the following transactions in a cash receipt Journal and post them into the concerned ledger accounts.

1-1-05	Sold goods for cash	Rs. 200
5-1-05	Received cash from Arjun Rs. 96 and allowed him discount	Rs. 4
10-1-05	Cash sales	Rs. 300
14-1-05	Received from Bhima Rs. 98 in full settlement of claim	Rs. 100
15-1-05	Received on cash sales	Rs. 500
20-1-95	Received cash from Nakula Rs. 145 and allowed cash discount of	Rs. 5

Solution

Cash Receipt Journal

Date	*Particulars*	*Lf*	*Cash Discount*	*Amount*
1-1-05	Sales a/c			200
5-1-05	Arjuna's a/c		4	96
10-1-05	Sales a/c			300
14-1-05	Bhima's a/c		2	98
15-1-05	Sales a/c			500
20-1-05	Nakula's a/c		5	145
			11	1,339

Ledger Accounts

[Posted at the end of the Month] **Discount A/c**

To Sundries a/c	11		

[Posted at the end of the month] **Cash A/c**

To sundries a/c	1,339		

Sales A/c **[Posted daily]**

		By Cash a/c	200
		By Cash a/c	300
		By Cash a/c	500

Arjun's A/c **[Posted Daily]**

		By Cash a/c	96
		By Discount a/c	4

Bhima's A/c **[Posted Daily]**

		By Cash	98
		By Discount	2

Nakula's A/c **[Posted Daily]**

		By Cash	145
		By Discount	5

Note :-

When the cash book is maintained in the form of ledger account i.e., with receipts and payments column, the monthly total is not posted to cash account because the cash book itself serves the purpose of cash account.

Posting from Cash Payment Journal.

The various accounts appearing in the cash payment Journal or credit items of cash book are posted daily into various accounts on their debit sides. The total of this Journal is posted monthly into the cash and discount accounts. Cash discount received on payment is in the nature of revenue. Hence, this is credited into discount account and debited to the person to whom the payment is made.

Problem 23

Enter the following transactions in a cash payment journal and post them into concerned ledger accounts.

1-2-05.	Purchased goods for cash	Rs. 5,000
10-2-05.	Paid Rent for the month of January	Rs. 500
15-2-05.	Paid to Nandagopal Rs. 280 ; Cash discount	Rs. 20
20-2-05.	Paid to Madangopal Rs. 145 ; Cash discount	Rs. 5
25-2-05.	Purchased goods for cash	Rs. 2000.
28-2-05.	Paid salary	Rs. 1,500

Solution

Cash Payment Journal

Date	*Particulars*	*Lf*	*Cash Discount*	*Amount*
1-2-05	Purchases a/c			5,000
10-2-05	Rent			500
15-2-05	Nandagopal		20	280
20-2-05	Madangopal		5	145
25-2-05	Purchases			2,000
28-2-05	Salary			1,500
			25	9,425

Ledger A/c

Discount A/c [Posted at the end of the month]

			By Sundries	25

Cash A/c [Posted at the end of the month]

			By Sundries	9,425

Purchases A/c

1-2-05	To Cash a/c	5,000		
25-2-05	To Cash a/c	2,000		

Rent Ac

	To Cash a/c	500		

Nandagopal's A/c

	To Cash a/c	280		
	To Discount a/c	20		

Madangopal's A/c

To Cash a/c	145		
To Discount a/c	5		

Salaries A/c

To Cash	1,500		

Recording of Discounts Subsequently Disallowed

A trader may at times wrongly deduct a cash discount though it might not have been allowed to him. In such a situation the discount amount deducted should be rectified by passing the following entry.

Discount received Dr.
To Creditor's a/c

Creditor here stands for the person to whom the payment is made by the trader.

Similarly, when the customer deducts any discount which is not actually allowed by the trader, only the amount received is to be recorded without recording the discount so deducted. The customer is informed about the discount which is in fact disallowed.

Disallowing of Discount Due to Dishonours of Cheque :-

When a cheque is presented into the bank it may be dishonoured by the bank for some reasons. The discount of such dishonoured cheques should not be recorded in cash book. It must be instead recorded in the Journal. The following entries are passed to set right the discount on dishonours of a cheque.

For cancelling the discount received due to dishonour of cheques issued personally :-

Discount received a/c Dr.
To creditors a/c

For cancelling the discount allowed due to dishonour of cheque received previously :-

Debtor's a/c Dr
To Discount allowed a/c

Bank Overdraft :-

While balancing the cash book it was mentioned earlier that the debit side of the cash book (cash column) will always be more than or equal to credit side as it is not possible to pay or incur more expenses than what is available with the trader. However the bank column of cash book may at time show a credit balance by virtue of an overdraft facility sanctioned by the bank. An overdraft is a temporary arrangement provided by the banker to his customers to draw more than the amount deposited with the bank. The bank column of cash book may even show a credit balance when withdrawal is more than the deposits made into the bank.

KEY WORDS

1. **Cash book :-**
   It is a book in which receipts and payments of cash are recorded.
2. **Cash Receipt Journal :-**
   It records all cash received by the trader from different sources.
3. **Cash payment Journal :-**
   It records all cash payment made by the trader on several accounts.

4. **Single cash book :-**
   It is used to record all receipts and payment of cash. It contains columns for cash transactions only.
5. **Cash book with cash and discount column :-**
   It records both cash receipts and payments and also discount received and allowed.
6. **Three column cash book :-**
   In this book an additional column is included for bank account an either side of cash book in addition to cash and discount columns.
7. **Petty cash book :-**
   It is book which is used to record small items of expenses and to avoid overburdening of the main cash book.
8. **Analytical petty cash book :-**
   It is a modified type of petty cash book which contains columns for various items of expenses.

QUESTIONS

1. What do you mean by a cash book ?
2. Mention three objects of cash book .
3. Mention two methods of maintaining a cash book.
4. Give the proforma of a simple cash book.
5. What do you mean by a cash receipt journal ?
6. What do you mean by a cash payment Journal ?
7. Distingush between a cash receipt journal and cash payment journal.
8. List out the various types of cash book
9. What do you mean by petty cash book ?
10. What is imprest ?
11. Mention two types of petty cash book.
12. What do you mean by contra entry ?

Answer the following questions in about a page each.

1. What is a petty cash book ? How is it maintained ?
2. Explain the imprest system of petty cash.
3. What is the object of cash book ? Further, explain the imprest system of petty cash.
4. What is a petty cash ? How is it best recorded in the books of account ?
5. What is a three column cash book ? What is its advantage ? And how is posting done from the cash book ?
6. State the points of similarities between a journal and a cash book.
7. "A cash book is both a Journal and a ledger" Do you agree. Explain.
8. What is a cash receipt Journal. Give a ruling of a cash receipt Journal.
9. What is a cash payment Journal. Give a ruling of a cash payment Journal ?
10. What is a simple cash book. How is it balanced ?
11. What do you mean by a two column cash book ? How is it balanced ?

EXERCISE 1

(Simple Cash Book)

Enter the following transactions of Aruna in a single column cash book.

2005 Jan,		Rs.
1.	Commenced business with	15,000
2.	Paid into bank	13,000
3.	Purchased goods for cash	1,500
4.	Sold goods for cash	1,100
5.	Paid for stationary	60
6.	Received from Narain	1,500
7.	Paid to Gupta	500
8.	Purchased office furniture	600

EXERCISE 2

(Simple Cash Book)

Enter the following transactions in a cash book and balance it.

2005 Mar,		Rs.
1.	Shri Avinash started business with.	4,000
3.	He purchased goods for cash	2,155
9.	Received cash for sale of goods	1,495
10.	Opened an account with Canara Bank by paying in.	1,000
14.	Purchased office furniture for cash	135
21.	Received from Manohar by postal order	475
23.	Sent by M.O. Rs. 200 to Shankar and paid of M.O. commission for the same	4
27.	Cash sales	380
28.	Paid Advertisement charges	70
31.	Trunk call expenses	5

EXERCISE 3

(Two Column Cash Book)

From the following transactions prepare a double column cash book with cash and discount columns.

2005 Mar,		Rs.
1.	Opening balance of cash	4,500
3.	Received from Krishna	3,800
	Allowed him discount	200
5.	Received from Rama	2,900
	Allowed him discount	100
7.	Paid Hari	3,150
	Allowed discount	150

9.	Received from investment interest	2,500
12.	Paid Lal	2,000
17.	Sold goods for cash	1,850
20.	Received from Singh	1,150
25.	Purchased goods from Pitambar for cash	850
31.	Paid Salaries	1,900
31.	Paid Rent	1,500
31.	Paid Advertisement	450

EXERCISE - 4

(Two Column Cash Book)

Enter the following transactions in the appropriate type of cash book.

2004 July,

1. Started business with an Investment of Rs. 1,00,000
2. Deposited in state bank of India Rs. 95,000
4. Acquired a building by issuing a cheque Rs. 60,000
10. Paid the bill of the furniture by cheque Rs. 10,000.
15. Purchased Rs. 20,000 of merchandise by cheque.
18. Withdrew Rs. 2,000 from the bank.
20. Sold merchandise for Rs. 25,000 each.
22. Deposited Rs. 22,000 into the bank.
25. Bought Rs. 5,000 merchandise for cash.
26. Sold Rs. 8,000 merchandise by crossed cheque.
27. Paid Rs. 100 cheque as the premium for insuring building against fire.
28. Paid freight Rs. 50.
30. Withdrew from bank for personal use Rs. 500.
31. Paid electricity bill Rs. 90.
    [**Hint :** Prepare a two column cash book with cash and bank columns. Problem involves contra entries. Balance c/d under bank column is Rs. 32,400 and under cash column Rs. 4,860 Total of Bank column is Rs. 1,25,000 and cash column is 1,27,000].

EXERCISE 5

(Two Column Cash Book)

Write up the cash book from the following transactions.

1-1-05.	Balance of cash on hand	Rs. 2,000
3-1-05.	Received from Keshav Rs. 580 and allowed him discount	Rs. 20
6-1-05.	Bought goods for cash	Rs. 500
8-1-05.	Sold goods for cash	Rs. 800
12-1-05.	Paid Joshi Rs. 310 in full settlement of account for	Rs. 400
15-1-05.	Paid wages	Rs. 40
19-1-05.	Bought goods for cash	Rs. 300
21-1-05.	Sold goods for cash	Rs. 400

25-1-05.	Received from Gopal Rs. 190 in full settlement of account for	Rs. 200
28-1-05.	Paid Arun Rs. 360 and was allowed discount	Rs. 40
30-1-05.	Paid salaries	Rs. 100
30-1-05.	Paid office rent	Rs. 50
31-1-05.	Received commission	Rs. 100

EXERCISE 6

(Two Column Cash Book)

Enter the following Transactions in a cash book without bank columns.

2005 April,

1. Tulasiram commences business with cash Rs. 10,000. He pays Rs. 2,300 for goods purchased. Rs. 500 for furniture purchased. Rs. 400 for office equipment.
2. He paid for stationary Rs. 100 and postage Rs. 10.
3. He sold goods to Norton on credit Rs. 800.
4. He sold goods for cash Rs. 1,800.
5. He paid wages Rs. 15, and cartage Rs. 5.
6. He bought goods for cash Rs. 700 and pays a creditor 'S' Rs. 425 in full settlement of a claim of Rs. 460.
7. He received cash from Norton Rs. 789 in full settlement of debt.
8. He sold goods for cash Rs. 50.

6

CHAPTER

Bank Reconciliation

1. INTRODUCTION

Businessmen maintain current accounts in Bank. He makes payment through cheque. Similarly all receipt of cheques will be deposited in the bank. For this purpose a separate column is provided in cash book to record the transactions of the Bank account. The Bank column in the cash book therefore, refers to the transactions relating to bank deposits and with drawals.

Pass Book or Computerised Statement of Bankers

Banks maintain the accounts of individual customers in their personal ledgers. For verification of the bank balance of the customers banks issue pass books or computerised statements wherein the customers transactions as found in the bank ledgers are entered by the bankers. Periodically, the customers may check the balance entered in the pass book with that in the cash book. Other things remaining same, the balance found in the cash book as well as the pass book must tally. But they may not. Discrepancies could arise from various reasons.

Reasons for Disagreement in the Pass Book and Cash Book Balance

The following are the reasons for the disagreement in the pass book and cash book balance :

1. **Cheques deposited into the bank for collection.** The customer makes an entry in the cash book as soon as he deposits a cheque in the bank, whereas the bank gives credit to the customers only when the cheque is realised. In the meantime, if the customer wants to compare the balance in the bank with that in his cash book he finds a difference.
2. **Cheques issued but not presented for payment.** When the customer issues a cheque he immediately enters it in the bank column of the cash book. Entry will be made by the bank regarding that cheque only when the person to whom the cheque is issued presents it for encashment or gets it encashed through his banker. In the meantime there will be a discrepancy between the balance found in the cash book and that in the pass book.
3. **Interest allowed by the bank.** Bankers credit customers accounts with interest on current accounts. This will be entered in the pass book but a corresponding entry will not be found in the cash book for some time. The customers will make the entry only after seeing the pass book.

4. **Interest on overdrafts and other bank charges.** The bank may debit the customers account with interest on overdraft or for bank charges. These items will not be entered in the cash book immediately.
5. **Dishonour of cheques and bills deposited for collection.** The cheques or bills may be deposited by the customer into the bank for collection. These may be dishonoured by the party liable to make payment. The customer might have debited his bank account as soon as he deposited these instruments. He comes to know the fact of dishonour only when the bank informs him on getting the information a credit entry is passed in the cash book. Until this the cash balance will disagree with the pass book balance.
6. **Collection of Interest, Dividend etc by the bank.** Sometimes customers may keep their securities with the bank either for safe custody or as security against overdrafts. The bank may directly receive interest or dividend on these securities and this fact may not be known to the customers. In this case there will be an entry in the pass book but no corresponding entry in the bank column of the cash book of the customer.
7. **Direct payment by the bank on behalf of the customer.** At times customers may issue standing instructions to their bankers to make payments at stipulated intervals, towards insurance premium, rent, telephone bill, electricity bill etc. In such cases the banks will debit the customers account and such entries will not be found in the cash book.
8. **Error in the pass book.** The ledger clerks at the bank may commit mistakes in posting accounts of the customers. In such cases there will be wrong entries in the pass book which will naturally not correspond with entries in the cash book.
9. **Error in the cash book.** Similarly, mistakes might occur in the maintenance of the cash book. This would also result in differences between the balances of the cash book and the pass book.
10. **Mistakes and Frauds.** Mistakes are unintentional whereas frauds are intentional. Any fraud committed either by the bank officials or the accountants of the customers would also result in discrepancies between the balance of the cash book and the pass book. One object of preparing the Bank reconciliation statement is to detect such frauds or forgeries, if any, in the transaction of the bank account. For example, if a cheque is forged and the amount is withdrawn from the bank, this can easily be detected while preparing the Bank Reconciliation statement. In this case there will be a debit entry (reduced balance) in the pass book without having any relevance to business transactions and no entry will be found in the cash book. In this case the cash book balance will be more than the pass book balance. This will provide a clue to the fraud and further investigation must be made to find the person who has drawn the amount from the bank wrongfully.

Bank Reconciliation Statement

A bank reconciliation statement is a statement wherein the causes responsible for the difference between the cash book balance and the pass book balance are established and suitable adjustments are made to eliminate them so that the two balances can agree with each other.

Steps Involved in Preparing Bank Reconciliation Statement

The following steps are involved in preparing bank reconciliation statement.

1. The date on which the reconciliation statement is to be prepared should be selected. Usually the last date of the month is chosen for the purpose.

2. The balance as shown by any one book (*i.e.*, either the cash book or the pass book) should be taken as the base. It is the starting point. This balance is to be compared with the other balance.
3. The items which cause the difference should be as ascertained.
4. The effect of causes that lead to the difference is to be analysed.
5. The causes that have resulted from in an increase in the balance are to be deducted from the bank balance.
6. The starting balance is thus adjusted and the balance as per the other book is arrived at

The following proforma is suggested.

Bank Reconciliation Statement
as at-------

Particulars	*Rs.*	*Rs.*
Debit balance as per cash book or bank OD as per pass book.		XXX
Add:		
1. Cheques issued but not presented for payment	XXX	
2. Cheques received and entered in the cash book but not sent to bank for collection	XXX	
3. Direct payments by customers into bank a/c.	XXX	
4. Amount collected by bank as interest, dividend etc. entered only in pass book	XXX	
5. Cheques not entered in cash book deposited into bank	XXX	
6. Wrong credit made in the pass book	XXX	
7. Wrong credit in the cash book	XXX	
8. Cheques issued but dishonoured	XXX	
		XXX
Less:		
1. Cheques deposited but not credited in the pass book	XXX	
2. Cheques entered in the cash book but not deposited with the bank	XXX	
3. Bank charges interest etc. debited in the pass book not entered in cash book	XXX	
4. Cheques, Bill dishonoured not entered in cash book	XXX	
5. Payment made by bank under standing orders not entered in cash book	XXX	
6. Cheques discounted but dishonoured	XXX	
7. Wrong debit in the cash book	XXX	
8. Wrong debit in the pass book	XXX	XXX
Balance as per Pass Book/Cash Book		**XXX**

Problem 1

On 31st March 2002, the cash book of Rahul showed a bank overdraft of Rs. 7,640. On the same date Rahul received the Bank statement. On perusal of the statement, Rahul ascertained the following information :

1. Cheques deposited but not credited by the bank	10,000
2. Interest on securities collected by the bank but not recorded in the cash book	1,280
3. Dividend collected by the bank directly, but not recorded in the cash book	1,000
4. Cheques issued but not presented for payment	37,400

5. Bank charges not recorded in the cash book 340

From the above information, you are required to prepare a bank reconciliation statement to as certain the balance as per bank statement **(CS Foundation Course, December 2002).**

Solution

Bank Reconciliation Statement

	Particulars	*Rs.*	*Rs.*
	Overdraft as per Cash book		7,640
Add :	Cheques deposited but not credited by the bank	10,000	
	Bank charges not recorded in the cash book	340	
			10,340
			17,980
Less :	Interest on securities collected by the bank but not recorded in the cash book.	1,280	
	Dividends collected by the bank but not recorded in the cash book	1,000	
	Cheques issued but not presented for payment	37,400	
			39,680
	Credit balance as per bank statement		21,700

Problem 2

From the following information supplied by Anil. Prepare the Bank Reconciliation Statement as on 31st March 2001, after amending the cash book.

1. Bank overdraft as per cash book Rs. 16,500
2. Cheques issued but not presented for payment Rs. 8,750
3. Cheques deposited with the bank but not collected Rs. 10,500
4. Cheque recorded in the bank column of the cash book but not sent to the bank for collection Rs. 2,000
5. Bank charges debited in the bank statement Rs. 250
6. A bill for Rs 3,000 (discounted with the bank in February 2001) dishonoured on 31st March and noting charges paid by the bank Rs. 30
7. Premium on the life insurance policy of Anil paid by the bank as per standing instructions Rs. 1,800

(CS Foundation Course, June 2001)

Solution

Cash Book (Bank Column Only)

Particulars	*Amount*	*Particulars*	*Amount*
To Balance c/d	21,580	By Balance b/d	16,500
		By Bank charges	250
		By Acceptor of Bill	3,030
		By Drawing a/c (Premium on life Insurance policy paid)	1,800
	21,580		21,580

Bank Reconciliation Statement

Particulars	Rs.	Rs.
Overdraft as per cash book		21,580
Add : Cheques deposited with the bank but not collected	10,500	
Cheques recorded in the cash book but not sent to bank for collection	2,000	
		12,500
		34,080
Less : Cheques issued but not yet presented for payment		8,750
Overdraft as per pass book		25,330

Problem 3

Following are the transactions recorded in the bank column of the cash book of Shri Madhav for the month ending 31st December 1998.

Cash Book (Bank Column)

Date	Particulars	Amount	Date	Particulars	Amount
1998 Dec			1998 Dec		
19.	To Cash	54,000	1.	By Balance b/d	60,000
24.	To Buddha	36,000	8.	By Ram	3,000
26.	To Chaitanya	15,000	10.	By Lakshman	600
			19.	By Bharat	360
31.	To Balance c/d	11,460	24.	By Satrughna	52,500
		1,16,460			1,16,460

On the receipt of the Bank statement on 31st December 1998 Shri Madhav collected the following information.

(*a*) Credit transfer not recorded in the cash book Rs. 300.
(*b*) Interest on Government bond collected by the bank but not entered in cash book Rs. 1,620.
(*c*) Cheques for Rs. 20,000 deposited but the bank collected only Rs. 5,000.
(*d*) Dividend collected by the bank directly but not intimated the same to Shri Madhav Rs. 1,500.
(*b*) Bank charges recorded twice in the cash book Rs. 510.
(*f*) Interest on overdraft charged by the bank but not entered in the cash book Rs. 1,500.
(*g*) Cheques for Rs. 66,100 issued by the trader but presented to the bank for payment only Rs 10,000.

You are asked to amend the cash book and prepare a Bank Reconciliation Statement from the above information **(Calcutta University B. Com (Hons) 1999)**

Solution

Cash Book (Amended)
(Bank Column)

Particulars	Amount	Particulars	Amount
To Credit transfer	300	31-12-98	
To Interest on Govt. Bond	1,620	By Balance b/d	11,460
To Dividend	1,500	(Incorrect)	
To Bank charges	510	By Interest on overdraft	1,500
To Balance c/d	9,030		
(correct)			
	12,960		12,960

Bank Reconciliation Statement

	Particulars	Rs.
	Bank balance as per cash book (overdrawn)	9,030
Add :	Cheques deposited but not collected by bank (20000 – 5000)	15,000
		24,030
Less :	Cheques issued but not presented (66100–10000)	56,100
	Bank balance as per pass book (favourable)	32,070

Note :- It is assumed that bank charges of Rs 510 recorded twice in November, which has not been detected till 31-12-98. Therefore it is rectified on that date.

Problem 4

The cash book of a firm showed an overdraft of Rs. 30,000 on 31st March, 1999. A comparison of the entries in the cash book and pass book revealed that .

1. On 22nd March, 1999 cheques totalling Rs. 6,000 were sent to bankers for collection. Out of these a cheque for Rs. 1,000 was wrongly recorded on the credit side of the cash book and cheques amounting to Rs. 300 could not be collected by bank before 1st April 1999.
2. A cheque for Rs. 4,000 was issued to a supplier on 28th March 1999. The cheque was presented to bank on 4th April 1999.
3. There were debits of Rs. 2,600 in the pass book for interest on overdraft and bank charges but the same had not been recorded in the cash book.
4. A cheque for Rs. 1,000 was issued to a creditor on 27th March 1990 but by mistake the same was not recorded in the cash book. The cheque was however, duly encashed by 31st March 1999.
5. As per standing instructions the banker collected dividend of Rs. 500 on behalf of the firm and credited the same to its account by 31st March 1999. The fact was however, intimated to the firm on 3rd April 1999.

You are required to prepare a Bank Reconciliation Statement as on 31st March. 1999

(C S Foundation Course, June 1999).

Solution

Bank Reconciliation Statement as on 31-3-1999.

	Particulars	Rs.	Rs.
	Bank overdraft as per cash book		30,000
Add :-			
(i)	Cheques deposited but not collected	300	
(ii)	Interest on overdraft and bank charges not recorded in cash book	2,600	
(iii)	Cheques issued to creditors but not recorded in cash book	1,000	
			3,900
			33,900
Less :			
(i)	Cheques wrongly recorded on the credit side of the cash book (1000 × 2)	2,000	
(ii)	Cheques issued but not presented for payment	4,000	
(iii)	Dividend collected by bank but not yet recorded in cash book	500	
			6,500
	Bank overdraft as per pass book		27,400

Problem 5

Prepare a Bank Reconciliation of M/s Benarasi Kuthi as on 31st December 1997 from the following particulars.

(*a*) Bank overdraft as per cash book Rs. 8,900
(*b*) A cheque for Rs. 1,200 issued to supplier on 28th December but the cheque was not presented to bank till 5th January 1998.
(*c*) Cheque for Rs. 3,400 paid into bank, but cheque of Rs. 1,600 only were cleared and credited by the bankers.
(*d*) A bill for Rs. 4,000 discounted for Rs. 3,980 returned dishonoured by the bank, noting charges being Rs. 20.
(*e*) Dividends amounting to Rs. 500 had been paid direct to the bank and not entered in the cash book.
(*f*) A cheque of Rs. 1,200 was issued to creditor was inadvertently destroyed it. A duplicate cheque was issued and recorded in the cash book as a new payment.
(*g*) Interest for Rs. 100 charged by the bank recorded twice in the cash book.
(*h*) A cheque from a customer entered in the cash book as Rs. 75 has been correctly entered by the bank as Rs. 275. **(Calcutta University, B. Com (Pass) 1998)**

Solution

Bank Reconciliation Statement

Particulars	*Rs.*	*Rs.*
Bank overdraft as per cash book		8,900
Add :		
(*i*) Cheques deposited but not collected by bank (3400 – 1600)	1,800	
(*ii*) Bills discounted not entered in cash book (including noting charges)	4,020	
		5,820
		14,720
Less :		
(*i*) Cheque issued to supplier not presented for payment	1,200	
(*ii*) Dividends collected by bank not entered in cash book	500	
(*iii*) Cheque paid to creditor cancelling the old one but same was not cancelled in the cash book	1,200	
(*iv*) Interest on bank overdraft recorded twice in cash book	100	
(*v*) Cheque received from customer wrongly entered in the cash book (275 – 75)	200	
		3,200
Bank overdraft as per pass book		11,520

Problem 6

Following are the entries recorded in the bank column of the cash book of Mr. X for the month ending on 31-3-1997.

Cash Book (Bank Column)

Date	Particulars	Amount	Date	Particulars	Amount
15-3-97	To Cash	36,000	1-3-97	By Balance b/d	40,000
20-3-97	To Roy	24,000	4-3-97	By John	2,000
22-3-97	To Kapoor	10,000	6-3-97	By Krishnan	400
31-3-97	To Balance c/d	7,640	15-4-97	By Kavilash	240
			20-3-97	By Joshi	35,000
		77,640			77,640

On 31-3-97 Mr. X received the Bank statement. On perusal of the statement Mr. X ascertained the following information.

1. Cheque deposited but credited by the bank Rs. 10,000.
2. Interest on securities collected by the bank but not recorded in cash book Rs. 1,080.
3. Credit transfer not recorded in the cash book Rs. 200.
4. Dividend collected by the bank directly but not recorded in the cash book Rs. 1,000.
5. Cheques issued but not presented for payment Rs. 37,400.
6. Interest debited by the bank but not recorded in the cash book Rs. 1,000.
7. Bank charges not recorded in the cash book Rs. 340.

From the above information you are asked to prepare a bank reconciliation statement to ascertain the balance as per bank statement (C. A Foundation course May 1997).

Solution

Bank Reconciliation Statement

	Particulars	Rs.	Rs.
	Overdraft as per cash book		7,640
Add :	Cheques deposited but not credited by the bank	10,000	
	Interest debited by the bank but not recorded in the cash book	1,000	
	Bank charges not recorded in the cash book	340	
			11,340
			18,980
Less :	Interest on securities collected by the bank but not recorded in cash book	1,080	
	Credit transfer not recorded in the cash book	200	
	Dividend collected by the bank directly but not recorded in the cash book	1,000	
	Cheques issued but not presented for payment	37,400	
			39,680
	Credit balance as per Bank statement		20,700

Problem 7

In respect of Bank account No. 1, on 30th September 1996 my cash book showed a bank overdraft of Rs. 98,700. On going through the bank statement for reconciling the balance, I find the following :

Out of cheques drawn on 26th September 1996 those for Rs. 7,400 were cashed by the bankers on 2nd October 1996 and a crossed cheque of Rs. 1,500 given to Antony was returned by him and a bearer one was issued to him in lieu on 1st October 1996.

Cash and cheques amounting to Rs. 6,800 were deposited in bank on 29th September 1996 but cheques worth Rs. 2,600 were cleared by the bank on 1st october 1996 and one cheque for Rs 500 was returned by them as dishonoured on the later date.

According to my standing orders, the bankers have on 30th September 1996 paid Rs. 640 as interest to my creditors, paid quarterly premium on my policy amounting to Rs. 320 and have paid a second call of Rs. 1,200 on shares held by me and lodged with the bankers for safe custody. They have also received Rs. 300 as dividend on my shares and recovered an insurance claim of Rs. 1,600 ; their charges and commission on the above being Rs. 30. On receipt of information of the above transactions, I have passed necessary entries on 1st October 1996. My bankers seem to have given to me a wrong credit for Rs. 1,000 paid in by me in No 2 account and a wrong debit in respect of a cheque for Rs. 600 drawn against my No 2 account.

Prepare the Reconciliation statement of bank account No 1 as on 30th September 1996 (ICW A, Intermediate June 1997)

Solution

Bank Reconciliation Statement (A/c No. 1)

	Particulars		*Rs.*	*Rs.*
	Overdraft as per cash book			98,700
Add :	Cheques deposited but not cleared (2600 + 500)		3,100	
	Payments made by bank not entered in cash book :			
	Interest to creditors	640		
	Premium on policy	320		
	Call on shares	1,200		
			2,160	
	Bank Commission & charges		30	
	Amount wrongly debited bank to this account instead of No 2 a/c		600	
				5,890
				1,04,590
Less :	Cheques issued but not presented (7400 + 1500)		8,900	
	Amount received by bank but not entered in cash book :-			
	Dividend on shares	300		
	Insurance claim	1,600		
			1,900	
	Amount wrongly credited by the bank to this a/c instead of No. 2 a/c		1,000	
				11,800
	Bank overdraft balance per pass book			92,790

EXERCISE 1

From the following particulars prepare a Bank Reconciliation statement as on 31st December 1995 :-

Cash at bank as per cash book as on 31-12-95	Rs. 8,700
Cheques issued but not presented at the bank	Rs. 3,550
Interest credited by bank but not entered in cash book	Rs. 125
Bank charges not entered in cash book	Rs. 30
Cheques deposited but not credited by bank	Rs. 1,700
Direct deposit by a customer into the bank	Rs. 450
Cheques dishoured by bank but not entered in cash book	Rs. 250
Income Tax (advance) paid by the bank under standing order but not entered in cash book	Rs. 200

In balancing the pass book a credit balance of Rs 352 was cast as Rs 325.

(Calcutta University, B. Com (Pass) 1996).

Answer : Bank balance as per pass book Rs 10618

EXERCISE 2

According to the cash book of Gopi. There was a balance of Rs. 44,500 standing to his credit in bank on 30th June 1996. On investigation you find that :

(*i*) Cheques amounting to Rs 60,000 issued to creditors have not been presented for payment till that date.
(*ii*) Cheques paid into bank amounting to Rs. 1,05,000 out of which cheques amounting to Rs. 55,000 only collected by the bank upto 30th June 1996.
(*iii*) A dividend of Rs. 4,000 and rent amounting to Rs. 6,000 received by the Bank and entered in the passbook but not recorded in the cashbook.
(*iv*) Insurance premium (upto 31st December 1996) paid by the bank Rs. 2,700 not entered in the cash book.
(*v*) The payment side of the cashbook had been under cast by Rs. 50.
(*vi*) Bank charges Rs. 50, Shown in the pass-book had not been entered in the cash-book.
(*vii*) A bill payable for Rs. 2,000 has been paid by the bank but is not entered in the cash-book and the bill receivable for Rs. 6,000 has been discounted with the bank at a cost of Rs. 100 which has also not been recorded in cash book. You are required :
(*viii*) To make the appropriate adjustment in the cash book.
(*ix*) To prepare a statement reconciling with the Bank pass book

(C A Foundation Course November 1996).

Answer : Cash book (Bank balance column)
Balance c/d Rs. 55,600
Balance as per pass book Rs. 65,600

EXERCISE 3

On 31st December 1993, the Bank account of Suman Bros. according to the cash book showed an overdraft balance of Rs. 1,500. On the same date the bank statement showed a balance in their favour of Rs. 2,050. An examination of the Cash book and Bank statement reveals the following.

(*i*) The total of the credit side on one page of the cash book amounting to Rs. 10,200 was wrongly carried forward to the next page as Rs. 12,000.

(*ii*) A cheque for Rs. 1,500 deposited with the bank on 30th December 1993, was recorded in the bank statement on 4th January 1994.

(*iii*) An instalment payment of Rs. 150 made directly by the bank had not been recorded in the cash book.

(*iv*) Bank charges amounting to Rs. 75 had not been entered in the cash book.

(*v*) Two cheques amounting to Rs. 975 issued prior to 31st December 1993 were not presented to the bank for payment until after that date.

(*vi*) A deposit of Rs. 2,500 made by Suman Bros, was wrongly credited by the bank to Suman Bros a/c.

Ascertain the correct balance as per the cash book of Suman Bros and then prepare the Bank Reconciliation Statement. **(Calcutta University B. Com (Pass) 1994)**

Answer : Cash book (Bank column) Balance c/d Rs 225.
Bank balance as per pass book Rs 2050.

EXERCISE 4

From the following particulars prepare a Bank Reconciliation Statement as on 31st December 1993 :-

1. On 31st December, 1993 the cash book of a firm showed a bank balance of Rs.6,000 (Debit balance).
2. Cheques had been issued for Rs 5000, out of which cheques worth Rs 4000 only were presented for payment.
3. Cheques worth Rs. 1,400 were deposited in the bank on 28th December 1993 but had not been credited by the bank. In additions this one cheque for Rs. 500 was entered in the cashbook on 30th December 1993, but was banked on 3-1-1994.
4. A cheque from Susan for Rs. 400 was deposited in the bank on 26th December 1993 but was dishonoured and the advice was received on 2-1-1994.
5. Pass book showed bank charges of Rs. 20 debited by the bank.
6. One of the debitors deposited a sum of Rs. 500 in the bank account of the firm on 20th December 1993 but the intimation in this respect was received from the bank on 2-1-1994.
7. Bank passbook showed a credit balance of Rs. 5,180 on 31st December, 1993.

(C A Foundation course, June 1994)
Answer : Bank balance (Cr) as per pass book Rs. 5,180

EXERCISE 4

From the following particulars, calculate the cash book balance of a merchant as on 31st March 1991, by means of a Bank Reconciliation Statement.

(*i*) Balance as per Bank pass book (Dr) Rs. 4,475.70.

(*ii*) A cheque for Rs. 399.50 was deposited on 24th March but the same was returned by the bank on 29th for which no entry was made in the cash book.

(*iii*) A Bill for Rs. 1,020 received from a Debtor previously discounted for Rs. 1,000 was dishonoured and the bank debited the account of the merchant, but the same was not recorded in the cash book.

(*iv*) Two cheques issued on 27th March, but not encashed before 5th April : Rs. 640.40 and Rs. 498.30.

(*v*) A cheque for Rs. 300 was debited twice in the cash book.

(*vi*) Interest an overdraft for Rs. 56 and bank charges for Rs. 17 were not passed through the cash book.

(*vii*) Dividend of Rs. 200 collected by the bank on behalf of the merchant but the matter was not recorded in the cash book. **(Calcutta University B Com (Pass) 1991)**

Answer : Bank balance as per cash book (over drawn) Rs. 4,020.90

7

CHAPTER

Bills Transactions

1. INTRODUCTION

In the present day business competitive world, it has become a common practice to buy and sell goods an credit basis. In such situation the terms of credit sale is embodied in a document which constitutes an evidence of credit sale. A written document also avoids the possible misunderstanding between buyer and seller as credit is payable after a particular period. Again a written document will enable the seller to enforce the buyer to pay the amount on the due date. One such credit or commercial instrument which is more popularly used by most of the businessman is termed as *Bill of exchange*. In a bill of exchange, the seller order the buyer to pay the amount to him or any other person after a certain period of time. This order will be signed by the buyer as a token of his willingness to pay the amount on due date. A bill of exchange is referred to as a negotiable instrument. It means a document which can be transferred by one person to another so as to constitute the latter the true owner of the instrument, the other two instrument which have been considered as negotiable instruments in our country are the promissory notes and cheques. All these three instruments are governed by Negotiable Instruments Act of 1881.

2. DEFINITION AND CHARACTERISTICS OF A BILL OF EXCHANGE

Section 5 of the Negotiable Instruments Act of 1881 defines a bill of exchange as an instrument in writing containing an unconditional order, signed by the maker directing a certain person to pay certain sum of money only to or to the order of a certain person or to the bearer of the instrument.

Characteristic Feature of a Bill of Exchange

1. **It must be in writing.** In other words a bill of exchange cannot be oral. It must be in the form of written document. No particular words, are necessary nor is there any prescribed form in which a bill of exchange can be drawn. Writing a bill of exchange includes printing.
2. **It must be signed by the maker.** A bill which is not signed by the drawer is regarded in law as an incomplete instrument. Signature of the drawer may not be affixed to the document at the time it is drawn but till this is done the bill is incomplete and in effective in law signature of an authorised agent on behalf of the drawer is considered sufficient for this purpose.

3. **It must contain an order.** In other words mere request is not sufficient.
4. The order directing payment must be unconditional. In other words, payment should not on the face of the bill depend on the happening of the contingency or fulfilment of the contract. Thus an order directing payment to be made if a certain ship arrived or when sales are realised is not a valid bill of exchange.
5. The drawer must be certain. If the name of the drawer is not mentioned the bill is incomplete. There can be joint drawee of a bill but not alternate or successive drawee.
6. The sum payable must be certain. For example, a direction to pay Rs. 500 and all sums that may be due does not make a valid bill.
7. The amount directed to be paid must be expressed in terms of money only. In one of the legal case an order to pay a certain sum and also to deliver a Radio was held not to be valid bill.
8. The bill must be drawn and made payable either to a certain person or to his order or to bearer. The payee must be certain. A bill may be made payable to joint payees or to payees in the alternative.
9. A bill must be properly stamped when necessary according to the Indian Stamps Act. The stamp required to be affixed to a bill of exchange is ad valorem, i.e., according to value. The stamp varies according to the amount of the bill of exchange. The larger the amount, the higher will be the stamp duty required to be paid. However, a bill of exchange payable on demand is exempt from stamp duty.
10. While drawing a bill certain other formalities are to be strictly followed. They are as follows :

(*a*) **Date of Bill :** The date of bill determines the due date of the bill i.e., the date on which the amount becomes payable. The date is usually written on the right hand top corner of the bill.

(*b*) **Amount of the Bill :** The amount of the bill is drawn twice on a bill of exchange on the left hand top corner, the amount is written in figures and the same amount is written in words on the body of the bill of exchange.

(*c*) **Terms of the Bill :** It refers to the duration on the completion of which the value of the bill becomes payable. The terms of bill may relate to payment on demand or after the expiry of a certain duration.

A specimen of a Bill of exchange is shown below :

Bangalore
21st Feb., 1995.

Rs. 500

Stamp

Three months after date pay to Mr. Vivek Kamath or order the sum of rupees Five Hundred only, for value received

Ashok Kamat

To
Mr. Ramesh Kamat
Jayanagar
Bangalore

(*d*) **Money consideration :** A bill of exchange always implies money consideration. This is denoted by the words "for value received" in a bill of exchange.

3. PARTIES TO A BILL OF EXCHANGE

There are many parties to a bill of exchange they are as follows :

1. **The Drawer.** The person who makes or draws a bill of exchange is known as the drawer. It is the drawer who gives the order to the other person to pay the money to him or any other person. He constitutes the creditor as it is he who has to receive payment from his debtor. In the specimen of Bill of exchange given earlier Mr. Ashok Kamat is Drawer of the bill.
2. **The Drawee.** The person to whom the order is addressed and who is directed to pay the bill is known as the drawee. He constitutes the debtor as it is he who owes money to his creditor i.e., drawer. In the specimen given earlier Mr. Ramesh Kamat is the Drawee of the bill.
3. **Drawee in case of need.** Where it is found that the drawee on whom a bill is drawn is not able to accept or discharge the bill, the drawer generally mentions on the bill the name of another person to whom recourse may be had for payment. Such a person is called drawee in case of need.
4. **Acceptor.** He is the drawee of a bill of exchange who has signed the bill and deliver the same to the holder or any person on his behalf.
5. **Acceptor for honour.** Where the bill of exchange is dishonoured for non-acceptance or non-payment any person who comes forward and accepts it for saving the honour of any party already liable on the bill is called the acceptor for honour.
6. **Payee.** The person named in the bill of exchange to whom or to whose order the money is directed to be paid is known as the payee. In the specimen bill of exchange shown above, Mr. Vivek Kamath is the payee of the bill.

4. TYPES OF BILL OF EXCHANGE

The following are the different kinds of bills used in practice.

(*a*) **Inland bill :** It is a type of bill in which it is drawn and payable in India. In other words, a bill of exchange is said to be inland when both drawer and drawee live in India. The specimen given earlier is an example of an Inland bill.

(*b*) **Foreign bill :** A bill of exchange which is not inland is known as foreign bill. It is a type of bill of exchange which is drawn by a person living in one country upon a person living in another country. The following are the instances of a foreign bills :

(*i*) A bill drawn in India on a person resident outside and made payable outside India.
(*ii*) A bill drawn outside India on a person resident outside India.
(*iii*) A bill drawn outside India are made payable in India.
(*iv*) A bill drawn outside India and made payable outside India.

The method of drawing a foreign bill is different from that of an Inland bill. A specimen of a foreign bill is given below.

Specimen of a Foreign Bill

Bangalore
22nd Feb., 2005.

Rs. 1,000

Stamp

Sixty days after sight of this bill of exchange (second and third of the same tenor and date being unpaid) pay to Mr. Deepak Kamat, U.S.A. or order the sum of Rupees one thousand only for value received.

sd. Ashok Kamat

To
Mr. Edward Simon
U.S.A.

A foreign Bill of exchange differs from an Inland bill in three respects. Firstly, in case of a foreign bill, its period is counted from the date when it is seen and accepted by the drawer. This practice is followed with a view to exclude the days the bill will take in transit and to give the drawee full benefit of the period for which it is drawn. Secondly, a foreign bill is always drawn in sets of two or three. This practice is followed to avoid the possibility of delay in the event of loss or delay in transit. Different copies are sent by different mails so that if one set is lost, other sets may reach safely. Each one of the set is called a "via". However, the drawer is bound to accept and pay for only one "via". As soon as one "via" is paid other bills of exchange become in operative. Thirdly, a foreign bill has to he stamped twice, i.e., once in the country of the drawer and again in the foreign country.

(*c*) **Documentary bill of exchange :** A documentary bill is a type of bill of exchange which accompany the shipping documents to be delivered to the importer upon his acceptance or payment of the bill. Some shipping documents which usually accompany a bill of exchange are Bill of lading, Railway receipt, invoice Marine Insurance Policy etc. A documentary bill may be either D/A Bill or D/P Bill. When the shipping documents are delivered on the acceptance of the bill it is called documents against acceptance or D/A Bill. When the documents are delivered on payment of the bill, it is called documents against payment or D/P Bill.

(*d*) **Accommodation bill :** It is a type of bill of exchange which does not involved any trade transaction but which is drawn and accepted for the purpose of arranging temporary financial accommodation. This type of bills are not very popular.

(*e*) **Trade bill :** It is type of bill which comes into existence owing to a business transacted between two parties. This type of bill is more popular when compared to accommodation bill.

A trade bill differs from an accommodation bill in two respects. Firstly in a trade bill a business transaction is involved whereas in an accommodation bill no such business transaction is involved. Secondly a value of a trade bill is entirely belongs to the drawer of the bill, whereas in case of accommodation bill, it is shared by both the drawer and acceptor. A trade bill can be of two types, viz, (a) Demand bill and (2) time bill. A demand bill is a bill which is payable at any time on demand. A time bill is one which is payable after a specific future period such as 2 months or 3 months later. It is also called as usance bill.

5. ADVANTAGES OF A BILL OF EXCHANGE

The advantages of a bill of exchange can be enumerated as follows.

1. It enables the person to buy the goods on credit basis by giving acceptance on the bill. After selling the same goods he can repay the amount to the drawer on maturity date. Thus a bill of exchange increases the volume of business.
2. As there is a written acknowledgement the drawer can enforce the payment promptly as it is a legal document recognised by the Negotiable Instruments Act, 1881.
3. Being a negotiable instrument, the drawer can discount it with banker and get the discounted value of it to meet immediate cash requirements.
4. Through bill of exchange it is possible for a debtor to transfer his debts to his creditor. It thus avoids settlement of transaction through payment of cash. For example a person in Bangalore has bought goods from a trader in Belguam for Rs. 2,500, and has, at the same time sold goods to another person in the same place for Rs. 2,500, he can draw a Bill of exchange on his debtor in favour of his creditor for the amount due from him. Thus his debtor will be saved the trouble and expenses of sending money to Bangalore

and he himself will not have to re-transfer that sum to Belgaum as his debtor will pay his creditor in that place.

5. The debtor and creditor know the exact date of payment because of the maturity date appearing on the bill.
6. Through accommodation bill the temporary financial requirements can be arranged by drawing and accepting accommodation bills and subsequently discounting them with the bank.
7. A trade bill gives the drawee (Debtor) the full time i.e., upto maturity date to retain the value of goods with him. In other words, the Drawer (creditor) cannot enforce the drawee to pay the value of the bill until its maturity date.

6. BILLS RECEIVABLE, BILLS PAYABLE AND BILLS OF EXCHANGE

A bill of exchange from the drawer's point of view will be called as bills receivable as he has to receive the value of the bill from the drawee on the maturity date. The same bill of exchange from the drawee's point of view will be called by bill payable as he has to pay the value of the bill to the drawer on maturity date. From the third party's point of view, the same bill is called as bills of exchange because from his (third party's) point of view only a bill is exchanged between the drawer and drawee. In other words, a third party will neither receive nor pay the value of the bill. Thus it can be said that accounting entries are made in respect of a bill receivable and payable but not in relation to a bill of exchange.

7. ACCEPTANCE OF A BILL

The term acceptance of a bill refers to the willingness of the drawee to be a party to the bill. It constitutes the consent given by the drawee to pay the amount as directed by the drawee. After giving the acceptance on the bill the drawee becomes the acceptor. The bill of exchange requires acceptance unless it is payable on demand. Until the bill is accepted it will not become a full fledged instrument. In other words, till acceptance is given by the drawee it will remain only as a "Draft". After acceptance of a bill the obligation to pay the value of the bill arises from the point of acceptor. Hence it will be appropriate on the part of the drawee to ensure that the goods received and terms of bill are satisfactory before he gives acceptance on the bill. However, if the drawee comes to know that the drawee has altered the terms and conditions of the bill inadvertently, he can alter the bill with the consent of the drawer and then accept the bill. Such an acceptance is known as "Qualified Acceptance". A qualified acceptance may relate to any of the following.

(*a*) **Qualified as to time :** A qualified acceptance relating to time will arise when the drawee has reduced the period of payment of the bill and the drawer wants to increase the same with the consent of the drawer. For example, instead of allowing four months for the drawee to pay the bill, if the drawer writes as three months. Then the drawer can alter the duration from 3 months to four months and then accept the bill.

(*b*) **Qualified as to amount :** Such an acceptance is given to alter an increased amount included in the bill by the drawer, instead of correct amount.

(*c*) **Conditional acceptance :** It the drawer wants to pay the bill by extending the duration of the bill along with payment of interest for the extended period, such as acceptance is known as conditional acceptance.

(*d*) **Qualified acceptance as to place :** When the drawee wants to pay the value of the bill at a place which is convenient to him and alter the original place of payment of bill then such an acceptance is called qualified acceptance as to place. Usually the drawer does not mind this type of qualified acceptance unless it causes great inconvenience to him.

8. BILLS RECEIVABLE AND BILL PAYABLE BOOKS

Bills Receivable Book : As was mentioned in chapter 3, Bills receivable and bills payable are subsidiary books maintained by most of the traders along with other subsidiary books. When a trader enters into numerous transactions on the basis of bills of exchange, he has to keep a complete record of dates of drawing the bills, the terms, the date of maturity, etc. The drawer has to present the bill to the acceptor for payment on due date. Otherwise he will be liable for discharge of his liability. So to avoid this complication, the trader will maintain bills of exchange for recording all particulars about each bill received. A specimen form of a bill receivable book is shown below.

Bills Receivable Book

Sr. No	*Date Received*	*Person from whom Received*	*Acceptor*	*Date of Bill*	*Due Date*	*Amount*	*Remark*

Posting the entries from Bills Receivable book

The various transactions from the Bills receivable books are posted into the ledger accounts of the drawee and into the bills receivable account. On the credit side of every Drawee's a/c the transaction is posted as "To Bills Receivable Account". On the debit side of the bills receivable account, the total amount is recorded as "to sundries as per bills receivable book".

Problem 1

Prepare a bills receivable book from the following particulars and post them into the concerned ledger account.

2005 May,

1.	Received from Keshav his acceptance at three months	Rs. 600
7.	Accepted Madhav's draft at two months	Rs. 1,000
14.	Bought goods from Damodar and gave him acceptance of one month	Rs. 660
19.	Sold goods to Govind and drew on him at four months for	Rs. 2,580
24.	Received from Anand his pro-note at two months for	Rs. 500
28.	Ram Narayan received our promissory note at one month for	Rs. 500
30.	Received from Krishna Prasad his bill at six months for	Rs. 2,000

Solution

Bills Receivable Books

Date	*Received from*	*Terms*	*Due date*	*Amount*
May 1.	Keshav	3 months	Aug. 4	600
19.	Govind	4 months	Sept. 22	2,580
24.	Anand	2 months	July. 27	800
30.	Krishna Prasad	6 months	Dec. 3	2,000
				5,980

Keshav's A/c

	May 1, By B.R a/c	600

Govind A/c

	May 19, By B.R. a/c	2,580

Anand's A/c

	May 24, By B.R. a/c	800

Krishna Prasad

	May 30, By B.R. a/c	2,000

Bills Receivable Book

31 May, To Sundries 5,980

Bills Payable Book : A traders apart from maintaining a bills receivable book also maintains a bills payable book to recorded all acceptances given by him to his suppliers. A specimen of bills payable book is shown below :

Bills Payable Book

Sr. No	*Date*	*To whom given*	*Payee*	*Place of payment*	*Term*	*LF*	*Due on*	*Amount*

Posting of Entries from Bills payable books : In the personal accounts of various suppliers the entries are recorded on the debit side as "To Bills payable account". In the bills payable account the various acceptance given is posted on the credit side as By sundries as per bills payable book

Problem 2

From the particulars given in problem 1. Prepare a bills payable book and prepare the necessary ledger accounts.

Solution

Bills Payable Book

Date	*To whom given*	*Term*	*Due on*	*LF*	*Amt*
May 7.	Madhav	2 months	July 10		1,000
14.	Damodar	1 month	June 17		660
28.	Ram Narayan	1 month	July 1		500
					2,160

Madhav's A/c

May 7	To Bill payable a/c	1,000			

Damodar's A/c

May 14	To Bill payable a/c	660			

Ram Narayan's A/c

May 28	To Bills payable a/c	500			

Bills payable A/c

			May 31	By Sundress	2,160

Problem 3

(Preparation of bills receivable and bills payable books)
Record the following transactions in the bills receivable and bills payable books and post them into ledger.

2,003 May,

1.	Received from B Pershad his acceptance at 3 months	Rs. 600
7.	Accepted Gauri Shankar's draft at 2 months	Rs. 1,000
14.	Bought goods from H. Ahmad and gave him our acceptance at one month	Rs. 660
19.	Sold goods to Nisar and drew on him at 4 months	Rs. 2,580
24.	Received from Kamath his pronote at 2 months	Rs. 800
28.	Gave Prabhu our promissory note at one month for	Rs. 500
30.	Received from Rama his bill at 6 months for	Rs. 2,000

Solution

Bills Receivable Book

Date	*Received from*	*Terms*	*Due date*	*Amount*
1-5-03	B. Pershad	3 months	4-8-03	600
19-5-03	Nisar	4 months	22-9-03	2,580
20-5-03	Kamath	2 months	27-7-03	800
30-5-03	Rama	6 months	3-12-03	2,000
				5,980

Bills Receivable A/c

31-5-03	To Sundries	5,980		By Balance c/d	5,980

B. Pershad's A/c

	To Bal c/d	600	1-5-03	By B.R. a/c	600

Nisar's A/c

	To Bal. c/d	2,580	19-5-03	By B. R a/c	2,580

Kamath's A/c

	To Bal c/d	800	24-5-03	By B. R. a/c	800

Rama's A/c

	To Bal c/d	2,000	30-5-03	By B. R. a/c	2,000

Bill Payable Book

Date	To whom given	Term	Due on	LF	Amt
7-5-03	Gauri Shankar	2 months	10-7-03		1,000
14-5-03	Ahmad	1 month	17-6-03		660
28-5-03	Prabhu	1 month	1-7-03		500
					2,160

Bills Payable A/c

	To Balance c/d	2,160	31-5-03	By Sundries	2,160

Gauri Shankar A/c

7-5-03	To B.P a/c	1,000		By Balance c/d	1,000

Ahmad's A/c

14-5-03	To B.P a/c	660		By Balance c/d	660

Prabhu's A/c

28-5-03	To B.P a/c	500		By Balance c/d	500

Problem 4

Record the following transactions of Mehta in the concerned subsidiary books and post them into ledger.

2003 Jan,

1. Accepted a bill of Govind for Rs. 1,000
4. Received (for goods sold) a bill from Krishna Rs. 2,000
8. Accepted for goods purchased Jones bill Rs. 500
10. Drew a bill on Jones Rs. 300

Solution

Bills Receivable Book

Date	Received from	Terms	Due date	Amt.	Remark
4-1-03	Krishna			2,000	
10-1-03	Jones			300	

Bills Payable book

Date	To whom given	Term	Due date	Amt.	Remove
1-1-03	Govind			1,000	
8-1-03	Jones			500	

Govind A/c

1-1-03	To B.P a/c	1,000		By Balance c/d	1,000

Krishna A/c

			4-1-03	By B. R. a/c	2,000

Jones A/c

8-1-03	To B.P. a/c	500	10-1-03	By B R a/c	300
				By Balance	200
		500			500

Problem 5

Enter the following transactions in the Bills Receivable book and Bills Payable book and post them to ledger.

2,003 Jan,

1.	Received from Ram Lal his promissory note	Rs. 400
5.	Sent our acceptance to Sita Ram & sons	Rs. 300
8.	Sent our draft to Govind Rao who returned it to us duly accepted	Rs. 100
20.	Ramnath & Co. drew upon us for 4 months	Rs. 490

Solution

Bills Receivable Book

Date	*Received from*	*Terms*	*Due date*	*Amt.*	*Remarks*
1-1-03	Ram Lal			400	
8-1-03	Govind Rao			100	
				500	

Bills Receivable A/c

31-1-03	To Sundries	500		By Balance c/d	500

Ram Lal A/c

31-1-03	To Balance c/d	400	1-1-03	B.R. a/c	400

Govind Rao's A/c

31-1-03	To Balance c/d	100	8-1-03	By B.R a/c	100

Bills Payable Book

Date	*To whom given*	*Term*	*Due date*	*Amt*	*Remarks*
5-1-03	Sita Ram & Sons			300	
20-1-03	Ram Nath & Co.			490	
				790	

Bills Payable A/c

31-1-03	To Balance c/d	790	31-1-03	By sundries	790

Sitaram & Son's A/c

5-1-03	To B.P. a/c	300	31-1-03	By Balance c/d	300

Ram Nath & Co. A/c

20-1-03	To B.P a/c	490	31-1-03	By Balance c/d	490

9. MATURITY DATE AND GRACE DAYS

The date on which the bill becomes due for payment is known as maturity date. It is also called as due date of the bill. The calculation of due date does not arise in case of a bill which is payable on demand, i.e., demand bill. The due date is to be calculated in case of time bills as its proceeds is payable after a certain period of time. The calculation of due date starts from the date of drawing the bill but not on the date of accepting the bill. Usually a duration of three days are allowed to calculate the due date. Such an extended period is known as Grace days. If the maturity date falls on a public holiday it is paid on the following day of the due date.

10. DISHONOUR OF A BILL-NOTING AND PROTESTING

It refers to the act of refusing to accept a bill or to make payment on presentation. Thus a bill may be dishonoured either by non-acceptance or by non-payment. When the drawee of a bill dose not accept the same it is called dishonour by non-acceptance. When the drawee fails to pay the amount on the due date, it is called dishonour by non-payment. When a bill is dishonoured by the acceptor a notice of dishonour is to be served by the holder of bill to the drawer of the bill. The holder of a bill will be usually the payee or the endorsee of the bill. Before any action can be taken for dishonour of the instrument proper notice of dishonour as required by law is to be given to all the parties liable on the instrument. The following points regarding notice are to be noted.

(*a*) The notice must be given to the party or to his agent.
(*b*) It may be either oral or written.
(*c*) It must be given within a reasonable time after dishonour.
(*d*) It must be served personally or by registered post.
(*e*) It must be given at the place of business of the party during business hour and if the party has no place of business at his residence.

Noting and Protesting : Whenever a bill of exchange is dishonoured, there must be an evidence to the fact of dishonour by acceptor. This evidence is necessary to recover the amount through a court of law. The evidence is provided by a person known as Notary public who is attached to the High court of every state by the Government. Wherever a Bill of exchange is dishonoured, an attempt is made for claiming the bill through notary public. If the bill is not paid the notary public notes down the drawees reply on a slip of paper, which serves as an evidence in a court of law. This process of providing written evidence is known as "Noting the bill". A fee is to be paid to the notary public for this purpose which is known as noting charges. The amount is paid by the holder who can later on recover it from drawer and the drawer in his turn recover it from the drawee.

Protest of a bill is required in cash of foreign bill. It is a certificate issued on dishonour signed by the notary public. The certificate is to be appropriately stamped. Protest of a bill serve two purposes, viz (*a*) It is an evidence declared by the notary public for the dishonour by non-acceptance or non-payment of the bill and (b) it offers better security for the holder of the bill.

11. ENTRIES RELATING TO DRAWING AND ACCEPTING A BILL

In the Books of Drawer :

1. When goods are sold on credit basis :

    Buyer a/c Dr
    To Sales a/c

2. When a bill is drawn and accepted :

    Bills receivable a/c Dr
    To Acceptors a/c

Reason :

Bills receivable account is a real account The Bill Receivable come into the business of the drawer. So Bill receivable account is debited.

Acceptor's a/c is a personal account. The acceptor is the giver of the bill. So Acceptor's account is credited.

In the books of the acceptor :

1. When he buy's the goods on credit based.

    Purchases a/c Dr
    To Seller's a/c

2. When he accepts the bill drawn on him by the drawer.

    Drawer's a/c Dr
    To Bills payable a/c

Reason :

Bills of exchange from the point of acceptor is called Bills payable. It is a real account. It goes out of the business of the acceptor. So bill payable is credited.

Problem 6

On 1st April 2003, Satish sold goods to Umesh for Rs. 200 and drew a 3 months bill on him for the amount. Umesh accepted it and returns to Satish. Pass necessary entries in the books of both the parties.

Solution

Entries in the Books of Satish

Date	*Particulars*	*L.F.*	*Dr. Amount*	*Cr. Amount*
1-4-03	Umesh's a/c Dr		200	
	To Sales a/c			200
	(Being goods sold to Umesh on credit)			
	Bill receivable a/c Dr		200	
	To Umesh			200
	(Being the accepted bill received from Umesh)			

Entries in the Books of Umesh

Date	*Particulars*	*L.F.*	*Dr. Amount*	*Cr. Amount*
1-4-03	Purchases a/c Dr		200	
	To Satish			200
	(Being the goods purchased from Ramesh on credit)			
	Satish a/c Dr		200	
	To Bills payable a/c			200
	(Being acceptance given to Ramesh)			

ENTRIES WHEN A BILL IS DISCHARGED OR PAID OR HONOURED

In the Books of Drawer :

on the due date the drawer will present the bill to the drawee. If the payment is received by him from the acceptor, the following entry is passed.

Cash or Bank a/c Dr
To Bill receivable a/c

In the books of drawee :

Bills payable a/c Dr
To Cash or bank

Problem 7

On 1st January 2,003 Sitaram sold goods to Radheshyam for Rs. 1,000 and received a two months bill for the amount, the bill was duly discharged on maturity date. Pass necessary Journal entries in the books of both the parties.

Solution

Entries in the Books of Sita Ram

Date	*Particulars*	*L.F.*	*Dr. Amount*	*Cr. Amount*
1-1-03	Radheshyam's a/c Dr		1,000	
	To Sales			1,000
	(Being the goods sold to Radheshyam on credit)			
	Bills Receivable a/c Dr		1,000	
	To Radheshyam			1,000
	(Being the accepted bill received from Radheshyam)			
4-3-03	Cash a/c Dr		1,000	
	To Bills receivable a/c			1,000
	(Being the amount received)			

Entries in the books of Radheshyam

Date	*Particulars*	*L.F.*	*Dr. Amount*	*Cr. Amount*
1-1-03	Purchases a/c Dr To Sitaram's a/c (Being goods purchased on credit from Sitaram)		1,000	1,000
	Sitaram's a/c Dr To Bill payable a/c (Being the acceptance given to Sitaram)		1,000	1,000
4-3-03	Bills payable a/c Dr To Cash (Being cash paid on the bill on due date)		1,000	1,000

12. ENDORSEMENT OF A BILL

A bill of exchange can be transferred by the drawer to another person to settle the mutual claim between them. The process of transferring a bill of exchange by the drawer to another person is by signing on the back of it is known as endorsement of a bill. On endorsement of the bill the drawer transfers his right to another person. The drawer is called as endorser on the endorsement of the bill and the transferee is called as endorsee. Thus on endorsement we have two parties to a bill. There are two ways of transferring a bill by the drawer to another person. The first method of transferring is called as transfer by mere delivery. The second method is known as transfer by endorsement and delivery. Endorsement can be made by the transferee to another individual by signing on the back of the bill of exchange. This process can be continued by any number of time. Where a bill of exchange is signed by many endorsers, leaving no space for further endorsement a piece of paper could be used for further endorsement Such a piece of paper used for further endorsement is known as an "allonge".

Entries in the books of Endorser : or Drawer on Endorsement

Endorsee's a/c Dr
To B. R. a/c

Note : No entry will be passed in the books of the acceptor in respect of endorsement because he is not affected by the endorsement.

Entry in the books of endorsee on receiving the Endorsed Bill :-

Bills receivable a/c Dr
To Endorser's a/c

Problem 8

Jagan sells goods worth Rs. 500 to Gajanan on 1st October 2,004 and draws a bill on him for the amount for 2 months. On the same day the bill is endorsed by him to his creditor Mohan. The bill is only paid on maturity. Pass the Journal entries in the books of all the parties.

Solution

Entries in the Books of Jagan

Date	Particulars		L.F.	Dr. Amount	Cr. Amount
1-10-04	Gajanan's a/c	Dr		500	
	To Sales a/c				500
	(Being goods sold to Gajanan on credit)				
	Bills receivable a/c	Dr		500	
	To Gajanan				500
	(Being accepted bill received from Jagan)				
	Mohan's a/c	Dr		500	
	To Bills Receivable				500
	(Being bill endorsed to Mohan)				

Entries in the Books of Mohan

Date	Particulars		L.F.	Dr. Amount	Cr. Amount
	Bills Receivable a/c	Dr		500	
	To Jagan				500
	(Being endorsed bill received from Jagan)				
	Cash a/c	Dr		500	
	To Bills receivable				500
	(Being cash received on the bill on due date)				

Entries in the books of Gajanan

Date	Particulars		L.F.	Dr. Amount	Cr. Amount
	Purchases a/c	Dr		500	
	To Jagan				500
	(Being goods bought from Jagan on credit)				
	Jagan's a/c	Dr		500	
	To Bills payable				500
	(Being acceptance given to Jagan)				
	Bills payable a/c	Dr		500	
	To Cash				500
	(Being the cash paid on due date)				

13. DISCOUNTING OF A BILL

Whenever a Drawer feels for the immediate requirements of cash he can sell the bill to a bank. Being a negotiable instrument Bankers will be willing to buy the bills of genuine traders and pay for the value of the bill. For paying the bill before maturity date they will charge a discount which will be an income to the bank. The drawer will thus get only the discounted value of bill. The discount thus deducted by the bank should not be confused with the cash discount earlier.

Entry in the Books of Drawer on Discounting the Bill

Cash a/c Dr
Discount a/c Dr
To Bill Receivable a/c

Note :-

No entry will be passed in the books of the acceptor for the discounting of the bill because he is not at all affected by the discounting of the bill.

Problem 9

On 1st March 2,003 Ram drew a 3 months bill on Rahim for Rs. 500 which was duly accepted. Ram discounted it with his banker at 8% per annum. The bill was duly honoured on the due date. Pass Journal entries in the books of Ram and Rahim.

Solution

Entries in the Books of Ram

Date	*Particulars*	*L.F.*	*Dr. Amount*	*Cr. Amount*
1-3-03	Bills Receivable a/c Dr		500	
	To Rahim's a/c			500
	(Being the bill received from Rahim)			
	Cash a/c Dr		490	
	Discount a/c Dr		10	
	To Bills Receivable a/c			500
	(Being the bill discounted)			

Entries in the Books of Rahim

Date	*Particulars*	*L.F.*	*Dr. Amount*	*Cr. Amount*
1-3-03	Ram's a/c Dr		500	
	To Bills payable a/c			500
	(Being the acceptance given to Ram)			
4-6-03	Bills payable a/c Dr		500	
	To Cash a/c			500
	(Being the cash paid on the acceptance on the due date)			

Note :

1. No entry should be passed in the books of Ram (Drawer) for the honouring of the bill on the due date because the cash was received on the due date not by him but by the Banker.
2. Discount amount is calculated as shown below.

$$500 \times \frac{8}{100} \times \frac{3}{12} = \text{Rs. } 10$$

3. No entry should be passed in the books of Rahim for the discounting of bill because he is not affected by the discounting of the bill.

14. SENDING THE BILL TO THE BANK FOR COLLECTION

If the Drawer and drawee lives in different places, the drawer may collect the proceeds of the bill through his banker instead of going to the place of drawee. The banker renders this service to his customers in return for a collection charge. The drawer is thus relieved from the botheration of going to the place of drawee to collect the proceeds of the bill on due date. The banker does not credit the drawer's account on receiving the bill for collection Instead, the drawer's account is credited only on collection process of the bill is completed. The following entries are passed to record the transactions relating to **bills sent to the bank for collection.**

1. When the bill is sent to bank for collection

   Bill sent to Bank for collection Dr
   To Bills receivable a/c

2. When the bank collects the bill on due date

   Bank a/c Dr
   To Bills sent to bank for collection.

3. When the bank charges collection charges

   Collection charges a/c Dr
   To Bank

In the Book of Banker :

1. On receiving bills for collection
   Bills Receivable a/c Dr
   To Customer's for bill collection a/c.
2. On colleting the bill on due date
   Cash a/c Dr
   To Bills receivable a/c
3. On crediting the proceeds into drawers a/c
   Customer's Bill for Collection a/c Dr
   To customer's a/c

In the Books of Acceptor

1. On receipt of the bill from the bank
   Bills payable a/c Dr
   To Cash a/c

Problem 10

On 1st March 2004 Girish draws a bill on Mukesh for Rs. 500 and sends it to bank for collection. The bill is duly met. Pass the Journal entries in the books of both the parties.

Solution

In the Books of Girish

Date	*Particulars*	*L.F.*	*Dr. Amount*	*Cr. Amount*
	Bills Receivable a/c Dr To Mukesh (Being acceptance received from Mukesh)		500	 500

Date	Particulars		L.F.	Dr. Amount	Cr. Amount
	Bill sent to Bank for collection a/c	Dr		500	
	To Bills receivable a/c				500
	(Being bill sent to bank for collection)				
	Bank a/c	Dr		500	
	To Bill sent to bank for collection a/c				500
	(Being the bill collected by the bank)				

In the Books of Mukesh

Date	Particulars		L.F.	Dr. Amount	Cr. Amount
	Girish a/c	Dr		500	
	To Bills payable				500
	(Being acceptance given on the bill)				
	Bills payable a/c	Dr		500	
	To Cash a/c				500
	(Being cash paid to bank on maturity date)				

15. ENTRIES RELATING TO DISHONOUR OF BILLS

A bill of exchange can be dishonoured by the drawer under any of the following situations.

(*a*) When presented by the drawer on due date .
(*b*) When presented by the bank the discounted bill.
(*c*) When presented by the endorsee
(*d*) When presented by the bank the bill received for collecting it from acceptor.

Entries in the Books of Drawer on Dishonouring a Bill :

1. For recording dishonour of the bill

Acceptor's a/c Dr
To Bills Receivable a/c

Note : The above entry is the reverse entry passed at the time of receiving the bill.

2. When noting charges are to be paid by the drawer owing to dishonour of the bill.

Acceptor's a/c Dr
To Cash

Acceptor's a/c is debited because the drawer can recover noting charges from the accptor i.e., The Acceptor becomes debtor to the extent of noting charges. Cash a/c is credited as it goes out in the form of noting charges.

In the Books of Acceptor

1. On dishonour of the bill

Bills payable a/c Dr
To Drawers a/c

2. To Record noting charges on dishonouring bill

Noting charges a/c Dr
To Drawer's a/c

Problem 11

On 1-1-04 'A' drew a 2 months bill on 'B' for Rs. 500 and the latter accepted the same. On the due date the bill was dishonoured and noting charges of Rs. 10 was paid. Pass Journal entries in the books of both the parties.

Solution

In the Books of 'A'

Date	*Particulars*		*L.F.*	*Dr. Amount*	*Cr. Amount*
1-1-04	Bills Receivable a/c	Dr		500	
	To B's a/c				500
	(Being Bills Receivable received)				
4-3-04	B's a/c	Dr		510	
	To Bills Receivable a/c				500
	To Cash a/c				10
	(Being the bills dishonoured and noting charges paid)				

In the Books of 'B'

Date	*Particulars*		*L.F.*	*Dr. Amount*	*Cr. Amount*
1-1-04	A's a/c	Dr		500	
	To Bills payable				500
	(Being acceptance given on the bill)				
	Bills payable a/c	Dr		500	
	Noting charges a/c	Dr		10	
	To A's a/c				510
	(Being the dishonour of the bill and noting charges paid).				

(*b*) ***Dishonour of the bill when Discounted bill is presented by bank***

In the books of Drawer

On Dishonour of the bill

Acceptor's a/c Dr

To Cash a/c

Note **:** On d ishonour of the bill, the acceptor becomes liable for payment of the bill. So he becomes a debtor, to the drawer. Hence his account is debited. Cash account is credited because on dishonour of the bill the drawer has to pay cash to the banker. Cash goes out on dishonour of the bill. Hence cash account is credited.

In case noting charges are also paid, acceptor's account should be debited and cash account should be credited along with noting charges.

In the books of the Acceptor

1. On dishonour of the bill

Bills payable a/c Dr

To Drawer's a/c

2. When noting charges are payable
Noting charges a/c Dr
To Drawer's a/c

Problem 12

On 1st December 2,004 Akbar drew a 2 months bill on Babar for Rs. 500. After acceptance, the bill was discounted with his banker at 6%. The bill was dishonoured on the due date. Pass the necessary Journal entries in the books of both the parties.

Solution

In the books of Akbar

Date	*Particulars*		*L.F.*	*Dr. Amount*	*Cr. Amount*
1-12-04	Bill receivable a/c	Dr		500	
	To Babar's a/c				500
	(Being the Accepted bill received from Babar)				
	Cash a/c	Dr		495	
	Discount a/c	Dr		5	
	To Bill receivable a/c				500
	(Being the bill discounted)				
4-2-05	Babar's a/c	Dr		500	
	To Cash				500
	(Being the payment of cash to the Bank on the dishonour of bill by Babar)				

In the books of Babar

Date	*Particulars*		*L.F.*	*Dr. Amount*	*Cr. Amount*
1-12-05	Akbar's a/c	Dr		500	
	To Bill payable a/c				500
	(Being the acceptance given to Aakbar)				
4-2-05	Bills payable a/c	Dr		500	
	To Akbar's a/c				500
	(Being the dishonour of the accepted bill)				

(*c*) ***Dishonour of an Endorsed bill :-***

In the books of the Drawer

1. On Dishonour of the bill
Acceptors a/c Dr
To Endorsees a/c
2. When the Drawer pays to the Endorsee
Acceptor's a/c Dr
To Cash a/c

In the books of Acceptor

Same entries as were passed under situation (*b*) above

Problem 13

On 1-3-2,004, Srinivas drew a 3 months bill on Venkatesh for Rs. 500. After acceptance the bill was endorsed to Balaji. The bill was dishonoured on the due date. Pass the necessary entries in the books of Srinivas Venkatesh and Balaji.

Solution

In the books of Srinivas (Drawer)

Date	Particulars		L.F.	Dr. Amount	Cr. Amount
	Bills Receivable a/c	Dr		500	
	To Venkatesh				500
	(Being the bills received from Venkatesh)				
	Balaji a/c	Dr		500	
	To Bills Receivable a/c				500
	(Being the bill endorsed to Balaji)				
	Venkatesh a/c	Dr		500	
	To Balaji a/c				500
	(Being the dishonour of the bill after endorsement)				

In the books of Balaji (Endorser)

Date	Particulars		L.F.	Dr. Amount	Cr. Amount
	Bills receivable a/c	Dr		500	
	To Srinivas a/c				500
	(Being the bill received from Srinivas)				
	Srinivas a/c	Dr		500	
	To Bills receivable a/c				500
	(Being the dishonour of the bill by Venkatesh)				

In the books of Venkatesh (Acceptor)

Date	Particulars		L.F.	Dr. Amount	Cr. Amount
	Srinivas a/c	Dr		500	
	To Bills payable a/c				500
	(Being the acceptance given)				
	Bills payable a/c	Dr		500	
	To Srinivas a/c				500
	(Being the dishonour of acceptance)				

(*d*) ***Dishonour of a bill sent to bank for collection***

In the books of drawer

1. On dishonour of the bill

    Acceptor's a/c Dr

    To Bill sent to bank for collecting bill a/c.

2. When noting charges are paid

Acceptors a/c Dr

To Cash

In the books of Acceptor

Same entries as were passed under situation (*b*) above

Problem 14

On 1st January 2004, for goods sold Prakash draws a bill of exchange on Sridhar for Rs. 4000 for a period of three months. Sridhar accepts it and returns to Prakash. Prakash then endorses it to Nazeer Ahmed, on 1st Feb. 2,004. The bill is then discounted by Nazeer Ahmed on the same date with his banker at 5% per annum. On the due date the bill is dishonoured.

Pass the necessary Journal entries in the books of all the parties.

Solution

In the books of Prakash

Date	*Particulars*	*L.F.*	*Dr. Amount*	*Cr. Amount*
1-1-04	Bills Receivable a/c Dr		4,000	
	To Sridhar			4,000
	(Being accepted bill received)			
	Hussain's a/c Dr		4,000	
	To Bills receivable a/c			4,000
	(Being Bills receivable endorsed)			

In the books of Hussain

Date	*Particulars*	*L.F.*	*Dr. Amount*	*Cr. Amount*
	Bills receivable a/c Dr		4,000	
	To Prakash			4,000
	(Being bills receivable received on endorsement)			
	Nazeer Ahmed a/c Dr		4,000	
	To Bills receivable a/c			4,000
	(Being Bills receivable endorsed)			

In the books of Nazeer Ahmed

Date	*Particulars*	*L.F.*	*Dr. Amount*	*Cr. Amount*
1-2-04	Bills Receivable a/c Dr		4,000	
	To Hussain a/c			4,000
	(Being Bills receivable received on endorsement)			
	Cash a/c Dr		3,967	
	Discount a/c Dr		33	
	To Bills receivable			4,000
	(Being Bills discounted on due date)			

In the books of Sridhar

Date	Particulars		L.F.	Dr. Amount	Cr. Amount
1-1-04	Prakash a/c	Dr		4,000	
	To Bills payable a/c				4,000
	(Being Acceptance given)				
4-4-04	Bills payable a/c	Dr		4,000	
	To Prakash account				4,000
	(Being bills dishonoured).				

Problem 15

For goods supplied Anand draws a bill on Burman for Rs. 4,000. Burman accepts the bill and Anand discounts it with his banker receiving Rs. 3,960. On the due date the banker present the bill to Burman who dishonours it. Anand meets the bill after paying Rs. 25 for noting charges. Burman gives another bill for Rs. 4,100 interest being included. This is met by Burman on the due date. Journalise the transaction in the books of Anand and Burman.

Solution

In the books of Anand

Date	Particulars		L.F.	Dr. Amount	Cr. Amount
	Bills receivable a/c	Dr		4,000	
	To Burman's a/c				4,000
	(Being accepted bill received)				
	Cash a/c	Dr		3,960	
	Discount a/c	Dr		40	
	To Bills receivable a/c				4,000
	(Being the bill discounted with the Bank)				
	Burman a/c	Dr		4,000	
	Noting charges a/c	Dr		25	
	To Bank				4,025
	(Being bill dishonoured payment made to Bank)				
	Bills Receivable a/c	Dr		4,100	
	To Burman a/c				4,000
	To Noting charges a/c				25
	To Interest a/c				75
	(Being new bill received)				
	Cash a/c	Dr		4,100	
	To Bills receivable a/c				4,100
	(Being bill met by Anand on due date)				

In the books of Burman

Date	Particulars		L.F.	Dr. Amount	Cr. Amount
	Anand a/c	Dr		4,000	
	To Bills payable a/c				4,000
	(Being acceptance given)				
	Bills payable	Dr		4,000	
	To Anand a/c				4,000
	(Being bill dishonoured)				
	Anand a/c	Dr		4,000	
	Interest and noting charges a/c	Dr		100	
	To Bills payable a/c				4,100
	(Being new bill accepted)				
	Bills payable a/c	Dr		4,100	
	To Cash a/c				4,100
	(Being the bill met on due date)				

Problem 16

Mr. Arun draws a bill on Barun for Rs. 1,000. Barun accepts the bill and returns it to Arun. The latter endorses it to Tarun and Tarun endorses it to Karun. Karun discounts the bill for Rs. 980. At maturity the bill is dishonoured and the noting charges incurred by Karun's bankers amounts to Rs. 20. Journalise the entries in the books of the parties concerned to record the above transactions.

Solution

In the books of Arun

Date	Particulars		L.F.	Dr. Amount	Cr. Amount
	Bills Receivable a/c	Dr		1,000	
	To Barun				1,000
	(Being the accepted bill received)				
	Tarun's a/c	Dr		1,000	
	To Bills Receivable a/c				1,000
	(Barun's accepted bill endorsed)				

In the books of Barun

Date	Particulars		L.F.	Dr. Amount	Cr. Amount
	Arun's a/c	Dr		1,000	
	To Bills payable a/c				1,000
	(Being acceptance given on the bill)				
	Bills payable a/c	Dr		1,000	
	Noting charges a/c	Dr		20	
	To Arun's a/c				1,020
	(Being the bill dishonoured)				

In the books of Tarun

Date	Particulars		L.F.	Dr. Amount	Cr. Amount
	Bills Receivable a/c	Dr		1,000	
	To Arun's a/c				1,000
	(Being endorsement of bill received)				
	Karun's a/c	Dr		1,000	
	To Bills Receivable a/c				1,000
	(Bills receivable received from Arun endorsed to Karun)				

In the books of Karun

Date	Particulars		L.F.	Dr. Amount	Cr. Amount
	Bills receivable a/c	Dr		1,000	
	To Tarun's a/c				1,000
	(Endorsement of bills receivable received)				
	Bank a/c	Dr		980	
	Discount a/c	Dr		20	
	To Bills receivable a/c				1,000
	(Bills Receivable received from Karun discounted)				
	Tarun's a/c	Dr		1,020	
	To Cash a/c				1,020
	(Amount paid to Bank on bill dishonoured)				

Problem 17

On 1st May 2004, Hari sold goods to Srinivasan for Rs. 1,000 and drew a bill on him at three months after date for the amount. After the bill is duly accepted, Hari endorsed it to Narayan who discounted the bill with his bankers for Rs. 975. The bill was dishonoured on the due date noting charges paid by the bank being Rs. 10. Pass the necessary entries in the books of Hari, Srinivasan and Narayan.

Solution

In the books of Hari

Date	Particulars		L.F.	Dr. Amount	Cr. Amount
	Srinivasan a/c	Dr		1,000	
	To Sales a/c				1,000
	(Being goods sold to Srinivasan)				
	Bills Receivable	Dr		1,000	
	To Srinivasan a/c				1,000
	(Being Acceptance received on the bill)				

Date	Particulars		L.F.	Dr. Amount	Cr. Amount
	Narayan's a/c	Dr		1,000	
	To Bills Receivable				1,000
	(Being the bill endorsed to Narayan)				
	Srinivasan a/c	Dr		1,010	
	To Narayan's a/c				1,000
	To Noting charges				10
	(Being the dishonour of the bill)				

In the books of Narayan

Date	Particulars		L.F.	Dr. Amount	Cr. Amount
	Bills receivable a/c	Dr		1,000	
	To Hari's a/c				1,000
	(Being the endorsed bill received)				
	Bank a/c	Dr		975	
	Discount a/c	Dr		25	
	To Bills receivable a/c				1,000
	(Being the bills discounted)				
	Hari's a/c	Dr		1,010	
	To Bills Receivable a/c				1,000
	Noting charges				10
	(Being the bills dishonoured)				
	Bank a/c	Dr		1,010	
	To Cash a/c				1,010
	(Being payment to bank on dishonoured bill including noting charges)				

In the Books of Srinivasan

Date	Particulars		L.F.	Dr. Amount	Cr. Amount
	Purchases a/c	Dr		1,000	
	To Hari's a/c				1,000
	(Being goods purchased from Hari)				
	Hari's a/c	Dr		1,000	
	To Bills payable a/c				1,000
	(Being the acceptance given on the bill)				
	Bills payable a/c	Dr		1,000	
	Noting charges a/c	Dr		10	
	To Hari's a/c				1,010
	(Being the Bill dishonoured)				

Problem 18

On 1st January 2,004, X draws a bill on Y for 4 months of Rs. 1,000 and Y draws on X for a similar amount and term. Both the bills are accepted and discounted respectively at 6%. 'X' meets his own acceptance on maturity. But Y's acceptance is dishonoured. Y, then accepts a new bill at three months for the amounts due by him plus interest at 8% which is duly met on maturity.

Journalise the above transactions in the books of 'X' only.

Solution

In the books of X

Date	*Particulars*		*L.F.*	*Dr. Amount*	*Cr. Amount*
1-1-04	Bills Receivable a/c	Dr		1,000	
	To Y's a/c				1,000
	(Being the Accepted bill received)				
	Y's a/c	Dr		1,000	
	To Bills payable a/c				1,000
	(Being the acceptance given on the bill)				
	Bank a/c	Dr		980	
	Discount a/c	Dr		20	
	To Bills Receivable a/c				1,000
	(Being the bill discounted with the bank)				
4-4-04	Bills payable a/c	Dr		1,000	
	To Cash				1,000
	(Being the bill honoured)				
	Y's a/c	Dr		1,000	
	To Bills Receivable a/c				1,000
	(Being Y dishonoured his bill)				
	Bills Receivable a/c	Dr		1,020	
	To Y's a/c				1,000
	To Interest a/c				20
	(Being the new bill received from Y including interest)				

Problem 19

1. On 1st Jan 2,004 'A' draws a bill of exchange on 'B' and B accepts it for 3 months after date for Rs. 2,000.
2. On the same date 'A' discount the Bill, with his Bank and pays discount charges Rs. 100.
3. On the same date he remits half the proceeds of the bill to 'B'.
4. On 1st April 'A' remits the balance to enable 'B' to discharge the bill on the due date.
5. On 4th April 'B' meets the bill.

Record the necessary entries in the books of 'A' and 'B'.

Solution

In the books of 'A'

Date	Particulars	L.F.	Dr. Amount	Cr. Amount
1-1-04	Bills Receivable a/c Dr To B's a/c (Being the accepted bill received)		2,000	2,000
	Cash a/c Dr Discount a/c Dr To Bills Receivable a/c (Being the bill discounted with the bank)		1,900 100	2,000
	B's a/c Dr To Cash a/c To Discount a/c (Half of the proceeds of the bill given to B)		1,000	950 50
1-4-04	B's a/c Dr To Cash a/c (Payment made to 'B' to enable him to honour the bill on due date)		1,000	1,000
	Profit & loss a/c Dr To Discount a/c (Being discount transferred to P & C a/c)		50	50

In the books of B

Date	Particulars	L.F.	Dr. Amount	Cr. Amount
1-1-04	A's a/c Dr To Bills payable a/c (Being the acceptance given on the bill)		2,000	2,000
	Cash a/c Dr Discount a/c Dr To A's a/c (Being half of the proceeds of the bill received from A)		950 50	1,000
1-4-04	Cash a/c Dr To A's a/c (Being the amount received from A)		1,000	1,000
4-4-04	Bills payable a/c Dr To Cash (Being the bill honoured on due date)		2,000	2,000
	P & L a/c Dr To Discount a/c (Being the discount transferred to P & L a/c).		50	50

Problem 20

A bill of Rs. 1,000 was drawn by 'X' on 'Y'. It was dishonoured on maturity and noting charges paid by the holder amounted to Rs. 25. Show what entries would be passed in the books of 'X' on dishonour of the bill in each of the following cases.

1. If 'X' had retained the bill with him till maturity.
2. If 'X' had discounted the bill for Rs. 985.
3. If 'X' had endorsed the bill to 'Z' in satisfaction of a debt due to him.
4. If 'X' had sent the bill to his banker for collection.

Solution

In the books of X

Date	Particulars	L.F.	Dr. Amount	Cr. Amount
	Bills Receivable a/c Dr To Y's a/c (Being the accepted bill received)		1,000	 1,000

1. When 'X' had retained the bill with him till maturity

Date	Particulars	L.F.	Dr. Amount	Cr. Amount
	Y's a/c Dr To Bills Receivable a/c To Noting charges (Being the bill dishonoured)		1,025	 1,000 25

2. When 'X' had discounted the bill

Date	Particulars	L.F.	Dr. Amount	Cr. Amount
	Bank a/c Dr Discount a/c Dr To Bills Receivables a/c (Being the bills discounted)		985 15	 1,000
	Y's a/c Dr To Bank (Being payment made to Bank on dishonour including noting charges).		1,025	 1,025

3. When 'X' had endorsed the bill to Z in satisfaction of a debt due to him

Date	Particulars	L.F.	Dr. Amount	Cr. Amount
	Z's a/c Dr To Bills Receivable a/c (Being the bill endorsed)		1,000	 1,000
	Y's a/c Dr To Z's a/c Dishonour of bill after endorsing it to Z)		1,025	 1,025

4. If 'X' had sent the bill to his banker for collection

Date	Particulars		L.F.	Dr. Amount	Cr. Amount
	Bank a/c for collection of bill	Dr		1,000	
	To Bill Receivable a/c				1,000
	(Being Y's acceptance sent to bank for collection)				
	Y's a/c	Dr		1,025	
	To Bank a/c for collection of bill				1,025
	(Being dishonour for of the bill after it was sent for collection).				

Problem 21

'A' draws a bill of exchange on B for goods supplied for Rs. 10,000 dated 1st January 2,004 at 3 months. 'B' accepts the bill and thereafter on 4 the January 'A' discounts it with his bankers at 8% per annum. The bill is dishonoured on presentation on the due date and the banker's debit 'A' with Rs. 20 noting expenses, in addition to the value of the bills. 'B' pays 'A' cash Rs. 5,000 on 5th April and simultaneously accepts a fresh bill for the balance due by him including Rs. 300 for interest and noting expenses of the first bill. The bill is paid in time. Journalise the above transactions.

Solution

In the books of A

Date	Particulars		L.F.	Dr. Amount	Cr. Amount
1-1-04	Bills Receivable a/c	Dr		1,000	
	To B's a/c				1,000
	(Being the Accepted bill received from B)				
4-1-04	Bank a/c	Dr		9,800	
	Discount a/c	Dr		200	
	To Bills receivable a/c				10,000
	(Being the dishonour of B's acceptance on presentation by the bank and the noting charges Rs. 10 incurred by bank).				
5-1-04	Bank a/c	Dr		5,000	
	To B's a/c				5,000
	(Being the payment by B against the bill dishonoured)				
5-1-04	Bank a/c	Dr		300	
	To Interest				300
	(Being the interest charged in consideration of accepting a new bill)				
5-1-04	Bills Receivable a/c	Dr		5,320	
	To B's a/c				5,320
	(Being the bill accepted by B against old bill together with noting charge and interest).				
5-1-04	Bank a/c	Dr		5,320	
	To Bills Receivable a/c				5,320
	(Being the cash received)				

In the books of B

Date	Particulars	L.F.	Dr. Amount	Cr. Amount
1-1-04	A's a/c Dr To Bills payable a/c (Being acceptance given on the bill)		10,000	10,000
4-1-04	Bills payable a/c Dr Noting charges a/c Dr To A's a/c (Being dishonour of A's bill and Rs. 20 noting charges incurred by A).		10,000 20	10,020
5-1-04	A's a/c Dr To Bank (Being part payment against dishonouring A's bill)		5,000	5,000
5-1-04	Interest a/c Dr To A's a/c (Being interest payable for renewal of bill).		300	300
5-1-04	A's a/c Dr To Bills payable (Being the acceptance of a bill against the dues of bills cancelled together with noting and interest).		5,320	5,320
	Bills payable a/c Dr To Bank (Being payment of A's Bill)		5,320	5,320

Note **:-** Discount calculated in terms of months amounts to Rs. 200 (8% on 10,000 for 3 months). The due date of the bill considering 3 days of grace falls on 4th April and out of 10,020 (including noting charges) Rs. 5,000 is paid. The balance of Rs. 5,020 together with interest of Rs. 300 is covered by the second bill.

Problem 22

'A' draws upon 'B' three bills of exchange of Rs. 3,000/Rs. 2,000 and Rs. 1,000 respectively A week later his fresh bill was mutually cancelled, 'B agreeing to pay 50% of the amount in cash immediately and for the balance plus interest Rs. 100 he accepted a fresh bill drawn by 'A'. This new bill was endorsed to C who discounted the same with his bankers for 1,500. The second bill was discounted by 'A' at 5%. The bill on maturity was returned dishonoured (noting charge being Rs. 30) The third bill was retained till maturity when it was duly met.

Give the necessary journal entries recording the above transactions in the books of A and B.

Solution

In the books of A

Date	Particulars	L.F.	Dr. Amount	Cr. Amount
	Bills Receivable a/c Dr To B's a/c (Being 3 bills for Rs. 3,000 Rs. 2,000 and Rs. 1,000 drawn on B and duly accepted by him received.		6,000	6,000

Date	Particulars		L.F.	Dr. Amount	Cr. Amount
	B's a/c	Dr		3,000	
	To Bills Receivable a/c				3,000
	(Being bills received from B cancelled for renewal)				
	Bank a/c	Dr		1,500	
	Bills Receivable a/c	Dr		1,600	
	To B's a/c				3,000
	To Interest a/c				100
	(Being the amount received on cancellation of the first bill, 50% along with a new bill, for 50% of the amount plus interest Rs. 100).				
	C's a/c	Dr		1,600	
	To Bills Receivable a/c				1,600
	(B's acceptance endorsed in favour of C)				
	Bank a/c	Dr		1,900	
	Discount a/c	Dr		100	
	To Bills receivable a/c				2,000
	(Second bill for Rs. 2,000 discounted with the Bank @ 5%).				
	B's a/c	Dr		2,030	
	To Bank a/c				2,030
	(Second Bill for Rs. 2,000 discounted with the bank dishonoured, noting charges Rs. 30 paid by the Bank).				
	Bank a/c	Dr		1,000	
	To Bills receivable a/c				1,000
	(Being the amount received on maturity of the third bill)				

In the books of B

Date	Particulars		L.F.	Dr. Amount	Cr. Amount
	A's a/c	Dr		6,000	
	To Bills payable a/c				6,000
	(Being three acceptance given to 'A' for Rs. 3,000, Rs. 2,000, Rs. 1,000)				
	Bills payable a/c	Dr		3,000	
	To A's a/c				3,000
	(Being the cancellation of the first bill issued to A by mutual agreement)				
	A's a/c	Dr		3,000	
	Interest a/c	Dr		100	
	To Bank a/c				1,500
	To Bills payable a/c				1,600
	(Amount paid to A against cancelled bill and issue of new bill for Rs. 1,600 including interest Rs. 100)				

Date	Particulars		L.F.	Dr. Amount	Cr. Amount
	Bills payable a/c	Dr		2,000	
	Noting charge a/c	Dr		30	
	To A's a/c				2,030
	(Dishonour of the second bill issued to A)				
	Bills payable a/c	Dr		1,000	
	To Bank				1,000
	(Being payment of 3rd bill to A on due date)				

Note : It is assured that the bill for Rs. 1,600 has not yet fallen due for payment.

16. Renewal of a Bill

Whenever an acceptor finds it difficult to honour the cheques he may request the drawer to extend the time for payment of the bill. This is done to avoid the complication arising out of dishonour of the bill. If the drawer agrees to the request of the drawee he will allow the drawee to pay the value of the bill at a later date. For having extended the payment period the drawee is expected to pay an interest on the value of the bill for the extended period. Before the drawee agrees to issue the fresh bill for an extended period, the old bill is to be cancelled first. This process of cancelling an old bill and drawing a fresh bill in its place to give more time to the acceptor is called Renewing the bill. The following entries are passed in the books of drawer and drawee on renewal of a bill.

In the books of Drawer

1. For the cancellation of the old bill
   Acceptor's a/c Dr
   To Bills Receivable a/c
2. For recording the interest for the extended period
   (a) *If received in cash*
   Cash a/c Dr
   To Interest a/c
   (b) *If included in the new bill*
   Acceptor's a/c Dr
   To Interest a/c
3. For receiving the new bill
   Bill receivable a/c Dr
   Acceptor's a/c

In the books of Acceptor

1. For the cancellation of old bills
   Bills payable a/c Dr
   To Drawers a/c
2. For the Interest payable on the bill for extending the time.
   (a) *If paid in cash*
   Interest a/c Dr
   To Cash
   (b) *If interest is included in the new bill*
   Interest a/c Dr
   To Drawer's a/c

3. For accepting the new bill
   Drawer's a/c Dr
   To Bills payable a/c

Problem 23

'B' being unable to meet his acceptance for Rs. 1,000 due on 15th June approaches the drawer 'A' (who is in possession of the bill), on 13th June with a request to receive Rs. 400 in cash and drew on him for the balance plus Rs. 5 for interest at 3 months date and cancel the old bill for Rs. 1,000, 'A' agrees to this. Pass the entries in the books of A and B.

Solution

In the books of A

Date	*Particulars*	*L.F.*	*Dr. Amount*	*Cr. Amount*
	B's a/c Dr		1,000	
	To Bills Receivable a/c			1,000
	(Being the cancellation of old bill)			
	Cash a/c Dr		400	
	To B's a/c			400
	(Being payment received in part towards old bill)			
	Bills Receivable a/c Dr		605	
	To B's a/c			600
	To Interest a/c			5
	(Being new bill received after acceptance)			

In the books of B

Date	*Particulars*	*L.F.*	*Dr. Amount*	*Cr. Amount*
	Bills payable a/c Dr		1,000	
	To A's a/c			1,000
	(Being cancellation of old bill)			
	A's a/c Dr		400	
	To Cash a/c			400
	(Being payment made in part towards the old bill)			
	A's a/c Dr		600	
	Interest a/c Dr		5	
	To Bills payable a/c			605
	(Being acceptance given on new bill).			

Problem 24

Gopi sold goods to Raghava on 1st Sept. 2004 for Rs. 600. Raghava accepted a 3 months bill. On the due date Raghava requested that the bill be renewed for a further period of 2 months with an offer to pay interest at 9% immediately in cash. To this Gopi was agreeable. The second bill was met on the due date. Journalise in the books of both the parties.

Solution

In the Books of Gopi

Date	Particulars		L.F.	Dr. Amount	Cr. Amount
1 Sept. 04.	Raghava's a/c	Dr		1,600	
	To Sales				1,600
	(Being goods sold to Raghava on credit)				
	Bills receivable a/c	Dr		1,600	
	To Raghava				1,600
	(Being the accepted bill received)				
1 Nov. 04.	Raghava's a/c	Dr		1,600	
	To Bills Receivable a/c				1,600
	(Being cancellation of old bill)				
	Cash a/c	Dr		24	
	To Interest				24
	(Being interest at 9% for 2 months received)				
	Bills Receivable a/c	Dr		1,600	
	To Raghava				1,600
	(Being fresh bill received from Raghava)				
4-1-04	Cash a/c	Dr		1,600	
	To Bill Receivable a/c				1,600
	(Being the bill honoured)				

In the books of Raghava

Date	Particulars		L.F.	Dr. Amount	Cr. Amount
1 Sep. 04.	Purchases a/c	Dr		1,600	
	To Gopi's a/c				1,600
	(Being goods purchased from Gopi on credit)				
	Gopi's a/c	Dr		1,600	
	To Bills Payable a/c				1600
	(Being cancellation of old bill)				
	Interest a/c	Dr		24	
	To Cash a/c				24
	(Being interest paid at 9% for 2 months)				
	Gopi's a/c	Dr		1,600	
	To Bills Payable				1,600
	(Being Acceptance given on the new bill).				
4-1-76.	Bills Payable a/c	Dr		1,600	
	To Cash				1,600
	(Being bills payable honoured on due date)				

Problem 25

On 1st May 2003, Merchant & Co. sold to AB & Co. goods valued at Rs. 500 and drew upon them at 3 months for the amount. AB & Co. accepted the draft on presentation. When the bill was about to mature AB & Co. expressed their inability to meet it and offered to pay merchant & Co. Rs. 200 in cash and accept a fresh bill for the balance plus interest at 6% per annum of three months. Merchant & Co. agreed to the proposal and the bill was renewed. Make entries in the books of the parties to record the above transactions.

Solution

In the Books of Merchant & Co.

Date	*Particulars*		*L.F.*	*Dr. Amount*	*Cr. Amount*
	AB & Co. a/c	Dr		500	
	To Sales				500
	(Being goods sold to AB & Co. on credit)				
	Bills Receivable a/c	Dr		500	
	To AB & Co. a/c				500
	(Being the accepted bill received from AB & Co.)				
	AB & Co. a/c	Dr		500	
	To Bills Receivable a/c				500
	(Being the cancellation of old bill)				
	Cash a/c	Dr		200	
	To AB & Co.				200
	(Being cash received from AB & W)				
	Bills Receivable a/c	Dr		304.50	
	To AB & Co.				300
	To Interest $\frac{6}{100} \times \frac{3}{12} \times 300$				4.50
	(Being new bill accepted including Interest at 6% for 3 months.)				

In the books of AB & Co.

Date	*Particulars*		*L.F.*	*Dr. Amount*	*Cr. Amount*
	Purchases a/c	Dr		500	
	To Merchant & Co.				500
	(Being goods purchased from Merchant & Co. on credit)				
	Merchant & Co. a/c	Dr		500	
	To Bills Payable a/c				500
	(Being acceptance given to Merchant & Co.)				

Date	Particulars		L.F.	Dr. Amount	Cr. Amount
	Bills Payable a/c	Dr		500	
	To Merchant & Co.				500
	(Being acceptance cancelled)				
	Merchant & Co. a/c	Dr		200	
	To Cash				200
	(Being cash paid to merchant & Co.)				
	Merchant & Co. a/c	Dr		300	
	Interest a/c	Dr		4.50	
	To Bills Payable a/c				304.5
	(Being acceptance for a new bill given including interest).				

17. RETIRING A BILL UNDER A REBATE

Sometimes an acceptor may be willing to pay the value of bill much before the due date which is always welcome by the drawer. As the acceptor is willing to pay the bill before the due date, he is given a discount by the drawer which is termed as Rebate. Such transactions are recorded both in the books of drawer and drawee as shown below.

In the books of Drawer

Cash a/c Dr
Discount a/c Dr
To Bill Receivable a/c

In the books of Acceptor

Bills Payable a/c Dr
To Cash a/c
To Discount a/c

Problem 25

On 1-1-04, Naveen drew a bill on Sunil for Rs. 5,000 for three months. Before a month of the due date, Sunil retired his bill for which he was given a rebate of Rs. 100. Pass the Journal entries in the books of the parties concerned.

Solution

In the books of Naveen

Date	Particulars		L.F.	Dr. Amount	Cr. Amount
	Bills receivable a/c	Dr		5,000	
	To Sunil's a/c				5,000
	(Being the accepted bill received from Sunil)				
	Cash a/c	Dr		4,900	
	Discount a/c	Dr		100	
	To Bills receivable a/c				5,000
	(Being the cash received and rebate allowed.)				

In the books of Sunil

Date	Particulars		L.F.	Dr. Amount	Cr. Amount
	Naveens a/c	Dr		5,000	
	To Bills Payable a/c				5,000
	(Being acceptance given the bill)				
	Bills Payable a/c	Dr		5,000	
	To Cash				4,900
	To Discount				100
	(Being the bill retired and received discount of Rs. 100)				

18. ACCOMMODATION BILL

While discussing about the features of bill of exchange it was laid down that there must be a valid consideration in a bill transaction for making it a valid instrument. As compared to such a bill which is also called, as a trade bill, an accommodation bill is drawn and "accepted by businessman who feel the need for temporary financial accommodation. A bill which provides a short term financial accommodation by drawing and accepting it is known as accommodation bill". It is also known as finance bill. It is drawn and accepted either for the benefit of the drawer or for the mutual benefit of both the drawer and acceptor.

The significance of an accommodation bill could be explained by means of an example. Suppose Mr. 'A' is in need of some cash he can draw a Bill of exchange on B. Mr. B will accept it and return it to Mr. A. Mr. A will then discount it with a Banker, and the discounted value of bill can be used by him for meeting the expenses of his business. Before the due date arrives Mr. A will pay the full value of the bill to Mr. B. When the bank presents the bill to Mr. B on due date it will be honoured by B. As the language used in case of trade bill and accommodation bill is the same the banker cannot make out the difference between a trade bill and accommodation bill. Entries are passed in the books of both the parties exactly in the way already mentioned under the trade bill. The only additional entry to be passed is for sending the remittance to the other party and also debiting the other party with the requisite amount of discount.

Problem 26

On 1st Oct. 2004, Mr. A drew a bill for Rs. 9,000 on B payable after 3 months for their mutual accommodation. The bill was duly accepted and returned by Mr. B.M Mr. A discounted it with the bankers at 6% and remitted $\frac{1}{3}$rd of the proceeds to Mr. B. Before the due date, Mr. A sent him the balance but Mr. B dishonoured, the bill on the due date and Mr. A had to pay his bankers the amount of the bill along with charges Rs. 30. Mr. B accepted a fresh bill for the whole amount including an interest of Rs. 150 and noting charges payable after 2 months.

Pass the necessary Journal entries in the books of Mr. A and Mr. B.

Solution

In the books of 'A'

Date	*Particulars*		*L.F.*	*Dr. Amount*	*Cr. Amount*
	Bills receivable a/c	Dr		9,000	
	To B's a/c				9,000
	(Being the accepted bill received from B)				
	Cash a/c	Dr		8,865	
	Discount a/c	Dr		135	
	To Bills receivable a/c				9,000
	(Being Bills Receivable discounted with the Bank)				
	B's a/c	Dr		3,000	
	To Cash a/c				2,955
	To Discount a/c				45
	(Being $\frac{1}{3}$rd of the proceeds given to B)				
	B's a/c	Dr		6,000	
	To Cash				6,000
	(Balance of $\frac{2}{3}$ paid to B to enable him to settle the bill on maturity)				
	B's a/c	Dr		9,000	
	Noting charges a/c	Dr		30	
	To Bank a/c				9,030
	(Being the bill dishonoured by B)				
	Bills Receivable a/c	Dr		9,180	
	To B's a/c				9,000
	To Interest a/c				150
	To Noting charges a/c				30
	(Being fresh bill accepted by B)				
	Profit & Loss a/c	Dr		90	
	To Discount a/c				90
	(Being the discount transferred to P & L a/c)				

In the books of 'B'

Date	*Particulars*		*L.F.*	*Dr. Amount*	*Cr. Amount*
	A's a/c	Dr		9,000	
	To Bills Payable a/c				9,000
	(Being the acceptance given for the bill drawn by A)				
	Cash a/c	Dr		2,955	
	Discount a/c	Dr		45	
	To A's a/c				3,000
	(Being $\frac{1}{3}$rd of the proceeds received from A)				

Date	Particulars		L.F.	Dr. Amount	Cr. Amount
	Cash a/c	Dr		6,000	
	To A's a/c				6,000
	(Balance $\frac{2}{3}$rd of the value of bill received from A before due date)				
	Bills payable a/c	Dr		9,000	
	Noting charges	Dr		30	
	To A's a/c				9,030
	(Being bills dishonoured and noting charges payable)				
	A's a/c	Dr		9,030	
	Interest a/c	Dr		150	
	To Bills payable a/c				9,180
	(Being the fresh bill accepted)				
	Profit & Loss a/c	Dr		225	
	To Noting charges				30
	To Interest a/c				150
	To Discount a/c				45
	(Being the various expenses on bill transferred to profit & loos a/c).				

Problem 27

A draws a bill for Rs. 3,000 and B accepts the same for the mutual accommodation of both of them to the extent of two-thirds and one-third respectively.

A discounts the same for Rs. 2,820 and remits $\frac{1}{3}$ of proceeds to B. Before the due date A remits his portion to B in order to enable the latter to meet the bill. B meets the bill on the due date. Pass journal entries in the books of A and B.

Solution

In the books of A

Date	Particulars		L.F.	Dr. Amount	Cr. Amount
	Bills Receivable a/c	Dr		3,000	
	To B's a/c				3,000
	(Being the accepted bill received)				
	Cash a/c	Dr		2,820	
	Discount	Dr		180	
	To Bills Receivable a/c				3,000
	(Being Bills receivable discounted with the bank)				
	B's a/c	Dr		1,000	
	To Cash a/c				940
	To Discount a/c				60
	(Being $\frac{1}{3}$rd of the proceeds paid to B)				

Date	Particulars	L.F.	Dr. Amount	Cr. Amount
	B's a/c Dr To Cash a/c (Being Balance paid to B to settle the bill on due date)		2,000	2,000
	Profit & Loss a/c Dr To Discount (Being the discount transferred to Profit & Loss a/c).		120	120

In the books of B

Date	Particulars	L.F.	Dr. Amount	Cr. Amount
	A's a/c Dr To Bills Payable a/c (Being the acceptance given the bill)		3,000	3,000
	Cash a/c Dr Discount a/c Dr To A's a/c (Being $\frac{1}{3}$rd of the proceeds of the bill received from A)		940 60	1,000
	Cash a/c Dr To A's a/c (Being the amount received from A to honour the bill)		2,000	2,000
	Bills Payable a/c Dr To Cash (Being the bill honoured on the due date)		3,000	3,000
	Profit & Loss a/c Dr To Discount (Being the discount transferred to P & C a/c		60	60

Problem 28

For the mutual accommodation of X and Y, X draws a bill on Y for Rs. 5,000 and Y accepts the bill and returns it to X. X discounts the bill with his bankers and received Rs. 4,800. The proceeds are shared between X and Y in proportion of $\frac{2}{3}$ and $\frac{1}{3}$ respectively. On the due date X remits his proportion to Y who meets the bill. Pass Journal entries in the books of X and Y to record the above transactions.

Solution

In the books of X

Date	Particulars	L.F.	Dr. Amount	Cr. Amount
	Bills Receivable a/c Dr To Y's a/c (Being the accepted bill received from Y)		5,000	5,000

Date	Particulars		L.F.	Dr. Amount	Cr. Amount
	Bank a/c	Dr		4,800.00	
	Discount a/c	Dr		200.00	
	To Bills Receivable a/c				5,000.00
	(Being the Bill Discounted)				
	Y's a/c	Dr		1,666.67	
	To Cash a/c				1,600.00
	To Discount				66.67
	(Being $\frac{1}{3}$rd amount of discounted bill sent and proportionate discount charged to him).				
	Y's a/c	Dr		3,333.33	
	To Cash a/c				3,333.33
	(Being the balance amount remitted to Y)				

In the books of Y

Date	Particulars		L.F.	Dr. Amount	Cr. Amount
	X's a/c	Dr		5,000.00	
	To Bills payable a/c				5,000.00
	(Being the accepted bill received)				
	Cash a/c	Dr		1,600.00	
	Discount a/c	Dr		66.67	
	To X's a/c				1,666.67
	(Being $\frac{1}{3}$rd of proceeds of the Bill received)				
	Cash a/c	Dr		3,333.33	
	To X 'as a/c				3,333.33
	(Balance received from X)				
	Bills Payable a/c	Dr		5,000.00	
	To Cash				5,000.00
	(Being the bills payable honoured)				

Problem 29

Sun accepted a bill for Rs. 10,000 drawn by Moon for mutual accommodation. It was discounted for Rs. 9,600 and was sent to Sun. Just before maturity a cheque of Rs. 2,000 only was received from Moon by Sun and the Bill was duly honoured by Sun. Moon became insolvent and only 20 paise in the rupee was received as dividend from his estate.

Show personal accounts in the books of both the parties.

Solution

Moon's A/c

Date	Particulars	Amount	Date	Particulars	Amount
	To Bills payable	10,000		By Bank	4,800
				By Discount	200
				By Bank	2,000
				By Balance c/d	3,000
		10,000			10,000

Date	Particulars	Amount	Date	Particulars	Amount
	To Balance b/d	3,000		By Bank	600
				By Bad debts	2,400
		3,000			3,000

Sun's a/c

Date	Particulars	Amount	Date	Particulars	Amount
	To Bank	4,800		By Bills receivable	10,000
	To Discount	200			
	To Bank	2,000			
	To Balance c/d	3,000			
		10,000			10,000
	To Bank	600		By balance b/d	3,000
	To Deficiency a/c	2,400			
		3,000			3,000

KEY WORDS

1. **Acceptance of Bill**
   It refers to the consent given on the bill by the drawee.
2. **Accommodation bill**
   A bill which is used to raise finance temporarily for the mutual benefit of the drawer and drawee.
3. **Bill of Exchange :**
   An instrument in writing signed by the maker directing a certain person to pay a certain sum of money either to the drawer or to a payee.
4. **Discounting the bill :**
   The process of encashing a bill before its maturity is called discounting the bill.
5. **Drawer**
   The person who draws a bill is known as drawer.
6. **Drawee**
   The person on whom the bill is drawn is known as drawee.
7. **Documentary bill**
   A bill which accompanies the shipping documents to be delivered to importer upon his acceptance or payment of the bill.
8. **Dishonour of the bill :**
   The act of refusing to accept a bill or to make payment on presentation.
9. **Endorsement of bill :**
   The process of transferring the bill by one person to another person so as to constitute the latter the true owner of the bill.
10. **Foreign Bill :**
    A bill which is drawn and made payable in a country other than home country.
11. **Inland Bill :**
    A bill which is drawn and made payable within the boundaries of a country.

12. Noting the bill

It means a proper authentication by the notary public giving the material facts relating to dishonour of a bill.

13. Renewal of a bill :

It refers to the process of extending the period for the payment of the bill along with certain amount of interest.

14. Retiring a bill :

It refers to process of paying the bill much in advance of due date.

15. Trade bill :

A bill which arises in course of a trade transaction between two parties.

QUESTIONS

Answer the following questions in about four lines each :

1. Define a Bill of Exchange.
2. What do you mean by
   (*a*) Drawer of the bill ? (*b*) The Drawee of the bill ?
   (*c*) Drawee in case of need ? (*d*) Acceptor ?
   (*e*) Acceptor for honour ? (*f*) Payee?
3. What do you mean by Inland bill ?
4. What do you mean by foreign bill ?
5. Distinguish between an Inland bill and foreign bill ?
6. What do you mean by Documentary Bill of Exchange ?
7. What do you mean by trade bill ?
8. What do you mean by accommodation B.U. ?
9. Distinguish between a trade bill and accommodation bill.
10. What do you mean by acceptance of a bill ?
11. What do you mean by dishonour of a bill ?
12. What do you mean by noting and protesting a bill ?
13. What do you mean by Endorsement of a bill ?
14. What do you mean by Discounting a bill ?
15. What do you mean by Renewal of a bill ?
16. What do you mean by Retiring a bill ?

Answer the following questions in about a page each.

1. What is meant by due date of a bill ? How do you calculate it ? Give two examples.
2. Mention and explain the names of books of original entry for bill transaction.
3. What do you understand by the terms "dishonour" and discounting of bill of exchange by say 'A' a businessman ? What are the usual Journal entries recorded under these circumstances ?
4. Draw a bill of exchange and show the acceptance there on.
5. List the essentials of a Bill of Exchange.
6. Give the meaning of
   (*i*) Days of grace (*ii*) Accomodation bill (*iii*) Payee of a bill
   (*iv*) Noting (*v*) Endorsement.
7. What for are bills receivable and bills payable books maintained ? Explain postings from them ?
8. What are the advantage of making payment by bills of exchange ?

9. Study carefully the following in the books of Z and fill up the bank in each to make it complete and correct.

(*a*) Bills Receivable a/c Dr
To ________ a/c
(For bills received from A)

(*b*) B's a/c Dr
To ________ a/c
(For endorsing the above bill to B)

(*c*) ________ a/c Dr
To B's a/c
(For dishonour of the bills by A)

(*d*) X's a/c Dr
To ________ a/c
(For accepting X's bill)

(*e*) Bills payable Dr
To Cash a/c
(For honouring our acceptance to X)

(*f*) ________ a/c Dr
To O's a/c
(For bill received on endorsement by O)

(*g*) ________ a/c Dr
________ a/c Dr
To Bills Receivable a/c
(For discounting O's bills with the banker)

(*h*) O's a/c Dr
To ________ a/c
(For the above bill of 'O' dishonoured on the due date)

Answer

(*a*) A's a/c (*b*) Bills Receivable a/c (*c*) A's a/c
(*d*) Bills Payable a/c (*e*) Cash a/c (*f*) Bills Receivable
(*g*) Cash a/c Dr
Discount a/c
(*h*) Bank a/c

(9) Answer each of the following questions is not more than two sentence.
(*i*) Acceptance of a bill.
(*ii*) What are days of grace.
(*iii*) Who should honour the bill and why ?
(*iv*) What is noting of a bill ?

EXERCISE 1

(When the bill is drawn and honoured)

Arun sold to Basu goods worth Rs. 1,000 and drew upon him a bill at 3 months on 1-4-95 for the amount. Basu accepts it and returns it to Arun. Arun presents the Bill on maturity to Basu who makes the payment. Make entries in the books of both the parties.

EXERCISE 2

(When the Bill is Discounted and honoured)

Murthy sold to Ravindra goods worth Rs. 1,000 and drew upon him a bill at 3 months on 1-4-04 for the amount. Ravindra accepts it and returns it to Murthy. Murthy discounts the bill on 4-5-04 with his bankers at 6% per annum. On the date of maturity the bill was duly honoured.

Record these transactions in the books of the parties.

EXERCISE 3

(When the bill is endorsed and honoured)

Arunesh sold to Vikram goods worth Rs. 5,000 and drew upon him a bill at 3 months on 1-1-04 for the amount. Vikram accepts it and returns it to Arunesh on 20-1-04. Arunesh endorses the bill in favour of Kishore. The bill was duly honoured on the date of maturity.

Pass Journal entries in the books of the parties concerned.

EXERCISE 4

(When a bill is sent to bank for collection)

On 1-1-2004 Sudhindra sold goods to Amarendar worth Rs. 2,000 and drew upon the latter a bill for the amount at 3 months. On 4th March, he deposited the bill with his banker, Dena Bank, for collection. On the due date Amarendra refused to honour acceptance.

Enter these transactions in the books of the parties .

EXERCISE 5

(When endorsed and discounted)

Bharath draws a bill on Sharath which was accepted by Sharath payable at the Union Bank of India. What entries would be passed in the books of all the parties under each of the following circumstances.

(*a*) If the bill is retained till the due date and then realised it on maturity.

(*b*) If it is discounted with the banker for Rs. 5,800.

(*c*) It is endorsed it over to the creditor Sampath in settlement of their debt.

State what further entries would be Passed in the books of Sharath under each of the above circumstances, if the bill was dishonoured on the due date.

State what further entries would be Passed in the books of Sharath under each of the above circumstances, if the bill was dishonoured on the due date.

EXERCISE 6

(When more then one bill is drawn)

On 1-9-04 'X' received from 'A' three bill of exchange for Rs. 700, Rs. 600 and Rs. 500 for 3 months, 2 months and 1 months respectively.

On 1-10-04, the first bill is endorsed in favour of a creditor. On the same date the second bill was discounted through Bank at 5% plus Re. 1 for in incidental charges and the bills were dishonoured. Show the entries that would appear in the books of Mr. 'X'.

EXERCISE 7

(Endorsement, discount and dishonour of the bill)

X, draws a bill for Rs. 500 on Y, and Y accepts it and passes it on to 'X'. 'X' endorses it to Z and Z endorses it to 'A'. A discounts the bill for Rs. 490. On the date of maturity, the bill is dishonoured and the noting charges incurred by the bankers amounted to Rs. 10. Assuming that bill was taken over by 'X' an dishonour, you are asked to gives journal entries recording the above transactions in the books of all the parties.

EXERCISE 8

(Renewal of a bill)

Mahendra sold to Surendra on 1-5-04 goods valued at Rs. 1,000 and drew upon him at three months for the amount. Surendra accepted the bill. On maturity, Surendra expressed his inability to meet the bill and offered to pay Mahendra Rs. 400 in cash and accept a fresh bill for the balance plus interest at 5% per annum for three months. Mahendra agreed to the proposal and the bill was renewed.

Make entries in the books of both the parties recording the above transactions.

EXERCISE 9

(Retiring a bill under discount)

On October 2004 P drew a bill of Rs. 600 on Q at 3 months. On 10th November 2004 Q retired the bill under discount at 6% per annum.

Record there transactions in the books of P and Q.

EXERCISE 10

(Discount, dishonour, renewal and retirement of a bill)

On 1-1-04 Prashanth sold goods to Nishanth to the value of Rs. 3,000 and drew a bill on the latter at 3 months after date for the amount. Prashanth discounted the bill on 4-1-04 at 5% per annum. The bill was dishonoured and bank. Paid Rs. 15 as noting charges. On 7th September Nishanth paid Rs. 750 and the expenses, and gave Prashanth another bill at 3 months for the balance due together with interest at 6% per annum. One month before maturity of the second bill, Nishanth retired the same at a discount of 6% per annum.

Draft Journal entries in the books of the parties.

EXERCISE 11

(Accomodation bill)

For the mutual accomodation of Prakash and Kumar, Prakash draws a bill on Kumar for Rs. 1,500. Kumar accepts the bill and return it to Prakash who discount it for Rs. 1,464. The proceeds are shared between Prakash and Kumar in proportion to $\frac{2}{3}$rd and $\frac{1}{3}$rd respectively on the due date, Prakash remits his share to Kumar who honours the bill. Pass Journal entries in the books of both the parties.

EXERCISE 12

'X' draws a bill for Rs. 1,500 and Y accepts the same for the mutual accommodation of both of them to the extent of X – $\frac{2}{3}$rd and Y –$\frac{1}{3}$rd.'X' discounts the same for Rs. 1,410 and remits $\frac{1}{3}$rd of the proceeds to Y. Before the due date, Y draws another bill for Rs. 2,100 on 'X' in order to provide funds to meet the first bill. The second bill is discounted for Rs. 2,040 with the help of which the first bill is met and Rs. 360 is remitted to 'X'. Before the due date of the second bill X becomes Bankurpt and Y receives a dividend of 0.50 paise in a rupee in full satisfaction.

Pass the necessary Journal entries in the books of X and Y respectively.

EXERCISE 13

On 1-1-04, Navin drew a bill on Sunil for Rs. 5,000 and Sunil drew a bill on Navin for a similar amount ; both the bills being for a term of three months. Both the bills were discounted at the bank at 6% on the due date, Sunil met his bill. Navin however notified Sunil of his inability to meet the bill and Sunil therefore had to take it up. Navin paid Rs. 2,000 on 3-4-04 and accepted another bill drawn on him by Sunil at two months date for Rs. 3,050 including interest. This acceptance having been met by Navin on the due date. Pass Journal entries in the books of both the parties.

8

CHAPTER

Average Due Date

1. INTRODUCTION-MEANING OF AVERAGE DUE DATE

In a business enterprise large number of transactions between a seller and buyer takes place on credit basis. The settlement of credit involves payment of interest. In order to simplify the calculation of interest involved in such transaction the concept of average due date has been introduced. The term average due date means the date on which mutual claims of two parties can be settled without loss of interest to any one of the parties . It may be defined as the mean or equated date on which one payment may be made in lieu of several payment due on different dates without loss of interest to either party. To illustrate this, consider that 'X' owes a sum of Rs. 1,000 to 'Y' payable on 15th October 2,004 and another 1,000 due on 10th November 2,004. If 'X' pays Rs. 2,000 on the 28th October 2,004, there is no loss of interest either to 'X' or 'Y'. This is so because 'X' Pays the first sum of Rs. 1,000, 13 days late and the second sum of Rs. 1,000, 13 days earlier. From Y's point of view he receives the sum of Rs. 1,000, 13 days later. The date is choosen by the parties, i.e., debtor and creditor in such a way that it will not cause any loss of interest to the debtor. In simple words average due date is the arithmetic average of various due dates for various payments. The method of calculating average due date is called the equation of payments because it assumes that the interest on the amounts due on "average due date" is equal to the interest on the amounts that are not due on the "average due date".

2. SITUATIONS UNDER WHICH THE AVERAGE DUE DATE TECHNIQUE IS USED

The following are the different situations under which the technique of average due date is used.

1. To settle the mutual debts of two traders. For example, 'X' sells goods to 'Y' and Y sells goods to 'X' on different dates on credit basis. To settle this transactions average due date technique is used.
2. To settle the accounts between an agent and principal, as in the case of consignment accounts.
3. To calculate the interest on Partners' drawings, in a partnership business .
4. To calculate interest due from sundry debtors which is realised in various instalments on dissolution of the partnership firm.
5. To settle bills which are due on different dates.

3. STEPS IN CALCULATION OF AVERAGE DUE DATE WHEN DUE DATES ARE GIVEN

The following steps are involved in the calculation of average due date.

1. Choose one of the due dates (preferably the earliest due date, as the starting day or the base day or the '0' (Zero) day.
2. Ascertain the number of days that elapse between the starting day and each of the other due dates. This process involves counting the number of days from the starting date to the due date.
3. Multiply the concerned amount with the days calculated as per step 2 above.
4. Add up the products as obtained in step 3.
5. Add up the amounts of all transactions.
6. Divided the "product total" by the total amount and get the result approximated to a whole number. This gives the number of days, the average due date is away from the starting date.
7. Ascertain the average due date by adding to or subtracting from the starting date the number of days calculated as per step 6. The following formula is used for ascertaining the average due date.

$$\text{Average Due Date} = \text{Starting Date} \pm \frac{\text{Total of Products}}{\text{Total Amounts}}$$

Problem 1

Calculate average due date from the following due dates.

2004, 1st December	Rs. 860
2005, 15th January	Rs. 640
2005, 28th March	Rs. 380

Solution

Calculation of Average due Date

1st December 1994 is taken as starting date

Due date	*Amount*	*No. of Days from Dec. 1*	*Product*
1st Dec.	860	0	0
15th Jan.	640	45 (Dec. 30 day Excluding day plus Jan's 15 days	2,880
28th Mar	380	117 Dec = 30 days Jan = 31 days Feb = 28 days Mar = 28 days	44,400
	1,880		73,300

$$\text{Average due date} = \text{Starting Date} \pm \frac{\text{Total of Products}}{\text{Total Amount}}$$

$$= \text{Starting Date} \pm \frac{73300}{1880} = 39 \text{ days} = \text{1st Dec.} + 39 \text{ days}$$

Average due date is 9th January, i.e., 30 days of December + 9 days of January.

Problem 2

X owes Y the following sum of money due on the dates stated :

Rs. 400 due of 5th January 2,005
Rs. 200 due on 20th January 2,005
Rs. 800 due on 4th February 2,005
Rs. 100 due on 26th February 2,005
Rs. 50 due on 10th March 2,005

Calculate such a date when payment may be made by X in one instalment resulting in no loss to either parties.

Solution

Calculation of Average due Date taking 5th January as the starting date

Due date	*Amount*	*No. of Days from 5th Jan*	*Product*
Jan. 5	400	0	0
Jan. 20	200	15	3,000
Feb. 14	800	30	24,000
Feb. 28	100	52	5,200
Mar. 10	50	65	3,250
	1,550		35,450

$$\text{Average Due date} = \text{January } 5 \pm \frac{35450}{1550}$$

$$= \text{Jan. } 5 + 23 = \text{Jan. } 28$$

Problem 3

The following are the amounts due on different dates in between the same parties.

Amounts	**Due dates**
Rs. 500	3rd July
Rs. 800	2nd August
Rs. 1,000	11th September

Suggest a date on which all the bills may be paid out without any loss of interest to either party.

Solution

Calculation of Average due date taking 3rd July as the starting date

Due date	*Amount*	*No. of Days from 3rd July*	*Product*
3rd July	500	0	0
2nd Aug.	800	30	24,000
11th Sept.	1,000	70	70,000
	2,300		94,000

$$\text{Average Due Date} = \text{3rd July} + \frac{94000}{2300}$$

$$= \text{3rd July} + 41 \text{ days}$$

$$= 13 \text{ August}$$

Problem 4

Swaminathan owed to subramanium the following sums.

Rs. 5,000 on 20th January 2,005.
Rs. 8,000 on 3rd March 2,005
Rs. 6,000 on 5th April 2,005
Rs. 11,000 on 30th April 2,005
Ascertain the average due date

Solution

Calculation of Average due date taking 20th January as the starting date

Due Date	*Amount*	*No of Days from 20th Jan.*	*Product*
20th Jan.	5,000	0	0
3rd Mar.	8,000	42	3,36,000
5th Apr.	6,000	75	4,50,000
30th Apr.	11,000	100	11,00,000
	30,000		18,86,000

$$\text{Average Due Date} = \text{20th Jan.} + \frac{\text{Total Product}}{\text{Total Amount}}$$

$$= \text{20th Jan.} + \frac{18,86,000}{3,00,000} = \text{20th Jan.} + 63 \text{ days} = \text{24th March}$$

Problem 5

Raghunath sold goods to Gurunath during 2,002 as follows

Date of the Invoice	*Value of the goods sold*
15-5-02	4,000
22-5-02	2,500
29-5-02	4,500
5-6-02	3,250
11-6-02	3,000

The payment were agreed to be made by bills payable 90 days from the respective dates of the invoice. Gurunath wanted to make payment of the bill on a single date.

Calculate the average due date on which such a payment would be made without loss of interest to either party.

Solution

Calculation of Average due Date Taking 16-8-02 as the Starting Date

Date of Invoice	*Due Date*	*No. of days from 16-8-02*	*Amount*	*Product*
15-5-02	16-8-02	0	4,000	0
22-5-02	23-8-02	7	2,500	17,500
29-5-02	30-8-02	14	4,500	63,000
5-6-02	6-9-02	21	3,250	68,250
11-6-02	12-9-02	27	3,000	81,000
			17,250	2,29,750

$$\text{Average Due Date} = 16\text{-}8\text{-}02 + \frac{\text{Total Product}}{\text{Total Amount}}$$

$$= 16\text{-}8\text{-}02 + \frac{2{,}29{,}750}{17{,}250}$$

$$= 16\text{-}8\text{-}02 + 14 \text{ Days}$$

Average due date = 30-8-02

Problem 6

Gourang had accepted three bills of exchange in favour of Jayadev. The following are the particulars.

Amount	*Date of Acceptance*	*Term*
20,000	10th April	3 months
30,000	12th June	2 months
10,000	25th July	3 months

Gourang wishes to pay the whole of the amount on one day. When should he do so

Solution

Calculation of Average Due Date Taking 13th July as the Starting Date

Date of Acceptance	*Due Date*	*Amount*	*No. of Days from 13th July*	*Product*
10-Apv.	13th July	20,000	0	0
12- June	14th Aug.	30,000	32	9,60,000
25-July	28th Oct.	10,000	107	10,70,000
		60,000		20,30,000

$$\text{Average Due Date} = \text{13th July} + \frac{\text{Total Product}}{\text{Total Amount}}$$

$$= \text{13th July} + \frac{20{,}30{,}000}{60{,}000} = \text{13th July} + 34 \text{ days}$$

Average due date is 16th August.

Problem 7

Prasanna sold goods to Chandrashekar as detailed below :

Date of the Invoice	*Value of the goods sold*
5-5-04	Rs. 3,000
12-5-04	Rs. 1,500
19-5-04	Rs. 35,00
26-5-04	Rs. 2,250
1-6-04	Rs. 2,000
3-6-04	Rs. 1,000

The payment were agreed to be made by bills payable 90 days from the respective dates of the invoice. However Chandrashekar wanted to arrange for payment of all the bills to be made on a single date.

Calculate the date of which such a payment could be made without loss of interest to either party.

Solution

Calculation of Due Dates

The various due dates taking into account 90 days on Invoice date as maturity period are as follows :

Date of Invoice	*Due date*
5-5-04	6-8-04
12-5-04	13-8-04
19-5-04	20-8-04
26-5-04	27-8-04
1-6-04	2-9-04
3-6-04	4-9-04

Calculation of due date taking 6-8-04 as the starting date

Due date	*Amount*	*No. of Days from 6-8-04*	*Product*
6-8-04	3,000	0	0
13-8-04	1,500	7	10,500
20-8-04	3,500	14	49,000
27-8-04	2,250	21	47,250
2-9-04	2,000	27	54,000
4-9-04	1,000	29	29,000
	13,250		1,89,750

$$\text{Average Due date} = 6\text{-}8\text{-}04 + \frac{\text{Total Product}}{\text{Total Amount}}$$

$$= 6\text{-}8\text{-}04 + \frac{1{,}89{,}750}{13{,}250}$$

$$= 6\text{-}8\text{-}04 + 14 \text{ days}$$

Due date = 20th Aug. 2,004

Problem 8

Find out the average due date of the following bills held by a trader who wishes to settle them in one single amount.

Date of the bill	*Amount of the bill*	*Due date*
1-4-04	Rs. 400	6-6-04
30-4-04	Rs. 500	3-8-04
3-6-04	Rs. 200	6-7-04
15-6-04	Rs. 300	18-9-04

Solution

Calculation of due date taking 6th June as starting date

Due date	*Amount*	*No. of Days from 6 June 94*	*Product*
6-6-04	400	0	0
3-8-04	500	58	29,000
6-7-04	200	30	6,000
18-9-04	300	104	31,200
	1,400		66,200

$$\text{Average Due date} = \text{6th June} + \frac{\text{Total Product}}{\text{Total Amount}}$$

$$= \text{6th June} + \frac{66{,}200}{1{,}400}$$

$$= \text{6th June} + 47 \text{ days}$$

Due date = 23rd July, 2004

Calculation of Interest

Average due date is the "no loss to either party" date. Therefore by calculating average due date, such a point is established where there is no loss to both the parties it payment is made on that date. Conversely, if the payment is not made on that date then there is a loss to the party who receives the amount. The loss is equal to the interest due on the total sum borrowed for a period for which payment is delayed from the average due date. This involves two steps.

(*a*) The number of days from the average due date to the date of actual payment.

(*b*) The interest on the total sum borrowed for the days calculated as per step above at the agreed rate of interest.

Problem 9

X owes Y Rs. 670 on 1st Jan. 2005. Following further transactions have taken place between X and Y.

Jan. 10	'X' buys goods	Rs. 700
Feb. 2	'X' receives cash	Rs. 550
Mar. 2	'X' buy's goods	Rs. 400

'X' pays the whole amount on 31st March 2,005, together with interest at 5% per annum. Calculate the interest by the average due date method.

Solution

Calculation of Average due date taking Jan. 1, 2005

Due date	*Amount*	*No. of Days from Jan. 1*	*Product*
Jan. 1	670	0	0
Jan. 17	700	15	10,500
Feb. 2	550	32	17,600
Mar 5	400	63	25,200
	2,320		53,300

$$\text{Average Due date} = \text{Jan. } 1 + \frac{\text{Total Product}}{\text{Total Amount}}$$

$$= \text{Jan. } 1 + \frac{53{,}300}{2{,}300}$$

$$= \text{Jan. } 1 + 23$$

Average due date = 24th Jan.

Calculation of Interest

No of days for which interest is to be calculated.

January from 25th to 31st	= 7 days
February	= 28 days
March	= 31 days
Total	66 days

$$2{,}320 \times \frac{66}{365} \times \frac{5}{100} = \text{Rs. } 20.98$$

Problem 10

X owes Y the following sums of money from him on the dates stated

Rs. 300 due on March 10, 2,005
Rs. 1,000 due on April 2, 2,005
Rs. 4,000 due on April 30, 2,005
Rs. 100 due on June 10, 2,005

He wants to make the complete payment on 30th June 2,005. Calculate the interest at 5% p.a., with the help of average due date method.

Solution

Calculation of Average due Date Taking Starting Date as 10-3-2005.

Due date	*Amount*	*No. of Days from March 10*	*Product*
March 10	300	0	0
April 2	1,000	23	23,000
April 30	4,000	51	2,04,000
June 10	100	92	9,200
	5,400		2,36,200

$$\text{Average Due date} = \text{10th March} + \frac{\text{Total Product}}{\text{Total Amount}}$$

$$= \text{10th March} + \frac{2,36,000}{5,400}$$

$$= \text{10th March + 44 days}$$

Average due date = April 23rd.

Interest will be calculated on Rs. 5,400 for the days from the average due date to the settlement date i.e., from April 23rd to the June 30.

April – 7 days
May – 31 days
June – 30 days
68 days

$$5,400 \times \frac{68}{365} \times \frac{5}{100} = \text{Rs. } 50.30$$

Problem 11

Sridhar a partner in the firm has drawn out from the firm the following amounts

Year 2,004	*Rs.*
Jan. 31	300
Feb. 28	250
April 30	160
June 30	200
July 31	350
Sept. 30	200
Oct. 31	400
Dec. 31	500

Calculate the average due date and the interest payable.

Solution

Note **:** As the drawings are made at the end of the month, the average due date can be calculated in months.

Calculation of Average due date in months taking January 31st

Date of Drawing	*Amount*	*No. of months starting from Jan. 31*	*Product*
Jan. 31	300	0	0
Feb. 28	250	1	250
April 30	160	3	480
June 30	200	5	1,000
July 31	350	6	2,100
Sept. 30	200	8	1,600
Oct. 31	400	9	3,600
Dec. 31	500	11	5,500
	2,360		14,530

$$\text{Average Due Date} = \text{Jan. } 31 + \frac{\text{Total Product}}{\text{Total Amount}}$$

$$= \text{Jan. } 31 + \frac{14{,}530}{2{,}360}$$

$$= 6 \text{ Months}$$

$$\text{Interest for six months} = 2{,}360 \times \frac{6}{100} \times \frac{6}{12} = \text{Rs. } 70.80$$

Note **:** Interest rate is not given in the problem. According to Indian Partnership Act 1932, if the rate of interest on drawing is not given then 6% rate of interest is applicable. So in this problem 6% rate of interest is calculated.

2. STEPS INVOLVED IN CALCULATING AVERAGE DUE DATE WHEN THE DUE DATES ARE NOT GIVEN

In some cases the due date of payments of each transaction may not be given in the problem. Instead one common date of settling or closing all accounts is given. The following steps are involved in such situations.

1. Count the days of each transaction from the date of such transaction to the common date of settlement.
2. Rest of the procedure is same as explained earlier.

Problem 12

Vinod has to pay to Venugopal Rs. 6,000 on 1st July 2,004. In addition, the following transactions have taken place between them.

Aug. 20 Vinod purchased goods worth Rs. 2,000
Sept. 15 Vinod borrowed Rs. 1,500
Sept. 25 Vinod bought goods worth Rs. 3,000
Nov. 10 Vinod purchased goods worth Rs. 1,000.

Vinod desires to pay the whole amount on 31st Dec. 2004 along with interest at 6% per annum.

Find out (*a*) Average due date and (*b*) Interest by Average due date.

Solution

Calculation of Average Due Date

Date of Transaction	*No. of Days upto 31st Dec.*	*Amount of Transaction*	*Product*
1-7-04	183	6,000	10,98,000
20-8-04	133	2,000	2,66,000
15-9-04	107	1,500	1,60,500
25-9-04	97	3,000	2,91,000
10-11-04	51	1,000	51,000
		13,500	18,66,500

$$\text{Average due date} = \frac{\text{Total Product}}{\text{Total Amount}}$$

$$\frac{18{,}66{,}500}{13{,}500} = 138 \text{ days}$$

The arrange due date is 138 days behind 31st Dec. 2,004, i.e., 15th August 2004. Alternatively, cumulative days from 1st January to 31st December = 365.138 days are to be deducted from 365 days. It is 227 days (365 – 138 = 227). 227 days from January 1st is 15th August.

Calculation of Interest

Interest for 138 days are calculated as shown below :

$$1{,}3500 \times \frac{138}{365} \times \frac{6}{100} = \text{Rs. } 307$$

Problem 13

Vivek who is a partner of a firm is charged interest at 10% per annum on his drawings. Following are the amounts withdrawn by Vivek from 1. Jan. 2005 to 31. March 2005.

1st Jan. 2,005 Rs. 3,200
16th Jan. 2,005 Rs. 4,800
7th Feb. 2,005 Rs. 2,500
4th Mar 2,005 Rs. 1,000

Find out the average due date and calculate the interest.

Solution

Calculation of Average due date

Date of Drawing Interest	*Days upto 31st March 953*	*Amount*	*Product*
1st Jan. 2,005	89	3,200	2,84,800
16th Jan. 2,005	74	4,800	3,55,200
7th Feb. 2,005	52	2,500	1,30,000
4th Mar. 2,005	27	1,000	27,000
		11,500	7,97,000

$$\text{Average due date} = \frac{\text{Total Product}}{\text{Total Amount}}$$

$$= \frac{797000}{11500} = 69 \text{ days}$$

Average due date is 69 days after the first transaction, i.e., 1st January i.e. 11th March 2,005.

Note the difference between this problem and the previous problem. In the pervious problem the desire to pay or date of payment was given as 31st Dec. But in this problem the actual date of payment is not given. Hence the average due date is calculated after the first transction.

Calculation of Due Date when the Day of Maturity is a Holiday

As was mentioned in the previous chapter when the due date happens to be a public holiday, the payment is said to be due on the preceding business day. The term public holiday refers to Sundays and other days declared by central government in a notification in the official gazette to be a public holiday. In case of an emergency or unforeseen holiday then the due date shall be the next following day.

Problem 14

Raghuram bought goods from Harish, the due date for payment of cash being as follows.

March 15, 2005 Rs. 400 due on 18th April.
April 21, 2,005 Rs. 300 due on 24th May.
April 27, 2,005 Rs. 200 due on 30th June.
May 15, 2,005 Rs. 250 due on 18th July.

Harish agreed to draw a bill for the total amount due on the average due date. Ascertain that date.

Solution

Calculation of Average due Date

Due Date 2005	*No. of Days from 18th April*	*Amount*	*Product*
18th April	0	400	0
24th May	36	300	10,800
30th June	73	200	14,600
18th July	91	250	22,750
		1,150	48,150

$$\text{Average due date} = \text{18th April} + \frac{\text{Total Product}}{\text{Total Amount}}$$

$$\text{18th April} + \frac{48{,}150}{1{,}150} = 42 \text{ day}$$

Average due date is 30 May

Calculation of average due date when amount is lent in one instalment but repaid in various Instalments.

The procedure for calculating average due date under this situation can be summarised as shown below.

1. Calculate the number of days or months from the date of lending money to the date of such repayment.
2. Find the total of such days or months.
3. Divide the total as calculated in step 2 above by the number of instalments paid in order to repay the amount.
4. The result will be number of days or months by which average due date falls from the date of commencement of loan.

The following formula is used to calculate average due date.

$$\text{Average Due date} = \frac{\text{Sum of the days or months from the Date of lending to the date of repayment of each instalment}}{\text{Number of instalments}}$$

Problem 15

Ranga Rao lent Rs. 10,000 to Govind Rao on 1st January 2,005 which is repayable in 5 equal annual instalments commencing on 1st January 2,005. Find the average due date and calculate interest at 5% per annum which Ranga Rao will recover from Govind Rao.

Solution

Calculation of Average Due Date

$$\text{Average due date} = \text{Date of loan} + \frac{\text{Sum of the number of years/month date or days from the date of lending date to the date of repayment of each Loan + instalment}}{\text{Number of instalment}}$$

$$= \text{1st Jan. 95} + \frac{1+2+7+4+5}{5}$$

$$= \text{1st Jan. 95 + 3 years = 1st Jan. 2,008}$$

Calculation of Interest :

$$10{,}000 \times \frac{5}{100} = 500 \text{ and for 4 years it will be Rs. } 500 \times 4 = 2{,}000.$$

Problem 16

Janardhan rent Rs. 10,000 to Joseph on 1st Jan. 2005 which is repayable in five six monthly equal instalments commencing from 1st January 2,005. Calculate the average due date and interest at 5% per annum.

Solution

Calculation of Average due date

Calculation of sum of period from the date of lending to the date of each transaction.

1st payment is made after	12	months from the date of loan.
2nd payment is made after	18	months from the date of loan.
3rd payment is made after	24	months from the date of loan.
4th payment is made after	30	months from the date of loan.
5th payment is made after	36	months from the date of loan.
	120	

$$\text{Average due date} = \text{Date of loan} + \frac{\text{Sum of total months}}{\text{No of Instalments}}$$

$$= \text{1st Jan. 05} + \frac{120}{5} = \text{24 months}$$

$$= \text{1st Jan. 05 + 24 months or 2 years}$$

$$= \text{Average due date 1st Jan. 2007}$$

$$\text{Calculation of Interest } 10000 \times \frac{5}{100} \times 2 = \text{Rs. } 1{,}000$$

Calculation of average due date when two traders buy goods from one another on credit

Under this situation it involves reciprocal purchases. The formula for calculating average due date is as follows :

$$\text{Starting date} + \frac{\text{Difference in Products}}{\text{Difference in Amount}}$$

Problem 17

Arun had the following bills receivable and bills payable against Bhaskar

Bills Receivable			Bills payable		
Date	*Amount*	*Tenure (in months)*	*Date*	*Amount*	*Tenure (in months)*
1-5-04	4,000	4	10-5-04	2,000	2
31-5-04	800	3	21-5-04	6,000	4
12-6-04	3,000	2	30-5-04	1,600	3
15-6-04	5,200	3	6-6-04	2,400	2
7-7-04	2,000	2	17-6-04	3,000	3
10-7-04	5,000	1	30-6-04	1,000	1

Calculate the average due date. When the payment can be made or received without any loss of interest to either party.

Note : Gazetted holidays during the period are 15th August 2004 and 2nd October 2004.

Solution

Calculation of Average due date taking starting date as 13-7-04

Bills Receivable

Date	*Due Date*	*Amount*	*No. of Days from 13.7.04*	*Product*
1-5-04	4-9-04	4,000	53	2,12,000
31-5-04	3-9-04	800	52	41,600
12-6-04	14-8-04	3,000	32	96,000
15-6-04	18-9-04	5,200	67	3,48,400
7-7-04	20-9-04	2,000	59	1,18,000
10-7-04	13-8-04	5,000	31	1,55,000
		20,000		9,71,000

Bills Payable

Date	*Due Date*	*Amount*	*No. of Days from 13th July*	*Product*
10-5-04	13-7-04	2,000	0	0
29-5-04	1-10-04	6,000	80	4,80,000
30-5-04	3-9-04	1,600	52	83,200
6-6-04	9-8-04	2,400	27	64,800
17-6-04	20-9-04	3000	69	2,07,000
30-6-04	2-8-04	1,000	20	20,000
		16,000		8,55,000

$$\text{Average Due Date} = \text{Starting date} + \frac{\text{Difference in Products}}{\text{Difference in Amount}}$$

$$= \text{July 13} + \frac{9{,}71{,}000 - 8{,}55{,}000}{20{,}000 - 16{,}000} = \text{July 13} + \frac{1{,}16{,}000}{4000}$$

$$= \text{July 13} + 29 \text{ days}$$

$$= \text{August 11th}$$

Problem 18

Vishwanath had the following bills accepted by Jeswanth

Amount	*Date*	*Tenor*
Rs. 3,000	29-4-05	2 months
Rs. 2,500	15-5-05	90 days
Rs. 4,000	28-5-05	3 months
Rs .1,000	6-6-05	60 days

Jeswanth had also the following bills accepted by Vishwanath.

Amount	*Date*	*Tenor*
Rs. 2,000	8-5-05	2 months
Rs. 3,000	24-5-05	90 days
Rs. 1,500	2-6-05	3 months
Rs. 1,000	19-7-05	2 months

Subsequently they agreed to settle the bills by a single bill payable on the average due date. Find out the date.

Solution

Calculation of due date

Taking the tenor of the bill and commencing from the date of drawing the bills the due dates of the bills drawn by Vishwanath and Jeswanth are as follows :

Due date of bills drawn by Vishwanath	*Due dates of the bills drawn by Jeswanth*
2-7-05	11-7-05
16-8-05	25-8-05
31-8-05	5-9-05
8-8-05	22-9-05

Calculation of the Sum total and Product total of bills drawn by Vishwanath

Due date	*Amount*	*No. of days from 8-8-95*	*Product*
16-8-05	2,500	8	20,000
31-8-05	4,000	23	92,000
08-8-05	1,000	0	0
	7,500		1,12,000

Bills drawn by Jeswanth

Due date	*Amount*	*No of days from 8-8-95*	*Product*
25-8-05	3,000	17	51,000
5-9-05	1,500	28	42,000
22-9-05	1,000	45	45,000
	5,500		1,38,000

$$\text{Average due date} = \text{Starting date} \pm \frac{\text{Difference in Products}}{\text{Difference in Amounts}}$$

$$= 8\text{-}8\text{-}05 \pm \frac{1{,}12{,}000 - 1{,}38{,}000}{7{,}500 - 5{,}500}$$

$$= 8\text{-}8\text{-}05 + \frac{-26{,}000}{2{,}000} = -13$$

The average due date is 8th August mines 13 days, i.e., 26th July

QUESTIONS

1. What do you mean by average due date ?
2. List our any four situation under which average due date is calculated ?

EXERCISE 1

X owes Y the following sums of money due on the dates stated against each.

Rs. 200 on 6th March
Rs. 320 on 25th April
Rs. 80 on 3rd May
Rs. 400 on 17th May
Rs. 1,000 on 2nd August

Find the average due date for making a single payment.

EXERCISE 2

Calculate average due date from the following due dates.

	Rs.
2,004 1st December	860
2,005, 15th January	640
2,005, 28th March	380

EXERCISE 3

A trader has purchased goods the due date for payment of which are as follows.

1995, January 5th, Rs. 1,000 due on April 8th
April 15th, Rs. 3,000 due on June 18th
June 25th, Rs. 4,000 due on August 28th.

It has been arranged with the creditor that the trader should give a bill on the average due date for the total amount due. You are asked to ascertain the average due date.

EXERCISE 4

A partner has withdrawn the following sums of money during the half year ending 30th June 2005.

January 12	Rs. 600
January 18	Rs. 1,000
February 8	Rs. 500
March 14	Rs. 400
April 26	Rs. 1,000
May 3	Rs. 800
June 15	Rs. 700

Interest is to be charged at 5% per annum. Find the average due date and calculate the interest.

EXERCISE 5 .

A owes the following sums of money due on the dates stated below :

Rs. 400 due on 5th January 2,005
Rs. 200 due on 20th January 2,005
Rs. 800 due on 4th February 2,005
Rs. 100 due on 26th February 2,005
Rs. 50 due on 10th March 2,005

Calculate such a day when payment may be made by X in one instalment resulting in no loss to either party.

EXERCISE 6

Amarnath has purchased goods from Diwakar the due dates of which are as follows:

Rs. 500 due on 5th July 2,004
Rs. 850 due on 10th August 2,004
Rs. 350 due on 25th Sept. 2,004
Rs. 650 due on 10th Nov. 2,004

Amarnath desires to give a bill of exchange for the total amount due, such having payable on the average due date.

EXERCISE 7

Ram Mohan a partner in a firm has drawn the following amounts for the half year ended 30th June 2,004.

January 8th	Rs. 440
Feb. 12th	Rs. 400
March 15th	Rs. 500
April 10th	Rs. 480
May 6th	Rs. 400
June 8th	Rs. 400

Interest is to be charged at 5% per annum. Ascertain this date and the amount of interest.

EXERCISE 8

Rs. 18,000 lent by Kishore to Prabhu an 1st January 2,005, is repayable in 6 annual instalments commencing from 1st January, 1997. Calculate average due date. Calculate interest at 5% per annum charged by Kishore.

9

CHAPTER

Trial Balance

"TRY-ALL" Balances to check Arithmetical Accuracy

A trial balance is a statement of debit and credit balances extracted from all the ledgers with a view to ascertain arithmetical accuracy of the posting of all transactions into the respective ledgers. In other words trial balance means "Try-all" balances to check the correctness of the maintanenace of accounts. If no mistake is committed in posting transactions, the debit and credit balances must always be equal. However, such an agreement of the trial balance is not a conclusive proof of the accuracy of postings in the ledgers.

Detect Certain Mistakes

Apart from checking the arithmetical accuracy of the postings in the ledgers, a trial balance helps to detect certain mistakes in the maintenance of different ledgers. Certain errors can be detected by the preparation of a Trial balance whereas certain others cannot. This aspect is more fully discussed in chapter 10.

Facilitate Preparation of Final Accounts

Since a Trial balance contains the balances of all the ledgers, both debit and credit, it provides at a glance, the basic date relating to the type of transaction carried on in the business for the accounting period. Further, it facilitates the preparation of the final accounts (Trading, profit & loss account and Balance sheet) for a particular financial period.

Checking the Proper Preparation of Trial Balance :

It is possible to find out whether a Trial balance has been prepared properly with a cursory glance. For example if the furniture account is entered under the credit balances of a Trial balance, it is clear that the Trial balance has not been prepared properly. There are certain accounts which should always form part of debit balances (e.g. Purchases, Land & buildings furniture etc.) and certain others which should always form part of credit balances (e.g. capital, sales, bills payable etc.). There are also certain accounts which may appear in both debit and credit balances (e.g. Rent, interest, commission etc.). Some general principles which can help determine whether an account should be a debit balance or a credit balance are discoused here.

Real Accounts

The balances extracted from real accounts such as plant and machinery a/c, Land and Building a/c, Furniture and fixtures a/c, etc. form part of the "assets" of business concerns and they should always appear under debit balance in the Trial balance. For acquering the tangible assets which form real account, "Payment" has to be made. Therefore, they are debit or payment balances. REAL ACCOUNT CAN NEVER BE A CREDIT OR RECEIPT BALANCE. It will never appear under the liability side of the balance sheet.

Personal Account

For personal accounts, the balances may form either a debit balance or a credit balance depending upon whether the person has given more to the business or received more from the business. If he has given more, the business must have received more. The balance extracted from the personal ledger would form a credit balance and it is a "Liability" to the business. The sum total of all the credit balances extracted from the ledgers of personal accounts are grouped under one account called "Sundry creditors a/c and are placed under the "Credit balance" column of the Trial balance.

Similarly if a person has received more from the business, naturally the business must have paid him more than he has given to business. The balance extracted from his personal ledger would form a debit balance and it is an "asset" to the business. The sum total of all the debit balances extracted from the ledgers of personal accounts are totalled and grouped under one account called "Sundry Debtors a/c". A Bank account is treated as personal a/c. If the bank has received more from the business than it has given it becomes a bank balance, which is a debit balance. Whereas it the bank has given more than it received, it is termed as "overdraft" and would form a credit balance. Debit balance of personal a/c is an asset and credit balance of personal a/c is a liability. On the same analogy loans received or borrowed from individuals and institutions form part of credit balances, because the business has received the amount. This will be a liability item. Loans paid or disbursed to individuals or institutions will be a debit balance. This will constitute assets in the Balance Sheet.

Nominal Accounts

For nominal accounts, balances are not extracted from the respective accounts and only totals are made from the ledgers. Expenses are debit balances and incomes are credit balances. An account like interest may be an expenditure if it is paid for a loan borrowed, and an income if it is received for a loan disbursed. Therefore the interest a/c may appear under both debit and credit balances in a trial balance. In nominal accounts debit balances are expenses and credit balances are income.

The above discussion may be summarised as below:

DEBIT BALANCES ARE EITHER EXPENSES OR ASSETS OR CREDIT BALANCES ARE EITHER INCOMES OR LIABILITIES

Preporation of the Trial Balance

There are two methods to prepare the Trial Balance : .

(*a*) Balance method and
(*b*) Total amount method.

(a) **Balance method :** The word Trial balance itself suggests that balances are extracted from all the ledgers and grouped according to their balances. This is the normal and popular method of preparing the Trial balance.

(b) **Total Amount method :** Trial balances can also be prepared by keeping the totals of all the debit and credit balances of each account without balancing them.

Problem 1

From the following transactions of the business of Mr. Ashok prepare ledger accounts and Trial balance using (a) Balance method and (b) Total amount method.

1. Mr. Ashok started business with Rs. 50,000.
2. Purchased goods on credit from Mr. B for Rs. 20000.
3. Sold all the goods an credit to Mr 'C' for Rs. 27,000.
4. Transport charges Rs. 1,000.
5. Paid cash to Mr. 'B' Rs. 12,000 on account.
6. Received cash from Mr. 'C' Rs. 18,000 on account.
7. Withdrew cash Rs. 10,000 for personal use.

Solution

Cash A/c

To Capital a/c	50,000	By Transport charges	1,000
To Mr. C	18,000	By Mr. 'B' a/c	12,000
		By Drawings a/c	10,000
		By Balance c/d	45,000
	68,000		68,000

Capital A/c

To Cash a/c		By Cash	50,000
— Drawings	10,000		
To Balance c/d	40,000		
	50,000		50,000

Purchase A/c

To Mr. B's a/c	20,000	By Balance c/d	20,000

Mr B's A/c

To Cash a/c	1,200	By Purchases a/c	2,000
To Balance c/d	800		
	2,000		2,000

Sales A/c

To Balance c/d	2,700	By Mr. 'C' a/c	2,700

Mr C's A/c

To Sales a/c	2,700	By Cash	1,800
		By Balance c/d	900
	2,700		2,700

Transport a/c

To Cash	100	By Balance c/d	100

Trial Balance under Total Amount Method

	Dr.	Cr.
Cash	6,800	2,300
Capital	1,000	5,000
Purchases	2,000	—
Mr. B	1,200	2,000
Mr. C	2,700	1,800
Sales	—	2,700
Transport charges	100	—
	13,800	13,800

Trial Balance under Balance Method

	Dr.	Cr.
Cash	4,500	—
Capital	—	4,000
Purchases	2,000	—
Mr. B	—	800
Sales	—	2,700
Mr. C	900	—
Transport charges	100	—
	7,500	7,500

Problem 2

The following are the balances extracted from the books of Mr Bopanna. Prepare a Trial balance as at 31-12-2004.

	Rs.
Cash	2,000
Capital	80,000
Purchases	85,000
Sales	1,08,400
Purchases return	6,000
Sales Return	4,000
Transportation	1,800
Discount allowed	500
Printing	5,000
Sundry debtors	70,000
Sundry creditors	40,000
Investment	8,000
Plant & Machinery	15,000
Building	20,000
Furniture	6,000
Electricity	700
Postage	400
Drawings	8,000
Salaries	6,000
Travelling expenses	2,000

Solution

Trial Balance of Mr Bopanna as at 31st December 2004

	Dr. Balance	*Cr. Balance*
Cash	2,000	
Capital	—	80,000
Purchases	85,000	—
Sales	—	1,08,400
Purchase Returns	—	6,000
Sales Returns	4,000	—
Transportation	1,800	—
Discount allowed	500	—
Printing	5,000	—
Sundry Debtors	70,000	—
Sundry creditors	—	40,000
Investment	8,000	—
Plant & Machinery	15,000	—
Building	20,000	—
Furniture	6,000	—
Electricity	700	—
Postage	400	—
Drawing	8,000	—
Salaries	6,000	—
Travelling expenses	2,000	—
	2,34,400	2,34,400

Problem 3

The following is the trial balance of Mr. Chengoppa prepared by the account clerk who was newly recurited. He was unable to make the trial balance agree. Prepare the Trial balance as at 31st December 2,004 correctly.

Trial Balance of C as on 31-12-2004

Debit balance		*Credit Balance*	
Purchases	94,000	Capital	30,000
Purchase returns	2,000	Sales	1,61,800
Sundry debtors	23,000	Sales Return	1,400
Bills Receivable	12,000	Investment	14,000
Land & building	15,000	Cash	500
Furniture	2,000	Drawings	3,500
Printing & Stationary	500	Stock	16,000
Postage	200	Bank balance	10000
Telephone	1,200	Sundry creditors	20,000
Wages	5,000	Bills payable	5,000
Salaries	3,000		
Trade expenses	300		
Carriage	400		
Final	800		
Plant & Machinery	16,000		
	1,75,400		2,62,200

Solution

Trial Balance of Chengappa as at 31-12-2004

Debit balance		*Credit Balance*	
Purchases	94,000	Capital	30,000
Sundry Debtors	23,000	Sales	1,61,800
Investment	14,000	Sundry Creditors	20,000
Cash	500	Bills payable	5,000
Bank balance	10,000	Purchases returns	2,000
Bills Receivables	12,000		
Land & Building	15,000		
Plant & Machinery	16,000		
Furniture	2,000		
Printing & Stationery	500		
Postage	200		
Telephone bill	1,200		
Drawings	3,500		
Wages	5,000		
Salaries	3,000		
Trade expenses	300		
Carriage	400		
Final	800		
Sales returns	1,400		
Stock	16,000		
	2,18,800		2,18,800

Problem 4

Redraft the following incorrect Trial balance of Mr. Dhanpal as at 31st December 2004.

	Dr. Balance	*Cr. Balance*
Capital	—	90,000
Drawings	—	1,150
Buildings	12,000	—
Plant & Machinery	40,000	—
Sundry Debtors	16,000	—
Bank loan	—	40,000
Purchases	1,70,000	—
Sales	—	2,50,000
Commission received	160	—
Sundry creditors	1,600	—
Bills payable	1,250	—
Stock	1,10,000	—
Salaries and wages	10,000	—
Travelling expenses	3,000	—
Rent, Rates and Taxes	5,000	—
Repairs	9000	—
Bad debt	5,000	—
Sales return	—	650
Bills Receivable	—	1,210
	3,83,010	3,83,010

Solution

Trial Balance of Mr. Dhanpal as on 31st December 2004

	Dr. Balance	*Cr. Balance*
Capital	—	90,000
Drawings	1,150	—
Buildings	12,000	—
Plant & Machinery	40,000	—
Sundry Debtors	16,000	—
Bank Loan	—	40,000
Purchases	1,70,000	—
Sales	—	2,50,000
Commission received	—	160
Sundry Creditors	—	1,600
Bills payable	—	1,250
Stock	1,10,000	
Salaries & Wages	10,000	
Travelling expenses	3,000	
Rent, Rates and Taxes	5,000	
Repairs	9,000	
Bad debts	5,000	
Sales Returns	650	
Bills Receivable	1,210	
	3,83,010	3,83,010

QUESTIONS

SIMPLE QUESTIONS

1. What is a trial balance ?
2. State the objects of preparing a trial balance.
3. How do you locate any error in a trial balance ?
4. State two method of preparing a trial balance.

EXERCISE 1

Prepare a trial balance from the following items.

	Rs.
Capital	24,000
Opening stock	8,500
Furniture	2,600
Purchases	8,950
Cash	7,300
Carriage	300
Sales	22,500
Buildings	12,000
Returns inwards	1,900
Returns outwards	350

Trade expenses	1,000
Discount received	970
Salary	3,000
Office rent	2,270

Answer : Total of trial balance Rs. 47820.

EXERCISE 2

The following is a trial balance as on 31-12-2,004 prepared by an incompetent accountant. You are required to redraft it in its corrected form

	Debit	Credit
Capital	24,000	—
Stock on 1-1-2,004	8,500	—
Furniture	5,600	—
Purchases	—	8,950
Cash at bank	7,300	—
Carriage	300	—
Sales	—	24,770
Buildings	12,000	—
Returns inwards	350	—
Trade expenses	1,000	—
Discount received	970	—
	60,020	33,720

Answer : Total of trial balance Rs. 50,090

EXERCISE 3

Redraft correctly the trial balance given below :

Capital	8,000	Debtors	7,580
Bad debts received	250	Bank deposit	2,750
Creditors	1,250	Discount allowed	40
Returns outwards	350	Drawings	600
Bank overdraft	1,570	Returns inwards	450
Rent	360	Sales	14,690
Salaries	850	Bills payable	1,350
Trade expenses	300		
Cash in hand	210		
Stock on 1-1-2,004	2,450		
Purchases	11,870		
	27,460		27,460

Answer : Total of correct trial balance Rs. 27,460.

EXERCISE 4

From the following balances taken from the books of Everest as on 31st March 2,004. Prepare a Trial balance.

	Rs.
Sales	1,64,000
Opening stock	45,800
Depreciation	5,200
Sundry Creditors	22,200
Miscellaneous expenses	350
Sundry Debtors	30,000
Furniture	9,000
Bills Receivable	15,000
Plant and Machinery	60,000
Carriage inward	1,500
Cash at bank	17,000
Wages	15,000
Purchases	87,000
Salaries	10,000
Reserve for bad and doubtful debts	1,550
Bills payable	6,500
Commission received	2,500
Telephone	1,000
Capital	98,000
Repairs	350
Miscellaneous Receipt	2,450

Answer : Total of trial balance Rs. 2,97,200.

10

CHAPTER

Rectification of Errors

INTRODUCTION

When the debit balances and credit balances in a Trial Balance do not agree, it is necessary to locate the errors immediately. It is quite likely that the errors have been committed in the preparation of the Trial balance itself and not in the maintenance of account. To verify this the following steps may be taken.

1. Recheck the totals of the Trial balance.
2. Check whether all the ledger balances have been taken to the Trial balance.
3. Verify whether the balances taken from different ledgers to the trial balance are placed correctly under the debit or credit balance. For example, certain items of the credit balance like capital account, bills payble a/c, sales a/c etc., might have been wrongly entered under the debit balance. These should be located and corrected.
4. In case of a disagreement in the Trial balance, find out the difference between the two balances. If the debit balances is more than the credit balance, it is possible that certain items belonging to the credit balance may have been wrongly entered under the debit balance.

This type of errors are committed only when the person preparing the Trial balance is not well acquainted with the fundamental principles of accounting. The rectification of such errors, as we have seen is mase simply by transferring items of accounts entered wrongly in the trial balance to the proper side. No rectification of Journal entries is necessary.

Errors Committed in the Maintenance of Accounts

So far we have discussed the location of errors in the preparation of a Trial balance only. In actual practice, mistakes are generally committed in the maintenance of accounts at different levels as stated below.

(*a*) While transactions are initially recorded.
(*b*) While posting to different ledgers.
(*c*) While closing or balancing the ledgers.
(*d*) While totalling the books of original entry and ledgers.

Steps to Locate Errors :

1. All the totals of the books of original entry should be thoroughly checked once again.

2. All the entries relating to the postings from the books of original entry to different ledgers should be checked thoroughly in regard to the posting of the right amounts to the right account and on the right side (debit or credit).
3. The opening balances of all the ledgers should be checked against the previous balance.
4. The closing balances of all the ledgers should be checked by a process of retotalling and balancing.
5. For some accounts like sundry debtors and sundry creditors a/c, the sum total of various individual ledgers are extracted and placed in the Trial balance. In such cases it has to be ascertained whether the total of all the individual ledger accounts tallies with the collective total taken to the trial balance.

Type of Errors

The following are the major types of possible errors in the maintenance of accounts.

(*a*) Error of Principle.
(*b*) Error of ommission
(*c*) Error of commission
(*d*) Compensating errors

(a) **Error of Principle :** When a transaction is not properly recorded according to the fundamental principles of accounting, it is called an error of principle. Revenue expenditure recorded as capital expenditure is an example of this error. This type of error will not make the trial balance disagree.

Illustration 1

An amount of Rs. 5,000 was spent for the extension of office building. This was treated as "Repairs to Building".

Solution

Amount spent for extension of building should be treated as Building a/c (Real a/c) and not repairs to Building a/c (Nominal a/c). It is an error of Principle. If this mistake is not rectified this will reduce the profit of the business as the amount will be taken to profit and loss a/c. This mistake will be rectified through rectifying entry :

The original Journal entry was :

Repairs to Building a/c	Dr.	5,000	
To Cash a/c			5,000

The rectifying journal entry will be as

Buildings a/c	Dr.	5,000	
To Repairs to building a/c			5,000

In this way the wrong entry (Rs. 5,000) made in repairs to building a/c is cancelled and building a/c is added with an amount of Rs. 5,000.

(*b*) **Error of omission.** An error of omission may be either partially or totally omitted from the books of original entry. Similarly, an omission in posting the account in the respective ledgers may also amount to an error of omission.

Complete omission :

If a transaction is completely omitted in the original books, such an error will not affect the agreement of the trial balance.

Illustration 2

Goods sold to 'B' on credit for Rs. 2,000 were not taken into the books of accounts though the goods were delivered to Mr. 'B'.

Solution

Since the transaction is completely omitted a fresh Journal entry should be passed and posted to the respective ledgers. This will not affect the agreement of the Trial Balance. The Rectification entry is as follows :-

B's a/c	Dr.	2000	
To Sales a/c			2000
(Being goods sold on credit to B)			

Partial omission :-

An error of partial omission is made when the posting or a transaction is done only in one ledger and omitted in the other ledger. Such an error will affect the agreement of the trial balance. Errors of partial omission cannot be rectified through the rectification journal entry, as only one account is involved.

Illustration 3

Goods purchased on credit for Rs. 3,000 on 31-12-04 from Mr. C were entered in the purchase book and posted to the purchase a/c but omitted to be posted to the personal a/c of Mr. 'C' This mistake was rectified on 8-1-05.

Solution

This error should be rectified by posting the omitted entry in the C's personal account.

C's A/c

	8-1-05 By Sales a/c	3000

(*c*) **Errors of Commission :** These are the errors committed by clerical staff at different stages in maintaining various books of accounts. There are many ways in which mistakes are committed under this category.

1. **Recording a smaller amount in the books of original entry :**

Illustration 4

A credit purchase made on 21-1-04 from 'D' for Rs. 1,650 was wrongly recorded as Rs. 1,560 in the books of original entry. This error was rectified on 31-1-04.

Solution

In this case the mistake was committed on both debit and credit sides of the respective ledgers. Therefore, it did not affect the agreement of the Trial balance. In order to rectify this type of error a rectification entry is to be passed and posted to respective ledgers. When smaller amount is entered, it is necessary to find out the difference and rectification done accordingly. The Rectification entry is as follows :

Purchase a/c Dr. 90
To D's a/c 90

Purchase A/c

21-1-04	To D's a/c	1,560			
31-1-04	To D's a/c	90			

D's A/c

			21-1-99	By purchases a/c	1,560
			31-1-99	By purchases a/c	90

2. Recording a greater amount in the books of original entry

Illustration 5

On 21-1-04 purchases were written up in the books of original entry of 'D' as Rs. 1,750 instead of the actual figure of Rs. 1,650. This mistake was rectified on 31-1-04.

Solution

In this case the wrong entry made is greater them the actual amount. Therefore, this error requires a different treatment. In such cases the amount wrongly recorded should be reduced in the ledgers concerned. The original journal entry has to be reversed to the extent of the difference (Rs. 100) and then posted to the ledgers concerned. The following journal entry is passed and the postings made in the respective ledgers.

31-1-04 D's a/c Dr. 100
To Purchases a/c 100

Purchases A/c

21-1-04	To D's a/c	1750	31-1-04	By D's a/c	100

D's A/c

31-1-04	By purchases a/c	100	21-1-04	By purchases a/c	1750

3. Posting to the wrong account of the ledger. At times a wrong account of the ledger is posted. This mistake is similar to that of the error of principle. However this may not affect the profit and loss a/c as in the case of error of principle.

Illustration 6

The credit sales effected to A for Rs. 1,000 on 12-2-04 were wrongly debited to X. This error was rectified on 28-2-04.

Solution

This type of error will not affect the agreement of the trial balance. Nevertheless, the individual balance of the personal ledgers will not be correct. To rectify this type of error, a rectification entry is to be passed and posted to the respective ledgers. The entry as follows :

A's a/c Dr. 1000
To X's a/c 1000
(Being rectification entry made for wrongly debiting X instead of A)

X's A/c

12-10-4	To Sales	1000	By A's a/c	1000

Note :- The wrong debit given to X is nullified by posting an equal amount on the credit side of the ledger.

A's A/c

28-2-04	To X's a/c	1000	

4. **Posting a lesser amount in the ledger.** When a wrong amount is posted in one ledger. The Trial balance will not agree. In this case no rectification entry is to be passed. The difference should be rectified directly in the ledger.

Illustration 7

A salary of Rs. 4,800 paid in cash on 7-3-04 was wrongly posted as Rs. 4,300. This error was rectified on 31-3-04.

Solution

It is presumed that the amount has been correctly entered in the cash book. Since a smaller amount is posted to the salary account the difference (Rs. 500) should be added to the ledger on the same side (debit).

Salary A/c

7-3-04	To Cash	4,300	
31-3-04	To Cash	500	

5. **Posting a greater amount in the ledger.**

Illustration 8

A salary of Rs. 4800 paid in cash on 7-3-04 was wrongly posted as Rs. 5800. The necessary rectification was made on 31-3-04.

Solution

This type of error will make the Trial balance disagree. Since a greater amount is posted, the difference of amount Rs. 1,000 should be reduced, for which the entry should be made direct in the salary a/c on the opposite side (credit side).

Salary A/c

7-3-04	To Cash	5,800	31-3-04	By Cash	1,000

6. **Posting to the wrong side of the ledger.** Since the mistake is committed on only one side, the trial balance will not agree. The rectification of such errors should be taken up by making appropriate correction in the ledgers.

Illustration 9

An amount of Rs. 100 received in cash on 22-4-04 towards discount a/c was posted to the debit side of the discount a/c. This wrong posting was rectified on 30-4-04.

Solution

The discount a/c should have been credited by Rs. 100. Since it was wrongly debited it had not only reduced the credit balance but also increased the debit balance. In order to nullify the double effect an amount of Rs. 200 (which is double the amount posted to the wrong side) has to be entered on the correct side, i.e., the credit side of the discount a/c.

Discount A/c

22-4-04	To Cash	100	30-4-04	By Cash	200

7. Posting a lessor amount on the wrong side of the ledger. In this case two errors have been committed viz, a wrong amount was posted and that too on the wrong side. This type of error will make the Trial balance disagree. The rectification should be made by making direct entries in the ledgers.

Illustration 10

An amount of Rs. 49 received as interest in cash on 13-3-04 was debited to interest a/c as Rs. 29. The wrong entry was rectified in the interest a/c on 31-5-04.

Solution

There was a twin mistakes here. Interest received (Rs. 49) should have been posted to the credit side on 13-3-04, but was posted to the debit side. Also, the amount was wrongly taken as Rs. 29. In order to place the correct amount (Rs. 49), on the correct (credit) side and also to cancel the wrong debit a total amount of Rs. 78 (49 + 29) has been written up on the credit side to the interest a/c.

Interest A/c

13-3-04	To cash	24	31-5-04	By Cash	78

8. Posting a greater amount on the wrong side of the ledger. This type of error will affect the Trial Balance. The procedure of rectification is similar to the previous case.

Illustration II

An amount of Rs. 49 received as interest in cash on 13-3-2004 was debited to interest a/c as Rs. 94. This error was rectified on 31-5-04.

Solution

Interest A/c

13-3-04	To Cash	94	31-5-04	By Cash	143

9. Posting wrong amount to wrong a/c. If a wrong amount is posted to the wrong a/c, the trial balance will not agree. Rectification is taken up directly in the ledger account concerned.

Illustration 12

An amount of Rs. 200 paid towards wages on 29-4-04 was wrongly posted to salaries a/c as Rs. 2000. The error was rectified on 30-6-04.

Solution

Salaries A/c

29-4-04	To Cash	2000	30-6-04	By Cash	2000

Wages A/c

30-6-04	To Cash	200			

10. Posting to a wrong account and on the wrong side of the ledger. Since the wrong side of the ledger is posted, the trial balance will be affected. To rectify such errors, direct posting to the ledger concerned is necessary.

Illustration 13

A commission of Rs. 50 Received in cash on 7-6-04 was wrongly debited to the discount account. This was rectified at the end of the month.

Solution

Discount A/c

7-6-04	To Cash	50	30-6-04	By Cash	50

Commission A/c

			30-6-04	By cash	50

Explanation

In the first instance the wrong debit to the discount a/c is nullified by posting the same amount to the credit side of the discount a/c. Then the commission received Rs. 50 on 7-6-04 is correctly posted to the credit side of the commission a/c on 30-6-04.

11. Posting a wrong amount to the wrong a/c and to the wrong side of the ledger. Such errors can be rectified by direct posting into the ledgers concerned. Since the error committed involves the posting of a wrong amount as well its posting on the wrong side. Such errors will affect the agreement of the Trial balance. The rectification of such errors can be taken up by means of direct posting into the concerned ledgers.

Illustration 14

Rs. 100 cash paid for commission on 25-3-04 was wrongly posted to interest a/c as Rs. 110 under credit side. This was rectified on 30-4-04

Solution

Interest A/c

30-6-04	To Cash a/c	110	25-3-04	By Cash	110

Commission A/c

30-6-04	To Cash a/c	100			

12. Recording Transactions in the wrong book of original entry itself. This type of error will not affect the agreement of the Trial balance. Such errors are corrected by passing a rectification entry and posting it to the ledgers concerned.

Illustration 15

Goods purchased on credit from A for Rs. 2,500 on 2-2-04 were entered in the sales day book. The error was rectified on 28-2-04 by passing a rectification entry and posting to the ledger concerned.

Solution

Rectification entry

28-2-04	Purchases a/c	Dr..	2,500	
	Sales a/c	Dr.	2,500	
	To A's a/c			5,000
	(Being rectification entry passed for wrong entry made in the sales book on 2-2-04)			

Sales A/c

28-2-04	To A's a/c	2,500	2-2-04	By A's a/c	2,500

A's A/c

12-2-04	To Sales	2,500	28-2-04	By sales	2,500
			28-2-04	By Purchases	2,500

Purchase A/c

28-2-04	To A's a/c	2,500			

Explanation

Purchases made on 2-2-04 on credit from 'A' was wrongly treated as credit sales and instead of debiting the purchases a/c and crediting A's a/c, the sales a/c was credited and A's a/c was debited. A rectification entry has been passed by reversing the original entry and also the correct entry, i.e., purchase a/c debited to A's a/c has also been incorporated in the rectification entry. Further, the postings have been made in the ledgers concerned from the rectification entries.

13. Wrong totalling in the books of original entry (undercasting). Such errors will affect the agreement of the Trial balance. They should be rectified by making direct entries in the ledgers.

Illustration 16

The sales books was undercast by Rs. 100 during November 2004. This was rectified at the end of the year.

Solution

Sales A/c

			31-12-04	By Cash a/c	100

14. Wrong totalling in the books of original entry (overcasting).

Illustration 17

The actual total of the purchase book was Rs. 17,480 at the end of April 2004 but it was wrongly entered as Rs. 19,480. This was rectified at the end of the next month.

Solution

Purchases A/c

30-4-04	To Sundry creditors	19,480	31-5-04	By Cash	2,000

15 Wrong totalling of ledgers. The rectification procedure is similar to the previous case.

16. Entering the same transaction in two books of original entry. In this case one transaction is mistakenly treated as two different transactions and posting are also made accordingly. Therefore this type of error will not affect the trial balance. To rectify such errors a rectification entry is to be passed.

Illustration 18

A cash sale of Rs. 500 effected on 10-5-04 to 'A' is recorded in the cash book as well as in the sales book, treating it as a credit transaction in the latter and thereby posting it to the personal ledger of 'A'. This error was rectified on 31-5-04.

Solution

Sales a/c	Dr.	500	
To A's a/c			500

(Being the rectification of wrong entry made in sales book as credit transaction)

Sales A/c

31-4-04	To A's a/c	500	10-5-04	By cash	500
			10-5-04	By A's a/c	500

A's A/c

10-5-04	To Sales a/c	500	31-5-04	By Sales	500

Explanation

The transaction effected on 10-5-04 was a cash sale. This was mistakenly treated as a cash sale as well as credit sale. The effect of the credit sale should be nullified by debiting the sales a/c and crediting the personal a/c of 'A'.

17. Double posting in the Ledgers. Posting the same transaction twice in the ledger will affect the Trial balance. Rectification is by appropriate postings directly in the ledger.

Illustration 19

Rs. 1300 paid as wages on 14-7-04 was posted twice in the ledger. The error was rectified at the end of the next month.

Solution

Wages A/c

14-7-04	To Cash	1,300	31-8-04	By Cash	1,300
14-7-04	To Cash	1,300			

18. Over Balancing in the Ledger. Such error will affect the agreement of the Trial balance. Rectification is by direct posting to the appropriate side of the ledger.

Illustration 20

The individual ledger of B was wrongly balanced as Rs. 900 instead of the actual amount of Rs. 800 on 31-1-04. This was rectified on 7-2-04.

Solution

B's A/c

1-2-04	To Balance b/d	900	7-2-04	By Cash	100

19. Underbalancing in the ledger

Illustration 21

The personal ledger of B showed is wrong balance of Rs. 500 instead of Rs. 800 on 31-1-04.

Solution

B's A/c

1-2-04	To Balance b/d	500			
7-2-04	To Cash	300			

20. Errors committed when "Bringing down" in the Ledger. Errors of this type will affect the trial balance. Rectification is by a direct entry in the ledgers concerned.

Illustration 22

In the personal ledger of 'C' the balance of Rs. 800 on 31-1-04 was brought down on 1-2-04 as "To balance b/d Rs. 1,000". Rectification was done on 7-2-04.

Solution

C's A/c

1-2-04	To Balance b/d	1,000	7-2-04	Cash	200

(D) **Compensating errors :** Compensating errors occurs as a combination of different errors which are either compensated by another error or errors. Such errors will not affect the Trial balance.

Illustration 23

Mr. 'A' started a business with cash Rs. 10,000. He purchased goods for cash Rs. 3000 and posted to purchases a/c as Rs. 2500. Purchased Furniture for Rs. 2000 and posted to furniture a/c Rs. 2300. Sold all the goods for Rs. 3800. Post these transaction in the respective ledgers and prepare the trial balance.

Solution

Cash A/c

To Capital	10,000	By Purchases	3,000
To Sales	4,000	By Furniture	2,000
		By Balance c/d	9,000
	14,000		14,000
To Balance b/d	9,000		

Capital A/c

To Balance c/d	10,000	By Cash a/c	10,000
		By Balance b/d	10,000

Purchases A/c

To Cash (Wrong amount posted)	2,500		

Furniture A/c

To Cash (Wrong amount posted)	2,300	By Balance c/d	2,300
To balance b/d	2,300		

Sales A/c

		By Cash (Wrong amount posted)	3,800

Trial Balance

Debit balance		Credit Balance	
Cash	9,000	Capital	10,000
Purchases	2,500	Sales	3,800
Furniture	2,300		
	13,800		13,800

Note :-

It is obvious that mistakes were committed in the posting of purchases, furniture and sales a/c. However, the different mistakes compensate each other and thereby do not not affect the trial balance.

The following statement will indicate how the errors referred to above have compensating effects on the debit and credit balances.

Statement showing the Effects of Compensating Errors

Item No.	*Particulars*		*Debit Less*	*Debit More*	*Credit Less*	*Credit More*
(1)	Actual purchase	3,000				
	posted as	2,500				
			500			
(2)	Actual furniture	2,000				
	posted as	2,300				
				300		
(3)	Actual sales	4,000				
	posted as	3,800				
					200	
			500	300	200	

Suspense a/c

Inspite of the best efforts made to locate errors, it may not be possible, at times, to find them and the total of the trial balance will then continue to disagree. Since final accounts have to be prepared without delay at the end of the financial period, there may not be enough time to spot the cause of the error. A way out is to open a new account called "Suspense a/c" for the amount involved and enter it in the trial balance on the side where the total is smaller. For example, if the debit side of the Trial balance is less than the credit side, the suspense a/c is debited and vice versa. The suspense a/c is only an item of adjustment created in the books of accounts for the sole purpose of tallying the trial balance for a temporary period. It is not a permanent solution of the errors committed. Efforts should continue to be made to locate the errors. When the errors are located they should be rectified by making proper adjustments with the suspense account already credited.

As the suspense account is entered in the trial balance, it has to be incorporated in the final accounts. If the suspense account is kept on the debit side of the trial balance, it will be taken to the assets side and if it is on the credit side, it will be taken to the liabilities side of the balance sheet.

When the suspense a/c is placed in the balance sheet, a ledger for the suspense a/c should be opened and in the next financial period, as and when the errors committed in the previous financial period are located, rectification should be made by appropriately adjusting the suspense a/c. Ultimately, the ledger for the suspense a/c should be completely closed when all the errors committed in the previous period are located and corrected.

Problem 1

On 31st March 2003, the trial balance of Kunal did not agree. To prepare the final accounts, the proprietor put the difference in a newly opened suspense account, in the next accounting year, the following errors were located :

1. Rs. 18,500 paid for the purchase of as machine was charged to office expense account.
2. Cash sales of Rs. 3,550 was posted as Rs. 3505.
3. Purchase returns book was undercast by Rs. 100.
4. Goods amounting to Rs. 860 sold to Raman were correctly entered in the sales book but were posted as Rs. 866 to the buyer's account.

Pass Journal entries to rectify the above mentioned errors and prepare the suspense a/c assuming that all the errors have been located. (C. S. Foundation, June 2003).

Solution

Rectification Entries

Date	*Particulars*	*L.F.*	*Dr. Amount*	*Cr. Amount*
	Machine a/c Dr. To Office Expense a/c (Purchase of machine charged to expenses a/c error now rectified)		18,500	18,500
	Suspense a/c Dr. To Sales a/c (Being cash sales, error now recorded and rectified)		45	45
	Suspense a/c Dr. To Purchase Returns a/c (Undercast of purchases returns books, error now rectified)		100	100

Date	Particulars		L.F.	Dr. Amount	Cr. Amount
	Suspense a/c	Dr.		6	
	To Raman's a/c				6
	(Excess amount debited to Raman, error now rectified).				

Suspense A/c

To Sales	45	By Difference in Trial balance	151
To Purchase Returns	100	(Balancing figure)	
To Raman	6		
	151		151

Problem 2

A book-keeper finds that the trial balance is out by excess debit of Rs. 500. He puts the difference to a newly opened suspense a/c. Later on, he detects the following errors.

(*i*) Goods worth Rs. 15,000 purchased from Ravi but entered in the sales book.
(*ii*) Received a promissory note for Rs. 25,000 from Arun, but entered in the bill payable book.
(*iii*) An item of Rs. 3,500 relating to prepaid rent account was omitted to be brought forward.
(*iv*) An item of Rs. 2,000 in respect of purchase returns to Roshan had been wrongly entered in the purchased book.
(*v*) Rs. 5,000 paid to Hari against acceptance was debited to Harish.
(*vi*) A bill was received for repairs of furniture for Rs. 2,500. The amount was debited to furniture a/c.

Pass Journal entries to rectify the above errors and prepare the suspenses account

(C. S. Foundation. December 2002).

Solution

Rectification Entries

Date	Particulars		L.F.	Dr. Amount	Cr. Amount
(*i*)	Purchases a/c	Dr.		15,000	
	Sales a/c	Dr.		15,000	
	To Ravi				30,000
	(Goods purchased from Ravi entered in sales book, error now rectified)				
(*ii*)	Bills receivable a/c	Dr.		25,000	
	Bills payable a/c	Dr.		25,000	
	To Arun's a/c				50,000
	(Promissory note received from Arun entered in bills payable book, error now rectified)				
(*iii*)	Prepaid Rent a/c	Dr.		3,500	
	To Suspense				3,500
	(Prepaid rent account omitted to be brought forward, error now rectified)				
(*iv*)	Suspense a/c	Dr.		4,000	
	To Purchases a/c				2,000
	To Purchase returns a/c				2,000
	(Purchases returns to Roshan wrongly entered in purchases book error now rectified)				

Date	Particulars	L.F.	Dr.. Amount	Cr. Amount
(v)	Bills payable a/c Dr. To Harish (Cash paid to Hari against our acceptance debited to Harish, error now rectified)		5,000	5,000
(vi)	Repairs a/c Dr. To furniture a/c (Repairs to furniture debited to furniture a/c, error now rectified)		2,500	2,500

Suspenses A/c

To Purchases a/c	2,000	By Difference on Trial balance	500
To Purchase return a/c	2,000	By Prepaid rent a/c	3,500
	4,000		4,000

Problem 3

On 28th February 2002, the trial balance of Zahir did not agree. The proprietor put the difference in a newly opened suspense a/c. Subsequently the following errors were located.

(i) The purchases book for January 2002 has been cast Rs. 1,000 short.

(ii) A credit sale for Rs. 6,000 has been passed thought the purchase book. The customer's account has however, been correctly debited.

(iii) A credit purchase for Rs. 6,710 had been posted to the debit of the creditor's account as Rs. 6,170 ; Rajan being the concerned creditor.

Pass Journal entries to rectify the above mentioned errors. Also prepare the suspenses a/c assuming that there are no other errors **(C.S. Foundation June 2002).**

Solution

Rectification Entries

Date	Particulars	L.F.	Dr. Amount	Cr. Amount
	Purchases a/c Dr. To Suspense a/c (Undercasting of purchases book by Rs. 1,000 now rectified)		1,000	1,000
	Suspense a/c Dr. To purchases a/c To Sales a/c (A credit sale for Rs. 6,000 has been wrongly recorded in the purchases book but the customers has been correctly debited, error now rectified)		12,000	6,000 6,000
	Suspense a/c Dr. To Rajan (A credit purchase for Rs. 6,710 to the debit of Rejoin, the supplier, the error now rectified)		12,880	12,880

Suspense A/c

To purchases a/c	6,000	By difference in Trial Balance (Balancing figure)	23,880
To Sales a/c	6,000	By Purchases a/c	1,000
To Rejoin	12,880		
	24,880		24,880

Problem 4

On 31st March 2001, a book-keeper finds the difference in the trial balance and he puts it on the suspenses a/c. Later on he detects the following errors.

(*i*) Rs. 50,000 received from A was posted to the debit of his account.
(*ii*) Rs. 20,000 being purchases return were posted to the debit of purchases a/c.
(*iii*) Discount of Rs. 8,000 received were posted to the debit of discount a/c.
(*iv*) Rs. 9,060 paid for repairs of motor car was debited to motor car a/c as Rs. 7,060.
(*v*) Rs. 40,000 paid to B was debited to A's a/c.

Give Journal entries to rectify the above errors and ascertain the amount transferred to suspense a/c on 31st March 2001, by showing the suspenses a/c, assuming that the suspense a/c is balanced after the above corrections. **(C A. Foundation, May 2001).**

Solution

Rectification Entries

Date	*Particulars*	*L.F.*	*Dr. Amount*	*Cr. Amount*
1.	Suspense a/c Dr.		1,00,000	
	To A's a/c			1,00,000
	(Being the rectification of error by which amount received from A was wrongly debited to his account)			
2.	Suspenses a/c Dr.		40,000	
	To Purchases a/c			20,000
	To Purchases returns a/c			20,000
	(Being the rectification of error by which purchases return had been wrongly posted to the purchases a/c)			
3..	Suspense a/c Dr.		16,000	
	To Discount a/c			16,000
	(Being the rectification of error by which discount received was wrongly debited to discount a/c)			
4.	Motor car repairs a/c Dr.		9,060	
	To Motor car a/c			7,060
	To Suspenses a/c			2,000
	(Being the rectification of error by which motor car repairs expenses Rs. 9,060 wrongly debited to motor car a/c as Rs. 7,060			
5.	B's a/c Dr.		40,000	
	To A's a/c			40,000
	(Being the rectification of error by which amount paid to B had been wrongly debited to A)			

Suspense A/c

To A's a/c	1,00,000	By difference in trial balance (Balancing figure)	1,54,000
To Purchases a/c	20,000	By Motor car repairs a/c	2,000
To Purchase returns a/c	20,000		
To Discount a/c	16,000		
	1,56,000		1,56,000

Problem 5

Following mistakes occurred in a computerised accounting system.

(*a*) Payment of Rs. 10,000 to a party by cheque was recorded through the receipt column of the bank account.

(*b*) Receipt of Rs. 25,000 from a customer was entered through the payment column of the bank account.

(*c*) Purchase invoice of Rs. 51,000 was entered through the sales journal as Rs. 15,000.

(*d*) Sales bill of Rs. 46,000 was entered through the purchase journal as Rs. 64,000.

(e) Returns inwards of Rs. 6,000 was entered through the sales journal as Rs. 500. What will be changes in final accounts on rectification of the above mistakes ? Pass the rectification entries and pinpoint the charges (ICWA, Inter, December 2000).

Solution

Rectification Entries and Effects

Date	*Particulars*	*L.F.*	*Dr. Amount*	*Cr. Amount*
(*a*)	Sundry Debtors Dr.		20,000	
	To Bank a/c			20,000
	Effect : Liability to suppliers—reduced by Rs. 20,000; Bank balance reduced by Rs. 20,000; No impact on profit of loss			
(*b*)	Bank a/c Dr.		50,000	
	To Sundry Creditors a/c			25,000
	To Sundry Debtors (assuming the supplier party wrongly debited).			25,000
	Effect : Dues from customers reduced by Rs. 25,000 Bank balance increased by Rs. 50,000. Dues to supplier party increased by Rs. 25,000. No impact on profit or loss.			
(*c*)	Purchases a/c Dr.		51,000	
	Sales a/c Dr.		15,000	
	To Party a/c			51,000
	To Sundry a/c			15,000
	Effect : Liabilities to supplier increased by Rs. 51,000. Purchases increased by Rs. 51,000. Sundry debtors reduced by Rs. 15,000. Sales reduced by Rs. 15,000, profit reduced by Rs. 66,000.			

Date	Particulars		L.F.	Dr. Amount	Cr. Amount
(d)	Sundry creditor a/c	Dr.		64,000	
	Sundry debtors a/c	Dr.		46,000	
	To Purchases a/c				64,000
	To Sales a/c				46,000
	Effect : Personal account of the party reduced by Rs. 64,000, Sales increased by Rs 46,000, Sundry debtors increased by Rs. 46,000. Profit increased by Rs. 1,10,000.				
(e)	Returns Inwards a/c	Dr.		6,000	
	Sundry Creditor a/c	Dr.		60,000	
	To Sundry debtors a/c				6,000
	To Purchases a/c				60,000
	Effect : Amount due to supplier party reduced by Rs. 6,000 ; profit goes up by Rs. 54,000.				
(f)	Returns outwards a/c	Dr.		5,000	
	Sales a/c	Dr.		500	
	To Sundry debtors				500
	To Sundry creditors				5,000
	Effect : Amount due from supplier party-reduced by Rs. 5,000 : Purchases returns increased by Rs. 5,000. Sales reduced by Rs. 500 ; Sundry debtors reduced by Rs. 500 ; profit goes up Rs. 4,500.				

Problem 6

An account prepared a trial balance on 31st January 2000, which revealed a diference in the books of account. He put the difference in a newly opened suspense a/c. During February 2000, he detected the following errors.

(*i*) The total of the returns outward book, Rs. 4,200 had not been posted in the ledger.

(*ii*) A purchase of Rs. 3,500 from Y had not been entered in the purchases book. However, Y's a/c had been correctly credited with the amount.

(*iii*) A sale of Rs. 3,900 to Z had been credited to his account as Rs. 2,900.

(*iv*) furniture sold for Rs, 5,400 had been entered as Rs. 4,500 in sales book.

(*v*) Goods worth Rs. 500 taken by proprietor for personal use had not been recorded at all.

(*vi*) Wages paid for on installation of machinery Rs. 1,000 had been debited to wages a/c.

Pass Journal entries to rectify the above mentioned errors and prepare suspense a/c assuming that all the errors have been located

(CS foundation, June 2000).

Solution

Rectification Entries

Date	*Particulars*	*L.F.*	*Dr. Amount*	*Cr. Amount*
(*i*)	Suspense a/c Dr. To returns outward a/c (Total of returns outward book not posted earlier, error now rectified).		4,200	4,200
(*ii*)	Purchases a/c Dr. To Suspense a/c (Purchases from Y not entered in purchase book although Y's a/c had been correctly credited, error now rectified.		3,500	3,500
(*iii*)	Z's a/c Dr. To suspense a/c (Sale of Rs. 3,900 to Z credited to him as Rs. 2,900, error now rectified)		6,800	6,800
(*iv*)	Sales a/c Dr. Buyer of furniture a/c Dr. To Furniture (Sale of furniture for Rs. 5,400 wrongly recorded in sales book as Rs. 4,500 error now rectified)		4,500 900	5,400
(*v*)	Drawing a/c Dr. To purchases/Trading a/c (Drawings of goods not recorded earlier, error now rectified)		500	500
(*vi*)	Machinery a/c Dr. To wages a/c (Wages spent on installation of machinery wrongly debited to machinery wrongly debited to wages a/c, error now rectified		1,000	1,000

Suspenses A/c

To Difference in Trial Balance	6,100	By Purchases a/c	3,500
To Returns outward a/c	4,200	By Z's a/c	6,800
	10,300		10,300

QUESTIONS

1. What do you mean by an error ?
2. What do you mean by error of commission ?
3. What do you mean by error of omission ?
4. What do you mean by error of principle ?
5. What are compensating errors ?
6. What is a suspense account ?

EXERCISE 1

A merchant, while balancing his books of account finds that the trial balance shows excess credit of Rs. 1,700. Being required to prepare the final accounts, he places the difference to a newly opened suspense a/c which he carries forward. In the next accounting year, the following errors are discovered.

(*i*) Goods bought from Narayan amounting to Rs. 500 had been posted to the credit of Narayan as Rs. 5500.
(*ii*) A discounted bill receivable for Rs. 20,000 was returned by the bank, as having been dishonoured. The amount of the bill was credited to bank and debited to bills receivable a/c.
(*iii*) An item of Rs, 1,000 entered in the sales return book was posted to the debit of Pandey who had returned the goods.
(*iv*) Sundry items of furniture sold for Rs. 26,000 had been entered in the sales book. Ignore depreciation and profit or loss on the sale.
(*v*) Discount amounting to Rs. 200 from a creditor had been duly entered in the creditors a/c but not posted to discount a/c.

Draft journal entries necessary for rectifying the above mentioned errors. Prepare the suspense a/c and show the ultimate effect of the errors on the last years profit by preparing profit & loss adjustment a/c. **(C S Foundation. December 1999).**

Answer : (Total of suspense a/c Rs. 3,900)
Total of P & C Adj. a/c Rs. 2,600)

EXERCISE 2

Give Journal entries for the following transactions :

(*i*) Proprietor has drawn goods worth Rs. 500 but no record has been made in the books.
(*ii*) Wages for installation of machinery have been debited to wages a/c Rs. 400
(*iii*) Closing Stock was Rs. 10,000.
(*iv*) Sale of furniture Rs. 4,800 has been passed through sales a/c.
(*v*) Salaries outstanding were Rs. 600.
(*vi*) A credit purchase of Rs. 1,000 from A. Pathak has been credited to B. Pathak a/c.

(Calcutta University B. Com (Pass) 1996).

EXERCISE 3

On 28th February, 1999 the trial balance of X did not agree. 'X' put the difference in a newly opened suspense account. Subsequently, the following errors were located.

(*i*) The returns inward book for January 1999 had been cast Rs 1000 short.
(*ii*) A purchase of Rs 1671 had been posted to the debit of the creditor's a/c as Rs. 1,617, the creditor is Panna and Co.
(*iii*) A sale of Rs. 2,000 to Singhi and Co., was credited to the account of the customer.
(*iv*) A sale of Rs. 4,000 has been passed through the purchase book. The customer's account has, however been correctly debited.
(*v*) While carrying forward the total of sales book from one page to the next, the amount was written as Rs. 1,76,658 instead of Rs. 1,67,568.

Pass Journal entries to rectify the above mentioned errors. Also prepare the suspense a/c assuming that all the errors have been located. **(CS Foundation Course, June 1999).**

Answer : Total of suspense a/c Rs. 14,090

EXERCISE 4

A book-keeper finds the difference in trial balance amounting to Rs. 1,000 and puts it in the suspense account. Later on he detects the following errors.

(*i*) Purchased goods from Ravi Rs. 15,000 but entered into sales book.

(*ii*) Received one bill for Rs. 25,000 from Arun but recorded in bills payable book.

(*iii*) An item of Rs. 3,500 relating to prepaid rent account was omitted to be brought forward.

(*iv*) An item of Rs. 2,000 in respect of purchase returns, had been wrongly entered in the purchase book.

(*v*) Rs. 25,000 paid to Hari against our acceptance were debited to Harish a/c.

(*vi*) Bills received from Janaki for repair done to radio Rs. 2,500 and radio supplied for Rs. 45,000 were entered in the purchase book as Rs. 46,000.

Give rectifying Journal entries with full narration and prepare suspense a/c

(C A Foundation Course, May 1998)

Answer : (Total of Suspense a/c Rs. 5,000)

11
CHAPTER

Final Accounts of Sole Traders

1. INTRODUCTION

The main objective of an accounting system is to reveal the results and financial position of the business. With this objective in view every trader will prepare accounts at the end of each year. Such accounts which are prepared to know the profit or loss and the financial position are known as final accounts. Final accounts can also be prepared in between two accounting years, in which case it is called as interim final accounts. These accounts are called as final accounts as these constitutes the ultimate accounts of the business. Preparation of final accounts is the last step involved under the accounting cycle. The final accounts of a trading concern involves preparation of two statements known as (*a*) Income statement and (*b*) Position statement. The Income statement shows the details of incomes and expenditures and the profit earned or loss suffered by the business. The income statement of a trading concern consists of : (*a*) trading account (*b*) profit & loss account. In case of manufacturing concerns, it also includes preparation of manufacturing account in addition to the above accounts. The position statement also known as balance sheet discloses the financial position of the business. The preparation of final accounts depend upon the nature of the business. In a manufacturing concern all the four accounts are prepared whereas, in a trading concern only the first mentioned three accounts are prepared. In service rendering organisation like banking and insurance companies, the final accounts will include only two accounts viz, profit and loss account and balance sheet. However in this book only final account of a trader and a manufactures are prepared.

2. MEANING OF FINAL ACCOUNTS

The trading and profit and loss account and Balance Sheet prepared at the end of the year is collectively known as final accounts. It is not proper to call these accounts as final accounts because balance sheet is only a statement but not an account. However in actual practice these accounts and statements are together called as final accounts. The final accounts are prepared on the basis of various ledger balances incorporated in the trial balance and other adjustments made at the time of preparation of trial balance.

3. TRADING ACCOUNT

Trading account constitutes the first section of the income statement . It is an account which is prepared to ascertain the gross profit or loss of the business. It is called as trading account as it reveals the trading result of the business. As in the case of other ledger accounts, it also has two sides, viz debit side and credit side. On the debit side, the following items usually appear ; (*a*) opening stock (*b*) purchases of goods and returns outwards or purchase returns and (*c*) Direct expenses. On the credit side usually two items appear ; (*a*) Sales and Returns inwards or Sales returns and (*b*) Closing Stock. The excess of credit side over debit side is known as gross profit. On the other hand the excess of debit side over credit side is known as gross profit.

Debit side of the trading account :

1. Opening Stock of goods : The stock of goods unsold for the previous years is known as opening stock for the current year. This constitutes the first item on the debit side of the trading account. This may relate to opening stock of raw materials, semi-finished goods or work in progress and finished goods.

2. Purchases of goods : This includes only purchases of goods which are meant for resale. It includes both cash and credit purchases. Usually the total purchases of goods are recorded in the inner column of the trading account. The purchase returns, i.e., goods turned by the trader to the supplier owing to dissatisfaction are deducted from the total purchases and net purchases are then extended to column of the trading account. Sometimes the purchase returns are added in the credit side instead of deducting from the purchases. This is not recommended as it is not correct to show returns outwards on the credit side of the trading account. If the purchased goods are still in transit, such goods should not be recorded in the trading account. Instead a separate entry is to be passed by debiting "goods-in-transit a/c" and crediting suppliers account. The goods-in-transit represents an asset and suppliers account a liability in the balance sheet. Sometimes the trader may withdraw goods purchased for the business. In such a case the usual recording of the purchased goods is to be made in the trading account. A second entry is then to be passed for withdrawing the goods by debiting the drawings account (or capital a/c) of the proprietor and crediting the purchase account. It is to be emphasised that goods withdrawn should not be treated as a sale because goods are withdrawn at cost price and not at sale price.

The following transactions are to be excluded from treating as purchases.

(*a*) Purchase of assets other than goods which are meant for sale.
(*b*) Goods received on consignment.
(*c*) Receipt of Invoice in advance of actual delivery of goods.

3. Direct expenses : It refers to all those expenses which are incurred in acquring the goods and transporting the same to the godown for sales purpose. Direct expenses include the following.

(*a*) **Wages :** Wages are mostly incurred by a manufacturing concern and hence appear in a manufacturing account. When separate manufacturing account is prepared it is recorded on the debit side of trading account. Sometime the term "wages and salaries" are given together as an expense. This is also treated as a direct expense and therefore to be taken as trading item . But if it is worded as Salaries and wages" it is to be treated as indirect expense and hence should be taken into the debit side of profit & loss account.

(*b*) **Dock charges :** It is a charge levied on ships and the goods carried by the ship. It is payable to dock authorities before taking delivery of goods. It is a direct expense and hence a trading item of expense.

(*c*) **Duty :** Duty payable by a trader may relate to customer duty, excise duty and octroi duty. Customs duty is lived on an imported goods whereas excise duty is levied on the goods manufactured within the country. Octroi duty is payable when goods are bought from another state of the same country. The duty payable on purchased goods appear on the debit side of the trading account.

(*d*) **Freight, carriage inwards and cartage inwards :** All these refers to transport expenses incurried on purchased goods until they reach the premises of the trader All expenses incurred in transporting goods are treated as direct expenses and appear on the debit side of trading account. However, freight, carriage expenses or cartage paid on purchase of assets should be capitalised by debiting asset account and crediting cash account and not to take into trading account.

(*e*) **Royalty :** It is the amount paid to the owner of the property or right or patents for using the property, right or patent. This appears on the debit side of manufacturing account. When no manufacturing account is prepared, it is taken on the debit side of the trading account.

(*f*) **Gas, Coal, Electricity, Water :** All these expenses are related to manufacturing and as such taken on the debit side of manufacturing account. Where separate manufacturing account is not prepared, it is taken on the debit side of trading account.

(*g*) **Primary packing materials :** Primary packing materials such as bottles, tins, boxes etc. used to pack the finished goods such as ink, coffee powder, paint, Jam etc. and treated as direct expenses. Hence they are taken on the debit side of trading account.

Credit side of Trading Account

1. Sales : Sales of goods is always taken to mean purchased goods which are meant for sale. Therefore sale of any asset such as machinery, furniture etc., should not be included in the trading account. Sale of goods include both cash and credit sales. Whenever there are any sales returns or returns inwards, i.e., goods returned by customers owing to their dissatisfaction, they should be deducted from total sales and the net sales are then extended to outer column. Sometimes sales returns are shown on the debit side and added along with other items. This procedure is not correct although it gives the same amount of gross profit or gross loss. Any sale of goods under hire purchase system should be shown separately and not to be included in the trading account. Similarly goods sold on approval basis should also be shown separately and not to be taken to trading account. Sometimes the term adjusted sales" is given on the credit side of the trial balance. This means the value of closing stock is added to the sales and brought into books of accounts before preparing the trial balance. In such a situation the closing stock appear on the debit side of trial balance. As the closing stock is already added to sales it should not be recorded again on the credit side of the trading account. It should be recorded only on the asset side of the balance sheet. Any free distribution of samples to prospective customers and goods lost, damaged or destroyed are to be shown an the credit side of trading account. Alternatively, they may be deducted from purchases on the debit side.

2. Closing Stock : The unsold stock for the given period is known as closing stock. It is taken on the credit side of the trading account. It may relate to raw materials, work-in-progress, and finished goods.

The following is the proforma of a trading account.

Trading account for the period ending --------

Date	Particulars		Amount	Date	Particular		Cr.Amount
	To Opening stock		—		By Sales	—	
	To Purchases	—			Less returns outwards	—	—
	Less returns inwards	—	—		By Closing stock		—
	To Direct expenses :-		—		By Gross loss		—
	To Carriage inwards		—				
	To Freight		—				
	To Wages		—				
	To Duty		—				
	To Power, Fuel		—				
	To Packing Material		—				
	To Gross profit		—				

Problem 1

Prepare trading account in the books of Ravi from the following particulars for the period ending 31-3-2005

Opening Stock	Rs. 20,000
Closing stock	21,000
Returns Inwards	300
Purchases	45,200
Sales	60,300
Wages	8,000
Returns outwards	200

Solution

Trading A/c for the period ending 31-3-05

Particulars	Rs.	Rs.	Particulars	Rs.	Rs.
To Opening stock		20,000	By Sales	60,300	
To Purchases	45,200		Less returns inwards	300	60,000
Less returns outwards	200		By Closing stock		21,000
		45,000			
To Wages		8,000			
To Gross profit c/d		8,000			
		81,000			81,000

Problem 2

Prepare trading account in the books of Shri Anil Kumar from the following particulars for the period ending 31-12-04

Opening Stock	75,000
Closing Stock	84,200
Wages	80,000

Import Charges	15,000
Sales	5,49,000
Dock dues	820
Work expenses	4,200
Purchases	2,62,000
Duty and clearance charges	3,420
Freight	1,050

Solution

Trading for the period ending 31-12-04

Particulars	*Rs.*	*Particulars*	*Rs.*
To Opening stock	75,000	By Sales	5,49,000
To Purchases	2,62,000	By Closing stock	84,200
To Import charges	15,000		
To Duty & clearance charges	3,420		
To Freight	1,050		
To Dock dues & Octroi	820		
To Work expenses	4,200		
To Wages	80,000		
To Gross profit c/d	1,91,710		
	6,33,200		6,33,200

4. MANUFACTURING ACCOUNT

In case of a manufacturing concerns, first of all a manufacturing account is prepared, which is then followed by a trading account. A manufacturing account is prepared in order to know the cost of production of goods or services manufactured. The manufacturing account is prepared like any other account involving debit and credit side. The debit side of manufacturing account includes the following:

(*a*) Cost of raw materials consumed. This is ascertained by adding purchases of raw materials to opening stock of raw materials and deducting the closing stock of raw materials there from.

(*b*) Opening stock of work in progress which refer to semi-finished goods requiring further processing.

(*c*) Direct wages which means wages paid for employees who convert raw materials into finished goods.

(*d*) Direct expenses which refers to expenses of direct nature other than direct material cost and direct labour cost.

(*e*) Indirect expenses or factory expenses which are incurred in addition to direct expenses.

On the credit side two items will usually appear. They are (*a*) Sale of scrap, i.e., the sale value received after selling the scrapped materials and (*b*) Closing stock of work-in-progress. The excess of debit side over credit side is known as "cost of goods manufactured" and is transferred to trading account. A proforma of a manufacturing account is shown below.

Proforma of Manufacturing A/c

Manufacturing account for the year ended —

Particulars		*Dr. Amount*	*Particulars*	*Cr. Amount*
To opening stock of		—	By closing work-in progress	—
Raw materials	—		By Sale of scrap -	—
Add purchases	—		By Cost of production	
	—			
Less closing stock of raw materials	—		(transferred to Trading a/c	—
To Opening stock of work-in-progress		—		
To Carriage inwards		—		
To Direct wages		—		
To Direct expenses		—		
To Indirect expenses		—		
Rent		—		
Electricity		—		
Coat & coke		—		
Repairs of plant		—		
Depreciation of Plant		—		
Other indirect expenses		—		

Problem 3

Manufacturing account

Prepare a manufacturing account for the period ending 31st March 2005 from the following particulars

	Rs.
Opening stock of raw materials	10,000
Purchases of raw materials	60,000
Returns outwards of raw materials	500
Opening stock of work in-progress	7,000
Closing stock of work in-progress	8,000
Wages	4,500
Gas and water	1,000
Factory rent	500
Power	600
Consumable stores	700
Closing stock of raw materials	4,000
Closing stock work-in-progress	8,000

Solution

Manufacturing A/c for the year ended 31-3-2005

Particulars	*Rs.*	*Rs.*	*Particulars*	*Rs.*
To Opening Stock of			By Closing work-in progress	
Raw materials	10,000		work in progress	8,000
Add purchases of			By Cost of production	67,300
Raw materials	60,000		(Transferred to trading a/c)	--
	70,000			
less returns outwards	500			
	65,000			
less closing stock				
of Raw materials	4,000			
		61,000		
To Opening Stock of WIP		7,000		
To Wages		4,500		
To Gas and water		1,000		
To Factory Rent		500		
To Power		600		
To Consumable stores		700		
		75,300		75,300

Problem 4

Following are the balances as on 31-12-04 taken from books of Naresh. You are required to prepare (*a*) manufacturing account and (*b*) Trading account.

	Rs.
Opening stock	
Raw materials	4,000
Work-in-progress	6,000
Finished goods	9,000
Closing Stock	
Raw materials	3,000
Work in-progress	8,000
Finished goods	6,000
Purchases (Raw materials)	30,000
Wages	24,000
Carriage inwards	1,000
Rent (Factory)	3,200
Factory repairs	4,200
Plant repairs	7,800
Supervisor's remuneration	10,000
Work manager's salary	4,000
Sales	1,20,000

Solution

Manufacturing A/c for the year ending 31-12-04

Particulars	Amount	Amount	Particulars	Amount	Amount
To Opening stock	4,000		By Closing stock of work		
Add purchases	30,000		in progress		8,000
	34,000		By Cost of production		79,200
Less closing stock	3,000				
		31,000			
To Opening stock of work-in-progress		6,000			
To Wages		24,000			
To Carriage inwards		1,000			
To Factory rent		3,200			
To Factory repairs		4,200			
To Plant repairs		7,800			
To Supervisor's remuneration		10,000			
		87,200			87,200

Trading A/c

Particulars	Amount	Particulars	Amount
		By Sales	1,20,000
To Opening stock of Finished goods	9,000	By Closing stock of finished goods	6,000
Add cost of production Manufacturing a/c	79,200		
	88,200		
To Gross profit	37,800		
	1,26,000		1,26,000

5. PROFIT AND LOSS ACCOUNT

This account constitutes the second section of the income statement. The object of this account is to reveal the net profit or loss of the business. The gross profit as shown by the trading account is transferred to the credit side of the profit and loss account and the gross loss if there is any is recorded on the debit side of the profit & loss account. The profit and loss account is debited with the following expenses :

1. **Financial expenses :**
   (*a*) Interest on loan
   (*b*) Discount allowed
   (*c*) Interest on capital
   (*d*) Bad debts
   (*e*) Discount on bills discounted
   (*f*) Bank expenses
   (*g*) Charities and donations etc.

2. Administration expenses :

(*a*) Salaries of office staff
(*b*) Printing and stationery
(*c*) Office rent
(*d*) Postage and telegram expenses
(*e*) Office lighting expenses
(*f*) Trade expenses
(*g*) Audit
(*h*) Operating expenses of office
(*i*) Insurance & Taxes
(*j*) Repairs and Maintainenance expenses of office
(*k*) Legal charges
(*l*) Subscription of trade journals
(*m*) Telephone expenses

3. Selling and Distribution expenses :

(*a*) Carriage outward
(*b*) Advertisement expenses
(*c*) Export duty
(*d*) Commission to sales agent
(*e*) Salaries to salesmen
(*f*) Insurance of goods sold
(*g*) Packing expenses
(*h*) Sales tax
(*i*) Warehouse insurance
(*j*) Warehouse rent
(*k*) Delivery van expenses

4. Depreciation and other provision :

(*a*) Depreciation of various assets such as land and building, plant and machinery, furniture and fixtures.
(*b*) Provision for doubtful debts.
(*c*) Provision for discount on debtors
(*d*) Provision for other expenses

On the credit side of the profit and loss account, the following items are recorded.

1. Income received :

(*a*) Rent received
(*b*) Interest received
(*c*) commission received
(*d*) Discount received
(*e*) Income form investment
(*f*) Profit on sale of Asset
(*g*) Bad debts recovered

2. Reserve or provision for division on creditor's :

Reserve for discount on creditors

The excess of credit side over debit side reveals net profit and the excess of debit side over credit side reveals the net loss. The net profit or net loss is transferred to the proprietors capital account. A proforma of profit and loss account is shown below.

Profit & Loss A/c for the Period Ending

Particulars	*Amount*	*Particulars*	*Amount*
To Salaries	—	By Gross profit b/d	—
To Rent & Rates	—	By Interest received	—
To Printing & stationery	—	By Discount received	—
To Lighting	—	By Commission received	—
To Insurance	—	By Income from investment	—
To Depreciation	—	By Apprentice premium	—
To Repairs	—	By profit on sale of Investment	—
To Postage & telephone	—		
To Bank charges	—		
To Interest	—		
To Audit fee	—		
To Advertisement expenses	—		
To Discount allowed	—		
To Commission	—		
To Carriage outwards	—		
To Bad debts	—		
To Provision for doubtful debts	—		
To Loss on sale of assets	—		
To Loss by fire	—		
To Net profit	—		

Problem 5

Trading and Profit & Loss A/c

From the following trial balance of Shri Arvind prepare a trading and profit & loss account for the year ending 31st Dec. 2004.

Trial Balance as on 31-12-04

	Dr.	*Cr.*
To Purchases	21,750	
To Discount allowed	1,300	
To Wages	6,500	
To Sales		30,000
To Salaries	2,000	
To Travelling expenses	400	
To commission	425	
To Carriage inwards	275	
To Administration expenses	105	
To Trade expenses	600	
To Interest	250	
To Building	5,000	
To Furniture	200	
To Debtors	4,250	
To Capital		13,000
To Creditors		2,100
To Cash	2,045	
	45,100	45,100

Stock on 31-12-2004 was Rs. 6,000

Solution

Trading and Profit & Loss
(For the year ending 31-12-04)

Particulars	*Amount*	*Particulars*	*Amount*
To Purchases	21,750	By Sales	30,000
To Wages	6,500	By Closing stock	6,000
To Carriage inwards	275		
To Gross profit	7,425		
	36,000		36,000
To Discount	1,300	By Gross profit	7,475
To Salaries	2,000		
To Travelling expenses	400		
To Commission	425		
To Administration expenses	105		
To Trade expenses	600		
To Interest	250		
To Net profit	2,395		
	7,475		7,475

Problem 6

From the following balances extracted from the books of Naveen on 31st Dec. 2004, prepare a Trading and Profit and Loss a/c

Trading and Profit & Loss Account

Stock (opening)	Rs. 9,600
Wages and Salaries	3,200
Commission on purchases	200
Freight	300
Purchases less returns	11,850
Sales less returns	24,900
Trade expenses	20
Rent	200
Horse expenses	500
Repairs to plant	160
Income tax	550
Discount on purchases	400
Closing stock	3,500

Solution

Trading and Profit & Loss A/c
For the year ending 31-12-04

Particulars	*Amount*	*Particulars*	*Amount*
To Opening stock	9,600	By Sales	24,900
To Purchases less returns	11,850	By Closing stock	3,500

Particulars	Amount	Particulars	Amount
To Wages & Salaries	3,200		
To Commission on purchases	200		
To Freight	300		
To Gross profit	3,250		
	28,400		28,400
To Trade expenses	20	By Gross profit	3,250
To Rent	200	By Discount on Purchases	400
To Horse expenses	500		
To Repairs to plant	160		
To Net profit	2,770		
	3,650		3,650

Problem 7

The following particulars are extracted from the books of Dinesh. Prepare a trading and profit & loss account for the period ending 31-3-2005.

	Rs.
Factory fuel and power	542
office salaries	3,745
Factory lighting	392
Bad debts	300
Travelling expenses	925
Carriage on sales	960
Purchases	83,290
Wages	9,915
Rent and taxes	1,765
Office expenses	2,778
Carriage on purchases	897
Discount	422
Stock on 1-4-2004	21,725
Manufacturing expenses	2,680
Sales returns	7,422
Insurance	570
Sales	1,26,177
Purchase returns	3172
Commission	2,000
Rebate from Suppliers	1,000
Stock on 31-3-95	16,580

Solution

Trading and Profit & Loss A/c
(For the year ending 31-3-05)

Particulars	Amount	Amount	Particulars	Amount	Amount
To Opening stock		21,725	By Sales	1,26,177	
To Purchases	83,290		Less returns	7,422	
Less returns	3,172	80,118			1,18,755

Particulars	Amount	Amount	Particulars	Amount	Amount
To Factory fuel & power		542	By Closing stock		16,580
To Factory lighting		392			
To Wages		9,915			
To Carriage on purchases		897			
To Manufacturing expenses		2,680			
To Gross profit		19,066			
		1,35,335			1,35,335
To office salaries		3,745	By Gross Profit b/d		19,066
To Bad debits		300	By Commission		2,000
To Travelling expenses		925	By Rebate from Suppliers		1,000
To Carriage on sales		960			
To Rent & Taxes		1,765			
To Office expense		2,778			
To Discount		422			
To Insurance		570			
To Net profit		10,601			
		22,066			22,066

6. BALANCE SHEET

A balance Sheet is a statement which portrays the financial position of the business. It is so called because it is a sheet of all ledger balances pertaining to assets and liabilities for a given period of time. Its purpose is to known the exact financial position, i.e., solvency or insolvency of a business for a specified time. After the preparations of trial balance and trading and profit & loss account all nominal accounts gets closed. In the ledger only personal and real accounts will show the balances. In other words they constitute liabilities and assets. The balance sheet is prepared showing the classified list of such balances. It should be noted that a balance sheet is a position statement and strictly speaking it is not a part of the double entry ledger account. Therefore no transfer of the ledger account balances are necessary. Only the relevant particulars are extracted from the ledger while preparing a balance sheet.

Feature of a Balance Sheet :

1. It is part of final accounts and is prepared along with trading and profit and loss account.
2. It is prepared on a particulars date to show the financial position on that date but not for a period .
3. It is a statement but not an account. This statement has two sides known as asset side and liability side. If the value of assets are more than the liabilities (third party liabilities) it indicates a sound financial position. On the other hand if third party liabilities are more than assets it indicates a weak financial position.
4. The two sides of the Balance sheet i.e. asset side and liability side are always same.
5. The two sides of the Balance sheet is not prefixed with "To" and "By" as in the case of ledger accounts.

Arrangement of assets and liabilities in a balance sheet :

The process of arranging assets and liabilities in a definite order is known as " marshalling of balance sheet. There are two ways of arranging assets and liabilities. viz (1) In the order of permanency and (2) in the order of liquidity. Under the first method, the assets are arranged on the basis of them permanent use in the business. This method is usually followed by higher forms of business organisation such as joint stock companies. Under the second method, assets and liabilities are arranged according to ability to convert an asset easily in the form of cash so as to enable payments to liability holders. This arrangement is followed by sole traders and partnership firms. The usual method of arranging assets by a trader takes the following forms:

(*i*) **Liquid assets :** These are the assets which are in the form of cash or which can be converted into cash easily. Examples are cash in hand, cash at bank, bills receivable, short term debtors.

(*ii*) **Fixed Assets :** These are the assets which are meant for use in the business and not for sale in the ordinary course of business. Examples are land & building, plant and machinery, furniture and fixtures.

(*iii*) **Wasting assets :** Fixed assets which are consumed in course of exploitation as in mines are termed as wasting asset.

(*iv*) **Current or Floating assets :** These are the assets which are acquired for sale or held for its conversion into cash in course of time. Example of such assets are stock, debtors etc.

(*v*) **Intangible Assets :** There are the assets which are not visible and touchable but business is benefited by such assets. Examples of such assets are goodwill , patents, Trade marks.

(*vi*) **Fictitions assets :** The assets arise from abnormal expenses which are not yet written off and which are not representative of tangible value. Examples of such assets are expenditure incurried in developing a new product, special advertising expenses incurred to promote a product, preliminary expenses in the formation of a company. The benefit os such expenditure will arise in future accounting period. Therefore it is not desirable to charge the expenses entirely to the period in which it is incurred.

The liabilities are classified into :

(*i*) **Capital :** It is the amount introduced into the business by the proprietor. While recording capital on the liability, side certain adjustment are to be made. These adjustment relate to (*a*) additional capital introduced (*b*) profit earned in the business (*c*) Interest on capital. From the total of the above amount, the amount of capital with drawn during the year and net loss if there is any is to be deducted. The balance of capital now represent net liability due by business to the proprietor.

(*b*) **Fixed or long-term liabilities :** They represent a type of liability which his to be repayable over long period of time Examples are long term loans borrowed from banks, debentures in case of companies.

(*c*) **Current liabilities :** They represent a type of liability which is to be paid back on demand or in the short term, which is usually within a period of one year. One more criterion used to identify a liability as current liability is, it is to be discharged from a current asset. Examples of a current liabilities are sundry creditors, Bank overdraft etc.

(*d*) **Contingent liabilities :** They represent a type of liability which arises for payment on the happening of an event. Examples are discounting of a bill before maturity, compensation payable in a court of law.

Differences between a Trial Balance and Balance Sheet.

Trial Balance	*Balance Sheet*
1. It is the first step which is essential for the preparation of find account. In this regard it may be viewed as a "means" to achieve the end, i.e., to know the financial position of the business.	1. It is the ultimate step. Hence it is the end of accounting procedure.
2. It's purpose is to check the arithmetical accuracy of accounts	2. Its purpose is to know the financial position of the business.
3. It contains columns for debit and credit items.	3. It contains columns for assets and liabilities.
4. It contains all the three type of accounts viz, personal, real and nominal.	4. It contains accounts relating to personal and real
5. It does not disclose profit or loss.	5. It discloses profit or loss
6. It does not disclose closing stock.	6. It discloses closing stock.
7. It is not acceptable by tax and government authorities.	7. It is accepted by tax and government authorities.
8. It does to reveal outstanding and prepaid expenses or incomes.	8. Balance sheet discloses all such items.
9. It does not reveal various adjustments such as depreciation interest, repairs, etc.	9. It reveals all the adjustment. Infact without making all the adjustments it is not possible to prepare a balance sheet.

Form of a Balance sheet

There is no format laid down for preparing the balance sheet of a sole trading concern and partnership firm. However, higher forms of organisation such as joint stock companies must necessasity prepare balance sheet as per the statute regulating the business. A specimen form of balance sheet of a trader is given below :

Balance sheet of ______ as on ______

Liabilities	*Rs.*	*Assets*	*Rs.*
Capital a/c	××	Land & Buildings	××
Add additional capital invested	××	Plant & Machinery	××
Add Interest on Capital	××	Investment	××
	××	Furniture & fixture	××
Add net profit	××	Vehicles	××
	××	Goodwill	××
Less Drawings	××	Patents & Trade mark	××
	××	Patterns	××
Less Interest on Drawings	××	Closing stock	××
	××	Bills receivable	××
Less Net loss (if there is any)	××	Prepaid expenses	××
	××	Accrued income	××
Long term loan from Bank	××	Cash at bank	××
Loan on Mortgage	××	Cash in hand	××
Loan from wife	××	Fictious assets :-	
Sundry creditors	××	Preliminary expenses	××
Bills payable	××	Advertising expenses	××
Bank overdraft	××		
Outstanding expenses	××		
Income received in advance	××		

Problem 8

The business of Arun made a profit of Rs. 637 for the month ending Jan. 2005. From following balances, prepare a Balance sheet as on 31st January 2005.

	Rs.
Plant & Machinery	6,230
Cash in hand	895
Petty cash	56
Debtors	1,950
Bills receivable	2,730
Bank overdraft	4,000
Creditors	1,780
Bills payable	541
Capital	9,228
Furniture & Fixtures	670
Stock on 31-1-2005	3,700

Solution

Balance Sheet of Arun as on 31-1-2005

Liabilities		*Rs.*	*Assets*	*Rs.*
Bank overdraft		4,000	Cash in hand	895
Creditors		1,780	Petty cash	56
Bills payable		541	Bills Receivable	2,730
Arun's capital	9,228		Debtors	1,905
Add net Profit	637	9,865	Closing stock	3,700
			Plant machinery	6,230
			Furniture & Fixtures	670
		16,186		16,186

Problem 9

The following particulars are extracted from the books of Suresh for the period ending 31-3-2005 for which period his business earned a profit of Rs. 13,469.

	Rs.
Cash in hand	3,600
Plant & Machinery	8,500
Cash at Bank	9,327
Bills payable	2,800
Sundry debtors	5,678
Bills payable	2,800
Sundry creditors	4,736
Drawings	2,400
Capital	15,000
Stock on 31-3-2005	6,500

Prepare a Balance Sheet from the above particulars

Solution

Balance Sheet of Mr. Suresh
For the period ending 31-3-2005

Liabilities		*Rs.*	*Assets*	*Rs.*
Capital	15,000		Plant & Machinery	8,500
Less drawing	2,400		Sundry debtors	5,678
	12,600			
Add net profit	13,469		Stock	6,500
		26,069	Cash at Bank	9,327
Sundry creditors		4,736	Cash in hand	3,600
Bills payable		2,800		
		33,605		33,605

7. Capital and Revenue Expenditure

The study of capital and revenue expenditure is very essential in connection with the preparation of final accounts. This is so because only revenue expenditure will appear in profit and loss account, whereas capital expenditure will appear in the Balance sheet.

Capital Expenditure

It consists of such expenses whose benefit is not derived in one accounting year but spread over many years. Such expenditure is non-recurring in nature. They include the following:

(*a*) Investments made in procuring fixed assets such as land and building, plant and machinery, furniture and fixture which are meant for long term use and not meant for resale.

(*b*) Expenses incured in adding to the existing fixed assets. e.g., cost of constructing a factory shed.

(*c*) Expenses incurred for increasing the income earning capacity of business either by reducing cost or by increasing productivity. For example, cost of replacing manual labour by machines.

(*d*) For acquiring a valuable sight. For example cost of acquiring patent right or copyright.

All items of capital expenditure will appear on the assets side of balance sheet.

Revenue Expenditure :

It refers to a type of expenditure by the incurrence of which the benefit is designed for the same period for which the expenses arc incurred. It does not create any asset of an enduring nature. Such expenditure arc incurred for

(*a*) buying assets which are meant for resale at a profit or for converting them into finished goods.

(*b*) maintaining fixed assets in good working order, e.g., repairs.

(*c*) For meeting day to day expenses such as rent and taxes, wages and salaries, carriage etc.

Revenue expenditure will appear on the debit side of trading and profit & loss account.

Capital Receipts and Revenue Receipts

A capital receipt represents an amount contributed by the proprietor and loans provided by others to the business. It also represents the sale value of a fixed asset. A capital asset other than sale value of fixed assets create a liability either to owners or outsiders. Hence it is recorded on the liability side of the balance sheet.

Revenue receipt represents the income received on sale of goods or other income earned such as interest on investment, commission received, rent received etc. It appears on the credit side of trading and profit & loss account.

The classification on expenses and incomes into capital and revenue and correct recording of such items in the final account is very important. Otherwise it vitiates the result shown by final accounts. For example a capital expenditure wrongly taken to profit & loss account results in smaller profit than actual profit. Similarly, a revenue expenditure taken into balance sheet would inflate the profit or deflate the loss besides balance sheet showing wrong amount.

Differences between Revenue and Capital Expenditure

Capital Expenditure	*Revenue Expenditure*
1. It is incurred either for acquiring a new asset or improving the existing one	1. It is incurred for maintaining an existing fixed asset or to meet normal business expenses
2. It increases the causing capacity of the business	2. It helps in increasing the tempo of the business.
3. Its benefit is available over a long period of time.	3. Its benefit is available for the accounting period in which it is incurred

8. ADJUSTMENTS TO BE MADE WHILE PREPARING FINAL ACCOUNTS

Preparation of a balance sheet very often involves certain adjustment. Some important adjustments which are most commonly involved are as follows :

1. Outstanding expenditure. Sometimes a few expens like wages, salaries, rent etc. relating to a particular period is not paid during the same period, but paid in subsequent period. Such expenses relating to one period and paid on some future period is known as outstanding expenses. For example rent of January is paid in the month of February and similarly salaries and wages of one month is paid in the subsequent month. Sometime expenses like printing and stationery is also met with on subsequent period. All outstanding expenses must be recorded in the accounting year in which they are incurred irrespective of the fact whether they are incurred or not. In other words with a view to get a correct result of the business all expenses relating to a particular year is to be recorded in that year whether such expenses are paid or not. Otherwise it leads to overstating of profit and understating the liabilities. The following entry is passed to make an adjustment relating outstanding expenses.

Expenses a/c Dr.
To Outstanding Expenses

The outstanding expenses is to be added to the concerned expense on the debit side of the trading or profit account. It will appear on the liability side of balance sheet to indicate that on outstanding expenses is a liability.

In the next years a reverse entry as given below is passed.

Outstanding expense a/c Dr.
To Expense a/c

This entry will close outstanding expenses account and adjust the next year's expense account.

2. Prepaid expense. This is also known as expenses paid in advance or unexpired expense. Sometimes expenses such as insurance, telephone bill, taxes, rent are paid in advance in the current period relating to the future period. Such expenses are known as prepaid expenses. Prepaid expense is adjusted in the final accounts by passing the following entry.

Prepaid expenses a/c Dr.
To Expense a/c

The prepaid expense is deducted from the concerned expense account on the debit side of trading or profit & loss account. It appears in the balance sheet on the asset to indicate that the person who has received benefit to the extent of prepaid expense is a debtor of the business. If this adjustment is not made it would understate profit and will have the effect of reducing the value of asset.

In the next year, a reverse entry is passed as given below

Expense a/c Dr.
To Prepaid expense a/c

This entry will close prepaid expense account and will correct the next year's expense account.

3. Accrued Income. This is also known as outstanding income or income earned but not received. Sometimes a business would have earned some income such as commission, interest, dividend relating to a period but would not have actually received. Such income is called as accrued income. Such transaction is to be adjusted in the final accounts by passing the following entry.

Accrued income a/c Dr.
To Income a/c

The accrued income account will appear on the credit side of profit and loss account by means of adding it to the concerned income account. It will also appear on the asset side of balance sheet to indicate that this much amount is still due to business from others. If this adjustment is not made, it will understate the profit and asset would not have been recorded in the balance sheet.

In the next year a reverse entry is passed as shown below

Income a/c Dr.
To Accrued income a/c

This entry would cancel the income accrued account and will have the effect of setting right next year's income account.

4. Income received in advance. This is also known as income received but not earned. Sometimes a business receive some amount much before rendering service. Such incomes which are received in the current period relating to a future period is known as income received in advance. Examples of such transactions are insurance premium received by an insurance company. Advertisement expenses received by an advertising agency, apprentice premium received from learners etc. The following entry is made for adjusting income received in advance.

Income a/c Dr.
To Income received in advance a/c

The income received but not earned is to be deducted from respective incomes on the credit side of the profit & loss account. This item also appears on the liability side of the balance sheet to indicate that this much money is owed by business to others. If this adjustment is not made it amounts to overstating of profit and liability is understated.

5. Depreciation. It refers to decrease in the value of an asset owing to its constant use. The asset would lose its value owing to wear and tear of the asset or passage of time. If the asset is not depreciated it does not show its true value. Infact depreciation is a loss of value of asset and hence it is to be adjusted in the final accounts by passing the following entry.

Depreciation a/c Dr.
To Asset a/c

The depreciation being nominal account appears on the debit side of profit and loss account. The same amount of depreciation is deducted from the concerned asset on the asset side of balance sheet.

6. Bad debts. Debts which are irrecoverable are known as bad debts. It constitutes a loss to the business and hence it is to be adjusted in preparing final account by passing the following Journal entry.

Bad debts a/c Dr.
To debtor's a/c

The bad debts amount is debited to profit and loss account. It is deducted from sundry debtors on the asset side of the balance sheet.

Some times additional bad debts are anticipated for the current year in which case it is mentioned as one of the adjustments. Such additional bad debts are given outside the trial balance. This additional bad debts is also to be shown on the debit side of profit & loss account. On the asset side of the balance sheet only the amount given as adjustment is to be deducted from sundry debtors.

7. Reserve for doubtful Debts. In course of dealing with credit basis a trader may come to know that a part of debt is not likely to be recovered owing to failure on the part of some debtors. Such debts are called doubtful debts. This debts cannot be regarded as bad debts as its recovery is only uncertain. Doubtful debts are calculated as a certain percentage of debtors. A provision is made out of current years profit to meet losses arising out of doubtful debts. The following adjustment entry is passed to make provision for doubtful debts.

Profit & Loss a/c Dr.
To provision for doubtful debts a/c

The provision for doubtful debts is recorded in the profit & loss a/c depending upon the existence of old provision for doubtful debts.

(*a*) Where the total of bad debts for the year and the Provision for debits at the end of the year is more than old provision :-

In this situation the difference will appear on the debit side of profit & loss a/c. The following calculation is involved.

Bad debts of the year		××
Add new provision for doubtful debts		××
		××
Less old provision for doubtful debts		××
Amount to be shown on debt side of balance sheet.		××

(*b*) When the old provision for doubtful debts is more than the total of bad debts and new reserve :-

In this situation the difference will appear on the credit side of profit & loss account. The following calculations are involved :

Old provision for doubtful debts		××
Less bad debts for the year	××	
Less new provision for doubtful debts	××	××
Amount to be shown on the credit side of profit & loss a/c		××

In the balance sheet the new provision for doubtful debts is to be deducted from the sundry debtors.

8. Reserve for Discount on Debtors. Discount on debtors arise in case of credit sales. To encourage the debtors to pay the cash promptly, they may be allowed certain cash discount. But until they pay the cash it will be difficult to ascertain the discount to be allowed. So an estimate of discount on debtors is normally made and it is provided out of current year's profit. Such a discount which is created out of present year's profit in order to meet the loss arising out of discount is known as provision for discount on debtors". This adjustment is made by passing a journal entry as given below.

Profit & Loss a/c   Dr.
  To provision for discount on debtors

The provision for discount on debtors is recorded in the profit & loss account. It depends upon the old provision of discount on debtors created earlier. Thus,

(*a*) Where total of cash discount allowed during the current year and the new provisions is more than old provision the difference will appear on the debit side of profit and loss account. The following calculations are involved

Old provision for doubtful debts	××
Cash discount allowed during the year	××
Add new provisions for discount on debtors	××
	××
Less old provisions for discount on debtors	××
Amount to be shown on debit side of of Profit & Loss a/c	××

(*b*) Where the old provision for discount on debtors exceed the total of cash discount allowed during the year and the new provision for discount on debtors, then the difference will appear on the credit side of profit & loss a/c. The following calculations are involved:

Old provisions for discount on debtors		××
Less cash discount allowed during the year	××	
Less new provisions for discount on Debtors	××	××
Amount to be shown on the credit side of profit & loss account.		××

In the Balance sheet, the new provision for discount on debtors is shown on the asset side as a deduction from sundry debtors. The following calculations are involved.

Sundry debtors	××
Less bad debts given as adjustment	××
	××
Less new provision for doubtful debts	××
	××
Less new provision for discount on Debtors	××
Balance amount to be shown on one asset side of balance sheet.	××

9. Provision for discount on creditors. Whenever a business makes prompt payment to his creditor he will allow the cash discount to the business. So businessman can estimate the probable amount of discount which he can earn by paying the debts promptly to his creditors. The provision which is thus made in the current year relating to discount which is receivable in the subsequent year is known as provision for discount on creditors. On estimating the provision for discount on creditors as a percentage on creditors it is adjusted by passing the following entry.

Provision for discount on creditors a/c   Dr.
  To Profit & Loss a/c

The provision for discount on debtors is recorded in the profit and loss account depending upon the extent of old provision already created.

(*a*) Where the cash discount received during the year and the new provision exceeds the old provision the difference will appear on the credit side of profit & loss a/c. The following calculations are involved.

Cash discount received during the year	××
Add new provisions for discount on creditors	××
	××
Less new provision for discount on creditors	××
Amount to be shown on the credit side of profit & loss a/c	××

(*b*) Where the old provision it more than the total of cash discount received during the year and the new provision for discount on creditors, the difference will appear on the debit side of profit & loss account. The following calculations are involved.

Old provision for discount on creditors	××
Less cash discount received during the year	××
	××
Less new provisions for discount on creditors	××
Amount to be shown on the debit side of profit & loss a/c	××

In the balance sheet, the provision for discount on creditors is shown as a deduction from sundry creditors.

10. Interest on capital. Sometimes a proprietor may decide to charge interest on capital out of the profit earned by the business. The amount of interest on capital to be paid to proprietor in addition to profit which belongs to the proprietor. Interest on capital is provided under the assumption that had the same capital is invested in some other from it would have fetched some interest or dividend to the businessman. Provision of interest on capital is calculated at the time of preparation of final account by means of the following adjusting entry.

Interest an Capital a/c Dr.
To Capital a/c

Interest on capital appears in two places. Firstly, it is debited to profit and loss account as this constitutes an expense to the business. Secondly, interest on capital is added to capital on the liability side of the balance sheet.

11. Interest on drawing. Whenever a business withdraws any amount from the business, interest on such drawings may also be provided in the books of accounts. This is on the assumption that if the same amount is invested by the business on some other form of investment it would have earned either interest or dividend. Interest on drawing is calculated based on amount withdrawn and period for which it is withdrawn. Interest on drawings is calculated at the time of preparation of final accounts and is recorded through the following adjusting entry.

Drawing a/c Dr.
To Interest on Drawing a/c

Interest on drawings appear in two places firstly it appears on the credit side of profit & loss account as it is an income to the business. Secondly, the interest on drawings is to he deducted from proprietor's capital on the liability side of the balance sheet.

Problem 10

Santosh commenced business on January 1, 2004 with a capital of Rs. 40,000. At the end of the year the following balances where obtained from the books of accounts.

	Dr.	*Cr.*
Plant and Machinery	12,500	
Purchases	48,500	
Wages	7,050	
Returns outwards		500
Sales		60,000
Furniture & fixtures	2,500	
Freight	1,000	
Carriage outwards	250	
Rent and taxes	2,300	
Printing and stationery	400	
Debtors	10,300	
Creditors		5,000
Postage and telegrams	400	
Discounts		600
Rent received		600
Insurance	350	
Salaries	3,600	
Cash in hand	3,050	
Cash at bank	13,300	
Returns inwards	1,000	
Trade expenses	200	

The stock at 31st December 2004 was worth Rs. 7,300. Make the following adjustments.

(*a*) Write off bad debts Rs. 300 and provide reserve for doubtful debts at 5% on debtors.
(*b*) Create a reserve for discount on debtors and creditors at 2%.
(*c*) Plant and Machinery are to be depreciated at 10%, Furniture at 5%.
(*d*) Insurance was prepared to the extent of Rs. 50.

Prepare trading and profit & loss account for the year and balance sheet as on 31st December 2004.

Solution

Trading and Profit & Loss A/c for the year ended 31-12-2004

Particulars	*Amount*	*Amount*	*Particulars*	*Amount*	*Amount*
To Purchases	48,500		By Sales	60,000	
To less returns	500	48,000	By less returns	1,000	
To Freight		1,000			59,000
To Wages		7,050	By Closing Stock		7,300
To Gross Profit c/d		10,250			
		66,300			66,300
To Carriage outwards		250	By Gross profit b/d		1,050
To Rent & taxes		23,00	By Discount		600
To Printing & stationery		400	By Rent		600
To Trade expenses		200	By Reserve for discount on		
To Postage & telegrams		400	Creditors @ 2%		100
To Insurance	350				
To less prepared	50	300			
To Salaries		3,600			
To Bad debts		300			
To reserve for doubtful debts at 5%		500			
To reserve for discount on debtors at 2%		190			
To Depreciation on :					
Plant and Machinery		1,250			
Furniture		125			
To Net profit		1,735			
		11,550			11,550

Note : Calculation of reserve for Doubtful debts

Debtors	10,300
Less bad debts	300
	10,000

$$\frac{5}{100} \times 10,000 = 500$$

Calculation of reserve for discount on Debtors

Good debts (as calculated above)	1,000
less provision for doubtful debts	500
	9,500

$$\frac{2}{100} \times 9,500 = 190$$

Balance Sheet as on 31 December 2004

Liabilities		*Rs.*	*Assets*		*Rs.*
Capital a/c	40,000		Cash in hand		3,050
Add net profit	1,735		Cash at bank		13,300
		41,735	Sundry Debtors	10,300	
Creditors	5,000		Less bad debts	300	
Less reserve for discount	100			10,000	
		4,900	Less reserve for bad debts	500	
				9,500	
			Less reserve for discount	190	
					9,310
			Closing stock	2,500	
			less depreciation	125	
					2,375
			Plant & Machinery	12,500	
			Less depreciation	1,250	
					11,250
			Prepaid insurance		50
		46,635			46,635

Problem 11

The following balances were extracted from the books of Sri Janardhan, a Trader as at 31-3--2004.

	Dr.	*Cr.*
Capital of Sri Janardhan		19,400
Purchases and sales	41,400	55,140
Trade debtors and creditors	7,250	3,860
Stock on 1-4-2003	4,120	
Purchase returns		100
Sales returns	120	
Balances at Bank	3,920	
Drawing	4,600	
Motor van expenses	510	
Motor van	6,250	
Rent & Rates	750	
Salaries	8,120	
Reserve for doubtful debts		250
Bad debts	230	
General expenses	1,120	
Discount allowed	1,050	
Discount received		930
Insurance	240	
	79,680	79,680

The following are the adjustments to be made :

(a) Salaries and rent accrued but not paid Rs. 820 and Rs. 150 respectively.
(b) Insurance paid in advance Rs. 40.
(c) Maintain the reserve for doubtful debts at Rs. 300.
(d) Depreciation on Motor van to be made at 10%.
(e) The stock in trade on 31st March 2004 was valued at Rs. 5,040.

You are required to prepare a trading, profit & loss account for the year ending 31st March 2004 and balance sheet as on that date.

Solution

Trading, Profit & Loss A/c for the year ended 31-3-04

Particulars	*Amount*	*Amount*	*Particulars*	*Amount*	*Amount*
To Opening stock		4,120	By Sales	55,140	
To Purchases	41,400		Less Returns	120	
Less returns	100	41,300			55,020
To Gross profit c/d		14,640	By Closing stock		5,040
		60,060			60,060
To Salaries	8,120		By Gross profit b/d		14,640
Add accrued	820	8,940	By Discount received		930
Rent & Rates	750				
Add accrued	150	900			
To Motor van expenses		510			
To General expenses		1,120			
To Discount allowed		1,050			
To Insurance	240				
To Less prepaid	40	200			
To Reserve for bad debts	300				
To Add bad debts	230				
	530				
To Less old reserve	250	250			
To Depreciation on Motor van at 10%		625			
To Net profit		1,945			
		15,570			15,570

Balance Sheet as on 31-3-2004

Liabilities		*Rs.*	*Assets*		*Rs.*
Capital balance	19,400		Cash at bank		3,920
Less drawings	4,600		Closing stock		5,040
	14,800		S. Debtors	7,250	
Add net profit	1,945		Less reserve	300	
		16,745			6,950
Creditors		3,860	Motor van	6,250	
Expenses accrued but not paid			Less depreciation	625	
					5,625
Salary	810		Prepaid insurance		40
Rent	150	970			
		21,575			21,575

Problem 12

The following trial balance of Desai & Co. was taken on 31-12-2004. Prepare trading account, profit & loss account and balance sheet taking the following facts into consideration.

(a) Allow interest on capital at 6%.
(b) The Insurance premium of Rs. 120 has been paid for the half year ending 31-3-2004.
(c) Depreciate building and furniture by 10%.
(d) A sum of Rs. 40 due for wages has not been paid.
(e) Reserve 10% of the book debts, for bad and doubtful debts and 5% discount on debtors and creditors.
(f) Stock of goods on 31-12-2004 is Rs. 7,060.

Trial Balance as on 31-12-2004

	Dr.	*Cr.*
Capital		15,000
Drawings	750	
Stock (1-1-2004)	6,920	
Bills receivable	1,000	
Purchase returns		320
Sales returns	300	
Bills payable		1,180
Sales		8,300
Purchases	4,500	
Wages	70	
Discount		30
Salaries	200	
Union Bank Shares	3,000	
Insurance	120	
Buildings	3,000	
Furniture	700	
Sundry Debtors	6,000	
Sundry Creditors		1,300
Cash in hand	470	
Overdraft at bank		900
	27,030	27,030

Solution

Trading and Profit & Loss A/c for the year ended 31-12-2004

Particulars	*Amount*	*Amount*	*Particulars*	*Amount*	*Amount*
To Opening stock		6,920	By Sales	8,300	
To Purchases	4,500		By Sales		
Less returns	320		Less returns	300	8,000
		4,180	By closing stock		7,060
To Wages	70				
Add O/s	40	110			
To Gross profit c/d		3,850			
		15,060			15,060

Contd.

Particulars	Amount	Amount	Particulars	Amount	Amount
To Salaries		200	By Gross profit b/d		3,850
To Insurance	120		By Discount		30
Less prepared	60	60	By Reserve for discount on		
To Interest on capital			Creditors at 5%		65
6% on 15,000		900			
To Depreciation					
Buildings @ 10%		300			
Furniture @ 10%		70			
To Reserve for doubtful					
Debts @ 10% on debtors		600			
To Reserve for discount on					
Debtors @ 5% on good					
Debts i.e. 5,400		270			
To Net profit c/d		1,545			
		3,945			3,945

Balance Sheet as at 31-12-2004

Liabilities		Rs.	Assets		Rs.
Capital	15,000		Cash on hand		470
Add Interest	900		Bill receivable		1,000
Add net profit	1,545		Closing stock		7,060
	17,445		Union Bank Shares		3,000
Less Drawings	750		S. Debtors	6,000	
		16,695	Less reserve for D. D	600	
Creditors	1,300			5,400	
Less reserve for Discount	65	1,235	Less reserve for discount	270	
Bills payable		1,180			5,130
Bank overdraft		900	Buildings	3,000	
Outstanding wages		400	Less dep.	300	2,700
			Furniture	700	
			less dep.	70	630
			prepaid Insurance		60
		20,050			20,050

Problem 13

The following balance sheet of a sole trader is badly prepared. Redraft in proper form rectifying the errors.

Balance Sheet for year ended 31-3-2004

Liabilities	Rs.	Assets	Rs.
Stock in trade	4,063	Lease of premises	1,800
Cash in hand	164	Loan an mortgage	3,000
Petty cash	24	Sundry creditors	5,670
Sundry debtors	3,520	Depreciation of	

Contd.

Liabilities	Rs.	Assets	Rs.
Bank overdraft	1,525	Fixtures & fittings	40
Furniture & Fittings	800	Capital	2,500
Outstanding expenses	275		
P & L a/c Balance (loss)	2,639		
	13,010		13,010

Solution

Balance Sheet as at 31-3-2004

Liabilities	Rs.	Assets		Rs.
Capital a/c	2,500	Cash in hand		164
Loan on mortgage	3,000	Petty cash		24
Sundry creditors	5,670	Sundry debtors		3,520
Bank overdraft	1,525	Closing stock		4,063
Outstanding expenses	275	Furniture	800	
		Less Dep.	40	760
		Premises		1,800
		P & L a/c loss		2,639
	12,970			12,970

Note : Since the amount of loss is more than the capital, loss is shown on the asset side.

Problem 14

Following is the trial balance of Raman as on 31st December 2004. Prepare a trading and profit & loss account and a balance sheet after taking into account the adjustments given below:

Trial Balance

	Dr.	Cr.
Capital		30,000
Drawings	5,000	
Purchases	40,000	
Carriage outwards	500	
Purchases returns		1,000
Sundry expenses	800	
Bad debts	300	
Sales		60,000
Postage	200	
Wages	1,000	
Bills payable		3,000
Discount paid	500	
Land & buildings	18,000	
Plant & Machinery	7,500	
Creditors		8,500
Debtors	10,500	
Salary	1,500	
Investments	3,000	
Opening stock	13,200	
Cash	500	
	1,02,,500	1,02,500

Adjustments

1. Closing Stock 10,300
2. Create reserve for debtors at 5%
3. Depreciation on Plant & Machinery at 6%
4. Salary outstanding 400
5. Interest on Investment accrued 90
6. Wages paid in advance 50

Solution

Trading and Profit & Loss A/c for the year ended 31-12-2004.

Particulars	*Amount*	*Amount*	*Particulars*	*Amount*	*Amount*
To Opening stock		13,200	By Sales		60,000
To Purchases	40,000		By Closing stock		10,300
Less returns	1,000	39,000			
To Wages	1,000				
Less prepared	50	950			
To Gross profit c/d		17,150			
		70,300			70,300
To Salaries	1,500		By Gross profit		17,150
Add O/s	400	1,900	By Interest on		
To Carriage outwards		500	Investment accrued		90
To Bad debts		300			
To Postage		200			
To Discount		500			
To Depreciation on plant & Machinery at 6%		450			
To Reserve for debtors at 5%		525			
To Net profit c/d		12,065			
		17,240			17,240

Balance Sheet as on 31-12-2004

Liabilities		*Rs.*	*Assets*		*Rs.*
Capital	30,000		Cash		500
Add Net profit	12,065		Debtors	10,500	
	42,065		Less reserve	525	
Less drawings	5,000				9,975
		37,065	Closing stock		10,300
Creditors		8,500	Investments		3,000
Bills payable		3,000	Plant & Machinery	7,500	
Salary outstanding		400	less dep	450	
					7,050
			Land & buildings		18,000
			Interest on Investment accrued		90
			Wages prepaid		50
		48,965			48,965

Problem 15

The following trading and profit & loss accounts prepared by a Junior Accountant have to be redrafted correctly into final accounts after taking into account the items given at the end.

Trading Account

Particulars	Amount	Particulars	Amount
To Opening stock	7,352	By Closing stock	9,368
To Purchases	63,681	By Sales	1,70,852
To Sundry creditors	25,375	By Sundry debtors	40,659
To Carriage inwards	2,654	By Gross loss c/d	8,182
To Carriage outwards	394		
To Salaries	24,370		
To Wages	51,963		
To Rent rates & taxes	3,981		
To Factory expenses	35,368		
To Insurance	13,923		
	2,29,061		2,29,061

Profit & Loss A/c

Particulars	Amount	Particulars	Amount
To Gross loss	8,182	By Bank O.D.	17,681
To Interest on 10 am	6,180	By Interest on	
To Dividend from Investment	9,375	Bank O D	123
To Furniture purchased	17,681	By Net loss	39,914
To Telephone charges	985		
To Electric charges	2,756		
To Depreciation-Plant & Machinery	663		
Furniture	259		
To General charges	1,1637		
	57,718		57,718

The items to be taken into account — Rs.

(a) Capital — 1,42,692
(b) Loan — 20,000
(c) Plant — 2009
(d) Investments — 1,00,000

Solution

Trading and Profit & Loss A/c

Particulars	Amount	Particulars	Amount
To Opening Stock	7,352	By Sales	1,70,852
To Purchases	63,681	By Closing Stock	9,368
To Carriage Inwards	2,654		
To Wages	51,963		
To Factory expenses	35,368		
To Gross profit c/d	19,202		
	1,80,220		1,80,220

Particulars	*Amount*	*Particulars*	*Amount*
To Salaries	24,370	By Gross profit b/d	19,202
To Rent, Rates, Taxes	3,981	By Dividend from Investments	9,375
To Carriage outwards	394	By Net loss c/d	36,694
To Insurance	13,923		
To Telephone charges	985		
To Electric charges	2,756		
To General charges	11,637		
To Interest on loan	6,180		
To Interest on bank overdraft	123		
To Depreciation on			
Plant & Machinery	663		
Furniture	259		
	65,271		65,271

Balance Sheet

Liabilities		*Rs.*	*Assets*		*Rs.*
Sundry Creditors		25,375	Sundry debtors		40,659
Bank overdraft		17,681	Investments		1,00,000
Loan		20,000	Closing stock		9,368
Capital	1,42,692		Furniture		17,681
Less net loss	36,694		Plant & Machinery	2,009	
		1,05,998	Less dep	663	
					1,346
		1,69,054			1,69,054

Problem 16

Redrawing correctly the trial balance given below, prepare the final accounts.

Trial Balance

Particulars	*Dr. Amount*	*Particulars*	*Cr. Amount*
Capital	8,000	Debtors	7,500
Bad draft received	250	Bank deposit	2,750
Creditors	1,250	Discount allowed	40
Returns outwards	350	Drawings	600
Bank overdraft	1,570	Returns inwards	450
Rent	360	Sales	14,690
Salaries	850	Bills payable	1,350
Trade expenses	300		
Cash in hand	210		
Stock – 1 January 2004,	2,450		
Purchases	11,870		
	27,460		27,460

Solution

Redrafted Trial Balance

Particulars	*Amount*	*Particulars*	*Amount*
Rent	360	Capital	8,000
Salaries	850	Bad drafts received	250
Trade expenses	300	Creditors	1,250
Cash in hand	210	Returns outwards	350
Stock on 1-1-2004	2,450	Bank overdraft	1,570
Purchases	11,870	Sales	14,690
Debtors	7,580	Bills payable	1,350
Bank deposits	2,750		
Discount allowed	40		
Drawings	600		
Returns Inwards	450		
	27,460		27,460

Trading and Profit & Loss A/c

Particulars	*Amount*	*Amount*	*Particulars*	*Amount*	*Amount*
To Opening Stock		2,450	By Sales	14,690	
To Purchases	11,870		Less Returns	450	
Less Returns	350				14,240
		11,520	By Closing stock		NIL
To Gross profit		270			
		14,240			14,240
To Salaries		850	By Gross Profit		270
To Rent		360	By Bad debts reserve		250
To Trade expenses		300	By Net loss		1,030
To Discount		40			
		1,550			1,550

Balance Sheet

Liabilities		*Rs.*	*Assets*	*Rs.*
Bills payable		1,350	Cash in hand	210
Overdraft Bank		1,570	Bank deposit	2,750
Sundry creditors		1,250	Debtors	7,580
Capital a/c	8,000			
Less net loss	1,030			
	6,970			
Less drawings	600	6,370		
		10,540		10,540

Problem 17

From the following ledger balances of a trader, prepare trading, profit & loss a/c and Balance sheet as at 31st December 2004.

	Rs.
Opening Stock	48,000
Drawings	6,000
Sales	1,25,000
Sundry debtors	18,000
Capital	25,000
Wages	14,000
Salaries	2,800
Carriage on purchases	2,500
Rent	3,500
Purchases	60,000
Discount on purchases	2,000
Interest on Bank loan	100
Bills receivable	3,000
Plant & Machinery	10,000
Cash	1,000
Building	2,500
Bills payable	2,500
Bank loan	2,000
Reserve for bad debts	2,500
Returns outwards	750
Sundry Creditors	11,650

Adjustment

Rent at Rs. 100 per month is not paid for 2 months. Wages and salaries are unpaid to the extent of Rs. 750 and Rs. 225 respectively. Depreciate plant by 10%. Stock at close was Rs. 17,500. Write off Rs. 1,500 as bad debts and maintain a reserve of 5% on debtors.

Solution

Trading and Profit & Loss A/c
For the year ended 31st December 2004

Particulars	*Amount*	*Amount*	*Particulars*	*Amount*	*Amount*
To Opening Stock		48,000	By Sales		1,25,000
To Purchases	60,000		By Closing Stock		17,500
Less reserve	750				
	59,250				
Less discount on purchases	2,000	57,250			
To Carriage		2,500			
To Wages	14,000				
Add o/s	750	14,750			
To Gross profit c/d		20,000			
		1,42,500			1,42,500

Particulars	Amount	Amount	Particulars	Amount	Amount
To Salaries	2,800		By Gross Profit		20,000
Add outstanding	225	3,025	By Reserve for Bad Debts	2,500	
To Rent	3,500		Less new Reserve	825	
Add outstanding	200	3,700			1,675
To Interest on bank loan		100			
To Bad debts written off		1,500			
To Depreciation on Plant & machinery		1,000			
To Net profit c/d		12,350			
		21,675			21,675

Note : Calculation of reserve for bad debts

Sundry debtors	18,000
Less bad debts	1,500
	16,500

$$\frac{5}{100} \times 16{,}500 = \text{Rs. } 825$$

Balance Sheet as on 31-12-2004

Liabilities		Rs.	Assets		Rs.
Bills payable		2,500	Cash		1,000
Sundry creditors		11,650	Bills receivable		3,000
Outstanding creditors			Sundry debtors	1,800	
Wages	750		less bad debtors	15,00	
Salaries	225			16,500	
Rent	200	1,175	less reserve for bad Debts 825		
Bank loan		2,000			15,675
Capital	25,000		Closing Stock		17,500
Add net profit	12,350		Plant & Machinery	10,000	
	37,350		Less Dep. @ 10%	1,000	
Less drawing	6,000				9,000
		31,350	Buildings		2,500
		48,675			48,675

Problem 18

Following are the balances extracted from the books of Sri Nataraj.

Balance as on 31-12-2003

	Rs.
Nataraj's capital	30,000
Nataraj's Drawings	5,000
Furniture & fittings	2,600
Bank overdraft	4,200

Creditors	13,300
Premises	20,000
Stock (1-1-2003)	22,000
Debtors	18,600
Rent from tenants	1,000
Purchases	1,14,000
Sales	1,50,000
Sales returns	2,000
Discounts (Dr.)	1,600
Discount (Cr.)	2,000
Taxes & Insurance	2,000
General expenses	9,000
Salaries	2,200
Carriage on purchases	1,800
Provision for doubtful debts	600
Bad debts written off	800
Commission received	500

Adjustments :

Stock in hand on 31st Dec. 2003 was valued at Rs. 2,000. Rent Rs. 300 it still due from the tenants. Salaries Rs. 750 are yet unpaid. Write off Rs. 600 as bad debts. Depreciate business premises by Rs. 300 and fittings by Rs. 260. Make a provision of 5% on debtors for bad and doubtful debts. Prepare final accounts.

Solution

Trading and Profit & Loss A/c
For the year ended 31-12-2003

Particulars	*Amount*	*Amount*	*Particulars*	*Amount*	*Amount*
To Opening stock		22,000	By sales	1,50,000	
To Purchases		1,14,000	less returns	2,000	
To Carriage		1,800			1,48,000
To Gross profit c/d		30,200	By closing stock		20,000
		1,68,000			1,68,000
To Discounts		1,600	By Gross profit b/d		30,200
To Taxes & Insurance		2,000	By Discount		2,000
To General expenses		9,000	By Commission		500
To Salaries	2,200		By Rent	1,000	
Add o/s	750	2,950	Add accrued	300	
To Depreciation :-					1,300
Buildings	300				
Fitting	260	560			
To Bad debts	800				
Add additions	600	1,400			
To Provision for Bad debts (i.e. 5% on) 18,000)	900				
Less old provision	600	300			
To Net profit c/d		16,190			
		34,000			34,000

Balance Sheet as on 31-12-2005

Liabilities		*Rs.*	*Assets*		*Rs.*
Nataraj's capital	30,000		Debtors	18,600	
Add net profit	16,190		Less bad debts	600	
	46,190			18,000	
Less drawings	5,000		Less provision	900	
		41,190			17,100
Creditors		13,300	Closing stock		20,000
Bank OD		4,200			
Outstanding salaries		750	Furniture	2,600	
			Less Dep.	260	
					2,340
			Premises	20,000	
			Less Dep.	300	
					19,700
			Rent o/s from Tenants		300
		59,440			59,440

PROBLEMS ON BAD DEBTS AND RESERVE FOR DOUBTFUL DEBTS

Problem 19

On 1st January 2002, the bad debts reserve account showed a balance of Rs. 4,000. The had debts during the year amounted to Rs. 3,750. The sundry debtors on 31st December 2002 amount to Rs. 76000 and a new reserve of 5% was required. Make the necessary Journal entries and show how they will appear in the various ledger accounts concerned and the balance sheet.

Solution

Journal Entries

Date	*Particulars*	*L.F.*	*Dr.*	*Cr.*
31-12-02.	Reserve for bad debts To bad debts (Transfer of bad debts to reserve a/c)		3,750	3,750
	Profit & Loss a/c To Reserve for bad debts (Being the amount charged to P & L a/c for making up the reserve to 5% on Rs. 76,000).		3,550	3,550

Note :

5% on Rs. 76,000 will be 3,800. But there is a balance of Rs. 250 in reserve for bad debts a/c (4,000 balance - Rs. 3,750 bad debt of 2,002). So the difference required is Rs. 3,550.

Reserve for Bad Debts A/c

Date	Particulars	Amount	Date	Particulars	Amount
31-12-02	To Bad debts a/c	3,750	1-1-02	By balance b/d	4,000
	To Balance	3,800	31-12-02	By P & L a/c	3,550
		7,550			7,550

Bad Debts A/c

Date	Particulars	Amount	Date	Particulars	Amount
31-11-02	To Sundry customers	3,750		By reserve for Bad debts	3,750

Profit & Loss A/c

Date	Particulars	Amount	Date	Particulars	Amount
31-12-02	To reserve for Bad debts	3,750			

Balance Sheet

Liabilities	Rs.	Assets		Rs.
		Sundry debtors	76,000	
		less reserve for bad debts	3,800	
				72,200

Problem 20

In the Trial Balance of Sun Corporation Ltd., the following accounts appear.

Trial Balance

	Dr.	Cr.
Sundry debtors	60,000	
Reserve for doubtful debts		5,300
Bad debts	1,100	

Outside the Trial Balance two adjustment are given as under.

1. Write off further bad debts Rs. 1,000
2. Create a reserve for doubtful debts at 10% of sundry debtors.

Draft the concerned ledger accounts and show how they appear in P & L a/c and the balance sheet.

Solution

Reserve for Doubtful Debts

Particulars	Amount	Particulars	Amount
To Bad debts (1,100 + 1,000)	2,100	By Balance b/d	5,300
To Balance c/d	6,000	By P & L a/c	2,800
	8,100		8,100

Profit and Loss A/c

Particulars		Amount	Particulars	Amount
To Bad debts	2,100			
Add reserve for bad debts				
@ 10% on Rs. 60,000	6,000			
	8,100			
Less old reserve	5,300			
		2800		

Balance Sheet

Liabilities	Rs.	Assets		Rs.
		Sundry debtors	60,000	
		Less reserve		
		for Bad debts	6,000	
				54,000

Problem 21

The reserve for doubtful debts accounts shows a credit balance of Rs. 18,00 on 1st January 2001. During the year bad debts amount to Rs. 1,400. The debtors on 31st Dec. 2001 is Rs. 48,000 and 5% reserve for doubtful debts is required to be maintained. The bad debts during the year 2002 amounted to Rs. 2,670. On 31st December 2002, the debtors are Rs. 50,000 and 5% reserve for doubtful debts is required to be maintained. Write up the Bad debts account and reserve for doubtful debts a/c and also show how the above items will appear in the profit and loss account and the balance sheet of the respective year.

Solution

Bad Debts A/c

Date	Particulars	Amount	Date	Particulars	Amount
2001	To Sundry Debtors	1,400		By Reserve for Bad debts	1,400
		1,400			1,400
2002	To Sundry Debtors	2,670		By reserve for Bad debts	2,670
		2,670			2,670

Reserve for Doubtful Debts A/c

Date	Particulars	Amount	Date	Particulars	Amount
2001	To Bad debts	1,400	1-1-01	By balance b/d	1,800
	To Balance c/d	2,400	31-12-01	P & L a/c	2,000
		3,800			3,800
2002	To Bad debts	2,670	1-1-02	By Balance b/d	2,400
	To Balance c/d	2,500	31-12-02	By P & L a/c	2,770
		5,170			5,170

Profit & Loss A/c on 31-12-01

Particulars		Amount	Particulars	Amount
To Bad debts	1,400			
To Reserve Bad debts	2,400			
	3800			
Less Reserve	1,800			
		2,000		

P & L A/c as on 31-12-02

Particulars		Amount	Particulars	Amount
To Bad debts	2,670			
To Reserve for Bad debts-New	2,500			
	5,170			
Less old reserve	2,400			
		2,770		

Balance Sheet as on 31-12-2001

Liabilities	Rs.	Assets	Rs.
		Sundry debtors	48,000
		Less reserve for Bad debts	2,400
			45,600

Balance Sheet as on 31-12-02

Liabilities	Rs.	Assets	Rs.
		Sundry debtors	50,000
		Less Reserve for bad debts	2,500
			47,500

Problem 22

Following are the extracts from the trial balance of Mr. Vivek.

Trial Balance as on 31st Dec. 2004.

	Dr.	Cr.
Sundry debtors	20,000	
Bad debts	5,000	

Additional information

(*i*) After preparing the Trial Balance it is learnt that a debtor, Anand has become insolvent and therefore, the entire amount of Rs. 3,000 due from his was irrecoverable.

(*ii*) Create a provision for bad debt and doubtful debts.

You are required to pass necessary adjusting entries and show how the items will appear in the final accounts of Mr. Vivek.

Solution

Journal Entries

Date	*Particulars*	*L.F.*	*Dr. Amount*	*Cr. Amount*
	Bad Debts a/c Dr. To Anand's a/c (Being bad debts written off)		3,000	3,000
	Profit & Loss a/c Dr. To provision for bad & doubtful debts (Being 10% provision created for bad and doubtful debts)		1,700	1,700

Note : Calculation of provision of 10% on debtors

Good debtors	2,0000
Less bad debts	3,000
	17,000

$$17{,}000 \times \frac{10}{100} = 1{,}700$$

Profit & Loss A/c for 31-12-04

Particulars		*Amount*	*Particulars*	*Amount*
To Bad debts	5,000			
Add additional Bad debts	3,000			
Add provision for Bad debts	1,700			
		9,700		

Balance Sheet for 31-12-04

Liabilities	*Rs.*	*Assets*		*Rs.*
		Sundry Debtors	20,000	
		Less additional Bad debts	3,000	
			17,000	
		Less provision for Bad debts	1,700	
				15,300

Problem 23

On 31st December 2002, Mr. Arvind has to receive Rs. 3,600 from sundry debtors and creates reserve of 5% on this amount for doubtful debts. Actual bad debts, during the year 2003 amounted to Rs. 150. The debtors on 31st December 2004 are Rs. 8,500 on which he again create a reserve of 5% for doubtful debts. During 2004, actual bad debts are Rs. 500. His debtors on 31st December 2004 are Rs. 9,000 on which a reserve of 5% for doubtful debts is required to be maintained. During 2005 his bad debts are Rs. 150 only. His debtors on 31st December 2005 are Rs. 4,000 on which 5% reserve for doubtful debts is necessary. From the above particulars write up the reserve for doubtful debts a/c and show how it will appear in the profit & loss a/c and balance sheet.

Solution

Reserve for Doubtful Debts

Date	*Particulars*	*Amount*	*Date*	*Particulars*	*Amount*
2002	To Balance c/d	180		By P & L a/c	180
2003	To Bad debts	150		By Balance b/d	180
	To Balance c/d	425		By Balance b/d	395
		575			575
2004	To Bad debts	500		By Balance b/d	425
	To Balance c/d	450		By P & L a/c	525
		950			950
2005	To Bad debts	150		By Balance	450
	To P & L a/c	100			
	To Balance c/d	200			
		450			450

Profit & Loss A/c

Date	*Particulars*		*Amount*	*Date*	*Particulars*		*Amount*
2002	To Reserve for Doubtful debts		180				
2003	To Bad debts	150					
	Add new Reserve	425					
		575					
	Less old reserve	180	395				
2004	To bad debts	500					
	Add new reserve	450					
		950					
	Less old reserve	425					
			525				
2005					By Reserve for Doubtful debts		450
					Less bad debts	150	
					Reserve required	200	350
							100

Balance Sheet

Liabilities	*Rs.*	*Assets*		*Rs.*
2002		Sundry debtors	3,600	
		Less reserve for Bad debts	180	3,420
2003		Sundry debtors	8,500	
		Less reserve for Bad debts	425	8,075
2004		Sundry debtors	9,000	
		Less reserve for Bad debts	450	8,550
2005		Sundry debtors	4,000	
		Less returns for Bad debts	200	3,800

Problem 25

(Problems on reserve for discount on debtors)
The reserve for discount on debtors account showed a credit balance of Rs. 1,000 on 1-1-2002 During 2002 discount allowed amounted to Rs. 850. On 31-12-2002, Sundry debtors totalled Rs. 24,000 on which a reserve of 5% for the doubtful debts and $2\frac{1}{2}$% for discount was considered necessary. Show the reserve for discount on debtors account, the entry in the profit & loss account and how the reserve account will appear in the balance sheet.

Solution

Reserve for Discount on Debtors A/c

Particulars	*Amount*	*Particulars*	*Amount*
To Discount a/c	850	By Balance b/d	1,000
To Balance c/d	720	By P & L a/c	570
	1,570	$2\frac{1}{2}$% on good debtors	1,570

Profit & Loss a/c

Particulars	*Amount*	*Particulars*	*Amount*
To Reserve doubtful Debts (5% on 24,000)	1,200		
To Reserve for discount on debtors ($2\frac{1}{2}$% on Rs. 22,800 Good debtors)	570		

Balance Sheet

Particulars	*Amount*	*Particulars*	*Amount*
		Sundry debtors	24,000
		Less reserve for Bad debts	1,200
			22,800
		Less reserve for Discount	570
			22,230

Problem 26

The following items are found in the Trial balance of P on 31-12-2003.

Sundry	16,000
Bad debts written off	900
Discount allowed to customers (Debtors)	180
Reserve for bad and doubtful debts (31-12-2002)	650
Reserve for discount on debtors	320

You are required to provide for the bad and doubtful debts at 5% and for discount on debtors at 2%.

Give the necessary Journal entries and show the bad debts account and the Discount a/c Bad debts reserve a/c and the discount reserve account in the ledger. Also show how the item sundry debtors will appear in the balance sheet on 31st December 2003.

Solution

Journal Entries

Date	*Particulars*		*L.F.*	*Dr. Amount*	*Cr. Amount*
	Profit & Loss a/c	Dr.		1,104	
	To reserve for bad and doubtful debts				800
	To Reserve for discount on Debtors				304
	(Being the amount transferred to reserve)				
	Reserve for Bad and doubtful Debts a/c	Dr.		900	
	To Bad debts a/c				900
	(Being bad debts written off)				
	Reserve for discount on debtors a/c	Dr.		180	
	To discount a/c				180
	(Discount allowed to debtors)				

Bad Debtors A/c

Particulars	*Amount*	*Particulars*	*Amount*
To Sundry debtors	900	By reserve for Bad debts	900
	900		900

Reserve for Bad and Doubtful Debts A/c

Particulars	*Amount*	*Particulars*	*Amount*
To Bad debts a/c	900	By Balance b/d	650
To Balance c/d	560	By P & L a/c	800
	1,460		1,450

Discount Account

Particulars	*Amount*	*Particulars*	*Amount*
To Debtors a/c	180	By Reserve for Discount on Debtors	180
	180		180

Reserve for Discount on debtors A/c

Particulars	*Amount*	*Particulars*	*Amount*
To Discount a/c	180	By Balance b/d	320
To Balance c/d	444	By P & L a/c	304
	624		624

Balance Sheet

Liabilities	*Rs.*	*Assets*		*Rs.*
		Sundry debtors	16,000	
		Less reserve for Bad and D. D	800	
			15,200	
		Less reserve for Discount on Debtors	304	
				14,896

Problem 27

On 31st December 2003, the items "Sundry debtors" appeared in A's balance sheet as follows :

Sundry debtors	8,800	
Less bad debts reserve	440	
	8,360	
Less Discount reserve	418	
		7,942

During the year 2004, bad debts amounted to Rs. 1,160 and the discount allowed to Rs. 298. At the end of the year the total of the balances on debtors account amounted to Rs. 9,200. A reserve of 5% for bad debts and a 5% for discount provided. Show the ledger and profit & loss account and balance sheet entries for the above.

Solution

Bad Debts Reserve A/c

Date	*Particulars*	*Amount*	*Date*	*Particulars*	*Amount*
31-12-04	To Bad debts a/c	1,160	1-1-04	By Balance b/d	440
	To Balance c/d	460	31-12-04	By P & L a/c	1,180
		1,620			1,620

Reserve for Discount on Debtors A/c

Date	*Particulars*	*Amount*	*Date*	*Particulars*	*Amount*
31-12-04	To Discount a/c	298	1-1-04	By Balance	418
	To Balance c/d	437	31-12-04	By P & L a/c	317
		735			735

Profit & Loss A/c

Particulars		Amount	Particulars	Amount
To Bad debts	1,160			
Add new	460			
	1,620			
Less old reserve	440			
		1,180		
To Discount	298			
Add new reserve	437			
	735			
Less old reserve	418			
		317		

Balance Sheet

Liabilities	Rs.	Assets		Rs.
		Sundry Debtors	9,200	
		Less RBD	460	
			8,740	
		Less reserve for Discount	437	
				8,303

Note :- Reserve for bad debts

New reserve will be 5% on Rs. 9,200 = Rs. 460 whereas the actual bad debts is Rs. 1,160. As amount of Bad debts is far in excess of reserve amount Rs. 1,180 is charged to profit & loss account.

Problem 28

The reserve for discount on debtors account showed a credit balance of Rs. 2,000 on 1st January 2004. During 2004 discount allowed amounted to Rs. 1,700. On 31st December 2004, Sundry debtors totalled Rs. 48,000 on which a reserve of 5% for doubtful debts and $2\frac{1}{2}$% for discount was considered necessary. Show the reserve for discount on debtors account, the entry in the profit and loss account and how the reserve account will appear in balance sheet.

Solution

Reserve for Discount in Debtors A/c

Date	Particulars	Amount	Date	Particulars	Amount
31-12-04	To Discount allowed	1,700	1-1-04	By Balance	2,000
	To Balance c/d	1,140	31-12-04	By P & L a/c	840
		2,840			2,840

Profit & Loss A/c

Particulars		Amount	Particulars	Amount
To Discount on Debtors	1,140			
Less old Reserve	300			
		840		

Balance Sheet

Liabilities	Rs.	Assets	Rs.
Reserve for discount on debtors	1,140		

Note :-

Rs. 1,140 is 2% on net debtors of Rs. 45,000 i.e., 48,000 – 2,400 Reserve for bad debts. There is a balance of Rs. 300 in reserve for discount on debtors a/c. So for 2004, in Profit & Loss account Rs. 840 is charged.

Problem 29

From the following figures, you are required to prepare :

(*a*) Provision for Bad Debts a/c
(*b*) Bad Debts a/c
(*c*) Profit & Loss a/c

			Rs.
1-1-03	Provision for bad debts		1,800
31-12-03	Bad debts	(Dr)	980
	Bad debts	(Cr)	120
	Debtors		20,000

Adjustments :

1. Further bad debts Rs. 200
2. Make provision for bad debts at 5% on debtors

		Rs.
31-12-04	Bad debts	1,850
	Debtors	30,000
	Discount allowed to debtors	270

Adjustments :

1. Make provision for bad debts as 5%.
2. Make provision for discount for bad debts at 2%.

Solution

For the year 2003
Bad Debts (Dr)

Particulars	Amount	Particulars	Amount
To Balance b/d	980	By provision for	1,180
To Debtors a/c	200	Bad debts (Transfer)	
	1,180		1,180

Bad Debts (Cr)

Particulars	*Amount*	*Particulars*	*Amount*
To Provision for Bad debts (Transfer)	120	By Balance b/d	120
	120		120

Provision for Bad Debts

Particulars	*Amount*	*Particulars*	*Amount*
To Bad debts	1,180	By Balance b/d	1,800
To Balance c/d		By Bad Debts	120
$\frac{5}{100} \times 19{,}800$	990	By P & L a/c (Balancing figure)	250
	2,170		2,170

Profit & Loss A/c

Particulars	*Amount*	*Particulars*	*Amount*
To Provision for Bad debts	250		

For the years 2004

Bad Debts

Particulars	*Amount*	*Particulars*	*Amount*
To Balance b/d	1,850	By Provision for Bad debts (Transfer)	1,850
	1,850		1,850

Discount on Debtors

Particulars	*Amount*	*Particulars*	*Amount*
To Balance b/d	270	By P & L a/c	270

Provision for Bad Debts

Particulars	*Amount*	*Particulars*	*Amount*
To Bad debts	1,850	By Balance b/d	250
To Balance c/d		By P & L a/c	
$\frac{5}{100} \times 30{,}000$	1,500	(Balance in figure)	3,100
	3,350		3,350

Provision for Discount

Particulars	*Amount*	*Particulars*	*Amount*
To Balance c/d $\frac{2}{100} \times (30{,}000 - 1{,}500)$	570	By P & L a/c	570
	570		570

Profit & Loss A/c

Particulars	Amount	Particulars	Amount
To Provision for bad debts	3,100		
To Provision for discount on Debtors	570		
To Discount allowed to debtors	270		

Note :

Discount allowed to debtors will be taken to profit & loss account because there is no opening balance of provision for discount. From the next year discount allowed will be taken to provision for discount on debtors account instead of profit & loss account because in the next year there will be an opening balance of provision for discount account.

Problem 30

(RESERVE FOR DISCOUNT ON CREDITORS)

Reserve for discount on creditors showed a debited balance of Rs. 500 on 1st January 2004. During 2004, a discount received from creditor amounted to Rs. 450. On 31-12-2004, the total amount due to sundry creditors was Rs. 25,000 on which a reserve for discount at $2\frac{1}{2}\%$ is required to the created. Show the reserve for discount on creditors account, the entry in profit & loss account and how the reserve account will appear in balance sheet.

Solution

Reserve for Discount on Creditors A/c

Particulars	Amount	Particulars	Amount
To Balance b/d	500	By Discount a/c	450
To P & L a/c	625	By Balance c/d	675
	1,125		1,125

Profit & Loss A/c

Particulars	Amount	Particulars	Amount
		By Reserve for discount on creditors	625
			625

Balance Sheet

Liabilities	Rs.	Assets	Rs.
Sundry creditors	25,000		
Less reserve for discount	625		
	24,375		

Problem 31

On 1st January 2003, the reserve for discount on creditors was Rs. 1,200. The discount earned during the year amounted to Rs. 1,040. The creditors at 31st December 2003, were Rs. 50,000 and a new reserve of $2\frac{1}{2}\%$ is required. Show the Journal, ledger, profit & loss account and balance sheet entries relating to discount.

Solution

Journal

Date	Particulars	L.F.	Dr. Amount	Cr. Amount
	Reserve for discount on Creditors a/c Dr To Profit & loss a/c (Being discount expected from creditors @ $2\frac{1}{2}\%$ on Rs. 25,000 after adjustment)		1,090	1,090
	Discount a/c Dr To Reserve for discount an creditors (Being discount received from creditors)		1,040	1,040

Reserve for Discount an creditors A/c

Date	Particulars	Amount	Date	Particulars	Amount
1-1-03	To Balance b/d	1,200	31-12-03	By Discount	1,040
31-12-03	To P & L a/c	1,090		By Balance c/d	1,250
				(Amount received)	
		2,290			2,290

Profit & Loss A/c

Particulars	Amount	Particulars		Amount
		By Reserve for discount	1,250	
		Add discount received	1,040	
			2,290	
		less old reserve	1,200	
				1,090

Balance Sheet

Liabilities	Rs.	Assets	Rs.
Sundry creditors	25,000		
Less reserve for Discount	1,250		
	23,750		

Problem 32

A trader maintains a reserve for discount at 2% on sundry creditor. On 1st January 2003, the reserve stood at Rs. 500. During the year he received discount Rs. 350 and creditors at the end of the year amounted to Rs. 50,000. In 2004, the discounts received amounted to Rs. 250

and creditors at the end of the year were Rs. 40,000. Pass Journal entries, prepare ledger accounts and also show how the above items would appear in the profit & loss account and balance sheet of respective years.

Solution

Journal Entries

Date	Particulars	L.F.	Dr. Amount	Cr. Amount
31-12-2003	Discount a/c Dr.		350	
	To Reserve for Discount on Creditors a/c			350
	(Discount received during the year)			
	Reserve for Discount on Creditors a/c Dr.		850	
	To P & C a/c			850
	(Creation of reserve to maintain 2% on Rs. 50,000)			
31-12-2004	Discount a/c Dr.		250	
	To Reserve for discount on Creditors a/c			250
	(Being discount received)			
	Reserve for discount on creditors Dr.		50	
	To P & L a/c			50
	(Being additional amount charged to maintain 2% on Rs. 40,000)			

Reserve for discount on creditors A/c

Date	Particulars	Amount	Date	Particulars	Amount
1-1-03	To Balance b/d	500	31-12-03	By Discount	350
31-12-03	To P & L a/c	850		By Balance c/d	1,000
		1,350			1,350
1-1-04	To Balance b/d	1,000	31-12-04	By Discount	250
31-12-04	To P & L a/c	50		By Balance c/d	800
		1,050			1,050

Profit & Loss A/c — 2003

Particulars	Amount	Particulars		Amount
		By Discount	350	
		Add new reserve	1,000	
			1,350	
		Less old reserve	500	
				850

Profit & Loss A/c — 2004

Particulars	Amount	Particulars		Amount
		By Discount	250	
		Add new Reserve	800	
			1,050	
		Less old Reserve	1,000	
				50

Balance Sheet as on 31-12-2003

Liabilities	*Rs.*	*Assets*	*Rs.*
Sundry creditors	50,000		
Less reserve for Discount	1,000		
	49,000		

Balance Sheet as on 31-12-2004

Liabilities	*Rs.*	*Assets*	*Rs.*
Sundry creditors	40,000		
Less reserve for Discount	800		
	39,200		

Problem 33

Reserve for discount on creditors showed debit balance of Rs. 500 on 1st January 2004. During 2004, discounts received from creditors amounted to Rs. 450. On 31st December 2004, the total amount due to sundry creditors was Rs. 25,000 on which a reserve for discount at $2\frac{1}{2}\%$ is required to credited . Show the reserve for discount on creditors a/c and entry in the profit and loss account.

Solution

Journal Entries

Date	*Particulars*	*L.F.*	*Dr. Amount*	*Cr. Amount*
	Sundry creditors a/c Dr.		450	
	To Discount a/c			450
	(Being discount received)			
	Discount a/c Dr.		450	
	To Reserve for discount on creditors			450
	(Being discount received transferred to reserve for discount on creditors a/c)			
	Reserve for discount a/c Dr.		575	
	To Profit & Loss a/c			575
	(Being the amount charged to P & L a/c for maintaining a reserve for discount at 10% on creditors-Balancing figure of reserve for discount a/c).			

Reserve for Discount on Creditor's A/c

Particulars	*Amount*	*Particulars*	*Amount*
To Balance b/d	500	By Discount	450
To P & L a/c	575	By Balance c/d	625
(Balancing figure)		$2\frac{1}{2}\%$ on 25,000	
	1,075		1,075

Profit & Loss A/c

Particulars	Amount	Particulars		Amount
		By Discount received	450	
		Add reserve for discount on Cr $2\frac{1}{2}$%	625	
			1,075	
		Less old reserve	500	
				575

Balance Sheet

Liabilities	Rs.	Assets	Rs.
Sundry Creditors	25,000		
Less reserve for Discount	625		
	24,375		

Problem 34

A business house maintains provision of 5% against bad and doubtful debts and 3% for discount on debtors and a reserve for discount on creditors at 2%. On 1st April 2001 it had the following balances.

Provision for bad and doubtful debts	Rs. 500
Provision for discount on debtors	Rs. 285
Reserve for discount on creditors	Rs. 480

During the year 2001-02 bad debts, discount allowed to debtors and discount received from creditors amounted to Rs. 395, Rs. 880 and Rs. 984 respectively, while for 2002-03 they amounted to Rs. 180 Rs. 700, and Rs. 680 respectively. Sundry debtors were Rs. 12,000 on March 31, 2002 and Rs. 8,000 on March 31, 2003. Sundry creditors on these two dates were Rs. 21,000 and Rs. 19,500 respectively.

Show provision for bad and doubtful debts account, provision for discount on debtors account and reserve for discount on creditors a/c alongwith relevant portion of profit & loss a/c.

Solution

Provision for Bad & Doubtful Debts A/c

Date	Particulars	Amount	Date	Particulars	Amount
31-3-02	To Bad debts	395	1-4-01	By Balance b/d	500
	To Balance c/d	600	31-3-01	By P & L a/c (Balancing figure)	495
		995			995
31-3-03	To Bad debts	180	1-4-02	By Balance b/d	600
	To P & L a/c (Balance figure)	20			
	To Balance c/d	400			
		600			600

Provision for Discount on Debtors A/c

Date	*Particulars*	*Amount*	*Date*	*Particulars*	*Amount*
31-3-02	To Discount allowed	880	1-4-01	By Balance b/d	285
	To Balance c/d	342	31-1-01	By P & L a/c	937
				(Balancing figure)	
		1,122			1,122
31-3-03	To Discount allowed	700	1-4-02	By Balance b/d	342
	To Balance c/d	228	31-12-03	By P & L a/c	586
				(Balancing figure)	
		928			928

Reserve for Discount on Creditors A/c

Date	*Particulars*	*Amount*	*Date*	*Particulars*	*Amount*
1-4-01	To Balance b/d	480	31-3-02	By Discount Received	984
31-3-02	To P & L a/c	924		By Balance	420
	(Balancing figure)				
		1,404			1,404
1-4-02	To Balance b/d	420	31-3-03	By Discount	680
31-3-03	To P & L a/c	650		By Balance c/d	390
	(Balancing figure)				
		1,070			1,070

Profit & Loss A/c for the year ended 31-3-02

Particulars		*Amount*	*Particulars*		*Amount*
To Bad debts	395		By Discount received	984	
Add new provision			Add new reserve		
for D.D	600		for discount on creditors	420	
	995			1,404	
Less old provision	500	495	Less old reserve	480	
To Discount allowed	880			924	
Add new provision					
for discount	342				
	1,222				
Less old provision	285				
		937			

Profit & Loss A/c for year end 31-3-03

Particulars		*Amount*	*Particulars*		*Amount*
To Discount allowed	700		By old provision for Bad and		
Add new provision			doubtful Debts	600	
for discount	228		less bad debts	180	
	928			420	

Particulars	Amount	Particulars		Amount
Less old provision for discount 342		Less new provision	400	
				20
	586	By Discount received	680	
		Add new reserve for discount	390	
			1,070	
		Less old reserve	420	
				650

Meaning of Concept

1. **Final Account :** The ultimate accounts prepared by the businessman to know the result and financial position of the business.
2. **Trading Account :** It is an account which is prepared to ascertain gross profit or gross loss of the business.
3. **Manufacturing Account :** It is an account which is prepared to ascertain the cost of production of goods or services in a business.
4. **Profit & Loss Account :** It is an account which is prepared to know the net profit caused or net loss incurred by a business.
5. **Balance sheet :** It is a statement which is prepared to know the financial position of a business.
6. **Capital Expenditure :** It refers to a type of expenditure whose benefit is not derived in one accounting year but spread over many years.
7. **Revenue expenditure :** It refers to a type of expenditure whose benefit is derived for the same period for which the expenses are incurred.
8. **Capital Receipt :** It refers to an amount contributed by the proprietor and loans provided by others to the business. It also represent the sale value of a fixed asset.
9. **Revenue Receipt :** It refers to an amount received on sale of goods or other routine income earned in carrying on a business.
10. **Outstanding expenses :** An expense relating to a previous period which is not yet paid is outstanding expenses.
11. **Prepaid expense :** An expenses relating to a current period which is paid in advance is a prepaid expense.
12. **Accrued Income :** An income which is earned but not yet received is an accrued income.
13. **Depreciation :** It refers to a decrease in the value of an asset owing to its constant use.
14. **Bad debts :** Debts which are not recoverable is known as bad debts.
15. **Reserve for doubtful debts :** A provision made against a debt which is not likely to be received is a reverse for doubtful debts.
16. **Reserve for discount on Debting :** A provision created out of the divisible profit to meet the loss arising out of discount is a provision for discount on debtors.
17. **Provision for discount on Creditors.** Provision made in current year relating to discount which is receivable in the subsequent year is known of provision of discount on creditors.

QUESTIONS

Answer the following question in about 4 lines each.

1. Mention the three components of the final accounts of a sole trader.
2. What do you mean by Trading account ?
3. What do you mean by Gross profit ?
4. What do you mean by profit & loss account ?
5. What do you mean by net profit ?
6. What do you mean by manufacturing account ?
7. Distinguish between a manufacturing account and a Trading account ?
8. Distinguish between a trading account and a profit and loss account .
9. Give four examples of Financial expenses.
10. Give four examples of Administrative expenses.
11. Give four examples of selling and distribution on expenses.
12. Mention four items of income which appear on the credit side of profit & loss a/c.
13. What do you mean by balance sheet ?
14. State four features of balance sheet.
15. How are assets arranged in balance sheet ?
16. What do you mean by Marshalling of assets and liabilities in balance sheet.
17. What do you mean by capital expenditure ?
18. What do you mean by revenue expenditure ?
19. Why it is necessary to classify expenditure into capital and revenue at the time of preparing a balance sheet ?
20. What do you mean by capital receipt ?
21. What do you mean by a revenue receipt ?
22. Distinguish between a revenue receipt and a capital receipt.
23. What do you mean by outstanding expenses ? How it treated in preparing final accounts ?
24. What do you mean by prepaid expense ? How is treated in preparing final accounts?
25. What do you mean by accrued expenses ? How is treated in preparing final accounts ?
26. What do you mean by income received in advance? How is it treated in preparing final accounts ?
27. What do you mean by Depreciation ? How is it treated in preparing final accounts ?
28. What do you mean by bad debts? How is it treated in preparing final accounts ?
29. What do you mean by reserve for doubtful debts accounts ? How is it treated while preparing final accounts ?
30. What do you mean by reserve for discount an debtors
31. What do you mean by provision for discount on creditors ?
32. What do you mean by interest on capital ? How is it treated in preparing final accounts ?
33. What do you mean by interest on drawings ? How is it treated in preparing final accounts ?
34. Give the proforma of a trading account of a trader.
35. Give a proforma of a manufacturing a/c of a trader.
36. Give a proforma for a profit & loss account of a trader.
37. Give a proforma of a balance sheet of a trader.

EXERCISE 1

From the following balances extracted from the books of Ram on 31st December 2004, prepare trading account.

	Rs.
Opening stock	20,800
Closing stock	18,700
Purchases	85,000
Carriage on purchases	2300
Carriage on sales	3,000
Sales	1,40,000

EXERCISE 2

Prepare a trading and profit and loss account from the following particular.

	Rs.
Sales	1,60,000
Purchases	91,300
Wages	18,100
Factory rent	3,000
Selling Dept's sent	1,500
Opening stock	22,100
Purchases returns	4,000
Sales returns	5,000
Salaries (office)	6,000
General expenses	4,500
Discount on creditors	1,100
Discount to customers	1,800

EXERCISE 3

The following particulars are extracted from the books of Gopal for the year ending 31-12-04.

	Rs.
Opening stock (1-1-04)	10,000
Purchases	4,20,000
Purchase returns	2,000
Sales	76,000
Sales returns	4,000
Wages	6,000
Factory expenses	4,000
Closing stock (31-12-04)	8,000

EXERCISE 4

The information furnished below are taken from the books of Mr. Arun. Prepare trading a/c for the year ending 31-12-2004.

	Rs.
Sales	47,857
Sales returns	829
Factory rent	160
Electric power	34
Wages	3,764
Carriage inwards	360
Purchases	38,723
Purchase returns	823
Gas and water	91
Bad debts	125
Salaries	790
General expenses	1,255
Closing stock on 31-12-04	5,500

EXERCISE 5

From the following particulars extracted from the books of Mr. Hari, prepare profit and loss account for the period ending 31-12-2004.

	Rs.
Salaries & wages	3,950
Travelling expenses	1,250
Bad debts	1,820
Warehouse charges	675
Audit fee	1,000
Distribution expenses	1,250
Postage and telephone	620
Carriage outwards	1,050
Free samples distributed	2,020
Commission received	2,825
Rates & taxes	750
Interest paid to bank	890
Interest on Investments	500

EXERCISE 6

Prepare trading and profit & loss account for the year ending 31st December 2004 from the following information extracted from the books of Mr. Sampat.

	Rs.
Purchases	1,65,000
Sales	2,55,000
Returns Inwards	5,000
Returns outwards	3,000
Stock (1-1-2004)	25,000
Wages	20,000

Salaries	7,400
Carriage Inwards	4,000
Trade expenses	2,000
Sundry expenses	500
Postage	500
Insurance	2,000
Stationery	1,000
Rent & Taxes	2,000
Interest from Investments	600
Commission received	1,400
Carriage outwards	1,600
Travelling expenses	3000
Miscellaneous receipts	1,000

EXERCISE 7

From the following balances extracted from the books of Shankar on 31st December, 2004 Prepare a balance sheet.

	Rs.
Bills receivable	600
Plant	2,000
Cash in hand	200
Debtors	4,000
Stock	3,500
Bills payable	500
Loan	900
Creditors	2,330
Capital	6,570

EXERCISE 8

Prepare final accounts from the following information.

	Rs.
Capital	10,000
Machinery	3,500
Debtors	2,700
Drawings	900
Purchases	9,500
Creditors	1,400
Wages	5,000
Bank	1,500
Stock in trade	2,000
Rent	450
Sales	14,500
Sundry expenses	200
Carriage	150

Additionall information :-

	Rs.
1. Stock at the end	600
2. Rent outstanding	50
3. Wages prepared	200
4. Depreciation on Machinery at 10%	

EXERCISE 9

The following are the balances extracted from the books or Mr. Narahari.

	Rs.
Narahari's capital	30,000
Narahari's Drawings	5,000
Furniture & fittings	2,600
Bank overdraft	4,200
Creditors	13,300
Business premises	20,000
Stock on 1-1-2004	22,000
Debtors	18,000
Rent from tenants	1,000
Purchases	1,10,000
Sales	1,50,000
Sales returns	2,000
Discount - debits	1,600
Discount - credit	2,000
Taxes and Insurance	2,000
General expenses	4,000
Salaries	9,000
Commission - Debit	2,200
Carriage on purchases	1,800
Reserve for band and doubtful debts	500
Bad debts written off	800

Stock on hand on 31-12-04 estimated at Rs. 20,060. Write off depreciation, business premises Rs. 300 and furniture & fittings Rs. 260. Make a reserve of 5% on debtors for Bad and doubtful debts. Allow interest on capital at 5% and carry forward Rs. 700 for unexpired insurance.

Prepare Trading account, profit & loss account and balance sheet as on 31-12-2004.

EXERCISE 10

From the following balances extracted from the books of Mohan on 20-6-2004, prepare a trading account, profit & loss account and a balance sheet.

	Dr.	Cr.
Mohan's capital and drawings	10,550	1,19,400
Bills receivable	9,500	
Purchases and sales	2,55,590	3,56,430
Returns Inwards	2,780	
Stock on 1-1-2004	89,680	

Commission		5,640
Plant & Machinery	28,800	
Salaries	11,000	
Travelling expenses	1,880	
Debtors (including Laxminarain's dishonoured cheque Rs. 1,000)	62,000	
Stationery	2,000	
Telephone Charges	1,370	
Interest and discount	5,870	
Bad debts	3,620	
Fixtures & fittings	8,970	
Creditors		59,630
6% loan		20,000
Wages	40,970	
Cash in hand	530	
Cash at bank	18,970	
Insurance (including premium of Rs. 300 per annum paid upto 31-12-04)	400	
Rent and Taxes	5,620	
	5,61,100	5,61,100

Stock in trade on 30-6-04 was Rs. 1,28,960 write off Laxminarains cheque. Create is reserve of 5% on debtors.

Manufacturing wages include Rs. 1,200 for creditors of new machinery purchased last year. Depreciate plant and Machinery by 5% and fixture and fittings by 10% per annum. Commission accrued Rs. 600. Interest on loan for the last two months is not paid.

EXERCISE 11

Following are the balances in the ledger of Mr. Prakash for the year ending 31st Mar. 2004

	Rs.
Stock (1-4-04) :-	
Raw materials	10,000
Semi finished goods	5,000
Finished goods	26,000
Purchases :-	
Raw Materials	80,000
Finished goods	17,000
Carriage Inwards on raw materials	3,000
Manufacturing wages	10,000
Salaries of the superior	3,600
Rent of the factory	7,000
Gas and water	3,000
Return of raw materials	1,300
Feel and coal	3,300
Factory power	12,500
Fire insurance	1,300

Sales returns	12,000
Depreciation on factory buildings	1,000
Stock on 31-3-2004 :-	
Raw materials	8,000
Semi-finished goods	13,000
Finished goods	22,000
Sales	2,20,000
Carriage outwards	3,500
Office salaries	15,000

Prepare manufacturing account and trading and profit & loss account for the year ending 31st March 2004.

EXERCISE 12

Following are the balances as on 31st Dec. 2004 taken from the books of Ramdas. You are required to prepare (a) Manufacturing account (b) Trading a/c and (c) Profit and Loss a/c.

	Rs.
Opening stock :	
Raw materials	4,000
Work-in-progress	6,000
Finished goods	9,000
Closing stock :	
Raw materials	3,000
Work in progress	8,000
Finished goods	6,000
Purchases of raw materials	30,000
Factory expenses :	
Wages	24,000
Carriage inwards	1,000
Rent	3,200
Factory repairs	4,200
Plant repairs	7,800
Supervisors remuneration	10,000
Work's Manager's salary	4,000
Administration overheads	
Salaries	4,000
Other expenses	6,000
Selling overheads :	
Salaries	2,000
Commission	1,000
Advertising	5,000
Other expenses	1,600
Distribution overhead :	
Van expenses	1,800
Wages	1,000

EXERCISE 13

From the following balance and information you are required to prepare final accounts of Mr. Murthy for the year ending 31st March 2004.

	Rs.
Plant and Machinery	49,500
Depreciation on Plant and Machinery	5,500
Fixture & fittings	1,720
Fuel and power (Factory)	542
Office salaries	4,095
Salary outstanding	350
Lighting (Factory)	392
Travelling expenses	925
Carriage on Sales	960
Cash in hand	2,313
Sundry debtors	47,800
Purchases (adjusted)	66,710
Stock 31-3-2003	16,580
Wages	9,915
Rent & taxes	1,951
Rent outstanding	150
Office expenses	2,778
Carriage on purchases	897
Discount allowed	422
Drawings	6,820
Stock on 1-4-2004	21,725
Direct expenses	2,680
Sales returns	7,422
Insurance	570
Capital	93,230
Sales	1,26,177
Creditors	22,680
Returns outwards	3,172
Bills payable	6,422

Additional information

1. Depreciate Furnitures & Fixtures at 10%
2. Provision for bad debts at $2\frac{1}{2}$% on sundry debtors.
3. Insurance unexpired Rs. 70.
4. Outstanding wages Rs. 800.

EXERCISE 14

The following are the ledger balances extracted from the books of Mr. 'X'.

	Rs.
X's Capital	60,000
X's Drawings	10,000

Bank overdraft	8,400
Furniture & fixtures	5,200
Business premises	40,000
Creditor's	26,600
Stock on 1-1-04	44,000
Debtors	36,000
Rent from tenant	2,000
Purchases	2,20,000
Sales	3,00,000
Sales returns	4,000
Discount-debit	3,200
Discount-credit	4,000
Taxes and Insurance	4,000
General expenses	8,000
Salaries	18,000
Commission-debit	4,400
Carriage on purchases	3,600
Reserve for bad and doubtful debts	1,000
Bad debts written off	1,600

Stock in hand on 31-12-2004, was estimated at Rs. 40,120. Write off depreciation — Business premises Rs. 600 and furniture and fitting Rs. 520. Make a reserve of 5% on debtors for bad and doubtful debts. Allow interest on capital at 5% and carry forward Rs. 1400 for unexpired insurance.

Prepare Trading a/c, Profit & loss a/c and balance sheet as on 31-12-04.

EXERCISE 15

The following figure appear in the books of Y

		Rs.
Jan.1,	Bad and doubtful debts provision	1,200
	Discount allowed provision	560
Dec. 31,	Discount allowed during the year	930
	Bad debts written off	470
	Bad debts recovered	25
	Debtors	10,060

Write off further Rs. 240 (definitely bad) create a discount allowed provision of 2% Create a bad and doubtful debts provision of 10%.

Prepare provision for doubtful debts account; bad debts account and provision for discount account.

EXERCISE 16

On 1-1-04 Mr. A had a credit balance in the provision for bad and doubtful debts a/c amounting to Rs. 7,500 (Cr). During the year 31-12-04 bad debts written off amounted to Rs. 1,750 and total debtors a/c on 31-2-04 stood at Rs. 1,60,000. A provision of 5% on book debts is to be made. Prepare necessary accounts.

EXERCISE 17

Mr. Jayaram has on 1-1-04, a credit balance of Rs. 1,500 in provision for doubtful debts account. During the year he incurred bad debts of Rs. 1,250 and his debtors on 31st December 2004 amount to Rs. 45,000. He maintains the 5% provision on debtors.

Pass Journal entries and show the necessary accounts and the balance sheet.

EXERCISE 18

From the following information pass the necessary entries and show the accounts.

2004.

Jan. 1. Balance on provision for doubtful debts a/c	3,800
Dec. 3. Bad debts during the year	900
Dec. 3. Sundry debtors a/c	60,000

You are to provide the doubtful debts at 4% on debtors.

EXERCISE 19

Given the Abridged Trial balance of Mr. George as on 31-3-2005.

Sundry assets & liabilities	50,500	94,900
Bad debts	3,900	
Sundry debtors	45,000	
Provision for doubtful debts as on 1-4-2004		4,500
	99,400	99,400

You are required to (*a*) write off further bad debts Rs. 800 (*b*) provide for doubtful at $7\frac{1}{2}\%$ on debtors (*c*) Write Journal entries open ledger accounts and show the balance sheet.

EXERCISE 20

On 31st December 2004 the books of Mr. Ananth showed a balance of Rs. 30,000 on sundry debtors account. He decided to create a provision for discount on debtors at 2%.

During the year 2004 the total discounts allowed were Rs. 500. Sundry debtors at the end 2004 amounted to Rs. 28,000 and they maintain the provision for discount at the same rate.

You are required to show the Journal, ledger, profit & loss a/c and balance sheet entries for 2004.

EXERCISE 21

From the following information write up the relevant ledger accounts, the profit & loss account and show how the sundry debtors appear in the Balance sheet on 21-12-2004.

1-1-04.	Provision for doubtful debts	Rs. 750
1-1-04.	Provision for discount on debtors	200
31-12-04.	Sundry debtors	12,200
	Bad debts written off	690
	Discounts allowed	205

You are required to write off further bad debts Rs. 200 ; make provision for doubtful debts at 5% and for discount on debtors at 2%.

EXERCISE 22

The reserve for discount on creditors showed debit balance of Rs. 500 on 1-1-04. During 2004, discount received from creditors amounted to Rs. 450 on 31st December 2004, the total amount due to sundry creditors was Rs. 25,000 on which a reserve for discount at $2\frac{1}{2}$% is required to be credited. Show the reserve for discount on creditors a/c, and entry in the profit & loss a/c.

EXERCISE 23

A businessman allowed discount to his debtors Rs. 600 and received discount of Rs. 650 from his creditors in the year ending at 31st December 2004. On 31st Dec. 2004 his debtors and creditors respectively were Rs. 30,000 and Rs. 25,000. It was decided to create a provision for discount at 4% on creditors and 5% debtors.

Prepare discount account, provision for discount on creditors a/c and provision for discount on debtors a/c.

12

CHAPTER

Consignment

1. MEANING OF CONSIGNMENT

When a manufactures or a wholesaler undertakes to sell the goods in different parts of the country through another person, such a transaction is known is consignment. The person who sends the goods which are to be sold on his behalf is known as consignor and the person who sells on behalf of consignor is known as consignee. The goods are sold by the consignee at the risk of consignor. The consignee is paid certain amount as his remuneration for having sold goods on behalf of consignor. When goods are sent by consignor to the consignee it is termed as consignment outward. When goods are received by consignee the same is termed as consignment inward. The relationship between the consignor and consignee is that of principal and agent. Whenever goods are sent on consignment the ownership does not pass on to the consignee. The consignee it not liable to pay for the goods on its receipt. So a consignor will not send an invoice at the time of despatch of the goods. However in order to inform the consignee about the description, quantity and value of goods sent to him and for recording purposes, a proforma invoice is prepared by consignor and sent to the consignee. A proforma invoice is not actual invoice but it only gives an idea about the invoice.

In addition to the payment of commission which is calculated on the amount of sales he is also entitled to get some additional amount known as Del credere commission. This is paid when the consignee guarantees that the proceeds of sale in case of any credit sale shall be paid to the consignor. But the agent would not be liable if the customer refuses to pay because of a dispute. In order to give further encouragement to the consignee, to sell more quantity of goods consigned, sometimes, an extra commission is given to him. This is known as overriding commission. This commission is usually given when sales exceeds a specific amount. The consignee is also entitled to get all the expenses incurred by him reimbursed by the consignor.

2. FEATURES OF CONSIGNMENT

The important features of a consignment transaction can be summarised under the following points.

1. Consignment is not a sale transaction. It only refers to a mere transfer of physical possession of goods by the consignor to the consignee.

2. The relationship that exists between a consignor and consignee is that of principal and agent but not that of a seller and buyer. The transferee or consignee does not acquire the ownership of goods on consignment of goods to him. Infact, the consignee is not responsible for any loss or destruction of goods.
3. The consignee is not liable to pay for the value of goods received on consignment. The liability to pay arises only when the consignee has actually sold the goods.
4. The consignee is not responsible for any bad debts arising out of consignment transactions, unless he expressly assume liability for such losses. In such a situation he is known as del credere agent and receives extra commission for the risk involved in credit sales effected by him.
5. The consignor has to meet all the expenses incurred by the consignee right from the time he receives the consigned goods upto its sales. In other words the consignor has to pay the expenses of taking delivery of goods, storage charges, advertisement expenses etc. incurred by the consignee.
6. The consignee is liable to account for the goods he receives from consignor until they are sold.
7. The consignor will remunerate the consignee in the form of commission for having sold goods on his behalf.
8. Any unsold stock of goods sent on consignment is to be recorded on the asset side of the consignor's balance sheet as "Stock on consignment". This is because the unsold stock remains as the property of the consignor until sold.
9. The consignment transaction does not resemble to "Sale or returns basis". Hence consignment transaction is to be distinguished from "Sale or return" transaction. In a consignment transaction, the consignee will constitute an agent but in case of good sent on sale or return the person to whom goods are sent is only an optional buyer.
10. The consignee is liable pay the value of goods sold to the consignor after deducting his commission and other expenses incurred by him.

3. DIFFERENCES BETWEEN A SALE AND A CONSIGNMENT

Sale	*Consignment*
1. The ownership of goods is transferred from seller to the buyer in case of a sale transaction.	1. The consignor retains the ownership until the time they are sold by consignee.
2. The goods once sold cannot be returned back in a sale transaction unless the goods are defective or the seller agree to take them back.	2. Unsold stock belongs to the consignor. Hence it can be sent back to the consignor.
3. When gods are sold on credit basis the relationship between seller and buyer is that of creditor and debtor.	3. The relation between consignor and consignee is that of principal and agent.
4. When goods are lost after delivery the buyer is responsible for bearing its loss.	4. When goods are lost on consignment, the consignor is responsible for bearing its loss.

4. ACCOUNT SALES

On completion of consignment sale either in full or in part the consignee sends a statement to the consignor showing the gross sale proceeds, the expenses incurred by him, the commission due to him and the net amount due to consignor. Such a statement is called as "Accounts sales". A proforma of account sales is given below.

Account Sales

	Details (Rs.)	Amount (Rs.)
Sale of 50 TV's (Colour) @ Rs. 15,000 each		7,50,000
Sale of 10 TV's (Black & White) @ Rs. 8,000 each		80,000
		8,30,000
Less expenses		
Freight	Rs. 3,000	
Insurance	Rs. 50,000	
Rent	7,000	
		60,000
		7,70,000
Less commission @ 10%		83,000
		6,87,000
Less advance paid		2,00,000
Balance due		4,87,000

E & O E — For star & Co.

Bangalore 6th July 2004 — sd/-

5. JOURNAL ENTRIES IN THE BOOKS OF CONSIGNOR

To determine the profit or loss on consignment to a particular consignee, the consignor maintains an account called as consignment account. When the consignor sends goods to more than one consignee on consignment basis he has to prepare as many consignment accounts as there are consignees. Each consignment account is distinguished from other consignment account by adding the name of the consignee or place of consignment. For example, goods sent on consignment to Belgium may be styled as consignment to Belgium account or goods sent to Mr. Patel may be styled as "consignment to Mr. Patel account" :

The consignment account resemble to trading and profit & loss account. On the debts side of consignment account the following items are recorded : (*a*) cost of goods sent (*b*) expenses incurred in respect of goods received on consignment (*c*) commission due to consignee and (*d*) expenses incurred by consignee in respect of consigned goods. On the credit side of the consigniment account the following items are recorded : (*a*) sale proceeds of goods and (*b*) closing stock of goods consigned. The difference between the credit side and debit side indicates profit.

In addition to the above account the consignor will also maintains consignees account in order to know the amount due from consignee.

The following entries are passed by the consignor in his books.

1. When goods are sent out to consignee

   Consignment a/c Dr.

   To Goods sent on consignment.

2. Recording expenses incurred by consignor in respect of the goods consigned

   Consignment a/c Dr.

   To Bank

3. When a consignor Draws a bill on consignee as on advance on consignment.
    Bills Receivable a/c Dr.
        To Consignees personal account
4. When the said bill is discounted with bank
    Bank a/c Dr.
    Discount a/c Dr.
        To Bills receivable a/c
5. If consignee pays cash as advance
    Cash a/c Dr.
        To Consignees personal a/c
6. When the consignee reports sales by sending account sales.
    Consignee's personal a/c Dr.
        To Consignment a/c
7. For recording expenses incurred by consignee.
    Consignment a/c Dr.
        To Consignee's personal a/c
8. For recording commission payable to consignee
    Consignment a/c Dr.
        To Consignees personal a/c
9. When consignee sends the net proceeds
    Bank a/c Dr.
        To Consignee's personal a/c
10. For recording closing stock with the consignee
    Stock on Consignment a/c Dr.
        To Consignment a/c
11. At this stage the consignment account will show either profit or loss on consignment transaction.
    (a) For recording profit on consignment
    Consignment a/c Dr.
        To profit & loss a/c
    (b) For recording loss on consignment
    Profit & Loss a/c Dr.
        To Consignment a/c

In the next accounting period consignment account starts with a debit for unsold stock at the end of the previous accounting period.

12. The goods sent on consignment must be transferred to purchases account in case of trading business or to trading account in case of a manufacturing business. The entry is a follows.
    Goods sent on consignment a/c Dr.
        To Purchases a/c

Note :

Some times goods are invoiced at a higher price. In such a case consignment account will be debited and goods sent on consignment a/c is credited with the invoice value of goods. Before we arrive at the true amount of profit or loss a reverse entry with the excess (difference between Invoice price and cost price) amount is to be passed. The entry will be :-

Goods sent on consignment a/c Dr.
To consignment a/c

Similarly the unsold stock with consignee has to be adjusted. The entry will be :-

Consignment a/c Dr.
To Consignment stock suspense a/c

Valuation of Stock (Closing) or Unsold Stock

The goods that remain unsold at the end of a certain period are termed as unsold stock. It is necessary to take into account the unsold stock before the amount of profit or loss on consignment could be ascertained. The unsold stock is to be valued on the principal of cost price or market price which ever is less. But the cost price does not simply mean the cost of goods but a proportion of such other expenses which increases the value of goods should also be added to the cost of goods. Quite often expenses are incurred by consignee as well. Therefore, while calculating the value of unsold goods with the consignee, a proportion of such expenses should also be included. The unsold stock is credited to the consignment a/c. The consignment account as it represents an asset, is shown in the balance sheet of the consignor.

Normal loss

In certain classes of goods, some loss is natural as in the case of coal, oil etc., where some loss is bound to occur owing to loading, unloading, leakage etc. Such loss which is unavoidable is turned as normal loss. It should be allowed while calculating the value of unsold stock. For example if 20 tons of coal is consigned at Rs. 2,000 a ton, freight and other expenses being Rs. 10,000. If the consignee receives only 190 tons out of which 50 tons are lying unsold, the value of unsold stock will be

$$\frac{40{,}000 + 10{,}000}{190} \times 10{,}000 \times 50$$

$$= \frac{50{,}000}{190} \times 50 = 13{,}110$$

Abnormal loss

Losses which occur over and above the normal loss is known as abnormal loss. An abnormal loss may arise owing to accident, careless or mischief. The amount of such abnormal loss should be debited to profit & loss account and credited to consignment account in order to ascertain the true profit or loss on consignment. Even when such abnormal loss is covered by insurance, consignment account is credited with the full cost of the goods so lost and by debiting to the Abnormal loss account. The only difference is that the amount received from insurance company is debited to cash and credited to Abnormal loss account. Only the balance of abnormal loss is debited to profit & loss account. The same rule is applied when part of the goods are salvaged and sold for cash.

6. JOURNAL ENTRIES IN THE BOOKS OF CONSIGNEE

The following entries are passed in the books of consignee

1. When consignee received the goods :- No entry is passed by the consignee as he is holding the goods on behalf of the consignor. However, he may record the details of the goods received in a separate book called consignment inward book.
2. When advance is paid to the consignor.

   Consignment a/c Dr.

   To Bank or bills payable a/c
3. When expenses are incurred by consignee

   Consignor's a/c Dr.

   Bank a/c
4. For recording sale proceeds of goods

   Bank a/c or Debtors a/c Dr.

   To Consignor's a/c
5. For recording commission due to consignee

   Consignors a/c Dr.

   To Commission a/c
6. For recording bad debts when he is entitled to Del Credere commission.

   Bad debts a/c Dr.

   To Particular customers a/c

Note :

It is always appropriate to transfer bad debts to commission account. The entry being

Commission a/c Dr.

To Bad debts a/c

7. For recording payment to Consignor

   Consignor's a/c Dr.

   To Cash a/c

Note :

1. The commission received will be transfered to profit & loss a/c by the consignee at the end of the year.
2. The consignee will not ascertain profit or loss on consignment.
3. Consignee will not make any entry in respect of unsold stock.
4. On the last date of the accounting year, if there is any balance either debt or credit in the consignor's a/c (which is prepared by the consignee) it should be shown in the balance sheet under Sundry debtors or sundry creditors depending upon the nature of the balance.

7. METHODS OF PREPARING CONSIGNMENT ACCOUNT

There are three methods of preparing the consignment account. They are (1) Cost method (2) invoice price method and (3) zemorandum column method. These three methods differ owing to the different basis on which goods consigned is valued for record in the consignment account. These methods are briefly explained below :

(1) **Cost Method :-** As the name itself suggests under this method goods consigned are recorded at cost price. The accounting entries which are given under the books of consignment earlier exactly holds goods under this method. This difference between the credit side and the debit side of consignment account reveals the profit made under consignment transaction. The unsold stock has to be valued at cost plus rateable share of non-recurring expenses or market price which ever is lower. Non-recurring expenses are those expenses which are incurred to bring the goods to godown of the consignee. Some such

expenses which are commonly incurred by the consignee are packing and forwarding charges, railway freight, Insurance intransit, carriage and cartege expenses and so on. However, expenses which are incurred there afterwards are not to be considered for determining cost of goods remaining unsold. This is Because the cost of stock is not affected whether a particular expenses is paid by the consignor or by the consignee. Where in a problem, the nature of expense is not specified it should be assumed that expense paid by the consignor is of non-recurring nature where as the expenses paid by He consignee are recurring nature.

2. Invoice Price Method : Under this method the consignor prepares the proforma invoice and consignment account considering the market price of goods. When goods are sent on consignment it is recorded at the market price but not at the cost price. This method is followed so that the consignee does not come to know the amount of profit which the consignor earns out of consignment transaction. In order to know the profit or loss the sale proceeds have to be compared with cost of goods.

Subsequently, goods sent on consignment account is debited and consignment account is credited with the excess of invoice price over cost to adjust the two accounts. The excess of invoice price over cost is known as loading. The closing stock also is valued at the market price. But this requires an adjustment in consignment account which is done by passing the following entry.

Consignment a/c Dr. (Loading included in the value of closing stock)
To Consignment stock reserve account

In the following year consignment stock reserve account is transferred to consignment account. All other entries are same in the books of consignor as in the cost method.

3. Memorandum Column Method :- This method is a modification of cost price method. Under this method additional columns are provided in (*a*) consignment account and (*b*) goods sent on consignment account to make memorandum entries regarding " invoice price of goods consigned, sold and remaining unsold".

Problem 1

Sadiq of Srinagar purchased 1,000 meters of Kashmir silks at Rs. 6 per metre and sent it to Desai of Bombay to be sold on consignment. Sadiq paid Rs. 200 towards packing charges etc. Sadiq drew a bill upon Desai for Rs. 5,000. Desai received the consignment and paid Rs. 500 as freight charges, Desai sold 900 meters at Rs. 9 per metre and paid Rs. 250 as expenses. Desai took over the remaining quantity for Rs. 650. He is to be paid commission on gross sales at 5%.

Prepare ledger accounts in the books of both the parties.

Solution

In the books of Sadiq
Consignment to Bombay A/c

	Rs.		Rs.
To Goods sent on consignment a/c	6,000	By Desai's a/c	8,100
To Cash (Packing ate)	200	(Sale of 900 metres @ Rs 9 per metre)	
To Desai a/c (freight)	500	By Desai's a/c	650
To Desai a/c (commission)	405	(unsold stock taken over)	
To Desai a/c (expenses)	250		
To P & L a/c	1,395		
	8,750		8,750

Desai's A/c (Consignee)

	Rs.		Rs.
To Consignment a/c (Sales)	8,100	By B.R. a/c	5,000
To Consignment a/c (Balance of goods taken over)	650	By consignment account :-	
		Freight	500
		Expenses	250
		Commission	405
		By Bank (Final settlement)	2,595
	8,750		8,750

In the Books of Desai

Sadiq's A/c (Consignor)

	Rs.		Rs.
To Cash (freight)	500	By Cash (Sales)	8,100
To Cash (Expenses)	250	By Goods a/c	650
To Commission	405		
To Bills payable a/c	5,000		
To Bank (final settlement)	2,595		
	8,750		8,750

Problem 2

Ram sends consignment of the value of Rs. 5,000 to Shyam drawing on the latter for Rs. 4,000 as an advance against the goods consigned. Ram also pays Rs. 450 for freight. Shyam clears the goods paying Rs. 250 for duty, dock dues etc. He sells on credit basis half the lot for Rs. 4,000 and half of the remaining is sold for cash at Rs. 2,200. Shyams remuneration is $2\frac{1}{2}\%$ on gross proceeds.

Shyam sends out an Account sales and draft to Ram for balance as shown therein. Open the necessary accounts in Ram's books to record the above transactions.

Solution

Consignment A/c

	Rs.		Rs.
To Goods sent an Consignment a/c	5,000	By Shyam's a/c	
To Cash a/c (Freight)	450	Sale on cash	2,200
To Shyams a/c (Duty etc.)	250	Sale on credit	4,000
To Shyam's a/c (Commission)	155	By Consignment	
To Profit & Loss a/c	1,770	Stock a/c	
		Goods 1/4	1,250
		Freight 1/4	113
		Duty	62
	7,625		7,625

Shyam's A/c (Consignee)

	Rs.		Rs.
To Consignment a/c — Sales	6,200	By B. R. a/c	4,000
		By Consignment a/c :-	
		Duty	250
		Commission	155
		By Bank	
		(Final settlement)	1,795
	6,200		6,200

Problem 3

Ramesh & Co. of Bangalore consign 50 cases of articles at Rs. 200 per case to Bhandary & sons of Mangalore, spending Rs. 5 per case for packing and transport. Ramesh & Co. drew a bill on Bhandary & sons for Rs. 5,000, which the consignee accept. After 3 months Bhandary & sons send the following Account sales to the Consignee :

	Rs.	Rs.
By Sales of 50 cases		15,000
Less bills accepted	5,000	
Godown charges	100	
Commission at 5% on sales	750	5,850
Draft enclosed for balance		9,150

Prepare necessary accounts in the books of consignor

Solution

Consignment to Mangalore A/c

	Rs.		Rs.
To Goods sent on Consignment a/c	10,000	By Bhandary & Sons	15,000
(Rs. 200 × 50 cases)		— Sales	
To Cash — Expenses			
(Rs. 5 × 50 cases)	250		
To Bhandari & sons a/c			
– Godown charges	100		
– Commission	750		
To Profit & loss a/c	3,900		
	15,000		15,000

Bhandary & Sons (consignee)

	Rs.		Rs.
To Consignment a/c		By B. R a/c	5,000
— Sales	15,000	By Consignment a/c	
		Godown charges	100
		Commission	750
		By Bank a/c	9,150
	15,000		15,000

Problem 4

Messe Smith and company of Madras are piece goods merchants and commission agents. The following transactions are taken from their books. You are required to enter the transaction in their Journal and ledger (without opening the consignment Inwards account).

2004, March

10. Received a consignment of piece goods to be sold on account and risk of M/s Robinson and Co., Bombay Rs. 8,500.
12. Paid charges on above Rs. 650
18. Accepted Robinson and Co. draft for Rs. 6,000 as an advance against consignment.
20. Sold the entire consignment of goods Rs. 10,500.
28. Sent account sales to Robinson & Co., charging commission 5% and Del credere commission $2\frac{1}{2}$%.
30, Remitted to Robinson & Co. a demand draft for the balance due to them.

Solution

Journal Entries
In the Books of Smith & Co.

Date	*Particulars*		*L.F.*	*Dr. Amount*	*Cr. Amount*
2004 Mar.					
12.	Robinson & Co.	Dr.		650	
	To Bank				650
	(Being charges paid on goods received)				
18.	Robinson & Co.	Dr.		6,000	
	To Bills payable				6,000
	(Being Acceptance given)				
20.	Bank a/c	Dr.		10,500	
	To Robinson & Co.				10,500
	(Being gross sale proceeds of goods)				
28.	Robinson & Co.	Dr.		787.50	
	To Commission				525
	To Del Credere commission				262.50
	(Being 5% commission and $2\frac{1}{2}$% Del Credere Commission charged)				
30.	Robinson & Co.	Dr.		3,062.50	
	To Bank				3,062.50
	(Being demand draft sent for the balance)				

Robinson & Company A/c

Date	Particulars	Rs.	Particulars	Rs.
Mar. 12.	To Bank charges	650.00	By Bank	10,500.00
18.	To Bills payable — advance	6,000.00	— Gross Sale Proceeds	
28.	To Commission	525.00		
	To Del Credere Commission	262.50		
30.	To Bank-Balance sent	3,062.50		
		10,500.00		10,500.00

Problem 5

Mohan of Madras sends out a consignment of the value of Rs. 10,000 to Sankar of Calcutta drawing on the latter for Rs. 8,000 as an advance against the same Mohan pays Rs. 960 for freight etc. Sanker clear the goods paying Rs. 50 for duty, dock dues etc. He sells on credit half the lot for Rs. 8,400 and half of the remaining is sold for cash at Rs. 4,000. Sankar's commission is $2\frac{1}{2}$% an gross proceeds. Sankar sends out account sales and a draft to Madras for the balance as shown therein. Unsold part of the consignment is brought into books with proportionate expenses incurred by the consignor.

Draft the necessary ledger accounts in the books of Mohan.

Solution

Consignment to Calcutta A/c

	Rs.		*Rs.*
To Goods sent an consignment a/c	10,000	By Sankar's a/c	
To Cash-freight	960	Credit sale 1/2	8,400
To Sankar's a/c		Cash sale 1/4	4,000
— Dock dues	50	By Consignment stock a/c	
To Sankar's a/c		— Cost 1/4	2,500
— Commission @ $2\frac{1}{2}$% on sales	310	— Freight 1/4	240
To P & C a/c	3,820		
	15,140		15,140

In the books of Mohan
Sankar's A/c

	Rs.		*Rs.*
To Consignment a/c	12,400	By B.R. a/c	
— Gross sale proceeds		— Advance	8,000
		By consignment a/c	
		— Dock dues	50
		— Commission	310
		By Bank a/c	
		— Final settlement	4,040
	12,400		12,400

Problem 6

Prepare an account sales rendered by the agents Nataraj and sons, Bangalore from the given information

Manufactures	:	Parry & Co. Madras
Agents	:	Natraj & Sons, Bangalore

Consigned 100 tins of sweets at Rs. 120 per Tin

	Rs.
Manufactures expenses :	
Railway charges	75
Insurance charges	45

Agents expenses
— Carriage 35
— Godown rent 55
— Other expenses 25
Sold 50 tins at Rs. 155 per tin

On receipt of the goods, the agents accepted a three months draft for Rs. 5,000. Deducting the commission at 6% on sales, enclosed a bank draft for the balance due to the consignor.

Solution

Accounts Sales

	Rs.	Rs.
Gross sales proceeds of 50 tins at Rs. 155 each		7,750
Less expenses :		
— Carriage	35	
— Godown rent	55	
— Other expenses	25	
Less Commission at 6%	465	
Less Draft accepted	5,000	5,580
Balance as per ban draft enclosed		2,170

E. & O.E
Dated

For Nataraj & son
— Bangalore

Problem 7

Mr. A of Bangalore sent a consignment of goods to his agent Mr. B of Bombay on 1 September 2004 invoiced at Rs. 24,000 and paid Rs. 480 for railway freight and other expenses. The agent was allowed 5% on sales as his commission. On arrival of the consignment at Bombay the agent spent Rs. 640 towards advertising and other expenses. By December the sales by the agent amounted to Rs. 40,000. The unsold stock was valued at Rs. 5,200. On December 31, 2004 the agent forwarded to A an account sales for the above along with an acceptance for the a balance due by him. Journalise the transactions in the books of Mr. A and Mr. B.

Solution

In the Books of A Consignor

Date	Particulars	L.F.	Dr. Amount	Cr. Amount
	Consignment to Bombay a/c Dr. To Goods sent on consignment a/c (Being cost of goods consigned)		24,000	24,000
	Consignment a/c Dr. To Cash (Being freight and other expenses paid)		480	480
	Consignment a/c Dr. To B's a/c (Being advertising and other expenses paid by him)		640	640

Date	Particulars		L.F.	Dr. Amount	Cr. Amount
	To B's a/c	Dr.		40,000	
	To Consignment				40,000
	(Being gross sale proceeds)				
	Consignment stock a/c	Dr.		5,200	
	To Consignment a/c				5,200
	(Being unsold stock of consignment)				
	Consignment a/c	Dr.		2,000	
	To B's a/c				2,000
	(Being commission @ 5% due to Mr. B)				
	Consignment a/c	Dr.		18,080	
	To Profit & loss a/c				18,080
	(Being profit on consignment)				
	Bills receivable a/c	Dr.		37,360	
	To B's a/c				37,360
	(Being Acceptance received for the balance due from him)				

In the Books of B

Date	Particulars		L.F.	Dr. Amount	Cr. Amount
	A's a/c	Dr.		640	
	To Cash a/c				640
	(Being advertising and other expenses paid)				
	Cash a/c	Dr.		40,000	
	To A's a/c				40,000
	(Being Gross sale proceeds of goods)				
	A's a/c	Dr.		2,000	
	To Commission a/c				2,000
	(Being Commission due to him)				
	A's a/c	Dr.		37,360	
	To Bills payable a/c				37,360
	(Being acceptance given for the balance)				

Problem 8

Vanaspathy private limited, Poona consigned 10,000 kg of ghee costing Rs. 20 per kg to Ramesh & Co. of Madras on 1-1-2004. Vanspathy private limited paid Rs. 50,000 as freight and insurance. 50 kgs of ghee was destroyed in transit. The insurance claim was entitled at Rs. 4,500 and was paid directly to the consignors.

Ramesh & Co. took delivery of consignment on 20th January 2004 and accepted a bill drawn upon them by Vanaspathy private limited for Rs. 1,00,000 for 3 months. On 31st March Ramesh & Co. reported as follows :

(*i*) 500 kg were sold at Rs. 30 per kg

(*ii*) Their expenses were

	Rs.
Godown rent	2,000
Wages	20,000
Printing & stationery including Advertising	10,000

(*iii*) 250 kg were lost due to leakage which is quite normal.

Ramesh & Co. is entitled to a commission of $4\frac{1}{2}\%$ on the sales affected. Ramesh & Co. paid the amount due in respect of the consignment on 31st March itself. Show the consignment account, the account of Ramesh & Co. and the loss in Transit account in the books of Vanaspathy private limited for the year ended 31-3-2004.

Solution

In the Books of Vanaspathy Pvt. Ltd.

Consignment to Madras A/c.

		Rs.		Rs.
To Goods sent on consignment a/c		2,00,000	By Loss in transit — Cost of 250 Tins	6,250
To Cash-freight and Insurance		50,000	By Ramesh & Co. sales	2,25,000
To Ramesh & Co.			By Consignment stock	51,316
expenses	32,000		By loss on Consignment	9,559
To Commission on				
Sales–$4\frac{1}{2}\%$ on sales	10,125			
		42,125		
		2,92,125		2,92,125

Ramesh & Co.

	Rs.		Rs.
To Consignment a/c		By B. R.	1,00,000
— Sales	2,25,000	By Consignment a/c	
		— Expenses	32,000
		— Commission	10,125
		By Bank	82,875
	2,25,000		2,25,000

Loss in Transits

	Rs.		Rs.
To lonsignment to Madras a/c	6,250	By Insurance Claim	4,500
		By P & L a/c	1,750
	6,250		6,250

Working Note :- Cost of Closing stock

Cost of 10,000 kgs @ Rs. 20	2,00,000
Add freight & Insurance	50,000
Total cost of 10,000 kgs	2,50,000
Less cost of 250 kgs lost in transit	6,250
	2,43,750
Quantity available for resale :	9,500 kgs.

i.e., 9750 – 250 loss due to leakage

$$\text{Cost of stock} = \frac{2{,}000}{9{,}500} \times 2{,}43{,}750 = \text{Rs. } 51{,}316.$$

Problem 9

On 1st September 2004 'A' of Andhra Pradesh sent on consignment to 'B' of Banaglore 10 cases of tea costing Rs. 500 each invoiced proforma at Rs. 600 each. Freight and other charges on the consignment amount of Rs. 310.

On 1st December 2004, 'B' sent account sales with the necessary remittance showing that 4 cases had realised Rs. 600 each and 3 cases Rs. 700 each and 3 cases remained in stock unsold. The expenses in Bangalore came to Rs. 250 in respect of the entire consignment. Mr. 'B' is entitled to a commission @ 5%. On 27th December. Mr. B informed Mr. 'A' that 2 cases were damaged due to bad packing that they would be sold at Rs. 200 per case.

Both the firms close the books of account of 31st December. Prepare ledger account in the books of both the parties.

Solution

In the books of Mr. A

Consignment of Bangalore A/c

	Rs.		*Rs.*
To Goods sent on Consignment	6,000	By B's a/c	
To Cash-expenses	310	4 × 600 = 2,400	
To B's a/c -expenses	250	3 × 700 = 2,100	
To B's a/c-commission	225		4,500
To Stock reserve	100	By Goods sent on Consignment	
To P& L a/c	308	(loading)	1,000
		By Abnormal loss	662
		By Closing stock	
		Damaged 400	
		Normal 631	
			1,031
	7,193		7,193

B's A/c

	Rs.		*Rs.*
To Consignment to Bangalore-Sales	4,500	By Consignment a/c — Expenses	250
		By Consignment a/c — Commission	225
		By Bank	4,025
	4,500		4,500

In the Books of 'B'

A's A/c

	Rs.		Rs.
To Cash-expenses	250	By Cash — Sales	4,500
To Commission	225		
To Bank	4,025		
	4,500		4,500

Problem 10

On 4th September 2004, Deshmukh sent to Kumar on consignment basis goods costing Rs. 8,000 invoiced porforma at Rs. 10,000 and drew upon the latter a bill at Rs. 3 months for Rs. 5,000 which was immediately accepted by the latter. Freight and other expenses incurred by Deshmukh on the goods consigned amounted to Rs. 640.

On 21st December 2004 Deshmukh received an account sales from Kumar along with a bank draft for the amount to settle the account up to date. According to accounts sales received Kumar had sold three-fourths of the goods for Rs. 8,700 and had incurred selling expenses amounted to Rs. 327. Kumar charged commission @ 5%.

Both the parties closed their accounts on 31st December 2004. Show the Journal entries to record the above mentioned transactions in the books of both the parties. Also show important ledger account in Deshmukhs ledger. Deshmukh passed entries on the basis of invoice price of the goods consigned.

Solution

In the Books of Deshmukh

Date	*Particulars*	*L.F.*	*Dr. Amount*	*Cr. Amount*
Sept. 4.	Consignment a/c Dr.		10,640	
	To Goods sent on consignment a/c			10,000
	To Bank a/c			640
	(Being invoice price of goods sent to Kumar on consignment basis and expenses incurred on goods consigned).			
	Bills receivable a/c Dr.		5,000	
	To Kumar			5,000
	(Being acceptance received from Kumar)			
7.	Bank a/c Dr.		5,000	
	To Bills receivable a/c			5,000
	(Cash received on maturity of bill)			
21.	Kumar's a/c Dr.		8,700	
	To Consignment a/c			8,700
	(Being sale proceeds of 3/4 of goods sold by Kumar)			
	Consignment a/c Dr.		327	
	To Kumar			327
	(Being expenses incurred by Kumar)			

Date	Particulars		L.F.	Dr. Amount	Cr. Amount
	Consignment a/c	Dr.		435	
	To Kumar				435
	(Being commission payable by Kumar)				
	Bank a/c	Dr.		4,198	
	To Kumar				4,198
	(Being amount of bank draft received from Kumar in settlement of account. 1/4 of the advance remaining unadjusted.)				
31.	Goods sent on consignment	Dr.		2,000	
	To Consignment a/c				2,000
	(Loading in the invoice price of goods sent on consignment)				
	Stock on Consignment a/c	Dr.		2,660	
	To Consignment a/c				2,660
	(Invoice price of one-fourth of goods plus a proportionate expenses incurred by consignor				
	Consignment a/c	Dr.		500	
	To Stock reserve a/c				500
	(Loading in the invoice price of one-fourth of the goods)				
	Goods sent on consignment	Dr.		8,000	
	To Purchases/ Trading a/c				8,000
	(Being transfer of goods sent on consignment to trading a/c)				
	Consignment a/c	Dr.		1,458	
	To Profit & loss a/c				1,458
	(Being transfer of profit on consignment to profit & loss a/c)				

Consignment A/c

	Rs.		Rs.
To Goods sent on Consignment a/c	10,000	By Kumar — sales	8,700
To Bank-expenses	640	By Goods sent on consignment a/c	
To Kumar-expenses	327	(Loading)	2,000
To Kumar (commission)	435	By Stock on Consignment a/c	2,660
To Stock reserve	500		
To Profit & loss a/c	1,458		
	13,360		13,360

Kumar's A/c

	Rs.		Rs.
To Consignment a/c		By Bills receivable	5,000
— Sales	8,700	By Consignment a/c	
To Balance c/d	1,250	— Expenses	327
		By Consignment	
		— Commission	425
		By Bank a/c	4,198
	9,950		9,950

In the Books of Kumar

Date	Particulars	L.F.	Dr. Amount	Cr. Amount
Sept. 4.	Deshmukh's a/c Dr. To Bills payable a/c (Being acceptance given to Deshmukh)		5,000	5,000
Dec. 7.	Bills payable a/c Dr. To Bank (Payment made at maturity)		5,000	5,000
Dec. 21.	Cash a/c Dr. To Deshmukh's a/c (Being sale proceeds of goods sold)		8,700	8,700
	Deshmukh's a/c Dr. To Cash (Being expenses incurred on behalf of Deshmukh)		327	327
	Deshmukh's a/c Dr. To Commission a/c (Being commission earned on sale made)		435	435
	Deshmukh's a/c Dr. To Bank a/c (Being bank draft sent to Deshmukh)		4,198	4,198
	Commission received a/c Dr. To P & L a/c (Being commission transferred to P & L a/c.)		435	435

Problem 11

AB Ltd. of Calcutta consigned goods worth Rs. 15,000 (200 boxes) to CD Ltd. of Bombay at a proforma Invoice price which included a profit of 25% on sales and incurred an expenses of Rs. 1,200 for freight and insurance. The consignee incurred Rs. 2,000 as import duty, Rs. 400 for cartage and reimitted an amount of Rs. 8,000 as advance against the consignment. The consignee sold 160 boxes for Rs. 21,000, deducting 5% of gross proceeds as commission and remitted the balance owing by them by sight draft.

Show the account in both the consignor and the consignee's books.

Solution

In the books of Consignor
Consignment A/c

		Rs.		Rs.
To Goods sent on Consignment a/c $= \frac{25}{75} \times 15,000$ (5,000 + 15,000)		20,000	By CD Ltd. — Sale proceeds	21,000
To Bank a/c		1,200	By Consignment Stock a/c	4,000
To CD Ltd – Import duty – Cartage – Commission	 2,000 400 1,050	3,450	By Goods sent out on consignment a/c	5,000
To Consignment stock Reserve a/c		1,000		
To P & L a/c		4,350		
		30,000		30,000

Goods Sent on Consignment A/c

	Rs.		Rs.
To Consignment a/c	5,000	By Consignment a/c	20,000
To Trading a/c	15,000		
	20,000		20,000

CD Ltd A/c (Consignee)

	Rs.	—	Rs.
To Consignment a/c		By Bank -	
— Sale proceeds	21,000	— Advance	8,000
		By Consignment a/c :-	
		— Import duty	2,000
		— Cartage	400
		— Commission	1,050
		By Bank-remittance	9,550
	21,000		21,000

In the books of Consignee
AB Ltd A/c (Consignor)

	Rs.		Rs.
To Bank a/c	8,000	By Bank-Sales	21,000
— Advance			
To Bank-Import duty and cartage	2,400		
To Commission	1,050		
To Bank-reimttance	9,550		
	21,000		21,000

Problem 12

On 1st October 2004, 'C' of Calcutta consigned 'D' of Delhi 100 Radio sets. Cost of each set was Rs. 190 but C prepared proforma invoice Rs. 220 per set. C incurred expenses amounting to Rs. 500 on goods consigned. On 31st December 2004, D informed C that he had sold 68 sets @ Rs. 280 per set and 11 sets e Rs. 270 per set and had spent Rs. 1,520 on behalf of the consignor. One set has been accidentally damaged and sold for Rs. 50 according to instructions of the consignor. D was entitled to a commission of 6% on gross sales including Del Credere Commission. D could recover only Rs. 250 from a customer to whom one set has been sold on credit for Rs. 280. All other sales were made on cash basis. Show ledger accounts in the books of both the parties under (1) Cost method (2) Invoice method and (3) Memorandum column method.

Solution

Cost Method

In the Books of C
Consignment A/c

	Rs.		Rs.
To Goods sent on consignment a/c	19,000	By D's a/c-sales	
To Cash-expenses	500	= 68 × 280	19,040
To D's a/c — Expenses	1,500	= 11 × 270	2,970
To D's a/c — Commission	1,321	By Abnormal loss	195
To P & L a/c	3,764	By Consignment stock	3,900
	26,105		26,105

Abnormal Loss A/c

	Rs.		Rs.
To Consignment a/c	195	By D's a/c-sales	50
To D's a/c — Commissions	3	By P & L a/c	148
	198		198

D's A/c

	Rs.		Rs.
To Consignment a/c	22,010	By Consignment	1,520
To Abnormal loss a/c	50	By Consignment	1,321
		By Abnormal loss	3
		By Balance c/d	19,216
	22,060		22,060

Invoice method :

Consignment A/c

	Rs.		Rs.
To Goods sent on Consignment a/c	22,000	By D's a/c	22,010
To Cash-expenses	500	By Abnormal loss	195
To D's a/c — Expenses	1,520	By Goods sent on consignment	
To D's a/c — Commission	1,321	— Loading	3,000
To Stock reserve	600	By Stock on consigneement	4,500
To P & L a/c	3,764		
	29,705		29,705

Goods sent on consignment A/c

	Rs.		Rs.
To Consignment a/c — loading	3,000	By Consignment	22,000
To Trading a/c — transfer	19,000		
	22,000		22,000

Note : There will be no change in Abnormal loss account D's a/c

Memorandum Column Method

Consignment A/c

	Invoice price	Cost price		Invoice price	Cost price
To Goods sent On consignment	22,000	19,000	By D'a a/c Sales	17,380	22,010
To Cash — Expenses		500	By Abnormal loss	220	195
To D's a/c		1,520	By Consignment Stock a/c	4,400	3,900
To D's a/c — Commission		1,321			
To P & L a/c		3,764			
	22,000	26,105		22,000	26,105

Note :

Other account will be the same as in the above two methods.

In the Books of D

C's A/c

	Rs.		Rs.
To Cash-Expenses	1,520	By Cash — Normal cash sales	21,730
To Commission (1,321 + 3)	1,324	By Debtors (Credit sales)	280
To Balance c/d	19,216	By Cash — Sale of damaged set	50
	22,060		22,060

Debtor's A/c

	Rs.		Rs.
To C's (credit sales) a/c	280	By Cash a/c	250
		By Bad debts	30
	280		280

Meaning of Concepts

1. **Consignment :** It is a method of sale under which goods are sent by one person to another who sells them on behalf of the first person.
2. **Consignor :** The person who sends goods under consignment basis is known as consignor.
3. **Consignee :** The person to whom goods are sent under consignment basis is known as consignee.
4. **Del Credere Commission :** It is a form of commission given to the consignee when he takes up the responsibility of collecting entire amount of credit sales

5. **Overriding Commission :** A type of commission which is paid to the consignee when he exceeds a specific target of sales.
6. **Consignment Outwards :** It means goods sent by the consignor to the consignee for sale.
7. **Consignment Inwards :** It means goods received for sales by the consignee from the consignor.
8. **Account Sales :** It is a statement sent by the consignee to the consignor to report the sales expenses incurred by him and his own commission.
9. **Proforma Invoice :** A statement sent by consignor to consignee to indicate the value of goods sent under consignment.
10. **Cost Method :** A method of preparing consignment account under which goods consigned is valued at cost price.
11. **Invoice price Method :** A method of preparing consignment account under which goods consigned is valued at market price.

Memorandum Column Method

A method of preparing consignment account under which a column is provided for both Cost price and Invoice price.

QUESTIONS

Answer the following questions in about four lines each.

1. What do you mean by 'Consignment ?
2. Who is a consignor in a consignment sale ?
3. Who is a consignee in a consignment transaction ?
4. What do you mean by consignment outward ?
5. What do you mean by consignment inward ?
6. What do you mean by a proforma invoice ?
7. What do you mean by an account sales ?
8. Distinguish between an "invoice" and a proforma invoice".
9. Distinguish between an account sales and proforma invoice.
10. What do you mean by Del Credere commission ?
11. What do you mean by "overriding commission ?
12. State the relationship between the consignor and consignee.
13. What do you mean by normal loss ?
14. What do you mean by Abnormal loss ?
15. Distinguish between normal loss and abnormal loss.
16. What do you mean by cost method "of preparing consignment account" ?
17. What do you mean by " Invoice price" method of preparing consignment account ?
18. What do you mean by "Memorandum column" method of preparing consignment a/c ?

SHORT ANSWER TYPE QUESTIONS

1. Explain a proforma invoice as used in a consignment transaction.
2. Give the usual Journal entries recorded in the case of consignment in the books of the consignor and consignee.

3. Give specimen of the following with imaginary figures.
   (*i*) Proforma invoice (*ii*) Account sales
4. Consignment is not a sale "Explain the statement by bringing differences between a consignment and sale transaction."
5. Differentiate between.
   (*a*) Proforma invoice and account sales.
   (*b*) Sale and consignment.

EXERCISE 1

Mr. Banerjee of Calcutta sent 1,000 cases of Ayurvedic medicines to Rao Bros. of Bangalore at Rs. 100 per case. Expenses on the consignment incurred by the consignor amounted to Rs. 3,000. Rao Bros. in Bangalore were working as Del Credere agents. Their ordinary commission was 5% and Del Credere commission $7\frac{1}{2}\%$.

Exactly after six months an account sales was received by Banerjee giving the following information.

(*a*) Sale proceeds of Rs. 750 cases, Rs. 1,50,000
(*b*) Stock of unsold goods in hand 250 cases.
(*c*) Commission charged at agreed rates of 5% and $7\frac{1}{2}\%$.
(*d*) Consignee's expenses amounted Rs. 1,200.
(*e*) Bank draft for Rs. 1,00,000 was sent by Rao Bros. along with account sales.

You are required to give the necessary Journal entries in the books of the consignor to record the above transactions.

EXERCISE 2

Sen Bros. of Calcutta sent 100 chesting tea to Mr. Kannan of Madras, each chest costing Rs. 1,500. The expenses incurred by the consignor on the whole consignment amounted to Rs. 2,000. Mr. Kannan is allowed an ordinary commission of $7\frac{1}{2}\%$ and a Del Credere commission of 10%. On 30-6-2005, exactly six months after the consignment is despatched, Mr. Kannan sends an account sales showing the following information.

(*i*) Gross sales proceeds of 80 chests for Rs. 2,00,000.
(*ii*) Agents (Kannan's) expenses before sales Rs. 5,000.
(*iii*) A bank draft for the amount due from the agent was enclosed.

You are required to record the transactions in the books of Sen Bros. Show the balance of unsold shock in hand.

EXERCISE 3

On 1-1-2005 Arun consigned to Varun 2,000 kgs of Rice invoiced at Rs. 10 per kg. The cost of Rice was Rs. 7.50 per kg and expenses incurred there on amounted to Rs. 2 per kg. On 15th Feb. Varun reported the sale of 1,000 kgs at Rs. 16 per kg. The expenses incurred by Varun were :- Sales expenses Rs. 900, insurance Rs. 120, commission 3% The consignee enclosed a bill for the net amount due and reported a shortage of weight of 50 kgs on the whole consignment.

Show the necessary account in the books of Arun.

EXERCISE 4

C Ltd. of Bombay shipped on Nov. 2004 to their agents Badami Ltd of Rangoon 140 cases of goods costing Rs. 1,29,000. Badami Ltd were to sell all the goods on account of the consignors and were to receive a commission of 5% of the gross proceeds with a further 2% as Del Credere commission.

C Ltd incurred the following charges in connection with the consignment .

Carriage Rs. 280, Insurance and freight Rs. 3,290, Loading charges Rs. 210 and cable expenses Rs. 40.

Badami Ltd. sold the cases at an average Rs. 1,500 per case incurring Bad debts of Rs. 4,310 and paid the following.

Landing charges Rs. 470, warehousing and Insurance Rs. 1,300 and packing and selling expenses Rs. 1,580.

Prepare the necessary accounts in the books of C. Ltd. to record the above transactions.

EXERCISE 5

On 1-1-2005 Lila & Co. of Bangalore consigned 100 cases of milk powder to Shila & Co. Mangalore. The goods were charged at a proforma invoice. Value of Rs. 10,000 including a profit of 25% an invoice price. On the same date the consignors paid Rs. 600 for freight and Insurance. On 1-7-2005 the consignor paid excise duty Rs. 1,000 and other expenses of Rs. 200 and sent to the consignors a Bank draft Rs. 4,000 as advance. On 15th July, they sold 80 cases for Rs. 10,500 and sent a remittance for the balance due to the consignors after deducting commission of 5% on gross sale proceed.

Show ledger accounts in the consignors books.

EXERCISE 6

M/s Hero cycle of Bangalore sent in consignment to Ghorpade of Bellary 100 cycles invoiced at 1,500 each on January 1st 2004. On the same date they pay by cheque the following expenses thereon carriage Rs. 3,200, Insurance 8,000 and Sundries Rs. 1,800. On January 15, they receive a bill at 3 months from Ghorpade for Rs. 12,000. On March 4th Ghorpade sends an account sales showing that the cycles have realised Rs. 1,270 each and that he has deducted expenses of Rs. 4,200 (carriage Rs. 1,600, warehousing Rs. 1,800 and sundries Rs. 800) and commission at 10% on sales.

Enter the transactions in the books of both the parties and prepare the necessary accounts.

EXERCISE 7

Shri Tendulkar of Bombay consigned 500 bales of cloth at Rs. 2,000 each to Shri Murali of Bangalore paying freight Rs. 7,500 and other expenses Rs. 2,500. Shri Murali received the consignment by paying Rs. 5,000 for freight, octroi, carriage etc. Shri Murali sold 350 bales at Rs. 2,200 each for cash. He incurred Rs. 2,000 as selling and other expenses.

Shri Murali remitted the amount due to Shri Tendulkar after deducting all expenses and his commission @ $7\frac{1}{2}$% and Del credere commission @ $\frac{1}{2}$%.

Write necessary accounts in the books of both the parties and show the valuation of consignment stock.

EXERCISE 8

On 1st July 'A' had consigned to B goods costing Rs. 50,000, on which 'A' paid freight and Insurance amounting to Rs. 2,500. On 30th September, B's first account sales was received showing that he had effected sales of Rs. 32,000 of which Rs. 30,000 had been received in cash. His expenses to date were Rs. 2,000 and a commission of 5% on gross sales. On receipt of the account sales the consignment account was balanced off, stock being valued at Rs. 28,000. A further account sales was received on 31st December showing that the balance of goods had been sold for Rs. 36,000 and the cash collected. Debtors had also paid their dues less discount of 3%. The expenses of B was Rs. 2,500. The rate of his commission was the same as before. Write up the consignment account and B's account upto 31st December in the books of A assuming that 'B' remitted the balance due with each Account sales.

EXERCISE 9

Shri Jayaram of Madras Consigned 1,000 cases of tinned fruits (cost Rs. 7,000) to Ganesh of Bangalore on 1-1-2004, charging them at a proforma invoice price to show a profit of 25% on sales. Jayaram paid on the same date Rs. 600 in respect of freight etc. During the half year ending 30th June 2004, Ganesh incurred expenses of Rs. 200 on godown rent and sold 800 cases of the consignment for Rs. 8,000. Ganesh is entitled to 5% commission on sales which is duly charged. Record the transaction in the ledger of Shri Jayaram under Memorandum column method.

13 CHAPTER

Joint Venture

1. MEANING OF JOINT VENTURE

A Joint venture is a partnership formed for a particular venture or for any specified transaction. It may be defined as an agreement entered into between two as more persons to share profit or losses in respect of a business in which their individual trading capabilities can be profitably pooled. Ventures of this nature are temporary in nature and terminate on completion of the venture. This type of business may be limited to one transaction or may be extended to a number of transactions. It may even be limited by reference to a period of time. The parties to a Joint venture business are called as Co-ventures. They share profit or losses at an agreed proportion. If there is no agreement to the contrary, the co-ventures shore profits and losses equally.

Joint venture resembles to a partnership in respect of the nature of the business. But a joint venture is carried out without a firm name. Examples of business under-takings which are carried out under joint venture are construction contractors, consignment transaction, purchase and sale of business which are liquidated, under writing shares of the companies etc.; A Joint venture is under taken when it is not possible for an individual to contribute the required capital and to run the business efficiently.

2. FEATURES OF JOINT VENTURE

The important features of a Joint venture can be summarised under the following :

(*a*) It is a kind of partnership business.
(*b*) It is not undertaken on a permanent basis since termination is certain.
(*c*) The business is dissolved after the venture is terminated.
(*d*) Ascertainment of profit is simple.
(*e*) All the assets are ultimately received in cash and all liabilities are paid in cash.
(*f*) Many of the accounting concepts which are normally applicable are dispensed with as for example going concern concept.
(*g*) Though it resembles partnership, yet it does not use firm name.

3. DISTINCTION BETWEEN A JOINT VENTURE AND CONSIGNMENT

Points of Differences	*Joint venture*	*Consignment*
1. Parties	Parties to a Joint venture are called Co-ventures	Parties to a consignment are called consignor and consignee.
2. Relationship	The relationship between coventures is that of partners	The relationship between consignor and consignee is that of principal and agent
3. Powers	Co-ventures enjoy full powers relating to purchase and sale of goods, collection of debts etc.	Consignee being an agent of the principal has to obey the orders of the principal
4. Governing Act	It is governed by Partnership Act	It is governed by the law of agency
5. Sharing of Profits	Co-ventures have right to share profits	Consignee has no right to share profit. He gets his share of remuneration which is known as commission.
6. Scope	The scope of carrying a Joint venture is very wide. It can be applied to any type of business such as construction, films, underwriting shares purchase and sale of goods etc.	Its scope is narrow as it is concerned with the sale of movable goods
7. Capital Contribution	Capital is contributed by all the co-ventures to carry out joint venture business	Consignee does not contribute capital in a consignment business
8. Number of persons	The number of members in a Joint venture may be more them two	In consignment there are normally two persons, namely consignor and consignee

4. DISTINCTION BETWEEN A PARTNERSHIP AND A JOINT VENTURE

Points of Differences	*Joint venture*	*Partnership*
1. Name	It is carried out without any name	It is carried out always with a firm name
2. Duration of business	It is temporary in nature. It comes to an end as soon as the venture is completed	It is more permanent when compared to joint venture
3. Accounts	No need to keep separate set of accounting books as it is temporary in nature.	A separate set of accounting books is necessary
4. Freedom	Co-venturers can run similar business and compete with a Joint venture business.	Partners of a firm cannot carry on parallel business and should not compete with the business.
5. Dissolution	It comes to an end automatically as soon as the venture or duration is completed	It can be carried as by other partners by mutual agreement though the operation of the business is completed.

5. METHOD OF PREPARING ACCOUNTS

There are two methods of preparing and maintaining accounting books. They are : (*a*) Recording of transactions only in individual books of accounts of co-ventures and (*b*) Maintenance of a separate set of books to record transactions relating to Joint venture.

(*a*) **When Individual Books are Maintained by Co-ventures :-** Under this method each co-venturers will maintain a set of books. A Joint venture account and the accounts of co-ventures are prepared by every co-venture. The joint venture account is prepared to know the profit or loss on Joint venture. The co-ventures accounts are prepared to know balances of amounts to be paid by them or to be received from them. This method is followed when the transactions are not so numerous. The following entries are applicable under this method. The entries can be shown under the following :

I. Transactions Relating to a Venture

1. When cash is contributed or goods purchased for Joint venture
   Joint Venture a/c Dr.
   To Cash or Bank a/c
2. When goods are supplied from own stock
   Joint Venture a/c Dr.
   To Purchases a/c
3. When any expenses are met
   Joint Venture a/c Dr.
   To Cash a/c
4. When goods are sold for cash
   Cash a/c Dr.
   To Joint Venture a/c
5. When goods are sold on credit
   Debtors a/c Dr.
   To Joint Venture a/c
6. When cash is received from debtors
   Cash a/c Dr.
   To Debtors a/c
7. When any discount is allowed to debtors or when there is any Bad debts.
   Joint Venture a/c Dr.
   To Debtors a/c
8. When cash or Bills Receivable received from other co-ventures.
   Cash or Bills Receivable a/c Dr.
   To Co-ventures a/c
9. Where cash or Bills Payable is given to the co-venture.
   Co-venturer's a/c Dr.
   To Cash or Bills Payable a/c
10. When commission or salary is receivable
   Joint Venture a/c Dr.
   To Commission or Salary a/c

11. When unsold stock is taken into stock
    Stock a/c Dr.
    To Joint Venture a/c

II. Transaction Relating to Co-ventures

13. When any cash is contributed or goods are contributed or purchased by the co-ventures.
    Joint Venture a/c Dr.
    To Co-ventures a/c
14. When co-ventures pay any expenses of Joint ventures or any discount allowed by him or bad debts incurred
    Joint Venture a/c Dr.
    To Co-ventures
15. When co-venturers sells goods on cash or on credit.
    Co-venturers a/c Dr.
    To Joint Venture a/c
16. When salary or commission is paid to co-ventures
    Joint Venture a/c Dr.
    To Co-venturer's a/c
17. When a co-venture takes unsold stock
    Co-venturer's a/c Dr.
    To Joint Venture a/c

III. Transaction Relating to the Results of the Business

1. When there is profit
   Joint Venture a/c Dr.
   To Profit & Loss a/c (Venturer's share)
   To Co-venturer's a/c (Co-venturer's)
2. When there is loss
   Profit & Loss a/c (Venture's share) Dr.
   Co-venture a/c (Co-ventures share) Dr.
   To Joint Venture a/c

IV. Transactions Relating to Settlement of Account

1. When cash or bills is received
   Cash or Bills receivable a/c Dr.
   To Co-venture's a/c
2. When cash or bill is given
   Co-venture's a/c Dr.
   To Cash or bills payable a/c.

Problem 1

Ramaiah and Bhimaiah entered into a joint venture in an account. Profit were to be shared equally. Ramaiah was to purchase arecanut and send it to Bhimaiah who would sell it. On 1st, January 2001, Ramaiah purchased arecanut worth Rs. 10,000 and incurred Rs. 600 as expenses on forwarding it to Bhimaiah. He immediately drew upon Bhimaiah for Rs. 10,000 for 3 months. The bill was discounted at 6% per annum. Bhimaiah paid Rs. 1,000 as freight,

Rs. 500 as commission to agent and Rs. 200 as rent. The whole stock was disposed off for Rs. 16,000. He forwarded a draft to Ramaiah for the amount due on 30th April 2001.

Prepare ledger accounts in the books of both the parties.

Solution

In the books of Ramaiah

Joint venture A/c

		Rs.		*Rs.*
To Purchases a/c		10,000	By Bhimaiah's a/c	
To Cash-expenses		600	— Sales	16,000
To Discount a/c		150		
To Bhimaiah's a/c				
— Freight		1,000		
— Commission		500		
— Rent		200		
To Prompt transferred to				
Ramaiah's a/c	1,775			
Bhimaish'a/c	1,775			
		3,550		
		16,000		16,000

Bhimaiah's A/c

	Rs.		*Rs.*
To Joint venture a/c		By Joint venture a/c	
— Sales	16,000	— Freight	1,000
		— Commission	500
		— Rent	200
		By Bills receivable a/c	10,000
		By Joint venture a/c	
		— Prompt	1,775
		By Bank — Final settlement	2,525
	16,000		16,000

In the books of Bhimaiah

	Rs.		*Rs.*
To Ramaiah a/c		By Cash-sales	16,000
— Purchases	10,000		
— Expenses	600		
To Cash			
— Freight	1,000		
— Commission	500		
— Rent	200		
To Discount a/c	150		
To P & L a/c	1,775		
To Ramaiah's a/c (profit)	1,775		
	16,000		16,000

Ramaiah A/c

	Rs.		Rs.
To Bills payable a/c	10,000	By Joint venture account	
To Bank-final settlement	2,525	— Purchases	10,000
		— Expenses	600
		By Joint venture a/c	
		— Discount	150
		By Joint venture a/c	
		— Profit	1,775
	12,525		12,525

Problem 2

Sen Bros. entered into Joint venture with Gupta Bros. profits being divided in the ratio of 2 : 1. Sen Bros. bought goods worth Rs. 15,000 and despatched the same to Gupta Bros., to be sold by latter. Sen Bros., paid Rs. 1,099 for carriage, insurance and freight and drew a bill on Gupta Bros. for Rs. 6,000 an account. The bill was discounted by Sen Bros. paying discount Rs. 200. Gupta Bros. paid Rs. 600 for dock charges, godown, rent etc. The goods were sold for Rs. 25,000 and the selling expenses amounting to Rs. 500 were met by Gupta Bros. who forwarded a cheque for the balance due to Sen Bros., after charging their sales commission at 5% on gross sale proceeds.

Write up the accounts in the books of Sen Bros.

Solution

In the Books of Sen Bros.
Joint Venture A/c

	Rs.		Rs.
To Purchases a/c	15,000	By Gupta Bros.	25,000
To Cash a/c			
— Carriage freight and insurance	1,099		
To Discount a/c	200		
To Gupta Bros. a/c			
— Dock charges rent	600		
To Gupta Bros. a/c			
— Selling expenses	500		
— Commission 5% on Rs. 25,000	1,250		
To P & L a/c 2/3	4,234		
To Gupta Bros. 1/3	2,117		
	25,000		25,000

Gupta Bros. A/c

	Rs.		Rs.
To Joint venture a/c		By B.R. a/c	6,000
— Sales	25,000	By Joint venture a/c	
		— Dock charges	600

	Rs.		Rs.
		— Selling expenses	500
		— Commission	1,250
		— Profit	2,117
		By Bank a/c	
		(Balance received)	14,533
	25,000		25,000

Problem 3

Anand & Bose, enter into Joint venture for sale of Jaggery in Madras from Kanpur. Anand purchased 100 bags at Rs. 100 per bag to be sold by Bose at Madras, the latter to get 5% commission on sale proceeds. Anand spent Rs. 700 towards freight and Insurance. Bose sold the consignment for Rs. 15,000. He had incurred Rs. 500 towards brokerage and selling expenses. The partners settle their accounts after completion of the venture. The partners share profit equally.

Prepare ledger accounts in the books of Anand.

Solution

In the Books of Anand

Joint venture A/c

	Rs.		Rs.
To Purchases	10,000	By Bose a/c	
Rs. 100 × 100 bags		— Sales	15,000
To Cash			
— Freight and Insurance	700		
To Bose a/c			
— Commission	750		
— Brokerage and Selling expenses	500		
To P & L a/c			
— Prompt	1,525		
To Bose a/c			
— Profit	1,525		
	15,000		15,000

Bose A/c

	Rs.		Rs.
To Joint venture a/c		By Joint venture a/c	
— Sales	15,000	— Commission	750
		— Brokerage & selling expenses	500
		— Profit	1,525
		To Bank a/c	
		(Final settlement)	12,225
	15,000		15,000

Problem 4

Moon and company bought goods of the value of Rs. 7,500 and consigned them to Star & Co. to be sold by them on a Joint venture, profits being divided into $\frac{2}{3}$ and $\frac{1}{3}$. They also paid Rs. 550 for freight and Insurance and cartage and drew on Star & Co., for Rs. 3,000 on account. The bills was discounted by Moon & Co. for Rs. 2,900. Star & Co. paid Rs. 300 for storage, rent etc. The sales realised Rs. 12,500 and the sales expenses of Rs. 250 were paid by the star and Co. The latter forwarded a sight draft for the balance due to Moon and Co., after charging their sales commission at 5% on gross proceeds.

Write up the accounts in the books of the Moon and Co.

Solution

In the books of Moon & Co.

Joint Venture A/c

	Rs.		*Rs.*
To Bank a/c		By Star & Co.	
— Goods sent	7,500	— Sales	12,500
To Bank a/c			
— Freight, Insurance	550		
To Bank discount a/c	100		
To Star & Co.			
— Storage rent	300		
— Sales expenses	250		
— Commission 5%	725		
To P & L a/c			
— Profit 2/3	2,050		
To Star & Co.			
— Profit 1/3	1,025		
	12,500		12,500

Star & Co. a/c

	Rs.		*Rs.*
To Joint venture a/c		By B. R.	3,000
— Sales	12,500	By Joint venture a/c	
		— Storage rent	300
		— Sales expenses	250
		— Commission	725
		By Joint venture a/c	
		— Profit	1,025
		By B. R.	7,200
		(Balance)	
	12,500		12,500

Problem 5

X and Y entered into a Joint venture agreeing to share profits & losses equally. The following transactions took place.

X Purchased goods	Rs. 8,000
Y Paid carriage & freight	Rs. 500
Y Sold goods	Rs. 6,000
X Paid storage fees	Rs. 200
X Sold remaining goods	Rs. 5,000

Journalise the transactions in the books of X and prepare the Joint venture account and Y's account.

Solution

Journal Entries in the books of X

Date	Particulars		L.F.	Dr. Amount	Cr. Amount
	Joint venture a/c	Dr.		8,000	
	To Cash a/c				8,000
	(Being purchase of goods)				
	Joint venture a/c	Dr.		500	
	To Y's a/c				500
	(Being carriage and freight paid by him)				
	Y's a/c	Dr.		6,000	
	To Joint venture a/c				6,000
	(Being goods sold by him)				
	Joint venture a/c	Dr.		200	
	To Cash a/c				200
	(Being storage fee paid)				
	Cash a/c	Dr.		5,000	
	To Joint venture a/c				5,000
	(Being remaining goods sold)				
	Joint venture a/c	Dr.		2,300	
	To P & L a/c				1,150
	To Y's a/c				1,150
	(Being profit on Joint venture shared equally)				

Joint Venture A/c

	Rs.		Rs.
To Cash — Goods purchased	8,000	By Y's a/c	
To Y's a/c		— Sales	6,000
— Cartage and Freight	500	By Cash a/c	
To Cash — Storage fee	200	— Sales	5,000
To P & L a/c $\frac{1}{2}$ profit	1,150		
To Y's a/c $\frac{1}{2}$ profit	1,150		
	11,000		11,000

Y's A/c

	Rs.		Rs.
To Joint venture a/c — Sales	6,000	By Joint venture a/c — Cartage & Freight	500
		By Joint venture a/c — $\frac{1}{2}$ profit	1,150
		By Bank	4,350
	6,000		6,000

Problem 6

On 1-1-2004 'A' and 'B' entered into a Joint venture sharing the profits in the ratio of 3 : 2, after allowing a salary of Rs. 200 per month to 'B'. A sent out of his stock goods costing Rs. 50,000 to be sold by the latter and incurred expenses amounting Rs. 1,070. On 3rd January 2004, 'B' accepted a bill of exchange at 2 months for Rs. 30,000 drawn on A. On 6th January 2004. A discounted the bill @ 9% per annum. By 31st March 2004, B had sold goods for Rs. 60,050 after incurring expenses amounting to Rs. 1,145. 'B' agreed to take over the remaining goods for Rs. 2,000. B forwarded a cheque immediately to settle the account. Show the Journal and ledger account in the books of A and B.

Solution

Journal Entries in the Books of A

Date	Particulars		L.F.	Dr.. Amount	Cr. Amount
1-1-2004	Joint venture a/c	Dr.		51,070	
	To Purchases a/c				50,000
	To Cash a/c				1,070
	(Being cost of goods taken out of stock to Joint venture and expenses incurred there on)				
3-1-2004	Bills receivable a/c	Dr.		30,000	
	To B's a/c				30,000
	(Being acceptance received from B)				
6-1-2005	Bank a/c	Dr.		29,550	
	Joint venture a/c	Dr.		450	
	To Bills Receivable a/c				30,000
	(Being bills discounted and discount charged to Joint venture a/c)				
31-3-2005	B's a/c	Dr.		60,050	
	To Joint venture a/c				60,050
	(Being sales made by B on account of Joint venture a/c)				
	Joint venture a/c	Dr.		1,145	
	To B's a/c				1,145
	(Being expenses incurred by B on account of Joint venture)				

Date	Particulars	L.F.	Dr. Amount	Cr. Amount
	B's a/c Dr.		2,000	
	To Joint venture a/c			2,000
	(Being agreed value of goods taken over by B)			
	Joint venture a/c Dr.		600	
	To B's a/c			600
	(Being salary allowed to B for 3 months @ Rs. 200 per month)			
	Joint venture a/c Dr.		8,785	
	To B's a/c			3,514
	To P & L a/c			5,271
	(Being profit shared)			
	Bank a/c Dr.		26,791	
	To B's a/c			26,791
	(Being amount from B in final settlement)			

Joint Venture A/c

	Rs.		Rs.
To Purchases	50,000	By B's a/c	
To Cash — Expenses	1,070	— Sales	60,050
To B. R. a/c — Discounted	450	By B's a/c	
To B's a/c — Expenses	1,145	— Goods	
To B's a/c — Salary	600	Taken over by B	2,000
To B's a/c — 2/5th profit	3,514		
To P & L a/c — 3/5th profit	5,271		
	62,050		62,050

B's A/c

	Rs.		Rs.
To Joint venture		By B.R. a/c	30,000
— Sales	60,050	By Joint venture	
To Joint venture		— Expenses	1,145
— Goods taken over	2,000	By Joint venture	
		— Salary	600
		By Joint venture	
		— Profit	3,514
		By Bank	26,791
	62,050		62,050

Bills Receivable A/c

	Rs.		Rs.
To B's a/c	30,000	By Bank a/c	20,550
		By Joint venture a/c	
		— Discount	450
	30,000		30,000

In the books of B

Date	Particulars	L.F.	Dr. Amount	Cr. Amount
	Joint venture a/c Dr. To A's a/c (Being cost of goods supplied and expenses incurred by A)		51,070	 51,070
	A's a/c Dr. To Bills payable a/c (Being acceptance given to A)		30,000	 30,000
	Joint venture a/c Dr. To A's a/c (Being discount on acceptance)		450	 450
	Bills payable a/c Dr. To Cash a/c (Being payment of cash on maturity of bills)		30,000	 30,000
	Cash a/c Dr. To Joint venture a/c (Being sales made on account of Joint venture)		60,050	 60,050
	Joint venture a/c Dr. To Cash (Being expenses incurred an account of Joint venture)		1,145	 1,145
	Joint venture a/c Dr. To Salaries a/c (Being salary for 3 months @ Rs. 200 per month)		600	 600
	Purchases a/c Dr. To Joint venture a/c (Being goods taken over)		2,000	 2,000
	Joint venture a/c Dr. To B's a/c To P & L a/c (Being prompt transferred)		8,785	 5,271 3,514
	A's a/c Dr. To Bank a/c (Being find settlement of a/c)		26,791	 26,791

Joint Venture A/c

	Rs.		Rs.
To A's a/c — Goods & Expenses	51,070	By Cash	
To A's a/c — Discount	450	— Sales	60,050
To Cash — Expenses	1,145	By Purchases	2,000
To Salary	600		
To A' a/c — 3/5 profit	5,271		
To P & L a/c — 2/5 profit	3,514		
	62,050		62,050

A's A/c

	Rs.		Rs.
To Bills payable a/c	30,000	By Joint venture	51,070
To Bank	26791	By Joint venture — Discount	450
		By Joint venture	5,271
	56,791		56,791

Problem 7

X and Y entered into a joint venture involving the buying and selling of old railway material. The profit & loss was to be shared equally. The cost of the material purchased was Rs. 85,000 which was paid by X who drew a bill an Y at two months demand for Rs. 60,000. The bill was discounted by X at a cost of Rs. 480. The transaction relating to the venture was (*a*) X paid Rs. 600 for carriage Rs. 1,000 for commission on sales and Rs. 400 travelling expenses (*b*) Y paid Rs. 200 travelling expenses and Rs. 300 sundry expenses (*c*) sales made by X amounted to Rs. 40,000 and sales made by Y were Rs. 60,000. Goods costing Rs 2,000 and Rs. 3,000 (being unsold stock) was retained by X and Y respectively and these were charged to them at prices to show the same rate of gross profit that made on total sales (excluding these sales). X was credited with a sum of Rs. 800 to cover the cost of warehousing and insurance. The expenses in connection with the bill were to be treated as a charge against the venture.

You are required to (*a*) show the account in the books of each party to record his own transactions.

Solution

In the Books of X
Joint Venture A/c

		Rs.		Rs.
To Bank (materials purchased)		85,000	By B. R. a/c	60,000
To Discount on bills		480	By Bank — Sales	40,000
To Bank			By Purchases (See not 1)	2,500
— Carriage	600			
— Commission	1,000			
— Travelling	400	2,000		
— Warehousing and Insurance expenses		800		
To P & L a/c		8,735		
To Balance c/d		5,485		
		1,02,500		1,02,500

In the books of Y
Joint Venture A/c

		Rs.		Rs.
To B.P a/c		60,000	By Bank — Sales	60,000
To Bank a/c			By Purchases (See note)	3,750
— Travelling	200		By Balance c/d (Amt. due)	5485
— Sundry expenses	300	500		
To P & L a/c		8,735		
		69,235		69,235

Note : Calculation of gross profit & sales

Goods purchased	85,000
Less unsold stock Rs. (2,000 + 3,000)	5,000
Cost of goods sold	80,000
Sales	1,00,000
Less cost of goods sold	80,000
Profit	20,000

Rate of gross prompt on profit cost

$$\frac{20,000}{80,000} \times 100 = 25\%$$

Unsold stock taken by X = 2,000 + 25% of 2,000 = Rs. 2,500

Unsold stock taken by Y = 3,000 + 25% of 3,000 = Rs. 3,750

Problem 8

A of Aurangabad and B of Bangalore enter into a joint number to consign 100 Bales of cloth to C of Calcutta, to be sold on their joint risk which is in proportion of $\frac{3}{5}$ and $\frac{2}{5}$ respectively. A sends 60 bales at Rs. 1,200 each paying for freight and other charges Rs. 1800. B sends 40 bales at Rs. 1,100 each paying for freight and other charges Rs. 1,000. All the bales are sold by C for Rs.1,40,000 out of which C deducts Rs. 1,600 for his expenses and his commission at 3%. C remits a Bills Receivable for Rs. 70,000 to A and a Bills Receivable for the balance to B.

Prepare the Joint venture account and co-ventures account in the ledgers of both the co-ventures.

Solution

In the Books of 'A'
Joint Venture A/c

		Rs.		*Rs.*
To Purchases a/c		72,000	By C's a/c	1,40,000
To Bank a/c		1,800		
To B's a/c (Goods)		44,000		
To B's — Expenses		1,000		
To C's — Expenses	1,600			
— Commission $\frac{3}{100} \times 14,000$.	4,200	5,800		
To P & L a/c		9,240		
To B's a/c		6,160		
		1,40,000		1,40,000

B's A/c

	Rs.		Rs.
To C's a/c	64,200	By Joint venture	44,000
		By Joint venture	1,000
		By Joint venture — Profit	6,160
		By Balance	13,040
	64,200		64,200

In the Books of B
Joint Venture A/c

	Rs.		Rs.
To A's a/c — Goods	72,000	By C's Sale	1,40,000
To A's — Expenses	1,800		
To Purchases	44,000		
To Bank	1,000		
To C's a/c — Expenses	1,600		
— Commission	4,200		
To P & L a/c	6,160		
To A's a/c	9,240		
	1,40,000		1,40,000

A's A/c

	Rs.		Rs.
To C's a/c	70,000	By Joint Venture	72,000
To Balance c/d	13,040	By Joint Venture	1,800
		By Joint Venture — Profit	9,240
	83,040		83,040

Problem 9

X and Y enter into a Joint venture for trade of a particular commodity. The profits & losses are to be shared equally. X purchases goods worth Rs. 5,000 and pays expenses amounting to Rs. 250. Y incurs an expense of Rs. 650 and makes a cash sale of Rs. 3,000. He also takes for his person use goods worth Rs. 1,000. At the close of the period, stock in X's hand is valued at Rs. 1,100. This stock is taken over by him at Rs. 1,200.

Show the necessary accounts in the books of both the parties.

Solution

In the Books of X
Joint Venture A/c

		Rs.			Rs.
To Purchase a/c		5,000	By Y's A/c		
To Cash — Expenses		250	Sales	3,000	
To Y's a/c — Expenses		650	Add Drawings of goods	1,000	4,000
			By Purchases a/c		1,200
			By P & L a/c		350
			By Y's a/c		350
		5,900			5,900

Y's A/c

		Rs.		Rs.
To Joint a/c			By Joint venture a/c	
Sale proceeds	3,900		— Expenses	650
Drawing of goods	1,000		By Balance c/d	3,700
Share of loss	350			
		4,350		
		4,350		4,350

In the Books of Y

	Rs.		Rs.
To X's a/c		By Cash — Sales	3,000
— Purchases a/c	5,000	By X's a/c	
— Expenses	250	(Drawings of goods)	1,200
To Cash — Expenses	650	By Purchases a/c	1,000
		By P & L a/c	350
		By X's a/c	350
	5,900		5,900

X's A/c

	Rs.		Rs.
To Joint venture a/c		By Joint venture a/c	
— Drawing of material	1,200	— Purchases	5,000
— Share of loss	350	— Expenses	250
To Balance c/d	3,700		
	5,250		5,250

Problem 10

S and H entered into a Joint venture to construct a bridge. They did not open separate set of books. They shared profits and losses as 3 : 2. S contributed Rs. 1,50,000 for purchase of materials. H paid wages amounting to Rs. 80,000. Other expenses were paid as

S — Rs. 5,000
H — Rs. 15,000

H purchased one machine for Rs. 20,000. The machine was taken over by 'S' for Rs. 10,000. Total contract value of Rs. 300.000 was received by H.

Show the accounts on the books of both the parties.

Solution

In the Books of S

	Rs.		*Rs.*
To Bank — Material	1,50,000	By H's a/c	
To Bank — Expenses	5,000	— Sales	3,00,000
To H's a/c		By Machine	
— Wages	80,000	— Taken over	10,000
— Expenses	15,000		
— Machine	20,000		
To P & L a/c -3/5 profit	24,000		
To H's a/c - 2/5 profit	16,000		
	3,10,000		3,10,000

H's A/c

	Rs.		*Rs.*
To Joint venture a/c		By Joint Venture a/c	
— Sales	3,00,000	— Wages	80,000
		— Expenses	15,000
		— Machine	20,000
		By P & L a/c	16,000
		By Balance c/d	1,69,000
	3,00,000		3,00,000

In the Books of H
Joint venture A/c

	Rs.		*Rs.*
To Bank a/c		By Bank a/c	
— Wages	80,000	— Sales	3,00,000
— Expenses	15,000	By S's a/c	
— Machine	20,000	—Machine	10,000
To S's a/c			
— Materials	1,50,000		
— Expenses	5,000		
To P & L a/c 2/5 profit	1,6000		
To S's a/c 3/5 profit	24,000		
	3,10,000		3,10,000

S's A/c

	Rs.		Rs.
To Joint venture a/c — Machine	10,000	By Joint venture a/c — Materials	1,50,000
To Balance c/d	1,69,000	— Expenses	5,000
		By Joint venture a/c — Profit	24,000
	1,79,000		1,79,000

(*b*) **When separate set of Books are kept.** Under this method, a separate set of books are maintained to record joint venture transaction. These books are common to all co-ventures. Hence they are different from the books maintained by individual co-ventures. Under this method three different types of accounts are opened, viz (*a*) Joint venture account (*b*) Joint Bank account and (*c*) Individual accounts of all the co-ventures. The Joint venture account is in the nature of trading and profit & loss a/c. In this account all expenses are debited and sales, closing stock and other gains are credited. A Joint bank account representing the Joint account of all co-ventures is opened. This account is in the nature of bank column of cash book. All amounts contributed by them and other amounts received are deposited in this Joint account. All expenses of Joint venture is paid out of this account. The co-venturers accounts resemble to capital accounts of partners in a partnership firm. Under this method the following journal entries are applicable.

1. When any capital is contributed by co-venturer

   Joint Bank a/c Dr.
   To Co-venture's capital a/c

2. When any goods are contributed by co-ventures or when he pays every expenses

   Joint Venture a/c Dr.
   To Co-venture's capital a/c

3. When goods are purchased for Joint venture for cash

   Joint Venture a/c Dr.
   To Joint Bank a/c

4. When goods are purchased for Joint venture on credit.

   Joint Venture a/c Dr.
   To suppliers or creditors a/c

5. When any expenses is incurred on Joint venture.

   Joint Venture a/c Dr.
   To Joint Bank a/c

6. When goods are sold under Joint venture for cash.

   Joint Bank a/c Dr.
   To Joint venture a/c

7. When goods are sold under Joint venture on credit.

   Customer's a/c or Debtors a/c Dr.
   To Joint venture a/c

8. When cash or Bills payable is paid to suppliers or creditors.

   Creditors or suppliers a/c Dr.
   To Joint bank a/c or Bills Payable a/c.

9. When cash or Bills receivable is received from customers or debtors

   Joints bank a/c or B. R a/c Dr.
   To customers or debtors a/c

10. When any salary, commission or interest is payable to any co-ventures

    Joint venture a/c Dr.
    To Co-venture capital a/c

11. When any unsold stock is taken by Co-ventures

    Co-venture's capital a/c Dr.
    To Joint venture a/c

12. When profit is earned by Joint venture business.

    Joint venture a/c Dr.
    To Co-venture's capital a/c

13. When loss is incurred by Joint venture business.

    Co-venture's capital a/c Dr.
    To Joint venture a/c

Problem 11

Peter and Jason agree to import Burmese timber for joint venture business. Hence on May 1, 2005, they open Joint Bank account for Rs. 24,000 towards which Peter contributed Rs. 14,000 and Jason Rs. 10,000. They divide profits and losses in proportion to their capital contribution. They send a cheque to their agent in Burma for Rs. 23,000 to pay for the timber purchased and to meet the freight, insurance and other charges amounting to Rs. 4,000. On December 31,2005, the sales amounted to Rs. 24,000 and on December 23, Peter took over the unsold stocks of timber for Rs. 3,800. They then closed the Joint venture after mutually settling their balances.

Write all the ledger accounts relating to the above joint venture ?

Solution

Joint Venture A/c

Date		*Rs.*		*Rs.*
1-5-2005	To Bank a/c		By Cash —	24,000
	— Timber	19,000	Joint bank a/c	
	— Freight, Insurance	4,000	(Sales)	
23-12-2005	To Peter's a/c 14/24	2,800	By Peter's a/c	3,800
	To Jason's a/c 10/24	2,000	— Balance of Unsold timber	
			Taken over	
		27,800		27,800

Joint Bank A/c

Date		Rs.		Rs.
1-5-2005	To Peter a/c	14,000	By Joint venture a/c :	
	To Jason a/c	10,000	— Timber	19,000
21-12-2005	To Joint venture a/c		— Freight & Insurance	4,000
	— Sales	24,000	By Peter's a/c	13,000
			By Jason's a/c	12,000
		48,000		48,000

Peter's A/c

	Rs.		Rs.
To Joint venture	3,800	By Joint bank a/c	14,000
— Unsold timber		By Joint venture a/c	
To Joint bank a/c (final Settlement)	13,000	— Profit	2,800
	16,800		16,800

Jason's A/c

	Rs.		Rs.
To Joint bank a/c		By Joint Bank a/c	10,000
— Final settlement	12,000	By Joint venture a/c	
		— Profit	2,000
	12,000		12,000

Problem 12

A and B both building contractors, undertook a Joint venture involving the construction of a school building. The Joint bank account was opened in which A deposited Rs. 50,000 and B deposited Rs. 25,000. The contract amount was Rs. 2,50,000. The result of Joint venture was to be shared by A $\frac{2}{3}$rd and B $\frac{1}{3}$rd. The detail of the transaction were as under :

	Rs.
1. Salaries	8,000
2. Wages paid	46,000
3. Building materials purchased	1,10,000
4. Materials supplied by 'A'	9,000
5. Materials supplied by 'B'	8,000
6. Architects fees	7,000
7. Cartage	12,000
8. Concrete mixer plant purchased	25,000

The stock the building materials on the completion of the contract valued at Rs. 11,000 was taken over by 'A'. Concrete mixer plant was sold out for Rs. 2,000. Mr. A was to pay Rs. 12,000 per annum against establishment expenses to be charged to the Joint venture account. The contract lasted for 8 months. Prepare a Joint venture account, Joint bank account and Accounts of A and B.

Solution

Joint Venture A/c

		Rs.		Rs.
To Joint Bank a/c			By Joint bank	
Salaries	8,000		— Contract price	2,50,000
Wages	46,000		By A's a/c	11,000
Building			(Building Materials taken over)	
Materials	1,10,000		By Joint bank	2,000
Architect's			(Sale of concrete mixer)	
Fees	7,000			
Cartage	12,000			
Concrete Mixer	25,000	2,08,000		
To A's a/c — Materials supplied		9,000		
To A's a/c — Establishment		8,000		
To B's a/c — Materials Supplied		8,000		
To Profit				
— A		32,000		
— B		16,000		
		2,81,000		2,81,000

Joint Bank A/c

	Rs.		Rs.
To A's a/c	50,000	By Joint venture	
To B's a/c	25,000	— Material expenses	2,08,000
To Joint venture — contract price	2,50,000	By A's a/c	88,000
To Joint venture		By B's a/c	49,000
— Sale of concrete mixer	20,000		
	3,45,000		3,45,000

A's Capial A/c

	Rs.		Rs.
To Joint venture a/c	11,000	By Joint bank	50,000
To Joint bank a/c	88,000	By Joint venture	17,000
		By Joint venture — Profit	32,000
	99,000		99,000

B's Capital A/c

	Rs.		Rs.
To Joint Bank a/c	49,000	By Joint Bank	25,000
		By Joint venture	8,000
		By Joint venture — Profit	16,000
	49,000		49,000

Problem 13

D and E entered into a Joint ventures to construct a building of new company. Profit & losses were to be shared in the ratio of 3:2. D invested Rs. 2,00,000 and E Rs. 1,00,000. The money was deposited to a Joint bank account with arrangement of overdraft Rs. 2,00,000. 'D' also supplied materials valued Rs. 35,000. 'E' also supplied a machine valued Rs. 25,000. Building materials valued Rs. 4,00,000 and wages Rs. 1,00,000 were met from the joint bank account.

On completion of the construction the company paid Rs. 8,00,000, out of which Rs. 4,00,000 in cash (deposited into joint bank account) and the balance of Rs. 4,00,000 in fully paid shares of Rs. 10 each. These shares were sold at Rs. 5.50 each and proceeds taken by D and E in the ratio of 3 : 1. The machine supplied by E was taken by him at an agreed value of Rs. 15,000. Bank charged interest Rs. 1,000 for the overdraft.

Prepare necessary ledger accounts.

Solution

Joint Venture A/c

	Rs.		Rs.
To Co-ventures's a/c		By New Co. a/c	8,00,000
D —Materials	35,000	By Co-venture a/c	
E — Architects fee	15,000	E — Machine taken over	15,000
E — Machine supplied	25,000		
To Joint bank a/c			
— Building materials	4,00,000		
— Wages	1,00,000		
To Shares in new Co. a/c	20,000		
To Interest on over draft	1,000		
To Coventure's a/c — Prompt			
D — 3/5	1,31,400		
E — 2/5	87,600		
	8,15,000		8,15,000

Joint Bank A/c

	Rs.		Rs.
To Co-ventures a/c		By Joint venture a/c	
— D	2,00,000	— Materials	4,00,000
— E	1,00,000	— Wages	1,00,000
To Bank Loan a/c		By Interest on	
O.D	2,00,000	O.D	1,000
To New company a/c	4,00,000	By Overdraft repaid	2,00,000
		By Coventures a/c	
		— D	81,400
		— E	1,17,600
	9,00,000		9,00,000

D's A/c

	Rs.		Rs.
To Shares on new Co. a/c	2,85,000	By Joint Bank a/c	2,00,000
To Joint bank a/c	81,400	By Joint venture a/c	35,000
		By Joint venture a/c	1,31,400
	3,66,400		3,66,400

E's A/c

	Rs.		Rs.
To Shares in new Co. a/c	95,000	By Joint bank a/c	1,00,000
To Joint bank a/c	1,17,600	By Joint venture a/c	15,000
To Joint venture a/c	15,000	By Joint venture a/c	25,000
		By Joint venture a/c	87,600
	2,27,600		2,27,600

Shares in new Co. A/c

	Rs.		Rs.
To New Co. a/c	4,00,000	By Co-venture's a/c Rs. (2,85,000 + 95,000)	3,80,000
		By Joint venture a/c — Loss on shares	20,000
	4,00,000		4,00,000

New Co. A/c

	Rs.		Rs.
To Joint venture a/c	8,00,000	By Joint bank a/c	4,00,000
		By Shares in New Co. a/c	4,00,000
	8,00,000		8,00,000

Problem 12

A, B and C entered into a Joint venture and agreed to divide the profit as 'A' — 60%, B — 30% and C — 10%. They purchased by auction several new machineries for 50,000. 'A' contributed Rs. 30,000, B Rs. 20,000, and C Rs. 10,000 for carrying on the transactions relating to the venture. A Joint bank account was opened. The ventures were successful in selling all the Machineries for Rs. 1,25,000 excepting one machine which had to be scrapped and it fetched Rs. 750 only. 'A' spent Rs. 2,450 and the two other ventures spent Rs. 1,250 each in connection with the venture.

You are required to give the necessary entries to record the above transactions and close the accounts of the ventures.

Solution

Journal Entries

Date	*Particulars*	*L.F.*	*Dr. Amount*	*Cr. Amount*
	Joint Bank a/c Dr.		60,000	
	To 'A' a/c			30,000
	To B' a/c			20,000
	To C's a/c			10,000
	(Being the amount of capital contributed by venturers)			
	Joint venture a/c Dr.		50,000	
	To Joint bank a/c			50,000
	(Being the purchase of machineries)			
	Joint venture a/c Dr.		4,950	
	To A's a/c			2,450
	To B's a/c			1,250
	To C's a/c			1,250
	(Being the expenses paid)			
	Joint bank a/c Dr.		1,25,750	
	To Joint venture a/c			1,25,750
	(Being the sale proceeds)			
	Joint venture's a/c Dr.		70,800	
	To A's a/c			42,480
	To B's a/c			21240
	To C a/c			7080
	(Being the amount of profit transferred)			
	A's a/c		74900	
	B's a/c		42490	
	C's a/c		18330	
	To Joint bank a/c			135750
	(Being the amount with drawn)			

Joint Venture A/c

	Rs.		*Rs.*
To Joint bank	50,000	By Joint bank a/c	1,25,000
To A's a/c — Expenses	2,450	By Joint band a/c	750
To B's a/c — Expenses	1,250		
To C's a/c — Expenses	1,250		
To Profit transferred to			
— A	42,480		
— B	21,240		
— C	7,080		70,800
	1,25,750		1,25,750

Joint Bank A/c

	Rs.		*Rs.*
To A's a/c	30,000	By Joint venture a/c	50,000
To B's a/c	20,000	By A's a/c	74,930
To C's a/c	10,000	By B's a/c	42,490
To Joint venture a/c	1,25,750	By C's a/c	18,330
	1,85,750		1,85,750

A's A/c

	Rs.		*Rs.*
To Joint bank a/c	74,930	By Joint bank a/c	30,000
		By Joint venture a/c	2,450
		By Joint venture a/c	42,480
	74,930		74,930

B's A/c

	Rs.		*Rs.*
To Joint bank a/c	42,490	By Joint bank a/c	20,000
		By Joint venture a/c	1,250
		By Joint venture a/c	21,240
	42,490		42,490

C's A/c

	Rs.		*Rs.*
To Joint bank a/c	18,330	By Joint bank a/c	10,000
		By Joint venture a/c	1,250
		By Joint venture a/c	7,080
	18,330		18,330

Problem 13

A and B doing business separately as building contractors undertake jointly to construct a building for a newly started Joint stock company for a contract price of Rs. 1,00,000 payable as to Rs. 80,000 by instalments in cash and Rs. 20,000 in fully paid shares of the company. A bank account is opened in the Joint names ; A paying in Rs. 25,000 and B Rs. 15,000. They are to share profit & loss in the proportion of 2/3 and 1/3 respectively. Their transactions were as follows :

	Rs.
Paid wages	30,000
Bought Materials	70,000
Materials supplied by A	5,000
Materials supplied by B	4,000
Architects fee paid by A	2,000

The contract was completed and the price (Cash and shares) duly received. The Joint venture was closed by 'A' taking up all the shares of the company at an agreed valuation of Rs. 16,000 and B taking up the stock of materials at an agreed valuation of Rs. 3,000.

Show the necessary ledger accounts.

Solution

Joint Venture A/c

		Rs.			Rs.
To Joint Bank a/c			By Joint Bank a/c		80,000
— Wages	30,000		By Shares a/c		20,000
— Materials a/c	70,000	1,00,000	By B's a/c		
To A's a/c — Materials		5,000	Materials		3,000
To B.s a/c — Materials		4,000	By Loss transferred to		
To A's a/c — Architects fee		2,000	— A	8,000	
To Shares a/c — Loss		4,000	— B	4,000	
					12,000
		1,15,000			1,15,000

Joint Bank A/c

	Rs.		Rs.
To A's a/c	25,000	By Joint Venture a/c	
To B's a/c	15,000	— Materials	70,000
To Joint venture a/c	80,000	— Wages	30,000
		By A's a/c	8,000
		By B's a/c	12,000
	1,20,000		1,20,000

A's A/c

	Rs.		Rs.
To Shares a/c	16,000	By Joint Bank a/c	25,000
To Joint ventures a/c		By Joint venture a/c	5,000
— loss	8,000	By Joint venture a/c	2,000
To Joint Bank a/c	8,000		
	32,000		32,000

B's A/c

	Rs.		Rs.
To Joint venture a/c	3,000	By Joint bank a/c	15,000
To Joint venture a/c		By Joint venture a/c	4,000
— loss	4,000		
To Joint bank a/c	12,000		
	19,000		19,000

Share's A/c

	Rs.		Rs.
To Joint venture a/c	20,000	By A' a/c	16,000
		By Joint venture a/c (loss)	4,000
	20,000		20,000

Problem 14

A and B entered into a Joint venture of underwriting the subscription at par of 50,000 shares of Rs. 10 each of a Joint stock company. They agreed to share profit & losses in the ratio of 3/5 and 2/5 respectively. The consideration for guaranteeing the subscription was 500 other shares of Rs. 10 each fully paid to be issued to them. The public took up 48,000 of the shares and the remaining shares of the guaranteed issue were taken up by A and B who provided cash equally. The entire shareholding of the venture was then sold through other brokers - 60% at a price of Rs. 9.50 less brokerage 50 paise per share, 20% at Rs. 9.75 less brokerage, 50 paise per share and the balance were taken over by A and B equally at Rs. 9 per share.

Prepare a Joint venture a/c, the Joint Bank a/c and the Venturer's Personal a/c

Solution

Joint Venture A/c

		Rs.		Rs.
To Joint bank a/c			By Joint bank a/c	
— Cost of 2,000 shares		20,000	— Sale of 60% of shares	13,500
To Profit			By Joint bank a/c	
— A	1575		— Sale of 20% of shares	4,625
— B	1,050	2,625	By A's a/c — 1/2 of 20% of total shares	2,250
			By B's a/c — 1/2 of 20% of total share	2,250
		22,625		22,625

Joint Bank A/c

	Rs.		Rs.
To A's a/c — 50% of Contribution	10,000	By Joint venture a/c	20,000
To B's a/c — 50% of Contribution	10,000	By A's final settlement	9,325
To Joint venture a/c		By B's — Final settlement	8,800
— Sale of 1,500 shares	13,500		
To Joint venture a/c			
— Sale of 500 shares	4,625		
	38,125		38,125

A's A/c

	Rs.		Rs.
To Joint venture a/c	2,250	By Joint bank a/c	10,000
(250 shares taken)		By Joint venture a/c — 3/5 share	1,575
To Joint bank a/c	9325		
	11,575		11,575

B's A/c

	Rs.		Rs.
To Joint venture a/c 250 shares taken up	2,250	By Joint bank a/c	10,000
To Joint bank a/c	8,800	By Joint venture 2/5th share	1,050
	11,050		11,050

QUESTIONS

Answer the following questions in about four lines.

1. What do you mean by Joint venture ?
2. State any four features of Joint venture.
3. State any four differences between a consignment and Joint venture.
4. State any four difference between a partnership and Joint venture.
5. What is the relationship that exists between venturers in a Joint venture.
6. Mention 2 methods under which joint venture account are prepared.

EXERCISE 1

A and B enter into a Joint venture. They agree to share profits and losses as A — 75% and B — 25%. On 1-1-2004 'A' sends Rs. 50,000 to B. The latter purchases several varieties of silk goods and sends them on to A. The particulars of such purchases are given below :

1,000 Ladies garments @ Rs. 10 each Rs. 10,000, 2,000 silk shirts @ Rs. 15 each, Rs. 30,000, 500 silk children garments @ Rs. 20 each Rs. 10,000.

The expenses incurred by B amount to Rs. 500. A sells the first two varieties at double the price but in respect of children garments he made profit of Rs. 5,000 only. His expenses amounted Rs. 2,000.

Prepare a Joint venture a/c, ascertain the net profit, distribute the same between venturers and close the accounts.

EXERCISE 2

A in Bangalore enters into a Joint venture with B in Bombay to ship cotton bales to C in Japan. A sends cotton to the value of Rs. 30,000 pays railway freight etc. Rs. 1,500, and sundry expenses Rs. 1,575. B sends goods valued at Rs. 20,750 and pays freight and Insurance Rs. 1200. Dock dues Rs. 200, customs charges Rs. 500 and other sundry expenses Rs. 500. 'A' advance to 'B' Rs. 6,000 on account of the venture. 'B' receives account sales and remittance of the net proceeds from 'C' in Japan for the whole of the goods amounting to Rs. 80,000.

Show how the joint venture a/c and 'A' or 'B' a/c would appear in the books of A and B respectively.

EXERCISE 3

P and Q enter into a Joint venture. P supplies goods worth Rs. 6,000 and spends Rs. 100 on various expenses. Q sells the entire lot for Rs. 7,350 meeting selling expenses amounting to Rs. 180. Q remits to P the amount due.

Record the above mentioned transactions in the books of both the parties.

EXERCISE 4

In a Joint venture, 'A' contributes Rs. 5,000 and B contributes Rs. 10,000. Goods are purchased for Rs. 11,200. Expenses amount to Rs. 750. Sales amount to Rs. 13,050 the remaining goods were taken up by B at an agree price of Rs. 500. A and B share profit and losses in the ratio of 1 : 2 respectively. Accounts are duly settled.

Record the transactions in the separate set of books maintained for Joint venture.

EXERCISE 5

Ram and Shyam were partners in a Joint venture sharing profit & losses in the ratio of 3 : 2 respectively. Ram supplied goods to the value of Rs. 15,000 and incurred expenses amounting to Rs. 2,500. Shyam supplied goods to the value of Rs. 20,000 and incurred expenses amounting to Rs. 3,000.

Ram sold all the goods an behalf of the joint venture and realised Rs. 50,000. He was entitled to a commission of 5% on sales. Ram settled his accounts with Shyam by a bank draft.

Give Journal entries in the books of Ram and ledger accounts in the books of Shyam.

EXERCISE 6

A and B entered into a Joint venture to buy and sell certain second hand materials. B is to look after the repair and sale for which he is entitled to a commission of 2% on gross sales. The profits & losses are to be shared equally.

'A' purchased materials worth Rs. 31,200 and paid for carriage and repairs Rs. 4,800. 'B' purchased materials amounting to Rs. 13,800 and contributed out of his own stock, goods worth Rs. 10,000. He spent for carriage and repairs Rs. 9,460 and sent a Bill to A for Rs. 9,000 in advance.

'B' sold all the goods for Rs. 82,000. A is to be credited with Rs. 300 as rent for his storage. Write the necessary journal entries and open ledger accounts in the books of both the parties.

EXERCISE 7

A of Ahmedabad and B of Bangalore enter into a Joint venture to consign 100 sales of cloth to 'C' of Calcutta to be sold on then Joint risk. Profits & losses are to be shared in the ratio of 3 : 2 respectively. 'A' sends 90 bales at Rs. 1,200 each.paying freight and other charges

Rs. 1,800, 'B' sends 10 bales at Rs. 1,100 each, paying for freight and other charges Rs. 300. 'B' advances, Rs. 15,000 to 'A' on Joint venture a/c. All the bales are sold by C for Rs. 1,40,000 out of which he deducts Rs. 1,600 for his expenses and his commission at 3% on sales. 'C' remits Rs. 1,04,200 to 'A' and the remaining amount to 'B'.

Prepare Joint venture a/c, and co-venture's account in the books of both the parties.

EXERCISE 8

Akbar and Babar entered into Joint venture for buying and selling second hand materials. They agreed to share profits and losses in the ratio of 3 : 2.

Akbar purchased materials costing Rs. 75,000 and paid Rs. 300 for carriage, Rs. 1,000 as commission on sales and incurred Rs. 500 towards travelling expenses. He affected sales amounting to Rs. 60,000.

Babar paid Rs. 200 for sundry expenses and Rs. 500 for commission on sales. He effected sales amounting to Rs. 25,000. Goods costing Rs. 4,000 were unsold and the same were taken over by them in their profit sharing ratios.

You are required to show the necessary accounts in the books of Akbar and Babar.

EXERCISE 9

Ananth and Bhaskar entered into joint venture to divide profits in the ratio of 3 : 2 respectively by doing business under joint venture. They opened a Joint account in bank with Rs. 40,000 for Joint venture. In this account Ananth deposited Rs. 24,000 and Bhaskar deposited Rs. 16,000. They gave Rs. 10,000 to their agent, Ramesh for purchasing coal. They paid Rs. 1,000 for freight, Rs. 500 for insurance and Rs. 500 for Miscellaneous Expenses. They paid Rs. 1,000 commission. They sold coal for Rs. 40,000. Unsold coal was purchased by Ananth for Rs. 6,000. The Joint Bank account is closed. Prepare necessary accounts.

EXERCISE 10

S, B and G entered into a Joint venture to construct a building for Mohan for Rs. 5,00,000. This amount was to be paid as under.

Rs. 4,00,000 in cash and as 1,00,000 in debentures. They share profits & losses equally. S, B and G contributed Rs. 60,000 Rs. 75,000 and Rs. 40,000 in Joint venture. All these amount were deposited in Joint bank account. S paid Rs. 7,000 fee to the architect and 'B' purchased concrete mixer for Rs. 25,000. 'G' purchased a motor truck for Rs. 20,000 for the work of Joint venture. They purchased in cash a plant for Rs. 24,000 and material of Rs. 2,40,000. They paid Rs. 1,95,000 for wages. After construction of the house, unused materials of Rs. 14,000 was taken over by 'S' and 'B' took over unused concrete mixer for Rs. 12,000. 'G' took back the motor lorry for Rs. 8,000. Plant was sold Rs. 6,000. When full amount of contract was received, 'S' took over debentures for Rs. 80,000.

Prepare Joint venture a/c, Joint bank a/c, debentures a/c, and 'S', 'B' and 'G' a/c.

14

CHAPTER

Depreciation Accounting

MEANING OF DEPRECIATION

Depreciation is the gradual and permanent decrease in the value of an asset from any cause. It has been defined as the dimunition in intrinsic value of an asset due to its use or lapse of time. Pickles has defined it as the permanent and continuing diminution in the quality, quantity or value of an asset.

The American Institute of certified public accountants has defined Depreciation accounting as "System of accounting which aims to distribute the cost or other value of tangible capital assets less salvage (if any) over the estimated useful life of the asset in a systematic and rational manner". It is a process of allocation and not of valuation.

DEPLETION

Depletion or exhaustion refers to the reduction in the workable quantity of a wasting asset. For example, a forest gets depleted when timber is constantly used. Similarly a mine gets exhausted when the mineral contents are extracted and a time comes when it becomes valueless. This kind of loss is called depletion or exhaustion. Unlike depreciation, which is gradual, depletion is in steps and is not uniform over different periods.

OBSOLESCENCE

Obsolescence represents loss in the value of in asset on account of its becoming obsolete or out of date. Due to technological improvements or market changes production with in existing machine may become unprofitable. The loss arising due to these factors is known as "obsolescence". It differs from depreciation in that it is a sudden loss while depreciation is a gradual loss.

FLUCTUATION

Fluctuation is a temporary variation in the market price of an asset due to the operation of the forces of demand and supply. The main points of distinction between depreciation and fluctuation are as follows :

Depreciation	*Fluctuation*
1. Depreciation is the permanent fall in the book value of an asset	1. Fluctuation is the temporary variation or change in the market value of an asset
2. Depreciation is concerned with the books value of an asset	2. Fluctuation is concered with the market value of an asset
3. Depreciation always represents a fall in the value of an asset.	3. Fluctuation may represent either a fall or rise in the value
4. Depreciation is concerned with the fixed - assets	4. Fluctuation is concerned with the floating assets
5. Depreciation is due to wear and tear, efflux of time, obsolescence etc.	5. Fluctuation is due to the operation of the forces of demand and supply in the market.

CAUSES FOR DEPRECIATION

The following are the causes for depreciation :

(*a*) **Wear and Tear :** When an asset is used it gets worn out. Its parts get loose or broken. Its production capacity or usefulness get reduced. Eventually it may become scrap.

(*b*) **Effect of time :** Certain assets like lease, patents or copy rights lose their value owing to passage of time.

(*c*) **Depletion :** Valuable contents of an asset like mine or quarry get reduced as their resources are extracted year after year and in course of time the entire asset becomes valueless.

(*d*) **Obsolescence :** Due to technological advancement an improved model of an assets is invented making old one uneconomical. So it has to be discarded resulting in loss.

(*e*) **Accident :** When an accident occurs and an asset is damaged or destroyed its value gets reduce or lost.

(*f*) **Permanent fall in the market value :** If the market price of an asset falls on a permanent basis there results a corresponding decline in the value of the asset in use.

OBJECTS OR DEPRECIATION

Depreciation is provided for serving the following objectives

1. **For proper determination of profits.** When business is carried on by using an asset such an asset gets depreciated. Naturally the loss owing to depreciation should be set off against the income in order to determine the true profits.
2. **For ascertainment of cost of Production.** Depreciation is as much an item of production expense as wages, rent etc. though not visible. Hence for the correct ascertainment of cost of production depreciation should be taken into account.
3. **For replacement of Assets.** Providing depreciation ensures that amount required for replacement of an asset at the end of its useful life is made available without causing any stream on the finance of the business.
4. **For meeting legal requirement.** In case of Joint stock companies providing for depreciation is a statutory requirement before declaring dividend.

Factors to be taken into account while calculating depreciation :

The following factors are to be taken into account while providing depreciation.

(a) original cost of the asset.
(b) The estimated scrap or residual value of the asset.
(c) The estimated life of the asset.
(d) The chance of the asset becoming obsolete.
(e) The statute governing the provision of deprecation viz, the companies Act and the Income tax Act.
(f) Sometimes the interest that could have been earned had the money spent in acquiring the asset been invested in interest bearing securities is also taken into account.

METHODS OF RECORDING DEPRECIATION

Depreciation can be recorded in the books of accounts by two different methods :

(*a*) **When a provision for depreciation account is maintained :** Under this method the amount of depreciation to be charged in a particular year is debited to profit & loss account and credited to provision for depreciation account. The asset account appears in the books at original cost.

(*b*) **When provision for depreciation account is not maintained :** Under this method the amount of depreciation is debited to the depreciation account and credited to the asset account. The asset account thus appears in the books at written down value.

METHOD OF PROVIDING DEPRECIATION

The various method of providing depreciation are as follows :

(A) **Uniform charge method :**
- (*i*) Fixed Instalment method.
- (*ii*) Depletion method.
- (*iii*) Machine hour rate method.

(B) **Declining charge method :**
- (*i*) Diminishing balance method.
- (*ii*) Sum of years digits method.
- (*iii*) Double declining method.

(C) **Other method :**
- (*i*) Group depreciation method.
- (*ii*) Inventory system of depreciation.
- (*iii*) Depreciation fund method.
- (*iv*) Insurance policy method.
- (*v*) Annuity method.

(A) Uniform Charge Method

(*i*) **Fixed Instalment method :**

Under this method, the assets are depreciated at a fixed amount through out its life span. The amount of depreciation is calculated by dividing the value of an asset by the number of years of the estimated life of the machine. At the end of its life, the value of the asset will become zero. This method of depreciation is followed where the services rendered by the asset is uniform as in the case of furniture. The following formula is used for calculating depreciation.

$$\text{Depreciation} = \frac{\text{Original cost} - \text{Estimated scrap value}}{\text{Life of the asset in number of years}}$$

Advantages :

(*a*) It is simple to understand and apply.
(*b*) It is possible to reduce the value of the asset to zero under this method.
(*c*) For assets whose life is definite and assets not requiring much of repairs and maintenance, this method of depreciation is ideal.

Disadvantages :

(*a*) This method is not suitable for assets which require considerable expenditure on repairs and maintenance.
(*b*) This method ignores the degree of usage, age and efficiency of the asset.
(*c*) This method ignores interest on the amount invested in the purchase of the asset.

Problem 1

A company purchased a second hand plant for Rs. 30,000. It immediately spent on it Rs. 5,000. The plant was put to use on 1-1-1990. After having used it for 6 years, it was sold for Rs. 15,000. You are required to prepare the plant account for all the six years providing depreciation at 10% p. a. on original cost. **(Madras University, B Com. April 2000).**

Solution

Plant A/c

Date	*Particulars*	*Amount*	*Date*	*Particulars*	*Amount*
	To Cash a/c — Purchase	30,000	31-12-90	By Depreciation $35{,}000 \times \frac{10}{100}$	3,500
	To Cash a/c — Installation	5,000		By Balance c/d	31,500
		35,000			35,000
1-1-91	To Balance b/d	31,500	31-1-91	By Depreciation	3,500
				By Balance c/d	28,000
		31,500			31,500
1-1-92	To Balance b/d	28,000	31-11-92	By Depreciation	3,500
				By Balance c/d	24,500
		28,000			28,000
1-1-93	To Balance b/d	24,500	31-11-93	By Depreciation	3,500
				By Balance c/d	21,000
		24,500			24,500
1-1-94	To Balance b/d	21,000	31-12-94	By Depreciation	3,500
				By Balance c/d	17,500
		21,000			21,000
1-1-95	To Balance b/d	17,500	31-12-95	By Depreciation	3,500
	To P& C a/c (Profit of sale)	1,000		By Cash — Sales	15,000
		18,500			18,500

Working Note :-

Calculation of profit or loss on sale of plant :

Cost of Machine	35,000
Less : Depreciation upto 6 years = 3,500 × 6 years books value	21,000
	14,000
Less : Sale value	15,000
Profit on sale	1,000

Problem 2

A trader purchased a machine on 1st January, 1990 at a cost of Rs. 50,000. It was estimated Rs. 5,000 as its scrap value and the life of the machine for 5 years. On 1st January, 1992 the machine was sold at Rs. 30,000 and another machine of the same type was purchased at a cost of Rs. 25,000 on that day. The scrap value of the machine was estimated at Rs. 3,000 and the life of the machine was 10 years. The installation cost of 1st and 2nd machine were Rs. 5,000 and Rs. 1,000 respectively. Show the machine a/c and depreciation a/c for 1990, 1991 and 1992. **(Calcutta University B. com. (Pass) 1999)**

Solution

Machine A/c

Date	*Particulars*	*Amount*	*Date*	*Particulars*	*Amount*
1-1-90	To Bank a/c (cost)	5,000	31-12-90	By depreciation a/c	10,000
				By Balance c/d	45,000
	To Bank a/c (Installation)	5,000			
		55,000			55,000
1-1-91	To Balance b/d	45,000	31-12-91	By Depreciation a/c	10,000
				By Balance c/d	35,000
		45,000			45,000
1-1-92	To Balance b/d	35,000	31-12-92	By Bank a/c (sold)	30,000
	To Bank a/c (cost)	25,000		By P & L a/c (loss on sale)	5,000
	To Bank a/c (Installation)	1,000		By Depreciation a/c	2,300
				By Balance c/d	23,700
		61,000			61,000

Depreciation A/c

Date	*Particulars*	*Amount*	*Date*	*Particulars*	*Amount*
31-12-90	To Machine a/c	10,000		By P & L a/c	10,000
31-12-91	To Machine a/c	10,000		By P & L a/c	10,000
31-12-92	To Machine a/c	2,300		By P & L a/c	2,300

Working note :

1. **Depreciation of the first machine per year :**

$$= \frac{\text{Cost price} + \text{Installation charges} - \text{Scrap value}}{\text{No. of years}}$$

$$= \frac{50{,}000 + 5{,}000 - 5{,}000}{5} = 10{,}000$$

2. **Depreciation of the second machine per year**

$$= \frac{25{,}000 + 10{,}000 - 3{,}000}{10} = 2{,}300$$

3. **Profit or loss on sale of the first machine**

$$[55{,}000 - (10{,}000 \times 2)] = 30{,}000$$

$$= \text{Loss Rs. } 5{,}000$$

Problem 3

A company whose accounting year is the calender year, purchased on 1st April 1992 machinery costing Rs. 30,000.

It purchased further machinery on 1st October 1992, costing Rs. 20,000 and on 1st July 1993 costing Rs. 10,000. On 1st January 1994 one-third of the machinery installed on 1st April 1992 became obsolete and was sold for Rs. 3,000.

Show how machinery account would appear in the books of the company if that machinery was depreciated by fixed instalment method at 10 percent annum

(Madras University B Com, October 1999)

Solution

Machinery A/c

Date	*Particulars*	*Amount*	*Date*	*Particulars*	*Amount*
1-4-92	To Cash — Purchases	30,000	31-12-92	By Depreciation (2,250 + 500)	2,750
1-10-92	To Cash — Purchases	20,000		By Balance c/d	47,250
		50,000			50,000
1-1-93	To Balance c/d	47250	31-12-93	By Depreciation (3,000 + 2,000 + 500)	5,500
1-7-93	To Cash — Purchases	10,000		By Balance c/d	51,750
		57,250			57,250
1-1-94	To Balance b/d	51,750	1-1-94	By Cash — Sale of machine	3,000
				By Loss on sale	5,250
			31-12-94	By Depreciation (2,000 + 2,000 + 1,000)	5,000
				By Balance c/d	38,500
		51,750			51,750

Working Note — Calculation of Depreciation

Date	*Particulars*	*Machine I*		*Machine II*	*Machine III*
1-4-92	Purchase	30,000		—	—
1-10-92	Purchase	—		20,000	—
31-12-92	**Depreciation :-**				
	Machine — I = $30{,}000 \times \frac{10}{100} \times \frac{1}{12}$	2,250		—	—
	Machine — II = $20{,}000 \times \frac{10}{100} \times \frac{3}{12}$	—		500	—
		27,750		19,500	—
1-7-93	Purchase	—		—	10,000
31-12-93	**Depreciation**				
	Machine I = $30{,}000 \times \frac{10}{100} \times 1\text{Yr}$	3,000		—	—
	Machine II = $20{,}000 \times \frac{10}{100} \times 1\text{Yr}$	—		2,000	—
	Machine III = $10{,}000 \times \frac{10}{100} \times \frac{6}{12}$	—		—	500
		24,750		17,500	9,500
1-1-94		$\frac{1}{3} \times 24{,}750 = 8{,}250$	$\frac{2}{3} \times 24{,}750 = 16{,}500$		
	Loss : Sale of $\frac{1}{3}$rd Machine	3,000			
	Loss on Sale	5,250			
31-12-94	Depreciation :				
	Remaining = $\frac{2}{3} \times 30{,}000 = 20{,}000$				
	Machine I $\left(\frac{2}{3}\right)$ = $20{,}000 \times \frac{10}{100} \times 1\text{ Yr}$	—	2,000	—	—
	Machine II = $20{,}000 \times \frac{10}{100} \times 1\text{ Yr}$	—	—	2,000	—
	Machine III = $10{,}000 \times \frac{10}{100} \times 1\text{ Yr}$	—	—	—	1,000
		Nil	14,500	15,500	8,500

(*ii*) **Depletion Method :** This method is adopted in such cases where it is possible to estimate the probable quantity of output available. Examples such organisation are mines quarries etc. The following factors are taken into account while calculating depreciation.

(*a*) The total amount paid.
(*b*) Estimated quantity of output available.
(*c*) Actual quantity taken out during the said period.

The depreciation is calculated per unit. The formula used is

$$\text{Rate of Depreciation per unit} = \frac{\text{Total cost of the Asset}}{\text{Deworkable Deposit}}$$

The chief advantage of this method is depreication is related with the use of the asset.

(*iii*) **Machine Hour Rate Method :** Under this method depreciation is calculated on the basis time during, which the asset as used. Examples of assets which are depreciated under this method are machinery vehicles etc. The following formula is used to calculate depreciation.

$$\text{Depreciation} = \frac{\text{Original cost of Asset} - \text{Scrap value}}{\text{Life of Asset in Hours}}$$

The main advantage of this method is it is related to actual working time of the asset".

The main disadvantage of this method is that depreciation can be calculated only when the life of asset is measured in terms of hour.

(B) DECLINING CHARGE DEPRECIATION METHODS

The various methods under this category involves reduction in the amount of depreciation charged in subsequent years. These methods are as follows :

1. DIMINISHING BALANCE METHOD OR WRITTEN DOWN VALUE METHOD OR REDUCING BALANCE METHOD.

Under this method the depreciation is calculated every year on the diminishing value of the asset. For example. Suppose the original value of asset is say Rs. 10,000 and the rate of depreciation is say 10 per cent. Then according to this method the asset will be depreciated by Rs. 9,000 in the first year. The diminished value of the asset in the second year will become Rs. 9,000. Then the depreciation for the third year will be charged on 9,000 which works out to Rs. 900 and this practice is continued till the end.

Advantages :

(*a*) For assets like machinery which requires increasing expenditure by way of repairs and maintenance as the assets advance in age this method is the most suitable. This is because while the amount charged by way of depreciation gradually declines the amount charged by way of repairs gradually increase so that the combined charge on the profit by these items will be more of less the same. This makes comparision of profits between different period meaningful.
(*b*) This method is simple to understand and easy to follows :

Disadvantages :

(*a*) The amount of depreciation charged differ from year to year.
(*b*) It is not possible to reduce the value of the asset to zero.

Problem 4

On the 1st January 1992, a limited company purchased a machinery for Rs. 12,000 and on 30th June 1993 it acquired additional machinery at a cost of Rs. 2,000. On 31st March 1994, one of the original machines which had cost Rs. 500 was found to have become obselete and was sold as scrap for Rs. 50. It was replaced on that date by a new machine costing Rs. 800.

Depreciation to be provided @15% p.a. on the written down value. Show ledger accounts for the first three years. **(Madras University B. Com, May 1999)**

Solution

Machinery A/c

Date	*Particulars*	*Amount*	*Date*	*Particulars*	*Amount*
1-1-92	To Cash	12,000	31-11-92	By Depreciation	1,800
				By Balance c/d	10,200
		12,000			12,000
1-1-93	To Balance b/d	10,200	31-12-93	By Depreciation	1,680
30-6-93	To Cash	2,000		By Balance c/d	10,520
		12,200			12,200
1-1-94	To Balance b/d	10,520	31-12-94	By Cash	50
31-3-94	To Cash	500		(Sale of scrap)	
				By Depreciation on Scrap machine (upto March 94)	14
				By P & L a/c (Loss)	297
				By Depreciation on remaining machine	1,614
				By Balance c/d	9,345
		11,320			11,320

Working Note :-

1. Calculation of Depreciation

On 31-12-92 $= 12,000 \times \frac{15}{100} \times 1\text{yr}$ $= 1,800$

On 31-12-93 $= 12,000 - 1,800 = 10,200$

$= 10,200 \times \frac{15}{100}$ $= 1,530$

On 30-6-93 Additional machine

$= 2,000 \times \frac{15}{100} \times \frac{6}{12}$ $= 150$

1,680

Depreciation on Scrap machine

On 31-3-94 Cost of Original Machine 500

Less : Depreciation for 1992

$= 500 \times \frac{15}{100}$ 75

425

Less Depreciation for 1993

$= 425 \times \frac{15}{100}$ 64

	Book value on 1-1-94	361
	Less : Depreciation for 1994 (upto March 94)	
	$= 361 \times \frac{15}{100} \times \frac{3}{12}$	14
		347
	Book value on 31-3-94. Sale of scrap	50
	Loss	297
on 31-12-94	**Depreciation on Remaining Machine**	
	Cost of original machine on 1-1-94	
	= (10,200 – 1,530)	8,670
	Add :- Additional machine on 1-1-94 (2,000-150)	1,850
		10,520
	Less : Book value of scrap machine (sold)	361
		10,159
	$= 10,159 \times \frac{15}{100}$	1,524
	New additional machine on 31-3-1994	
	$= 800 \times \frac{15}{100} \times \frac{9}{12}$	90
	Depreciation on 31-12-94	1,614

Problem 5

X & Co., purchased a machine for Rs. 60,000 on 1st January 1994. On 1st July, 1975, X & Co., sold the machine for Rs. 45,000 and purchased another machine for Rs. 80,000. X & Co., charged depreciation @ 15% under diminishing balance method. The accounts of the business were closed every year on 31st December.

Short the Journal entries for 1994, 1995 and 1996 in the books of X & Co.,

(Calcutta University B. com (Pass) 1997)

Solution

Working Note

1. Depreciation for 1994 = $60,000 \times \frac{15}{100}$ = 9,000
2. Depreciation for 1995 = $(60,000 - 9,000) \times \frac{15}{100} \times \frac{6}{12}$ = 3,825
3. Loss on sale of machine = (60,000 – 9,000 – 3,825 – 45,000) = 2,175
4. Depreciation for 1995 for new machine = $80,000 \times \frac{15}{100} \times \frac{6}{12}$ = 6,000
5. Total Depreciation for 1995 (old + new) = 3,825 + 6,000 = 9,855
6. Depreciation for 1,996 = $(80,000 - 6,000) \times \frac{15}{100} \times \frac{6}{12}$ = 11,100

Journal Entries
In the Books of X & Co.

Date	*Particulars*		*Dr. Amount*	*Cr. Amount*
1-1-94	Machine a/c To Bank a/c (Being machine purchased for cash)	Dr.	60,000	60,000
31-12-94	Depreciation a/c To Machine a/c (Being depreciation charged on machinery @ 15% on diminishing balance method	Dr.	9,000	9,000
31-12-94	Profit & loss a/c To Depreciation a/c (Being depreciation transferred to Profit & Loss a/c)	Dr.	9,000	9,000
1-7-95	Depreciation a/c To Machine a/c (Being depreciation charged @ 15% on machine for 6 months)	Dr.	3,825	3,895
1-7-95	Bank a/c To Machine a/c (Being the machine sold for cash)	Dr.	45,000	45,000
1-7-95	Profit & loss a/c To Machine a/c (Being the loss on sale of Machinery transferred)	Dr.	2,175	2,175
1-7-95	Machine a/c To Bank a/c (Being new machine purchased for cash)	Dr.	80,000	80,000
31-12-95	Depreciation a/c To Machine a/c (Being depreciation charged on new machine @ 15% for 6 months)	Dr.	6,000	6,000
31-12-95	P & L a/c To Depreciation a/c (Being the depreciation transferred to P & L a/c)	Dr.	9,825	9,825
31-12-96	Depreciation a/c To Machine a/c (Being depreciation charged @ 15% on machine)	Dr.	11,100	11,100
31-12-96	Profit & Loss a/c To Depreciation (Being depreciation transferred to P & L a/c)	Dr.	11,100	11,100

(*i*) **Sum of years digits method :** Under this method also the depreciation goes on decreasing every year. The following formula is used.

$$\frac{\text{Remaining life of the asset(taking into account the current year)}}{\text{Sum of the digits of the life of the Assets in years}} \times \text{Cost of acquiring the asset}$$

(*c*) **Other methods :**

(*i*) **Group Depreciation method :-** Under this method, all assets having same average life expectancy are grouped together Depreciation is charged for the group of assets as a whole but not on each machine.

(*ii*) **Inventory system of depreciation :-** This method is adopted in case of assets whose value is small as in the case of tools, cattle etc. The following procedure is followed in calculating depreciation.

	Value of asset at the beginning of the year	XX
Add :	Additions during the year	XX
		XX
Less :	Value of asset at the end year	XX
	Depreciation for the year	XX

(*iii*) **Depreciation fund method or sinking fund method :-** Under this method to facilitate ready replacement of asset without facing a financial problem, the depreciation amount is set aside from the divisible profit every year and a fund known as depreciation fund is created. The fund is invested in good securities. At the time of replacing the asset the securities are sold out and the sale proceeds are utilised for the purchase of the new asset. The following journal entries are passed :

(A) **All the end of first year :**

1. For setting aside the amount of depreciation :
   Depreciation a/c Dr.
   To Depreciation fund a/c
2. For investing the amount of depreciation :
   Depreciation fund Investment a/c Dr.
   To Bank a/c

Note : The depreciation a/c is shown on the debit side of P & L a/c. The Depreciation fund a/c is shown on the liability side of Balance Sheet and Depreciation Fund Investment a/c is shown on the asset side of Balance sheet.

(B) **In the second and subsequent years :**

(*i*) For interest received on Investment
Bank a/c Dr.
To Interest on Depreciation fund Investment a/c

(*ii*) For transferring interest to depreciation fund account.
Interest on depreciation fund —
Investment a/c Dr.
To Depreciation fund a/c

Note : The above two entries may be combined as follows :

Bank a/c Dr.
To Depreciation fund a/c

(*iii*) For annual instalment of depreciation
Depreciation a/c Dr.
To Depreciation Fund a/c

(*iv*) For investing the amount of depreciation and interest received on investment
Depreciation fund investment a/c Dr.
To Bank a/c

(C) **At the end of the last year :** In the last year entries Nos (*i*), (*ii*) and (*iii*) are repeated. The following additional entries are passed.

(*i*) For sale of investment
Bank a/c Dr.
To Dep. fund Investment a/c

(*ii*) For transfer of profit or loss on sale of investment

(*a*) **In case of profit :**
Dep. fund Investment a/c Dr.
To Dep. fund a/c

(*b*) **In case of loss :**
Dep. fund a/c Dr.
To Dep. fund Investment a/c

(*iii*) For recording sale of old asset
Bank a/c Dr.
To Old asset a/c

(*iv*) For transferring depreciation fund a/c to old asset a/c
Depreciation fund a/c Dr.
To Old asset a/c

(*v*) The balance is the old asset a/c represents profit & loss. It will be transferred to P & L a/c.

(*vi*) For purchase of new asset
New asset a/c Dr.
To Bank

Problem 6

A company purchased a machinery for Rs. 25,000 on 1-1-1994. It was decided to make provision of depreciation by means of Depreciation fund. The final investments were expected to fetch interest at 3% p.a. According to depreciation table Rs. 8,088.25 to be invested annually. At the end of the third year the investments realised Rs. 16,400.

Pass Journal entries to record the above transactions and prepare depreciation fund a/c and depreciation fund Investment a/c.

Solution

Journal Entries

Date	*Particulars*		*Dr. Amount*	*Cr. Amount*
1994 Jan. 1	Machinery a/c To Bank a/c (Being machinery purchased)	Dr.	25,000.00	25,000.00
Dec. 31	Depreciation a/c To Depreciation fund a/c (Being the annual depreciation charged).	Dr.	8,088.25	8,088.25
Dec. 31	Depreciation fund Investment a/c To Bank (Being the amount of depreciation fund invested)	Dr.	8,088.25	8,088.25

Date	Particulars		Dr. Amount	Cr. Amount
1995 Dec. 31	Bank a/c	Dr	242.65	
	To Depreciation fund a/c			242.65
	(Being the interest received on Investment credited to fund a/c)			
	Depreciation a/c	Dr.	8,088.25	
	To Depreciation fund a/c			8,088.25
	(Being the annual depreciation amount set aside)			
	Depreciation fund Investment a/c	Dr.	8,330.90	
	To Bank a/c			8,330.90
	(Being amount invested including current years. depreciation of 8088.25 and interest of Rs. 242.65)			
1996 Dec. 31	Bank a/c	Dr.	492.57	
	To Depreciation fund a/c			492.57
	(Being interest received credited to fund a/c)			
	Depreciation a/c	Dr.	8,088.28	
	To Depreciation fund a/c			8,088.28
	(Being annual depreciation)			
	Bank a/c	Dr.	16,400.00	
	To Depreciation fund Investment a/c			16,400.00
	(Being investments realised)			
	Depreciation fund a/c	Dr.	19.15	
	To Depreciation fund Investment a/c			19.15
	(Being the loss on sale of investment transferred)			
	Depreciation fund a/c	Dr.	25,000.00	
	To Machinery a/c			25,000.00
	(Being machinery written off by transfer to fund a/c)			
	Profit & loss a/c	Dr.	19.15	
	To Depreciation fund a/c			19.15
	(Being balance in depreciation fund a/c transferred to P & L a/c)			

Machinery A/c

Date	Particulars	Amount	Date	Particulars	Amount
1-1-94	To Bank	25,000	31-12-94	By Balance c/d	25,000
1-1-95	To Balance b/d	25,000	31-12-95	By Balance c/d	25,000
1-1-96	To Balance b/d	25,000	31-12-96	By Depreciation fund a/c (Transfer)	25,000
		25,000			25,000

Depreciation on A/c

Date	Particulars	Amount	Date	Particulars	Amount
31-12-94	To Dep. fund a/c	8,088.25	31-12-94	By P & L a/c	8,088.25
31-12-95	To Dep. fund a/c	8,088.25		By P & L a/c	8,088.25
31-12-96	To Dep. fund a/c	8,088.25		By P & L a/c	8,088.25

Depreciation Fund A/c

Date	Particulars	Amount	Date	Particulars	Amount
31-12-94	To Balance c/d	8,088.25	31-12-94	By Depreciation a/c	8,088.25
31-12-95	To Balance c/d	16,419.15	1-1-95	By balance b/d	8,088.25
				By Interest on dep. Fund Investment $8{,}088.25 \times \frac{3}{100}$	242.65
				By Depreciation	8,088.25
		16,419.15			16,419.15
31-12-96	To Machinery a/c	25,000.00	1-1-96	By Balance b/d	16,419.15
	To Dep. fund Investment a/c (loss transferred)	19.15		By Interest on Dep. fund Investment $16{,}419.15 \times \frac{3}{100}$	492.57
				By Depreciation (See note -1)	8,088.28
				By P & C a/c (See note-2)	19.15
		25,019.15			25,019.15

Depreciation Fund Investment A/c

Date	Particulars	Amount	Date	Particulars	Amount
31-12-94	To Bank	8,088.25	31-12-94	By Balance c/d	8,088.25
1-1-95	To Balance b/d	8,088.25	31-12-95	By Balance c/d	16419.15
31-12-95	To Bank (8,088.25 + 242.65)	8,330.90			
		16,419.15			16,419.15
1-1-96	To Balance b/d	16,419.15	31-12-96	By Bank	16,400.00
				By Dep. fund a/c (loss on realisation)	19.15
		16,419.15			16,419.15

Interest on Depreciation Fund Investment A/c

Date	Particulars	Amount	Date	Particulars	Amount
31-12-94	To Dep. fund a/c	242.65	31-12-94	By Bank a/c	242.65
31-12-95	To Dep. fund a/c	492.57	31-12-95	By Bank a/c	492.57

Working notes :-

1. In order to make the amount Rs. 25,000, the investment made is Rs. 8,088.28 instead of Rs. 8,088.25.
2. Balance in the Depreciation fund a/c is transferred to P & L a/c. This balance is arrived at as follows :

	Value of Investment realised	16,400.00
Add :	Investment for 1996	8,088.25
Less :	Balance in fund a/c	24,980.85
	Value of Machinery	25,000.00
	Balance in fund a/c	19.15

Problem 7

A concern maintains sinking fund for replacement of machinery. The balance in the relevant account on 1-1-98 are :

	Rs.
Sinking fund	2,50,000
10% sinking fund Investment (Nominal : Rs. 3,00,000)	2,50,000
Machinery at cost	3,00,000

Annual contribution to sinking fund is Rs. 20,000. The investment are sold on 1-1-99 at a net price of 80% of the nominal value. The old machinery is sold for Rs. 30,000 on 1-1-99 and new machinery is purchased for Rs. 3,40,000.

Show ledger accounts in the books of the concern (Calcutta University B.com (Hons.) 2000).

Solution

Sinking Fund

Date	Particulars	Amount	Date	Particulars	Amount
31-12-98	To Balance c/d	2,95,000	1-1-98	By Balance b/d	2,50,000
			31-12-98	By Interest a/c	25,000
				By P & L a/c	20,000
		2,95,000			2,95,000
1-1-99	To Sinking fund Investment a/c (Balance transferred)	55,000	1-1-99	By Balance b/d	2,95,000
		2,95,000			2,95,000

10% Sinking Fund Investments A/c

Date	*Particulars*	*Amount*	*Date*	*Particulars*	*Amount*
1-1-98	To Balance b/d	2,50,000	31-12-98	By Balance c/d	2,95,000
31-12-98	To Bank a/c (Annual contribute ion together with (interest)	45,000			
		2,95,000			2,95,000
1-1-99	To Balance b/d	2,95,000	1-1-99	By Bank a/c (asset old)	2,40,000
				By Sinking fund a/c (loss on sale)	55,000
		2,95,000			2,95,000

Machinery A/c

Date	*Particulars*	*Amount*	*Date*	*Particulars*	*Amount*
1-1-98	To Balance b/d	3,00,000	31-12-98	By Balance c/d	3,00,000
1-1-99	To Balance b/d	3,00,000	1-1-99	By Bank a/c (sold)	30,000
	To Bank a/c (Purchase)	3,40,000		By Sinking fund a/c	2,40,000
				By P & L a/c (Loss on sale)	30,000
				By Balance c/d	3,40,000
		6,40,000			6,40,000

(*iv*) **Insurance Policy method :** Under this method in order to provide for replacement of the asset at the and of its useful life an amount equal to annual depreciation charged is used to pay premium on insurance policy. At the end of the period the insurance company agrees to pay policy value, which is used in purchasing a new asset. The following entries are involved :

(A) **First and subsequent years :** In the beginning of the year for paying insurance premium.

Depreciation Insurance policy a/c Dr.
    To Bank a/c

At the end of the year

Profit & loss a/c Dr.
    To depreciation reserve a/c

(B) **At the end of the last year :** When money is received from Insurance Co.

Bank a/c Dr.
    To Depriciation Insurance Policy a/c :

For transfer of profit on insurance policy

Dep. Insurance policy a/c Dr.
    To Depreciation reserve a/c

For transfer of accumulated depreciation to the asset a/c

Depreciation reserve a/c Dr.
To Asset a/c

When new asset is purchased

New asset a/c Dr.
To Bank

Problem 8

A firm purchases a lease for 3 years for 30,000 on 1-1-1997. It decided to provide for its replacement by means of Insurance policy for Rs. 30,000. The annual premium is Rs. 9,500 on 1-1-2000. The lease is renewed for a further period of 3 years for Rs. 30,000. Pass the necessary Journal entries and prepare various ledger accounts to record the above transactions.

Solution

Journal Entries

Date	*Particulars*		*Dr. Amount*	*Cr. Amount*
1-1-97	Depreciation Insurance policy a/c	Dr	9,500	
	To Bank			9,500
	(Being the insurance premium paid)			
31-12-97	P & L a/c	Dr	9,500	
	To Depreciation reserve a/c			9,500
	(Being depreciation provided out of profit)			
1-1-98	Dep Insurance policy a/c	Dr	9,500	
	To Bank a/c			9,500
	(Being depreciation provided out of profit)			
31-12-98	P & L a/c	Dr	9,500	
	To Dep reserve a/c			9,500
	(Being depreciation provided out of profit)			
31-12-99	Bank a/c	Dr	30,000	
	To Dep. Insurance policy a/c			30,000
	(Being the receipt of the policy amount on maturity)			
	Dep Insurance policy a/c	Dr	1,500	
	To Dep. reserve a/c			1,500
	(Being the transfer of profit on Insurance policy)			
	Depreciation Reserve a/c	Dr	30,000	
	To Lease a/c			30,000
	(Being transfer of accumulated depreciation to lease a/c)			
1-1-2000	New Lease a/c	Dr	30,000	
	To Bank a/c			30,000
	(Being lease renewed for further 3 years)			

Lease A/c

Date	Particulars	Amount	Date	Particulars	Amount
1-1-97	To Bank	30,000	31-12-97	By Balance c/d	30,000
1-1-98	To Balance b/d	30,000	31-12-98	By Balance c/d	30,000
1-1-99	To Balance b/d	30,000	31-12-99	By Depreserve a/c	30,000

Depreciation Reserve A/c

Date	Particulars	Amount	Date	Particulars	Amount
31-12-97	To Balance c/d	9,500	31-12-97	By P& L a/c	9,500
31-12-98	To Balance c/d	19,000	1-1-98	By Balance b/d	9,500
			31-12-98	By P & L a/c	9,500
		19,000			19,000
31-12-99	To Lease a/c	30,000	1-1-99	By Balance b/d	19,000
				By P & L a/c	9,500
				By Insurance policy a/c	1,500
		30,000			30,000

Dep Insurance Policy A/c

Date	Particulars	Amount	Date	Particulars	Amount
1-1-97	To Bank — Premium	9,500	31-12-97	By Balance c/d	9,500
1-1-98	To Balance b/d	9,500	31-12-98	By Balance c/d	19,000
	To Bank — Premium	9,500			
		19,000			19,000
1-1-99	To Balance b/d	19,000	31-12-99	By Bank — Policy realised	30,000
	To Bank — Premium	9,500			
31-12-99	To Dep. Reserve a/c	1,500			
		30,000			30,000

(*v*) **Annuity method :** This method is based on the presumption that when an asset is used in a business the total loss to the business during the life of the asset is not only the original cost of the asset but also the interest which could have been otherwise earned had the money spent in the acquisition of the asset was invested in interest bearing securities. So under this system not only the original cost of the asset but also the interest on the money invested on the asset is written off as depreciation over the life of the asset. The amount of depreciation is uniform and is determined on the basis of annuity table. The following Journal entries are passed.

1. When the asset is purchased
   Asset a/c Dr.
   To Bank
2. When interest is charged to the asset
   Asset a/c Dr.
   To Interest a/c

3. When depreciation is charged
   Depreciation a/c Dr.
   To Asset a/c
4. When interest a/c is transferred to P & L a/c
   Interest a/c Dr
   To P & L a/c
5. When depreciation a/c is transferred to P & L a/c.
   P & L a/c Dr
   To Depreciation a/c

Problem 9

Vikrant tyres took a property on lease for Rs. 60,000 for 5 years on 1-1-95. It was decided to charge depreciation on Annuity method. As per annuity table Re. 1 for 5 years at 5% p.a. would be Re. 0.230975.

Show the lease account and Interest a/c for 5 years.

Solution

Working Note

Annual charge to depreciation is

Re. 0.230975 × Rs. 60,000 = Rs. 13,858.50

Lease A/c

Date	Particulars	Amount	Date	Particulars	Amount
1-1-95	To Bank a/c	60,000.00	31-12-95	By depreciation	13,858.50
31-12-95	To Interest a/c $= 60{,}000 \times \frac{5}{100}$	3,000.00		By Balance c/d	49,141.50
		63,000.00			63,000.00
1-1-96	To Balance b/d	49,141.50	31-12-96	By depreciation	13,858.50
	To Interest $= 49{,}141.50 \times \frac{5}{100}$	2,457.10		To Balance c/d	37,740.10
		51,598.60			51,598.60
1-1-97	To Balance b/d	37,740.10	31-12-97	By Depreciation	13,858.50
31-12-97	To Interest $= 37{,}740.10 \times \frac{5}{100}$	1,887.00		By Balance c/d	25,768.60
		39,627.10			39,627.10
1-1-98	To Balance b/d	25,768.60	31-12-98	By Depreciation	13,858.50
31-12-98	To Interest $= 25{,}768.60 \times \frac{5}{100}$	1,288.45		By Balance c/d	13,198.55
		27,057.05			27,057.05
1-1-99	To Balance b/d	13,198.55	31-12-99	By Depreciation	13,858.50
31-12-99	To Interest $= 13{,}198.55 \times \frac{5}{100}$	659.50			
		13,858.50			13,858.50

Interest A/c

Date	Particulars	Amount	Date	Particulars	Amount
31-12-95	To P & L a/c	3,000.00	31-12-95	By Lease a/c	3,000.00
31-12-96	To P & L a/c	2,457.10	31-12-96	By Lease a/c	2,457.10
31-12-97	To P & L a/c	1,887.00	31-12-97	By Lease a/c	1,887.00
31-12-98	To P & L a/c	1,288.45	31-12-98	By Lease a/c	1,288.45
31-12-99	To P & L a/c	659.95	31-12-98	By Lease a/c	659.95

CHANGE OF METHOD

In order to get consistency in the profit and loss a/c it is necessary to follow the same method of depreciation through out the life of the business. Sometimes the method of depreciation is changed and such a change may be effected either from the year of change or with retrospective effect.

Problem 10

X company purchased a machine on 1st April 1995, for 1,60,000 on October 1 1996, another machine was purchased for Rs. 1,04,000. On October 1, 1997 the first machine was sold for Rs. 1,20,000. On the same date another machine was purchased for Rs. 1,00,000. On October 1 1998, the second machine was sold for Rs. 92,000.

Rate of depreciation was 10% on original cost annually on 31st March. In 1998, the method of charging depreciation was changed to diminishing balance method, the rate being 15%.

Prepare machine account for the years ending 31st March 1996, 1997, 1998 and 1999.

(Delhi University, B.Com (Hons.) 1999).

Solution

Machinery A/c for 31-3-1996

Date	Particulars	Amount	Date	Particulars	Amount
1-4-95	To Vendor's a/c	1,60,000	31-3-96	By Depreciation a/c on machine — I (10% p.a. SLM)	16,000
			31-3-96	By Balance c/d Machine I	1,44,000
		1,60,000			1,60,000

Machinery A/c for 31-3-97

Date	Particulars	Amount	Date	Particulars	Amount
1-4-96	To Balance b/d Machine I	1,44,000	31-3-97	By Depreciation a/c	
				Machine I (@ 10% p.a. SLM)	16,000
1-10-96	To Vendor a/c Machine II	1,04,000		Machine II (@ 10% p.a. S.L.M for 6 months)	5,200
			31-3-97	By Balance c/d	
				Machine I	1,28,000
				Machine II	98,800
		2,48,000			2,48,000

Machinery A/c for 31-3-98

Date	Particulars	Amount	Date	Particulars	Amount
1-4-97	To Balance b/d		1-10-97	By Depreciation a/c	
	Machine I	1,28,000		Machine I	8,000
	Machine II	98,000		(@ 10% p.a. SLM for 6 months)	
1-10-97	To Vendor's a/c				
	Machine III	1,00,000	1-10-97	By Bank a/c	1,20,000
				By Depreciation a/c	
				Machine II	10,400
				(@ 10% p.a. SLM)	
				Machine III	5,000
				(@ 10% p.a. SLM for 6 months)	
			31-3-98	By Balance c/d	
				Machine II	88,400
				Machine III	95,000
		3,26,800			3,26,800

Machinery A/c for 31-3-99

Date	Particulars	Amount	Date	Particulars	Amount
1-4-98	To Balance b/d		1-10-98	By Depreciation a/c	
	Machine I	Nil		Machine II	6,630
	Machine II	88,400		(@ 15% p.a. DBM for 6 months)	
	Machine III	9,50,00			
1-10-98	To Profit on sale of		1-10-98	By Bank a/c	92,000
	Machine II a/c	10,230	31-3-99	By Depreciation a/c	
				Machine III	14,250
				(@ 15% p.a. DBM)	
			31-3-99	By Balance c/d	
				Machine III	80,750
		1,93,630			1,93,630

Note :

It is mentioned in the problem that depreciation method is changed from 1st April 1998. So DBM @ 15% p.a. is applied on machine II as well which is sold on 1-10-98 making a profit on its sale of Rs. 10,230.

Problem 11

Deva Ltd. charges depreciation on its plant and machinery @ 10% per annum on the diminishing balance method. On 31st March 2,000 the company decides to adopt straight line method of changing depreciation with retrospective effect from 1st April 1996, the rate of depreciation being 15%. On 1st April the plant and Machinery account stood in the books at Rs. 2,91,600. On 1st July 1999, a sum of Rs. 65,000 was realised by selling a machine, cost of which on 1st April 1996 was Rs. 90,000. On 1st January 2000 a new machine was acquired at a cost of Rs. 1,50.000.

Show the plant and machinery a/c in the books of the company for the year ended 31st 2000 (CS foundation June 2000).

Solution

Plant and Machinery A/c

Date	*Particulars*	*Amount*	*Date*	*Particulars*	*Amount*
1-4-99	To Balance b/d	2,91,600	1-7-99	By Bank	65,000
1-7-99	To P & L a/c (Profit on sale)	1,030		By Depreciation a/c (On machinery sold)	1,640
1-1-2000	To Bank — Purchase of new machine	1,50,000	31-3-2000	By P & L a/c (additional depreciation)	55,490
				By Depreciation a/c (Old Machine)	46,500
				By Depreciation a/c (on new machine)	5,625
				By Balance c/d	2,68,375
		4,42,630			4,42,630

Working Notes :

1. If cost of machinery is 100 on 1st April 1996, written down value of Machinery on 1st April 1999 @ 10% depreciation on diminishing balance method will be = Rs. 100-10-9-8.1 = Rs. 72.9.
2. **Calculation of profit or loss on sale of machinery :**

Cost of machinery on 1-4-1996	90,000
Written down value on 1-4-1999 $= 90{,}000 \times \frac{72.9}{100}$	65,610
Less : Depreciation from 1st April 1999 till 1st July 1999 $= 65{,}610 \times \frac{3}{12} \times \frac{10}{100}$	1,640
Written down value on 1-7-99	63,970
Sale proceeds	65,000

Profit on sale = Rs. 65,000 – 63,970 = Rs. 1,030

3. **Additional Depreciation :**

Written down value of machinery on 1st April 1996	2,91,600
Cost on 1st April 1996 $= 2{,}91{,}600 \times \frac{100}{72.9}$	4,00,000
Less : Cost of machinery sold	90,000
Cost of remaining machinery	3,10,000
Written down value of remaining machinery on 1st April 1999 $= 3{,}10{,}000 \times \frac{72.9}{100}$	2,25,900

	Cost of remaining machines as on 1-4-96 =	3,10,000
Less :	Depreciation for three years @ 15% p.a. on straight the method	
	$= 3,10,000 \times \frac{45}{100} =$	1,30,500
	Written down value as per new method	1,70,500

Additional depreciation to be debited to profit and loss account.
$= 2,25,990 - 1,70,500 =$ Rs. 55,490

4. Depreciation on Rs. 3,10,000 @ 15% for full year = Rs. 46,500
5. Depreciation on Rs. 1,50,000 @ 15% for three months.

$$= 1,50,000 \times \frac{15}{100} \times \frac{3}{12} = \text{Rs. } 5,625$$

Accounting Standard 6 (Revised) Depreciation Accounting

Accounting standard-6 applies to all depreciable assets except the following items to which special considerations apply :

1. Forest, plantation or similar regenerative natural resources.
2. Wasting assets including expenditure on the exploration for and extraction of mineral oil, natural gas and similar non- regenerative resources.
3. Expenditure on research and development.
4. Goodwill.
5. Livestock.

And also land unless it has. a limited useful life for the enterprise.

Definitions :

(*a*) **Depreciation :** Depreciation is a measure of the wearing out, consumption or other loss of value of a depreciable asset arising from use, efflusion of time or obsolescence through technology and market changes. Depreciation is allocated so as to charge a fair proportion of the depreciable amount in each accounting period during the expected useful life of the asset. Depreciation includes amortisation of assets whose useful life is predetermined.

Depreciable assets :

Depreciable assets are assets which

(*i*) are expected to be used during more than one accounting period.
(*ii*) have a limited useful life and
(*iii*) use held by an enterprise for use in the production or supply of goods and services, for rental to others or for administrative purposes and not for the purpose of sale in the ordinary course of business.

Useful Life :

Useful life is either (*i*) The period over which a depreciable asset is expected to be used by the enterprise or (*ii*) The number of production or similar units expected to be obtained from the use of the asset by the enterprise.

Depreciable amount :

Depreciable amount of a depreciable asset is its historical cost or other amount substituted for historical cost in the financial statements, less the estimated residual value.

Accounting standard :

1. The depreciable amount of a depreciable asset should be allocated on a systematic basis to each accounting period during the useful life of the asset.
2. The depreciation method selected should be applied consistently from period to period. A change from one method of providing depreciation to another should made only if the adoption of the new method is required by statute or for compliance with an accounting standard or if it is considered that the change would result in more appropriate preparation or presentation of the financial statements of the enterprise. When such a change in the method of depreciation is made. Depreciation should be recalculated in accordance with the new method form the date of the asset coming into use. The deficiency of surplus rasing from retrospective recomputation of depreciation in accordance with the new method should be adjusted in the accounts in the year in which the method of depreciation is charged. In case the change in the method results in deficiency in depreciation in respect of past years, the deficiency should be charged in the statement of profit and loss. In case the change in the method results in surplus, the surplus should be credited to the statement of profit and loss. Such a change should be treated as a change in accounting policy and its effect should be quantified and disclosed.
3. The useful life of a depreciable asset should be estimated after considering the following factors :
   (*i*) Expected physical wear and tear.
   (*ii*) Obsolescence.
   (*iii*) Legal or other limits on the use of the asset.
4. The useful lives of major depreciable assets or classes of depreciable assets may be revienied periodically. Where there is a revision of the estimated useful life of an asset, the unamortised depreciable amount should be charged over the revised remaining useful life.
5. Any addition or extension which becomes an integral part of the existing asset should be depreciated over the remaining useful life of that asset. The depreciation on such addition or extension may also be provided at the rate applied to existing asset. Where an addition or extension retains a separate identity and is capable of being used after the existing asset is disposed of depreciation should be provided independently on the basis of an estimate of its own useful life.
6. Where the historical cost of a depreciable asset has undergone a change due to increase or decrease in the long term liability on account of exchange fluctuations, price adjustments, changes in duties or similar factors the depreciation on the revised unamortised depreciable amount should be provided prospectively over the residual useful life of the asset.
7. Where the depreciable assets are revalued the provision for depreciation should be based on the revalued amount and on the estimate of the remaining useful lives of such assets. In the case the revaluation has a material effect on the amount of depreciation, the same should be disclosed separately in the year in which revaluation is carried out.
8. If any depreciable asset is disposed of discarded, demolished or destroyed the net surplus or deficiency, if material, should be disclosed separately.
9. The following information should be disclosed in the financial statements.
   (*i*) The historical cost or other amount substituted for historical cost of each class of depreciable assets.

(*ii*) Total depreciation for the period for each class of assets and
(*iii*) The related accumulated depreciation.

10. The following information should also be disclosed in the financial statements along with the discloser of other accounting polices.
    (*i*) Depreciation method used.
    (*ii*) Depreciation rates.

QUESTIONS

1. What is depreciation ?
2. What is depletion ?
3. What is obsolescence ?
4. What is “straight line method” of charging depreciation ?
5. What do you mean by “diminishing balance method” ?
6. Give the meaning of “Revaluation method” of depreciation.
7. What is “Annuity method” of depreciation ?
8. What is “Sinking fund ” method of depreciation ?
9. What is “Insurance policy method” of depreciation ?
10. Write a note on “ Machine hour method” of depreciation ?

EXERCISE 1

(Straight Line Method)

Jain Bros acquired a machine on 1st July 2000 at a cost of Rs. 14,000 and spent Rs. 1,000 on its installation. The firm writes off depreciation at 10% of the original cost every year. The books are closed on 31st December every year. On 31st March 2003 the machine is sold for Rs. 9,500. Show the machinery account and depreciation account.

Answer : Machinery a/c total for the year 2003 is Rs. 1,1250.

EXERCISE 2

(Diminishing Balance Method)

The Machinery account of a factory showed a balance of Rs. 3,80,000 on 1st January 1997. The accounts are closed every year on 31st December. Depreciation is written off @ 10% on diminishing balance. On 1st June 1997 new machinery was acquired at a cost of Rs. 57,783 and on the same date a machine which had cost Rs. 12,000 on 1st January 1992 was sold for Rs. 1,500 and another machine which had cost Rs. 1,200 on 1st January 1993 was scraped without realising any thing. Show the machinery a/c for the year 1997

(University of Madras B. com May 1998)

Answer. Total of Machinery a/c for 1993 Rs. 4,37,783.

EXERCISE 3

(Annuity Method)

On 1st January 1999 a company purchased a lease for a term of 4 years costing Rs. 20,000. You find from the annuity tables that in order to write off the lease on annuity method at 5% interest per annum, the amount to be written off annually as depreciation amounts to Rs. 5,640.34. Show the lease a/c for 4 years.

Answer. Total of lease a/c for the year 2003 is Rs. 5,640.24

EXERCISE 4

(Sinking Fund Method)

Mysore tyres company Ltd. Purchased a machinery on 1-1-2000 for Rs. 50,000 and decided to make a provision or it replacement by means of depreciation fund. The investment yield 4% per annum According to the sinking fund tables Rs. 11,774.50 are to be invested annually. At the and of the fourth year the investments realised Rs. 36,700.

Show the depreciation find a/c, depreciation fund investment a/c and the machinery a/c.

Answer. Total of depreciation fund a/c on 2002 is Rs. 36,755.30

EXERCISE 5

(Insurance Policy Method)

A firm purchased in machine for Rs. 1,00,000 on 1-1-2000. It was dicided to replace the machine at the end of the 4th year. For this purpose an insurance policy was taken, the annual premium being Rs. 22,000.

Prepare (1) Insurance policy a/c (2) Depreciation fund a/c (3) Machinery account.

Answer. Total of Insurance policy a/c on 2003, Rs. 100,000.
Total of Depreciation fund a/c on 2003 Rs. 100,000.

15
CHAPTER

Accounting of Non-Trading Concerns

INTRODUCTION

Non-trading concerns are those organisations which are formed not for earning profits but to render a type of service or promote certain activities such as education, health, sports, arts, science, cooperation, etc. They do not engage in trading or manufacturing activities. Hence they are called non-trading concerns. Though their object is not to earn profit, still it is necessary to maintain a set of accounting books in order to avoid misappropriation of funds contributed by the numbers of such organisations. In other words the purpose of accounting in a non-trading concern is to safeguard the interest of its members. However, the accounting books and types of accounts prepared in such organisations differ from those of trading concerns. The following are some of the distinctive features of such organisations :-

1. They mostly deal on cash basis rather than credit basis. Hence accounts are based on cash basis as compared to accrued or mercantile basis under trading concerns.
2. The usual accounts prepared by non-trading concerns differ from the types of accounts prepared by trading concern.
3. Some transactions of non-trading concerns are peculiar in nature when compared to trading concerns.
4. The object of preparing accounts in non-trading concern is different when compared to trading concerns.
5. The set of accounting books maintained by non-trading concerns differ from those of trading concerns and they are termed as accounts of non-trading concerns.
6. The maintenance of accounts is not compulsory in case of registered organisations.
7. The classification of expenses into capital and revenue assumes more importance in preparing accounts of non-trading concerns.

Some examples of non-trading concerns are educational institutions, libraries, religious organisations, clubs, sports and recreational, cooperative societies, hospitals, literary associations, scientific and cultural organisations, charitable organisations and professional persons, such as Doctors, Engineers, Lawyers, Auditors, sports persons, etc.

Capital and Revenue Items

A classification of expenses into capital and revenue is necessary to prepare the accounts of non-trading concerns. All revenue items of expenses and revenue incomes are taken in preparing the trading and Profit and Loss Account and all items of capital expenses and capital revenues in preparing the balance sheet of trading concerns, the some principle is adopted and used in preparing accounts of non-trading concerns. So the classification of items into revenue and capital is very important as any error in this regard will distort the accounting of non-trading concerns.

Capital Expenditure

It refers to expenditure or investment made in procuring a fixed asset. The benefit of incurring capital expenditure is felt in the future period. It is incurred for ; (*a*) servicing of fixed assets ; (*b*) increasing business assets ; (*c*) for increasing earning capacity of the business. The following tests are to be applied for considering an expenditure as capital expenditure.

(*a*) It should be incurred to purchase or produce an asset of fixed nature.
(*b*) It should be incurred to acquire capital or loan.
(*c*) It should be incurred for replacement of fixed assets.
(*d*) It should be incurred for maintaining the quality of fixed assets. Such as :-
  (*i*) increasing the efficiency of fixed assets ;
  (*ii*) increasing the life span of fixed assets ;
  (*iii*) increasing the capacity of fixed assets.

Some examples of capital expenditure are as follows :-

(*a*) Expenditure resulting in acquisition of fixed assets such as land and building, plant and machinery, furniture and fixture etc.
(*b*) Expenditure incurred for acquiring the right to carry on business such as patents, copy-right, goodwill etc.
(*c*) Expenditure resulting in extension and improvement of fixed assets such as amount spent on increasing the seating capacity of a college, expenses incurred in increasing the plant capacity, etc.
(*d*) Expenditure incurred in acquiring and installation of fixed assets such as import duty, registration fee, cost of errecting machinery etc. Such expenses are called capitalised expenses.
(*e*) Expenditure incurred for rehabilitating or reconditioning of fixed assets.

Revenue Expenditure

It is an expenditure which is incurred in day-to-day running of a business. Such expenses are incurred as a matter of routine activity. As compared to capital expenditure, revenue expenditure is incurred to benefit current period. Such expenditure is incurred to maintain revenue earning capacity of the business. Its distinctive features are as follows :-

(*a*) They are incurred in the normal course of running the business.
(*b*) They fluctuate from period to period.
(*c*) They are incurred for relatively short period of time.
(*d*) They are recurring in nature.
(*e*) They maintain the efficiency of business.
(*f*) They appear in the trading and Profit and Loss Account of the business.

The examples of revenue expenditure are : rent and rates, postage and telegram, printing and stationery, heating and lighting, materials purchased for the business, depreciation on assets, loss on account of fire and such other reasons, selling expenses etc.

Deferred Revenue Expenditure

Any revenue expenditure whose benefit is derived for a long period of time is known as deferred revenue expenditure. Such expenses are of large amount and it will not be entirely charged to Profit and Loss Account of the year during which it is incurred. This is so because it will minimise the profit of the year considerably and hence they are charged to Profit and Loss Account of certain future period. The balance of such expense will appear on the asset side of the Balance Sheet of the concerned year. Examples of such expenses are preliminary expenses, commission and brokerage on issue of shares, discount on issue of shares and debentures, heavy advertisement expenses and so on.

Differences between capital and revenue expenditure

Points of Difference	*Capital Expenditure*	*Revenue Expenditure*
1. Purpose of spending	Spent for purchasing fixed assets.	Spent for purchase of raw materials.
2. Increase in value of assets	It increases the value of fixed assets.	It does not increase the value of fixed assets.
3. Earning capacity	It increases the earning capacity of business.	It maintains the earning capacity of business.
4. Nature of expense	It is a capital expenditure for the person incurring the expense but revenue expenditure for the person who receives the amount as for example, furniture purchased by the buyer is capital expenditure and for the seller it is revenue expenditure.	Such expenses are revenue expenses for the buyer and revenue a income for the seller.
5. Frequency of incurrence	They are non-recurring in nature.	They are recurring in nature.

Capital Receipt

The amount received by the sale of fixed assets or investments or by the issue of share capital, debenture, or raising loans are termed as capital receipt.

Revenue Receipt

The amount received in the course of running the business is known as revenue receipt. Examples of revenue receipts are sale proceeds of goods, interest received on deposits or loans granted, dividend received from investment.

Books of Accounts maintained by Non-Trading Concerns

The important books of accounts maintained by a non-trading concern are as follows :-

(1) **Register of Members.** this book contains the particulars of members such as their names, addresses, occupation and the membership fee received and the date on which it is received.

2. **Minutes Book.** This book contains the proceedings of the meetings of members held from time to time.
3. **Cash Receipt Journal.** This book contains particulars of cash received towards entrance fee, subscription, donations, receipts for special programme such as dance, music etc. Accordingly, this book may be ruled so as to provide columns for each of the above mentioned items.
4. **Cash Payment Journal.** This book contains the particulars of cash paid towards wages, salaries, honorarium, sports materials, entertainment, electricity bill etc. Accordingly, this book may be ruled so as to provide columns for each of the above mentioned items.
5. **Ledger.** This book contains the accounts relating to various receipts and expenditure.

Accounting Procedure

As in the case of trading concerns three steps are involved in the preparation of accounts of non-trading concerns. They are :

1. Recording the transactions in the subsidiary books such as register of members, minutes book, cash receipt journal and cash payment journal.
2. Posting to ledger accounts from the various journals. Separate account is maintained for each and every item of receipts and expenditure.
3. Preparation of final accounts. They comprise
   (*a*) Income and expenditure account ;
   (*b*) Receipts and payments account ; and
   (*c*) Balance Sheet.

Final accounts are prepared with the help of : (*i*) Balance Sheet of the last year ; (*ii*) Receipts and Payments account ; and (*iii*) Additional information regarding accrued incomes and outstanding expenses.

Receipts and Payments Account

It forms part of the final accounts of a non-trading concerns. This account is prepared from cash receipts journal and cash payments journal. It is also termed as summary statement of cash book because it contains the summary transactions of cash book. This account is prepared to get a better idea about the nature of transactions. As is known, the cash receipt journal records the subscription received on different months. The total of such subscription received for the year will be recorded on the receipt side of the Receipts and Payments accounts. Similarly, the cash payment journal records various expenses such as wages, rent, electricity charges etc., in the chronological order of spending. The total of such payments are recorded in the payment side of receipts and payments account. This gives at a glance the total payments incurred under each head. Thus receipts and payments account summarises the various receipts and payments of cash, the details of which are found in cash receipts and cash payments journal. The features of Receipts and Payments account are as follows :

1. It is a real account and hence the rule of real account, viz., debit what comes in and credit what goes out is applicable.
2. The receipts are recorded on the debit side and payments are recorded on the credit side.
3. It begins with opening cash (and bank) balance and ends with closing cash (bank) balance.

4. All cash transactions relating to both revenue and capital nature are recorded in this account.
5. All cash transactions to whatever period they might relate – previous years, current year or the next year – will be recorded in this account.
6. It records only cash receipts and cash payments. Non-cash expenses are not recorded and income earned but not received are also not recorded in this account.

The closing balance of cash as revealed by Receipts and Payments account does not mean that the income for the year has exceeded the expenditure by an amount equal to the balance of cash in hand. It may be even possible that with more cash balance income may be less than expense. A large cash balance may result from sale of an asset, say, machinery. But it only means conversion of one asset into another form. Therefore it is necessary to distinguish income from receipts of cash and expenses from payment of cash. In order to know the income earned by non-trading concerns, an income and expenditure account is to be prepared.

Differences Between Receipts and Payments Account and Cash Account

Receipts and Payments Account	*Cash Account*
1. It is prepared only by non-trading concerns	1. It is prepared by both trading and non-trading concerns.
2. Entries are recorded under different headings.	2. Entires are not recorded under different headings.
3. It is prepared at the end of the year.	3. Transactions are recorded throughout the year.
4. Entries are not recorded in chronological order.	4. Transactions are recorded in a chronological order.

Income and Expenditure Account

This forms the second component of the final accounts of non-trading concerns. This account resembles to the Profit and Loss Account of a trading concern. It is an account which records the summary of all income and expense for the whole year. It is prepared at the end of the year. In it are recorded all revenue items of incomes and expenses but not the capital items of Receipts and Payments. The balance at the end represents the excess of income over the expenditure or vice-versa.

The following are the distinctive features of Income and Expenditure Account :-

1. It is a nominal account. As such, the rules of nominal account, viz., debit all expenses and losses and credit all incomes and gains are applicable.
2. All expenses are recorded on the debit side and all incomes are recorded on the credit side of income and expenditure account.
3. It reveals the result of working of a non-trading concern for an accounting year, *i.e.*, an excess of income over expenditure or vice-versa.
4. The revenue income and revenue expenses relating to the same period for which this account is prepared are considered and not of previous or future year.
5. Adjustments such as provision for bad debts, and depreciation are recorded in it.
6. Adjustments relating to outstanding expenses are to be added and prepaid expenses are to be deducted from the concerned expense. Similarly outstanding incomes are to be added and income received in advance is to be deducted from the concerned item of revenue.

Differences between Receipts and Payments Account and Income and Expenditure Account :

Points of Difference	*Receipts and Payment Account*	*Income and Expenditure Account*
1. Nature of Account	It is a real account.	It is a nominal account.
2. Type of Account	It is more or less like a cash account.	It is more or less like a Profit and Loss Account.
3. Recording of Transactions	Receipts are recorded on the debit side and payments are recorded on the credit side.	Expenses and losses are recorded on the debit side and incomes are recorded on the credit side.
4. Nature of Transactions	Capital expenses and capital revenues are recorded.	Revenue expenses and revenue incomes are recorded.
5. Opening and Closing Cash Balance	It begins with cash balance and ends with closing cash balance.	It does not begin with opening balance and does not end with closing cash balance.
6. Types of Transactions	Only cash transactions are recorded.	Both cash and non-cash transactions are recorded.
7. Expenses	All cash expenses made during the year are recorded in it whether they relate to previous year, current year or next year.	All revenue expenses of concerned year are recorded. Revenue expenses of previous year or next year is not recorded.
8. Incomes	Incomes received during the year whether it belongs to previous year, current year or next year.	Current year's income is recorded whether it is received or not.
9. Unearned Income	Only incomes earned and received is recorded. Unearned income is not recorded.	Both earned and un-earned income are recorded.
10. Recording of Adjustments.	Adjustments are not recorded in it.	Adjustments are recorded in it.

Balance Sheet

It is prepared in usual way as in the case of trading concerns incorporating all assets and liabilities. The important sources for preparing a Balance Sheets are : (*a*) Previous year's balance sheet ; (*b*) Stock Register maintained for recording assets and (*c*) Receipts and Payments account. The various items of Balance Sheet of a non-trading concerns are as follows :-

1. **Capital Fund.** It resembles the capital amount of a trading concerns. It is represented by an excess of assets over liabilities as on the beginning of the accounting year. This item appears on the liability side of the Balance Sheet. To this fund the current years profit or loss is transferred.
2. **Special Fund.** This represents the fund received for a special purpose such as endowment, tournament etc. Such funds are separately shown on the liability side. Incomes received in respect of special funds are added to that funds and the expenses incurred there on are deducted from relevant fund without recording them in income and expenditure account.
3. **Creditors.** If the amount paid to creditors appears on the payment side of Receipts and Payments Account ; then this amount should be deducted from the amount of opening creditors. The amount of new credit purchases is to be added to the above balance. The amount thus arrived at is recorded on the liability side of the Balance Sheet.

4. **Other Liabilities.** Other opening balances of liabilities should be recorded after adding and deducting relevant payment.
5. **Cash Balance.** The closing balance of cash account from the Receipts and Payments Account is recorded on the asset side of Balance Sheet.
6. **Other Assets.** The opening balances of other assets should be recorded after adding additions if any and deducting depreciation and sale of asset on the asset side.
7. **Expenses.** All prepaid expenses are recorded on the asset side and outstanding expenses on the liability side.

Items Peculiar to Various Non-Trading Concerns

1. **Legacy.** It is the amount which is given to a non-trading concern by a written will, *i.e.*, an authorisation to pay the amount on the death of maker of will. It resembles to a donation. As it is not recurring nature it is recorded on the receipt side of Receipts and Payments Account. This item is not treated as an income. However, legacy of small amount may be treated as an income.
2. **Donations.** It is offered as a gift to a non-trading concern by an individual firm or companies. It appears on the receipt side of Receipts and Payments Account. Donations are of different types and so the method of treatment differs.
   (*a*) ***Specific Donation.*** Any donation received for a specific purpose such as donation for building, donation for library etc., is known as specific donation. Such donation should be capitalised and appears on the liability side of the Balance Sheet.
   (*b*) ***General Donation.*** This item is taken into the receipt side of Receipts and Payments Account. It may be of big amount or small amount. The former is taken into the liability side of Balance Sheet as it is not of recurring nature. The latter is treated as an income and hence taken into Income and Expenditure Account as donation of such type may be expected every year.
3. **Endowment Fund.** It is a big amount given to non-trading concerns so as to have a strong base for its functioning. It may be either deposited with the bank or invested in investments. Such fund is shown on the liability side of Balance Sheet. The income earned from such funds such as interest or dividend is taken on the income side of Income and Expenditure Account.
4. **Entrance Fee.** Entrance fee received once in the life time of membership is treated as capital receipt. Hence it is to be taken on the receipt side of Receipts and Payments Account. However, entrance fee received every year as in the case of sports or recreation club owing to change in membership is treated as income and hence taken to the income side of Income and Expenditure Account.
5. **Sale of Old Assets.** The sale proceeds of old assets appear on the Receipt side of Receipts and Payments Account. Any loss or income on sale of such asset is taken into the Income and Expenditure Account.
6. **Sale of Old Newspaper.** The sales amount of old newspaper appears on the receipt side of Receipts and Payments Account. It is to be transferred to Income and Expenditure Account on the income side. This is so because sale of old newspapers is a regular feature.
7. **Sale of Sports Materials.** This item appears in the Receipts and Payments Account. It is transferred to Income and Expenditure Account on the income side.
8. **Payment of Honorarium.** It is spent on cultural programme. Such amount is recorded in the expenditure side of the Income and Expenditure Account.

9. **Life Membership.** It refers to lumpsum amount paid by a member instead of paying in instalments. Such amount should be credited to capital fund.

Preparation of Income and Expenditure Account from Receipts and Payments Account

The following steps are involved in preparing Income and Expenditure Account from Receipts and Payments Account :

1. Do not take the following items from the Receipts and Payments Account into the Income and Expenditure Account.
   (*a*) Opening and closing cash and bank balance ;
   (*b*) Revenue income and expenses relating to previous or subsequent year.
   (*c*) Receipts and Payments in respect of real and personal accounts.
   (*d*) Revenue receipts to be capitalised.
2. Take the following items into Income and Expenditure Account.
   (*a*) Revenue receipts for current year as per Receipts and Payments Account.
   Add : Outstanding income for current year.
   Add : Received in advance in the last year.
   (*b*) Revenue expenses for current year
   Add : Unpaid expenses for current year
   Add : Paid in advance in the last year.
3. Adjustment in respect of bad debts or depreciation should also be made.
4. Show the amount of profit (along with its computation) arising out of trading activities on the credit side of the Income and Expenditure Account and losses therefrom on the debit side.
5. Close the Income and Expenditure Account by finding the balance. If the total of credit side exceeds the total of debit side, show the excess of income over expenditure on the debit side. If the total of debit side exceeds the total of credit side, show the excess of expenditure over income on the credit side of the Income and Expenditure Account.

Problem 1

From the following information calculate the amount of subscription received in advance during 1998-99.

(*i*) Subscription received during the year 1998-99 Rs. 52,500.
(*ii*) There were two members paying subscription at the rate of Rs. 250 per annum each.
(*iii*) Some members have paid their annual subscription in advance during the year.
(*iv*) As on 1st April, 1998 no subscription had been received in advance but subscription were outstanding to the extent of Rs. 1,000 as on 31st March, 1998.
(*v*) Subscription accrued as on 31st March, 1999 Rs. 1,500

(University of Delhi, B-com (Hons., 1999)

Solution

Balance Sheett as on 1-4-98

	Rs.		*Rs.*
		Subscription accured	1,000

Receipts and Payments A/c for 1998-99

	Rs.		Rs.
To subscription received	52,500		

Income and Expenditure A/c for 1998-99

	Rs.		Rs.
		By subscription received	52,500
		Less : Outstanding last year	1,000
			51,500
		Add : Accrued as on 1999	1,500
			53,000
		Less : Subscription received in advance	3,000
			50,000

Working Note

Income for 1998-99 should be Rs. 50,000 (200 × 250)
Subscription received in advance as balancing figure of Rs. 3,000.

Balance Sheet as on 31-3-99

	Rs.		Rs.
Subscritpion received in advance	3,000	Subscription accured	1,500

Problem 2

On the basis of the following information ascertain the subscriptions actually received in 1999.

Subscription as per Income and Expenditure A/c for the year 1999.	5,000
Subscription received in advance on 31-12-199	200
Subscription outstanding on 31-12-199	800
Subscription in arrears on 1-1-1999	400

(Osmania University B-com March, 2000)

Solution

	Subscription as per Income and Expenditure A/c		5,000
Add :	Subscription in arrears on 1-1999	400	
	Subscription received in advance on 31-12-1999	200	
			600
			5600
Less :	Subscription outstanding on 31-12-99		800
	Subscription received during the year		4800

Problem 3

Calculate the amount of stationery consumed during the calender year 1997.

Stock of stationery as on 1-1-1997	3,000
Creditors for stationery on 1-1-1997	2,000
Advance paid for stationery carried from 1996.	200
Amount paid for stationery during the year	10,800
Stock of stationery on 31-12-1997	500
Creditors for stationery for 31-12-1997	1,300
Advance paid for stationery on 31-12-1997	1,300

(Delhi University B-com (Hons.) 1998)

Solution

Income and Expenditure A/c

		Rs.		*Rs.*
To Stationery A/c				
Stock of stationery as on 1-1-97	3,000			
Add : Purchases during the year	9,000			
	12,000			
Less : Stock of stationery as on 31-12-97	500			
		11,500		

Working Note :-

Calculation of Stationery Purchases during the year.

Amount paid for the stationery during the year	10,800
Less : Creditors of last year	2,000
	8,800
Less : Advance paid for it as on 31-12-97	1,300
	7,500
Add : Advance paid for it last year	200
Add : Creditors for it as on 31-12-97	1,300
	9,000

Problem 4

From the following particulars find out the capital fund.

Buildings	10,000
Investments	2,000
Outstanding subscription	3,500
Cash at Bank	3,000
Rent outstanding	500
Prepaid Insurance	200
Creditors	7,000

(Osmania University B-Com October, 1998)

Solution

Balance Sheet

	Rs.		Rs.
Creditors	7,000	Cash at Bank	3,000
Outstanding Rent	500	Buildings	10,000
Capital Fund	11,200	Investments	2,000
		Outstanding Subscriptions	3,500
		Prepaid Insurance	200
	18,700		18,700

Problem 5

(PREPARATION OF INCOME AND EXPENDITURE ACCOUNT)

From the following particulars relating to a charitable hospital prepare an Income and Expenditure A/c for the year ended 31-3-98 and a Balance Sheet as on that date.

Receipts and Payments A/c

	Rs.		Rs.
To Balance b/d 1-4-1997	7,500	By Medicines purchased	3,000
To Subscriptions	48,000	By Doctors honorarium	90
To Donations	15,000	By Salaries	2,700
To Interest on investment @ 6% p.a.	6,000	By Newspapers & Journals	140
To Charity show proceedings	10,000	By Surgical equipment	1,500
To Sale of newspaper	450	By Charity show expenses	1,600
To Life membership fee	9,150	By Sundry expenses	820
		By Shares purchased	4,180
		By Balance c/d 31-3-1998	7,100
	96,100		96,100

Additional Details :-

	1-4-1997 Rs.	31-3-1998 Rs.
Subscription due	500	400
Subscription received in advance	1000	500
Stockof medicine	21,200	31,600
Equipment	25,000	30,000
Building	50,000	48,000

(Osmania University B-com October, 2000)

Solution

Balance Sheet as on 1-4-1997

	Rs.		Rs.
Subscription received in advance	1,000	Cash in hand	7,500
Capital fund	2,03,200	Investments	1,00,000
(Balancing figure)		Subscritpion due	500
		Stock of Medicines	21,200
		Equipment	25,000
		Building	50,000
	2,04,200		2,04,200

Income and Expenditure A/c for the year ending 31-3-1998

	Rs.		Rs.
To Medical Expenses : Opening stock 21,200 Add : Purchases 30,000 51,200 Less : Closing stock 31,600	19,600	By Subscription 48,000 Less : Last years subscription due 500 47,500 Add : Subscription received in advance on 1-4-1998 1,000 48,500 Add : Current year's subscription due 400 48,900 Less : Subscription received in advance 500	48,400
To Doctor's honorarium	9,000		
To Salaries	27,000		
To Newspapers and Journals	1,400		
To Charity show expenses	1,600		
To Sundry expenses	820		
To Depreciation on : Building (50,000 – 48,000)	2,000		
To Equipment (25,000 + 15,000 – 30,000)	10,000	By Donation	15,000
		By Interest on investment	600
		By Charity show proceeds	1,000
To Excess of income over expenditure	8,430	By Sale of old newspapers	45
	79,850		79,850

Balance Sheet as on 31-3-1998

	Rs.		Rs.
Subscription received in advance	500	Cash in Hand	7,100
Capital fund 2,03,200		Investment	1,00,000
Add : Life Membership fee 9,150		Shares	4,180
Excess of income over expenditure 8,430		Subscription due	400
		Stock of Medicines	31,600
	2,20,780	Equipment	30,000
		Building	48,000
	2,21,280		2,21,280

Problem 6

The following is the Receipts and Payments Account of a club for the year ending 31st December, 1996.

Recipts	Rs.	*Payments*	Rs.
To Balance b/d		By Rates and taxes	2,520
Cash	340	By Printing & Stationery	940
Bank	16,240	By Magic show expenses	3,060
To Subscriptions	20,400	By Groundmen's wages	1,680
To Dinner receipts	7,300	By Dineer expenses	7,200
To Proceeds of magic share	3,500	By Canteen payments	12,000
To Bank interest	460	By Repairs	640
To Canteen receipts	15,000	By Billiards table (less stable proceeds of old billiards table Rs. 2,500)	12,500
		By Balance c/d	
		Cash	700
		Bank	22,000
	63,240		63,240

You are given the following additional information :-

	31-12-1995	31-12-1996
	Rs.	Rs.
(a) Subscription due	2,400	1,800
(b) Club premises at cost	58,000	—
(c) Depreciation on club premises	37,600	—
(d) Billiards table at cost	15,000	—
(e) Depreciation on Billiards table	13,500	—
(f) Canteen stock	1,420	1,740

(g) Depreciation is to be provided at 5% per annum on written down value of the club premises and at 10% per annum on Billiards table for whole of the year.

You are required to prepare Income and Expenditure A/c and the Balance Sheet

(Sri Venkateshwara University B.Com, September, 2000)

Solution

Balance Sheet as on 31-12-95

	Rs.		*Rs.*
Capital Fund (Balancing figure)	44,800	Cash	340
		Bank	16,240
		Subscipttion Receivable	2,400
		Club Premises (58,000 – 37,600)	20,400
		Billiards table (15,000 + 2,500 – 13,500)	4,000
		Canteen Stock	1,420
	44,800		44,800

Income and Expenditure A/c

	Rs.			*Rs.*
To Rates & Taxes	2,520	By subscription	20,400	
To Printing and Stationery	940	Add : Receivable	1,800	
To Magic Show expenses	3,060		22,200	
To Groundmen Wages	1,680	Less : Previous year's		
To Dinner expenses	7,200	Subscription	2,400	19,800
To Canteen payments	11,680	By Dinner receipts		7,300
To Repairs	640	By Magic show proceeds		3,500
To Depreciation on club premises	1,020	By Bank interest		460
To Depreciation on billiards table (400 + 1,250)	1,650	By Canteen receipts		15,000
To Excess of income over expenditure)	15,670			
	46,060			46,060

Balance Sheet as on 31-12-1996

		Rs.			Rs.
Capital fund	44,800		Cash Balance		700
Add : Excess of income			Bank		22,000
over expenditure	15,670		Subscription receivable		1,800
		60,470	Club premises	20,400	
			Less : Depreciation	1,020	
					19,380
			Billiards Table		14,850
			Canteen Stock		1,740
		60,470			60,470

Working Notes

1. Canteen Stock Consumption

= Opening stock + payments – closing stock

= 1,420 + 12,000 – 1,740 = 11,680

2. Closing value of billiards table

Opening value + sale price of table (15,000 + 2,500)	17,500
Less : Depreciation	13,500
	4,000
Add : Purchase table cost	12,500
	16,500
Less : Depreciation $\frac{10}{100} \times 16{,}500$	1,650
Closing Value	14,850

3. Calculation of Closing Club Premises

Club premises	58,000
Less : Depreciation	37,600
	20,400
Less : Current year's depreciation $20{,}400 \times \frac{5}{100}$	1,020
	19,380

Problem 7

The following is the Receipts and Payments A/c of Ruby club for the year ended on March 31, 1999.

Recipts		Rs.	*Payments*		Rs.
To Balance b/d		4,200	By Rent		14,000
To Donations		14,000	By Salary		
: Subscriptions :			31-3-1998	2,500	
31-3-1998	2,100		31-3-1999	8,400	11,200
31-3-1999	39,900		By Sports materials		12,600
31-3-2000	2,800		By Interest (6% loan)		1,050
		44,800	By Match expenses		5,600
To Interest on investments		2,800	By Newspapers		1,400
To Entrance fees		9,800	By Balance		29,750
		75,600			75,600

Other Information :

As on 31st March, 1999, subscription Rs. 2,800 ; entrance fees Rs. 1,400, Rent Rs. 1,400, Salary Rs. 2,800 and repairs Rs. 700 were outstanding. Donations include Rs.7,000 for Match Fund as Special donations.

On Ist April, 1998, the club had ; Building Rs. 28,000 ; Sports Materials Rs. 14,000 ; Furniture Rs. 14,000 ; Match fund investments Rs. 21,000 (interest accrued on that Rs. 700 for the year ended 31st March, 1999). Match fund Rs. 21,000.

Depreciation on Sports Materials for current year was charged Rs. 6,600.

Prepare Income and Expenditure Account for the year ended on 31st March, 1999 and a Balance Sheet as at that date. (Delhi University ; B-Com (Pass) 2000)

Solution

Balance Sheet as on 31-3-1998

	Rs.		Rs.
Salaries Outstanding	2,800	Cash in hand	4,200
Match fund	21,000	Subscription due	2,100
Loan $1,050 \times \frac{100}{6}$	17,500	Building	28,000
Capital fund	42,000	Sports materials	14,000
(Balancing figure)		Furniture	14,000
		Match Fund investment	21,000
	83,300		83,300

Income and Expenditure A/c for the year ended 31st March, 1999

		Rs.			Rs.
To Rent	14,000		By Donation	14,000	
Add Outstanding	1,400		Less : Received for Match		
		15,400	fund	7,000	
To Salaries	8,400				7,000
Add Outstanding	2,800		By Subscription	39,900	
		11,200	Add : Outstanding	2,800	
To Interest on loan		1,050			42,700
To Newspapers		1,400	By entrance fees	9,800	
To repair expense (due)		700	Add : Outstanding	1,400	
To Depreciation on sports materials		6,600			11,200
To excess of income over expense		24,550			
(Balancing figure)					
		60,900			60,900

Balance Sheet as on 31st March, 1999

		Rs.			Rs.
Subscription received in advance		2,800	Match fund investment		21,000
Match fund :-			Interest on Match fund		
As on 1-4-98	21,000		Investment accrued		700
Add : Donations	7,000		Sports Materials :		
Add : Interest received	2,800		As on 1-4-98	14,000	
Add : Interest still due	700		Add : Purchases	12,600	
	31,500			26,600	
Less : Expenses	5,600		Less Depreciation	6,600	
		25,900			20,000
Outstanding Expenses :-			Cash in hand		29,750
Rent		1,400	Subscription due		2,800
Salaries		2,800	Entrance fee due		1,400
Loan		17,500	Building		28,000
$\left(1{,}050 \times \frac{100}{6}\right)$			Furniture		14,000
Repair		700			
Capital fund :					
Opening Balance	42,000				
Add : Surplus	24,550				
		66,550			
		1,17,650			1,17,650

Problem 8

The following is the receipts and payments account of a charitable hospital for the year ended 31st March, 2002.

Recipts	Rs.	Payments	Rs.
To Balance b/d :-		By Medicines	1,500
Cash in Hand	50	By Honorarium to Doctors	500
Cash at Bank	300	By Salaries	1,375
To Subscriptions	2,500	By Sundry expenses	25
To Donations	725	By Equipments purchased	750
To Interest for full year on investment @ 7% per annum	350	By Charity show expenses	50
To Charity show receipts	500	Balance c/d :-	
		Cash in hand	25
		Cash at bank	200
	4,425		4,425.

Additional Information

	On 31-3-2001 (Rs. in thousand)	On 31-3-2002 (Rs. in thousand)
Subscription Outstanding	25	50
Subscriptions received in advance	50	[illegible]
Stock of medicines	[illegible]	50
Amounts due to suppliers of medicines	[illegible]	25
Value of equipments	[illegible]	750
Value of b[illegible]	500	600
[illegible]	400	[illegible]
[illegible]ies	1,050	[illegible]

You are required to prepare Income and Expenditure Account for the year ended 31st March, 2002 and the Balance Sheet as on that date. (C.S. Foundation, June 2002)

Solution

Working Notes

1. Calculation of Subscriptions Earned (Rs. in thousands)

Subscription received during the year		2,500
Add : Outstanding as on 31-3-2002		50
Add : Received in advance as on 31-3-2002		50
		2,600
Less : Outstanding on 31-3-2001	25	
Less : Received in advance on 31-3-2001	25	
		50
		2,550

2. Calculation of Medicines Used

Payments to Suppliers	1,500
Add : Due to suppliers on 31-3-2002	600
	2,100
Less : Due to suppliers on 31-3-2001	400
Medicines purchased during the year	1,700
Add : Stock of medicines on 31-3-2001	500
	2,200
Less : Stock of medicines on 31-3-2002	750
	1,450

3. Depreciation on Equipments

Balance on 1-4-2001	1,050
Add : Purchases during the year	750
	1,800
Less : Balance as on 31-3-2002	1,500
Depreciation during the year	300

4. Amount of Investments

$$\text{Rs. } 3,50,000 \times \frac{100}{7} = \text{Rs. } 50,00,000$$

5. Calculation of capital fund

Balance Sheet as at 31-3-2001

	Rs.		Rs.
Subscription received in advance	50	Subscription receivable	25
Creditors for Medicines	400	Stock of medicines	500
Capital Fund	8,475	Equipments	1,050
(Balancing figure)		Buildings	2,000
		Investments	5,000
		Cash in hand	50
		Cash at bank	300
	8,925		8,925

Income and Expenditure A/c
For the year ended 31st March, 2002

Expenditure		*Rs.*	*Income*		*Rs.*
To Medicines used		1,450	By Subscriptions		2,550
To Honorarium to Doctors		500	By Donations		725
To Salaries		1,375	By Interest on investments		350
To Sundry expenses		25	By Income from charity show :-		
To Depreciation on :			Proceeds	500	
Equipment	300		Less : Expenses	50	
Buildings	100				450
		400			
To Surplus i.e., excess of income over expenditure		325			
		4,075			4,075

Balance Sheet as at 31st March, 2002

		Rs.			*Rs.*
Suppliers of Medicines		600	Buildings	2,000	
Subscription received in advance		25	Less : Depreciation	100	
Capital fund :-					1,900
Opening Balance	8,475		Equipments	1,050	
Add : Surplus for the year	325		Add : Additions	750	
		8,800		1,800	
			Less Depreciation	300	
					1,500
			Investments		5,000
			Stock of medicines		750
			Subscription outstanding		50
			Cash at Bank		200
			Cash in Hand		25
		9,425			9,425

Problem 9

The following is the Receipts and Payments Account of a club for the year ended 31st December, 1999.

Receipts		*Rs.*	*Payments*	*Rs.*
To Balance at Bank on 1-1-1999		2,040	By Salaries	8,320
To Entrance Fees		2,000	By Rent	3,720
To Subscriptions :			By Electricity	2,560
1997 —	500		By Postage & Stattionery	660
1998 —	6,100		By Insurance Premium	360
1999 —	700		By General Expenses	920
		7,300	By Part Payment on Account of new furniture	9000
To Sale of Investments		15,000	By Balance at bank	4,800
To Loan from Krishna on 1-7-1999 at 10% interest p.a.,		4,000		
		30,340		30,340

The following information is also available

1.	31-12-98	31-12-99
	Rs.	Rs.
Rent Due	360	720
Electricity	1,280	400
Subscription Due	500	800
Insurance paid in advance	100	140.

2. The cost of the investment sold was Rs. 10,000. The surplus is to be treated as income.
3. Furniture was valued at Rs. 6,000 on 31-12-1998. On 30th June, 1999 the club purchased additional new furniture at a cost of Rs. 10,400. Depreciation at the rate of 10% per annum is to be provided.
4. The entrance fees are not to be captialised.

Prepare Income and Expenditure Account for the year ended 31st December, 1999 and a Balance Sheet as on that date. (Sri Venkateshwara University B-Com, April, 2000)

Solution

Balance Sheet as on 1-1-1999

	Rs.		*Rs.*
Outstanding Rent	360	Cash	2,040
Outstanding Electricity	1,280	Subscription receivable (1998)	500
Capital Fund	17,000	Furniture	6,000
		Investment	10,000
		Prepaid Insurance	100
	18,640		18,640

Income and Expenditure A/c

Expenditure		*Rs.*	*Income*		*Rs.*
To Salaries		8,320	By Entrance Fee		20
To Rent	3,720		By Subscription	6,100	
Add : Outstanding	720		Add : Receivable	800	
	4,440				6,900
Less : Rent Due	360		By Profit on sale of investment		5,000
		4,080	By Excess of expenditure over income		3,400
To Electricity	2,560				
Add : Outstanding	400				
	2,960				
Less : Previous years expenses	1,280				
		1,680			
To Postage and Stationery		660			
To Insurance Premium	360				
Add : Previous year prepaid	100				
	460				
Less : Prepaid current year	140				
		320			

	Rs.		Rs.
To General Expenses	920		
To Depreciation on Furniture			
$6,000 \times \frac{10}{100} = 600$			
$10,400 \times \frac{10}{100} \times \frac{6}{12} = 520$			
	1120		
To Interest on loan	200		
$4,000 \times \frac{10}{100} \times \frac{6}{12}$			
	17,300		17,300

Balance Sheet as on 31-12-1999

		Rs.			Rs.
Outstanding Rent		120	Cash Balance		4,800
Outstanding Electricity		400	Furniture	6,000	
Loan from Krishna	4,000		Add : Additional Furniture	10,400	
Add outstanding interest	200			16,400	
		4,200	Less : Depreciation	1,120	
Outstanding creditors (10,400 – 9,000)		1,400			15,280
			Subscription Receivable		800
			Prepaid insurance		140
Capital Fund	17,000				
Less : Excess of expenses over income	3,400				
		13,600			
Subscription received (2000)		700			
		21,020			21,020

Problem 10

The following is the Income and Expenditure A/c of the Neelagiri's Sports Club for the year ended 31st Decembner, 1997.

Expenditure	*Rs.*	*Income*	*Rs.*
To Salaries	6,000	By Admission fees	15,000
To Printing & Stationery	2,500	By subscriptions	25,000
To Advertising	1,000	By Rent receivable	4,800
To Insurance Charges	900		
To Electricity	500		
To Depreciation on sports equipment	12,000		
To Excess of income over expenditure	21,900		
	44,800		44,800

Receipts and Payments A/c of
Neelagiri Sports Club for the year ended 31-12-1997

Recipts		Rs.	Payments	Rs.
To Balance b/d		5,000	By Salary (including advertising)	7,500
To Admission Fees			By Advertising	1,000
1996	2,500		By Insurance charges	1,200
1997	13,500		(Partly for next year)	
		16,000	By Printing & Stationery	2,500
To Subscription :			By Electricity	500
1996 —	1,000		By Purchase of head assets	20,000
1997 —	23,000		By Balance c/d	17,900
1998 —	2,000			
		26,000		
To Rent received		3,600		
		50,600		50,600

On 1st January, 1997 ; the club had the following assets :-

(*a*) Land & Buildings Rs. 60,000
(*b*) Sports equipment 30,000
(*c*) Furniture 4,500

Prepare (*a*) Opening Balance Sheet as on 1-1-1997
(*b*) Closing Balance Sheet as on 31-12-1997.

(Osmania University B-com, March, 1999)

Solution

Balance Sheet of
Neelagiri Sports Club as on 1-1-1997

	Rs.		Rs.
Capital fund	1,03,000	Cash	5,000
(Balancing figure)		Outstanding Admission Fees	2,500
		Outstanding Subscriptions	1,000
		Sports equipments	30,000
		Furniture	4,500
		Land & Buildings	60,000
	1,03,000		1,03,000

Balance Sheet as on 31-12-1997

		Rs.			Rs.
Subscription received in advance		2,000	Cash		17,900
Capital fund	1,03,000		Outstanding Admission Fee		1,500
Add : Excess of income			Outstanding Subscriptions		2,000
over expenditure	21,900		Rent Receivable		1,200
		1,24,900	Prepaid Insurance		300
			Advance Salary		1,500
			Sports equipment	30,000	
			Less : Depreciation	12,000	
					18,000
			Furniture		4,500
			Land & Building		60,000
			Fixed Assets		20,000
		1,26,900			1,26,900

Problem 11

A summary of Receipts and Payments Account of Sri Sai Siva Hospital for the year ended on 31-3-1998 is given below :-

Receipts and Payments A/c

Recipts	*Rs.*	*Payments*	*Rs.*
To Balance (1-4-97)	280	By Payment to medicines	1,200
To subscriptions	2,000	By Honorarium to Director	400
To Interest on Investment @ 7% p.a.	280	By Salaries	1,100
To Donations	580	By Sundry Expenses	20
To Charity Show Proceeds	400	By Purchase of equipment	600
		By Charity show expenses	40
		By Balance	180
	3,540		3,540

Addittional Information

	1-4-97 Rs.	31-3-98 Rs.
Subscription Due	20	40
Subscription received in advance	40	20
Stock of Medicines	400	600
Amount due to medicine suppliers	320	480
Value of equipmentt	840	1,200
Value of Buildings	1,600	1,520

Donations are to be capitalised. Prepare Income and Expenditure Account for the year ended 31-12-98 and the Balance Sheet as on that date.

(Sri Ventakateshwara University B.Com, April, 1999)

Solution

Income and Expenditure A/c of Sri Sai Siva Hospital

Expenditure		*Rs.*	*Income*		*Rs.*
To Medicines	1,200		By Subscription	2,000	
Add : Opening Stock	400		Add : Received in advance in 97	40	
	1,600			2,040	
Less : Closing Stock	600		Add : Receivable on 31-3-98	40	
	1,000			2,080	
Less : Due on 1997	320		Less : Due in 97	20	
	680			2,060	
Add : Due in 1998	480	1,160	Less : Due in 98	20	2,040
To Honorarium to Director		400			
To Salaries		1,100	By Interest on investment		280
To Charity Show Expenses		40	By Charity Show Proceeds		400
To Sundry Expenses		20	By Excess of Expenditure over Income		320
To Depreciation on equipment		240			
To Depreciation on building		80			
		3,040			3,040

Balance Sheet as on 01-04-1997

	Rs.		Rs.
Subscriptions in Advance	40	Cash in Hand	280
Due to Medicines	320	Investments $280 \times \frac{100}{7}$	4,000
Capital Fund (Balancing figure)	6,780	Subscription Due	20
		Stock of Medicines	400
		Equipment	840
		Buildings	1,600
	7,140		7,140

Balance Sheet as on 31-3-1998

		Rs.		Rs.
Subscriptions in advance		20	Cash in Hand	180
Due to medicines suppliers		480	Investments	4,000
Capital fund	6,750		Subscription due	40
Add : Donations	580		Stock of medicines	600
	7,360		Equipment	1,200
Less : Deficiency	320		Buildings	1,520
		7,040		
		7,540		7,540

Problem 12

(Preparation of Receipts and Payments Account)

Prepare Receipts and Payments Account for the year ending 31st March, 1999 and also the Balance Sheet as on that date from the following :

Income and Expenditure A/c
For the year ending 31st March, 1999

Expenditure		*Rs.*	*Income*	*Rs.*
Salaries		29,500	Interest	10,000
Stationery		5,000	Donations	15,000
Taxes and Rent		2,500	Subscriptions	25,000
Insurance		1,200	Miscellaneous Receipts	300
Other expenses		1,800		
Depreciation on				
Properties	3,750			
Furniture	120			
Books	100			
		3,970		
Surplus		6,330		
		50,300		50,300

Other Information

	31-3-98 Rs.	31-3-99 Rs.
Cash in hand and at bank	?	23,700
Investment in Shares and Debentures (Face value Rs. 3,00,000)	2,80,000	2,80,000
Subscription outstanding	7,000	10,000
Subscription received in advance	1,200	1,600
Salaries outstanding	500	1,000
Furniture	2,000	1,980
Properties	3,00,000	2,96,250
Interest on investments accrued	1,000	1,000
Books	3,500	3,900
Stationery payment due	200	300
Stock of stationery	1,000	800

(Delhi University B-Com (Hons.) 2000

Solution

Receipts and Payments A/c
For the Year Ending 31st March, 1999

Recipts		*Rs.*	*Payments*		*Rs.*
To Balance b/d		15,800	By Salaries	29,500	
Cash and Bank			Add : Outstanding last year	500	
(Balancing figure)				30,000	
To Interest	10,000		Less : Outstanding		
Add : Received for			this year	1,000	
last year	1,000				29,000
	11,000		Stationery	5,000	
Less : Accumulated			Add : Paid for		
this year	1,000		last year	200	
		10,000		5,200	
To Donations		15,000	Less : Last years	1,000	
To Subscriptions	25,000			4,200	
Add : Due last year	7,000		Less : Outstanding this year	300	
	32,000			3,900	
Less : Received on			Add : Stock of this year	800	
advance last year	1,200				4,700
	30,800				
Less : Due this year	10,000		By Taxes & Rent		2,500
	20,800		By Insurance		1,200
Add : Received in			By other expenses		1,800
advance this year	1,600		By Furniture purchased		100
		22,400	By Books purchased		500
To Miscellaneous Receipts		300	By Cash and Bank		23,700
		63,500			63,500

Balance Sheet as at 31st March, 1999

		Rs.			*Rs.*
Accumulated Capital Fund :-			Properties :-		
As on 1-4-98	6,08,400		As on 1-4-98	3,00,000	
Add : Surplus this year	6,370		Less : Depreciation	3,750	
		6,14,730			2,96,250
Subscription received in advance		1,600	Furniture :-		
Salaries due		1,000	As on 1-4-98	2,000	
Stationery Expenses Outstanding		300	Add : Purchases	100	
				2,100	
			Less : Depreciation	120	
					1,980
			Books :-		
			As on 1-4-98	3,500	
			Add : Purchases	500	
				4,000	
			Less : Depreciation	100	
					3,900

	Rs.		Rs.
		Investment in shares and debentures (face value 3,00,000)	2,80,000
		Cash and Bank	23,700
		Subscription Due	10,000
		Interest on investment accrued	1,000
		Stock of Stationery	800
	6,17,630		6,17,630

Working Notes

Balance Sheet as on 31st March, 1998

	Rs.		Rs.
Accumulated Capital Fund (Balancing figure)	6,08,400	Cash and Bank	15,800
Subscription received on advance	1,200	Investment in Shares & Debentures (Face value Rs. 3,00,000)	2,80,000
Salaries Outstanding	500	Subscription Due	7,000
Stationery Expenses Outstanding	200	Furniture	2,000
		Properties	3,00,000
		Interest on investment accrued	1,000
		Books	3,500
		Stock of Stationery	1,000
	6,10,300		6,10,300

Furniture A/c

	Rs.		Rs.
To Balance b/d	2,000	By Depreciation	120
To Bank Purchases (Balancing figure)	100	By Balance c/d	1980
	2,100		2,100

1. Accumulated capital fund is the balancing figure of last years Balance Sheet.
2. Cash and Bank balance as on 1-4-98 is the Balancing figure of this year's Receipts and Payments Account.
3. Interest income of this year Rs. 10,000 is presumed to be on investment in shares and debentures of face value of Rs. 3,00,000.
4. Books purchased should be Rs. 500, then only its balance after depreciation can be Rs. 3,900 as given.

Problem 13

The Income and Expenditure Account of Bharat Club for the year ended 31st March, 2000 was as follows :-

Expenditure	*Rs.*	*Income*	*Rs.*
To Salaries	1,20,000	By Subscriptions	1,70,000
To Printing	6,000	By Entrance fees	4,000
To Postage	500	By Contribution for dinner	36,000
To Telephone	1,500		
To General expenses	12,000		
To Interest charges	5,500		
To Audit fees	2,500		
To Annual dinner expenses	25,000		
To Depreciation on Sports equipment	7,000		
To Surplus	30,000		
	2,10,000		2,10,000

The Income and Expenditure Account has been prepared after taking into consideration the following information :

	As on 31-3-1999 Rs.	As on 31-3-2000 Rs.
Subscriptions Outstadning	16,000	18,000
Subscriptions received in advance	13,000	8,400
Salaries outstanding	6,000	8,000
Audit fees outstanding	2,000	2,500
Buildings	1,90,000	1,90,000
Sports equipment	52,000	63,000

During the year 1998-99, the Bharat Club raised a bank loan of Rs. 30,000 which was outstanding on 31st March, 2000 also. Cash in hand on 31st March, 2000 was Rs. 28,500.

Prepare Receipts and Payments Account of the Bharat Club for the year ended 31st March, 2000 and the Balance Sheet as on that date. (C.S. Foundation, June 2000)

Solution

Working Notes

1. Subscriptions Received during 1999-2000

Subscription as per Income and Expenditure Account		1,70,000
Add : Outstanding Subscriptions on 31-3-1999		16,000
Add : Subscription received in advance as on 31-03-2000		8,400
		1,94,400
Less : Outstanding subscriptions as on 31-3-2000	18,000	
Less : Subscriptions received in advance as on 31-3-1999	13,000	
		31,000
Subscriptions received during the year		1,63,400

2. Salaries Paid during 1999-2000

Salaries as per Income and Expenditure A/c	1,20,000
Add : Outstanding Salaries as on 31-3-1999	6,000
	1,260,000
Less : Outstanding Salaries as on 31-3-2000	8,000
Salaries paid during the year	1,18,000

3. Audit Fees Paid During 1999-2000

	Rs.
Audit fees as per Income and Expenditure Account	2,500
Add : Outstanding Audit Fees as on 31-3-1999	2,000
	4,500
Less : Outstanding Audit Fees as on 31-3-2000	2,500
Audit fees paid during the year	2,000

4. Sports Equipment Account

	Rs.		Rs.
To Balance b/d	52,000	By Depreciation	7,000
To Cash Purchases (Balacning figure)	18,000	By Balance c/d	63,000
	70,000		70,000

5. Balance Sheet as on 31st March, 1999

	Rs.		Rs.
Subscription received in advance	13,000	Cash in hand (as per Receipts and Payments A/c)	13,600
Salaries Outstanding	6,000	Subscription Outstanding	16,000
Audit Fee Outstanding	2,000	Sports Equipment	52,000
Bank Loan	30,000	Buildings	1,90,000
Capital Fund (Balancing figure)	2,20,600		
	2,71,600		2,71,600

Receipts and Payments A/c of Bharat Club
For the year ended 31st March, 2000

Recipts	Rs.	*Payments*	Rs.
To Balance b/d (Balancing figure)	13,600	By Salaries (W N – 2)	1,18,000
To Subscriptions (W N – 1)	1,63,400	By Printing	6,000
To Entrance Fee	4,000	By Postage	500
To Contribution for dinner	36,000	By Telephone	1,500
		By General Expenses	12,000
		By Interest charges	5,500
		By Audit Fees (W N – 3)	2,000
		By Annual dinner expenses	25,000
		By Sports equipment Purchased (W N - 4)	18,000
		By Balance c/d	28,500
	2,17,000		2,17,000

Balance Sheet as on 31st March, 2000

		Rs.		Rs.
Capital Fund	2,20,600		Buildings	1,90,000
Add : Surplus for the year	30,000		Sports Equipment	63,000
		2,50,600	Subscription Outstanding	18,000
Bank Loan		30,000	Cash in Hand	28,500
Subscription received in advance		8,400		
Salaries Outstandings		8,000		
Audit Fees Outstandings		2,500		
		2,99,500		2,99,500

Problem 14

(Preparation of Receipts & Payments Account and Income and Expenditure Account)

Universal Brotherhood Club does not maintain complete double entry books of accounts. From the following details, prepare a Receipts and Payments Account and an Income and Expenditure Account for the year ending 31st December, 1999 and a Balance Sheet as on that date.

	1-1-99 Rs.	31-11-99 Rs.
Outstanding Subscriptions	14,000	19,600
Advance Subscriptions	2,800	5,600
Outstanding Salaries	1,400	700
Salary Advance	—	700
Cash in hand and at Bank	14,000	?
5% Investment	14,000	7,000
Furniture	2,800	1,400
Sports goods	5,600	11,200.

Subscription for the year amount to Rs. 70,000 salaries paid Rs. 15,400. Face value of investments was Rs. 16,800. 50% of investments was sold at 80% of face value. Interest on investmentt left unsold was received. Rs. 1,400 Furniture was sold for Rs. 700 at the beginning of the year. Sports goods were purchased at the end of the year. Charge 20% depreciation on sports goods and 10% on furniture. Sports expenses amount to Rs. 14,000. Miscellaneous expenses are Rs. 4,200 and rent amounts to Rs. 8,400.

(Calcutta University B-Com (Hons)., 2000)

Solution

Working Notes

1. **Balance Sheet as on 1-1-99**

	Rs.		*Rs.*
Advance Subscription	2,800	Outstanding Subscription	14,000
Outstanding Salaries	1,400	Cash	14,000
Capital Fund (Balancing figures)	46,200	5% Investments	14,000
		Furniture	2,800
		Sports Goods	5,600
	50,400		50,400

2. **Subscription Received**

$$= 70{,}000 - (19{,}600 + 2{,}800) + (14{,}000 + 5{,}600)$$

$$= 67{,}200.$$

3. **Loss on Sale of Investment**

$$= 7{,}000 - \left(16{,}800 \times \frac{50}{100} \times \frac{80}{100}\right) = 280$$

4. **Depreciation on Sports Goods**

$$5{,}600 \times \frac{20}{100} = 1{,}120$$

5. Depreciation on Furniture

$$(2{,}800 - 1{,}400) \times \frac{10}{100} = 140$$

In the books of Universal Brotherhood
Receipts and Payments A/c

Recipts	*Rs.*	*Payments*	*Rs.*
To Cash in hand	14,000	By Salaries	15,400
To Subscriptions	67,200	By Sports expenses	14,000
To Sale of Investments	6,720	By Miscellaneous Expenses	4,300
To Sale of furniture	700	By Rent	8,400
To Interest in Investments	420	By Purchase of Sports goods	5,600
		By Cash in Hand	41,440
	89,040		89,040

Income and Expenditure A/c
For the year ended 31-11-1999

Expenditure	*Rs.*	*Income*	*Rs.*
To Salaries	14,000	By Subscriptions	70,000
(15,400 + 700) – (1,400 + 700)		By Interest in Investment	420
To Sports Expenses	14,000		
To Miscellaneous Expenses	4,200		
To Rent	8,400		
To Loss on Furniture	700		
To Loss on Investment	280		
To Depreciation on Sports goods	11,200		
To Depreciation on Furniture	140		
To Capital Fund (Surplus Transferred)	27,580		
	70,420		70,420

Balance Sheet as on 31-12-99

		Rs.			*Rs.*
Capital Fund	46,200		Furniture	1,400	
Add : Surplus	27,580		Less : Depreciation	140	
		73,780			1,260
Subscription received in advance		5,600	5% Investment		7,000
Outstanding Salaries		700	(Face Value Rs. 8,400)		
			Sports Goods	11,200	
			Less : Depreciation	1,120	
					10,080
			Cash in Hand		41,440
			Accrued Subscriptions		19,600
			Salary Paid in Advance		700
		80,080			80,080

QUESTIONS

SIMPLE QUESTIONS

1. What are non-trading concerns ?
2. What do you mean by capital expenditure ?
3. State the differences between Receipts and Payments Accounts and Cash Book.
4. Give four examples of capital expenditure.
5. What do you mean by revenue expenditure ?
6. What do you mean by deferred revenue expenditure ?
7. Define capital receipt.
8. What is meant by capital fund ?
9. State the differences beteen capital and revenue expenditure.
10. State the features of Income and Expenditure Account.
11. Sttate the differences between Profit & Loss Account and Income and Expenditure Account.

EXERCISE 1

From the following particulars, calculate the actual amount of subscriptions received during the year 1998 :

Subscription as per Income and Expenditure Account	45,000
Subscription due for the year 1997	4,000
Subscription due for the year 1998	6,000
Subscriptions received in advance during 1998	5,000
Subscriptions received in advance during 1998	5,000
Subscriptions received in advance during 1999	4,600

(Osmania University, B-com, October, 1999)

Answer :- Subscriptions received during the year Rs. 43,400.

EXERCISE 2

(Income and Expenditure Account and Balance Sheet)

Following is the Receipts and Payments Account of India Medical Soceity, for the year ended March 31, 1998.

Receipts and Payments A/c
For the year ended on 31st March, 1998

Recipts	*Rs.*	*Payments*	*Rs.*
To Balance b/d	7,000	By Medicine Suppliers	30,000
To Subscription	50,000	By Honorarium to Doctors	10,000
To Donations	14,500	By Sundry expenses	2,000
To Interest on Investment 10% p.a.	10,000	By Salaries	30,000
To Charity Show Proceeds	15,000	By Equipments	12,000
		By Charity Show expenses	4,000
		By Balance c/d	8,500
	96,500		96,500

Additional Information

	1-4-97	31-3-98
	Rs.	Rs.
(i) Subscription in arrears	NIL	2,000
(ii) Stock of Medcines	10,000	15,000
(iii) Medicine Suppliers (Cr.)	8,000	12,000
(iv) Value of Equipments	23,000	30,000
(v) Value of Buildings	50,000	47,500

Donations are not received for any purpose.

You are requested to prepare :-

1. Income and Expenditure Account for the year ended on March 31, 1998 ; and
2. Balance Sheet as on that date.

(Delhi University B-com 2000 (External))

Answer : Surplus as shown by Income and Expenditure A/c Rs. 9,000
Balance Sheet ; Total Rs. 2,03,000

EXERCISE 3

The following is the Receipts and Payments Accounts of the Calcutta club for the year ending 31-12-92.

Recipts	*Rs.*	*Payments*	*Rs.*
Opening Balances :-		Salaries	6,000
Cash	1,025	Sports Expenses	6,900
Stamps	50	Electricity	1,000
Bank F.D.R.	10,000	Telephone	1,200
Bank - S.B. A/c	4,200	Postage Expenses	200
Bank Current A/c	2,100	General Body Expenses	700
Subscriptions		Printing & Stationery	850
1996	1,010	Building Purchases A/c	12,000
1997	18,900	Repairs	400
1998	900	Closing Balances :	
Donations	7,000	Cash	1,740
Bank interest received	1,340	Stamps	25
Receipts from Sports	2,600	Bank F.D. A/c	11,000
Telephone recoveries	900	Bank S.B. A/c	4,310
		Bank Current A/c	3,700
	50,025		50,025

A building costing Rs. 1,00,000 was purchased during last year and Rs. 88,000 was paid for it.

Subscription outstanding for 1997	1,100
Salaries Outstanding	200
Interest accrued on bank deposit but not received	200

From the above, prepare Income and Expenditue Account for the year 1997 and also the Balance Sheet as on 31-12-1997 of the Calcutta Club.

(Osmania University B-Com, October, 1998)

Answer : Excess of Income over Expenditure as shown by Income and Expenditure A/c Rs. 14,590.
Total of Balance Sheet Rs. 1,22,075.

EXERCISE 4

The accounts set out below have been put up to you for audit. If you do not approve it, amend it and prepare Balance Sheet at end.

EAST CLUB'S INCOME AND EXPENDITURE A/c FOR THE YEAR ENDING 31-3-1995

Expenditure		*Rs.*	*Income*	*Rs.*
Entrance Fees (21 at Rs. 10)		210	Salaries and Wages	675
Life Membership fees		260	Secretary's Salary	350
Annual Subscription	1,565		Rent Rates	1,265
Add : Paid in Advance	65		Printing and Postage	37
		1,630	Repairs to Premises	124
Interest on C.P. Notes		70	Interest on Bank Loan	57
Sundry Receipts		60	Balance c/d	960
Balance of last year		1,238		
		3,468		3,468

Treasurer's Note

The subscriptions in arrears amounted to Rs. 120. Sundry bills are Rs. 42 were outstanding. Secretary's salary has not been paid. The 3.5% C.P. Notes (Face Value Rs. 2,000) were bought at Rs. 20. Lease of the club premises costed Rs. 2,124. Cash Balance on 1-4-1994 was Rs. 1,238 and on 31-3-1995 Rs. 1,190. Bank loan taken was Rs. 1,000.

(Osmania University B-com, April 1998)

Answer : Excess of Expenditure over Income Rs. 645.
Total of Balance Sheet Rs. 3,834.

EXERCISE 5

The following shows the position of the Calcutta Library as at 1st January 1997.

	Rs.		*Rs.*
Capital Fund	1,50,000	Building	50,000
Outstanding Expenses	5,000	Furniutre	5,000
		Library	25,000
		Investments	50,000
		Outsanding subscriptions	20,000
		Cash in Hand	5,000
	1,55,000		1,55,000

An analysis of the cash book during the year gives the following particulars :

Recipts	*Rs.*	*Payments*	*Rs.*
To Subscription	75,000	By Salaries	3,600
To Donations	50,000	By Purchase of Books	40,000
To Interest on Investment	600	By Rent and Taxes	3,600
To Sale of old Furniture	500	By Outstanding Expenses	5,000
To Proceeds of lectures etc.	8,000	By Insurance Premium	1,500
		By Printing & Stationery	450
		By Purchase of Furniture	7,500
		By Investment	75,000
		By Sundry expenses	450
		By Balance	2,000

The following adjustments are required :-

(*a*) Outstanding subscriptions Rs. 15,000

(*b*) Outstanding liabilities for expenses Rs. 7,500

(*c*) Insurance premium amouting to Rs. 300 was paid in advance.

(*d*) Depreciate on Building at 5% ; Library at 10% and Investment at 5%.

Prepare Income and Expenditure Account for the year ended 31st December, 1997 and a Balance Sheet as at that date. **(Calcutta University ; B.Com (Hons.) 1998)**

Answer : Capital Fund (Surplus) 67,050
Balance Sheet Total Rs. 2,74,550

EXERCISE 6

The following is the Receipts and Payments Account of Bengal Club for the year ended 31st December, 1996.

Recipts	*Rs.*	*Payments*	*Rs.*
To Balance	2,100	By General expenses	1,600
To subscriptions	17,500	By Salaries	4,500
To Donations for Building	5,000	By Electric charges	1,200
To entrance Fees	2,500	By Books	6,500
To Interest on Investment	1200	By Printing and Stationery	700
To Sale of Old Furniture (Costing Rs. 1,400)	1,250	By News papers and magazines	3,200
To Sale of Old Newspaper	150	By Sports Expenses	600
		By Balance	2,400
	28,700		28,700

Prepare an Income and Expenditure A/c for the year ended 31st December, 1996 taking out account the following information :

(*a*) Subscriptions include Rs. 500 relating to 1995 and subscriptions Rs. 700 for 1996 are still outstanding. Subscriptions realised in advance this year amounted to Rs. 1,900.

(*b*) 60% of the Entrance fees is to be capitalised.

(*c*) Salaries outstanding Rs. 200

(*d*) Depreciate Books and Sports Equipments at 10%.

(*e*) Interest on Investment accrued Rs. 400. (Calcutta University B-Com (Pass) 1997

Answers : Excess of income over expenditure has shown by income and expenditure Rs. 4,850.

EXERCISE 7

From the following Trial Balance and the necessary information given below for Saraswati Public School, prepare Income and Expenditure for the year 1994-95 and a Balance sheet as on 31-3-195.

Debit Balance	*Rs.*	*Credit Balance*	*Rs.*
Buildings	2,50,000	Admission fees	5,000
Furniture	4,000	Tution & Other fees	2,00,000
Library Books	6,000	Creditors for Suppliers	6,000
Investments at 9%	2,00,000	Rent for the hall	4,000
Salaries	2,00,000	Miscellaneous Receipts	12,000
Stationery	15,000	Government Grants	1,40,000
General expenses	8,000	General Fund	4,00,000
Annual sports expenses	6,000	Donation for Library Books	25,000
Cash at Bank	21,000	Sale of furniture	8,000
	8,00,000		8,00,000

Tution and other fes yet to be received for the year are Rs. 10,000. Salaries yet to be paid amounted to Rs. 12,000. Furniture costing Rs. 15,000 was purchased on 1-1-94. Book value of furnitture sold (on 30-9-94) was Rs. 20,000 on 1-4-94. Depreciate furniture att 10%. Library books at 15% and Buildings at 5%. **(Osmania University B-com October, 1997)**

Answer : Excess of income over expenditure as per Income and Expenditure Account Rs. 1,13,250.
Total of Balance Sheet Rs. 5,56,250.

16

CHAPTER

Accounting Standards

INTRODUCTION

Accounting as a "language of business communicates the financial result of an enterprise to various interested parties by means of financial statements which have to exhibit a "true and fair" view of its state of affairs. Like any other language, accounting has its own complicated set of rules. However these rules have to be used with a reasonable degree of flexibility in response to specific circumstances of an enterprise and also in line with the changes in the economic environment, social needs, legal requirement and technological developments. Therefore, these rules cannot be absolutely rigid unlike those of the physical sciences. This however does not imply that accounting rules can be applied arbitrarily, for they have to operate within the bounds of nationality.

MEANING OF STANDARD

Standard refers to written statements issued by a competent authority in respect of measurement, treatment and disclosure of accounting transactions for ensuring uniformly in accounting practices and reporting. It implies a set of guide lines or a code of conduct which should be followed while treating various items which go to make up the financial statement.

Need for Accounting Standards :- The world is becoming smaller and smaller with the passage of time. Trade and commerce has expanded rapidly due to advances in the field of communication and transportation. The increasing scale of international trade and investment has given rise to a demand for unifermily in the accounting system, the accounting procedure and presentation of results which varies from country to country. Thus the overall direction of the accountant should be towards uniformly so that business profits may become comparable leading to better analysis and comparison of performance.

In response to the long felt need for standardisation of accounting on a global scale; the International Accounting Standards Committee (IASC) was formed in 1973. This leading professional accounting Institute of nine developed countries was set up for securing more sophistication and precision in accounting procedures worldwide.

Recognising the need to harmonise the diverse accounting policies and practices in India, the Institute of Chartered Accountants of India constituted on Accounting Standards Board (ASB) on 21st April 1977. The main function of ASB is to formulate accounting standards so that such standard may be established by the council of the Institute of Chartered Accountants of India. While formulating the accounting standards, ASB will take into consideration the applicable laws, customs, usages and business environment.

Purposes of Setting Accounting Standards

1. To facilitate presentation of information to the user's on the basis of sound accounting practice.
2. To ensure application of uniferm accounting policies while preparing and presentation of financial statements.
3. To facilitate comparison of accounts which becomes more reliable when accounts are prepared using accounting standards.
4. To facilitate judgement by professional accountants whether various items are treated consistently while preparing financial statements.

Advantages of Accounting Standards

1. Accounting standard implies preparation of financial statements applying uniform accounting policies and principles. This ensures easy comparison of accounts.
2. Accounts prepared by adhering to accounting standards are more reliable.
3. As accounting standards of a country are based on International Accounting Standards, the Accounting Standards ensure incorporation of the latest trends in accounting while preparing financial statements.
4. Accounting standards by raising the standard of auditing makes Chartered Accountants more sincere and commitment to their profession.
5. Accounts prepared on the basis of accounting standards are readily accepted by government official and tax authorities.
6. Accounts prepared on the basis of Accounting standard is benefited by Investors, and researchers.

Procedure for Issuing Accounting Standards

The following procedure will be adopted for formulating Accounting Standards

1. Accounting Standard Board will determine broad areas in which accounting standards need to be formulated and the priority in regard to the selection thereof.
2. In the preparation of accounting standards, ASB will be assisted by study groups constituted to consider specific subjects. In the formation of study groups, provision will be made for wide participation by the members of the Institute and others.
3. ASB will also consult the representatives of the Government, public sector undertakings, industry and other organisation for ascertaining their viewers.
4. On the basis of the deliberations of study group and consultation with various representatives as mentioned in the above point, an exposure draft of the proposed standard will be prepared and issued for comments by members of the Institute and the public at large.
5. After taking into consideration the comments received, the draft of the proposed standard will be finalised by ASB and submitted to the Council of the Institute.
6. The Council of the Institute will consider the final draft of the proposed standard and if found necessary, modify the same in consultation with ASB. The Accounting standard on the relevant subject will then be issued under the authority of the council.

Contents of Accounting Standard

The draft of the proposed standard will include the following points.

(*a*) A statement of concepts and fundamental accounting principles relating to the standard.
(*b*) Definition of the terms used in the standard.
(*c*) The manner in which the accounting principles have been applied for formulating the standard.
(*d*) The presentation and disclosure requirements in complying with the standard.
(*e*) Class of Enterprise to which the standard will apply.
(*f*) Date from which the standard will be effective.

Compliance with the Accounting Standards

It is the duly to members of the Institute of chartered accountant of India to ensure that the accounting standards are implemented in the presentation of financial statements covered by their audit reports. In the event of any deviation from the standards, it will also be thier duty to make adequate disclosures in their reports so that the users of such statements may be aware of such deviations.

Nature of Accounting Standards

The accounting standards may be recommendatory or mandatory in nature. In the initial years the standards will be recommendatory in character and the Institute will give wide publicity among the users and educate members about the utility of Accounting Standards, and the need for compliance with the above discolour requirements. Once, an awareness about these requirements is ensured steps will be taken to enforce compliance with the accounting standards in the manner stated in the above paragraph.

List of Accounting Standards Formulated by the ASB.

AS - 1 : Disclosure of Accounting Policies.
AS - 2 : Valuation of inventories.
AS - 3 : Changes in financial position
AS - 4 : Contingencies and events occurring after the balance sheet date.
AS - 5 : Prior period and extraordinary items and changes in accounting policies.
AS - 6 : Depreciation accounting
AS - 7 : Accounting for construction contracts.
AS - 8 : Accounting for research and development.
AS - 9 : Revenue recognition
AS - 10 : Accounting for fixed assets.
AS - 11 : Accounting for the effects of changes in foreign exchange rates.
AS - 12 : Accounting for government grants
AS - 13 : Accounting for investment
AS - 14 : Accounting for amalgamation
AS - 15 : Accounting for retirement benefit in the financial statements of employers.

Scope of Accounting Standards in India

The scope of accounting standards can be enumerated under the following points.

1. Accounting standards are made to conform with the laws, customs, usage and business enviornment of our country.

2. The Accounting standards in India is based on the local regulation which govern the preparation and presentation of financial statements in our country.
3. The Accounting standards are intended to apply only to items which are material. Any limitation with regard to the applicability of a specific standard will be made clear by the Institute of Chartered Accountants of India form time to time. The date from which a particular standard will come into effect, as well as the class of enterprises to which it will apply, will also be specified by the Institute of chartered Accountants of India.
4. In order to achieve uniformity in the presentation of financial statement the Institute of Chartered Accounts will persuade the appropriate authorities, the Government, industrial and business community to adopt these standards.
5. Accounting standards are designed to concentrate on basic matters It covers only essential aspects and the intention is to simplify them. They are flexible in nature.

Mandatory Accounting Standard.

Following accounting standards are mandatory.

(1) AS - 1 Disclosure of Accounting Policies

(*a*) All significant accounting policies adopted in the preparation and presentation of financial statements should be disclosed.

(*b*) The disclosure of the significant accounting Policies as such should form part of the financial statements and the significant accounting policies should normally be disclosed at one place.

(*c*) Any change in the accounting policies which has a material effect in the current period or which is reasonably expected to have a material effect in later periods should be disclosed. In the case of change in accounting policies which has a material effect in the current period, the amount by which any item in the financial statement is affected by such change should also be disclosed to the extent ascertainable where such amount is not ascertainable wholly or in part, the fact should be indicated.

(*d*) If the fundamental accounting assumptions are followed in financial statements, specific disclosure is not required. If a fundamental accounting assumption is not followed the fact should be disclosed.

(2) AS - 4 Contingencies and events accruing after the balance sheet date.

1. Contingent liabilities do not form part of the totals of the balance sheet. It will become an actual liability only on the happening of a certain event which may or may not happen Hence it is sufficient if these are disclosed by way of a note in the balance sheet.
2. These are to be disclosed in the following manner ;

   (*a*) Claims against the company not acknowledged as debts.

   (*b*) Uncalled liability on shares partly paid.

   (*c*) Arrears of dividends on cumulative preference share.

   (*d*) Estimated amount of contracts remaining to be executed on capital account and not provided for

   (*c*) Other money for which the company is contingent by liable (i e liability on bill receivable previously discounted).
3. The amounts of any guarantee give on the behalf of the directors or other officers of the company must be stated and where practicable the general nature and amount of each such contigent liability, if material is also to be specified.

4. In respect of assets of fixed cumulative dividend the following are to be disclosed.
   (*a*) the period for which dividends are in arrears
   (*b*) The amount of dividends in arrears
   (*c*) Deduction of income tax.
   (*d*) In case of tax-free dividends, the amounts must be shown free of income tax.

   The above information should be given in respect of each class of preference shares separately.
5. Contegent liabilities have two characteristic as follows : Uncertainly as to whether the amount will be payable at all and uncertaintly about the amount involved. Hence it is sufficient if these are disclosed by way of a note in the balance sheet.

(3) **AS - 5 Net profit or loss for the period, prior period items and changes in the Accounting policies**

These items arise due to changes in the accounting policies and are generally non-recurring in nature.

Prior period items are material changes in credit which arise in the current period as a result of errors and omission in the preparation of financial statements of one and more priority period.

Extra ordinary items gain all losses that arise from the events and transactions which are distinct from the normal activities of business. They also include material adjustments which are necessitated by circumstances arises for no recurring items.

Events Occurring After Balance Sheet Date

These are the significant events favourable or unfavourable that occur after balance sheet date and before date on which financial statement are approved by appropriate authority.

These events may indicate the need for adjustment of statement itself. This is applicable where the events are related to some condition existing on Balance Sheet date.

The event following the conditions arising subsequent to Balance Sheet date need to be disclosed separately without altering the statement is not considered desirable.

The manner of disclosure in respect of events can be by a coverage in the notes on the accounts or in the report. The disclosure should furnish information regarding.

(*a*) Nature of event and
(*b*) Estimate of financial effect.
If estimates are not possible a statement to that affect should be included.

(4) **AS 12 - Accounting for Government Grants**

This standard requires that Government grant should be recognised as revenue only when :

(*a*) There is reasonable certainty that the enterprise will comply with conditions attached.
(*b*) There is reasonable certainty that the grants will be received.
The financial statement should disclose.

(*a*) Accounting policy adopted for the grants.
(*b*) Nature and extent of grants.

The grants can be categorised as :

(*a*) Related to specific fixed assets
(*b*) Related to revenue
(*c*) Related to promoters contribution

There are two approaches for accounting, viz,

(a) 'Capital' approach — This approach treats grants as equivalent to shareholders funds. It considers grant as incentives provided by government without related cost.
(b) "Income approach" — This approach recognises grant as income related to appropriate period an systematic and rational basis.

QUESTIONS

SIMPLE QUESTIONS

1. What do you mean by Accounting standard.
2. State any four advantages of accounting standards.
3. State any four objectives of accounting standards.
4. List out the contents of accounting standards.

SHORT ANSWER QUESTIONS

1. Explain the need for accounting standards.
2. Explain the various mandatory accounting standards.

17

CHAPTER

Partnership Accounts — Past Adjustment and Guarantee

1. DEFINITION AND FEATURES OF PARTNERSHIP

Section 4 of the Indian Partnership Act 1932 defines a partnership as "the relation between the partners who have agreed to share the profits of business carried on by all or any of them acting for all". The persons entering into partnership is individually called as partners and collectively a firm.

FEATURES OF PARTNERSHIP

1. There must be a minimum of 2 persons to form a partnership. However the maximum is fixed at 10 persons in case a firm carries on banking business and 20 in case of other business.
2. An agreement is essential to form a partnership business.
3. It can be carried on by all the partners or some of the partners on behalf of all partners.
4. The business must be carried on for earning profit.
5. The business must be carried for a lawful purpose.
6. The liability of partners in a firm is unlimited.
7. Partners cannot transfer their ownership without obtaining the consent of other partners.
8. Utmost good faith among partners is one the important features of partnership.

2. TYPE OF PARTNERS

Partners in a partnership may be of the following types.

1. **Active or Working Partner :** An active partner is one who not only contributes capital but also takes active part in the business.
2. **Dormant or Sleeping Partners :** He is a partner who contributes only capital but does not take any part in the partnership business.
3. **Nominal Partner :** He is a partner who neither contributes capital nor takes active part in the business. But he lends his name and reputation to the business.

4. **Partner in Profit :** He is a partner who shares only profit but not loss of the firm. However, he is liable to other for the debt of the firm.
5. **Partner by Estoppel :** He is a partner who neither contributes capital nor claims any right in the firm. But he creates an impression among outsiders that he is one of the partner of the firm. He is liable to outsiders for the debt of the firm.
6. **Partner by Holding out :** His is a partner who does not contradict his partnership when declared to be a partner in a firm. He is liable to outsiders for the debt of the firm.
7. **Secret Partner :** He is partner who does not want his name to be disclosed to outsiders though he is an actual partner.
8. **Minor Partner :** He is a partner who has no capacity to enter into partnership agreement but admitted to the benefit of the firm.

3. PARTNERSHIP AGREEMENT

Partnership comes into existence as result of an agreement. The agreement may be oral or written. The written agreement of the partners is known as partnership agreement or Articles of partnership.

Contents of Partnership Agreement

1. The name of the firm.
2. The nature of the partnership business.
3. The names and addresses of partners.
4. The rights, duties and liabilities of partners.
5. The duration of partnership.
6. The amount of capital contributed by the partner and the interest payable thereon.
7. Profit sharing ratio.
8. Salary, commission and interest on capital.
9. Drawings of partners and interest thereon.
10. Loans given by partners and interest thereon .
11. Valuation of goodwill on reconstitution of the firm.
12. Valuation of assets and liabilities on reconstitution of the firm.
13. Arbitration clause.
14. Duration of notice required for retirement.
15. The manner of settlement of accounts on retirement or death of a partner.
16. The mode of dissolution of the partnership.
17. Maintenance of accounts and its audit.

Rules applicable in the absence of Partnership Deed

When the partnership deed is silent on any of the above matters, the following rules of partnerships Act is applicable.

1. Partners to share profit & loss equally.
2. Partners are not entitled to interest on their capital.
3. No interest is charged on partners drawings.
4. No salary or commission is payable for the efforts of partners.
5. 6% interest is payable on loan given by the partner.

Partnership Accounts Vs Sole Proprietorship Accounts

The partnership accounts does not differ much from the accounts of a sole traders. As in the case of sale trader, partnership firm will also prepare capital accounts of partners a profit & loss appropriation a./c and a Balance Sheet at the end of accounting year. However partnership accounts differ from sole trading accounts in two respects.

(*a*) A sole trader prepare his capital account and a drawings account. Whereas a partner may prepare capital a/c, current a/c, drawings a/c, loan a/c.

2. The various adjustments in a sole trader's account is made by opening a profit & loss a/c. Whereas in partnership accounts such adjustments are made by preparing a profit & loss appropriation a/c, which is an extension of P & L a/c.

Special Aspects of Partnership Accounts

While preparing partnership accounts the following aspects deserve special mention.

Capital Accounts

The capital contributed by a partner (in the form of cash, kind or both) is recorded in the capital account. Thêre are two methods of maintaining capital accounts of partners viz (*a*) fixed capital method and (*b*) fluctuating capital method.

(*a*) **Fixed capital method :** Under this method the original capital amount of partners remain fixed unless there are any additions to or withdrawal from the capital. When a partner contributes the capital his capital a/c is credited with the amount contributed by him. The various adjustments relating to drawings, interest on capital, salary, commission, profit, or loss etc. are not made in capital a/c. Instead a separate account known as a current a/c is opened and all adjustment are made in it. Thus under method two accounts are maintained, viz, (*a*) capital a/c (*b*) current a/c.

A proforma of fixed capital a/c and current a/c of a partner are given below.

Partners Fixed Capital A/c

	Rs.		*Rs.*
To Cash a/c To Asset a/c (When capital is withdrawn)	X X X X	By Cash a/c By Asset a/c (When original capital is contributed)	X X X X
To Balanced c/d (Balancing figure)	X X	By Cash a/c By Asset a/c (When additional capital is contributed	X X X X

Partners Current A/c

	Rs.		*Rs.*
To Drawing a/c	X X	By Balance B/d	X X
To Interest on drawings	X X	By Interest on capital a/c	X X
To Profit & Loss Appropriation a/c — Loss	X X	By Salary	X X
To Balance c/d (If credit side is greater)		By Commission	X X
		By Profit & Loss Appropriation a/c — Profit	X X
		By Balance c/d (If debit side is greater)	X X

Some times drawings a/c is maintained separately independent of current account. In such a case the amount withdrawn whether in cash or kind is debited to drawings account and the balance is transferred to partners current account. A specimen form of drawings account is shown below.

Partner's Drawings A/c

	Rs.		*Rs.*
To Cash or Bank (When cash is withdrawn)	X X	By Partner current a/c (Total Drawings transferred to current a/c)	X X
To Purchases a/c (When goods are withdrawn)	X X		
To Asset a/c (When asset is withdrawn)	X X		

(*b*) **Fluctuating or Floating Capital Method :-** Under this method the capital amount of partners keep fluctuating from year to year. This is so because all adjustments in respect of salary, commission, interest on capital, profit etc. are all recorded in the capital a/c. Since all adjustments are made in the capital account there is no need to prepare a current account under this method. A proforma of fluctuating capital is given below.

Partner's Capital A/c

	Rs.		*Rs.*
To Drawings a/c	X X	By Cash or bank a/c	X X
To Interest on drawings	X X	By Asset a/c	X X
To P & L Appropriation a/c — Loss		By Interest on capital a/c	X X
To Balance c/d (If credit side is greater than debit side)	X X	By Salaries a/c	X X
		By Commission a/c	X X
		By P & L Appropriation a/c — Profit	X X
		By Balance c/d (If debit side is greater than credit side)	X X
	X X		X X

Difference Between Fixed and Fluctuation Capital Methods

(*a*) Capital balance under fixed method remains constant throughout. Whereas under fluctuating method the capital balance differs from year to year.

(*b*) The capital balance under fixed method will always show credit balance. Whereas under fluctuating method capital balance may be a debit balance because of heavy withdrawal and losses.

(*c*) Under fixed capital method, capital a/c and current a/c are prepared. Whereas under fluctuating capital method only capital a/c is prepared.

3. Partners Drawings Account

Sometimes partners withdraw cash in anticipation of their share of profit for their private use. Drawings can be in the form of cash or goods or assets. The following entries are recorded.

(*a*) For withdrawal of Cash :

Partner's Drawings a/c Dr.
    To Cash or Bank a/c

(*b*) For withdrawal of goods :

Partners Drawings a/c Dr.
    To Purchases a/c

(*c*) For withdrawal of assets :

Partner's Drawings a/c Dr.
    To Asset a/c

At the end of the year the balance in the drawings a/c is transferred to partner's capital a/c.

3. Interest on Capital a/c :- When partners agree to allow interest on their capital, it is calculated on the opening balance of capital. Such rate of interest is fixed by partnership agreement. Interest on capital is mostly allowed when there is disproportionate contribution of capital. Naturally, a partner who contributes more capital but get less share of profit owing to sharing profit & loss on equal basis must get benefit by way of charging interest on his capital. The interest on capital is either credited to capital a/c (where fluctuating capital method is followed) or credited to current a/c (where fixed capital method is adopted). The following entry is recorded.

Interest on capital a/c Dr.
    To Partner's capital a/c

At the end of the year the interest on capital is charged to debit side of P & L Appropriation a/c.

4. Interest on Drawings :- When the partners draw any amount from the firm it is treated as a temporary loan due from the partner to the firm. Interest on drawings is charged as per partnership deed from the date of drawing to the account ending period. The following entries are passed to record the interest on drawings.

(*a*) Partners drawings a/c Dr
    To Interest on drawings
    (Being the interest on drawings charged)

(*b*) Interest on drawings a/c Dr
    To P & L Appropriation a/c
    (Being interest on drawings transferred to P & L Appropriation a/c).

Method of Calculating Interest on Drawings

The following methods are used to calculate interest on drawings :

1. When the withdrawal is made only once during the accounting period and the date of withdrawal is mentioned

In this case interest is calculated on the amount withdrawn at the agreed rate from the date of drawing upto the accounting period.

Problem 1

Mr. 'A' a partner has withdrawn Rs. 1,000 on 1st April 2003. Interest on drawings chargeable is 5% p.a. The books are closed on 31st December every year. Calculate interest on A's drawings.

Solution

$$10{,}000 \times \frac{9}{12} \times \frac{5}{100} = \text{Rs. } 37.50$$

2. When different sums are drawn at different time during the same accounting year and the interval between two withdrawal is not uniform :-

Two alternate methods are available for calculation of interest on drawings.

(*a*) **First method :-** Interest on drawings in calculated on each amount withdrawn for the period of drawings. The total interest is obtained by adding interest on various drawings.

Problem 2

Mr. 'A' a partner withdrew the following amounts on :

31st	March	2003	Rs. 10,000
30th	June	2003	Rs. 5,000
31st	Oct.	2003	Rs. 2,000

The accounting period is 31st December every year. Calculate interest on Mr. 'A' drawings if the rate of interest is 6%.

Solution

$$10{,}000 \times \frac{9}{12} \times \frac{6}{100} = 450$$

$$5{,}000 \times \frac{6}{12} \times \frac{6}{100} = 150$$

$$2{,}000 \ \frac{2}{12} \times \frac{6}{100} = 20$$

Total interest 620

Second Method : Product method :

The following steps are involved :

(*a*) Multiply the amount withdrawn by the number of months that elapses between the date of withdrawal and the date of accounting period.

(*b*) Add all the product so obtained.

(*c*) Charge interest at the agreed rate for one month.

Problem 3

Calculate the total interest on drawings under the product method for problem 1

Solution

Amount	*No of months that elapse between the date of withdrawal to the date of accounting period.*	*Product*
10,000	9	90,000
5,000	6	30,000
2,000	2	4,000
		1,24,000

$$1{,}24{,}000 \times \frac{6}{100} \times \frac{1}{12} = \text{Rs. } 620$$

Case – 3. If uniform amount is with drawn at each time and the interval between two withdrawal is also uniform.

Under this situation any one of the following three methods can be followed.

Method 1

Under this method interest is calculated from the date of withdrawal to the end of accounting period. After adding the interest on all the withdrawals the total interest can be obtained.

Problem 4

Mr. 'A', a partner withdrew Rs. 2,000 at the beginning of every month for the year ending 31st December 2003. Interest on drawings is calculated at 6% per annum. Calculate interest on Mr. 'A's drawings.

Solution

Calculation of Interest on Drawing

Jan.	$2000 \times \frac{6}{100} \times \frac{12}{12}$	= 120
Feb.	$2000 \times \frac{6}{100} \times \frac{11}{12}$	= 110
Mar.	$2000 \times \frac{6}{100} \times \frac{10}{12}$	= 100
Apr.	$2000 \times \frac{6}{100} \times \frac{9}{12}$	= 90
May	$2000 \times \frac{6}{100} \times \frac{8}{12}$	= 80
June	$2000 \times \frac{6}{100} \times \frac{7}{12}$	= 70
July	$2000 \times \frac{6}{100} \times \frac{6}{12}$	= 60
Aug.	$2000 \times \frac{6}{100} \times \frac{5}{12}$	= 50
Sept.	$2000 \times \frac{6}{100} \times \frac{4}{12}$	= 40
Oct.	$2000 \times \frac{6}{100} \times \frac{3}{12}$	= 30
Nov.	$2000 \times \frac{6}{100} \times \frac{2}{12}$	= 20
Dec.	$2000 \times \frac{6}{100} \times \frac{1}{12}$	= 10
		Total 780

Method 2 - Product Method

The steps outlined under method-2, Case-2 are applicable to this method.

Problem 5

Work out the total interest payable to Mr. 'A' for problem No. 3

Solution

Calculation of Total Interest

Months of withdrawal	*Amount of Drawings*	*No. of months that elapses between the date of withdrawal and the end of accounting year*	*Product*
Jan.	2000	12	24,000
Feb.	2000	11	22,000
Mar.	2000	10	20,000
Apr.	2000	9	18,000
May	2000	8	16,000
June	2000	7	14,000
July	2000	6	12,000
Aug.	2000	5	10,000
Sept.	2000	4	8,000
Oct.	2000	3	6,000
Nov.	2000	2	4,000
Dec.	2000	1	2,000
			1,56,000

$$\text{Interest per month} = 1{,}56{,}000 \times \frac{6}{100} \times \frac{1}{12} = \text{Rs. } 780$$

Method 3

Under this method, interest on drawings is calculated by applying following steps :

(*a*) Calculate the average of the longest period (i.e., The period involved in the first withdrawal and the shortest period (i.e. the period involved in the last withdrawal).

(*b*) Find out the total drawings.

(*c*) Calculate the interest using the rate of interest on the drawings.

Problem 6

Calculate the interest on drawings for problem No. 3

Solution

Average of longest period and shortest period.

$$\frac{12+1}{2} = 6\tfrac{1}{2} \text{ months}$$

$$\text{Total Drawing} = 2{,}000 \times 12 = 24{,}000$$

$$\text{Interest on drawings} = 24{,}000 \times \frac{6\frac{1}{2}}{12} \times \frac{6}{100}$$

$$= 24{,}000 \times \frac{13}{2} \times \frac{1}{12} \times \frac{6}{100} = \text{Rs. } 780$$

5. Salary and Commission of Partners

Those partners who contribute skill and ability to a firm are entitled to salary or commission provided there is an agreement for such payment. The salary or commission is not paid in cash instead it is credited to the partners current a/c or capital a/c. As salary or commission is paid out of divisible profit it is debited to profit & loss appropriation account. The entry is as follows.

P & L Appropriation a/c Dr.
To Salary a/c or commission a/c

When Salary or commission is withdrawn the following Journal entry is passed

Salary a/c or Commission a/c Dr.
To Cash a/c

6. Partners Loan a/c

Whenever a firm is in need of additional funds it can obtain from partners instead of resorting to external source. The loan contributed is different from capital contribution. The entry to record loan contributed by a partner is as follows :

Cash a/c Dr
To Partner's loan a/c

The loan amount is shown separately on the liability side of the balance sheet.

7. Interest on Partner's Loan a/c

Whenever a partner lends a loan to a firm he is entitled to get interest on loan as per the agreement entered into by partners. Where no such agreement is entered into the partner is eligible to get interest at 6% p.a. The interest on loan is an appropriation of profit. Hence the following journal entry is passed to record interest on loan of a partner.

Interest on Loan a/c Dr
To P & L Appropriation a/c

PROFIT & LOSS APPROPRIATION ACCOUNT

The net profit as arrived at by preparing profit & loss a/c is used for various dispositions, division and appropriation, such as paying salary or commission, interest on capital, interest on drawings etc. All there are accounted through profit & loss appropriation a/c.

Beginning with net profit (Cr.) or net loss (Dr.) the account is credited with interest on drawing and debited with salary or commission paid to partners interest on partners capital etc. The balance representing net profit or loss will be transferred to partners capital or current a/c in their profit sharing ratios and the account is closed.

Problem 7

Mr. N and K commenced business with capital investment of Rs. 4,00,000 and Rs. 3,00,000 respectively on Jan. 1st 2003. They agreed to share the profit in the ratio of 3 : 2 . For the year ending December 31st 2003 they earned a profit of Rs. 1,20,000 before allowing (*i*) Interest on capital at 5% (*ii*) Interest on drawings (N-Rs. 1,200 and K-Rs. 1,000 (*iii*) Partners Salary to 'K' Rs. 30,000. Their drawings during the year amounted to 'N' Rs. 70,000 and 'K' Rs. 40,000.

Prepare Profit & Loss Appropriation a/c

Solution

Profit & Loss Appropriation A/c

	Rs.			Rs.
To K's capital a/c — Salary	30,000	By P & L a/c		1,20,000
To Interest on capital		By Interest on		
N — $\left(\frac{5}{100} \times 4{,}00{,}000\right)$	20,000	N —	1,200	
K — $\left(\frac{5}{100} \times 3{,}00{,}000\right)$	15,000	K —	1,000	2,200
To Net profit transferred to Partners capital account				
N	34,320			
K	22,880			
	1,22,200			1,22,200

Difference between Profit & Loss a/c and Profit & Loss Appropriation a/c.

P & L a/c	*P & L App. a/c*
1. P & L a/c is an extension of trading a/c. Hence it is starts with gross profit or loss as shown by the trading a/c	1. It is an extension P & L a/c. It starts with net profit or net loss as shown by P & L a/c
2. The P & L a/c contains general expenses which are in the nature of administration expenses, selling & distribution expenses and financial expenses and incomes from general business.	2. It includes special transactions such as interest on capital salaries or commission, interest on partners loan etc.
3. The purpose of P & L a/c is to know the net profit or loss of the partnership	3. The purpose of P & L Appropriation a/c is to distribute profit or loss of the firm. among partners.

PAST ADJUSTMENTS

Some times partnership accounts must have been closed without taking into account certain transactions or by recording wrong amount of such transactions. Those transactions relate to interest on capital, interest on drawings, salary or commission of partners etc. When such ommissions or commissions are discovered subsequently they are to be adjusted accordingly.

If such adjustments are carried out in the same accounting year they are recorded properly in the profit & loss appropriation account and the balance is transferred to partners current a/c (under fixed capital method) or partner's capital a/c (under fluctuation capital method).

Where the mistakes are discovered in the subsequent accounting year such adjustments one made in an account known as Profit & Loss Adjustment a/c but not in Profit & Loss appropriation a/c. The balance from Profit & Loss adjustment a/c is then transferred to partners current a/c (under fixed capita method) or partner's capital a/c (under fluctuation capital method).

Problem 8

A, B and C started a partnership from 1-4-98. A contributed Rs. 3,000 on 1-4-98. B contributed Rs. 2,000 on 1-4-98 and thereafter increases his capital to Rs. 2,500 from 1-8-98 and then after 8 months on 1-12-98 he withdrew Rs. 1,500. 'C' contributing Rs. 4,000 on 1-4-98. Withdrew Rs. 2,500 after 6 months on 1-10-98.

At the end of the year on 31-3-99 they made a profit of Rs. 910. Show how the partners would divide this profit on the basis of the effective capital employed by each partner during the whole year 1998-99. **(Calcutta University, B. Com (Pass) 2000).**

Solution

Calculation of Effective Capital Employed

$$A = 3{,}000 \times 12 \text{ months} = 36{,}000$$

$$B = (2{,}000 \times 4 \text{ months}) + (2{,}500 \times 4) + (1{,}000 \times 4) = 22{,}000$$

Note :- Rs. 1,000 is the difference between Rs. 2,500 and 1,500 of withdrawings

$$C = (4{,}000 \times 6 \text{ months}) + (1{,}500 \times 6 \text{ months}) = \text{Rs. } 33{,}000$$

Note :- Rs. 1,500 is the difference between Rs. 4,000 and Rs. 2,500 of withdrawing).

Division of Profit for the year

Profit sharing ratios of partners

36,000 : 22,000 : 33,000

36 ; 22 ;. 33

A's share of profit $910 \times \frac{36}{91} = \text{Rs. } 360$

B's share of profit $910 \times \frac{22}{91} = \text{Rs. } 220$

C's share of profit $910 \times \frac{33}{91} = \text{Rs. } 330$

Problem 9

The partners A and B decided to appropriate profit of the firm on the following terms.

(*a*) Interest is payable on capitals at 5% p.a.

(*b*) Both A and B will get remuneration at Rs. 200 and Rs. 100 per month respectively.

(*c*) Interest will be paid on the loan of Rs. 5,000 contributed by 'A' on 1-4-1997 at 6% per annum.

(*d*) Interest will be paid on drawings of partners at 4% per annum (Drawings of A and B during the year 1998 were Rs. 6,000 and 4,000 respectively).

(*e*) Profit sharing ratio between A and B will be 3 : 2

(Osmania University, B. Com. March 2000).

Solution

Profit & Loss Appropriation a/c

		Rs.			Rs.
To Interest on capital			By Balance b/d		70,000
A —	2,500		By Interest on drawings		
B —	2,000	4,500	A —	240	
To Salary			B	160	400
A —	2400				
B —	1,200	3,600			
To Interest on 'A's loan		300			
To Net profit transferred					
to A's capital a/c		37,200			
B's capital a/c		24,800			
		70,400			70,400

Problem 10

Sanjay, Madhav and Bijoy are partners in a registered firm. Balances of their capital accounts as on 1st April 1998 were Rs. 25,000, Rs. 15,000 and Rs. 5,000 respectively. The partnership agreement provides :

(*i*) Bijoy shall be credited with a salary of Rs. 3,00 per month.

(*ii*) Interest on capitals allowed @ 10% per annum and interest on drawings is charged at 15% per annum.

(*iii*) After providing (*i*) and (*ii*) mentioned above and after making a provision for extra remuneration mentioned in this para (*iii*) Bijay shall be entitled to 5% of all the profit in excess.

(*iv*) Madhav of Rs. 7,000 is to have $\frac{1}{5}$th of the profit after charging all amounts under (*i*) to (*iii*) above and in this para (*iv*). The balance of profits is to be divided between Sanjay and Bijoy in the ratio of 7 : 1 respectively.

Bijoy contributed additional capital of Rs. 5,000 on 1st October 1998. Sanjay has withdrawn Rs. 2,000 on 1st August 1998 and Rs. 1,600 on 31st December 1998, whereas Bijoy did not withdraw any amount. Madhav has withdrawn Rs. 400 at the end of each partner.

The net profit for the year ended 31st March 1999 before making above adjustments was Rs. 40,500.

You are required to prepare profit & loss appropriation account for the year ended 31st March 1999 and the partner's capital accounts **(C.S. Foundation June 1999)**

Solution

Profit & Loss Appropriation A/c
For the year ending 31st March 1999

		Rs.			Rs.
To Bijoy's capital a/c — Salary		3,600	By Net profit b/d		40,500
To Interest on capital			By Interest on Drawing :-		
— Sanjay	2,500		Sanjay	260	
— Madhav	1,500		Madahv	90	350
— Bijoy	750	4,750			
To Bijoy's capital a/c (See note below)		1,214			
To Madhav's capital a/c — Share Profit $31{,}286 \times \frac{1}{6}$		5,214			
To Sanjay's capital a/c $26{,}072 \times \frac{7}{8}$		22,813			
To Bijoy's capital $26{,}072 \times \frac{1}{8}$		3,259			
		40,850			40,850

Sanjay's Capital A/c

	Rs.		Rs.
To Drawings	3,600	By Balance b/d	25,000
To Interest on Drawings	260	By Interest on Capital	2,500
To Balance c/d	46,453	By P & L Appropriation a/c — Profit	22,813
	50,313		50,313

Madhav's Capital A/c

	Rs.		Rs.
To drawings	1,600	By Balance b/d	15,000
To Interest on Drawings	90	By Interest on Capital	1,500
To Balance c/d	20,024	By P & L Appropriation a/c — Profit	5,214
	21,714		21,714

Bijoy's capital A/c

	Rs.		Rs.
To Balance c/d	18,823	By Balance b/d	5,000
		By Cash	5,000
		By Salary — P& L Appropriation a/c	3,600
		By Interest on capital	750
		By P & L Appropriation a/c (Extra remuneration)	1,214
		By P & L Appropriation a/c — Profit	3,259
	18,823		18,823

Note : Calculation of Extra remuneration

$$\text{Rs. } 40{,}850 - (3{,}600 + 4{,}750 + 7{,}000) \times \frac{5}{105}$$

Problem 11

The partners A and B decided to appropriate profits of the firm on the following terms :

(*a*) Interest is payable on capital at 5% per annum.
(*b*) Both A and B will get remuneration at Rs. 2,000 and Rs. 1,000 per month respectively.
(*c*) Interest is payable on loan contributed by A at 6% p. a (A contributed loan of Rs. 20,000 to the firm on 1-7-1997).
(*d*) Interest on drawings of partners is 4% per annum (Drawings of A and B during 1997 were Rs. 6,000 and Rs. 4,000 respectively.
(*e*) Profit having ratio between A and B is 3 : 2.

For the year ending on 31-12-97 the total net profit of the firm is shown at Rs. 70,000. On 1-1-97 the capital balances of A and B were Rs. 50,000 and Rs. 40,000 respectively.

Show Journal entries, Profit & Loss Appropriation a/c, and capital accounts in the firms books **(Calcutta University, B. Com. (Hons.) 1998)**

Solution

Journal Entries

Date	*Particulars*		*Dr. Amount*	*Cr. Amount*
	P & L a/c	Dr.	70,000	
	To P & L Appropriation a/c			70,000
	(Being the net profit transferred to P & L Appropriate)			
	P & L App. a/c	Dr.	4,500	
	To Interest on A's capital			2,500
	To Interest on B's capital			2,000
	(Being interest on partners capital allowed)			
	P & L App. a/c	Dr.	36,000	
	To Salary to A			24,000
	To Salary to B			12,000
	(Being salary payable to partners)			

Date	*Particulars*		*Dr. Amount*	*Cr. Amount*
	P & L App. a/c	Dr	600	
	To Interest on A's loan a/c			600
	(Being interest payable on A's loan a/c)			
	P & L App. a/c	Dr	29,100	
	To A's capital a/c			17,460
	To B's capital a/c			11,640
	(Being profit transferred to capital a/c)			
	A's capital a/c	Dr	120	
	B's capital a/c	Dr	80	
	To P & L App. a/c			200
	(Being interest drawings charged)			

P & L Appropriation A/c

		Rs.			*Rs.*
To Interest on capital			By P & L a/c		70,000
— A	2,500		By Interest on Drawings		
— B	2,000	4,500	— A	120	
To partners's Salary			— B	80	200
— A	24,000				
— B	12,000	36,000			
To Interest on loan					
— A		600			
Profit transferred to					
— A	17,460				
— B	11,640	29,100			
		70,200			70,200

A's Capital A/c

	Rs.		*Rs.*
To Drawings	6,000	By Balance b/d	50,000
To Interest on Drawing	120	By P & L App. a/c	
To Balance c/d	88,440	— Interest on capital	2,500
		— Salary	24,000
		— Interest on loan	600
		— Profit	17,460
	94,560		94,560

B's Capital A/c

	Rs.		Rs.
To Drawings	4,000	By Balance b/d	40,000
To Interest on Drawings	80	By P & L App. a/c	
To Balance c/d	61,560	— Interest on capital	2,000
		— Salary	12,000
		— Profit	11,640
	65,640		65,640

Working Notes :

1. Interest on capital :

$$A — 50,000 \times \frac{5}{100} = 2,500$$

$$B — 40,000 \times \frac{5}{100} = 2,000$$

2. Partners salary ; $A = 2,000 \times 12 = 24,000$
   $B = 1,000 \times 12 = 12,000$

3. Interest on Loan :

$$A = 2,000 \times \frac{6}{100} \times \frac{6}{12} = 600$$

4. Interest on Drawings

$$A = 6,000 \times \frac{4}{100} \times \frac{6}{12} = 120$$

$$B = 4,000 \times \frac{4}{100} \times \frac{6}{12} = 80$$

(Interest on drawings has been charged for 6 months)

5. Share of profit

$$A = 29,100 \times \frac{3}{5} = 17,460$$

$$B = 29,100 \times \frac{2}{5} = 11,640$$

Problem 12

Papia, Diya, and Ria are three partners in a firm. They drew Rs. 10,000, Rs. 8,000 and Rs. 6,000 respectively. Interest on capital and Interest on drawings are fixed at 12% and 10% respectively. Profit during the year 1995 was Rs. 85,000, out of which Rs. 20,000 is to be transferred to General Reserve Account. Papia and Diya are entitled to receive salary of Rs. 4,500 and Rs. 3,000 p. a. respectively. Ria is entitled to receive commission at 10% on distributable profit on 1st January 1995. The balances of their capital Accounts were Rs. 60,000, Rs. 50,000 and Rs. 40,000 respectively.

You are required to show profit and loss appropriation a/c for the year ended 31st December, 1995 and the capital accounts by partners in the books of the firm.

(Calcutta University B. Com (Pass) 1996)

Solution

Profit & Loss Appropriation A/c

		Rs.		Rs.
To Interest on capital			By P & L a/c	85,000
— P	7,200		(net profit)	
— D	6,000		By Interest on Drawing :	
— R	4,800	18,000	P's a/c	500
To Salary			D's a/c	400
— P	4,500		R's a/c	300
— D	3,000	7,500		
To Commission — R		4,070		
To General Reserve		20,000		
— Transfer				
To Partners capital a/c				
— Profit transferred				
— P	12,210			
— D	12,210			
— R	12,210			
		36,630		
		86,200		86,200

P's Capital A/c

	Rs.		Rs.
To Drawings a/c	10,000	By Balance b/d	60,000
To Interest on Drawings	500	By Interest on capital	7,200
To Balance c/d	73,410	By Salary	4,500
		By Profit	12,210
	83,910		83,910

D's Capital A/c

	Rs.		Rs.
To Drawings a/c	8,000	By Balance b/d	50,000
To Interest on Drawings	400	By Interest on capital	6,000
To Balance c/d	62,810	By Salary	3,000
		By Profit	12,210
	71,210		71,210

R's Capital A/c

	Rs.		Rs.
To Drawings a/c	6,000	By Balance b/d	40,000
To Interest on Drawings	300	By Interest on capital	4,800
To Balance c/d	54,780	By Commission	4,070
		By profit	12,210
	61,080		61,080

PAST ADJUSTMENTS

Sometimes partnership accounts must have been closed without taking into account certain transactions or by recording wrong amount of such transactions. Those transactions relate to interest on capital, interest on drawings, salary or commission of partners etc. When such ommission or commission are subsequently discovered they are to be adjusted accordingly. This can be done by three methods.

1. Method — 1 By Means of Profit & Loss Appropriation Account :

This method is followed if the adjustments are carried out in the same accounting year. The following steps are involved.

(*a*) Transfer from capital accounts of partners amount already credited (in case of profits) or debited (in case of loss) back to profit & loss appropriation a/c by means of a Journal entry.

(*b*) Open Profit & Loss Appropriation accounts and enter there in the omitted items.

(*c*) Finally, transfer net profit or loss resulting from these adjustments to partners capital accounts.

Problem 13

A B and C are in partnership on 31st March 2003. Their capital accounts after making adjustments for profit and drawings for the year stood at Rs. 80,000. Rs. 60,000 and Rs. 40,000 respectively.

Subsequently it was discovered that interest on capital and on drawings had been omitted to be charged at 5% p.a. The drawings during the year were : A Rs. 20,000. B Rs. 15,000 and C Rs. 9,000 and the interest on drawings chargeable to the partners were A Rs. 500 B Rs. 360 and C Rs. 200. The profit for the year amounted to Rs. 1,20,000 which was shared by the partners in the ratio of 3 : 2 : 1.

Give the necessary adjusting journal entries to rectify the above omission.

Solution

Calculation of Interest on partners capital.

Before as certaining the interest on partners capital it is necessary to arrive at partners capitals as on 1-4-2002 (opening balance). This can be done by means of the following table.

	A	B	C
Capital as on 31-3-2003	80,000	60,000	40,000
Less ; Profit already Credited (Rs. 1,20,000 in the ratio of 3;2;1)	60,000	40,000	20,000
	20,000	20,000	20,000
Add : Drawing during the year	20,000	15,000	9,000
Capital as on 1-4-2002	40,000	35,000	29,000
Interest on capital	2,000	1,750	1,450

Profit & Loss Appropriation a/c

		Rs.			Rs.
To Interest on capital			By P & L a/c		1,20,000
— A	2,000		By Interest on Drawings		
— B	1,750		— A	500	
— C	1,450	5,200	— B	360	
To Profit transferred to			— C	200	1,060
A's Capital a/c		57,930			
B's Capital a/c		38,620			
C's Capital a/c		19,310			
		1,21,060			1,21,060

Journal Entries

Date	Particulars		Dr. Amount	Cr. Amount
	A's Capital a/c	Dr.	60,000	
	B's Capital a/c	Dr.	40,000	
	C's Capital a/c	Dr.	20,000	
	To P & L App. a/c			1,20,000
	(Being the net profit already credited to partners in the ratio of 3:2:1 Written back)			
	A's Capital a/c	Dr.	2,000	
	B's Capital a/c	Dr.	1,750	
	C's Capital a/c	Dr.	1,450	
	To P & L App. a/c			5,200
	(Being interest on capital previously omitted now charged)			
	P & L App. a/c	Dr.	1,060	
	To A's Capital a/c			500
	To B's Capital a/c			360
	To C's Capital a/c			200
	(Being interest charged on drawings)			
	P & L App. a/c	Dr.	1,15,860	
	To A's Capital a/c			57,930
	To B's Capital a/c			38,620
	To C's Capital a/c			19,310
	(Being net profit on adjustment of omitted items credited to partners capital a/c)			

2. Method — 2 By Means of Profit & Loss Adjustment A/c

Where the mistakes are discovered in the subsequent accounting year, such adjustment are made in an account known as Profit and Loss Adjustment a/c. This method involve the following steps.

(a) Pass entries for items omitted debiting or crediting capital accounts and debiting or crediting profit & loss adjustment a/c.

(b) Then transfer the net balance in profit & loss adjustment a/c to partners capital accounts.

Problem 14

Given below is the profit & loss appropriation account of X and Y for the year ended 31st March 2003.

Profit & Loss Appropriation A/c

		Rs.		Rs.
To Interest on capital			By Net profit b/d	40,000
X — 8% on Rs. 40,000		3,200	By Interest on drawings :	
Y — 8% on Rs. 30,000		2,400	X — 6% on Rs. 8,000	240
To Salary — X		4,800	Y — 6% on Rs. 6,000	180
To Net profit			(for 6 months)	
X — $\frac{1}{2}$ —	15,010			
Y — $\frac{1}{2}$ —	15,010	30,020		
		40,420		40,420

The entries were duly passed in the books, after which the following discrepancies were subsequently discovered.

(*a*) Interest on capital should have been allowed at 6% p.a. and that on drawings should have been charged at 8% p.a.

(*b*) 'X' was not entitled to get any salary but Y was entitled to get a monthly salary of Rs, 250.

(*c*) Profit should have been shared in the opening capital ratio.

You are required to redistribute the profit correctly.

Solution

Profit & Loss Adjustment A/c

		Rs.			Rs.
To Interest on capital at 6% p.a			By X's capital a/c		22,770
X —	2,400		— Amount written back		
Y —	18,00	4,200	(Rs. 3,200 + 4,800 + 15,010 - 240)		
To Y 's (Salary) a/c		3,000	By Y's capital a/c		
To Net profit transferred			— Amount written back		
to capital accounts			(Rs. 2,400 + 15,010 – 180)		
X $\frac{4}{7}$ =	19,603		By Interest on drawings		
Y $\frac{3}{7}$ =	13,757	33,360	at 8% p.a. for 6 months		
			X —	320	
			Y —	240	
					560
		40,560			40,560

Method - III By Means of a Single Consolidated Entry

Under their method the net difference in the credit (or debit) already given and the credit (or debit) should be given to the capital accounts of partners is found out. The capitals of partners with excess credit are debited and those with shortage are credited by passing a single consolidated entry.

Problem 15

A, B and C are partners in a firm. The profit of the firm for the year ended 31st march 2003 is Rs. 30,000 which has been duly distributed amongst the partners in the agreed ratio of 3:1 :1 respectively. It was discovered on 10th April 2003 that the under mentioned transactions were not passed through the books of the firm for the year ended 31st March 2003.

(*a*) Interest an capital at 6% p.a. the capital of A, B and C being Rs. 50,000 Rs. 40,000 and Rs. 30,000 respectively.
(*b*) Interest on drawings : A Rs. 350 B Rs. 250 : C Rs. 150.
(*c*) Partnership salaries : A Rs 5,000 : B Rs. 7,500.
(*d*) Commission due to A (for some special transactions) Rs. 3,000.

You are required to suggest a single Journal entry to be made to rectify the position of partners.

Solution

Statement Showing the Adjustment of Capital.

	A		*B*		*C*		*Total*	
	Dr.	Cr.	Dr.	Cr.	Dr.	Cr.	Dr.	Cr.
Interest on capital	—	3,000	—	2,400	—	1,800	7200	—
Interest on drawings	350	—	250	—	150	—	—	750
Salary	—	5,000	—	7,500	—	—	12,500	—
Commission	—	3,000	—	—	—	—	3,000	—
Loss distributed in profit Sharing ratio	13,170	—	4,390	—	4,390	—	—	21,950
	13,520	11,000	4,640	9,900	4,540	1,800	22,700	22,700
Debited or credited	2,520	—	—	5,260	2,740	—	—	—

Journal Entry

Date	*Particulars*		*Dr. Amount*	*Cr. Amount*
	A's Capital a/c	Dr.	2,520	
	C's Capital a/c	Dr.	2,740	
	To B's capital a/c			5,260
	(Being the entry to rectify omissions in preparing partners capital accounts.			

Problem 16

X, Y and Z & Co. is a partnership firm having three partners X, Y and Z. Their capital account stood at Rs. 30,000 Rs. 15,000 and Rs. 15,000 respectively on April 1, 2002. The partnership deed provided that.

(*a*) Z should be allowed a remuneration of Rs. 3,000 p.a.
(*b*) Interest at 5% per annum has to be allowed on capital
(*c*) Balance of profit & loss is to be divided in the proportion of 2 : 2 : 1.

Ignoring the above terms the profit of Rs. 18,000 for the year ended 31st March 2003 was divided equally.

You are required to pass the Journal entry to rectify the error.

Solution

Statement Showing Adjustment of Capitals

	X		Y		Z	
	Dr.	Cr.	Dr.	Cr.	Dr.	Cr.
Remuneration credited to Z	—	—	—	—	—	3,000
Interest on capital at 5% per annum	—	1,500	—	750	—	750
Final Balance of profit transferred in 2 ; 2 ; 1 ratio (18,000 – 1,500 – 750 – 3,750 = 12,000)	4,800	—	4,800	—	2,410	
Net amount to be credited	6,300	—	5,550	—	6,150	
Less amount already credited	—	6,000	—	6,000	—	6,000
	—	(+) 300	—	(–) 450	—	+ 150

Journal Entry

Date	*Particulars*	*Dr. Amount*	*Cr. Amount*
	Y's Capital a/c Dr.	450	
	To X's Capital a/c		300
	To Z's Capital a/c		150
	(Being unrecorded interest and salary now accounted).		

Guarantee of Profit :-

In order to induce a person to become a partner a guarantee is given to him by other partners that his share of profit will not be less than a certain amount. It is also further agreed that if in a year his share of profit exceeds the minimum limit he would refund the excess which is wrongly credited earlier to his account. Where such an agreement is entered into the following steps are involved.

(*a*) Profit should be divided as if no guarantee is given.

(*b*) The amount by which the actual share falls short of the guaranteed share should be credited to the partner for whom the guarantee is given and debited to the other partners in their mutual profit sharing ratio. The following entry is passed.

Existing Partner's Capital a/c Dr.
  To New Partner's a/c

(*c*) For recouping the excess in subsequent years a reverse entry is passed which is as follows

New Partners Capital a/c Dr.
  To Existing Partner's Capital a/c

Sometimes only one partner may give guarantee to new partner when share of profit of new partner fall below the guaranteed amount . In such a case the following entry is passed.

Capital a/c of the Guarantor Dr.
  To New Partner's Capital a/c

The amount to be recorded is the excess of the guaranteed amount over the actual share of the partner.

Problem 17

With effect from 1st April 2002. D the manager in the firm of A, B and C who were sharing profit & losses in the rates of 5 : 3 : 2 respectively was admitted as a partner in the firm with $\frac{1}{11}$th share of profit. It was agreed that should D's share of profits exceed his remuneration as the manager, A will bear the burden of such an excess. As the manager D was entitled to a salary of Rs. 1,000 PM plus a commission of 2% of net profit remaining after charging his salary but before charging his commission.

Profit & Loss a/c for the year ended 31st March 2003 should a profit of Rs. 2,20,000. Show how the profit will be distributed among the four partners.

Solution

The main point of management is that B and C are not to suffer due to D's becoming a partner. Suppose D is still the manager then

Profit as given	2,20,000
Less salary which D would have received	12,000
	2,08,000
Less D's commission @ 2% on Rs. 2,08,000	4,160
Net profit	2,03,840

	A $\frac{5}{10}$	B $\frac{3}{10}$	C $\frac{2}{10}$	D (as manager)
Distribution	1,01,920	61,152	40,768	16,160

Under the new arrangement 'D' will receive $\frac{1}{11}$th of Rs. 2,20,000, i.e., Rs. 20,000. It means that D will get Rs. 3,840 more than what he would have got as manager. This will be deducted from A's share. Hence the profit of Rs. 2,20,000 will be distributed as follows.

A — Rs. 98,080
B — Rs. 61,152
C — Rs. 40768
D — Rs. 20,000

Final Accounts of a Partnership Firm

The final accounts of a partnership firm consists of

(*a*) Trading and profit & loss a/c and (*b*) Balance sheet. It is prepared as in the case of sole trading concern.

Problem 18

From the information given prepare trading and profit & loss account for the year ended 31st March 1998 and the Balance sheet as on that date of X, Y and Z, a partnership firm.

Trial Balance as an 31st March 1998

	Dr. Balance	Cr. Balance
Capital accounts (fixed)		
X		80,000
Y		70,000
Z		60,000
Sales		8,50,000
Opening stock (1-4-1997) :		
Raw materials	30,000	
Finished goods	40,000	
Work in progress	50,000	
Wages	2,80,000	
Drawings a/c :		
X	12,000	
Y	11,500	
Z	11,000	
Plant & Machinery	80,000	
Loan accounts :-		
X		5,000
Y		45,000
Z		40,000
Furniture & fixture	14,000	
Loose tools	15,000	
Purchases	3,40,000	
Salaries	1,17,000	
Rent Rate & Taxes	22,500	
Electric charges	12,115	
Postage & Telegrams	1,505	
Insurance premium	3,081	
Printing & stationery	2,316	
General charges	27,283	
Sundry debtors	1,00,000	
Sundry creditors		35,000
Cash in hand & Bank	67,500	
Provision for Bad & doubtful debits		6,800
	12,36,800	12,36,800

Additional information : -

(*a*) As at 31st March 1998 stock in hand was valued at.

(*i*) Raw Materials Rs. 45,000

(*ii*) Finished goods Rs. 75,000

(*iii*) Work in progress Rs. 57,000

(*b*) Outstanding salaries Rs. 2,500, wages Rs. 1,500.

(*c*) Insurance premium covered a period of 13 months.

(*d*) Depreciate plant & Machinery at 10% furniture at 5%.

(*e*) Write off Rs. 4,000 as bad debts and maintain provision for bad debts at 2%.

(*f*) Partners were entitled to 5% interest on their capitals and 6% interest was charged on their loan amount. Their drawings are to be charged at an average rate of 3% per annum.

(Osmania University B. Com. October 2000)

Solution

Trading and Profit & Loss A/c
For the year ending 31-3-1998

Particulars		*Amount*	*Particulars*		*Amount*
To opening stock :-			By sales		8,50,000
Raw materials		30,000	By Closing stock :-		
Work in progress		50,000	Raw materials		45,000
Finished goods		40,000	Work-in-progress		57,000
To Purchases		3,40,000	Finished goods		75,000
To Wages	2,80,000				
Add on/s	1,500				
		2,81,500			
To Gross profit		2,85,500			
		10,27,000			10,27,000
To Salaries	1,17,000		By Gross profit		2,85,500
Add o/s	2,500	1,19,500	By Provision for Doubtful debts		4,880
To Rent rates and			(6,800 – 1,920)		
taxes		22,500	By Interest on Drawings		
To Electric charges		12,115	X—		360
To Postage & Telegram		1,505	Y—		345
To Insurance premium	3081		Z—	330	1,035
Less prepaid	237	2,844			
To Printing and stationery		2,316			
To General charges		27,283			
To Depreciation :-					
on plant & machinery		8,000			
on furniture		700			
To Bad Debts		4,000			
To Interest on capital :					
X—	4,000				
Y—	3,500				
Z—	3,000	10,500			
To Interest on loan					
X—	3,000				
Y—	2,700				
Z—	2,400	8,100			
To Net profit transferred to					
X—	24,018				
Y—	24,017				
Z—	24,017	72,052			
		2,91,415			2,91,415

Balance sheet as on 31-3-1998

Liabilities		*Amount*	*Assets*		*Amount*
Sundry creditors		35,000	Cash in hand & at Bank		67,500
o/s Salaries	2,500		Sundry debtors	1,00,000	
o/s Wages	1,500	4,000	Less bad debts	4,000	
Loan account :				96,000	
X	50,000		Less: provision for		
Add o/s interest	3,000		doutful debts	1,920	
		53,000			94,080
Y—	45,000		Closing stock		1,77,000
Add o/s Interest	2,700	47,700	Loose tools		15,000
Z—	40,000		Prepaid Insurance		237
Add o/s Interest	2,400		Furniture & fixtures	14,000	
		42,400	Less : Depreciation	700	
Capital accounts :					13,300
X's capital	80,000		Plant & Machinery	80,000	
Add Interest			Less depreciation	8,000	
On capital	4,000				72,000
To Net profit	24,018				
	1,08,018				
Less drawings	12,000				
	96,018				
Less : Interest on drawing	360				
		95,658			
Y's capital	70,000				
Add : Interest on Capital	3,500				
To Net profit	24,017				
	97,517				
Less : drawings	11,500				
	86,017				
Less Interest on drawings	345				
		85,672			
Z's capital	60,000				
Add : Interest on Capital	3,000				
Add Net profit	24,017				
	87,017				
Less : drawings	11,000				
	76,017				
Less : Interest on drawings	330				
		75,687			
		4,39,117			4,39,117

Problem 19

From the following details of a partnership firm prepare Manufacturing. Trading and profit & loss account and P & L Appropriation a/c for the year ending 31st March 1998 a Balance sheet as on 31st March 1998.

	Dr. Balance	Cr. Balance
Opening stock :		
Raw material	60,000	
Work-in-progress	5,000	
Finished goods	20,000	
Purchases :		
Raw materials	2,10,000	
Finished goods	10,000	
Cash	2,000	
Factory rent	12,000	
Office rent rate & taxes	3,000	
Factory salary	18,000	
Office salary	12,000	
Debtors and creditors	78,000	56,000
Sales		3,30,000
Selling expenses	8,000	
Interest on Loan paid	4,000	
Discount allowed	3,000	
Discount received		1,100
Capital and Salary (Drawn)		
Sita	6,000	68,000
Gita	3,000	30,000
Loan		50,000
Wages	30,000	
Interest on Partners Capital (Drawn)		
Sita	500	
Gita	600	
Machinery	45,000	
Furniture	5,000	
	5,35,100	5,35,100

(a) Provide 10% Depreciation on Machinery and Furniture.

(b) Loan carries 10% interest and the amount is brought forward from earlier year.

(c) Provide 6% interest on partners capital.

(d) Closing stock are :

Materials	50,000
Work-in-progress	10,000
Finished goods	35,000

(e) Salary outstanding as on 31st March 1998 :

Factory	2,000
Office	1,000

(f) Sita and Gita share profits and losses as 3 : 2 after charging salary @ Rs. 500 and Rs. 250 PM to Sita and Gita respectively.

(g) Outstanding factory Rent Rs. 1,000

(ICWA, Inter, June 1999)

Solution

Manufacturing A/c
For the year ended 31st March 1998.

Particulars		Amount	Particulars	Amount
To Opening stock			By Closing stock :	
Raw materials	60,000		Raw materials	50,000
Work-in-progress	5,000	65,000	Work-in-progress	10,000
To Purchase of Raw materials		2,10,000	By Cost of production c/d	2,82,500
To Wages		30,000		
To Factory expenses : (18,000 + 2,000)		20,000		
Factory rent (12,000 + 1,000)		13,000		
Depreciation on Machinery (10%)		4,500		
		3,42,500		3,42,500

Trading A/c
For the year ended 31st March 1998

Particulars	Amount	Particulars	Amount
To Opening stock of Finished goods	20,000	By Sales	3,30,000
To Purchase of finished goods	10,000	By Closing stock of finished goods	35,000
To Cost of production b/d	2,82,500		
To Gross profit c/d	52,500		
	3,65,000		3,65,000

Profit & Loss A/c
For the year ended 31st March 1998

Particulars	Amount	Particulars	Amount
To office salaries (12,000 + 1,000)	13,000	By Gross profit	52,500
		Discount received	1,000
To Office rent rates & Taxes	3,000		
To Selling expenses	8,000		
To Discount allowed	3,000		
To Interest on loan $\frac{10}{100} \times 50,000$	5,000		
To Depreciation on Furniture 10%	500		
To Net profit c/d	21,100		
	53,600		53,600

Profit & Loss Appropriation A/c
For the year ended 31st March 1998

Particulars		*Amount*	*Particulars*	*Amount*
To Interest on Capital			By Net profit b/d	21,100
Sita	4,080			
Gita	1,800	5,880		
To Partner's salary				
Sita	6,000			
Gita	3,000	9,000		
To Share of profit				
Sita $\frac{3}{5}$ —	3,732			
Gita $\frac{2}{5}$ —	2,488	6,220		
		21,100		21,100

Balance Sheet
As at 31st March 1998

Liabilities		*Amount*	*Assets*		*Amount*
Capital accounts :			Machinery	45,000	
Sita	68,000		Less : Depreciation	4,500	
Add Salary	6,000				40,500
Add Interest on capital	4,080		Furniture	5,000	
Add Share of profit	3,732		Less : Depreciation	500	
	81,812				4,500
Less : Drawings	6,500		**Stock :**		
(6,000 + 500)		75,312	Finished goods		35,000
Gita	30,000		Work -in- progress		10,000
Add Salary	3,000		Raw materials		50,000
Add Interest on Capital	1,800		Debtors		78,000
Add Share of profit	2,488		Cash		2,000
	37,288				
Less : Drawings	3,600				
(3,000 + 600)		33,688			
Loan		50,000			
Sundry creditors		56,000			
Liabilities for expenses :					
Salaries o/s	3,000				
Factory rent o/s	1,000				
Interest on Loan	1,000				
(5,000 – 4,000)		5,000			
		2,20,000			2,20,000

Problem 20

The Trial Balance of Ram and Shyam as on 31-3-1999 is given below.

	Dr. Balance	*Cr. Balance*
Ram's capital a/c		80,000
Shyam's capital a/c		1,00,000
Stock on 1-4-1998 :-		
Raw Materials	2,500	
Finished goods	6,500	
Purchases	64,500	
Sales		1,19,000
Sales returns	2,000	
Wages	16,000	
Manufacturing expenses	14,000	
Salaries	6,000	
Insurance	1,500	
Postage	100	
Advertisement	1,000	
Bad debts	300	
Bills payable		12,000
Discount		500
Land & Buildings	90,000	
Plant & Machinery	70,000	
Furniture	1,000	
Sundry debtors	25,400	
Sundry creditors		42,000
Drawings :		
Ram	1,800	
Shyam	1,400	
Cash in hand	500	
Cash at Bank	49,000	
	3,53,500	3,53,500

Ram and Shyam share profit in the ratio of 4 : 6

Prepare trading and profit & loss a/c for the year ended 31-3-1999 and also the Balance Sheet on that date after taking in to consideration the following information.

1. Ram withdrew goods worth Rs. 4,000 for Personal use.
2. Stock on 31-3-1999 valued at
   Raw materials Rs. 5,000
   Finished goods Rs. 15,000
3. Provide depreciation on land and building @ 5%, on furniture @ 10%, and on plant and machinery @ 75%.
4. Outstanding wages Rs. 2,000, Salaries Rs. 2,500.
5. Write off Rs. 1,000 as further bad debts and provide 5% for doubtful debts on debtors.
6. Insurance paid for 15 months upto 30-6-99.
7. Manager of the business is to be paid a commission of 5% on the profit after providing for such commission **(Omania University B. Com. October 1999)**

Solution

Trading and Profit & Loss A/c
for the year ended 31-3-1999.

Particulars		*Amount*	*Particulars*		*Amount*
To Stock on 1-4-98			By Sales	1,19,000	
Raw materials	2,500		Less returns	2,000	
Finished goods	6,500	9,000			1,17,000
To Purchases	64,500		By Stock 31-3-94		
Less : Goods			Raw materials		5,000
Withdrawn			finished goods		1,5000
by Ram	4,000	60,500			
To Wages	16,000				
Add : o/s wages	2,000	18,000			
To Manufacturing expenses		14,000			
To Gross profit c/d		35,500			
		1,37,000			1,37,000
To Salaries	6000		By Gross profit b/d		35,500
Add o/s	2,500	8,500	By Discount received		500
To Insurance	1,500				
less prepaid	300	1,200			
To Postage		100			
To Advertisement		1,000			
To Bad debts	300				
Add : Additional					
Bad Debts	1000	1,300			
To Provision for doubtful					
Debts		1,220			
To Depreciation on :					
Building -	4,500				
Furniture -	100				
Plant & Machinery	5,250	9,850			
To Commission to Manager					
$12{,}830 \times \frac{5}{105}$		610			
To Balance c/d		12,220			
		36,000			36,000
To Salary (Shyam)		6,000	By Balance b/d		12,220
To Interest on capital			By Net loss transferred		
Ram -	6,400		to Ram	3,272	
Shyam -	8,000		Shyam	4,908	
		14,400			8,180
		20,400			20,400

Balance Sheet as on 31-12-1999

Liabilities		Amount	Assets		Amount
Sundry creditors		42,000	Cash in hand		500
Bills payable		12,000	Cash at bank		49,000
o/s expenses :-			Sundry debtors	25,400	
Wages		2,000	Less : Bad debts	1,000	
Salaries		2,500		24,400	
Commission to manager		610	Less : Provision		
Ram's capital	80,000		for doubtful debts	1,220	
Add Interest on					23,180
Capital	6,400		Closing stock		20,000
	86,400		Prepaid insurance		300
Less : Net loss	3,272		Furniture	1,000	
	83,128		Less : depreciation	100	900
Less drawings	5,800		Land & buildings	90,000	
(1,800 + 4,000)		77,328	less depreciation	4,500	85,500
			Plant & Machinery	70,000	
			Less depreciation	5,250	64,750
Shyam's capital	10,000				
Add Interest on Capital	8,000				
Add Salary	6,000				
	1,14,000				
Less : Net loss	4,908				
	1,09,092				
Less Drawings	1,400				
		1,07,692			
		2,44,130			2,44,130

QUESTIONS

Simple Questions

1. Define partnership.
2. List the essential features of partnership.
3. What is a partnership deed ?
4. In the absence of a partnership deed what are guidelines laid down by the Indian partnership Act 1932 ?
5. What do you mean by fixed capital method of maintaining partners capital account ?
6. What is fluctuating capital method of maintaining partners capital account ?
7. What are drawings ? How are they accounted ?
8. How do you close the drawings account of a partner ?
9. How is interest on partner drawings accounted ?

EXERCISE 1

On 1st April 2002 X and Y started business in partnership agreeing to share profits and losses equally. X contributed Rs. 30,000 while Y contributed Rs. 20,000 by way of capital. It was agreed that interest be allowed on capital @ 6% per annum and charged on drawings @ 8% per annum. X withdrew Rs. 200 at the end of every month whereas Y withdrew Rs. 450 in the middle of every month.

Profit before the above adjustments for the year ended 31st March 2003 amounted to Rs. 8,970. Show the necessary ledger accounts assuming.

(*a*) Capital accounts are fluctuating.
(*b*) Capital accounts are fixed.

Answer : When capital account are fluctuating :-
Total of X's capital a/c 34,937.
Total of Y's capital a/c 24,337.
When capital accounts are fixed-
Total of X' current a/c Rs. 4,937.
Total of Y's current a/c Rs. 5,616.

EXERCISE 2

On 1st April 2002 the capital accounts of X, Y and Z stood at Rs. 30,000 Rs. 20,000 and Rs. 10,000 respectively. They shared profits and losses equally. Profit and loss account for the year ended 31st March 2003 revealed a net profit of Rs. 12,000 which was transferred to capital account of the partners equally.

It was decided that during 2003 - 04 profits should be distributed equally after allowing interest on capital @ 6% per annum with effect from 1st April 2002. While going through the books of account for 2002 - 03 it was discovered that repair charges for X's personal scooter amounting to Rs. 90 had been charged to repairs account.

Show the Journal entries necessary to adjust the current account.

Answer : Net profit after adjustment Rs. 8,490, each partner's share is Rs. 2,830.
Net adjustments to be made X + 540, Y + 30, Z - 570

EXERCISE 3

X, having a capital of Rs. 60,000 takes Y and Z into partnership on Jan. 1, 2003 on the following terms.

Y to bring in Rs. 20,000 as capital : Interest on capital to be allowed 5% Y to receive a salary of Rs. 6,000 annually.

'Z' is guaranteed by 'X' that his minimum share of profits shall be Rs 6,500 per annum : and profits shall be shared as X $\frac{1}{2}$, Y $\frac{1}{3}$, Z $\frac{1}{6}$.

In the first year of partnership, the business shows a profits of Rs. 4,000 before charging Y's salary or interest on capital. They had withdrawn during the year : X Rs. 10,000 : Y Rs. 8,000 (including salary) Z Rs. 6,000.

Show the position of partner's accounts on 31-12-2003 after adjustment. No interest on drawing is to be allowed.

Answer : X's share of loss Rs. 1,500
Y's share of loss Rs. 1,000
Z's share of loss Rs. 5,00
Total of X's capital Rs. 60,000
Total of Y's capital Rs. 27,000
Total of Z's capital Rs. 6,500

EXERCISE 4

After including the profit for the year ended 31st December 2003 and dealing with drawings, the capital capital accounts of A. B and C stood at Rs. 40,000. Rs. 30,000 and Rs. 20,000 respectively.

Subsequently the following ommissions were noticed and it was decided to bring them into account :-

(*a*) Interest on capitals at 5% per annum

(*b*) Interest on drawings A-Rs. 250 B-190 C-190 C-130.

(*c*) Commission to the Manager at 5% on the net profit and interest on drawings after charging such interest on capital.

The profit for the year in arriving at the above figure of capital amounted to Rs. 60,000 and their drawings had been. A 10,000. B 7,500 and C Rs. 4,500 they shared profits * losses as to A $\frac{1}{2}$, B$\frac{1}{3}$, C$\frac{1}{6}$.

Give the adjusted capital accounts of the partner with entries necessary for such adjustment.

Answer : Commission Rs. 2,760
A's share of profit Rs. 27,605
B's share of profit Rs. 18,403
C's share of profit Rs 9,202
Total of A's capital Rs. 48,605
Total of B's capital Rs. 36,778
Total of C's capital Rs. 24,427

EXERCISE 5

(FINAL ACCOUNTS)

From the following trial balance of M/s R & L sharing profit & losses in the rates of 3 : 5 prepare Trading and Profit and Loss a/c and Balance Sheet as at 31st December 2003.

Trial Balance

	Dr. Balance	*Cr. Balance*
R's capital		35,000
L's capital		30,000
R's Drawings	1,000	
L's Drawings	8,800	

	Dr. Balance	*Cr. Balance*
Sundry debtors	45,000	
Plant and Machinery	15,000	
Fixtures & fittings	11,000	
Stock on 1-1-2003	30,000	
Cash in hand	350	
Cash at bank	10,000	
Purchases	50,000	
Wages	16,000	
Salaries	12,000	
Bills payable		12,000
Bill Receivable	14,000	
Insurance	350	
Returns from customers	1,200	
Carriage Inwards	400	
Returns to creditors		1,000
Commission and Travelling expenses	850	
Rent rates & taxes	5,500	
Discount	200	
Trade expenses	600	
Bad debts	250	
Sundry creditors		39,000
Loan account		10,000
Sales		1,03,500
	2,30,500	2,30,500

1. Allow interest on partner's capital at 5% per annum.
2. Interest on drawings : 'R' 275 and 'L' Rs. 190 per annum.
3. Depreciate plant and Machinery by 10% and fixture and fittings by 5%.
4. Provide for bad and doubtful debts at 5% on sundry debtors.
5. Outstanding liabilities were in respect of wages Rs. 300. Salaries Rs. 175 and Rent Rs. 200.
6. Insurance was prepaid to the extent of Rs. 75.
7. Stock at the end was valued at Rs. 50,000.

Answer : Gross profit Rs. 56,600.
Net profit 'R'- Rs. 17,679.
Net profit 'C' - Rs. 11,786.
Balance sheet total Rs. 1,41,125.

EXERCISE 6

Chandra and Dinakar were in partnership sharing profits and losses in the proportion of 3 : 2 respectively. The partnership deed provided inter alia :

1. That Dinakar should receive a salary of Rs. 250 PM.
2. That interest at 5% P.A. should be allowed on capitals and should be charged at 5% on drawings.

The following is the list of balances drawn from the books of partnership as on 31st December 2003.

Debit Balance	*Amount*	*Credit Balance*	*Amount*
Chandra's drawings	2,900	Chandra's capital	30,000
Dinkar's drawings	3,000	Dinkar's capital (5000 introduced on 1-7-2003)	25,000
Office furniture	1,800	Purchase returns	1,500
Purchases	30,800	Sales	75,000
Oil and fuel	1,700	Bills payable	12,000
Rent, rates, Insurance	2,500	Sundry creditors	18,200
Wages	13,200	Discount	2,130
Cartage	1,100	Reserve for Doubtful debts	4,060
General expenses	870	Reserve for discount	3,940
Travelling expenses	1,340		
Sales returns	1,300		
Advertisement	1,875		
Plant	17,500		
Stock (1-1-2003)	8,600		
Debtors	30,600		
Commission	1,260		
Accounting charges	1,000		
Bills receivable	18,000		
Cash in hand	285		
Cash at Bank	15,000		
Office salaries	6,800		
Motive power	2,400		
Good will	8,000		
	1,71,830		1,71,830

Adjustments

1. On 31st December 2003 the stock on hand was valued at Rs. 11,400.
2. Write off Rs. 400 from office furniture and 10% off on plant as Depreciation.
3. Wages outstanding Rs. 400 and Insurance prepaid Rs. 375.
4. They agreed to bring down the goodwill to Rs. 6,000 and decided to maintain reserve for doubtful debts at 10%.
5. There was no need for discount on debtors any more.
6. Interest on drawings, chandra Rs. 60 and Dinkar Rs. 75.

You are required to prepare trading and profit & loss account for the year ending 31st December 2003 and Balance sheet as on that date.

Answer : Chandra profit Rs. 6,336
Dinkar's profit Rs. 4,224
Total of Balance sheet Rs. 16,185.

18

CHAPTER

Partnership Accounts—Admission of a Partner

INTRODUCTIONS

Whenever a partnership firm is to be expanded a new partner may be admitted with the mutual consent of the existing partners. A new partner will strengthen the existing firm by contributing capial requirement or to influence the business or provide special skill to the business. The following adjustments are involved on admission of a partner.

1. Distribution of Reserves or accumulated profit among existing partners.
2. Revaluation of Assets and Liabilities of the firm.
3. Adjustment relating to goodwill.
4. Calculation of new profit sharing ratios.
5. Adjustments of capital of existing partners.

1. Distribution of Reserves or Accumulated Profit among Existing Partners

The Reserve created out of profit or any undistributed profit must be transferred to the old partners in the old profit sharing ratio before the admission of a new partner. This is because, the reserve or profit balance was built up before the admission of a partner and new partner will not get any share from such Reserve or profit. Similarly, accumulated loss if any is transferred to old partners in their old profit-sharing ratio. The new partner will not share any loss of the firm which existed at the time of his admission.

2. Revaluation of Assets and Liabilities

A new partner will not get any benefit out of increase in the value of assets or decrease in the value of liabilities. Similarly, he will not stand to lose because of depreciation in the value of asset or appreciation in the value of liabilities. Therefore at the time of admission, the assets and liabilities are revalued with a view to know the profit or loss on such revaluation. This is done by preparing an account known as revaluation account. The revaluation of assets and liabilities and liabilities can be done by two methods, viz.

(*a*) When revised values are shown in the books of the firm.
(*b*) When the revised values are not shown in the books of the firm.

(*a*) **When Revised Values are shown in the Books of the Firm or Revaluation Method :**

Under this method, a revaluation account is prepared to record the revised values of assets and liabilities. A revaluation account is a account in which increase or decrease in the value of assets and liabilities are recorded in order to ascertain the profit or loss on revaluation. On revaluation, any increase in the value of assets or decrease in the value of liabilities is recorded on the credit side of the account, while any decrease in value of assets or increase in liabilities is entered on the debit side. The difference represent profit if the credit side is greater and loss if the debit side is greater and is transferred to capital accounts of the old partners in the old profit sharing ratio.

(*b*) **When Revised Values are not Recorded in the Books of the Firm OR Memorandum Revaluation Method :**

Where it is decided that the revised values of assets and liabilities are not be shown in the new Balance Sheet, then all those entries which were passed in the revaluation account is reversed. For example, if building account is credited to revaluation it will now be debited. This process of reversing entries gives rise to a new revaluation account known as Memorandum Revaluation Account. The balance from the Memorandum Revaluation Account is transferred to all partners capital accounts including new partners capital account in the new profit sharing ratio.

3. Adjustment Relating to Goodwill

Goodwill is the extra value attached to a business over and above the value of its tangible assets. The following factors determine the goodwill.

(*a*) Reputation of a business.
(*b*) Quality of goods or services dealt by the business.
(*c*) Location of the business.
(*d*) Trade mark, patent, possessed by the business.
(*e*) Fair dealings
(*f*) Business experience.

Methods of Valuation of Goodwill

There are four methods of valuation of goodwill. They are as follows :-

1. Average profit method ;
2. Super profit method ;
3. Capitalisation method ; and
4. Annuity method.

1. Average Profit Method

Under this method, the value of goodwill is calculated on the basis of the average profit for the past few years multiplied by the number of years in which the anticipated profit will be available.

Example

If the goodwill is valued at 2 years purchase of the average profits of the past 3 years and if the past profits were :

2000 — Rs. 5,200
2001 — Rs. 5,900
2002 — Rs. 6,900

$$\text{Average Profit for the 3 years} = \frac{5{,}200 + 5{,}900 + 6{,}900}{3}$$

$$= \frac{18{,}000}{3} = \text{Rs. } 6{,}000.$$

2 years purchase of above average = 2 × Rs. 6,000 = Rs. 12,000.
= Value of goodwill is Rs. 12,000.

2. Super Profit Method

Super profit refers to the excess profit earned by a business over and above the normal return on investment expected to be earned in a similar business or industry. This super profit is assumed to represent the goodwill of the business. Usually the super profit is multiplied by the number of years in which the super profit is expected in future to arrive at the goodwill.

Example

Suppose a business earns a profit of Rs. 18,000 on an investment of Rs. 1,00,000 while the normal return in a similar business is 10%.

The annual profit of the business		Rs. 18,000
Less : Normal return		Rs. 10,000
	Super Profit	Rs. 8,000

If the goodwill is valued at 5 years purchase of super profit, the value of goodwill is 8,000 × 5 = 40,000.

3. Capitalisation Method

This method involves the following steps :

(*a*) Find out the total value of the firm. That is found out by using the following formula

$$\frac{\text{Average annual profit of the firm}}{\text{Normal rate of return in the same industry}} \times 100$$

(*b*) Find out the net value of assets. This is found out by applying the formula
Total Assets – Total Liabilities

(*f*) Find out the value of goodwill by using the following formula :
Total value of the firm – Net value of assets of the firm

Example

Given, Average annual profit Rs. 15,000
Normal rate of return in the same industry is 15%.
Net value of assets Rs. 50,000.

Step - 1

$$\text{Total value of the firm} = \frac{\text{Average annual profit}}{\text{Normal rate of return}} \times 100$$

$$= \frac{15{,}000}{15} \times 100 = 1{,}00{,}000$$

Step - 2

Net value of assets as given = Rs. 50,000

Step - 3

Goodwill = Total value of the firm – Net value of assets
= Rs. 1,00,000 – Rs. 50,000
= Rs. 50,000.

4. Annuity Method

This method is used on time value of money. The value of money that will be received over a period of time will depend upon rate of interest. Suppose, if the super profit earned is Rs. 3,000 which can be maintained for 5 years and the rate of interesst is 15% then the discounted value of super profit to be earned in different future years will be as follows :-

Year	*Super Profit*	*Discount factor @ 15%*	*Discounted Value of Super Profit*
1	3,000	0.8676	2,608.80
2	3,000	0.7561	2,263.30
3	3,000	0.6575	1,972.50
4	3,000	0.5718	1,715.40
5	3,000	0.4972	1,491.60
			10,056.60

So under annuity method discounted value of super profit becomes Rs. 10,056.60 not Rs. 15,000 (3,000 × 5 years)

Need for Valuation of Goodwill at the time of Admission of a Partner

On admission, a partner will not only acquires a right over the assets and liabilities of the firm but also a share in the future profits of the firm. The old partners who have sacrificed their share in profits in favour of the new partner and also been responsible for putting the business into the current position should be compensated for the loss. Hence, valuation of goodwill becomes necessary at the time of admitting a new partner.

Treatment of Goodwill on Admission of a New Partner

On admission of a new partner, goodwill can be treated in any one of the following ways :-

1. **When goodwill is paid privately to the partners :** When the incoming partner pays the amount of goodwill to the existing partners privately no entry will appear in the books of the firm.

2. When goodwill is brought, recorded in the books and retained in the business :

The following entries are recorded :

(a) Bank a/c Dr.
To Goodwill a/c
(Being cash brought in by the new partner towards goodwill)

(b) Goodwill a/c Dr.
To Old partners capital a/c
(Being goodwill shared by the old partners in the sacrifice ratio)

3. When the required amount of goodwill is brought in by the new partner and the same is withdrawn by the old partners :

(a) Bank a/c Dr.
To Goodwill a/c
(Being goodwill brought in by new partner)

(b) Goodwill a/c Dr.
To Old Partners Capital a/c
(Being goodwill brought in by new partner credited to old partners capital accounts in sacrifice ratio)

(c) Old Partners Capital a/c Dr.
To Bank a/c
(Being the amount withdrawn)

4. When the new partner does not bring in goodwill but the same is raised to its full value and allowed to remain in the books :

Para 16 of Accounting Standard - 10 (AS - 10) on "Accounting of Fixed Assets" issued by the Institute of Chartered Accountants of India states that the goodwill can be recorded in the books only when some consideration in money or money's worth has been paid for it. Therefore, only purchased goodwill should be recorded in the books of the firm. In case of admission of a partner, goodwill connot be raised in the books of the firm because no consideration in money or money's worth is paid for it. However, if the partners decide to raise the goodwill to its full value and allowed to remain in the books, the following entries are recorded.

Goodwill a/c Dr.
To Old Partner Capital a/c
(Being goodwill raised to its full value and distributed among old partners in their old profit sharing ratio)

Note : Here the goodwill account will appear on the asset side of the Balance Sheet.

5. When the goodwill raised in the books of the firm is written off immediately :

(a) Goodwill a/c Dr.
To Old Partners Capital a/c
(Being goodwill raised to its full value by crediting old partners in the old profit sharing ratio)

(b) All Partners Capital a/c Dr.
To Goodwill a/c
(Being goodwill created, written off amongst all the partners including the new partner in the new profit sharing ratio)

Note : In this case "Goodwill account" will not appear in the Balance Sheet.

6. **When existing goodwill is revalued :** Sometimes when the incoming partner is unable to bring in goodwill, then goodwill appearing in the Balance Sheet is revalued. If the present value of goodwill is higher than the amount appearing in the Balance Sheet, the difference is credited to the old partners in the old profit sharing ratio. The entries are reversed in case of fall in the value of goodwill. Goodwill then appears in the Balance Sheet at its new value.

Goodwill to be Inferred or Hidden Goodwill

Sometimes the value of goodwill has to be inferred from the agreement of capital and profit sharing ratio among the partners. Suppose X and Y share profit on the ratio of 2 : 1 and their capitals stands at Rs. 20,000 and Rs. 10,000 and they admit Z who brings Rs. 14,000 and is given $\frac{1}{4}$th share in future profit. Now Z's capital should be $\frac{1}{4}$th of the total capital or in other words, the combined capital of X and Y should be 3 times that of Z's capital. Since the existing total capital of X and Y is only Rs. 30,000 there is goodwill of Rs. 12,000. On the same capital consideration, goodwill may be attached to a particular partner on formation of partnership. For example, if X and Y form partnership agreeing to share profit equally but they contribute Rs. 12,000 and Rs. 9,000 respectively, it can be inferred that a goodwill of Rs. 3,000 attaches to X.

Treatment of Goodwill in Case of Change in the Profit Sharing Ratio.

Whenever there is a change in profit sharing ratio of the existing partners, there arises the need for valuation of goodwill. A change in profit sharing ratio results in gain to the partner and loss to the other. As a result, the partner who gains from the new ratio has to compensate the partner who loses. The gaining partner, in respect of share of profit may buy his share of profit from any one or more partners, as the case may be. The partners who sell the share may sacrifice in equal or unequal proportions. The amount of goodwill credited to partners from whom the gaining partner purchases has share is always in proportion to sacrifice made. The journal entry for this purpose is to debit the partners capital account (one who gains) with the proportionate share of goodwill and credit the capial account or accounts of the partners (who lose) with the same amount.

Problem 1

On 1st April, 2003 ; X, Y and Z who were sharing profits and losses in the ratio of 5 : 3 : 2 respectively decided to become equal partners. Goodwill of the firm was valued at Rs. 45,000. It was also decided to appreciate the book value of Land and Buildings by Rs. 14,000. No goodwill account appeared in the books of the firm and none was opened on change in profit sharing ratio. Pass journal entries to make the necessary adjustment.

Solution

Calculation of Loss or Gain in the Ratios

$$\text{Old profit sharing ratio} = \frac{5}{10} : \frac{3}{10} : \frac{2}{10}$$

$$\text{New profit sharing ratio} = \frac{1}{3} : \frac{1}{3} : \frac{1}{3}$$

$$\text{A loses} = \frac{5}{10} - \frac{1}{3}$$

$$= \frac{15-10}{30} = \frac{5}{30}$$

$$\text{B Gains} = \frac{1}{3} - \frac{3}{10}$$

$$= \frac{10-9}{30} = \frac{1}{30}$$

$$\text{C Gains} = \frac{1}{3} - \frac{2}{10}$$

$$= \frac{10-6}{30} = \frac{4}{30}$$

A will be credited with $\frac{5}{30} \times 45{,}000 = 7{,}500$

B will be debited with $\frac{1}{30} \times 45{,}000 = 1{,}500$

C will be debited with $\frac{4}{30} \times 45{,}000 = 6{,}000$

Journal Entries

Date	*Particulars*		*Dr. Amount*	*Cr. Amount*
	Land & Buildings a/c	Dr.	14,000	
	To Revaluation a/c			14,000
	(Being the appreciation in the value of Land & Building)			
	Revaluation a/c	Dr.	14,000	
	To X's Capital a/c			7,000
	To Y's Capital a/c			4,200
	To Z's Capital a/c			2,800
	(Being transfer of profit on revaluation to partners capital accounts in old profit sharing ratio)			
	Y's Capital a/c	Dr.	1,500	
	Z's Capital a/c	Dr.	6,000	
	To X's Capital a/c			7,500
	(Being adjustment for goodwill on change in profit sharing ratio)			

Problem 2

Alok and Bibhas are partners sharing profits and losses in the ratio of 7 : 5. On 1-4-1999 they admitted Dilip into their patnership. The new profit sharing ratio to be 5 : 3 : 2. Value of goodwill as per their books is Rs. 8,000 whereas for the purpose of admitting Dilip it was agreed upon at Rs. 20,000. Dilip agreed to pay the required premium for a goodwill in cash. Show the journal entry appropriating the premium money.

(Calcutta University (B-Com Pass), 2000)

Solution

Increase in the value of goodwill on admission is (Rs. 20,000 – 8,000) = Rs. 12,000.

Therefore, dilip will bring $12{,}000 \times \frac{2}{10}$ = Rs. 2,400

This will be divided between Alok and Bibhas in their sacrificing ratio.

$$\text{Alok} = \frac{7}{12} - \frac{5}{10}$$

$$= \frac{35-30}{60} = \frac{5}{60}$$

$$\text{Bishas} = \frac{5}{12} - \frac{3}{10}$$

$$= \frac{25-18}{60} = \frac{7}{60}$$

= i.e., : 5 : 7

A's share of goodwill = $2{,}400 \times \frac{5}{12}$ = Rs. 1,000

B's share of goodwill = $2{,}400 \times \frac{7}{12}$ = Rs. 1,400

Journal Entires

Date	*Particulars*	*Dr. Amount*	*Cr. Amount*
	Cash a/c Dr.	2,400	
	To Good will a/c		2,400
	(Being cash brought in by dilip as premium for goodwill for $\frac{2}{10}$th share of future profit)		
	Goodwill a/c Dr.	2,400	
	To Alok's Capital a/c		1,000
	To Bibhas's Capital a/c		1,400
	(Being the premium for goodwill divided between A and B in their sacrifice ratio 5 : 7)		

Problem 2

Tumpa and Tutul are in partnership sharing profits and losses as 3 : 2. On 1st January, 1997; they admit Keya at a pemium of Rs. 30,000 for one-fourth share of the profit. As between Tumpa and Tutul, they agree to share future profits and losses equally.

Pass journal entries recording the above transactions.

(Calcutta University B.Com (Hons.) 1997)

Solution

Calculation of Sacrifice Ratio

Suppose total profit = 1

Keya's share is $\frac{1}{4}$

So, the re-amaining profit $1 - \frac{1}{4} = \frac{3}{4}$ is to be shared by Tumpa and Tutul equally

i.e., $\frac{3}{4} \times \frac{1}{2} = \frac{3}{8}$ each

Sacrifice ratio = Old ratio – New ratio

$$\text{Tumpa} = \frac{3}{5} - \frac{3}{8}$$

$$= \frac{24-15}{40} = \frac{9}{40}$$

$$\text{Tutul} = \frac{2}{5} - \frac{3}{8}$$

$$\frac{16-15}{40} = \frac{1}{40}$$

So, the sacrifice ratio is 9 : 1.

Journal Entries

Date	*Particulars*	*Dr. Amount*	*Cr. Amount*
	Cash a/c Dr. To Goodwill a/c (Being cash brought in by Keya as goodwill)	30,000	 30,000
	Goodwill a/c Dr. To Tumpa's Capital a/c To Tutul's Capital a/c (Being the distribution of goodwill between old partners in their sacrifice ratio 9 : 1).	30,000	 27,000 3,000

Contribution and Purchase of Share of Profit

A new partner may either purchase his share of profit from one or more of the existing partners or he may contribute to the assets of the firm. In the former case, the total capital of the firm does not change. The amount brought in by the new partner is paid to the partners from whom share is purchased. In the latter case, the total capital of the firm is augmented by the amount brought in by the new partner. Suppose, A and B share profit and loss in the ratio of 2 : 1 and their capitals stand at Rs. 10,000 and 5,000 respectively. If C is admitted and he buys $\frac{1}{5}$th share from A, 'C' will bring Rs. 3,000 $\left(\text{Rs. } 15{,}000 \times \frac{1}{5}\right)$ in cash which will be withdrawn by A. The new balances of the capital accounts of A, B and C will be Rs. 7,000 ; Rs. 5,000 ; and Rs. 3,000 respectively. If C contributes to the capital for $\frac{1}{5}$th share of profit, he will bring Rs. 3,750 $\left(15{,}000 \times \frac{5}{4} \times \frac{1}{5}\right)$. The total capital of the new firm will be Rs. 18,750.

Problem 3

P and Q are partners in a firm sharing profits and losses in the ratio of 3 : 2. They admit R as a partner on 1-1-99 on the basis of his buying $\frac{1}{5}$ of P's share and $\frac{1}{6}$ of Q's share. On 1-1-99 they permit R to purchase in further $\frac{1}{10}$th of their remaining shares. How much did R pay each of the others on each occassion for goodwill, assuming that the goodwill of the firm was Rs. 30,000 on the first occassion and Rs. 40,000 on the second occassion. What is the ultimate share of each partner in the business ? (Calcutta University, B-Com (Hons.), 2000)

Solution

Goodwill and New Profit Sharing Ratio as on 1-1-97

$$\text{P's share of the goodwill} = 30{,}000 \times \frac{3}{5} = \text{Rs. } 18{,}000$$

$$\text{Q's share of the goodwill} = 30{,}000 \times \frac{2}{5} = \text{Rs. } 12{,}000$$

$$\text{Therefore amount paid by R to P for goodwill} = 18{,}000 \times \frac{1}{5} = \text{Rs. } 3{,}600.$$

$$\text{Amount paid by R to Q for goodwill} = 12{,}000 \times \frac{1}{6} = \text{Rs. } 2{,}000$$

Profit Sharing Ratio on 1-1-97

$$P = \frac{3}{5} - \left(\frac{3}{5} \times \frac{1}{5}\right)$$

$$= \frac{3}{5} - \frac{3}{25} = \frac{15-3}{25} = \frac{12}{25}$$

$$Q = \frac{2}{5} - \left(\frac{2}{5} \times \frac{1}{6}\right)$$

$$= \frac{2}{5} - \frac{2}{30} = \frac{12-2}{30} = \frac{10}{30}$$

$$R = \left(\frac{3}{5} \times \frac{1}{5}\right) + \left(\frac{2}{5} \times \frac{1}{6}\right)$$

$$= \frac{3}{25} + \frac{2}{30} = \frac{18+10}{150} = \frac{28}{150}$$

$$P : Q : R$$

$$\frac{12}{25} : \frac{10}{30} : \frac{28}{150}$$

or $$\frac{72}{150} : \frac{50}{150} : \frac{28}{150}$$

Goodwill on 1-1-1999

Increase in the value of goodwill = 40,000 – 30,000 = Rs. 10,000

Q Purchases $\frac{1}{10}$ of remaining shares of P & Q

i.e., $10{,}000 \times \left(\frac{72}{150} + \frac{50}{150}\right) \times \frac{1}{10}$ = Rs. 813

P gets $813 \times \frac{72}{122}$ = Rs. 480

Q gets $813 \times \frac{150}{122}$ = Rs. 333.

New Profit Sharing Ratio :-

$$P = \frac{72}{150} - \left(\frac{72}{150} \times \frac{1}{10}\right)$$

$$= \frac{72}{150} - \frac{72}{1{,}500} = \frac{720-72}{1{,}500} = \frac{648}{1{,}500}$$

$$Q = \frac{50}{150} - \left(\frac{50}{150} \times \frac{1}{10}\right) = \frac{50}{150} - \frac{50}{1{,}500}$$

$$= \frac{500-50}{1{,}500} = \frac{450}{1{,}500}$$

$$R = \frac{28}{150} + \left(\frac{72+50}{150} \times \frac{1}{10}\right) = \frac{28}{150} + \frac{122}{1{,}500}$$

$$\frac{280+122}{1{,}500} = \frac{402}{1{,}500}$$

i.e., 648 : 450 : 402.

4. Calculation of New Profit Sharing Ratio

When a new partner is admitted into a partnership firm, he acquires a share in the profit. From the point of view of old partners they surrender or sacrifice a portion of profit in favour of new partner. So it is implied that on admission of a partner we have to calculate the sacrifice ratio for the sake of distributing goodwill among old partners. Sacrifice ratio is the difference between old profit sharing ratio and the new profit sharing ratio.

Sacrifice ratio = Old profit sharing ratio – New profit sharing ratio.

However, calculation of sacrifice ratio depends upon the data provided.

New profit sharing ratio is calculated where capital amounts are to be adjusted. On admission of a new partner, the profit sharing ratios differ having sacrificed a portion of profit by old partners in favour of new partner. Thereafter the profit or loss is shared by all partners in the new profit sharing ratios.

Problem 4

A and B are partners in a firm sharing profits and losses in the ratio of 3 : 2. C joins the firm for a quarter share in the future profits. Ascertain the future profit sharing ratio of the partners in each of the following cases :-

(*a*) If C acquires his share of profit from the original partners in their profit sharing ratio.
(*b*) If C acquires his share of profits from the original partners in equal proportion.
(*c*) If C acquires his share only from B.
(*d*) If C acquires his share of profits from the original partners in the ratio of 2 : 3.

Solution

(*a*) A $\frac{3}{5}$ B $\frac{2}{5}$ C $\frac{1}{4}$

$$A = \frac{3}{5} - \left(\frac{3}{5} \times \frac{1}{4}\right) = \frac{3}{5} - \frac{3}{20}$$

$$= \frac{12-3}{20} = \frac{9}{20}$$

$$B = \frac{2}{5} - \left(\frac{2}{5} \times \frac{1}{4}\right)$$

$$= \frac{2}{5} - \frac{2}{20} = \frac{8-2}{20} = \frac{6}{20}.$$

New Ratios A $\frac{9}{20}$: B $\frac{6}{20}$: C $\frac{1}{4}$ or $\frac{5}{20}$

Or A : B : C : 9 : 6 : 5.

(*b*) $$A \frac{3}{5} : B \frac{2}{5} : C \frac{1}{4} = \frac{1}{8} + \frac{1}{8}$$

$$A = \frac{3}{5} - \frac{1}{8} = \frac{24-5}{40} = \frac{19}{40}$$

$$B = \frac{2}{5} - \frac{1}{8} = \frac{16-5}{40} = \frac{11}{40}$$

New Ratios = A : B : C

$$= \frac{19}{40} : \frac{11}{40} : \frac{1}{4} \text{ or } \frac{10}{40}$$

(c) $A = \frac{2}{5}$; $B = \frac{2}{5}$; $C \frac{1}{4}$

$$B = \frac{2}{5} - \frac{1}{4}$$

$$= \frac{8-5}{20} = \frac{3}{20}$$

New Ratios = A B C

$$= \frac{3}{5} \quad \frac{3}{20} \quad \frac{1}{4}$$

or $\frac{12}{20} \quad \frac{3}{20} \quad \frac{5}{20}$

(d) $A \frac{3}{5} : B : \frac{2}{5} : C \frac{1}{4}$

Share from = $A \frac{1}{4} \times \frac{2}{5} = \frac{2}{20}$

$$B \frac{1}{4} \times \frac{3}{5} = \frac{3}{20}$$

$$A = \frac{3}{5} - \frac{2}{20} = \frac{12-2}{20} = \frac{10}{20}$$

$$B = \frac{2}{5} - \frac{3}{20} = \frac{8-3}{20} = \frac{5}{20}$$

$$C = \frac{1}{4} \text{ or } \frac{5}{20}$$

A : B : C = 10 : 5 : 5.

Problem 5

Vinod, Pramod and Subodh are partners who are sharing in the ratio of 5 : 3 : 2. They admit Nakul as a partner giving him $\frac{1}{4}$th share in the future profits which he acquires equally from Vinod and Pramod only. Find out the future profit ratio for all partners.

Solution

Nakul's share is $\frac{1}{4}$th of which he obtains $\frac{1}{8}$th from Vinod and $\frac{1}{8}$th from Pramod. Vinod's share after giving $\frac{1}{8}$th share to Nakul is :

$$\text{Vinod} = \frac{5}{10} - \frac{1}{8} = \frac{20-5}{40} = \frac{15}{40}$$

$$\text{Pramod} = \frac{3}{10} - \frac{1}{8} = \frac{12-5}{40} = \frac{7}{40}.$$

Subodh's share remain altered which is $\frac{2}{10}$ or $\frac{8}{40}$.

Nakul's share is $\frac{1}{4}$ or $\frac{10}{40}$.

Problem 6

P and Q are partners sharing profits and losses in the proportion of 3 : 2 respectively. They agree to admit 'R' into the partnership and offer him $\frac{1}{6}$th share in future profits which he obtains $\frac{1}{24}$th from P and $\frac{1}{8}$th from Q. Calculate the new profit sharing ratio.

Solution

New profit Sharing ratio = Old ratio – Sacrifice ratio

$$P = \frac{3}{5} - \frac{1}{24} = \frac{72-5}{120} = \frac{67}{120}$$

$$Q = \frac{2}{5} - \frac{1}{8} = \frac{16-5}{40} = \frac{11}{40} \text{ or } \frac{33}{120}$$

$$R : \frac{1}{6} \text{ or } \frac{20}{120}$$

P : Q : R = 67 : 33 : 20.

Problem 7

X and Y are partners sharing profits and losses in the ratio of 4 : 3. They admit Z into partnership. The new profit sharing ratio of the partners is 5 : 3 : 2. Calculate the sacrifice ratio.

Solution

Sacrifice ratio = Old ratio – New profit sharing ratio

$$X = \frac{4}{7} - \frac{5}{10} = \frac{40-35}{70} = \frac{5}{70}$$

$$Y = \frac{3}{7} - \frac{3}{10} = \frac{30-21}{70} = \frac{9}{70}$$

So, sacrifice ratio of X : Y = 5 : 9.

Problem 8

Rama and Sharma are equal partners in a firm. They admit Ravi for $\frac{1}{3}$rd share in the future profits which he acquires $\frac{1}{4}$th from Rama and $\frac{3}{4}$th from Sharma. Find out the new profit sharing ratio of partners.

Solution

Calculation of actual sacrifice made by Rama and Sharma :

$$\text{Rama} = \frac{1}{3} \times \frac{1}{4} = \frac{1}{12}$$

$$\text{Sharma} = \frac{1}{3} \times \frac{3}{4} = \frac{3}{12}.$$

Calculation of New Profit Sharing Ratio

New ratio = Old ratio – Sacrifice ratio

$$\text{Rama} = \frac{1}{2} - \frac{1}{12} = \frac{6-1}{12} = \frac{5}{12}.$$

$$\text{Sharma} = \frac{1}{2} - \frac{3}{12} = \frac{6-3}{12} = \frac{3}{12}$$

$$\text{Ravi} = \frac{1}{3} \text{ or } \frac{4}{12}$$

Rama, Sharma, Ravi = 5 : 3 : 4.

5. Adjustment of Capitals of Old Partners

When it is decided that the capital amount of partners must be according to the new profit sharing ratio, it involves adjustment of capital which is proportionate to the new profit sharing ratio. This can be done under the following ways :-

(a) The new partners capital and his share of profit can be taken as the basis and capitals of other partners adjusted accordingly.

(b) The capital of new partner can be determined on the basis of the capitals of existing partners after making all adjustments required at the time of admission. In the process of adjusting the capitals of the partners, sometimes, there may be surplus amount which can either be withdrawn or transferred to their respective current account. Where there is deficit in the capital because of capital adjustments, the partners must contribute the deficit or the same could be made good by transferring the same to the current accounts.

Problem 9

On the admission of C the following were the balances in the capital accounts of partners after making all the adjustments : A Rs. 20,200 ; B Rs. 11,600 ; and C Rs. 6,000.

It was decided to adjust the capital accounts of the partners according to the new profit sharing ratio, i.e., 3 : 2 : 1 and with C's capital as the base by opening current account.

Pass entries and prepare capital account.

Solution

Note : Before giving entires we must find out what should be the balance in the capital accounts of A and B with C's. Capital as the base. C's share in profit = $\frac{1}{6}$

C's capital = Rs. 6,000

For $\frac{1}{6}$th share; C's capital is Rs. 6,000. So the capital of the firm is Rs. 6,000 × 6 = Rs. 36,000

A's capital should be $\frac{3}{6} \times 36{,}000$ = Rs. 18,000

B's capital should be $\frac{2}{6} \times 36{,}000$ = Rs. 12,000.

Calculation of Proportionate Capitals :

		A	B	C
	Actual capitals	20,200	11,600	6,000
	Capitals as per ratio	18,000	12,000	6,000
∴	Surplus/Deficit	+ 2,200	– 400	

Journal Entires

Date	*Particulars*		*Dr. Amount*	*Cr. Amount*
	A's Capital a/c	Dr.	2,200	
	To A's Current a/c			2,200
	(Being transfer of surplus in A's capital account over his ratio to his current account)			
	B's Current a/c	Dr.	400	
	To B's Capital a/c			400
	(Being shortage in B's capital adjusted in his current account)			

A's Capital A/c

Particulars	Amount	Particulars	Amount
To A's Current a/c	2,200	By Balance C/d	20,200
To Balance c/d	18,000		
	20,200		20,200

B's Capital A/c

Particulars	Amount	Particulars	Amount
To Balance C/d	12,000	By Balance b/d	11,600
		By B's Current a/c	400
	12,000		12,000

C's Capital A/c

Particulars	Amount	Particulars	Amount
To Balance c/d	6,000	By Balance b/d	6,000
	6,000		6,000

A's Current A/c

Particulars	Amount	Particulars	Amount
To Balance c/d	2,200	By A's Capital a/c	2,200
	2,200		2,200

B's Current A/c

Particulars	Amount	Particulars	Amount
To B's Capital a/c	400	By Balance c/d	400
	400		400

ENTRIES INVOLVED AT THE TIME OF ADMISSION OF A PARTNER

1. **For distribution of Reserve fund among old partners**

   Reserve Fund a/c Dr.
   To Old Partners Capital a/c

2. **For distribution of credit balance (i.e., profit) of Profit and Loss Account among old partners**

   Profit and Loss a/c Dr.
   To Old Partners Capital a/c

3. **For distributing debit balance (i.e., loss) of Profit and Loss Account among old partners**

   Old Partners Capital a/c Dr.
   To Profit and Loss a/c.

4. For recording decrease in the value of assets and increase in the value of liabilities :

Revaluation a/c Dr.
To Asset a/c
To Liability a/c

5. For recording increase in the value of assets and decrease in the value of liabilities

Asset a/c Dr.
Liability a/c Dr.
To Revaluation a/c.

6. For transfer of profit on revaluation.

Revaluation a/c Dr.
To Old Partner's Capital a/c

7. For transfer of loss on revaluation

Old Partners Capital a/c Dr.
To Revaluation a/c

8. For recording capital introduced by new partner :

(*a*) When cash is introduced :
Cash or Bank a/c Dr.
To New Partner's Capital a/c

(*b*) When assets are introduced :
Assets a/c Dr.
To New Partners Capital a/c

(*c*) When assets and liabilities are introduced :
Assets a/c Dr.
To Liabilities a/c
To New Partner's Captial a/c

9. For recording goodwill brought in cash by the New Partner

Cash or Bank a/c Dr.
To Goodwill a/c

10. For distributing goodwill among the old partners

Goodwill a/c Dr.
To Old Partner's Capital a/c

11. For recording goodwill amount withdrawn by the old partners

Old Partners Capital a/c Dr.
To Goodwill a/c

12. For recording the goodwill created in the business :

Goodwill a/c Dr.
To Old Partners Capital a/c

Note : Goodwill is distributed in the old ratio. Goodwill appears as an asset in the Balance sheet.

13. For Writing Off Goodwill among Old Partners

All Partners Capital a/c Dr.
To Goodwill a/c

Note : The goodwill is written off to all partners in their new profit sharing ratio. In this case the goodwill does not appear in the Balance Sheet.

14. For adjustment of surplus in capital account.

(*a*) If the surplus amount is withdrawn by partners
Old Partners Capital a/c Dr.
To Cash or Bank a/c

(*b*) If the surplus amount is transferred to the current account :
Old Partners Capital a/c Dr.
To Old Partners Current a/c

15. For adjusting deficit in the capital accounts :

(*a*) When deficit is brought in the form of cash
Cash or Bank a/c Dr.
To Old Partner's Capital a/c

(*b*) When deficit is made good by transfer to their current accounts
Old Partners Current a/c Dr.
To Old Partners's Capital a/c

Problem 10

A and B sharing profits in the ratio of 3 : 1. Their Balance Sheet as on 31st December 1999 is as under :

Liabilities	*Amount*	*Assets*	*Amount*
Creditors	37,500	Cash at Bank	22,500
General Reserve	4,000	Bills Receivable	3,000
Capital Accounts		Stock	20,000
A —	30,000	Debtors	16,000
B —	16,000	Furniture	1,000
		Building	25,000
	87,500		87,500

On 1-1-2000 they admit C as a new partner on the following arrangements.

(*a*) C to bring Rs. 10,000 as capital for $\frac{1}{5}$th share of profit.

(*b*) The new firm to have goodwill Rs. 10,000

(*c*) Stock and furniture to be reduced by 10% a reserve of 5% on debtors for doubtful debts to be created.

(*d*) Building to be appreciated at 20%.

Give necessary ledger accounts and Balance Sheet

(University of Madras, B-Com, April, 2001)

Solution

Revaluation A/c

	Amount		Amount
To Stock $\left(20{,}000 \times \frac{10}{100}\right)$	2,000	By Building $\left(\frac{20}{100} \times 25{,}000\right)$	5,000
To Furniture $\left(1{,}000 \times \frac{10}{100}\right)$	100		
To Reserve for doubtful debts	800		
To Profit transferred to			
A's Capital a/c	1,575		
B's Capital a/c	525		
	5,000		5,000

A's Capital A/c

	Amount		Amount
To Balance C/d	42,075	By Balance b/d	30,000
		By General Reserve a/c	3,000
		By Revaluation a/c	1,575
		By Goodwill a/c	7,500
	42,075		42,075

B's Capital A/c

	Amount		Amount
To Balance c/d	20,025	By Balance b/d	16,000
		By General Reserve a/c	1,000
		By Revaluation a/c	525
		By Goodwill a/c	2,500
	20,025		20,025

C's Capital A/c

	Amount		Amount
To Balance c/d	10,000	By Cash a/c	10,000
	10,000		10,000

Cash A/c

	Amount		Amount
To Balance b/d	22,500	By Balance c/d	32,500
To C's Capital a/c	10,000		
	32,500		32,500

Balance Sheet

Liabilities	*Amount*	*Assets*		*Amount*
Creditors	37,500	Cash at Bank		32,500
Capital Accounts :		Bills Receivable		3,000
A	42,075	Stock	20,000	
B	20,025	Less : 10% reduced	2,000	
C	10,000			18,000
		Debtors	16,000	
		Less : Reserve for bad debts 5% on 16,000	800	
				15,200
		Furniture	1,000	
		Less : 10% reduced	100	
				900
		Building	25,000	
		Add : Appreciation 20% on Rs. 25,000	5,000	
				30,000
		Goodwill		10,000
	1,09,600			1,09,600

Note : Goodwill of Rs. 10,000 is shared between old partners in their profit sharing ratio of 3 : 1 and the same is shown in Balance Sheet on the Asset side.

Problem 11

The following is the Balance Sheet of Surya, Chandra and Pawan sharing profits and losses in the proportion of $\frac{6}{14}, \frac{5}{14}$ and $\frac{3}{14}$ respectively.

Liabilities	*Amount*	*Assets*	*Amount*
Creditors	37,800	Cash	3,780
Bills Payable	12,600	Debtors	52,920
General Reserve	21,000	Stock	58,800
Surya's Capitals	70,800	Furniture	14,700
Chandra's Capitals	59,700	Land & Buildings	90,300
Pawan's Capitals	29,100	Goodwill	10,500
	2,31,000		2,31,000

They agreed to take Dharma into partnership and give him $\frac{1}{8}$th share on the following terms :

1. Furniture to be depreciated by Rs. 1,840
2. Stock to be depreciated by 10%.
3. A provision of Rs. 2,640 be made for outstanding repairs.
4. That the value of land and buildings having appreciated up to Rs. 1,19,700.
5. The value of goodwill be brought up to Rs. 28,140.
6. Dharma should bring Rs. 29,400 as his capital.
7. After making the above adjustments the capital accounts of old partners be adjussted on the basis of the proportion of Dharma's capital to his share in the business, i.e., actual cash to be paid off or brought in by the old partners as the case may be.

Show the necessary accounts and prepare the balance sheet of the new firm.

(Sri Venkateshwara University, B.Com, September, 2000)

Solution

Revaluation A/c

	Amount		Amount
To Furniture a/c	1,840	By Land & Building	29,400
To Stock a/c	5,880		
To Outstanding Repairs a/c	2,640		
To Profit transferred to			
Surya's Capital	8,160		
Chandra's Capital	6,800		
Pawan's Capital	4,080		
	29,400		29,400

Surya's Capital A/c

	Amount		Amount
To Cash a/c	7,320	By Balance b/d	70,800
To Balance c/d	88,200	By General Reserve A.c	9,000
		By Goodwill a/c	7,560
		By Revaluation a/c	8,160
	95,520		95,520

Chandra's Capital A/c

	Amount		Amount
To Cash a/c	6,800	By Balance b/d	59,700
To Balance c/d	73,500	By General Reserve a/c	7,500
		By Goodwill a/c	6,300
		By Revaluation a/c	6,800
	80,300		80,300

Pawan's Captial A/c

	Amount		Amount
To Balance c/d	44100	By Balance b/d	29,100
		By General Reserve a/c	4,500
		By Goodwill a/c	3,780
		By Revaluation a/c	4,080
		By Cash a/c	2,640
	44,100		44,100

Dharma's Capital A/c

	Amount		Amount
To Balance c/d	29,400	By Bank a/c	29,400
	29,400		29,400

Cash A/c

	Amount		Amount
To Balance b/d	3,780	By Surya's Capital a/c	7,320
To Dharama's Capital a/c	29,400	By Chandra's Capital a/c	6,800
To Pawan's Capital a/c	2,640	By Balance c/d	21,700
	35,820		35,820

Working Notes :

Calculation of new profit sharing ratio :

Old profit and loss account ratio = $\frac{6}{14} : \frac{5}{14} : \frac{3}{14}$

Dharma's Share = $\frac{1}{8}$th

Remaining ratio = $1 - \frac{1}{8} = \frac{7}{8}$

Surya's new ratio = $\frac{7}{8} \times \frac{6}{14} = \frac{42}{112}$

Chandra's new ratio = $\frac{7}{8} \times \frac{5}{14} = \frac{35}{112}$

Pawan's new ratio = $\frac{7}{8} \times \frac{3}{14} = \frac{21}{112}$

Dharam's new ratio = $\frac{1}{8}$ or = $\frac{14}{112}$

∴ New profit sharing ratio is 42 : 35 : 28 : 14

Or 6 : 5 : 3 : 2.

For 2 share of Dharma, his capital is Rs. 29,400

For 1 share = 14,700

∴ 6 share, Surya's Capital = 6 × 14,700 = Rs. 88,200

5 Share, Chandra's Capital = 5 × 14,700 = Rs. 73,500

3 Share, Pawani Capital = 3 × 14,700 = 44,100.

Balance Sheet
Of Surya, Chandra, Pawan & Sharma

Liabilities	Amount	Assets	Amount
Creditors	37,800	Cash	21,700
Bills Payable	12,600	Debtors	52,920
Outstanding repairs	2,640	Stock in trade (58,800 – 5,880)	52,920
Capital Accounts :-		Furniture	12,860
Surya	88,200	(14,700 – 1,840)	
Chandra	73,500	Land & Building	1,19,700
Pawan	44,100	(90,300 + 27,400)	
Dharma	29,400	Goodwill	28,140
	2,88,240		2,88,240

Problem 12

A and B shared profits in the ratio of 2 : 1 respectively. On 31st March 2000, their Balance Sheet stood as follows :

Liabilities	*Amount*	*Assets*	*Amount*
Sundry Creditors	35,500	Cash at Bank	22,500
General Reserve	6,000	Bills Receivable	3,000
A's Capital	30,000	Sundry Debtors	16,000
B's Capital	16,000	Stock	15,000
		Furniture	6,000
		Machinery	25,000
	87,500		87,500

On 1st April 2000, C was admitted into partership on the following terms :

(1) That C brings in Rs. 10,000 as his capital for $\frac{1}{4}$th share in future profit.

(2) That a goodwill account be, raised in the books of the firm at Rs. 15,000.

(3) That the value of machinery be raised to Rs. 30,000.

(4) The stock and furniture be depreciated by 10% and a provision for doubtful debts be created at 5% on Sundry Debtors.

(5) That the capital accounts of the partners be readjusted on the basis of their profit sharing ratio and any additional amount be debited or credited to their current accounts.

Prepare the necessary ledger accounts and opening Balance Sheet of the new firm

(C.S. Foundation, June 2000)

Solution

Revaluation A/c

	Amount		*Amount*
To Stock a/c	1,500	My Machinery	5,000
To Furniture a/c	600		
To Provision for Doubtful Debts	800		
To Profit transferred to			
A's Capital a/c	1,400		
B's Capital a/c	700		
	5,000		5,000

A's Capital A/c

	Amount		*Amount*
To A's Current a/c	25,400	By Balance b/d	30,000
To Balance c/d	20,000	By General Reserve	4,000
		By Goodwill a/c	10,000
		By Revaluation a/c	1,400
	45,400		45,400

A's Current A/c

	Amount		Amount
To Balance c/d	25,400	By A's Capital a/c	25,400
	25,400		25,400

B's Capital A/c

	Amount		Amount
To B's Current a/c	13,700	By Balance b/d	16,000
To Balance c/d	10,000	By General Reserve a/c	2,000
		By Goodwill a/c	5,000
		By Revaluation a/c	700
	23,700		23,700

B's Current A/c

	Amount		Amount
To Balance c/d	13,700	By B's Capital a/c	13,700
	13,700		13,700

C's Capital A/c

	Amount		Amount
To Balance c/d	10,000	By Bank a/c	10,000
	10,000		10,000

Cash A/c

	Amount		Amount
To Balance b/d	22,500	By Balance c/d	32,500
To C's Capital a/c	10,000		
	32,500		32,500

Working Note :

Calculation of New Profit Sharing Ratio :

C gets $\frac{1}{4}$th share

$$\text{Remaining share} = 1 - \frac{1}{4} = \frac{3}{4}$$

$$\text{A's Share} = \frac{3}{4} \times \frac{2}{3} = \frac{6}{12}$$

$$\text{B's Share} = \frac{3}{4} \times \frac{1}{3} = \frac{3}{12}$$

$$\text{C's Share} = \frac{1}{4} \text{ or } = \frac{3}{12}$$

New Profit Sharing Ratio = 6 : 3 : 3

or : 2 : 1 : 1.

Total Capital :

C brings Rs. 10,000 for $\frac{1}{4}$th share.

Hence Total capital must be $10,000 \times 4 = 40,000$

$$\text{A's Capital} = \frac{1}{2} \text{ of } 40,000 = \text{Rs. } 20,000$$

$$\text{B's Capital} = \frac{1}{4} \text{ of } 40,000 = \text{Rs. } 10,000$$

$$\text{C's Capital} = \frac{1}{4} \text{ of } 40,000 = \text{Rs. } 10,000$$

Balance Sheet of A, B and C as on

1st April, 2000

Liabilities	*Amount*	*Assets*		*Amount*
Sundry Creditors	35,500	Cash at Bank		32,500
A's Capital a/c	20,000	Bills Receivable		3,000
B's Capital a/c	10,000	Sundry Debtors	16,000	
C's Capital a/c	10,000	Less : Provisions for		
A's Current a/c	25,400	Bad debts	800	
B's Current a/c	13,700			15,200
		Stock		13,500
		Furniture		5,400
		Machinery		30,000
		Goodwill		15,000
	1,14,600			1,14600

Problem 13

The following was the Balance Sheet of A, B, C sharing profits and losses in proportion of 6 : 5 : 3 respectively.

Liabilities		*Amount*	*Assets*	*Amount*
Creditors		18,800	Cash at Bank	8,890
Bills Payable		6,400	Debtors	26,460
Reserve		7,000	Stock	29,400
Capital Accounts :-			Furniture	7,350
A –	39,900		Land & Buildings	50,400
B –	33,600			
C –	16,800			
		90,300		
		1,22,500		1,22,500

They agreed to take 'D' into partnership and gave him $\frac{1}{8}$th share of profit on the following terms :

(*a*) That 'D' brings in Rs. 16,000 as his capital.

(*b*) That furniture be written down by Rs. 920 and stock be depreciated by 10%.

(*c*) That provision of Rs. 1,320 be made for outstanding repair bills.

(*d*) That the value of land and buildings be Rs. 65,100

(*e*) That the value of goodwill be fixed at Rs. 8,820.
(*f*) That the capitals of A, B and C be adjusted on the basis of D's capital by opening current accounts.

Give necessary journal entries and the Balance Sheet of newly constituted firm.

(Osmania University, B.Com, October, 1998)

Solution

Journal Entries

Date	*Particulars*		*Dr. Amount*	*Cr. Amount*
	Reserve a/c	Dr.	7,000	
	To A's Capital a/c			3,000
	To B's Capital a/c			2,500
	To C's Capital a/c			1,500
	(Being the transfer of reserve to old partners in the old ratio)			
	Land & Building a/c	Dr.	14,700	
	To Revaluation a/c			14,700
	(Being the increase in the value of land and buildings)			
	Revaluation a/c	Dr.	5,180	
	To Furniture a/c			920
	To Provision against stock			2,940
	To Provision for repairs			1,320
	(Being the fall in the value of assets and creation of liability in respect of repairs)			
	Revaluation a/c	Dr.	9,520	
	To A's Capital a/c			4,080
	To B's Capital a/c			3,400
	To C's Capital a/c			2,040
	(Being the transfer of profit on revaluation to the old partners)			
	Goodwill a/c	Dr.	8,820	
	To A's Capital a/c			3,780
	To B's Capital a/c			3,150
	To C's Capital a/c			1,890
	(The value of goodwill credited to the old partners in the old ratio of 6 : 5 : 3)			
	Bank a/c	Dr.	16,000	
	To D's Capital a/c			16,000
	(Being the amount brought in by 'D' as capital)			
	A's Capital a/c	Dr.	2,760	
	B's Capital a/c	Dr.	2,650	
	To A's Current a/c			2,760
	To B's Current a/c			2,650
	(Being the transfer of respective surplus to current account of the partners)			
	C's Current a/c	Dr.	1,770	
	To C's Capital a/c			1,770
	(Being the deficiency of C's capital transferred to his current account)			

Working Note :

Calculation of New Profit Sharing Ratio :

'D' gets $\frac{1}{8}$th share. Hence the balance is $1 - \frac{1}{8} = \frac{7}{8}$

$$\text{A's Share} = \frac{7}{8} \times \frac{6}{14} = \frac{42}{112}$$

$$\text{B's Share} = \frac{7}{8} \times \frac{5}{14} = \frac{35}{112}$$

$$\text{C's Share} = \frac{7}{8} \times \frac{3}{14} = \frac{21}{112}$$

$$\text{D's Share} = \frac{1}{8} \text{ or } = \frac{14}{112}$$

Hence the ratios are : 42 : 35 : 21 : 14

or 6 : 5 : 3 : 2

Total capital of the firm on the basis of D's capital.

For 2 parts : 16,000

$$\text{For 16 parts : } \frac{16{,}000 \times 16}{2} = 1{,}28{,}000$$

$$\text{A's Share of Capital} = 1{,}28{,}000 \times \frac{6}{16} = \text{Rs. } 48{,}000$$

$$\text{B's Share of Capital} = 1{,}28{,}000 \times \frac{5}{16} = \text{Rs. } 40{,}000$$

$$\text{C's Share of Capital} = 1{,}28{,}000 \times \frac{3}{16} = \text{Rs. } 24{,}000$$

$$\text{D's Share of Capital} = 1{,}28{,}000 \times \frac{2}{16} = \text{Rs. } 16{,}000$$

Balance Sheet of A, B, C and D

Liabilities		*Amount*	*Assets*		*Amount*
Creditors		18,800	Goodwill		8,820
Bills Payable		6,400	Land and Buildings		65,100
Provision for Repairs		1,320	Furniture	7,350	
Capital Accounts :			Less : Depreciation	920	
A –	48,000				6,430
B –	40,000		Stock	29,400	
C –	24,000		Less : Provisions	2,940	
D –	16,000				26,460
		1,28,000	Debtors		26,460
Current Accounts :			Cash at Bank		24,890
A –	2,760		C's Current a/c		1,770
B –	2,650				
		5,410			
		1,59,930			1,59,930

Problem 14

Following is the Balance Sheet of Active and Sharp who shared profits and losses in the ratio of 3 : 2

Liabilities	*Amount*	*Assets*	*Amount*
Active's Capital	30,000	Goodwill	10,000
Sharp's Capital	25,000	Sundry Assets	50,000
Sundry Creditors	10,000	Cash	5,000
	65,000		65,000

Blunt was admitted as partner on the date of Balance Sheet. The new ratio for sharing profits and losses will be 5 : 3 : 2. Blunt pays Rs. 20,000 as capital but nothing for goodwill which has to be valued on the basis of 2 years purchase of 3 years profits. The profit for the 3 years were Rs. 10,000, Rs. 12,000 and Rs. 14,000. Draw up the Balance Sheet after giving journal entries and ledger accounts relating to Blunts admission.

(University of Madras B.Com, April, 2000)

Solution

Calculation of Goodwill

Goodwill is average of 3 years profit of 2 years purchase

$$\text{Average Profit} = \frac{10{,}000 + 12{,}000 + 14{,}000}{3} = 12{,}000$$

$$\text{2 years purchase} = 12{,}000 \times 2 = 24{,}000$$

Goodwill as per above calculation = 24,000

Goodwill as per Balance Sheet = 10,000

Goodwill raised = 14,000

$$\text{Active's Share of goodwill} = \frac{3}{5} \times 14{,}000 = 8{,}400$$

$$\text{Sharp's Share of goodwill} = \frac{2}{5} \times 14{,}000 = 5{,}600.$$

Journal Entries

Date	*Particulars*		*Dr. Amount*	*Cr. Amount*
	Cash a/c	Dr.	20,000	
	To Blunt's Capital a/c			20,000
	(Being capital contributed by Blunt)			
	Goodwill a/c	Dr.	14,000	
	To Active's Capital a/c			8,400
	To Sharp's Capital a/c			5,600
	(Being the goodwill raised in the books and shared between old partners)			

Active's Capital A/c

	Amount		Amount
To Balance c/d	38,400	By Balance b/d By Goodwill a/c	30,000 8,400
	38,400		38,400

Sharp's Capital A/c

	Amount		Amount
To Balance c/d	30,600	By Balance b/d By Goodwill	25,000 5,600
	30,600		30,600

Blunt's Capital A/c

	Amount		Amount
To Balance c/d	20,000	By Cash	20,000
	20,000		20,000

Balance Sheet of Active, Sharp, Blunt

Liabilities	*Amount*	*Assets*		*Amount*
Sundry Creditors	10,000	Goodwill (10,000 + 14,000)		24,000
Capital Accounts :				
Active	38,400	Sundry Assets		50,000
Sharp	30,600	Cash :		
Blunt	20,000	Opening Balance	5,000	
		Blunt's Capital	20,000	
				25,000
	99,000			99,000

Problem 15

X and Y are partners sharing profits and loss in the ratio of 1 : 1. Their Balance Sheet as on 31-3-1999 is as under :

Liabilities	*Amount*	*Assets*	*Amount*
Sundry Creditors	1,00,000	Cash	50,000
Capitals :		Sundry Debtors	50,000
X –	2,00,000	Stock	1,00,000
Y –	2,00,000	Plant and Machinery	2,00,000
		Land and Buildings	1,00,000
	5,00,000		5,00,000

'Z' is admitted as partner with effect from 1-4-1999 on the following terms :

(a) Plant and Machinery shall be valued at Rs. 2,50,000.
(b) The value of land and building shall be increased by 50%.
(c) The value of stock shall be reduced to 80%.
(d) Goodwill has been valued at Rs. 60,000 and Z shall bring in Rs. 18,000 as his share of Goodwill.
(e) Z shall bring in Rs. 80,000 as his capital.
(f) The whole amount brought in by Z shall remain in the business.
(g) New Profit Sharing Ratio, $X = \frac{4}{10}$; $Y = \frac{3}{10}$; $Z = \frac{3}{10}$

Write up necessary accounts and show the opening Balance Sheet of the New Firm

(Sri Venkateshwara University, B.Com October, 1999)

Solution

Revaluation A/c

	Amount		*Amount*
To Stock	20,000	By Plant and Machinery	50,000
To Profit		By Land and Buildings	50,000
X's Capital	40,000		
Y's Capital	40,000		
	100,000		100,000

Goodwill A/c

	Amount		*Amount*
To X's Capital a/c	6,000	By Cash a/c	18,000
To Y's Capital a/c	12,000		
	18,000		18,000

X's Capital A/c

	Amount		*Amount*
To Balance c/d	2,46,000	By Balance b/d	2,00,000
		By Revaluation a/c	40,000
		By Goodwill a/c	6,000
	2,46,000		2,46,000

Y's Capital A/c

	Amount		*Amount*
To Balance c/d	2,52,000	By Balance b/d	2,00,000
		By Revaluation a/c	40,000
		By Goodwill	12,000
	2,52,000		2,52,000

Z's Capital A/c

	Amount		Amount
To Balance c/d	80,000	By cash	80,000
	80,000		80,000

Cash A/c

	Amount		Amount
To Balance b/d To Goodwill To Z's capital	50,000 18,000 80,000	By Balance c/d	1,48,000
	1,48,000		1,48,000

Working Note :

Calculation of sacrifices ratio for distributing goodwill :

$$\text{X's Sacrifice Ratio} = \frac{1}{2} - \frac{4}{10}$$

$$= \frac{5-4}{10} = \frac{1}{10}$$

$$\text{Y's Sacrifice Ratio} = \frac{1}{2} - \frac{3}{10}$$

$$= \frac{5-3}{10} = \frac{2}{10}$$

∴ Sacrifice Ratio of X & Y : 1 : 2.

Balance Sheet of X, Y and Z as on 1-4-1999

Liabilities	*Amount*	*Assets*		*Amount*
Sundry Creditors	1,00,000	Cash		1,48,000
Capital Accounts :		Sundry Debtors		50,000
X –	2,46,000	Stock	1,00,000	
Y –	2,52,000	Less : Depreciation	20,000	
Z –	80,000			80,000
		Plant and Machinery	2,00,000	
		Add : Appreciation	50,000	
				2,50,000
		Land and Buildings	1,00,000	
		Add : Appreciation	50,000	
				1,50,000
	6,78,000			6,78,000

Problem 16

The Balance Sheet of Aritra and Amartya as on 31st December, 1996 is given below. They share profits and losses in the ratio of 2 : 1.

Liabilities	*Amount*	*Assets*	*Amount*
Aritra's Capital	50,000	Land and Buildings	50,000
Amartya's Capital	40,000	Furniture	10,000
General Reserve	12,000	Stock	12,000
Sundry Creditors	11,000	Debtors	30,000
		Cash	8,000
		Profit and Loss a/c	3,000
	1,13,000		1,13,000

On 1st January, 1997 they agree to admit Akash as a new partner of the firm on the following terms and conditions :-

(*a*) Akash will be entitled to $\frac{1}{4}$th share of the future profits of the firm.
(*b*) The goodwill of the firm shall be valued at Rs. 36,000 and Akash will pay his share of goodwill in cash.
(*c*) Furniture is to be depreciated by 10%.
(*d*) Land and Buildings is to be appreciated by 15%.
(*e*) Stock is to be reduced by Rs. 500.
(*f*) Provision for doubttful debts is to be created @ 5% on Sundry Debtors.
(*g*) Akash will contribute $\frac{1}{3}$rd of the adjusted combined capitals of Aritra and Amartya as his capital.

You are required to prepare revaluation account, the capital accounts and Balance Sheet of the new firm.

(Calcutta University, B.Com (Pass), 1997)

Solution

Revaluation A/c

	Amount		*Amount*
To Furniture a/c	1,000	By Land and Buildings	7,500
To Stock a/c	500		
To Provision for Bad Debts a/c	1,500		
To Partners Capital a/c			
Aritra	3,000		
Amartya	1,500		
	7,500		7,500

Aritra's Capital A/c

	Amount		*Amount*
To Profit and Loss a/c	2,000	By Balance b/d	50,000
To Balance c/d	65,000	By General Reserve a/c	8,000
		By Goodwill a/c	6,000
		By Revaluation a/c	3,000
	67,000		67,000

Amartya's Capital A/c

	Amount		Amount
To Profit and Loss a/c	1,000	By Balance b/d	40,000
To Balance c/d	47,500	By General Reserve a/c	4,000
		By Goodwill a/c	3,000
		By Revaluation a/c	1,500
	48,500		48,500

Akash's Capital A/c

	Amount		Amount
To Balance c/d	37,500	By Cash a/c	37,500
	37,500		37,500

Cash A/c

	Amount		Amount
To Balance b/d	8,000	By Balance c/d	54,500
To Akash's Capital a/c	37,500		
To Goodwill a/c	9,000		
	54,500		54,500

Working Notes :

Goodwill and its distribution

Goodwill brought by Akash $= \frac{1}{4} \times 36{,}000 =$ Rs. 9,000

Calculation of New Ratio :

$$A = \frac{2}{3} \times \frac{3}{4} = \frac{6}{12}$$

$$B = \frac{1}{3} \times \frac{3}{4} = \frac{3}{12}$$

$$C = \frac{1}{4} \text{ or } = \frac{3}{12}$$

Calculation of Sacrifice Ratio :

Sacrifice Ratio = Old Ratio – New Ratio

$$A = \frac{2}{3} - \frac{6}{12}$$

$$= \frac{8-6}{12} = \frac{2}{12}$$

$$B = \frac{1}{3} - \frac{3}{12}$$

$$= \frac{4-3}{12} = \frac{1}{12}.$$

Goodwill is shared in the sacrifice ratio of 2 : 1.

(2) Capital contribution by Akash

$= \frac{1}{3}$rd of Aritra's Capital + Amartya's Capital

$= \frac{1}{3} \times (65{,}000 + 47{,}500) =$ Rs. 37,500.

Balance Sheet of the Firm as on 1-1-1997

		Amount			*Amount*
Sundry Creditors		11,000	Land and Buildings	50,000	
Capital Accounts :-			Add : Increase	7,500	
Aritra –	65,000				57,500
Amartya –	47,500		Furniture	10,000	
Akash –	37,500		Less : Depreciation	1,000	
		1,50,000			9,000
			Stock	12,000	
			Less : Decrease	500	
					11,500
			Debtors	30,000	
			Less : Provision for Bad Debts	1,500	
					28,500
			Cash		54,500
		1,61,000			1,61,000

Problem 17

A, B and C were in partnership sharing profits and losses as to A $\frac{1}{2}$: B $\frac{1}{3}$: C $\frac{1}{6}$. As from 1st January, 1996 they admitted D into partnership on the following terms :

D to have $\frac{1}{6}$th share which he purchased entirely from A paying A Rs. 8,000 for that share of goodwill. Of this amount, A had withdrawn Rs. 6,000 and put the balance in the firm as additional capital. As a condition to admission of D as a partner D also brought Rs. 5,000 capital into the firm. It was further agreed that the investments should be valued at its market value of Rs. 3,600 and plant be valued at Rs. 5,800.

The Balance Sheet of the old firm on 31-12-1995 as as follows :

Cash at Bank Rs. 8,000 ; Debtors Rs. 12,000 ; Stock Rs. 10,000 ; Investment at cost Rs. 6,000 ; Furniture Rs. 2,000 ; Plant Rs. 7,000 ; Creditors Rs. 21,000 ; Capital ; A Rs. 12,000 ; B Rs. 8,000 ; and C Rs. 4,000.

The Profit for the year 1996 were Rs. 12,000 and the drawings were : A Rs. 6,000 ; B Rs. 6,000 ; C Rs. 3,000 ; and D Rs. 3,000.

You are required to journalise the opening adjustments, prepare Opening Balance Sheet of the new firm as on 1st January, 1996 and give the capital account of each partner as on 31st December, 1996. **(C.A. Foundation, November, 1997)**

Solution

Journal Entires

Date	Particulars		Dr. Amount	Cr. Amount
	Revaluation a/c	Dr.	3,600	
	To Investment a/c			2,400
	To Plant a/c			1,200
	(Being revaluation of investment and plant recorded)			
	A's Capital a/c	Dr.	1,800	
	B's Capital a/c	Dr.	1,200	
	C's Capital a/c	Dr.	600	
	To Revaluation a/c			3,600
	(Being loss on revaluation transferred to old partners in 3 : 2 : 1 ratio).			
	Bank a/c	Dr.	13,000	
	To D's Capital a/c			5,000
	To Goodwill a/c			8,000
	(Being capital and goodwill contributed by D)			
	Goodwill a/c	Dr.	8,000	
	To A's Capital a/c			8,000
	(Being goodwill transferred to A)			
	A's Capital a/c	Dr.	6,000	
	To Bank a/c			6,000
	(Being goodwill withdrawn by A)			

A's Capital A/c

	Amount		Amount
To Drawings a/c	6,000	By Balance b/d	12,000
To Revaluation a/c	1,800	By Goodwill a/c	8,000
To Bank a/c	6,000	By Profit and Loss a/c	4,000
To Balance c/d	10,200		
	24,000		24,000

B's Capital A/c

	Amount		Amount
To Drawings a/c	6,000	By Balance b/d	8,000
To Revaluation a/c	1,200	By Profit and Loss a/c	4,000
To Balance c/d	4,800		
	12,000		12,000

C's Capital A/c

	Amount		Amount
To Drawings	3,000	By Balance b/d	4,000
To Revaluation a/c	600	By Profit and Loss a/c	2,000
To Balance c/d	2,400		
	6,000		6,000

D's Capital A/c

	Amount		Amount
To Drawings a/c	3,000	By Cash a/c	5,000
To Balance c/d	4,000	By Profit and Loss a/c	2,000
	7,000		7,000

Cash A/c

	Amount		Amount
To Balance b/d	8,000	By A's Capital a/c	6,000
To D's Capital a/c	5,000	By A's Drawings a/c	6,000
To Goodwill a/c	8,000	By B's Drawings a/c	6,000
To Profit and Loss a/c — Profit	12,000	By C's Drawings a/c	3,000
		By D's Drawing a/c	3,000
		By Balance c/d	9,000
	33,000		33,000

Balance Sheet of New Firm as on 1st January, 1996

Liabilities	*Amount*	*Assets*	*Amount*
Creditors	21,000	Plant	5,800
Capital Accounts :		Furniture	2,000
A –	10,200	Investments	3,600
B –	4,800	Stock	10,000
C –	2,400	Debtors	12,000
D –	4,000	Cash	9,000
	42,400		42,400

Problem 18

Tom and Bom are equal partners in a firm. The Balance Sheet of the firm as on 31st March, 1997 is given below :

Liabilities	*Amount*	*Assets*	*Amount*
Capital Accounts :		Plant and Machinery	50,000
Tom	50,000	Furniture and Fixture	25,000
Bom	50,000	Stock in Trade	20,000
Sundry Creditors	20,000	Sundry Debtors	5,000
Bills Payable	5,000	Cash at Bank	25,000
	1,25,000		1,25,000

On 1st April, they agreed to admit Com as $\frac{1}{3}$rd partner to increase the capital base to Rs. 1,50,000.

Show the necessary journal entries, capital accounts, and the Balance Sheet of the firm after Com's admission **(I.C.W.A. Inter, December, 1997)**

Solution

Journal Entries

Date	Particulars		Dr. Amount	Cr. Amount
	Bank a/c	Dr.	75,000	
	To Com's Capital a/c			75,000
	(Being cash brought in by new partner as capital)			
	Com's Capital a/c	Dr.	25,000	
	To Tom's Capital a/c			12,500
	To Com's Capital a/c			12,500
	(Being the amount of premium for goodwill adjusted with capital accounts of new partner and credited to old partners in the sacrifice ratio 1 : 1)			
	Tom's Capital a/c	Dr.	12,500	
	Bom's Capital a/c	Dr.	12,500	
	To Bank a/c			25,000
	(Beeing the amount of premium of goodwill withdrawn by the old partners)			

Tom's Capital A/c

	Amount		Amount
To Bank a/c	12,500	By Balance b/d	50,000
To Balance c/d	50,000	By Com's Capital a/c	12,500
	62,500		62,500

Bom's Capital A/c

	Amount		Amount
To Bank a/c	12,500	By Balance b/d	50,000
To Balance c/d	50,000	By Com's Capital a/c	12,500
	62,500		62,500

Com's Capital A/c

	Amount		Amount
To Tom's Capital a/c	12,500	By Bank a/c	75,000
To Bom's Capital a/c	12,500		
To Balance c/d	50,000		
	75,000		75,000

Working Notes :-

New Partner's Share of Profit = $\frac{1}{3}$

Total Capital Base = Rs. 1,50,000

New Partner Com's Capital = $\frac{1}{3} \times 1,50,000 = 50,000.$

Total amount of capital brought by Com = Rs. 7,5000.

The balance amount Rs. 25,000 as the premium of goodwill which is withdrawn by the old partners in their sacrifice ratio which is equal ratio.

Balance Sheet of the Firm on 1-4-97

Liabilities	*Amount*	*Assets*	*Amount*
Capital Accounts :-		Plant and Machinery	50,000
Tom	50,000	Furniture and Fixture	25,000
Bom	50,000	Stock in Trade	20,000
Com	50,000	Sundry Debtors	5,000
Sundry Creditors	20,000	Cash at Bank	75,000
Bills Payable	5,000		
	1,75,000		1,75,000

QUESTIONS

Simple Questions

1. State the adjustments required to be made in the books of a firm on admission of a new partner.
2. What is revaluation account ? When is it prepared ?
3. How is "revaluation account" prepared ?
4. How do partners share the General Reserve at the time of admission of a new partner ? Give the journal entries with narration.
5. What is goodwill ?
6. State any four factors which determine goodwill.
7. When does the need to value goodwill arise ?
8. List out the methods of valuing goodwill.
9. What is "Average Profit Method" of valuing goodwill ?
10. What is "Super Profit Method" of valuing goodwill ?
11. Why goodwill should be taken into account when a new partner is admitted ?
12. What is sacrifice ratio ?

EXERCISE 1

The following is the Balance Sheet of A, B and C sharing profit and losses in the proportion of 6 : 5 : 3 respectively.

Liabilities	*Amount*	*Assets*	*Amount*
Creditors	18,900	Cash	1,890
Bills Payable	6,300	Debtors	26,460
General Reserve	10,500	Stock	29,400
A's Capital	35,400	Furniture	7,350
B's Capital	29,850	Land and Building	45,150
C's Capital	14,550	Goodwill	5,250
	1,15,500		1,15,500

They agree to take 'D' into partnership and give him $\frac{1}{8}$th share on the following terms :

(*a*) That furniture be depreciated by Rs. 920.
(*b*) That stock be depreciated by 10%.
(*c*) That a provision of Rs. 1,320 be made for outstanding repair bills.
(*d*) That the value of land and buildings having appreciated be brought up to Rs. 59,850.
(*e*) That the value of goodwill be brought up to Rs. 14,070.
(*f*) That 'D' should bring in Rs. 14,700 as his capital.
(*g*) That after making above adjustments the capital accounts of old partners be adjusted on the basis of proportion of D's capital to his share in the business (i.e.,) actual cash to be paid off or brought in by the old partners as the case may be.

Pass journal entries and prepare revaluation, partner's capital account and Balance sheet of new firm. **(University of Madras, B.Com, April, 1998)**

Answer : Balance Sheet Total Rs. 1,44,120.

EXERCISE 2

Vani and Rani are partners sharing profits and losses in 3 : 2 ratio. They admit Mani as a partner who has to contribute Rs. 5,000 as her capital and premium for goodwill for a $\frac{1}{5}$th share. She being unable to bring any cash for capital, requested Vani to grant Rs. 3,000 as loan and Rani Rs. 2,000 as loan. Since she could not bring her share of goodwill also, it was raised in the books at Rs. 15,000. Vani and Rani had capitals of Rs. 18,000 and Rs. 12,000 respectively pass necessary journal entries in the books of the firm and show the Balance Sheet of the new firm, assuming that the firm's total capitals in the profit sharing ratio, partners either bringing in or taking out. (Osmania University, B-Com, March, 1998)

Hint :-

1. Calculate new profit sharing ratio. It is Vani $\frac{12}{25}$; Rani $\frac{8}{25}$; Mani $\frac{5}{25}$.
2. Calculate total capital based on Mani's capital. It is Rs. 25,000. Vani's capital is Rs. 12,000. Rani's Capital is Rs. 8,000 and Mani's Capital is Rs. 5,000.
3. Prepare opening Balance Sheet to know cash balance. It is Rs. 30,000 (18,000 + 12,000).
4. Balance Sheet total Rs. 25,000, after admission of Mani)
5. Loan taken by Mani from Vani and Rani is treated as private loan and not passed through books of accounts.

EXERCISE 3

A, B and C are partners sharing profits and losses in the ratio of 2 : 2 : 1. Their Balance Sheet as on 31-3-1998 is as under :

Liabilities		*Amount*	*Assets*	*Amount*
Sundry Creditors		12,850	Land and Buildings	25,000
Outstanding Liabilities		1,500	Furniture	6,500
General Reserve		6,500	Stock	11,750
Capitals :			Sundry Debtors	5,500
A –	12,000		Cash in Hand	1,100
B –	12,000			
C –	5,000			
		29,000		
		49,850		49,850

They agreed to take 'D' as partner from 1-4-98 on the following terms :

(a) D shall bring in Rs. 5,000 as his capital.
(b) Value of stock shall be increased by Rs. 2,500.
(c) Rs. 550 shall be written off as bad debts.
(d) Furniture to be depreciated by 10%.
(e) Value of land and building shall be increased by 20%.
(f) Value of the goodwill of the firm is Rs. 15,000.
(g) New profit sharing ratio of A, B, C, D is 5 : 5 : 3 : 2 respectively.
(h) After admission goodwill account is to be written back.
(i) Outstanding liabilities include Rs. 1,000 due to X which has been paid by A. It is not recorded in the books.

Prepare necessary accounts and new Balance Sheet

(Sri Venkateshwara University, B.Com, April, 1999)

Answer :- Total of Balance Sheet Rs. 61,150.

EXERCISE 4

On 31st March, 1996, the Balance Sheet of M/s P, R and S sharing profit and losses in the ratio of 6 : 5 : 3 stood as follows :

Liabilities	*Amount*	*Assets*	*Amount*
Sundry Creditors	37,800	Cash	3,780
Bills Payable	12,600	Sundry Debtors	52,920
General Reserve	21,000	Stock	58,800
Capital Accounts :		Furniture	14,700
P –	70,800	Land and Building	90,300
R –	59,700	Goodwill	10,500
S –	29,100		
	2,31,000		2,31,000

They agree to admit Q into partnership giving him $\frac{1}{8}$th share, on 1-4-1996 on the following terms :

1. Furniture be depreciated by Rs. 1,840.
2. Stock shall be valued 10% less than the Balance Sheet Value.
3. A provision of Rs. 2,640 be made for outstanding repair bill.
4. The value of land and building having appreciated be brought up to Rs. 1,19,700.
5. Value of goodwill be brought up to Rs. 28,140.
6. Q should bring in cash Rs. 29,400 as his capital.

After making the above adjustments the capital accounts of the old partners be adjusted on the basis of proportion of Q's capital to his share in the business by bringing in or taking out cash.

You are required to prepare revaluation account ; capital accounts of partners, cash account and Balance Sheet as on 1-4-1996 after Q's admission

(CA, Foundation, May, 1996) **Answer :** Total of Balance Sheet Rs. 2,88,240.

EXERCISE 5

Arul and Babu are partners sharing profits in the ratio of 3 : 2. On January 1, their Balance Sheet stood as follows :

Liabilities	*Amount*	*Assets*	*Amount*
Capital :		Goodwill	800
Arul –	10,000	Sundry Assets	17,200
Babu –	6,000		
Reserve a/c	2,000		
	18,000		18,000

On the above data they decided to admit Charle in the firm with $\frac{1}{3}$rd share of profit. Charle's share of goodwill was reckoned at Rs. 600 out of which he brought Rs. 400 only. He, however, brought in cash his share of capital Rs. 8,000. It was decided that goodwill should appear in the Balance Sheet at Rs. 12,00. Pass journal entries and prepare New Balance Sheet. **(University of Madras, B.Com, September, 1997)**

Answer : Total of Balance Sheet Rs. 27,000

EXERCISE 6

Arup and Birup are partners in a firm sharing profits and losses in the ratio of 3 : 2 respectively. Their Balance Sheet as on 31st December, 1994 was as follows :

Liabilities		*Amount*	*Assets*	*Amount*
Capital Accounts :			Plant and Machinery	60,000
Arup –	70,000		Building	30,000
Birup –	40,000		Stock in trade	25,000
		1,10,000	Debtors	40,000
Reserve fund		12,000	Cash at Bank	5,000
Sundry Creditors		38,000		
		1,60,000		1,60,000

They agreed to take Chiramp as a new partner with effect from 1st January, 1995 ; under the folloiwng terms :

(*a*) That Chiramp was to bring Rs. 16,000 as premium for goodwill for $\frac{1}{5}$th share of the future profits of the firm.

(*b*) He was also required to contribute $\frac{1}{2}$ of the adjusted combined capital of Arup and Birup as his capital.

(*c*) Stock-in-trade is to be revalued at Rs. 24,000.

(*d*) Plant and Machinery is to be revalued at Rs. 75,000.

(*e*) Provision for doubtful debts is to be created @ 5% on Sundry Debtors.

You are required to prepare revaluation account, the capital accounts of the partners and the Balance Sheet of the new firm. **(Calcutta University, B.Com (pass), 1995)**

Answer : Total of Balance Sheet Rs. 2,61,500.

EXERCISE 7

A and B are in partnership sharing profits and losses in the proportion of $\frac{3}{4}$ and $\frac{1}{4}$ respectively. Their Balance Sheet on 31st March, 1995 was as follows :

Cash Rs. 1,000 ; Sundry Debtors Rs. 25,000 ; Stock Rs. 22,000 ; Plant and Machinery Rs. 4,000 ; Sundry Creditors Rs. 12,000 ; Bank overdraft Rs. 15,000 ; A's capital Rs. 15,000 ; B's capital Rs. 10,000.

On 1st April 1995, they admitted C into partnership on the following terms :

(*a*) C to provide $\frac{1}{3}$ of the goodwill for Rs. 2,000 and provide Rs. 10,000 as capital. Goodwill not to appear in books.

(*b*) Future profits and losses are to be shared by A, B and C equally.

(*c*) Plant and Machinery is to be reduced by 10% and Rs. 500 is to be provided for estimated bad debts. Stock is to be taken at a valuation of Rs. 24,940.

(*d*) By bringing in or withdrawing cash and capitals of A and B are to be made proportionate to that of C on their profit sharing basis.

Set out entries relating to the above arrangement in the firm's journal, give the partner's capital accounts and submit the opening Balance Sheet of the new firm.

(C.A. Foundation, November, 1995)

Answer : Total of Balance Sheet Rs. 57,000

EXERCISE 8

Jyoti and Bikas are partners sharing profits and losses in the ratio of 3 : 2. Their Balance Sheet as on 31-12-1992 was as given below :

Liabilities	*Amount*	*Assets*	*Amount*
Sundry Creditors	25,000	Plant and Machinery	45,000
Reserve Fund	82,500	Building	80,000
Jyoti's Capital a/c	60,000	Stock	50,000
Bikas's Capital a/c	40,000	Sundry Debtors	30,000
		Bank Balance	2,500
	2,07,500		2,07,500

On 1-1-93 they agreed to admit Arun as a partner on the following terms :

1. Plant and machinery is to be depreciated @ 10%. Building is to be appreciated by 25% stock is to be valued at Rs. 60,000 and a provision for bad debts on debtors @ 5% is to be created.
2. Reserve fund is to be appreciated by the old partners.

3. Arun is to pay Rs. 15,000 as premium for goodwill for his $\frac{1}{5}$th share in the future profits of the firm. He is also to bring in as his capital $\frac{1}{4}$th of the combined capital of Jyoti and Bikas after the above adjustments.

Prepare (*i*) Revaluation Account ; (*ii*) Partners Capital Accounts ; and (*iii*) A Balance of the New Firm. **(Calcutta University, B.Com (Pass), 1993)**

Answer : Total of Balance Sheet Rs. 3,01,875.

EXERCISE 9

Gopal and Govind are partners sharing profits and losses in the ratio of 60 : 40. The firms Balance Sheet as on 31-3-92 was as follows :-

Liabilities	*Amount*	*Assets*	*Amount*
Capital Accounts :		Fixed Assets	3,00,000
Gopal	1,20,000	Investments	50,000
Govind	80,000	Current Assets	2,00,000
Long Term Loan	2,00,000	Loans and Advances	1,00,000
Current Liabilities	2,50,000		
	6,50,000		6,50,000

Due to financial difficulties, they have decided to admit Guru as a partner in the firm from 1-4-1992 on the following terms :

Guru will be paid 40% of the profit.

Guru will bring in cash Rs. 1,00,000 as capital.

It is agreed that goodwill of the firm will be valued at 2 years purchase of 3 years normal average profit of the firm and Guru will bring in cash his share of goodwill. It was also decided that the partners will not withdraw their share of goodwill nor goodwill appear in the books of account.

The profits of the previous three years were as follows :

For the year ended 31-3-1990, profit Rs. 20,000 (includes insurance claim received of Rs. 40,000). For the year ended 31-3-1991 loss Rs. 80,000 (includes voluntary retirement compensation paid Rs. 1,10,000).

For the year ended 31-3-1992 profit of Rs. 1,05,000 (includes a profit of Rs. 25,000 on the sale of assets)

It was decided to revalue the assets on 31-3-1992 as follows :-

Fixed Assets (net)	4,00,000
Investments	NIL
Current Assets	1,80,000
Loans and Advances	1,00,000

The new profit sharing ratio after the admission of Guru was 35 : 25 : 40.

Pass journal entries on admission, show goodwill calculation and prepare revaluation account, partners capital accounts and Balance Sheet as on 1-4-1992 after admission of Guru.

(C.A. Foundation, June, 1993)

Hint : Goodwill 2 years purchase of Average Profit = Rs. 60,000
Goodwill brought by Guru 40% of 60,000 = Rs. 24,000.
Total of Balance Sheet = Rs. 8,04,000.

19

CHAPTER

Partnership Accounts — Retirement of a Partner

INTRODUCTION

A partner in a firm may retire from a firm, (*a*) With the consent of all partners (*b*) in accordance with partnership agreement (*c*) by giving a notice to other partners in case of partnership-at-will. When a partner retires the contractual relationship among the partners comes to an end. This leads to a temporary closure of business and the firm is reconstituted on retirement. The retiring partner has a claim over the following items.

(*a*) The amount of capital as shown by his capital a/c and interest if any on the same till the date of retirement.

(*b*) The credit balance of his current a/c.

(*c*) Share of profit to the date of retirement.

(*d*) Share in the accumulated profit and reserve.

(*e*) Share in the goodwill of the firm.

(*f*) Share of profit on revaluation of assets and liabilities.

(*g*) Salary or commission if any due to the retiring partner.

(*h*) His share of Joint Life Policy.

However the following deductions are made from the amount due to the retiring partner.

(*a*) Debit balance of profit & loss account.

(*b*) Drawings and interest on drawings.

(*c*) Loss on revaluation of assets and liabilities.

(*d*) Debit balance of current account.

The resulting balance is the amount which is ultimately payable to the retiring partner.

Adjustment Involved at the Time of Retirement of a Partner

The following adjustment are involved at the time of retirement of a partner.

1. Reserve and undistributed profit.
2. Revaluation of assets and liabilities .
3. Calculation of gaining ratio and new ratio.
4. Treatment of Goodwill.

5. Settlement of amount due.
6. Adjustment of remaining partners capital accounts in accordance with their profit sharing ratio.

1. Reserve and Undistributed Profit

The undistributed profit or reserve is to be distributed among the partners in their old profit sharing ratio. When the continuing partners continue to share in the same profit sharing ratio, only retiring partner's share may be transferred to his capital a/c.

2. Revaluation of Assets and Liabilities

When a partner retires, the assets and liabilities are revalued by preparing a revaluation account. The profit on revaluation is credited to all the partners in their old profit sharing ratio. Similarly any loss on revaluation is debited to all the partner in their old profit sharing ratio. This revaluation account is closed by transferring profit or loss to the partners 'capital accounts.

Where adjustments are made for profit or loss on revaluation without altering the values of assets and liabilities a memorandum revaluation account is opened. The profit or loss on revaluation is calculated without actually debiting or crediting any asset or liability. In case of profit the following entries are passed

Memorandum Revaluation a/c Dr.
    To All partners capital a/c

On retirement of the partner, the following entry is passed.

Remaining Partners Capital a/c Dr.
    To Memorandum Revaluation a/c

Memorandum revaluation a/c is transferred to the remaining partner's capital a/c in the new profit sharing ratio.

3. Calculation of Gaining and New Ratio

On retirement of a partner his share in the profit will be taken up by the continuing partners The ratio in which they so benefit is the gain or benefit ratio expressed in the form of an equation :

Gain ratio = New ratio – Old ratio

Having gained a share in the profit, new profit sharing ratio is calculated for continuing partners. New profit sharing ratio is calculated by adding gain ratio to the old ratio. Expressed in the form of an equation,

New profit sharing ratio = Old Rates + gain ratio

Problem 1

J. K. and L are partners sharing profit & losses in the ratio of 5 : 4 : 2. 'K' retires from partnership. The new profit sharing ratio of J and L are $\frac{6}{10}$ and $\frac{4}{10}$. Calculate the ratio in which the remaining partners benefit.

Solution

Gain ratio = New ratio – Old ratio

$$J = \frac{6}{10} - \frac{5}{11} = \frac{66-50}{110} = \frac{16}{110}$$

$$L = \frac{4}{10} - \frac{2}{11}$$

$$\frac{44-20}{110} = \frac{24}{110}$$

Gain ratio of J : L 16 : 24 or 2 : 3

Problem 2

C, D, E are partners sharing profit and losses in the ratio of 2 : 2 : 1. C retire. His share is taken up by D and E in the ratio of 3 : 2 Calculate the new profit sharing ratio of remaining partners.

Solution

First we must calculate the actual gains of continuing partners.

$$\text{D Gains} = \frac{2}{5} \times \frac{3}{5} = \frac{6}{25}$$

$$\text{E Gains} = \frac{1}{5} \times \frac{2}{5} = \frac{2}{25}$$

New profit sharing ratio = old share + share gained

$$D = \frac{2}{5} + \frac{6}{25} = \frac{10+6}{25} = \frac{16}{25}$$

$$E = \frac{1}{5} + \frac{2}{25} = \frac{5+2}{25} = \frac{7}{25}$$

Problem 3

A, B and C are partners sharing profits and losses in the ratio of 3 : 2 : 1. C retires and his share is gained by A = $\frac{1}{24}$ and B = $\frac{1}{8}$. Calculate the new profit sharing ratios of A and B.

Solution

New profit sharing ratio = Old ratio + Gain ratio

$$A = \frac{3}{6} + \frac{1}{24} = \frac{12+1}{24} = \frac{13}{24}$$

$$B = \frac{2}{6} + \frac{1}{8}$$

$$\frac{8+3}{24} = \frac{11}{24}$$

New profit sharing rates of A and B = 13 : 11.

4. Treatment of Goodwill

1. Goodwill of the firm may be raised to its full value in the books of the firm :

   Goodwill a/c Dr.
   To All partners capital a/c

Note :- Good will is credited to all partners in their old profit sharing ratio. The goodwill a/c will appear in the balance sheet.

2. Good will may be raised to its full value but it may be immediately written off by the continuing partners. The following entries are recorded.

   Goodwill a/c Dr.
   To All partners capital a/c
   (in their old profit sharing ratio)

   Continuing partners capital a/c Dr.
   (In their new profit sharing ratio)
   To Goodwill a/c

3. Good will a/c is raised to the extent of retiring partners share but not to the full value.

   Goodwill a/c Dr.
   (with the share of retiring partners)
   To Retiring partners capital a/c

Note : In this case it is advisable to write off goodwill a/c to old partners capital accounts in their new profit sharing ratio.

   Continuing partners capital a/c Dr.
   (in their new profit sharing ratios)
   To Good will a/c.

4. Sometimes goodwill of the retiring partners is ascertained and his capital account is credited and the continuing partners capital accounts are debited in their new profit sharing ratio or in the ratio in which they gain.

   Continuing partners capital a/c Dr.
   (in new profit sharing ratios)
   To Retiring partners capital a/c

Note : Here goodwill is not opened in the books of the firm. This method is followed when the problem says that no goodwill a/c is to be raised.

5. In case there exists already goodwill a/c the same is revalued like any other asset and adjustment is made through revaluation a/c.

Problem 4

A, B and C are partners sharing profits and losses in the ratio of 3 : 2: 1. On 31-12-2003, B retires. On account of B's retirement the goodwill of the firm was valued at Rs. 18,000. Find the amount to be credited to retiring partner in each of the following circumstances.

(*a*) Goodwill is raised to its full value and maintained in the books.
(*b*) Goodwill is raised to its full value and written off.
(*c*) Only B's share of goodwill is raised and then written off.
(*d*) B is given his share without raising it.

Solution

(*a*) **Goodwill is raised and maintained.**

		Rs.	Rs.
Goodwill a/c	Dr.	18,000	
To A's Capital a/c			9,000
To B's Capital a/c			6,000
To C's Capital a/c			3,000
(Being goodwill raised in the books to its full value by crediting all partners including retiring partner in the old profit sharing ratio).			

(*b*) **Goodwill raised and written off :**

		Rs.	Rs.
Goodwill a/c	Dr.	18,000	
To A's Capital			9,000
To B's Capital			6,000
To C's Capital			3,000
(Being goodwill raised to its full value by crediting all partners including retiring partner in the old profit sharing ratio).			

		Rs.	Rs.
A's Capital a/c	Dr.	13,500	
C's Capital a/c	Dr.	4,500	
To Goodwill a/c			18,000
(Being goodwill written off among continuing partners in the new profit sharing ratio i.e., 3 : 1).			

(*c*) **When retiring partner's share is raised and subsequently written off**

		Rs.	Rs.
Goodwill a/c	Dr.	6,000	
To B's Capital a/c			6,000
(Being retiring partners share of goodwill credited to his account).			

		Rs.	Rs.
A's Capital a/c	Dr.	4,500	
B's Capital a/c	Dr.	1,500	
To Goodwill a/c			6,000
(Being retiring partner's share written off among continuing partners in gain ratio; i.e., 3 : 1)			

Working Note : *Calculation of Gain Ratio :*

Gain Ratio = New ratio – Old ratio

$$A = \frac{3}{4} - \frac{3}{6}$$

$$\frac{9-6}{12} = \frac{3}{12}$$

$$C = \frac{1}{4} - \frac{1}{6}$$

$$\frac{3-2}{12} = \frac{1}{12}$$

A : C = 3 : 1

(*d*) **Goodwill given to the retiring partner without raising it**

		Rs.	Rs.
A's Capital a/c	Dr.	4,500	
C's Capital a/c	Dr.	1,500	
To B's Capital a/c			6,000
(Being retiring partners goodwill adjusted in continuing partners capital accounts in the benefit ratio i.e., 3 : 1			

5. Settlement of Amount Due

The retiring partners account is settled as per the terms of agreement. Where terms of agreement is silent it is settled by mutual agreement. The payment can be made in any of the following methods.

(*a*) **Lumpsum payment method.** If the firm has adequate funds, the retiring partner's account is settled immediately by paying lumpsum amount. On payment, his capital account is debited and bank account is credited.

(*b*) **Instalment payment method.** Where the firm face financial problems the retiring partner is not paid in full or part immediately. In such a case the capital balance is transferred to his loan a/c and the same is credited with interest at the agreed rate on the outstanding balance and debited with payment an account until the balance is extinguished. The instalment payment can take two forms. viz.

(*i*) **Decreasing payment method :** Under this method, the total amount due is divided in a number of equal instalments and the instalment plus interest on the outstanding balance is paid out.

(*ii*) **Equal payment method :** Under this method the total amount to be paid is divided in a number of equal instalments in such a way that the amount plus interest on outstanding balance is always equal.

6. Adjustment of Capital Accounts of Continuing Partners

Sometimes continuing partners decide that their capital should be in the new profit sharing ratios. In such a case the total capital of the firm is fixed and is divided among the continuing partners in their new profit sharing ratios. The other way of allocating capital is on the basis of the total of the balances of capital accounts of the continuing partners after making all adjustments on retirement of a partner. The adjustments of capital account is made by bringing in or payment of cash to the continuing partner.

Purchase of Retiring Partners Share by Continuing Partners

Sometimes the continuing partners may purchase the retiring partners share in an agreed ratio. In such a case the retiring partners capital account is closed by trasnferring to the continuing partners capital accounts in the ratio in which they agreed to purchase his share. In this situation the retiring partner has to look to the continuing partners in their individual capacities for the satisfaction of his claim. Hence the new firm is not responsible for retiring partners.

Entries on Retirement of a Partner :

1. Transfer the reserve account and credit balance of Profit & Loss account.
   Reserve a/c or P & L a/c Dr.
   To All partners capital a/c
2. Transfer the debit balance of Profit & Loss a/c if any to all partner's capital accounts.
3. Revalue assets and liabilities through revaluation. The profit on revaluation is transferred to partners capital accounts.
   Revaluation a/c Dr.
   To Partner's capital a/c
4. Record the loss on revaluation by transferring it to partners capital accounts
   Partners capital a/c Dr.
   To Revaluation a/c
5. Ascertain the goodwill payable to the retiring partner.
   Goodwill a/c Dr.
   To Retiring partner's capital a/c
6. Ascertain the share of profit payable to the retiring partner till the date of retirement.
   Profit & Loss a/c Dr.
   To Retiring partners capital a/c
7. It salary and Interest on capital are to be allowed to the retiring partners
   Salary a/c Dr.
   Interest on capital a/c Dr.
   To Retiring partners capital a/c
8. If interest if to be charged on his drawings, ascertain the same
   Drawing a/c Dr.
   To Interest on drawings a/c
9. Transfer the debit balance of drawings account of the retiring partner to his capital a/c
   Capital a/c Dr.
   To Drawings a/c
10. Now the capital account of the retiring partner shows the balance due and payable to him. If the same is paid
    Capital a/c Dr.
    To Bank
11. If the amount payable to the retiring partner is not paid out immediately transfer the same to his loan a/c.
    Capital a/c Dr.
    To Loan a/c

Problem 5

R, S and P are partners with capitals Rs. 50,000, Rs. 30,000, and Rs. 20,000, share profits in the ratio of 5 : 3 : 2. As from 1st January 1999. S retires and the following revaluations were made :

(*a*) Land and building to be increased by Rs. 48,000

(*b*) Stock, furniture, and Machinery values to be reduced by Rs. 4,000, Rs. 1000, and Rs. 4,600 respectively.

(*c*) Create a Reserve of Rs. 200 for doubtful debts.

(*d*) Goodwill of the firm is agreed at Rs. 30,000.

Prepare S's a/c and find out the amount due (University of Madras B. Com, May 2001).

Solution

Revaluation A/c

	Amount		*Amount*
To Stock a/c	4,000	By Land & Buildings a/c	48,000
To Furniture a/c	1,000		
To Machinery a/c	4,600		
To Provision for doubtful Debts	200		
To Profit transferred to			
R's capital a/c	19,100		
S's capital a/c	11,460		
P's capital a/c	7,640		
	48,000		48,000

S's Capital A/c

	Amount		*Amount*
To Balance c/d	50,460	By Balance b/d	30,000
(Amount due to S)		By Revaluation a/c	11,460
		By Goodwill a/c	9,000
		$\frac{3}{10} \times 30,000$	
	50,460		50,460

Problem 6

On 31-3-1998 the balance sheet of M/S A, B and C, sharing profit and losses in proportion to their capitals stood as follows :

Liabilities		*Amount*	*Assets*		*Amount*
Creditors a/c		1,08,000	Cash at bank		80,000
Capital accounts :-			Debtors	1,00,000	
A	4,50,000		less : Reserve	2,000	
B	3,00,000				98,000
C	1,50,000		Stock		90,000
		9,00,000	Machinery		2,40,000
			Land & Buildings		5,00,000
		10,08,000			10,08,000

On that date 'B' wants to retire from the firm and the remaining partners decide to carry on the firm. The following adjustments of assets and liabilities have been agreed upon before the ascertainment of the amount payable to 'B'.

(*i*) That out of the amount of insurance premium which was debited annually entirely to Profit and Loss a/c Rs. 10,000 be carried forward for unexpired insurance on 31-3-1998.

(*ii*) That the land and buildings be appreciated by 10%.

(*iii*) That the reserve for doubtful debts to brought upto 5% on debtors.

(*iv*) That the machinery be depreciated by 5%.

(*v*) That a provision for Rs. 15,000 be made in respect of an outstanding bill for repairs.

(*vi*) That the goodwill of the entire firm be fixed at Rs. 1,80,000 and B's share of the same be adjusted in the accounts of A and C who will share future profit in 3 : 1 ratio respectively (no goodwill account being raised) and

(*vii*) That "B" be paid Rs. 50,000 in cash and the balance be transferred to his loan a/c.

Prepare Revaluation a/c, Capital accounts of the partners and the Balance Sheet of the newly constituted firm **(Osmania University, B.Com, March 2000)**

Solution

Revaluation A/c

		Amount		Amount
To Provisions for Doubtful debts a/c		3,000	By Unexpired Insurance a/c	10,000
To Machinery a/c		12,000	By Land & Buildings a/c	50,000
To Provision for o/s Repair bill		15,000		
To Capital a/c				
A —	15,000			
B —	10,000			
C —	5,000	30,000		
		60,000		60,000

A's Capital A/c

	Amount		Amount
To B's Capital a/c	45,000	By Balance b/d	4,50,000
To Balance c/d	4,20,000	By Revaluation a/c	15,000
	4,65,000		4,65,000

B's Capital A/c

	Amount		Amount
To Bank a/c	50,000	By Balance b/d	3,00,000
To B's loan a/c	3,20,000	By Revaluation a/c	10,000
		By A's Capital a/c	45,000
		By C's Capital a/c	15,000
	3,70,000		3,70,000

B's Loan a/c

	Amount		Amount
To Balance c/d	3,20,000	By B's Capital a/c	3,20,000

C's Capital a/c

	Amount		Amount
To B's Capital a/c	15,000	By Balance b/d	1,50,000
To Balance c/d	1,40,000	By Revaluation a/c	5,000
	1,55,000		1,55,000

Balance Sheet of A & C as on 31-3-1998

Liabilities	Amount	Assets		Amount
Creditors a/c	1,08,000			
		Cash at bank (80,000 - 50,000)		30,000
O/S Repair bills	15,000			
A's Capital a/c	4,20,000	Debtors	1,00,000	
C's Capital a/c	1,40,000	Less : Provision	5,000	95,000
B's loan a/c	3,20,000	Stock		90,000
		Unexpired Insurance		10,000
		Machinery	2,40,000	
		Less depreciation	12,000	2,28,000
		Land & building	5,00,000	
		Add appreciation	50,000	5,50,000
	10,03,000			10,03,000

Problem 7

Following is the balance sheet on 31st March 1998 of M/S A, B, and C who share profits in the ratio of 4 : 2 : 1 respectively.

Liabilities		Amount	Assets	Amount
Capital accounts			Goodwill	10,000
A	30,000		Stock	15,000
B	20,000		Sundry Debtors	11,000
C	15,000		Land & building	20,000
		65,000	Plant & Machinery	26,500
Sundry creditors		15,000	Motor vehicle	10,000
Bills payable		3,000	Cash	1,000
General Reserve		10,500		
		93,500		93,500

On the above date A retired and the following arrangements were agreed upon.

(*a*) Goodwill of the firm is to be valued at Rs. 24,000.

(*b*) The assets and liabilities are to be valued as under : Stock Rs. 12,000, Sundry debtors Rs. 10,500, land & buildings Rs 22,600, plant and the machinery Rs. 25,000 and sundry creditors Rs. 14,000.

(*c*) B and C were to introduce Rs. 20,000 and Rs. 5,000 respectively into the business and Rs. 16,200 was to be paid in three equal instalments together with interest at 9% p.a.

(*d*) B and C agree not to retain goodwill in books.

Give Journal entries to record the above transactions, The Balance Sheet of the firm after A's retirement and A's loan a/c until it is paid off.

(University of Delhi B.Com. (Pass) 2000)

Solution

Journal Entries

Date	*Particulars*		*Dr. Amount*	*Cr. Amount*
	General Reserve a/c	Dr.	10,500	
	To A's Capital a/c			6,000
	To B's Capital a/c			3,000
	To C's Capital a/c			1,500
	(Being reserve distributed)			
	Goodwill a/c	Dr.	14,000	
	To A's Capital a/c			8,000
	To B's Capital a/c			4,000
	To C's Capital a/c			2,000
	(Being the value goodwill increased)			
	Revaluation a/c	Dr.	5,000	
	To Stock a/c			3,000
	To Debtors a/c			500
	To Plant & Machinery a/c			1,500
	(Being decrease in the value assets)			
	Land & building a/c	Dr.	2,600	
	Sundry creditors a/c	Dr.	1,000	
	To Revaluation a/c			3,600
	(Being gain on revaluation of land and building and sundry creditors)			
	A's Capital a/c	Dr.	800	
	B's Capital a/c	Dr.	400	
	C 's Capital a/c	Dr.	200	
	To Revaluation a/c			1,400
	(Being loss on revaluation of assets and liabilities transferred to the capital account of all partners).			
	Cash a/c	Dr.	25,000	
	To B's Capital a/c			20,000
	To C's Capital a/c			5,000
	(Being additional capital brought in by B and C)			
	A's Capital a/c	Dr.	43,200	
	To Cash a/c			16,200
	To A 's loan a/c			27,000
	(Being Rs. 16,200 immediately paid to A and the balance due to him i.e., Rs. 27,000 transferred to his loan a/c)			
	B's Capital a/c	Dr.	16,000	
	C's Capital a/c	Dr.	8,000	
	To Capital a/c			24,000
	(Being goodwill written off entirely by B and C after A's retirement)			

Revaluation A/c

	Amount		Amount
To Stock a/c	3,000	By Land & building	2,600
To Debtors a/c	500	By Sundry creditors	1,000
To Plant & Machinery	1,500	By Loss transferred to Capital a/c	
		A	800
		B	400
		C	200
	5,000		5,000

A's Capital A/c

	Amount		Amount
To Revaluation	800	By Balance b/d	30,000
To Cash	16,200	By Goodwill account	8,000
To A's loan a/c	27000	By General Reserve	6,000
	44,000		44,000

B's Capital A/c

	Amount		Amount
To Revaluation a/c	400	By Balance b/d	20,000
To Goodwill	16,000	By Goodwill a/c	4,000
To Balance c/d	30,600	By General Reserve	3,000
		By Cash a/c	20,000
	47,000		47,000

C's Capital A/c

	Amount		Amount
To Revaluation a/c	200	By Balance b/d	15,000
To Goodwill	8,000	By Goodwill a/c	2,000
To Balance c/d	15,300	By General Reserve	1,500
		By Cash a/c	5,000
	23,500		23,500

Cash A/c

	Amount		Amount
To Balance b/d	1,000	By A's Capital a/c	16,200
To B's Capital a/c	20,000	By Balance c/d	9,800
To C's Capital a/c	5,000		
	26,000		26,000

Balance Sheet of B and C as on 31st March 1998

Liabilities	Amount	Assets	Amount
B's Capital a/c	30,600	Cash	9,800
C's Capital a/c	15,300	Stock (15,000 – 3,000)	12,000
Sundry creditors (15,000 – 1,000)	14,000	Sundry debtors	10,500
Bills payable a/c	3,000	Land & building (20,000 + 2,600)	22,600
A's loan	27,000	Plant & Machinery (26,500 – 1,500)	25,000
		Motor vehicle	10,000
	89,900		89,900

A's Loan A/c

Date	Particulars	Amount	Date	Particulars	Amount
31-3-98	To Balance c/d	27,000	31-3-98	By A's Capital a/c	27,000
31-3-99	To Cash a/c (9,000 + 2,430)	11,430	1-4-98	By Balance b/d	27,000
			31-3-98	By Interest a/c $27{,}000 \times \frac{9}{100}$	2,430
31-3-99	To Balance c/d	18,000			
		29,430			29,430
31-3-2000	To Cash a/c (9,000 + 1,620)	10,620	1-4-99	By Balance b/d	18,000
	To Balance c/d	9,000	31-3-2000	By Interest $18{,}000 \times \frac{9}{100}$	1,620
		19,620			19,620
31-3-2000	To Cash	9,810	1-4-2000	By Balance b/d	9,000
			31-3-2000	By Interest $9{,}000 \times \frac{9}{100}$	810
		9,810			9,810

Problem 8

Arvind, Balajee and Sankar were carrying on business in partnership, sharing profits in the proportion of 4 : 3 : 2. Their Balance Sheet on 31st December 1999 stood as follows.

Liabilities		Amount	Assets		Amount
Sundry creditors		41,400	Cash at bank		33,000
Capital accounts			Sundry debtors	30,000	
Arvind	1,20,000		Less provision for Doubtful debts	600	29,400
Balajee	90,000		Stock		48,000
Sankar	60,000	2,70,000	Plant& Machinery		51,000
			Land & Building		1,50,000
		3,11,400			3,11,400

Balajee retired from the business on the same date and the following adjustments of the assets and liabilities had been agreed upon before ascertaining the amount payable by the firm to Balajee.

(*a*) That the reserve for doubtful debts to be brought up' to 5% on debtors.
(*b*) Land & buildings to be appreciated by 20%.
(*c*) Stock be reduced by Rs. 3,500
(*d*) Provision of Rs. 4,000 be made in respect of outstanding andit fees.
(*e*) The goodwill of the firm be fixed at Rs. 64,800 and Balajees share of the same be adjusted into the accounts of Arvind and Sankar who decided to continue the business sharing profit or losses in the proportion of 5 : 3 respectively.
(*f*) The capital of the new firm be fixed at Rs. 1,68,000 between Arvind and Sankar in proportion to their new profit sharing ratio and actual cash be brought in or paid off by or to the continuing partners as the case may be.
(*g*) Balajee agreed to leave the amount due to him by the firm as loan to the new firm carrying interest at the rate of 9%.

Show the necessary accounts and prepare the balance sheet of the new firm following the retirement of Balajee. **(Sri Venkateshwara University B.Com, April 2000)**

Solution

Revaluation A/c

	Amount		Amount
To Reserve for doubtful debts (1,500 — 600)	900	By Land and Buildings	30,000
To Depreciation on stock	3,500		
To O/S Audit fees	4,000		
To Profit transferred to			
Arvind's capital	9,600		
Balajee's capital	7,200		
Sankar Capital	4,800		
	30,000		30,000

Arvind's Capital A/c

	Amount		Amount
To Balajee's Capital a/c	13,500	By Balance b/d	1,20,000
To Bank a/c	11,100	By Revaluation a/c	9,600
To Balance c/d	1,05,000		
	1,29,600		1,29,600

Balajee's Capital A/c

	Amount		Amount
To Balajee's loan a/c	1,18,800	By Balance b/d	90,000
		By Revaluation a/c	7,200
		By Arvind's Capital a/c	13,500
		By Sankar Capital a/c	8,100
	1,18,800		1,18,800

Sankar's Capital A/c

	Amount		Amount
To Balajee's capital a/c	8,100	By Balance b/d	60,000
To Balance c/d	63,000	By Revaluation a/c	4,800
		By Bank a/c	6,300
	71,100		71,100

Bank A/c

	Amount		Amount
To Balance b/d	33,000	By Arvind's Capital a/c	11,100
To Sankar capital a/c	6,300	By Balance c/d	28,200
	39,300		39,300

Balance Sheet
Of Arvind and Sankar as on 31-12-1999

Liabilities	Amount	Assets		Amount
Sundry creditors	41,400	Cash at bank		28,200
Balajees loan a/c	1,18,800	Sundry debtors	30,000	
Capital accounts		Less provision for D.D	1,500	
Arvind —	1,05,000			28,500
Sankar —	63,000	Stock	48,000	
O/S Audit fees	4,000	Less Depreciation	3,500	
				44,500
		Plant & Machinery		51,000
		Land & Building	1,50,000	
		Add appreciation	30,000	
				1,80,000
	3,32,200			3,32,200

Problem 9

X, Y and Z are partners sharing profit and losses in the ratio of 5 : 3 : 2 respectively. The Balance Sheet of their firm as on 31st December 1998 was as follows.

Liabilities		Amount	Assets		Amount
Capital Accounts			Land & Building		80,000
X	50,000		Furniture		2,000
Y	30,000		Stock		10,000
Z	20,000		Debtors	25,000	
		1,00,000	Less provision for D.D.	2,000	
General Reserve		20,000			23,000
			Bank		5,000
		1,20,000			1,20,000

Y retires on that date subject to the following conditions.

(*a*) The goodwill of the firm is to be valued at Rs. 20,000.

(*b*) Furniture is to be depreciated by 10% and land & building to be appreciated by 10%.
(*c*) Provision for doubtful debts is to be increased to Rs. 3,000.
(*d*) Amount due to Y is to be transferred to his loan account.

X and Z agreed to continue the business and share the future profits and losses in the ratio of 3 : 2 respectively. Changes in the value of assets and liabilities are to be recorded in the books.

Show Revaluation a/c, Partners Capital Accounts and the newly constructed Balance Sheet of the firm (Calcutta University, B. Com (Pass) 2000).

Solution

Revaluation A/c

		Amount		*Amount*
To Furniture a/c		200	By Land & building a/c	8,000
To Provision for doubtful Debt		1,000		
To Profit transferred to				
X	3,400			
Y	2,040			
Z	1,360			
		6,800		
		8,000		8,000

X's Capital A/c

	Amount		*Amount*
To Balance c/d	73,400	By Balance b/d	50,000
		By General reserve a/c	10,000
		By Goodwill a/c	10,000
		By Revaluation a/c	3,400
	73,400		73,400

Y's Capital A/c

	Amount		*Amount*
To Y's loan a/c	44,040	By Balance b/d	30,000
		By General reserve a/c	6,000
		By Goodwill a/c	6,000
		By Revaluation a/c	2,040
	44,040		44,040

Z's Capital A/c

	Amount		*Amount*
To Balance c/d	29,360	By Balance c/d	20,000
		By General reserve a/c	4,000
		By Good will a/c	4,000
		By Revaluation	1360
	29,360		29,360

Balance Sheet of New Firm

Liabilities	Amount	Assets		Amount
X's Capital a/c	73,400	Goodwill		20,000
Z's Capital a/c	29,360	Land & Building	80,000	
Y's Loan a/c	44,040	Add : Appreciation	8,000	
				88,000
		Furniture	2,000	
		Less depreciation	200	
				1,800
		Stock		10,000
		Debtors	25,000	
		Less : Provision for D.D.	3,000	
				22,000
		Bank		5,000
	1,46,800			1,46,800

Problem 10

A, B and C were carrying on business in partnership sharing profit in the ratio of 5 : 3 : 2 respectively. on 31st March 2,000. Their Balance Sheet stood as follows.

Liabilities	Amount	Assets	Amount
Capital accounts		Buildings	75,000
A	1,00,000	Furniture	22,550
B	60,000	Stock	69,840
C	35,000	Trade debtors	26,900
Trade creditors	31,180	Bills receivable	10,000
Outstanding expenses	2,745	Cash at bank	24,635
	2,28,925		2,28,925

'C' retired on the above mentioned date on the following terms :

(i) Buildings be appreciated by 25%.
(ii) Furniture be depreciated by 10%.
(iii) Provision for doubtful debts @ 5% of trade debtors be created.
(iv) Goodwill account be raised with Rs. 60,000 the agreed value of firm's goodwill.
(v) The amount finally due to C be paid immediately. A and B bringing in Rs. 20,000 each to facilitate the payment.

A and B agreed to share profit in future in the ratio of 3 : 2 respectively immediately after C's retirement. They wrote off goodwill account.

Prepare Revaluation a/c, Partners capital accounts and cash book. Also drawn the Balance sheet immediately after the above mentioned transactions have been completed

(C.S. Foundation, December 2000)

Solution

Revaluation A/c

	Amount		Amount
To Furniture	2,255	By Building a/c	18,750
To Provision for D. D	1,345		
To Profit transferred to			
A's Capital a/c	7,575		
B's Capital a/c	4,545		
C's capital a/c	3030		
	18750		18,750

A's Capital A/c

	Amount		Amount
To Good will a/c	36,000	By Balance b/d	1,00,000
To Balance c/d	1,21,575	By Revaluation a/c	7575
		By Goodwill a/c	30,000
		By Bank a/c	20,000
	1,57,575		1,57,575

B's Capital A/c

	Amount		Amount
To Goodwill a/c	24,000	By Balance b/d	60,000
To Balance c/d	78,545	By Revaluation a/c	4,545
		By Goodwill a/c	18,000
		By Bank a/c	20,000
	1,02,545		1,02,545

C's Capital A/c

	Amount		Amount
To Bank a/c	50,030	By Balance b/d	35,000
		By Revaluation a/c	3,030
		By Goodwill	12,000
	50,030		50,030

Cash Book
(Bank Column Only)

	Amount		Amount
To Balance b/d	24,635	By C's Capital a/c	50,030
To A's Capital a/c	20,000	By Balance c/d	14,605
To B's Capital a/c	20,000		
	64,635		64,635

Balance Sheet
Of A and as on 1st April 2,000

Liabilities	*Amount*	*Assets*		*Amount*
A's Capital a/c	1,21,575	Buildings		93,750
B' Capital a/c	78,545	Furniture		20,295
Trade creditors	31,180	Stock		69,840
O/S expenses	2,745	Trade debtors	26,900	
		Less provision for D. D	1,345	
				25,555
		Bills receivable		10,000
		Cash at Bank		14,605
	2,34,045			2,34,045

Problem 11

X, Y and Z are partners in a firm sharing profit & losses as 3 : 2 : 1 respectively. The Balance Sheet of the firm as on 31st December 1997 was as follows :

Liabilities		*Amount*	*Assets*		*Amount*
Capital a/cs			Factory building		60,000
X —	45,000		Machinery		25,000
Y —	30,000		Furniture		15,000
Z —	25,000		Stock		20,000
		1,00,000	Debtors	15,000	
General Reserve		24,000	Less provision for D. D	500	
Sundry creditors		14,000			14,500
			Cash in hand		3,500
		1,38,000			1,38,000

Y retired from the business on the same date and X and Z continued in partnership sharing profit and losses in the ratio of 3 : 1 subjects to the following adjustment.

(*a*) Goodwill valued Rs. 18,000 is not to be raised in the book.
(*b*) Factory building to be appreciated by Rs. 10,000 and stock to be appreciated by 5%.
(*c*) Machinery and furniture are to be depreciated by 10%.
(*d*) The provision for doubtful debts is to be raised to Rs. 1,000.
(*e*) A provision of Rs. 600 is to be made for outstanding expenses.
(*f*) A typewriter costing Rs. 3,600 was purchased on 1-10-97 but not recorded in the book.

X and Z are to bring in cash in their profit sharing ratio to pay off Y's dues on retirement and leave a sum of Rs. 7,500 as working capital.

Prepare Revaluation a/c, Partners capital accounts and the new Balance Sheet of the firm

(Calcutta University, B.Com Pass 1998)

Solution

Revaluation A/c

		Amount		Amount
To Depreciation on machinery a/c		2,500	By Factory buildings a/c	10,000
To Depreciation on Furniture a/c		1,500	By Stock a/c	1,000
To Provision for D. D (1,000 – 500)		500	By Typewriter	3,600
To Provision for O/S expenses		600		
To Partners Capital a/c				
X	4,750			
Y	3,167			
Z	1,583	9,500		
		14,600		14,600

X's Capital A/c

	Amount		Amount
To Y's Capital a/c	4,500	By Balance b/d	45,000
To Balance c/d	95,625	By General Reserve a/c	12,000
		By Revaluation a/c	4,750
		By Cash a/c	38,375
	1,00,125		1,00,125

Y's Capital A/c

	Amount		Amount
To Cash a/c	47,167	By Balance b/d	30,000
		By General Reserve a/c	8,000
		By Revaluation a/c	3,167
		By X's Capital a/c	4,500
		By Z's Capital a/c	1,500
	47,167		47,167

Z's Capital A/c

	Amount		Amount
To Y's Capital a/c	1,500	By Balance b/d	25,000
To Balance c/d	41,875	By General Reserve	4,000
		By Revaluation a/c	1,583
		By Cash a/c	12,792
	43,375		43,375

Working Note :

(*i*) Total goodwill of the firm is Rs. 18,000. Y's

Share of the same is $18{,}000 \times \frac{2}{6} = 6{,}000$. It is credited to Y and debited to X and Z in their gaining ratio 3 : 1.

(*ii*) Y is to be paid	Rs. 47,167
Add : Cash for working capital	4,000
	51,167

X brings in $51{,}167 \times \frac{3}{4} = 38{,}375$

Z brings in $51{,}167 \times \frac{1}{4} = 12{,}792$

Balance Sheet of X and Z

Liabilities		*Amount*	*Assets*		*Amount*
Capital Accounts			Factory building	60,000	
X —	95,625		Add appreciation	10,000	70,000
Z —	41,875		Machinery	25,000	
		1,37,500	Less depreciation	2,500	22,500
Sundry creditors		14,000	Furniture	15,000	
Provision for O/S		600	Less depreciation	1,500	13,500
Expenses			Typewriter		3,600
			Stock	20,000	
			Add appreciation	1,000	21,000
			Debtors	15,000	
			Less provision	1,000	14,000
			Cash in hand		7,500
		1,52,100			1,52,100

Problem 12

Amala, Kamala and Vimala carrying on business in partnership were sharing in 4 : 3 : 2 ratio on 31-3-95. The following is their position :-

Liabilities	*Amount*	*Assets*		*Amount*
Sundry creditors	13,800	Plant & Machinery	15,000	
Reserve	4,200	Less depreciation	4,000	
Capital : Amala	28,000			11,000
Kamala	14,000	Debtors		28,000
Vimala	7,000	Cash		11,800
		Buildings	17,200	
		Less depreciation	1,000	
				16,200
	67,000			67,000

Kamala retired on 30-6-95 on the following terms

(*a*) Plant to be appreciated by Rs. 7,000

(*b*) Provision for doubtful debts to be made at 7%

(*c*) Rs. 5,000 to be paid to kamala and balance taken as loan @ 10%.

(*d*) Average profit for last 3 year were Rs. 7,000 p.a.

Show Kamala's account **(Osmania University B.Com, March 1998)**

Solution

Working Note

(*i*) **Distribution of profit on revaluation of assets :**

Appreciation on Plant	7,000
Less provision for doubtful debts	1,960
Profit	5,040

Kamala's share $5,040 \times \frac{3}{9} = 1,680$

(*ii*) Share in reserve $4,200 \times \frac{3}{9} = 1,400$

(*iii*) Share in profit $7,000 \times \frac{3}{9} \times \frac{3}{12} = 583$

Kamala's Capital A/c

	Amount		Amount
To Cash a/c	5,000	By Balance b/d	14,000
To Kamala's loan a/c	12,663	By Reserve a/c	1,400
		By Revaluation a/c	1,680
		By P & L a/c	583
	17,663		17,663

Problem 13

A, B and C were in partnership sharing profit in the proportion of 5 : 4 : 3. The balance sheet of the firm as on 31st March 1998 was as under :-

Liabilities	*Amount*	*Assets*	*Amount*
Capital accounts		Goodwill	40,000
A	1,35,930	Fixtures	8,200
B	95,120	Stock	1,57,300
C	61,170	Sundry debtors	93,500
Sundry creditors	41,690	Cash	34,910
	333910		333910

A had been suffering from ill health and gave notice that he wished to retire. An agreement was therefore entered into as on 31st March 1998, the terms of which were as follows :-

(*i*) The Profit and Loss account for the year ended 31st March 1998 which showed a net profit of Rs. 48,000 was to be reopened. B was to be credited with Rs. 4,000 as bonus in consideration of the extra work which had devolved upon him during the year. The profit sharing ratio was to be revised as from 1st April 1997 to 3 : 4 : 4.

(*ii*) Goodwill was to be valued at 2 years purchase of the average profit of the preceding five years The fixtures were to be valued by an independent valuer. A provision of 2% was to be made for doubtful debts and the remaining assets were to be taken at their book values.

The valuations arising out of the above agreement were goodwill Rs. 56,800 and fixtures Rs. 10,980.

B and C agreed as between themselves to continue the business sharing profit in the ratio of 3 : 2 and decided to eliminate goodwill from the Balance Sheet, to retain the fixtures on the books at the revised value and to increase the provision for doutful debts to 6%.

You are required to submit the journal entries necessary to give effect to the above arrangements and to draw the capital account of the partner after carrying out all adjusting entries as stated above **(C.A. Foundation, May 1998)**

Solution

Journal Entries

Date	*Particulars*		*Dr. Amount*	*Cr. Amount*
	A's Capital a/c	Dr.	20,000	
	B's Capital a/c	Dr.	16,000	
	C's Capital a/c	Dr.	12,000	
	To P & L adjustment a/c			48,000
	(Being profit written back for making adjustment)			
	P & L adjustment a/c	Dr.	4,000	
	To B's Capital a/c			4,000
	(Bonus credited to B's capital a/c)			
	P & L Adjustment a/c	Dr.	44,000	
	To A's capital a/c			12,000
	To B's capital			16,000
	To C's capital			16,000
	(Being profit distributed in the new ratio)			
	Goodwill a/c	Dr.	16,800	
	Fixtures a/c	Dr.	2,780	
	To Revaluation a/c			19,580
	(Being increase in the value of assets)			
	Revaluation a/c	Dr.	1,870	
	To Provision for bad debts a/c			1,870
	(Being provision for bad debts credited)			
	Revalutiaon a/c	Dr.	17,710	
	To A's Capital a/c	Dr.		4,830
	To B's Capital a/c			6,440
	To C's Capital a/c			6,440
	(Being profit on revaluation transferred)			

Date	Particulars		Dr. Amount	Cr. Amount
	B's capital a/c	Dr.	36,324	
	C's Capital a/c	Dr.	24,216	
	To Goodwill a/c			56,800
	To Provision for Bad debts a/d			3,740
	(Writing off goodwill and raising provision for bad debts)			

A's Capital A/c

	Amount		Amount
To P & L adj. a/c	20,000	By Balance b/d	1,35,930
To A's Loan a/c	1,32,760	By P & L adj a/c	12,000
		By Revaluation	4,830
	1,52,760		1,52,760

B's Capital A/c

	Amount		Amount
To P & L adj a/c	16,000	By Balance b/d	95,120
To Goodwill a/c and		By P & L Adj a/c	4,000
Provision for bad Debts a/c	36,324	By P & L Adj a/c	16,000
To Balance a/d	69,236	By Goodwill a/c and Fixtures	6,440
	1,21,560		1,21,560

C's Capital A/c

	Amount		Amount
To P & L Adj a/c	12,000	By Balance b/d	61,170
To Goodwill a/c and		By P & L Adj a/c	16,000
Provision for bad debts	24,216	By Goodwill a/c and Fixture a/c	6,440
To Balance c/d	47,394		
	83,610		83,610

Problem 14

(Problems on retirement and admission of a partner)

Durga and Kali were working in partnership sharing profits equally. On 31st December 1997. Durga decided to retire and in her place it was decided that Lakshmi her daughter would be admitted as partner from January 1, 1998 and her share in profit will be $\frac{1}{3}$.

The Balance sheet of the firm as on December 31, 1997 was as follows :-

Liabilities	Amount	Assets	Amount
Sundry creditors	22,050	Goodwill	22,500
Capital :-		Land & buildings	60,075
Durga	81,450	Motor car	18,000
Kali	72,000	Furniture	13,950
		Sundry debtors	36,225
		Cash and Bank balance	24,750
	1,75,500		1,75,500

It was further decide as follows :-

(a) Goodwill should be raised to Rs. 30,000
(b) The motor car would be taken over by Durga at its book value.
(c) The value of Land and buildings would be increased by Rs. 12,420.
(d) Kali and Lakshmi would introduce sufficient capital to pay off Durga and to leave thereafter a sum of Rs. 11,025 as working capital in a manner that the capitals of the new partner will be in proportion to their profit - sharing ratio.
(e) The capital payable by Lakshmi was to be gifted to her by her mother.
(f) The new partners decided not to show goodwill as an asset.

The partners introduces the capital on January 10, 1998. Show the accounts of the partners, the cash a/c and the Balance Sheet **(Calcutta University, B.Com (Hons.) 1999)**

Solution

Durga's Capital A/c

	Amount		Amount
To Motor car a/c	18,000	By Balance b/d	81,450
To Lakshmi's capital	47,215	By Goodwill a/c	3,750
To Cash a/c	26,195	By Revaluation a/c	6,210
	91,410		91,410

Kali's Capital A/c

	Amount		Amount
To Goodwill a/c	20,000	By Balance b/d	72,000
To Balance c/d	74,430	By Goodwill a/c	3,750
		By Revaluation	6,210
		By Cash a/c	12,470
	94,430		94,430

Lakshmi's Capital A/c

	Amount		Amount
To Goodwill a/c	10,000	By Durga's capital a/c	47,215
To Balance c/d	37,215		
	47,215		47,215

Cash A/c

	Amount		Amount
To Balance b/d	24,750	By Durga's capital a/c	26,195
To Kali's capital a/c	12,470	By Balance c/d	11,025
	37,220		37,220

Working Note :

Total capital of the new firm :-

Land & building	72,495
Furniture	13,950
Sundry Debtors	36,225
Cash	11,025
	1,33,695
Less creditors	22,050
	1,11,645

$$\text{Capital of Kali} = 1,11,645 \times \frac{2}{3} = 74,430$$

$$\text{Capital of Lakshmi} = 1,11,645 \times \frac{1}{3} = 37,215$$

Capital gifted by Durga to Lakshmi :

37,215 + Goodwill written off Rs. 10,000 = 47,215

Cash brought in by Kali = (74,430 + goodwill written off Rs. 20,000) – (72,000 + 3,750 + 6,210)

= 12,470

Balance Sheet of Kali and Lakshmi as on 1-1-98

Liabilities	*Amount*	*Assets*		*Amount*
Sundry Creditors	22,050	Land & building	60,075	
Capital :-		Add increase	12,420	
Kali	74,430			72,495
Lakshmi	37,215	Sundry debtors		36,225
		Cash		11,025
	1,33,695			1,33,695

Problem 15

A, B and C were partners entitled to $\frac{1}{2} : \frac{1}{3}$ and $\frac{1}{6}$ share of profits respectively . A summary of their Balance sheet as on 31-12-1998 was as follows.

Liabilities		*Amount*	*Assets*	*Amount*
Sundry creditors		15,000	Goodwill	50,000
Capital			Block account	60,000
A	70,000		Cash	55,000
B	50,000			
C	30,000			
		1,50,000		
		1,65,000		1,65,000

The following steps were taken on 1st January 1999.

(*a*) C retired and his interest in firm was valued at Rs. 40,000. It was purchased by A and B from their private resources in their profit sharing proportion.

(*b*) D was admitted and became entitled to $\frac{1}{6}$ share of profit on the condition that A and B should be credited in profit ratio for goodwill amounting Rs. 30,000. He should bring in capital equal to $\frac{1}{5}$ of the combined capital of A and B after adjustments.

Prepare partners capital accounts and show the opening balance sheet of the reconstituted firm as on 1-1-1999. **(University of Madras B.Com, October 1999)**

Solution

Working Notes :

1. Calculation of goodwill amount of C :

C's interest on the firm	Rs. 40,000
Less C's capital a/c as balance	Rs. 30,000
Excess given to Mr. C is treated as goodwill.	10,000

2. C's share of Rs. 40,000 is purchased by A & B. Therefore it is shared by A & B and brought in cash to firm as follows:-

$$A — 40,000 \times \frac{3}{5} = 24,000$$

$$B — 40,000 \times \frac{2}{5} = 16,000$$

3. Old ratio of A : B: C is $\frac{1}{2} : \frac{1}{3} : \frac{1}{6}$ or $\frac{3}{6} : \frac{2}{6} : \frac{1}{6}$

new ratio of A & B is 3 : 2 or $\frac{3}{5} : \frac{2}{5}$.

Capital A/c's on retirement

A's Capital A/c

	Amount		*Amount*
To Balance c/d	94,000	By Balance b/d	70,000
		By Cash a/c	24,000
	94,000		94,000

B's Capital A/c

	Amount		*Amount*
To Balance c/d	66,000	By Balance b/d	50,000
		By Cash a/c	16,000
	66,000		66,000

C's Capital A/c

	Amount		*Amount*
To Cash a/c	40,000	By Balance b/d	30,000
		By Goodwill a/c	10,000
	40,000		40,000

On admission of Mr. D

Working Notes :

1. Goodwill amount of Rs. 30,000 is raised and credited to A & B in their old ratio of 3 : 2.

$$\text{A's share} = 30{,}000 \times \frac{3}{5} = \text{Rs. } 18{,}000$$

$$\text{B's share} = 30{,}000 \times \frac{2}{5} = \text{Rs. } 12{,}000$$

2. **Total Goodwill :-**

Goodwill in Balance Sheet	Rs. 50,000
Add Excess given to Mr. C on retirement	10,000
Total goodwill	60,000

This Rs. 60,000 goodwill is written off to A & B in their old ratio, 3 : 2.

$$A = 60{,}000 \times \frac{3}{5} = 36{,}000$$

$$B = 60{,}000 \times \frac{2}{5} = 24{,}000$$

A's Capital A/c

	Amount		*Amount*
To Goodwill a/c	36,000	By Balance b/d	94,000
To Balance c/d	76,000	By Goodwill a/c	18,000
	1,12,000		1,12,000

B's Capital A/c

	Amount		*Amount*
To Goodwill a/c	24,000	By Balance b/d	66,000
To Balance c/d	54,000	By Goodwill a/c	12,000
	78,000		78,000

D's Capital A/c

	Amount		*Amount*
To Balance c/d	26,000	By Cash	26,000

Working Note :

Capital of new partner D is $\frac{1}{5}$th of combined capital of A & B.

A's Capital balance (after D' admission)	76,000
B's Capital balance (after D's admission)	54,000
	1,30,000

$$\text{D's Capital} = \frac{1}{5} \times 1{,}30{,}000 = 26{,}000$$

New Balance sheet

Liabilities	*Amount*	*Assets*		*Amount*
Sundry creditors	15,000	Goodwill		30,000
A's Capital a/c	76,000	Block account		60,000
B's Capital a/c	54,000	Cash :		
D's Capital a/c	26,000	Balance of Cash	55,000	
		Cash brought by D as capital	26,000	81,000
	1,71,000			1,71,000

Problem 16

K, L and M are partners sharing profits and losses in the ratio 5 : 3 : 2. Due to illness L wanted to retire from the firm on 31-3-99 and admit his son N in his place

Liabilities		*Amount*	*Assets*	*Amount*
Capital :			Goodwill	30,000
K	40,000		Furniture	20,000
L	60,000		Sundry debtors	50,000
M	30,000		Stock in trade	50,000
		1,30,000	Cash & Bank balance	50,000
Reserve		50,000		
Sundry Creditors		20,000		
		2,00,000		2,00,000

On retirement of 'L' assets were revalued :

Goodwill Rs. 50,000, furniture Rs. 10,000, Stock-in-trade Rs. 30,000.

50% of the amount due to 'L' was paid off in cash and the balance was retained in the firm as capital of N.

On admission of the new partner, goodwill has been written off.

M is paid off his extra balance to make capital proporationate.

Pass necessary journal entries and prepare Balance Sheet of M/s K M N as on 1-4-1999. Show necessary working. **(C.A. Foundation, November 1999)**

Solution

Journal Entries

Date	*Particulars*		*Dr. Amount*	*Cr. Amount*
	Reserve a/c	Dr.	50,000	
	To K's Capital a/c			25,000
	To L's Capital a/c			15,000
	To M's Capital a/c			10,000
	(Being reserve transferred to capital accounts of K, L and M).			
	Goodwill a/c	Dr.	20,000	
	To Revaluation a/c			20,000
	(Being revaluation of goodwill on L's retirement)			

Date	Particulars		Dr. Amount	Cr. Amount
	Revaluation a/c	Dr.	30,000	
	To Furniture a/c			10,000
	To Stock in trade a/d			20,000
	(Being revaluation of furniture and stock-in trade recorded)			
	K's Capital a/c	Dr.	5,000	
	L's Capital a/c	Dr.	3,000	
	M's Capital a/c	Dr.	2,000	
	To Revaluation a/c			10,000
	(Being loss on revaluation transferred to partners capital accounts).			
	L's Capital a/c	Dr.	72,000	
	To Cash a/c			36,000
	To N Capital a/c			36,000
	(Being 50% of the amount due to L was paid off in cash and the balance was retained in the firm as capital of N)			
	K's Capital a/c	Dr.	25,000	
	M's Capital a/c	Dr.	10,000	
	N Capital a/c	Dr.	15,000	
	To Goodwill a/c			50,000
	(Being goodwill written off as agreed after retirement of L and admission of N in the new profit sharing ratio)			
	M's Capital a/c	Dr.	14,000	
	To Bank a/c			14,000
	(Being amount paid to M to make his capital proportionate).			

K's Capital A/c

	Amount		Amount
To Revaluation	5,000	By Balance b/d	40,000
To Goodwill a/c	25,000	By Reserve a/c	25,000
To Balance a/c	35,000		
	65,000		65,000

L's Capital A/c

	Amount		Amount
To Revaluation a/c	3,000	By Balance b/d	60,000
To Cash a/c	36,000	By Reserve a/c	15,000
To N Capital a/c	36,000		
	75,000		75,000

M's Capital A/c

	Amount		Amount
To Revaluation a/c	2,000	By Balance b/d	30,000
To Goodwill a/c	10,000	By Reserve a/c	10,000
To Bank (Balance figure)	14,000		
To Balance c/d	14,000		
	40,000		40,000

N's Capital A/c

	Amount		Amount
To Goodwill a/c	15,000	By L's Capital a/c	36,000
To Balance c/d	21,000		
	36,000		36,000

Balance Sheet
Of M/S K, M, N as on 1st April 1999.

Liabilities		*Amount*	*Assets*	*Amount*
Capital accounts			Furniture	10,000
K	35,000		Sundry Debtors	50,000
M	14,000		Stock in trade	30,000
N	21,000	70,000		
Sundry creditors		20,000		
		90,000		90,000

Problem 17

P and Q are working in partnership sharing profits and losses equally on 31-12-96. P decided to retire ; in his place, his son R was admitted as partner from 1st Jan. 1997 with $\frac{1}{3}$ rd share in profit as partner from 1st January 1997. The Balance Sheet of the firm as on 31-12-96 was as follows :

Liabilities		*Amount*	*Assets*	*Amount*
Sundry Creditors		14,700	Goodwill	15,000
Capital :			Land & buildings	40,050
P	54,000		Motor car	12,000
Q	48,300		Furniture	9,300
		1,02,300	Sundry Debtors	24,150
			Cash at Bank	16,500
		1,17,000		1,17,000

It was decided as follows :

(*a*) The goodwill should be raised to Rs. 20,000.

(*b*) The Motor car could be taken over by P at its book value.

(c) The value of land and buildings would be increased by Rs. 8,280.
(d) Q and R would introduce sufficient to pay off P and to leave there after a sum of Rs. 7,350 as bank balance in a manner to make their capitals in proportion to their share of profits.
(e) The capital payable by R was to be gifted to him by his father.
(f) The new partners decide not to show good will as an asset.

The above arrangements were duly complied with. Show the partners capital accounts and the bank account **(University of Madras B.Com, May 1999)**

Solution

P's Capital A/c

	Amount		*Amount*
To Motor car a/c	12,000	By Balance b/d	54,000
To R's Capital a/c	31,477	By Goodwill a/c	2,500
To Cash a/c — P	17,163	By Revaluation a/c	4,140
	60,640		60,640

Q's Capital A/c

	Amount		*Amount*
To Goodwill a/c (written off)	13,333	By Balance b/d	48,300
To Balance c/d	49,620	By Goodwill a/c	2,500
		By Revaluation a/c	4,140
		By Cash-shortage brought in by Q	8,013
	62,953		62,953

R's Capital A/c

	Amount		*Amount*
To Goodwill a/c (written off)	6,667	By P's Capital a/c — P's Capital gifted to R	31,477
To Balance c/d	24,810		
	31,477		31,477

Bank A/c

	Amount		*Amount*
To Balance b/d	16,500	By P's capital a/c (balance in P's a/c given as cash)	17,163
To QS Capital a/c (Balance cash brought in by Q) (Balance figure)	8,013	By Balance c/d	7,350
	24,513		24,513

Working Notes :

1. Calculation of Capital of Q & R (after P's retirement and R's admission)

Goodwill (15,000 + 5,000)	20,000
Land & Building (40,050 + 8,280)	48,330
Furniture	9,300
Sundry Debtors	24,150
Cash at Bank (to be required)	7,350
	1,09,130
Less Creditors	14,700
	94,430

$$\text{Q's Capital} = 94,430 \times \frac{2}{3} = 62,953$$

$$\text{R's Capital} = 94,430 \times \frac{1}{3} = 31,477$$

2. The increased value of goodwill Rs. 5,000 (20,000 - 15,000) is first credited to old partners P and Q in their old ratio 1 : 1.
3. Entire goodwill amount of Rs. 20,000 (15,000 + 5,000) is decided to be written off after admission of partner 'R'. Therefore the goodwill amount of Rs. 20,000 is debited to new partners of R and Q in the new ratio of $\frac{1}{3}$rd and $\frac{2}{3}$rd.

Problem 18

Gita and Mita are equal partners. Gita by agreement, retires and Lata joins the firm on the basis of $\frac{1}{3}$ share of profit on 1-4-1998. The balances of the books as on 31st March 1998 were.

	Dr	*Cr*
Goodwill	10,000	
Fixed assets at cost	1,20,000	
Current assets :		
Stock	60,000	
Debtors	40,000	
Bank balance	8,000	
Creditors		20,000
Provision for depreciation		12,000
Capital accounts :		
Gita		1,04,000
Mita		1,02,000
	2,38,000	2,38,000

Goodwill and fixed assets valued at Rs. 30,000 and Rs. 1,40,000 respectively and it was agreed to be written off accordingly before admission of Lata as partner. Sufficient money is to be introduced so as to enable Gita to be paid off and leave Rs. 5,000 cash at bank : Mita and Lata are to provide such sum as to make their capitals proportionate to their share of profit. Assuming the agreement was carried out show the journal entries required and prepare the Balance Sheet after admission of Lata **(ICWA Inter, June 1998)**

Solution

Working Notes :

1. Capitals of Mita and Lata in the new firm :-

Goodwill	30,000	
Fixed assets	1,40,000	
Stock	60,000	
Debtors	40,000	
Cash at Bank	5,000	
		2,75,000
Less : Liabilities i.e., creditors		20,000
Capital		2,55,000

Mita's share of capital $\frac{2}{3} \times 2,55,000 = 1,70,000$

Lata's share of capital $\frac{1}{3} \times 2,55,000 = 85,000$

2. Amount to be brought in by Mita :

Opening capital	1,02,000
on Ravaluation Profit	26,000
	1,28,000
Capital required in the new firm	1,70,000
Amount to be brought in	42,000

Journal Entries

Date	*Particulars*		*Dr. Amount*	*Cr. Amount*
	Goodwill a/c	Dr.	20,000	
	Fixed asset a/c	Dr.	20,000	
	Provision for depreciation	Dr.	12,000	
	To Gita's capital a/c			26,000
	To Mita's capital a/c			26,000
	(Increase in value of goodwill and fixed assets credited to Gita and Mita in profit sharing ratios)			
	Bank a/c	Dr.	1,27,000	
	To Mita's Capital a/c			42,000
	To Lata's Capital a/c			85,000
	(Amount brought in by Mita and Lata in cash to make their capital Rs. 1,70,000 and Rs. 85,000).			
	Gita's Capital a/c	Dr.	1,30,000	
	To Bank a/c			1,30,000
	(Amount due to Gita paid off)			

Bank A/c

	Amount		*Amount*
To Balance b/d	8,000	By Gita's Capital a/c	1,30,000
To Mita's Capital a/c	42,000	By Balance c/d	5,000
To Lata's Capital a/c	85,000		
	1,35,000		1,35,000

Balance Sheet of Mita and Lata as on 1-4-1998

Liabilities	*Amount*	*Assets*	*Amount*
Capitals :		Goodwill	30,000
Mita	1,70,000	Fixed assets	1,40,000
Lata	85,000	Stock	60,000
Sundry creditors	20,000	Sundry debtors	40,000
		Cash at bank	5,000
	2,75,000		2,75,000

Problem 19

A, B and C are in partnership sharing profits and losses equally. On December 31st 1996, the firms Balance Sheet was a follows :

Liabilities		*Amount*	*Assets*	*Amount*
Capitals			Sundry assets	88,000
A	40,000		Cash	10,000
B	30,000			
C	20,000	90,000		
Sundry creditors		8,000		
		98,000		98,000

On that date C decided to retire. The value of Goodwill (Which does not appear in the above Balance Sheet) was agreed to be Rs. 12000. Sundry assets were taken to have increased in value Rs. 24000 on revaluation.

Draw up the readjusted P Balance Sheet showing the amount due to C.

On C's retirement D comes in as a partner. He pays no premium but brings Rs. 18,000 in cash as capital. Profit and losses are now to be shared by A, B and D in the ratio 3 : 3 : 2.

Draw up the Balance Sheet on D's admission after restoring the sundry assets to their original value and wiping out goodwill **(Calcutta University B.Com (Hons.) 1997)**

Solution

Statement Showing Amount Due to C

	A	B	C
Capital balance	40,000	30,000	20,000
Add goodwill (equally)	4,000	4,000	4,000
Add Profit on Revaluation	8,000	8,000	8,000
	52,000	42,000	32,000

Balance Sheet after C's Retirement

Liabilities		*Amount*	*Assets*		*Amount*
Capital :			Goodwill		12,000
A	52,000		Sundry assets	88,000	
B	42,000		Add : increase in value	24,000	
		94,000			1,12,000
C's Loan		32,000	Cash		10,000
Sundry creditors		8,000			
		1,34,000			1,34,000

Statement showing capital of partners after D's admission

	A	B	C
Capital	52,000	42,000	18,000
Less : loss on revaluation (3 : 3 : 2)	9,000	9,000	6,000
	43,000	33,000	12,000
Less : Goodwill written off (3 : 3 : 2)	4,500	4,500	3,000
	38,500	28,500	9,000

Balance Sheet after D's admission

Liabilities		*Amount*	*Assets*		*Amount*
Capital			Sundry assets		88,000
A	38,500		Cash	10,000	
B	28,500		Add cash Brought in by D	18,000	
D	9,000				28,000
		76,000			
C's loan		32,000			
Sundry creditors		8,000			
		1,16,000			1,16,000

QUESTIONS

Simple Questions

1. State the steps involved on retirement of a partner.
2. What is the nature of a retiring partners liability ?
3. What is gaining ratio ?
4. State the methods of treating goodwill on retirement of a partner.
5. What are the amount which become due to a retiring partner ?
6. State the accounting treatment of goodwill when it already appears in the balance sheet ?

EXERCISE 1

A, B and C carrying on business in partnership were sharing profits and losses in 3 : 2 : 1 ratio on 31-3-1996. The following is their position.

Liabilities		*Amount*	*Assets*		*Amount*
Sundry creditors		13,590	Plant & Machinery	15,000	
Reserve fund		4,200	Less depreciation	4,000	11,000
Capital :- A	15,000		Debtors		18,000
B	10,000		Cash		7590
C	10,000		Buildings	17,200	
		35,000	Less depreciation	1,000	16,200
		52,790			52,790

Show the Balance Sheet after B's retirement on 30-6-96 on the following terms :

(*a*) Machinery to be appreciated by Rs. 7,000.
(*b*) Provision for doubtful debts to be made at 5%.
(*c*) Goodwill of the firm to be valued at Rs. 9,000 for his retirement.
(*d*) Rs. 5,000 to be paid to B and the balance taken as loan @ 10% in interest.
(*e*) Average profit for last 3 years were Rs. 6,000 per annum

(Osmania University, B.Com, October 1997)

Answer : Total of balance sheet of A & Rs 54,390.

EXERCISE 2

On 31st March 1990 the Balance Sheet of M/S Ram, Hari & Mohan sharing profits and losses in the ratio of 2 : 3 : 2 stood follows :

Liabilities		*Amount*	*Assets*	*Amount*
Capital accounts :			Lands & buildings	10,00,000
Ram	10,00,000		Machinery	17,00,000
Hari	15,00,000		Closing stock	5,00,000
Mohan	10,00,000		Sundry debtors	6,00,000
		35,00,000	Balance	2,00,000
Sundry creditors		5,00,000		
		40,00,000		40,00,000

On 31st March 1997 Hari desired to retire from the firm and the remaining partners decided to carry on. It was agreed to revalue the assets and liabilities on that date on the following basis.

1. Land & Building be appreciated by 30%.
2. Machinery be depreciated by 20%.
3. Closing stock to be valued at Rs 4,50,000.
4. Provision for bad debts be made at 5%.
5. Old credit balance of sundry creditors Rs. 50,000 be written back.
6. Joint Life Policy of the partners surrendered and cash obtained Rs. 3,50,000.
7. Goodwill of the entire firm be valued at Rs. 6,30,000 and Hari's share of the goodwill be adjusted in the accounts of Ram and Mohan who share the future profits & losses in the ratio of 3 : 2. No goodwill account be raised.
8. The total capital of the firm is to be the same as before retirement. Individual capital be in their profit sharing ratio.
9. Amount due to Hari is to be settled on the following basis; 50% on retirement and the balance 50% within one year.

Prepare Revaluation account, Capital accounts of partners, cash account, and Balance Sheet as on 1-4-1997 of M/S Ram and Mohan **(C.A. Foundation, May 1997)**

Answer : Total of Balance Sheet of Ram and Mohan Rs. 48,95,000.

EXERCISE 3

Bijan, Kujan and Srijan were partners in a firm. They share profits & losses in the ratio of 3 : 2 : 1. Their Balance Sheet as at 31st December 1995, was as follows.

Liabilities		*Amount*	*Assets*		*Amount*
Sundry creditors		12,000	Cash		900
Bills payable		5,500	Sundry debtors	5,000	
Capital accounts			Less provision	400	4,600
Bijan	36,000		Closing stock		5,000
Kujan	24,000		Furniture		10,000
Srijan	12,000		Plant & Machinery		25,000
		72,000	Building		50,000
Reserve		6,000			
		95,500			95,500

On 31st December 1995, Bijan retired. The terms of retirement provided the following.

(*a*) Goodwill of the firm is to be valued at Rs. 12,000 but no goodwill accounts is to be raised in the books.
(*b*) The value of furniture and plant and machinery are to be depreciated by 20% and 10% respectively.
(*c*) The value of stock and building are to be appreciated by 10% and 20% respectively.
(*d*) Provision for doubtful debts is to be maintained at Rs. 300.
(*e*) The amount due to be transferred to a separate loan account.

Show the Revaluation accounts and Partners Capital accounts incorporating all the above charges

(Calcutta University B.Com (Pass) 1996)

Answer : Bijan's Loan a/c Balance Rs. 48,050
Kujan's capital Balance Rs. 24,033
Srijan's capital Balance Rs. 12,017

EXERCISE 4

The Balance Sheet of Messrs A, B and C who are sharing profits & losses equally, stood as follows on 31st December 1989.

Liabilities		*Amount*	*Assets*		*Amount*
Sundry creditors		18,000	Cash at bank		10,000
Bills payable		12,000	Debtors	80,000	
Reserve		18000	Less : Reserve	2,000	
Capital :-					78,000
A	1,20,000		Stock		40,000
B	1,00,000		Truck		60,000
C	1,00,000		Machinery		1,00,000
		3,20,000	Buildings		80,000
		3,68,000			3,68,000

On 1st April 1990, Mr. C retired from the business and the following revaluation were agreed upon by the business.

(a) Building to be appreciated b 15%.
(b) Truck and machinery to be depreciated by 10%.
(c) Reserve for doubtful debts was to be raised to 5%.
(d) Stock to be revalued at Rs. 46,000.
(e) The goodwill of the firm was to be valued at 3 times the average profits of the last 5 years. The profits and losses were 1985 profit Rs. 40,000; 1956 profits Rs. 60,000; 1987 loss 20,000, 1998 profit Rs. 1,00,000 ; 1989 loss Rs. 30,000.
(f) Mr. C was entitled to receive his share of profit up to the date of his retirement. Such profit was based on the average profits of the last 5 years.

Find out the amount payable Mr. 'C' at the time of retirement. Show the necessary accounts and prepare the Balance Sheet of the continuing partners on 1-4-1996 assuming that Rs. 18,500 was paid immediately and the balance in 4 equal annual instalments at 8% interest. Prepare Mr. C's loan a/c till it is finally closed **(University of Mysore, B.Com, April 1994)**

Answer : Total of Balance Sheet of A and B Rs. 3,70,000.

EXERCISE 5

The following is the Balance Sheet of A, B and C who were sharing profits in the ratio of 2 : 2 : 1 on March 31 1994 :

Liabilities	*Amount*	*Assets*	*Amount*
Creditor	12,000	Plant & Machinery	49,000
5% Mortgage loan	16,600	Furniture	4,800
Capital accounts :		Stock in trade	22,800
A	33,600	Sundry debtors	21,600
B	25,200	Cash in hand	1,200
C	12,000		
	99,400		99,400

On 1-4-1995, C retired from the business and claimed his share in the secret reserve/profit arising out of the following.

1. During the year 1994-95 purchase of machinery at a cost of Rs. 5,000 was charged to purchases account. The installation charge of Rs. 300 to erect the machinery being charged to machinery repairs account.
2. Rs. 1,200 received from Raman towards rent of property which was credited to his personal account instead of rent account so as to reduce his debit balance from Rs. 1,600 to Rs. 400 debit.
3. Interest on mortgage loan was paid in advance upto 31-3-1996 and the whole amount was charged to interest account in 1994-95.

After rectifying the above errors, it was mutually decided as under :

(a) The goodwill of the firm be valued at 3 times the average profits of the last 3 years. Such profits should be the correct profits and not the books profit. The book profits for the last 3 years were :
1992 - 93 Rs. 13,830, 1993-94 Rs. 32,000, 1994-95, Rs. 12,020.
(b) Machinery be depreciated by 10% and the provision for bad and doubtful debts be made at 5% on debtors.
(c) There is a liability for Rs. 483 for bills discounted.

(*d*) Goodwill should appear in the books to the extent of the retiring partner's share therein.

(*e*) C should be paid half his dues in cash which shall be brought in by A and B in their profit sharing proportion and the other half should be left in the business as C's loan.

Show ledger account and Balance Sheet of A and B

(Manonmanian Sundrahar University, November 1996)

Answer : Total of Balance Sheet 1,13,196.

EXERCISE 6

Ajay, Bikash and Kamal were partners sharing profit and losses in the ratio of 3 : 2 : 1. Their Balance Sheet as on 31-3-1992 stood as follows :

Liabilities		*Amount*	*Assets*		*Amount*
Sundry creditors		12,500	Cash at bank		1,500
General Reserve		18,000	Debtors	15,000	
Capital accounts			Less : R B D	2,500	
Ajay	40,000				13,500
Bikash	21,000		Stock		12,500
Kamal	20,000		Joint Life Policy		8,000
		81,000	Office equipment		14,000
			Furniture		12,000
			Buildings		50,000
		1,11,500			1,11,500

Bikash retires on 1-4-92 subject to the following conditions.

1. A typewriter purchased on 1-10-91 for Rs. 2,000, debited to office expenses a/c is to be brought into account charging depreciation at the rate of 10% p.a.
2. Building revalued at Rs. 75,000. Furniture is to be written down by Rs. 2,000 and stock is reduced to Rs. 10,000.
3. Reserve for Bad debt is to be calculated @ 5% on debtors.
4. Goodwill of the firm is valued at Rs. 18,000. But no goodwill account is to be raised.
5. Life policy is to be shown at surrender value. The surrender value is Rs. 7,500.
6. Amount due to Bikash is to be transferred to Loan a/c.
7. Ajay and Kamal will share profit & losses in the ratio of 2 : 1 and their capital is to be adjusted in the profit sharing ratio. You are required to prepare : Revaluation a/c Partner's capital account and Balance Sheet immediately after retirement

(Calcutta University B. Com (Hons.) 1994).

Answer : Total of balance sheet Rs. 1,34,150

EXERCISE 7

(RETIREMENT AND ADMISSION)

Dowels & Co. is a partnership firm with partner Mr. A, Mr. B and Mr. C sharing profits and losses in the ratio of 10 : 6 : 4. The Balance Sheet of the firm as at 31st March, 1996 is as under.

Liabilities		*Amount*	*Assets*	*Amount*
Capital			Land	10,000
Mr. A	80,000		Buildings	2,00,000
Mr. B	20,000		Plant & Machinery	1,30,000
Mr. C	30,000		Furniture	43,000
		1,30,000	Investment	12,000
Reserve		20,000	Stock	1,30,000
Long term debt		3,00,000	Debtors	1,39,000
Bank overdraft		44,000		
Trade creditors		1,70,000		
		6,64,000		6,64,000

It was mutually agreed that Mr. B will retire from partnership and in his place Mr. D will be admitted as a partner with effect from 1st April 1996. For this purpose the following adjustments are to be made.

1. Goodwill is to be valued at Rs. 1 Lakh but the same will not appear as an asset in the books of the reconstituted firm.
2. Buildings and Plant and Machinery are to be depreciated by 5% and 20% respectively Investments are to be taken over by the retiring partner at Rs. 15,000. Provision of 20% is to be made on debtors to cover doubiful debts.
3. In the reconstituted firm, the total capital will be Rs. 2 Lakhs which will be contributed by Mr. A Mr. C and Mr. D in their new profit sharing ratio, which is 2 : 2 : 1.
4. The surplus funds, if any, will be used for repaying the bank overdraft.
5. The amount due to the retiring partner shall be transferred to his loan account. You are to prepare.
   (*a*) Revaluation a/c
   (*b*) Partners capital accounts
   (*c*) Bank a/c and
   (*d*) Balance Sheet of the reconstituted firm as on 1st April 1996

(C.A Foundation, November 1996)

Answer : Total of Balance Sheet Rs. 6,92,760.

EXERCISE 8

X and Y carried on business of X, Y and Co. as equal partners It was agreed that X should retere on 31-12-97 and his son 'Z' should join Y in partnership on 1-1-98 and should be entitled to $\frac{1}{3}$rd of the profits of the firm, the style of the firm remaining unchanged. The balances in the firms books on 31-12-97 were as follows.

Liabilities	*Amount*	*Assets*	*Amount*
Sundry creditors	980	Goodwill	1,000
Capitals		Freehold premises	2,070
X	3,400	Furniture	1,420
Y	2,820	Sundry debtors	1,610
		Bank Balance	1,100
	7,200		7,200

For the purpose of X's retirement and Z's admission goodwill was written up to Rs. 2,200 and freehold premises to Rs. 2,400. Other terms agreed were that enough money should be introduced to enable X to be paid out and leave Rs. 1,000 cash for working capital and that Y and Z should respectively provide such sum as would make their capitals proportionate to their shares in profit. X agreed to make Z a gift by transfer from his capital a/c half the amount which Z had to provide.

Y and Z paid cash due from them on 7-1-1998 and the amount due to X was paid out on the same day.

Prepare ledger accounts and Balance Sheet to recorded the above transactions.

20

CHAPTER

Partnership Accounts — Death of a Partner

The accounting treatment of death of a partner is more or less the same when compared to retirement of partner. But it differs from the following.

1. A partner retires usually at the close of the accounting period. So his share of capital and goodwill with profit is credited at the time of his retirement.
   A partners death cannot be predicted. So his share of profit, goodwill, salary, interest on capital and other remuneration payable to him is to be calculated to the date of his death.
2. In case of retirement of a partner a loan account in the name of the partner retiring is opened.
   In case of death of partner the firm opens the accounts in the name of executors of the deceased partner.

EXECUTORS ACCOUNT

Executors are legal inheritors of the deceased partner and the amount due to deceased partner is transferred to an account opened in the name of person entitled to his share called "Executors" account.

In arriving at amount due to deceased partner the following items are to be considered.

(*a*) Capital as on date of last Balance Sheet.
(*b*) Share in profit or loss on revaluation of assets and liabilities.
(*c*) Share in goodwill of the firm.
(*d*) Proportionate share in profit or loss upto date of death.
(*e*) Interest on drawings & capital.
(*f*) Share in accumulated profit or losses.

ADJUSTMENT OF ACCOUNTS ON THE DEATH OF A PARTNER :

1. To Adjust the profit due to the deceased partner.
   Profit & loss a/c   Dr
         To Deceased partner's capital a/c

2. To Adjust the goodwill amount due to the deceased partner.
   Goodwill a/c Dr
   To Deceased partner's capital a/c
3. To Transfer the drawings account of the deceased partner to his capital a/c
   Deceased partner's capital a/c Dr
   To Deceased partners drawings a/c
4. To Adjust interest on capital on deceased partner.
   Interest on capital a/c Dr
   To Deceased partners capital a/c
5. To Transfer the amount due to the partner to the executors of deceased partners loan a/c
   Deceased partners capital a/c Dr
   To Executors of deceased partners loan a/c
6. To Settle the deceased partners capital a/c
   Deceased partners a/c Dr
   To Bank a/c
7. To Pay the deceased partner's Executor in part :-
   Executor's of the deceased partner's loan a/c
   To Bank a/c Dr
8. To Credit the executors of the deceased partners loan account with interest on unpaid balance :-
   Interest a/c Dr
   To Executors of deceased partner's loan a/c
9. To Write off the goodwill paid to the deceased :
   Continuing partner's capital a/c Dr
   To Goodwill a/c
   (in the gaining ratio)

Problem 1

A, B and C were in partnership sharing profits equally. C died on 31st March 1999. The Balance Sheet of the firm as at 31st December 1998 was as under.

Liabilities		*Amount*	*Assets*	*Amount*
Sundry creditors		15,600	Cash in hand & at bank	4,000
General Reserve		6,000	Debtors	18,000
Investment fluctuation Fund		2,100	Stock	28,000
Reserve for doubtful debts		1,800	Investment (at cost)	8,000
			Freehold property	30,000
			Goodwill	13,500
Capitals				
A	30,000			
B	25,000			
C	21,000			
		76,000		
		1,01,500		1,01,500

On the date of death it was found that :-

(*a*) Freehold property was worth Rs. 57,000.
(*b*) Debtors were all good.
(*c*) Stocks were valued at Rs. 25,000.
(*d*) Investments valued at Rs. 7,500 and was taken over by 'A'.
(*e*) A liability for Workman Compensation for Rs. 3,000 was to be provided.
(*f*) Goodwill was to be valued at one year purchase of average profit of last 5 years.
(*g*) C's share of profit upto the date of death was to be calculated on the basis of last years.

Profit : The profit for 5 years were :-

Year	:	1994	1995	1996	1997	1998
Profit (Rs.)	:	11,500	12,500	8,000	10,000	12,000

Prepare (*i*) Revaluation a/c (*ii*) Capital a/c of C (*iii*) Balance Sheet of remaining partners.

(University of Madras B. Com., May 2001)

Solution

Revaluation A/c

		Amount			Amount
To Stock a/c		3,000	By Freehold property		27,000
To Workman's Compensation a/c		3,000	By Reserve for doubtful Debts		1,800
To Profit transferred to			By Investment fluctuation		
Partner's capital a/c			Fund	2,100	
A —	8,133		Less : Loss in Investment	500	
B —	8,133		(8,000 – 7,500)		1,600
C —	8,134	24,400			
		30,400			30,400

A's Capital A/c

	Amount		Amount
To Goodwill a/c	900	By Balance b/d	30,000
To Investment a/c	7,500	By General Reserve a/c	2,000
To Balance c/d	31,733	By Revaluation	8,133
	40,133		40,133

B's Capital A/c

	Amount		Amount
To Goodwill a/c	900	By Balance b/d	25,000
To Balance c/d	34233	By General Reserve a/c	2,000
		By Revaluation a/c	8,133
	35,133		35,133

C's Capital A/c

	Amount		Amount
To Goodwill a/c	900	By Balance b/d	21,000
To C's Executor's Loan a/c	31,234.	By General Reserve	2,000
		By Revaluation a/c	8,134
		By Profit	1,000
	32,134		32,134

Balance Sheet

Liabilities		Amount	Assets	Amount
Sundry Creditors		15,600	Cash at bank	4,000
Workmen's compensation		3,000	Debtors	18,000
Capital accounts :-			Stock	25,000
A —	31,733		Freehold property	57,000
B —	34,233		Goodwill	10,800
		65,966	P & L a/c	1,000
C's Executor's Loan a/c		31,234	(C's share)	
		1,15,800		1,15,800

Working Notes :

1. Since all debtors are good, Reserve for doubtful debts is not required and must be transferred to Revaluation a/c.
2. The market value of investment has gone down by Rs. 500. This loss in investment is adjusted in 'Investment fluctuation fund". Then the balance fund Rs. 1600 (2,100 – 500) is transferred to "Revaluation a/c". The revised investment value Rs. 7,500 is taken by Mr. A. Therefore it is debited to A's capital a/c.
3. **Calculation of Goodwill :**

$$= \frac{\text{Total profit of 5 years}}{5} \times \text{one year purchase}$$

$$= \frac{11{,}500 + 12{,}500 + 8{,}000 + 10{,}000 + 12{,}000}{5} \times 1$$

$$= \text{Rs. } 10{,}800$$

Goodwill in Balance Sheet is Rs. 13,500. Therefore the difference of Rs. 2,700 (13,500 – 10,800) is debited to all partners in their equal ratio

$$= \frac{2{,}700}{3} = \text{Rs. 900 to each partners.}$$

4. Calculate of C's share of profit to the date of death-on the basis of last years profit. Last year's profit (1998) = 12,000

Profit for 3 months $= 12{,}000 \times \frac{3}{12} = \text{Rs. } 3{,}000$

i.e., upto 31-3-1999.

C's share i.e., equal share $= \frac{3000}{3} = \text{Rs. } 1{,}000$

Problem 2

The following was the Balance Sheet of Om 4 Co. in which X, Y and Z were partners sharing profits & losses in the ratio of 1 :2 : 2 as on 31 -3- 1999. Mr. Z died on 31st December 1999. His account has to be settled under the following terms.

Balance Sheet of Om & Co. as on 31-3-1999

Liabilities		*Amount*	*Assets*	*Amount*
Sundry creditors		20,000	Goodwill	30,000
Bank Loan		50,000	Building	1,20,000
General Reserve		30,000	Computers	80,000
Capital Accounts			Stock	20,000
X	40,000		Sundry debtors	20,000
Y	80,000		Cash at Bank	20,000
Z	80,000		Investments	10,000
		2,00,000		
		3,00,000		3,00,000

Goodwill is to be calculated at the rate of two years purchase as on the basis of average of last three year's profit and losses. The profit and losses for the three years were as detailed below.

Year ending on	Profit / loss
31-3-1999	30,000
31-3-1998	20,000
31-3-1997	(10,000) loss

Profit for the period from 1-4-1999 to 31-12-1999 shall be ascertained proportionately on the basis of average profits and losses of the preceding three years.

During the years ending on 31-3-1999, a car costing Rs. 40,000 was purchased on 1-4-1998 and debited to travelling expenses account on which depreciation is to be calculated at 20% p.a. This asset is to be brought into account at the depreciated value.

Other values of assets were agreed as follows.

Stock at Rs. 16,000 : Building at Rs. 140,000 computers at Rs. 50,000 : Investment at Rs. 6,000 sundry Debtors were considered good. You are asked to prepare partners capital accounts and Balance Sheet of the firm Om & Co. on 31-12-1999 assuming that other items of assets and liabilities remained the same. (C.A. Foundation, May 2000).

Solution

Working Notes

1. Calculation of goodwill :

(*a*) *Adjusted profit for the year ended 31-3-1999 :*

Profit (given)		30,000
Add back : Cost of car wrongly written off	40,000	
Less : Depreciation for the year 1998 - 99 (20% on Rs. 40,000)	8,000	32,000
		62,000

(b) *Average of last three year's profit and losses :-*

Year ending on	Profit / loss
31-3-1997	(10,000)
31-3- 1998	20,000
31-3-1999	62,000
	72,000

$$\text{Average profit} = \frac{72,000}{3} = 24,000$$

(c) *Goodwill at 2 years purchase :-*

Rs. 24,000 × 2 = Rs. 48,000

(d) *Z's Share of profit for the period from 1-4-1999 to 31-12-1999.*

$$\text{Rs. } 24,000 \times \frac{9}{12} \times \frac{2}{5} = \text{Rs. } 7,200$$

Revaluation A/c

	Amount			Amount
To Stock a/c	4,000	By Building a/c		20,000
To Computers a/c	30,000	By Loss transferred to		
To Investments a/c	4,000	X	3,600	
		Y	7,200	
		Z	7,200	18,000
	38,000			38,000

X's Capital A/c

	Amount		Amount
To Revaluation a/c	3,600	By Balance b/d	40,000
To Balance c/d	52,400	By General Reserve	6,000
		By Goodwill $\left(18,000 \times \frac{1}{5}\right)$	3,600
		By Car a/c	6,400
	56,000		56,000

Y's Capital A/c

	Amount		Amount
To Revaluation a/c	7,200	By Balance b/d	80,000
To Balance c/d	1,04,800	By General Reserve	12,000
		By Goodwill – $18,000 \times \frac{2}{5}$	7,200
		By Car a/c	12,800
	1,12,000		1,12,000

Z's Capital A/c

	Amount		Amount
To Revaluation a/c	7,200	By Balance b/d	80,000
To Z's Executor's a/c	1,12,000	By General Reserve	12,000
		By Goodwill 18,000 × $\frac{2}{5}$	7,200
		By Car a/c	12,800
		By P & L suspense a/c	7,200
	1,19,200		1,19,200

Balance sheet of Om & Co. as at 31-12-99

	Amount		Amount
Sundry creditors	20,000	Goodwill	48,000
Bank Loan	50,000	Building	1,40,000
Capital accounts		Car	32,000
X	52,400	Stock	16,000
Y	1,04,800	Computers	50,000
		Investment	6,000
Z's Executor's a/c	1,12,000	Sundry debtors	20,000
		Cash at Bank	20,000
		P & L suspense a/c	7,200
	3,39,200		3,39,200

Problem 3

A deceased partner is to be paid Rs. 60,000 on 1-4-1994. The amount is to be paid to his executor in 3 yearly instalments together with interest @ Rs. 10 p. a. shows the executors of deceased account for 3 years. **(Osmania University B. Com., March 1999)**

Solution

A's Executor's loan A/c

Date	Particulars	Amount	Date	Particulars	Amount
31-3-95	To Bank a/c	26,000	1-4-94	By A's Capital a/c	60,000
	To Balance c/d	40,000	31-3-95	By Interest a/c	6,000
		66,000			66,000
31-3-96	To Bank a/c	24,000	1-4-95	By Balance b/d	40,000
	To Balance c/d	20,000	31-3-96	By Interest a/c	4,000
		44,000			44,000
31-3-97	To Bank a/c	22,000	1-4-96	By Balance b/d	20,000
			31-3-97	By Interest a/c	2,000
		22,000			22,000

Problem 4

X, Y and Z were trading in partnership sharing profits & losses as 4 : 3 : 3 respectively. The accounts of the firm are made up to 31st December every year.

The deed provided that, on the death of a partner, goodwill is to be valued at 3 years average profits of 3 years ending up to the date of death, after deducting interest at 8% on capital employed and a fair remuneration to each partner. The profits are assumed to be earned evenly through the year.

On 30th June 1995, X died and it was agreed to adjust goodwill in the capital accounts without showing any amount of goodwill in the Balance Sheet. It was agreed that for the purpose of valuation of goodwill, fair remuneration to each partner would be Rs. 15,000 p.a. and the capital employed would be Rs. 1,56,000 and Y and Z were to continue the partnership sharing profit & losses equally after the death of X.

The following were the amounts of profits of various years before charging interest on capital employed.

1992	Rs. 67,200
1993	Rs.75,600
1994	Rs. 72,000
1995	Rs. 62,400

Compute the value of goodwill and show the entry in the books of the firm (ICWA, Inter December 1996).

Solution

Calculation of Goodwill

1. Average profit for the year ending on :

$$30\text{-}6\text{-}93 \quad \frac{67{,}200 + 75600}{2} = 71{,}400$$

$$30\text{-}6\text{-}94 \quad \frac{75{,}600 + 72{,}000}{2} = 73{,}800$$

$$30\text{-}6\text{-}95 \quad \frac{72{,}000 + 62400}{2} = 67{,}200$$

$$2{,}12{,}400$$

$$\text{Average profit} = \frac{2{,}12{,}400}{3} = \text{Rs. } 70{,}800$$

2. $\text{Expected return} = \left(\frac{8}{100} \times 1{,}56{,}000\right) + 45{,}000$

$= 12{,}480 + 45{,}000 = 57{,}480$

3. Goodwill $(70{,}800 - 57{,}480) \times 3 = 39{,}960$

4.

	X	Y	Z
Goodwill raised 4 : 3 : 3	15,984	11,988	11,988
Less : written off in 1 : 1	—	19,980	19,980
	15,984	(7,992)	(7,992)

Journal Entry

Date	Particulars		Dr. Amount	Cr. Amount
	Y's Capital a/c	Dr	7,992	
	Z's Capital a/c	Dr	7,992	
	To X's Capital a/c			15,984
	(Being adjustment entry passed)			

Problem 5

A, B and C are partners sharing profits at $\frac{2}{5}\frac{2}{5}\frac{1}{5}$ respectively and their balance sheet on 31-12-2000 should the following position

	Amount		Amount
Creditors	29,000	Cash at Bank	4,000
Capital accounts		Debtors	30,000
A	30,000	Stock	45,000
B	20,000	Plant & Fixtures	20,000
C	20,000		
	99,000		99,000

C dies on 1-9-2001 and the deed provides that the estate of the deceased shall be entitled to a share of the profits up to the date of death based on the profit of the previous years together with a share in respect of goodwill to be calculated on the basis of 2 year's purchase of the average net profits of the previous 3 years. The net profits of the years 1998, 1990 and 2,000 were Rs. 20,000, Rs. 22,000 and Rs. 18,000 respectively. C had withdrawn Rs. 1,500 from the date of the last Balance Sheet to the date of his death and 6% interest was agreed to be credited to the capital of each partner.

It was agreed between the surviving partners and executors of the deceased that the amount due to the latter be paid to them within 3 years by 6 monthly instalments of Rs. 5,500 each : interest at 6% being calculated on the balance due. Show the executors of C (deceased) Loan a/c.

Solution

Working notes

C's share of profit :

It is based on last year's profit, i.e. 2000 (i.e., Rs. 1,8000)

$$18{,}000 \times \frac{1}{5} \times \frac{8}{12} = 2{,}400$$

C's share of goodwill

1998	-	20,000
1999	-	22,000
2000	-	18,000
		60,000

Average profit $= \frac{60,000}{3} = 20,000$

2. Years purchase = 20,000 × 2 = 40,000

C's share $= \frac{1}{5} \times 40,000 = 8,000$

Interest on Capital

$$20,000 \times \frac{6}{100} \times \frac{8}{12} = 800$$

C's Capital A/c

	Amount		*Amount*
To Drawings	1,500	By Balance b/d	20,000
To C's Loan	29,700	By P & L a/c	2,400
		By Goodwill a/c	8,000
		By Interest	800
	31,200		31,200

Balance Sheet

	Amount			*Amount*
Creditors	29,000	Cash at Bank	4,000	
C's loan a/c	29,700	Less : Cash drawn	1,500	2,500
Capital a/c		Debtors		30,000
A -	30,000	Stock		45,000
B -	20,000	Plant		20,000
		Goodwill		8,000
		P & L a/c	2,400	
		Interest	800	3,200
	1,08,700			1,08,700

Executors's of C (deceased) Loan A/c

Date	*Particulars*	*Amount*	*Date*	*Particulars*	*Amount*
2002 Feb. 28	To Bank	5,500	2001 Sept.		
	" Balance c/d	25,091		By C's capital a/c	29,700
			2002 Feb.	By Interest $29,700 \times \frac{6}{100} \times \frac{6}{12}$	891
		30,591			30,591

Date	Particulars	Amount	Date	Particulars	Amount
2002 Aug. 31	To Bank	5,500	2002 March 1,	By Balance b/d	25,091
	To Balance c/d	20,344	Aug. 31,	" Interest	753
				$25,091 \times \frac{6}{100} \times \frac{6}{12}$	
		25,844			25,844
2003 Feb. 28	To Bank	5,500	2002 Step. 1	By Balance b/d	20344
	To Balance c/d	15,454	2003	By Interest	610
			Feb.	$20,344 \times \frac{6}{100} \times \frac{6}{12}$	
		20,954			20,954
2003 Aug.	To Bank	5,500	2003 Mar. 1	By Balance b/d	15454
	To Balance c/d	10,418	Aug.	By Interest	464
				$15,454 \times \frac{6}{100} \times \frac{6}{12}$	
		15,918			15,918
2004 Feb. 28,	To Bank	5,500	2003 Sept. 1,	By Balance b/d	10,418
	To Balance c/d	5,230	2004 Feb.	By Interest	312
				$10,418 \times \frac{6}{100} \times \frac{6}{12}$	
		10,730			10,730

Problem 6

E, F and G are in partnership sharing profits equally. E dies on 31-3-2003 and the partnership deed provided among other things that :-

1. The share of a deceased partners capital account shall be taken at the balance of his capital a/c as at the the date of the last financial year less the withdrawal a/c if any made to the date of death.
2. That his share of profits to the date of death shall be calculated on the basis of the average of the three preceding years.
3. That the goodwill of the firm shall be taken at one year's purchase of the average profit of the five preceding years.
4. That the firms freehold property shall be taken at an independent valuation.
   The firm's last Balance Sheet was as under.

	Amount		Amount
Creditors	18,900	Cash on hand	500
Capital accounts		Cash at bank	4,500
E - 30,000		Debtors	10,000
F - 20,000		Stock	15,000
G - 20,000		Freehold property	40,000
	70,000	Goodwill	18,900
	88,900		88,900

The freehold property was valued at Rs. 58,000. The profit for the five years ending 31-12-2002 were.

1998 — 11,500
1994 — 14,000
2000 — 9,000
2001 — 8,000
2002 — 10,000

Pass the Journal entries and show E's capital a/c and the Balance Sheet of the surviving partners. Show also how the Balance Sheet will appear if the goodwill a/c is wiped off from the books of the firm.

Solution

Working notes

1. E's share of profit

2002 — 10,000
2001 — 8,000
2000 — 9,000
27,000

$$\text{Average profit } \frac{27,000}{3} = 9,000$$

$$\text{E's share } 9,000 \times \frac{1}{3} \times \frac{3}{12} = 750$$

2. E's share of goodwill

2002 — 10,000
2001 — 8,000
2000 — 9,000
1999 — 14,000
1998 — 11,500
52,500

$$\text{Average profit} = \frac{52500}{5} = 10,500$$

Goodwill in the Balance Sheet = 18,900
Present value of goodwill = 10,500
8,400

Journal Entries

Date	Particulars		Dr. Amount	Cr. Amount
	P & L a/c	Dr	750	
	To E's Capital a/c			750
	(Being E's share of profit credited)			
	E's Capital a/c	Dr	2,800	
	F's Capital a/c	Dr	2,800	
	G's Capital a/c	Dr	2,800	
	To Goodwill a/c			8,400
	(Being depreciation in the value of goodwill adjusted to partner's Capital's)			
	Freehold property a/c	Dr	18,000	
	To E's Capital a/c			6,000
	To F's Capital a/c			6,000
	To G's Capital a/c			6,000
	(Being appreciation in the value of freehold premises credited).			
	E's Capital a/c	Dr	33,950	
	To Executor's a/c of (deceased) Loan a/c			33,9150
	Being amount due to E transferred to his Executor's loan a/c			

E's Capital A/c

	Amount		Amount
To Goodwill a/c	2,800	By Balance b/d	30,000
To Executors of E		By P & L a/c	750
(Deceased) loan a/c	33,950	By Freehold property	6,000
	36,750		36,750

F's Capital A/c

	Amount		Amount
To Goodwill a/c	2,800	By Balance b/d	20,000
To Balance c/d	23,200	By Freehold property a/c	6,000
	26,000		26,000

C's Capital A/c

	Amount		Amount
To Goodwill a/c	2,800	By Balance b/d	20,000
By Balance c/d	23,200	By Freehold property a/c	6,000
	26,000		26,000

Balance Sheet

		Amount		*Amount*
Creditors		18,900	Cash on hand	500
Executors of E			Cash at Bank	4,500
(Deceased) Loan a/c		33,950	Debtors	10,000
Capital accounts			Stock	15,000
F	23,200		Freehold property	58,000
G	23,200		Goodwill	10,500
		46,400	P & L a/c	750
		99,250		99,250

If the continuing partners decide for writing off the goodwill amount from the books of the firm the following journal entry will be passed

Date	*Particulars*		*Dr. Amount*	*Cr. Amount*
	F's Capital a/c	Dr	5,250	
	G's Capital a/c	Dr	5,250	
	To Goodwill a/c			10,500
	(Entry for writing off the goodwill amount from the firms books)			

Balance Sheet of F and G

	Amount		*Amount*
Creditors	18,900	Cash at bank	4,500
Capitals		Cash at office	500
F - (23,000 - 5,250)	17,750	Debtors	10,000
G - (23,000 - 5,250)	17,750	Stock	15,000
Loan a/c of the		Freehold property	58,000
Executors of E	33,950	P & L a/c	750
	88,750		88,750

JOINT LIFE POLICY

The main aim of taking a Joint Life Policy on the lives of all the partners is to provide necessary funds to pay out the amount due to the executors of a deceased partner. When such a policy is taken the amount of the policy becomes payable as soon as any of the partner dies. Thus the financial resources of the firm are not adversely affected.

Treatment of Joint Life Policy

Joint life policy may be treated in any of the following ways

1. **When premium paid is treated as an expense :-** The premium paid annually is treated as an expense and hence debited to profit & Loss a/c. Whenever a partner dies the amount of the policy received is credited to Joint Life Policy. The amount in the Joint Life Policy account is transferred to all the partners Capital accounts in the profit sharing ratio. The following entries are involved.

1. On payment of premium of the Joint life policy :-
   (*a*) Joint life insurance premium a/c Dr
   To Bank a/c
   (Being the amount of premium paid on Joint Life Policy)
   (*b*) Profit & Loss a/c Dr
   To Joint Life Insurance Premium a/c
   (Being the amount of premium charged to P & L a/c)
2. On receipt of the policy money :
   Bank a/c Dr
   To All Partner's Capital a/c
   (Being the policy money distributed among all partners in the profit sharing ratio)

2. **When premium paid is treated as an asset and surrender value is taken into accounts :-** Under this method as and when premium is paid, the same is debited to Joint Life Policy account. At the end of the year the book value of the policy is adjusted to surrender value by transferring to Profit & Loss account. The balance in Life Policy a/c is shown as an asset in the Balance Sheet. The amount received on maturity of policy in excess of surrender value will be net gain and will be divided among all the partners in their profit sharing ratio. The following entries are recorded.
   (*a*) Joint Life Policy a/c Dr
   To Bank a/c
   (Being the premium paid on policy)
   (*b*) Profit & Loss a/c Dr
   To Joint Life Policy a/c
   (Being the adjustment of book value with the surrender value, i.e., excess of life policy over the surrender value).
   (*c*) Bank a/c
   To Joint Life Policy a/c
   (Being amount received on maturity of policy)
   (*d*) Joint Life Policy a/c Dr
   To all partners Capital a/c
   (Being the amount received minus the surrender value on that date dis tributed among the partners).

3. **When premium paid is treated as an asset and Life Insurance Policy reserve account is maintained** Under this method the following procedure is followed.
   (a) The premium paid is debited to Joint Life Policy a/c and credited to Bank a/c
   Joint-Life Policy a/c Dr
   To Bank a/c
   (For the premium paid)
   (*b*) In order to keep the working capital intact the amount of premium payable is provided out of divisible profits.
   Profit & Loss a/c Dr
   To Jointly Life Policy Reserve a/c
   (For reserve provided equal to the amount of premium paid out of divisible. Profits).
   (c) In order to bring down the policy account to its surrender value.
   Joint Life Policy Reserve a/c Dr (with the difference between cost) and surender value

To Joint life policy a/c.

(For the excess of J. L. P. a/c over surrender value written of J L P R a/c).

(*d*) The policy a/c will then appear at its surrender value on the asset side and Policy Reserve a/c will appear on the liabilities side of the Balance Sheet at the same figure until it is realised.

(*e*) When a partner dies the policy amount is received.

Bank a/c Dr

To Joint Life Policy a/c

(For the amount of policy realised on the death of a partner.

(*f*) For transferring the balance standing in the former a/c to latter a/c.

Joint Life Policy Reserve a/c Dr

To Joint Life Policy a/c

(For the balance in the Joint Life Policy Reserve a/c transferred)

(*g*) For paying the amount of policy

Joint Life Policy a/c Dr

To partners capital a/c

(For the balance in Joint Life Policy a/c transferred to capital accounts of all the partners).

Problem 7

The firm of X, Y and Z took out a joint survivorship policy on 5th January 2,000 for Rs. 20,000 in order to provide a fund for repayment of a deceased partner's share. The last annual premium of Rs. 500 was paid on 5th January 2003 and X died on 10th February 2003. Assume that the surrender value of the policy was as follows : In 2000 - Nil, in 2001 - Rs. 125, and in 2002 - Rs. 225. The policy amount was realised in full on the death of Y and you are required to show the entries relating to the policy, all these years and the final adjustment on the death of Y, following best method desirable. The partners shared profits in the proportion of $\frac{1}{2}:\frac{1}{4}$ and books were closed on 31st December every year.

Solution

Journal Entries

Date	*Particulars*		*Dr. Amount*	*Cr. Amount*
2000	Joint Life Policy a/c	Dr	500	
	To Bank			500
	(Being the payment of premium)			
	Profit & Loss a/c	Dr	500	
	To Joint life policy reserve a/c			500
	(Being the provision of premium made out of divisible profit).			
	Joint Life Policy reserve a/c	Dr	500	
	To Joint life policy			500
	(Being the entry for bringing down the latter a/c to its surrender value)			
2001	Joint Life Policy a/c	Dr	500	
	To Bank a/c			500
	(Being the payment of premium)			

Date	Particulars		Dr. Amount	Cr. Amount
	P & L a/c To Joint Life Policy Reserve a/c (Being the provision of premium made out of divisible profits)	Dr	500	500
	Joint Life Policy Reserve a/c To Joint life policy a/c (500 - 125) (for bringing down the latter account to its surrender value)	Dr	375	375
2002	Joint Life Policy a/d To Bank a/c (Being the payment of premium)	Dr	500	500
	Joint Life Policy Reserve a/c To Joint life policy a/c (provision for premium made out of divisible profit)	Dr	500	500
	Joint Life Policy Reserve a/c To Joint life policy a/c (125 + 500 = 625 - 225) (For bringing down the latter a/c to its surrender value)	Dr	400	400
2003	Joint Life Policy a/c To Bank a/c (Being the payment of premium)	Dr	500	500
	Bank a/c To Joint Life Policy a/c (Policy amount realised on the death of Y)	Dr	20,000	20,000

Joint Life Policy a/c

Date	Particulars	Amount	Date	Particulars	Amount
2000 Jan. 5,	To Bank a/c	500	2000 Dec. 31,	By J. L. P. R. a/c	500
2001 Jan. 5,	To Bank a/c	500	2001 Dec. 31,	By J. L. P. R. a/c " Balance c/d	375 125
		500			500
2002 Jan. 1, 5	To Balance b/d To Bank a/c	125 500	2002 Dec. 31,	By J. L. P. R. a/c By Balance c/d	400 225
		625			625
2003 Jan. 1, 5	To Balance b/d To Bank a/c	225 500	2003 Feb. 10,	By J. L. P. R. a/c By Bank	225 20,000
Feb. 10,	To X 19500 × $\frac{1}{2}$	9,750			
	By Y 19500 × $\frac{1}{4}$	4,875			
	By Z 19500 × $\frac{1}{4}$	4,875			
		20,225			20,225

Joint Life Policy Reserve a/c

Date	Particulars	Amount	Date	Particulars	Amount
	To Joint Life Policy a/c	500	2000, Dec. 31,	By P & L a/c	500
	To Joint Life Policy a/c	375	2001, Dec. 31,	By P & L a/c	500
	To Balance c/d	125			
		500			500
	To Joint Life Policy a/c	400	2002, Jan. 1,	By Balance b/d	125
	To Balance c/d	225	Dec. 31,	By P & L a/c	500
		625			625
	To Joint Life Policy a/c	225	2003, Jan. 1,	By Balance b/d	225

Problem 8

Sohan and Mohan were partners in a firm sharing profits and losses in the ratio of $\frac{2}{3}$ and $\frac{1}{3}$ respectively. They close their books on 31st December each years. They effected a Joint Assurance Policy on their lives on 10th February 2,000 for a sum of Rs. 80,000. The annual premium on the policy amounting to Rs. 2,000 was payable on 10th February each year. The yearly surrender value of the policy was nil in 2,000, Rs. 260 in 2001, Rs. 500 in 2002, and Rs. 700 in 2,003. Mohan died on 7th March 2004 and the policy amount was received on 20th April 2,004.

Pass the necessary Journal entries to record the above transaction and open the necessary accounts.

Solution

Journal Entries

Date	Particulars		Dr. Amount	Cr. Amount
2,000 Fer. 10,	Joint Life Policy a/c	Dr	2,000	
	To Bank a/c			2,000
	(For the payment of annual premium)			
Dec. 31,	P& L a/c		2,000	
	To Joint Life Policy reserve a/c			2,000
	(provision of premium out of p & L a/c)			
Dec. 31,	J. L. P. R. a/c	Dr	2,000	
	To J. L. P a/c			2,000
	(For bringing down the latter a/c to its surrender value).			
2001, Feb. 10,	Joint life policy a/c	Dr	2,000	
	To Bank a/c			2,000
	(For the payment of annual premium)			

Date	*Particulars*		*Dr. Amount*	*Cr. Amount*
Dec. 31,	P & L a/c To Joint Life Policy Reserve a/c (For the provision of premium out of p& L a/c)	Dr	2,000	2,000
Dec. 31,	Joint Life Policy Reserve a/c (2,000-260) To Joint Life Policy a/c (for bringing down the latter a/c to its surrender value)	Dr	1,740	1,740
2002	Joint Life Policy a/c To Bank a/c (For the payment of annual premium)	Dr	2,000	2,000
Dec. 31,	P & L a/c To Joint Life Policy Reserve a/c (For the provision of premium out of P & L a/c)	Dr	2,000	2,000
	Joint Life Policy Reserve a/c To Joint Life Policy a/c (260 + 2,000 - 500) (For bringing down the value of latter a/c to its surrender value)	Dr	1,760	1,760
2,003 Fer. 10,	Joint Life Policy a/c To Bank a/c (For the payment of annual premium)	Dr	2,000	2,000
Dec. 31,	P & L a/c To Joint Life Policy Reserve a/c (For a reserve equal to the premium paid provided out of profits)	Dr	2,000	2,000
	Joint Life Policy Reserve a/c To Joint Life Policy a/c (500 + 2,000 - 700) (For bringing down the value of latter a/c to its surrender value).	Dr	1,800	1,800
2004, Feb. 10,	Joint Life Policy a/c To Bank (For the payment of annual premium)	Dr	2,000	2,000
Apr. 10,	Bank a/c To Joint Life Policy a/c (For the amount of policy received on the death of Mohan)	Dr	80,000	80,000

Joint Life Policy A/c

Date	*Particulars*	*Amount*	*Date*	*Particulars*	*Amount*
2000 Feb. 10	To Bank	2,000	2000 Dec. 31,	By J. L. P. R. a/c	2,000
2001 Feb. 10,	To Bank	2,000	Dec. 31,	By J. L. P. R. a/c By Balance	1,740 260
		2,000			2,000
2002 Jan. 1, Feb. 10,	To Balance b/d To Balance	260 2,000	2002 Dec. 31,	By J. L. P. R. a/c By Balance c/d	1,760 500
		2,260			2,260

Date	Particulars	Amount	Date	Particulars	Amount
2003			2003		
Jan. 1,	To Balance b/d	500	Dec. 31,	By J. L. P. R. a/c	1,800
Feb. 10,	By Bank	2,000		By Balance c/d	700
		2,500			2,500
2004			2004		
Jan. 1,	To Balance b/d	700	Apr. 20,	By Bank	80,000
Feb. 10,	To Bank	2000		By J. L. P. R. a/c	700
Apr. 20,	To Sohan's Capital a/c	52,000			
	By Mohan's Capital a/c	26,000			
		80,700			80,700

Joint life policy reserve A/c

Date	Particulars	Amount	Date	Particulars	Amount
2000			2000		
Dec. 31,	To Joint life Policy	2,000	Dec. 31,	By P & L a/c	2,000
2001			2001		
	To Joint life Policy a/c	1,740	Dec. 31,	By P & L a/c	2,000
Dec. 31,	By Balance c/d	260			
		2,000			2,000
2002			2002		
	To Joint life Policy a/c	1,760	Jan. 1,	By Balance b/d	260
Dec. 31,	To Balance c/d	500	Dec. 31,	To P & L a/c	2,000
		2,260			2,260
2003			2003		
Dec. 31,	To Joint life Policy .	1,800	Jan. 1,	By Balance b/d	500
	To Balance c/d	700		By P & L a/c	2,000
		2,500			2,500
2004.	To Joint life Policy a/c	700	2004 Jan.	By Balance b/d	700

4. **Individual policies on the life of each partner :-** It instead of one Joint Life Policy, a number of individual policies are taken on the death of a partner the amount of the policy on the life of the deceased partner will be received in cash. The other policies will be shown at their respective surrender value while ascertaining the amount due to the executors of the deceased partner.

Problem 9

X, Y, and Z are partners in a firm sharing profits & losses in the ratio of 5 : 4: 3. The firm had insured the partners lives severally. A's life for Rs. 20,000, B's life for Rs. 16,000 and C's life for Rs. 14,000. The premium were charged to the firms Profit & Loss a/c. The surrender values of these policies were 20% of the policy amount.

Y died on 1-9-2002. Calculate Y's share in policies.

Solution

Claim on Y's policy	Rs. 16,000
Surrender value of X's and Z's	
Life policies 20%	Rs. 6,800
(4,000 + 2,800)	22,800

Y's share - 22,800 × $\frac{4}{12}$ = Rs. 7,600

QUESTIONS

Simple Questions

1. What is an executor's account ?
2. How do you close Revaluation a/c on the death of a partner ?
3. Who is an Executor ?
4. Why is an Executor's a/c prepared ?
5. What are the items to be considered in arriving at the amount due to the deceased partner ?
6. What is a Profit & Loss suspense a/c ?
7. What do you mean by a Joint Life Policy ?
8. State the method of treating joint Life Policy on the death of a partner.

EXERCISE 1

Shiv, Sai and Ananth are partners in a firm sharing profits and losses in the ratio of 5 : 3 : 2. Their Balance Sheet on 31st Dec. 2002 was as follows.

	Amount		*Amount*
Capital accounts		Buildings	35,000
Shiv	50,000	Plant & Machinery	25,000
Sai	30,000	Furniture & Fixture	20,000
Ananth	20,000	Stock	20,000
Creditors	15,000	Debtors	15,000
Bills Payable	5,000	Bank	5,000
	1,20,000		1,20,000

On 1st June 2003, Ananth died. According to the Articles of partnership the executors of the deceased partner are entitled to claim.

1. The Capital of Ananth.
2. Salary of Rs. 100 per month.
3. Interest on capital at 6% per annum.
4. His share of goodwill. The goodwill of the firm amounted to Rs. 5,000.
5. His share of profit to the date of death which shall be calculated on the basis of the average profits of three preceding years.

2,000	Rs. 4,000
2,001	Rs. 5,400
2,002	Rs. 5,000

The drawings of the deceased partner upto the date of death amounted to Rs. 3,400.

Prepare Ananth's Executor's a/c.

Answer : Amount payable to Ananth's Executor Rs. 19,000.

EXERCISE 2

Hema, Malini and Agnihotri are partners in a business sharing Profits & Losses in the ratio of 2 : 2 : 1, respectively. Their Balance Sheet as on 31st December 2,002 was as follows :-

	Amount		*Amount*
Creditors	50,000	Cash at bank	10,000
Capital a/c s		Bills receivable	15,000
Hema	30,000	Debtors	40,000
Malini	50,000	Stock	30,000
Agnihotri	20,000	Furniture	15,000
		Buildings	40,000
	1,50,000		1,50,000

Mrs. Agnihotri died on 30th April 2003 and the Partnership deed provided interalia the following.

1. The deceased partner will be entitled to her share of profits upto the date of death calculated on the previous year's profits.
2. She will be entitled to her share of the goodwill of the firm calculated on the basis of three years purchase of average profit of the last four years. The profit for the past four years are given below :

1,999	-	80,000
2,000	-	50,000
2,001	-	40,000
2,002	-	30,000

The drawings of the deceased partner upto the date of her death amounted Rs. 2,000.
Interest on capital was to be allowed at 6% per annum.
Surviving partners agreed that Rs. 10,400 should be paid to the executors immediately and the balance in 2 yearly instalments with interest at 6% on the outstanding balance.
Show Agnihotri's capital a/c, and the account of the executors of the deceased.

Answer : Amount due to Agnihotri Rs. 50,400
Last instalment paid Rs. 21,200.

EXERCISE 3

Raju, Hari and Ananth were partners sharing profits in the ratio of 5 : 3 : 2. Their Balance Sheet as on 31-12-2002 is as follows.

	Amount		*Amount*
Capital :-		Cash	12,400
Raju	26,000	Stock	36,800
Hari	20,000	Debtors	34,000
Ananth	18,000	Investments	28,000
Creditors	38,000	Furniture	14,000
Bills payable	28,000	Bills receivable	21,800
Reserve	15,000	Goodwill	10,000
P & L a/c	12,000		
	1,57,000		1,57,000

Ananth died on 1-10-2003. Profit of the deceased partner to the date of death to be calculated on the basis of the average of the three preceding years.

The goodwill of the firm to be taken at 2 year's purchase of the average profits of the preceding four years profits for the past four years were :

1999	-	6,800
2000	-	3,600
2001	-	4,200
2002	-	3,600

Bad debts Rs. 2,000
Reserve for doubtful debts 5%
Depreciate stock 5%
Depreciate furniture 15%
Appreciate Investments 10%
Prepaid Rent amounted to Rs. 400

Prepare Revaluation a/c, Capital account of partners and the Balance Sheet assuming the executors of Ananth agreed to keep the amount as loan at 8%.

Answer : Total of Balance sheet Rs. 1,52,330

EXERCISE 4

Mr. kumar Mr. Khan and Mr. Kiran are partners sharing Profits and Losses in the ratio of 2 : 3 : 5 respectively. Their Balance Sheet as on 1-1-2003 was as under :-

	Amount		*Amount*
Bills payable	3,000	Goodwill	10,000
Bank O/D	2,000	Cash	8,000
Sundry creditors	8,000	Stock	22,000
Capital		Sundry debtors	9,000
Kumar	15,000	Buildings	38,000
Khan	22,000	Furniture	6,000
Kiran	45,000	Machinery	12,000
General Reserve	10,000		
	1,05,000		1,05,000

Mr. Kumar died on 30-9-2003. The partnership deed provided that.

(*a*) The heirs of the deceased partner shall get his share in the goodwill as valued on the date of death. The goodwill on 30-9-2003 was valued at Rs. 50,000.

(*b*) The heirs shall get the share of profit upto the date of death of the partner, calculated on the basis of the profits for the immediate previous years of death (The profit in 2002 was Rs. 24,000).

(*c*) The Deceased partner is entitled to get interest on capital at 8% per annum.

Mr. Kumar had drawn Rs. 1,800 upto his death. It was decided to settle his entire capital account through Bank Overdraft.

Mr. Khan and Kiran who contributed with equal share decided to maintained goodwill at its full value.

Give journal entries and show the capital account of Mr. Kumar and show the Balance Sheet immediately after settling kumar's a/c.

Answer : Balance sheet total Rs. 1,47,700.

EXERCISE 5

Following is the Balance Sheet of Prakash, Prasad and Prashanth who share profits in the ratio of 2 : 2 : 1 on 31-12-2002.

	Amount		*Amount*
Creditors	27,000	Cash	11,700
Bank O/D	7,000	Investments	22,000
Bills Payable	14,000	Bills Receivable	4,000
Reserve fund	2,000	Debtors	21,600
Capitals		Stock	13,700
Prakash	12,000	Furniture	8,000
Prasad	16,000	Machinery	15,000
Prashanth	18,000		
	96,000		96,000

On 1-7-2003 Prasad died and his dependent are entitled to get the following.

1. His share of Capital and Reserve fund.
2. His share of profit upto the date of death calculated on the basis of average profit of last 2 years.
3. His share of goodwill to be valued at 3 times the average profit of last four years.

Profit for last four years were :

1999 — 3,600
2000 — 2,400
2001 — 2,800
2002 — 3,200

4. His share in the profits or losses arising out of Revaluation of assets and liabilities are as under :-

Stock Rs. 14,800, Investments Rs. 13,900 Machinery Rs. 12,700. Reserve for Bad Debts Rs. 750. Prepare Revaluation a/c, Partners Capital accounts and the Balance Sheet of surviving partners.

Answer : Total of Balance Sheet Rs. 90,200.

EXERCISE 6

P, Q and R sharing profit & losses in the ratio of 5 : 3 : 2 took out a Joint Life Policy for Rs 15,000 paying annual premium of Rs. 600 starting from 1st January 1995. The surrender value of the policy was as follows :-

1995 - Nil, 1996 - Rs. 200 1997 - Rs. 500 1998 - Rs. 850

Q died on 6th June 1999 and the policy amount was realised. The books of the firm were closed on 31st December every year.

Show the Joint Life Policy and Joint Life Policy Reserve account for all the years

(Bangalore University, B. Com. April 2002)

EXERCISE 7

X, Y and Z were partners sharing profit in the ratio of 3 : 2 : 1. They took a Joint Life Policy for Rs. 24,000 on 1-1-1996, by paying annual premium of Rs. 2,000. The firm closes its books on 31st December each year. The values were, 1996 - Rs. Nil, 1997 - Rs. 480, 1998 - Rs. 1,080 and 1999 - Rs. 1,600. 'Y' died on 30-9-2000 and the policy was received on 18-11-2000. Prepare (a) Joint Life Policy a/c (b) Joint Life Policy Reserve a/c.

(Bangalore University B. Com. April 2001)

EXERCISE 8

'M', 'N' and 'O' sharing profit and losses in the ratios of 2 : 2 : 1 took a Joint Life Policy for Rs. 1,00,000 on 1-1-92, paying an annual premium of Rs. 5,000.

The surrender values were as follows :

1992 ; Nil, 1993 - Rs 1,500, 1994 Rs. 4,000 1995 Rs. 6,000.

'M' died on 31st July 1996 and the Insurance Co. paid the claim on 5th September 1996, Books of accounts are closed on 31st December annually.

Show (*i*) Joint Life Policy a/c (*iii*) Joint life Policy Reserve a/c from 1992 to 1996

(Bangalore University B. Com. Nov. 1997)

21

CHAPTER

Partnership Accounts—Amalgamation

MEANING

When two or more organisations, carrying on similar business combine to form a new firm, such a combination is called amalgamation.

Types of Amalgamation

Amalgamation may take place in any of the following ways :

(a) Two or more sole traders may amalgamate into a partnership firm.

(b) A sole trading concern may amalgamate with a partnership firm. this is similar to admission of a new partner.

(c) Amalgamation between two or more partnership firms.

Objects of Amalgamation

(a) To secure economies associated with large scale production.

(b) To obtain a larger share of market for a product, thus create a monopoly.

(c) To obtain diversity of products.

(d) To avoid competition

(e) To secure skill and efficiency of persons carrying on different business.

ACCOUNTING PROCEDURE INVOLVED UNDER AMALGAMATION IN THE BOOKS OF OLD FIRM

1. Transfer all reserves and surplus and losses if any appearing in the Balance Sheet to capital accounts of partners in the profit sharing ratio.

   (a) For Transfer of Reserves and Accumilated Profit

   Reserve Fund a/c Dr.
   To Capital a/c

   (b) For transfer of debit balance of profit and loss account

   Capital a/c Dr.
   To Profit and Loss a/c

2. Revalue assets and liabilies of the amalgamating unit when they are taken over at a value other than book value. This is done by preparing a Revaluation account.
3. Transfer the profit or loss on Revaluation of assets and liabilities to the capital accounts.

   (a) In case of profit
   Revaluation a/c Dr.
   To Capital a/c

   (b) In case of loss
   Capital a/c Dr.
   To Revaluation a/c

4. The assets and liabilites of the amalgamating units which are not taken over will be transferred to capital accounts of the partners in the ratio of their capitals.
5. When goodwill is created or raised in the books of amalgamating unit
   Goodwill a/c Dr.
   To Capital a/c
6. Close the assets and liabilities which have been taken over by the new firm. The entry is

   (a) New Firm's a/c Dr.
   To Various Assets a/c
   (For transfer of assets)

   (b) Various liabilities a/c Dr.
   To New Firm a/c
   (For transferring liabilities)

6. Close the firms account and capital accounts of partners by the following entry
   Capital account Dr.
   To New Firm a/c

IN THE BOOKS OF NEW FIRM

1. Record the assets and liabilities taken over
   Assets a/c Dr.
   To Liabilities a/c
   To Capital account
2. For writing off goodwill
   Capital accounts Dr.
   To Goodwill

Note : Goodwill is written off in the New Profit Sharing Ratio.

3. Capital account of partners should be adjusted to the requirement of the new firm

   (a) If surplus is withdrawn

   Capital a/c Dr.
   To Bank a/c

   (b) If deficit is made good by bringing in cash

   Bank a/c Dr.
   To Capital account
   (For cash introduced to bring the capital to the required level)

Problem 1

The Balance Sheets of 'AB' and 'CD', the two partnership firms on the date of amalgamation were as follows :-

Liabilities	*Amount*	*Amount*	*Assets*	*Amount*	*Amount*
	AB	CD		AB	CD
Sundry Creditors	43000	42000	Cash at Bank	6,000	2,000
Reserve Fund	—	23000	Sundry Debtors	40,000	49,000
Capitals			Stock	60,000	40,000
A	50,000	—	Investments	16,000	—
B	30,000	—	Furniture	1,000	2,000
C	—	38,000	Leasehold Premisses	—	24,000
D	—	22,000	Goodwill	—	8,000
	1,23,000	1,25,000		1,23,000	1,25,000

It was agreed that the balance sheet of 'AB' should be adjusted as follows before amalgamation

(*a*) That Rs. 800 is to be reserved for doubtful debts.
(*b*) Stock and furniture be depreciated by 10%.
(*c*) Investments to be taken over at Rs. 20,000.
(*d*) Rs. 600 be reserved for discount on creditors.

The following adjustments were agreed upon in 'CD' Balance Sheet

(*a*) Debtors, stock and furniture be taken at book values.
(*b*) Leasehold premises and goodwill be valued at Rs. 36,000 and Rs. 12,000 respectively.

The capitals of A, B, C and D in the new firm were fixed at Rs. 50,000 ; Rs. 30,000 ; Rs. 60,000 ; and Rs. 40,000 respectively.

1. Pass journal entires (*a*) in the books of A and B ; and (*b*) in the books of C and D to give effect to the above arrangement.
2. Show the Balance Sheet of each firm as adjusted.
3. Prepare Balance Sheet of the new firm as amalgamated

(Bangalore University, B.Com, April, 2001)

Solution

In the Books of A & B

Date	*Particulars*		*Dr. Amount*	*Cr. Amount*
	Revaluation a/c	Dr.	6,900	
	To Reserve for doubtful debts			800
	To Stock			6,000
	To Trade Fixtures			100
	(For decrease in the value of assets and provisions made)			
	Investments a/c	Dr.	4,000	
	Reserve for Discount on Creditor	Dr.	600	
	To Revaluation a/c			4,600
	(Being the increase in the value of investment and provision on creditors made)			

Date	Particulars		Dr. Amount	Cr. Amount
	A's Capital a/c	Dr.	1,150	
	B's Capital a/c	Dr.	1,150	
	To Revaluation a/c			2,300
	(Loss on revaluation transferred)			
	Bank a/c	Dr.	2,300	
	To A's Capital a/c			1,150
	To B's Capital a/c			1,150
	(Being the amount brought in by A & B to make up their capital as agreed)			

In the Books of C and D

Date	Particulars		Dr. Amount	Cr. Amount
	Leasehold premises a/c	Dr.	12,000	
	Goodwill a/c	Dr.	4,000	
	To Revaluation a/c			16,000
	(Being the value of lease and goodwill adjusted)			
	Revaluation a/c	Dr.	16,000	
	To C's Capital a/c			8,000
	To D's Capital a/c			8,000
	(Profit on revaluation transferred)			
	Reserve fund a/c	Dr.	23,000	
	To C's Capital a/c			11,500
	To D's Capital a//c			11,500
	(Being reserve transferred)			
	Bank a/c	Dr.	2,500	
	To C's Capital a/c			2,500
	(Being the amount brought in by C to make up his capital to Rs. 40,000 as agreed)			
	D's Capital a/c	Dr.	1,500	
	To Bank a/c			1,500
	(Being the amount withdrawn by him to bring down his capital to Rs. 40,000 as agreed)			

A's Capital A/c

	Amount		Amount
To Revaluation a/c	1,150	By Balance b/d	50,000
To Balance c/d	50,000	By Bank a/c	1,150
	51,150		51,150

B's Capital A/c

	Amount		Amount
To Revaluation a/c	1,150	By Balance b/d	30,000
To Balance c/d	30,000	By Bank	1,150
	31,150		31,150

C's Capital A/c

	Amount		Amount
To Balance c/d	60,000	By Balance b/d	38,000
		By Revaluation a/c	8,000
		By Reserve fund	11,500
		By Bank	2,500
	60,000		60,000

D's Capital A/c

	Amount		Amount
To Bank a/c	1,500	By Balance b/d	22,000
To Balance c/d	40,000	By Revaluation a/c	11,500
		By Reserve fund	8,000
	41,500		41,500

Adjusted Balance Sheet of A & B

		Amount			Amount
Creditors	43,000		Cash at Bank		83,000
Less : Discount	600		Debtors	40,000	
		42,400	Less : Reserve	800	
A's Capital		50,000			39,200
B's Capital		30,000	Stock		54,000
			Investments		20,000
			Office furniture		900
		1,22,400			1,22,400

Adjusted Balance Sheet of C & D

	Amount			Amount
Sundry Creditors	42,000	Cash at Bank		3,000
C's Capital a/c	60,000	Debtors	50,000	
D's Capital a/c	40,000	Less : Reserve	1,000	
				49,000
		Stock		40,000
		Trade fixtures		2,000
		Leasehold		36,000
		Goodwill		12,000
	1,42,000			1,42,000

Balance Sheet of New Firm

		Amount			Amount
Sundry Creditors	85,000		Cash at Bank		11,300
Less : Discounts	600	84,400	Sundry Debtors	90,000	
			Less : Reserve	1,800	88,200
Capital Accounts :-					
A	50,000		Stock		94,000
B	30,000		Investment		20,000
C	60,000		Office furniture		900
D	40,000	1,80,000	Trade fixtures		2,000
			Leasehold		36,000
			Goodwill		12,000
		2,64,400			2,64,400

Problem 2

Two firms 'P' & 'Q' & 'R' & 'S' agreed to amalgamate their business. Their positions as on December 31, 1998 were as follows :

Liabilities	*Amount* P & Q	*Amount* R & S	*Assets*	*Amount* P & Q	*Amount* R & S
Creditors	1,04,000	52,000	Cash at Bank	1,56,000	65,000
Capitals :			Debtors	1,30,000	1,40,000
P	1,82,000	—	Stock in Trade	42,000	26,000
Q	1,30,000		Office building	78,000	—
R	—	91,000	Furniture	10,000	13,000
S	—	65,000			
	4,16,000	2,08,000		4,16,000	2,08,000

Creditors and Debtors were not taken over by the new firm PQRS. Office buildings were retained by P and Q but new firm agreed to pay a monthly rent of Rs. 400. The cash required for working of the new firm was estimated at Rs. 1,30,000 to be provided by the partners in their new profit sharing proportions as under :

P $\frac{3}{10}$ Q $\frac{3}{10}$ R $\frac{2}{10}$ S $\frac{2}{10}$

1. Write the books of P & Q and R & S.
2. Prepare the amalgamated Balance Sheet of PQRS

(Bangalore University, B.Com, April, 1999)

Solution

In the Books of P & Q

Date	Particulars		Dr. Amount	Cr. Amount
	P's Capital a/c	Dr.	2,12,333	
	Q's Capital a/c	Dr.	1,51,667	
	To Cash a/c			1,56,000
	To Debtors a/c			1,30,000
	To Buildings a/c			78,000
	(Being assets not taken over by new firm transferred to partners capital accounts in the ratio of 7 : 5).			
	Creditors a/c	Dr.	1,04,000	
	To P's Capital a/c			60,667
	To R's Capital a/c			43,333
	(Being creditors not taken over by the new firm transferred to capital account of partners in the capital ratio of 7 : 5)			
	P's Capital a/c	Dr.	30,334	
	Q's Capital a/c	Dr.	21,666	
	To PQRS			52,000
	(Being capital accounts closed by transfer to new firm PQRS)			
	PQRS a/c	Dr.	52,000	
	To Stock a/c			42,000
	To Furniture a/c			10,000
	(Being assets taken over by the new firm)			

In the Books of R & S

Date	Particulars		Dr. Amount	Cr. Amount
	R's Capital a/c	Dr.	98,583	
	S's Capital a/c	Dr.	70,417	
	To Cash a/c			65,000
	To Debtors a/c			1,04,000
	(Being the assets not taken over transferred to capital accounts in 7 : 5 ratio)			
	Creditors a/c	Dr.	52,000	
	To R's Capital a/c			30,333
	To S's Capital a/c			21,667
	(Being creditors not taken over by the new firm transferred to capital accounts in the ratio of 7 : 5.)			
	PQRS a/c	Dr.	39,000	
	To Stock a/c			26,000
	To Furniture a/c			13,000
	(Being the assets taken over by the new firm)			
	R's Capital a/c	Dr.	22,750	
	S's Capital a/c	Dr.	16,250	
	To PQRS a/c			39,000
	(Being capital accounts closed by transfer to the new firm)			

Balance Sheet of PQRS

Dr.	*Amount*	*Cr.*	*Amount*
P's Capital a/c (30,334 + 39,000)	69,334	Cash at Bank	1,30,000
Q's Capital a/c (21,666 + 39,000)	60,666	Stock	68,000
R's Capital a/c (22,750 + 26,000)	48,750	Furniture	23,000
S's Capital a/c (16,250 + 26,000)	42,250		
	2,21,000		2,21,000

Working Note :-

It is assumed that Bank Balance have not been taken over, hence cash required for the new firm is to be contributed by partners in their new profit sharing ratio PQRS : 3 : 3 : 2 : 2.

Problem 3

The Balance Sheet of 'A' & 'B' and 'C' & 'D' as on 31st December, 1997 were as follows :-

Liabilities	*Amount* A & B	*Amount* C & D	*Assets*	*Amount* A & B	*Amount* C & D
Capitals					
A	20,000	—	Land & Building	20,000	24,000
B	20,000	—	Machinery	14,000	16,000
C	—	20,000	Furniture	6,000	7,000
D	—	20,000	Debtors	12,000	17,000
Creditors	30,000	20,000	Cash at Bank	6,000	2,000
Loan	—	20,000	Stock	16,000	20,000
Outstanding expenses	4,000	6,000			
	74,000	86,000		74,000	86,000

The two firms decided to amalgamate to form ABCD on 1st January, 1998. The partners continue to share profits equally as they were doing before the merger. Prior to amalgamation the following Revaluation of assets and liabilities should be made.

	A and B	C and D
Land & Building	20,000	20,000
Machinery	14,000	16,000
Furniture	5,000	5,000
Debtors	11,000	14,000
Stock	16,000	16,000
Outstanding Expenses	4,000	7,000

In addition the following things are to be carried out :

(*a*) The new firm will not take over the loan of 'C' and 'D'.

(*b*) The goodwill of 'A' and 'B' and that of C and D should be valued initially at Rs. 20,000 and Rs. 10,000 respectively but for the purpose of the new firm the combined goodwill of the firm should be Rs. 24,000.

(c) Each partner should have Rs. 28,000 as capital in the new firm and that cash should be brought if necessary. Show :

1. The two revaluation accounts
2. Capital accounts before and after amalgamation.
3. The opening Balance Sheet of new firm.

(Bangalore University, B.Com, November, 1998)

Solution

In the Books of A & B

Revaluation A/c

	Amount		*Amount*
To Furniture a/c	1,000	By Loss on Revaluation transferred	
To Debtors	1,000	to capital accounts	
		A	1,000
		B	1,000
	2,000		2,000

Capital Accounts

Liabilities	*Amount*	*Amount*	*Assets*	*Amount*	*Amount*
	A	B		A	B
To Revaluation a/c loss	1,000	1,000	By Balance b/d	20,000	20,000
To New firm's capital a/c	29,000	29,000	By Goodwill a/c	10,000	10,000
	30,000	30,000		30,000	30,000

In the books of C & D

Revaluation A/c

	Amount		*Amount*
To Land	4,000	By Loss transferred to	
To Furniture	2,000	C's Capital a/c	7,000
To Debtors	3,000	D's Capital a/c	7,000
To Stock	4,000		
To Outstanding expenses	1,000		
	14,000		14,000

Capital Accounts

	Amount	*Amount*		*Amount*	*Amount*
	C	D		C	D
To Revaluation a/c	7,000	7,000	By Balance b/d	20,000	20,000
To New firm's capital a/c	28,000	28,000	By Goodwill a/c	5,000	5,000
			By Loan a/c	10,000	10,000
	35,000	35,000		35,000	35,000

Capital Accounts (on Amalgamation)

Particulars	Amount	Amount	Particulars	Amount	Amount
	A	B		A	B
To Goodwill	1,500	1,500	By Balance b/d	29,000	29,000
To Balance c/d	28,000	28,000	By Bank a/c	500	500
	29,500	29,500		29,500	29,500
	C	D		C	D
To Goodwill a/c	1,500	1,500	By Balance b/d	28,000	28,000
To Balance c/d	28,000	28,000	By Bank a/c	1,500	1,500
	29,500	29,500		29,500	29,500

Balance Sheet of ABCD

Libilities	Amount	Assets	Amount
Creditors	50,000	Bank	12,000
Outstanding expenses	11,000	Debtors	25,000
Capital Accounts :		Stock	32,000
A	28,000	Furniture	10,000
B	28,000	Machinery	30,000
C	28,000	Land	40,000
D	28,000	Goodwill	24,000
	1,73,000		1,73,000

Working Note :

1. Treatment of Goodwill. The difference between original value and revised value of goodwill i.e., Rs. 6,000 is to be written off amongst all partners equally.
2. The partners capital must be Rs. 28,000 each and deficit must be made good in cash.
3. Bank balance is arrived at as follows :

Balance taken over (A Rs. 6,000 + C Rs. 2,000)	8,000
Cash introduced by partners (A Rs. 500 + B Rs. 500 + C Rs. 1,500 + D Rs. 1,500)	4,000
	12,000

Problem 4

On 1st January 2003, AB and CD who had previously engaged in competitive business agrees to amalgamate. The Balance Sheet of the two firms on 31st December, 2002 were as follows :

Liabilities	Amount	Amount	Assets	Amount	Amount
	AB	CD		AB	CD
Creditors	3,000	25,000	Stock	50,000	75,000
Bills Payable	6,000	—	Debtors	30,000	45,000
Bank Overdraft	—	10,300	Premises	20,000	—
A's Capital	50,000	—	Machinery	5,000	20,000
B's Capital	50,000	—	Bank	1,500	—
C's Capital	—	52,500	Furniture	500	300
D's Capital	—	52,500	War Bonds	2,000	—
	1,09,000	1,40,300		1,09,000	1,40,300

A valuation of assets of both business was made and it was agreed that the premises and machinery belonging to AB should be taken over by new firm at Rs. 25,000 and Rs. 10,000 respectively. CD were to be credited with Rs. 5,000 as the value of certain patent right they possessed which became the property of the partnership and which was not included in the Balance Sheet. All the other assets were taken at the values stated in the respective Balance Sheet, except War Bonds belonging to AB which was not taken over. Both firms agreed to discharge their own liabilities and it was agreed that A and B should introduce cash to make their capitals equal to total of CD.

Pass journal entries in the books of the old firms and the opening entries in the books of the new firm. Prepare the Balance Sheet of the new firm.

Solution

In the Books of A and B

Date	*Particulars*		*Dr. Amount*	*Cr. Amount*
	Premises a/c	Dr.	5,000	
	Machinery a/c	Dr.	5,000	
	To Revaluation a/c			10,000
	(Being increase in the value of premises and machinery)			
	Revaluation a/c	Dr.	10,000	
	To A's Capital a/c			5,000
	To B's Capital a/c			5,000
	(Being profit on revaluation shared equally)			
	Creditors a/c	Dr.	3,000	
	Bills payable a/c	Dr.	6,000	
	To A's Capital a/c			4,500
	To B's Capital a/c			4,500
	(Being liabilities not taken over transferred to partners capital account in profit sharing ratio)			
	A's Capital a/c	Dr.	1,000	
	B's Capital a/c	Dr.	1,000	
	To National War Bonds a/c			2,000
	(Being Assets not taken over by the new firm transferred to capital accounts)			
	ABCD	Dr.	1,17,000	
	To Bank a/c			1,500
	To Stock a/c			50,000
	To Debtors a/c			30,000
	To Premises a/c			25,000
	To Machinery a/c			10,000
	To Furniture a/c			500
	(Being the various assets taken over by the new firm transferred to new firm's account)			
	A's Capital a/c	Dr.	58,500	
	B's Capital a/c	Dr.	58,500	
	ToABCD			1,17,000
	(Being transfer of capital to new firm)			

Working Note :

1. A's capital is arrived at as follows :

Opening Balance	50,000
Add : Profit on revaluation	5,000
liabilities transferred	4,500
	59,500
Less : National War Bonds	1,000
	58,500

2. Similarly B's Capital is calculated

In the Books of C & D

Date	*Particulars*		*Dr. Amount*	*Cr. Amount*
	Patent rights a/c	Dr.	5,000	
	To Revaluation a/c			5,000
	(Being patent rights brought into account)			
	Revaluation a/c	Dr.	5,000	
	To C's Capital a/c			2,500
	To D's Capital a/c			2,500
	(Being profit on revaluation shared equally)			
	Creditors a/c	Dr.	25,000	
	Overdraft a/c	Dr.	10,300	
	To C's Capital a/c			17,650
	To D's Capital a/c			17,650
	(Being transfer of liabilities not taken over to accounts of C and D)			
	ABCD a/c	Dr.	1,45,300	
	To Stock a/c			75,000
	To Debtors a/c			45,000
	To Machinery a/c			20,000
	To Patents a/c			5,000
	To Furniture a/c			300
	(Being assets taken over by the new firm)			
	C's Capital a/c	Dr.	72,650	
	D's Capital a/c	Dr.	72,650	
	To ABCD			1,45,300
	(Being transfer of capital to new firm)			

In the Books of ABCD

Date	*Particulars*		*Dr. Amount*	*Cr. Amount*
	Bank a/c	Dr.	1,500	
	Stock a/c	Dr.	50,000	
	Debtors a/c	Dr.	30,000	
	Premises a/c	Dr.	25,000	
	Machinery a/c	Dr.	10,000	
	Furniture a/c	Dr.	500	
	To A's Capital a/c			58,500
	To B's Capital a/c			58,500
	(Being assets taken over from A and B)			

Date	Particulars		Dr. Amount	Cr. Amount
	Stock a/c	Dr.	75,000	
	Debtors a/c	Dr.	45,000	
	Machinery a/c	Dr.	20,000	
	Patents a/c	Dr.	5,000	
	Furniture a/c	Dr.	300	
	To C's Capital a/c			72,650
	To D's Capital a/c			72,650
	(Being Assets of C and D taken over)			
	Bank a/c	Dr.	28,300	
	To A's Capital a/c			14,150
	To B's Capital a/c			14,150
	(Being cash brought by A and B to make their capital equal to that of C and D).			

Balance Sheet of ABCD as on 1-1-2003

		Amount		Amount
Capital Accounts			Cash at Bank (28,300 + 1,500)	29,800
A	72,650		Debtors	75,000
B	72,650		Stock	1,25,000
C	72,650		Patent rights	5,000
D	72,650	2,90,600	Premises	25,000
			Machinery	30,000
			Furniture	800
		2,90,600		2,90,600

Problem 5

The following were the Balance Sheet as at 31st December, 2002 of the two firms M/s A and B and M/s X and Y.

Liabilities	A & B Amount	X & Y Amount	Assets	A & B Amount	X & Y Amount
Sundry Creditors	20,000	25,000	Cash at Bank	5,600	6,700
Mrs. A's Loan	5,000	—	Stock	20,400	18,300
Capitals			Debtors	15,000	20,000
A	40,000	—	Furniture	4,000	5,000
B	20,000	—	Premises	40,000	—
X	—	24,000	Investments	—	15,000
Y	—	16,000			
	85,000	65,000		85,000	65,000

The two firms decided to amalgamate their business as from 1st January, 2003. For this purpose it was agreed that

(*a*) Mrs. A's loan should be repaid and that the investment of Mr. X and Y be not taken over by the new firm.
(*b*) Goodwill of M/s A and B was fixed at Rs. 8,000 and that of M/s X and Y at Rs. 10,000. Goodwill a/c in the new firm was to be written off.
(*c*) Premises were revalued at Rs. 50,000 but the stock of M/s A and B was found overvalued by Rs. 4,000. The stock of M/s X and Y was undervalued by Rs. 2,000.
(*d*) A provision of 5% was created for bad debts of both the firms.
(*e*) The total capital of the new firm was to be Rs. 80,000 and the capital of each partner was to be in his profit sharing ratio which was to be 3 : 2 : 3 : 2.

Close the books of both the firms and pass opening entries of M/s A B X Y. Also give the Balance Sheet of the newly constitute firm.

Solution

In the Books of A & B

Revaluation A/c

		Amount		*Amount*
To Stock		40,000	By Premises	10,000
To Provision for bad debts		750		
To Profit transferred to Capital Accounts :-				
A	2,625			
B	2,625	5,250		
		10,000		10,000

Capital Accounts

	Amount A	*Amount* B		*Amount* A	*Amount* B
To New Firm's a/c	46,625	26,625	By Balance b/d	40,000	20,000
			By Revaluation a/c	2,625	2,625
			By Goodwill	4,000	4,000
	46,625	26,625		46,625	26,625

In the books of X & Y

Revaluation A/c

		Amount		*Amount*
To Provision for Bad Debts		1,000	By Stock	2,000
To Profit transferred to capital accounts				
X	500			
Y	500	1,000		
		2,000		2,000

Capital Accounts

	Amount X	Amount Y		Amount X	Amount Y
To Investment (1 : 1)	7,500	7,500	By Balance b/d	24,000	16,000
To New firm's a/c	22,000	14,000	By Revaluation a/c	500	500
			By Goodwill	5,000	5,000
	29,500	21,500		29,500	21,500

Working Note :

1. **Treatment of Goodwill :** Goodwill is not to appear in the books of the new firm. Hence each partner is credited with this share of goodwill in the old profit sharing ratio and the goodwill account is closed by debiting partner in new profit sharing ratio (Rs. 18,000 in 3 : 2 : 3 : 2 ratio)
2. Capital of the firm is to be Rs. 80,000 in 3 : 2 : 3 : 2 ratio. The excess or deficit in capitals is to be transferred to current account opened in the name of each partner.

In the Books of the New Firm

Date	Particulars		Dr. Amount	Cr. Amount
	Cash a/c	Dr.	600	
	Stock a/c (20,400 – 4,000)	Dr.	16,400	
	Sundry Debtors a/c	Dr.	15,000	
	Furniture a/c	Dr.	4,000	
	Premises a/c	Dr.	50,000	
	Goodwill a/c	Dr.	8,000	
	To Sundry Creditors			20,000
	To Provision for bad debts			750
	To A's Capital a/c			46,625
	To B's Capital a/c			26,625
	(Being Assets and liabilities taken over from A and B at revised values)			
	Cash a/c	Dr.	6,700	
	Stock a/c (18,300 + 2,000)	Dr.	20,300	
	Debtors a/c	Dr.	20,000	
	Furniture a/c	Dr.	5,000	
	Goodwill a/c	Dr.	10,000	
	To Sundry Creditors			25,000
	To Provision for Bad Debts			1,000
	To X's Capital a/c			22,000
	To Y's Capital a/c			14,000
	(Being Assets & liabilities takn over from X and Y at revised values)			
	A's Capital a/c	Dr.	5,400	
	B's Capital a/c	Dr.	3,600	
	C's Capital a/c	Dr.	5,400	
	D's Capital a/c	Dr.	3,600	
	To Goodwill a/c			18,000
	(Being total goodwill written off in new profit sharing ratio)			

Date	Particulars		Dr. Amount	Cr. Amount
	A's Capital a/c	Dr.	17,225	
	B's Capital a/c	Dr.	7,025	
	To A's Current a/c			17,225
	To B's Current a/c			7,025
	(Being excess in A and B's capital account transferred to their current account)			
	X's Current a/c	Dr.	7,400	
	Y's Current a/c	Dr.	5,600	
	To X's Capital a/c			7,400
	To Y's Capital a/c			5,600
	(Being deficit in capital accounts transferred to current accounts)			

Balance Sheet of ABXY as on 1-1-2003

	Amount			Amount
Creditors	45,000	Cash at Bank		7,300
Capitals :		Stock		36,700
A	24,000	Debtors	35,000	
B	16,000	Less : Reserve	1,750	
X	24,000			33,250
Y	16,000	Furniture		9,000
Current Account :		Premises		50,000
A	17,225	Current Accounts :		
B	7,025	X	7,400	
		Y	5,600	13,000
	1,49,250			1,49,250

Problem 6

(Accounting record when amalgamation is made during the year)

A and B who make up their yearly accounts to 31st December, decided to amalgamate with C and D who make up their accounts to 30th June of each year. The amalgamation was to take place as from 1st July, 2003 and the first accounts of the new firm. A, B, C and D were to be drawn up to 30th June, 2004. As stock had not been taken at the date of merger, it was agreed that A and B should have 10% of their net assets for that period in lieu of actual profits. Profits were shared as follows :

A and B : A : B : 3 : 2 : C and D : C; 1 : D : 2

It was agreed in the new firm that as between A and B : C and D the same ratios were to continue, A and B taking half of the profits and C and D half.

The Trial Balance of the new firm at 30th June, 2004 was as follows :

Trial Balance

	Dr.	Cr.
Creditors		14,000
Captials		
A		12,000
B		8,000
C		6,000
D		6,000
Sales A & B : $\frac{1}{2}$ year to 30-6-2003		10,000
ABCD year to 30-6-2004		48,000
Sundry Assets	40,000	
Purchases	36,000	
Selling expenses	12,000	
Stock A & B on 1-1-2003	10,000	
C & D on 1-7-2004	6,000	
	1,04,000	1,04,000

Assuming that the closing stock to be Rs. 20,000, show the Trading and Profit & Loss a/c of ABCD for the period to 30th June, 2004 and Balance Sheet at that date.

Solution

Trading and Profit & Loss A/c

		Amount		Amount
To Stock (10,000 + 6,000)		16,000	By Sales (10,000 + 48,000)	58,000
To Purchases		36,000	By Stock	20,000
To Gross Profit c/d		26,000		
		78,000		78,000
To Selling expenses		12,000	By Gross Profit b/d	26,000
To Balance c/d		14,000		
		26,000		26,000
To A & B (10% of Rs. 10,000)			By Balance b/d	14,000
A	600			
B	400			
		1000		
To A and B $\left(\frac{1}{2}\right.$ of Rs. 13,000 :$\left.\right)$				
A	3,900			
B	2,600			
		6,500		
To C & D $\left(\frac{1}{2}\right.$ of Rs. 13,000$\left.\right)$				
C	3,250			
D	3,250			
		6,500		
		14,000		14,000

Balance Sheet as on 30-6-2004

		Amount		Amount
Creditors		14,000	Sundry Assets	40,000
Capital Accounts :			Stock	20,000
A	12,000			
B	8,000			
C	6,000			
D	6,000			
		32,000		
Current Accounts :-				
A	4,500			
B	3,000			
C	3,250			
D	3,250			
		14,000		
		60,000		60,000

Working Notes :-

(1) The net profit of Rs. 14,000 is to be distributed as follows between A and B :

(*a*) 10% of Rs. 10,000 (net assets in lieu of profits) Rs. 1,000 in the ratio of 3 : 2. So A gets Rs. 600 and B Rs. 400.

(*b*) Of the remaining profit (Rs. 14,000 – Rs. 1,000) Rs. 13,000 50% is to be shared between A and B in the ratio of 3 : 2. So A gets $\left(6{,}500 \times \frac{3}{5}\right)$ Rs. 3,900 and B gets Rs. 2,600.

(*c*) Between C and D remaining Rs. 6,500 shared equally.

(*d*) Profits are to be transferred to the current account of respective partners.

Problem 7

(Amalgamation of a Sole Trader and Partnership Firm)

A and B are partners in a business sharing profits & losses in the ratio of 4 : 3. Their Balance Sheet on 31st March, 2003 was as follows :

	Amount		Amount
Bills Payable	12,000	Plant	46,000
Creditors	37,500	Horses and Cart	7,700
A's Capital	80,000	Furniture	2,800
B's Capital	65,000	Debtors	81,000
		Stock	37,900
		Cash in Hand	500
		Cash at Bank	18,600
	1,94,500		1,94,500

They amalgamated with 'C' who had been carrying on similar business. The Balance Sheet showed ; Debtors Rs. 28,000 ; Stock Rs. 12,300 ; Plant Rs. 21,500 ; Furniture Rs. 1,200 ;

Horses and Carts Rs. 3,600 and Creditors Rs. 15,850. C is to bring cash to make his capital Rs. 60,000 after making a reserve of 5% on Debtors and reducing the value of stock by 10%. The Goodwill of the firm A and B is valued at Rs. 14,000 and revaluation of their plant and Horses and Carts are made at Rs. 47,500 and Rs. 9,700 respectively at which amounts the new firm A, B and C is to take them over. Profits are shared equally in the new firm. A is to draw out a sum which will leave his capital same as B's.

Record the above transactions in the books of the old firm and prepare the Balance Sheet of the new firm as on 1st April, 2003

Solution

In the books of C

Balance Sheet as on 31st March, 2003

	Amount		*Amount*
Creditors	15,850	Debtors	28,000
C's Capital a/c	50,750	Stock	12,300
(Balancing figure)		Plant	21,500
		Furniture	1,200
		Horses and Carts	3,600
	66,600		66,600

Revaluation A/c

	Amount		*Amount*
To Reserve on Debtors	1,400	By C's Capital a/c	5,190
To Stock	3,790		
	5,190		5,190

In the books of A & B

	Amount		*Amount*
To Profit on revaluation		By Plant	1,500
transferred to capital accounts		By Horses and Carts	2,000
A	10,000	By Goodwill	14,000
B	7,500		
	17,500		17,500

Capital Accounts

	Amount	*Amount*		*Amount*	*Amount*
	A	B		A	B
To Bank a/c	17,500	—	By Balance b/d	80,000	65,000
(Excess withdrawn)			By Revaluation a/c profit	10,000	7,500
To Balance c/d	72,500	7,2500			
	90,000	72,500		90,000	72,500

Balance Sheet as on 1st April, 2003

		Amount			Amount
Creditors		53,350	Plant		69,000
Bills Payable		12,000	Horses & Cart		13,300
Capital Accounts :			Furniture		4,000
A	72,500		Debtors	1,09,000	
B	72,500		Less : Reserve	1,400	
C	60,000				1,07,600
		2,05,000	Stock		46,410
			Goodwill		14,000
			Cash		16,040
		2,70,350			2,70,350

Working Notes :

1. Amount of cash to be introduced by 'C' is arrived at as follows :

Capital as per Balance Sheet	50,750
Less : Loss on revaluation	5,190
	45,560
Cash required	6,000
Cash to be introduced	14,440

2. Bank Balance is arrived at as follows :

As per Balance Sheet of A and B	19,100
Add : Cash introduced by C	14,440
	33,540
Less : Excess capital withdrawn by A	17,500
Balance at end	16,040

QUESTIONS

Simple Questions

1. What do you mean by amalgamation ?
2. Mention different types of amalgamation.
3. State the objects of amalgamation.

EXERCISE 1

X and Y amalgmate their business on 1st January, 2001, their Balance Sheet being as follows :-

Balance Sheet of X

	Amount		Amount
Creditors	25,000	Cash at Bank	2,500
Loan from Mrs. 'X'	7,500	Debtors	20,000
Capital	35,000	Stock	15,000
		Furniture & Fixture	2,000
		Plant	28,000
	67,500		67,500

Balance Sheet of Y

	Amount			Amount
Creditors	40,000	Stock		25,000
Capital	23,000	Debtors	25,000	
		Less : Reserve	1,000	24,000
		Bills Receivable		2,000
		Plant		12,000
	63,000			63,000

The following adjustments were agreed upon :

(*a*) The goodwill of X and Y was agreed at Rs. 7,500 and Rs. 5,000 respectively.
(*b*) The plant of X was to be depreciated by 10% and that of Y to be taken at book value.
(*c*) 5% reserve for doubtful debts was to be created on debtors of both the partners.
(*d*) X's stock was to be appreciated by 15% and Y's to be depreciated by 5%.
(*e*) X's fixture were taken over at Rs. 2,300 and the creditor of each were brought by 5% reserve for discount.
(*f*) The private liability of X and the Bills Recoverable of Y were not brought in.
(*g*) 'Y' is to be credited with Rs. 3,000 for patent right which he possesses and which are not to be deemed as partnership property.
(*h*) X brought in his Bank Balance and Y was to bring in the necessary amount in cash in order to equal his capital to that of X.

Pass the journal entries that are necessary for incorporating the various adjustments above in the books of X and Y separately and prepare Balance Sheet in the books of amalgamated firm.

Answer : Total of Amalgamated Balance Sheet Rs. 1,61,750.

EXERCISE 2

The following two firms carrying on separate business decide to amalgamate on the terms as under :

1. That the new partnership to take over the stock of both the firms at 10% less than book values and that 5% reserve for doubtful debts be credited before taking over the book debts.
2. That the leasehold premises of X and Y be taken over at Rs. 12,000 and the trade fixtures of A and B and X and Y be taken over at Rs. 1,500 and Rs. 2,000 respectively.

3. The liabilities of both the firms are taken over less 5% Reserve for discounts.
4. X and Y who were sharing profits $\frac{2}{3}$ and $\frac{1}{3}$ should divide between themselves half the share of net profit in the new firm and should contribute capital of Rs. 30,000 in the like proportion.
5. That the firm of A and B (equal partners) be credited with Rs. 10,000 for goodwill and must provide cash to make their capital equal to half the joint capital of the new partnership and take half share in profits.

Balance Sheet of A & B

		Amount			*Amount*
Creditors		11,000	Cash at Bank		1,500
Capitals :			Debtors	10,000	
A	10,000		Less : Reserve	500	
B	10,000				9,500
		20,000	Stock		18,000
			Trade Fixtures		2,000
		31,000			31,000

Balance Sheet of X and Y

		Amount		*Amount*
Creditors		30,000	Cash at Bank	5,500
Capitals :			Debtors	12,000
X –	14,000		Stock	15,000
Y –	7,000	21,000	Trade Fixutres	3,000
			Leasehold property	15,500
		51,000		51,000

Pass the necessary entries in the books of both the firms to give effect to the above arrangement and show the opening Balance Sheet in the Amalgamated firm.

Answer : Total of Balance Sheet of amalgamated firm Rs. 98,950.

EXERCISE 3

The following were the Balance Sheet of the firms of C and D and X and Y respectively on December, 2002 on which date they decide to amalgamate their business.

Balance Sheet of C and D

	Amount			*Amount*
Creditors	26,000	Cash at Bank		5,000
Bills payable	5,000	Debtors	30,000	
Reserve	4,000	Less : Reserve	1,000	
C's Capital a/c	50,000			29,000
D's Capital a/c	40,000	Stock		40,000
		Freehold property		51,000
	1,25,000			1,25,000

Balance Sheet of X and Y

	Amount		Amount
Creditors	27,000	Cash at Bank	6,000
Capitals :		Bills Receivable	4,000
X	30,000	Debtors	24,000
Y	20,000	Stock	30,000
		Office furniture	2,000
		Motor van	5,000
		Goodwill	6,000
	77,000		77,000

The terms of amalgamation were as follows :

1. The new firm was to take over the assets and liabilities of both the concern subject to C and D meeting their Bills Payable which were immediately due.
2. C and D's assets were valued thus :-
   Debtors Rs. 26,000 ; Stock Rs. 35,000 ; Freehold property Rs. 65,000 and Goodwill Rs. 8,000.
3. X and Y's assets were valued thus :
   Debtors 22,000 ; Stock 34,000 ; Office furniture Rs. 1,000 ; and Goodwill at Rs. 3,000.
4. Y took over the Motor Vans at an agreed value of Rs. 3,000 and also Rs. 5,000 from the bank balance.
5. The capitals of the partners in the new firm were fixed at : C Rs. 40,000 ; D Rs. 30,000 ; X Rs. 20,000 ; and Y is 10,000 and any excess or any partners capital account after the above adjustment was to be temporarily held over on a separate current account of the partner concerned.
6. C and D were sharing profits in proportion to capitals X and Y equally.
   Close the books of old firms and open the books of Amalgamated firms.

Answer : Balance Sheet Total of Amalgamated firm Rs. 1,99,000.

22

CHAPTER

Partnership Accounts — Dissolution

DISSOLUTION OF PARTNERSHIP

Dissolution of partnership refers to a process under which the activities of a partnership firm are wound up.

Dissolution of the Firm vs. Dissolution of Partnership

1. Dissolution of partnership among all the partners of a firm is called "dissolution of the firm" whereas dissolution of partnership involves breaking of partnership relation between a few and not all partners.
2. Dissolution of partnership is temporary whereas dissolution of partnership firm is permanent.
3. Dissolution of partnership does not necessarily involve dissolution of firm, whereas dissolution of firm does necessarily involve dissolution of partnership.

Modes of Dissolution of a Firm

According to Sections 40 to 44 of the Indian Partnership Act 1932, a firm can be dissolved in any one of the following circumstances :

1. **Dissolution by Agreement :** A firm may be dissolved with the consent of all the partners or in accordance with a contract among them.
2. **Dissolution by Notice :** Any partner can dissolve the partnership by giving in writing to all the other partners if the partnership is at will.
3. **Contingent Dissolution :** This happens under the following circumstances :
   (*a*) By the expiry of the term for which the firm was constituted.
   (*b*) By the completion of the adventure for which the firm was constituted.
   (*c*) On the death of a partner.
   (*d*) On the insolvency of a partner.
4. **Compulsory Distribution :** This happens under the following circumstances :-
   (*a*) By the adjudication of all the partners or all but one partner as insolvent.
   (*b*) By the happening of an event which makes it unlawful for carrying on the business.

5. **Dissolution of Court :** A court may dissolve the firm under any one of the following ground :
   (*a*) Where a partner has become insane.
   (*b*) Where a partner becomes permanently incapable of doing business.
   (*c*) Where a partner is guilty of misconduct carrying on the business.
   (*d*) Where a partner wilfully commits breach of agreement.
   (*e*) Where a partner transfers all his shares to a third party.

Mode of Settlement of Accounts on Dissolution

Section 48 of the Indian Partnership Act lays down the following rules for the settlement of accounts on dissolution.

(*a*) **Payment of Losses :** Losses are to be paid first out of profits, next out of capital and lastly, by the partners individually in proportion to their profit sharing ratio.

(*b*) **Distribution of Assets :** The assets of the firm, including the amount contributed by the partners to make up the deficiency of capital are to be applied in the following order :
   (*a*) Debts to third parties
   (*b*) Partners loans and advances, and
   (*c*) Capital.

The balance if any, is to be distributed among the partners in proportion to their profit sharing ratio.

(*c*) **Payment of firms debts and personal debts :** The property of the firm shall be applied in the first instance in payment of debts of the firm and if any surplus remains, it will be applied in payment of personal debts. Again partner's personal property shall be applied first in payment of personal debts and if there is any surplus, it will be applied in payment of firm's debts.

ACCOUNTING ENTRIES ON DISSOLUTION

1. Transfer all the Assets at book values except cash, bank, losses and expenses a/c :
   Realisation a/c Dr.
   To Assets account
2. Transfer all third party liabilities to the credit side of Realisation a/c :
   Liabilities a/c Dr.
   To Realisation a/c
3. Transfer created funds such as Reserve for Doubtful debts, Depreciation fund etc., to the credit side of Realisation a/c
   Reserve for doubtful debts (Dep. Fund) a/c Dr.
   To Realisation a/c
4. Transfer the credit balance of profit, Reserve etc., to the credit side of partners capital a/c
   P & L a/c / Reserve a/c Dr.
   To Partner's Capital a/c
5. Transfer the debit balance of loss or expenses account.
   Partner's Capital a/c Dr.
   To P & L a/c or Expenses a/c

6. Recording cash realised on Sale of Assets :
   Bank a/c Dr.
   To Realisation a/c

Note : No entry is passed for recording loss or profit on realisation of any asset.

7. Recording cash paid on external liabilities
   Realisation a/c Dr.
   To Bank a/c

Note : No entry is passed for recording any profit on payment of any liability

8. Recording cash received on realisation of any unrecorded asset :
   Bank a/c Dr.
   To Realisation a/c
9. Recording payment for any unrecorded liabilities
   Realisation a/c Dr.
   To Bank a/c
10. Recording any asset taken over by any partner
    Partner's Capital a/c Dr.
    To Realisation a/c
11. Recording any liability taken over by any partner
    Realisation a/c Dr.
    To Partner's Captial a/c
12. Recording expenses of Realisation
    (*a*) If paid by the firm :
    Realisation a/c Dr.
    To Bank a/c
    (*b*) If payable in the form of commission to a partner
    Realisation a/c Dr.
    To Partner's Capital a/c
    (*c*) Payable personally by any partner :
    No entry
    (*d*) Paid personally by a partner but out of firm's cash :
    Partner's Capital a/c Dr.
    To Cash a/c
13. Record Profit on Realisation :
    Realisation a/c Dr.
    To Partner's Capital a/c
14. Record Loss on Realisation :
    Partner's Capital a/c Dr.
    To Realisation a/c
15. Record repayment of partner's loan :
    Partner's Loan a/c Dr.
    To Bank a/c
16. Any amount received from partner against debit balance in his capital a/c
    Bank a/c Dr.
    To Partner's Capital a/c
17. Amount paid to partners in settlement of accounts
    Partner's Capital a/c Dr.
    To Bank a/c

Problem 1

P, Q and R are partners sharing profits and losses equally on 31st March, 2001, their Balance sheet stood as follows :

Liabilities	*Amount*	*Assets*	*Amount*
Bills Payable	16,000	Cash in Bank	15,000
Creditors	1,19,000	Debtors	1,25,000
Loan from Q	25,000	Stock	2,90,000
General Reserve	30,000	Furniture	40,000
P's Current a/c	15,000	Machinery	1,20,000
Q's Current a/c	15,000	R's Current a/c	30,000
P's Capital a/c	2,00,000		
Q's Capital a/c	1,00,000		
R's Capital a/c	1,00,000		
	6,20,000		6,20,000

The firm was dissolved on the above mentioned date. P agreed to pay creditors at par. Q took over the entire furniture for Rs. 36,000. The remaining assets were sold for Rs. 5,53,000. Bills payable were retired for a discount of Rs. 100 received for payment before the due date of maturity. Expenses of dissolution amounted to Rs. 1,200.

Prepare important ledger accounts and cash book. The current accounts and the capital accounts may be prepared in columnar form. **(C.S. Foundation, June, 2001)**

Solution

Realisation A/c

Particulars	*Amount*	*Particulars*	*Amount*
To Debtors a/c	1,25,000	By Bills payable a/c	16,000
To Stock a/c	2,90,000	By Creditors a/c	1,19,000
To Furniture a/c	40,000	By A's Current a/c	
To Machinery a/c	1,20,000	— Furniture a/c	36,000
To P's Current a/c	1,19,000	By Bank a/c	
Creditors a/c		(Debtors, Stock and Machinery)	5,53,000
To Bank (Bills payable 16,000 – 100)	15,900		
To Bank-expenses a/c	1,200		
To P's Current a/c	4,300		
To Q's Current a/c	4,300		
To R's Current a/c	4,300		
	7,24,000		7,24,000

Loan from Q

Particulars	*Amount*	*Particulars*	*Amount*
To Bank a/c	25,000	By Balance b/d	25,000
	25,000		25,000

P's Current A/c

Particulars	Amount	Particulars	Amount
To P's Capital a/c Transfer	1,48,300	By Balance b/d	15,000
		By General Reserve	10,000
		By Realisation a/c — Creditors	1,19,000
		By Realisation a/c — Profit	4,300
	1,48,300		1,48,300

P's Capital A/c

Particulars	Amount	Particulars	Amount
To Bank	3,48,300	By Balance b/d	2,00,000
		By P's Current a/c	1,48,300
	3,48,300		3,48,300

Q's Current A/c

Particulars	Amount	Particulars	Amount
To Realisation a/c	36,000	By Balance b/d	15,000
		By General Reserve	10,000
		By Realisation a/c – Profit	4,300
		By Q's Capital a/c — Transfer	6,700
	36,000		36,000

Q's Capital A/c

Particulars	Amount	Particulars	Amount
To Q's Current a/c	6,700	By Balance b/d	1,00,000
To Bank	93,300		
	1,00,000		1,00,000

R's Current A/c

Particulars	Amount	Particulars	Amount
To Balance b/d	30,000	By General Reserve	10,000
		By Realisation a/c — Profit	4,300
		By R's Capital a/c — Transfer	15,700
	30,000		30,000

R's Capital A/c

Particulars	Amount	Particulars	Amount
To R's Current a/c	15,700	By Balance b/d	1,00,000
To Bank	84,300		
	1,00,000		1,00,000

Bank A/c

Particulars	Amount	Particulars	Amount
To Balance b/d	15,000	By Realisation a/c – Bills Payable	15,900
To Realisation a/c	5,53,000	By Realisation a/c – Expenses	1,200
		By Loan from Q	25,000
		By P's Capital a/c	3,48,300
		By Q's Capital a/c	93,300
		By R's Capital a/c	84,300
	5,68,000		5,68,000

Problem 2

A's and B were partners sharing profits in the ratio of 3 : 2. On 1st July, 1998, their Balance Sheet was as under :

Liabilities		Amount	Assets	Amount
Sundry Creditors		20,000	Stock	12,000
Capital			Debtors	15,000
A	5,000		Furniture	600
B	3,000		Cash	400
		8,000		
		28,000		28,000

The firm was dissolved on the above date. The assets realised only Rs. 16,000. Expenses came to Rs. 500. A's Private Estate could pay only Rs. 1,000. B has no surplus. Close the books of the firm by showing relevant ledger accounts.

(University of Madras, B. Com., May 2000)

Solution

Realisation A/c

Particulars	Amount	Particulars	Amount
To Stock a/c	12,000	By Cash – Assets realised a/c	16,000
To Debtors a/c	15,000	By Loss transferred to partners capitals	
To Furniture a/c	600		
To Cash – Expenses a/c	500	$A = \frac{3}{5} \times 12{,}100$	7,260
		$B = \frac{2}{5} \times 12{,}100$	4,840
	28,100		28,100

Partner's Capital A/c

Particulars	Amount	Amount	Particulars	Amount	Amount
	A	B		A	B
To Realisation — Loss	7,260	4,840	By Balance b/d	5,000	3,000
			By Cash – Private estate	1,000	—
			By deficiency a/c (Balancing figure)	1,260	1,840
	7,260	4,840		7,260	4,840

Cash A/c

Particulars	Amount	Particulars	Amount
To Balance b/d	400	By Realisation a/c	500
To Realisation a/c — Assets Realised	16,000	By Sundry Creditors a/c	
To A's Capital a/c — Private estate	1,000	(Balancing figure–given to creditors)	16,900
	17,400		17,400

Sundry Creditors

Particulars	Amount	Particulars	Amount
To Cash a/c	16,900	By Balance b/d	20,000
To Deficiency a/c	3,100		
	20,000		20,000

Deficiency A/c

Particulars	Amount	Particulars	Amount
To A's Capital a/c	1,260	By Sundry Creditors a/c	3,100
To B's Capital a/c	1,840		
	3,100		3,100

Problem 3

A, B and C were equal partners. Their Balance sheet on 31-12-2000 stood as under, when the firm was dissolved ;

Liabilities	Amount	Assets	Amount
Sundry Creditors	32,000	Machinery	12,000
A's Capital	4,000	Furniture	3,000
B's Capital	3,000	Sundry Debtors	5,000
		Stock	4,000
		Cash at Bank	2,800
		C's Capital	12,200
	39,000		39,000

The Assets realised as under :-

Machinery Rs. 6,000 ; Furniture Rs. 1,000 ; Sundry Debtors Rs. 4,000 ; and Stock Rs. 3,000.

The expenses of realisation came to Rs. 1,400.

A's personal properties are not sufficient to pay his personal liabilities, whereas in B's and C's private estate there is a surplus of Rs. 2,400 and Rs. 3,000 respectively.

Show necessary accounts closing the books of the firm. **(C.A., Foundation, May 2001)**

Solution

Realisation A/c

Particulars	*Amount*	*Particulars*	*Amount*
To Sundry Assets :		By Bank a/c – Machinery a/c	6,000
Machinery a/c	12,000	— Furniture a/c	1,000
Furniture a/c	3,000	— Debtors a/c	4,000
Debtors a/c	5,000	— Stock a/c	3,000
Stock a/c	4,000	By Loss on Realisation a/c	
To Bank a/c – Expenses	1,400	transferred to Capital Accounts :	
		A' a/c	3,800
		B' a/c	3,800
		C' a/c	3,800
	25,400		25,400

Bank A/c

Particulars	*Amount*	*Particulars*	*Amount*
To Balance b/d	2,800	By Realisation a/c	1,400
To Realisation a/c	14,000	By Creditors a/c (Balancing figure)	20,800
To B's Capital a/c	2,400		
To C's Capital a/c	3,000		
	22,200		22,200

Creditors A/c

	Amount		*Amount*
To Bank a/c	20,800	By Balance b/d	32,000
To Deficiency a/c	11,200		
	32,000		32,000

Partners Capital A/c

Particulars	*A*	*B*	*C*	*Particulars*	*A*	*B*	*C*
To Balance b/d	—	—	12,200	By Balance b/d	4,000	3,000	—
To Realisation a/c	3,800	3,800	3,800	By Bank a/c	—	2,400	3,000
To Deficiency a/c	200	1,600	—	By Deficiency a/c	—	—	13,000
	4,000	5,400	16,000		4,000	5,400	16,000

Deficiency A/c

Particulars	*Amount*	*Particulars*	*Amount*
To C's Capital a/c	13,000	By Creditors a/c	11,200
		By A's Capital a/c	200
		By B's Capital a/c	1,600
	13,000		13,000

Problem 4

Nihar, Nikhil, and Narayan were partners in a firm sharing profits in the ratio of 2 : 2 : 1. The firm was dissolved on 1st January, 1998 and on that date their Balance sheet were as under :

Liabilities	*Amount*	*Assets*	*Amount*
Capitals :		Fixed Assets	25,000
Nihar	20,000	Debtors	10,000
Nikhil	15,000	Stock	4,000
Reserve Fund	10,000	Narayan's Capital	1,000
Creditors	6,000	Cash at Bank	11,000
	51,000		51,000

Prepare realisation a/c, Capital accounts and Bank a/c after taking into consideration of the following :-

(*a*) Nikhil took over creditors at Rs. 5,000
(*b*) Fixed Assets were sold at Rs. 26,000
(*c*) Debtors were bad in full
(*d*) Nihar took over stock at Rs. 3,500
(*e*) Narayan was allowed the right to use the firm name for his business for which he paid Rs. 6,000. **(Calcutta University, B. Com (Pass), 1999)**

Solution

Realisation A/c

Particulars	*Amount*	*Particulars*	*Amount*
To Fixed Assets a/c	25,000	By Creditors a/c	6,000
To Debtors a/c	10,000	By Bank a/c :	
To Stock a/c	4,000	Fixed Assets a/c	26,000
To Nikhil's Capital – Creditors	5,000	Goodwill purchased by Narayan	6,000
		By Nihar's Capital a/c – Stock	3,500
		By Loss on realisation transferred to	
		Nihar a/c	1,000
		Nikhil a/c	1,000
		Narayan a/c	500
	44,000		44,000

Nihar's Capital A/c

Particulars	Amount	Particulars	Amount
To Realisation a/c	3,500	By Balance b/d	20,000
To Realisation a/c	1,000	By General Reserve	4,000
To Bank a/c	19,500		
	24,000		24,000

Nikhil's Capital A/c

Particulars	Amount	Particulars	Amount
To Realisation a/c	1,000	By Balance b/d	15,000
To Bank a/c	23,000	By Reserve a/c	4,000
		By Realisation a/c	5,000
	24,000		24,000

Narayan's Capital A/c

Particulars	Amount	Particulars	Amount
To Balance b/d	1,000	By Reserve a/c	2,000
To Realisation a/c	500		
To Bank a/c	500		
	2,000		2,000

Bank A/c

Particulars	Amount	Particulars	Amount
To Balance b/d	11,000	By Nihar's a/c	19,500
To Realisation a/c	32,000	By Nikhil's a/c	23,000
		By Narayan's a/c	500
	43,000		43,000

Problem 5

A, B and C commenced business on 1-4-96 with a capital of Rs. 25,000 ; Rs. 20,000 and Rs. 15,000 respectively. Profits and losses are shared in the ratio of 4 : 3 : 3. Capitals carried interest @ 5% p.a. During the year ended on 31-3-97 they made a profit of Rs. 12,000 (before allowing interest on capitals). Drawings of each partner were Rs. 2,500 per year.

On 31-3-97 the firm was dissolved. Creditors on that date were Rs. 6,000. The assets realised Rs. 60,000. Give necessary accounts to close the books

(Sri Ventakteshwara University, B. Com, April, 1999)

Solution

Profit & Loss Adjustment A/c

Particulars		Amount	Particulars	Amount
To Interest on Capital a/c			By Net Profit	12,000
A' a/c	1,250			
B' a/c	1,000			
C' a/c	750			
		3,000		
To Profit transferred to				
A' a/c	3,600			
B' a/c	2,700			
C' a/c	2,700			
		9,000		
		12,000		12,000

A's Capital A/c

Particulars	Amount	Particulars	Amount
To Drawings a/c	2,500	By Balance b/d	25,000
To Balance c/d	27,350	By Interest on capital a/c	1,250
		By P & L adjustment a/c	3,600
	29,850		29,850

B's Capital A/c

Particulars	Amount	Particulars	Amount
To Drawings	2,500	By Balance b/d	20,000
To Balance c/d	21,200	By Interest on capital	1,000
		By P & L Adjustment a/c	2,700
	23,700		23,700

C's Capital A/c

Particulars	Amount	Particulars	Amount
To Drawings	2,500	By Balance b/d	15,000
To Balance c/d	15,950	By Interest on capital a/c	750
		By P & L adjustment a/c	2,700
	18,450		18,450

Balance Sheet of ABCD as on 31-3-97

Liabilities	Amount	Assets	Amount
A's Capital a/c	27,350	Sundry Assets (Balancing figure)	70,500
B's Capital a/c	21,200		
C's Capital a/c	15,950		
Creditors a/c	6,000		
	70,500		70,500

Realisation A/c

Particulars	*Amount*	*Particulars*	*Amount*
To Sundry Assets a/c	70,500	By Creditors a/c	6,000
To Cash (Balancing figure)	6,000	By Cash a/c	60,000
		By Loss transferred to	
		A's Capital a/c	4,200
		B's Capital a/c	3,150
		C's Capital a/c	3,150
	76,500		76,500

A's Capital A/c

Particulars	*Amount*	*Particulars*	*Amount*
To Realisation a/c – loss	4,200	By Balance b/d	27,350
To Cash a/c	23,150		
	27,350		27,350

B's Capital A/c

Particulars	*Amount*	*Particulars*	*Amount*
To Realisation a/c – loss	3,150	By Balance b/d	21,200
To Cash	18,050		
	21,200		21,200

C's Capital A/c

Particulars	*Amount*	*Particulars*	*Amount*
To Realisation a/c	3,150	By Balance b/d	15,950
To Cash a/c	12,800		
	15,950		15,950

Bank A/c

Particulars	*Amount*	*Particulars*	*Amount*
To Realisation a/c	60,000	By Realisation a/c	6,000
		By A's Capital a/c	23,150
		By B's Capital a/c	18,050
		By C's Capital a/c	12,800
	60,000		60,000

Problem 6

A, B and C were partners sharing profits and losses in the ratio of 3 : 2 : 1. On 31-12-95 their Balance Sheet was as follows :

Liabilities	Amount	Assets		Amount
Sundry Creditors	15,400	Cash at Bank		3,500
Bills payable	3,600	Stock		19,800
A's Loan	10,000	Debtors	15,000	
Capital Accounts :		Less : Provision	1,000	
A	20,000			14,000
B	16,000	Joint Life Policy		4,000
C	8,000	Plant & Machinery		43,000
Reserve fund	12,000			
	85,000			85,000

The firm was dissolved on 1-1-96. Joint Life Policy was taken over by A at Rs. 5,000 ; Stock Realised Rs. 18,000 ; Debtors realised Rs. 14,500 ; Plant & Machinery was sold for Rs. 36,000 ; Liabilities were paid in full. In addition, one bill for Rs. 700 under discount was dishonoured and had to be paid by the firm. Give the necessary ledger accounts to close the books of the firm. **(University of Madras, B. Com, April, 1999)**

Solution

Realisation A/c

Particulars	Amount	Particulars	Amount
To Stock a/c	19,800	By Provision for Bad Debts a/c	1,000
To Debtors a/c	15,000	By Sundry Creditors a/c	15,400
To Joint life policy a/c	4,000	By Bills payable a/c	3,600
To Plant & Machinery a/c	43,700	By A's Capital a/c	5,000
To Bank :-		(Joint life policy)	
Sundry Creditors a/c	15,400	By Bank :	
Bills payable a/c	3,600	Stock a/c	18,000
To Bank a/c		Debtors a/c	14,500
(payment of dishonoured bill)	700	Plant & Machinery a/c	36,000
		By Loss on realisation transferred to capital a/c	
		$A = 8{,}700 \times \frac{3}{6}$	4,350
		$B = 8{,}700 \times \frac{2}{6}$	2,900
		$C = 8{,}700 \times \frac{1}{6}$	1,450
	1,02,200		1,02,200

A's Capital A/c

Particulars	Amount	Particulars	Amount
To Realisation (Joint life policy) a/c	5,000	By Balance b/d	20,000
To Realisation – loss a/c	4,350	By Reserve a/c	6,000
To Bank (loan a/c)	10,000	By A's loan a/c	10,000
To Bank a/c	16,650		
	36,000		36,000

B's Capital A/c

Particulars	*Amount*	*Particulars*	*Amount*
To Realisation – loss a/c	2,900	By Balance b/d	16,000
To Bank a/c	17,100	By Reserve a/c	4,000
	20,000		20,000

C's Capital A/c

Particulars	*Amount*	*Particulars*	*Amount*
To Realisation – loss a/c	1,450	By Balance b/d	8,000
To Bank a/c	8,550	By Reserve a/c	2,000
	10,000		10,000

Bank A/c

Particulars	*Amount*	*Particulars*	*Amount*
To Balance b/d	3,500	By Realisation :	
To Realisation a/c		— Creditors a/c	15,400
— Stock a/c	18,000	— Bills payable a/c	3,600
— Debtors a/c	14,500	By A's Capital a/c	10,000
— Plant & Machinery a/c	36,000	— loan a/c	
		By Realisation a/c	
		— Bills Discounted a/c	700
		By A's Capital a/c	16,650
		By B's Capital a/c	17,100
		By C's Capital a/c	8,550
	72,000		72,000

Problem 7

Ram and Hanuman are partners in a firm, they share profits and losses in the ratio of 1 : 2. On 1st April, 1999, they decided to dissolve the partnership and on that date the Balance Sheet of the firm was as under :

Liabilities	*Amount*	*Assets*		*Amount*
Sundry Creditors a/c	50,000	Cash at Bank		10,000
General Reserve a/c	60,000	Sundry Debtors	50,000	
Hanuman's Loan a/c	30,000	Less : Provision for		
Capital Accounts :-		Doubtful Debts	2,000	48,000
Ram a/c	1,50,000	Stock a/c		1,02,000
Hanuman a/c	1,00,000	Furniture a/c		30,000
		Machinery & Plant a/c		80,000
		Land & Building a/c		1,20,000
	3,90,000			3,90,000

The sales of firm's properties realised Rs. 1,00,000 from Stock ; Rs. 34,000 from Furniture and Rs. 1,00,00 from Land and Building. Rs. 45,000 were collected from Debtors and Creditors were paid off at a discount of Rs. 1,000.

Machinery and Plant are taken over by Ram at their book value. The expenses of realisation amounted to Rs. 4,000.

Pass Jounral entries to close the books of the firm and prepare necessary ledger accounts.

(C.A. Foundation, May 1999)

Solution

Journal Entries

Date	*Particulars*		*Dr. Amount*	*Cr. Amount*
	Realisation a/c	Dr.	3,82,000	
	To Sundry Debtors a/c			50,000
	To Stock a/c			1,02,000
	To Furniture a/c			30,000
	To Machinery & Plant a/c			80,000
	To Land & Building a/c			1,20,000
	(Being assets transferred to realisation a/c)			
	Sundry Creditors a/c	Dr.	50,000	
	Provision for Doubtful Debts a/c	Dr.	2,000	
	To Realisation a/c			52,000
	(Being sundry creditors and provision for doubtful debts transferred to realisation a/c)			
	Bank a/c	Dr.	2,79,000	
	To Realisation a/c			2,79,000
	(Being amount realised by sale of furniture, land & building, stock and collection from debtors)			
	Ram's Capital a/c	Dr.	80,000	
	To Realisation a/c			80,000
	(Being machinery and plant taken over by Ram at Book Value)			
	Realisation a/c	Dr.	4,000	
	To Bank a/c			4,000
	(Being expenses of realisation paid)			
	Realisation a/c	Dr.	49,000	
	To Bank a/c			49,000
	(Being sundry creditors paid off)			
	Ram's Capital a/c	Dr.	8,000	
	Hanuman's Capital a/c	Dr.	16,000	
	To Realisation a/c			24,000
	(Being loss on realisation transferred to capital accounts of partners)			
	Hanuman's Loan a/c	Dr.	30,000	
	To Bank a/c			30,000
	(Being Hanuman's loan paid off)			

Date	Particulars		Dr. Amount	Cr. Amount
	General Reserve a/c	Dr.	60,000	
	To Ram's Capital a/c			20,000
	To Hanuman's Capital a/c			40,000
	(Being the general reserve transferred to partner's capital accounts)			
	Ram's Capital a/c	Dr.	82,000	
	Hanuman's Capital a/c	Dr.	1,24,000	
	To Bank a/c			2,06,000
	(Being partners capital amount paid off)			

Realisation A/c

Particulars	Amount	Particulars		Amount
To Sundry Debtors a/c	50,000	By Sundry Creditors a/c		50,000
To Stock a/c	1,02,000	By Provision for Doubtful Debts a/c		2,000
To Furniture a/c	30,000	By Bank :-		
To Machinery & Plant a/c	80,000	Stock	1,00,000	
To Land & Building a/c	1,20,000	Furniture	34,000	
To Bank – Expenses a/c	4,000	Land & Building	1,00,000	
To Bank – Sundry Creditors a/c	49,000	Debtors	45,000	
				2,79,000
		By Ram's Capital a/c — Machinery & Plant taken over.		80,000
		By Loss transferred to Capital a/c :-		
		Ram	8,000	
		Hanuman	16,000	
				24,000
	4,35,000			4,35,000

Ram's Capital A/c

Particulars	Amount	Particulars	Amount
To Realisation a/c – Machinery & Plant	80,000	By Balance b/d	1,50,000
To Realisation a/c	8,000	By General Reserve	20,000
To Bank a/c	82,000		
	1,70,000		1,70,000

Hanuman's Capital A/c

Particulars	Amount	Particulars	Amount
To Realisation a/c – loss	16,000	By Balance b/d	1,00,000
To Bank a/c	1,24,000	By General Reserve	40,000
	1,40,000		1,40,000

Bank A/c

Particulars	*Amount*	*Particulars*	*Amount*
To Balance b/d	10,000	By Realisation a/c – Sundry Creditors	49,000
To Realisation a/c – Sale of Assets	2,79,000	By Realisation a/c – Expenses	4,000
		By Hanuman's Loan a/c	30,000
		By Ram's Capital a/c	82,000
		By Hanuman's Capital a/c	1,24,000
	2,89,000		2,89,000

INSOLVENCY OF A PARTNER – GARNER vs. MURRAY CASE

If a partner's capital account shows a debit balance on dissolution and he is unable to make good the deficiency, he is said to be insolvent. In Garner vs. Murray case, it was ruled that in the absence of any agreement to the contrary, the deficiency in the insolvent partner's capital account must be borne by the other solvent partners in proportion to their capitals as they stood just prior to dissolution and before the realisation of assets. The two important points arising out of this ruling is that :

(*a*) Solvent partners should bring in cash equal to their respective share of loss on realisation.

(*b*) Deficiency in the capital account of the insolvent partner is to be shared by solvent partners in the capital ratio.

Determination of Capital Ratios under Fixed and Fluctuating Capital Method

Partners can maintain their capitals either under fixed or fluctuating capital method. Under fixed capital method, original capital remains unaltered unless additional capital is invested or withdrawn. Adjustment relating to drawings, interest on capital or drawings, share in profit or loss, salary, commission etc., are not made in the capital account but in a separate "current account" opened for the purpose, in the name of each partner. Hence in case of fixed capital method, the ratio for sharing deficiency is the fixed capital ratio itself.

Fluctuating capital method is a system of maintaining capital accounts in which all adjustments relating to partners interest, drawings, commission, salary etc., are made in the capital account itself. So in case of fluctuating capital method the deficiency shall be shared in capital ratio after adjustments for reserves, drawings, accumulated profit / loss, partners salary etc., are made.

Problem 8

The position of X, Y and Z on June 30, 1998 was as follows :

Liabilities	*Amount*	*Assets*	*Amount*
Sundry Creditors a/c	63,000	Cash a/c	25,000
X's Loan a/c	40,000	Sundry Assets a/c	1,70,000
X's Capital a/c	64,000	Z's Capital a/c	78,000
Y's Capital a/c	36,000		
Profit & loss a/c	70,000		
	2,73,000		2,73,000

Profits and losses are shared : X $\frac{4}{7}$; Y $\frac{1}{7}$ and Z $\frac{2}{7}$. Z became insolvent and the firm was dissolved on the above date. Sundry Assets realise Rs. 1,40,000. Sundry creditors are paid Rs. 60,000 in full settlement. Expenses amount to Rs. 8,000.

Assume the capitals are not fixed. Close the books of the firm by opening necessary ledger accounts. **(Delhi University, B. Com, 2000)**

Solution

Realisation A/c

Particulars	*Amount*	*Particulars*	*Amount*
To Sundry Assets a/c	1,70,000	By Sundry Creditors a/c	63,000
To Cash :-		By Cash a/c	1,40,000
— Creditors a/c	60,000	— Assets realised	
— Expenses a/c	8,000	By Loss on realisation transferred to	
		X's Capital a/c	20,000
		Y's Capital a/c	5,000
		Z's Capital a/c	10,000
	2,38,000		2,38,000

X's Capital A/c

Particulars	*Amount*	*Particulars*	*Amount*
To Realisation a/c – loss	20,000	By Balance b/d	64,000
To Z's capital a/c	47,150	By P & L a/c	40,000
To Cash a/c	36,850		
	1,04,000		1,04,000

Y's Capital A/c

Particulars	*Amount*	*Particulars*	*Amount*
To Realisation a/c – loss	5,000	By Balance b/d	36,000
To Z's Capital a/c	20,850	By P & L a/c	10,000
To Cash	20,150		
	46,000		46,000

Z's Capital A/c

Particulars	*Amount*	*Particulars*	*Amount*
To Balance b/d	78,000	By P & L a/c	20,000
To Realisation a/c – loss	10,000	By X's Capital a/c	47,150
		By Y's Capital a/c	20,850
	88,000		88,000

Cash A/c

Particulars	Amount	Particulars	Amount
To Balance b/d	25,000	By Realisation a/c	
To Realisation a/c	1,40,000	— Creditors a/c	60,000
		— Expenses a/c	8,000
		By X's loan a/c	40,000
		By X's Capital a/c	36,850
		By Y's Capital a/c	20,150
	1,65,000		1,65,000

Working Note :

1. The deficiency of Z is transferred to X and Y's capital accounts in the ratio of their capital which stood before the date of dissolution. i.e, 1,04,600 : 46,000

$$\text{X's share} = \frac{104}{150} \times 68{,}000 = 47{,}150 \text{ App.}$$

$$\text{Y's Share} = \frac{46}{150} \times 68{,}000 = 20{,}850 \text{ App.}$$

	X	Y
Capital balance as per Balance Sheet	64,000	36,000
Add : P & L a/c	40,000	10,000
	1,04,000	46,000

2. Cash brought by X and Y equal to their share of realisation loss, i.e., Rs. 20,000 and Rs. 5,000 have not been shown above.

Problem 9

A, B, C and D were partners sharing profits and losses in the ratio of 3 : 3 : 2 : 2 respectively. The following is their Balance Sheet as at 31st March, 2000.

Liabilities		Amount	Assets		Amount
Creditors		31,000	Cash in Hand		4,000
A's loan		20,000	Debtors	32,000	
Capital Accounts :-			Less : Provision	1,000	31,000
A	40,000		Stock		20,000
B	30,000		Furniture		8,000
		70,000	Scooter		14,000
			Capital Accounts :-		
			C	12,000	
			D	32,000	
					44,000
		1,21,000			1,21,000

It was decided to dissolve the firm with effect from 31st March, 2000. B was appointed to liquidate the assets and pay the creditors. He was to bear the expenses of realisation which amounted to Rs. 500.

B was also entitled to receive 5% commission on the amount payable to A (including for his loan, but excluding the cash brought by A towards his share of loss on realisation) after charging such commission. A has agreed to bear this commission wholly himself.

The assets realised Rs. 54,000. Creditors were paid in full. In addition, a sum of Rs. 5,000 was also paid to staff on retrenchment in full settlement of their claims.

D was insolvent and the partners accepted Rs. 7,400 from his estate in full settlement.

Applying the rule in Garner Vs. Murray, prepare the necessary Ledger accounts.

(Delhi University, B.Com. (Hons., 2000)

Solution

Realisation A/c

Particulars	*Amount*	*Particulars*	*Amount*
To Sundry Assets :		By Sundry Liabilities :	
Debtors a/c	32,000	Provision for Doubtful Debts a/c	1,000
Stock a/c	20,000	Creditors a/c	31,000
Furniture a/c	8,000	A's loan a/c	20,000
Scooter a/c	14,000	By Cash a/c	54,000
To Cash a/c		— Assets realised	
Creditors	31,000	By Loss transferred to capital	
To Cash — Staff	5,000	accounts :	
To Cash a/c		A's a/c	7,200
A's loan repaid	20,000	B's a/c	7,200
		C's a/c	4,800
		D's a/c	4,800
	1,30,000		1,30,000

A's and B's Capital A/c

Liabilities	A	B	*Assets*	A	B
To Realisation a/c – Loss	7,200	7,200	By Balance b/d	40,000	30,000
To Cash a/c — Expenses	—	500	By A's Capital a/c	—	1,714
To D's Capital a/c	16,800	12,600	(B's Commission)		
To B's Capital a/c	1,714	—	(See Note 4)		
To Cash a/c	14,286	11,414			
	40,000	31,714		40,000	31,714

C's and D's Capital A/c

Particulars	C	D	*Particulars*	C	D
To Balance b/d	12,000	12,000	By Cash a/c	—	7,400
To Realisation a/c – loss	4,800	4,800	By A's Capital a/c	—	16,800
			(See Note 3)		
			By B's Capital a/c	—	12,600
			(See Note 3)		
			By Cash a/c	16,800	—
	16,800	36,800		16,800	36,800

Cash A/c

Particulars	*Amount*	*Particulars*	*Amount*
To Balance b/d	4,000	By B's Capital a/c – expenses	500
To Realisation a/c	54,000	(See Note – 2)	
To D's Capital a/c	7,400	By Realistion a/c – Creditors paid	31,000
To C's Capital a/c	16,800	By Realisation a/c	5,000
(See Note – 6)		By Realisation a/c – A's loan	20,000
		By A's Capital a/c	14,286
		By B's Capital a/c	11,414
	82,200		82,200

Working Notes :

1. A's loan has been treated through realisation a/c :
2. Expenses Rs. 500 are paid by the firm but borne by B.
3. Loss on D's insolvency Rs. 29,400 is transferred to the capital accounts of A and B in the ratio of their capitals just before dissolution *i.e.*, 4 : 3 according to the Garner Vs. Murray rule.
4. B's commission (C) is calculated as under :

$$C = \frac{5}{100}(36{,}000 - C)$$

$$20\,C = 36{,}000 - C$$

$$C = \frac{36{,}000}{21} = \text{Rs. } 1{,}714.$$

as amount payable to A including has loan is

Rs. 40,000 + Rs. 20,000 – Rs. 7,200 – Rs. 16,800 *i.e.*, Rs. 36,000 and B's commission is 5% of the amount payable to A after commission as A has agreed to bear this commission himself.

5. Amount of share of loss on realisation debited to the accounts of A and B has not been shown in above accounts as cash brought in by A and B for applying the Garner Vs. Murray rule. See note number 3 above.
6. C is not insolvent. So he brings in money due from loan.

Problem 10

X, Y and Z trading under the name of XYZ & Co., and sharing profits & losses in $\frac{1}{2}$, $\frac{1}{3}$ and $\frac{1}{6}$ respectively, dissolved the firm as from 1st January, 1996 on which date their Balance Sheet showed the following position :

Liabilities		*Amount*	*Assets*	*Amount*
Creditors		40,000	Land & Building	57,000
Bills payable		7,000	Stock	50,000
X's loan a/c		10,000	Sundry Debtors	50,000
Capital Accounts :			Bank	3,000
X	90,000		Y's Current a/c	2,000
Y	10,000		Z's Current a/c	5,000
Z	10,000		P & L a/c	1,500
		1,10,000		
X's Current a/c		1,500		
		1,68,500		1,68,500

Land & Building were sold for Rs. 40,000 and Stock and Debtors realised Rs. 30,000 and 42,000 respectively. The expenses of realisation came to Rs. 1,200. Z became insolvent and a dividend of 50 paise in the rupee is received from his private estate.

Pass the Journal entries to close the books of the firm applying the ruling in Garner vs. Murray Case **(Osmania University, B. Com, March, 1999)**

Solution

Journal Entries

Date	Particulars		Dr. Amount	Cr. Amount
	Realisation a/c	Dr.	1,57,000	
	To Land & Buildings a/c			57,000
	To Stock a/c			50,000
	To Sundry Debtors a/c			50,000
	(Being assets transferred to realisation a/c)			
	Creditors a/c	Dr.	40,000	
	Bills payable a/c	Dr.	7,000	
	To Realisation a/c			47,000
	(Being liabilities transferred to realisation a/c)			
	Bank a/c	Dr.	1,12,000	
	To Realisation a/c			1,12,000
	(Being assets realised)			
	Realisation a/c	Dr.	47,000	
	To Bank a/c			47,000
	(Being liabilities paid off)			
	Realisation a/c	Dr.	1,200	
	To Bank a/c			1,200
	(Being expenses on realisation)			
	X's Current a/c	Dr.	23,100	
	Y's Current a/c	Dr.	15,400	
	Z's Current a/c	Dr.	7,700	
	To Realisation a/c			46,200
	(Being loss on Realisation shared among X, Y and Z in the ratio of 3 : 2 : 1)			
	X's Capital a/c	Dr.	22,350	
	Y's Capital a/c	Dr.	17,900	
	Z's Capital a/c	Dr.	12,950	
	To X's Current a/c			22,350
	To Y's Current a/c			17,900
	To Z's Current a/c			12,950
	(Being debit closing balance in partners current accounts transferred to capital accounts)			
	Bank a/c	Dr.	38,500	
	To X's Capital a/c			23,100
	To Y's Capital a/c			15,400
	(Being solvent partners X and Y brought cash equal to their share of loss on realisation)			

Date	Particulars		Dr. Amount	Cr. Amount
	Bank a/c	Dr.	1,475	
	Deficiency a/c	Dr.	1,475	
	To Z's a/c			2,950
	(Being 0.50 paise recovered from Z on his insolvency)			
	X's Capital a/c	Dr.	1,327.50	
	Y's Capital a/c	Dr.	147.50	
	To Deficiency a/c			1,475
	(Being deficiency shared between X and Y in the capital ratio *i.e.*, 9 : 1)			
	X's Capital a/c	Dr.	89,422.50	
	Y's Capital a/c	Dr.	7,352.50	
	To Bank a/c			96,775
	(Being solvent partners capital balance paid off)			

Working Note :-

Realisation A/c

Particulars	Amount	Particulars	Amount
To Land & Building a/c	57,000	By Creditors a/c	40,000
To Stock a/c	50,000	By Bills Payable a/c	7,000
To Sundry Debtors a/c	50,000	By Bank a/c	1,12,000
To Bank a/c	47,000	By X's Current a/c	23,100
To Bank a/c	1,200	By Y's Current a/c	15,400
		By Z's Current a/c	7,700
	2,05,200		2,05,200

X's Current A/c

Particulars	Amount	Particulars	Amount
To Realisation a/c	23,100	By Balance b/d	1,500
To P & L a/c	750	By Capital a/c	22,350
	23,850		23,850

X's Captial A/c

Particulars	Amount	Particulars	Amount
To Current a/c	22,350.00	By Balance b/d	90,000.00
To Deficiency a/c	1,327.50	By Bank	23,100.00
To Bank a/c	89,422.50		
	1,13,100.00		1,13,100.00

Y's Current A/c

Particulars	Amount	Particulars	Amount
To Balance b/d	2,000	By Capital a/c	17,900
To Realisation a/c	15,400		
To P & L a/c	500		
	17,900		17,900

Y's Capital A/c

Particulars	Amount	Particulars	Amount
To Current a/c	17,900.00	By Balance b/d	10,000.00
To Deficiency a/c	147.50	By Bank	15,400.00
To Bank a/c	7,352.50		
	25,400.00		25,400.00

Z's Current A/c

Particulars	Amount	Particulars	Amount
To Balance b/d	5,000	By Capital a/c	12,950
To Realisation a/c	7,700		
To P & L a/c	250		
	12,950		12,950

Z's Capital A/c

Particulars	Amount	Particulars	Amount
To Current a/c	12,950	By Balance b/d	10,000
		By Bank a/c	1,475
		By Deficiency	1,475
	12,950		12,950

Bank A/c

Particulars	Amount	Particulars	Amount
To Balance b/d	3,000	By Realisation a/c	47,000
To Realisation a/c	1,12,000	By Realisation a/c	1,200
To X's Capital a/c	23,100	By X's Loan a/c	10,000
To Y's Capital a/c	15,400	By X's Capital a/c	89,423
To Z's Capital a/c	1,475	By Y's Capital a/c	7,352
	1,54,975		1,54,975

Problem 11

A, B and C are partners sharing profits & losses in the ratio of 6 : 3 : 5. Their Balance Sheet as in 31-3-1999 was as follows :

Liabilities	Amount	Assets	Amount
Sundry Creditors	30,000	Buildings	10,000
Mortage Loan	4,000	Furniture	5,000
Capitals :		Stock	23,100
A's a/c	26,000	Sundry Debtors	30,000
C's a/c	15,500	Cash	2,500
		B's Capital	4,900
	75,500		75,500

The firm was dissolved on the above data and the assets realised as follows :-

Buildings Rs. 6,000 ; Stock Rs. 15,000 ; Furniture Rs. 2,000 ; Sundry Debtors Rs. 20,000.

The expenses of realisations amounted to Rs. 2,000. Creditors received 75 paise in a rupee in full settlement of their claim. Mortage loan was paid in full. B had become inssolvent and 50 paise in a rupee was received from his estate.

Write up necessary accounts to close the books as per Garner vs. Murray case judgement **(Sri Venkateshwara University, B. Com, October, 1999)**

Solution

Realisation A/c

Particulars		Amount	Particulars	Amount
To Buildings a/c		10,000	By Sundry Creditors a/c	30,000
To Furniture a/c		5,000	By Mortgage on Loan a/c	400
To Stock a/c		23,100	By Cash a/c :	
To Debtors a/c		30,000	Buildings a/c	6,000
To Cash a/c :			Furniture a/c	2,000
Creditors	22,500		Stock a/c	15,000
Mortgage	4,000		Debtors a/c	20,000
		26,500	By Loss transferred to Capital a/c	
To Cash a/c :		2,000	A' a/c	8,400
— Realisation expenses			B' a/c	4,200
			C' a/c	7,000
		96,600		96,600

A's Capital A/c

Particulars	Amount	Particulars	Amount
To Realisation a/c – loss	8,400	By Balance b/d	26,000
To B's Capital a/c – loss	2,851	By Cash a/c	8,400
To Cash a/c	23,149		
	34,400		34,400

B's Capital A/c

Particulars	*Amount*	*Particulars*	*Amount*
To Balance b/d	4,900	By Cash	4,550
To Realisation a/c – loss	4,200	By A's Capital a/c	2,851
		By B's Capital a/c	1,699
	9,100		9,100

C's Capital A/c

Particulars	*Amount*	*Particulars*	*Amount*
To Realisation a/c – loss	7,000	By Balance b/d	15,500
To B's Capital a/c	1,699	By Cash a/c	7,000
To Cash a/c	13,801		
	22,500		22,500

Cash A/c

Particulars	*Amount*	*Particulars*	*Amount*
To Balance b/d	2,500	By Realisation a/c	26,500
To A's Capital a/c	8,400	By Realisation a/c – Expenses	20,000
To B's Capital a/c	4,550	By A's Capital a/c	23,149
To C's Capital a/c	7,000	By B's Capital a/c	13,801
To Realisation a/c – Assets sold	43,000		
	65,450		65,450

Insolvency of all the Partners

Insolvency of all the partners result in the insolvency of the firm. As a result, the liabilities of the firm cannot be paid in full. The following steps are involved

1. Open realisation account and transfer only assets. Creditors should not be transferred to realisation a/c.
2. Credit realisation a/c with the amount realised from assets.
3. Debit realisation a/c with the expenses of realisation.
4. Balance the realisation a/c and transfer the balance to the capital accounts of partners in their profit sharing ratio.
5. A separate account is to be opened for recording external liabilities and creditors under the head creditors a/c and credit with such liabilities and debit with actual payment. The balance is deficiency and is transferred to the debit of partner's capital account.
6. Close partners capital accounts in the normal way except that beginning with one with the worst position, the credit balance of which is transferred to the debit balance of another which automatically closes all the accounts.
7. Prepare cash account. After recording the amounts which are received from the estate of the partners the entire cash should be distributed among the creditors rateably.

Problem 12

X, Y and Z were partners in a business. Their Balance Sheet as on 31st March, 1999 was as follows :

Liabilities		*Amount*	*Assets*	*Amount*
Capital			Properties	4,00,000
X	1,60,000		Fixtures	1,60,000
Z	1,00,000		Machine	4,00,000
		2,60,000	Book Debts	2,00,000
X's Loan		2,00,000	Stock	1,60,000
Creditors		10,00,000	Cash	10,000
			Y's Capital (Overdrawn)	1,30,000
		14,60,000		14,60,000

Due to bad financial position of the partners, the firm was dissolved and all partners were declared bankrupt.

The assets were realised as follows :-

Book Debts 45% less, Properties Rs. 1,60,000, Stock Rs. 1,00,000, Machine Rs. 2,00,000 and Fixtures Rs. 40,000. Realisation expenses amount Rs. 10,000.

The private financial position of partners was as follows :

	Private Assets	Private Liabilities
X	2,50,000	2,50,000
Y	2,00,000	1,80,000
Z	2,30,000	2,50,000

Prepare :

Realisation a/c, Bank a/c, Creditors a/c, Deficiency a/c, and Partners Capital accounts.

(Delhi University, B. Com (Hons.), 1999)

Solution

Realisation A/c

Particulars	*Amount*	*Particulars*	*Amount*
To Assets :		By Cash a/c	
Properties a/c	4,00,000	Debtors a/c	1,10,000
Fixtures a/c	1,60,000	Properties a/c	1,60,000
Machines a/c	4,00,000	Stock a/c	1,00,000
Debtors a/c	2,00,000	Machines a/c	2,00,000
Stock a/c	1,60,000	Fixtures a/c	40,000
To Cash a/c – Expenses	10,000	By Loss transferred to capital accounts	
		X	2,40,000
		Y	2,40,000
		Z	2,40,000
	13,30,000		13,30,000

X's Capital A/c

Particulars	*Amount*	*Particulars*	*Amount*
To Realisation a/c – loss To Deficiency a/c – Final amount not paid	2,40,000 1,20,000	By Balance b/d By Loan a/c	1,60,000 2,00,000
	3,60,000		3,60,000

Y's Capital A/c

Particulars	*Amount*	*Particulars*	*Amount*
To Balance b/d To Realisation a/c – loss	1,30,000 2,40,000	By Cash a/c By Deficiency a/c – Amount not received from him	20,000 3,50,000
	3,70,000		3,70,000

Z's Capital A/c

Particulars	*Amount*	*Particulars*	*Amount*
To Realisation a/c – loss	2,40,000	By Balance b/d By Deficiency a/c – Amount received from him	1,00,000 1,40,000
	2,40,000		2,40,000

Creditors A/c

Particulars	*Amount*	*Particulars*	*Amount*
To Cash a/c To Final payment	6,30,000 3,70,000	By Creditors a/c	10,00,000
	10,00,000		10,00,000

Cash A/c

Particulars	*Amount*	*Particulars*	*Amount*
To Balance b/d	10,000	By Realisation a/c – Expenses	10,000
To Realisation a/c		By Creditors a/c	6,30,000
Debtors a/c	1,10,000		
Properties a/c	1,60,000		
Stock a/c	1,00,000		
Machines a/c	2,00,000		
Fixtures a/c	40,000		
To Y's Capital a/c	20,000		
	6,40,000		6,40,000

Deficiency A/c

Particulars	Amount	Particulars	Amount
To Y's Capital a/c	3,50,000	By Creditors a/c	3,70,000
To Z's Capital a/c	1,40,000	By X's Capital a/c	1,20,000
	4,90,000		4,90,000

Problem 13

Below is the Balance Sheet of A, B and C as on 31st March, 2003.

Liabilities		Amount	Assets	Amount
Sundry Creditors		20,000	Cash	3,120
Loan		10,000	Stock	15,630
Capital Accounts :			Debtors	4,720
A	8,000		Furniture	9,530
B	6,000		Profit & loss a/c	12,000
C	1,000			
		15,000		
		45,000		45,000

The firm was dissolved due to insolvency of all the partners. Stock was sold for Rs. 10,900 while furniture fetched Rs. 4,000. Rs, 4,100 were received from debtors. Expenses to be Rs. 220.

Nothing could be recovered from B and C but A's private estate showed a surplus of Rs. 600.

Close the books of the firm.

Solution

Realisation A/c

Particulars	Amount	Particulars	Amount
To Stock a/c	15,630	By Cash a/c – Assets	19,000
To Debtors a/c	4,720	By A's Capital a/c	3,700
To Furniture a/c	9,530	By B's Capital a/c	3,700
To Cash – Expenses a/c	220	By C's Capital a/c	3,700
	30,100		30,100

A's Capital A/c

Particulars	Amount	Particulars	Amount
To P & L a/c	4,000	By Balance b/d	8,000
To Realisation a/c – Loss	3,700	By Cash a/c	600
To Deficiency a/c	900		
	8,600		8,600

B's Capital A/c

Particulars	Amount	Particulars	Amount
To P & L a/c	4,000	By Balance b/d	6,000
To Realisation a/c – Loss	3,700	By Deficiency a/c	1,700
	7,700		7,700

C's Capital A/c

Particulars	Amount	Particulars	Amount
To P & L a/c	4,000	By Balance b/d	1,000
To Realisation a/c – loss	3,700	By Deficiency a/c	6,700
	7,700		7,700

Cash A/c

Particulars	Amount	Particulars	Amount
To Balance b/d	3,120	By Realiation a/c – expenses	220
To Realisation a/c – Assets	19,000	By Loan	7,500
To A's Capital a/c	600	By Sundry Creditors	15,000
	22,720		22,720

Loan A/c

Particulars	Amount	Particulars	Amount
To Cash	7,500	By Balance b/d	10,000
To Deficiency a/c	2,500		
	10,000		10,000

Sundry Creditors A/c

Particulars	Amount	Particulars	Amount
To Cash a/c	15,000	By Balance b/d	20,000
To Deficiency a/c	5,000		
	20,000		20,000

Deficiency A/c

Particulars	Amount	Particulars	Amount
To B's Capital a/c	1,700	By Loan a/c	2,500
To C's Capital a/c	6,700	By Sundry Creditors a/c	5,000
		By A's Capital a/c	900
	8,400		8,400

QUESTIONS

Simple Questions

1. What is meant by "Dissolution of partnership firm" ?
2. What is dissolution of partnership ?
3. Distinguish between dissolution of the firm and dissolution of partnership.
4. What is "Realisation a/c" ?
5. Who is an insolvent partner ?
6. What is the principle involved in the case of Garner vs. Murray ?

EXERCISE 1

The following is the Balance Sheet of A and B as on 31st December, 1995.

Liabilities	*Amount*	*Assets*		*Amount*
Sundry Creditors	30,000	Cash in Hand		500
Bills payable	8,000	Cash at Bank		8,000
Mrs. A's loan	5,000	Stock in trade		5,000
Mrs. B's loan	10,000	Investment		10,000
Reserve fund	10,000	Debtors	20,000	
Investment fluctuation fund	1,000	Less : Provision	2,000	
A's Capital	10,000			18,000
B's Capital	10,000	Plant		20,000
		Buildings		15,000
		Goodwill		4,000
		P & L a/c		3,500
	84,000			84,000

The firm was dissolved on 31st December, 1995 and the following was found.

(*a*) A promised to pay Mrs. A's loan and took away stock-in-trade at Rs. 4,000.
(*b*) B took away half the investments at 10% discount.
(*c*) Debtors realised Rs. 19,000.
(*d*) Creditors and Bills payable were due on an average basis one month after 31st December, but they were paid immediately on 31st December at 6% discount per annum.
(*e*) Plant realised Rs. 25,000 ; Building Rs. 40,000 ; Goodwill Rs. 6,000 and remaining investments at Rs. 4,500.
(*f*) There was an old typewriter in the firm which had been written off completely from the books. It is now estimated to realise Rs. 300. It was taken away by B at the estimated price.
(*g*) Realisation expenses were Rs. 1,000.

You are required to give Journal entries and ledger accounts.

(University of Madras, B. Com., September, 1997)

Answer : Profit transferred to A's Capital is Rs. 15,745 & B's Capital is Rs. 15,745. Total of cash a/c Rs. 1,03,000.

EXERCISE 2

Sandhya, Pratima, and Nirmala were partners in a firm sharing profits & losses in the ratio of 2 : 2 : 1. They decided to dissolve their firm on 31st December, 1996 on which date the Balance Sheet of the firm was as follows :

Liabilities	*Amount*	*Assets*		*Amount*
Capitals :		Machinery		28,000
Sandhya	30,000	Furniture		15,000
Pratima	20,000	Investments		12,000
Nirmala	15,000	Stock		7,000
Sundry Creditors	8,000	Sundry Debtors	13,000	
Bills payable	7,000	Less : Provision for		
Workmen's compensation fund	3,000	Bad Debts	1,000	
				1,2000
		Cash at Bank		6,000
		Advertisement expense		3,000
	83,000			83,000

The assets realised the following amounts :- Machinery Rs. 30,000 ; Furniture Rs. 18,000 ; Stock Rs. 4,000 ; and Debtors in full with the exception of one item of Rs. 1,500 which was bad.

Sandhya took over the investments at book value. Discount amounting to Rs. 300 were allowed by creditors while paying their claims. Nirmala was allowed the right to use the firm name for her business for which she paid Rs. 8,000 in cash.

The expenses of realisation amounted to Rs. 800.

Prepare Realisation a/c, cash book and capital accounts of the partners.

(Calcutta University, B.Com (Pass), 1997)

Answer : Total profit on realisation 12,000 ; cash book total Rs. 77,500.

Note : It is assumed that bills payable has been paid in full and nothing paid to workmen's compensation since there is no accident and claim by any worker.

EXERCISE 3

Daniel, Eshwar, Frank, and Harish were partners sharing profits and losses in 3 : 2 : 3 : 2 ratio. Their Balance Sheet on the date of dissolution was as follows :

Liabilities		*Amount*	*Assets*	*Amount*
Sundry Creditors		6,000	Assets	17,000
Reserve fund		4,000	Frank's capital	6,360
Capital :-			Harish's Capital	1,640
Daniel	10,000			
Eshwar	5,000			
		15,000		
		25,000		25,000

On the above date, Frank became insolvent and was able to contribute only 50 paise in a rupee. Assets realised Rs. 12,500 and realisation expenses amounted to Rs. 400. Prepare necessary ledger accounts to close the books of the firm applying Garner Vs. Murray rule.

(Osmania University, B. Com, March, 1997)

Answer : Total loss on realisation : Rs. 4,900
Total of Bank a/c : Rs. 20,085.

EXERCISE 4

Nishikanta and Sashikanta were partners in a firm. They shared profits & losses equally. On 31st December, 1993 they decided to dissolve the firm. On that date their Balance Sheet stood as follows :-

Liabilities	*Amount*	*Assets*	*Amount*
Sundry Creditors	32,000	Cash	1,500
Capital Accounts :-		Debtors	12,500
Nishikanta	52,000	Stock	25,000
Sashikanta	30,000	Building	60,000
		Furniture	15,000
	1,14,000		1,14,000

The Assets realised as under :

Debtors – Rs. 9,000 ; Stock – Rs. 15,000 ; Building – Rs. 40,000 ; Furniture – Rs. 12,000. The creditors were paid off at Rs. 28,000 and expenses of liquidation amounted to Rs. 5,000.

Prepare realisation a/c, cash a/c, and capital account. **(Calcutta University, B. Com, 1995)**

Answer : Total loss on realisation : Rs. 37,500
Total of cash a/c : Rs. 77,500.

EXERCISE 5

A, B, C and D were partners in a firm sharing profits in the ratio of 3 : 3 : 2 : 2. The following is their Balance Sheet as at 30-6-97.

Liabilities		*Amount*	*Assets*		*Amount*
Sundry Creditors		15,500	Cash at Bank		2,000
A's Loan		10,000	Debtors	16,000	
Partner's Capital a/c :			Less : Provisions	500	
A	20,000				15,500
B	15,000		Stock in trade		10,000
		35,000	Furniture & Fittings		4,000
			Trade Marks		7,000
			Drawings Accounts :		
			C	16,000	
			D	6,000	
					22,000
		60,500			60,500

The firm was dissolved as in the above date. B being appointed to realise the assets and pay off the liabilities, he is entitled to receive 5% as his remuneration on the amount finally paid to the other partners towards their capital. The expenses of realisation were to be borne by B. The assets realised as follows :-

Sundry Debtors Rs. 11,000 ; Stock Rs. 8,000 ; Furniture etc., Rs. 1,000 and Trade Marks Rs. 4,000.

Sundry Creditors were paid off in full including a contingent liability amounting to Rs. 2,500 in respect of bills discounted materialised. Expenses of realisation amounting to Rs. 500 were paid by the firm. As C was insolvent, only 3,700 could be recovered from his private estate. Close the books of the firm applying the rule in the case of Garner Vs. Murray.

(Calcutta University, B.Com (Hons.), 1998)

Answer : Loss on realisation ; Rs. 15,000
Total of cash a/c ; Rs. 38,700.

EXERCISE 6

Ram, Shyam and Shesh were partners sharing profits in the ratio of 2 : 1 : 2. They appointed Shesh to realise the assets and distribute the proceeds. Shesh is to receive 5% remuneration on all the realisation other than amount received from partners and is to bear all expenses. The Balance Sheet of the firm on 1994 was as follows :-

Liabilities	*Amount*	*Assets*		*Amount*
Sundry Creditors	30,000	Goodwill		3,000
Outstanding expenses	1,300	Debtors	31,500	
Capitals :-		Less : Reserve	1,500	
Ram	20,000			30,000
Shyam	1,000	Stock		35,200
Shesh	16,000			
	68,200			68,200

Shesh reports the result of realisation as follows : Debtors Rs. 21,500 ; Stock Rs. 27,000 ; and Goodwill Rs. 200. Creditors were paid at a discount of 2%. Besides outstanding expenses of Rs. 1,200 and outstanding creditors not provided for Rs. 825 were also paid. Shyam was insolvent and his estate yields only Rs. 500. Prepare Realisation a/c, capital accounts, and Bank a/c. (Follow the Principle in Garner Vs. Murray decision).

(Bangalore University, B.Com, October, 1995)

Answer : Loss on realisation a/c – Ram Rs. 8,864, Shyam Rs. 8,864, Shesh Rs. 4,432.
Total of cash a/c Rs. 62,496.

EXERCISE 7

The following is the Balance Sheet of A, B, C and D on 31st March, 1994. They shared profits and losses in the ratio of 4 : 3 : 2 : 1.

Liabilities	*Amount*	*Assets*	*Amount*
Creditors	10,000	Goodwill	10,000
Capitals :-		Fixed Assets	40,000
A	30,000	Current Assets	12,000
B	20,000	D's Capital a/c	1,000
C	3,000		
	63,000		63,000

D has no separate assets and liabilities. The partners decided to wind up the business. Fixed assets realised Rs. 30,000 and current assets realised Rs. 10,000. The goodwill is valueless. Realisation expenses amount to Rs. 3,000. C can contribute only Rs. 500 from his separate resources.

Prepare the necessary ledger accounts. Apply Garner Vs. Murray decision assuming that both C and D have become insolvent. **(Bangalore University, B.Com, April, 1995)**

Answer : Total loss on realisation a/c Rs. 25,000.
Total of cash a/c 58,000.

EXERCISE 8

(When all partners are insolvent)

The Balance Sheet of X, Y and Z who were sharing profits and losses in the ratio of 3 : 1 : 1 stood as follows on December 31, 2003, the date of dissolution.

Liabilities	*Amount*	*Assets*	*Amount*
Bank Overdraft	60,000	Cash in hand	1,000
Sundry Creditors	45,000	Bills Receivable	4,000
X's Capital	15,000	Debtors	25,000
Z's Capital	10,000	Stock	40,000
		Plant	30,000
		Goodwill	10,000
		Y's Capital	20,000
	1,30,000		1,30,000

The assets were realised for Rs. 73,750 and after paying Rs. 2,000 for realisation expenses, the creditors were paid 75 paise in a rupee. Show the final adjustment amongst the partners assuming that all partners are insolvent.

Answers : Loss on realisation a/c X – Rs. 18,750 ; Y – Rs. 6,250 ; Z – Rs. 6,250.
Deficiency a/c Rs. 30,000.

EXERCISE 9

The Balance Sheet of Ramesh, Suresh, and Satish, who were sharing profits and losses in $\frac{3}{5}$, $\frac{2}{5}$ and $\frac{1}{5}$ ratios, stood as follows on 31-12-89.

Liabilities	Amount	Assets	Amount
Bank overdraft	28,000	Cash in hand	500
Creditors	24,500	Bills Receivable	2,000
Ramesh's Capital	7,500	Debtors	12,000
Suresh's Capital	5,000	Stock	19,000
		Machinery	16,000
		Goodwill	5,000
		Suresh's Capital	10,500
	65,000		65,000

The assets realised Rs. 39,875. The expenses amounted to Rs. 1,000. The liabilities were paid 75 paise in a rupee.

Prepare dissolution accounts, assuming that all the partners are insolvent.

(Bangalore University, B.Com, October, 1990)

Answer : Total loss on realisation a/c ; 15,125
Total of cash a/c Rs. 40,375
Total of Deficiency a/c Rs. 15,100

23

CHAPTER

Dissolution of Partnership — Piecemeal

Distribution of Cash

Under dissolution of partnership discussed in the previous chapter, it was assumed that all the assets were realised on the date of dissolution and accounts settled on the same date. However, normally sale of assets and realisation of cash is a long drawn process spread over a period of time during which the assets are gradually realised in stages and their proceeds used in payment of liabilities and partners capitals. Such a process of gradual distribution of money is known as "piecemeal distribution".

The cash received on gradual sale of assets shall be applied in making settlement in the following order :

1. Realisation expenses
2. To pay external liabilities of firm in the following order :
   (*a*) secured creditors ;
   (*b*) preferential creditors or income tax dues etc.,
   (*c*) unsecured creditors ;
   (*d*) contingent liabilities, if any.
3. To pay each partner rateably what is due to him from the firm for advances or loans.
4. In paying each partner rateably what is due to him on account of capital.
5. The residue, if any is divided among the partners in the proportion in which they are entitled to share profits.

Distribution Amongst Partners

In regard to return of capital to the partners, the important point for consideration is the ratio in which the capitals have to be repaid, whether the capital contribution ratio or profit sharing ratio. Where the capitals are in profit sharing ratio, their proceeds will be distributed in the profit sharing ratio, but where the capital ratios and profit sharing ratios are different, a suitable method has to be deviced which ensures that final deficit or loss on realisation is in profit sharing ratio and that such distribution does not result either in over payment or under payment to partners. Two such methods which ensure just and equitable distribution of cash amongst partners are : (*a*) Surplus or proportion capital method ; (*b*) Maximum possible loss method or Notional loss method.

1. Surplus or Proportionate Capital Method

Under this method, where the capitals of the partners are not in the profit sharing ratio they are brought into profit sharing ratio by paying one who has the capital in excess of what is required according to his share in the profits. For example, if X and Y are two partners having capitals of Rs. 20,000 and Rs. 10,000 and sharing profits in the ratio of 3 : 2 and the assets realised (*i*) Rs. 4,000 ; (*ii*) Rs. 2,000 and (*iii*) Rs. 1,000, then the distribution will be as under partners :

	X	Y
Profit sharing ratio	3	2
Capitals	20,000	10,000
Taking Y's capital as the basis, X's capital according to his share in profit should be $10{,}000 \times \frac{3}{2}$	15,000	10,000
Excess capital	5,000	

This means that Y will not be paid unless X is paid out Rs. 5,000. Once X is paid Rs. 5,000, all realisations can be paid in the profit sharing ratio because then the capitals of partners will be in the profit sharing ratio. The distribution will be as under :

	X	Y
Capitals	20,000	10,000
Ist Instalment paid to X	(–) 4,000	—
	16,000	10,000
IInd Instalment of Rs. 2,000 of which Rs. 1,000 is paid to X	1,000	—
	15,000	10,000
The balance Rs. 1,000 will be paid in the profit sharing ratio of 3 : 2	600	400
	14,400	9,600
IIIrd instalment of Rs. 1,000 paid for X and Y in the ratio of 3 : 2	600	400
Balance unpaid (loss)	13,800	9,200

It can be seen that the loss of Rs. 13,800 and Rs. 92,00 to X and Y respectively is in the profit sharing ratio of 3 : 2.

Problem 1

The firm BBM was dissolved on 31-3-1998 at which date its Balance Sheet stood as follows :

Liabilities	*Amount*	*Assets*	*Amount*
Creditors	1,50,000	Fixed Assets	33,75,000
Bank Loan	3,75,000	Cash at Bank	1,50,000
Brahma's Loan	7,50,000		
Capital :			
Brahma	11,25,000		
Bishnu	7,50,000		
Maheshwar	3,75,000		
	35,25,000		35,25,000

Partners share profits equally. Vyas & Co., a firm of Chartered Accountants is retained to realise the assets and distribute the cash after discharge of liabilities. Their fees which are to include all expenses is fixed at Rs. 75,000. No loss is expected on realisation since fixed assets include valuable land and building.

Realisations	Amount in Rs.
Serial No. 1	3,75,000
Serial No. 2	11,25,000
Serial No. 3	11,25,000
Serial No. 4	22,50,000
Serial No. 5	22,50,000

Vyas & Co., decided to pay off the partners in proportionate capital method. You are required to prepare a statement showing the distribution of cash.

(Calcutta University, B.Com (Hons.), 1999)

Solution

Statement showing distribution of cash

		Creditors	Bank Loan	Brahma's Loan	Brahma	Bishnu	Maheshwar
31-3-98	Balance due	1,50,000	3,75,000	7,50,000	11,25,000	7,50,000	3,75,000
Ist	Paid to creditors, Bank loan & Brahma's loan 2 : 5 : 10	44,118	1,10,294	2,20,588	—	—	—
	Balance due	1,05,882	2,64,706	5,29,142	11,25,000	7,50,000	3,75,000
IInd	Paid to Creditors, Bank Loan & Brahma's Loan Balance due	1,05,882	2,64,706	5,29,142	2,25,000	—	—
	Balance due				9,00,000	7,50,000	3,75,000
IIIrd	Paid to Brahma, Bishnu, Maheshwar				6,00,000	4,50,000	75,000
	Balance due				3,00,000	3,00,000	3,00,000
IVth	Paid to Brahma, Bishnu, Maheshwar				7,50,000	7,50,000	7,50,000
	Surplus				4,50,000	4,50,000	4,50,000
Vth	Paid to Brahma, Bishnu, Maheshwar				7,50,000	7,50,000	7,50,000
	Surplus				12,00,000	12,00,000	12,00,000
	(Cash at Bank – Fees to Vyas & Co. = 1,50,000 – 75,000 = 75,000 paid to Brahma, Bishnu Maheshwar.)				25,000	25,000	25,000
					12,25,000	12,25,000	12,25,000

Notes :-

1. The first instalment is paid towards Creditors, Bank Loan, and Brahma's Loan.
2. Brahma is paid up to Rs. 3,75,000 being his surplus capital in comparison with Bishnu's capital at first.
3. Thereafter Brahma and Bishnu are paid Rs. 3,75,000 each being their surplus capital in comparison with Maheshwar.
4. Thereafter they are all paid equally.
5. Cash at Bank is paid at last after paying fees to Vyas & Co.

Problem 2

Following is the Balance Sheet of M/s A, B and C who share profits & losses in the ratio of 2 : 2 : 1.

Liabilities	*Amount*	*Assets*	*Amount*
Sundry Creditors	15,000	Cash in hand	2,000
Capitals :-		Sundry Debtors	12,000
A	15,000	Stock	22,000
B	12,000	Furniture	10,000
C	4,000		
	46,000		46,000

The firm was dissolved and the assets were realised gradually Rs. 10,000 ; Rs. 15,000 and Rs. 9,000 as the first, second, and third instalments.

Show how each instalment is to be distributed under proportionate capital method.

(University of Madras, B.Com, April, 1999)

Solution

Statement Showing Distribution of Cash

	Creditors	A	B	C
Balance	15,000	15,000	12,000	4,000
Cash in hand paid to creditors	2,000	—	—	—
	13,000	15,000	12,000	4,000
Ist Instalment :	10,000	—	—	—
	3,000	15,000	12,000	4,000
IInd Instalment : Paid to creditors paid to 'A'	3,000	3,000		
	NIL	12,000	12,000	4,000
Paid to 'A'				
Paid to 'B'		4,000	4,000	—
		8,000	8,000	4,000
Paid A, B and C in the ratio of 2 : 2 : 1		400	400	200
		7,600	7,600	3,800
III Instalment paid A, B and C in the ratio of 2 : 2 : 1		3,600	3,600	1,800
Loss		4,000	4,000	2,000

Problem 3

P, Q and R share profits of a firm in the ratio of $\frac{1}{2}$, $\frac{1}{4}$ and $\frac{1}{4}$ respectively. On the date of dissolution their Balance Sheet stood as follows :

Liabilities	*Amount*	*Assets*	*Amount*
Creditors	10,000	Sundry Assets	60,000
P's loan	5,000	Cash in hand	1,000
Q's loan	3,000		
P's capital	20,000		
Q's capital	15,000		
R's capital	8,000		
	61,000		61,000

The Assets realised Rs. 45,000 which were received in instalments of Rs. 15,000 ; Rs. 16,000 and Rs. 14,000. Show how proceeds should be distributed as and when received by following the proportionate capital method. (University of Madras, B.Com, October, 1999)

Solution

Statement Showing Distribution of Cash

		Creditors	P's loan	Q's loan	P	Q	R
Balance due		10,000	5,000	3,000	20,000	15,000	8,000
Cash in hand :-	1,000						
Paid to Creditors	1,000	1,000	—	—	—	—	—
	NIL	9,000	5,000	3,000	20,000	15,000	8,000
Ist Instalment :-	15,000						
Paid to Creditors	9,000	9,000	—	—	—	—	—
	6,000						
Paid to P and Q in the loan ratio of 5 : 3	6,000		3,750	2,250	—	—	—
	NIL	NIL	1,250	750	20,000	15,000	8,000
IInd Instalment :	16,000						
Paid to partner's loan	2,000		1,250	750	—	—	—
	14,000		NIL	NIL	20,000	15,000	8,000
Paid to Q	5,000					5,000	
				NIL	20,000	10,000	8,000
Paid to P & Q Rs. 4,000 and Rs. 2,000 to make their capital 2 : 1 : 1					4,000	2,000	—
				NIL	16,000	8,000	8,000
Balance of 3,000 given to all partners in the ratio of 2 : 1 : 1				NIL	1,500	750	750
				NIL	14,500	7,250	7,250
IIIrd Instalment	14,000						
Paid to P, Q and R in the ratio of 2 : 1 : 1	14,000				7,000	3,500	3,500
	NIL	Loss in realisation			7,500	3,750	3,750

Working Note :

Under proportionate capital method, capital of partners are changed according to profit sharing ratio.

	P	Q	R
Profit Ratio	$\frac{1}{2}$	$\frac{1}{4}$	$\frac{1}{4}$
	2	1	1
Capital Balance	20,000	15,000	8,000
Taking R's capital as basis proportionate capital would be	$\frac{8,000}{1} \times 2$	$\frac{8,000}{1} \times 1$	—
	16,000	8,000	8,000
Excess capital paid	4,000	7,000	NIL
Proportionate capital between P and Q taking P as base	—	$\frac{4,000}{2} \times 1$	—
	—	2,000	—
Excess capital to be paid	—	5,000	—

First, Rs. 5,000 is given to Mr. Q. And then to P & Q in the ratio of 2 : 1 up to reaching Rs. 16,000 and Rs. 8,000. Lastly, to P, Q & R in their ratio 2 : 1 : 1.

Problem 4

Orange, Apple and Banana were in partnership sharing profits and losses in the ratio 3 : 2 : 1. They decided to dissolve the partnership and to distribute the sale proceeds as and when realised.

The partner's capital were Orange Rs. 10,000, Apple Rs. 9,000 and Banana Rs. 5,000, Apple's loan (Cr.) amounted to Rs. 3,000

Sundry Creditors amounted to Rs. 6,000. The assets were realised as under :-

	Stock	*Furniture*	*Debtors*	*Expenses*
July	3,000	300	2,000	500
August	2,000	100	1,500	200
September	2,500	—	2,000	300
October	3,000	—	1,500	200

You are required to draw up a statement. Showing the distribution of cash by following the proportionate capital method. **(University of Madras, B.Com, May, 1999)**

Solution

Working Note :

(1) **Calculation of Net realisation**

July = 3,000 + 300 + 2,000 – 500 = 4,800

August = 2,000 + 100 + 2,500 – 200 = 3,400

September = 2,500 + NIL + 2,000 – 300 = 4,200

October = 3,000 + NIL + 1,500 – 200 = 4,300

(2) **Calculation of Proportionate Capital :**

	Orange	Apple	Banana
Profit Sharing Ratio	3	2	1
Capital Balance	10,000	9,000	5,000
Based on Orange, proportionate capitals are			
$\frac{10,000 \times 2}{3} = 6,667$			
$\frac{10,000 \times 1}{3} = 3,333$	10,000	6,667	3,333
Excess capital paid	—	2,333	1,667

Between Apple and Banana :

Based on Apple, proportionate capital would be

	Apple	Banana
$\frac{9,000}{2} \times 1$	9,000	4,500
Excess capital paid		500

Statement Showing Distribution of Cash

		Creditors	Apple's Loan	Orange	Apple	Banana
Balance due		6,000	3,000	10,000	9,000	5,000
July Realisation	4,800					
Paid to Creditors	4,800	4,800	—	—	—	—
	NIL	1,200	3,000	10,000	9,000	5,000
August Realisation	3,400					
Paid to Creditors	1,200	1,200	—	—	—	—
	2,200	NIL	3,000	10,000	9,000	5,000
Paid Apple's Loan	2,200		2,200	—	—	—
	NIL		800	10,000	9,000	5,000
September Realisation	4,200					
Paid Apple's Loan	800		800	—	—	—
	3,400		NIL	10,000	9,000	5,000
Paid to Banana	500			—	—	500
	2,900			10,000	9,000	4,500
Paid to Apple & Banana	2,900			—	1,933	967
	NIL			10,000	7,067	3,533
October Realisation	4,300					
Paid to Apple & Banana	600			—	400	200
	3,700			10,000	6,667	3,333
Paid to all partners in the ratio of 3 : 2 : 1	3,700			1,850	1,233	667
			Loss	8,150	5,434	2,716

Problem 5

P, Q and R were partners sharing profits and losses in the ratio of 2 : 2 : 1. The partnership was dissolved on December 31, 1997 and their Balance Sheet on that date was as follows :-

Liabilities	*Amount*	*Assets*	*Amount*
Sundry Creditors	6,000	Cash in Hand	2,000
Capital Accounts :		Other Assets	38,000
P	16,000		
Q	10,000		
R	3,000		
Profit & Loss a/c	5,000		
	40,000		40,000

The assets were realised gradually : Rs. 10,000 was received in first instalment, Rs. 10,000 the second time and Rs. 13,000 finally. Show how the cash was distributed.

(University of Madras, B.Com, May, 1998)

Solution

Working Note :

Statement of Capital Distribution

	P	Q	R
Capital as per Balance Sheet	16,000	10,000	3,000
Add : P & L a/c Rs. 5,000 (2 : 2 : 1)	2,000	2,000	1,000
	18,000	12,000	4,000
Capital as per Profit Ratio 2 : 2 : 1 taking R as base	8,000	8,000	4,000
$P = \frac{4,000}{1} \times 2$			
$Q = \frac{4,000}{1} \times 2$			
	10,000	4,000	—
Capital as per profit ratio of P & Q (2 : 2) taking Q as basis	4,000	4,000	—
$P = \frac{4,000}{2} \times 2$			
Surplus	6,000	—	—

Statement of Distribution of Cash

		Creditors	P	Q	R
Balance		6,000	16,000	10,000	3,000
Add P & L a/c		—	2,000	2,000	1,000
		6,000	18,000	12,000	4,000
Cash in hand	2,000				
Paid to Creditors	2,000	2,000	—	—	—
	NIL	4,000	18,000	12,000	4,000
Ist Instalment	10,000				
Paid to Creditors	(–) 4,000	4,000	6,000		—
Paid to P	(–) 6,000				
	NIL	NIL	12,000	12,000	4,000

		Creditors	P	Q	R
IInd Instalment	10,000				
Paid to P	(–) 4,000		4,000	4,000	—
Paid to Q	(–) 4,000				
	2,000		8,000	8,000	4,000
Paid to P, Q and R (2 : 2 : 1)	2,000		800	800	400
	NIL		7,200	7,200	3,600
IIIrd Instalment	13,000				
Paid to P, Q and R (2 : 2 : 1)	13,000		5,200	5,200	2,600
	NIL	Loss	2,000	2,000	1,000

2. Maximum Loss Method Or Notional Loss Method

Maximum possible loss is the difference between capital payable and the assets realised at any particular date of distribution. In other words, it is the net balance due to the partners after having paid them the amount realised on certain date. Under this method, the unrealised value of assets after each realisation is considered to be valueless and loss is charged to each partner in the profit sharing ratio. Each partner's share of the deficiency is deducted from the amount of his share capital and the balance will be the amount payable to him. If a partner's capital account thereby shows a debit balance, it is assumed that such partner is insolvent and this deficiency is charged to the capital accounts of the other partners in the proportion of their capital as per Garner Vs. Murray principle. During the next period the opening balance would be the amount of original capital less the amount already paid. This process is, repeated on each realisation till all the assets are disposed off. After the final distribution the amount due to each partner, unpaid will be in the profit & loss sharing ratio.

Problem 6

P, Q and R were partners sharing profits and losses in the ratio of 3 : 2 : 1 respectively. On 31st March, 1999, their Balance Sheet stood as follows :-

Liabilities	*Amount*	*Assets*	*Amount*
Bills payable	10,000	Cash in hand	2,500
Trade Creditors	20,000	Other Assets	1,05,000
P's loan a/c	10,000		
P's capital a/c	25,000		
Q's capital a/c	25,000		
R's capital a/c	17,500		
	1,07,500		1,07,500

The firm was dissolved on that date. The collections and expenses during the subsequent months were as follows :

	Amount realised Rs.	Expenses Rs.
April, 1999	23,000	200
May, 1999	23,950	1,250
June, 1999	40,480	480
July, 1999	18,400	400

On 31st March, 1999, there was a bill discounted amounting to Rs. 1,000 due on 3rd May, 1999. The bill was met on the due date.

Cash was distributed on the first of every month. All the assets had been sold by the end of July and hence final settlement was made on 1st August, 1999.

Prepare a statement showing distribution of cash under the maximum loss method.

(C.S. Foundation, December, 1999)

Solution

Statement Showing Distribution of Cash – Maximum Loss Methhod

	Bills Payable	Trade Creditors	P's Loan	P	Q	R
Balance on Ist April, 1999.	10,000	20,000	10,000	25,000	25,000	17,500
Cash available = 1,500 (2,500 – 1,000) distributed in the ratio of 1 : 2	500	1,000	—	—	—	—
	9,500	19,000	10,000	25,000	25,000	17,500
1st May, 1999. Cash available = 22,800 (23,000 – 200) distributed in the ratio of 1 : 2	7,600	15,200	—	—	—	—
	1,900	3,800	10,000	25,000	25,000	17,500
1st June, 1999. Cash available = 23,700 (23,950 – 1,250 + 1,000) payment of liabilities & loan	1,900	3,800	10,000	—	—	—
	NIL	NIL	NIL	25,000	25,000	17,500
Cash left = (23,700 – 1,900 – 3,800 – 10,000) = 8,000 Maximum loss = (25,000 + 25,000 + 17,500 – 8,000) = Rs. 59,500 transferred to capitals in profit sharing ratio				29,750	19,833	9,917
Rs. 4,750 debited to Q and R in the ratio of 250 : 175				–4,750	5,167	7,583
Cash paid ®				+ 4,750	– 2,794	– 1,956
				NIL	2,373	5,627
Ist July 1999 :- Balance Left				25,000	22,627	1,187
Cash available 40,000 (40,480 – 480) Maximum loss (59,500 – 40,000) = 19,500 distributed among partners				9,750	6,500	3,250
Cash paid				15,250	16,127	8,623
1st August, 1999 Balance left				9,750	6,500	3,250
Cash available (18,400 – 400) = 18,000 Actual loss (19,500 – 18,000) = 1,500 transferred to capital accounts				750	500	250
Cash paid				9,000	6,000	3,000

Working Note :

1. On 1st April, 1999 Rs. 1,000 is deducted from the cash available treating it as provision for bills discounted.
2. The same amount of Rs. 1,000 is added to the cash available on 1st June, 1999 since the bill was met.

Problem 7

A, B and C were partners sharing in the ratio of 4 : 3 : 1. Their Balance Sheet as on 31st March, 1998 was as follows :

Liabilities	*Amount*	*Assets*	*Amount*
Creditors	26,250	Buildings	60,000
Bank loan (secured)	8,750	Plant	20,000
Loan from A	10,000	Stock	55,000
Capital accounts :		Debtors	60,000
A	70,000		
B	30,000		
C	50,000		
	1,95,000		1,95,000

They decided to dissolve the firm. The assets were realised gradually and the net amount were distributed immediately as given below :-

1998 May	20,	Rs. 22,000	Expenses paid 2,000
July	30,	16,800	Expenses paid 1,800
September	20,	38,000	Expenses paid 3,000
November	15,	45,000	Expenses paid 5,000
December	31,	72,000	Expenses paid 7,000

Show the piecemeal distribution of cash and loss to be born by the partners.

(Delhi University, B.Com (Hons.), 1998)

Solution

Statement Showing Distribution of Cash

		Bank loan	Creditors	A's loan	A	B	C
Balance due		8,750	26,250	10,000	70,000	30,000	50,000
20-5-98							
Amount realised	22,000						
Less : Expenses	2,000						
Paid Bank loan and Creditors	20,000	8,750	11,250	—	—	—	—
		NIL	15,000	10,000	70,000	30,000	50,000
30-5-98							
Amount realised	16,800						
Less : Expenses	1,800						
Paid Creditors	15,000		15,000	—	—	—	—
			NIL	10,000	70,000	30,000	50,000

		Bank loan	Creditors	A's loan	A	B	C
20-9-98							
Amount realised	38,000						
Less : Expenses	3,000						
	35,000						
Paid A's loan	10,000			10,000	—	—	—
Maximum loss				NIL	70,000	30,000	50,000
(70,000 + 30,000 + 50,000 – 25,000) = 1,25,000 transferred to capitals in profit sharing ratio i.e., 4 : 3 : 1					62,500	46,875	15,625
				NIL	7,500	– 16,875	34,375
– 16,875 debited to A and C in the ratio of 7 : 5					– 9,844	+ 16,875	– 7,031
					– 2,344	NIL	27,344
– 2,344 debited to C					+ 2,344		– 2,344
					NIL	NIL	25,000
Cash paid					NIL	NIL	
Balance left							25,000
15-11-98					70,000	30,000	25,000
Cash available	45,000						
Less : Expenses	5,000						
	40,000						
Maximum loss (70,000 + 30,000 + 25,000 – 40,000) = 55,000 distributed among partners in profit sharing ratio i.e., 4 : 3 : 1					4,2500	31,875	10,625
					27,500	– 1,875	14,375
– 1,875 debited to A and C in the ratio of 7 : 5					– 1,094	+ 1,875	– 781
Cash paid					26,406	NIL	13,594
Balance left					43,594	30,000	11,406
31-12-98							
Amount realised	72,000						
Less : Expenses	7,000						
	65,000						
Actual loss	85,000						
Transferred in the ratio of 4 : 3 : 1	20,000				– 10,000	– 7,500	– 2,500
Cash paid					33,594	22,500	8,906

Problem 8

A, B and C are partners sharing profits and losses in the ratio of 5 : 3 : 2. Their capitals were Rs. 9,600 ; Rs. 6,000 and Rs. 8,400 respectively.

After paying creditors, the liabilities and assets of the firm were :

Liability for interest on loan from :

Spouses of partners	Rs. 2,000
Partners	Rs. 1,000
Investments	Rs. 1,000
Furniture	Rs. 2,000
Machinery	Rs. 1,200
Stock	Rs. 4,000

The assets realised in full in the order in which they are listed above. B is insolvent.

You are required to prepare a statement showing the distribution of cash as and when available, applying maximum possible loss procedure. **(C.A., Inter November, 1999)**

Solution

Statement Showing Distribution of Cash

		Interest on loan from partner's spouses	Interest on loan from partners	A	B	C
Balance due		2,000	1,000	9,600	6,000	8,400
(1) Sales of Investment	1,000					
Paid to partner's spouse	1,000	1,000	—	—	—	—
	NIL	1,000	1,000	9,600	6,000	8,400
(2) Sale of furniture	2,000					
Paid to partner's spouse and partners	2,000	1,000	1,000	—	—	—
	NIL	NIL	NIL	9,600	6,000	8,400
(3) Sale of Machinery	1,200					
Maximum possible loss is 22,800 (9,600 + 6,000 + 8,400 – 1,200) Allocated to partners in the profit sharing ratio of 5 : 3 : 2				11,400	6,840	4,560
				– 1,800	– 840	3,840
Deficiency of A and B written off against C				1,800	840	– 2,640
Balance in capital				NIL	NIL	1,200
(4) Sale of stock	4,000					
Maximum possible loss	18,800			9,600	6,000	7,200
(22,800 – 4,000) distributed to partners in the ratio of 5 : 3 : 2				– 9,400	– 5,640	– 3,760
Amount of credit and cash paid				200	360	3,440
Balance in capital a/c Unpaid-loss				9,400	5,640	3,760

Problem 9

Ram, Shyam and Bharath are partners in RSB Associates sharing profits & losses in the ratio of 5 : 4 : 3. They agree to dissolve the firm on 1-1-2000.

Balance Sheet as on 1st January, 2000

Liabilities	*Amount*	*Assets*	*Amount*
Capital account		Plant	2,50,000
Ram	6,00,000	Furniture	50,000
Shyam	4,50,000	Stock	7,50,000
Bharath	3,00,000	Debtors	7,25,000
Loan from Shyam	45,000		
Sundry Creditors	3,80,000		
	17,75,000		17,75,000

The following realisations were made :

1st Instalment	Rs. 2,50,000
2nd Instalment	Rs. 1,50,000
3rd Instalment	Rs. 1,05,000
4th Instalment	Rs. 4,50,000
5th Instalment	Rs. 4,20,000

Expenses of realisation amounted to Rs. 25,000 which was kept as reserve before distribution of proceeds until the 3rd instalment when the actual loss of Rs. 20,000 was met. Prepare a statement of distribution. **(I.C.W.A., Inter June, 2000)**

Solution

Statement Showing Distribution of Cash

		Expenses	Creditors	Loan from Shyam	R	S	B
Balance Due		25,000	3,80,000	45,000	6,00,000	4,50,000	3,00,000
Ist Instalment	2,50,000						
Expenses (kept as reserve)	– 25,000	25,000	2,25,000	—	—	—	—
Paid Creditors	– 2,25,000						
	NIL	NIL	1,55,000	45,000	6,00,000	4,50,000	3,00,000
IInd Instalment	1,50,000						
Paid Creditors	– 1,50,000		1,50,000	—	—	—	—
			5,000	45,000	6,00,000	4,50,000	3,00,000
IIIrd Instalement (1,05,000 + 5,000 being the difference between 25,000 – 20,000)	1,10,000						
Paid Creditors	– 5,000						
Paid Loan	– 45,000		5,000	45,000	—	—	—
Cash available	60,000		NIL	NIL	6,00,000	4,50,000	3,00,000
Maximum loss (6,00,000 + 4,50,000 + 3,00,000 – 60,000) = 12,90,000 Distributed among partners in the ratio of 5 : 4 : 3					5,37,500	4,30,000	3,22,500
					62,500	20,000	– 22,500
Deficiency of Bharath shared by Ram and Shyam in 4 : 3					– 12,855	– 9,645	+ 22,500

	Expenses	Creditors	Loan from Shyam	R	S	B
Cash paid				49,645	10,355	—
Balance due				5,50,355	4,39,645	3,00,000
IVth Instalment 4,50,000 Maximum possible loss (5,50,355 + 4,39,645 + 3,00,000 – 4,50,000) = 8,40,000 distributed among partners				3,50,000	2,80,000	2,10,000
Cash paid				2,00,355	1,59,645	90,000
Balance due				3,50,000	2,80,000	2,10,000
Vth Instalment 4,20,000 Maximum possible loss (3,50,000 + 2,80,000 + 2,10,000 – 4,20,000) 4,20,000 distributed among partners in the ratio of 5 : 4 : 3				1,75,000	1,40,000	1,05,000
Cash paid				1,75,000	1,40,000	1,05,000

QUESTIONS

EXERCISE 1

(Proportionate capital method)

Nishanth, Manu and Nischal are partners sharing profits and losses in the ratio of $\frac{1}{2}$, $\frac{1}{3}$ and $\frac{1}{6}$. Their Balance Sheet was as follows :-

Liabilities	*Amount*	*Assets*	*Amount*
Capitals :-		Assets less liabilities	4,000
Nishanth	1,500		
Manu	1,500		
Nischal	1,000		
	4,000		4,000

The firm was dissolved and the Assets were realised as under : I Realisation – Rs. 500, II Realisation – Rs. 750 and III Realisation – Rs. 1,250.

Prepare a statement showing how the distribution should be made under surplus capital method. **(Bangalore University, B.Com, April, 2001)**

EXERCISE 2

P, Q and R were partners in a firm sharing profits and losses in the ratio of 2 : 1 : 1 respectively. On the date of dissolution their Balance Sheet was as follows :

Liabilities	Amount	Assets	Amount
Creditors	28,000	Sundry Assets	80,000
P's Capital	20,000		
Q's Capital	20,000		
R's Capital	12,000		
	80,000		80,000

The Assets realised as follows :-

I Instalment Rs. 28,000
II Instalment Rs. 20,000
III Instalment Rs. 20,000.

Prepare a statement showing distribution of cash under proportionate capital method.

(Bangalore University, B.Com, April, 2002)

EXERCISE 3

M, N and P are partners in a firm sharing profit and loss in the ratio of 4 : 2 : 1. Their Balance Sheet as on 31st December, 1998 stood as follows :

Liabilities	Amount	Assets	Amount
Sundry Creditors	20,000	Cash	3,500
Capitals :		Buildings	36,500
M	35,000	Plant & Machinery	10,000
N	21,000	Furniture	6,000
P	14,000	Stock	20,000
		Profit & Loss	14,000
	90,000		90,000

They decided to dissolve the firm on the above date and the amount realised as under ;-

Realisation	Building	Plant & Machinery	Furniture	Stock	Expenses
I	10,000	3,000	2,000	15,000	1,500
II	15,000	5,000	2,000	3,000	1,800
III	10,000	1,000	500	2,500	200

Prepare a statement showing the distribution of cash among the partners.

(Bangalore University, B.Com, April, 1999)

EXERCISE 4

Chetali, Reshmi and Ipsita were partners in a firm sharing profits and losses in the ratio of 3 : 2 : 1. The partnership was dissolved in 30th September, 1995 when the Balance Sheet was as follows :

Liabilities	*Amount*	*Assets*	*Amount*
Capital :		Cash	8,000
Chetali	12,000	Debtors	19,000
Reshmi	11,000	Stock	40,000
Ipsita	3,000		
Loan :			
Chetali	6,000		
Reshmi	10,000		
Creditors	25,000		
	67,000		67,000

It was agreed that net realisation should be distributed in due order at the end of each month. The realisation and expenses were as follows :

	Debtors *Rs.*	*Stock* *Rs.*	*Expenses* *Rs.*
October, 1995	5,000	8,000	2,000
November, 1995	3,000	8,000	1,000
December, 1995	5,000	12,000	1,000
January, 1996	2,000	10,600	2,000
February, 1996	3,000	1,000	500

The stock was completely disposed off. It was agreed that Ipsita should take over the remaining debts of Rs. 100.

Show the distribution of cash as and when realised. **(Calcutta University, B.Com, 1996)**

Answers : Loss on realisation, Chetali Rs. 3,900 ; Reshmi ; Rs. 2,600 ; Ipsita ; Rs. 1,300.

EXERCISE 5

(Maximum loss method)

The following is the Balance Sheet of A, B and C who share profits and losses equally.

Liabilities	*Amount*	*Assets*	*Amount*
Capital Accounts		Sundry Assets	1,20,000
A	58,000	Cash at Bank	8,000
B	40,000	P & L a/c	12,000
C	22,000		
Creditors	20,000		
	1,40,000		1,40,000

The firm was dissolved on 1-12000 and the assets were realised as follows :-

Ist Instalment Rs. 12,000 ; IInd Instalment Rs. 18,000 ; IIIrd Instalment Rs. 30,000 ; IVth Instalment Rs. 36,000.

Show the distribution of cash under maximum loss method.

(Bangalore University, B.Com, April, 2001)

EXERCISE 6

A, B and C were partners sharing profits and losses in the ratio of 3 : 2 : 1. Their Balance Sheet on 31-3-1999 was as follows :-

Liabilities		*Amount*	*Assets*	*Amount*
Creditors		7,500	Cash at Bank	5,000
Mr. B's loan		1,500	Other Assets	43,000
Mr. A's loan		5,000	P & L a/c	6,000
Capitals :				
A	20,000			
B	13,000			
C	7,000			
		40,000		
		54,000		54,000

The firm was dissolved and the assets were realised in stages. The amount collected were to be distributed at the end of every month. The realisation were :

During April, 1999 – Rs. 9,000
During May, 1999 – Rs. 12,000
During June, 1999 – Rs. 15,000
During July, 1999 – Rs. 5,000

The expenses of realisation were estimated at Rs. 2,000 while the actual expenses incurred amounted to Rs. 2,400.

Prepare a statement of distribution of cash under Maximum Loss Method.

(Bangalore University, B.Com, April, 2000)

EXERCISE 7

A, B and C are partners sharing profits equally. The Balance Sheet as on 31st December, 1998 stood as follows :

Liabilities	*Amount*	*Assets*	*Amount*
Capital		Cash in hand	1,000
A	6,000	Other fixed and current assets	12,000
B	2,000		
C	1,000		
Sundry Creditors	4,000		
	13,000		13,000

On the above date the firm was dissolved and assets were realised as follows : Ist Instalment Rs. 6,700 ; IInd Instalment Rs. 2,830 ; C took away stock worth Rs. 170 and IIIrd Instalment Rs. 4,700.

Realisation expenses were estimated at Rs. 400 but it actually amounted to Rs. 500. The firm was forced to pay Rs. 1,000 out of IIIrd Instalment for which no provision was made as the same was not expected. You are required to prepare a statement showing distribution of cash among partners, using maximum loss method.

(Bangalore University, B.Com, November, 1999)

24

CHAPTER

Partnership Account — Sale of Business to a Company

A partnership firm is converted into a limited company in order to overcome the disadvantages of partnership such as unlimited liability, lack of perpetual existence and small amount of capital. Sometimes, the business of the firm is sold to a new company formed for the purpose when a partnership business is converted into a limited company the partnership firm is dissolved and the assets and liabilities of the firm will be taken over by the company. Therefore, the same procedure as applicable to the dissolution of a firm is also followed in the case of conversion of a partnership into a limited company or sale of the business of the firm to the newly formed company.

PURCHASE CONSIDERATION

On sale of business to a company the partnership firm will receive the value of the business from the company. The price so received is known as purchase consideration. From the point of view of the partnership firm it is known as sale price. Purchase consideration can be determined under any of the following methods.

1. **Net Assets method :** The excess of assets over liabilities taken over constitutes purchase consideration.
2. **Total Payment method :** The purchase consideration is paid as a lumpsum price agreed upon. The lumpsum payable may be in the form of cash, debentures and shares.

ACCOUNTING PROCEDURE

In the books of Vendor firm

The following entries are passed in the books of vendor firm.

1. The account of asset taken over by the company will be closed by transfer to Realisation a/c at Book Values

   Realisation a/c   Dr.

       To Sundry assets

2. The accounts of iiabilities taken over by the company will be closed by transfer to the realisation a/c

Liabilities a/c	Dr.	
To Realisation a/c		

3. Record the purchase consideration due

Purchasing company	Dr.	
To Realisation a/c		

4. Record the receipt of purchase consideration

Cash a/c	Dr.	
Debenture a/c	Dr.	
Shares a/c	Dr.	
To Purchasing company's a/c		

5. Sell the assets not taken over by the purchasing company.

(*a*) If the assets are realised in cash

Cash a/c	Dr.	
To Realisation a/c		

Note : The above entry is passed if the asset is transferred to realisation a/c

OR

Cash a/c	Dr.	
To Concerned asset a/c		

Note : The above entry is passed if the asset is not transferred to realisation a/c

(*b*) If the assets is realised at a valued higher then book value

Cash a/c	Dr.	(With the realised value)
To Concerned asset a/c		(With book value)
To Realisation a/c		(With profit)

(*c*) If the asset is realised at lesser than book value

Cash a/c	Dr.	(With the realised value)
Realisation a/c		(With loss)
To Concerned asset a/c		(With book value)

6. It assets are taken over by a partner.

(*a*) When assets are taken over at book value

Partner's capital a/c	Dr.	
To Asset a/c		

(*b*) When assets are taken over at higher value

Partner's capital a/c	Dr.	(With agreed value)
To Asset a/c		(With book value)
To Realisation a/c		(With profit)

(c) When asset are taken over at a lesser value

Partners capital a/c	Dr.	(With agreed value)
Realisation a/c	Dr.	(With loss)
To Asset a/c		(With books value)

7. Settle the liabilities not taken over by the purchasing Company.

(*a*) If the liability is paid in cash

Realisation a/c	Dr.	
To Cash a/c		

Note : The above entry is passed if liability is transferred to realisation a/c

Or

Liability a/c	Dr.	
To Cash a/c		

Note : The above entry is passed if liability is not to realisation a/c.

(*b*) If the liability is taken over by a partner

Liability a/c Dr.

To Partner's capital a/c

(*c*) If the liability paid is less than book value

Liability a/c Dr.

To Partner's Capital a/c

To Realisation a/c

(*d*) It the liability paid is more then book value

Liability a/c Dr.

Realisation a/c Dr.

To Partner's Capital a/c

8. Record the expenses incurred on Realisation of assets.

(*a*) When paid by partnership firm :

Realisation a/c Dr.

To Cash a/c

(*b*) When paid by the purchasing company : No entry is passed in the books of partnership firm as it is not affected by this transaction

(*c*) When it is paid by the purchasing company as part of purchase consideration.

Realisation a/c Dr.

To Cash a/c

9. At this stage the Realisation a/c will show profit or loss on Realisation of assets.

(*a*) For transfer of profit :

Realisation a/c Dr.

To All partners capital a/c

(*b*) For transfer of loss :

All partners capital a/c

To Realisation a/c

10. Transfer general reserve and undisturbed profit to partners capital accounts

General Reserve a/c Dr.

To Partner's capital a/c

11. Pay off partners loan

Partners loan a/c Dr.

To Cash

12. Pay off partner's Capital a/c balance in the ratio of their final capital balances.

Partners Capital a/c Dr.

To Shares in the purchasing Co.

To Debentures in the purchasing Co.

To Cash

ADDITIONAL TRANSACTIONS TO BE CONSIDERED

1. When the partnership from sells the shares and debentures received by it from the purchasing company.

(*a*) When sold at the same value :

Cash a/c Dr.

To Shares a/c

To Debentures a/c

(*b*) When sold at higher value :

Cash a/c Dr. (With actual cash received)
  To Shares a/c (With the sale price)
  To Debenture a/c
  To Realisation a/c (With profit)

(*c*) When sold at lower value :

Cash a/c Dr. (With actual cash)
Realisation a/c Dr. (With loss)
  To Debenture a/c (With sale price)
  To Shares a/c

2. When any asset is either sold nor taken over by any partner nor taken over by the purchasing company : Such assets must be distributed amongst partners in their profit sharing ratio. The entry is.

   Partners Capital a/c Dr.
     To Assets a/c

3. When the liabilities are neither taken over by the purchasing company nor paid in cash nor taken over by any of the partners :

   Such liabilities are distributed among partners in their final capital balances. The entry is

   Liability a/c Dr.
     To Partner's capital a/c

4. When formation expenses of the purchasing company is met by the partnership firm it is treated as realisation expenses. The following entry is passed

   Realisation a/c Dr.
     To Cash a/c

ENTRIES IN HE BOOKS OF PURCHASING COMPANY

1. On acquisition of business :

   Business purchase a/c Dr.
     To Vendor firm a/c

2. Record the assets and liabilities taken over

   Various assets a/c Dr.
     (except goodwill)
   Goodwill a/c Dr.
     (If credit exceeds debit)
     To Liabilities taken over
     To Vendor firm a/c
     To Capital Reserve (If the debit exceeds credit)

3. Payment of purchase consideration to the vendor firm

   Vendor firm a/c Dr.
     To Cash a/c
     To Debenture a/c
     To Shares Capital a/c
     To Share Premium a/c

4. When the purchase company meets the realisation expenses ;
   Goodwill a/c Dr.
   To Cash a/c
5. When the formation expenses are met by the purchasing company
   Preliminary expenses a/c Dr.
   To Cash

Problem 1

P and Q were partners sharing profits in the ratio of 2 : 1 respectively. Their Balance Sheet on 31-12-2001, on which date they converted their business into a company was as follows :

Liabilities	*Amount*	*Assets*	*Amount*
Creditors	60,000	Cash	14,000
Loan	20,000	Debtors	52,000
Capital :		Stock	32,000
P	40,000	Machinery	10,000
Q	20,000	Freehold premises	32,000
	1,40,000		1,40,000

The Company took over all the assets and liabilities except cash and loan for a purchase price of Rs. 1,20,000 payable as to Rs. 24,000 in cash and the balance in share.

Prepare the ledger accounts in the books of the firm

(Bangalore University B. Com. April 2002)

Solution

Payment of Purchase Consideration

Payment in cash	24,000
Payment in shares (1,20000 – 24,000)	96,000
	1,20,000

In the Books of the Firm

Realisation A/c

Particulars	*Amount*	*Particulars*	*Amount*
To Debtors a/c	52,000	By Creditors a/c	60,000
To Stock a/c	32,000	By Loan a/c	20,000
To Machinery a/c	10,000	By Purchasing Co. a/c	1,20,000
To Freehold premises	32,000		
To Cash a/c — Loan	20,000		
To Profit transferred to			
P's a/c	36,000		
Q's a/c	18,000		
	2,00,000		2,00,000

P's Capital A/c

Particulars	Amount	Particulars	Amount
To Shares	64,000	By Balance b/d	40,000
To Cash a/c	12,000	By Realisation a/c	36,000
	76,000		76,000

Q's Capital A/c

Particulars	Amount	Particulars	Amount
To Shares a/c (76,000 : 38,000)	32,000	By Balance b/d	20,000
		By Realisation a/c	18,000
To Cash	6,000		
	38,000		38,000

Cash A/c

Particulars	Amount	Particulars	Amount
To Balance b/d	14,000	By Realisation a/c (loan)	20,000
To Purchasing Co. a/c	24,000	By P's Capital a/c	12,000
		By Q's Capital a/c	6,000
	38,000		38,000

Purchasing Co. A/c

Particulars	Amount	Particulars	Amount
To Realisation a/c	1,20,000	By Cash a/c	24,000
		By Shares a/c	96,000
	1,20,000		1,20,000

Problem 2

X, Y and Z are in partnership sharing profits & losses in the ratio of 4 : 3 : 1 respectively. On 31st March 2001, they agreed to sell their business to a limited company. Their position on that date was as follows :

Liabilities	Amount	Assets	Amount
Capital a/cs		Freehold properly	18,000
X	20,000	Machinery	12,000
Y	15,000	Book Debts	15,000
Z	13,000	Stock	13,000
		Cash	2,000
Loan from Bank	4,000		
Sundry creditors	8,000		
	60,000		60,000

The company took the following assets at the values shown below :

Freehold property Rs. 22,000. Machinery Rs. 11,000. Book debts Rs. 14,000, Stock Rs. 12,000 and Goodwill Rs. 4,000.

The company also agreed to pay the creditors which was agreed at Rs. 7,700. The company paid Rs. 1,150 shares of Rs. 10 each fully paid and the balance in cash. The expenses amounted to Rs. 500.

Prepare Realisation a/c, Cash a/c, and Capital account in the books of the firm

(Bangalore University, B. Com. April 2001)

Solution

Calculation of Purchase Consideration

Freehold property	22,000
Machinery	11,000
Book Debts	14,000
Stock	12,000
Goodwill	4,000
	63,000
Less : Liabilities taken over-creditors	7,700
	55,300

Note :

1. Cash at Bank is not taken over by the purchasing company. So it is not taken into account in calculating purchase consideration.
2. Loan from Bank are discharged by the vendor firm. So this is not taken into account in calculating purchase consideration.
3. Purchase consideration is settled as follows

Shares 1,150 shares of Rs. 10 each	11,500
Cash (55,300 – 11,500)	43,800
	55,300

Realisation A/c

Particulars	*Amount*	*Particulars*	*Amount*
To Freehold property	18,000	By Loan from Bank a/c	4,000
To Machinery a/c	12,000	By Sundry creditors a/c	8,000
To Book debts a/c	15,000	By Purchasing Co. a/c	55,300
To Stock a/c	13,000		
To Bank a/c :			
Loan from bank a/c	4,000		
To Realisation expenses a/c	500		
To Profit transferred to			
X — $4800 \times \frac{1}{2}$	2,400		
Y — $4800 \times \frac{3}{8}$	1,800		
Z — $4800 \times \frac{1}{8}$	600		
	67,300		67,300

A's Capital A/c

Particulars	*Amount*	*Particulars*	*Amount*
To Shares a/c	4,880	By Balance b/d	20,000
To Cash a/c	17,520	By Realisation a/c	2,400
	22,400		22,400

B's Capital A/c

Particulars	*Amount*	*Particulars*	*Amount*
To Shares a/c	3,660	By Balance b/d	15,000
To Cash a/c	13,140	By Realisation a/c	1,800
	16,800		16,800

C's Capital A/c

Particulars	*Amount*	*Particulars*	*Amount*
To Shares	2,960	By Balance b/d	13,000
To Cash a/c	10,640	By Realisation a/c	600
	13,600		13,600

Cash A/c

Particulars	*Amount*	*Particulars*	*Amount*
To Balance b/d	2,000	By Realisation a/c — Expenses	500
To Purchasing Co.	43,800	By Loan from Bank	4,000
		By A's Capital a/c	17,520
		By B's Capital a/c	13,140
		By C's Capital a/c	10,640
	45,800		45,800

Purchasing Co. A/c

Particulars	*Amount*	*Particulars*	*Amount*
To Realisation a/c	55,300	By Shares a/c	11,500
		By Cash a/c	43,800
	55,300		55,300

Problem 3

Following was the balance sheet of M/S A and B on 31-12-2000.

Liabilities		*Amount*	*Assets*		*Amount*
Current Liabilities		30,000	Fixed Assets		1,00,000
General Reserve		36,000	Stock		60,000
Capital's			Debtors	25,000	
A	1,00,000		Reserve for Bad and doutful debts	1,000	24,000
B	64,000		Bill Receivable		20,000
		1,64,000	Bank		26,000
		2,30,000			2,30,000

P Ltd., acquired this business on the above date and the terms were :

(*a*) Fixed assets to be valued at 20% more then the book value.
(*b*) Stock to be valued at 90% of book value.
(*c*) Reserve for bad and Doubtful Debts to be 10% on debtors.
(*d*) The purchase consideration was to be settled by the issue of 20,000 equity shares of Rs. 10 each valued at Rs. 12 each.

Pass Journal entries in the books of P Ltd. **(Bangalore University B. Com. April 2000)**

Solution

Working Notes

1. Calculation of Purchase Consideration

Fixed assets — (1,00,000 + 20,000)	1,20,000
Stock — (60,000 – 6,000)	54,000
Debtors — (25,000 — 2,500)	22,500
Bill Receivable	20,000
Bank	26,000
	2,42,500
Less : Liabilities	30,000
	2,12,500

The purchase consideration payable in the firm of shares is Rs. 2,40,000. The difference of 27,500 (2,40,000 – 2,12,500) is premium payable on shares.

Realisation A/c

Particulars	*Amount*	*Particulars*	*Amount*
To Fixed assets a/c	1,00,000	By Current liabilities	30,000
To Stock a/c	60,000	By Reserve for bad and doubtfull debts a/c	1,000
To Debtors a/c	25,000	By Purchasing Co. a/c	2,40,000
To Bill Receivable a/c	20,000		
To Bank a/c	26,000		
To Bank a/c — Creditors	30,000		
To Profit (transferred to			
A's a/c	5,000		
B's a/c	5,000		
	2,71,000		2,71,000

A's Capital A/c

Particulars	*Amount*	*Particulars*	*Amount*
To Shares a/c	1,40,500	By Balance b/d	1,00,000
		By Reserve fund a/c	18,000
		By Realisation a/c	5,000
		By Cash a/c	17,500
	1,40,500		1,40,500

B's Capital A/c

Particulars	Amount	Particulars	Amount
To Shares a/c	99,500	By Balance b/d	64,000
		By Reserve fund a/c	18,000
		By Realisation a/c	5,000
		By Cash a/c	12,500
	99,500		99,500

Cash A/c

Particulars	Amount	Particulars	Amount
To A's Capital	17,500	By Realisation a/c	30,000
To B's Capital a/c	12,500	— Current liabilities	
	30,000		30,000

P' Ltd. Co.

Particulars	Amount	Particulars	Amount
To Realisation a/c	2,40,000	By Shares a/c	2,12,500
		By Premium a/c	27,500
	2,40,000		2,40,000

Journal Entries

Date	Particulars		Dr. Amount	Cr. Amount
	Reserve fund a/c	Dr.	36,000	
	To A's Capital a/c			18,000
	To B's Capital a/c			18,000
	(Being Reserve fund distributed)			
	Realisation a/c	Dr.	2,20,000	
	To Fixed assets			1,00,000
	To Stock			60,000
	To Debtors			25,000
	To Bill Receivable			20,000
	To Bank			26,000
	(Being assets transferred to realisation a/c			
	Current liabilities a/c	Dr.	30,000	
	Reserve for Bad and Doutful debt a/c	Dr.	1,000	
	To Realisation a/c			31,000
	(Being liabilities & RBD transferred to Realisation a/c)			
	Realisation a/c	Dr.	30,000	
	To Current liabilities			30,000
	(Being current liabilities paid)			
	P Ltd. a/c	Dr.	2,40,000	
	To Realisation a/c			2,40,000
	(Being purchase consideration due)			

Date	Particulars		Dr. Amount	Cr. Amount
	Realisation a/c	Dr.	10,000	
	To A's Capital a/c			5,000
	To B's Capital a/c			5,000
	(Being profit on realisation transferred)			
	Cash a/c	Dr.	35,000	
	To A's capital a/c			17,500
	To B's capital a/c			17,500
	(Being Cash brought in by A and B)			
	A's Capital a/c	Dr.	1,40,500	
	B's Capital a/c	Dr.	99,500	
	To Shares			2,40,000
	(Being final settlement among partners)			

Problem 4

Venkat and Suresh are equal partners and desire to convert their partnership into a Ltd. Co. Their Balance Sheet as on 31-12-1995 is as under.

Liabilities	Amount	Assets	Amount
Sundry creditors	37,000	Stock	20,000
Loan	25,000	Debtors	47,000
General reserve	15,000	Machinery	15,000
Capital :		Building	35,000
Venkat	20,000		
Suresh	20,000		
	1,17,000		1,17,000

The following terms were agreed upon.

(*a*) The loan creditor has agreed to take preference shares in the New Co.
(*b*) The creditors were to be paid in cash.
(*c*) Machinery and building were to be taken at the agreed values of Rs. 20,000 and Rs. 55,000 respectively.
(*d*) 9% Debentures to be issued for cash to the extent of Rs. 1,00,000.
(*e*) The goodwill of the firm is to be valued at Rs. 20,000.
(*f*) The Co. is to allot equity shares to the vendor for the purchase consideration.

You are required to give the Realisation a/c, Partners Capital a/c and the Opening Balance sheet of the new company. **(Bangalore University B. Com. November 1999)**

Solution

Realisation A/c

Particulars	Amount	Particulars	Amount
To Stock a/c	20,000	By Creditors a/c	37,000
To Debtors a/c	47,000	By Loan a/c	25,000
To Machinery a/c	15,000	By Purchasing Co. a/c	1,62,000
To Buildings a/c	35,000		

Particulars	Amount	Particulars	Amount
To Cash a/c — Creditors	37,000		
To Purchasing Co. (Shares issued in satisfaction of loan)	25,000		
To Profit transferred to A - 22,500 B - 22,500	45,000		
	2,24,000		2,24,000

A's Capital A/c

Particulars	Amount	Particulars	Amount
To Equity shares a/c	50,000	By Balance b/d	20,000
		By Realisation a/c	22,500
		By General reserve a/c	7,500
	50,000		50,000

B's Capital A/c

Particulars	Amount	Particulars	Amount
To Equity shares a/c	50,000	By Balance b/d	20,000
		By Realisation a/c	22,500
		By General reserve a/c	7,500
	50,000		50,000

Balance sheet of ---- Co.

Liabilities	Amount	Assets	Amount
Share Capital :		Stock a/c	20,000
Preference share		Debtors a/c	47,000
Capital	25000	Machinery a/c	20,000
Equity share		Buildings a/c	55,000
Capital	1,00,000	Goodwill a/c	20,000
9% Debentures a/c	1,00,000	Cash at Bank	63,000
	2,25,000		2,25,000

Problem 5

King Queen and Jack are sharing profits and losses in the ratio of 3 : 2 : 1. They are also entitled to interest on loan at 10% p.a.; but not interest on capital.

The partners decided to dissolve the firm on 31-3-2000 Balance sheet was drawn up to 31-12-1999 which is reproduced below :

Liabilities	*Amount*	*Assets*	*Amount*
Capital :		Buildings a/c	2,10,000
King	1,68,000	Furniture a/c	35,000
Queen	1,15,500	Motor cycle a/c	1,40,000
King's loan	77,000	Stock a/c	1,92,500
Sundry creditors	2,80,000	Sundry debtors a/c	1,40,000
Bank overdraft	1,05,000	Jack's Capital a/c	28,000
	7,45,000		7,45,000

Between the Balance Sheet date and the date of dissolution purchases amounted to Rs. 1,05,000 and sales Rs. 1,57,500. In addition to payments made to creditors, a sum of Rs. 42,000 and Rs. 21,000 were paid on account of salaries and general expenses.

Each partner withdrew Rs. 2,800 per month. On 31-3-2000, Debtors, Creditors and Stock amounted to Rs. 2,10,000 Rs. 2,45,000 and Rs. 1,57,500 respectively.

In course of proceedings the partners decided to transfer the entire business to a private limited company with all assets, liabilities and partners loan for a consideration of Rs. 3,15,000. Dissolution expenses amounted to Rs. 9,800 was borne by king.

You are advised to present the Balance Sheet as at 31-3-2000 along with necessary ledger accounts of the firm viz K Q J & Co. **(ICWA Inter, December 2000)**

Solution

Sundry Debtors A/c

Particulars	*Amount*	*Particulars*	*Amount*
To Balance b/d	1,40,000	By Bank	87,500
To Sales	1,57,500	(Balancing figure)	
		By Balance c/d	2,10,000
	2,97,500		2,97,500

Sundry creditors A/c

Particulars	*Amount*	*Particulars*	*Amount*
To Bank a/c (Balancing figure)	1,40,000	By Balance b/d	2,80,000
		By Purchases a/c	1,05,000
To Balance c/d	2,45,000		
	3,85,000		3,85,000

Bank A/c

Particulars	*Amount*	*Particulars*	*Amount*
To Sundry Debtors	87,500	By Balance c/d	1,05,000
To Balance c/d	2,45,700	By Sundry creditors a/c	1,40,000
		By Salaries a/c	42,000
		By General expenses a/c	21,000
		By Drawings a/c	25,200
	3,33,200		3,33,200

Profit & Loss A/c

Particulars	Amount	Particulars	Amount
To Opening stock	1,92,500	By Sales	1,57,500
To Purchases a/c	1,05,000	By Closing stock	1,57,500
To Salaries	42,000	By Balance c/d	45,500
To General expenses	21,000		
	3,60,500		3,60,500
To Balance b/d	45,500	By Net loss :	
To Interest on Loan	1,925	King	23,712
		Queen	15,808
		Jack	7,905
	47,425		47,425

King's Capital A/c

Particulars	Amount	Particulars	Amount
To P & L a/c	23,712	By Balance b/d	1,68,000
To Drawing (2,800 × 3)	8,400		
To Balance c/d	1,35,888		
	1,68,000		1,68,000

Queen's Capital A/c

Particulars	Amount	Particulars	Amount
To P & L a/c	15,808	By Balance b/d	1,15,000
To Drawing (2,800 × 3)	8,400		
To Balance c/d	91,292		
	1,15,000		1,15,000

Jacks Capital A/c

Particulars	Amount	Particulars	Amount
To Balance b/d	28,000	By Balance c/d	44,305
To P & L a/c	7,904		
To Drawings	8,400		
	44,305		44,305

Balance Sheet

Liabilties		*Amount*	*Assets*	*Amount*
King		1,35,888	Building	2,10,000
Queen		91,292	Furniture	35,000
Sundry Creditors		2,45,000	Motor cycle	1,40,000
Bank Overdraft		2,45,700	Stock in trade	1,57,500
Kings loan		77,000	Sundry debtors	2,10,000
Jack's capital a/c	44,305		Jack's capital	44,305
Interest on Loan	1,925			
		78,925		
		7,96,805		7,96,805

Problem 6

Arun, Barun and Karun were carrying business as oil dealers and they share profit $\frac{7}{15}$, $\frac{5}{15}$ and $\frac{3}{15}$ respectively. On 31st March 1996 they dissolve partnership. The Balance Sheet of the firm on that date was as follows :

Liabilties	*Amount*	*Assets*	*Amount*
Sundry creditors	12,500	Land & Building	37,500
Loan from Arun at 5%	30,000	Plant	11,250
Capitals :		Furniture	5,000
Arun	45,000	Stock	53,250
Barun	30,000	Sundry debtors	15,000
Karun	12,500	Cash at Bank	8,000
	1,30,000		1,30,000

Arun and Barun wanted Karun to join them in floating the concern as a private limited company but Karun refused and Arun and Barun arranged to pay Karun out and then form the company.

The arrangement between Arun, Barun and Karun were as follows : Arun and Barun took over the liabilities at book figure plus Rs. 2,500 allowed for realisation expenses : They also took over the cash at bank and the furniture was sold for cash realising Rs. 3,700. The other assets, Arun and Barun agreed to take over as follows :

Land & building Rs. 50,000 ; Plant less 10% ; Stock less 20% ; Debtors at Rs. 10,575.

Arun and Barun having paid the realisation expenses Rs. 2,500 and having paid out Karun by providing the required cash in the same proportion as they share the profits and losses inter be proceed to sell the assets as they stand to A B & Company Private Ltd., for Rs. 60,000 cash and Rs. 60,000 in fully paid shares. The latter Arun and Braun take in the same proportion as they share profits and losses.

Arun and Barun pay off the liabilities and close the partnership books.

You are required to show (*a*) The Bank a/c (*b*) The Capital Accounts (*c*) The Realisation account and (*d*) A B & Company private limited accounts.

Assume that all the above transactions are put through on March 31, 1996 (Calculation to be made to the nearest rupee) **(ICWA, Inter June 1997)**

Realisation A/c

Particulars	Amount	Particulars	Amount
To Sundry assets :		By Sundry creditors a/c	12,500
Land & Building a/c	37,500	By Bank a/c	3,700
Plant a/c	11,250	— Furniture sold a/c	
Furniture a/c	5,000	By A B Co. Ltd. :	
Stock a/c	53,250	Land & Building a/c	50,000
Debenture a/c	15,000	Plant at 9%	10,125
To A B Pvt. Ltd :	12,500	Stock at 80%	42,600
Creditors taken over a/c		Debtors a/c	10,575
To Bank a/c	2,500	By Loss on realisation	
— Realisation expenses		Transferred to	
		Arun $\frac{7}{15}$	3,500
		Barun $\frac{5}{15}$	2,500
		Karun $\frac{3}{15}$	1,500
	1,37,000		1,37,000

Arun's Capital A/c

Particulars	Amount	Particulars	Amount
To Realisation a/c — (Loss)	3,500	By Balance b/d	45,000
To Share capital a/c	35,000	By Bank a/c	1,050
To Bank — Final payment	11,458	(brought to pay Karun)	
		By A B Co. Ltd	3,908
		(Profit) $\frac{7}{12}$	
	49,958		49,958

Barun's Capital A/c

Particulars	Amount	Particulars	Amount
To Realisation a/c — Loss	2,500	By Balance b/d	30,000
To Share Capital a/c	25,000	By Bank a/c	750
To Bank final Payment	6,042	(Brought to pay Karun)	
		By A B Co. Ltd.	2,792
		Profit $\frac{5}{12}$	
	33,542		33,542

Karun's Capital A/c

Particulars	Amount	Particulars	Amount
To Realisation a/c — Loss	1,500	By Balance b/d	12,500
To Bank a/c (Karun's due paid off)	11,000		
	12,500		12,500

Bank A/c

Particulars	Amount	Particulars	Amount
To Balance b/d	8,000	By Realisation a/c — Expenses	2,500
To Realisation a/c — Furniture sold	3,700	By Karuns capital	11,000
To A's Capital a/c	1,050		
To B's Capital a/c	750		
	13,500		13,500

Particulars	Amount	Particulars	Amount
To A B & Co. Ltd.	60,000	By A B Co. c/d a/c (Sundry creditors)	12,500
		By A's loan a/c — Paid fully	30,000
		By A's Capital a/c	11,458
		By B's Capital a/c	6,042
	60,000		60,000

A B Realisation A/c

Particulars	Amount	Particulars	Amount
To Realisation a/c (Assets taken over)	1,13,300	By Realisation a/c (creditors)	12,500
To Bank a/c (creditors paid)	12,500	By Purchase consideration a/c	1,20,000
To A's capital a/c	3,908		
To B's capital a/c	2,792		
	1,32,500		1,32,500

A B & Co. Ltd A/c

Particulars	Amount	Particulars	Amount
To A & B Realisation — Purchase Consideration	1,20,000	By Bank a/c	60,000
		By Equity share Capital a/c	60,000
	1,20,000		1,20,000

EXERCISE 1

The Balance Sheet of A B C firm stood as follows on 31-12-2003.

Liabilities		*Amount*	*Assets*		*Amount*
Creditors		20,000	Cash at Bank		9,000
Bills payable		5,000	Debtors	25,000	
Capitals accounts			Less Reserve	2,000	
A	24,000				23,000
B	24,000		Stock		26,000
C	14,000		Machinery		19,000
		62,000	Furniture		10,000
		87,000			87,000

It was decided to sell the business to P Q R & Co. Ltd. On the company agreeing to allot 7,500 fully paid shares of Rs. 10 each and Rs. 1,800 in cash in full satisfaction of the purchase consideration. The company assumed liabilities except the Bills Payable and took over all the assets except Bank Balance. The expenses amounted to Rs. 800 which were paid by A B C firm. The partners shared profit & losses in the proportion of $\frac{1}{2}$ $\frac{1}{3}$ and $\frac{1}{6}$ respectively.

Pass Journal entries and prepare accounts showing the final settlement as regards the partners assuming that the shares were duly allotted.

Answer : Total profit Rs. 18,000
Total of Bank a/c Rs. 800.

EXERCISE 2

The New Co. Ltd. , is formed to take over the partnership business of A and B as at 31-12-2002. The partners share profits and losses in the ratio of 7 : 5. The Balance sheet of A and B as at 31-12-2002 is

Liabilities		*Amount*	*Assets*		*Amount*
Bills payable		7,000	Goodwill		2000
Loan		5,000	Land & Buildings		18,000
Capitals :			Machinery		12,000
A	10,000		Stock		2,000
B	8,000		Debtors	7,500	
		18,000	Less : Reserve	500	7,000
Creditors		15000	Bills Receivable		2,500
			Cash		1,500
		45,000			45,000

The Assets are taken over at Book Values except Land & Buildings and stock which were taken over at Rs. 20,000 and Rs. 2,500 respectively. The liabilities are taken over at Book Values. The purchase consideration for the net assets taken over is fixed at Rs. 30,000 Payable as follows :

Rs. 1,500, in equity shares of Rs. 10 each fully paid, Rs. 12,000 in 4% debentures and Rs. 3,000 in cash. Close the books of the firm

Answer : Profit on Realisation Rs. 12,000
Total of cash a/c Rs. 300

EXERCISE 3

The Balance Sheet of A B C firm stood as follows on 31-12-2003.

Liabilities		*Amount*	*Assets*		*Amount*
Creditors		17,000	Cash at bank		6,200
Bills payable		1,200	Sundry debtors	20,000	
Capital a/cs			Less Reserve	1,000	
					19,000
A	20,000		Stock		22,000
B	20,000		Machinery & plant		15,000
C	10,000		Fixtures		1,500
		50,000	Goodwill		4,500
		68,200			68,200

It was decided to sell the business to X Y Z Co. Ltd., on the company agreeing to allot 6,000 fully paid shares of Rs. 10 each in full satisfaction of the purchase consideration. The company assumed the liability except the bills payable and took over all the assets excepting the bank balance. The partners shared profits & losses in proportion of $\frac{1}{2}$, $\frac{1}{3}$ and $\frac{1}{6}$ respectively.

Pass Journal entries and prepare accounts showing the final settlement as regards the partners assuming that shares were duly allotted.

Answer : Profit on Realisation Rs. 15,000
Bank a/c Total Rs. 6,200

EXERCISE 4

Khalsa Co. Ltd., was formed to acquire the business of X and Y who share profit and losses in the ratio of 2 : 1 respectively. The firm's Balance Sheet on 31-12-2003 was as follows :

Liabilities	*Amount*	*Assets*	*Amount*
Creditors	10,800	Land & Building	20,000
Bills payable	3,600	Machinery	10,000
Loan	1,600	Stock	12,000
Capitals		Debtors	14,800
X	30,000	Investment	2,400
Y	22,000	Goodwill	4,000
		Cash at Bank	4,800
	68,000		68,000

The company agreed to take over the assets at book values, with the exception of Land and Buildings and stock which where taken over at Rs. 22,500 and Rs. 10,000 respectively The investments were retained by the firm and sold for Rs. 2,000. The firm also paid off the loan. The value of goodwill is fixed at Rs. 14,400.

The purchase consideration is discharged by the issue of 5,000 equity shares of Rs. 10 each fully paid and the balance in cash. Show ledger accounts to close the books of the firm.

Answer : Profit on Realisation Rs. 10,500
Total of cash a/c Rs. 14,100

EXERCISE 5

X, Y and Z were in partnership sharing profits & losses equally their balance sheet as at 31-12-2003 was as under.

Liabilities	Amount	Assets	Amount
Creditors	36,000	Debtors	68,000
Capital a/c		Stock	82,000
X	80,000	Bank	6,000
Y	30,000		
Z	10,000		
	1,56,000		1,56,000

X Y Z Co. with an authorised capital of Rs. 1,00,000 divided into 10,000 equity shares of Rs. 10, was formed to take over the business of X, Y and Z, as a going concern as from 1-1-2004. It was agreed that :

1. The X Y Z Co. Ltd should take over all the assets of the firm at book values, except the bank balance.
2. The company should also assume the liability.
3. The value of goodwill was to be Rs. 30,000.
4. The purchase consideration was payable by the allotment of 9,000 equity shares of Rs. 10 each and the balance in cash.

Set out the realisation a/c and the capital accounts of the partners.

Answer : Profit on realisation Rs. 30,000 ; Total of cash a/c Rs. 60,000

EXERCISE 6

Rama Rao and Ranga Rao are equal partners and desire to convert then partnership into a limited company. Their Balance Sheet as at 31-11-2003 is as under

Liabilities	Amount	Assets	Amount
Creditors	37,000	Stock	20,000
Loan	25,000	Debtors	47,000
General Reserve	15,000	Machinery	15,000
Capital		Building	35,000
Rama Rao	20,000		
Ranga Rao	20,000		
	1,17,000		1,17,000

The following terms were agreed upon :

(*a*) The loan creditors has agreed to take preference shares in the new company.
(*b*) The Creditors were to be paid in cash.
(*c*) Machinery and Buildings were to be taken at the agreed value of Rs. 20,000 and Rs. 55,000 respectively.
(*d*) 9% Debentures were to be issued for cash to the extent of Rs. 1,00,000.
(*e*) The good will of the firm is to be valued at Rs. 20,000.
(*f*) The company is to allot equity shares to the vendors for the purchase consideration.

You are required to give the realisation a/c, the partners capital accounts and the opening Balance sheet.

Answer : Profit on realisation Rs. 45,000
Total of opening balance sheet Rs. 2,25,000

25

CHAPTER

Single Entry System

MEANING AND FEATURES

As the name itself indicates it is a system of accounting under which only one aspect of every transaction is recorded. This is as compared to double entry system under which both the aspects (debit and credit) of transactions are recorded. However it is not proper to interpret single entry system to imply recording of only one aspect of a transaction. Truly speaking single entry system does not convey any definite system of accounting. Rather it refers to lack of adoption of a definite system. Under this system, the businessman keeps records which he considers absolutely essential for himself. This is so because the actual single entry system will differ from business to business. In other words, no uniform principle is applied to treat transactions under this system of accounting.

Different meanings are attributed to this system by different authors. A few such interpretations of the meaning of single entry system are as follows :

1. It is a system of accounting which is designed to indicate accounts for incomplete records.
2. The method of single entry involves maintaining only personal accounts of the debtors and creditors though cash book is maintained sometimes. As complete set of accounting books are not maintained and the two-fold aspects of each transaction is ignored this method of book keeping is incomplete and unsatisfactory. Accurate information of the operation of the business is also lacking under this system.
3. Single entry is indicative simply one entry for every transaction. However it is not so applied and hence a misnomer.
4. It is a system which is used to indicate partial observance of the rules of double entry. In this connection this system is termed as incomplete or defective or unscientific double entry system.
5. It is a combination of "single entry" and "double entry" but involving "no entry" in itself. It entails double entry as regards personal accounts and single entry as regards cash transaction of nominal and real items. and no entry for items like depreciation, accrued expenses etc. As it is a mixture of single entry and double entry system of book keeping it is also known as composite or hybrid system.

DEFINITION OF SINGLE ENTRY

Kohler in his book "Dictionary for Accountants" defines it as a "System of book keeping in which as a rule only records of cash and Personal accounts are maintained ; it is always incomplete double entry varying with circumstances.

Carter in his book "Advanced Accounts" defines this system as a "method or variety of methods employed for recording of transactions which ignores the two-fold aspects and consequently fails to provide the businessman with the information necessary for him to be able to ascertain the position".

Single entry system is practised under the following circumstances.

(*a*) Where a business lacks accounting knowledge of double entry system.

(*b*) Where business establishments are small in size such as sole trading concern and partnership firm which cannot afford to adopt double entry system.

(*c*) When uncertain events such as riots, accidents, flood, earthquakes etc. destroy the books of accounts thereby forcing to adopt single entry system to find out lost information such as stock, purchases, sales etc.

Features of Single Entry System

1. There is no definite or uniform pattern of single entry system. It can be adopted in any convenient form so as to suit the requirements of the business.
2. All transactions relating to business and personal are recorded in the books of accounts without distinguishing them as business and personal transactions.
3. Under this system only few books such as cash book and personal ledgers are maintained. Transactions relating to real and nominal accounts are ignored.
4. As all accounts are not prepared it is difficult to prepare trial balance and as such it is not possible to verify the arithmatical accuracy of accounts.
5. This system of accounting is employed only by small sized business but not by large sized companies. This is because higher forms of business organisation are governed by their respective Acts according to the requirements of which accounts are to be prepared.
6. For knowing the information one has to refer to the original receipt or invoice as for example to know the credit purchases the proprietor has to see purchase bills.

Advantages and Disadvantages of Single Entry System

The advantages of this system of book keeping may be summarised as under.

1. When the business transactions are few in number, this system will be more economical.
2. By adopting this system it is possible to avoid the complexity of double entry system and to overcome some of the limitation of the double entry system.
3. When the books of accounts are destroyed by unforeseeable events, this system helps in ascertaining lost information such as stock, purchases, or sales etc.
4. It is simple method of account keeping and easy to understand.
5. It is most suited to small sized business enterprise .

The disadvantages of this system as compared to double entry system are as follows :

1. **Encourages frauds and misappropriation :** Under this system transactions are partially recorded both in respect of : (*a*) number of transactions and (*b*) two-fold aspect of the transactions. This prevents the preparation of trial balance and hence it is not possible to test the arthmatical accuracy of the accounts. This leads to frauds and misappropriations.

2. **Difficult to know Gross Profit :** As it is difficult to prepare a trading account in the absence of a trial balance, it is difficult to ascertain gross profit and its rate on sales.
3. **Difficult to Know net Profit :** As nominal accounts are not maintained it is difficult to prepare a profit & loss account Hence the result of the business cannot be ascertained. In the absence of net profit information, it is difficult to know the progress of business over a period of time.
4. **Difficult to know the financial Position :** As the real accounts are not maintained it becomes difficult to prepare a Balance Sheet. Hence under this system, the financial position of a business cannot be known. It is difficult to know as to how capital is utilised in the form of assets and liabilities.
5. **Difficult to plan and control business activities :** As it is not possible to appraise the profitable and finanical position of the business, it is not possible for a businessman to plan, make decisions and exercise control over the business.
6. **Difficulty in valuing the assets of the business :** Whenever a businessman wants to sell his business it will become a problem to value tangible asset like stock and intangible asset like goodwill.
7. **Not Suitable for large Sized Organisations :** Large sized organisations such as Joint stock companies cannot employ single entry system as they have to prepare accounts according to the requirements of Companies Act.
8. **Difficulty to ascertain the efficiency of business :** As the profitability liquidity, and solvency position cannot be compared between similar business or over a period of time it is not possible to ascertain the efficiency of the business.
9. **Not acceptable by Income tax authorities :** Because of the unscientific method of ascertaining profit, this system is not accepted by income tax authorities.
10. **Difficult to rectify errors :** Rectification of errors is not possible as in the case of double entry system.
11. **Does not provide Correct information :** Any information obtained under this system will not be free from doubts.

Types of Single Entry System

Under single entry system there are no hard and fast rules relating to the maintenance accounts. As there is no uniform pattern available for adopting this system, the businessman follow their own type suiting to their convenience. From this point of view there are three types of single entry system. They are as follows :

1. **Pure single entry :** It is a type under which only a ledger containing personal accounts of debtors and creditors are maintained ignoring all other types of accounts. No subsidiary book is maintained under this type. As it fails to provide information relating to cash, expense and income, this type is not found in actual practice. The two-fold aspect of each transaction is completely ignored under this types. Hence it is not possible to prepare final accounts under this types.
2. **Conventional or simple single entry :** It is a type under which personal and cash accounts are both maintained. But the posting from cash book are made only to personal accounts and no other account is posted .

3. **Quasi-single entry :** It is a type which lies in between pure single entry and complete double entry. Under this type, personal accounts, cash book and some subsidiary books are maintained. But posting from these books are made to personal accounts only. Hence based on existing ledger accounts, trial balance and final accounts cannot be prepared. Still it is possible to prepare final accounts by incorporating unposted accounts through analysis of cash book and other subsidiary books. This process is known as conversion of single entry into double entry. This is the most popular type of single entry system.

Difference between Single Entry and Double Entry System of Book Keeping :

Points of Differences	*Double Entry System*	*Single Entry System*
1. Record of transactions	Both the aspects of a transaction are recorded	Some transactions are not recorded while in some cases only one aspect is recorded.
2. Subsidiary books	Various subsidiary books are maintained	Excepted cash book no subsidiary books are maintained.
3. Ledger Accounts	There is always a ledger which contains personal, real and nominal accounts.	There may be no ledger and even if it is maintained it contains only personal accounts.
4. Trial Balance	It is possible to prepare a trial balance. Hence it is possible to know accuracy of books of accounts.	It is not possible to prepare a trial balance under this system. Hence it is not possible to check the accuracy of accounts.
5. Final Accounts	Final accounts are prepared in a scientific manner	It is not possible to prepare final accounts. Only a rough estimate of profit or loss is made and a statement of affairs is prepared which is a Balance Sheet. It does not present an accurate picture of financial position.
6. Reliability	Books maintained are realiable as they are based on scientific principles.	Books maintained are not reliable as they are not based on scientific principles.
7. Suitability	This system of accounting is suitable for all types of business.	This system is useful only for small sized business.
8. Evidence	In case of necessity the books of accounts is treated as proof in court of law.	The books under this system can not serve the purpose of proof in a court of law.

Ascertainment of Profit and Loss and Financial Positions on the basis of Statement of Affairs :

There are two methods of ascertaining profit under single entry system. They are as follows.

1. **Synthetic Method :** This method is also called by different names such as capital

comparison method increase in net worth method or statement of affairs method. This involves preparation of two statements, viz, (a) Statement of affairs and (b) Statement of Profit & Loss.

(a) Statement of Affairs

This statement is prepared in order to know the capital amount of the businessman. For arriving at the profit or loss for any given period, it is necessary to compile two statement of affairs-one at the commencement of the period and the other at the close of the period. The opening statement of affairs helps in ascertaining opening capital and closing statement of affairs in ascertaining the closing capital of the businessman. This statement resembles to a Balance Sheet as it contains assets and liabilities. It is prepared from the records that are maintained and from information that are available form other internal source. Sometime the required information can also be estimated. This statement indicates the financial position of the business. The following procedure is involved in preparing a statement of affairs.

(*a*) The Cash Book is balanced and the book balances reconciled with physical balance.
(*b*) The physical balance of stock is counted and valued.
(*c*) The value of plant and machinery, furniture and such other assets are ascertained from existing records as are available or estimated.
(*d*) The list of debtors and creditors are made out from the ledger accounts.
(*e*) All outstanding liabilities for expenses and accounts of prepaid expenses are listed.
(*f*) The assets and liabilities having thus determined, are arranged in the form of Balance Sheet.

Differences between Statement of Affairs and a Balance Sheet

Points of Differences	*Statement of Affairs*	*Balance sheet*
1. Purpose	**1.** The purpose of preparing a statement of affairs is to find out capital as on a particulars date.	**1.** The purpose of preparing a Balance Sheet is to know the financial position of the business.
2. Accuracy	**2.** It does not reveal accurate view of the state of financial position of the business.	**2.** It reveals the true and fair view of the financial position of the business.
3. Basis of preparation	**3.** It is prepared on the basis of balances of accounts, valuation calculation enquiry and estimates.	**3.** It is prepared only on the basis of the balance of accounts
4. System of Book keeping	**4.** It is prepared under single entry system of book keeping.	**4.** It is prepared under double entry system of book keeping
5. Capital	**5.** Capital is ascertained by preparing a statement of affairs. Separate capital account is not maintained.	**5.** Capital amount is konown by preparing a seperate capital a/c

(b) Statement of Profit and Loss

The difference between closing capital and opening capital during a given period represents profit for that year. For example, if the closing capital is Rs. 20,000 and the opening capital is Rs. 15,000, the difference of Rs. 5,000 is profit. Where the businessman has withdrawn any capital or adds further amount of capital, it requires further adjustments. In such a case the following procedure is adopted to calculate the profit for the year.

(*a*) Consider the capital at the end of the year.
(*b*) Add drawings of the proprietor during the year.
(*c*) Deduct additional capital introduced by the proprietor during the year.
(*d*) Deduct opening capital of the proprietor.

The amount so arrived at is known as profit for the year. If the balance happens to be negative it indicates loss for the year. The following proforma is applicable ;

Statement Showing Ascertainment of Profit

Particulars	*Rs.*	*Rs.*
Closing capital		XX
Add : Drawings		XX
		XX
Less : Additional capital introduced	XX	
Less opening Capital	XX	XX
Profit / Loss		XX

It there are any adjustment that are to be made they too must be considered before arriving at the profit or loss amount. The various adjustments which are normally involved are : (*a*) salary to partner in case of partnership firm (*b*) interest on capital and drawings (*c*) Depreciation (*d*) Reserve for doubtful debts (*e*) Income received in advance (*f*) Prepaid expenses etc. Finally, a statement of affairs is to be prepared once again incorporating all these adjustments.

Ascertainment of result of the business under this method does not provide the information as to how profit or loss is earned or incurred. It does not consider the sales revenue, cost of production, gross profit, administration and selling expenses, This method fails to explain as to how the profit is earned.

2. Analytical Method or Conversion Method :

This method provides not only the amount of profit but also the composition thereof. Hence the method is termed as analytical method. This method involves preparation of final accounts to know not only the result but also the financial position of the business.

BOOKS OF ACCOUNTS

The number of books kept and the manner in which entries are made therein vary according to the degree of completeness of records desired. However cash book is maintained in most cases. The personal accounts of debtors and creditors are also maintained to know amount due from and due to debtors and creditors. In most of the cases real and nominal accounts are not maintained. Hence a physical verification has to be made to ascertains the assets of the business. To know the sources of income and expenses, cash book is to be analysed.

Transactions relating to credit sales and credit purchases are recorded in personal accounts as sales book and purchase book is not maintained. Similarly, returns inwards and returns outwards are also recorded in personal accounts as no separate book is maintained to record these transaction. The acceptance given on bills are recorded again in the personal account because a separate bills receivable book is not maintained . On maturity of the bills when payment is received it is recorded in the cash book. No separate record is maintained for transactions like outstanding expenses, income received in advance, depreciation on fixed assets etc.

Problem 1

Mr. Narayan maintains his books by single entry system. From the following particulars regarding his assets and liabilities and additional information provided to you ascertain the profit earned by him during 2004 :

Particulars	*31-12-2003* *Rs.*	*31-12-04* *Rs.*
Cash	1,010	1,118
Stock	11,165	12,815
Debtors	4,075	5,130
Furniture	5,000	—
Creditors	7,240	6,940

Furniture is depreciated by Narayan @ 10% per annum on diminishing balance method. Narayan withdraws every month Rs. 500 for his household expenses.

Solution

Statement of Affairs as on 31-12-03

	Amount		*Amount*
Creditors	7,240	Cash	1,010
Capital	14,010	Stock	11,165
(Balancing figure)		Debtors	4,075
		Furniture	5,000
	21,250		21,250

Statement of Affairs as on 31-12-04

	Amount			*Amount*
Creditors	6,940	Cash		1,188
Capital	16,693	Stock		12,815
(Balancing figure)		Debtors		5,130
		Furniture	5,000	
		Less : Depreciation	500	
				4,500
	23,633			23,633

Statement of Profit & Loss
For the year ended 31-12-04

Capital as on 31-12-04	16,693
Add : Drawings 500 × 12	6,000
	22,693
Less : Capital as on 31-12-03	14,010
Profit for the year	8,683

Problem 2

Ranganath had Rs. 3,00,000 in bank on 1st January 2002 when he started his business. He closed his accounts on 31st March 2003. His single entry books (in which he did not maintain any account for the bank) showed his position as follows.

Particulars	*31-3-2002* *Rs.*	*31-3-03* *Rs.*
Cash in hand	2,000	3,000
Stock in trade	19,000	29,000
Debtors	1,000	2,000
Creditors	5,000	3,000

On 1st April 2002, he began drawing Rs. 700 per month for this personal expenses from the cash book of the business. His account in the bank had the following entries.

Dates	*Deposits*	*Withdrawals*
1-1-2002	3,00,000	–
1-1-2002 to 31-3-2002	–	2,23,000
1-4-2002 to 31-3-2003	2,30,000	2,70,000

The above withdrawals included payments by cheques of Rs. 2,00,000 and Rs. 60,000 respectively during the period from 1-1-2002 to 31-3-2002. and from 1st March 2003 for the purchase of machinery for the business. The deposits after 1-1-2002 consisted wholly of sale price received from customers by cheques.

Draw up Ranganath's statement of affairs as at 31-3-2002 and 31-3-2003 respectively and work out his profit or loss for the year ended 31-3-2003.

Solution

Statement of Affairs as on 31-3-2002

	Amount			*Amount*
Sundry creditors	5,000	Cash in hand		2,000
Capital	2,94,000	Cash at bank	3,00,000	
(Balancing figure)		Less withdrawl	2,23,000	77,000
		Stock in trade		19,000
		Debtors		1,000
		Machinery		2,00,000
	2,99,000			2,99,000

Statement of Affairs as on 31-3-2003

	Amount		Amount
Sundry creditors	3,000	Cash in hand	3,000
Capital	3,28,000	Cash at bank	37,000
(Balancing figure)		(See note 2)	
		Stock in trade	29,000
		Sundry debtors	2,000
		Machinery	2,60,000
		(2,00,000 + 60,000)	
	3,31,000		3,31,000

Statement of Profit & Loss
For the year ended 31-3-2003

Capital as on 31-3-2003	3,28,000
Add : Drawings during the year (700 × 12)	8,400
	3,36,400
Less : Capital as on 31-3-2002	2,94,000
Profit for the year	42,400

Note : 1 As the rate of depreciation is not given, it is not calculated.

Note : 2 Cash at Bank for 31-3-2003 is calculated as under :

Opening balance	77,000
Add : Deposits	2,30,000
	3,07,000
Less : Withdrawals	2,70,000
Cash at bank	37,000

Conversion of Single Entry into Double Entry

Conversion of single entry into double entry involve the following steps :

1. Prepare a statement of affairs as at the beginning of the period to ascertain the opening capital.
2. Prepare a cash or Bank a/c to know :
   - Opening cash balance
   - Closing cash balance
   - Drawings
   - Cash purchases
   - Sundry expenses

   } If the debit side is more than credit side

   - Additional capital
   - Cash sales
   - Sundry income

   } It the credit side is more than debt side

3. Prepare (a) Bill Receivable a/c (b) Bills Payable a/c (c) Total Debeits a/c (d) Total creditors a/c

Bills receivable a/c is prepared to know :

- Opening balance of Bill Receivable
- Closing balance of Bill Receivable
- B. R. received from debtors during the trading period.
- Cash received against Bill Receivable (i.e., Bill Receivable honoured)

A profoma of Bills receivable a/c is shown below :

Bills Receivable A/c

	Amount		*Amount*
To Balance b/d	X X	By Cash received (i.e., Bill Receivable honoured)	X X
To Sundry Debtors (Bill Receivable received from Debtors during the Trading period)	X X	By Sundry debtors (Bill Receivable dishonoured)	X X
		By Sundry creditors (Bill Receivable endorsed to creditors)	X X
		By Balance	
	X X		X X

A bills payable a/c is prepared to known :

- Opening balance of Bills Payable
- Closing balance of Bills Payable
- Bill Payable accepted or issued to creditors during the trading.
- Cash paid against bills payable

A specimen of bills payable account is shown below.

Bills Payable A/c

	Amount		*Amount*
To Cash (Bill Payable honoured)	X X	By Balance b/d	X X
To Sundry creditors (Bill Payable dishonoured)	X X	By Sundry creditors (Bill Payable issued to creditors during the period)	X X
To Balance c/d	X X		
	X X		X X

A Total debtors a/c is prepared to know

- Credit sales
- Closing balance of debtors
- Opening balance of debtors
- Cash received from debtors

A Specimen of total debtors a/c is shown below :

Total Debtors A/c

	Amount		*Amount*
To Balance b/d	X X	By Cash (received	
To Credit sales	X X	from Debtors)	X X
To Bill Receivable (dishonoured)	X X	By Bill Receivable (received	
To Creditors (Bill Receivable	X X	form Debtors)	X X
endorsed to creditors		By Sales returns	X X
dishonoured)		By Bad debts	X X
Cash (paid to		By Discount allowed	
(Debtors)	X X	to debtors	X X
To Interest charged		By Balance c/d	X X
Debtors	X X		

A total creditors accounts is prepared to know :

- Credit Purchases
- Opening balance of creditors
- Closing balance of creditors
- Cash paid to creditors

A Specimen of total creditors a/c is shown below

Total Creditors A/c

	Amount		*Amount*
To Cash (paid to creditors)	X X	By Balance b/d	X X
To B/P issued to creditors	X X	By Credit purchases	X X
To B/R endorsed to creditors	X X	By Bill Payable Dishonoured	X X
To Purchases returns	X X	By Debtors (Bill Receivable	
To Discount received from creditors	X X	endorsed to creditors dishonoured	X X
To Balance c/d	X X	By Cash received from creditors	X X
		By Interest credited to creditors	X X

4. Necessary adjustment must be made for items as prepaid or outstanding expenses, accrured interest, depreciation atc.
5. Prepare final accounts in the usual manner.

Problem 3

From the following particulars prepare Bills Receivable a/c and Total Debtors a/c for the year ended 31-12-1999

Total Debtors on 1-1-1999	36,000
Bills Receivable on 1-1-1999	10,000
Sales (including cash sales Rs. 20,000 made during the year)	3,00,000
Cash received from debtors	2,00,000
Bills receivable on 31-12-1999	15,000

Returns Inwards	15,000
Discount allowed to debtors	10,000
Bad debts written off	3,000
Bills Receivable endorsed to creditors	10,000
Cash received on bill matured	15,000

(University of Madras B. Com. April 2001)

Solution

Total Debtors A/c

Date	*Particulars*	*Amount*	*Date*	*Particulars*	*Amount*
1-1-99	To Balance b/d	36,000		By Cash received from debtors	2,00,000
	To Credit sales (3,00,000 – 20,000)	2,80,000		By Returns Inwards	15,000
				By Discount allowed	10,000
				By Bad debts	3,000
				By B. R. a/c	30,000
			31-12-99	By Balance c/d	58,000
		3,16,000			3,16,000

Bills Receivable A/c

Date	*Particulars*	*Amount*	*Date*	*Particulars*	*Amount*
1-1-99	To Balance b/d	10,000		By Cash received against bill	15,000
	To Debtors a/c (B. R. received from debtors)	30,000		By Bill Endorsement to creditor	10,000
			31-12-99	By Balance c/d	15,000
		40,000			40,000

Problem 4

Mr. Sankar did not maintain his books under double entry systems as well as his bank a/c. From the following information prepare his profit and loss a/c for the year ended 30-6-1999 and his Balance Sheet as on that date.

(*a*)

Assets and Liabilities	*30-6-1998* *Rs.*	*30-6-1999* *Rs.*
Stock in trade	19,800	1,13,200
Creditors	31,000	14,500
Debtors	1,18,000	1,25,000
Building	90,000	90,000
Furniture	11,000	11,500
Air Conditioner	15,000	15,000

(*b*) Creditors as at 30-6-1998 includes Rs. 15,000 for purchase of Air conditioner

	Rs.
(*c*) Cash transaction :	
Cash at July 1, 1998	15,000
Collecting form customers	1,60,800
Payment to creditors (Trade)	1,44,000
Rent & taxes	11,500
Salaries	1,12,500
Sundry Expenses	18,000
Sundry Income	16,500
Drawings by Sankar	30,000
Loan from Mrs. Babu	23,000
Capital introduced	12,000
Cash Sales	11,500
Cash Purchases	15,000
Paid to Air Conditioner	15,000

(*d*) Bad debts written off Rs. 1,200

(University of Madras, B. Com. April 2001)

Solution

Working Notes :

1. Calculation of credit sales :

Debtors A/c

	Amount		*Amount*
To Balance b/d	1,18,000	By Cash received from customers	1,60,800
To Credit sales (Balancing figure)	1,69,000	By Bad debts	1,200
		By Balance c/d	1,25,000
	2,87,000		2,87,000

2. Calculation of credit Purchases :

Creditors A/c

	Amount		*Amount*
To Cash paid to creditors	1,44,000	By Balance b/d (15,000 for A C + 16,000)	31,000
To Cash paid to Air Conditioner	15,000	By Credit purchases (Balancing figure)	1,42,500
To Balance c/d	14,500		
	1,73,500		1,73,500

3. Calculation of opening capital :

Opening Statement of Affairs

Particulars	*Amount*	*Particulars*	*Amount*
Creditors	31,000	Stock in trade	19,800
Capital (Balancing figure)	2,37,800	Debtors	1,18,000
		Building	90,000
		Furniture	11,000
		Air Conditioner	15,000
		Cash	1,5000
	2,68,800		2,68,800

4. Calculation of closing cash balance :

Cash A/c

Particulars	Amount	Particulars	Amount
To Balance b/d	15,000	By Payment to creditors	1,44,000
To Collection form customers	1,60,800	By Rent and tax	11,500
To Sundry Income	16,500	By Salaries	1,12,500
To Loan from Mrs. Basu	23,000	By Sundry expenses	18,000
To Cash sales	11,500	By Drawings	30,000
To Capital introduced	12,000	By Cash purchase	15,000
To Balance c/d	1,07,700	By Paid for Air conditioner	15,000
(Balancing figure)		By Purchase of furniture	500
		(See note -5)	
	3,46,500		3,46,500

5. Calculation of purchase of furniture

Opening balance of furniture is	11,000
Closing balance of furniture is	11,500
Difference is purchase of furniture	500

Trading and Profit & Loss A/c

Particulars		Amount	Particulars		Amount
To Opening stock		19,800	By Sales :		
To Purchase :			Cash	11,500	
Cash	1,500		Credit	1,69,000	
Credit	1,42,500				1,80,500
		1,57,500	By Closing stock		1,13,200
To Gross profit		1,16,400			
		2,93,700			2,93,700
To Rent & taxes		11,500	By Gross profit		1,16,400
To Salaries		1,12,500	By Sundry Income		16,500
To Sundry expenses		18,000	By Net loss		10,300
To Bad debits		1,200			
		1,43,200			1,43,200

Balance Sheet

Particulars		Amount	Particulars	Amount
Capital	2,37,800		Closing stock	1,13,200
Less Net loss	10,300		Debtors	1,25,000
	2,27,500		Building	90,000
Less Drawings	30,000		Furniture	11,500
	1,97,500		Air-conditioner	15,000
Add Capital introduced	12,000			
		2,09,500		
Creditors		14,500		
Loan from Mrs. Babu		23,000		
Bank OD		1,07,700		
		3,54,700		3,54,700

Problem 5

Mr. Srinivas did not maintain his Books of Accounts property. From the following data supplied to you, prepare Final accounts for the year ended 31-12-1999.

	Rs.
Opening stock	10,000
Creditors on 1-1-1999	4,000
Cash on hand on 1-1-1999	6,000
Furniture on 1-1-1999	2,000
Salaries	6,800
Rent	2,400
Other expenses	4,800
Cash sales	8,000
Credit sales	80,000
Cash received from debtors	64,000
Cash paid to creditors	36,000
Cash purchases	4,000
Credit purchases	60,000
Closing stock	8,000
Debtors on 31-12-1999	24,000
Debtors on 1-1-1999	10,000
Drawings	10,000
Discount allowed to debtors	2,000

(Bangalore University, B. Com. April 2002)

Solution

Working Notes

1. Calculation of opening capital balance :

Opening Statement of Affairs

Particulars	*Amount*	*Particulars*	*Amount*
Creditors	4,000	Cash in hand	6,000
Opening capital (Balancing figure)	24,000	Debtors	10,000
		Stock	10,000
		Furniture	2,000
	28,000		28,000

2. Calculation of closing cash balance

Cash A/c

Particulars	*Amount*	*Particulars*	*Amount*
To Balance b/d	6,000	By Office salaries	6,800
To Cash sales	8,000	By Rent	2,400
To Cash received from Debtors	64,000	By Other expenses	4,800
		By Cash paid to creditors	36,000
		By Cash purchases	4,000
		By Drawings	10,000
		By Balance given	14,000
	78,000		78,000

3. Calculation of opening balance of debtors

Total Debtors A/c

Particulars	Amount	Particulars	Amount
To Balance b/d — Opening balance (Balancing figure)	10,000	By Cash received from debtors	64,000
		By Discount allowed to debtors	2,000
		By Balance c/d	24,000
To Credit sales	80,000		
	90,000		90,000

4. Calculation of closing balance of creditors

Total Creditors A/c

Particulars	Amount	Particulars	Amount
To Cash paid to creditors	36,000	By Balance b/d	4,000
To Balance c/d (Balancing figure)	28,000	By Credit purchasers	60,000
	64,000		64,000

Trading and Profit & Loss A/c

Particulars		Amount	Particulars		Amount
To Opening stock		10,000	By Sales :		
To Purchases			— Cash	8,000	
— Cash	4,000		— Credit	80,000	
— Credit	60,000				88,000
		64,000	By Closing stock		8,000
To Gross profit c/d		22,000			
		96,000			96,000

Particulars	Amount	Particulars	Amount
To Office salaries	6,800	By Gross profit b/d	22,000
To Rent	2,400		
To Other expenses	4,800		
Discount allowed	2,000		
To Not profit c/d	6,000		
	22,000		22,000

Balance Sheet as on 31-12-1999

Leablel		Amount	Assest	Amount
Creditors		28,000	Cash in hand	14,000
Capital			Debtors	24,000
Opening balance	24,000		Closing stock	8,000
Add net profit	6,000		Furniture	2,000
	30,000			
Less Drawings	10,000			
		20,000		
		48,000		48,000

Problem 6

With the information given by a businessman prepare a profit and loss account for the year ended 31st December 1999 and the Balance Sheet as on that date :

Receipts for the year ended 31st December 1999 :

	Rs.
From sundry debtors	17,625
Cash sales	4,125
Paid by proprietor	2,500
	24,250

Payment made in the year ended 31-12-1999.

	Rs.
New plant purchased	625
Drawings	1,500
Wages	6,725
Salaries	1,125
Interest paid	75
Telephone	125
Rent	1,200
Light and power	475
Sundry expenses	2,125
Sundry creditors	7,625
	21,600

Assets and Liabilities	*31-12-98* *Rs.*	*31-12-99* *Rs.*
Sundry Creditors	2,525	2,400
Sundry debtors	3,750	6,125
Bank	625	—
Stock	6,250	3,125
Plant	7,500	7315

(University of Madras, B. Com. May 2001)

Solution

Working Notes

1. Calculation of Purchases

Total Creditors A/c

	Amount		*Amount*
To Payment to creditors	7,625	By Balance b/d	2,525
To Balance c/d	2,400	By Credit purchases (Balancing figure)	7,500
	10,025		10,025

2. Calculation of sales

Total Debtors A/c

	Amount		*Amount*
To Balance b/d	3,750	By Cash received from Debtors	17,625
To Credit sales (Balancing figure)	20,000	By Balance c/d	6,125
	23,750		23,750

3. Calculation of Depreciation on plant :

Plant on 1-1-99	7,500
Add : New plant purchased	625
	8,125
Less : Plant on 31-12-99	7,315
Depreciation for the year	810

4. Calculation of closing Bank balance

Bank A/c

	Amount		*Amount*
To Balance b/d	625	By Cash payment	21,600
To Cash received During the year	24,250	By Balance c/d	3,275
	24,875		24,875

5. Calculation of Opening Capital

Opening Statement of Affairs

	Amount		*Amount*
Creditors	2,525	Bank	625
Capital (Balancing figure)	15,600	Debtors	3,750
		Stock	6,250
		Plant	7,500
	18,125		18,125

Trading and Profit & Loss A/c

	Amount			*Amount*
To Opening stock	6,250	By Sales		
To Purchases	7,500	— Cash	4,125	
To Wages	6,725	— Credit	20,000	
To Power	475			24,125
To Gross profit	6,300	By Closing stock		3,125
	27,250			27,250
To Salaries	1,125	By Gross profit b/d		6,300
To Interest	75			
To Telephone	125			
To Rent	1,200			
To Sundry expenses	2,125			
To Depreciation	810			
To Net profit	840			
	6,300			6,300

Balance Sheet as on 31-12-1999

		Amount			Amount
Capital	15,600		Bank		3,275
Add net profit	840		Debtors		6,125
	16,440		Closing stock		3,125
Less : Drawings	1,500		Plant : On 1-1-98	7,500	
	14,940		Add : new plant	625	
Add Additional Capital	2,500			8,125	
		17,440	Less : Depreciation	810	
Sundry Creditors		2,400			7,315
		19,840			19,840

Problem 7

Mr. Venkat keeps his books by single entry. From the following particulars prepare his Trading profit and loss account for the year ending 31-3-1998 and the Balance Sheet as on that date. On 1st April 1997, he had stock worth Rs. 30,000, Creditors Rs. 250,00, Debtors. Rs. 60,000, Business Premises Rs. 50,000, Office Furniture Rs. 5,000 and Bank Overdraft Rs. 15,000.

On the analysis of his cash book for the year you find :

Received from debts	80,000
Cash sales	25,000
Rent & Taxes paid	1,500
Drew for personal use	2,000
Paid to creditors	40,000
Cash purchases	10,000
Interest on overdraft	1,000
Salary and wages	9,000
General expenses	800

A scruiting of the personal accounts showed that he had allowed Rs. 4,000 as discount to his customers and had earned Rs. 3,000 as discount from his supplies.

On 31st March 1998 he had stock Rs. 50,000, Debtors Rs. 65,000, Creditors Rs. 20,000. Business Premises Rs. 50,000, Office Furniture Rs. 5,000. He also owed Rs. 400 for expenses. Charge 5% depreciation on furniture and premises. Provide Rs. 4,000 for doubtful debts and allow 5% interest on capital. **(Osmania University B. Com. October 2000)**

Solution

Working Notes

(*a*) Calculation of Credit Sales

Total Debtors A/c

Particulars	*Amount*	*Particulars*	*Amount*
To Balance b/d	60,000	By Bank	80,000
To Credit sales	89,000	By Discount allowed	4,000
		By Balance c/d	65,000
	1,49,000		1,49,000

(*b*) Calculation of Credit Purchases :

Total Creditors A/c

Particulars	*Amount*	*Particulars*	*Amount*
To Bank	40,000	By Balance b/d	25,000
To Discount received	3,000	By Credit Purchases	38,000
To Balance c/d	20,000		
	63,000		63,000

(*c*) Calculation of Opening Capital Balance

Opening Statement of Affairs

Particulars	*Amount*	*Particulars*	*Amount*
Bank overdraft	15,000	Debtors	60,000
Sundry creditors	25,000	Stock	30,000
Capital	1,05,000	Business premises	50,000
(Balancing figure)		Office furniture	5,000
	1,45,000		1,45,000

(*d*) Calculation of Closing Cash Balance

Cash A/c

Particulars	*Amount*	*Particulars*	*Amount*
To Cash received from debtors	80,000	By Balance b/d	15,000
To Cash sales	25,000	By Rent & Taxes	1,500
		By Drawings	2,000
		By Payment to creditors	40,000
		By Cash purchases	10,000
		By Interest on O.D.	1,000
		By Salary and wages	9,000
		By General expenses	800
		By Balance c/d	25,700
	1,05,000		1,05,000

Trading and Profit & Loss A/c

Particulars		*Amount*	*Particulars*		*Amount*
To Opening stock		30,000	By Sales :		
To Purchases			Cash	25,000	
— Cash	10,000		Credit	89,000	
— Credit	38,000				1,14,000
		48,000	By Closing stock		50,000
To Gross profit		86,000			
		1,64,000			1,64,000
To Rent & taxes		1,500	By Gross profit		86,000
To Interest on Overdraft		1,000	By Discount received		3,000
To Salary & wages		9,000			
To general expenses		800			
To Discount allowed		4,000			
To Outstanding expenses		400			
To Depreciation on furniture		250			
To Depreciation on premises		2,500			
To Provision for Doubtful debts		4,000			
To Interest on capital		5,250			
To Net profit transferred to capital a/c		60,300			
		89,000			89,000

Balance Sheet as on 31-3-1998

Liabilities		*Amount*	*Assests*		*Amount*
Creditors		20,000	Cash at bank		25,700
Outstanding expenses		400	Sundry debtors	65,000	
Capital	1,05,000		Less provision for D. D.	4,000	61,000
Add Net Profit	60,300		Closing stock		50,000
Add Interest on capital	5,250		Furniture	5,000	
	1,70,550		Less Depreciation	250	
Less Drawings	2,000				4,750
		1,68,550	Business premises	50,000	
			Less depreciation	2,500	
					47,500
		1,88,950			1,88,950

Problem 8

Mr. Yugandhar keeps incomplete books. With the help of the following information Prepare his trading and profit & loss account for the Year ended 30th June 1998 and Balance Sheet as on that date.

His Position on 1st July 1997

Stock Rs. 13,000 : Creditors Rs. 12,500 : Debtors Rs. 32,000 : Buildings Rs. 20,000, Bank overdraft Rs. 5,000 and furniture Rs. 2,000.

Analysis of Cash Book :

Received from debtors Rs. 38,000, Cash sales Rs. 11,000 : Paid to creditors Rs. 24,000 : Cash purchases Rs. 7,000 : Interest on overdraft Rs. 300 : Wages Rs. 1,350 : Salaries Rs. 3,000 : General expenses Rs. 1,100, Drawings Rs. 600.

He allowed discount Rs. 2,250 and received discount Rs. 1,750 in the year. Stock on 30th June 1998 could not be known but Mr. Yugandhar informs that he has sold goods at cost plus 25%. Debtors and creditors were Rs. 36,600 and Rs. 13,750 respectively on 30th June 1998

(Sri Venkateshwara University B. Com. September 2000)

Solution

Working Notes

1. Calculation of Credit Sales

Total Debtors A/c

Particulars	*Amount*	*Particulars*	*Amount*
To Balance b/d	32,000	By Cash	38,000
To Credit sales	44,850	By Discount allowed	2,250
(Balancing figure)		By Balance c/d	36,600
	76,850		76,850

Total Creditors

Particulars	*Amount*	*Particulars*	*Amount*
To Cash paid	24,000	By Balance b/d	12,500
To Discount received	1,750	By Credit purchases	27,000
To Balance c/d	13,750		
	39,500		39,500

3. Calculation of closing cash balance :

Cash A/c

Particulars	*Amount*	*Particulars*	*Amount*
To Received from Debtors	38,000	By Bank overdraft	5,000
To Cash sales	11,000	By Paid to creditors	24,000
		By Purchases	7,000
		By Interest on bank Overdraft	300
		By Wages	1,350
		By Salaries	3,000
		By General expenses	1,100
		By Drawings	600
		By Balance c/d	6,650
	49,000		49,000

4. Calculation of Value of Closing Stock :

Trading A/c

Particulars		*Amount*	*Particulars*		*Amount*
To Opening stock		13,000	By Sales :		
To Purchases :			— Cash	11,000	
— Cash	7,000		— Credit	44,850	
— Credit	27,000				55,850
		34,000	By Closing stock		2,320
To Profit		11,170	(Balancing figure)		
$55850 \times \frac{25}{125}$					
		58,170			58,170

Note : Calculating of profit :

Let cost price = Rs. 100

Add profit = Rs. 25

Selling price = Rs. 125

If the selling price is 125 profit is 25

If the selling price is 55850 → ?

$$55{,}850 \times \frac{25}{125} = \text{Rs. } 11{,}170$$

5. Calculation of opening capital balance

Opening Statement of Affairs

Particulars	*Amount*	*Particulars*	*Amount*
Creditors	12,500	Stock in trade	13,000
Bank O.D.	5,000	Buildings	20,000
Capital	49,500	Furniture	2,000
(Balancing figure)		Debtors	32,000
	67,000		67,000

Trading and Profit & Loss A/c

Particulars		*Amount*	*Particulars*		*Amount*
To Opening stock		13,000	By Sales		
To Purchases :			— Credit	44,850	
— Cash	7,000		— Cash	11,000	
— Credit	27,000				55,850
		34,000	By Closing stock		2,320
To Wages		1,350			
To Gross profit		9,820			
		58,170			58,170

Particulars	Amount	Particulars	Amount
To Salaries	3,000	By Gross profit	9,820
To General expenses	1,100	By Discount received	1,750
To Discount allowed	2,250		
To Interest on overdraft	300		
To Net profit	4,920		
	11,570		11,570

Balance Sheet Cash as on 30-6-1998

Liabilities		Amount	Assets	Amount
Creditors		13,750	Cash	6,650
Capital	49,500		Buildings	20,000
Add net profit	4,920		Debtors	36,600
	54,420		Closing stock	2,320
Less Drawings	600			
		53,820		
		67,570		67,570

Problem 9

The following information is obtained from the books of Mr. Vinay, who maintained the same under single entry system.

1. Receipts for the year ending 31-12-2000 :

	Rs.
From Debtors	88,125
Cash sales	20,625
Paid by Mr. Vinay	12,500

2. Payments during the year :

New plant bought	3,125
Drawings	7,500
Salaries	5,625
Wages	33,625
Interest paid	375
Rent paid	6,625
Light and power	2,375
Sundry expenses	10625
Sundry creditors	38,125

Mr. Vinay banks all receipts and makes payments by means of cheques.

3.

Assets and Liabilities	*1-1-2000 Rs.*	*31-12-2000 Rs.*
Sundry creditors	12,625	12000
Sundry debtors	18,750	30,625
Bank	3,125	?
Stock	31,250	15,625
Plant	37,500	36,575

Prepare Trading and Profit & Loss a/c and Balance Sheet

(Bangalore University, B. Com. April 2001)

Solution

Working Notes :

1. Calculation of Credit purchases

Total Creditors

Particulars	*Amount*	*Particulars*	*Amount*
To Bank — Paid to creditors	38,125	By Balance b/d	12,625
To Balance c/d	12,000	By Credit Purchases (Balancing figure)	37,500
	50,125		50,125

2. Calculation of Credit Sales

Total Debtors

Particulars	*Amount*	*Particulars*	*Amount*
To Balance b/d	18,750	By Bank — Received from debtors	88,125
To Credit sales (Balancing figure)	1,00,000	By Balance c/d	30,625
	1,18,750		1,18,750

3. Calculation of Opening Capital

Opening Statement of Affairs

Particulars	*Amount*	*Particulars*	*Amount*
Sundry creditors	12,625	Bank	3,125
Capital	78,000	Stock	31,250
		Sundry debtors	18,750
		Plant	37,500
	90,625		90,625

4. Calculation of closing bank balance

Bank A/c

Particulars	*Amount*	*Particulars*	*Amount*
To Balance b/d	3,125	By New plant	3,125
To Received from Debtors	88,125	By Wages	33,625
To Cash sales	20,625	By Interest paid	375
To Paid by vinay	12,500	By Rent	6,625
		By Sundry expenses	10,625
		By Drawings	7,500
		By Salary	5,625
		By Light & power	2,375
		By Paid to sundry creditors	38,125
		By Balance c/d	16,375
	1,24,375		1,24,375

5. Calculation of Depreciation on plant

Plant A/c

Particulars	*Amount*	*Particulars*	*Amount*
To Balance b/d	37,500	By Depreciation (Balancing figure)	4,050
To Bank-new Plant	3,125	By Balance c/d	36,575
	40,625		40,625

Trading and Profit & Loss A/c

Particulars	*Amount*	*Particulars*	*Amount*
To Opening stock	31,250	By Sales	
To Purchases — Credit	37,500	— Cash	20,625
To Wages	33,625	— Credit	1,00,000
To Light & Power	2,375	By Closing stock	15,625
To Gross profit	31,500		
	1,36,250		1,36,250
To Salaries	5,625	By Gross profit	31,500
To Sundry expenses	10,625		
To Rent	6,625		
To Interest	375		
To Depreciation on Plant	4,050		
To Net profit	4,200		
	31,500		31,500

Balance Sheet as on 31-12-2000

Liabilities		*Amount*	*Assets*		*Amount*
Sundry Creditors		12,000	Plant	37,500	
Capital :			Add :		
Opening balance	78,000		Additions	3,125	
Add : Additions	12,500			40,625	
	90,500		Less : Dep	4,050	
					36,575
Add : Net profit	4,200		Sundry debtors		30,625
	94,700		Stock		15,625
Less : Drawings	7,500		Bank		16,375
		87,200			
		99,200			99,200

Problem 10

Mr. Ananda Kumar a small producer of Machine parts, has supplied the following details of his business transactions :

	Rs.
Cash and discount credited to debtors	64,200
Discount received	200
Expenses paid in cash	3,400
Bad debts	500
Cash drawn from bank	4,500
Expenses paid by cheque	3,500
Cash collections from debtors	20,300
Cash deposit in bank	15,500
Cash drawings	1,500
Cheques collected from debtors	43,200
Drawings by cheques	4,200
Cash in hand on 30-9-1995	2,200
Discount allowed	700
Cheques paid to creditors	53,400
Total sale	69,100
Cash purchases	2,100
Cash paid to creditors	6,300

	As on 1-10-94	As on 30-9-95
	Rs.	Rs.
Debtors	?	15,000
Cash and Bank balance	13,900	5,300
Stock	8,700	10,500
Plant	56,00	4,600
Furniture	2,200	2,200
Creditors	6,000	9,400
Liabilities for expenses	500	800

You are required to prepare trading and profit & loss account for the year ending 30-9-95 and a Balance Sheet as on that date (University of Madras, B. Com. October 2000).

Solution

Working Notes :

1. Calculation of credit purchase

Creditors A/c

Particulars	*Amount*	*Particulars*	*Amount*
To Discount received	200	By Balance b/d	6,000
To Cash paid to creditors	6,300	By Credit purchase	63,300
To Cheques paid to creditor	53,400	(Balancing figure)	
To Balance c/d	9,400		
	69,300		69,300

2. Calculation of opening balance of Debtors

Debtors A/c

Particulars	*Amount*	*Particulars*	*Amount*
To Opening balance b/d (Balancing figure)	12,900	By Discount allowed	700
To Credit sales (69,100 - 2,300)	66,800	By Cash collection	20,300
		By Cheque collected	43,200
		By Bad debts	500
		By Balance c/d	15,000
	79,700		79,700

3. Calculation of Opening Capital

Opening Statement of Affairs

Particulars	*Amount*	*Particulars*	*Amount*
Creditors	6,000	Debtors	12,900
Liability for expenses	500	Cash & bank	13,900
Opening balance of Capital	36,800	Stock	8,700
		Plant	5,600
		Furniture	2,200
	43,300		43,300

4. Calculation of cash sales and opening balance of bank. As cash transactions and cheque transaction are separately given a two column cash book (i.e., cash & bank column) is prepared

Cash Book — Cash & Bank Columns

Particulars	*Cash*	*Bank*	*Particulars*	*Cash*	*Bank*
To Balance b/d (13,900 – 10,000)	3,900	—	By Cash deposited into bank (Contra)	15,500	—
To Balance b/d (Balancing figure)	—	10,000	By Cash drawn firm bank (Contra)	—	4,500
To Cash collection from Debtors	20,300	—	By Expenses paid in cash	3,400	
To Cheque collection from debtors	—	43,200	By Expenses paid by cheque	—	3,500
To Cash drawn From Bank (Contra)	—	15,500	By Cash drawn by proprietor	1,500	—
			By Cheques drawn by proprietor	—	4,200
			By Cheque paid to creditors	—	53,400
			By Cash paid to creditor	6,300	
			By Cash purchases	2,100	
			By Balance c/d (5,300 – 2,200)	2,200	3,100
	31,000	68,700		31,000	68,700

5. Calculation of depreciation on plant

Opening balance of plant	5,600
Less closing balance	4,600
Depreciation	1,000

Trading & Profit & Loss A/c

		Amount		*Amount*
To Opening stock		8,700	By Sales	
To Purchases			— Cash	2,300
— Cash		2,100	— Credit	66,800
— Credit		63,300	By Closing stock	10,500
			By Gross profit c/d	5,500
		79,600		79,600
To expenses paid in cash	3,400		By Gross profit	5,500
To Expenses paid in cheques	3,500		By Discount received	200
Add : o/s Liability		6,900	By Net loss	3,700
for expenses	800			
	7,700			
Less : o/s liability for expenses (opening)	500			
		7200		
To Bad debts		500		
To Discount allowed		700		
To Depreciation on plant		1,000		
		9,400		9,400

Balance Sheet as on 30-9-95

Liabilities		*Amount*	*Assets*	*Amount*
Creditors		9,400	Debtors	15,000
o/s Liability for expenses		800	Cash	2,200
Capital :			Bank	3,100
Opening balance	36,800		Stock	10,500
Less : Net loss	3,700		Plant (5,600 – 1,000)	4,600
	33,100		Furniture	2,200
Less Drawings :				
— Cash 1,500				
— Cheque 4,200	5,700			
		27,400		
		37,600		37,600

Problem 11

The following is the Balance Sheet of P and Q as on 1-4-1997.

Liabilities	*Amount*	*Assests*	*Amount*
Creditors	18,000	Cash at Banks	20,000
Bills payable	8,000	Bills Receivable	7,500
Capital accounts		Debtors	19,500
P 50,500		Stock of goods	30,000
Q 50,500		Plant & Machinery	20,000
	1,01,000	Land & Buildings	30,000
	1,27,000		1,27,000

	Rs.
Other transactions :	
Purchase	1,50,000
Discount received on purchases	500
Sales	1,90,000
Discount allowed on sales	1,000
Bills receivable received during the year	45,000
Bills payable issued during the year	77,500
Stock of goods on 31-3-1998	35,000

You are required to write off depreciation of plant and machinery Rs. 2,000 and to provide for depreciation of Rs. 1,500 on land & Buildings and for discount of Rs. 1,000 on debtors.

Prepare trading, profit & loss a/c for the year ended 31-3-1998 and the Balance sheet as on that date, dividing the profit equally between the partners, paid & P & Q after taking note of the cash transactions for the year 1997 - 98 Which are given ahead.

Details of cash transactions :

Date	*Particulars*	*Amount*	*Date*	*Particulars*	*Amount*
1-4-97	To Balance b/d	20,000		By Salaries	6,000
	To Receipts from Debtors	1,35,000		By Wages	7,400
	To Bills receivable	45,000		By Bills payable	36,600
				By Payment to Creditors	77,500
				By Drawings by 'P'	7,500
				By Drawings by 'Q'	7,500
			31-3-98	By Balance c/d	57,500
		2,00,000			2,00,000

(Osmania University, B. Com. March 2000)

Solution

Working Notes

(*a*) Calculation of closing balance of Debtors

Total Debtors A/c

Particulars	*Amount*	*Particulars*	*Amount*
To Balance b/d	19,500	By Bank	1,35,000
To Sales	1,90,000	By Discount allowed	1,000
		By Bills receivable	45,000
		By Balance c/d	28,500
	2,09,500		2,09,500

(*b*) Calculation of closing balance of Bill Receivable

Bills Receivable A/c

Particulars	*Amount*	*Particulars*	*Amount*
To Balance b/d	7,500	By Bank a/c	45,000
To Sundry debtors a/c	45,000	By Balance c/d	7,500
	52,500		52,500

(*c*) Calculation of closing balance of creditors

Total creditors

Particulars	*Amount*	*Particulars*	*Amount*
To Bank	77,500	By Balance b/d	18,000
To Discount received	500	By Purchase	1,50,000
To Bills payable	77,500		
To Balance c/d	12,500		
	1,68,000		1,68,000

(*d*) Calculation of closing of Bills Payable

Bills Payable A/c

Particulars	*Amount*	*Particulars*	*Amount*
To Bank a/c	36,600	By Balance b/d	8,000
To Balance c/d	48,900	By Sundry creditors a/c	77,500
	85,500		85,500

Trading and Profit & Loss A/c

Particulars	Amount	Particulars	Amount
To Opening stock	30,000	By Sales	1,90,000
To Purchases	1,50,000	By Closing stock	35,000
To Wages	7,400		
To Gross profit c/d	37,600		
	2,25,000		2,25,000
To Salaries	6,000	By Gross profit b/d	37,600
To Discount allowed	1,000	By Discount received	500
To Depreciation on :			
plant & Machenery	2,000		
Land & Buildings	1,500		
To Discount on debtors	1,000		
To Net Profit transferred to			
P's Capital	13,300		
Q's Capital	13,300		
	38,100		38,100

Balance Sheet as on 31-3-1998

Liabilities		Amount	Assests		Amount
Sundry creditors		12,500	Cash at Bank		57,500
Bills payable		48,900	Bills Receivable		7,500
P's Capital	50,500		Sundry debtors	28,500	
Add net profit	13,300		Less Discount on Debtors	1,000	
	63,800			27,500	
Less Drawings	7,500	56,300	Stock		35,000
Q's Capital	50,500		Plant & Machinery	20,000	
Add Net profit	13,300		Less Depreciation	2,000	
	63,800				18,000
Less drawings	7,500	56,300	Land & Building	30,000	
Less Depreciation	1,500				28,500
		1,74,000			1,74,000

Problem 12

A retail tradesman asks you to prepare account of his business as on December 31st 1996. From the following information obtained from the records prepare accounts on December 31st Keeping in view the fact that he uses scooter for the personal purposes and should be charged with $\frac{1}{3}$ of expenses.

Cash received from the debtors	45,000
Private dividend paid into the bank	600
Cash paid to creditors	36,600
Private payments	7,800

Cash sales	64,230
Cash purchases	48,000
indirect expenses	16,200

Assets and liabilities at the beginning end at the end of the period is as follows :

	Opening Rs.	Closing Rs.
Stock	6,000	9,000
Scooter	150,00	?
Trade debtors	4,200	6,000
Creditors	8,190	9,000
Cash in hand	8,190	9,000
Cash at Bank	90	120
	2,400	3,600

Depreciation scooter at 20% p.a. Expenses outstanding in respect of scooter is Rs. 600 and scooter expenses already included in indirect expenses Rs. 1,800

(Sri Venkateshwara University B. Com. April 2000).

Solution

Working Notes

(*a*) Calculation of opening capital

Opening Statement of Affairs

Particulars	*Amount*	*Particulars*	*Amount*
Creditors	8,190	Cash in hand	90
Capital	19,500	Cash at bank	2,400
		Stock	6,000
		Scooter	15,000
		Debtors	4,200
	27,690		27,690

(*b*) Calculation of credit purchases

Creditors A/c

Particulars	*Amount*	*Particulars*	*Amount*
To Cash paid	36,600	By Balance b/d	8,190
To Balance c/d	9,000	By Credit purchases	37,410
	45,600		45,600

(*c*) Calculation of credit sales

Debtors A/c

Particulars	*Amount*	*Particulars*	*Amount*
To Balance b/d	4,200	By Cash received	45,000
To Credit sales	46,800	By Balance c/d	6,000
	51,000		51,000

Trading and Profit & Loss A/c

Particulars		Amount	Particulars	Amount
To Opening stock		6,000	By Sales	
To Purchases :			— Cash	64,230
— Cash		48,000	— Credit	46,800
— Credit		37,410	By Closing stock	9,000
To Gross profit		28,620		
		1,20,030		1,20,030
To Indirect expenses	16,200		By Gross profit	28,620
Less Scooter expenses	1,800			
		14,400		
To Scooter expenses	1,800			
Add o/s	600			
	2,400			
Less $\frac{1}{3}$	800	1,600		
To Depreciation on Scooter	3,000			
Less $\frac{1}{3}$ personal use	1,000			
		2,000		
To Net profit		10,620		
		28,620		28,620

Balance Sheet as on 31-12-96

Liabilities		Amount	Assests		Amount
Creditors		9,000	Cash in hand		120
of/s Scooter expenses		600	Cash at bank		3,600
Capital	19,500		Stock in trade in trade		9,000
Add N.P.	10,620		Debtors		6,000
	30,120		Scooter	15,000	
Add Dividend	600		Less Dep.	3,000	
	30,720				12,000
Less Drawings	9,600	21,120			
(7800 + 1000 + 800)					
		30,720			30,720

Problem 13

Mr. Prakash is a small trader. He maintains no books but only an account with a bank in which all takings are lodged after meeting business expenses and his personal drawings and in which all payment for business, purchase are passed through.

You are required to ascertain his trading result for the year end 31-3-1999 and Balance Sheet as on that date from the following information.

(a) The bank statement shows deposits during the year of Rs. 12,020 and withdrawals of Rs. 11,850.

(b) The Assets and liabilities on 31-3-99 were ;
Stock -Rs. 1,100, book debts - Rs. 1,150 ; Bank balance - Rs. 320, furniture Rs. 2,000 and trade creditors Rs. 400

(c) In the absence of reliable information estimates are supplied on the following matters : Stock and book debts have each increased by Rs. 100 during the year. There was no purchase or sale of furniture during the year. The trade creditors were Rs. 200 on 1-4-98. During the year the personal expenses amounted to Rs. 800 and business expenses Rs. 700

(Bangalore University B. Com. April 2000)

Solution

Working Notes :

(*a*) Calculation of Credit Purchases

Sundry Creditors A/c

Particulars	*Amount*	*Particulars*	*Amount*
To Bank - cheques paid	11,850	By Balance b/d	200
To Balance c/d	400	By Credit purchases (Balancing figure)	12,050
	12,250		12,250

(*b*) Calculation of cash collection form debtors

Cash A/c

Particulars	*Amount*	*Particulars*	*Amount*
To Sundry debtors – Collection from debtors (Balancing figure	13,520	By Business Expenses	700
		By Drawings	800
		By Bank deposit	12,020
	13,520		13,520

(*c*) Calculation of credit sales

Sundry Debtors A/c

Particulars	*Amount*	*Particulars*	*Amount*
To Balance b/d	1,050	By Cash-collection from debtors	13,520
To Credit sales	13,620	By Balance c/d	1,150
	14,670		14,670

(*d*) Calculation of opening capital

Opening Statement of Affairs

Particulars	*Amount*	*Particulars*	*Amount*
Sundry creditors	200	Furniture	2,000
Capital	4000	Stock (1,100 – 100)	1,000
		Sundry Debtors (1,150 – 100)	1,050
		Bank	150
	4,200		4,200

Trading and Profit & Loss A/c

Particulars	*Amount*	*Particulars*	*Amount*
To Opening (1100 - 100)	1,000	By Credit sales	13,620
To Credit purchases	12,050	By Closing stock	1,100
To Gross profit	1,670		
	14,720		14,720
To Business expenses	700	By Gross profit b/d	1,670
To Net profit	970		
	1,670		1,670

Balance Sheet as on 31st Dec. 1999

Liabilities		*Amount*	*Assests*	*Amount*
Creditors		400	Furniture	2,000
Capital	4,000		Stock	1,100
Add Net Profit	970		Sundry debtors	1,150
	4,970		Bank	320
Less Drawings	800			
		4,170		
		4,570		4,570

Problem 14

From the information supplied below by Vinay Ventures, prepare profit & loss account for the year ended 31-12-1999 and a Balance Sheet as on that date.

	1-1-1999	31-12-1999
Sundry fixed Assets	1,80,000	2,00,000
Stock in hand	1,40,000	1,90,000
Cash in hand	82,000	48,000
Cash at Bank	22,000	80,000
Sundry Debtors	?	2,60,000
Sundry creditors	1,20,000	98,000
OS Expenses	10,000	6,000

During the year the following transactions took place :

	Rs.
1. Collection from debtors and discount allowed to them	24,50,000
2. Returns Inward	60,000
3. Bad debts	10,000
4. Sales (cash and credit)	30,00,000
5. Return outward	30,000
6. Paid to supplies by cheque	23,62,000
7. Collection form debtors and deposited into the bank	24,30,000

8.	Cash purchases	1,00,000
9.	Salaries and wages paid by cheque	1,80,000
10.	Miscellaneous cash expense	50,000
11.	Drawings in cash	94,000
12.	Assets purchased by cheque	20,000
13.	Cash withdrawals from bank	2,10,000
14.	Cash sales deposited into bank	?
15.	Discount received	40,000

(ICWA, Inter June 2000)

Solution

Working Notes :

(*a*) Calculation of opening capital

Opening Statement of Affairs

Particulars	*Amount*	*Particulars*	*Amount*
Sundry creditors	1,20,000	Sundry Assets	1,80,000
O/s Expenses	10,000	Sundry Debtors	1,80,000
Capital	4,74,000	Stock in trade	1,40,000
(Balancing figure)		Cash at Bank	22,000
		Cash in hand	82,000
	6,04,000		6,04,000

(*b*) Calculation of Opening Balance of debtors

Total Debtors A/c

Particulars	*Amount*	*Particulars*	*Amount*
To Balance b/d	1,80,000	By Bank	24,30,000
(Balancing figure)		By Discount allowed	20,000
To Credit sales	26,00,000	By Return inward	60,000
		By Bad debit	10,000
		By Balance c/d	2,60,000
	27,80,000		27,80,000

(*c*) Calculation of credit purchases

Total Debtors A/c

Particulars	*Amount*	*Particulars*	*Amount*
To Bank	23,62,000	By Balance b/d	1,20,000
To Discount	40,000	By Credit purchases	24,10,000
To Returns	3,000	(Balancing figure)	
To Balance c/d	98,000		
	25,30,000		25,30,000

(*d*) Calculation of Cash sales

Cash and Bank A/c

Particulars	*Cash*	*Bank*	*Particulars*	*Cash*	*Bank*
To Balance b/d	82,000	22,000	By Sundry Creditors		23,62,000
To Sundry Debtors	—	24,30,000	By Purchases	1,00,000	
To Cash sales (Balance figure)		4,00,000	By Salary & wages		1,80,000
			By Misc expenses	50,000	
To Bank	2,10,000		By Drawings	94,000	
			By Cash		2,10,000
			By Fixed assets		20,000
			By Balance c/d	48,000	80,000
	2,92,000	28,52,000		2,92,000	28,52,000

Trading and Profit & Loss A/c

		Amount			*Amount*
To Opening stock		1,40,000	By Sales		
To Purchases :			— Cash	4,00,000	
— Cash	1,00,000		— Credit	26,00,000	
— Credit	24,10,000			30,00,000	
	25,10,000		Less return Inwards	60,000	
Less Return Outward	30,000				29,40,000
		24,80,000	By Closing stock		1,90,000
To Gross profit c/d		5,10,000			
		31,30,000			31,30,000
To Salaries & Wages		1,80,000	By Gross profit		5,10,000
To Miscellanies (50,000 + 6,000 – 10,000)		46,000	By Discount received		40,000
To Discount allowed		20,000			
To Bad debits		10,000			
To Net profit		2,94,000			
		5,50,000			5,50,000

Balance Sheet as on 31-12-1999

		Amount		*Amount*
Capital a/c			Sundry Assets (1,80,000 + 20,000)	2,00,000
Opening balance	4,74,000		Stock in trade	1,90,000
Add Net profit	2,94,000		Sundry debtors	2,60,000
	7,68,000		Cash at Bank	80,000
Less Drawings	94,000		Cash in hand	48,000
		6,74,000		
Sundry creditors		98,000		
O/s expenses		6,000		
		7,78,000		7,78,000

QUESTIONS

Simple Questions

1. What is single entry system of book keeping ?
2. State the chief characteristic features of single entry system of books keeping.
3. State the advantages of single entry system.
4. State the demerits of single entry system.
5. What are the books of accounts maintained under single entry ?
6. What is "Statement of affairs" ?
7. How is profit ascertained under single entry system ?
8. Distinguish between single entry and double entry.
9. Distinguish between statement of affairs and Balance Sheet.
10. What do you mean by pure single entry system ?
11. What do you mean by simple single entry system ?
12. What do you mean by quasi single entry system.
13. State the methods of ascertaining profit under single entry.

EXERCISE 1

From the following particulars prepare total creditors account.

Credit purchases	2,40,000
Cash purchases	50,000
Payment to creditors	2,10,000
Discount allowed by them	5,000
Bills payable accepted	30,000
Creditors at the beginning of the year	90,000

(Osmania University, B. Com. March 1999)

Answer : Closing Balance of creditors Rs. 85,000

EXERCISE 2

Mr. Ravi did not maintain his books under Double entry system as well as his bank a/c. From the following information prepare his trading and profit & loss account for the year ended 30-6-1998 and his Balance Sheet as on that date

(*a*) Assets and Liabilities

	30-6-97 Rs.	30-6-98 Rs.
Stock-in-trade	19,800	1,13,200
Creditors	31,000	14,500
Debtors	1,18,000	1,25,000
Buildings	90,000	90,000
Furniture	11,000	11,500
Air-conditioner	15,000	15,000

(*b*) Creditors as on 30-6-97 includes Rs. 15,000 for the purchase of Air-conditioner

(c) Cash transactions :

	Rs.
Cash on July 1 1997	15,000
Collection form customers	1,60,800
Payments to creditors (trade)	1,44,000
Rent & taxes	11,500
Salaries	1,12,500
Sundry expenses	18,000
Sundry income	16,500
Drawings by Ravi	30,000
Loan from Mrs. Padma	23,000
Cash sales	11,500
Capital introduced	12,000
Cash purchases	15,000
Paid to Air-Conditioner	15,000

(d) Bad debts written off Rs. 1,200

(University of Madras B. Com. May 2000)

Answer : G P 1,16,400, N P 1,200, B/S total 3,54,700

EXERCISE 3

Your are given

(a) The Balance sheet of A on 1st April 1996.

(b) The cash transaction for the year upto 31st March 1997.

(c) A summary of the remaining transactions

(a) **Balance Sheet of A on 1st April 1996**

	Amount		*Amount*
Bank overdraft	500	Cash in hand	70
Sundry creditors	3,600	Bills Receivable	2,500
Bills payable	1,600	Sundry debtors	3,900
Capital	20,000	Stock of goods	7,530
		Plant & Machinery	4,700
		Land & Buildings	7,000
	25,700		25,700

(b) **Cash Transactions for the year up to 31st March 1997**

	Amount		*Amount*
To Balance b/d	70	By Bank overdraft	500
To Receipts from Debtors	29,000	By Salaries	4,900
To Bills receivable	10,000	By Wages	1,580
To Cash sales	3,700	By Bills payable	14,300
		By Payment to Creditors	14,700
		By Office expenses	800
		By Drawings	4,500
		By 6% Investments	
		Purchased at per on 1st Oct. 96	1,000
		By Balance c/d	
		— Cash 40	
		— Bank 450	490
	42,770		42,770

(c) A summary of the remaining transactions

	Rs.
Credit Sales	40,700
Discount allowed to customer	200
Credit purchases	30,000
Discount received	100
Bills payable issued to creditors	15,000
Stock of goods on 31-3-97	5,300
Bills receivable received	10,900

Provide for doubtful debts at 5% on sundry debtors. Provide for depreciation on plant & Machinery at 5% and on hand & Buildings at $2\frac{1}{2}$%. Prepare trading and profit & loss a/c for the year ending 31-3-97 and the Balance Sheet as on that date

(Osmania University, B. Com. March 1999)

Answer : Gross profit Rs. 10,590
Net profit Rs. 4,185
Total of B/S Rs. 25,785

EXERCISE 4

Mahesh Keeps his books by single entry. Form the following information Prepare trading, profit & loss account for the year ended on 31-3-99 and the Balance Sheet as on that date. Also show cash book with Bank column, total debtors a/c, total creditors a/c,

	Rs.
Analysis of Cash book :	
Receipts form debtors	64,000
Additional capital introduced on 1-1-99	8,000
Loan from Ramesh @ 16% p.a. on 1-10-98	10,500
Paid to creditors	57,700
General expenses	3,900
Salaries paid	3,000
Drawings	4,000
Amount deposited in the bank during the year	50,000
Withdrawls from the bank during the year	36,000
Balances Existed on 1-4-98 :	
Sundry Debtors	15,300
Sundry Creditors	11,500
Bank overdraft	8,000
Buildings	42,510
Stock	21,800
Cash balance	600
Balance existed on 31-3-99	
Sundry debtors	16,000
Sundry creditors	11,900
Stock	26,000

Depreciate building by 5% provide for interest on the loan from Ramesh.

(Sri Venkateshware University B. Com Oct. 1999)

Answer : Gross profit Rs. 60,700
Net profit Rs. 935
B/S total Rs. 88,875

EXERCISE 5

Mr. Ramkumar keeps his books by single entry and the position of his business as on 1st January 1998 is as follows :

Capital Rs. 70,000 Sundry creditors Rs. 10,000 Bills Payable Rs. 7,000, Freehold premises Rs. 50,000 : Stock Rs. 25,000 ; Debtors Rs. 15,000, furniture Rs. 2,000, B.R. Rs. 5,000

His transactions during the year were as follows :

Receipts	*Amount*	*Payments*	*Amount*
Sundry debtors and B. R.	15,000	Bank OD as on (1-1-97)	10,000
Cash Sales	80,000	Drawings	23,000
		Expenses	5,000
		Payment to creditors and bills payable	20,000
		Balance :	
		Cash in hand	2,000
		Cash at Bank	35,000
	95,000		95,000

You are asked to prepare a trading and profit and loss account for the year ended 31st December 1998 and a Balance Sheet as on that date.

The following additional information is supplied.

Closing stock Rs. 30,000 closing debtors Rs. 20,000 : Bills Receivable Rs. 5,000 No addition has bee made during the year to freehold premises and furniture but they are to be depreciated as under :

Freehold premises 10% and furniture 15%.

A Bad and doubtful debts provision at $2\frac{1}{2}$% is to be raised against closing debtors. There were balances of bills payable account Rs. 3,000 and creditors account Rs. 4,000. Expenses to [or 2.5 %] the extent of Rs. 200 were outstanding.

(Bangalore University B. Com. November 1999)

Answer : Gross profit Rs. 95,000
Net profit Rs. 84,000
Total of B/S Rs. 1,38,200

EXERCISE 6

Rama commenced business as a cloth merchant on 1-4-98 with a capital of Rs. 10,000. On the some date he purchased furniture for cash Rs. 3,000. From the following particulars obtained from his books kept by single entry, you are required to prepare a trading and profit & loss a/c for the year ending 31-3-99 and a Balance Sheet as on that date.

Sale (inclusive of cash Rs. 47,000)	1,17,000
Purchases (Inclusive of cash Rs. 14,000)	95,000
Rama's Drawings	11,200
Salaries to staff	12,000

Bad debts written off	500
Business expenses	10,700

Rama took cloth worth Rs. 500 from the shop for private use and paid Rs. 200 to his son but omitted to record these transactions in his book on 31-3-99, his sundry debtors were Rs. 5,200 and sundry creditors Rs. 13,600. Stock on hand on 31-3-99 was Rs. 16,500.

(University of Madras B. Com. April 1999)

Answer : Gross profit Rs. 39,000
Net profit Rs. 15,800
Total of B/S Rs. 27,500

EXERCISE 7

Mohan a retail trader keeps his books under single entry system. From the following information prepare trading and profit & loss a/c for the year ended on 31-3-98 and the Balance sheet as on that date. An analysis of cash book revealed the following

		Rs.
Cash balance (1-4-97)		524
Cash sales		33,312
Purchase of new machine		2,000
Sundry expenses		3,252
Wages paid		5,334
Loan from bank		2,800
Drawings		4,160
Rent paid		1,800
Receipts form customers		14,324
Payment to creditors		32,032
Other information :	1-4-97	31-3-98
Machinery	9,000	10,100
Sundry debtors	3,256	3,720
Of/S Expenses	240	300
Stock	4,320	4,930
Creditors	1,720	1,848
Rent outstanding		500

During the year Mohan received discount from Creditors Rs. 1,308 and he has allowed Rs. 630 as discount to debtors. Provide Rs. 840 for doubtful debts

(Sri Venkateshwara university B. Com. April 1999)

Answer : Gross profit Rs. 10,538
Net profit Rs. 3,864
Total of B/S Rs. 20,292

EXERCISE 8

Mr. X keeps his records under single entry system. From the following prepare trading and profit & loss a/c for the year ended 31-3-1996 together with Balance Sheet as on that date. Cash book analysis shows the following.

		Rs.
Interest charges		100
Personal with drawls		2,000
Staff salaries		8,500
Other business expenses		7,900
Payment to creditors		15,000
Balance at bank as on 31-3-96		2,425
Cash in hand on 31-3-96		75
Receipts form debtors		25,000
Cash sales		15,000
Further details available are :	As on 1-4-95	As on 31-3-96
Stock on hand	9,000	10,220
Creditors	8,000	5,500
Debtors	22,000	30,000
Furniture	1,000	1,000
Office premises	15,000	15,000

Provide 5% interest on X's Capital balance as on 1-4-1995. Provide Rs. 1,500 for doubtful debts, 5% depreciation on all fixed assets, 5% group incentive commission to staff has to be provided for on net profit after meeting all expenses and commission.

(University of Madras, B. Com. April 1998)

Answer : Gross profit Rs. 36,720
Net profit Rs. 15,400
Total of B/S Rs. 56,420

EXERCISE 9

X and Y are equal partners in a business in which the books are maintained using single entry system. On 1st April 1999, their statement of Affairs was as under.

	Amount		*Amount*
Bills payable	12,400	Cash in hand	540
Sundry Creditors	40,000	Cash at bank	27,760
Capital accounts		Bills receivable	9,200
X Rs. 1,60,000		Sundry debtors	67,600
Y Rs. 1,60,000		Stock	97,300
	3,20,000	Furniture & fixture	10,000
		Plant & Machinery	1,60,000
	3,72,400		3,72,400

On 31st March 2000, following was the state of affairs :

Cash in hand Rs. 800, Cash at bank Rs. 31,600, Sundry creditors Rs. 42,400, Stock Rs. 1,33,400 Sundry debtors : Rs. 60,600 bills payable Rs. 13,200 : Bill receivable Rs. 17,600 plant and machinery and furniture and fixture are to be depreciated by 10%.

Ascertain the profit for the year ended 31st March 2000 and draw up the statement of Affairs as on that date showing the accounts of the partners in detail, assuming X withdrew Rs. 30,000 and Y with drew Rs. 26,000 during the year. **(C. S. Foundation December 2000)**

Answer : Total profit of the firm Rs. 77,400
Each partner gets Rs. 38,700

EXERCISE 10

Kannan a retail merchant commenced business with a capital of Rs. 15,000 on 1st Jan. 1995. Subsequently on 1st May 1995, he invested a further sum of Rs. 7,000 as Capital in the same business. During the year he has withdrawn Rs. 3,000 for his personal use. On 31-12-1995 his assets and liabilities were : cash at bank Rs. 6,000, Debtors Rs. 8,000, stock of goods Rs. 32,000 furniture Rs. 4,000 and sundry creditors Rs. 10,000.

Ascertain the profit or loss for the year 1995. **(University of Madras B. Com. April 2000)**

Answer : Profit for the year Rs. 21,000

26
CHAPTER

Self Balancing Ledgers

INTRODUCTION

In a big business concern, where the volume of business transactions is large, it is not possible to maintain all accounts in one ledger. Besides, in case of disagreement of trial balance it requires a lot of time and effort to track down the error. Hence the "Self Balancing System" has been devised.

Self balancing system is a system in which ledgers are maintained in such a manner as to contain all the material needed for preparing a trial balance separately for each ledger without the help of other ledgers.

Advantages of Self Balancing Ledgers

1. Errors can be easily detected with least possible time and effort.
2. Frauds can be minimised to a great extent.
3. Helps in preparation of interim accounts.
4. Promotes division of work and fixing responsibilities there of. It fixes responsibility of the ledger keeper, as to the balancing of the ledger or ledger under his charge and the person responsible for the mistake can be called upon to work overtime to locate it.

Ledgers Maintained Under Self Balancing System

The following ledgers are maintained under Self Balancing System.

1. Sales or sold or Debtors Ledger.
2. Purchase or brought or Creditor Ledger.
3. General or Nominal Ledger.

Self Balancing of Debtors Ledger

A Debtors Ledger or Sales Ledger is maintained for recording transactions pertaining to personal accounts of trade debtors only. It contains entries with trade traders relating to (*a*) Credit Sales (*b*) Drawing of Bill (*c*) Receipts from Debtors (d) Discount allowed and (*e*) Sales Returns.

Following entries are required to be passed to make debtors ledger Self-Balancing.

1. For credit sales, Bills Receivable dishonoured, interest and expenses charged to debtors during the period.
   Debtors Ledger Adjustment a/c Dr.
   (in general ledger)
   To General Ledger Adjustment a/c
   (in debtors ledger)
2. For receipts from debtors, discount allowed to them, Bills Received, Sales Returns and bad debts written off :
   General Ledger Adjustment a/c Dr.
   (in debtors ledger)
   To Debtors Ledger Adjustment a/c
   (in general ledger)

Items such as trade discount, reserve for bad debts, bad debts recovered, Endorsement of Bills Receivable, Cash sales, Discount of bills receivable, provision for discount on creditors etc. do not affect adjustment account and hence do not require Self Balancing Entries.

A Specimen of Adjustment Account is given below :-

In Debtors Ledger
General Ledger Adjustment A/c

Particulars	*Amount*	*Particulars*	*Amount*
To Debtors ledger Adjustment a/c (in general ledger) :-		By Balance b/d	X X
		By Debtors ledger adjustment a/c (in general ledger) :-	
Cash received	X X	Sales	X X
Discount	X X	Cheques dishonoured	X X
Bills receivable	X X	Bills renewed	X X
Allowances to Debtors	X X	Noting Charges	X X
Returns in ward	X X	Interest charged	X X
Bad Debts	X X	Carriage charged	X X
To Bank (cheque received) transfer	X X	Expenses charged	X X
To Balance c/d	X X	Refund to debtors	X X
		Discount disallowed	X X

Self Balancing of Creditors Ledger

A creditors ledger or purchase ledger is meant for recording personal accounts of trade creditors only and contains items relating to transactions as : (*a*) Credit purchases (*b*) Acceptance of a bill (*c*) Payment of creditors (*d*) Discount received (*e*) Purchase returns etc.

The following entries are passed to make the purchase ledger Self-Balancing.

(*i*) For credit purchases, Bill Payable dishonoured, interest and expenses charged by creditors.
General Ledger Adjustment a/c Dr.
(in creditors ledger)
To Creditors Ledger Adjustment a/c
(in general ledger)

(*ii*) For total cash paid to creditors, discount received, bills accepted, purchase returns etc.
Creditors ledger adjustment a/c Dr.
(in general ledger)
To General ledger adjustment a/c
(in creditors ledger)

A specimen of general ledger adjustment a/c is given below.

In the Creditors Ledger-General Ledger Adjustment A/c

Particulars	*Amount*	*Particulars*	*Amount*
To Balance b/d	XX	By creditors ledger adjustment a/c (in general ledger) :	
To Creditors ledger adjustment a/c (in general ledger) :		Cash paid	XX
Purchases	XX	Discount received	XX
Interest payable	XX	Bills payable	XX
Carriage charged	XX	Returns outward	XX
B/P dishonoured	XX	Allowances	XX
		Transfer	XX
		By balance c/d	XX
Noting charges	XX		
Refund from Creditors	XX		
Discount disallowed	XX		
Cheques dishonoured	XX		

Self Balancing of General Ledger

It contains all personal and nominal accounts as will as such personal accounts except trade creditors and trade debtors. In order to make the general ledger self balancing, the adjustment in respect of trade creditors and trade debtors must be made by opening two adjustment accounts viz, debtors ledger adjustment account and creditors ledger adjustment account at the end of the general ledger. These adjustment accounts in the general ledger are nothing but a summary of transaction already posted in the debtors ledger or creditors ledger as the case may be.

A specimen of creditors ledger adjustment a/c and debtors ledger adjustment a/c is given below.

In General Ledger-Creditors Ledger Adjustment A/c

Particulars	*Amount*	*Particulars*	*Amount*
To General ledger adjustment a/c (in general ledger) :		By Balance b/d	XX
		By General ledger adjustment a/c (in creditors ledger) :	
Cash paid	XX	Purchases	XX
Discount	XX	Noting charges	XX
Bills payable	XX	B/P dishonoured	XX
Returns outward	XX	Interest payable	XX
Allowances	XX	Carriage charged	XX
Transfer	XX	Refund from Creditors	XX
To balance c/d	XX	Discount allowed	XX
		Cheque dishonoured	XX

In General Ledger
Debtors Ledger Adjustment A/c

Particulars	*Amount*	*Particulars*	*Amount*
To Balance b/d	XX	By General ledger Adjustment a/c (in Debtors ledger)	
To General ledger Adjustment a/c (in debtors ledger):		By Cash received	XX
Sales	XX	By Discount allowed	XX
Cheques dishonoured	XX	By B/R	XX
B/R dishonoured	XX	By Returns inward	XX
Bills renewed	XX	By Allowances	XX
Noting charges	XX	By Bad debts	XX
Interest charged	XX	By Bank transfer (cheque received)	XX
Carriage charged	XX		
Expenses charged	XX	By Balance c/d	XX
Refund to debtors	XX		
Discount allowed	XX		

Transfer Entries in Ledgers

It is possible that purchases are made from and sales made to the same person. In which case he is a debtor as will as creditor. Under such circumstances balances of one account may be transferred to another account in order to find out net amount payable or recoverable. Usually the balance in smaller account is transferred to account with larger balance.

Example

If A's account in the Debtors Ledger shows a balance of Rs. 10,000 and in Creditors Ledger Rs. 5,000, the latter will be transferred to the former : In the normal course the following entry is required.

Date	*Particulars*		*Dr. Amount*	*Cr. Amount*
	A's a/c (in creditors ledger)	Dr.	5,000	
	To A's a/c (in debtors ledger)			5,000
	(Being the transfer of A's credit balance in creditors ledger to debtors ledger)			

Under the Self Balancing System the following two entries are required :

Date	*Particulars*		*Dr. Amount*	*Cr. Amount*
	Creditors ledger a/c (in general ledger)	Dr.	5,000	
	To General ledger adj. a/c (in creditors ledger)			
	(Being adjusting entry to balance creditors ledger)			
	General ledger adj. a/c (in debtors ledger)	Dr.	5,000	
	To Debtors ledger adj. a/c (in general ledger)			5,000
	(Adjusting entry to balance debtors ledger)			

Problem 1

From the following particulars given below you are required to prepare the Bought Ledger Adjustment a/c

Creditors on 1-1-1999	11,800
Credit purchases	19,300
Cash paid to creditors	16,500
Discount allowed by them	700
Bills payable issued	5,300
Transfer to sales ledger	1,100
Cash purchases	8,200

(University of Madras B. Com. April 2001)

Solution

In General Ledger
Bought Ledger Adjustment A/c

Particulars	*Amount*	*Particulars*	*Amount*
To General ledger		By Balance b/d	11,800
Adjustment a/c :-		By General ledger	
— Cash paid to Creditors	16,500	Adjustment a/c :-	
— Discount	700	— Credit purchases	19,300
— Bills payable	5,300		
To Transfer to sales ledger	1,100		
To Balance c/d	7,500		
	31,100		31,100

Note : Cash purchase is not to be considered in bought ledger a/c.

Problem 2

In the General Ledger of Dinesh company Ltd, prepare Sales Ledger Adjustment a/c from the following particulars.

		Rs.
1999		
Jan. 1,	Balance of Sundry debtors	80,000
Dec. 31,	Credit purchases	45,000
	Credit sales	1,96,000
	Received cash from debtors	1,56,000
	Allowed discount	4,000
	Received bills receivable	30,000
	Returns inward	17,500
	Returns outward	6,000
	Rebate allowed to debtors	5,500
	Bad debts	9,000
	B.R. dishonoured	7,500

(University of Madras, B. Com., May 2001)

Solution

In General Ledger
Sales Ledger Adjustment A/c

Particulars	*Amount*	*Particulars*	*Amount*
1-1-99			
To Balance b/d	80,000	By General ledger	
To General ledger		Adjustment a/c	
Adjustment a/c :-		— Cash received from debtors	1,56,000
— Cash sales	1,96,000	— Discount allowed	4,000
— BR dishonoured	7,500	— Bills receivable	30,000
		— Returns inwards	17,500
		— Rebate	5,500
		— Bad debts	9,000
		By Balance c/d	61,500
	2,83,500		2,83,500

Note : Credit purchase and return outward is not to be considered in sales ledger adjustment a/c.

Problem 3

From the following information of "Prasanna Enterprises" you are required to prepare the Sales Ledger Adjustment account and Bought Ledger Adjustment account.

	Rs.
1998 1st January - Debtors	15,400
1998 1st January - Creditors	14,600
Credit purchases	60,790
Credit sales	70,200
Discount received from creditors	700
Cash received from debtors	56,450
Cash paid to creditors	45,740
Returns Inwards	2,300
Returns Outwards	3,100
Discounts allowed to debtors	500
Interest debited to debtors a/c	250
Allowances from suppliers	350
Bills receivable received	10,270
Bills payable accepted	9,750
Bad debts	230
Bills receivable dishonoured	2,100
Bills payable dishonoured	750

(University of Madras, B. Com. April 2000)

Solution

In General Ledger
(i) Sales Ledger Adjustment A/c

Particulars	Amount	Particulars	Amount
1-1-1998			
To Balance b/d	15,400	By General Ledger	
To General Ledger		Adjustment a/c :	
Adjustment a/c :		— Cash received from debtors	56,450
— Credit sales	70,200	— Discount allowed	500
— Bills Receivable		— Bills Receivable	10,270
dishonoured	2,100	— Returns Inwards	2,300
— Interest debited		— Bad Debts	230
to debtors	250	By Balance c/d	18,200
	87,950		87,950

(ii) Bought Ledger Adjustment A/c

Particulars	Amount	Particulars	Amount
To General ledger		**1-1-98**	
Adjustment a/c :		By Balance b/d	14,600
— Discount received	700	By General ledger	
— Cash paid to creditors	45,740	Adjustment a/c :	
— Credit purchase	60,790	— Bills payable Dishonour	750
— Returns Outward	3,100	Credit purchase	60790
— Allowance from Supplier	350		
— Bills payable	9,750		
To Balance c/d	16,500		
	76,140		76,140

Problem 4

From the following information, prepare the Bought Ledger Adjustment account as they would appear in the General Ledger of Bharath Traders for the year ended 31-12-1998.

Opening Balance 1-1-1998 :-

Bought ledger	(Dr.)	Rs. 2,500
Bought ledger	(Cr)	Rs. 38,000
Sales ledger	(Dr.)	Rs. 45,000
Sales ledger	(Cr)	Rs. 750

Purchases	1,90,000
Sales	2,60,000
Purchase returns	7,500
Sales returns	3,500
Cash Received from Debtors	2,20,000
Bills Receivable received	12,000
Bills Payable accepted	6,500

Bills Receivable endorsed to creditors	4,000
Endorsed bills dishonoured	1,500
Discount allowed on Debtors	8,000
Cash paid to creditors	17,5000
Discount received thereon	5,000
Cash refunded to Debtors	500
Bills Payable dishonoured	1,000
Transfer from Bought Ledger to Sales ledger	500
Transfer from Sales Ledger to Bought ledger	100

Closing Balance on 31-12-1998 :
Bought Ledger (Dr.) Rs. 2,000
Sales ledger (Cr) Rs. 1,300

(Osmania University B. Com. October 2000)

Solution

In the General ledger
Bought Ledger Adjustment A/c

Particulars	*Amount*	*Particulars*	*Amount*
To Balance b/d	2,500	By Balance b/d	38,000
To General Ledger Adjustment a/c :		By General ledger Adj a/c :	
— Purchase Returns	7,500	— Purchases	1,90,000
— Cash paid	1,75,000	— Endorsed bill dishonoured	1,500
— Discount received	5,000	— Bills payable dishonoured	1,000
— Bills Payable	6,500	By Balance c/d	2,000
— B/R endorsed	4,000		
— Transfer	500		
— Transfer	100		
To Balance c/d	31,400		
	2,32,500		2,32,500

Sales Ledger Adjustment A/c

Particulars	*Amount*	*Particulars*	*Amount*
To Balance b/d	45,000	By Balance b/d	750
To General Ledger Adjustment a/c :		By General ledger Adjustment a/c :	
— Sales	2,60,000	— Sales returns	3,500
		— Cash received	2,20,000
— Cash received	2,20,000	— Discount allowed	8,000
— Cash Refunded	500	— Bills receivable	12,000
— Endorsed Bill Dishonoured	1,500	— Transfer	500
To Balance c/d	13,000	— Transfer	100
		By Balance c/d	62,150
	3,07,000		3,07,000

Problem 5

Mr. Hari keep his accounts under the Self Balancing System. You are required to prepare the adjustment accounts in the General Ledger :-

		Rs.
1-1-1998		
	Debtors balance (debit)	42,840
	Debtors balance (credit)	2,140
	Provision for Bad Debts	6,300
	Creditors balance (credit)	50,700
	Creditors balance (debit)	1,480
31-3-1998		
	Purchases	1,30,580
	Purchases returns	4,640
	Cash and cheque received from debtors	1,41,020
	Cash paid to creditors	1,18,730
	Cash discount received	3,640
	Interest charged by creditors	360
	Bad debts written off	3,150
	Sales	1,77,160
	Sales returns	2,740
	Bills receivable	10,600
	Bills payable accepted	10,800
	Cash discount allowed	4,740
	Cheques from debtors dishonoured	3,000
	Bills receivable dishonoured	1,400
	Bills receivable discounted (discount Rs. 100)	4,800
	Debtors balance (credit)	1,140
	Creditors balance (debit)	3,700
	Interest charged to debtors	1,140

(Sri Venkateshwara University B. Com. September 2000)

Solution

In the General Ledger
Debtors Ledger Adjustment A/c

Particulars	*Amount*	*Particulars*	*Amount*
To Balance b/d	42,840	By Balance b/d	2,140
To General ledger		By General ledger	
Adjustment a/c :-		Adjustment a/c:-	
— Sales	1,77,160	— Cash received	1,41,020
— Cheque		— Bad debts	3,150
— Dishonoured	3,000	— Sales returns	2,740
— B/R dishonoured	1,400	— Bills receivable	10,600
— Interest charged		— Discount allowed	4,740
to customers	1,140	By Balance c/d	62,290
To Balance c/d	1,140		
	2,26,680		2,26,680

Creditors Ledger Adjustment A/c

Particulars	Amount	Particulars	Amount
To Balance b/d	1,480	By Balance b/d	50,700
To General Ledger		By General ledger	
Adjustment a/c :		Adjustment a/c :	
— Purchase returns	4,640	— Purchases	1,30,580
— Cash paid	1,18,730	— Interest charged by creditors	360
— Discount received	3,640	By Balance c/d	3,700
— Bills payable	10,800		
To Balance b/d	46,050		
	1,85,340		1,85,340

Problem 6

From the following information available from the books of a Trader from 1-1-2000 to 31-3-2000, You are required to draw up the Debtors Ledger Judgement account in the General Ledger :

(*a*) **Total sales amounted to Rs. 1,80,000 including the sale of old zerox machine for Rs. 4,800 (Book value Rs. 8,000). The total Cash Sales were 80% less than the Total Credit Sales.**

(*b*) **Cash collections from debtors amounted to 70% of the aggregate of the opening debtors and credit sales for the period. Debtors were allowed a cash discount of Rs. 20,000.**

(*c*) **Bills Receivable drawn during the three months totalled Rs. 30,000 of which bills amounting to Rs. 10,000 were endorsed in favour of suppliers. Out of the endorsed bills, one bill for Rs. 6,000 was dishonoured for non-payment as the party became insolvent his estate realised nothing.**

(*d*) **Cheques received from customers Rs. 8,000 were dishonoured, a sum of Rs. 2,000 was irrecoverable ; Bad debts written off in the earlier years realised Rs. 11,000.**

(*e*) **Sundry debtors as on 1-1-2000 stood at Rs. 50,000.** **(C A, Foundatiom, May 2000)**

Solution

Working Notes :

1. Calculation of Credit Sales

Let credit sales	=	100
Add cash sales 80% less then Credit sales	=	20
Total sales		120
Total sales		1,80,000
Less sale of old zerox machine Included in total sales		4,800
Actual total sales		1,75,200
For a total sale of 120 : The amount of actual sales is		1,75,200
For 100 ?		

$$\frac{100}{120} \times 1{,}75{,}200 = \text{Rs. } 1{,}46{,}000$$

2. Calculate of Collection

$\frac{70}{100}$ of opening debtors + credit sales

$= \frac{70}{100}$ (50,000 + 1,46,000)

$= \frac{70}{100} \times 1,96,000 =$ Rs. 1,37,200

General Ledger

Debtors Ledger Adjustment A/c

Date	*Particulars*	*Rs.*	*Date*	*Particulars*	*Rs.*
2000			2000		
Jan. 1,	To Balance b/d	50,000	Mar. 31	By General ledger	
Mar. 31	To General ledger			Adjustment a/c	
	Adjustment a/c :			— Collections	1,37,200
	— Credit sales	1,46,000		— Discount	20,000
	— BR dishonoured	6,000		— Bad Debts	8,000
	— Cheque dishonoured	8,000		(6,000 + 2,000)	
				By Balance c/d	14,800
		2,10,000			2,10,000

Problem 7

From the following particulars, prepare the necessary Ledger Adjustment Accounts.

	Rs.
Jan. 1, 1998 :	
Balance on Bought Ledger (Dr.)	870
Balance on Bought Ledger (Cr)	11,940
Balance on Sales Ledger (Dr.)	14,620
Balance on Sales Ledger (Cr)	240
Jan. 31, 1998 :	
Purchases	66,180
Purchase Returns	2,560
Sales	87,490
Sales Returns	1,170
Cash received from customers	76,250
Discount allowed thereon	2,820
Cash paid to suppliers	58,430
Discount received thereon	1,660
Cash paid to customers	130
Bills Receivable	4,120
Bills Payable	2,250
Bills Receivable Dishonoured	250
Bought Ledger Balance (Dr.)	770
Sales Ledger Balance (Dr.)	18,350

(University of Madras B. Com. May 2000)

Solution

In General Ledger
Sales Ledger Adjustment A/c

Date	Particulars	Rs.	Date	Particulars	Rs.
1-1-98	To Balance b/d	14,620	1-1-98	By Balance b/d	240
	To General ledger Adjustment a/c :			By General ledger Adjustment a/c :	
	— Sales	87,490		— Sales returns	1,170
	— BR Dishonoured	250		— Bills receivable	4,120
	— Cash paid to Customers	130		— Cash received	76,210
	To Balance c/d	420		— Discount allowed	2,820
				By Balance c/d	18,350
		1,02,910			1,02,910

Bought Ledger Adjustment A/c

Date	Particulars	Rs.	Date	Particulars	Rs.
1-1-98	To Balance b/d	870	1-1-98	By Balance b/d	11,940
	To General Ledger Adjustment a/c :			By General ledger Adjustment :	
	— Purchase returns	2,560		Purchases	66,180
	— Cash paid	58,430		By Balance c/d	770
	— Bills payable	2250			
	— Discount received	1,660			
	To Balance c/d	13,120			
		78,890			78,890

Notes :

1. In Self Balancing two opening balances are given debt balance is recorded on debit side. Credit balance is recorded on credit side.
2. Whereas in case of closing balance debit balance will be recorded on credit side.

In the sales Ledger
General Ledger Adjustment A/c

Date	Particulars	Rs.	Date	Particulars	Rs.
1-1-98	To Balance b/d	240	1-1-98	By Balance b/d	14,260
	To Sales ledger Adjustment a/c :			By Sales ledger Adjustment a/c :	
	— Sales Returns	1,170		— Sales	87,490
	— Bills Receivable	4,120		— B.R. Dishonour	250
	— Cash Received	76,210		— Cash paid to customer	130
	— Discount allowed	2,820		By Balance c/d	420
31-1-98	To Balance c/d	18,350			
		1,02,910			1,02,910

In the Bought Ledger
General Ledger Adjustment A/c

Date	Particulars	Rs.	Date	Particulars	Rs.
1-1-98	To Balance b/d	11,940	1-1-98	By Balance b/d	870
	To Bought Ledger Adjustment a/c			By Bought ledger Adjustment a/c :	
	— Purchases	66,180		— Purchases Returns	2,560
31-1-98	To Balance c/d	770		— Cash paid	58,430
				— Bills payable	2,250
				— Discount received	1,160
				By Balance c/d	13,120
		78,890			78,890

Problem 8

The particular given below are from the books of trader for the month of January 1998.

1998		Rs.
Jan. 1,	Opening balance	60,000
31,	Total sales for the month	1,80,000
31,	Sales Returns	1,000
31,	Cash received from Debtors	80,000
31,	Bills Receivable	30,000
31,	B/R Dishonoured	3,000
31,	Discount allowed to Debtors	800
31,	Bad debts	750
31,	Transfer from another ledger	1500

The trader wishes to maintain his books on Self Balancing System".

You are required to Journalise the above transactions and also pass the Self-Balancing journal entries in the books of the trader. **(Osmania University B. Com. March 2000)**

Solution

Date	Transaction	Usual Entry			Self Balancing Entry		
1998 Jan. 31,	Credit Sales	Customers a/c	Dr. 1,80,000		Sales Ledger Adj. a/c	Dr. 18,000	
		To sales		1,80,000	To Gen. Ledger Adj a/c		1,80,000
31,	Sales Returns	Sales Returns a/c	Dr. 1,000		General Ledger Adj a/c	Dr. 1,000	
		To Customer a/c		1,000	To Sales Ledger Adj. a/c		1,000
31,	Cash received from Customers	Cash a/c	Dr. 80,000		Gen. Ledger Adj a/c	Dr. 80,000	
		To Customers a/c		80,000	To Sales Ledger Adj a/c		80,000
31,	Bills receivable from customers	B.R. a/c	Dr. 30,000		Gen. Ledger Adj a/c	Dr. 30,000	
		To Customers a/c		30,000	To sales Ledger Adj a/c		30,000
31,	Bills Receivable dishonoured	Customers a/c	Dr. 3,000		Sales Ledger Adj a/c	Dr. 3,000	
		To B R a/c		3,000	To General Ledger Adj a/c		3,000
31,	Discount allowed to Customers	Discount allowed a/c	Dr. 800		Gen. Ledger Adj	Dr. 800	
		To Customers a/c		800	To Sales Ledger Adj a/c		800

Date	Transaction	Usual Entry	Self Balancing entry
31,	Bad Debts	Bad Debts a/c Dr. 750 To Customers a/c 750	Gen. ledger adj a/c Dr. 750 To Sales ledger Adj a/c 750
31,	Transfer from another ledger	Suppliers a.c Dr. 1,500 To Customers a/c 1,500	Purchase ledger Adj a/c Dr. 1,500 To Gen. ledger Adj a/c 1,500 General ledger Adj a/c Dr. 1,500 To Sales ledger Adj a/c 1,500

Problem 9

From the following details in Bought Ledger and Sold Ledger write general Adjustment Account as on 31st December 1999.

	Rs.
Debtors (1st January, 1999) debit	36,000
Debtors (1st January, 1999) credit	800
Creditors (1st January, 1999) credit	54,000
Creditors (1st January 1999) debit	500
Purchases	1,00,000
Purchase Returns	1,200
Sales	1,56,000
Cash paid to creditors	42,000
Bills received from debtors	18,000
Bills Dishonoured	600
Bills accepted for creditors	15,000
Discount allowed to debtors	500
Discount allowed to debtors but later on disallowed	100
Cash received from debtors	17,800
Discount allowed by creditors	900
Cash paid to debtors	50
Transfer from Debtors to Creditors Ledger	2,400
Cash Purchases	9,000
Cash sales	15,000
Bad Debts written off	500

(Sri Venkateshwara University B. Com. April 2000)

In General Ledger
Debtors Adjustment A/c

Particulars	Amount	Particulars	Amount
To Balance b/d	36,000	By Balance b/d	800
To General Ledger Adjustment a/c :-		By General Ledger Adjustment a/c :-	
— Sales	1,56,000	— B/R received	18,000
— B/R Dishonoured	600	— Discount allowed	500
— Discount allowed but later on dishonoured	100	— Cash received	17,800
— Cash paid	50	— Transfer from debtors to creditors	2,400
		— Bad Debts	500
		By Balance c/d	1,52,750
	1,92,750		1,92,750

Creditors Ledger Adjustment A/c

Particulars	*Amount*	*Particulars*	*Amount*
To Balance b/d	500	By Balance b/d	54,000
To General Ledger Adjustment a/c :		By General ledger Adjustment a/c	
— Purchase returns	1,200	— Purchases	1,00,000
— Cash paid	42,000		
— Bills payable	15,000		
— Discount received	900		
— Transfer from Debtors to creditors	2,400		
To Balance c/d	92,000		
	1,54,000		1,54,000

Problem 10

Prepare the General ledger adjustment account as will appear in the debtors and creditor's ledger from the information given below :

	Dr. Rs.	Cr Rs.
Balance on 1-4-98		
Debtors's ledger	47,200	240
Creditor's ledger	250	26,300
Transactions for the year ended 31-3-1999 :		
Total Sales	1,20,000	
Cash Sales	8,100	
Total Purchases	89,500	
Credit Purchases	67,000	
Creditors paid off (in full settlement of Rs. 40,000)	39,500	
Received from Debtors (in full settlement of Rs. 59,000)	58,200	
Returns from Debtors	2,600	
Returns to Creditors	1,800	
Bills accepted for Creditors	5,500	
Bills Payable matured	8,000	
Bills accepted by customers	20,100	
Bills Receivable dishonoured	1,500	
Bills Receivable discounted	5,000	
Bills Receivable endorsed to creditors	4,000	
Endorsed bills dishonoured	1,000	
Bad debts written off (after bad debts recovered Rs. 300)	2,200	
Provision for Doubtful Debts	550	
Transfer from Debtor's ledger to Creditor's ledger	1,100	
Transfer from Creditors ledger to Debtor's ledger	1,900	
Balances on 31-3-99 :		
Debtor's ledger (cr)	380	
Creditor's ledger (Dr.	420	

(CA Foundation, May 1999)

Solution

In Debtors Ledger
General Ledger Adjustment A/c

Date		*Rs.*	*Date*		*Rs.*
1-4-98	To Balance b/d	240	1-4-98	By Balance b/d	47,200
	To Debtors Ledger Adjustment a/c :			By Debtors ledger Adjustment a/c :	
	— Bank	58,200		— Credit sales	1,12,000
	— Discount	800		— B R dishonoured	1,500
	— Returns	2,600		By Balance c/d	380
	— B R	20,100			
	— Bad debts written off	2,500			
	— Transfer from Debtors ledger to creditor's ledger	1,100			
	— Transfer from creditors ledger to debtors ledger	1,900			
	To Balance c/d	74,640			
		1,62,080			1,62,080

In Creditors Ledger
General Ledger Adjustment A/c

Date		*Rs.*	*Date*		*Rs.*
1-4-98	To Balance b/d	26,300	1-4-98	By Balance b/d	280
	To Creditors Ledger Adjustment a/c :			By Creditors ledger Adjustment a/c :	
	— Purchases	67,000		— Bank	39,500
	— Endorsed BR. Dishonoured	1,000		— Discount received	500
31-3-99	To Balance c/d	420		— Returns	1,800
				— BP.	550
				— BR. Endorsed	4,000
				By Transfer from Creditors ledger to debtor's ledger	1,900
				By Transfer form Debtor's ledger to Creditor's ledger	1,100
				By Balance c/d	40,140
		94,720			94,720

SECTIONAL BALANCING SYSTEM

Sectional balancing System is a system where total debtors account and total creditors account are maintained in the General Ledger along with the Individual Customers Accounts in the Sales Ledger and individual creditors accounts in the purchase ledger. Control or total account is an account which receive debits and credits in total or in aggregate of all the transactions, which have been debited or credited to the Individual Ledger Accounts.

If the total balances of individual customers is equal to the balances in the total debtors account, the Sales Ledger Account is correctly posted and similarly if the balance in the total creditors account is equal to the total of the individual creditors balance both the creditors ledger and total creditors accounts are correct. Since only General ledger is Self Balancing and not debtors and creditors account, this system is known as Self Balancing System.

Differences Between Self Balancing and Sectional Balancing System

1. Under the self balancing system all the three ledger, viz, Debtors, Creditors and General Ledger is made self balancing, while under Sectional Balancing System only the general Ledger is made self balancing.
2. Under the Sectional Balancing System control accounts are kept in the General Ledger merely as memorandum accounts and they do not form part of the double entry system. On the other hand under the Self Balancing System, control or adjustment accounts maintained forms part of the double entry.

Problem 11

From the following summary of the transactions of Electronics company Ltd. for the month of January 2004 prepare.

(*a*) Debtors ledger control account
(*b*) Creditors ledger control account

Transactions pertaining to sundry debtors :	
Balance of debtors control a/c as	Rs.
On Dec. 31, 2003	30,000
Credit Sales	3,00,000
Sales Returns	3,000
Cash received from Debtors	1,33,000
Discount allowed to Debtors	13,000
Bills drawn on Debtors	66,000
Bills Receivable discounted	30,000
Bills Receivable honoured	23,000
Bills Receivable dishonoured	2,000
Noting charges paid	30
Bills Receivable endorsed	6,600
Discounted Bills dishonoured	3,300
Endorsed bills dishonoured	600
Provision made for Bad and Doubtful debts	6,000
Provision made for discount on Debtors	1,200
Bad debts written off	333
Transactions pertaining to sundry creditors :	
Balance of creditors ledger control account as on December 31, 2003	20,000
Credit Purchases	2,22,000
Purchases Returns	2,000
Cash paid to creditors	1,20,000
Discount received from creditors	12,000
Bills Accepted	44,000
Bills Payable honoured	4,000

Bills Payable dishonoured	400
Noting charges paid by creditors	40
Bills Receivable endorsed by creditors	6,600
Endorsed bills dishonoured	600
Provision made for discount on creditors	6,000

Solution

Debtors Ledger Control A/c

Particulars	*Amount*	*Particulars*	*Amount*
To Balance b/d	30000	By Sales Returns	3,000
To Credit sales	3,00,000	By Bank	1,33,000
To B. R. dishonoured	2,000	By Discount	13,000
To Cash (Noting Charges)	30	By B R.	66,000
To Bank (Bill dishonoured)	3,300	By Bad Debts	333
To Creditors (Bill endorsed dishonoured)	600	By Balance c/d	1,20,597
	3,35,930		3,35,930

Note :

The following transactions do not affect Adjustment a/c.

Bills discounted bills endorsed, provision for doubtful debts, provision for discount on debtors etc.

Creditors Ledger Control A/c

Particulars	*Amount*	*Particulars*	*Amount*
To Purchase Returns	2,000	By Balance b/d	20,000
To Bank	1,20,000	By Credit Purchases	2,22,000
To Discount	12,000	By B/P dishonoured	400
To B/P	44,000	By Cash (noting charges)	40
To B/R endorsed	6,600	By B/R endorsed dishonoured	600
To Balance c/d	58,440		
	2,43,040		2,43,040

Problem 12

Write up (1) Debtors control a/c and (2) Creditor's control a/c recording the following transactions for the year ended 30th June 2003, bringing down the balances on that date :

	Rs.
Sales	2,04,500
Purchases	1,40,000
Cash received from debtors	1,55,000
Cash paid to creditors	1,37,000
Allowances to customers on goods damaged	2,000
Cash received in respect of debts previously written off	1,300
Bad Debts written off	1,000

Amount due to suppliers as shown by Creditors Ledger offset against amount due from the same concern as shown by Debtors Ledger	1,400
Cash received in respect of Dr. balance in creditors ledger	1,100
Returns Inward	9,900
Bills Receivable	40,000
Bills Dishonoured	2,500
Returns Outward	1,500
Discount Received	3,000
Discount Allowed	2,500

On 1st July 2002 the Debtors Ledger Balances were Rs. 18,300 debit, and Rs. 190 Credit while the creditors ledger balances on the same date were Rs. 16,500 credit and Rs. 1,000 debit. On 30th June there were no credit balances in debtors ledger except those outstanding on 1st July 2002 and no debit balances in the creditors ledger.

Solution

Debtor's Ledger Control A/c

Particulars	*Amount*	*Particulars*	*Amount*
To balance b/d	18,300	By Balance b/d	190
To Sales	2,04,500	By Bank	1,55,000
To Bills dishonoured	2,500	By Allowances	2,000
To Balance c/d	190	By Bad Debts	1,000
		By Returns	9,900
		By BR.	40,000
		By Discount	2,500
		By Transfer	1,400
		By Balance c/d	13,500
	2,25,490		2,25,490

Creditors Ledger control A/c

Particulars	*Amount*	*Particulars*	*Amount*
To Balance b/d	1,100	By Balance b/d	16,500
To Cash	1,37,000	By Purchases	1,40,000
To Transfer	1,400	By Cash	1,100
To Returns	1,500		
To Discount	3,000		
To Balance c/d	13,600		
	1,57,600		1,57,600

QUESTIONS

Simple questions

(*a*) What do you mean by Self Balancing Ledger ?
(*b*) State four advantages of Self Balancing Ledger.
(*c*) Mention the three ledger maintained under Self Balancing Ledgers.
(*d*) What is Sectional Balancing System.
(*e*) Distinguish between Self Balancing and Sectional Balancing System.

EXERCISE 1

From the following particulars, prepare Sales Ledger adjustment a/c in the General Ledger of a company.

1997		
Jan. 1,	Balance of sundry debtors	80,000
Dec. 31,	Credit sales	1,96,000
	Cash received from debtors	1,56,000
	Allowed discount	4,000
	Received Bills Receivable	30,000
	Returns inward	6,000
	Rebate allowed to debtors	5,500
	Bad debts	9,000
	BR dishonoured	7,500
	Bad debts previously written off now recovered	2,400

(University of Madras, B. Com., April 1999)

Answer : Sales ledger Adj a/c balance Rs. 73,000.

EXERCISE 2

From the following information, prepare Sales Ledger Adjustment account for the month of ended 31st January 1998.

		Rs.
Jan. 1	Debtors balance (Dr.)	45,000
	Debtors balance (Cr)	500
	Credit sales	80,000
	Cash sales	40,000
	Cash received (including B.R. Rs. 4,000)	40,000
	Bad debts	1,200
	Provision for Bad Debts	1,800
	Sales Returns	2,000
	Credit Purchase	48,000
	Purchases Returns	1,000
	Balance of debtors 31st Jan. (Cr)	800

(Osmania University B. Com., Oct. 1999)

Answer : Balance in sales ledger adj a/c Rs. 86,100.

EXERCISE 3

Prepare Purchase and Sales Ledger Adjustment accounts as they would appear in the normal ledger as on 30-11-98 from the following

	Rs.
Balances as on 1-11-98 :	
Purchase Ledger (Dr.)	700
Purchase Ledger (Cr)	30,640
Sales Ledger (Dr.)	66,930
Sales Ledger (Cr)	1,865
Transactions during November 1998 :	
Total Sales	1,35,000
Credit Sales	1,16,000
Cash Purchases	11,800
Credit Purchases	72,700
Sales Returns	500
Provision for bad and doubtful debts	270
Bad debts written off	1,000
Amount received against bad debts	
Written off last year	600
Purchase Returns	2,500
Receipts from Debtors	83,000
Payments to Creditors	57,500
Discounts allowed	650
Discounts received	320
Interest charged to debtors	592
Bills Receivable received	10,000
Bills Payable accepted	8,000
Bills Receivable dishonoured	2,500
Notary charges debited	10
Cash paid to customers	137
Balance as on 30-11-98 :	
Purchase ledger (Dr.)	980
Sales ledger (Cr)	266

(Sri Venkateshwara University B. Com. October 1999)

Answer : Balance of debtor's ledger adj. a/c Rs. 89,420 and creditors ledger adj. a/c Rs. 35,300.

EXERCISE 4

The Undermentioned particulars have been extracted from the books of D. D. Boot company. You are required to prepare the Sales Ledger Adjustment account as on 30th June 1995.

	Rs.
Debtors on 1st July 1994	55,842
Credit sales	98,602
Cash received from debtors	88,753

Discount allowed to debtors	480
Acceptance received from debtors	7,120
Returns from debtors	5,430
Bills Receivable dishonoured	1,120
Bad debts written off	3,890
Sundry charges debited to customers	378
Transfer to Bought Ledger	100

(University of Madras B. Com., April 1998)

Answer : Balance of Sales Ledger Adj. a/c Rs. 50,169

EXERCISE 5

From the following particulars prepare Debtors Ledger Adjustment a/c and Creditors Ledger Adjustment a/c in the General Ledger.

Opening Balances of debtors :	
On 1-1-1997 (Dr.)	Rs. 40,000
On 1-1-1997 (Cr)	500
Opening Balances of creditors :	
On 1-1-1997 (Dr.)	Rs. 1,000
On 1-1-1997 (Cr)	45,000
Transactions during the year :	Rs.
Bills Receivable received	12,000
Credit Purchases	2,00,000
Credit Sales	2,82,000
Purchase Returns	8,500
Cash Sales	1,00,000
Cash Purchases	50,000
Cash Received from debtors	2,32,000
Discount allowed to debtors	8,000
Cash paid to creditors	1,60,000
Discount allowed by creditors	5,000
Bills payable issued	7,500
Bad debts written off	2,000
Bills receivable dishonoured	2,700
Transfer from Bought ledger to Sales ledger	1,300
Bad debts recorded	3,500
Sales returns	3,500

(Osmania University B. Com., March 1999)

Answer : Balance in Debtors Ledger Adj a/c Rs 65,400 and Creditors Ledger Adj a/c Rs. 61,700.

EXERCISE 6

A, B, C Company Ltd. maintains its books under Self Balancing system. From the following particulars prepare necessary adjustment accounts in General Ledger for the month of January.

Balances as on 1-1-1999.
Debtors balance as per General Ledger
Adjustment a/c 49,500 (Cr)
Creditors balance as per General Ledger.
Adjustment a/c 28,000 (Dr.)
Transactions during the month :

	Rs.
Sales (20% on cash)	50,000
Purchases (50% on credit)	30,000
Payments to creditor	7,500
Discount allowed	1,500
Discount received	500
Receipts from customers	20,000
Bad debts	500
Bills payable accepted	5,000
Bills receivable received	3,000
Bills receivable dishonoured	400
Transfer from sales ledger to purchase Ledger	200
Transfer from purchase ledger to Sales ledger	100

Discount allowed to debtors amounting to Rs. 300 was recorded as discount received from creditors.

(Sri Venkateshwara University B. Com. April 1999)

Answer : Balance in Debtors Ledger Adjustment a/c Rs. 64,300 and Creditors Ledger Adjustment a/c Rs. 30,000

EXERCISE 7

From the following details write up General Ledger adjustment accounts and the Bought and Sales Ledger Adjustment accounts as on 31st December 1997.

Debtors (1-1-97) Dr.	17,425
Debtors (1-1-97) Cr	320
Creditors (1-1-97) Cr	27,408
Creditors (1-1-97) Dr.	204
Purchases	25,200
Sales	28,209
Sales Returns	208
Purchase returns	714
Cash paid to creditors	12,700
Bills received from debtors	9,300
Bills dishonoured	200
Bills accepted from creditors	7,400
Discount allowed to debtors	215
Discount allowed to debtors but later disallowed	100
Cash received from debtors	8,700
Discount allowed by creditors	1,020

Cash paid to debtors	25
Transfer from debtors to creditors	
Ledger	1,242
Case purchases	4,320
Cash sales	7,400
Bad debts written off	215

(University of Madras B. Com. May 1998)

Answer : Balance in Sales Ledger Adjustment a/c Rs. 25,759 and Bought Ledger Adjustment a/c Rs. 29,328

27

CHAPTER

Royalty Accounts

INTRODUCTION

when a owner of a property enters into an agreement with another person authorising him to make use of the right of property in return for a consideration payable periodically it is known as royalty agreement. The person who lets out his right to another is known as Lessor and he person to whom such right is given is known as lessee. The right of property thus granted is known as lease. Common examples of lease are mine leased out by landlord, copyright by an Author, patent right by a patentee.

TERMS USED IN ROYALTY ACCOUNTS

1. **Royalty :** Royalty is a periodical payment based on output or sale, for the use of a certain asset or right like mine, copyright or patent to its owner.
2. **Minimum Rent or Dead Rent :** Minimum rent is the minimum sum guaranteed to the holder of royalty rights. It is called fixed rent or dead rent. If the royalty earned is less than the stipulated amount usually accompanied by a provision that if the sum due (as calculated as so much per unit) does not reach the minimum, such deficiency may be carried forward and deducted from future royalties.
3. **Short working :** Short working is the excess of minimum rent over royalty. When royalty does not work upto a minimum fixed, then the difference between such fixed minimum and royalty amount is known as short workings. That agreement may contain conditions for recovery of short workings from future royalties.
4. **Recoupment of short working :** Recouping is the act of recovering short workings from royalties. The terms of recoupment may be limited to a certain period from the date of agreement or from the date of deficiency of rent.

ADDITIONAL POINTS TO BE BORNE IN MIND IN CONNECTION WITH ROYALTY ACCOUNTS.

1. **Amount payable to lessor in a year :** The amount payable by lessee to the lessor may relate to any of the following :
   (*a*) The amount of minimum rent when royalty is less than minimum rent for that year.

OR

(*b*) The amount of minimum rent plus that portion of surplus royalty which is left after the recoupment of short working.

OR

(*c*) The amount of royalty, if the royalty for the year is more than minimum rent and there is no short working to be recovered out of the surplus royalty.

2. **Abnormal fall in output or sales :** When sales or output decrease in any year owing to abnormal conditions such as strike, lock out; occurrence of fire etc., the lessor may not demand lessee to pay minimum rent. In such a case the lessee may be allowed some deduction in the minimum rent payable for that year by means of inserting a clause in the royalty agreement.
3. **Surplus Royalty left after recoupment of Short Working :** Where surplus royalty is left after recoupment of short working, then that surplus royalty should be paid along with minimum rent to the landlord.
4. **Irrecoverable Short Working :** Where short working is not recovered within the prescribed period of recoupment then the irrecoverable short working should be transferred to profit & loss a/c in the books of both the lessor and lessee. In the books of lessee it is treated as loss and hence debited to profit & loss a/c, credit being given to short working a/c. In the books of lessor, it is treated as a gain and hence credited to P & L a/c, debit being given to short working allowable a/c or short working reserve a/c.
5. **When there is no Provision for recoupment of Short Working :** When there is no provision for the recoupment of short working, then such short working of each of the years is to be treated as irrecoverable short working and hence transferred to profit & loss a/c for the years in which short working arise.
6. **Damage payable by the lessor to the lessee :** In case of copyright the author (lessor) may be required to revise the manuscript by the publisher (lessee) for further publication. Where the author fails to do so he may be asked to pay damages to the publisher. This is recorded in the books of both the parties.

To the lessee it is a gain and hence the following entry is passed

Lessor's (Author's) a/c Dr.
  To Damages Receivable a/c

The amount of damages is not actually received in cash. Instead it is set off against the royalty payable to the lessor. So no entry is passed in the books of lessee for the actual receipt of damages.

As regards lessor, the damage payable is a loss and the following entry is recorded.

Damages payable a/c Dr.
  To Lessee's a/c

As damages are set off against royalty receivable no entry is passed for actual payment of royalty

7. **Income Tax deducted at Source by the Lessee on the amount due to The Lessor :** The income tax deducted at sources is recorded in both the books of lessor and lessee. In the books of Lessee the following entry is passed :

Lessors a/c Dr.
  To Income tax payable a/c

The above entry is recorded for deducting the income tax. When it is paid to Government. The following entry is recorded.

Income tax payable a/c Dr.
To Bank a/c

In the books of lessor the following entry is passed for income tax deducted at source.

Income tax payable a/c Dr.
To Lesse's a/c

ENTRIES IN THE BOOKS OF LESSEE

(A) When minimum rent a/c is not opened the following entries are passed :-

1. When Royalty is less than minimum rent and short working accumulated.
Royalty a/c Dr. (with the actual Royalty)
Short working a/c Dr. (with the shortage)
To Landlord (with the minimum Rent) or Lessor's a/c
2. When Royalty is paid
Lessor's a/c Dr. (with minimum rent)
To Bank a/c
3. When the royalty is transferred :
P & L a/c or Production a/c Dr. (with actual royalty)
To Royalty a/c

Note : The above entries are repeated every year. But when the production exceeds the minimum rent the following entries are passed.

4. Royalty a/c Dr.
To Landlord a/c

Note :- As the royalty is more than the minimum rent the short working does not arise instead the lessee will recoup the short working that had resulted in the past. The entry is

5. Lessor's a/c Dr. (with the amount recouped)
To Short working
6. For Writing of Short Working : When the right to recoup expires and the lessee is not able to recoup the short working the amount of short working is a loss to him and it is closed by transferring to P & L a/c. The entry is
Profit & loss a/c Dr.
To Short working a/c

(B) Entries when minimum rent is opened :

1. When royalty is less than minimum rent :
(*a*) For recording the minimum rent payable to lessor :
Minimum rent a/c Dr. (with minimum rent payable)
To Lessor's a/c
(*b*) For accumulating short working :
Royalty a/c Dr. (with actual royalty)
Short working a/c Dr. (with the amount of short working)
To Minimum rent a/c (with the amount of minimum rent)
(*c*) For the payment of Royalty :
Landlord's a/c Dr. (With the amount of minimum rent)
To Bank a/c

(*d*) When the Royalty is transferred)
P & L a/c or production a/c Dr.
To Royalty a/c
(*e*) For transfer of irrecoverable short working to profit & loss a/c
Profit & Loss a/c Dr.
To Short working a/c

2. **When Royalty is more than minimum rent :-** The minimum rent a/c is not opened and rest of the entries are same as was passed under method (A).

In the Books of Lessor

The entries in the books of lessor is opposite to the entries passed in the books of lessee. They are as follows :-

1. When production is less :
Lessee's a/c Dr. (with minimum rent)
To Royalty a/c (with actual royalty)
To Short working a/c (with the difference)
2. When payment is received :
Bank a/c Dr.
To Lessee's a/c
3. When Royalty is transferred :
Royalty a/c Dr.
To P & L a/c
4. When short working is recouped :
Short working a/c Dr.
To lessee's a/c
5. When short working is closed on the expiry of right
Short workings a/c Dr.
To P & L a/c

Problem 1

Ramu took a lease of mine for a period of 20 years. Royalty payable is Re 1 per ton subject to a minimum rent of Rs. 12,000 per annum. The short workings are recoupable during the first three years of the lease. The output was : 1994 - Nil, 1995 - 4,000 tons 1996 - 20,000 tons, 1997 - 40,000 tons. Give the Journal entries in the books of Ramu.

(University of Madras B. Com. May 1998)

Solution

Royalty Table

Year	Output (Tons)	Royalty (Rs.)	Minimum rent	Short working	Recouped	Loss	Payment to landlord
1994	Nil	—	12,000	12,000	—	—	12,000
1995	4,000	4,000	12,000	8,000	—	—	12,000
1996	20,000	20,000	12,000	—	8,000	12,000	12,000
1997	40,000	40,000	12,000	—	—	—	40,000

Note : Payment to Landlord is royalty or minimum rent which over is higher after deducting recouped amount if any.

Journal Entries in The books of Ramu
"With minimum Rent a/c method"

Date	Particulars		Dr. Amount	Cr. Amount
1994	Minimum Rent a/c	Dr.	12,000	
	To Landlord a/c			12,000
	(Being the minimum rent due)			
	Royalty a/c	Dr.	Nil	
	Short working a/c		12,000	
	To Minimum Rent a/c			12,000
	(Being first year's short working)			
	Landlord a/c	Dr.	12,000	
	To Cash a/c			12,000
	(Being the amount paid to Landlord)			
1995	Minimum Rent a/c	Dr.	12,000	
	To Landlord's a/c			12,000
	(Being minimum rent due)			
	Royalty a/c	Dr.	4,000	
	Short working a/c	Dr.	8,000	
	To Minimum rent a/c			12,000
	(Being royalty payable after taking short working into a/c)			
	Landlord's a/c	Dr.	12,000	
	To Cash a/c			12,000
	(Being the amount paid to Landlord)			
	Profit & Loss a/c	Dr.	4,000	
	To Royalty a/c			4,000
	(Being the actual royalty transferred)			
1996	Royalty a/c	Dr.	20,000	
	To Short working a/c			8,000
	To Landlord a/c			12,000
	(Being The royalty payable after adjusting earlier short working)			
	Landlord's a/c	Dr.	12,000	
	To Cash a/c			12,000
	(Being the amount paid to landlord)			
	Profit & Loss a/c	Dr.	12,000	
	To Short working a/c			12,000
	(Being the Unrecouped short working of 4,000 of 1st year, 8,000 of IInd years transferred to P & L a/c)			
	Profit & Loss a/c	Dr.	20,000	
	To Royalty a/c			20,000
	(Being the royalty transferred)			

Date	Particulars		Dr. Amount	Cr. Amount
1997	Royalty a/c To Landlord a/c (Being Royalty due)	Dr.	40,000	40,000
	Landlord a/c To Cash a/c (Being Landlord paid)	Dr.	40,000	40,000
	Profit & Loss a/c To Royalty a/c (Being the royalty transferred)	Dr.	40,000	40,000

Problem 2

The Bengal mines Co. Ltd. took from Mr. Dass a lease of a mine for a period of 25 years from 1-1-86 on a royalty or Rs. 5 per ton of mineral-got with a dead rent of Rs. 20,000 and power to recoup short working during the first five years of the lease. The annual output were as follows :- 1986 - 2,000 tonnes, 1987 - 3,000 tonnes 1988 - 4,000 tonnes, 1989 - 4,500 tonnes, 1990 - 5,000 tonnes.

Give Journal entries in the Books of the Bengal company and in the books of Dass.

(University of Madras B. Com. September 1997)

Solution

Calculation of Royalty

Year	Production	Royalty	Minimum Rent	Short Working	Short Working Recoupned	Loss	Amount paid to Landlord
1986	2,000	10,000	20,000	10,000	—	—	20,000
1987	3,000	15,000	20,000	5,000	—	—	20,000
1988	4,000	20,000	20,000	—	—	—	20,000
1989	4,500	22,500	20,000	—	2,500	—	20,000
1990	5,000	25,000	20,000	—	5,000	7,500	20,000

In The Books of Bengal Mines Co. Ltd.

Journal Entries

Date	Particulars		Dr. Amount	Cr. Amount
1986	Minimum Rent a/c To Mr. Dass (landlord) a/c (Being the minimum rent due)	Dr.	20,000	20,000
	Royalty a/c Short working a/c To Minimum rent a/c (Being Royalty payable @ Rs. 5 per tonne on 2,000 tonnes)	Dr. Dr.	10,000 10,000	20,000

Date	Particulars		Dr. Amount	Cr. Amount
	Mr. Dass a/c To Bank a/c (Being the minimum Rent paid to Landlord)	Dr.	20,000	20,000
	Profit & Loss a/c To Royalty a/c (Being actual royalty transferred to P & L a/c)	Dr.	10,000	10,000
1987	Minimum rent a/c To Mr. Dass (Landlord) (Being the minimum rent due)	Dr.	20,000	20,000
	Royalty a/c Short working a/c To Minimum rent a/c (Being the royalty payable to Mr. Dass @ 5 per tonne on 3,000 tonnes)	Dr. Dr.	15,000 5,000	20,000
	Mr. Dass a/c To Bank a/c (Being the minimum rent paid to Landlord)	Dr.	20,000	20,000
	Profit & Loss a/c To Royalty a/c (Being actual royalty transferred to P & L a/c)	Dr.	15,000	15,000
1988	Minimum Rent a/c To Mr. Dass (Landlord) (Being the minimum rent due)	Dr.	20,000	20,000
	Royalty a/c To Minimum rent a/c (Being Royalty payable to Landlord @ Rs 5 per tonne on 4,000 tonnes)	Dr.	20,000	20,000
	Mr. Dass a/c To Bank a/c (Being minimum rent paid to landlord)	Dr.	20,000	20,000
	Profit & Loss a/c To Royalty a/c (Being actual royalty transferred to P & L a/c)	Dr.	20,000	20,000
1989	Royalty a/c To Short working a/c To Mr. Dass a/c (Being royalty payable to landlord @ Rs. 5 per tonne on 4,500 tonnes after adjusting earlier short working)	Dr.	22,500	2,500 20,000
	Mr. Dass a/c To Bank a/c (Being the minimum rent paid to Mr. Dass)	Dr.	20,000	20,000

Date	Particulars		Dr. Amount	Cr. Amount
	Profit & Loss a/c	Dr.	22,500	
	To Royalty a/c			22,500
	(Being the royalty transfer to P & L a/c)			
1990	Royalty a/c	Dr.	25,000	
	To Short working a/c			5,000
	To Mr. Dass a/c			20,000
	(Being royalty payable to Landlord @ Rs. 5 per tonne on 5,000 tonnes after adjusting earlier short working)			
	Mr. Dass a/c	Dr.	20,000	
	To Bank a/c			20,000
	(Being the minimum rent paid to Landlord)			
	Profit & Loss a/c	Dr.	7,500	
	To Short working			7,500
	(Being the balance in short working now being irrecoverable transferred to P & L a/c)			
	Profit & Loss a/c	Dr.	25,000	
	To Royalty a/c			25,000
	(Being the Royalty transferred to P & L a/c)			

In the Books of Landlord (Mr. Dass)

Date	Particulars		Dr. Amount	Cr. Amount
1986	Bengal Mine Co. a/c	Dr.	20,000	
	To Royalty a/c			10,000
	To Short working a/c			10,000
	(Being the Royalty due @ 5 per tonne for 2,000 tonnes)			
	Bank a/c	Dr.	20,000	
	To Bengal Mines Co. a/c			20,000
	(Being Minimum rent received)			
	Royalty a/c	Dr.	10,000	
	To profit & Loss a/c			10,000
	(Being the royalty transferred to P & L a/c)			
1987	Bengal Mine Co. a/c	Dr.	20,000	
	To Royalty a/c			15,000
	To Short working a/c			5,000
	(Being royalty due @ 5 per tonne for 3000 tonnes)			
	Bank a/c	Dr.	20,000	
	To Benagal Mine Co. a/c			20,000
	(Being minimum rent received)			
	Royalty a/c	Dr.	20,000	
	To Profit & Loss a/c			20,000
	(Being royalty transferred to P & Loss a/c)			

Date	Particulars		Dr. Amount	Cr. Amount
1989	Bengal Mine is a/c	Dr.	20,000	
	Short Working a/c	Dr.	2,500	
	To Royalty a/c			22,500
	(Being royalty due @ 5 per tonne for 4,500			
	Bank a/c	Dr.	20,000	
	To Bengal Mines Co. a/c			20,000
	(Being minimum rent received)			
	Royalty a/c	Dr.	22,500	
	To Profit & Loss a/c			22,500
	(Being Royalty transfer to P & L a/c)			
1999	Bengal Mines Co. a/c	Dr.	20,000	
	Short working	Dr.	5,000	
	To Royalty a/c			25,000
	(Being Royalty due @ 5 per tonne for 5,000 tonnes)			
	Bank a/c	Dr.	20,000	
	To Bengal Mine Co. a/c			20,000
	(Being minimum rent received)			
	Royalty a/c	Dr.	25,000	
	To P & L a/c			25,000
	(Being royalty transferred to P & L a/c).			
	Short working suspense a/c	Dr.	7,500	
	To P & L a/c			7,500
	(Being the irrecoverable short working transferred).			

Problem 3

Dinesh Ltd. Patented to manufacture water filters, granted the licence to Prakash Ltd., for ten years to manufacture and sell the water filters on the following terms.

(*i*) Prakash Ltd., to pay a royalty of Rs. 10 for every water filter sold with a minimum payment of Rs. 40,000 per annum, accounts to be settled annually on 31st December.

(*ii*) The short working in any year may be recouped from any excess of royalties over the minimum rent in the next two years subject to a maximum of Rs. 16,000 per annum.

The number of water filters sold for the first five years was as follows :

Year	Water filters sold
31st Dec. 1991	800
1992	4,400
1993	10,400
1994	1,600
1995	8,800

The following accounts are to be prepared in the books of Prakash Ltd.

1. Minimum rent a/c
2. Royalty a/c
3. Short working a/c

(Sri Venkateshwara University B. Com. September 2000)

Solution

Royalty Table

Year	*Sales*	*Royalty*	*Minimum Rent*	*Short Working*	*Short Working recouped*	*Short Working not recouped*	*Amount paid to Landlord*
1991	800	8000	40,000	32,000	—	—	40,000
1992	4,400	44,000	40,000	—	4,000	—	40,000
1993	10,400	10,400	40,000	—	28,000	—	76,000
1994	1,600	16,000	40,000	24,000	—	—	40,000
1995	8,800	88, 000	40,000	—	24,000	—	64,000

Minimum Rent A/c

Date		*Rs.*	*Date*		*Rs.*
1991	To Landlord a/c	40,000	1991	By Royalty a/c	8,000
				By Short workings a/c	32,000
		40,000			40,000
1992	To Landlord a/c	40,000	1992	By Royalty a/c	40,000
1994	To Landlord a/c	40,000	1994	By Royalty a/c	16,000
				By Short working a/c	24,000
		40,000			40,000

Royalty A/c

Date		*Rs.*	*Date*		*Rs.*
1991	To Minimum Rent a/c	8,000	1991	By P & L a/c	8,000
1992	To Minimum Rent a/c	44,000	1992	By P & L a/c	44,000
1993	To Landlord a/c	1,04,000	1993	By P & L a/c	1,04,000
1994	To Minimum Rent a/c	16,000	1994	By P & L a/c	16,000
1995	To Landlord a/c	88,000	1995	By P & L a/c	88,000

Short Workings A/c

Date		*Rs.*	*Date*		*Rs.*
1991	To Minimum Rent a/c	32,000	1991	By Balance c/d	32,000
1992	To Balance b/c	32,000	1992	By Land lord a/c	4,000
				By Balance c/d	28,000
		32,000			32,000
1993	To Balance b/d	28,000	1993	By Landlord a/c	28,000
1994	To Minimum Rent	24,000	1994	By Balance c/d	24,000
1995	To Balance b/d	24,000	1995	By Landlord a/c	24,000

Problem 4

The Bihar Coal Co. Ltd., undertook a lease of a coal mine on a royalty of 50 paise per ton of coal raised with a dead rent of Rs. 30,000 per annum and power to recoup short workings during the first five years of the lease. The output for the first three years was a follows :

I - year - 15,000 tons, II - year - 50,000 tons, III year - 75,000 tons.

Write up Minimum Rent a/c, Royalties a/c, and Short Workings a/c.

(University of Madras B. Com. October 2000)

Solution

Royalty Table

Year	*Output*	*Royalty*	*Minimum rent*	*Short working*	*S.W Recouped*	*Paid to Landlord*
I	15,000	7,500	30,000	22,500	—	30,000
II	50,000	25,000	30,000	5,000	—	30,000
III	75,000	37,500	30,000	—	7,500	30,000

Minimum Rent A/c

Date		*Rs.*	*Date*		*Rs.*
I Year	To Landlord a/c	30,000	I Year	By Royalty a/c	7,500
				By Short working a/c	22,500
		30,000			30,000
II Year	To Landlord a/c	30,000	II Year	By Royalty a/c	25,000
				By Short working a/c	5,000
		30,000			30,000

Royalty A/c

Date		*Rs.*	*Date*		*Rs.*
I Year	To Minimum rent a/c	7,500	I Year	By P & L a/c	7,500
II Year	To Minimum rent a/c	25,000	II Year	By P & L a/c	25,000
III Year	To Landlord	30,000	III Year	By P & L a/c	37,500
	To Short working a/c	7,500			
		37,500			37,500

Short working A/c

Date		*Rs.*	*Date*		*Rs.*
I Year	To Minimum rent	22,500	I Year	By Balance c/d	22,500
II Year	To Balance b/d	22,500	II Year	By Balance c/d	27,500
	To Minimum rent a/c	5,000			
		27,500			27,500
III Year	To Balance b/d	27,500	III Year	By Royalty (recouped)	7,500
				By Balance c/d	20,000
		27,500			27,500

Problem 5

Bengal Coal company Ltd., are the lessee of a mine on a royalty or Rs. 5 per ton of coal raised with a dead rent of Rs. 30,000 per annum and power to recoup short workings during the first five years of the lease. The output for the first six years were as follows :

I - 1,500 tons, II - 5,000 tons, III- 7,500 tons, IV - 4,000 tons, V - 6,000 tons, VI - 10,000 tons.

Prepare (*a*) Royalty a/c (*b*) Short workings a/c.**(University of Madras B. Com. April 2000)**

Solution

Royalty Table

Year	*Sales*	*Royalty*	*Minimum Rent*	*Short Working*	*Recouped*	*Loss*	*Payment to Landlord*
I	1,500	7,500	30,000	22,500	—	—	30,000
II	5,000	25,000	30,000	5,000	—	—	30,000
III	7,500	37,500	30,000	—	7,500	—	30,000
IV	4,000	20,000	30,000	10,000	—	—	30,000
V	6,000	30,000	30,000	—	—	30,000	30,000
VI	10,000	50,000	30,000	—	—	—	50,000

Royalty A/c

Date		*Rs.*		*Rs.*
I Year	To Minimum rent a/c	7,500	By P & L a/c	7,500
II Year	To Minimum rent a/c	25,000	By P & L a/c	25,000
III Year	To Landlord a/c	30,000	By P & L a/c	37,500
	To Short working a/c	7,500		
		37,500		37,500
IV Year	To Minimum rent a/c	20,000	By P & L a/c	20,000
V Year	To Landlords a/c	30,000	By P & L a/c	30,000
VI Year	To Landlords a/c	50,000	By P & L a/c	50,000

Short workings A/c

Date		*Rs.*		*Rs.*
I Year	To Minimum rent a/c	22,500	By Balance c/d	22,500
II Year	To Balance b/d	22,500	By Balance c/d	27,500
	To Minimum rent a/c	5,000		
		27,500		27,500
III Year	To Balance b/d	27,500	By Royalty recouped	7,500
			By Balance c/d	20,000
		27,500		27,500
IV Year	To Balance b/d	20,000	By Balance c/d	30,000
	To Minimum rent	10,000		
		30,000		30,000
V year	To Balance b/d	30000	By P & L a/c — loss (not recouped)	30,000
		30,000		30,000

Problem 6

(Royalty during a period of strike)

On 1-1-95 Mohini Coal Co. Ltd., leased a coal mine from A.R. Ltd., at Royalty of Rs. 10 per ton with a minimum rent of Rs. 15,000 per annum and power to recoup each year's short workings out of the excess royalty of next 2 years. In the event of a strike, the minimum rent would be reduced in proportion to time actually worked.

The annual output was a follows

Year	Tons	
1995	800	
1996	1,350	
1997	1,800	
1998	1,050	(Strike for 4 months)
1999	1,500	

Write up royalty a/c, short workings a/c, and A. R. Ltd. a/c in the books of Mohini Coal Co. Ltd.

(Calcutta University B. Com. (Pass) 2000)

Solution

Royalty Table

Year	*Output*	*Royalty*	*Minimum Rent*	*Short Working*	*Short recouped*	*Short working Lapsee*	*Payment*
1995	800	8,000	15,000	7,000	—	—	15,000
1996	1,350	13,500	15,000	1,500	—	—	15,000
1997	1,800	18,000	15,000	—	3,000	4,000	15,000
1998	1,050	10,500	10,000	—	500	1000	1,000
1999	1,500	15,000	15,000	—	—	—	15,000

Note :- Minimum rent in 1998 $\left(15000 \times \frac{8}{12}\right) = 10,000$

In the books of Mohini Coal A/c

Royalty A/c

Date		Rs.		Rs.
1995	To A.R. Ltd. a/c	8,000	By P & L a/c	8,000
1996	To A.R. Ltd. a/c	13,500	By P & L a/c	13,500
1997	To A.R. Ltd. a/c	15,000	By P& L a/c	18,000
	To Short working a/c	3,000		
		18,000		18,000
1998	To A.R. Ltd. a/c	10,000	By P & L a/c	10,500
	To Short working	500		
		10,500		10,500
1999	To A.R. Ltd. a/c	15,000	By P & L a/c	15,000

A.R. Ltd. A/c (Landlord)

Date		Rs.		Rs.
1995	To Bank a/c	15,000	By Royalty a/c	8,000
			By Short working a/c	7,000
		15,000		15,000
1996	To Bank a/c	15,000	By Royalty a/c	13,500
			By Short working a/c	1,500
		15,000		15,000
1997	To Bank a/c	15,000	By Royalty a/c	15,000
1998	To Bank a/c	10,000	By Royalty a/c	10,000
1999	To Bank a/c	15,000	By Royalty a/c	15,000

Short Working A/c

Date		Rs.		Rs.
1995	To A.R. Ltd. a/c	7,000	By Balance c/d	7,000
1996	To Balance b/d	7,000	By Royalty a/c (recovery)	3,000
	To A. R. Ltd. a/c	1,500	By P & L a/c (loss)	4,000
			By Balance c/d	1,500
		8,500		8,500
1997	To Balance b/d	1,500	By Royalty a/c (recovery)	500
			By P & L a/c	1,000
		1,500		1,500

Problem 7

Murthy took a lease of mines from Avinash with effect from 1st 1959 for a period of 20 years. The terms of agreement provided for the payment of royalty at Re 0.60 per ton raised subject to a minimum rent of Rs. 24,000 per annum, with a right to recoup short workings within a period of 3 years immediately succeeding the year in which the short working arises. It was further agreed that the minimum rent should be reduced proportionately, in case of strikes or lock out's in any year.

You are furnished with the following details :

Year	Tons raised
1993	46,000
1994	37,400
1995	30,800
1996	38,000
1997	41,200
1998	45,200

There was a strike in the year 1995 from October to December. The balance of short working as on 1-1-93 was Rs. 9,800 of which Rs. 4,400 arose in 1990 and the balance in 1991. Prepare Royalties a/c, short workings a/c and Avinash a/c in the books of Murthy for the above said years. **(Sri Venkateshwara University B. Com. April 2000)**

Solution

Royalty Table

Year	Output	Royalty	Minimum Rent	Short working	Surplus	Short working recouped	short working not recouped	Amount paid to Landlord
1990	—	19,600	24,000	4,400	—	—	—	24,000
1991	—	18,600	24,000	5,400	—	—	—	24,000
1992	—	24,000	24,000	—	—	—	—	24,000
1993	46,000	27,600	24,000	—	3,600	3,600	800	24,000
1994	37,400	22,400	24,000	1,560	—	—	5,400	24,000
1995	30,800	18,480	18,000	—	480	480	—	18,000
1996	38,000	22,800	24,000	1,200	—	—	—	24,000
1997	41,200	24,720	24,000	—	720	720	360	24,000
1998	45,200	27,120	24,000	—	3,120	1200	—	25,920

Note : In 1990 the short working was 4,400 and in 1991 Rs 5,400. Before 1993 the output raised is not known. So Royalty is calculated according to the short workings. In 1992 the minimum rent is equal to Royalty.

Royalty A/c

Date		*Rs.*		*Rs.*
1990	To Landlord a/c	19,600	By P & L a/c	19,600
1991	To Landlord a/c	18,600	By P & L a/c	18,600
1992	To Landlord a/c	24,000	By P & L a/c	24,000
1993	To Landlord a/c	24,000	By P & L a/c	27,600
	To Short working a/c	3,600		
		27,600		27,600
1994	To Landlord a/c	22,400	By P & L a/c	22,400
1995	To Landlord	18,000	By P & L a/c	18,480
	To Short working	480		
		18,480		18,480
1996	To Landlord a/c	22,800	By P & L a/c	22,800
1997	To Landlord a/c	24,000	By P & L a/c	24,720
	To Short working	720		
		24,720		24,720
1998	To Landlord a/c	25,920	By P & L a/c	27,120
	To Short working	1,200		
		27,120		27,120

Landlord's A/c

Date		Rs.		Rs.
1990	To Bank a/c	24,000	By Royalty a/c	19,600
			By Short working a/c	4,400
		24,000		24,000
1991	To Bank a/c	24,000	By Royalty a/c	18,600
			By Short working a/c	4,400
		24,000		24,000
1992	To Bank a/c	24,000	By Royalty a/c	24,000
1993	To Bank a/c	24,000	By Royalty a/c	24,000
1994	To Bank a/c	24,000	By Royalty a/c	22,440
			By Short working a/c	1,560
		24,000		24,000
1995	To Bank a/c	18,000	By Royalty a/c	18,000
1996	To Bank a/c	24,000	By Royalty a/c	22,800
			By Short working	1,200
		2,4000		2,4000
1997	To Bank a/c	24,000	By Royalty a/c	24,000
1998	To Bank a/c	25,920	By Royalty a/c	25,920

Short working A/c

Date		Rs.		Rs.
1990	To Landlord a/c	4,400	By Balance c/d	4,400
1991	To Balance b/d	4,400	By Balance c/d	9,800
	To Landlord a/c	5,400		
		9,800		9,800
1992	To Balance b/d	9,800	By Balance c/d	9,800
1993	To Balance b/d	9,800	By Royalty a/c	3,600
			By P & L a/c	8,00
			By Balance c/d	5,400
		9,800		9,800
1994	To Balance b/d	5,400	By P & L a/c	5,400
	To Landlord a/c	1,560	By Balance c/d	1,560
		6,960		6,960
1995	To Balance b/d	1,560	By Royalty	480
			By Balance c/d	1,080
		1,560		1,560
1996	To Balance b/d	1,080	By Balance c/d	2,280
	To Landlord a/c	1,200		
		2,280		2,280
1997	To Balance b/d	2,280	By Royalty a/c	720
			By P & L a/c	360
			By Balance c/d	1,200
		2,280		2,280
1998	To Balance b/d	1,200	By Royalty a/c	1,200

Problem 8

(Royalty in case of publications)

Mr. Chandra wrote a text boo on Business Management and got it published through Veda Books House on 1-1-95 on the following terms :

He was to receive a royalty of Rs. 10 per copy sold subject to a minimum rent of Rs. 50,000 per annum allowing the Book house to recover any short working during the first four years. Other details are.

Year	*No. of Copies printed*	*Closing Stock*
1995	3,000	1,000
1996	4,000	2,000
1997	8,000	3,000
1998	5,000	1,500
1999	6,000	500

Pass Journal entries in the books of Veda Book House for the five years.

(Bangalore University B. Com., April 2000)

Solution

In the Books of Veda Book House

JOURNAL ENTRIES

Date	*Particulars*		*Dr. Amount*	*Cr. Amount*
1995	Minimum Rent a/c	Dr.	50,000	
	To Chandra (Author)			50,000
	(Being minimum rent due)			
	Royalty a/c	Dr.	20,000	
	Short working a/c	Dr.	30,000	
	To Minimum rent a/c			50,000
	(Being excess of minimum rent over royalty)			
	Chandra a/c	Dr.	50,000	
	To Bank a/c			50,000
	(Being minimum rent paid)			
	P & L a/c	Dr.	20,000	
	To Royalty a/c			20,000
	(Royalty transferred to P & L a/c)			
1996	Minimum rent a/c	Dr.	50,000	
	To Chandra a/c			50,000
	(Being the minimum rent due)			
	Royalty a/c	Dr.	20,000	
	Short working a/c	Dr.	30,000	
	To Chandra a/c			50,000
	(Being excess of minimum rent over royalty)			
	Chandra a/c	Dr.	50,000	
	To Bank a/c			50,000
	(Being minimum rent paid)			

Date	Particulars		Dr. Amount	Cr. Amount
	P & L a/c To Royalty a/c (Being Royalty transferred to P & L a/c).	Dr.	20,000	20,000
1997	Royalty a/c To Chandra a/c (Being royalty due to Chandra)	Dr.	50,000	50,000
	Chandra a/c To Bank a/c (Being royalty paid)	Dr.	50,000	50,000
	Profit & Loss a/c To Royalty a/c (Being royalty transferred to P & L a/c)	Dr.	50,000	50,000
1998	Royalty a/c To Chandra a/c (Being royalty due to Chandra)	Dr.	35,000	35,000
	Chandra a/c To Bank a/c (Being the royalty paid)	Dr.	35,000	35,000
	P & L a/c To Royalty a/c (Being royalty transferred to P & L a/c)	Dr.	35,000	35,000
	Profit & loss a/c To Short working a/c (Being Unrecouped Short working transferred to P & L a/c)	Dr.	60,000	60,000
1999	Royalty a/c To Chandra a/c (Being royalty due to Chandra)	Dr.	55,000	55,000
	Chandra a/c To Bank a/c (Being royalty paid)	Dr.	55,000	55,000
	P & L. a/c To Royalty a/c (Being the transfer of royalty to P & L a/c)	Dr.	55,000	55,000

Note : **Since there is no excess of royalty over the minimum rent during any of the first four years the entire amount of accumulated short working, viz, Rs. 60,000 is transferred to P & L a/c and Chandra is paid the full royalty in the fifth year.**

Problem 9

(When closing stock is given)

On 1-1-90 Bengal Coal Mines Co. Ltd. obtained a lease of coal mines from 'A' at a royalty of Rs. 4 per ton of coal raised subject to a minimum rent of Rs. 10,000 p.a. The Short working can be recouped in the first 4 years of the lease.

From the following prepare Royalty a/c, Short working a/c and 'A's a/c in the books of the company.

Year	1990	1991	1992	1993	1994
Sales	1,100	1,750	2,300	2,900	3,500
Closing Stock (Tonnes)	150	250	200	300	400

(Sri Venkateshwara University, B. Com. Oct. 1999)

Solution

Calculation of Output

Output (in tonnes)	=	Sales	+	Closing stock	–	Opening stock	
1990	=	1,100	+	150	–	0	= 1,250
1991	=	1,750	+	250	–	150	= 18,50
1992	=	2,300	+	200	–	250	= 2,250
1993	=	2,900	+	300	–	200	= 3,000
1994	=	3,500	+	400	–	300	= 3,600

Royalty Table

Year	*Output*	*Royalty*	*Min. Rent*	*Short Working*	*S.W. Recouped*	*S.W, Not Recouped*	*Paid to Landlord*
1990	1,250	5,000	10,000	5,000	—	—	10,000
1991	1,850	7,400	10,000	2,600	—	—	10,000
1992	2,250	9,000	10,000	1,000	—	—	10,000
1993	3,000	12,000	—	—	2,000	2000	10,000
1994	3,600	14,400	—	—	—	—	14,400

In the Books of Bengal Coal Mine
Royalty A/c

Date		Rs.		Rs.
1990	To Minimum Rent a/c	5,000	By P & L a/c	5,000
1991	To Minimum Rent a/c	7,400	By P & L a/c	7,400
1992	To Minimum Rent a/c	9,000	By P & L a/c	9,000
1993	To Short working a/c	2,000	By P & L a/c	12,000
	To A's a/c	10,000		
		12,000		12,000
1994	To A's a/c	14,400	By P & L a/c	14,400

Short working A/c

Date		Rs.		Rs.
1990	To Minimum Rent a/c	5,000	By Balance c/d	5,000
1991	To Balance b/d	5,000	By Balance c/d	7,600
	To Minimum Rent a/c	2,600		
		7,600		7,600

Date		Rs.		Rs.
1992	To Balance b/d	7,600	By Balance c/d	8,600
	To Minimum rent a/c	1,000		
		8,600		8,600
1993	To Balance b/d	8,600	By Royalty a/c	2,000
			By P & L a/c	6,600
		8,600		8,600

A's A/c

Date		Rs.		Rs.
1990	To Cash a/c	10,000	By Minimum Rent a/c	10,000
1991	To Cash a/c	10,000	By Minimum Rent a/c	10,000
1992	To Cash a/c	10,000	By Minimum Rent a/c	10,000
1993	To Cash a/c	10,000	By Royalty a/c	10,000
1994	To Cash a/c	14,400	By Royalty a/c	14,400

Problem 10

(Royalty subject to deducting Income tax)

Mobil India Ltd., commenced production on 1st October 1997 under a collaboration agreement with Mobil Inc U.S.A . As per the agreement mobile India Ltd. is to pay a royalty at 5% of sales during each quarter of a calendar year subject to deduction of income tax @ 30% subject to a minimum remittance of $ 1,000 per quarter. Short working are recoupable from out of royalty payable in subsequent two quarters and not beyond. Quarter - wise sales are as under

Quarter ending	Sales Rs
31-12-97	5,00,000
31-3-98	8,00,000
30-6-98	14,00,000
30-9-98	16,00,000
31-12-98	10,00,000
31-3-99	18,00,000

Rate of exchange upto 31-3-98 Was $ 1 = Rs. 35 and there after $ 1 = Rs 42. Remittance of each quarter was made within one month from the end of the quarter.

Show Royalty a/c, Mobile Inc. a/c and Short working account in the books of Mobile India Ltd. **(CA, Inter May 2000)**

Solution

Calculation of Minimum Remittance :

For quarter upto 31-3-1998

From 31-12-97 to 31-3-1998 = $ 1,000 × 35 = 35,000

For quarter beyond 31-3-98 = $ 1,000 × 42 = Rs 42,000

Income Tax deduction is 30%. The minimum amount of Rs. 35,000 and Rs. 42,000 are after deduction of income tax. Hence the amounts are equal to 70%.

For 70% the amount are Rs. 35,000 and Rs. 42,000

For 100% → ?

$$= \frac{35,000 \times 100}{70} = \text{Rs. } 50,000$$

$$= \frac{42,000 \times 100}{70} = \text{Rs. } 60,000$$

Royalty Table

Quarter ended	*Sales (Rs.)*	*Royalty (Rs.)*	*Minimum Remittance*	*Short workings*	*Recouped*	*Writer off*
31-12-97	5,00,000	25,000	50,000	25,000	—	—
31-3-98	8,00,000	40,000	50,000	10,000	—	—
30-6-98	14,00,000	70,000	60,000	—	10,000	15,000
30-9-98	16,00,000	80,000	60,000	—	10,000	—
31-12-98	10,00,000	50,000	60,000	10,000	—	—
31-3-99	18,00,000	90,000	60,000	—	10,000	—

In the books of Mobile India Ltd.

Royalty A/c

Date		*Rs.*	*Date*		*Rs.*
1997			1997		
Dec. 31	To Mobile Inc.	25,000	March 31	By P & L a/c	65,000
1998					
Mar 31	To Mobile Inc.	40,000			
		65,000			65,000
1998			1999		
June 30,	To Mobile Inc.	70,000	Mar. 31,	By P & L a/c	2,90,000
Sept. 30,	To Mobile Inc.	80,000			
Dec. 31,	To Mobile Inc.	50,000			
1999					
Mar. 31,	To Mobile Inc.	90,000			
		2,90,000			2,90,000

Short Working A/c

Date		*Rs.*	*Date*		*Rs.*
1997			1998		
Dec. 31,	To Mobile Inc.	25,000	Mar. 31,	By Balance c/d	35,000
1998					
Mar. 31,	To Mobile Inc.	10,000			
		35,000			35,000
1998			1998		
April, 1	To Balance b/d	35,000	June 30	By Mobile Inc.	10,000
Dec. 31,	To Mobile Inc.	10,000		By P & L a/c	15,000
			Sept. 30,	By Mobile Inc.	10,000
			1999		
			Mar. 31,	By Mobile Inc.	10,000
		45,000			45,000

Mobile Inc.

Date		Rs.	Date		Rs.
1997			1997		
Jan. 31,	To Tax deducted	15,000	Dec. 31,	By Royalty a/c	25,000
	To Bank a/c	35,000		By Short working a/c	25,000
Mar. 31,	To Balance c/d	50,000	1998		
			Mar. 31,	By Royalty a/c	40,000
				By Short working a/c	10,000
		1,00,000			1,00,000
1998			1998		
Apr. 30,	To Tax Deducted	15,000	Apr. 1	By Balance b/d	50,000
	To Bank a/c	35,000	June 30.	By Royalty a/c	70,000
June 30,	To Short working	10,000	Sept. 30.	By Royalty a/c	80,000
July 31.	To Tax Deducted	18,000	Dec. 31.	By Royalty a/c	50,000
	To Bank a/c	42,000		By Short working a/c	10,000
			1999		
Sept. 30.	To Short working	10,000	Mar. 31.	By Royalty a/c	90,000
Oct. 31.	To Tax Deducted	21,000			
	To Bank a/c	49,000			
1999					
Jan. 31.	To Tax Deducted	18,000			
	To Bank a/c	42,000			
Mar. 31.	Short working	10,000			
	To Balance c/d	80,000			
		3,50,000			3,50,000

Problem 11

(Payment to Landlord after deducting income tax)

The following information has been obtained from the books of a lessee relating to the years 1989 - 90 to 1992 - 93.

Payment to Landlord : (After deducting tax @ 20 %)

1989 - 90	Rs.12,000
1990 - 91	12,000
1991 - 92	12,000
1992 - 93	19,200

Short working recovered :

1990 - 91	2,500
1991 - 92	1,000

Short working written off

1991-92	500

Short working a/c balance brought forward on 1st April 1989 - Rs. 800 (which arose in 1987-88).

According to the terms of agreement short working is recoverable within the next two years following the year in which short working arises.

You are required to prepare the Royalty a/c and the landlord's a/c for the years ended 31st March 1993. **(ICWA Inter June 1993)**

Solution

Calculation of Royalty

	1989-90 Rs.	1990-91 Rs.	1991-92 Rs.	1992-93 Rs.
Payment to Landlord	12,000	12,000	12,000	19,200
Add : Tax deducted $\frac{20}{80}$	3,000	3,000	3,000	4,800
	15,000	15,000	15,000	24,000
Short working adjusted	– 4,000	+ 2,500	+ 5,000	Nil
Royalty	11,000	17,500	16,000	24,000

In the books of Lessee
Royalty A/c

Date		Rs.		Rs.
1989-90	To Landlord	11,000	By P & L a/c	11,000
1990-91	To Landlord	15,000	By P & L a/c	17,500
	To Short working	2,500		
		17,500		17,500
1991-92	To Landlord	15,000	By P & L a/c	16,000
	To Short working	1,000		
		16,000		16,000
1992-93	To Landlord	24,000	By P & L a/c	24,000

Landlord's A/c

Date		Rs.		Rs.
1989-90	To Income tax	3000	By Royalty a/c	11,000
	To Bank a/c	12,000	By Short working a/c	4,000
		15,000		15,000
1990-91	To Income tax	3,000	By Royalty a/c	15,000
	To Bank a/c	12,000		
		15,000		15,000
1991-92	To Income tax	3,000	By Royalty a/c	15,000
	To Bank a/c	12,000		
		15,000		15,000
1992-93	To Income tax	4,800	By Royalty a/c	24,000
	To Bank a/c	19,200		
		24,000		24,000

Sub-Lease :

When a lessee under the terms of the original lease is empowered to sublet a part of the land to another person, a sub lease arises. In such a case, the status of the original lessee will be two fold : (*a*) as lessee paying royalties to the landlord and (*b*) as a sub-lessor receiving royalties from the sub-lessee. As a lessee he maintains the following accounts :

1. Royalties payable a/c
2. Short working
3. Landlord's a/c

As a sub-lessor he maintains :

1. Royalties Receivable a/c
2. Short workings a/c
3. Sub-lessee's a/c

A point to be noted in case of sub-lease is that production or sales by the sub-lessee under sub-lease will be considered to be production or sales under the original lease and royalties payable to the original landlord will be calculated on the basis of total production or sales of both the lessee and the sub-lessee.

Problem 12

(Sub-lease)

Homeo Research Laboratories (P) Ltd., developed soft skinobit, a new cosmetic and got it patented.

On 31-3-1996 it issued licence to M/S. M Bhattacharya & Sons for commercial production and sale of the product. Later in the day, M Bhattacharya & Sons granted a sub-licence to Chowdhary Bros., for the same purpose. The terms are stated below :

Licence :- Royalty - Rs. 5 per unit produced

Minimum Rent - Rs. 36,000 p.a.

Sub-licence :- Royalty - Rs. 7.50 per unit sold

Minimum Rent - Rs. 14,000 p.a.

Recoupment of short working ; if the royalty for any year falls short of the minimum rent, the short working can be recouped out of royalties in excess of the minimum rent for either of the two immediately following years applicable to both parties.

From the following particulars prepare Royalty accounts and short workings accounts in the books of M/S M. Bhattacharya & Sons for the entire period.

	M/S M. Bhattacharya & Sons		*Chowdhary Bros.*	
	Sales (Units)	*Closing Stock (Units)*	*Production (Units)*	*Closing Stock (Units)*
Year I	2,500	500	2,100	200
Year II	5,800	600	1,800	400
Year III	4,800	1,000	2,000	700

(Calcutta University B. Com. (Hons.) 1999)

Solution

In The Books of M/S Bhattacharya & Sons

Statement Showing Royalty Payable

Year	*Production = Sales + es Stock – op Stock*	*Sub Lease Production*	*Total Production*	*Royalty*	*Min. Rent*	*Short Working*	*Recovery*	*Lepse*	*Payment*
I	3,000	2,100	5,100	25,500	36,000	10500	—	—	36,000
II	5,900	1,800	7,700	38,500	36,000	—	2,500	—	36,000
III	5,200	2,000	7,200	36,000	36,000	—	—	8,000	36,000

Statement Showing Royalty Receivable

Year	*Sales = + op Stock – es Stock*	*Royalty*	*Min. Rent*	*Short Working Suspense*	*Recovery*	*Lepse*	*Receipts*
I	1,900	14,250	14,000	—	—	—	14,250
II	1,600	12,000	14,000	2,000	—	—	14,000
III	1,700	12,750	14,000	1,250	—	—	14,000

Royalty Payable A/c

Date	*Particulars*	*Rs.*	*Particulars*	*Rs.*
1997	To Homeo Research Lab Ltd. a/c	25,500	By Royalty received a/c	10,500
			By P & L a/c	15,000
		25,500		25,500
1998	To Homeo Research Lab Ltd. a/c	38,500	By Royalty Received a/c	9,000
			By P & L a/c	29,500
		38,500		38,500
1999	To Homeo Research Lab Ltd. a/c	36,000	By Royalty Received a/c	10,000
			By P & L a/c	26,000
		36,000		36,000

Royalty Receivable A/c

Date	*Particulars*	*Rs.*	*Particulars*	*Rs.*
1997	To Royalty payable a/c	10,500	By Chowdhary Bros. a/c	14,250
	To P & L a/c	3,750		
		14,250		14,250
1998	To Royalty payable a/c	9,000	By Chowdary Bros. a/c	12,000
	To P & L a/c	3,000		
		12,000		12,000

Date	Particulars	Rs.	Particulars	Rs.
1999	To Royalty payable a/c	10,000	By Chowdhary Bros. a/c	12,750
	To P & L a/c	2,750		
		12,750		12,750

Short Working A/c

Date	Particulars	Rs.	Particulars	Rs.
1997	To Homeo Research Lab Ltd., a/c	10,500	By balance c/d	10,500
1998	To Homeo Research Lab Ltd.,	10,500	By Homeo Research Lab Ltd., a/c	2,500
			By Balance c/d	8,000
		10,500		10,500
1999	To Homeo Research Lab Ltd.	8,000	By P & L a/c	8,000

Short Working Suspense A/c

Date	Particulars	Rs.	Date	Particulars	Rs.
1997	To Balance c/d	2,000	1997	By Chowdhary Bros. a/c	2,000
1998	To Balance c/d	3,250	1998	By Balance b/d	2,000
				By Chowdhary Bros. a/c	1,250
		3,250	1999	By Balance b/d	3,250

Problem 13

On 1-1-1989 Abhijit Chakarborthy obtained a mining lease and from that date he sub-leased a part of the mine to Satyajit Saha. Show ledger accounts in the books of Abhijit Chakraborthy from the following date.

	Lease Tons	Sub-lease Tons/
1989	1,500	1,000
1990	4,000	4,500
1991	18,000	10,000
1992	15,000	3,000 (Strike)
1993	8,000	15,000
Royalty per ton	Rs. 3.00	Rs. 4.00
Minimum rent p.a.	Rs. 35,000	Rs. 25,000
Short working recoverable in the following	3 years	2 years

In case of strike, royalty earned will discharge all rental obligations for the year only.

(Calcutta University B. Com. Hons. 1995)

Solution

In The Books of Abhijit Chakraborthy

Statement Showing Royalty Payable

Year	Output (Tons)	Royalty @ Rs. 3	Min. Rent	Short Working	Short Working recouped	Short Working Lepase	Payment
1989	2,500	7,500	35,000	27,500	—	—	35,000
1990	8,500	25,500	35,000	9,500	—	—	35,000
1991	28,000	84,000	35,000	—	37,000	—	47,000
1992	18,000	54,000	35,000	—	—	—	54,000
1993	23,000	69,000	35,000	—	—	—	69,000

Statement Showing Royalty Receivable

Year	Output (Tons)	Royalty @ Rs. 4	Min. Rent	Short Working suspense	Short Working recouped	Short Working Lepase	Reciepts
1989	1,000	4,000	25,000	21,000	—	—	25,000
1990	4,500	18,000	25,000	7,000	—	—	25,000
1991	10,000	40,000	25,000	—	15,000	6,000	25,000
1992	3,000	12,000	12,000	—	—	7000	12,000
1993	15,000	60,000	25,000	—	—	—	60,000

Royalty Payable A/c

Date		Rs.		Rs.
1989	To Landlord a/c	7,500	By Royalty Receivable a/c	3,000
			By P & L a/c	4,500
		7,500		7,500
1990	To Landlord a/c	25,500	By Royalty Receivable a/c	13,500
			By P & L a/c	12,000
		25,500		25,500
1991	To Landlord a/c	84,000	By Royalty Receivable a/c	30,000
			By P & L a/c	54,000
		84,000		84,000
1992	To Landlord a/c	54,000	By Royalty Receivable a/c	9,000
			By P & L a/c	45,000
		54,000		54,000
1993	To Landlord a/c	69,000	By Royalty Receivable a/c	45,000
			By P & L a/c	24,000
		69,000		69,000

Landlord A/c

Date		Rs.		Rs.
1989	To Bank a/c	35,000	By Royalty payable a/c	7,500
			By Short working a/c	27,500
		35,000		35,000
1990	To Bank a/c	35,000	By Royalty payable a/c	25,500
			By Short working a/c	9,500
		35,000		35,000
1991	To Short working	37,000	By Royalty payable a/c	84,000
	To Bank	47,000		
		84,000		84,000
1992	To Bank a/c	54,000	By Royalty payable a/c	54,000
1993	To Bank a/c	69,000	By Royalty payable a/c	69,000

Short Working A/c

Date		Rs.		Rs.
1989	To Landlord a/c	27,500	By Balance c/d	27,500
1990	To Balance b/d	27,500	By Balance c/d	37,000
	To Landlord a/c	9,500		
		37,000		37,000
1991	To Balance b/d	37,000	By Landlord a/c	37,000

Bills Receivable A/c

Date		Rs.		Rs.
1989	To Royalty payable a/c	3,000	By S. Sinha a/c	4,000
	To P & L a/c	1,000		
		4,000		4,000
1990	To Royalty payable a/c	13,500	By S. Sinha a/c	18,000
	To P & L	4,500		
		18,000		18,000
1991	To Royalty payable a/c	30,000	By S. Sinha a/c	40,000
	To P & L a/c	10,000		
		40,000		40,000
1992	To Royalty payable a/c	9,000	By S. Sinha a/c	12,000
	To P & L a/c	3,000		
		12,000		12,000
1993	To Royalty payable a/c	45,000	By S. Sinha a/c	60,000
	To P & L a/c	15,000		
		60,000		60,000

S. Sinha A/c

Date		Rs.		Rs.
1989	To Royalty Receivable a/c	4,000	By Bank a/c	25,000
	To Short working suspense a/c	21,000		
		25,000		25,000
1990	To Royalty Receivable a/c	18,000	By Bank a/c	25,000
	To Short working suspense a/c	7,000		
		25,000		25,000
1991	To Royalty Receivable a/c	40,000	By Short working Suspense a/c	15,000
			By Bank a/c	25,000
		40,000		40,000
1992	To Royalty Receivable a/c	12,000	By Bank a/c	12,000
1993	To Royalty Receivable a/c	60,000	By Bank a/c	60,000

Short Working Suspense A/c

Date		Rs.		Rs.
1989	To Balance c/d	21,000	By S. Sinha a/c	21,000
1990	To Balance c/d	28,000	By Balance b/d	21,000
			By S. Sinha a/c	7,000
		28,000		28,000
1991	To S. Sinha a/c	15,000	By Balance b/d	28,000
	To P & L a/c	6,000		
	To Balance c/d	7,000		
		28,000		28,000
1992	To P & L a/c	7,000	By Balance b/d	7,000

QUESTIONS

Simple Questions

1. What is Royalty ?
2. What is minimum rent ?
3. State the basis on which royalty is calculated in the following cases.
   (*i*) Author of a books (*ii*) Owner of a mine
   (*iii*) A scientist holding patent (*iv*) Owner of an oil well.
4. What is "Short working" ?
5. What is meant by recouping of short workings ?
6. What do you mean by sub-lease ?

EXERCISE 1

Andhara Coal Co. Ltd., leased a colliery on 1-1-1998 to 'X' at a minimum rent of Rs. 15,000 merging into a Royalty of Re 1 per ton with a stipulation to recoup short working over the first three years of the lease. The output for the first four years of the lease was 8,000, 13,000, 21,000 and 18,000 tons respectively. Prepare short workings accounts in the books of Mr. X . **(Osmania University B. Com. October 2000)**

Answer : Total of Short working for III year Rs. 9,000.

EXERCISE 2

Misra Mining Company Ltd., takes a lease of Coal mine for 8 years form 1-1-90 on a minimum rent of Rs. 12,000 p.a. The Royalty is 75 paise per ton of coal raised and it is payable half yearly on 30th June and 31st December of each years. Short working can be recouped during the first three years of lease only.

The company closes books on 31st December each year. Coal raised is as follows :-

	Tons
Half year ending 30-6-90	6,000
Half year ending 31-12-90	8,000
Half year ending 30-6-91	10,000
Half year ending 31-12-91	6,000
Half year ending 30-6-92	7,000
Half year ending 31-12-92	9,000

Prepare Royalty a/c landlord a/c. Short working a/c, in the books of Misra mining to.

(Sri Venkateshwara University B. Com. April 1999)

Answer :	Total of Royalty a/c For 1992	Rs. 12,000
	Total of Landlords a/c for 1992	Rs. 12,000
	Total of Short working a/c for 1992	Rs. 2,250

EXERCISE 3 (ROYALTY WHEN THERE IS STRIKE)

Murugan Coal Works took a Coal mine under a lease which provided for the payment of Royalties at 50 paise per tonne with a minimum rent of Rs. 17,000 per annum. Each year's excess of minimum rent over the actual royalties was recoverable during the subsequent three years.

The lease, however stipulated that if in any year the normal rent was not allowed due to strike, the minimum rent was to be regarded as having been reduced proportionality having regarded to the length of the stoppage. The output was as follows :

Year	Production (Tonnes)
30-12-90	4,000
31-12-91	28,000
31-12-92	30,000
31-12-93	46,000
31-12-94	30,000
31-12-95	50,000

During the year 1994, there was a stoppage (due to strike) lasting three mother. Write up (*a*) Royalties a/c (*b*) Short workings a/c. **(University of Madras, B. Com. May 2000)**

Answer :	Total of M. R. a/c for 1992	Rs. 17,000
	Total of Landlord's a/c for 1995	Rs. 25,000
	Total of Short workings a/c for 1995	Rs. 2,000

EXERCISE 4

The Ranee colliery Co. Ltd., has taken a property on lease from Atma Ram on Royalty of one rupee per ton with a minimum rent of Rs. 30,000 per annum. Each year's Excess of minimum rent over Royalties is recoverable out of the Royalties of the next five years.

In the event of a strike and the minimum rent not being reached the lease provided that the actual Royalties earned for the year discharge all rental obligations for that years. The results of the working were as follows :-

Year	1991	92	93	94	95	96	97	98
Actual								
Royalty (in Rs.)	NiL	9,750	27,750	33,750	42,000	52,500	28,500	45,000

The year 1997 was a strike year. You are required to write up the necessary ledger accounts in the books of the Ranee Colliery Co. Ltd.

(Osmania University B. Com. March 2000)

Answer :	Total of M. R. a/c for 1993	Rs. 30,000
	Total of Royalties for 1998	Rs. 45,000
	Total of Short working for 1998	Rs. 2,250

EXERCISE 5

The Eastern Coal Co. Ltd., holds a lease of coal mines for a period of 10 years commencing from 1st January 1991. According to the lease, the company is to pay a Royalty of Rs. 2 per ton of coal raised with a minimum rent of Rs. 30,000 per year. Short working can, however be recovered out of the Royalty in excess of the minimum rent of the next two years only. In the event of a strike and minimum rent not being reached the actually Royalty calculated will meet the rental obligation. The output for the 6 years has been as under.

Year	output (Tons)
1991	10,000
1992	12,000
1993	25,000
1994	30,000
1995	12,000 (Strike)
1996	14,000

Write up the necessary ledger accounts in the books of Eastern Coal Co. Ltd., for the 6 years **(Calcutta University B. Com. 1998)**

Answer :	Total of Royalty a/c for 6th year	28,000
	Total of Landlords a/c for 6th year	30,000
	Total of Short working a/c for 6th year	2,000

EXERCISE 6

Vikas publishers Published a book written by Swamy on the terms that he will get a Royalty of Rs. 3 per copy sold subject to a minimum of Rs. 5,000 p.a. and the Short working of each year could be recovered in next three years.

The Copies Sold were :

1990 - 800, 1991 - 1,500, 1992 - 2,000, 1993 - 3,000.

Show the irrecoverable short workings if any. **(Osmania University B. Com. October 1999)**

Answer : Uncoverable Short working Rs. 600

EXERCISE 7 (SUB-LEASE)

Janaki obtains a lease from Indira to work a mine. The terms being a Royalty of Rs. 10 per ton merging into a minimum rent of Rs. 2,000 per year, there being granted to the lessee the right to recoup Short working during the first 4 years of the lease.

Janaki Sublets Part of the Property to Tulasi the terms being a Royalty of Rs. 12.50 per tonne merging into a minimum rent of Rs. 9,600 p.a. Tulasi has a right of recoupment in the two years following the short working. The results of the working is as follows.

Year (Tons)	*Janaki (Tons)*	*Tulasi (Tons)*	*Total*
1.	1,100	400	1,500
2.	1,160	540	1,700
3.	1,300	700	2,000
4.	1,400	900	2,300
5.	1,800	1,200	3,000
6.	800	1,200	2,000

Write up the Royalty payable and Royalty receivable accounts in the books of Jankai.

(Osmania University B. Com. March 1998)

Answer : Total of Royalty payable a/c in VI year Rs. 23,000.

Total of Royalty receivable a/c in VI year Rs. 15,000.

28

CHAPTER

Hire Purchase System

INTRODUCTION

Hire purchase is a method of sale under which the seller undertakes to sell the goods with an agreement to receive cash price in convenient instalments. The physical possession of goods is delivered at the time of agreement. Hire purchase is a compromise between cash sale and credit sale. In case of cash sale the physical possession of the goods as well as the ownership is transferred to the buyer on receiving the price of goods. In case of credit sale though ownership and physical possession of goods is transferred to the buyer, the seller will receive the price of goods at a later date. In case of Hire purchase system, the buyer gets only physical possession of goods but not the ownership. The price of goods is agreed to be payable in easy instalments with interest.

Definition

The Hire purchase act 1972, defines hire purchase agreement as an agreement under which goods are let on hire and under which the hirer has an option to purchase them in accordance with the terms of the agreement and includes an agreement under which (*i*) Possession of goods is delivered by the owner, thereof to a person on condition that such person pays the agreed amount in periodical instalments (*ii*) The property in goods is to pass to such person on the payment of the last of such instalment and (*iii*) Such person has a right to terminate the agreement at any time before the property so passes.

Cash Price

Cash price of an article is the amount which the seller is prepared to accept if the full payment of the article is made in a lump sum immediately on sale.

Hire Purchase Price

Hire purchase prise means the total amount payable by hire purchaser to hire vendor under a contract of hire purchase. Thus, hire purchase price consist of cash price of the goods plus interest on outstanding balances for different period of time.

Down Payment

Down payment refers to the payment required to be made under instalment payment system or hire purchase system immediately on signing the contract.

Hire Purchaser

Hire purchaser is the party who has agreed to buy goods on hire purchase basis.

Hire Vendor

Hire is the party who has agreed to sell some goods on hire purchase basis.

Features of Hire Purchase System

1. The hire purchaser takes possession of the goods on the date of signing the contract.
2. He agrees to pay the seller the price of the goods in certain number of instalments.
3. The ownership of the goods passes on to the hire purchaser only after he pays the last instalment as specified in the contract. Until then the ownership has with the seller while the goods lie in the possession and enjoyment of the hire purchaser.
4. If the hire purchaser fails to make instalment payments as specified the hire seller can take away the goods and the hire purchaser loses all the instalments already paid as they are treated as hire charges.
5. The hire purchaser is also free to return the goods and terminate the contract before the payment of full price.

Differences between Sale and Hire Purchase System :

Sale	*Hire Purchase*
1. Ownership is immediately transferred	1. Ownership is transferred only when a certain agreed number of instalment is paid.
2. The buyer is the owner.	2. The hire purchaser is a bailee.
3. Buyer cannot terminate the contract.	3. Hire purchaser has an option to terminate the contract.
4. If the amount payable is by instalment the amount payable is reduced.	4. The amount is treated as hire charges.

Accounting Procedure

Hire purchase transactions are recorded both by the hire purchaser and hire vendor.

In the books of Hire purchaser. There are two methods of recording transactions in the books of hire purchaser, viz.

I. When the Asset is recorded at full Cash Price : Under this method it is assumed that the hire purchaser has acquired ownership of the asset. The entries to be passed are as follows :

1. **At the time of entering into agreement or at the time of purchase**

   (*a*) ***When the asset is bought :***

   Asset a/c Dr.
   To Hire Vendor

   (*b*) ***On down payment :***

   Hire vendor Dr.
   To Bank

2. **At the end of each instalment :**

   (*a*) ***When the interest becomes due :***

   Interest a/c Dr.
   To Hire Vendor a/c

(*b*) ***When the first instalment is paid***

Hire Vendor a/c Dr.

To Cash a/c

(*c*) ***For charging depreciation on asset :***

Depreciation a/c Dr.

To Asset a/c

(*d*) ***For transferring interest and Depreciation to Profit & loss a/c***

Profit & Loss a/c Dr.

To Interest a/c

To Depreciation a/c

2. **When the Asset is recorded at Cash Price actually Paid :** This method is based on the assumption that the hire purchaser does not become the owner of the asset until he makes the payment of final instalment. The following entries are recorded under this method.

(A) **On Signing the agreement :**

(*a*) ***At the time of purchase of asset :***

Asset a/c Dr.

To Hire Vendor

(*b*) ***When down payment is made :***

Hire Vendor a/c Dr.

To Bank a/c

(B) **At the end of each Instalment :**

(*a*) ***When hire purchase instalment becomes due***

Asset a/c Dr. (With the amount of cash price inclouded in the instalment)

Interest a/c Dr. (Interest included in the instalment)

To Hire Vendor a/c (With the amount of Instalment)

(*b*) ***When instalment is paid :***

Hire Vendor a/c Dr.

To Bank

(*c*) ***For depreciating the asset :***

Depreciation a/c Dr.

To Asset a/c

(*d*) ***For transfer of interest and depreciation to Profit & Loss a/c***

Profit & Loss a/c Dr.

To Interest a/c

To Depreciation a/c

In The Books of Hire Vendor

(A) **AT the time of entering into agreement :**

(*a*) ***On sale asset under hire purchase :***

Hire Purchaser a/c Dr.

To Sales a/c

(*b*) ***On receiving down payment :***

Bank a/c Dr.

To Hire Purchaser

(B) **At The end of each Instalment :**

(*a*) ***When Interest is due :***

Hire Purchaser a/c Dr.

To Interest a/c

(*b*) ***When Instalment is received :***

Cash a/c Dr.

To Hire Purchaser a/c

(*c*) ***For transfer of interest to P & L a/c***

Interest a/c Dr.

To P & L a/c

Important Points in Relation to Hire Purchase System

1. Calculation of Interest : The hire-purchase transaction involves payment of interest by hire-purchaser to hire-vendor on the outstanding balance of cash price of the asset. The calculation of interest depends upon the following circumstances.

(A) **When Cash Price, each instalment amount, and rate of interest is given**

The following steps are involved.

(*a*) Ascertain the outstanding balance of cash price at the beginning of each instalment.

The outstanding balance of the first instalment is ascertained by deducting the down payment from the cash price of the asset.

For the second year, add the interest for the first instalment to the unpaid balance of the cash value of the asset at the beginning of the second instalment. From this total, deduct the total amount paid (Cash value plus interest) at the end of the first instalment. The balance represents the outstanding of the cash value of the asset at the beginning of the second instalment.

The above procedure is repeated for various instalment. The interest is calculated on the outstanding balance of cash price of the asset at the beginning of the concerned instalment at the given rate of interest.

The interest for the last instalment is calculated by applying the following formula :-

Last instalment amount – Unpaid balance of the cash value of the asset at the beginning of the last instalment.

Problem 1

Given the following date

Cash price	Rs. 68,500
Down payment	15,000
Balance payable in 3 instalments	20,000

Interest payable 6% per annum.

Calculate the interest payable by the Hire Purchaser to the Hire Vendor.

Solution

Calculation of Interest

	Cash price	68,500
Less :	Down payment	15,000
	Unpaid cash balance at the beginning of Ist instalment	53,500
Add :	Interest	3,210
	$53{,}500 \times \frac{6}{100}$	56,710
Less :	1st Instalment amount paid	20,000
	Unpaid cash balance at the beginning of IInd instalment	36710
Add :	Interest	
	$36{,}710 \times \frac{6}{100}$	2,203
		38,913
Less :	IInd Instalment paid	20,000
	Unpaid cash balance at the beginning of IIIrd Instalment	18,913
Add :	Interest (20,000 – 18,913)	1,087
		20,000
Less :	IIIrd Instalment paid	20,000
		NIL

(B) **When the total cash price amount payable towards the asset at the end of each instalment and the rate of interest is given :** Under this situation interest is calculated for each of the instalment including the last instalment on the unpaid balance of the cash price of the asset at the beginning of the concerned instalment at the given rate of interest.

The unpaid Cash balance at the beginning of each instalment is calculated as follows :

Unpaid cash balance as the beginning of the first instalment :

	Total cash price	X X
Less :	down payment	X X
	Unpaid cash balance at the beginning of the Ist instalment	X X

Unpaid cash balance at the beginning of the second Instalment :

	Unpaid cash balance at the beginning of the 1st Instalment	X X
Less :	Cash paid at the end of 1st Instalment	X X
	Unpaid Cash balance at the beginning of IInd Instalment.	X X

The above procedure is to be repeated for other instalments.

Problem 2

Given the following date :-

Cash price of a TV	Rs. 40,000
Down payment	10,000

Balance to be paid in 3 annual instalments plus interest on the outstanding balance at 10% p.a.

Calculate the interest payable by the Hire Purchaser to Hire Vendor.

Solution

Calculation of Interest

Interest for the first Instalment

	Total cash price of T.V	40,000
Less :	Down payment	10,000
	Unpaid cash balance at the beginning of Ist instalment	30,000

Interest $\frac{10}{100} \times 30{,}000 = $ Rs. 3,000

Interest for the second instalment :

	Unpaid cash balance at the beginning of 1st instalment	30,000
Less :	Amount paid at the end of Ist Instalment $\left(\frac{30{,}000}{3}\right)$	10,000
	Unpaid-cash balance at the beginning of IInd instalment	20,000

Interest $\frac{10}{100} \times 20{,}000 = 2{,}000$

Interest for the last instalment :

	Unpaid cash balance at the beginning of III instalment	20,000
Less :	Amount paid at the end of 2nd instalment	10,000
		10,000
	Interest for the last instalment $\frac{10}{100} \times 10{,}000$	1,000

(*c*) **When total cash price and each instalment is given but not the rate of interest :** The following steps are involved

1. Ascertain the total interest for all the instalment. The total interest for all the instalments is the difference between the total hire purchase price and the total cash price.
2. Apportion the total interest for all the instalment among various instalments in the ratio of the total hire purchase price outstanding at the beginning of each instalment.

Problem 3

Rajaram purchased on hire purchase system a machine, from Vishwanathan , on 1-4-1995 for a sum of Rs. 80,000. Rs. 20,000 is to be paid on signing the contract and the remaining amount in three equal annual instalments of Rs. 20,000 each. The cash price of the machine is Rs. 74,500. Calculate interest for the first three financial years.

(Osmania University B. Com. March 1999).

Solution

Calculation of Interest

Hire purchase price	= 80,000
Less cash price	= 74,500
	5,500

Calculation of Hire Purchase Price outstanding at the beginning of each Instalment :

	Total Hire purchase price	80,000
Less :	Down payment	20,000
	Hire purchase price outstanding at the beginning of 1st instalment	60,000
Less :	Total amount of 1st instalment paid	20,000
	Hire purchase price outstanding at the beginning of 2nd instalment	40,000
Less :	Total amount IInd instalment paid	20,000
	Hire purchase price outstanding at the beginning of 3rd instalment	20,000

Calculation of Interest for each instalment :

Ratio of outstanding hire purchase price at the beginning of 1st, IInd and IIIrd instalment

60,000 : 40,000 : 20,000

or 6 : 4 : 2

or 3 : 2 : 1

or $\frac{3}{6}$ $\frac{2}{6}$ $\frac{1}{6}$

Interest for Ist instalment $\frac{3}{6} \times 5{,}500 = 2{,}750$

Interest for IInd instalment $\frac{2}{6} \times 5{,}500 = 1{,}833$

Interest for IIIrd instalment $\frac{1}{6} \times 5{,}500 = 917$

Total 5,500

(D) **When cash price of the Asset is not given but each instalment amount and interest are given :** The procedure involved in calculation of interest for each instalment and cash price of the asset is known as "reverse order" or back calculation method. Suppose there are three instalments their the following steps are involved.

(*a*) Consider the last instalment amount. From it deduct the last instalment interest. The interest is calculated by applying the following formula.

$$\frac{\text{Rate of Interest}}{100 + \text{Rate of Interest}} \times \text{Total amount at the end of last instalment}$$

The balance obtained from the above calculation represent the total amount due at the beginning of the last instalment.

(*b*) Add the total amount due at the beginning of the last instalment to the second instalment amount. This represents the total amount due at the end of second instalment. Deduct the interest of second instalment from the total amount due at the end of the second instalment. The interest is calculated by applying the following formula.

$$\frac{\text{Rate of Interest}}{100 + \text{Rate of Interest}} \times \text{Total amount due at the end of IInd instalment}$$

The balance obtained denotes the total amount due at the beginning of the second instalment.

(*c*) Add the total amount due at the beginning of the second instalment to the first instalment. This total represents the amount due at the end of first instalment. From this total deduct the interest of first instalment. The interest is calculated by applying the following formula.

$$\frac{\text{Rate of Interest}}{100 + \text{Rate of Interest}} \times \text{Total amount due at the end of Ist instalment}$$

The balance thus obtained indicate the amount due at the beginning of first instalment.

(*d*) Add down payment to the total amount due at the beginning of the first instalment. The total so obtained will be the cash price of the asset.

Problem 4

From the following, Calculate the cash price

Hire purchase price of the asset	Rs. 50,000
Down payment	10,000
Form annual instalments at the end of each year	10,000
Rate of interest	5% p.a.

(Osmania University B. Com. October 2000)

Solution

FIRST STEP :

4th Instalment amount	10,000
Less : Interest $10{,}000 \times \frac{5}{105}$	477
Total amount due at the beginning of 4th instalment	9,523

SECOND STEP :

Add : 3rd instalment amount	10,000
	19,523
Less : Interest $19523 \times \frac{5}{105}$	930

THIRD STEP :

	18,593
Add : 2nd Instalment amount	10,000
	28,593
Less : Interest $28593 \times \frac{5}{105}$	1,361

FOURTH STEP :

	27,232
Add : 1st instalment amount	10,000
	37,232
Less : Interest $37{,}232 \times \frac{5}{105}$	1,772
	35,460

LAST STEP :

Add : Down payment	10,000
Cash price	45,460

The above calculation can be presented in the from of table shown below.

Number of Instalment	*Closing balance*	*Amount of Instalment*	*Total*	*Interest* $\frac{5}{105}$	*Opening Balance*
4	Nil	10,000	10,000	477	9,523
3	9,525	10,000	19,525	930	18,593
2	18,593	10,000	28,593	1,361	27,232
1	27,232	10,000	37,232	1,772	35,460

Cash price = Down payment + 35,460
= 10,000 + 35,460
= 45,460

2. **Calculation of Depreciation :** Though ownership is transferred on the payment of last instalment, the hire purchaser has to depreciate the asset either on the original value of asset or diminishing balance method. Depreciation is always provided on the basis of cash price of the asset purchased. The entry passed to record depreciation is as follows :

   Depreciation a/c Dr.
   To Asset a/c

3. **Calculation of cash price of the Asset :** Cash price when not given is to be found out. Cash price of the asset is essential in order to charge interest and also to provide for depreciation. Cash price of the asset can be calculated under any of the following two methods.

   (*a*) By adopting reverse order method which was explained earlier.
   (*b*) By consulting to annuity table given the rate of interest and the instalments payable annually and in equal amounts the following formula is applicable.

   = Present value of a rupee × Amount of each annual instalment

Problem 5

On 1st April 2000 Anil bought a Machinery from Sunil for a cash price of Rs. 74,500. Anil made a down payment of Rs. 20,000 and agreed to pay the balance in three annual instalment of Rs. 20,000 each along with interest at the rate of 5% per annum. Depreciate the machinery at 10% per annum on diminishing balance method.

Pass the necessary Journal entries and open the ledger accounts in the books of both the parties.

Solution

Working Note

1. Calculation of interest

Cash price	74,500
Less : Down payment	20,000
	54,500
Add : Interest on 54,500 @ 5%	2,725
	57,225
Less : Amount paid on 31-3-2001	20,000
	37,225
Add : Interest on Rs. 37,225 @ 5%	1,861
	39,086

Less : Amount paid on 31-3-2002	20,000
	19,086
Add : Interest (20,000 - 19,086)	914
	20,000
Less : Amount paid on 31-3-2003	20,000
	Nil

2. Calculation of Depreciation :

Cash price of Machine on 1-4-2000	74,500
Less : Depreciation on 31-3-2001	7,450
	67,050
Less : Depreciation on 31-3-2002	6,705
	60,345
Less : Depreciation on 31-3-2003	6,034
	54,311

In the Books of Anil

Date	*Particulars*		*Dr. Amount*	*Cr. Amount*
2,000 April 1,	Machinery a/c To Sunil's a/c (Being purchase of machinery at cash price of Rs. 74,500 on hire purchase system)	Dr.	74,500	74,500
	Sunil's a/c To Bank a/c (Being down payment made)	Dr.	20,000	20,000
2001 March 31,	Interest a/c To Sunil's a/c (Being interest due)	Dr.	2,725	2,725
	Sunil's a/c To Bank a/c (Being payment of 1st instalment)	Dr.	20,000	20,000
	Depreciation a/c To Machinery (Being depreciation on machinery @ 10% per annum)	Dr.	7,450	7,450
	P & L a/c To Interest a/c To Depreciation (Transfer of interest a/c and Depreciation a/c to P & L a/c)	Dr.	10,175	2,725 7,450
2002 March 31,	Interest a/c To Sunil's a/c (Being Interest due)	Dr.	1,861	1,861

Date	Particulars		Dr. Amount	Cr. Amount
	Sunil's a/c	Dr.	20,000	
	To Bank a/c			20,000
	(Being payment of IInd instalment)			
	Depreciation a/c	Dr.	6,705	
	To Machinery a/c			6,705
	(Being depreciation on machinery @ 10% per annum on diminishing balance method)			
	Profit & Loss a/c	Dr.	8,566	
	To Interest a/c			1,861
	To Depreciation a/c			6,705
	(Transfer of interest a/c and depreciation a/c to P & L a/c)			
2003 March 31,	Interest a/c	Dr.	914	
	To Sunil's a/c			914
	(Interest due to Sunil's a/c)			
	Sunil's a/c	Dr.	20,000	
	To Bank a/c			20,000
	(Being payment of last instalment)			
	Depreciation a/c	Dr.	6,035	
	To Machinery a/c			6,035
	(Being depreciation on machinery charged)			
	Profit & Loss a/c	Dr.	6,949	
	To Interest a/c			914
	To Depreciation a/c			6,035
	(Transfer of interest and depreciation a/c to P & L a/c)			

Ledger A/c's

Machinery A/c

Date	Particular	Rs.	Date	Particular	Rs.
2000 Apr. 1,	To Sunil's a/c	74,500	2001 31st Mar.	By Depreciation	7,450
				By Balance c/d	67,050
		74,500			74,500
2001 Apr. 1,	To Balance	67,050	2002 31st Mar.	By Depreciation a/c	6,705
				By Balance c/d	60,345
		67,050			67,050
2002 Apr. 1,	To Balance b/d	60,345	2003 31st Mar.	By Depreciation a/c	6,035
				By Balance c/d	54,310
		60,345			60,345

Sunil's A/c

Date	Particular	Rs.	Date	Particular	Rs.
2000 Apr. 1,	To Bank a/c	20,000	2000 Apr. 1,	By Machinery a/c	74,500
2001 Mar. 31,	To Bank a/c	20,000	2001 Mar. 31,	By Interest a/c	2,725
	To Balance c/d	37,225			
		77,225			77,225
2002 Mar. 31,	To Bank a/c	20,000	2001 Apr. 1,	By Balance b/d	37,225
	To Balance c/d	19,086	2002 Mar. 31,	By Interest a/c	1861
		39,086			39,086
2003 Mar. 31,	To Bank a/c	20,000	2002 Apr. 1,	By Balance b/d	19,086
			2003 Mar. 31,	By Interest a/c	914
		20,000			20,000

In the Books of Sunil

Date	Particulars	Dr. Amount	Cr. Amount
2000 Apr. 1,	Anil's a/c Dr.	74,500	
	To Sales a/c		74,500
	(Being sale of machinery to Anil on hire purchase system)		
	Bank a/c Dr.	20,000	
	To Anil's a/c		20,000
	(Being down payment received)		
2001 Mar. 31,	Anil's a/c Dr.	2,725	
	To Interest a/c		2,725
	(Being interest due from Anil)		
	Bank a/c Dr.	20,000	
	To Anil's a/c		20,000
	(Being 1st instalment received)		
	Interest a/c Dr.	2,725	
	To P & L a/c		2,725
	(Transfer of interest a/c to P& L a/c)		
2002 Mar. 31,	Anil's a/c Dr.	1,861	
	To Interest a/c		1,861
	(Interest due from Anil)		
	Bank a/c Dr.	20,000	
	To Anil's a/c		20,000
	(Being II instalment received)		

Date	*Particulars*		*Dr. Amount*	*Cr. Amount*
	Interest a/c	Dr.	1,861	
	To P & L a/c			1,861
	(Transfer of interest a/c to P & L a/c)			
2003 Mar. 31,	Anil's a/c	Dr.	914	
	To Interest a/c			914
	(Being interest due from Anil)			
	Bank a/c	Dr.	20,000	
	To Anil's a/c			20,000
	(Being the last instalment received)			
	Interest a/c	Dr.	914	
	To P & L a/c			914
	(Transfer of interest to P & L a/c)			

Anil's A/c

Date		*Rs.*	*Date*		*Rs.*
2000 Apr. 1,	To Sales	74,500	2000 Apr. 1,	By Bank a/c	20,000
2001 Mar. 31,	To Interest	2,725	2001 Mar. 31,	By Bank a/c	20,000
				By Balance c/d	37,225
		77,225			77,225
2001 Apr. 1,	To Balance b/d	37, 225	2002 Mar. 31,	By Bank a/c	20,000
				By Balance c/d	19,086
2002 Mar. 31,	To Interest a/c	1,861			
		39,086			39,086
2002 Apr. 1,	To Balance b/d	19,056	2003 Mar. 31,	By Bank a/c	20,000
2003 Mar. 31,	To Interest a/c	914			
		20,000			20,000

Problem 6

The Madras company purchased machinery from the Bombay company on hire purchase agreement on 1st January 1996, paying cash of Rs. 10,000 and agreeing to pay three further instalments of Rs. 10,000 each on the 31st December of every year. The cash price of the machinery is Rs. 37,250 and the Bombay Company charges interest at 5% per annum. The Madras Company writes off 10% every year on cash value of the machinery on the reducing instalment system. **(University of Madras B. Com. October 1999)**

Solution

Working Note :

1. Calculation of Interest :

		Instalment	Interest	Cash price
Total Cash price	37,250			
Less : down payment	10,000	10,000	—	10,000
	27,250			
Add : Interest				
$27{,}250 \times \frac{5}{100}$	1,362	10,000	1,362	8,638
	28,612			
Less : 1st Instalment	10,000			
	18,612			
Add : Interest	930	10,000	930	9,070
$18{,}612 \times \frac{5}{100}$	19,542			
Less : IInd Instalment	10,000			
	9,542			
Add : Interest (10000 – 9542)	458	10,000	458	9542
	10,000			
Less : IInd Instalment	10,000			
	Nil	40,000	27,510	37,250

2. Calculation of Depreciation

Cash price	37,250
I year = $37{,}250 \times \frac{10}{100}$	3,725
Depreciation	33,525
II Year Depreciation $33{,}525 \times \frac{10}{100}$	3,352
	30,172
III Year Depreciation $30{,}172 \times \frac{10}{100}$	3,017
	27,155

In the Books of Madras Company

Date	Particulars		Dr. Amount	Cr. Amount
1-1-96	Machine a/c	Dr.	37,250	
	To Bombay Co. a/c			37,250
	(Being machine purchased under hire purchase system)			
	Bombay Co. a/c	Dr.	10,000	
	To Cash a/c			10,000
	(Being down payment made)			
31-12-96	Interest a/c	Dr.	1,362	
	To Bombay Co. a/c			1,362
	(Being interest of the 1st year due)			

Date	Particulars	Dr. Amount	Cr. Amount
	Bombay Company a/c Dr. To Cash a/c (Being the 1st instalment paid)	10,000	 10,000
	Depreciation a/c Dr. To Machine a/c (Being depreciation on machine charged)	3,725	 3,725
	P & L a/c Dr. To Interest a/c To Depreciation a/c (Being interest and depreciation transferred to P & L a/c)	5,087	 1,362 3,725
31-12-97	Interest a/c Dr. To Bombay Company a/c (Being 2nd years interest due)	930	 930
	Bombay Co. a/c Dr. To Cash a/c (Being the 2nd instalment paid)	10,000	 10,000
	Depreciation a/c Dr. To Machine a/c (Being depreciation charged at 10% on diminishing balance method)	3,352	 3,352
	P & L a/c Dr. To Interest To Depreciation (Being interest and depreciation charged to P & L a/c)	4,282	 930 3,352
31-12-98	Interest a/c Dr. To Bombay Co. a/c (Being 3rd years a interest due)	456	 456
	Bombay Co. a/c Dr. To Cash a/c (Being the 3rd instalment paid)	10,000	 10,000
	Depreciation a/c Dr. To Machinery a/c (Being depreciation charged at 10% on diminishing balance method)	3,017	 3,017
	P & L a/c Dr. To Interest a/c To Depreciation a/c (Being the interest and depreciation transferred to P & C a/c)	3,473	 456 3,017

Machinery A/c

Date	Particular	Rs.	Particular	Rs.
1996	To Bombay Co.	37,250	By Depreciation a/c	3,725
			By Balance c/d	33,525
		37,250		37,250
1997	To Balance b/d	33,525	By Depreciation a/c	3,352
			By Balance c/d	30,173
		33,525		33,525
1998	To Balance b/d	30,173	By Depreciation a/c	3,017
			By Balance c/d	27,156
		30,173		30,173

Bombay Co. A/c (Hire vendor)

	Rs.		Rs.
To Cash down payment	10,000	By Machinery a/c	37,250
To Cash a/c	10,000	By Interest a/c	,1362
To Balance c/d	18,612		
	38,612		38,612
To Cash a/c	10,000	By Balance b/d	18,612
To Balance c/d	9,542	By Interest a/c	930
	19,542		19,542
To Cash a/c	10,000	By Balance b/d	9,542
		By Interest a/c	458
	10,000		10,000

Problem 7

Cholan firm purchased a machinery costing Rs. 60,000 from Pardiyan firm on hire purchase system. It was agreed to pay the amount at Rs. 20,000 per year in three annual instalments with interest at 5%. Show machinery account and Pardiyan's firm account in the books of cholan firm. **(University of Madras B. Com. May 2001)**

Solution

Calculation of Interest

Cash price	60,000
Less : Down payment	—
	60,000
Add : Interest $60,000 \times \frac{5}{100}$	3,000
	63,000
Less : Ist Instalment paid (20,000 + 3,000)	23,000
	40,000
Add : Interest $40,000 \times \frac{5}{100}$	2,000

	42,000
Less : IInd Instalment paid (20,000 + 2,000)	22,000
	20,000
Add : Interest $20{,}000 \times \frac{5}{100}$	1,000
	21,000
Less : IIIrd Instalment paid (20,000 + 1,000)	21,000
	Nil

In The Books of Cholan firm

Machinery A/c

	Rs.		Rs.
To Pardiyan firm a/c	60,000		

Pardiyan firm A/c (Hire vendor)

	Rs.		Rs.
		I year	
To Cash a/c	23,000	By Machinery a/c	60,000
To Balance c/d	40,000	By Interest a/c	3,000
	63,000		63,000
		II year	
To Cash a/c	22,000	By Balance b/d	40,000
To Balance c/d	20,000	By Interest	2,000
	42,000		42,000
		III year	
To Cash a/c	21,000	By Balance b/d	20,000
		By Interest	1,000
	21,000		21,000

Problem 8

On 1st January 1994 Sai Ram brother acquired a machine on hire purchase. The terms of the contract were as follows : Vendor's name is Avanti Ltd.

1. The Cash price of the machine was Rs. 56,000
2. Rs. 16,000 was to be paid on signing the contract.
3. The balance was to be paid in annual instalments of Rs. 10,000 plus interest .
4. Interest chargeable on outstanding balance was at 5% p.a. Depreciation at 10% p.a. is to be written off on the straight line method.

You are required to show the necessary accounts in the books of Sai Ram brother

(Sri Venkateshwara University B. Com. April 2000)

Solution

Calculation of Interest

	Cash price	56,000
Less :	Down payment	16,000
		40,000
Add :	Interest $40{,}000 \times \frac{5}{100}$	2,000
		42,000
Less :	Ist Instalment paid	12,000
		30,000
Add :	Interest $30{,}000 \times \frac{5}{100}$	1,500
		31,500
Less :	IInd Instalment paid	11,500
		20,000
Add :	Interest $20{,}000 \times \frac{5}{100}$	1,000
		21,000
Less :	IIIrd Instalment paid	11,000
		10,000
Add :	Interest $10{,}000 \times \frac{5}{100}$	1,000
		11,000
Less :	IVth Instalment paid	11,000
		Nil

In the Books of Sai Ram Bros.

Machinery

Date		Rs.	Date		Rs.
1-1-94	To Bank	16,000	31-12-94	By Depreciation	5,600
31-12-94	To Avanti Ltd. a/c	10,000		By Balance c/d	20,400
		26,000			26,000
1-1-95	To Balance b/d	20,400	31-12-95	By Depreciation	5,600
	To Avanti Ltd. a/c	10,000		By Balance c/d	24,800
		30,400			30,400
1-1-96	To Balance b/d	24,800	31-12-96	By Depreciation	5,600
	To Avanti Ltd. a/c	10,000		By Balance c/d	29,200
		34,800			34,800
1-1-97	To Balance b/d	29,200	31-12-97	By Depreciation	5,600
	To Avanti Ltd. a/c	10,000		By Balance c/d	33,600
		39,200			39,200

Avanti Ltd. A/c

Date		Rs.	Date		Rs.
31-12-94	To Bank a/c	12,000	31-12-94	By Machinery a/c	10,000
				By Interest	2,000
		12,000			12,000

Date		Rs.	Date		Rs.
31-12-95	To Bank a/c	11,500	31-12-95	By Machinery a/c	10,000
				By Interest	1,500
		11,500			11,500
31-12-96	To Bank a/c	11,000	31-12-96	By Machinery a/c	10,000
				By Interest	1,000
		11,000			11,000
31-12-97	To Bank a/c	10,500	31-12-97	By Machinery a/c	10,000
				By Interest	500
		10,500			10,500

Depreciation A/c

Date		Rs.	Date		Rs.
31-12-94	To Machinery	5,600	31-12-94	By P & L a/c	5,600
31-12-95	To Machinery a/c	5,600	31-12-95	By P & L a/c	5,600
31-11-96	To Machinery a/c	5,600	31-11-96	By P& L a/c	5,600
31-12-97	To Machinery a/c	5,600	31-12-97	By P & L a/c	5,600

Interest A/c

Date		Rs.	Date		Rs.
31-12-94	To Avnti Ltd. a/c	2,000	31-12-94	By P & L a/c	2,000
31-12-95	To Avanti Ltd. a/c	1,500	31-12-95	By P & L a/c	1,500
31-12-96	To Avanti Ltd. a/c	1,000	31-12-96	By P & L a/c	1,000
31-12-97	To Avanti Ltd. a/c	500	31-12-97	By P & L a/c	500

Problem 9

On 1st April 1998 a transport Company ordered a motor vehicle whose cash price was Rs. 3,50,000. The Company entered into a hire purchase agreement to pay Rs. 1,00,000 immediately and Eight quarterly instalment of Rs. 36,740 each the first instalment being payable on 30th June 1998. The rate of interest was 15% per annum. The Company depreciated the motor vehicle @ 10% per annum on the diminishing balancing method.

Prepare the motor vehicle account in the books of the hire purchaser for the two years ended 31st March 2000 assuming that on every payment the hire purchaser debited the motor vehicle a/c with that portion of the payment which was made towards cash price. Also assume the account is closed on 31st March every year.

(CS Foundation, December 2000)

Solution

Working Notes :

1. Calculation of Interest

Date	Particulars	Rs.
1998		
Apr. 1,	Cash price	3,50,000
	Less : Down payment	1,00,000
		2,50,000
June 30,	Add : Interest on Rs. 2,50,000 for 3 months @ 15% p.a.	9,375
		2,59,375
	Less : First instalment	36,740
		2,22,635
Sept. 30,	Add : Interest on Rs. 2,22,835 for 3 months @ 15% p.a.	8,349
		2,30,984
	Less : Second instalment	36,740
		1,94,244
Dec. 31,	Add : Interest on Rs. 1,94,244 for 3 months @ 15% p.a.	7,284
		2,01,528
	Less : third Instalment	36,740
		1,64,788
1999		
March 31,	Add : Interest on Rs. 1,64,788 for 3 months @ 15% p.a.	6,180
		1,70,968
	Less : Fourth instalment	36,740
		1,34,228
June 30,	Add : Interest on Rs. 1,34,228 for 3 months @ 15% p.a.	5,034
		1,39,262
	Less : fifth instalment	36,740
		1,02,522
Step. 30,	Add : Interest on Rs. 1,02,522 for 3 months @ 15% p.a.	3,845
		1,06,367
	Less : Sixth instalment	36,740
		69,627
Dec. 31,	Add : Interest on Rs. 69,627 for 3 moths @ 15% p.a.	2,611
		72,238
	Less : Seventh instalment	36,740
		35,498
2000		
March 31,	Add :Interest (36,740 – 35,498)	1,242
		36,740
	Less : Last instalment	36,740
		Nil

2. Calculation of Depreciation

Particulars	Rs.
Cash price	3,50,000
Less : Depreciation for the year ended 31st March 1999	35,000
	3,15,000
Less : Depreciation for the year ended 31st March 2000	31,500
	2,83,500

3. Payment towards cash price :

		Rs.
1998		
Apr. 1,	Down payment	1,00,000
Jun. 30,	Rs. (36,740 – 9,375)	27,365
Sep. 30,	Rs. (36,740 – 8,349)	28,391
Dec. 31,	Rs. (36,740 – 7,284)	29,456
1999		
Mar. 31,	Rs. (36,740 – 6,180)	30,560
Jun. 30,	Rs. (36,740 – 5,034)	31,706
Sep. 30,	Rs. (36,740 – 3,845)	32,895
Dec. 31,	Rs. (36,740 – 2,611)	34,129
2000		
Mar. 31,	Rs. (36,740 – 1,242)	35,498
		3,50,000

Motor Vehicle A/c

Date		*Rs.*	*Date*		*Rs.*
1998			1999		
Apr. 1,	To Hire vendor	1,00,000	Mar. 31,	By Depreciation	35,000
Jun. 30,	To Hire vendor	27,365		By Balance	1,80,772
Sept. 30,	To Hire vendor	28,391			
Dec. 31,	To Hire vendor	29,456			
1999					
Mar. 31,	To Hire vendor	30,560			
		2,15,772			2,15,772
1999			2000		
Apr. 1,	To Balance b/d	1,80,772	Mar. 31,	By dep a/c	31,500
Jun. 30,	To Vendor	31,706		By Balance c/d	2,83,500
Sept. 30,	To Hire vendor	32,895			
Dec. 31,	To Hire vendor	34,129			
2000					
Mar. 31,	To Hire vendor	35,498			
		3,15,000			3,15,000

Problem 10

On 1-1-1993, Ramaswamy Company purchased a car from Alagappan and company. At the time of agreement a sum of Rs. 24,000 was paid out car as cash down price of the car and the balance would be payable in 3 equal annual instalments with interest at 5% p.a. The amount of last instalment including interest was Rs. 33,600. Depreciation was to be provided at 10% p.a. on the reducing balances.

Prepare.

(*a*) Motor can a/c (b) Alagappan a/c in the books of Ramaswamy Company.

(University of Madras B. Com. October 2000)

Solution

Working Note :

The total cash price is not given. The instalment include interest. By following reverse order method the cash price is determined.

Particulars	*Instalment*	*Interest*	*Cash Price*
III Instalment	33,600	$33{,}600 \times \frac{5}{105} = 1{,}600$	32,000
II Instalment	33,600	$(32{,}000 + 33{,}600) \times \frac{5}{105} = 3{,}124$	30,476
I Instalment	33,600	$(32{,}000 + 30{,}476 + 33{,}600) \times \frac{5}{105} = 4{,}575$	29,025
Down payment	24,000	No Interest	24,000
	1,24,800	9,299	1,15,500

In the Books of Ramaswamy Company

(Hire Purchaser) (*a*) Motor car A/c

Date		*Rs.*	*Date*		*Rs.*
1-1-93	To Alogappan a/c	1,15,500	31-12-93	By Depreciation a/c 1,15,500 @ 10%	11,550
				By Balance c/d	1,03,950
		1,15,500			1,15,500
1-1-94	To Balance b/d	1,03,950	31-12-94	By Depreciation a/c 1,03,950 @ 10%	10395
				By Balance c/d	93,555
		1,03,950			1,03,950
1-1-95	To Balance b/d	93,555	31-12-95	By Depreciation 93,555 @ 10%	9,355
				By Balance c/d	84,200
		93,555			93,555

Alapaggan A/c (Hire vendor)

Date		*Rs.*	*Date*		*Rs.*
1-1-93	To Cash	24,000	1-1-93	By Car a/c	1,15,500
	To Cash	33,600	31-12-93	By Interest a/c	4,575
	To Balance c/d	62,476			
		1,20,076			1,20,076
31-12-94	To Cash	33,600	1-1-94	By Balance b/d	62,476
	To Balance c/d	32,000	31-12-94	By Interest	3,124
		65,600			65,600
31-12-95	To Cash	33,600	1-1-95	By Balance b/d	32,000
				By Interest	1,600
		33,600			33,600

Repossession of Goods on Default

When a hire purchaser fails to pay any instalment payment the hire vendor has the right to take back the possessions of the asset. As regards the entries in the books of hire purchaser it depends upon the method followed i.e., when asset is recorded at the full cash price or when the asset is recorded at the cash price actually paid. Further the accounting entries also depends upon whether the hire vendor has taken complete possession or only partially. The various instalments paid till then is treated as hire charges and the ownership is again acquired by the hire vendor.

Entries in the Books of Hire Purchaser

(A) **When the Asset is recorded at full Cash Price**

1. In the year of repossession, all the usual entries except the entry for the payment of the instalment should be made.
2. When there is complete repossession, the hire purchaser should close the hire vendor's a/c by transferring the entire balance in the hire vendor's a/c to the asset a/c. The entry is as follows :
   Hire Vendor a/c Dr.
   To Asset a/c
3. Any balance left in the asset should be treated as a loss and the same must be transferred to P & L a/c. In this process the asset a/c is closed. The entry is as follows :
   P & L a/c Dr.
   To Asset a/c

(B) **When The Asset is recorded at the cash price actually paid :**

The only entries required under this method are as follows :

(*a*) Entry for charging depreciation, Viz,

Depreciation a/c Dr.
To Asset a/c

(*b*) The final balance in the asset a/c is to be treated as loss and as such transferred to P & L a/c. The entry is

P & L a/c Dr.
To Asset a/c

Entries in the Books of Hire Vendor

1. During the year of repossession all entries except the entry for the receipt of instalment money are recorded.
2. On complete repossession the hire vendor cannot get the balance from hire Purchaser. So the hire purchaser's a/c is to be closed by transferring, the credit balance to an account known as "Repossessed stock a/c. The entry is :
   Repossessed Stock a/c Dr. (With the entire balance)
   To Hire purchaser's a/c
3. When hire vendor incurs any expenses in repairing the repossessed stock, the following entry is passed.
   Repossessed Stock a/c Dr.
   To Cash a/c

4. When the repossessed goods are sold after repairing.
   Cash a/c Dr.
   To Repossessed stock a/c
5. The balance in the repossessed stock a/c is to be treated as profit or loss on repossession and hence it is to be transferred to P & L a/c.
   (a) ***In case of profit :***
   Repossessed stock a/c Dr.
   To P & L a/c
   (b) ***In case of loss :***
   P & L a/c Dr.
   To Repossessed Stock a/c
6. In case of repossession of part of the stock, the hire vendor should not close hire purchaser's a/c. Instead :
   (a) ***An entry is to be passed for taking over part of the goods.***
   Repossessed stock a/c Dr.
   To Hire purchaser's a/c
   (b) ***The hire purchaser's a/c should be balanced and the balance should be carried forward.***
   (c) ***The repossessed stock a/c should be balanced and the balance to be carried forward.***

Problem 11

(Repossession of goods)

On 1st April 1997, Singh acquired a truck from a dealer on hire purchase basis, cash price of which was Rs. 8,00,000. The terms of payment being Rs. 2,00,000 cash down, Rs. 2,45,000 at the end of the first year : Rs 2,30,000 at the end of the second year and Rs. 2,15,000 at the end of the third year. The dealer charged interest @ $7\frac{1}{2}$% per annum.

Singh depreciated the truck at 10% per annum on the written down value method. After having made down payment and having paid the first instalment on 31st March 1998, he could not pay the second instalment on 31st March 1999. The hire vendor took possession of the truck and after spending Rs. 20,000 on repairs of the truck, sold it way for Rs. 4,57,500.

Prepare ledger account in the books of both the parties.

(CS Foundation December 1999)

Solution

In the Books of Singh

Truck A/c

Date	*particulars*	*Rs.*	*Date*	*particulars*	*Rs.*
1997 Apr. 1,	To Hire vendor a/c	8,00,000	1998 Mar. 31,	By Depreciation By Balance c/d	80,000 7,20,000
		8,00,000			8,00,000
1998 Apr. 1,	To Balance b/d	7,20,000	1999 Mar. 31,	By Depreciation a/c By Hire vendor a/c By P & L a/c - loss transferred	72,000 4,30,000 2,18,000
		7,20,000			7,20,000

Hire Vendor A/c

Date		Rs.	Date		Rs.
1997 Apr. 1,	To Bank a/c	2,00,000	1997 Apr. 1,	By Truck a/c	8,00,000
1998 Mar. 31,	To Bank	2,45,000	1998 Mar. 31,	By Interest on Rs. 6,00,000 @ $7\frac{1}{2}$ % p.a.	45,000
	To Balance c/d	4,00,000			
		8,45,000			8,45,000
1999 Mar. 31,	To Truck a/c transfer	4,30,000	1998 Apr. 1,	By Balance b/d	4,00,000
			1999 Mar. 31,	By Interest (on Rs. 4,00,000 @ $7\frac{1}{2}$%)	30,000
		4,30,000			4,30,000

In the books of Hire Vendor
Singh's A/c

Date		Rs.	Date		Rs.
1997 Apr. 1,	To Sales a/c	8,00,000	1997 Apr. 1,	By Bank a/c	2,00,000
1998 Mar. 31,	To Interest a/c	45,000	1998 Mar. 31,	By Bank a/c	2,45,000
				By Balance c/d	4,00,000
		8,45,000			8,45,000
1998 Apr. 1,	To Balance b/d	4,00,000	1999 Mar. 31,	By Goods Repossessed a/c	4,30,000
1999 Mar. 31,	To Interest a/c	30,000			
		4,30,000			4,30,000

Goods Repossessed A/c

Date		Rs.	Date		Rs.
1999 Mar. 31,	To Singh a/c	4,30,000	1999 Mar. 31,	By Bank— Sales	4,57,500
	To Bank — Repairs	20,000			
	To P & L a/c — Profit Transferred	7,500			
		4,57,500			4,57,500

Problem 12

On 1-1-1998 Mr. Ram a Television dealer bought 5 television sets from A. M. Electronics on hire purchase. The cash price of each set was Rs. 20,000. It was agreed that Rs. 25,000 should be paid immediately and the balance in three instalments of Rs. 30,000 each at the end of each year.

The vendor charges interest at 10% p.a. The buyer depreciates TV sets at 20% p.a. on the diminishing balance method.

Ram paid cash down and two Instalments but failed to pay the last instalment. Consequently, the vendor repossessed three sets, leaving two sets with the buyer and adjusting the value of 3 sets against the amount due. The sets repossessed were valued on the basis of 30% depreciation p.a. on the written down value. These sets were sold by the vendor for Rs. 30,000 after necessary repair amounting to Rs. 5,000.

Open the necessary ledger accounts in the books of both the parties.

(Osmania University B. Com. October 2000)

Solution

Working Note :

1. Value of three sets on repossession :

	1998 Rs.	1999 Rs.	2000 Rs.
Cost/ written down value	60,000	42,000	29,400
Depreciation for the year @ 30 %	18,000	12,600	8,820
	42,000	29,400	20,580

2. Value of two Sets Still in Possession :

Cost/written down value	40,000	32,000	25,600
Depreciation for the year @ 20%	8,000	6,400	5,120
	32,000	25,600	20,480

In the Books of Mr. Ram

Television A/c

Date		Rs.	Date		Rs.
1998 Jan. 1,	To A. M. Electronics Ltd.	1,00,000	1998 Dec. 31,	By Depreciation a/c	20,000
				By Balance c/d	80,000
		1,00,000			1,00,000
1999 Jan. 1,	To Balance b/d.	80,000	1999 Dec. 31,	By Depreciation a/c	16,000
				By Balance c/d	64,000
		80,000			80,000
2000 Jan. 1,	To Balance b/d	64,000	2000 Dec. 31,	By Depreciation a/c	12,800
				By A. M. Electronics Ltd. (TV repossessed)	20,580
				By P & L a/c (loss on default)	10,140
				By Balance c/d (written down value of TV on possession)	20,480
		64,000			64,000

A. M. Electronics Ltd. A/c

Date		Rs.	Date		Rs.
1998			1998		
Jan. 1,	To Bank a/c	25,000	Jan. 1,	By T.V. a/c	1,00,000
Dec. 31,	To Bank a/c	30000	Dec. 31,	By Interest	7,500
	To Balance c/d	52,500		$\frac{10}{100} \times 75,000$	
		1,07,500			1,07,500
1999			1999		
Dec. 31,	To Bank a/c	30,000	Jan. 1,	By Balance b/d	52,500
	To Balance c/d	27,750	Dec. 31,	By Interest a/c	5,250
		57,750			57,750
2000			2000		
Dec. 31,	To T.V. a/c	20,580	Jan. 1,	By Balance b/d	27,750
	To Balance c/d	9,420	Dec. 31,	By Interest a/c	2,250
		30,000			30,000

In the Books of A. M. Electronics Ltd.
Ram's A/c

Date		Rs.	Date		Rs.
1998			1998		
Jan. 1,	To Sales a/c	1,00,000	Jan. 1,	By Bank a/c	25,000
Dec. 31,	To Interest a/c	75,00	Dec. 31,	By Bank a/c	30,000
				By Balance c/d	52,500
		1,07,500			1,07,500
1999			1999		
Jan. 1,	To Balance b/d	52,500	Dec. 31,	By Bank a/c	30,000
Dec. 31,	To Interest a/c	5,250	Jan. 1,	By Balance c/d	27,750
		57,750			57,750
2000			2000		
Jan. 1,	To Balance b/d	27,750	Dec. 31,	By Repossession stock a/c	20,580
Dec. 31,	To Interest a/c	2,250		By Balance c/d	9,420
		30,000			30,000

Repossessed Stock A/c

Date		Rs.	Date		Rs.
2000			2000		
Dec. 31,	To A. M. Electronics Ltd.	20,580	Dec. 31,	By Bank a/c	30,000
	To Bank — Repairs	5,000			
	To P & L a/c (Profit)	4,420			
		30,000			30,000

Problem 13

D. Ltd. sold three machines costing Rs. 10,000 each to P on hire purchase system on 1-1-96. P paid Rs. 6,000 on the above date to receive delivery of the machines and agreed to pay half-yearly instalments of Rs. 6,000 each.

P could not pay the third instalment in time where upon D Ltd. repossesses one machine and P retained the other two machines. The value of the returned machine was agreed to be cash price less 40%. The purchaser charges depreciation @ 10% p.a. on reducing balance method.

D Ltd., sold the repossessed machine for Rs. 4,500 on 31st December 1997 after incurring repairs of Rs. 200.

You are required to show :

1. D Ltd. a/c and Machinery a/c in the books of hire-purchaser : and
2. P's a/c and Goods Repossessed a/c in the books D Ltd.

(University of Delhi, B. Com. Pass 2000)

Solution

In the books of P (Hire Purchaser)
Machinery A/c

Date		*Rs.*	*Date*		*Rs.*
1-1-96	To D Ltd. (Vendor)	30,000	31-12-96	By Depreciation a/c	3,000
				By Balance c/d	27,000
		30,000			30,000
1-1-97	To Balance b/d	27,000	30-6-97	By Depreciation a/c (On one machine Note 1)	450
				By D Ltd. a/c (Note 2)	6,,000
				By P & L a/c (loss on default)	2,550
			31-12-97	By Depreciation a/c	1800
				By Balance c/d (Note -3) (2 Machines)	16,200
		27,000			27,000

D Ltd. A/c (Vendor)

Date		*Rs.*	*Date*		*Rs.*
1-1-96	To Bank a/c	6,000	1-1-96	By Machinery a/c — Total cash price	30,000
30-6-96	To Bank a/c	6,000	30-6-96	By Interest a/c	2,000
31-12-96	To Bank a/c	6,000	31-12-96	By Interest a/c	1,600
	To Balance c/d	15,600			
		33,600			33,600

In the books of D (Hire vendor)
P's A/c

Date		Rs.	Date		Rs.
1-1-96	To Sales a/c	30,000	1-1-96	By Bank a/c	6,000
30-6-96	To Interest a/c	2,000	30-6-96	By Bank a/c	6,000
31-12-96	To Interest a/c	1,600	31-12-96	By Bank a/c	6,000
				By Balance c/d	15,600
		33,600			33,600
1-1-97	To Balance b/d	15,600	30-6-97	By Goods Repossessed a/c	6,000
30-6-97	To Balance	1,200		By Balance c/d	10,800
		16,800			16,800

Goods Repossessed A/c

Date		Rs.	Date		Rs.
30-6-97	To P's a/c	6,000	31-12-97	By Bank a/c	4,500
	To Bank a/c — Repairs	200		By P & L a/c loss on c/d	1,700
		6,200			6,200

Working Notes :

1. Depreciation for $\frac{1}{2}$ year will be provided only on one machine being repossessed. On other two Machines, depreciation will be provided up to 31-12-97.
2. **Value of 2 Machines left with buyer :**

Cash price = 2 × 10,000	Rs. 20,000
— Dep 1 year	2,000
	18,000
— Dep II year	1,800
	16,200

3. **Calculation of total interest payable :**

Total instalment amount (6,000 × 5)	30,000
Add : Amount paid on signing the contract	6,000
	36,000
Less : Cash price (10,000 × 3)	30,000
Total interest payable	6,000

Total interest payable over whole period of 5 instalments has been apportioned in the ratio of the Hire Purchaser price during these 5 period, i.e., 30,000, 24,000, 18,000, 12,000, and 6,000 or 5 : 4 : 3 : 2 : 1. So interest charged and included in each instalment will be

$$\text{I - } 6{,}000 \times \frac{5}{15} = \text{Rs. } 2{,}000$$

$$\text{II - } 6{,}000 \times \frac{4}{15} = \text{Rs. } 1{,}600$$

$$\text{III - } 6{,}000 \times \frac{3}{15} = \text{Rs. } 1{,}200$$

$$\text{II - } 6{,}000 \times \frac{2}{15} = \text{Rs. } 800$$

$$\text{I - } 6{,}000 \times \frac{1}{15} = \text{Rs. } 400$$

4. D Ltd. a/c credit balance Rs. 10,800 is still payable.
5. Agreed price at which machine is repossessed is Rs. 1,000. Less 40%, i.e., 6,000
6. It is assumed that account are closed every year on 31st December.
7. Instalments fall due at the and of each half yearly.

Problem 14

On 1st October 1999 five trucks were purchased by Kartar on the hire purchase system. The cash price of each truck was Rs. 5,50,000. The payment was to be made as follows :-

— 10% of cash price at the time of delivery

— 25% of cash price at the end of each one of the subsequent four half years.

The payment due on 30th September 2000 could not be made and hence trucks were seized by the hire vendor but after negotionon, Kartar was allowed to keep three trucks on the condition that the value of the other two trucks would be adjusted against the amount due the trucks being valued at cost less 25% depreciation and Kartar would pay the balance in five half yearly instalments together interest @ 10% per annum. Both the parties close their books of accounts on 31st March every year, Kartar charges 15% depreciation on trucks on the original cost.

In October 2000, the hire vendor spent Rs. 60,000 on getting the seized trucks throughly over-hauled and sold them for Rs. 9,50,000.

Prepare for two accounting years ended 31st March 2001 :-

(*i*) Trucks account in Kartar's ledger assuming that Kartar debited it with full cash price in the beginning of the contract and

(*ii*) The personal account of Kartar and goods repossessed account in hire vendor's ledger.

(CS., Foundation June 2001)

Solution

Working Notes :

1. **Calculation of Interest :** Total interest is 10% of the cash price

$$\frac{10}{100} \times 27{,}50{,}000 = \text{Rs. } 2{,}75{,}000$$

As there are four equal instalments, the interest will be apportioned in the ratio of 4 : 3 : 2 :1.

Interest included in the first instalment

$$= 2{,}75{,}000 \times \frac{4}{10} = \text{Rs. } 1{,}10{,}000$$

Interest included in the second instalment

$$= 2{,}75{,}000 \times \frac{3}{10} = \text{Rs. } 82{,}500$$

2. Calculate of Depreciation : Depreciation provided on 31st March 2000

= On Rs. 27,50,000 @ 15% p.a. for 6 months

$$= 27{,}50{,}000 \times \frac{15}{100} \times \frac{6}{12} = \text{Rs. } 2{,}06{,}250$$

Depreciation provided on 30th Sept. 2000 on two trucks.

= On Rs. 11,00,000 @ 15% p.a. for 6 months

$$= 11{,}00{,}000 \times \frac{15}{100} \times \frac{6}{12} = \text{Rs. } 82{,}500$$

Depreciation provided on 31st March 2001

= On Rs. 16,50,000 @ 15% p.a. for full year

$$= 16{,}50{,}000 \times \frac{15}{100} = \text{Rs. } 2{,}47{,}500$$

(*iii*) **Agreed Value of 2 trucks seized by hire vendor**

= Cash price less 25% = 75% of cash price

$$= 11{,}00{,}000 \times \frac{75}{100} = \text{Rs. } 8{,}25{,}000.$$

(*iv*) **Calculation of loss on default :** Written down value of 2 trucks

= Cash price less depreciation for 1 year

= 11,00,000 – 1,65,000 = 9,35,000

Less :agreed value of trucks taken always = 8,25,000

Loss on default 1,10,000

(*v*) **Calculation of payment made by Kartar on 31st March 2001.**

Amount due on 1st October 2000

= (18,97,500 + 82,500 - 8,25,000)

= Rs. 11,55,000

$\frac{1}{5}$ of Rs. 11,55,000 = 2,31,000

Add : Interest on Rs. 11,55,000 @ 10% p.a. for 6 months

$11{,}55{,}000 \times \frac{10}{100} \times \frac{6}{12} =$ 57,750

Total amount paid 2,88,750

In the books of Kartar

Trucks A/c

Date		*Rs.*	*Date*		*Rs.*
1999			2000		
Oct. 1,	To Hire Vender	27,50,000	Mar. 31	By Depreciation for 6 months @ 15% p.a. on original cost	2,06,250
				Balance c/d	25,43,750
		27,50,000			27,50,000

Date		Rs.	Date		Rs.
2000 Apr 1	To Balance b/d	25,43,750	2000 Sept. 30,	By Depreciation a/c — 6 months @ 15% p.a. on original Cost of 2 trucks	82,500
				By Hire vendor (Note – III)	8,25,000
				By P & L — Loss on default (Note – IV)	1,10,000
			2001 Mar. 31,	By Depreciation a/c — full year on 3 trucks	2,47,500
				By Balance c/d	12,78,750
		25,43,750			25,43,750

In hire vendor's ledger

Kartar's A/c

Date	Particulars	Amount	Date	Particulars	Amount
1999 Oct. 1	To sales a/c	27,50,000	1999 Oct. 1	By Bank	2,75,000
2000 Mar. 31	To Interest a/c	1,10,000	2000 Mar. 31	By Bank	6,87,500
				Balance c/d	18,97,500
		28,60,000			28,60,000
2000 Apr. 1	To Balance b/d	18,97,500	2000 Sept. 30	By Goods Repossessed	8,25,000
2000 Sept. 30	To Interest a/c	82,500			
2001 Mar. 31	To Interest a/c on Rs 11,55,000 for 6 month @ 10% p.a.	57,750	2001 Mar. 31	By Bank (2,31,000 + 57,750)	2,88,750
				Balance c/d	9,24,000
		20,37,750			20,37,750

Goods Repossessed A/c

Date		Rs.	Date		Rs.
2000 Sept. 30,	Kartar's a/c	8,25,000	2000 Oct.	By Bank — Sale proceeds	9,50,000
Oct.	To Bank a/c — Expenses on an over Lauling	60,000			
	To P & L a/c — Profit	65,000			
		9,50,000			9,50,000

HIRE PURCHASE TRADING ACCOUNT

When many articles of comparatively small value is sold on hire purchase basis it becomes of difficult to calculate interest in respect each and every article sold. In such a case a Hire purchase trading a/c is maintained to ascertain the profit or loss on hire purchase business. The following entries are involved.

1. **On sale of goods on hire purchase :**
   Hire purchase trading a/c Dr.
   To Goods sold on hire purchase a/c
   (with the hire purchase price of goods sold)
2. **On receipt of instalments :**
   Cash a/c Dr.
   To Hire purchase trading a/c
   (with the amount received)
3. **On default of payment and repossession of goods**
   Goods repossessed a/c Dr.
   To Hire purchase trading a/c
   (with the estimated value of goods repossessed)
4. **At the end of the accounting year ; for instalments due but not received :**
   Instalment due a/c Dr.
   To Hire purchase trading a/c.
5. **At the end of the year, for instalments which are yet to fall due in respect of goods sold.**
   Hire Purchase Stock a/c Dr.
   To Hire Purchase Trading a/c.
6. **To Remove the loading in hire- purchase sales :**
   Goods sold on Hire Purchase a/c
   To Hire Purchase Trading a/c
   (With the difference between hire-purchase price and cost price of goods sold).
7. **To remove loading in hire purchase stock, i.e., in amount of instalments not yet due in respect of goods sold**
   Hire Purchase Trading a/c Dr.
   To Stock Reserve a/c
   (with the loading in the hire purchase stock at end).
8. **To transfer profit :**
   Hire Purchase Trading a/c Dr.
   To profit & loss a/c
   (with balance in hire purchase trading a/c).
9. **To transfer loss :**
   Profit & loss a/c Dr.
   To Hire Purchase Trading a/c

Note :-

Instalments due a/c. Hire Purchase Stock a/c and Stock Reserve a/c will be transferred to the hire purchase trading a/c of the next accounting period. During the current year they will appear in the balance sheet.

Problem 15

Arvin sells goods on hire purchase basis at a profit of 50% on cost. Following particulars are given to you relating to the business during 1999 :-

Hire purchase stock (at selling price) as 1-1-1999 9,000

Instalments due on 1st Jan. 1997	5,000
Goods sold on hire purchase during the year (at selling price)	87,000
Cash received from hire purchase customers during the year	60,000
Goods repossessed (Instalments due Rs. 2,000) valued at	500
Hire purchase stock (at selling price) as on 31st December 1999	30,000
Instalments due on 31st December 1999	9,000

Prepare Hire purchase trading account showing the profit earned for 1999.

(University of Madras, B. Com. May 2001)

Solution

Hire Purchase Trading A/c

Date		*Rs.*	*Date*		*Rs.*
1-1-99	To Hire purchase opening stock	9,000		By Cash received	60,000
	To Instalment due (opening)	5,000		By goods repossessed (at net value)	500
	To Goods sold on hire purchase	87,000	31-12-99	By Hire Purchase Closing Stock	30,000
	To Stock Reserve (closing stock of hire purchase stock loading) $30{,}000 \times \frac{50}{150}$	10,000		By Instalment due (closing)	9,000
	To Profit (Balancing figure)	20,500		By Stock reserve (Opening stock of hire purchase Stock — Loading) $9{,}000 \times \frac{50}{150}$	3,000
				By Goods sold on H.P. (loading) $87{,}000 \times \frac{50}{150}$	29,000
		1,31,500			1,31,500

Note :

Loading profit is given at 50% on cost. Whereas opening stock, goods sold on H. P, closing stock are given on selling price. Therefore $\frac{50}{150}$ on cost = $\frac{50}{100}$ on selling price charged.

Goods Sold on HP A/c

	Rs.		Rs.
To H.P. Trading a/c (loading) $87{,}000 \times \frac{50}{150}$	29,000	By H. P. Trading a/c	87,000
To Purchases (Balancing figure)	58,000		
	87,000		87,000

Stock Reserve A/c

	Rs.		Rs.
To H.P. Trading a/c (Opening Stock of H.P. stock loading)	3,000	By H.P. Trading a/c (Closing stock of hire purchase stock loading)	10,000

Problem 16

Brave-well Traders sell on Hire purchase terms consumer durables . Details of its activities during 1998 are given below :

Product	*Television*	*Washing machine*	*Motorcycle*
No. of units sold	100	80	40
Cost per unit	10,000	12,000	18,000
Price per unit payable on delivery	2,500	4,000	6,000
Balance in	10 monthly instalments of Rs. 1,250 each	32 bi-monthly instalments of Rs. 500 each	12 Quarterly instalment of Rs. 2,000 each
No of instalments received in 1998	980	1,600	110

Two washing machines on which only six instalments in all and one motor cycle on which 3 instalments were received were repossessed as the customers defaulted in payment of subsequent instalments. These were taken back at original cost less 30%.

Prepare Hire purchase trading a/c of Bravewell Traders for the year 1998.

(Calcutta University B. Com. (Hons.) 1999)

Solution

Working Notes :

1. **Calculation of Hire Purchase Sales :**

Down payment :-

T.V. (100 × 2,500) = 2,50,000
W. M. (80 × 4,000) = 3,20,000
M. C. (40 × 6,000) = 2,40,000

Add : Instalments received :-

T. V. (980 × 1,250) = 12,25,000
W. M. (1,600 × 500) = 8,00,000
M. C. (110 × 2,200) = 2,42,000

30,77,000

2. **Calculation of Return price :**

Cost of two washing machines

12,000 × 2 = 24,000

Cost of one motor cycle = 18,000

42,000

Less : 30% of cost 12,600

29,400

3. Calculation of Hire Purchase Closing Stock :

$$= \frac{\text{Cost Price}}{\text{Selling Price}} \times \text{Instalment not due}$$

$$\text{T.V.} = \frac{10{,}000}{15{,}000} \times (100 \times 10) - 980 \times 1{,}250 \quad = \quad 16{,}667$$

$$\text{W. M} = \frac{12{,}000}{20{,}000} \times (78 \times 32) - (1{,}600 - 6) \times 500 \quad = \quad 2{,}70{,}600$$

$$\text{M. C.} = \frac{18{,}000}{30{,}000} \times (39 \times 12) - (110 - 3) \times 2{,}000 \quad = \quad 4{,}33{,}200$$

$$7{,}20{,}467$$

In the Books Bravewell Traders Hire Purchase Trading A/c

	Rs.		*Rs.*
To General Trading a/c :		By H. P. Sales a/c	30,77,000
T.V. 10,000 × 100	10,00,000	By General Trading a/c	29,400
W. M. 12,000 × 80	9,60,000	(Return of W. M. and M. C)	
M. C. 18,000 × 40	7,20,000	By H.P. Closing stock	7,20,467
To General P & L a/c	11,46,867	c/d (at cost)	
— Profit			
	38,26,867		38,26,867

Problem 16

Bhaskar commenced business on 1-4-1993. He effected cash sales as well as hire purchase sales, the latter being cash price plus 12.5%. For the year ended March 31, 1994 following were his business

Particulars :	Rs.
Purchases	55,000
Cash Sales	12,000
Receipts from debtors	22,500
Closing stock at cost	19,000
Hire purchase sales	31,500

Prepare Trading account, Hire purchase Trading a/c for 1993-94.

(Osmania University B. Com. March 1998)

Solution

Working Notes :

1. Calculation of Unrealised Profit :

Let cost price =	Rs. 100
Add : Profit =	Rs. 12.50
Selling price	Rs. 112.50

If selling price is Rs. 112.50 – Cost is Rs, 100.

If selling price is Rs. 31,500 → ?

$$\frac{31,500}{112.50} \times 100 = 28,000$$

Selling price	= 31,500
Cost	= 28,000
Unrealised profit	3,500

2. Ascertainment of Instalment due :

Goods sent on H. P.	31,500
Less : Cash received	22,500
Instalment due	9,000

Hire Purchase Trading A/c

	Rs.		Rs.
To Goods sent on H.P.	31500	By Cash a/c	22,500
To Profit & loss a/c	3,500	By Instalment due a/c	9,000
		By Goods sent on H.P.	3,500
	35,000		35,000

General Trading A/c

		Rs.		Rs.
To Purchases	55,000		By Cash sales a/c	12,000
Less : Cost of goods Sold on H.P.	28,000		By Closing stock a/c	19,000
		27,000		
To Gross Profit		4,000		
		31,000		31,000

STOCK AND DEBTORS SYSTEM

This is a method which is also used to record transactions relating to numerous articles which are of comparatively small value sold on hire purchase basis. Under this method the following accounts are maintained.

(*a*) Hire Purchase Stock a/c
(*b*) Hire Purchase Debtors a/c
(*c*) Hire Purchase Adjustment a/c

The following entries are involved under this method

(*a*) **On Sale of Goods :**

Hire Purchase Stock a/c	Dr.	(with H.P. price)
To Goods Sold on H.P. a/c		(with cost price of goods sold)
To H.P. Adjustment a/c		(with excess of hire purchase price over cost price of goods sold)

(*b*) **When Instalments fall due :**

H.P. Debtors a/c	Dr.	(with amount of instalments falling due)
To H.P. Stock a/c		

(*c*) **When Cash received in Payment of Instalment :**

Cash a/c	Dr.	(with amount actually received)
To H.P. Debtors a/c		

(*d*) **When goods are repossessed in default**

Repossessed Stock a/c	Dr.	(Estimated value)
H. P. Adjustment a/c	Dr.	(Loss on revaluation)
To H.P. Debtors a/c		(Total instalment due)

(*e*) **At the end of the year :**

H.P. Adjustment a/c	Dr.	(With loading in the closing stock with H.P. customers)
To stock Reserve a/c		

(*f*) **For Transfer of Profit :**

H.P. Adjustment a/c	Dr.	(With amount of profit)
To P & L a/c		

(*g*) **For Transfer of Loss :**

P & L a/c	Dr.	
To H.P. Adjustment a/c		

(*h*) **For Transfer of Cost of Goods Sold on Hire Purchase :**

Goods sold on hire purchase a/c	Dr.	(With balance in goods on H.P. a/c)
To Trading a/c or purchase a/c		

Note :

Hire purchase stock a/c, Hire Purchase Debtors a/c and stock reserve a/c shows balances which are carried froward to the books of the next year. In the next year Stock Reserve a/c is transferred to Hire Purchase adjustment a/c, the entry being. (with opening balance of stock reserve)

Stock Reserve	Dr.
To H.P. Adjustment a/c	

Problem 17

Simpson Company Ltd., which sells a patent product on hire purchase terms, has the following transactions for the year to 31st December 1998. The gross profit is 25% on selling price.

1998		Rs.
Jan. 1,	Stock out on hire at H.P. price	40,000
	Stock on hand (at shop)	5,000
	Instalment due (customers still paying)	3,000
Dec. 31,	Stock out on hire at H.P. price	46,000
	Stock on hand (at shop)	7,000
	Instalments due (customers still paying)	5000
	Cash received in instalment during the year	80,000

Prepare necessary accounts to find out gross profit of Simpson Company Ltd., for the year to 31st December 1998. **(University of Madras B. Com. May 2000)**

Solution

Hire Purchase Stock A/c

Date		Rs.	Date		Rs.
1-1-98	To Stock out on hire To Shop Stock a/c (Balancing figure)- Goods sold on H.P. **Transfer to shop** Profit 88,000 × $\frac{25}{125}$ = 22,000 Cost = 66,000 88,000	40,000 88,000	 31-12-98	By H.P. Debtors a/c (Transfer from H.P. debtors a/c) By Stock out on hire	82,000 46000
		1,28,000			1,28,000

Hire Purchase Debtors A/c

Date		Rs.	Date		Rs.
1-1-98	To Balance b/d To H.P. stock a/c (Balancing figure)	3,000 82,000	 31-12-98	By Cash received in Instalments By Balance c/d	 80,000 5,000
		85,000			85,000

Shop Stock A/c

Date		Rs.	Date		Rs.
1-1-98	To Balance b/d To Purchases (Balancing figure)	5,000 68,000	 31-12-98	By H.P. Stock (cost only) [Transfer from H.P. Stock a/c] By Balance c/d	66,000 7,000
		73,000			73,000

Hire Purchase Adjustment A/c

Date		Rs.	Date		Rs.
	To H.P. Stock a/c (closing stock loading) 46,000 × $\frac{25}{100}$ To Gross profit a/c	11500 20,500		By H.P. Stock a/c (loading) 88,000 × $\frac{25}{100}$ By H.P. stock a/c (Op. stock loading) 40,000 × $\frac{25}{100}$	22,000 10,000
		32,000			32,000

Problem 18

X sells goods at hire purchase system, the price being cost plus 50%. From the following calculate profit by preparing ledger accounts on stock and debtors system for the year ended 31st March 2000.

1999		
April 1,	Stock at cost price	3,60,000
	Stock out with hire-purchase-customers at selling price	1,80,000
	Instalments due	1,00,000
2000		
Mar. 31,	Cash received from customers	12,00,000
	Goods repossessed (Rs. 40,000) valued at	12,000
	Instalment due at the end of the year	1,80,000
	Stock at the shop at the end of the year, at cost	4,00,000
	Instalments not yet due on 31-3- 2000	6,00,000
	Purchases made during the year.	12,00,000

(CS Foundation June 2000)

Solution

Hire Purchase Stock A/c

Date		Rs.	Date		Rs.
1999 Apr. 1,	To Balance b/d	1,80,000	1999 Apr. 1,	By H.P. Debtors a/c	13,20,000
2000 Mar. 31,	To Goods sent on H.P. a/c	17,40,000	2000 Mar. 31,	By Balance c/d	6,00,000
		19,20,000			19,20,000

Hire Purchase Debtors A/c

Date		Rs.	Date		Rs.
1999 Apr. 1,	To Balance b/d	1,00,000	1999 Apr. 1,	By Cash a/c	12,00,000
				By Goods Repossessed a/c	1,20,000
2000 Mar.31,	To H.P. Stock a/c	13,20,000		By H.P. Adjustment a/c	28,000
			2000 Mar. 31,	By Balance c/d	1,80,000
		14,20,000			14,20,000

Goods Sold on H.P. A/c

Date		Rs.	Date		Rs.
				By Hire Purchase Stock a/c	17,40,000
2000 Mar. 31,	To H.P. Adjustment a/c	5,80,000			
	To Trading a/c — Transfer	11,60,000			
		17,40,000			17,40,000

Hire Purchase Adj. A/c

Date		Rs.	Date		Rs.
2000 Mar.31,	To H.P. Debtors a/c (Loss on default by customers)	28,000	2000 Mar. 31,	By H.P. Stock Reserve a/c $1{,}80{,}000 \times \frac{50}{150}$	60,000
	To H.P. Stock Reserve a/c $(6{,}00{,}000 \times \frac{50}{150})$	2,00,000		By Goods sold on H. P. a/c $17{,}40{,}000 \times \frac{50}{150}$	5,80,000
	To P & L a/c — Transfer of profit	4,12,000			
		6,40,000			6,40,000

Working Notes :

Calculation of goods sold during the year at purchase price :

	Opening stock at cost	3,60,000
Add :	purchase	12,00,000
		15,60,000
Loss :	closing stock	4,80,000
	Cost of goods sold	11,60,000

$$\text{H.P. Price} = 11{,}60{,}000 \times \frac{150}{100} = \text{Rs. } 17{,}40{,}000$$

QUESTIONS

Simple Questions

1. Define Hire purchase system of sale.
2. What do you mean by cash price ?
3. What do you mean by hire purchase price ?
4. What is down payment ?
5. State four features of hire purchase system.
6. State four points of difference between hire purchase and a sale transaction.

EXERCISE 1

Mr. Ashish Purchased a motor bike on hire purchase system on 1-4-1996. Total cash price of motor bike was Rs. 63,920 payable Rs. 15,920 down and 3 instalment of Rs. 16,000 each plus interest at 5% payable at the end of each year. Depreciation is to be charged at 10% p.a. on straight line method.

Pass entries in the books of Mr. Ashish.**(Bangalore University B. Com. April 2001)**

EXERCISE 2

On 1st April 1998 a machinery was purchase on H.P. System. The cash price of machinery was Rs. 34,860. The amount payable was Rs. 10,000 on signing the contract and Rs. 10,000 annually for three years at the end of each year. The hire vendor has charged 10% interest per annum. Show the hire vendor a/c in the books of the buyer.

(University of Madras, B. Com., April 1999)

Answer : Interest Rs. 5,140.
Cash Price Rs. 34,860
Total of HIre Vendor a/c for the last year Rs. 10,000.

EXERCISE 3

On 1st January 1998 'Y' bought a water cooler from 'X' under the hire purchase system. The cash price of which being Rs. 10,450 as per the following terms :

(*a*) Rs. 3,000 to be paid on signing the agreement.
(*b*) Balance to be paid in three instalments of Rs. 3,000 each at the end of every year.
(*c*) Rate of interest payable at Rs. 10% p.a.

Prepare the Hire Vendor account to show the interest payable as per the terms

(Osmania University, B. Com., October 1999)

Answer : Total of Hire Vendor a/c for the last year is Rs. 3,000.

EXERCISE 4

Ravi and Company purchased a machine on hire-purchase system on 1-1-96. Its cash price is Rs. 45,000. The payment is to be made in 4 half yearly instalments of Rs. 12,500 each. Rate of interest is 8% per annum. Machine was destroyed by an accident on 1-1-98 and Ravi and Company received Rs. 35,000 from Insurance Company. The company charges depreciation on machinery @ 10% per annum on fixed instalment method. Ravi and Company closes books on 31st December each year.

Prepare machine account interest a/c, Depreciation a/c and Hire Vendor a/c in the books of Ravi and Co.

(Sri Venkateshwara University, B. Com. October 1999)

Answer : Total of hire vendor's a/c for the last year Rs. 25,000.
Total of Interest a/c Rs. 1,828 for the last year
Total of Machinery a/c for the last year Rs. 36,000

EXERCISE 5

(Repossession)

'P' Purchased a truck for Rs. 56,000. Payment to be made Rs, 15,000 down and 3 instalment of Rs. 15,000 each at the end of each year. Rate of interest is charged at 5% p.a. Buyer depreciates assets at 10% on written down value method. Because of financial difficulties P, after having made down payment and first instalment at the end of 1st year, could not pay second instalment and seller took possession of the truck. Seller after spending Rs. 350 on repairs of the asset, sold it away for Rs. 30,110. Show the ledger accounts in the books of both, the parties.

(University of Madras, B. Com. May 1998)

Answer : Total of hire vendor a/c :-
Ist year - 58,050, IInd year - 29,453
Total of truck a/c Rs. 50,400
Total of P's a/c :-
Ist year - 58,050, II year - 29,453
Total of goods repossessed a/c Rs. 30,110.

EXERCISE 6

From the following particular calculate

(*i*) Value of plant taken back by the vendor.
(*ii*) Value of plant left with the purchaser
(*iii*) Profit or loss on plant taken back.
(*iv*) Profit or loss on plant repossessed when sold by vendor .

Particulars :-

(*i*) X purchased 3 plants form Y costing Rs. 1,00,000 each.
(*ii*) Purchaser charged depreciation @ 20% on diminishing balance method.
(*iii*) 2 plants were seized by the vendor when second instalment was not paid at the end of second year and vendor valued the plants at cost less 30% depreciation annually charged at diminishing balance method.
(*iv*) The vendor spent Rs. 40,000 on over hauling the plants and sold for Rs. 1,60,000.

(Delhi University B. Com. (Hons. 1999)

Answer : 1. Value of plants taken by vendor Rs. 98,000.
2. Value of plant (i) left with the purchaser Rs. 64,000.
3. Loss to the purchaser on plants taken back by the vendor Rs. 30,000
4. Profit to the vendor on plant repossessed when resold Rs. 22,000.

EXERCISE 7

(Stock and Debtors System)

Prepare H.P. Trading a/c to find profit or loss of the trader from the following H.P. transactions.

H. P. Price = Cost + 60%

Jan. 1,	Stock with H.P. customers at H.P. price	6,480
Dec. 31,	Goods sold on H.P. basis during the year	26,136
	Cash received from H.P. customers during the year	8,400
	Stock with H.P. customers at H. P. price	22,696

(Delhi University B. Com. (Hons.) 1997)

Answer : Net Profit on preparing H.P. Trading a/c Rs. 3,720
Total of H.P. Debtors a/c Rs. 9,920
Total of H.P. Stock a/c Rs. 32,616
Total of H.P. Adj. a/c Rs. 12,231

EXERCISE 8

A limited company sells a patent product on hire purchase terms. It has the following transactions for the year ending 31st March 1994.

		Rs.
1993 1st Apr.,		
	Stock out on hire at hire purchase price	1,20,000
	Stock on hand (at shop)	15,000
	Instalments due (customers still paying)	9,000

1994
31st Mar.,

Stock out on hire at hire purchase price	1,38,000
Stock on hand (at shop)	21,000
Instalments due (customers still paying)	15,000
Cash received in instalments during the year	2,40,000

The business follows the practice of charging gross profit at 25% of selling price.

Prepare the necessary ledger accounts to record thee transactions in the books of the limited company in a manner as to show the cost of purchase made, and the profit earned by the company during the year. **(Delhi University B. Com. (Hons.) 1994)**

Answer : Total of H.P. Stock a/c Rs. 3,84,000
Total of H.P. Debtors a/c Rs. 2,55,000
Total of H.P. Adjustment a/c Rs. 96,000
Total of shop Stock a/c Rs. 2,19,000

29

CHAPTER

Instalment System

INTRODUCTION

Instalment system of selling is a contract of sale under which the purchaser gets the possessions of goods immediately on payment of down price and agrees to pay the price of the goods in a certain number of instalments. As the ownership of the goods passes to the purchaser on the date of contract itself the seller cannot take away the goods in the case of failure to pay the instalments. The features of instalment system are as follows :

1. The instalment purchaser gets possession of the goods as well as ownership on signing the contract.
2. The instalment purchaser agrees to pay the price of the goods in certain number of instalments.
3. In case of his failure to do so, the seller cannot take away the goods as the ownership has already passed on to the instalment purchaser. The seller can sue for the amount due.
4. The instalment purchaser cannot returns the goods to the seller if he is not satisfied with the goods as the ownership passes on from the seller to the buyer.

Differences between Hire Purchase and Instalment System

Hire Purchase System	*Instalment System*
1. It is an agreement of hiring.	**1.** It is an agreement of out right purchase.
2. The ownership remains with the hire vendor until the last instalment is paid.	**2.** Ownership passes to the seller immedi ately on signing the agreement.
3. The hire purchaser may return back the goods if he is dissatisfied with the goods.	**3.** Goods cannot be returned unless there is some fault with the seller.
4. The seller can take possession of goods if hirer commits a default.	**4.** The seller cannot take the possession of goods on default. Instead he can sue for the price.
5. The buyer cannot hire-out, sell, pledge, assign, or transfer goods	**5.** The buyer may dispose of and give good title to any bonafide purchaser.

Interest Suspense account

Under Instalment system the instalment price of goods includes interest payable or receivable on all instalments. The total interest cannot be treated as expenditure or income till it is actually paid or received. So a separate account known as interest suspense account is created and the total interest is transferred to it.

ENTRIES IN THE BOOKS OF INSTALMENT PURCHASER

1. On delivery of Asset to the Instalment Purchaser

Asset a/c	Dr.	(with cash price)
Interest Suspense a/c	Dr.	(with total interest)
To Vendor's a/c	Dr.	(with total payment)

2. For the down payment made

Vendor's a/c	Dr.
To Bank a/c	

3. For transferring each instalment interest from the interest suspense a/c to interest a/c

Interest a/c	Dr.
To Interest Suspense a/c	

4. For payment of first instalment

Vendor's a/c	Dr.
To Bank a/c	

5. For charging of depreciation

Depreciation a/c	Dr.
To Asset a/c	

6. For transfer of interest and the depreciation for the accounting year to the Profit & Loss a/c

Profit & Loss a/c	Dr.
To Interest a/c	
To Depreciation a/c	

Note :

(1) Entries (3) To (6) will be repeated in subsequent years for different instalments.

(2) Balance of the interest suspense a/c will appear on the asset side of the balance sheet.

Entries in the books of the vendor

1. On the date of sale :

Purchaser a/c	Dr.	(with the total payment)
To Sales a/c		(with cash price)
To Interest Suspense a/c		(with total interest)

2. For receiving down payment :

Bank a/c	Dr.
To Purchaser a/c	

3. At the end of each instalment :

(*a*) For transferring each instalment interest from the interest suspense a/c to interest a/c

Interest Suspense a/c Dr.
To Interest a/c

(b) For the receipt of instalment money :

Bank a/c Dr.
To Purchaser a/c

(c) For transferring the interest to profit and loss a/c

Interest a/c Dr.
To Profit & Loss a/c

Note :

(*i*) Entries 3 (*a*) (*b*) (*c*) will be repeated for subsequent instalments.

(*ii*) Balance of Interest Suspense a/c will appear on the liability side of the Balance Sheet.

Problem 1

Based on the date given below give entries in the books of both the parties under instalment system.

Purchaser	—	Gopal
Seller	—	Arvind
Goods sold	—	Machinery
Date of contract	—	1st April 2000
Cash price	—	Rs. 74,500

Instalment payable - Rs. 20,000 by way of down payment, balance in three annual instalment of Rs. 20,000 each.

Rate of interest - 5% per annum.

Depreciation on machinery - 10% per annum on diminishing balances.

Also show important ledger accounts.

Solution

Working Note :

1. Calculation of interest

Cash price	74,500
Less : Down payment	20,000
	54,500
Add : Interest on 54,500 For one year at 5%	2,725
	57,225
Less : Amount paid on 31-3-2001	20,000
	37,225
Add : Interest on Rs. 37,225 at 5%	1,861
	39,056
Less : Amount paid on 31-3-2002	20,000
	19,056
Add : Interest (20,000 - 19,086)	914
	20,000
Less : Amount paid on 31-3-2003	20,000
	Nil

In The Books of Gopal

Date	Particulars		Dr. Amount	Cr. Amount
2000 Apr. 1,	Machinery a/c	Dr.	74,500	
	Interest Suspense a/c	Dr.	5,500	
	To Arvind's a/c			80,000
	(Purchase of Machinery under instalment system)			
	Arvind's a/c	Dr.	20,000	
	To Bank a/c			20,000
	(Being down payment made)			
2001 Mar. 31,	Arvind's a/c	Dr.	20,000	
	To Bank a/c			20,000
	(Being the 1st instalment paid)			
	Interest a/c	Dr.	2,725	
	To Interest Suspense a/c			2,725
	(Transfer of first year's interest from interest suspense a/c to interest a/c)			
	Depreciation a/c	Dr.	7,450	
	To Machinery a/c			7,450
	(Depreciation on Machinery @ 10% p.a.)			
	Profit & Loss a/c	Dr.	10,175	
	To Interest a/c			2,725
	To Depreciation a/c			7,450
	(Transfer of interest and depreciation to P & L a/c)			
2002 Mar. 31,	Arvind's a/c	Dr.	20,000	
	To Bank a/c			20,000
	(Being the payment of IInd instalment)			
	Interest a/c	Dr.	1,861	
	To Interest Suspense a/c			1,861
	(Transfer of 2nd years interest from interest suspense a/c)			
	Depreciation a/c	Dr.	6,705	
	To Machinery a/c			6,705
	(Being Machinery depreciated)			
	P & L a/c	Dr.	8,566	
	To Interest a/c			1,861
	To Depreciation a/c			6,705
	(Transfer of interest and depreciation to P & L a/c)			
2003 Mar. 31,	Arvind's a/c	Dr.	20,000	
	To Bank's a/c			20,000
	(Being the payment of IIIrd instalment)			
	Interest a/c	Dr.	914	
	To Interest Suspense a/c			914
	(Transfer of the year's interest form interest suspense a/c)			

Date	Particulars		Dr.. Amount	Cr. Amount
	Depreciation a/c	Dr.	6,034.50	
	To Macheinery a/c			6,034.50
	(Depreciation on Macheinery)			
	Profit & Loss a/c	Dr.	6,948.50	
	To Interset a/c			914
	To Depreciation a/c			6,034.50
	(Transfer of interest and depriciation to P & L a/c)			

Machinery A/c

Date		Rs.	Date		Rs.
2000 Apr. 1,	To Arvind's a/c	74,500	2001 Mar. 31	By Depreciation a/c	7,450
				By Balance c/d	67,050
		74,500			74,500
2001 Apr. 1,	To Balance b/d	67,050	2002 Mar. 31	By Depreciation a/c	6,705
				By Balance c/d	60,345
		67,050			67,050
2002 Apr. 1,	To Balance b/d	60,345	2003 Mar. 31	By Depreciation	6,034.50
				By Balance c/d	54,310.50
		60,345			60,345

Arvind's A/c

Date		Rs.	Date		Rs.
2000 Apr. 1,	To Bank a/c	20,000	2000 Apr. 1	By Machinery a/c	74,500
2001 Mar. 31,	To Bank a/c	20,000		By Interest Suspense a/c	5,500
	To Balance c/d	40,000			
		80,000			80,000
2002 Mar. 31,	To Bank a/c	20,000	2001 Apr. 1,	By Balance b/d	40,000
	To Balance c/d	20,000			
		40,000			40,000
2003 Mar. 31,	To Bank a/c	20,000	2002 Apr. 1,	By Balance b/d	20,000

Interest Suspense A/c

Date		Rs.	Date		Rs.
2000 Apr. 1,	To Arvind's a/c	5,500	2001 Mar. 31	By Interest a/c	2,725
				By Balance	2,775
		5,500			5,500

Date		Rs.	Date		Rs.
2001 Apr. 1,	To Balance b/d	2,775	2002 Mar. 31	By Interest a/c By Balance c/d	1,861 914
		2,775			2,775
2002 Mar. 1,	To Balance b/d	914	2003 Mar. 31	By Interest a/c	914

Interest A/c

Date		Rs.	Date		Rs.
2001 Mar. 31	BY P & L a/c	2,725	2001 Mar. 31	To Interest Suspense a/c	2,725
2002 Mar. 31	By P & L a/c	1,861	2002 Mar. 31	To Interest Suspense a/c	1,861
2003 Mar. 31	By P & L a/c	914	2003 Mar. 31	To Interest Suspense a/c	914

In the Books of Arvind

Date	Particulars		Dr.. Amount	Cr. Amount
2000 Apr. 1,	Gopal's a/c To Sales a/c To Interest Suspense a/c (Being sale of machinery under instalment system)	Dr.	80,000	 74,500 5,500
	Bank a/c To Gopal a/c (Being down payment received)	Dr.	20,000	 20,000
2001 Mar. 31,	Bank a/c To Gopal's a/c (Being 1st instalment received)	Dr.	20,000	 20,000
	Interest Suspense a/c To Interest a/c (Transfer of interest for the year from interest suspense a/c)	Dr.	2,725	 2,725
	Interest a/c To Profit & Loss a/c (Transfer of interest a/c to P & L a/c)	Dr.	2,725	 2,725
2002 Mar. 31,	Bank a/c To Gopal a/c (Being 2nd instalment received)	Dr.	20,000	 20,000

Date	Particulars		Dr. Amount	Cr. Amount
	Interest Suspense a/c	Dr.	1,861	
	To Interest a/c			1,861
	(Entry for year's interest)			
	Interest a/c	Dr.	1,861	
	To P & L a/c			1,861
	(Transfer of interest a/c to Profit & Loss a/c)			
2003 Mar. 31,	Bank a/c	Dr.	20,000	
	To Gopal's a/c			20,000
	(Being last instalment received)			
	Interest Suspense a/c	Dr.	914	
	To Interest a/c			914
	(Entry for years interest)			
	Interest a/c	Dr.	914	
	To P & L a/c			914
	(Transfer of interest to P & L a/c)			

Ledger A/c

Gopal's A/c

Date		Rs.	Date		Rs.
April 1,	To Sales a/c	74,500	April 1,	By Bank a/c	20,000
	To Interest Suspense a/c	5,500	2001 Mar. 31	By Bank a/c	20,000
				By Balance c/d	40,000
		80,000			80,000
2001 Apr. 1,	To Balance b/d	40,000	2002 Mar. 31	By Bank a/c	20,000
				By Balance c/d	20,000
		40,000			40,000
2002 April 1,	To Balance b/d	20,000	2003 Mar. 31	By Bank a/c	20,000

Interest Suspense A/c

Date		Rs.	Date		Rs.
2001 Mar. 31	To Interest a/c	2,725	2001 April 1,	By Gopal's a/c	5,500
	To Balance c/d	2,775			
		5,500			5,500
2002 Mar. 31	To Interest a/c	1,861	2002 Apr. 1	By Balance b/d	2,775
	To Balance c/d	914			
		2,775			2,775
2003 Mar. 31	To Interest a/c	914	2003 Apr. 1,	By Balance b/d	914

Interest A/c

Date		*Rs.*	*Date*		*Rs.*
2001 Mar. 31	To P & L a/c	2,725	2001 Mar. 31	By Interest Suspense a/c	2,725
2002 Mar. 31	To P & L a/c	1,861	2002 Mar. 31	By Interest Suspense a/c	1,861
2003 Mar. 31	To P & L a/c	914	2003 Mar. 31	By Interest Suspense	914

Problem 2

On 1st January 1994, The Sarat & Co. bought machinery from Sakthi Ltd, on the instalment system. The cash price of machinery was Rs. 22,500. An amount of Rs. 6,000 was to be paid on the signing of the agreement and the balance in three instalments of Rs. 6,000 each at the end of each year. 5% interest is charged by the Sakthi Ltd. per annum. The company has decided to write off 10% depreciation annually on diminishing balance method.

Show the ledger accounts in the books of Sarat & Co.

(Sri Venkateshwara University B.Com. September 2000)

Solution

Working Note

Cash price	22,500
Less : Down payment	6,000
	16,500
Add : Interest @ 5% on 16,500	825
	17,325
Less : Ist Instalment paid	6,000
	11,323
Add : Interest @ 5% on 11,323	566
	11889
Less : IInd Instalment paid	6,000
	5,889
Add : Interest (6,000 - 5,889)	111
	6,000
Less : IIIrd Instalment paid	6,000
	Nil

Sakthi Company A/c (Vendor)

Date		*Rs.*	*Date*		*Rs.*
1-1-94	To Bank a/c	6,000	1-1-94	By Machinery a/c	22,500
			31-12-94	By Interest Suspense a/c	1,500
	To Bank a/c	6,000			
31-12-94	To Balance	12,000			
		24,000			24,000

Date		Rs.	Date		Rs.
31-12-95	To Bank a/c	6,000	31-12-95	By Balance b/d	12,000
	To Balance c/d	6,000			
		12,000			12,000
31-12-96	To Bank a/c	6,000	31-12-96	By Balance b/d	6,000

Machinery A/c

Date		Rs.	Date		Rs.
1-1-94	To Sakthi Co. a/c	22,500	31-12-94	By Depreciation a/c	2,250
				By Balance c/d	20,250
		22,500			22,500
1-1-95	To Balance b/d	20,250	31-12-95	By Depreciation	2,025
				By Balance c/d	18,225
		20,250			20,250
1-1-96	To Balance b/d	18,225	31-12-96	By Depreciation	1,822
				" Balance c/d	16,403
		18,225			18,225

Interest Suspense A/c

Date		Rs.	Date		Rs.
1-1-94	To Sakthi Co. a/c	1,500	31-12-94	By Interest a/c	825
				Balance c/d	675
		1,500			1,500
1-5-95	To Balance b/d	675	31-12-95	By Interest a/c	566
				By Balance c/d	109
		675			675
1-196	To Balance b/d	109	31-12-96	By Interest a/c	109

Interest A/c

Date		Rs.	Date		Rs.
31-12-94	To Interest Suspense a/c	825	31-12-94	By P & L a/c	825
31-12-95	To Interest Suspense a/c	566	31-12-95	By P & L a/c	566
31-12-96	To Interest Suspense a/c	109	31-12-96	By P & L a/c	109

Problem 3

The Mopeds Limited sold a motor cycle on instalment system to Electrical Limited. The cash price was Rs. 7,450. Rs. 2,000 was to be paid on delivery and the balance in three instalments of Rs. 2,000 each at the end of each year. The Mopeds Limited charge interest at the rate of 5% per annum.

Show the account of Mopeds limited in the books of Electronics Ltd.

(Osmania University B.Com, April 1999)

Solution

Calculation of interest

	Cash price	7,450
Less :	Down payment	2,000
		5,450
Add :	Interest @ 5% on 5,450	272
		5,722
Less :	Ist Instalment	2,000
		3,722
Add :	Interest @ 5% on 3,722	186
		3,908
Less :	IInd Instalment	2,000
		1,908
Add :	Interest (2,000 – 1,908)	92
		2,000
Less :	IIIrd Instalment	2,000
		Nil

In the books of Electronics Ltd.

Mopeds Limited Account

Date		*Rs.*	*Date*		*Rs.*
Ist year	To Bank a/c	2,000	I year	By Motor Cycle a/c	7,450
	To Bank a/c	2,000		By Interest Suspense a/c	550
	To Balance c/d	4,000			
		8,000			8,000
II year	To Bank a/c	2,000	II year	By Balance b/d	4,000
	To Balance c/d	2,000			
		4,000			4,000
III year	To Bank a/c	2,000	III year	By Balance b/d	2,000

Problem 3

Caravan Company purchases a motor car from Madurai Motor Company on the instalment system on January 1, 1991, paying cash Rs 10,000 and agreeing to pay three further instalments of Rs. 10,000 each on December 31, every year. The cash price of the car is Rs. 37,250 and the Madurai Motor Company charges interest at 5% per annum. Caravan Co. writer off 10% per annunm as depreciation on the written down value system. Journalise the transactions in the books of Caravan Company. **(University of Madras B.Com, April 1998)**

Solution

Calculation of interest

	Cash price	37,250
Less :	Down payment	10,000
		27,250
Add :	Interest @ 5% on 27,250	1,362
		28,612
Less :	Ist instalment paid	10,000
		18,612
Add :	Interest @ 5% on 18,612	930
		19,542
Less :	IInd instalment paid	10,000
		9,542
Add :	Interest (10,000 - 9,542)	458
		10,000
Less :	IIIrd Instalment paid	10000
		Nil

Calculation of Depreciation

Cash price	37,250.00
I year less depreciation	3,725.00
	33,525.00
II year Less Depreciation	3,352.50
	30,172.50
III year Less : Depreciation	3,017.25
	27,155.25

In the Books of Caravan Company (Buyer)

Journal Entries

Date	*Particulars*		*Dr. Amount*	*Cr. Amount*
1-1-91	Motor Car a/c	Dr.	37,250	
	Interest Suspense a/c	Dr.	2,750	
	To Madurai Motor Co. a/c			40,000
	(Being the Motor car purchased under instalment system)			
	Madurai Motor Co. a/c	Dr.	10,000	
	To Cash a/c			10,000
	(Being the down payment made)			
31-12-91	Madurai Motor Co. a/c	Dr.	10,000	
	To Cash a/c			10,000
	(Being the instalment paid)			
	Interest a/c	Dr.	1,362	
	To Interest Suspense a/c			1,362
	(Being the transfer of first year interest)			

Date	Particulars		Dr. Amount	Cr. Amount
	Depreciation a/c	Dr.	3,725	
	To Motor car a/c			3,725
	(Being Depreciation on 37,250 @ 10%)			
	Profit & Loss a/c	Dr.	5,087	
	To Interest a/c			1,362
	To Depreciation a/c			3,725
	(Being the interest and depreciation transferred to P & L a/c at the end of the year).			
31-12-92	Madurai Motor Co. a/c	Dr.	10,000	
	To Cash a/c			10,000
	(Being the IInd Instalment paid)			
	Interest a/c	Dr.	930	
	To Interest Suspense a/c			930
	(Being the transfer of second years interest)			
	Depreciation a/c	Dr.	3,352	
	To Motor car a/c			3,352
	(Being the depreciation on 33,525 @ 10%)			
	P & L a/c	Dr.	4,283	
	To Interest a/c			930
	To Depreciation a/c			3,352
	(Being the interest and depreciation transferred to P & L a/c)			
31-12-93	Madurai Motor Co. a/c	Dr.	10,000	
	To Cash a/c			10,000
	(Being the IIIrd instalment paid)			
	Interest a/c	Dr.	458	
	To Interest suspense a/c			458
	(Being the transfer of third year's interest)			
	Depreciation a/c	Dr.	3,017	
	To Motor car a/c			3,017
	(Being the Depreciation on 30,172)			
	P & L a/c	Dr.	3,475	
	To Interest			458
	To Depreciation			3,017
	(Being the interest and depreciation transferred to P & L a/c).			

Problem 5

Raghu Purchased on instalment basis a machine, from yughander on 1-4-1995 for a sum of Rs. 80,000. Rs. 20,000 is to be paid on signing the contract and the rest in three instalments of Rs. 20,000 each . The cash price of the machine is Rs. 74,500. Find interest for the first 3 financial years. **(Osmania University B.Com, March 1997)**

Solution

Total Instalment sum	= 80,000
Less cash price	= 74,500
	5,500

1995- 96 Amount outstanding for interest after down payment	Rs. 60,000
1996-97 Amount outstanding for interest after the 1st instalment	Rs. 40,000
1997-98 Amount outstanding for interest after the 2nd instalment	Rs. 20,000

The interest for all the three years is Rs. 5,500 which should be divided in the ratio of 3 : 2 : 1.

Hence the interest comes to :-

	Rs.
$1995 - 96 = 5{,}500 \times \frac{3}{6}$ =	2,750
$1996 - 97 = 5{,}500 \times \frac{2}{6}$ =	1,833
$1997 - 98 = 5{,}500 \times \frac{1}{6}$ =	917
	5,500

QUESTIONS

Simple Questions

1. What do you mean by Instalment system ?
2. State the features of instalment system.
3. Mentions 4 points of differences between Hire purchase and instalment system.
4. What is a interest suspense a/c.

EXERCISE 1

Under an instalment system the purchaser paid Rs. 10,000 as down payment and paid Rs. 6,200, Rs. 5,800 and Rs. 5,400 at the end of 1st, 2nd and 3rd years respectively which included interest at 8%. Find the cash price of the asset.

(Osmania University B.Com, March 1998)

Answer

Closing Balance	*Amt. of Instalment*	*Total*	*Interest* $\frac{8}{108}$	*Opening Balance*
Nil	5,400	5,400	400	5,000
5,000	5,800	10,800	800	10,000
10,000	6,200	16,200	1,200	15,000

Cash price = Down payment + 15,000

= 10,000 + 15,000

= 25,000

EXERCISE 2

Mr. Raman bought a machine on instalment basis by paying Rs. 2,000 on 1-1-1995. The date of signing the agreement and the balance in four half-yearly instalments of Rs. 4,000 each, interest charged @ 10% p.a. Show how interest suspense a/c appear in Raman's book.

(Osmania University B.Com, October 1998)

Answer :		
	Interest of Last Instalment	Rs. 190
	Interest of 3rd Instalment	Rs. 372
	Interest of 2nd Instalment	Rs. 545
	Interest of 1st Instalment	Rs. 709
	Total of Interest Suspense a/c of 1st year	Rs. 1,816
	Total of Interest Suspense a/c of 2nd year	Rs. 562

EXERCISE 3

Mr. James purchased a colour T. V. Costing Rs. 20,000 on 1-4-95 from Uday Electronics under instalment system, the terms being Rs. 5,000 down and the balance in three equal annual instalments together with interest @ 20% p.a. on the outstanding cash price. Depreciation was to be charged at 15% p.a. under straight line method. Prepare necessary ledger accounts in the books of James till 31-3-1998. **(Bangalore University B.Com, April 2000)**

EXERCISE 4

Osaka Co. Purchased a truck under instalment system for a cash price of Rs. 46,500. Rs. 1,500 is to be paid on signing the agreement the balance is payable in three instalments of Rs. 15,000 cash together with interest. Depreciation is to be charged @ 10% per annum on the reducing balance method. Prepare the truck a/c of the 1st three and calculate the total interest. **(Bangalore University B.Com, April 1999)**

EXERCISE 5

Mr. 'X' bought on 1st Jan. 1995 an Ambassador car from Bengal distributors Ltd. The agreements provided payment of Rs. 60,000 on delivery and 3 instalments of Rs. 60,000 each to be paid on 31st Dec. every year. The cash price of the car was Rs. 2,23,500. The vendors charged interest at 5% p.a. yearly balance.

Show Bengal Distributors Ltd. a/c in the books of X using instalment payment.

(Bangalore University B.Com, April 1998)

EXERCISE 6

Sita Tailoring House purchases a few sewing machines from Krishna Brothers of Lucknow under instalment purchase system on 1st Jan. 1995. As per the agreement payments were made as under :

	Rs.
On 1-1-95	4,000
On 31-12-95	4,700
On 31-12-96	4,500
On 31-12-97	2,500
On 31-12-98	1,000

Each instalment includes interest @ 10% p.a. Provide depreciation 15% p.a. on the written down value of the machine. Open necessary accounts in the books of Sita Tailoring House.

(Allahabad University B.Com, 1999)

30

CHAPTER

Departmental Accounts

INTRODUCTION

Departmental accounts are accounts which relate to each of the several departments or division of a business and are prepared when it is disired to know the trading result of each department or class of goods separately. Departmental accounts are prepared to ascertain at any time the earning capacity of each department and to detect any leakage or short comings in the efficiency of the department. Departmental accounts are nothing more than as many trading and profit & loss accounts as there are departments.

Advantages of Departmental Accounts

1. To make sure whether the department makes a profit or incurs a loss.
2. Compare results with those of other departments and take corrective action.
3. Formulating policy to expand business on proper lines.
4. Rewarding departmental managers properly on the basis of the results.

Difference between a Branch and a Department

The chief point of distinction is that while a branch represents the business unit of an organisation located at different point of the city or state, departments are divisions of the business located under the same roof.

Methods employed in departmental accounting :

Accounts of departments can be maintained in any of the following methods.

1. **Independent Method :** In this method accounts are maintained separately for each department, treating them as independent units. However at the end of the period profit & loss account of each department is consolidated into one profit & loss account for the whole business.
2. **Columnar Method :** In this method common books of accounts are maintained for the entire organisation with appropriate columns for different departments.

Allocation of Indirect expenses under departmental accounts :

The important problem in the preparation of departmental accounts is allocation of expenses. Direct expenses of a particular department are charged to the department for which they are incurred. But indirect expenses are to be apportioned to various departments on a suitable basis. In allocating expenses the following rules shall apply :

(*a*) Those expenses which are specifically incurred for a particular department should be charged to that department.

(*b*) Those expenses which are generally incurred but can be charged to specific department must be done so.

(*c*) Such expenses which cannot be directly related to a particular department shall be apportioned on a reasonable basis. Some bases of allocation of expenses to various departments is given below :

1. **Expenses on Purchase :** Some of expenses incurred directly on purchases such as carriage inwards, freight, duties, Octroi, etc. should be apportioned in the ratio of net departmental purchases (purchase less returns). In this connection inter departmental purchases are not to be considered.
2. **Expenses on Sales :** Selling expenses such as sales commission, discount on sales, carriage outwards, bad debts etc., which depend directly on sales may be allocated in the sales ratio between departments.
3. **Expenses on Land and Building :** Such expenses on Land and Building as rent rates, taxes, depreciation, repairs, insurance on building etc. should be allocated based on the space occupied by each department.
4. **Electricity Charges :** Power consumption for lighting, heating air-conditioning etc., should be divided on the basis of meter reading of each department or power points or space occupied by each department as the case may be.
5. **Expenses on Machinery :** Expenses on machinery including depreciation, repairs etc. should be charged on the basis of assets employed in each department. In some cases expenses on machinery are allocated in the ratio of sales or wages or space occupied by machines in each department.
6. **Labour welfare expenses :** These expenses are apportioned on the basis of number of employees working in each department.

Some expenses like Income tax, dividend paid, general managers salary, legal charges, sundry office expenses etc., which cannot be specifically allocated should be charged entirely to general profit & loss account to which profit of the various departments are transferred.

Inter-Departmental Transfers

The transfer of goods and the exchange of services between departments are called inter departmental transactions or inter department transfer.

While preparing the departmental trading and profit & loss a/c, the department receiving the goods or services should be debited with the value of the goods or services so supplied and department providing such goods or services should be credited with the said amount.

However if the transfer takes place at a price other than the cost price and the same remains in the stock on date of final accounts, the following adjustments is required.

First unrealised profit on opening stock is to be ascertained. Then the same is to be deducted from the unrealised profit on closing stock and the balance transferred to the debit of "General Profit and Loss a/c. If the loading on closing stock is less than that of opening stock then it shall be entered on the credit side of general profit & loss account.

Problem 1

The following purchases were made by a business having three departments :-

Department X 1,000 units
Department Y 2,000 units } at a total cost of Rs 1,00,000
Departments Z 2,400 units

Stock of January 1, were :

Department X 120 units
Department Y 80 units
Department Z 152 units

The sales were :

Department X 1,020 units at Rs. 20 each.
Department Y 1,920 units at Rs. 22.50 each.
Department Z 2496 units at Rs. 25 each.
The rate of gross profit is the same in each case.

Prepare the departmental trading account (University or Madras B. Com. April 2001).

Solution

Working Notes

1. Calculation of cost of Purchase :

	Dept. A		*Dept.* B		*Dept.* C
Ratio of quantity	1,000 Units		2,000 Units		2,400 Units
or	5	:	10	:	12
Ratio of sale price	Rs. 20		Rs. 22.50		Rs. 25
or	4	:	4.5	:	5
Composite Ratio	$5 \times 4 = 20$	:	$10 \times 4.5 = 45$	:	$12 \times 5 = 60$

Total purchase cost of Rs. 1,00,000 is divided into composite ratio, i.e., 20 : 45 : 60

$$\text{Dept A} = \frac{1,00,000}{125} \times 20 = \text{Rs. } 16,000$$

$$\text{Dept B} = \frac{1,00,000}{125} \times 45 = \text{Rs. } 36,000$$

$$\text{Dept C} = \frac{1,00,000}{125} \times 60 = \text{Rs. } 48,000$$

2. Calculation of purchase rate per unit :

$$\text{Dept A} = \frac{16,000}{1,000 \text{ Units}} = \text{Rs. } 16$$

$$\text{Dept B} = \frac{36,000}{2,000 \text{ Units}} = \text{Rs. } 18$$

$$\text{Dept C} = \frac{48,000}{2,400 \text{ Units}} = \text{Rs. } 20$$

3. Calculation of closing stock units :

= Opening stock + Purchases – Sales = Closing stock

Dept A = 120 + 1,000 – 1,020 = 100 Units

Dept B = 80 + 2,000 – 1,920 = 160 Units

Dept C = 152 + 2,400 – 2,496 = 56 Units

4. Valuation of closing stock at purchase cost :

Dept A = 100 × 16 = Rs. 1,600

Dept B = 160 × 18 = Rs. 2,880

Dept C = 56 × 20 = Rs. 1,120

5. Valuation of opening sock at purchase cost :

Dept A = 120 × 16 = Rs. 1,920

Dept B = 80 × 18 = Rs. 1,440

Dept C = 152 × 20 = Rs. 3,040

6. Valuation of sales units at selling price :

Dept A = 1,020 × 20 = Rs. 20,400

Dept B = 1,920 × 22.50 = Rs. 43,200

Dept C = 2,496 × 25 = Rs. 62,400

Departmental Trading A/c

	A	B	C		A	B	C
To Opening stock	1,920	1,440	3,040	By Sales	20,400	43,200	62,400
To Purchases	16,000	36,000	48,000	By Closing stock	1,600	2,880	1,120
To Gross profit	4,080	8,640	12,480				
	22,000	46,080	63,520		22,000	46,080	63,520

Problem 2

The trading and profit and loss account of a concern having three departments is as follows for the year ending 31-3-1999

Purchase	*Rs.*	*Sales*	*Rs.*
(A) Television	1,40,700	Television (A)	1,50,000
(B) Radios	90,600	Radio (B)	1,00,000
(C) Spare parts for services	64,400	Receipts from servicing (C)	25,000
Salaries and wages	48,000	Closing stock :-	
Rent	10,800	Television (A)	60,100
Sundry expenses	11,000	Radio (B)	20,300
Profit	34,500	Spare parts (C)	44,600
	4,00,000		4,00,000

Prepare departmental accounts for the departments A, B and C taking into account the following information.

(*a*) T.V. and Radios are sold in the shop and servicing is done in the workshop.
(*b*) Salaries and wages comprise the following :

Shop $\frac{3}{4}$: Workshop $\frac{1}{4}$

It was decided to allocate shop salaries and wages in the ratio of 1 : 2 between A and B.
(*c*) Workshop rent is Rs. 500 per month Rent of the shop is divided equally between A and B.
(*d*) Sundry expenses are to be distributed on the basis of turnover of each department.

(University of Madras B.Com, April 2001)

Solution

Working Notes :

1. Total salaries and wages = Rs. 48,000. It is divided between shop and workshop in $\frac{3}{4}$ & $\frac{1}{4}$

$$\text{Shop} = 48{,}000 \times \frac{3}{4} = \text{Rs. } 36{,}000$$

$$\text{Workshop} = 48{,}000 \times \frac{1}{4} = \text{Rs. } 12{,}000$$

Further shop salaries and wages of Rs. 36,000 is divided between A & B in 1 : 2.

$$A = 36{,}000 \times \frac{1}{3} = \text{Rs. } 12{,}000$$

$$B = 36{,}000 \times \frac{2}{3} = \text{Rs. } 24{,}000$$

2. Rent for workshop = Rs. 500 PM × 12 = Rs 6,000 the balance rent Rs. 4,800 (10,800 – 6,000), is divided equally between A & B . Therefore

$$A = \text{Rs. } 4{,}800 \times \frac{1}{2} = \text{Rs. } 2{,}400$$

$$B = \text{Rs. } 4{,}800 \times \frac{1}{2} = \text{Rs. } 2{,}400$$

3. Sundry expenses are divided into "Turnover ratio". The turnover ratio is :

A	:	B	:	C
1,50,000	:	1,00,000	:	25,000
6	:	4	:	1

$$A = \text{Rs. } 11{,}000 \times \frac{6}{11} = \text{Rs. } 6{,}000$$

$$B = \text{Rs. } 11{,}000 \times \frac{4}{11} = \text{Rs. } 4{,}000$$

$$C = \text{Rs. } 11{,}000 \times \frac{1}{11} = \text{Rs. } 1{,}000$$

Departmental Trading and Profit & Loss A/c
For the year ending 31-3-1999

	A	B	C		A	B	C
To Purchases	1,40,700	90,600	64,400	By Sales	1,50,000	1,00,000	25,000
To Gross profit	69,400	29,700	5,200	By Closing stock	60,100	20,300	44,600
	2,10,100	1,20,300	69,600		2,10,100	1,20,300	69,600
To Salaries & Wages	12,000	24,000	12,000	By Gross profit	69,400	29,700	5,200
To Rent	2,400	2,400	6,000	By Loss	—	700	13,800
To Sundry expenses	6,000	4,000	1,000				
To Profit	49,000	—	—				
	69,400	30,400	19,000		69,400	30,400	19,000

Total Profit (or) Loss

Department A — Profit = 49,000

Department B — Loss = 700

Department C — Loss = 13,800

Profit 34,500

Problem 3

M/s Z & Co. had two departments. You are requested to prepare the trading and profit & loss a/c for each department for the year ended on 31st March 1993, on the basis of the following information.

	Dept A Rs.	Dept B Rs.
Opening stock (1-4-1992)	25,000	20,000
Purchases	2,30,000	1,90,000
Sales	6,33,000	4,92,000
Sales return	3,000	2,000
Closing stock (31-3-1993)	30,000	18,000
Wages	80,000	60,000
Salaries	40,000	25,000

Other Common expenses :

Rent	Rs. 15,000
Electricity	6,000
Depreciation	18,000
Selling expenses	8,000

Some other relevant information are given below :

	Dept A	Dept B
Light points	18	9
Value of Asets (Rs.)	1,50,000	1,20,000
Floor area (sq ft.)	300	200

(Calcutta University, B.Com. (Pass) 1994)

Solution

Note :

1. Rent has been divided in the ratio of floor area i.e., 3 : 2.
2. Electricity has been divided in the ratio of light points, i.e., 2 : 1.
3. Depreciation has been divided in the ratio of value of assets i.e., 5 : 4.
4. Selling expenses in the ratio of net sales, i.e., 9 : 7.

Departmental Trading and P & L A/c

For the year ended 31-12-93

	Dept A	*Dept B*		*Dept A*	*Dept B*
To Opening stock	25,000	20,000	By Sales a/c	6,33,000	4,92,000
To Purchase a/c	2,30,000	1,90,000	By Closing stock a/c	30,000	18,000
To Sales returns	3,000	2,000			
To Wages a/c	80,000	60,000			
To Gross profit c/d	3,25,000	2,38,000			
	6,63,000	5,10,000		6,63,000	5,10,000
To Sales a/c	40,000	25,000	By Gross profit b/d	3,25,000	2,38,000
To Rent a/c	9,000	6,000			
To Electricity a/c	4,000	2,000			
To Depreciation a/c	10,000	8,000			
To Selling expenses	4,500	3,500			
To Net profit	2,57,500	1,93,500			
	3,25,000	2,38,000		3,25,000	2,38,000

Problem 4

The following balances as at 31-12-1997 have been extracted from the books of Sri Rajit & Co. Which has two departments

	Dept A	Dept B	General
Opening stock as at 1-1-1997	12,500	10,000	—
Purchases	1,15,000	1,45,000	—
Purchases returns	2,500	500	—
Sales	3,16,500	2,46,000	—
Sales returns	1,500	1,000	—
Wages	90,000	80,000	
Miscellaneous charges	17,500	16,000	—
Sundry debtors			95,000
Sundry creditors			86,000
Plant & Machinery			1,20,000
Leasehold			40,000
Buildings			60,000
Furniture & fittings			24,000
Office and selling expenses			64,000
Cash in hand on 31-12-97			4,000
Cash at bank on 31-12-97			55,000
Capital			2,50,000

Plant & Machinery is to be depreciated by 10%, buildings by 2%, furniture and fittings by 5%. Leaseholds are to be depreciated by Rs. 8,000. The stock on hand on 31st December 1997 were as follows.

Department - A	Department - B
Rs.	Rs.
26,000	24,000

All unallocted expenditure is to be apportioned in the ratio of the net sales of each department.

Prepare in colummar a form trading and profit & loss a/c of the two departments and balance sheet of the combined business as a whole on 31-12-1997.

(Calculate University, B. Com. (Pass) 1998)

Solution

Working Notes

1. Trial Balance shows a debit balance of Rs. 48,500. So the difference is put on the liability side of the balance sheet.
2. Ratio of net sales = (3,16,500 – 1,500) ; (2,46,000 – 1,000)
   = 9 ; 7
3. **Depreciation Lease :**

$$\text{Dept A} = 8{,}000 \times \frac{9}{16} = 4{,}500$$

$$\text{B} = 8{,}000 \times \frac{7}{16} = 3{,}500$$

4. **Depreciation on Plant & Machinery :**

$$\text{Dept A} = 1{,}20{,}000 \times \frac{10}{100} \times \frac{9}{16} = 6{,}750$$

$$\text{B} = 1{,}20{,}000 \times \frac{10}{100} \times \frac{7}{16} = 5{,}250$$

5. **Depreciation on Building :**

$$\text{Dept A} = 60{,}000 \times \frac{2}{100} \times \frac{9}{16} = 675$$

$$\text{B} = 60{,}000 \times \frac{2}{100} \times \frac{7}{16} = 525$$

6. **Depreciation on Furniture :**

$$\text{Dept A} = 24{,}000 \times \frac{5}{100} \times \frac{9}{16} = 675$$

$$\text{B} = 24{,}000 \times \frac{5}{100} \times \frac{7}{16} = 525$$

7. **Office and selling expenses :**

$$\text{Dept A} = 64{,}000 \times \frac{9}{16} = 36{,}000$$

$$\text{B} = 64{,}000 \times \frac{7}{16} = 28{,}000$$

Departmental Trading and Profit & Loss A/c

	A	B		A	B
To Opening stock a/c	12,500	10,000	By Purchase Returns a/c	2,500	500
To Purchases a/c	1,15,000	1,45,000	By Sales a/c	3,16,500	2,46,000
To Sales returns a/c	1,500	1,000	By Closing stock a/c	26,000	24,000
To Wages a/c	90,000	80,000			
To Gross profit c/d	1,26,000	34,500			
	3,45,000	2,70,500		3,45,000	2,70,500
To Miscellaneous charges. a/c	17,500	16,000	By Gross profit b/d	1,26,000	34,500
To Office & selling expen.a/c	36,000	28,000	By Net loss	—	19,300
To Depreciation on lease hold a/c	4,500	3,500			
To Depreciation on Plant & Machinery	6,750	5,200			
To Depreciation on Buildings	675	525			
To Depreciation on Furniture	675	525			
To Net profit	59,900	—			
	1,26,000	53,800		1,26,000	53,800

Balance sheet

Particulars		*Amount*	*Particulars*		*Amount*
Capital	2,50,000		Leasehold	40,000	
Add NP of dept A	59,900		Less Dep	8,000	
	3,09,900				32,000
Less : loss of Dept B	19,300		Building	60,000	
		2,90,600	Less Dep	1,200	
					58,800
Sundry creditors		86,500			
Suspense		48,500	P & M	1,20,000	
(Difference in the Trial Balance)			Less Dep	12,000	
					1,08,000
			Furniture	24,000	
			Less Dep	1,200	
					22,800
			Stock A —	26,000	
			B —	24,000	50,000
			Debtors		95,000
			Cash at Bank		55,000
			Cash on Hand		4,000
		4,25,600			4,25,600

Problem 5

(Inter Departmental Transfer)

A firm had two departments, cloth and ready made clothes. The clothes were made by the firm itself out of cloth supplied by the cloth department at its selling price. From the following figures prepare Departmental Trading and profit and loss account for the year 1995.

	Cloth Dept Rs.	Redymade Cloth Dept Rs.
Opening stock	3,00,000	50,000
Purchases	20,00,000	15,000
Sales	22,00,000	4,50,000
Transfer to ready-made department	3,00,000	—
Expenses :		
Manufacturing	—	60,000
Selling	20,000	6,000
Closing stock	2,00,000	60,000

The stock in the readymade clothes department may be considered as consisting of 75% cloth and 25% other expenses. The cloth department earned gross profit at the rate of 15% in 1994. General expenses of the business as a whole came to Rs. 1,10,000.

(University of Madras, B. Com. October 2000).

Solution

Working Notes :

1. **Transfer :** Transfer of stock to Readymade from cloth Department : Receiving department (Readymade) is debited with Rs. 3,00,000 and giving department (cloth) is credited with Rs. 3,00,000.
2. Rate of Gross profit for cloth department in 1994 is 15% (given).
3. Rate of gross profit for cloth department for 1995 is calculated as :

$$\frac{\text{Gross Profit in cloth}}{\text{Sales in Cloth}} \times 100$$

$$= \frac{4,00,000}{22,00,000 + 3,00,000} \times 100$$

$$= \frac{4,00,000}{25,00,000} \times 100 = 16\%$$

4. **1995. Opening Stock Loading**

Readymade opening stock	50,000
Less ; Expenses 25% (given)	
$50,000 \times \frac{25}{100}$	12,500
Remaining 75% is cloth	37,500

$\therefore$ G. P. 15% on 37,500 = $37,500 \times \frac{15}{100}$ = 5,625

(Opening stock of 1995 is nothing but closing stock of 1994. Therefore G. P. 15% of 1994 is taken).

5. 1995. Closing Stock Loading :

Readymade closing stock	60,000
Less : Expenses 25%	
$60{,}000 \times \frac{25}{100}$	15,000
Remaining 75% is cloth	45,000

∴ G. P. 16% (Working note 3) on : 45,000

$$45{,}000 \times \frac{16}{100} = 7{,}200$$

6. Since goods are transferred from cloth department to readymade department, the opening and closing stock of readymade department represent goods of cloth department. Therefore, stock reserve is calculated on the stock of readymade department applying G. P. rate of cloth department.

Departmental Trading and Profit & Loss A/c

	Cloth	*Readymade*		*Cloth*	*Readymade*
To Opening stock a/c	3,00,000	50000	By Sales	22,00,000	4,50,000
To Purchases a/c	20,00,000	15,000	By Transfer to Ready-made From cloth	3,00,000	—
To Transfer to Readymade from Cloth	—	3,00,000	By Closing stock	2,00,000	60,000
To Manufacturing Expenses	—	60,000			
To Gross profit c/d	4,00,000	85,000			
	27,00,000	5,10,000		27,00,000	5,10,000
To Selling expense a/c	20,000	6,000	By Gross profit b/d	4,00,000	85,000
To Net profit a/c	3,80,000	79,000			
	4,00,000	85,000		4,00,000	85,000

General Profit & Loss A/c

Particulars	*Amount*	*Particulars*		*Amount*
To General expenses a/c	1,10,000	By Net Profit :		
To Stock Reserve a/c (Closing Stock loading)	7,200	Cloth	3,80,000	
		Readymade	79,000	4,59,000
To Profit	3,47,425	By Stock Reserve a/c		5,625
	4,64,625			4,64,625

Problem 6

On the basis of the following trail balance and additional information provided to you thereafter, prepare departmental trading account and general profit and loss account for the year ended 31st March 2001 and balance sheet as at that date :

Trial Balance as at 31st March 2001

Particulars	*Debit* *Rs.*	*Credit* *Rs.*
Capital account		3,00,000
Land & Building	2,25,000	—
Furniture	35,000	—
Opening Stock :		
Department - A	1,20,000	—
Department - B	2,40,000	—
Purchases :		
Department - A	12,00,000	
Department - B	17,00,000	
Sales		
Department - A	—	20,00,000
Department - B	—	32,00,000
General expense	14,00,000	—
Debtors	2,10,000	—
Creditors	—	1,00,000
Drawings	2,80,000	
Bank	1,90,000	—
	56,00,000	56,00,000

Additional Information :

(*i*) Closing stock of department A is Rs. 1,30,000 which includes goods purchased from department - B and invoiced at Rs. 50,000. Department - B transfers goods to department -A at cost plus 25%.

(*ii*) Closing stock of Departments B is Rs. 2,60,000 which includes goods transferred by department - A at an invoice price of Rs. 1,08,000 which is arrived at by department - A by adding 20% to the cost of the goods.

(*iii*) Sales of department -A and department - B include goods transferred to the other department at Rs. 2,00,000 and Rs. 3,00,000 respectively.

(*iv*) Depreciation is to be provided on land and building @ 5% per annum and on furniture @ 10% per annum (C.S. Foundation, June 2001).

Solution

Working Notes :

1. Stock Reserve required :

$$\text{Dept A} = \text{Rs. } 50,000 \times \frac{25}{125} = \text{Rs. } 10,000$$

$$\text{Dept B} = \text{Rs. } 1,08,000 \times \frac{20}{120} = \text{Rs. } 18,000$$

2. Purchases from outsiders by :

Department A = 12,00,000 – 3,00,000 = 9,00,000

Department B = 17,00,000 – 2,00,000 = 15,00,000

3. Sales to outsiders by :

Dept A = 20,00,000 – 2,00,000 = Rs 18,00,000
Dept B = 32,00,000 – 3,00,000 = Rs 29,00,000

4. Depreciation on Land & Building = 5% of Rs 2,25,000 = Rs 11,250
Depreciation on Furniture = 10% of Rs 35,000 = Rs 3,500

Departmental Trading A/c
For the year ended 31st March 2001

	Dept A	*Dept B*		*Dept A*	*Dept B*
To Opening Stock a/c	1,20,000	2,40,000	By Sales a/c	18,00,000	29,00,000
To Purchases a/c	9,00,000	15,00,000	By Transfers a/c	2,00,000	3,00,000
To Transfers a/c	3,00,000	2,00,000	By Closing Stock a/c	1,30,000	2,60,000
To Gross Profit a/c	8,10,000	15,20,000			
	21,30,000	34,60,000		21,30,000	34,60,000

General Profit & Loss A/c

Particulars	*Amount*	*Particulars*	*Amount*
To General expenses	14,00,000	By Gross profit b/d	
To Depreciation on :		Dept A	8,10,000
Land & Building	11,250	Dept B	15,20,000
Furniture	3,500		
To Stock Reserve on transfers unsold			
Dept A	10,000		
Dept B	18,000		
To Net Profit	8,87,250		
	23,30,000		23,30,000

Balance Sheet at 31st March 2001

Liabilities		*Amount*	*Assets*		*Amount*
Capital a/c	3,00,000		Land & Building	2,25,000	
Add : Net profit	8,87,250		Less : Dep	11250	
	11,87,250				2,13,750
Less : Drawings	2,80,000				
		9,07,250	Furniture	35,000	
Creditors		1,00,000	Less Dep.	3,500	
					31,500
			Stock	3,90,000	
			Less : Stock Reserve	28,000	
					3,62,000
			Debtors		2,10,000
			Bank		1,90,000
		10,07,250			10,07,250

Problem 7

Bubbles Ltd., has three operating departments. The details of operations of each department during 1998 had been as follows :

	Dept I	*Dept II*	*Dept III*
Sales to customers	4,00,000	6,00,000	8,00,000
Purchases from outsiders	3,00,000	4,00,000	5,00,000
Opening stock (out of local purchase)	80,000	1,00,000	1,20,000
Transfer to Dept III	1,35,000	—	—
Closing stock	50,000	50,000	1,00,000
Common expenses :			
Selling Commission Rs.	36,000		
Depreciation	45,000		
Administration expenses	1,60,000		
Interest on capital	90,000		

Stock of Dept III includes 20% transfer from Dept I. Prepare departmental profit & loss a/c and ascertain the net profit of the company after considering the following details :

	Dept I	*Dept II*	*Dept III*
Fixed assets installed (Rs.)	3,60,000	2,00,000	1,60,000
Capital employed (Rs.)	2,00,000	3,00,000	3,00,000
Administration expenses to be shared	$\frac{4}{10}$	$\frac{3}{10}$	$\frac{3}{10}$

Department I transfer supplies to Dept III at normal selling price less 10%.

(Calcutta University, B. Com. (Hons.) 1991)

Solution

Working Notes :

Ratio of Sales to customers is 2 : 3 : 4
Ratio of fixed asset is 9 : 5 : 4
Ratio of capital employed is 2 : 3 : 3

1. Department I transfer goods to dept III at 10% below sale Price :
   Suppose sales 100, then transfer price is (100 – 10) = 90
   Therefore sale price of goods transferred to Dept III is

$$1{,}35{,}000 \times \frac{100}{90} = 1{,}50{,}000$$

2. Goods sold by dept I = 4,00,000 + 1,55,000 = 5,50,000
   Cost of goods sold is

$$80{,}000 + 3{,}00{,}000 - 50{,}000 = 3{,}30{,}000$$

   Profit margin is

$$5{,}50{,}000 - 3{,}30{,}000 = 2{,}20{,}000$$

   So percentage of profit on sale is

$$\frac{2{,}20{,}000}{5{,}50{,}000} \times 100 = 40\%$$

3. Cost price of goods supplied by Dept I to Dept III is 1,50,000 – 40% of 1,50,000

$$= 1,50,000 - 60,000 = \text{Rs. } 90,000$$

Hence Loading on goods transferred is

$$1,35,000 - 90,000 = \text{Rs. } 45,000$$

Rate of loading on transfer price is

$$\frac{45,000}{1,35,000} \times \frac{1}{3} = 33\frac{1}{3}\%.$$

4. Unsold stock of Dept. III included goods supplied by dept 1 at transfer price is

$$1,00,000 \times \frac{20}{100} = 20,000.$$

5. Unrealised profit on unsold stock (stock reserve) is

$$\frac{20,000 \times 33\frac{1}{3}}{100} = \text{Rs. } 6,667$$

Departmental Trading and P & L a/c

	I	II	III		I	II	III
To Opening stock	80,000	1,00,000	1,20,000	By Transfer	1,35,000	—	—
To Purchases	3,00,000	4,00,000	5,00,000	By Sales	4,00,000	6,00,000	8,00,000
To Transfer	—	—	1,35,000	By Closing stock	50,000	50,000	1,00,000
To Gross profit c/d	2,0,5000	1,50,000	1,45,000				
	5,85,000	6,50,000	9,00,000		5,85,000	6,50,000	9,00,000
To Selling Commission a/c	8,000	12,000	16,000	By Gross profit b/d	2,05,000	1,50,000	1,45,000
To Depreciation a/c	22,500	12,500	10,000				
To Adm. Expenses	64,000	48,000	48,000				
To Interest on Capital a/c	22,500	22,500	33,750				
To Stock reserve a/c	6,667	-	-				
To Net profit	81,333	55,000	37,250				
	2,05,000	1,50,000	1,45,000		2,05,000	1,50,000	1,45,000

Problem 8

Senthil Ltd. has three departments C, D and E. From the following information prepare a departmental trading and profit & loss a/c.

	C Rs.	D Rs.	D Rs.
Opening Stock	3,000	4,000	6,000
Consumption of direct materials	8,000	12,000	—
Wages	5,000	10,000	—
Closing stock	4,000	14,000	8,000
Sales	—	—	34,000

Stock in each department are valued at cost to the department concerned. Stocks of 'C' department are transferred to 'D' at a margin of 50% above departmental cost. Stock of 'D' department is transferred to "E" department at a margin of 10% above departmental cost. Other expenses were; salaries Rs. 20,000, printing and stationery Rs. 1,000. Rent Rs. 6,000, Interest paid Rs. 4,000 and depreciation Rs. 3,000.

Allocate expenses in the ratio of departmental gross profit Opening figures of reserve for unrealised profits on departmental stocks were :

Department 'D' – Rs. 1,000
Department 'E' – Rs. 2,000

Prepare departmental trading and profit and loss a/c.

(University of Madras, B. Com. April 2,000)

Solution

Working Notes :

1. Calculation of Stock Transfer

(*a*) Transfer From dept. C to Dept. D (i.e., entire stock is transferred)

	Opening stock	3,000
	Material	8,000
	Wages	5,000
		16,000
Less :	Closing stock	4,000
	Cost of value of goods transferred	12,000
Add :	Loading 50% of cost 12,000 × $\frac{50}{100}$	6,000
	Transfer value from C to D	18,000

(*b*) **Transfer from Department D to Dept. E**

	Transfer value from Dept C (as above)	18,000
	Opening stock of D	4,000
	Materials	12,000
	Wages	10,000
		44,000
Less :	Closing stock of D	14,000
		30,000
Add :	Loading 10% of cost 30,000 × $\frac{10}{100}$	3,000
	Transfer value from D to E	33,000

2. Unrealised profit on closing stock : Goods are transferred from A to B and B to C. Therefore unrealised profit on closing stock of B and C is calculated below :
Of 'B' Rs 14,000 unrealised profit in closing stock of 'B' Rs. 14,000.
Proportionate amount of goods out of transfer :

$$= \frac{\text{Transfer A to B}}{\text{Total cost in Dept B}} \times \text{Closing stock}$$

$$= \frac{18,000}{\underset{\text{(Material)}}{12,000} + \underset{\text{(Labours)}}{10,000} + \underset{\text{(Transfer)}}{18,000}} \times 14,000$$

$= 6,300$

Unrealised profit is 50% on cost is $\frac{50}{150}$ on sales

$$= 6,300 \times \frac{50}{150} = 2,100$$

Unrealised profit in closing stock of Dept. C

Closing stock of 'C' = Rs. 8,000

(*i*) Margin of 10% on cost from B to C is $\frac{10}{110}$ on sales

$$= 5{,}000 \times \frac{10}{110} = 727 = \qquad 727$$

(*iii*) Proportion of profit in transferred goods available in closing stock of 'C'.

Cost of Rs. 7,273 (i.e., 8,000 – 727)

$$= \frac{18{,}000}{40{,}000} \times 7{,}273 = 3{,}273$$

$$= 7{,}273 \times \frac{50}{150} = \qquad \underline{1{,}091}$$

$$\underline{1{,}818}$$

Total unreaslied profit (2,100 + 1,818) = 3,918

Note :

1. Since value of stock transfers from C to D and D to E are not given, therefore entire stock is transferred.
2. All expenses are divided in the Gross Profit Ratio i.e.,

6,000 : 3,000 : 3,000

or 2 : 1 : 1

Departmental Trading and Profit & Loss a/c

	C	*D*	*E*	*Total*		*C*	*D*	*E*	*Total*
To Op. stock	3,000	4,000	6,000	13,000	By Sales	—	—	34,000	34,000
To Material Consumption	8,000	12,000	—	20,000	By Transfer	18,000	33,000	—	51,000
To Wages	5,000	10,000	—	15,000	By Closing Stock	4,000	14,000	8,000	26,000
To Transfer	—	18,000	33,000	51,000					
To Gross profit	6,000	3,000	3,000	12,000					
	22,000	47,000	42,000	1,11,000		22,000	47,000	42,000	1,11,000
To Salaries	1,000	500	500	2,000	By Gross profit b/d	6,000	3,000	3,000	12,000
To Printing	500	250	250	1,000	By Net loss	2,000	1,000	1,000	4,000
To Rent	3,000	1,500	1,500	6,000					
To Interest	2,000	1,000	1,000	4,000					
To Depreciation	1,500	750	750	3,000					
	8,000	4,000	4,000	16,000		8,000	4,000	4,000	16,000

General Profit & Loss a/c

Particulars		*Amount*	*Particulars*		*Amount*
To Net loss			By Stock Reserve (Op stock loading)		
Dept C	2,000		Dept D —	1,000	
Dept D	1,000		Dept E —	2,000	3,000
Dept E	1,000	4,000	By P & L a/c		4,918
To Stock reserve (Closing stock loading)		3,918	(Total loss transferred)		
		7,918			7,918

Problem 9

Sunrise Ltd., has two departments X and Y. From the following particulars, prepare departmental trading accounts and profit and loss account for the year ended 31st March 1999.

	Dept. X Rs.	Dept. Y Rs.
Opening stock (at cost)	40,000	24,000
Purchases	1,84,000	1,36,000
Carriage Inwards	4,000	4,000
Wages	24,000	16,000
Sales	2,80,000	2,24,000
Purchased goods Transferred.		
By Dept. Y to Dept. X	20,000	—
By Dept. X to Dept. Y	—	16,000
Finished goods transferred		
By Dept. Y to Dept. X	70,000	—
By Dept. X to Dept. Y	—	80,000
Return of finished goods		
By Dept. Y to Dept. X	20,000	—
By Dept. X to Dept. Y	—	14,000
Closing stock :-		
Purchased goods	9,000	12,000
Finished goods	48,000	28,000

Purchased goods have been transferred mutually at their respective departmental purchase cost and finished goods at departmental market price and that 20% of the closing finished stock with each department represents finished goods received from the other department. **(C.S. Foundation, June 1999)**

Solution

Working Notes :

1. Calculation of unrealised profit in closing stock

	Dept. X	Dept. Y
Sales	2,80,000	2,24,000
Add : Transfer of finished goods	80,000	70,000
	3,60,000	2,94,000
Less : Returns of finished goods	20,000	14,000
	3,40,000	2,80,000
Gross profit	85,000	84,000
Rate of gross profit	25%	30%

2. Finished goods from other department included in closing stock :

	Dept. X	Dept. Y
Stock of finished goods	48,000	28,000
Stock realised to other department (20% of finished)		
Stock	9,600	5,600
Amount of unrealised profit	30% of 9,600 = 2,880	25% of 5,600 = 1,400

Departmental Trading A/c for The year ended 31-3-1999

	X	Y		X	Y
To Opening stock a/c	40,000	24,000	By Sales	2,80,000	2,24,000
To Purchases a/c	1,84,000	1,36,000	By Transfer :		
To Carriage a/c	4,000	4,000	Purchase goods	16,000	20,000
To Wages a/c	24,000	16,000	Finished goods	80,000	70,000
To Transfer :			By Returns :		
Purchased goods	20,000	16,000	Finished goods	14,000	20,000
Finished goods	70,000	80,000	By Closing Stock :		
To Returns :			Purchased goods	9,000	12,000
Finished goods	20,000	14,000	Finished goods	48,000	28,000
To Gross profit	85,000	84,000			
	4,47,000	3,74,000		4,47,000	3,74,000

Profit & Loss A/c

Particulars	*Amount*	*Particulars*	*Amount*
To Provision for unrealised		By Gross profit	
Profit incuded in closing stock		Dept X	85,000
Dept X	2,880	Dept Y	84,000
Dept Y	1,400		
To Net profit	1,64,720		
	1,69,000		1,69,000

Problem 10

From the following trial balance, prepare departmental trading and profit & loss a/c for the year ended 31st March 1990 and balance sheet as at that date

		Dr.	*Cr.*
Stock 1-4-89	Dept A	17,000	
	Dept B	14,500	
Purchase	Dept A	35,400	
	Dept B	30,200	
Sales	Dept A		60,800
	Dept B		51,250
Wages	Dept A	8,200	
	Dept B	2,700	
Rent, rates, taxes & insurance		9,390	
Sundry expenses		3,600	
Salaries		3,000	
Lighting and heating		2,100	
Discount allowed		2,220	
Discount received			650
Advertising		3,680	
Carriage inwards		2,340	
Furniture & fittings		3,000	
Plant & Machinery		21,000	

	Dr	Cr
Sundry Debtors	6,060	
Sundry Creditors		18,600
A's Capital a/c		47,660
A's Drawings	4,500	
Cash in Hand	170	
Cash at Bank	9,900	
	1,78,960	1,78,960

The following information in also provided :

(a) Internal transfer of goods from Dept A to Dept B Rs. 420.

(b) The items rent, taxes and insurance, sundry expanses, lighting and heating, salaries and carriage inwards to be apportioned $\frac{2}{3}$ to Dept A and $\frac{1}{3}$ to Dept B.

(c) Advertising to be apportioned equally.

(d) Discount allowed and received are apportioned on the basis of departmental sales and purchases (excluding transfer) correct to nearest Rs. 10.

(e) Depreciation at 10% per annum on furniture and fitting and on plant and Machinery. This is to be charged $\frac{3}{4}$ to Dept A and $\frac{1}{4}$ to Dept B.

(f) Services rendered by B Dept. to A Dept. Included in wages Rs. 500.

(g) Stock as at 31-3-90 A Dept Rs. 16,740 and B Dept Rs. 12,050.

(h) Fixed assets remain unchanged during the year.

(University of Madras B. Com. October 1999)

Solution

Working Notes :

Goods or service transfer from one department to another department. Debit receiving Dept and credit giving Dept i.e., debit 'B' Dept and credit 'A' Dept with 420.

Services (included in wages) B to A debit 'A' dept and credit 'B' Dept with Rs. 500.

2. Carriage inward, Rent & Rates, Sundry expenses, Salaries, lighting are divided between A and B in the ratio of 2 : 1, Advertisement equally, depreciation 3 : 1, Discount allowed in sales ratio (60,800 : 51,250). Discount received in the purchase ratio, i.e., (35,400 : 30,200).

Departmental Trading & Profit & Loss A/c

	Dept A	*Dept B*		*Dept A*	*Dept B*
To Opening stock a/c	17,000	14,500	By Sales a/c	60,800	51,250
To Purchases a/c	35,400	30,200	By Transfer -		
To Wages a/c	8,200	2,700	Goods (A to B)	420	—
To Carriage Inward	1,560	780	Wages (B to A)	—	500
To Transfer :			By Closing stock	16,740	12,050
— Goods (A to B)	—	420			
— Wages (B to A)	500	—			
To Gross profit	15,300	15,200			
	77,960	63,800		77,960	63,800

	Dept A	Dept B		Dept A	Dept B
To Rent & Rates	6,260	3,130	By Gross profit	15,300	15,200
To Sundry expenses	2,400	1,200	By Discount received	350	300
To Salaries	2,000	1,000	By Net loss	1,250	—
To Lighting	1,400	700			
To Discount allowed	1,200	1,020			
To Advertisement	1,840	1,840			
To Depreciation :					
On Furniture	225	75			
On Plant	1,575	525			
To Net profit	—	6,010			
	16,900	15,500		16,900	15,500

General P & L A/c

Particulars	Amount	Particulars	Amount
To Net loss :		By Net Profit :	
Dept A	1,250	Dept B	6,010
To Net profit	4,760		
	6,010		6,010

Balance Sheet as on 31-3-1990

Liabilities		Amount	Assets		Amount
Capital	47,660		Furniture	3,000	
Add Net Profit	4,760		Less Dep	300	
	52,420				2,700
Less : Drawings	4,500		Plant & Machinery	21,000	
		47,920	Less : Dept	2,100	
Sundry Creditors		18,600			18,900
			Sundry Debtors		6,060
			Cash in hand		170
			Cash at Bank		9,900
			Closing stock		
			Dept A	16,740	
			Dept B	12,050	
					28,790
		66,520			66,520

Problem 11

Bose & Co. has two departments P and Q. Department P sells goods to department Q at normal selling prices. From the following particulars prepare departmental trading and profit & loss account of the year ended 31-3-96 and also ascertain the net profit to be transferred to balance sheet.

	Dept — P	Dept — Q
Opening stock	5,00,000	Nil
Purchases	28,00,000	3,00,000
Goods from P	—	8,00,000
Wages	3,50,000	2,00,000
Travelling expenses	20,000	1,60,000
Closing stock at cost to the department	8,00,000	2,09,000
Sales	30,00,000	20,00,000
Printing and stationery	30,000	25,000

The following expenses incurred for both the departments were not apportioned between the department.

(*a*) Salaries - Rs. 3,30,000
(*b*) Advertisements expenses - Rs. 1,20,000
(*c*) General expenses - Rs. 5,00,000
(*d*) Depreciation is to be charged @ 30% on the machinery value of Rs. 96,000.

The advertisement expenses of the departments are to be apportioned in the turnover ratio. Salaries and depreciation are apportioned in the ratio of 2 : 1 and 1 ; 3 respectively. General expenses are to be apportioned in the ratio of 3 ; 1.

(Calcutta University, B. Com. (Hons.) 1997)

Solution

Working Notes :

1. Percentage of Gross Profit on Sales of Dept 'P'

$$\frac{9,50,000}{(30,00,000+8,00,000)} \times 100 = 25\%$$

2. Closing stock of Dept 'Q' consist of own purchases and goods received from Dept 'P' in the ratio of 3,00,000 ; 800,000, i.e., 3 ; 8.

Therefore portion of goods received from dept 'P' in the closing stock of Dept Q is

$$2,09,000 \times \frac{8}{11} = \text{Rs. } 1,52,000$$

So stock reserve is $1,52,000 \times \frac{25}{100} = \text{Rs. } 38,000$

Department Trading and Profit & Loss A/c

	P	Q		P	Q
To Opening stock a/c	5,00,000	—	By Goods to 'Q'	8,00,000	—
To Purchases a/c	28,00,000	3,00,000	By Sales	30,00,000	20,00,000
To Goods from 'P'	—	8,00,000	By Closing stock	8,00,000	2,09,000
To Wages a/c	3,50,000	2,00,000			
To Gross profit c/d	9,50,000	9,09,000			
	46,00,000	22,09,000		46,00,000	22,09,000

	P	Q		P	Q
To Depreciation a/c	7,200	21,600	By Gross Profit b/d	9,50,000	9,09,000
To Travelling expenses a/c	20,000	1,60,000			
To Printing & stationery	30,000	25,000			
To Salaries	2,20,000	1,10,000			
To Advt. expenses	72,000	48,000			
To General expenses	3,75,000	1,25,000			
To Stock Reserve	38,000	—			
To Net Profit	1,87,800	4,19,400			
	9,50,000	9,09,000		9,50,000	9,09,000

QUESTIONS

Simple Question

1. What are departmental accounts ? Why are they prepaid ?
2. State the difference between a branch and a department.
3. What are the different methods adopted in departmental accounting ?
4. State the rules regarding allocation of expenses.
5. What is the general basis on which the following expenses are allocated while preparing departmental accounts.
   (*a*) Bad debits
   (*b*) Lighting and heating expenses
   (*c*) Rent
   (d) Works manager's salary
   (*e*) Insurnace premium on premises
   (*f*) Discount allowed by creditors
   (*g*) Labour welfare expenses.
6. What is inter departmental transfer ? How is it dealt with ?
7. State the advantages of preparing departmental accounts ?

EXERCISE 1

Mixed goods were purchased for Rs. 1,00,000 and later they were assorted into three categories X, Y, Z as follows :

X 1,000 - Selling price Rs. 20 each
Y 2,000 - Selling price Rs. 22.50 each
Z 2,400 - Selling price Rs. 25 each

All categories yield the same rate of profit. Calculate the purchase price of each category.

(University of Madras B. Com. April 1998)

Answer : Purchase price of X = Rs. 16,000
Y = Rs. 36,000
Z = Rs. 48,000

EXERCISE 2

From the data prepare departmental trading, profit & loss a/c and thereafter the combined income account revealing the concern's true result for the year ended 31st December 1989 :

	Department	
	A (Rs.)	B (Rs.)
Stock (January)	40,000	—
Purchase from outside	2,00,000	20,000
Wages	10,000	1,000
Transfer of goods from Department A	—	50,000
Stock (Dec. 31) at cost to the department	30,000	10,000
Sales to outsiders	2,00,000	71,000

B's entire stock represents goods from Dept. A which transfer them at 25% above its cost. Administrative and selling expenses amount to Rs. 15,000 which are to be allocated between departments A and B in the ratio 4 : 1 respectively

(University of Madras, B. Com. May 1999)

Answer : Gross Profit of Dept A — Rs. 30,000
Gross Profit of Dept B — Rs. 10,000
Net Profit — Rs. 23,000

EXERCISE 3

Vijoya Ltd., has three department I, N, and K for the year ended 31-12-1999. The information is given below.

	I Rs.	*N* Rs.	*K* Rs.
Stock on 1-1-99	13,500	18,000	27,000
Materials consumed	36,000	54,000	—
Manufacturing expenses	22,500	45,000	—
Stock on 31-12-99	18,000	63,000	36,000
Unrealised profit in Stock on 1-1-99	—	4,500	6,000
Sales	—	—	1,53,000

Each department values its stocks at cost to the department concerned. Whereas department I transferred goods to department N at a margin of 30% above departmental cost, department N transferred to department K at 25% above departmental cost.

Other expenses were : staff remuneration Rs. 6,000, stationery Rs. 4,500, Rent Rs. 27,000, Depreciation Rs. 18,000 and Advertising Rs. 13,500. These expenses are to be shared by the department in the ratio of gross profit.

Prepare departmental trading and profit & loss a/c.

(Calcutta University B. Com. (Hons.) 2000)

Answer : Net Loss of Dept I — Rs. 4,500
N — Rs. 8,650
K — Rs. 1,850
Net loss Rs. 16,180

EXERCISE 4

Prepare departmental trading account and general profit & loss a/c and balance sheet as on 31st December 1995.

	Rs.	Rs.
Capital	—	3,00,000
Land & Building	1,25,000	
Furniture	25,000	
Opening Stock :		
Dept A	30,000	
Dept B	40,000	
Purchases :		
Dept A	10,00,000	
Dept B	15,00,000	
Sales		
Dept A		20,00,000
Dept B		32,00,000
General expenses	14,00,000	
Debtors	2,00,000	
Creditors		1,00,000
Drawings	2,80,000	
Bank	10,00,000	
	56,00,000	56,00,000

Additional information :

(*a*) Closing stock of department A is Rs. 1,30,000. It includes stock of Rs. 40,000 which B department has sent to 'A' Department at cost.

(*b*) Closing stock of 'B' Department Rs. 2,60,000. It includes stock of Rs. 90,000 which A department has sent to 'B' Department at cost.

(*c*) Sales of 'A' department include goods of Rs. 2,00,000 transferred to B department. Sales of B department include goods of Rs. 3,00,000 transferred to 'A' department. Both of these transfers have been made at market price.

(*d*) Opening stock of A Dept includes goods of Rs. 10,000 taken from B department at cost and closing stock of B department includes goods of Rs. 15,000 taken from A department at cost.

(*e*) Depreciation on Land and Buildings @ 5% per year and on furniture @ 10% per year.

(University of Madras B. Com September 1997)

Answer :

Gross profit 'A'	Rs. 11,00,000
Gross profit 'B'	Rs. 19,20,000
Net profit	Rs. 15,52,000
Balance Sheet Total	Rs. 17,31,250

EXERCISE 5

From the following particulars, prepare the departmental trading and profit & loss a/c and a balance sheet as at 31st Dec. 2003.

Particulars	*Rs.*
Capital a/c	30,000
Sales — Dept A	70,000
— Dept B	30,000
Sundry Creditors	13,500
Stock 1st Jan. 2003	
Dept A	3,400
Dept B	1,100
General Reserve	750
Sundry Debtors	28,000
Furniture & Fittings	1,080
Rent Rates and Insurance	1,800
Marine Insurance	2,400
Purchase duty etc. :	
Dept A	43,000
Dept B	25,000
Office salaries	17,220
Printing and Stationery	2,700
Postage & Telegram	600
Exchange and discount (Dr)	1,500
Investments	6,900
Cash in hand	2,500
Cash at Bank	7,050

Apportion the expenses in proportion to the turnover of each department :
Closing stock-dept A Rs. 4,000. Dept B - Rs. 1,680.

Provide : Depreciation on furniture 10%, provision for doubtful debts Rs. 300 and 2% on debtors for discount. Increase general reserve by Rs. 3,000. Allocate provision for bad debts in the ratio of 7 : 3.

Answer :	Gross profit of Dept A	Rs. 27,600
	Gross profit of Dept B	Rs. 5,580
	Net profit of Dept A	Rs. 9,246
	Net profit loss of Dept B	Rs. 2,286
	Total of Balance sheet	Rs. 50,248

31

CHAPTER

Branch Accounting

Definition of Branch

Whenever a business grows into a large size it may diversify its activities by opening separate establishments in the same locality or in different parts of a country. Such an establishment of a business is known as a branch. The parent establishment which supervises and controls the branches is known as Head office.

Type of Branches

From the accounting point of view branches may be classified into three types : (*a*) Dependent branches (*b*) Independent branches and (*c*) Foreign branches.

Dependent Branch

A dependent branch is one which depends entirely on Head office for its supplies of goods as well as cash for expenses. The accounts of dependent branches are maintained by Head office. The features of dependent branches are as follows.

(*a*) The branch sells only those goods which are supplied by the head office and are not allowed to make purchases from open market.

(*b*) All branch expenses of regular nature such as rent, staff salary, etc. are paid by the head office, while certain petty expenses such as cartage, postage etc. are met by the branch Manager out of the petty cash account maintained either on simple or imprest it system.

(*c*) The branch is normally expected to sell goods only for cash but may also sell on credit in exceptional circumstances.

(*d*) Such branches are required to deposit cash collected either by way of cash sales or from debtors into the bank account opened in the name of the branch.

(*e*) The branch does not maintain any accounting records. But in order to furnish information to the head office it may maintain a petty cash book, a stock register and a debtors ledger when goods are sold on credit basis.

Accounts Maintained by Head Office Relating to Dependent Branch

There are four methods of maintaining accounts by head office in respect of dependent branches. They are as follows : (1) Debtors system (2) Final account system (3) Stock and Debtors system and (4) wholesale branch system.

1. **Debtors System:** This system is adopted when the size of the branch is small involving few transactions. Under this system the head office prepares only one account known as "branch a/c" for each branch. Under this system the head office may supply goods to branches either at cost price or at invoice price. The branch may sell the goods supplied by the head office either on cash basis or on cash and credit basis.

When a Branch Sells goods supplied by Head office for Cash

Under this type the relationship between the branch and Head office is that of debtor and creditor. The following entries are passed in the books of Head office.

1. When Head office supplies goods to the branch :
   Branch a/c Dr.
   To Goods sent to Branch a/c
2. If the branch returns some goods to Head office :
   Goods sent to Branch a/c Dr.
   To Branch a/c
3. When Head office meets the expenses of branch
   Branch a/c Dr.
   To Bank a/c
4. When the branch deposits the sale proceeds with the bank in the name of Head Office :
   Bank a/c Dr.
   To Branch a/c
5. To record stock of goods unsold by the branch
   Branch Stock a/c Dr.
   To Branch a/c
6. For recording profit made by the branch :
   Branch a/c Dr.
   To Profit & Loss a/c
7. For recording loss incurred by a branch
   Profit & Loss a/c Dr.
   To Branch a/c
8. Branch stock a/c appears in the balance sheet of the Head office. In the beginning of the next year this account is transferred to branch account by means of the following entry.
   Branch a/c Dr.
   To Branch Stock a/c
9. For closing goods sent to branch a/c : Goods sent to branch a/c must be transferred at the end of the year to purchases a/c in the case of a trading concern and to trading a/c in the case of a manufacturing concern.
   Goods sent to Branch a/c Dr.
   To Purchases a/c or Trading a/c

A profoma of branch a/c incorporating the above entries will appear as shown below.

In the books of H.O.
Branch A/c

Particulars		Amount	Particulars		Amount
To Balance b/d			By Balance b/d		X X
(opening balance of assets)			(Opening balances of liabilities)		
— Cash in hand	X X		By Bank a/c — Remittance from		X X
— Stock	X X		branch — cash sales & cash		
— Furniture	X X		collected from branch debtors		
— Petty cash	X X		By Goods sent to branch		X X
— Prepaid rent etc.	X X		Returns from the branch		
		X X	By Balance c/d		
To Goods sent to Branch		X X	(Closing balance of assets)		
To Bank (expenses Paid by H.O)		X X	— Cash in hand	X X	
To Net profit		X X	— Stock	X X	
			— Debtors	X X	
			— Furniture	X X	
			— Prepaid rent etc.	X X	
					X X
			By Loss		X X

Problem 1

The Bombay Textiles Ltd., opened a branch at Delhi on 1st January 1988.

From the following particulars, prepare all the accounts effected for 1988 and 1989 in the books of the head office.

	1998 *Rs.*	*1989* *Rs.*
Goods sent to Delhi	45,000	1,35,000
Cash sent to branch for - Rent	6,000	6,000
Salaries	4,800	6,800
Other expenses	2,000	3,000
Cash received from branch	70,000	1,60,000
Stock on 31st December	7,000	26,000
Petty cash in hand on 31st December	120	260

(University of Madras, B. Com. October 1999)

Solution

In the Books of H.O.
Branch A/c — 1988

Particulars	Amount	Particulars	Amount
To Goods sent to Branch	4,500	By Cash a/c	
To Cash a/c		— Cash received from branch	70,000
— Rent	6,000	By Balance c/d :	
— Salaries	4,800	— Stock	7,000
— Other expenses	2,000	— Petty cash	120
To Profit & loss a/c — Profit	19,320		
	77,120		77,120

Goods Sent to Branch A/c

Particulars	*Amount*	*Particulars*	*Amount*
To Purchases a/c (Balancing figure)	45,000	By Branch a/c	45,000
	45,000		45,000

Stock of Branch A/c

Particulars	*Amount*	*Particulars*	*Amount*
To Branch a/c	7,000	By Balance c/d	7,000

Branch A/c — 1989

Particulars	*Amount*	*Particulars*	*Amount*
To Balance b/d		By Cash to H.O.	
— Stock 1-1-89	7,000	— Cash received from branch	1,60,000
— Petty cash 1-1-89	120	By Balance c/d	
To Goods sent to Branch	1,35,000	— Stock	26,000
To Cash a/c		— Petty cash	260
— Rent	6,000		
— Salaries	6,800		
— Other expenses	3,000		
To Profit & Loss a/c — Profit	28,340		
	1,86,260		1,86,260

Goods Sent to Branch A/c

Particulars	*Amount*	*Particulars*	*Amount*
To Purchases a/c (Balancing figure)	1,35,000	By Branch a/c	1,35,000
	1,35,000		1,35,000

Problem 2

Bangalore Traders invoiced goods to its Mysore branch at cost. All the expenses are paid direct from the Head office. Petty cash expenses are met by the branch manager. Branch is advised to sell for cash only and deposit the days sale in the Head office account with a local bank. From the following details ascertain the profit of the Mysore Branch through debtors system.

Stock on Jan. 1, 2003	Rs. 2,100
Petty cash on Jan. 1, 2003	50
Furniture on Jan., 1, 2003	250
Goods supplied from H.O.	7,800
Goods returned to H.O.	300
Cash sales	15,250
Salaries and wages	1,860

Advertisement	240
Rent & Rates	360
Stock on Dec. 31, 2003	1,950
Petty cash on Dec. 31, 2003	30
Furniture on Dec. 31, 2003	230

Solution

In The Books of Bangalore Traders
Mysore Branch A/c

Particulars		*Amount*	*Particulars*		*Amount*
To Balance b/d			By Bank-Cash remitted to H.O.		15,250
— Stock	2,100		By Goods sent to Branch		300
— Debtors	50		— Returns to H.O.		
— Furniture	250		By Balance c/d		
		2,400	— Stock	1,950	
To Goods sent to Branch a/c		7,800	— Petty cash	30	
To Bank a/c			— Furniture	230	
— Salaries		1,860			2,210
— Advt.		240			
— Rent & Rates		360			
To P & L a/c — Profit		5,100			
		17,760			17,760

When Branch Sells H.O. Goods for Cash and Credit

Under this situation the branch sells the goods supplied by Head office both on cash and credit basis. The total proceeds remitted by branch to Head office comprises of cash sales and cash received from debtors. In order to provide information about credit sales a branch maintains a debtors ledger and transactions relating to credit sales, returns from credit customers, discount allowed to debtors, bad debts and cash collected from sundry debtors are recorded to arrive at the closing balance.

The Head office will prepare branch account as was explained under the first situation, i.e., branch selling goods for cash. But it records only transactions relating to opening and closing debtors without recording returns from debtors, bad debts, discount.

The following additional entries are involved under this situation.

(*a*) For cash received from branch debtors during the year.

Bank a/c Dr.
To Branch a/c

Note : The entry is similar to cash sales.

(*b*) For recording the total amount due from branch debtors at the end of the year.

Branch Debtors a/c Dr.
To Branch a/c

Note : Branch Debtor a/c will appear in the balance sheet of the head office and will be transferred to the Branch a/c in the beginning of the next accounting period.

Problem 3

Good Luck Ltd., opened a branch on 1st January 1995 at Calcutta. The following information is supplied to you. Give journal entries and prepare Branch account.

	Rs.
Goods sent to branch	50,000
Sales : Cash	20,000
Credit	36,000
Cash received from debtors	32,000
Discount allowed to them	600
Cash sent to branch for expenses	7,000
Stock on 31st December 1995	8,000

(University of Madras, B. Com. October 2000)

Solution

Journal Entries

Date	*Particulars*		*Dr. Amount*	*Cr. Amount*
	Branch a/c	Dr.	50,000	
	To Goods sent to branch a/c			50,000
	(Being goods sent to Calcutta branch a/c)			
	Branch a/c	Dr.	7,000	
	To Bank a/c			7,000
	(Being branch expenses met by H. O.)			
	Cash a/c	Dr.	52,000	
	To Branch a/c			52,000
	(Being the sale proceeds remitted to H.O. a/c)			
	Closing Stock a/c	Dr.	8,000	
	Closing Debtors a/c	Dr.	3,400	
	To Branch a/c			11,400
	(Being closing stock a/c and closing debtors a/c recorded)			
	Branch a/c	Dr.	6,400	
	To P & L a/c			6,400
	(Being profit earned by Calcutta branch a/c)			

In the books of Goods Luck Ltd.
Calcutta Branch A/c

Date	*Particulars*	*Amount*	*Date*	*Particulars*	*Amount*
	To Goods Sent to Branch	50,000		By Cash a/c	
	To Bank-Expenses	7,000		— Cash sales	20000
	To P & L a/c — Profit	6,400		— Cash from Debtors	36,000
			31-12-95	By Closing Stock a/c	8,000
				By Closing Debtors a/c	3,400
		63,400			63,400

Branch Debtors A/c

Particulars	*Amount*	*Particulars*	*Amount*
To Credit Sales	36,000	By Cash received from Debtors	32,000
		By Discount allowed	600
		By Closing Debtors (Balancing figure)	3,400
	36,000		36,000

Problem 4

From the following particulars relating to Trichy Branch prepare the Branch a/c in the books of head office for the year ended 31-12-1998.

	Rs.
Sock on 1-1-98	30,000
Debtors on 1-1-98	12,000
Petty cash on 1-1-98	200
Goods sent to branch	50,000
Goods returned to H.O.	600
Sales at Branch :	
Cash	30,000
Credit	42,000
Sales returns at branch	250
Bad debts written off	300
Discount allowed to customers	100
Branch expenses paid by H.O.	3,000
Petty cash sent to branch	500
Petty expenses at branch	400
Furniture purchased by the branch	1,000
Stock on 31-12-1998	12,500

(University of Madras, B. Com. April 2000)

Solution

In the Books of H.O.
Trichy Bank A/c

Particulars	*Amount*	*Particulars*	*Amount*
To Opening balance		By Cash to H.O.	29,000
— Stock	30,000	(See Note -1)	
— Debtors	12,000	By Goods returned to H.O.	600
— Petty Cash	200	By Closing balance	
To Goods sent to Branch	50,000	— Stock	12,500
To Bank a/c		— Debtors	53,350
— Petty cash sent to branch	500	(See Note 2)	
To Profit & Loss a/c	1,050	— Petty cash	300
— Profit		(See Note 3)	
		— Furniture	1,000
	96,750		96,750

Working Note :

1. Cash Sent to H.O.

Cash Sales	30,000
Collection from debtors	Nil
	30,000
Less : Furniture purchased by Branch	1,000
Cash sent to H.O.	29,000

2. Branch Debtors A/c

Particulars	*Amount*	*Particulars*	*Amount*
To Opening Balance	12,000	By Sales Returns	250
To Credit sales	42,000	By Bad debts written off	300
		By Discount allowed	100
		By Closing Debtors (Balancing figure)	53,350
	54,000		54,000

3. Petty Cash a/c

Particulars	*Amount*	*Particulars*	*Amount*
To Opening balance	200	By petty expenses at branch	400
To Cash sent to Branch	500	By Closing petty cash (Balancing figure)	300
	700		700

Problem 5

From the following details relating to Delhi branch for the year ending March 31st 1997. Prepare the Branch a/c in the books of Head office. Show your workings clearly.

	Rs.
Stock on 1-4-1996	25,000
Debtors on 1-4-1996	10,000
Furniture on 1-4-1996	6,000
Petty cash on 1-4-1996	1,000
Insurance prepaid on 1-4-1996	300
Salaries outstanding on 1-4-1996	4,000
Goods sent to branch during 96-97	2,00,000
Cash sales during the year	2,70,000
Cash received from debtors	65,000
Cash paid by debtors direct to H.O.	5,000
Goods returned from branch	2,000
Goods returned by debtors	1,000
Cash sent to branch for expenses :-	

Rent Rs. 800 PM	9,600	
Salary Rs. 4000 PM	48,000	
Petty cash	2,000	
Insurance (up to June 97)	1,200	
		60,800
Petty cash expenses		2,200
Discount allowed to debtors		500
Stock on 31-3-97		15,000

Goods costing Rs. 2,500 were damaged in transit and a sum of Rs. 2,000 was recovered from the insurance company in full settlement of the claim. Provide depreciation on furniture @ 10% p.a. **(University of Madras B. Com. May 1999)**

Solution

Working Notes :

1. **Branch Debtors A/c**

Particulars	*Amount*	*Particulars*	*Amount*
To Opening Balance	10,000	By Cash from Debtors (65,000 + 5,000)	70,000
To Credit Sales (3,50,000 – 2,70,000)	80,000	By Sales Return	1,000
		By Discount	500
		By Closing Debtors	18,500
	90,000		90,000

2. **Petty Cash A/c**

Particulars	*Amount*	*Particulars*	*Amount*
To Opening balance	1,000	By Expenses by branch	2,200
To Cash given by H.O.	2,000	By Closing petty cash	800
	3,000		3,000

3. **Closing Furniture :**

Opening balance of furniture	6,000
Less : depreciation at 10%	600
	5,400

4. Insurance is upto June 1997. Therefore 3 months prepaid Insurance from 1-4-97 to 30-6-1997 is $1{,}200 \times \frac{3}{12}$ = Rs. 300 is taken as closing balance.

5. Salary outstanding for one month is taken as closing balance.

6. Salary outstanding for one month is taken as closing balance, i.e.,

Total salary paid	48,000
Less : opening o/s salary	4,000
	44,000
Add : Closing o/s salary	4,000
	48,000

Branch A/c

Particulars	Amount	Particulars	Amount
To Opening Balance		By Opening Balance	
— Stock	25,000	(Liability)	
— Debtors	10,000	— Outstanding Salary	4,000
— Furniture	6,000	By Cash sent to H.O.	
— Petty Cash	1,000	— Cash sales	
— Prepaid Insurance	300	— Collection from Debtors	70,000
To Goods sent to branch	2,00,000	(65,000 + 5,000)	
To Cash sent to branch:		By Goods returned to H.O.	2,000
— Rent	9,600	By Closing Balance	
— Salary	48,000	— Stock	15,000
— Petty cash	2,000	— Debtors	18,500
— Insurance	1,200	— Petty cash	800
To Closing balance (Liability)		— Furniture	5,400
To Salary o/s	4,000	— Prepaid Insurance 1,200 × $\frac{3}{12}$	300
To Profit	80,900		
	3,88,000		3,88,000

Problem 6

From the following transactions prepare the Bangalore Branch account for the year ended 31st December, 1996 in the books of the Head office Chennai.

Stock at branch 1-1-96	36,200
Stock at branch 31-12-96	33,140
Branch debtors 1-1-96	11,300
Branch debtors 31-12-96	6,040
Petty cash at the branch 1-1-96	220
Petty cash at the branch 31-12-96	140
Goods sent to branch	1,56,680
Branch expenses met by H. O.	7,000
Cash sent by H.O., to branch to meet Petty expenses	1,040
Cash sales	1,68,200
Cash received from branch debtors	27,700

(University of Madras B. Com. April 1998).

Solution

In the books of H.O. (Chennai)
Bangalore Branch A/c

Date	Particulars	Amount	Date	Particulars	Amount
	To Balance b/d			By Cash	
	— Stock	36,200		— Cash sales's	1,68,200
	— Debtors	11,300		— Cash received	
	— Petty cash	220		form debtors	27,700
	To Goods sent to branch	1,56,680	31-12-96	By Balance c/d	
	To Cash-expenses	7,000		— Stock	33,140
	— Petty cash	1,040		— Debtors	6,040
	To Profit & Loss a/c	22,780		— Petty cash	140
		2,35,220			2,35,220

Goods supplied by H.O. to branch at Invoice Price

Some times the head office supplies goods to the branch at a price higher than cost price this is known as invoice price or loading. The main purpose of sending goods at invoice price are two :

(*a*) Avoid disclosing profit made on sales to the branch manager so that he should not start similar business of his own and divert the customers to his own business (*b*) to exercise better control over branch stock. It there is a discrepancy, it will call for investigation.

Entries in the accounts books when goods are sent at Invoice Price

The head office will make entries on the basis of selling price or invoice price of goods sent but in order to ascertain the true profit, adjustment entries will have to be made for the differences between the invoice value of goods sent to the branch and their cost. Similarly, stock at branch will be valued at invoice price but adjustment will be necessary to ensure that stock does not appear in the balance sheet at more than the cost. The entries relating to these transactions are as follows :

(*a*) For adjusting the loading included in the opening stock.
Stock Reserve a/c Dr.
To Branch a/c
(With the difference between the invoice price and cost price of opening stock).

(*b*) For adjusting loading included in the goods supplied to branch.
Goods sent to branch a/c Dr.
To Branch a/c
(With the difference between the invoice price and cost price of goods sent by H.O. to the branch).

(*c*) For adjusting loading included in the goods returned by the branch to the Head office
Branch a/c Dr.
To Goods sent to branch a/c
(With the difference between the invoice price and cost price of the goods returned by the branch).

(*d*) For adjusting loading included in the closing stock :
Branch a/c Dr.
To stock Reserve a/c
(With the difference between the invoice price and cost price of the closing stock).

Problem 7 (Calculation of loading)

Calculate loading in the following cases

(*a*) Goods are invoiced at cost plus 10%. The invoice price of goods is Rs. 3,33,300.

(*b*) Goods are invoiced at a profit of 20% on sales. The cost price of goods sent is Rs. 1,48,800.

(*c*) Goods are invoiced at coat plus 15%. The cost of goods sent is Rs. 75,400.

Solution

(*a*) 110% is represented by 3,33,300

$$100\ \%\ ? = \frac{100 \times 3{,}33{,}300}{110} = \text{Rs. } 3{,}03{,}000$$

Loading = Invoice price – Cost price
= 3,33,300 – 3,03,000
= Rs. 30,300

(*b*) If the sale price is Rs. 100 profit is Rs. 20 and the cost price is Rs. 80.
If the cost is Rs. 80. The profit is Rs. 20
∴ If the cost is Rs. 148,800, the profit is ?

$$= \frac{1,48,800 \times 20}{80} = \text{Rs. } 37,200$$

∴ The sale price should be Rs. 1,86,000 if there is to be a profit of 20% on sales.

(*c*) If the cost price is Rs. 100, the loading is Rs. 15.
If the cost is Rs. 75,400 loading should be ?

$$= \frac{75400 \times 15}{100} = \text{Rs. } 11,310$$

Problem 8

Goldie Ltd. invoices goods to its branch at selling price which is cost plus 60%. From the following particulars, prepare branch account for the year ended 31st March 2002.

Stock at branch on 1st April 2001 at invoice price	2,40,000
Branch debtors on 1st April 2001	2,13,750
branch furniture on 1st April 2001	2,00,000
Transactions during the year 2001-2002 :	
Invoice price of goods sent to branch	31,20,000
Cash sales at branch	21,60,000
Credit sales at branch	6,24,000
Cash expenses for the branch - directly met by Head office	1,62,600
Discount allowed to branch debtors	6,000
Bad debts written off	3,750
Stock at branch on 31st March 2002 at invoice price	3,36,000
Branch debtors on 31st March 2002	1,08,000
Depreciate furniture @ 15% per annum.	

(C.S. Foundation, June 2002)

Solution

Working Notes :

Branch Debtors A/c

Particulars	*Amount*	*Particulars*	*Amount*
To Balance b/d	2,13,750	By Bad debts a/c	3,750
To Credit sales	6,24,000	By Discount a/c	6,000
		By Bank (Collection being balancing figure)	7,20,000
		By Balance c/d	1,08,000
	8,37,750		8,37,750

2. Calculation of stock reserve in opening stock

$$2,40,000 \times \frac{60}{160} = \text{Rs. } 90,000$$

3. Calculation of stock reserve in closing stock

$$3,36,000 \times \frac{60}{160} = \text{Rs. } 1,26,000$$

4. Loading on goods sent to branch

$$31,20,000 \times \frac{60}{160} = \text{Rs. } 11,70,000$$

Branch A/c

Particulars	*Amount*	*Particulars*	*Amount*
To Balance b/d :		By Stock reserve (Opening)	90,000
Stock	240,000		
Debtors	2,13,750	By Bank :	
Furniture	2,00,000	Cash sales	21,60,000
To Goods sent to		from debtors	7,20,000
Branch a/c	31,20,000	By Goods sent to	
To Bank-expenses	1,62,600	Branch a/c (Loading)	11,70,000
To Stock reserve		By Balance c/d	
(Closing)	1,26,000	Stock	3,36,000
To Profit & Loss a/c		Debtors	1,08,000
— Profit	6,91,650	Furniture	1,70,000
		(2,00,000 – 30,000)	
	47,54,000		47,54,000

Problem 9

A Head office in Madras sends goods to its branch at Madurai marked 20% above cost. From the following particulars, show how the branch a/c will appear in the Head office books.

		Rs.
Stock on 1-7-99 at the branch		1,800
Debtors on 1-7-99 at the branch		3,000
Petty cash on 1-7-99 at the branch		30
Goods supplied to branch		30,000
Remittances from branch :		
Cash sales	6,000	
money received from Debtors	21,000	
		27,000
Cheques sent to branch :		
Salary	900	
Rent & taxes	150	
Petty cash	110	
		1,160
Stock at branch on 31-12-99		3,000
Debtors at branch on 31-12-99		4,800
Petty cash at branch on 31-12-99		20

(University of Madras B. Com. April 2001)

Solution.

In the books of H.O
Madurai Branch A/c

Particulars	Amount	Particulars	Amount
To Opening balance b/d		By Cash to H.O :	
— Stock	1,800	Cash sales	6,000
— Debtors	3,000	Cash received	
— Petty cash	30	From debtors	21,000
To Good's sent to branch	30,000	By Stock reserve (Opening)	300
To Bank :			
— Salary 900		$1,800 \times \frac{20}{120}$	
— Rent & taxes 150		By Loading in goods	
— Petty cash 110		Sent to branch	5,000
	1,160	$30,000 \times \frac{20}{120}$	
To Stock reserve (Closing)	500	31-12-99	
		By Closing balances	
$3,000 \times \frac{20}{120}$		— Stock	3,000
To Profit & loss a/c	3,630	— Debtors	4,800
		— Petty cash	20
	40,120		40,120

Problem 10

A business firm opened a branch at Nagpur on 1st April 1999. The goods were sent by the head office to the branch at cost plus 25%. The following are the particulars of the transactions relating to the branch for the accounting year ended 31st March 2000 :

Goods sent to branch at invoice price	3,51,000
Sales : Cash	1,25,000
Credit	1,75,000
Cash collected from branch debtors	1,56,000
Discount allowed	4,000
Stock on 31-3-2000 at invoice price	55,500
Cash sent to branch for :	
Wages	3,000
Freight	11,000
Other expenses	600

Spoiled goods written off, at invoice price 500. Prepare branch account showing, profit earned or loss in cased during the year ended 31st March 2,000. Also show memorandum branch debtors account ascertaining closing balance of branch debtors.

(C.S. Foundation, June 2,000)

Solution

Branch A/c

Particulars	Amount	Particulars	Amount
To Goods sent to branch	3,51,000	By Bank	
		— Cash sales	1,25,000
To Bank - Expenses	20,000	— From debtors	1,56,000
To Stock Reserve (closing)	11,100	By Goods sent to branch	
		(stock reserve)	70,200
To Profit & Loss a/c	39,600	To Closing Balance	
		— Stock	55,500
		— Debtors	15,000
	4,21,700		4,21,700

Branch Debtors A/c

Particulars	Amount	Particulars	Amount
To Credit sales a/c	1,75,000	By Bank a/c	1,56,000
		By Discount a/c	4,000
		By Balance c/d	15,000
	1,75,000		1,75,000

Problem 11

A company has a branch at Delhi. From the following particulars, calculate the profit earned by branch :

	Rs.
Stock on 1-1-94 (Invoice price)	20,000
Goods sent to branch during 1994 at invoice price	1,10,000
Expense at b ranch during 1994	6,000
Sales during 1994	1,20,000

Goods are invoiced to the branch at cost plus 25%. The sale price is cost plus 50%. Also ascertain the stock reserve that should be maintained in respect of unrealised profit on stock.

(University of Madras, B. Com. April 1999)

Solution

Note : In this problem, we are asked to calculate profit earned by the branch. The profit earned can be known by preparing a trading a/c.

Branch Trading A/c

Particulars	Amount	Particulars	Amount
To Opening stock (Invoice price)	20,000	By Sales a/c	1,20,000
To Goods sent to Branch (Invoice price)	1,10,000	By Closing stock a/c (Invoice price)	30,000
To Expenses	6,000		
To Profit	14,000		
	1,50,000		1,50,000

Calculation of Closing Stock at Branch (Invoice Price)

Opening stock		20,000
Goods sent to branch		1,10,000
		1,30,000
Less : (Cost of goods sold at branch) Invoice price :		
Sales at branch =	1,20,000	
Less : Profit at cost plus 50%		
or $\frac{50}{150}$ on sales		
$= \frac{15}{150} \times 1,20,000 =$	40,000	
Cost price of sale	80,000	
Add : H.O. Loading cost plus 25% i.e., 25% on cost		
$80,000 \times \frac{25}{100} =$	20,000	1,00,000
Branch closing stock at Invoice price		30,000

Note : Since opening stock, goods sent to branch are shown in H.O., at invoice price, the cost of sales at branch should also be shown at H.O. Invoice price, Hence the H.O. loading is added with cost price of sale.

Unrealised profit on closing stock is

$$30,000 \times \frac{25}{100} = \text{Rs. } 6,000$$

Problem 12

Knight Ltd. invoices goods to its branch at selling price which is cost plus 60%. From the following figures, prepare branch account in the books of the head office.

Stock at branch on 1st April 1998, at invoice price	16,000
Branch debtors on 1st April 1998	14,250
Invoice price of goods sent to branch	2,08,000
Cash sales at branch	1,44,000
Credit sales at branch	41,600
Cash expenses for the branch directly met by the head office	10,840
Discount allowed to branch debtors	650
Stock at branch 31st March 1999 at invoice-price	22,400
Branch debtors on 31st March 1999	7,200

(C.S. Foundation, December 1999)

Solution

Branch A/c

Particulars	*Amount*	*Particulars*	*Amount*
To Opening Balance		By Stock Reserve a/c	6,000
— Stock	16,000	— (opening)	
— Debtors	14,250	By Bank ;	
To Goods sent to Branch a/c	2,08,000	— Cash sales	1,44,000
To Bank expenses	10,840	— Collection from Drs	48,000
To Branch Stock Reserve a/c	8,400	By Goods sent to Branch	78,000
To P & L a/c	48,110	(loading)	78,000
(profit)		By Balance c/d	
		— Stock	22,400
		— Debtors	7,200
	3,05,600		3,05,600

2. **Final Account System** : Under this system, the Head office will prepare a trading and profit & loss a/c to know the profit or loss of the branch. The returns from the branch is not shown on credit side of trading a/c. Instead it is deducted from goods sent to branch on the debit side of the trading a/c. A branch a/c may also be prepared. The branch a/c in this case takes the form of personal a/c. It is prepared to know the final balance due from or due to branch.

Problem 12

From the following information, prepare a trading and profit and loss account of branch and also show the branch account as it would appear in the head office.

Branch Cash A/c

Particulars	*Amount*	*Particulars*	*Amount*
To Balance	7,500	By Petty cash	3,000
To Receipt form debtors	37,500	By Stock	62,000
To Cash sales	25,000	By Balance	5,000
	70,000		70,000

Branch Debtors A/c

Particulars	*Amount*	*Particulars*	*Amount*
To Balance	3,000	By Cash	37,500
To Sales	45,000	By Discount allowed	1,000
		By Bad debts	1,500
		By Balance	8,000

Branch A/c

Date		Rs.	Date		Rs.
1-1-2003	To Balance b/d :			By Balance b/d :	
	— Cash	7,500		— Expenses o/s	1,000
	— Debtors	3,000		Bank	62,000
	— Furniture	7,500	31-12-03	By Balance c/d	20,500
	— Stock	10,000			
31-12-03	To Goods transferred	45,000			
	To Furniture purchased	2,500			
	To Sundry expenses	8,000			
		83,500			83,500

Closing stock at branch was Rs. 4,000 and expenses outstanding were Rs. 900. Depreciation at 10% of the book value has to be provided on furniture :

Solution.

Branch Trading and Profit & Loss A/c

Particulars		Amount	Particulars	Amount
To Opening Stock		10,000	By Sales	
To Goods transferred From H.O.		45,000	— Cash	25,000
To Gross Profit c/d		19,000	— Credit	45,000
			By Closing Stock	4,000
		74,000		74,000
To Expenses :			By Gross profit b/d	19,000
Petty cash expenses	3,000			
Sundry expenses	8,000			
Add o/s in the end	900			
	11,900			
Less o/s in the beginning	1,000	10,900		
To Discount		1,000		
To Bad Debits		1,500		
To Depreciation 7,500 + 2,500 = 10,000 @ 10%		1,000		
To Net Profit		4,600		
		19,000		19,000

Branch A/c

Particulars	Amount	Particulars	Amount
To Balance b/d	20,500	By Closing Balance	
To O/s expenses	900	— Cash	5,000
To Net Profit	4,600	— Debtors	8,000
		— Furniture	9,000
		— Stock	4,000
	26,000		26,000

Problem 13

Aruna carries on business at Bangalore and makes up his annual accounts on 31st December. In 2003 he opened a branch at Mumbai and on 30th June Keshava joined him in partnership having the charge of the branch which was opened on that date and introduced Rs. 2,500 cash as his capital.

As regards branch it was agreed that:

(*a*) Keshava should obtain from Bangalore all supplies of goods.
(*b*) Such goods should be invoiced proforma at the fixed branch selling price of cost plus 25%.
(*c*) All sales should be for cash.

On 31st December 2003 the following balances appear in the firms books .

Particulars	*Dr.*	*Particulars*	*Cr*
Purchases	19,410	Sales	19,720
Branch goods a/c	6,225	Branch Sales a/c	5,450
Stock on 1-1-2203	4,700		
Salaries -H.O	1,740	Goods sent to branch	4,980
Salaries - Branch	371	Branch adjustment a/c	1,245
Bad debts	14	Proceeds - H.O, stock	
Rates & Taxes	466	Fire claims	220
Rates & taxes (branch)	280	Discount received	280
Repairs & renewals	172	Rent received by the	
Repairs & renewals		Branch	52
(Branch)	75	Provision for property	
General expenses	260	repairs	500
General expenses		Aruna's capital	12,500
(Branch)	43	Keshava's capital	2,500
Premises	8,910	Aruna's current a/c	50
Motor Van	480	Creditors	2,222
Fixtures	1,500		
Fixtures (branch)	280		
Drawing - Aruna	2,300		
-Keshva	312		
Debtors	320		
Bank	1,811		
Cash	50		
	49,719		49,719

Stock on 31-12-2003 were : H.O. (Bangalore) cost Rs. 4,120, branch (Mumbai) at selling price Rs. 770. Provide 5% for doubtful debts. Depreciate fixtures 5% p.a. and Motor van 25%. The provision for property repairs to be retained. Prepare trading profit & loss a/c for the year ended 31st December 2003 and a balance sheet as on that date.

Solution

Trading and Profit & Loss A/c

Particulars	Bangalore	Mumbai	Particulars	Bangalore	Mumbai
To Stock	4,700	—	By Sales	19,720	5,450
To Purchases	19,410	—	By Goods sent to branch	4,980	—
To Goods sent to Branch 6,225			By Fire claim	220	—
Less · Adj $\frac{1}{5}$ 1,245	—	4,980	By Stock	4,120	—
To Gross profit	4,930	1,086	By Stock 770 Less : Adj $\frac{1}{5}$ 154	—	616
	29,040	6,066		29,040	6,066
To Salaries	1,740	371	By Gross profit	4,930	1,086
To Rates & taxes	466	280	By Discount	280	
To Repairs & renewals	172	75	By Rent received	—	52
To General expenses	260	43			
To Depreciation :					
-Fixture	75	—			
-Motor van	120	—			
To Bad debts	14				
To Doubtful debts	16	—			
To Net profit	2,347	362			
	5,210	1,138		5,210	1,138

Balance Sheet as on 31st Dec. 2003

Particulars			Amount	Particulars		Amount
Capitals :				Premises		8,910
Aruna - 12,500				Motor van	480	
Keshva - 2,500			15,000	Less depreciation	120	360
Current a/c:				Fixtures	1,500	
	Aruna	**Keshav**		Less depreciation	75	1,425
Balance	50	—		Fixtures - branch	280	
Add Net Profit	2,347	362		Less : Depreciation	75	273
	2,397	362		Debtors	320	
Less : Drawings	2,300	312		Less : DD	16	304
	97 +	50	147	Stock H.O.	4,120	
Provision for repairs			500	—Branch	616	4,736
Creditors			2,222	Bank		1,811
				Cash		50
			17,869			17,869

3. **Stock and Debtors Method :** Under this method the head office maintains the following accounts instead of preparing one branch account.

1. **Goods Sent to Branch a/c :** In this account transactions relating to goods sent by head office to branch and the goods returned by branch to head office at invoice price is recorded. The adjustment entries relating to loading are also recorded This account is closed by transferring the balance to the trading a/c or the purchases a/c .
2. **Branch Debtors a/c :** In this account transactions relating to branch debtors such as opening balance of debtors, credit sales, sales returns, cash collected from debtors, bad debts written off, discount allowed to debtors and allowances given to debtors are recorded.
3. **Branch stock a/c :** In this account transactions relating to opening stock, closing stock, goods sent to branch, good returned by the branch to the head office, cash sales, credit sales to customers, returns inwards etc. are recorded. The difference in this account represent shortage or surplus stock and is transferred to branch adjustment a/c.
4. **Branch cash a/c :** In this account transactions relating to cash sent by head office to the branch, cash realised by the branch from cash sales, cash collected by the branch from debtors, expenses paid by the branch out of cash received from the head office and cash remitted by the branch to head office are recorded.
5. **Branch Expenses a/c :** In this account transactions relating expenses paid in cash such as rent, salary, petty expenses etc. and non-cash expenses such as bad debt written off discount allowed etc. are recorded. The balance in this account is transferred to branch profit & loss account.
6. **Branch Profit and Loss a/c :** This account shows the net profit or net loss of the branch. This amount of profit or loss is transferred to general profit & loss a/c

Entries in the Books of H.O. Under Stock and Debtors Method

1. For goods sent to the branch at invoice price
   Branch stock a/c Dr.
   To goods sent to branch a/c
2. For goods returned by the branch to the head office (at invoice price).
   Goods sent to the branch a/c Dr.
   To Branch stock a/c
3. For cash sales at the branch (at invoice price)
   Cash a/c Dr.
   To Branch stock a/c
4. For credit sales at the branch (at invoice price)
   Branch debtors Dr.
   To Branch stock a/c
5. For goods returned by branch debtors to the branch at invoice price
   Branch stock a/c Dr.
   To Branch debtors a/c
6. For goods returned by branch debtors directly to the head office at invoice price
   Good sent to branch Dr.
   To Branch debtors
7. For goods sent by one Branch to another : It will be recorded as if the branche, has first returned the goods to the Head office and then the head office has sent goods to another branch. For example if branch 'X' sends goods to Branch 'Y' The following entries will be passed.

(*a*) Goods sent to X branch a/c Dr.
To 'X' Branch a/c
(*b*) 'Y' Branch Stock a/c Dr.
To Goods sent to 'Y' Branch a/c

8. For bad debts
Branch Profit & Loss a/c Dr.
To Branch Debtors

9. For Expenses at Branch
Branch Expenses a/c Dr.
To Bank

10. For abnormal shortage (or pilferage or loss) of stock
Branch Adj a/c Dr. (with the amount of loading)
Branch P & L a/c Dr. (with shortage at cost)
To Branch Stock a/c (with the shortage at invoice price)

Note :

(*a*) For surplus at branch, a reverse entry will be passed.

(*b*) No entry is required for normal loss of stock. The branch stock balance will be shown at the net amount as found by the physical verification.

(*c*) Any amount received from the Insurance company for abnormal loss of stock (if insured) will be debited to branch cash account and credited to profit & loss a/c.

11. For adjustment of profit included in opening stock :
Stock Reserve a/c Dr.
To Branch Adjustment a/c

12. For adjustment of profit included in closing stock.
Branch Adjustment a/c Dr.
To Stock Reserve a/c

13. For adjustment of profit included in the good sent to branch by H.O.
Good sent to Branch a/c Dr.
To Branch Adjustment a/c

14. For transferring the balance in goods sent to the branch a/c
Goods sent to Branch a/c Dr.
To Purchases a/c

15. (*a*) For transfer of gross profit
Branch Adjustment a/c Dr.
To Branch Profit & Loss a/c
(*b*) In case of loss, the entry will be reversed.

16. (*a*) For transfer of net profit at the branch
Branch P & L a/c Dr.
To General P & L a/c
(*b*) In case of net loss, the entry will be reversed.

Problem 14

Dolphin Computer World Ltd., with its head office in Delhi invoiced goods to its branch at Agra at 20% less the catalogue price which is cost plus 50% with instruction that cash sales were to be made at invoice price and credit sales at catalogue price less discount at 15% on

prompt payments. From the particulars available from the branch, prepare the branch stock a/c, Branch adjustment a/c, and Branch profit & loss a/c for the year ended 31st March 2002, (showing workings) in the head office books :

	Rs.
Stock on 1st April 2001 (Invoice price)	24,000
Debtors on 1st April 2001	20,000
Good received from head office (Invoice price)	2,64,000
Cash sales	92,000
Credit sales	2,00,000
Cash received from debtors	1,71,270
Discount allowed to debtors	26,730
Expenses at the Branch	12,000
Remittances to Head office	2,40,000
Debtors on 31st March 2002	22,000
Cash in hand on 31st March 2002	11,270
Stock on 31st March 2002 (Invoice price)	30,000

It was further reported that a part of the stock was lost by fire (not covered by insurance) during the year whose value is to be ascertained and a provision should be made for discount to be allowed to debtors as on 31st March 2002, on the basis of year's trend of prompt payments. **(University of Delhi, B. Com. (Hons.) 2002)**

Solution

Agra Branch Stock A/c

Particulars	*Amount*	*Particulars*	*Amount*
To Balance b/d	24,000	By Branch Cash a/c — Cash sales	92,000
To Goods sent to Branch	2,64,000	By Branch debtors a/c — Credit sales	2,00,000
To Branch adj. a/c — Difference between Catalogue price and Invoice price of Credit sales 2,00,000 Minus $\left(2,00,000 \times \frac{120}{150}\right)$	40,000	By Branch adj a/c (See note below) — Loading on stock destroyed by fire	1,000
		By Branch P & L a/c — Cost of stock destroyed by fire (See note below)	5,000
		By Balance c/d	30,000
	3,28,000		3,28,000

Note : The balancing figure in Agra branch stock a/c of 6,000 is considered as stock lost by fire. Out of this Rs. 1,000 is treated as loading on stock destroyed by fire.

Branch Adjustment A/c

Particulars	Amount	Particulars	Amount
To Stock reserve on Closing stock $30,000 \times \frac{20}{120}$	5,000	By Stock reserve on Opening stock $24,000 \times \frac{20}{120}$	4,000
To Agra branch stock a/c — Loading on stock Destroyed by fire $\frac{20}{120} \times 6,000$	1,000	By Goods sent to Branch a/c $2,64,000 \times \frac{20}{120}$	44,000
To Branch P & C a/c — Gross profit	82,000	By Agra branch stock a/c — Difference between Catalogue price and invoice price of goods sold on credit	40,000
	88,000		88,000

Branch Profit & Loss A/c

Particulars		Amount	Particulars	Amount
To Branch expenses a/c			By Branch Adjustment a/c — Gross profit	82,000
— Expenses	12,000			
— Discount allowed	26,730	38,730		
To Agra branch stock a/c (goods destroyed by fire)		5,000		
To Provision for discount (See note below)		2,970		
To General P & L a/c Net profit		35,300		
		82,000		82,000

Working Note :

Provision For Discount on Debtors :

Cash received from debtors	1,71,270
Discount allowed for profit payment	26,730
	1,98,000
Debtors before allowing discount on 31-3-2002	22,000
For a debtor of 1,98,000, discount allowed is	26,730

For a debtor of 22,000 →

$$\frac{22,000 \times 26,730}{1,98,00} = \text{Rs. } 2,970$$

Problem 15

A Head office in mumbai has a branch office at Chennai. Goods are sent at cost plus 33.33% profit. From the following particulars prepare branch stock a/c, Branch debtors a/c, Branch. Expenses account and branch adjustment a/c

		Rs.
Stock on 1-1-99 (Invoice price)		15,000
Debtors on 1-1-99		11,400
Goods invoiced to branch during the year (invoice price)		67,000
Sales at branch — Cash	31,000	
— Credit	37,400	68,400
Cash received form debtors		4,000
Bad debts written off		250
Discount allowed to customers		300
Expenses at branch		6,700
Stock on 31-12-1999 (Invoice price)		

(University of Madras, B. Com. April 2001)

Solution

In the Books of H.O.
Branch Stock A/c

Date		Rs.	Date		Rs.
1-1-99	To Opening Stock	15,000		By Sales	
	To Goods Sent to Branch	67,000		— Cash	31,000
				— Credit	37,400
				By Shortage (Balancing figure)	200
			31-12-99	By Closing stock	13,400
		82,000			82,000

Branch Debtors A/c

Date		Rs.	Date		Rs.
1-1-99	To Balance b/d	11,400		By Cash received from debtors	40,000
	To Credit sales	37,400		By Bad debts	250
				By Discount allowed	300
			31-12-99	By Balance c/d	8,250
		48,800			48,800

Branch Expenses A/c

Particulars	Amount	Particulars	Amount
To Bad debts	250	By Branch adjustment a/c — Transfer	7,250
To Discount allowed	300		
Cash — expenses	6,700		
	7,250		7,250

Good Sent to Branch A/c

Particulars	*Amount*	*Particulars*	*Amount*
To Branch adj. a/c — Loading $67{,}000 \times \frac{25}{100}$	16,750	By Branch stock a/c	67,000
To Purchases (Balancing figure)	50,250		
	67,000		67,000

Branch Adjustment A/c

Particulars	*Amount*	*Particulars*	*Amount*
To stock reserve a/c on closing stock $13{,}400 \times \frac{25}{100}$	3,350	Stock reserve a/c on opening stock $15{,}000 \times \frac{25}{100}$	3,750
To Shortage — Loading $200 \times \frac{25}{100}$	50	By Goods sent to branch — Loading $67{,}000 \times \frac{25}{100}$	16,750
To Gross profit	17,100		
	20,500		20,500

Branch Profit & Loss A/c

Particulars	*Amount*	*Particulars*	*Amount*
To Branch expenses a/c	7,250	By Goods profit b/c	17,100
To Shortage (cost) (200 - 50 loading)	150		
To Net profit	9,700		
	17,100		17,100

Working Notes :

Loading $33\frac{1}{3}\%$ on cost price is equal to 25% on invoice price.

Problem 16

EBONY Stores Ltd., with its head office at Delhi invoiced goods to its branch at Jaipur at 20% less than list price which is cost plus 100% with instructions that cash sales were to be made at invoice price and credit sales at catalogue price (i.e., list price)

From the following particular available form the branch prepare branch stock account branch adjustment account, branch profit and loss account and branch debtors account for the year ending December 31, 2000.

		Rs.
Stock on 1st January, 2000 (Invoice price)		60,000
Debtors on 1st January, 2000		50,000
Goods received from head office (Invoice price)		6,60,000
Sales :		
Cash	2,30,000	
Credit	5,00,000	7,30,000
Cash received from debtors		4,28,200
Expenses at branch		86,800
Remittances to Head office		6,00,000
Debtors on 31st December 2000		12,200
Stock at invoice price on 31st December 2000		8,800

(University of Delhi B. Com. (Hons.) 2001)

Solution

In The Books of EBONY STORES LTD.
Branch Stock A/c

Particulars	*Amount*	*Particulars*	*Amount*
To Balance b/d	60,000	By Branch cash a/c - cash sales	2,30,000
To Goods sent to branch	6,60,000	By Branch Debtors a/c	
To Branch adj. a/c		— Credit sales	5,00,000
(Excess sale price on loaded price of credit sales)		By shortage (Balancing figure)	81,200
List price of credit Sales = 5,00,000		By Balance c/d	8,800
Less : Invoice Price of credit sales $\frac{160}{200} \times 5{,}00{,}000 =$ 4,00,000			
	1,00,000		
	8,20,000		8,20,000

Note :

Let cost price = Rs. 100

Then List price shall be Rs. 200 (cost plus 100%) Then invoice price shall be Rs. 160 = (List price - 20% of List price).

Branch Debtors A/c

Particulars	*Amount*	*Particulars*	*Amount*
To Balance b/d	50,000	By Cash	4,28,200
To Branch stock a/c		By Branch Adjustment a/c	1,09,600
— Credit sales	5,00,000	Discount/Bad debts (Balancing figure)	
		By Balance c/d	12,200
	5,50,000		5,50,000

Branch Expenses A/c

Particulars	Amount	Particulars	Amount
To Branch cash a/c	86,800	By Branch Adjustment a/c	86,800
	86,800		86,800

Branch Adjustment A/c

Particulars	Amount	Particulars	Amount
To Stock Reserve (in closing stock) $\frac{60}{160} \times 8,800$	33,00	By Stock Reserve a/c (in opening stock) $\frac{60}{160} \times 60,000$	22,500
To Branch Stock a/c Loading on shortage $\frac{60}{160} \times 81,200$	30,450	By Goods Sent to Branch a/c — Loading $\frac{60}{160} \times 6,60,000$	2,47,500
To Balance c/d	3,36,250	By Branch stock a/c — Excess of sale price on loading price of credit sales	1,00,000
	3,70,000		3,70,000
To Branch Expenses a/c	86,800	By Balance b/d	3,36,250
To Branch Stock a/c — Cost of shortage (81,200-30,450)	50,750		
To Branch Debtors a/c (Discount, bad debits)	1,09,600		
To Net Profit Transferred to General Profit & Loss a/c	89,100		
	3,36,250		3,36,250

Problem 17

Omkar Corporation Ltd. has Two branches - one at Jaipur and another at Lucknow. Goods are invoiced to branched at cost plus 50%. Branch remit all cash received to head office and all expenses are met by the H.O. From the following particulars, prepare the necessary accounts on the "Stock and Debtors system" to show the profit earned at the Jaipur Branch.

	Rs.
Stock on 1st January 1997	9,300
Debtors on 1st Janurary 1997	6,800
Goods sent to branch (at cost)	34,000
Sales at branch :	
Cash	25,010
Credit	31,000
Cash collection form debtors	30,400
Goods returned by Branch to H.O.	1,200
Goods transferred from Lucknow branch to Jaipur branch	1,500

Shortage of stock	2,100
Shortage of stock at branch	450
Discount allowed to customers	200
Expenses at branch	5,400

(University of Delhi, B. Com. (Pass) 2000)

Solution

In The Books of Omkar Corporation Ltd.
Jaipur Branch A/c
Branch Stock A/c

Particulars	*Amount*	*Particulars*	*Amount*
To Balance b/d	9,300	By Cash — Cash Sales	25,010
To Goods sent to branch at invoice price	51,000	By Branch Debtors a/c — Credit Sales	31,000
To Goods sent to branch at invoice price — Goods from Lucknow branch	1,500	By Goods Returned by branch at invoice price	1,200
		By Branch Adjustment a/c (spoilage)	450
		By Balance c/d	4,140
	61,800		61,800

Branch Debtors A/c

Particulars	*Amount*	*Particulars*	*Amount*
To Balance b/d	6,800	By Cash a/c	30,400
To Branch Stock a/c (Credit sales)	31,000	By Discount a/c	200
		By Balance c/d	7,200
	37,800		37,800

Branch Adjustment A/c

Particulars	*Amount*	*Particulars*	*Amount*
To Stock Reserve on Goods sent by branch to H.O. $\frac{1}{3} \times 1{,}200$	400	By Stock Reserve on Opening stock $\frac{1}{3} \times 9{,}300$	3,100
To Loading on spoilage $\frac{1}{3} \times 450$	150	By loading on goods sent to branch a/c $\frac{1}{3} \times 51{,}000$	17,000
To Stock reserve on Closing stock $\frac{1}{3} \times 4{,}140$	1,380	By Loading on goods to Jaipur branch a/c from Lucknow $\frac{1}{3} \times 1{,}500$	500
To branch stock a/c – Spoilage cost 450 – 150	300		
To Discount a/c	200		
To Branch Expenses a/c	5,400		
To Net profit transferred to General P & L a/c 12,770	12,770		
	18,670		18,670

Note :

1. Goods received from Lucknow branch are treated as goods received from H.O., i.e., goods are routed through the H.O.
2. Shortage of stock of Rs. 2,100 has not been charged to the branch. It is H.O. loss.

Problem 18

'X' Trading Ltd., has its head office at Mumbai with branch at Calcutta. Goods are invoiced by the Head office to the branch at cost plus 25%.

From the following particular prepare in the books of Head office : (1) Branch Stock a/c (2) Goods Sent to Branch a/c (3) Branch Adjustment a/c (4) Branch Debtors a/c and (5) Branch Profit & Loss a/c.

			Rs.
Branch stock at Invoice Price on 1-1-98			25,000
Branch debtors on 1-1-98			20,000
Goods sent to branch during the year at invoice price			1,50,000
Invoice price of goods returned by branch			15,000
Branch sales	Cash sales	60,000	
	Credit	90,000	
			1,50,000
Cash received on ledger account			85,000
Bad debts written off			1,000
Discount allowed			2,000
Branch expenses			16,500
Branch stock at invoice price on 31-12-98			18,000

(Calcutta University, B. Com. (Pass) 1999)

Solution

In The Books of 'X' Trading Ltd.
Calcutta Branch A/c

Particulars	*Amount*	*Particulars*	*Amount*
To Balance b/d	25,000	By Goods Sent to Branch	
To Goods Sent to Branch	1,50,000	— Returns	15,000
To Branch Adj. a/c	8,000	By Branch Cash	60,000
(Surplus stock)		— Cash Sales	
		By Branch Debtors — Credit sales	90,000
		By Balance c/d	18,000
	1,83,000		1,83,000

Goods Sent to Calcutta Branch A/c

Particulars	*Amount*	*Particulars*	*Amount*
To Loading on Goods Sent	30,000	By Branch Stock a/c	1,50,000
$\frac{1}{5} \times 1{,}50{,}000$		By Loading on Returns $\frac{1}{5} \times 15{,}000$	3,000
To Branch stock a/c — Returns	15,000		
To Trading a/c (Transfer)	1,08,000		
	1,53,000		1,53,000

Stock Adjustment A/c

Particulars	*Amount*	*Particulars*	*Amount*
To Stock Reserve on Closing Stock $\frac{1}{5} \times 18{,}000$	3,600	By Stock Reserve on opening stock $\frac{1}{5} \times 25{,}000$	5,000
To Loading on Goods Returned $\frac{1}{5} \times 15{,}000$	3,000	By Loading on Goods Sent to Branch $\frac{1}{5} \times 1{,}50{,}000$	30,000
To Branch P & L a/c — Gross profit	36,400	By Branch Stock a/c (surplus)	8,000
	43,000		43,000

Branch Debtors A/c

Particulars	*Amount*	*Particulars*	*Amount*
To Balance b/d	20,000	By Cash a/c	85,000
To Branch Stock a/c — Credit Sales	90,000	By Branch P & L a/c (Bad Debts)	1,000
		By Branch P & L a/c (Discount allowed)	2,000
		By Balance c/d	22,000
	1,10,000		1,10,000

Branch P & L a/c

Particulars	*Amount*	*Particulars*	*Amount*
To Branch Cash — Expenses	16,500	By Branch Adj. a/c — Gross profit	36,400
To Branch debtors — Bad Debtors	1,000		
To Branch debtors — Discount allowed	2,000		
To General P & L a/c Net profit	16,900		
	36,400		36,400

Problem 19

Auto Distributors Ltd., has two branches at Masjid and Jogeshwari. Goods are invoiced to branches at cost plus 50%. Both the branches remit all cash received to the head office and all expenses are also met by head office from the following particulars. Prepare :

1. Branch Stock a/c.
2. Branch Stock Adjustment a/c.
3. Branch Debtors a/c.
4. Goods Sent to Branch a/c/
5. Branch Profit & Loss a/c for the year ended 31st December 1998.

	Masjid Rs.	Jogeshwari Rs.
Stock on 1-1-98 (at invoice price)	18,600	31,200
Debtors on 1-1-98	13,600	17,400
Goods returned to H.O.	3,000	—
Transfer form Jogeshwari to Masjid	4,200	4,200
Goods invoiced (cost price)	68,000	72,000
Cash sales	50,020	70,000
Credit sales	62,000	60,200
Collection from debtors	60,800	59,600
Returns from debtors	2,400	3,000
Shortage of stock	900	—
Surplus in stock	—	600
Discount allowed to customers	400	700
Expenses at branches	10,800	13,400

(University of Bombay B. Com. October 1999)

Solution

In the Books of Auto distributors Ltd.
Branch stock A/c

Particulars	*Masjid*	*Jogeshwari*	*Particulars*	*Masjid*	*Jogeshwari*
To Balance b/d	18,600	31,200	By Branch Cash sales	50,020	70,000
To Goods sent to Branch (Invoice price)	102,000	1,08,000	By Branch Debtors — Credit sales	62,000	60,200
To Branch Debtors — Returns	2,400	3,000	By Goods sent to branch — Returns	3,000	—
To Goods sent to branch transfer	4,200	—	By Goods sent to branch — transfer	—	4,200
To Surplus	—	600	By shortage	900	—
			By Balance c/d (Balancing figure)	11,280	8,400
	1,27,200	1,42,800		1,27,200	1,42,800

Branch Debtors A/c

Particulars	*Masjid*	*Jogeshwari*	*Particulars*	*Masjid*	*Jogeshwari*
To Balance b/d	13,600	17,400	By Branch Cash	60,800	59,600
To Branch Stock a/c Credit Sales	62,000	60,200	By Branch Stock – returns	2,400	3,000
			By Branch Stock returns		
			By Branch P & L a/c (Discount)	400	700
			By Balance c/d (balance figure)	12,000	14,300
	75,600	77,600		75,600	77,600

Branch Stock Adjustment A/c

Particulars	Masjid	Jogeshwari	Particulars	Masjid	Jogeshwari
To Goods sent to Branch — loading in return	1,000		By Stock Reserve (loading in opening stock)	6,200	10,400
To Goods sent to branch-in loading	—	1,400	By Good Sent to branch — Loading in goods sent	34,000	36,000
To Branch stock a/c — Loading in shortage	300		— By Goods sent to branch — loading in goods transferred	1,400	—
To Stock reserve — Loading in closing Stock	3,760	2,800	By Branch stock a/c loading in surplus	—	200
To Cross profit	36,540	42,400			
	41,600	46,600		41,600	46,600

Branch Profit & Loss A/c

Particulars	Masjid	Jogeshwari	Particulars	Masjid	Jogeshwari
To Shortage (lost)	600	—	By Branch stock Adj. a/c — Gross profit	36,540	42,400
To Branch debtors — Discount	400	700	By Surplus (cost)	—	400
To Branch Expenses	10,800	13,400			
To General P & L a/c	24,740	28,700			
	36,540	42,800		36,540	42,800

Goods Sent to Branch A/c

Particulars	Masjid	Jogeshwari	Particulars	Masjid	Jogeshwari
To Branch stock a/c — Returns	3,000	—	By Branch stock — Goods sent to branch	1,02,000	1,08,000
To Branch Stock — Transfer	—	4,200	By Branch stock — Transfer	4,200	—
To Branch Stock Adj. a/c — Loading in goods sent	34,000	36,000	By Branch stock Adj. a/c — Loading in returns	1,000	—
To Branch Stock Adj. a/c (loading in goods transferred)	1,400	—	By Branch stock Adj. a/c (Loading in goods transferred)	—	1,400
To Trading a/c	68,800	69,200			
	1,07,200	1,09,400		1,07,200	1,09,400

4. Wholesale Branch System

When an organisation supplies goods to retailers at a wholesale price, the branch earns two types of profit, viz, wholesale profit and retail profit. Wholesale profit it the difference between wholesale price and cost price and retail profit is the difference between wholesale price and retail price. The Head office follows this system to know the retail profit earned by retail branch. Under this system the Head office supplies goods to branch at wholesale price and the branch sells it at a retail price.

Accounting Treatment

The Head office prepares branch trading and profit & loss a/c at the wholesale price and not at the cost price. No difficulty is encountered as long as the branch sells all the goods supplied by Head office. But if there is unsold stock at the end of the year, then it will be valued at wholesale price and not at cost price. To know the correct profit or loss, the unsold stock is to be valued at cost price by creating stock reserve for the unrealised profit. The following entry is passed.

Head Office P & L a/c Dr.
To Stock Reserve a/c

Problem 20

A Head office sends goods to its branch at 20% less than the list price. Goods are sold at cost plus 100%. From the following particulars, ascertain the profit made at the head office and the branch on the wholesale basis.

	Head office Rs.	*Branch* Rs.
Purchases	2,00,000	—
Goods sent to branch (Invoice price)	80,000	—
Sales	1,70,000	80,000

Assume that the head office is selling goods to customers at catalogue price.

Solution

Working Notes :

1. **Calculation of invoiced price of goods sold by the branch :**
The sale price is 200 (i.e., 100 + 100)
The price at which goods are invoiced by the head office to the branch is Rs. (200 – 40) = 160
For 200 sale price, the goods solds by the branch is Rs. 80,000
For 160 sale price → ?
$$\frac{160}{200} \times 80{,}000 = \text{Rs. } 64{,}000$$
2. **Calculation of invoice price of the closing stock**

Invoice price of the goods sent by the H.O. to the branch	80,000
Less : Invoice price of goods sold by the branch	64,000
Invoice price of closing stock with the branch	16,000

3. **Calculation of stock Reserve in the Branch Closing Stock**

Invoice price of closing stock with the branch	16,000
Less : Cost price of closing stock with the branch	10,000
$16{,}000 \times \frac{100}{160}$	
Stock Reserve	6,000

4. Calculation of Cost Price of Goods Sold by the Head office

For 200 sale price : Cost price is Rs. 100

for 1,70,000 ?

$$\frac{1,70,000 \times 100}{200} = \text{Rs. } 85,000$$

5. Calculation of Cost Price of Goods Sent by the H.O., to the Branch

For 160 (200 – 40) List price : The cost price is Rs. 100

For 80,000 → ?

$$\frac{100}{160} \times 80,000 = \text{Rs. } 50,000$$

6. Calculation of closing stock with the Head office

Cost price of goods purchased by H.O.		2,00,000
Less : Cost price of goods sent by H.O. to Branch	50,000	
Less cost price of goods sold by the head office	85,000	
		1,35,000
Cost of closing stock with the H.O.		65,000

In The Books of H.O

Head Office Trading A/c

Particulars	*Amount*	*Particulars*	*Amount*
To Purchases	2,00,000	By Goods sent to Branch	80,000
To Gross Profit c/d	1,15,000	By Sales a/c	1,70,000
		By Closing Stock	65,000
	3,15,000		3,15,000
To Stock Reserve	6,000	By Gross Profit b/d	1,15,000
To Net Profit	1,09,000		
	1,15,000		1,15,000

Branch Trading A/c

Particulars	*Amount*	*Particulars*	*Amount*
To Goods sent to Branch	80,000	By Sales a/c	80,000
To Gross Profit	16,000	By Closing Stock	16,000
	96,000		96,000

Problem 21

X Ltd., has a retail branch at Kolkota. Goods are sold to customers at cost plus 100%. The wholesale price is cost plus 80%. Goods are invoiced to Kolkota at wholesale price. From the following particulars, find out the profit made at Head office and Kolkota for the year 2002-03.

	Head office	*Kolkota*
Stock on 1st April 2002	Rs. 25,000	—
Purchases	1,50,000	—
Goods sent to branch (at invoice value)	54,000	
Sales	1,53,000	50,000
Stock on 31st March 2003	60,000	9,000

Sales at Head office are made only on wholesale basis and that at branch to consumers. Stocks at branch is valued at invoice price.

Solution

Trading A/c of the year ended 31-3-2003

Particulars	*H.O.*	*Kolkota*	*Particulars*	*H.O.*	*Kolkota*
To Opening Stock	25,000	—	By Sales	1,53,000	50,000
To Purchases	1,50,000	—	By Goods sent to branch	54,000	—
To Goods received from H.O.	—	54,000	By Closing Stock	60,000	9,000
To Gross profit	92,000	5,000			
	2,67,000	59,000		2,67,000	59,000
To Stock Reserve against branch stock $\frac{80}{180} \times 9,000$	4,000	—	By Gross Profit	92,000	5,000
To Net profit	88,000	5,000			
	92,000	5,000		92000	5,000

INDEPENDENT BRANCH

Independent branch means a branch which maintains its own set of books. The characteristics of the accounting system of an independent home branch can be summarised as follows :

1. Such a branch keeps a complete set of its books. Besides receiving goods from the head office, it may also purchase goods form outside parties. It maintains its own bank account. It may remit money from time to time to the Head office as per the head office instruction.
2. It prepares its own trial balance and final accounts and sends their copies to the Head office for their incorporation in the Head office books.
3. It maintains a Head office account in its books. This is of the nature of a personal account. All transactions relating to the head office are recorded in this accounts. The Head office also maintains a branch account in its books. It is also of the nature of a personal account. It records all transactions relating to the branch in this account.
4. For inter-branch transactions, there are two alternatives available.
   (*a*) Each branch may open a separate account for each of the branches. Such accounts are of the nature of personal account.
   (*b*) A branch may record transactions with the other branch of the same pattern as if the transactions are with the head office. In other words, all transactions relating to the other branches regarding receipt of goods or cash and sending of goods or cash are to be treated at par with the receipt of goods or cash from or to the Head office. At the end of a period, the branch sends a summary of the different transactions entered with different branches. The Head office maintains account of each of the branches in which necessary adjustment entries may be passed and accounts of different branches reconciled.

5. On receipt of trail balances and final accounts from each of the branches, the head office reconciles the balance as shown in the head office account in the books of the branch with the balance as shown by the branch account in the books of Head office. Necessary adjustment entries for reconciliation of differences are passed generally in the books of Head office.
6. Having reconciled the branch balance, the head office passes the incorporation entries for incorporating various branch balances in its books.

Though the branch is independent, some transactions between the head office and branch are recorded in the books of both head office and branch. Such entries are as follows :

Entries in The Books of Branch

1. Goods supplied by Head office :
   Goods received from H.O. a/c Dr.
   To H.O. a/c
2. Cash remittance form H.O., to branch :
   Bank a/c Dr.
   To H.O. a/c
3. Cash remittance from branch to H.O. :
   H.O. a/c Dr.
   To Bank a/c
4. Remittance sent by branch but not received By H.O.
   Remittance in transit a/c Dr.
   To H.O. a/c
5. Assets purchased by branch but the asset a/c is to be kept in H.O.
   H.O. a/c Dr.
   To Bank a/c
6. Depreciation with respect to the above asset :
   Depreciation a/c Dr.
   To H.O. a/c
7. Head office expenses chargeable to branch
   H.O. Expenses a/c Dr.
   To H.O. a/c
8. Inter branch transactions - goods sent by one branch to another :
   Receiving Branch :
   Goods from H.O. a/c Dr.
   To H.O. a/c
   Supplying Branch :
   H.O. a/c Dr.
   To Goods sent to H.O. a/c

Entries in the Books of Head office

1. Goods supplied by head office :
   Branch a/c Dr.
   To Goods sent to branch a/c
2. Cash remittance from H.O., to branch :
   Branch a/c Dr.
   To Bank a/c

3. Cash remitted from branch to H.O.
   Bank a/c Dr.
   To Branch a/c
4. Goods sent by H.O. but not received by the branch
   Goods in transit a/c Dr.
   To Branch a/c
5. Asset purchased by branch but the asset a/c is to be kept in H.O.
   Branch asset a/c Dr.
   To Branch a/c
6. Depreciation with respect of the above asset :
   Branch a/c Dr.
   To Branch asset a/c
7. Head office expenses chargeable to branch :
   Branch a/c Dr.
   To P & L a/c
8. Inter-branch transactions - goods sent by one branch to another.
   Receiving branch a/c Dr.
   To Supplying Branch a/c

INCORPORATION OF BRANCH TRIAL BALANCE IN THE HEAD OFFICE

Head office and its various branches functions as one organisation and it is therefore, necessary that the head office should prepare only one combined balance sheet for the benefit of the shareholders and the outsiders. For this purpose, the head office is required to incorporate the branch trial balance in its books. The process by which consolidated balance sheet of the whole business is prepared is known as incorporation of the branch trial balance. The following are the two methods available for incorporating trial balance in the Head office.

First Method

Under this method branch trading and profit and loss a/c is prepared incorporating all revenue items. Assets, liabilities and profit are also incorporated in order to prepare the consolidated balance sheet. The following Journal entries are passed under this method.

1. For incorporating debit side items of trading account such as opening stock, net purchases and direct expenses :
   Branch Trading a/c Dr.
   To Branch a/c
2. For incorporating credit side items of trading account such as net sales and closing stock.
   Branch a/c Dr.
   To Branch Trading a/c
3. For incorporating gross profit
   Branch Trading a/c Dr.
   To Branch P & L a/c
4. For incorporating gross loss
   Branch P & L a/c Dr.
   To Branch Trading a/c

5. For incorporating total of various expenses and losses which appear on the debit side of profit and loss account :
   Branch P & L a/c Dr.
   To Branch a/c
6. For incorporating total of incomes and gains which appear on the credit side of P & L a/c
   Branch a/c Dr.
   To Branch P & L a/c
7. For incorporating net profit
   Branch P & L a/c Dr.
   To General P & L a/c
8. For Incorporating profit & loss
   General P & L a/c Dr.
   To Branch P & L a/c
9. For incorporating total of various branch assets.
   Branch assets a/c Dr.
   To Branch a/c
10. For incorporating total of various branch liabilities
   Branch a/c Dr.
   To Branch liabilities a/c

Second Method

Under this method, branch trading and profit & loss a/c is prepared as a memorandum account and entry for incorporating the net profit or loss is passed in the books of Head office. No entries are passed for incorporating branch assets and liabilities in the books of head office with the result that branch a/c in the books of head office will show equal amount of assets and liabilities, i.e., total assets = total liabilities.

Problem 22

From the following information show :

(*a*) The journal entries to incorporate the trial balance of the branch in the H.O., books and

(*b*) The branch current account after incorporation of the branch.

Agra branch trial balance as at December 31, 1999 is as under.

Particulars	*Amount*	*Particulars*	*Amount*
Purchases	17,350	Sales	38,200
Goods form H.O.	8,100	H.O., Current a/c	7,560
Selling expenses	4,260	Creditors	2,340
Administrative expenses	2,040		
Sundry expenses	1,380		
Petty cash	50		
Cash at Bank	1,250		
Debtors	6,400		
Stock on 1-7-99	7,270		
	48,100		48,100

Stock on land at the branch on 31st December 1999, Rs. 8,200. Agra branch current a/c in the H.O. books showed a balance of Rs. 8,440. While the goods sent to Agra branch a/c showed a balance of Rs. 8,980 by the closing date. A provision for doubtful debts is to be raised, calculated at $1\frac{1}{2}\%$ on debtors. **(University of Madras, B. Com. May 2001)**

Solution

Branch Trading A/c

Particulars	*Amount*	*Particulars*	*Amount*
To Opening Stock a/c	7,270	By Sales a/c	38,200
To Purchases	17,350	By Closing Stock a/c	8,200
To Goods from H.O.	8,100		
To Gross Profit c/d	13,680		
	46,400		46,400
To Expenses a/c	7,776	By Gross Profit b/d	13,680
To Net Profit	5,904		
	13,680		13,680

Branch A/c

Particulars	*Amount*	*Particulars*	*Amount*
To Opening balance	8,440	By Branch Trading a/c	32,720
To Branch Trading a/c	46,400	By Branch P & L	7,776
To Branch Creditors	2340	By Branch Petty Cash	50
To Provision for Doubtful Debts	96	By Bank - Cash at Bank	1,250
		By Branch debtors	6,400
		By Branch closing Stock	8,200
		By Goods in Transit	880
	57,276		57,276

Incorporating Journal Entries in the H.O. Books

Date	*Particulars*	*Dr. Amount*	*Cr. Amount*
	Branch trading a/c Dr.	32,720	
	To Branch a/c		32,720
	(Being the debit side of branch trading a/c incorporated :		
	Opening stock (1-7-99) 7,270		
	Purchase 17,350		
	Goods from H.O. 8,100		
	32,720		
	Branch a/c Dr.	46,400	
	To Branch trading a/c		46,400
	(Being the credit side of branch trading a/c incorporated :		
	Sales 38,200		
	Closing stock 31-12-99 8,200		
	46,400		

Date	Particulars		Dr. Amount	Cr. Amount
	Branch Trading a/c	Dr.	13,680	
	To Branch P & L a/c			13,680
	(Being the gross profit transferred)			
	Branch P & L a/c	Dr.	7,776	
	To Branch a/c			7,776
	(Being the debit side of P & L a/c incorporated)			
	Selling expenses 4,260			
	Administrative expenses 2,040			
	Sundry expenses 1,380			
	Provision for doubtful debts 96			
	7,776			
	Branch P & L a/c	Dr.	5,904	
	To General P & L a/c			5,904
	(Being net profit transferred)			
	Branch Petty Cash a/c	Dr.	50	
	Branch Cash at Bank a/c	Dr.	1,250	
	Branch Debtors a/c	Dr.	6,400	
	Branch Closing Stock a/c	Dr.	8,200	
	To Branch a/c			15,900
	(Being the asset side of branch balance sheet incorporated)			
	Branch a/c	Dr.	2,436	
	To Branch Creditors a/c			2,340
	To provision for Doubtful Debts a/c			96
	(Being the liability side of branch balance sheet incorporated)			
	Goods in Transit a/c	Dr.	880	
	To Branch a/c			880
	Goods sent to Agra Branch = 8,980			
	Less : Goods from H.O., given in Trial Balance = 8,100			
	880			
	Difference is treated as goods in transit			

Problem 23

From the following balances and additional information, in the books of Head office you are required to prepare for ascertaining profit - loss at branch :

(*i*) Branch a/c

(*ii*) Branch Trading, Profit & Loss a/c to ascertain the result of trading at branch.

(*iii*) Journal entries to incorporate the above figures.

Balances as on 31st March 2,000

Particulars	*Amount*	*Particulars*	*Amount*
Purchases	3,56,000	Bills payable	7,000
Stock 1-4-1999	1,20,000	Creditors	30,000
Salaries	20,000	Goods supplied To Head office	1,20,000
Commission	10,000	Sales	7,60,000
Head office a/c	64,800		
Cash received from Head office	1,80,000		
Bills Receivable	4,000		
Debtors	70,000		
Rent and expense	28,600		
Plant	28,000		
Cash in hand	35,600		
	9,17,000		9,17,000

Additional information :

1. The Branch account in H.O., books as on 31st March 2000 stood at Rs. 9,200 (Debit balance).
2. On 25th March 2000. the H.O., sent goods for Rs. 45,000 to the branch, received on 2nd April 2000.
3. A Cash remittance of Rs. 29,000 by branch on 28th March was received by H.O. on 3rd April 2000.
4. Closing stock as on 31st March 2,000 valued at Rs. 54,000.

(Delhi University, B. Com. (Hons.) 2000)

Solution

Branch A/c

Particulars	*Amount*	*Particulars*	*Amount*
To Balance b/d	9,200	By Goods in Transit a/c	45,000
To Branch Trading a/c :		By Cash in Transit a/c	29,000
— Sales	7,60,000	By Branch Trading a/c	
— Goods supplied to H.O. a/c	1,20,000	— Opening Stock	1,20,000
To Branch P & L a/c	Nil	— Purchases	3,56,000
To Branch Liabilities a/c		— Goods from H.O. a/c	1,80,000
— Bills payable	7,000	By Branch P &L a/c	
— Creditors	30,000	— Salaries	20,000
		— Commission	10,000
		— Rent & expenses	28,600
		By Branch Asset a/c	
		— Bills receivable	4,000
		— Debtors	70,000
		— Plant	28,000
		— Cash at bank	35,600
	9,26,200		9,26,200

Branch Trading A/c

Particulars	*Amount*	*Particulars*	*Amount*
To Opening Stock	1,20,000	By Sales a/c	7,60,000
To Purchase a/c	3,56,000	By Closing Stock	54,000
To Goods from H.O.	1,80,000		
	6,56,000		
Less : Goods supplied to H.O.	1,20,000		
	5,36,000		
To Gross profit	2,78,000		
	8,14,000		8,14,000
To Salaries a/c	20,000	By Gross Profit b/d	2,78,000
To Commission a/c	10,000		
To Rent & Expenses a/c	28,600		
To Net Profit	2,19,400		
	2,78,000		2,78,000

Journal Entries in H.O. Books

Date	*Particulars*	*Dr. Amount*	*Cr. Amount*
	Goods in transit a/c Dr.	45,000	
	Cash in transit a/c Dr.	29,000	
	To Branch a/c		74,000
	(Being in transit items to reconcile the mutual balances)		
	Branch Trading a/c Dr.	6,56,000	
	To Branch a/c		6,56,000
	(Being debit items of trading a/c incorporated)		
	Branch a/c Dr.	8,80,000	
	To Branch Trading a/c		8,80,000
	(Being items of sales and goods supplied to H.O.)		
	Branch P & L a/c Dr.	58,600	
	To Branch a/c	58,600	
	(Being items of salaries, commission, rent and expenses incorporated)		
	Branch Asset a/c Dr.	1,37,600	
	To Branch a/c		1,37,600
	(Being the following branch assets incorporated)		
	Bills Receivable 4,000		
	Debtors 70,000		
	Plant 28,000		
	Cash at Bank 35,600		
	Branch a/c Dr.	1,00,000	
	To Branch Liabilities a/c		1,00,000
	(Being the following branch liabilities incorporated :		
	Bills payable 70,000		
	Creditors 30,000		

Problem 24

VIP Traders Ltd., has the Head office at Churchgate and branch at Virar. The branch is authorised to have independent transactions. It maintains complete set of accounts.

Trial Balance of Virar Branch as at 31st March 1999.

	Debit *Rs.*	*Credit* *Rs.*
Sales	—	3,60,000
Purchases	1,30,000	—
Goods from Head office	1,24,000	—
Stock	60,000	—
Wages	66,000	—
Carriage	25,200	—
Salaries	18,000	—
Rent	9,600	—
Office expenses	9,200	—
Cash in box	4,000	—
Debtors / Creditors	3,200	24,000
Head office	—	94,000
	4,78,000	4,78,000

On 31st March 1999 stock was valued at Rs. 98,000. The Head office revealed Debit balance in branch account Rs. 1,08,000.

The analysis revealed :

(*a*) Rs. 8,000 remitted by Virar branch on 29th March 1999 was received by head office on 2nd April 1999.

(*b*) Goods worth Rs. 6,000 sent by head office on 28th March 1999 was received by Virar branch on 3rd April 1999.

You are required to :

(*i*) Pass Journal entries incorporating branch account.

(*ii*) Prepare Virar branch account in the books of Churchgate head office.

(*iii*) Prepare Branch Trading, Profit and Loss a/c for the year ended 31st March 1999.

(*iv*) Branch Balance Sheet as at 31st March 1999.

(University of Bombay B. Com. April 1999)

Solution

Journal Entries in The Books of Churchgate H.O.

Date	*Particulars*	*Dr. Amount*	*Cr. Amount*
	Cash in Transit a/c Dr. To Virar Branch a/c (Being cash sent by branch in transit on 31-3-99)	8,000	8,000
	Goods in Transit a/c Dr. To Virar Branch a/c (Being goods sent to branch in transit on 31-3-1999)	6,000	6,000

Date	Particulars		Dr. Amount	Cr. Amount
	Virar Branch a/c	Dr.	16,000	
	To General P & L a/c			16,000
	(Being net profit of P & L a/c taken to general P & L a/c)			
	Branch Stock a/c	Dr.	98,000	
	Branch Debtors a/c	Dr.	32,000	
	Branch Cash a/c	Dr.	4,000	
	To Virar Branch a/c			1,34,000
	(Being branch assets recorded).			
	Virar Branch a/c	Dr.	24,000	
	To Branch Creditors a/c			24,000
	(Being branch liabilities recorded in H.O.)			

In The Books of Churchgate H.O.

Virar Branch A/c

Particulars	Amount	Particulars	Amount
To Balance b/d (Balancing figure)	1,08,000	By Branch Stock	98,000
To General P & L a/c	16,000	By Branch Debtors	32,000
To Branch Creditors	24,000	By Branch Cash	4,000
		By cash in Transit	8,000
		By goods in Transit	6,000
	1,48,000		1,48,000

Branch Trading and P & L A/c for the year ending 31-3-99

Particulars	Amount	Particulars	Amount
To Opening Stock	60,000	By Sales a/c	3,60,000
To Purchases a/c	1,30,000	By Closing Stock	98,000
To Goods form H.O.	1,24,000		
To Wages a/c	66,000		
To Carriage inward	25,200		
To Gross Profit	52,800		
	4,58,000		4,58,000
To Salaries a/c	18,000	By Gross Profit b/d	52,800
To Rent a/c	9,600		
To Office Expenses a/c	9,200		
To Net Profit a/c	16,000		
	52,800		52,800

Balance Sheet as on 31-3-99

Particulars		Amount	Particulars	Amount
Creditors		24,000	Stock	98,000
H.O. a/c	1,08,000		Debtors	32,000
Add : Net Profit	16,000	1,24,000	Cash	4,000
			Cash in Transit	8,000
			Goods in Transit	6,000
		1,48,000		1,48,000

Problem 25

From the following information, prepare :

(*a*) Reconciliation of head office account in branch books and the branch account in the head office books and

(*b*) The trading and profit & loss account of the head office for the year ended 31st December 2001.

	Head office Rs.	*Branch Rs.*
Opening stock	10,000	4,500
Purchases	1,15,000	—
Sales	2,05,000	1,55,000
Other expenses	15,200	6,200
Closing stock	5,200	3,100

The branch books show the head office account at Rs. 9,000 (Cr.) and the head office books show the branch account at Rs. 24,000 (Dr.). The branch receives all its supplies from the head office which are invoiced at 25% over cost. During the year, the Head office credits its sales account with the invoice price of the goods sent to the branch.

The head office billed the branch for Rs. 12,000 on 31st December 2001 representing the Branch's share of the expenses in curried by the Head office. The said expenses had not been recorded in the books of the branch.

The expenses of the branch are met by the head office from time to time for which amounts are sent in advance to the branch. A sum of Rs. 3000 sent to the branch by the head office on 29th December 2001 in this connection, was received by the Branch on 3rd January 2002.

(ICWA Intermediate. Stage II, December 2002)

Solution

Reconciliation A/c of the Branch
(In H.O. Books)

Particulars	*Amount*	*Particulars*	*Amount*
To Balance b/d (as per H.O., books)	24,000	By Remittance in transit (transit to branch)	3,000
		By H.O. Expenses (Entry not yet made in branch books)	12,000
		By Balance (as per Branch books)	9,000
	24,000		24,000

Reconciliation a/c of the H.O. A/c
(In Branch Books)

Particulars	*Amount*	*Particulars*	*Amount*
To Balance b/d (as per H.O., books)	24,000	By Balance b/d (as per branch book)	9,000
		By Expenses	12,000
		By H.O. Cash in Transit	3,000
	24,000		24,000

Trading and Profit & Loss A/c

Particulars	H.O.	Branch	Total	Particulars	H.O.	Branch	Total
To Opening Stock	10,000	4,500	14,500	By Sales	1,00,500	1,55,000	2,55.500
To Purchases—H.O.	1,15,000	—	1,15,000	By Good Sent to Br.	1,04,500	—	1,04,500
To Goods from H.O.	—	1,04,500	1,04,500	By Closing Stock	5,200	3,100	8,300
To Gross Profit	85,200	49,100	1,34,300				
	2,10,200	1,58,100	3,68,300		2,10,200	1,58,100	3,68,300
To Expenses	15,200	6,200	21,400	By Gross Profit	85,200	49,100	1,34,300
To H.O. Expenses	—	12,000	12,000	By Opeing Stock	900	—	900
To Stock Reserve	620	—	620	(Reserve) $4,500 \times \frac{1}{5}$			
(Closing) $3,100 \times \frac{1}{5}$							
To Net Profit	70,280	30,900	1,01,180				
	86,100	49,100	1,35,200		86,100	49,100	1,35,200

Problem 26

Imphal branch of a business having H.O., in Calcutta, prepare its accounts independently. The position as on 31-12-98 is depicted below.

	Calcutta H.O.		Imphal Branch	
	Dr. (Rs.)	Cr (Rs.)	Dr. (Rs.)	Cr (Rs)
Bills receivable / bills Payable	—	11,800	6,000	—
Debtors / creditors	78,500	39,600	58,400	29,200
Stock	1,42,000	—	72,000	—
Cash at bank	1,07,400	—	44,200	—
Fixed asset	4,53,500	—	1,59,400	—
Profit & loss a/c	—	1,46,600	—	30,600
Capital	—	8,82,000	—	—
Branch a/c	2,98,600	—	—	—
H.O. a/c	—	—	—	2,80,200
	10,80,000	10,80,000	3,40,000	3,40,000

It is revealed that the above accounts for the year ended 31-12-98 were prepared without considering the following fact :

(a) Goods worth Rs. 4,400 had been despatched by the H.O., to Imphal on 27-12-98 but the goods did not reach there till 2-1-99.

(b) As per convention the branch should be charged with Rs. 3,000 for administrative services rendered by the H.O.

(c) The branch had sent a Bank draft to the H.O., on 30-12-98 for Rs. 10,000. But the draft reached H.O., after 31-12-98.

(d) Stock stolen in transit Rs. 4,000 (Uninsured). The stock was invoiced by the H.O., to the branch and charged to the branch a/c. But the Branch Manager refused to consider it in the Branch books.

(e) Depreciation on some branch assets (of which accounts are maintained in H.O. Books) not provided for Rs. 2,500.

(f) The balance of branch profit should be transferred to the H.O. Books.

Show the necessary adjustment entries in the books of the H.O., and the branch. Prepare the Balance Sheet of the business as on 31-12-98 (Calcutta University B. Com. (Hons.) 1999).

Solution

In the Books of H.O.
Journal Entries

Date	Particulars		Dr. Amount	Cr. Amount
	Goods in Transit a/c	Dr.	4,400	
	To Imphal Branch a/c			4,400
	(Being the goods in transit adjusted)			
	Abnormal Loss a/c	Dr.	4,000	
	To Imphal Branch a/c			4,000
	(Being the loss in transit adjusted)			
	Branch P & L a/c	Dr.	2,500	
	To Branch Asset a/c			2,500
	(Being the adjustment for depreciation)			
	Profit & Loss a/c	Dr.	4,000	
	To Abnormal Loss a/c			4,000
	(Being the transfer of abnormal loss to P & L a/c).			
	Branch P & L a/c	Dr.	3,000	
	To P & L a/c			3,000
	(Being the adjustment for branch expenses paid)			
	Branch P & L a/c	Dr.	25,100	
	To General P & L a/c			25,100
	(Being the adjustment for net profit of branch)			

In the books of Imphal Branch
Journal Entries

Date	Particulars		Dr. Amount	Cr. Amount
	Cash-in-Transit a/c	Dr.	10,000	
	To Calcutta H.O. a/c			10,000
	(Being the cash in transit adjusted)			

Balance Sheet of Calcutta H.O. and Imphal Branch as on 31-12-98

Particulars		Amount	Particulars		Amount
Capital		8,82,000	**Fixed asset :**		
Profit & Loss a/c			Calcutta		4,53,500
Calcutta	1,45,600		Imphal	1,59,400	
Imphal	25,100		Less dep.	2,500	
		1,70,700			1,56,900
Creditors			**Stock :**		
Calcutta	39,600		Calcutta	1,42,000	
Imphal	29,200		Add : Goods in transit	4,400	
		68,800			1,46,400

Particulars	Amount	Particulars		Amount
Bills Payable :		Imphal		72,000
Calcutta	11,800	**Debtors**		
		Calcutta	78,500	
		Imphal	58,400	
				1,36,900
		Bills Receivable :		
		Imphal		6,000
		Cash at Bank		
		Calcutta		1,07,400
		Imphal	44,200	
		Add : Cash in Transit	10,000	
				54,200
	11,33,300			11,33,300

Problem 27

Give Journal entries to rectify or adjust the following in the books of both the head office and the branch :

(*i*) Goods costing Rs. 16,000, purchased by branch but payment made by head office. The head office has debited the amount to its own purchase account.

(*ii*) Branch paid Rs. 30,000 as salary to a visiting head office official. The branch has debited the amount to salaries account.

(*iii*) Depreciation, Rs. 50,000 in respect of branch assets whose accounts are kept in head office books is to be recorded by both the parties.

(*iv*) Expenses Rs. 70,000 to be charged to the branch for work done on its behalf by the head office. **(C.S. Foundation, December 2000)**

Solution

Journal Entries in The Books of H.O.

S.No.	Particulars	Dr. Amount	Cr. Amount
1.	Branch a/c Dr. To Purchases a/c (Purchases made by the branch and paid for by the head office wrongly debited to hėad office purchases account error now rectified).	16,000	16,000
2.	Salaries a/c Dr. To Branch a/c (Salary paid by branch to a visiting head office official)	30,000	30,000
3.	Branch a/c Dr. To Branch Fixed Asset a/c (Depreciation on branch fixed assets, account for which are maintained in the head office books)	50,000	50,000
4.	Branch a/c Dr. To Administrative Expenses a/c (Branch is charged for work done by head office on behalf of the branch)	70,000	70,000

Journal Entries In The Books of Branch

S.No.	Particulars	Dr. Amount	Cr. Amount
1.	Purchases a/c Dr. To Head Office a/c (Purchases for which payment has been made by head office)	16,000	16,000
2.	Head office a/c Dr. To salaries a/c (Salary paid to a visiting head office official wrongly debited to salaries a/c, error now rectified).	30,000	30,000
3.	Depreciation a/c Dr. To Head Office a/c (Depreciation on fixed asset whose accounts are maintained in the books of head office)	50,000	50,000
4.	Head Office Expenses a/c Dr. To Head Office a/c (Charge by head office for work done by it on behalf of the branch)	70,000	70,000

FOREIGN BRANCH

When a branch is located in a foreign country it is called a foreign branch. Such branch will keep its books of accounts in foreign currency. The main problem which the head office faces under this type of branch is to convert the branch trial balance from the foreign currency to the currency of that country where a head office is working in order to incorporate, the branch trial balance in the books of head office. Otherwise for all purposes this type of branch is treated as an independent branch.

Techniques for Foreign Currency Translation — Accounting Standard — II (AS - II)

The following terms are used in AS - II along with their meaning.

1. **Reporting currency :** It is the currency used in presenting the financial statements.
2. **Foreign currency :** It is a currency other than the reporting currency of an enterprise.
3. **Exchange rate :** It is the rates for exchange of two currencies as applicable to the realisation of a specific asset or the payment of a specific liability of the recording of a specific transaction or a group of inter-related transactions.
4. **Average rate :** It is the mean of the exchange rates in force during a period.
5. **Forward rate :** It is the exchange rate established by the terms of an agreement for exchange of two currencies at a specified future date.
6. **Closing rate :** It is the exchange rate at the balance sheet date.
7. **Monetary Items :** It refers to money held and assets and liabilities to be received or paid in fixed or determinable amounts of money, e.g., cash receivables, payables.
8. **Non-Monetary items :** It refers to asset and liabilities other than monetary items, e.g., fixed assets, stock, investment in equity shares.
9. **Settlement date :** It is the date at which a receivable is due to be collected or payable is due to be paid.

10. Recoverable amount : It is the amount which the enterprise expects to recover from the future use of an asset, including its residual value on disposal.

Paragraphs 19 to 25 of AS - II deals with translation of the financial statements of foreign branches. There paragraphs are reproduced below.

1. **Paragraph 19 :** Revenue items, except opening and closing inventories and depreciation, should be translated into reporting currency of the reporting enterprise at average rate. In appropriate circumstances, weighted average rate may be applied, e.g., where the income or expenses are not earned or incurred evenly during the accounting period (such as in the case of seasonal business) or where there are exceptionally wide fluctuations in exchange rate during the accounting period.

Opening and closing inventories should be translated at the rates prevalent at the commencement and close respectively of the accounting period.

Depreciation should be translated at the rates used for the translation of the values of the assets on which depreciation is calculated.

Illustration

Branch revenue items are as follows :

	(000)
Sales	$ 517
Wages and Salaries	115
Opening Stock	85
Goods from H.O.	255
Closing Stock	67

Monthly exchange rates for $ 1,000 :

Jan.	Rs. 20,500	Feb.	Rs 20,200	March	Rs. 19,900
Apr.	Rs. 20,100	May	Rs. 20,500	June	Rs. 20,300
July	Rs. 20,200	Aug.	Rs. 20,700	Sept.	Rs. 20,900
Oct.	Rs. 21,200	Nov.	Rs. 21,500	Dec.	Rs. 21,900

Translation

Average rate = $ 1,000 = Rs. 20,658

Opening rate = $ 1000 = Rs. 20,500

Closing rate = $ 1000 = Rs. 21,900

Sales $ 517 × 20,658 = Rs. 1,06,80,186

Wages & salaries $ 115 × 20,658 = Rs. 23,75,670

Opening stck $ 85 × 20,500 = Rs. 17,42,500

Goods form H.O., to be taken at the rupee value recorded at Closing stock

$ 67 × 21,900 = Rs. 14,67,300

Note : In case of wide fluctuation in exchange rate or seasonal business, weighted average should be taken.

2. **Paragraph 20 :** Monetary items should be translated using the closing rate. However in circumstances where the closing rate does not reflect with reasonable accuracy the amount in reporting currency that is likely to be realised from a rate that reflects approximately the likely realisation as aforesaid should be used.

3. **Paragraph 21 :** Non-monetary items other then inventories and fixed assets should be translated using the exchange rate at the time of the transaction.
4. **Paragraph 22 :** Fixed assets are normally translated at the original rate consistent with the historical cost concept. However, if there is change in the value of foreign currency, liabilities due to increase or decrease in the exchange rate, adjustment is necessary to the cost of fixed assets and so depreciation also charges.

Illustration

Fixed assets at the branch \$ 55,000. Life 10 years. Exchange rate at the time of purchase on 1-1-2001 = Rs. 12,500. Loan taken to purchase the fixed assets \$ 45,000 (at the rate \$ 1,000 = Rs. 12,500) on the same date. As on 31-12-2001, the exchange rate was \$ 1,000 = Rs. 13,900, as on 31-12-2002, the exchange rate was \$ 1,000 = Rs. 14,700 and as on 31-12-2003 exchange rate was & 1,000 = Rs. 16,800.

Average rates for \$ 1,000 : 2001, Rs. 12,700, 2002 – Rs. 14,200, 2003 – Rs. 15,400.

Annual loan instalments \$ 4,500 along with 18% interest p.a. were paid at year end every year.

Translation For 2001 :

		(Rs. 000)
	Fixed assets at original exchange rate \$ 1,000 = Rs. 12,500	6,87,500
Add :	Adjustment for increase in foreign currency liability \$ 45 × (13,900 – 12,500)	63,000
	Adjusted value of fixed assets	750,500
	Depreciation Rs. $\frac{7,50,500}{10}$	75,050
	Long terms loan (\$ 45,000 – \$ 4,500) × Rs. 13.90	= 5,62,950
	Interest \$ 45,000 × $\frac{18}{100}$ Rs. 12.70	= 1,02,870

Translation for 2002

	Fixed asset : (Adjusted value less depreciation i.e.) 7,50,500 – 75,050	6,75,450
Add :	Adjustment for increase in foreign currency liability \$ 40.5 (14,700 – 13,900).	32,400
	Adjusted value of fixed assets	7,07,850
	Depreciation $\frac{7,07,850}{9}$ =	78,650
	Long terms loan (\$ 40,500 – \$ 4,500) × RS. 14.70	= 5,29,200
	Interest \$ 40,500 × $\frac{18}{100}$ Rs. 14.20	= 30,618

Translation for 2,003

	Fixed asset : Adjusted value less depreciation 7,07,850 – 78,650	= 6,29,200
Add :	Adjustment for increase in foreign currency loan \$ 36 × (16,800 – 14,700)	75600
	Adjusted value of fixed assets	7,04,800

Depreciation $\frac{7,04,800}{8}$ = 88,100

Long term loan (\$ 36,000 – 84,500) × Rs. 16.8 = 5,29,200

Interest \$ 36000 × $\frac{18}{100}$ × Rs. 154 = 99,792

5 **Paragraph 23 :** Balance in head office account whether debit or credit should be reported at the amount of the balance in the branch account in the books of head office after adjusting for unresponded transactions.

6. **Paragraph 24 :** The net exchange difference resulting from the transaction of items in the financial statements of a foreign branch should be recognised as income or expense for the period, except to the extent adjusted in the carrying amount of the related fixed assets in accordance with paragraph 22 above.

7. **Paragraph 25 :** Contingent liability should be translated into the reporting currency of the enterprise at the closing rate.

Problem 28

The London Branch of Bangalore Export House sent the following Trail Balance as on 31-12-2003.

	Dr. £	*Cr.* £
Fixed assets	17,500	—
Loan (taken to purchase fixed assets)	—	13,000
Depreciation	2,500	
Stock on 1-1-2003	8,200	
Goods form H.O.	58,800	
Sales	—	1,05,200
Salaries & wages	15,200	
Interest	2,880	
Cash at Bank	1,700	
Debtors	21,200	
H.O. Accounts	—	9,780
	1,27,980	1,27,980

Fixed assets were purchased on 1-1-2003 when £1 = 25.50, life was estimated to be 10 years. To finance the fixed assets a loan amounting to £ 22,000 was taken @ 18% interest p.a. Annual loan instalment of 3000 and interest were payable every December.

Exchange rates :

Average of 2001	£ 1 = Rs. 25.70
31-12-2001	£ 1 = Rs. 26.10
Average of 2002	£ 1 = Rs. 26.20
31-12-2002	£ 1 = Rs. 26.40
Average of 2003	£ 1 = Rs. 36.50
31-12-2003	£ 1 = Rs. 42.20

In the head office books London Branch a/c appeared as follows :

London Branch a/c

Particulars	£	Rs.	Particulars	£	Rs.
To Balance b/d	7,000	1,84,800	By Bank	56,020	20,44,730
To Goods	58,800	21,46,200	By Balance	9,780	4,12,716
To P & L a/c Exchange gain	—	1,26,446			
	65,800	24,57,446		65,800	24,57,446

Closing Stock : £ 2,400

You are required to show :

(1) Branch Fixed Asset a/c (2) Branch Loan a/c (3) Branch Trail Balance in rupee terms (4) Branch P & L a/c (5) Adjustment Entries to incorporate branch balances in the H.O., loans.

Solution

1. Branch Fixed Assets A/c

	Particulars	£	Rs.	Date	Particulars	£	Rs.
1-1-2001	To Balance b/d	25,000	6,37,500	31-12-2001	By Depreciation a/c	2,500	65,070
	To Adjustment	—	13,200		By Balance c/d	22,500	5,85,630
		25,000	6,50,700			25,000	6,50,700
1-1-2002	To Balance b/d	22,500	5,85,630	31-12-2002	By Depreciation a/c	2,500	65,703
	To adjustment	—	5,700		By Balance c/d	20,000	5,25,627
		22,500	5,91,330			22,500	5,91,330
1-1-2003	To Balance b/d	20,000	5,25,627	3-12-2003	By Depreciation a/c	25,00	97303
	To Adjustment	—	2,52,800		By Balance c/d	17,500	6,81,124
		20,000	7,78,427			20,000	7,78,427

2. Branch Loan A/c

	Particulars	£	Rs.	Date	Particulars	£	Rs.
31-12-2001	To Bank a/c	6,960	1,81,656	1-12-2001	By Balance b/d	22,000	5,61,000
	To Balance c/d	19,000	4,95,900		By Adjustment a/c	—	13,200
					By Interest a/c	3,960	1,03,356
		25,960	677,556			25,960	6,77,556
31-12-2002	To Bank	6,420	1,69,488	1-1-2002	By Balance b/d	19,000	4,95,900
	To Balance c/d	16,000	4,22,400		By Adjustments a/c	—	5,700
					By Interest a/c	3,420	90,288
		22,420	5,91,888			22,420	5,91,888
31-12-2003	To Bank a/c	5,880	2,48,136	1-1-2,003	By Balance b/d	16,000	4,22,400
	To Balance c/d	13,000	5,48,600		By Adjustment a/c	—	2,52,800
					By Interest a/c	2,880	1,21,536
		18,880	7,96,736			18,880	7,96,736

3. Trial Balance

	Dr.	Cr.
Fixed assets	6,81,124	—
18% Loan	—	5,48,600
Depreciation	97,303	—
Stock (8,200 × 26.4)	2,16,480	—
Goods form H.O.	21,46,200	—
Sales (1,05,200 × 36.5)	—	38,39,800
Salaries and wages (15,200 × 36.5)	5,54,800	—
Interest	1,21,536	—
Cash at Bank (1,700 × 42.20)	71,740	—
Debtors (21200 × 42.20)	8,94,640	—
H.O. a/c	—	4,12,716
Exchange loss (Balancing figure)	17,293	—
	48,01,116	48,01,116

4. Branch P & L A/c

Particulars	Amount	Particulars	Amount
To Opening Stock	2,16,480	By Sales	38,39,800
To Goods from H.O.	21,46,200	Closing stock	1,01,280
To Salaries & Wages	5,54,800	(2,400 × 42.2)	
To Depreciation	97,303		
To Interest a/c	1,21,536		
To Exchange loss	17,293		
To H.O. a/c-profit	7,87,468		
	39,41,080		39,41,080

5. Incorporation Entries

Date	Particulars		Dr. Amount	Cr. Amount
	Branch a/c	Dr.	7,87,468	
	To Branch P & L a/c			7,87,468
	Branch a/c	Dr.	5,48,600	
	To 18% Loan			5,48,600
	Fixed Assets a/c	Dr.	6,81,124	
	Closing Stock a/c	Dr.	1,01,280	
	Cash & Bank a/c	Dr.	71,740	
	Debtors a/c	Dr.	8,94,640	
	To Branch a/c			17,48,784

Branch A/c

Particulars	Amount	Particulars	Amount
To Balance b/d	4,12,716	By Sundries	17,48,784
To 18% Loan	5,48,600		
To Branch P & L a/c	7,87,468		
	17,48,784		17,48,784

QUESTIONS

Simple Questions

1. What is a branch ?
2. State the features of dependent branch.
3. State the features of independent branch.
4. State the different systems of books keeping that can be followed in case of dependent branch.
5. What is loading ? Why is it adopted.
6. Distinguish between "cost price" and "loaded price".
7. What is the significance of stock reserve account ?
8. What is the meaning of (*a*) Cash in transit and (*b*) Goods-in-transit.
9. What are inter-branch transactions ?
10. State the features of independent branch.
11. How are abnormal losses treated under "stock and debtors system" while preparing branch accounts.

EXERCISE 1

(When Branch Sells only H.O. Goods for Cash)

Bangalore traders invoiced goods to its Mysore Branch at cost. All the expenses are paid direct from the Head office. Petty cash expenses are met by the branch manager. Branch is advised to sell for cash only and deposit the days sale in the Head office a/c with a local bank. From the following details ascertain the profit of the Mysore Branch through Debtors system.

	(Rs. 000)
Stock 1-1-2003	Rs. 2,100
Petty cash 1-1-2003	50
Furniture 1-1-2003	250
Goods supplied from H.O.	7,800
Goods returned to H.O.	300
Cash sales	15,250
Salaries & wages	1,860
Advertisement	240
Rent and rates	360
Stock 31-12-2003	1,950
Petty cash 31-12-2003	30
Furniture 31-12-2003	230

Answer : Profit (Rs. 000) 5,100

EXERCISE 2

(When Branch Sells Goods for Cash and Credit)

Fancy Clothes Ltd., opened a branch on 1st January 1998 at Delhi. The figures given below are for the year 1998.

Goods sent to Branch	25,000
Sales : Cash	10,000
Credit	18,000
Cash received from debtors	16,000
Discount allowed to them	300
Cash sent to branch for expenses	3,500
Stock on 31st December 1998	4,000

Give Journal entries and prepare branch account.

(University of Madras, B. Com, May 2000)

Answer : Profit Rs. 3,200
Closing Debtors Rs. 1,700

EXERCISE 3

(When Goods are Sent to Branch at Invoice Price)

Goods are invoiced to the branch by the head office at Rs. 9,200, so as to include 25% profit on cost. From the following particulars prepare (*a*) Branch profit & loss account (*b*) Branch account.

	Rs.
Sales by the branch	8,460
Cash remitted by the branch	8,060
Returns to H.O.	200
Expenses paid by H.O. for branch	200
Furniture purchased by H.O. for branch	800
Stock at the end (invoice price)	600
Write off furniture at 10%	

(University of Madras, B. Com, May 2001)

Answer : Net profit Rs. 1,460

EXERCISE 3

(Stock and Debtors System)

A Head office in Chennai has a branch office at madurai. Goods are sent at cost plus $33\frac{1}{3}\%$ profit. From the following particulars prepare Branch Stock, Branch Debtors account, Branch Expenses account and Branch Adjustment account.

		Rs.
Stock on 1-1-1997 (Invoice price)		15,000
Debtors on 1-1-1997		11,400
Goods invoiced to branch to branch during the year (Invoice price)		67,000
Sales at branch : Cash	31,000	
Credit	37,400	68,400
Cash received from debtors		40,000
Bad debts written off		250
Discount allowed to customers		300
Expenses at branch		6,700
Stock on 31-12-97 (Invoice price)		13,400

(University of Madras B. Com, May 1998)

Answer : Branch Stock a/c : Shortage of 200 is the balancing figure.
Branch Adj. a/c : Net profit Rs. 9,700.

EXERCISE 4

Crossroad Stores of Mumbai (H.O.) has a branch at Pune. It charges goods to its branch at cost plus $33\frac{1}{3}\%$.

Following information is available for the transactions of the Pune Branch.

	Rs.
Balance as on 1-1-1999 :	
Debtors	50,000
Stock at invoice price	4,00,000
Branch cash	10,000
Transactions during the year 1999 :	
Goods sent to branch at invoice price	8,00,000
Credit sales at branch	6,00,000
Cash sales at branch	4,00,000
Goods returned by branch at invoice price	40,000
Cash remitted to Branch for expenses	80,000
Goods returned by customers	10,000
Discount allowed to customers	2,000
Cash received from debtors	5,50,000
Bad debts at branch	8,000
Goods filfered at invoice price	12,000
Goods lost in fire at invoice price	4,000
Insurance company paid to H.O. for loss by fire	2,000

Branch remitted the entire cash to H.O., after keeping balance Rs. 10,000 with branch as on 31st December 1999.

Give necessary ledger a/c in the books of head office at Mumbai using Stock and Debtors system. **(University of Bombay, B. Com, April 2000)**

Answer : Goods Sent to Branch a/c

— Balancing figred transferred to trading a/c Rs. 5,70,000.

Branch adjustment a/c

— Balancing figure transferred to branch P & L a/c Rs. 2,47,500.

Branch Expenses a/c

— Balance transferred to P & L a/c — Rs. 90,000

— Branch P & L a/c — Profit Rs. 1,47,500

EXERCISE 5

Mr. 'X' has a branch at Delhi and Haridwar and the goods are invoiced at a profit of 20% on invoice price. Following information is available of the transactions at Delhi Branch for the year ending 31st March 1998 :

	As on 1-4-1997 (Rs.)	*As on 31-3-1998 (Rs.)*
Stock at Invoice price	40,000	?
Debtors	12,000	11,000
Petty cash	150	250
Transactions during the year :-		
Goods sent to branch at invoice price		4,20,000
Goods returned to H.O.		15,000
Case sales		1,05,000
Credit sales		1,80,000
Normal loss at invoice price		350
Goods pilfered at invoice price		3,000
Goods lost by fire at invoice price		4,000
Insurance Co. paid to H.O., for loss by fire at Delhi		3,000
Cash sent for petty expenses		32,000
Bad debts at Delhi branch		400
Goods transferred to Haridwar branch under instructions from H.O. at Invoice price		12,000
Insurance charges paid by H.O.		200
Goods returned by Debtors		500

Note : Goods transferred to Haridwar branch were in transit (given above) on 31st March 1998.

Prepare various ledger accounts in the books of head office under stock and debtors system.

(University of Delhi B. Com. (Hons.) 1998)

Answer : Net profit Rs. 21,520.

EXERCISE 6

ANT Co. of Calcutta has a branch at Mumbai. Goods are invoiced to the branch at cost plus $33\frac{1}{3}$%. Branch remits all cash receipts to the Head office and all expenses are paid by the head office. From the following particulars, prepare Branch Stock a/c, Branch Adjustment a/c, Branch Debtors a/c, and Branch Profit & Loss a/c in the books of ANT Co.

	Rs.
Stock on 1-1-96 at Branch (cost price)	96,000
Stock on 31-12-96 at branch (invoice price)	1,00,000
Goods sent to branch at invoice price	3,80,000
Cash sales	2,20,000
Credit sales	1,80,000
Discount allowed to customers	4,000
Goods returned by branch at invoice price	5,000
Bad debts written off	2,000
Branch expenses	24,800
Cash received from customers	1,64,000

(Calcutta University, B. Com. (Pass) 1997)

Answer : Net profit of branch Rs. 66,950

EXERCISE 7

A trader has its branch at Calcutta to which the goods are invoiced at cost plus 20%. Prepare Branch a/c under Stock and Debtors System in the books from the following :

Opening stock at branch	24,000
Cash sales at branch	17,500
Credit sales	41,000
Collection from debtors	37,900
Goods received from H.O.	30,000
Branch expenses :	
Paid by H.O.	3,000
Paid by branch	6,000
Expenses unpaid	1,400
Closing stock at branch	18,000
Closing balance of debtors	9,160
Goods in transit from H.O.	3,600

(University of Delhi B. Com. (Hons.) 1997)

Answer : Net profit Rs. 18,100

EXERCISE 8

(Final A/c System)

The following is the Trial Balance of Calcutta Branch as at 31st March 1995.

	Dr. (*Rs.*)	*Cr.* (*Rs.*)
Bombay head office	32,400	—
Stock - 1st April 1994	60,000	—
Purchase	1,78,000	—
Goods received from H.O.	90,000	—
Sales	—	3,80,000
Goods supplied to H.O.	—	60,000
Salaries	15,000	—
Debtors	37,000	—
Creditors	—	18,500
Rent	9,600	
Office expenses	4,700	
Cash in hand and at bank	17,800	
Furniture	14,000	
	4,58,500	4,58,500

Closing stock was valued at Rs. 27,000. The Branch account in the books of the H.O. stood at Rs, 4,600 (Debit balance) on 31st March 1995. On 28th March 1995, the head office forwarded goods to the value of Rs. 25,000 to the branch where they were received on 3rd April 1995.

Required :

(*a*) Branch Trading and Profit & Loss a/c

(*b*) Journal entries necessary to incorporate the above figures.

(*c*) Calcutta Branch a/c in the books of the H.O.

(University of Delhi B. Com. (Hons.) 1995)

Answer : Net profit Rs. 1,09,700

EXERCISE 9

Kota Branch with its Head office at Delhi supplies partly from head office and partly from outside suppliers. The branch keeps a separate set of books on 30th June 1,992. The following trial balance were extracted

	Head office		Branch	
	Dr. (Rs.)	Cr (Rs.)	Dr. (Rs.)	Cr (Rs)
Share capital	—	30,000		—
Fixed assets	16,000	—	8,000	—
Profit & loss a/c on 1-7-1991	—	4,000		—
Opening stock (at cost)	14,000	—	1,900	—
Debtors and creditors	17,000	10,000	1,500	2,050
Cash	3,000	—	1,000	—
Purchased & sales	1,20,000	1,40,000	6,750	22,500
Sundry expenses	15,000	—	2,250	—
Goods form H.O.	—	12,000	11,500	—
Current a/c	11,000	—	—	8,350
	1,96,000	1,96,000	32,900	32,900

Fixed assets are to be depreciated by 10%

Stock on 30th June 1992 :

Head office Rs. 10,000

Branch Rs. 2,100

Prepare the company's profit & loss a/c for the year ended 30th June 1992 and its Balance sheet on the same date. **(Mahatma Gandhi University B. Com. October 1996)**

Answer : Net profit of H.O. 11,400, Net profit of branch 1,400
Total of Balance Sheet Rs. 58,850

EXERCISE 10

(Independent Branch)

A firm has its head office in Mumbai and an independent branch in Calcutta. The following were the balances as on 31st March 1999.

	H.O.	Branch
Liabilities :		
H.O. a/c	—	1,28,020
P & L a/c	14,660	3,060
Creditors	1,23,960	31,920
Capital	3,00,000	—
	4,38,620	163,000
Assets :		
Fixed assets	2,36,000	1,16,000
Stock	35,200	20,740
Debtors	17,820	24,840
Cash	19,740	1,420
Branch a/c	1,29,860	—
	4,38,620	1,63,000

Information to be adjusted was as follows :

(*i*) Branch had sent a cheque for Rs. 1,000 to H.O. On 25th March but not received and recorded by H.O., till next month.
(*ii*) Depreciation of branch assets, of which accounts were maintained by the head office, not provided for Rs. 250.
(*iii*) It was agreed that branch should be charged with Rs. 300 for administrative service, rendered by the head office during the year.
(*iv*) Goods worth Rs. 840 forwarded by H.O., to branch on 27th March but not received and recorded by branch till next month.

Prepare Balance Sheet of the firm for the whole business as on 31st March 1999 after passing journal entries for recording adjustments and profits in the books of Head office and branch.

(University of Delhi B. Com. (Hons.) 1999)

Answer : Total of Balance Sheet Rs. 4,73,350.

EXERCISE 11

M/s Vivek Agencies Limited have Head Office at Parle and Branch Office at Virar. Both offices maintain independent books of accounts. Their Trial Balance on 31st March 1998 was as follow :

	Parle		*Virar*	
	Dr. (Rs.)	*Cr (Rs.)*	*Dr. (Rs.)*	*Cr (Rs)*
Share capital	—	20,000	—	—
Fixed assets	64,000	—	32,000	—
Profit & Loss a/c		16,000		—
Stocks	56,000	—	7,600	—
Purchases/sales	4,80,000	5,60,000	27,000	90,000
Goods from H.O.	—	48,000	—	—
Goods from branch	—	—	46,000	—
Administration expenses	60,000	—	9,000	—
Branch a/c	44,000	—	—	—
H.O. a/c	—	—	—	33,400
Debtors/Creditors	68,000	40,000	6,000	8,200
Cash on hand	12,000	—	4,000	—
	7,84,000	7,84,000	1,31,600	1,31,600

Additional information :

(*i*) Stock on 31-3-1998 at Parle Rs. 40,000, Virar Rs. 8,400
(*ii*) Depreciate fixed assets @ 10%.
(*iii*) Difference in H.O., and Branch a/c to be treated cash in transit.

You are required to prepare in books of head office.

(*i*) Branch a/c (*ii*) Columnar Profit & Loss a/c (*iii*) Balance Sheet

(University of Bombay, B. Com. April 1998).

Answer : Net Profit Parle Rs. 45,600, Net Profit of Virar Rs. 5,600
Total of Balnce Sheet Rs. 2,35,400

EXERCISE 12

(Foreign Branch)

Carlin & Co., has head office at New York (U.S.A) and branch at Mumbai (India). Mumbai branch furnishes you with its trial balance as on 31st March 1999 and the additional information given thereafter.

	Dr.	Cr
	(Rupees in thousands)	
Stock on 1st April 1998	300	—
Purchases and sales	800	1,200
Sundry debtors and Creditors	400	300
Bills of Exchange	120	240
Wages and salaries	560	—
Rent rates, & taxes	360	—
Sundry charges	160	—
Computers	240	—
Bank balance	420	—
New York office a/c	—	1,620
	3,360	3,360

Additional information :

(*a*) Computers were acquired from a remittance of US $ 6,000 received from New York head office and paid to the suppliers. Depreciate computers at 60% for the year.

(*b*) Unsold stock of Mumbai branch was worth Rs. 4,20,000 on 31st March 1999.

(*c*) The rates of exchange may be taken as follows

(*i*) On 1-4-1998 @ Rs. 40 per US $.

(*ii*) On 31-3-1999 @ Rs. 42 per US $.

(*iii*) Average exchange rate for the year @ Rs. 41 per US $.

(*iv*) Conversion in $ shall be made up to two decimal accuracy.

You are asked to prepare in US Dollars the revenue statement for the year ended 31st March 1999 and the Balance sheet as on that date of Mumbai branch as would appear in the books of New York head office of Carlin & Co. You are informed that Mumbai branch account showed a debit balance of U.S. $ 39,609.18 on 31-3-1999 in New York books and there were no items pending reconciliation. **(C.A. Inter May 1999)**

Answer : Net Loss Rs. 17,685.38
Balance Sheet Total Rs. 34,780.9

32

CHAPTER

Insurance Claims

INTRODUCTION

A contract of insurance is a contract under which one party known as insurer undertakes to indemnify the other party known as insured on the happening of an unforeseen event in consideration for a fixed amount known as premium. Though the liability of the insurer to indemnify arises on the happening of an event the liability is limited to the amount of actual loss suffered by the insured. However in case of under insurance, the insurance liability is limited to the extent of the coverage.

CLAIMS UNDER FIRE INSURANCE

A fire insurance policy is taken to cover the following types of risk.

(*a*) Loss on stock.

(*b*) Loss of fixed assets such as building, machinery, furniture.

(*c*) Loss of profit arising owing to dislocation caused by fire.

1. CLAIM FOR LOSS OF STOCK

When the subject matter of fire insurance is subjected to risk of loss the claim for such loss can be calculated as follows :

1. **Where proper stock records are maintained and such records are not destroyed by fire.** The following steps are involved.

   (*a*) Ascertain the value of stock on the date of occurrence of fire by referring to stock record.

   (*b*) Ascertain the amount of stock lost by fire. The following formula is used.

Amount of stock lost by fire = Value of stock on the date of fire – Value of stock saved or salvaged

   (*c*) Apply the average clause if applicable. The following formula is used.

$$\text{Claim} = \text{Loss suffered} \times \frac{\text{Sum Insured}}{\text{Actual Insurable Value}}$$

2. **Where proper records are not maintained or such records are destroyed by fire :** As records are not maintained it is some what difficult to know the value of stock lost and consequently the claim on such loss of stock. The following steps are involved :

(*a*) Determine the estimated value of stock on the date of occurrence of fire by preparing a memorandum trading account for the period of commencement of accounting year to the date of occurrence of fire. This is shown under the following proforma.

Memorandum Trading A/c

Particulars	*Amount*	*Particulars*	*Amount*
To Opening stock	XX	By Sales	XX
To Purchases	XX	By Closing stock	XX
To Manufacturing expenses	XX	(Balancing figure)	
To Gross profit			
(Calculated as a Percentage on Sales)			
	XX		XX

(*b*) Ascertain the amount of stock lost by the occurrence of fire : The following formula is used

Amount of stock lost by fire = Value of stock as shown by Memorandum Trading a/c – Value of stock saved or salvaged

(*c*) Apply the average clause, if applicable

TERMS OR CONCEPTS TO BE NOTED UNDER FIRE INSURANCE POLICIES

1. **Amount of Indemnity :** It represents the amount which will be made good by the Insurer on destruction of stock by the occurrence of fire. Under no circumstance insured will get more amount owing to loss suffered by him though the insured value of the property is high.
2. **Period of indemnity :** It relates to the duration which dislocates business owing to occurrence of fire. This period differs with the nature of the business and the time involved in getting the new machinery or equipment. Generally the period of indemnity does not exceed one year.
3. **Average clause :** An average clause is applicable when an insured has underinsured his goods. In such a case the insurer pays only proportionally but not the entire amount of loss suffered by him. The following formula is used.

$$\text{Claim} = \text{Loss suffered} \times \frac{\text{Sum Insured}}{\text{Actual Insurable Value}}$$

Illustration

Value of goods Rs. 30,000
Goods insured for Rs. 20,000
Actual loss suffered Rs. 15,000
Determine the claim

Solution

$$\text{Claim} = \text{Loss suffered} \times \frac{\text{Sum Insured}}{\text{Actual Insurable Value}}$$

$$= 15{,}000 \times \frac{20{,}000}{30{,}000} = \text{Rs. } 10{,}000$$

However if the goods is totally destroyed the average clause will not be applicable. In this case the amount of claim is restricted to Rs. 20,000.

4. **Normal Percentage of gross profit on sales :** While preparing the Memorandum Trading account it was mentioned that the estimated value of goods destroyed by fire is calculated by considering the normal percentage of gross profit on sales. The normal percentage of gross profit is calculated on the basis of gross profit ratio of the previous year. Where gross profit ratio is given for more then one year we have to take average of gross profit as the normal rate of gross profit on sales.

Where the gross profit ratio for the previous years show a rising trend, we have to consider the trend and accordingly decide the normal rate of gross profit.

In ascertaining the gross profit of the previous year necessary adjustments are to be made in respect of opening stock or closing stock. Where stock values are over or under valued, they must be adjusted and shown at cost price.

Similarly, where any slow moving material is included in the opening stock or closing stock of any previous year such item must be eliminated from the stock taken into memorandum trading account in order to get the normal gross profit.

5. **Salvage :** Sometimes a portion of the stock may be saved from fire either in undamaged or partly damaged condition. Such stock are known's "salvaged" stock. Usually when the goods insured are destroyed by fire the Insurer has a right to take possession of the salvaged stock. In case the salvaged stock is retained by the insured the amount of insurance claim is to be reduced by the value of Salvage.

Problem 1

A fire accurred on the Premises of a Merchant on 1-7-99 and a considerable part of the stock was destroyed. The value of stock saved from the fire was Rs. 45,000 (at cost) on 1-4-99. The stock was valued at Rs. 3,67,400 (which is 10% above cost). The purchases from 1-4-99 to the date of fire were Rs. 10,00,000 and the sales were Rs. 15,65,000. On investigation of books of account it was understood that the average gross profit during the last 5 years were 36%. Find the fire claim amount. (University of Madras, B. Com. May 2001).

Solution

Memorandum Trading A/c

Particulars	*Amount*	*Particulars*	*Amount*
To Opening stock $367400 \times \frac{100}{110}$	3,34,000	By Sales By Stock on the date of fire	15,65,000 3,32,400
To Purchases	10,00,000		
To Gross profit $\frac{36}{100} \times 15{,}65{,}000$	5,63,400		
	18,97,400		18,97,400

Amount of claim :

Stock on the date of fire	3,32,400
Less : Salvaged value	45,000
Amount of claim	2,87,400

Working Notes :

1. Stock are valued at 10% above cost

Let the cost be =	100
Add : 10% to cost	10
	110

$$\text{Original value of stock} = 3{,}67{,}400 \times \frac{100}{110}$$
$$= 3{,}34{,}000$$

2. Gross profit 36% means, 36% on sales.

Problem 2

A fire occured on 30th Sept. 1998 in the godown of Srinivasan. From the following particulars calculate the amount of claim.

Stock on 1-1-98 Rs. 17,000, Purchases from 1-1-98 to the date of fire Rs. 1,70,000 : Sales from 1-1-98 to the date of fire Rs. 2,00,000 : Wages and manufacturing expenses Rs. 17,000 : Stock salvaged Rs. 4000 : The rate of gross profit on cost 30%.

(University of Madras, B. Com. April 2000).

Solution

Memorandum Trading A/c

Particulars	*Amount*	*Particulars*	*Amount*
To Opening stock	17,000	By Sales up to fire	2,00,000
To Purchases up to date of fire	170,000	By Stock on the date of fire	50,154
To Wages & manufacturing expenses	17,000		
To Gross profit $\frac{30}{100}$ on cost or $\frac{30}{130}$ on sales	46,154		
	2,50,154		2,50,154

Stock on the date of fire =	50,154
Less : Salvaged value =	400
	46,154

Problem 3

A fire occured in the premises of Malcom Marshall & Co., on 15-5-1999 causing destruction of a large part of the stock. The firm had taken a fire insurance policy for Rs. 5,47,200 to cover the loss of stock by fire. From the record saved the following particulars were ascertained :

Purchase for the year 1998	Rs. 30,01,600
Sales for the year 1998	Rs. 37,12,000
Purchases from 1st January 1999 to 15th May 1999	Rs. 5,82,000
Sales from 1st January 1999 to 15th May 1999	Rs. 7,68,000
Stock on 1st January 1998	Rs. 4,60,800
Stock on 31st December 1998	Rs. 7,74,400
Wages paid during 1998	Rs. 3,20,000
Wages paid during 1st January 1999 to 15th May 1999	Rs. 57,600
Stock salvaged was	Rs. 89,600

In 1998 some goods were destroyed by fire. The cost of such goods was Rs. 1,60,000. These goods were not covered by any insurance policy.

In valuing stock on 31st December 1998 stock costing Rs. 34,000 were found to be poor selling line and Rs. 6,000 in relation to such stock were written off. A portion of these goods (original cost Rs. 5,000) were sold in April 1999 at a loss of Rs. 1,000 on original cost. The remainder of this stock was now estimated to be worth the original cost. Subject to the above exception, gross profit has remained at a uniform rate throughout.

You are required to ascertain the insurance claim available to the firm

(Calcutta University B. Com. (Hons.) 2000).

Solution

Memorandum Trading A/c

Particulars	*Amount*	*Particulars*	*Amount*
To Opening Stock	4,60,800	By Sales	37,12,000
To Purchases	30,01,600	By Abnormal Loss	1,60,000
To Wages	3,20,000	By Closing Stock	7,80,400
To Gross Profit c/d	8,70,000	(7,74,400 + 6,000)	
	46,52,400		46,52,400

$$\text{Rate of gross profit on sale} = \frac{\text{Gross Profit}}{\text{Sales}} \times 100$$

$$= \frac{8{,}70{,}000}{37{,}12{,}000} \times 100$$

$$= 23.43\%$$

Memorandum Trading A/c

Particulars	*Amount*	*Particulars*	*Amount*
To Opening Stock	7,46,400	By Sales	7,64,000
(7,80,400 – 34,000)		7,68,000 – (5,000 – 1,000)	
To Purchases	5,82,400	By Closing Stock	8,01,463
To Wages	57,600		
To Profit	1,79,063		
(23.43% on sales)			
	15,65,463		15,65,463

Statement Showing Insurance Claim

	Amount of regular stock in godown	8,01,463
Add :	Amount of irregular stock (34,000 – 5,000)	29,000
		8,30,463
Less :	Value of stock salvaged	89,600
	Net value of stock destroyed	7,50,863

$$\text{Amount of insurance claim} = \frac{7,50,863}{8,30,463} \times 5,47,200$$

$$= \text{Rs. } 4,94,750$$

Problem 4

On 1st October 2000, the godown of X Y Z Ltd., was destroyed by fire. The record of the company revealed the following

	Rs.
Stock as on 1st April 1999	9,50,000
Stock as on 31st March 2000	8,00,000
Purchases for the year ended 31st March 2000	31,00,000
Sales for the year ended 31st March 2000	40,00,000
Purchases from 1st April 2000 to the date of fire	7,50,000
Sales from 1st April 2000 to the date of fire	10,00,000

While valuing stock on 31st March 2000, a sum of Rs. 10,000 was written off on the goods cost of which was Rs. 48,000. A part of this stock was sold in June 2000 at a loss of Rs. 4,000 on the original cost of Rs. 24,000. The remainder of this stock was now estimated to be worth the original cost subject to the above exception gross profit remained at a uniform rate throughout.

Stock salvaged was Rs. 50,000. The godown was fully insured. Calculate the amount of the insurance claim for the loss. **(C. S. Inter, December 2000)**

Solution

Trading A/c for the year ended 31-3-2002

Particulars	*Amount*	*Particulars*		*Amount*
To Opening stock	9,50,000	By Sales		40,00,000
To Purchases	31,00,000	By Closing stock		
To Gross profit	7,60,000	Normal	7,62,000	
(Balancing figure)		Abnormal	48,000	
				8,10,000
	48,10,000			48,10,000

$$\text{Rate of gross profit} = \frac{7,60,000}{40,00,000} \times 100 = 19\ \%$$

Memorandum Trading A/c from 1-4-2000 to 1-10-2000

	Normal Items	Abnormal Items	Total		Normal Items	Abnormal Items	Total
To Opening stock	7,62,000	48,000	8,10,000	By Sales	9,80,000	20,000	10,00,000
To Purchases	7,50,000	—	7,50,000	By Loss on sale	—	4,000	4,000
To Gross profit 19% of 9,80,000	1,86,200	—	1,86,200	By Closing stock	7,18,200	24,000	7,42,200
	16,98,200	48,000	17,46,200		16,98,200	48,000	17,46,200

Note : The sales under abnormal items is the difference of 24,000 and 4,000 = 20,000

Claim to be made

Value of stock on hand on the date of fire =	7,42,200
Less : Stock salvaged =	50,000
Claim to be made	6,92,200

Problem 5

A fire occured on 15th December 1999 in the premises of A B C & Co. Ltd.,. From the following figures, calculate the amount of claim to be lodged with the insurance company for loss of stock.

	Rs.
Stock at cost as on 1st April 1998	20,00,000
Stock at cost as on 1st April 1999	30,00,000
Purchases for the year ended 31st March 1999	40,00,000
Purchases from 1st April 1999 to 15th December 1999	88,00,000
Sales for the year ended 31st March 1999	60,00,000
Sales from 1st April 1999 to 15th December 1999	1,05,00,000

During the accounting year 1999 - 2000 cost of purchases cost by 10% above the previous year's level's while selling prices went up by 5%.

Salvage value of stock after fire was Rs. 2,00,000. The policy was for Rs. 55,00,000 and was subject to the average clause **(CS, Inter, June 2000)**

Solution

Trading A/c for the year ended 31-3-1999

Particulars	*Amount*	*Particulars*	*Amount*
To Opening Stock	20,00,000	By Sales	60,00,000
To Purchases	40,00,000	By Closing Stock	30,00,000
To Gross Profit	30,00,000		
	90,00,000		90,00,000

$$\text{Rate of gross profit} = \frac{30,00,000}{60,00,000} \times 100 = 50\%$$

Memorandum Trading A/c
From 1st April 1999 to 15th December 1999

	Actual	*At last year rates*		*Actual*	*At last year rates*
To Opening stock	30,00,000	30,00,000	By Sales	1,05,00,000	1,00,00,000
To Purchases	88,00,000	80,00,000	By Closing stock		
To Gross profit			at last year rates	—	60,00,000
— 50% of sales	—	50,00,000	(Balancing figure)	—	60,00,000
— Actual	53,00,000	—	— Actual on FiFo basis $\frac{60,00,000 \times 110}{100}$	66,00,000	
	1,71,00,000	1,60,00,000		1,60,00,000	1,60,00,000

Amount to be claimed

Stock on date of fire	66,00,000
Less : Salvaged stock	2,00,000
Loss suffered	64,00,000

Average clause :

$$64,00,000 \times \frac{55,00,000}{66,00,000} = 5333,333$$

Problem 6

A fire occured in the premises of a company on 15-10-97. From the following particulars, ascertain the loss of stock and prepare a claim for insurance.

	Rs.
Stock on 1-1-96	30,600
Purchases form 1-1-96 to 31-12-96	1,22,000
Sales from 1-1-96 to 31-12-96	1,80,000
Stock on 31-12-96	27,000
Purchases form 1-1-97 to 15-10-97	1,47,000
Sales from 1-1-97 to 15-10-97	1,50,000

The stock were always valued at 90% of cost. The stock saved from fire was worth Rs. 18,000. The amount of policy was Rs. 63,000. There was an average clause in the policy.

(University of Madras B. Com. April 1999)

Solution

Trading A/c for the period 1-1-96 to 31-12-96

Particulars	*Amount*	*Particulars*	*Amount*
To Opening Stock $\frac{30,600 \times 100}{90}$	34,000	By Sales	180000
To Purchases	1,22,000	By Closing Stock $\frac{27,000 \times 100}{90}$	30,000
To Gross Profit	54,000		
	2,10,000		2,10,000

$$\text{Rate of gross profit} = \frac{\text{Gross Profit}}{\text{Sales}} \times 100$$

$$= \frac{54{,}000}{1{,}80{,}000} \times 100 = 30\%$$

Note : Since stocks are valued at 90% of cost we have to charge to original value.

Memorandum Trading A/c
From 1-1-97 to 15-10-97

Particulars	*Amount*	*Particulars*	*Amount*
To Opening stock	30,000	By Sales	1,50,000
To Purchases	1,47,000	By Stock on the date of fire	72,000
To Gross Profit $1{,}50{,}000 \times \frac{30}{100}$	45,000		
	2,22,000		2,22,000

Loss of stock :

	Stock on the date of fire =	72,000
Less :	Stock saved =	18,000
	Actual loss of stock on fire	54,000

Claim under average clause :

$$\frac{\text{Amount Insured}}{\text{Stock on the date of fire}} \times \text{Actual loss}$$

$$= \frac{63{,}000}{72{,}000} \times 54{,}000 = \text{Rs. } 47{,}250$$

Problem 7

A fire occured in the premises of a business on 21st June 1999 and a considerable part of the stock was destroyed. The stock salvaged was Rs. 1,12,000. The Firm had taken a fire insurgence policy for Rs. 6,84,000 to cover the loss of stock by fire.

You are required to ascertain the insurance claim due from the insurance company for the loss of stock by fire. The following particulars are available.

	Rs.
Purchases for the year ended 31-3-1999	37,52,000
Sales for the year ended 31-3-1999	46,40,000
Purchases from 1st April 1999 to 21-6-1999	7,28,000
Sales from 1-4-1999 to 21-6-1999	9,60,000
Stock on 1-4-1998	5,76,000
Stock on 31-3-1999	9,68,000
Wages paid during the year ended 31-3-1999	4,00,000
Wages paid from 1-4-1998 to 21-6-1999	72,000

In September 1998, the firm had consigned goods worth Rs. 2,00,000 which were lost in an accident. As there was no insurance, the loss was borne by the firm in full.

Stock at the end of each year till the end of accounting year 1997-98 had been valued at cost less 10%. However with effect from 31st March 1999, there was a change in the valuation of closing stock which was ascertained by adding 10% to its cost.

(C.S. Inter, December 1999)

Solution

Trading A/c
For the year ended 31-3-1999

Particulars	*Amount*	*Particulars*	*Amount*
To Opening Stock	6,46,000	By Sales	46,40,000
$5,76,000 \times \frac{100}{90}$		By Loss of stock in accident	2,00,000
To Purchases	37,52,000	By Closing Stock	8,80,000
To Wages	4,00,000	$9,68,000 \times \frac{100}{110}$	
To Gross Profit	9,28,000		
	57,20,000		57,20,000

$$\text{Rate of gross profit} = \frac{9,28,000}{46,40,000} \times 100 = 20\%$$

Memorandum Trading A/c
From 1-4-99 to 21-6-99

Particulars	*Amount*	*Particulars*	*Amount*
To Opening Stock	8,80,000	By Sales	9,60,000
To Purchases	7,28,000	By Closing Stock	9,12,000
To Wages	72,000	(Balancing figure)	
To Gross Profit — 20% on sales	1,92,000		
	18,72,000		18,72,000

Loss of Stock

Closing stock as on 21-6-1999	9,12,000
Less : Stock salvaged	1,12,000
	8,00,000

Applying average clause

$$= \text{Loss suffered} \times \frac{\text{Sum Insured}}{\text{Actual Insurable value}}$$

$$= 8,00,000 \times \frac{6,84,000}{9,12,000} = \text{Rs. } 6,00,000$$

Problem 8

On 16th August 1997, a fire occured in the godown of Ganges Jute Mill and the godown was destroyed. From the following information prepare a statement showing the claim to be lodged to the Insurance company.

	Rs.
Stock on 1st January 1996	36,000
Wages paid -1996 (out of this Rs. 1,000 Paid for construction of a stage for performing a cultural programme by the Staff Recreation Club of Jute Mill)	6,000
Carriage inward - 1996	3,000
Purchases for the year ended 31-12-96	1,42,000
Sales for the year ended 31-12--96	2,03,400
Closing stock on 31-12-96	32,000
Purchases from 1-1-97 to 16-8-1997	74,000
Sales from 1-1-97 to 16-8-1997	82,600

An item of stock purchased in 1995 at a cost of Rs. 10,000 was valued at Rs. 6,000 on 31st January 1995. Half of this stock was sold in 1996 for Rs. 3,400; The remaining stock was valued at Rs. 2,000 on 31st December 1996. One fourth of the original stock was sold in April 1997 for Rs. 2,600. The remaining Stock was considered to be worth 40% of its original cost. Stock of the value of Rs. 15,000 was salvaged. The amount of the policy was for Rs. 42,000. There was an average clause in the policy. **(Calcutta University B. Com. (Hons.) 1998)**

Solution

Memorandum Trading A/c
For the year ended 31-12-96

Particulars		*Amount*	*Particulars*		*Amount*
To Opening stock	36,000		By Sales	2,03,400	
Less : Abnormal Items	6,000		Less : Abnormal Loss	3,400	
		30,000			2,00,000
To Purchases		1,42,000	By Closing Stock	32,000	
To Wages	6,000		Less : Abnormal items	2,000	
Less : construction wages	1,000	5,000			30,000
To Carriage Inward		3,000			
To Gross Profit		50,000			
		2,30,000			2,30,000

$$\text{Percentage of gross profit on sales} = \frac{50,000}{2,00,000} \times 100 = 25\%$$

Trading A/c
For the period 1-1-97 to 16-8-97

Particulars	*Amount*	*Particulars*		*Amount*
To Opening Stock (Normal)	30,000	By Sales	82,600	
To Purchases	74,000	Less : abnormal items	2,600	80,000
To Gross Profit (25% on sales)	20,000	By Closing Stock		44,000
	1,24,000			1,24,000

Claim to be lodged with Insurance company

Closing stock as on 16-8-97	44,000
Less : Stock salvaged	15,000
	29,000

$$\text{Applying average clause} = \text{Loss suffered} \times \frac{\text{Sum Insured}}{\text{Actual Insurable Value}}$$

$$= 29{,}000 \times \frac{42{,}000}{44{,}000} = 27{,}682$$

Problem 9

A fire occured on 15th December 1996 in the premises of Risky Co. Ltd.,. From the following figures, Calculate the amount of claim to be lodged with the insurance company for loss of stock.

	Rs.
Stock at cost on 1st April 1995	20,000
Stock at cost on 31st March 1996	30,000
Purchases during the year ended 31st March 1996	40,000
Purchases from 1st April 1996 to 15th December 1996	88,000
Sales during the year ended 31-3-96	60,000
Sales from 1-4-1996 to 15-12-96	1,05,000

During the current year cost of purchases have risen by 10% above last year's levels. Selling prices have gone up by 5%. Salvage value of stock after fire was Rs. 2,000.

(C.S. Inter, December 1997)

Solution

Trading A/c
For the year ending on 31st March 1996

Particulars	*Amount*	*Particulars*	*Amount*
To Opening Stock	20,000	By Sales	60,000
To Purchases	40,000	By Closing Stock	30,000
To Gross Profit — 50% on sales	30,000		
	90,000		90,000

Memorandum Trading A/c
From 1st April 1996 to 15th December 1996.

	Actual	*At last year's rates*		*Actual*	*At last year's rates*
To Opening Stock	30,000	30,000	By Sales	1,05,000	1,00,000
To Purchases	88,000	80,000	By Closing Stock	66,000	60,000
To Gross Profit	53,000	50,000			
	1,71,000	1,60,000		1,71,000	1,60,000

Amount of claim :

Value of closing stock	66,000
Less : Salvage value	2,000
Amount of claim	64,000

Problem 10

On 1st April 1996 a company took an insurance policy for Rs. 4,50,000 in respect of goods stored in its godown. On 12th June 1996, there was a loss of goods due to fire. Goods salvaged were valued at Rs. 14,500. Find out the amount of the claim for loss of goods taking into account the following additional information also;

(*i*) The company has a policy of selling goods at price to give profit margin of 25% of the cost.

(*ii*) The company values its stock at cost price or market price whichever is lower. On 31st March 1996, the closing stock was valued at Rs. 4,28,000, which included damaged goods costing Rs. 10,000 valued at Rs. 8,000.

(*iii*) Purchases during the current period till 12th June 1996, amounted to Rs. 11,00,000 during the same period the company made sales amounting to Rs. 12,54,800 which included the sales of 60% of damaged goods at book value. **(C.S. Inter, June 1997)**

Solution

Memorandum Trading A/c up to 12-6-967

	Normal Items	*Abnormal Items*		*Normal Items*	*Abnormal Items*
To Opening Stock	4,20,000	8,000	By Sales	12,50,000	4,800
To Purchases	11,00,000	—	By Closing Stock	5,20,000	320
To Gross Profit Sales	2,50,000	—			
	17,70,000	8,000		17,70,000	8,000

Statement of claim :

Value of stock : Normal item	5,20,000
Abnormal item	3,200
	5,23,200
Less : Value of stock salvaged	14,500
	5,08,700

Amount of claim on applying average clause

$$= 5,08,700 \times \frac{4,50,000}{5,23,200}$$

$$= \text{Rs. } 4,37,529$$

2. CLAIM FOR LOSS OF FIXED ASSETS

For indemnifying the loss, the value of any fixed asset has to be taken as its value as at the date of fire. If any loss is suffered in respect of such asset due to under insurance, the same has to be treated as a capital loss and as such, it should be written off against the capital reserve of the company.

The amount of claim has to be determined in the same manner as it is done in case of loss of stock. But no trading account is required to be prepared in this case.

Problem 11

'A' Co. Ltd., insured its Machinery for Rs. 2,50,000 whereas its value to the company was Rs. 3,00,000. The insurance policy contained an average clause.

A fire broke out in the production department and destroyed the Machinery, the value of that salvaged being Rs. 30,000. You are required to prepare a statement showing the amount of claim to be lodged with the insurance company.

Solution

Statement showing the amount of claim for loss of Machinery

Value of Machinery as on the date of fire	3,00,000
Less : Value of Machinery salvaged	30,000
Value of Machinery lost	2,70,000

$$\text{Applying average clause} = \text{Loss suffered} \times \frac{\text{Sum Insured}}{\text{Actual Insurable Value}}$$

$$= 2,70,000 \times \frac{2,50,000}{3,00,000} = \text{Rs. } 2,25,000$$

3. CLAIMS FOR LOSS OF PROFIT OR CONSEQUENTIAL LOSS

Insurance policy can also be taken to meet losses arising on account of dislocation of business caused by fire. The occurrence of fire has both direct and indirect impact on the business. The loss of stock has direct impact while dislocation of business has indirect impact. It is not easy to restore normalcy in the business unless new assets replace lost assets. During this phase of business sales are affected and consequently profit earning ability also declines, fixed cost remaining the same. Thus consequential loss has two-fold implications viz, (*a*) Profit lost which otherwise would have been earned under normal condition (*b*) non recovery of fixed cost. A policy of loss of profit or consequential loss policy covers the risk against such loss of expected profit.

The consequential loss policy vary depending upon circumstances of each case. The following conditions are commonly seen in such a policy.

1. The duration of period of indemnity is fixed in the policy. Accordingly the period of indemnity or the period of dislocation, whichever is less, is the period for which expected profit that is lost should be considered. For example, if the indemnity period is 4 months and the dislocation continues for 6 months, the loss of profit for the indemnity period of 4 months should be considered. On the other hand, if the dislocation continues for 2 months in the same case, the loss of profit for the dislocation period of 2 months should be considered.
2. The claim is calculated by way of a percentage which the turnover is expected to earn. This percentage is applied on the loss of turnover caused by fire during indemnity period or the dislocation period which ever is less. The resultant figure give the amount of claim subject to "Special Circumstances clause" and "Average clause" if any .

3. The insured gross profit ratio is calculated on the basis of the trading results of the last accounting year. The following formula is used.

$$\text{G. P. Ratio} = \frac{\text{Net Profit + Insured Fixed Costs}}{\text{Sales}} \times 100$$

Note : Insured fixed cost is a cost which the insured desires to recover in the event of damage.

In case of net loss the following formula is used.

$$\text{G.P. Ratio} = \frac{\text{Insured Fixed Costs – Net Loss}}{\text{Sales}} \times 100$$

4. The loss of turnover in the dislocation period subject to the maximum of the period of indemnity is ascertained by comparing the actual turnover for the period with the sales for the corresponding period in the preceding year known as the standard sales. Thus, the loss of turnover is the difference between the actual sales for the dislocation period (or the indemnity period which ever is less) and the standard sales for the corresponding period in the preceding year. For example, if a fire occurs on 31st January 2003 and the period of indemnity is for 3 months while the dislocation period is 6 months a comparison has to be made between the actual sales for the indemnity period of 3 months, i.e., February, March , April 2002.
5. There is usually a clause for indemnity to cover an increase in the cost of working with the definite object of avoiding or reducing the loss of sales which would have taken place without such increased cost of working. The following limitations are to be considered in determining the amount of claim.
   (*a*) Where all the insurable fixed costs are not covered by the policy, a proportion of the increased cost is allowed as claim which has to be calculated by applying the following formula :

$$\text{Increased Working Cost} \times \frac{\text{Net Profit + Insured Fixed Cost}}{\text{Net Profit + All Insurable Fixed Cost}}$$

   (*b*) The amount of claim can never exceed the sum produced by applying the gross profit ratio to the reduction of turnover avoided with increased cost of working, i.e., the maximum saving of liability of the insurer.
   (*c*) It there is any savings in insured fixed charges, the same has to be deducted from the amount of claim for increased cost of working.

Illustration

Gross profit ratio of a business is 20%	
Net profit for the last accounting year	Rs. 20,000
Insured standing charges	Rs. 30,000
Uninsured standing charges	Rs. 10,000
Increased cost of working	Rs. 12,000
Saving in insured fixed cost	Rs. 500
Reduction in sales avoided through increased cost of working	Rs. 30,000

Determine the amount of claim.

Solution

Note : The amount of claim for increased working cost will be restricted to the minimum of the following two items.

1. Proportion of increased cost of working :

$$\text{Increased Working Cost} \times \frac{\text{Net Profit + Insured Fixed Cost}}{\text{Net Profit + All Insured Fixed Cost}}$$

$$= 12{,}000 \times \frac{20{,}000 + 30{,}000}{20{,}000 + 40{,}000}$$

$$= 12{,}000 \times \frac{50{,}000}{60{,}000} = \text{Rs. } 10{,}000$$

2. Maximum saving of liability of the insurer =

$$\text{Reduction in turnover avoided} \times \text{Gross Profit Ratio}$$

$$= 30{,}000 \times \frac{20}{100} = \text{Rs. } 6{,}000$$

Therefore, the amount of claim for increased cost of working will be restricted to Rs. 6,000

Now, the amount of claim for increased cost of working	Rs. 6,000
Less : Saving in insured fixed cost	500
Amount of net claim	5,500

6. In consequential loss policy special clause known as special circumstances clause is included. It states that such adjustment shall be made as may be necessary to provide for the trend of the business for variations in or special circumstances affecting the business. This clause would affect the calculation of the gross profit ratio, the loss of sales and the increased cost of working. So while calculating the gross profit ratio, ;the loss of turnover and the increased cost of working, care should be taken to adjust such factor.

For example, if the gross profit ratio for the last accounting year is 20% and there is a possibility of an increase of 2% in the current year which is stipulated in the policy through special circumstances clause, the adjusted gross profit ratio is 20 : 22.

7. In case of Average clause, the amount of the claim should be proportionally reduced.

Steps involved in calculating the amount of claim for loss of profit :

1. Fix the period of claim by taking the period of indemnity or the period of dislocation, whichever is less.
2. Ascertain the loss of turnover in the claim period with due regard to the special circumstances clause, if any.
3. Calculate the gross profit ratio based on the trading result of the last accounting year with due regard to the special circumstance clause.
4. Compute the gross profit lost during the period of claim by applying gross profit ratio to the loss of turnover during the period of claim.
5. Add thereto increased cost of working, if any, keeping in view of the restrictions stated in clause (5) to arrive at the amount of gross claim.
6. Ascertain the amount of net claim by applying the "average clause" if any.

Problem 12

On 1st August 2,000, a fire occured in the premises of A B C Ltd. The company has a loss of profit policy for Rs. 12,00,000. Sales from 1st August 1999 to 31st July 2,000 were Rs. 1 crore : the sales from 1st August 1999 to 30th November 1999 being Rs. 30,00,000

During the indemnity period, which lasted four months, sales amounted to Rs. 4,00,000 only . The company closes its books of account every year on 31st March. The profit & loss account for the year ended 31st March 2000 is given below.

Profit and Loss A/c

Particulars	*Amount*	*Particulars*	*Amount*
To Opening Stock	10,00,000	By Sales	95,00,000
To Purchases	60,00,000	By Closing Stock	5,00,000
To Manufacturing Expenses	6,70,000		
To Variable Selling Expenses	9,05,000		
To Fixed Expenses	7,25,000		
To Net Profit	7,00,000		
	1,00,00,000		1,00,00,000

As compared with the sales for the first four months of the accounting year 1999 - 2000. The sales for the first four months of the accounting year 2000 - 2001 were found to be up by 20%.

Calculate the amount of claim for loss of profit assuming that the policy has an "average clause". **(C. S. Inter, June 2001)**

Solution

Calculation of Short Sales

	(Rs. in Lakhs)
Sales from 1st Aug., 1999 to 30th Nov., 1999	30
Add : 20% increase (20% of 30 Lakhs)	6
	36
Less : Sales from 1st Aug., 2000 to 30th Nov. 2000	4
Short Sales	32

Calculation of gross profit

$$\text{G. P. Ratio} = \frac{\text{Net Profit + Fixed Cost for 1999 - 2000}}{\text{Sales for 1999 - 2000}} \times 100$$

$$= \frac{7,00,000 + 7,25,000}{95,00,000} \times 100 = 15\%$$

Loss of profit = 15% of Rs. 32 lakhs = Rs. 4,80,000

Calculation of adjusted annual turnover :

Annual turnover, i.e., Sales for 12 months (from 1-8-1999 to 31-7-2000)	100
Add : 20% annual turnover	20
Adjusted annual turnover	120

Application of average clause :

Gross profit on Rs. 1,20,00,000 @ 15% = Rs. 18 lakhs

But the policy has been taken for Rs. 12 lakhs only

Hence average clause will apply

$$\text{Amount of claim} = 4{,}80{,}000 \times \frac{12{,}00{,}000}{18{,}00{,}000}$$

$$= \text{Rs. } 3{,}20{,}000$$

Problem 13

From the following details determine the amount of claim under a loss of profit insurance policy :

Indemnity period	6 months
Date of fire	1-4-2004
Dislocation up to	1-8-2004
Sum insured	Rs. 60,000
Sales for the last accounting year	Rs. 2,40,000
Net profit for the last accounting year	Rs. 26,000
Standing charges for the last accounting Year, i.e., 2003. (all insured)	Rs. 34,000
Sales for the dislocation period i.e., 1-4-2004 to 1-8-2004	Rs. 30,000
Sales for the corresponding period in the preceding year, i.e., 1-4-2003 to 1-8-2003	Rs. 1,00,000

The policy contains "Special circumstances clause" which stipulates for increase of turnover. (Standard and Annual) by 10% as there is a upward trend in the business.

Solution

Computation of the Amount of Claim.

1. Period of claim = Dislocation period being less than indemnity period, i.e., 4 months from 1-4-2004 to 1-8-2004.
2. Loss of turnover in the dislocation period :Standard turnover for the corresponding period in the preceding year, i.e., 1-4-2003 to 1-8-2003

Standard turnover for the corresponding period in the preceding year, i.e., 1-4-2003 to 1-8-2003	Rs. 1,00,000
Add : Agreed increase of 10% for upward trend	10,000
Adjusted standard turnover	1,10,000
Less : Actual turnover in the dislocation period	30,000
Loss of turnover in the dislocation Period	80,000

3. Gross profit ratio based on the trading results of the last accounting year, i.e., 2003.

$$\text{G. P.} = \frac{\text{Net Profit} + \text{Insured fixed cost}}{\text{Sales}} \times 100$$

$$= \frac{26,000 + 34,000}{2,40,000} \times 100$$

$$= \frac{60,000}{2,40,000} \times 100 = 25\%$$

4. Gross profit lost during the dislocation period —

Loss of gross profit = Loss of turnover × Gross Profit Ratio

$$= 80,000 \times \frac{25}{100} = \text{Rs. } 20,000$$

5. Application of average clause :

Annual turnover preceding the date of fire	3,20,000
Add : Agreed increase of 10 % for upward trend	32,000
Adjusted annual turnover	3,52,000

Insurable value of the loss of profit

$$= \frac{25}{100} \times 3,52,000 = \text{Rs. } 88,000$$

Applying average clause :

$$\text{Amount of Net claim} = \text{Loss suffered} \times \frac{\text{Sum Insured}}{\text{Actual Insurable Value}}$$

$$= 20,000 \times \frac{60,000}{88,000} = \text{Rs. } 13,636$$

Alternatively the amount of claim may be calculated as follows

Loss of turnover in the dislocation period = Rs. 80,000

Amount of claim will be restricted to the lower of the two percentages calculated below :

1. $\frac{\text{Net Profit + Insured Fixed Cost}}{\text{Sales in previous year}} \times 100$

$$= \frac{26,000 + 34,000}{2,40,000} \times 100 = 25\%$$

2. $\frac{\text{Amount of the policy}}{\text{Sales in the 12 month preceding the date of fire as adjusted for any trend}} \times 100$

$$= \frac{60,000}{3,52,000} \times 100 = 17.04\%$$

$$\therefore \quad \text{Claim} = \frac{17.04}{100} \times 80,000 = \text{Rs. } 13,636$$

QUESTIONS

Simple Questions

1. What is a contract of fire insurance ?
2. What is an average clause ?
3. What do you mean by salvage ?
4. What are abnormal items ? How are they treated in ascertaining the amount of claim ?

EXERCISE 1

A fire occured on the premises of a merchant on 15th June 1999 and a considerable part of the stock was destroyed. The value of the stock saved was Rs. 9000.

The books disclosed that on 1st April 1999, the stock was valued at Rs. 73,500. Purchases to the date of the fire amounted to Rs. 2,09,880 and sales to Rs. 3,13,000. On the investigation it was found that during the part five years the average gross profit on the sales was 36%.

You are required to compute the claim to be made from the insurance company in respect of goods damaged by the fire. **(University of Madras B. Com. October, 2000)**

Answer : Claim is for Rs. 74,060

EXERCISE 2

A fire occured in the godown of Mr. X on 31-8-1999 and destroyed all the goods in the godown. From the following information find out the value of stock lost by fire.

Stock on 1-1-99	Rs. 25,000
Purchases from 1-1-99 to 31-8-99	Rs. 80,000
Sales from 1-1-99 to 31-8-99	Rs. 1,20,000
Goods are sold 25% profit on sales	

(Calcutta University B. Com. (Pass) 2000)

Answer : Stock lost by fire Rs. 15,000

EXERCISE 3

A fire occured on the premises of merchant on 18th December 1998 and a considerable part of the stock was destroyed. The books disclosed that on 1st April 1998 the stock was valued at 66,850, the purchases to the date of fire amounted to Rs. 1,85,000 and the sales to Rs. 2,82,500. Goods costing Rs. 500 were taken for personal use and goods sold for Rs. 2,500 were returned to the merchant. On investigation it is found that during the past fire years the average gross profit on the cost was 25%. The value of the stock salvaged was Rs. 8,200.

Compute the claim to be made with the insurance company

(University of Madras, B. Com. May 2000)

Answer : Amount to claimed Rs. 19,150

EXERCISE 4

There is a fire in godown of spark Ltd. on 1-7-97. Stock worth . 30,000 was saved. The insurance policy was for Rs. 50,000 and it was included that average clause will be applied.

(*i*) An average gross profit of 20% on sale is maintained by the company.
(*ii*) The stock is valued at 10% above cost.

The purchases and sales for first 6 months of the year were Rs. 2,10,000 and Rs. 4,50,000 respectively. Stock on January 1, 1997 was Rs. 1,48,500, the wages for that period amount to Rs. 90,000

Find out the amount of insurance claim. **(Calcutta University B. Com. (Pass) 1998)**

Answer : Amount of claim Rs. 30,000

EXERCISE 5

A fire occured on 30th September 1995 in the godown of Mr. Anand. From the following figure ascertain the claim to be lodged, stock on 1-1-95 Rs. 17,000 : Purchases from 1st January to date of fire Rs. 1,70,000 : Sales from 1st January to date of fire Rs. 2,00,000. The rate of gross profit is 25% on cost. The stock salvaged was valued at Rs. 4,000.

(University of Madras B. Com. April 1998)

Answer : Amount of claim Rs. 40,000

EXERCISE 6

A fire occured in the premises of Agni on 25th August 1997 when a large part of the stock was destroyed. Salvage was Rs. 15,000.

Agni gives you the following information for the period January 1, 1997 to August 25th 1997.

(*a*) Purchases Rs. 85,000
(*b*) Sales Rs. 90,000
(*c*) Goods costing Rs. 5,000 were taken by agni for personal use.
(*d*) Cost price of stock on January 1, 1997 was Rs. 40,000.

Over the past few years Agni has been selling goods at a consistent gross profit margin of $33\frac{1}{3}\%$.

The Insurance policy was for Rs. 50,000. It included an average clause.

Agni asks you to prepare a statement of claim to be made on the insurance company.

(C.A. Inter November 1997)

Answer : Amount to be claimed Rs. 37,500

EXERCISE 7

(Consequential Loss Policy)

The premises of company were partly destroyed by fire which took place on 1st March 2004 and as a result of which the business was disorganised from 1st March 2004 to 31st July. Accounts are closed on 31st December every year. The Company is insured under a loss of profits policy for Rs. 75,000. The period of indemnity specified in the policy is 6 months. From the following information you are required to compute the amount of claim under the loss of profit policy.

	Rs.
Turnover for the year 2003	4,00,000
Net profit for the year 2003	24,000
Insured standing charges	48,000
Turnover during the period of dislocation i.e., from 1-3-2004 to 31-7-2004	80,000
Standard turnover for the corresponding period in the preceding year, i.e., from 1-3-2003 to 31-7-2003	2,00,000
Annual turnover for the year immediately preceding the fire, i.e., from 1-3-2003 to 28-2-2004	4,40,000
Increased cost of working	15,000
Saving in insured standing charges	3,000
Reduction in turnover avoided through increase in working cost	40,000

Owing to reasons acceptable to the insurer the "special circumstances clause" stipulated for :

(*a*) Increase of turnover (Standard and annual) by 10% and
(*b*) Increase of rate of gross profit by 2%

Answer : Amount of claim Rs. 25,568

EXERCISE 8

C Ltd., has a "loss of profit insurance policy of Rs. 21,00,000. The period of indmnity is three months. A fire occured on 31st March 2004. The following information is available.

	Rs.
Sales :	
For the year ended 31st December 2003	70,00,000
For the period from 1st April 2003 to 31st March 2004	80,00,000
For the period from 1st April 2003 to 30th June 2003	18,00,000
For the period from 1st April 2004 to 30th June 2004	1,20,000
Standing charges	16,00,000
Profit for 2003	5,00,000
Saving in standing charges because of fire	50,000
Additional expenses to reduce loss of turnover	1,00,000

Assuming no adjustment has to be made for the upward trend in turnover, compute the claim to be made on the insurance company.

Answer : Amount of claim Rs. 4,28,750

33

CHAPTER

Insolvency Accounts

MEANING OF INSOLVENT

An Insolvent is a person whose liabilities exceed the assets and against whom an order of adjudication has been passed by a competent court. The Insolvency proceedings in India are governed by two Acts, viz (*a*) The Presidency Towns insolvency act 1909 which applies to the Presidency Towns of Mumbai, Calcutta and Chennai : and (*b*) the Provincial Insolvency Act 1920 which applies to the rest of the country.

Components of Insolvency Accounts

Insolvency accounts comprises of (1) Statement of affairs and (2) Deficiency account.

STATEMENT OF AFFAIRS

A statement of affairs is a statement prepared by an insolvent showing his financial position and also his deficiency as on the date of adjudication. This statement is prepared and submitted by a person to the court on passing an adjudication order by the court. A proforma of statement of affairs is shown below :

Statement of Affairs as on ---

Gross Liabilities Rs.	*Liabilities (as stated and estimated by the Debtor*		*Expected to rank Rs.*	*Assets (as stated and estimated by the debtor)*	*Book value Rs.*	*Estimated to produce Rs.*
	Unsecured creditors			Property as per List 'E'		
X X X	as per list 'A'		X X X	Cash in Hand	X X X	X X X
	Fully secured Creditors			Cash at Bank	X X X	X X X
X X X	as per list 'B'	X X X		Stock in Trade	XX X	X X X
	Estimated Value of			Furniture	X X X	X X X
	Securities	X X X		Plant & Machinery	X X X	X X X
	Surplus	X X X		Buildings	X X X	X X X
				Book Debts as per List 'F'		
				Good	XXX	XXX

Gross Liabilities Rs.	*Liabilities (as stated and estimated by the Debtor*		*Expected to rank Rs.*	*Assets (as stated and estimated by the debtor)*	*Book value Rs.*	*Estimated to produce Rs.*
	Less : Amount			Doubtful	XXX	XXX
	there of carried			Bad	XXX	XXX
	to list 'C'	XXX		Bill of exchange etc. as		
	Balance thereof	XXX	NIL	per list 'G'	XXX	XXX
	to contra			Surplus from securities		
	Partly secured			in the hand of fully		
	Creditors as			Secured creditors as per		XXX
	per list 'C'	XXX		contra		XXX
	Less : Estimated			Less : Preferential creditors		XXX
	value of securities	XXX		as per contra		
			XXX	Deficiency as per list 'H'		XXX
	Preferential creditors					
	as per list 'D'	XXX				
	Less : Deducted per					
	contra	XXX	Nil			

FEATURES OF STATEMENT OF AFFAIRS

1. The liabilities are shown on the left hand side and the assets on the right hand side. The difference between the two sides constitutes the deficiency.
2. Liabilities are classified into four types and shown under four headings viz, (*a*) Unsecured creditors as per list 'A' (*b*) Fully secured creditors as per list 'B' (*c*) partly secured creditors as per list 'C' and (*d*) Preferential creditors as per list 'D'.
4. Unsecured creditors are not backed by any security. They include sundry creditors, bills payable, Bank OD, contingent liability.
5. Fully secured creditors are backed by securities. The excess of the estimated value of the securities over the amount due is the surplus securities. If any portion of surplus securities is charged to partly secured creditors, that portion is deducted from the surplus securities. The remaining surplus securities are added along with the assets on the assets side of the statement of affairs.
   The amount of fully secured creditors will not appear in the amount expected to rank column. This is because the amount of fully secured creditors expected to rank are set off against the estimated value of the asserts in the particulars column.
6. Partly secured creditors are those which are not backed by full security. In other words, the estimated value of securities is less than the amount of liability.
7. Preferential creditors are those who have priority over other unsecured creditors. Under the Presidency Town Insolvency act the following payments shall be considered to be preferential.
   (*a*) Dues to government - central, state or local. Examples are Income Tax, Sales Tax property Tax etc.
   (*b*) Salary due to any clerk for any services rendered during four months before the date of presentation of insolvency petition-subject to a maximum of either 4 months salary or Rs. 300 which ever is less.

(*c*) Wages due to any servant or labourer for services rendered to the insolvent during four months before the presentation of insolvency petition subject to a maximum of either 4 months wages or Rs. 100 whichever is less.

(*d*) Rent due to landlord, subject to only one month rent irrespective of the amount.

The following are Preferential Creditors Under Provincial Insolvency Act :

(*a*) All debts due to Government or local authorities in respect of rates and taxes.

(*b*) Salary due to any clerk for services rendered to the insolvent during the 4 months before the presentation of the insolvency petition subject to the maximum of either 4 months salary or Rs. 20 which even is less.

(*c*) Wages due to any labourer or servant subject to maximum of either 4 months wages or Rs. 20 which ever is less.

The gross amount of the preferential creditors are shown in the "gross liabilities". The amount of these liabilities expected to rank are shown on the particulars column and from this amount is deducted preferential creditors as per contra. The implication of this procedure is that as these liabilities have priority of payment over other unsecured creditors, they are not entered on the liabilities side in the "amount expected to rank" column, but are shown as deduction from assets available on the asset side of the statement of affairs.

8. The assets are classified into three categories, viz (*a*) Property as per list 'E'. (*b*) Book debts as per list 'F' and (*c*) Bills receivable etc. as per list 'G'. These assets are shown on the credit side of the statement.
9. The difference between the two sides of statement denotes "deficiency" which is placed under list 'H'.

Differences between Statement of Affairs and Balance Sheet

1. A balance sheet is prepared from balances taken from books of accounts. A statement of affairs is not prepared from balances of accounts.
2. A statement of affairs in case of insolvency is to be prepared in prescribed form. There is no prescribed form of balance sheet in case of a sole trading or partnership firm.
3. A statement of affairs is prepared on the date on which an order of adjudication is passed against a debtor; a balance sheet is prepared usually at the end of each accounting year.
4. A statement of affairs include both personal and business assets and liabilities of the debtor, while a balance sheet includes assets and liabilities of the business only.
5. In a balance sheet only the book values of the assets and liabilities are shown, but in a statement of affairs not only the book values but also the realisable payable values are shown.

Deficiency Account

Deficiency account is a statement which explains how the deficiency as shown in the statement of affairs has arisen.

A deficiency account is prepared to show how the capital introduced by the proprietor came to be lost along with the amounts belonging to creditors. This account explains the deficiency appearing in the statement of affairs.

A preforma of deficiency account is shown below.

Deficiency A/c – List H

Particulars	*Amount*	*Particulars*	*Amount*
Excess assets over liabilities, i.e., capital	X X	Excess of liabilities over assets (if any) Drawing	X X
Net profit arising from business	X X	Interest on Drawings	X X
Income or profit form other sources	X X	Net loss from business	X X
Profit on realisation of assets	X X	Bad debts	X X
Interest on capital	X X	Losses on realisation of assets	X X
Private assets brought into business	X X	Private liabilities brought into the business	X X
Deficiency as shown in the statement of affairs	X X	Surplus if any as shown in the Statement of Affairs	

Treatment of Loan Payable to the Wife of a Businessman on Insolvency

If the loan given by the wife is out of her personal property or Stridhan she will rank as a creditor and the loan amounts to be included in list 'A' as unsecured creditors. But if the loan is given out of the money given to her by her husband, then it is considered as additional capital introduced by the proprietor.

Treatment of Private Assets and Liabilities of a Sole Trader when he becomes Insolvent

In case of insolvency of sole trader, no distinction is made between business assets and liabilities and the private assets and liabilities of the proprietor. So his private business assets and liabilities are shown alongside business assets and liabilities in the statement of affairs.

Difference between Insolvency of an Individual and Partnership

When an individual is adjudicated insolvent no distinction is made between his business and private assets and liabilities in meeting his business liabilities and private liabilities. However this is not so in the case of a firm. The partners private assets are first used to pay his private liabilities and if there is any surplus of assets it is used in meeting the firms liabilities. Similarly the assets of the firm are applied first for paying the liabilities of the firm and if there is any surplus in the firms assets each partners share in the surplus asset is used for paying his private liabilities.

Problem 1

Mr. Gowda files his insolvency petition on 1-1-2000. He had the following assets and liabilities (estimated to realise and expected to rank are given in brackets).

	Rs.	Rs.
Cash at Bank		1,000
Stock	(7,00,000)	8,00,000
Electrical equipment	(2,00,000)	2,00,000
Furniture	(20,000)	40,000
Machinery	(2,50,000)	3,10,000

Buildings	(70,000)	80,000
Book Debts :		
Good	—	300,000
Bad and doubtful	(40,000)	1,00,000
Investments	(2,00,000)	2,00,000
Mortgage on electrical equipment	—	2,00,000
Loan secured by Investment	—	5,00,000
Loan secured by first Charge on stock	—	1,00,000
Loan unsecured	—	10,00,000
Preferential creditors	—	40,000
Liabilities on B/R discounted	(40,000)	100,000

He commenced business with capital of Rs. 6,00,000. Profit up to 31-12-99 was Rs. 591,000 after allowing interest on capital of Rs. 60,000. He had withdrawn Rs. 10,40,000. Prepare statement of affairs and deficiency a/c. (Bangalore University, B. Com. April 2003).

Solution

Working Note :

1. **Calculation of unsecured creditors expected to rank :**

Unsecured loan	10,00,000
Liabilities on B/R discounted	40,000
expected to rank	10,40,000

2. **Calculation of Gross liabilities on unsecured creditors**

Unsecured loan	10,00,000
Amount of bills discounted	1,00,000
	11,00,000

3. **Book value of Stock Under List 'E' is arrived at after making proportionate reduction for security held by loan creditors.**

$$\frac{8,00,000}{7,00,000} \times 1,00,000 = 1,14,286$$

Rest of the stock Rs. 6,85,714 (8,00,000 — 1,14,286) is shown on the asset side.

Statement of Affairs of Mr. Gowda

Gross Liability	*Liabilities*	*Exected to rank*	*Assets*	*Book value*	*Estimated to produce*
	Unsecured creditors as per		Prosperty as per list E		
			Cash at Bank	1,000	1,000
11,00,000	List 'A'	10,40,000	Stock	6,85,714	6,00,000
	Fully secured creditors		Furniture	40,000	20,000
	as per		Ma chinery	3,10,000	2,50,000
3,00,000	List B 3,00,000		Buildings	80,000	70,000
	Less estimated value		Book Debts as per		
	of security 3,00,000	Nil	List 'F'		
	Partly secured creditors		Good	3,00,000	3,00,000
	as per list 'C' 5,00,000		Bad and doubtful	1,00,000	40,000
	Less : Estimated		Bills of exchange as		
	value of		per List 'G'		—

Gross Liability	Liabilities		Exected to rank	Assets	Book value	Estimated to produce
	Security	2,00,000	3,00,000	Surplus as per contra		—
	Preferential creditors					12,81,000
	as per list 'D'	40,000		Preferential creditors		
	Deducted as per			deducted as per contra		40,000
	Contra	40,000	—			12,41,000
				Deficiency as per list 'H'		99,000
			13,40,000			13,40,000

Deficiency A/c

Particulars	Amount	Particulars	Amount
Excess of assets over Liabilities, i.e., capital (1,00,000 – 40,000)	6,00,000	Drawing	10,40,000
Interest on capital	60,000	Bad debts (1,00,000 – 40,000)	60,000
Net profit	5,91,000	Loss on realisation of Assets :	
Deficiency as per statement of affairs	99,000	Buildings (80,000 – 70,000)	10,000
		Machinery (3,10,000 – 2,50,000)	60,000
		Furniture (40,000 – 20,000)	20,000
		Stock (8,00,000 – 7,00,000)	1,00,000
		Bills discounted (1,00,000 – 40,000)	60,000
	13,50,000		13,50,000

Problem 2

Mr. A. B. Rajanna, a trader, had submitted his petition for insolvency to the court on 31-3-2002. On that date, the position of his business was as under.

	Rs.
Land valued at	22,000
Secured creditors (first mortgage on land)	16,000
Partly secured creditors (Second mortgage on land)	8,400
Unsecured creditors	32,000
Bank overdraft (unsecured)	16,000
Liability for bills discounted (estimated to rank Rs. 1700)	4,000
Tax due to Municipality	240
Two months wages due to a worker	400
Furniture (Estimated sale price Rs. 12,000)	16,000
Cash balance	400
Investments (Estimated sale price Rs. 1,600)	4,000
Machineries (Estimated sale price Rs. 13,400)	30,000
Debtors :	
Good	7,000
Doubtful (Estimated to realise Rs. 1,640)	3,640
Bills receivable (Estimated to realise Rs. 2,000)	4,000

When A. B. Rajanna commenced business six years ago he had a capital of Rs. 76,000. But even if he had earned a profit of Rs. 16,000 in the first two years, he had to suffer from the following losses in the following years :

Loss through betting	Rs. 16,000
Loss form trading	Rs. 20,000

Further, he had (with drawn) Rs. 42,000 from the firm for his personal use.

Prepare a statement of affairs and deficiency a/c of Mr. A. B. Rajanna (Bangalore University B. Com. April 2002).

Solution

Mr. A. B. Rajanna's Statement of Affairs as on 31-3-2002

Gross Liability	*Liabilities*	*Exected to rank*	*Assets*	*Book value*	*Estimated to produce*
	Unsecured creditors as		property as per list 'E'		
52,360	Per List 'A'	50,060	Cash balance	400	400
	(see note below)		Furniture	16,000	12,000
	Fully secured creditors		Investment	4,000	1,600
	as Per list 'B' 16,000		Machinery	30,000	13,400
	Less : Estimated value				27,400
	of security being		Book debts as per list 'F'		
	the first mortgage		Good	7,000	7,000
	on land 22,000				
	Surplus transferred				
	to partly secured		Doubtful	3,640	1,640
	Creditors		Bad	—	—
	6,000		Bills of exchange as per		
8,400	Partly secured Creditors				
	as per list 'C' 8400		List 'G'	4,000	2,000
	Less : Estimated value			65,040	38,040
	of security being		Surplus form securities		
	Second mortgage on		in the hands of fully		
	land 6,000		Secured creditors as		Nil
		2,400	per contra		38,040
	Preferential creditors				
	for rent taxes, salaries		Deduct preferential		280
250	Wages etc. 280		Creditors per contra		37,760
	Deducted per contra				
	280		Deficiency as per list 'H'		14,700
77,040		52,460			52,460

Working Note :

1. Unsecured creditors under expected to rank column is the total of unsecured creditors 32,000 + bank OD Rs. 16,000 + liability for bills discounted Rs. 1,700 + Rs. 360 excess of preferential claim on the assumption that under the provincial insolvency act, a labour gets only 20 wages as a preferential claim.
2. Unsecured creditors (gross column) is the total of 32,000 + 16,000 + 40,000 + 360 = 52,360.

Deficiency A/c as per list H

Particulars	*Amount*	*Particulars*	*Amount*
Excess of assets over Liabilities	76,000	Net loss from business	20,000
Net profit	16,000	Bad debts as per List 'F'	2,000
Deficiency as per Statement of affairs	14,700	Drawings	42,000
		Loss on realisation :	
		Furniture	4,000
		Investment	2,400
		Machineries	16,600
		bills receivable	2,000
		Loss through dishonour of discounted bills	1,700
		Loss through betting	16,000
	1,06,700		1,06,700

Problem 3

On 1st January 1997 sundar commenced business with Rs. 6,350. He earned a total profit of Rs. 5,534 during 1997 and 1998. The loss he suffered in 1999 was Rs. 2,500. His total drawing were Rs. 9,000.

Prepare statement of affairs and deficiency account from the following information.

Cash Rs. 230, stock Rs. 1,000, debtors good -Rs. 7,000. Doubtful Rs. 1,800, Bad debts Rs. 1,500, furniture Rs. 564. Investment in shares Rs. 500 unsecured creditors Rs. 13,000 secured creditors Rs. 2,500. Value of securities held by creditors Rs. 3,500, Preferential creditors Rs. 190.

Stock realises Rs. 666, furniture Rs, 282, Investment realised the book value. Doubtful debts realised Rs. 600.

(University of Madras B. Com., October 2000).

Solution

Statement of Affairs of Mr. Sunder

Gross Liability	*Liabilities*		*Exected to rank*	*Assets*	*Book value*	*Estimated to produce*
	Unsecured creditors as			property as per list 'E'		
13,000	Per List 'A'		13,000	Cash in hand	230	230
	Fully secured			Stock in trade	1,000	666
	Creditors as per			Furniture & fittings	564	282
2,500	List B	2,500		investment	500	500
	Estimated Value of				2,294	1,678
	Securities	3,500		Debtors as per		

Gross Liability	Liabilities		Exected to rank	Assets	Book value	Estimated to produce
				List 'F'		
	Balance	1,000		Good	7,000	7,000
	To contra			Doubtful	1,800	600
	Partly secured			Bad	1,500	—
	Creditors as per list CNil			Bills of exchange	—	—
	Preferential			as per list		
	Creditors as per			Surplus from		1,000
190	List D	190		secured creditors		
				(as per contra)		
	Deducted as				12,594	10,278
	per contra	190	—	Deduct preferential		
	as per contra		—	creditors		190
				Deficiency as per list 'H'		10,088
						2,912
15,690			13,000			13,000

Deficiency A/c as per List H

Particulars	Amount	Particulars	Amount
Excess of assets over Liabilities i.e., capital on 1-1-97	6,350	Net loss during 1999	2,500
Net profit arising for 1,997/19,998	5,554	Bad debts as per list 'F' (1,500 + 1,200)	2,700
Deficiency as per statement of affairs	2,912	Drawing	9,000
		Other losses ;	
		Stock in trade (1,000 - 666)	334
		Furniture & fittings (564- 282)	282
	14,816		14,816

Problem 4

Sarma filed on insolvency petition on 30th June 1995. His books showed the following balances.

Trial Balance

	Debit	Credit
Cash in hand	100	
Fixture and fittings (estimated to produce Rs. 800)	2,500	
Stock in Trade (estimated to produce Rs. 12,000)	18,000	
Sundry creditors ;		
Trade creditors		20,000
Bills payable		20,000
Mrs. Sarma's loan		2,000
Sundry debtors		
Good	10,000	

	Debit	Credit
Doubtful (estimated at 50%).	20,000	
Bad	20,000	
Bank overdraft		12,000
Capital		16,600
	70,600	70,600

Liability on bills discounted Rs. 5,000 and expected to rank Rs. 1,000. The amount due to Mrs. Sarma was a loan out money given to her by Sarma.

His household furniture was valued at Rs. 2,500. He owned a Moped valued at Rs. 7,500 having a mortgage on it of Rs. 6,000 at 8%. Interest paid up to the preceding 31st December.

Preferential creditors amounted to Rs. 350 (included in sundry creditors) and Rs. 150 for taxes on the moped.

Prepare a statement of affairs and deficiency account (Sri Venkteshwara University B. Com. September 2000).

Solution

Working Notes :

1. Calculation of Unsecured creditors

Sundry creditors	20,000
Bills payable	20,000
Loan form wife	2,000
Bank O.D.	12,000
	54,000
Less : Preferential creditors	350
	53,650
Add : Bills discount dishonour	1,000
	54,650

2. Calculation of Fully Secured Creditors
   Mortgage on the property @ 8% on Rs. 6,000

   6 Months interest due $= \frac{6}{12} \times \frac{8}{100} \times 6{,}000 = 240$

   Total amount due = 6,000 + 240 = 6,240

   ∴ Surplus = 7,500 – 6,240 = 1,260

3. $\frac{\text{Total preferential crebetors}}{350 + 150 = 500}$

4. Calculation of surplus realised from personal assets

Household furniture	2,500
Moped	7,500
	10,000
Less : Mortgage and Interest (6,000 + 240)	6,240
	3,760
Less : Taxes on Moped	150
Surplus	3,610

Statement of Affairs of Sarma as on 30th June 1995

Gross Liability	*Liabilities*	*Exected to rank*	*Assets*	*Book value*	*Estimated to produce*
	Unsecured creditors		Properties as per list 'E'		
58,650	as per list 'A'	54,650	Cash in hand	100	100
	Fully secured creditors		Fixtures & fittings	2,500	800
	as per list 'B' 6,240		Stock	18,000	12,000
	Less : Value of		Household furniture	–	2,500
	Security 7,500		Debtors as per list 'F'		
	Surplus as per 1,260		Good	10,000	10,000
	Contra		Doubtful	20,000	10,000
	Partly secured creditors—	Bad debts	20,000	—	
	as per list 'C'				35,400
	Preferential creditors		Add : Surplus as per		
			contra		1,260
	as per list 'D' 500				36,660
	Deduct as per 500		Less : preferential		
	Contra		creditors as per contra		500
					36,160
			Deficiency as per list H		18,490
		54,650			54,650

Deficiency A/c as per List H

Particulars	*Amount*	*Particulars*	*Amount*
Excess of assets over		Loss on sale of assets	
Liabilities being		Debtors	30,000
Capital	16,600	Stock	6,000
Surplus from sale		Furniture	1,700
Of personal assets	3,610	Discounted bills	
Deficiency as per		Dishonoured	1,000
Statement of			
Affairs	18,490		
	38,700		38,700

Problem 5

Mr. Arora finds himself insolvent on 31st December 1998. You are instructed to prepare his statement of affairs and deficiency account from the following information.

	Rs.
Sundry debtors :	
Good	20,000
: Doubtful (estimated Rs. 10,000)	30,500
Shares in 'B' Ltd., (estimated to realise Rs. 75,000)	90,000
Creditors on open account	96,500
Creditors holding first charge on shares in 'B' Ltd.	35,000
Creditors holding second charge on Shares in 'B' Ltd.	40,000

(To the extent of Rs. 30,000)	
Bills payable	8,000
Creditors for salaries wages etc. (of which Rs. 2,500 are Preferential)	1,000
Cash in hand	160
Stock in trade (estimated to realise Rs. 28,000)	32,840
Bills receivable (estimated to produce Rs. 9,000)	12,000
Speculation losses	20,000

Mr. Arora started business on 1-1-1996 with a capital of Rs. 80,000. He earned a profit of Rs. 15,000 in the first year, lost Rs. 20,500 in the second year and Rs. 28,300 in the third year, after allowing Rs. 3,600 as interest on capital per annum. His drawings amounted to Rs. 26,000. He has household furniture of estimated value of Rs. 6,000 and there is a private creditor for Rs. 10,000 (Bangalore University B. Com. April 2,000)

Solution

Statement of affairs of Mr. Arora as on 31-12-98

Gross Liability	*Liabilities*	*Exected to rank*	*Assets*	*Book value*	*Expected to realise*
	Unsecured creditors as		property as per list 'E'		
1,21,000	Per list 'A'	1,21,000	Cash in hand	160	160
	Fully secured creditors		Stock	32,840	28,000
	as per list 'B' 35,000		House hold furniture	—	6,000
	Less : Estimated value		Book debts as per list 'F'		
	of security 75,000		Good	20,000	20,000
	40,000				
	Less : Transferred		Doubtful	30,500	10,000
	To List 'C' 30,000		Bills of exchange as per		
	Surplus as per contra				
	10,000		List 'G'	12,000	9,000
				95,500	73,160
	Partly secured creditors		Surplus security		10,000
					83,160
	as per list 'C' 40,000		Less preferential creditors		
	Less : Estimated value		as per contra		2,500
	of security 30,000	10,000			80,660
	Preferential creditors as		Deficiency as per list 'H'		50,340
2,500	Per list 'D' 2,500				
	Deducted per				
	contra , 2,500				
		1,31,000			1,31,000

Working Note :

Calculation of unsecured Creditors :

Creditors + B. P. + Private Creditors + Salary and wages

96,500 + 80,00 + 10,000 + 6,500 = 1,21,000

Deficiency A/c

Particulars	*Amount*	*Particulars*		*Amount*
Capital as on 1-1-96	80,000	Net loss from business from 1-1-1996 to 31-12-1998		48,800
Net profit from business From 1-1-1996 to 31-12-98	15,000	Bad debts		20,500
Interest on capital	10,800	Household expenses (Drawings) (26,000 + 14,000)		40,000
Deficiency	50,340	Other losses :		
		Shares in B Ltd.	15,000	
		Stock	4,840	
		Bills Receivable	3,000	
		Speculation loss	20,000	42,840
		Excess of private liabilities over private assets (10,000 - 6,000)		4,000
	1,56,140			1,56,140

Note : Difference in trial balance Rs. 14,000 is taken as additional drawings.

Problem 6

Bharadwaj finds himself insolvency on 1-1-97. You are required to prepare his statement affairs as at that date and the deficiency account for the three year ended on that date. The information you are able to obtain as to his position is as follows :

Sundry debtors =	
Good Rs. 20,000	
Doubtful Rs. 81,000 (Estimated to produced Rs. 40,000)	
Shares of Kakatiya Ltd.	2,20,000
(Estimated to produce Rs. 1,82,000)	
Creditors open account	1,90,000
Creditors holding a first charge on investment	80,000
Creditors holding a second charge on	
Investments to the extent of Rs. 60,000,	70,000
Bills receivable discounted (of which Rs. 7,000 is likely to be dishonoured)	12,000
Creditors for rent, taxes etc. (of which Rs. 3,000 is preferential)	6,000
Furniture (estimated to realise Rs. 6,000)	8,000
Cash in hand	240
Stock in trade (estimated to realise Rs. 60,000)	71,760
Bills receivable (estimated to realise Rs. 14,000)	26,000
Loss on betting	30,000

He started business on 1-1-1994 with capital of Rs. 1,00,000. In the first two year there was a profit of Rs. 55,000 and in the third year there was a loss of Rs. 10,000. He has been allowed interest at 6% per annum on his original capital for each of the three years. Withdrawals for the whole period amounted Rs. 52,000.

(Sri Venkateshwara University B. Com. April 2000)

Solution

Statement of Affairs of Bhardwaj as on 1-1-97

Gross Liability	*Liabilities*		*Exected to rank*	*Assets*	*Book value*	*Estimated to produce*
	Unsecured creditors			Assets & properties		
2,05,000	as per list A		2,00,000	as per List 'E'		
	Fully secured creditors			Furniture	8,000	6,000
	as per list 'B'	80,000		Cash	240	240
	Less : Value of			Stock	71,760	60,000
	Security	1,82,000		Jewellery from wife	—	8,000
		1,02,000		Book Debts as per list 'F'		
	Less carried to list 'C'			Good	20,000	20,000
		60,000		Doubtful	81,000	40,000
	Surplus as per contra			Bills of exchange as per		
		42,000	—	List 'G'	26,000	14,000
	Partly secured creditors					
	as per list 'C'	70,000				
	Less value of security					
		60,000	10, 000			
	Preferential creditors as					1,48,240
	per list 'D'	3,000		Add surplus as per contra		42,000
	Deducted as per contra					1,90,240
		3,000	—	Less deduct as per contra		3,000
	Deduct as per					1,87,240
	contra	3,000		Deficiency as per list 'H'		22,760
			2,10,000			2,10,000

Deficiency A/c

Particulars	*Amount*	*Particulars*	*Amount*
Capital	1,00,000	Net Loss	10,000
Net Profit	55,000	Bad Debts	41,000
Interest on capital	18,000	Household expenses	
6,000 × 3		Including purchase of	
Jewellery form wife	8,000	Jewellery	52,000
Deficiency	22,760	Loss on assets	63,760
		Liability on bills discounted	7,000
		Loss on stock exchange	30,000
	2,03,760		2,03,760

Working Note :

Unsecured creditors :

Creditors	1,90,000
Rent & Rates	3,000
B/R discounted dishonour	7,000
	2,00,000

Problem 7

The Assets of Mr. X of Mumbai on 30th June 1990 as shown by his books were Rs. 28,000 and his liabilities were Rs. 22,000. He filed his petition in the insolvency court and estimated his deficiency to be Rs. 15,000. After making the above estimate, he found the following items were not passed through his books of account.

(*a*) Interest at 6% on his capital from 1-1-1990.

(*b*) A contingent liability for Rs. 1,250 on bills discounted by him for Rs. 5,000.

(*c*) Amount duc for wages Rs. 300; Salaries Rs. 200, Rent Rs. 100 Rates and Taxes Rs. 150 (All are preferential).

Prepare his statement of Affairs and Deficiency a/c.

(University of Madras, B. Com. April 1999)

Solution

Statement of Affairs of Mr. 'X' as on 30-6-90

Gross Liability	*Liabilities*		*Expected to rank*	*Assets*	*Book value*	*Expected to produce*
	Unsecured Creditors as per			Property as per list 'E'	28,000	7,000
22,000	List 'A'		22,000	Debtors as per list 'F'	—	—
5,000	Liability for bills			Bills receivable as per		
	Discount		1,250	List 'G'	—	—
			23,250			7,000
	Fully secured					
	creditors as per			Deducted for preferential		
—	List 'B'		—	creditors as per contra		750
	Partly secured					6,250
	creditors as per					
—	List 'C'		—	Deficiency as per list H		17,000
	Preferential					
	creditors as per					
750	List 'D'	750				
	Deducted as					
	per contra	750				
27,750			23,250			23,250

Deficiency A/c

Particulars	*Amount*	*Particulars*	*Amount*
Excess of assets over Liabilities	6,000	Loss on realisation	
		of assets (28,000 – 7,000)	21,000
(28,000 – 22,000)		Bills discount	1,250
Deficiency as per		Preferential creditors	
Statement of affairs	17,000	Not yet considered	750
	23,000		23,000

Working notes :

1. **Value of Assets Expected to Produce :**

Total liabilities (given)	22,000
whereas total deficiency estimated by Mr. 'X' (given)	15,000
Balance is assumed to realise through sale of assets.	7,000

2. **Total Preferential Creditors as per list 'D'**
   Wages + Salary + Rent + Rates & Taxes
   300 + 200 + 100 + 150 = 750
3. **Interest on Capital at 6%**

When outside liabilities are not being paid in full, the interest on capital should not be considered.

Problem 8

Vamsee Krishna of Delhi commenced business on 1-1-90 with a capital of Rs. 16,250. His profits for three years were Rs. 8,850. He did not maintain proper books for the next 2 years. His drawings averaged Rs. 1,200 per annum. He filed his insolvency petition on 31-12-94. On that date his affairs were as follows :

Building : Cost Rs. 15,000 estimated to realise		5,000
Machinery : Cost Rs. 7,000 estimated to realise		2,500
Book Debts : Good	3,000	
Doubtful	1,000	
(Estimated to realise 250)		
Bad	2,500	6,500
Bills receivable discounted and Expected to Rank		1,250
Preferential creditors		250
Party secured creditor (security : Life policy worth Rs. 2,000)		5,750
Mortgage on building		2,500
Unsecured creditors		10, 000
Household furniture		750
Household Debts		500
Stock cost Rs. 4,000 estimated to realise		2 ,750
Furniture cost Rs. 500 estimated to realise		200
Cash		50

Mrs. Vamsee Krishna gave up her Jewellery worth Rs. 625 to the official receiver. Prepare statement of Affairs and Deficiency a/c (Sri Venkateshwara University B. Com. April 1999).

Solution

Working Notes :

1. **Calculation of Unsecured creditors :**

Creditors	10,000
Household debt	500
Liability on bills discounted	1,250
	11,750

2. **Calculate of Surplus From Private Assets :**

Household furniture	750

Insurance policy	2,000
Jewellery	625
	3,375
Less : Household debts	500
	2,875

3. **Trial Balance**

	Debit	Credit
Buildings	15,000	
Machinery	7,000	
Debtors (3,000 + 1,000 + 2,500)	6,500	
Preferential creditors		250
Party secured creditors		5,750
Mortgage on building		2,500
Unsecured creditors		10,000
Stock	4,000	
Furniture	500	
Cash	50	
Drawings (1,200 × 5)	6,000	
Capital		16,250
Trade profits		8,850
Trade loss (Balancing figure)	4,550	
	43,600	43,600

4. Liabilities on bills discounted and private assets and private liabilities are not considered for the purpose of Trial Balance.

Statement of Affairs of Vamsee Krishna as on 31-12-94

Gross Liability	Liabilities		Expected to rank	Assets	Book value	Expected to produce
11,750	Unsecured creditors as per list 'A'		11,750	Assets and properties as Per list 'E'		
	Fully secured creditors			Machinery	7,000	2,500
2,500	as per List 'B'			Household furniture	750	750
	Mortgage loan	2,500		Stock	4,000	2,750
	Less security	5,000		Furniture	500	200
	Surplus as per Contra	2,500		Cash	50	50
				Jewellery	625	625
	Partly secured creditors as per list 'C'	5,750		Book debts as per list 'F'		
	Less surplus as per contra	2,000	3,750	Good	3,000	3,000
				Doubtful	1,000	250
	Preferential creditors			Bad debts	2,500	—
250	as per list 'D'	250		Bills of exchange as per List 'G'	—	—
	Deducted as per contra	250	—			10,125
				Add : surplus as per contra		2,500
						12,625

Gross Liability	*Liabilities*	*Expected to rank*	*Assets*	*Book value*	*Expected to produce*
			Less : Deducted as per contra		250 12,375
			Deficiency as per List II		3,125
20,250		15,500			15,500

Deficiency A/c

Particulars	*Amount*	*Particulars*	*Amount*
Capital	16,250	Drawings (1,200 × 5)	6,000
Net Profit	8,850	Bad Debts	3,250
Surplus on private assets	2,875	Loss on sale of assets :	
Deficiency as per Statement of affairs	3,125	Buildings	10,000
		Machinery	4,500
		Stock	1,250
		Furniture	300
		Loss on Bills Discounted	1,250
		Trade loss	4,550
	31,600		31,600

Problem 9

Sri Rakesh Sharma of Neelagiri finds himself insolvent on 1st January 1996. You are instructed to prepare his Statement of Affairs as at that date and Deficiency Account for the Three years ended on that date. The information you are able to obtain as to his position is as follows :

Sundry debtors : Good	10,000
: Doubtful (estimated to produce Rs. 20,000)	40,500
Share in Malhotra Ltd. (estimated to produce Rs. 91,000)	1,10,000
Creditors on open account	95,000
Creditors holding a first charge on Investment	40,000
Creditors holding a second charge on Investment to the extent of Rs. 30,000)	35,000
Bills receivable discounted (of which Rs. 3,500 is likely to be dishonoured)	6,000
Creditors for Rent, Taxes, etc. (of which Rs. 1,500 is preferential)	3,000
Furniture (Estimated to realise Rs. 3,000)	4,000
Cash in hand	120
Stock in trade (Estimated to realise Rs. 30,000)	35,880
Bills receivable (Estimated to realise Rs. 7,000)	13,000
Loss on Stock Exchange	15,000

He started business on 1-1-1994 with a capital of Rs. 50,000. In the first two years there was a profit of Rs. 27,500 and in the third year there was a loss of Rs. 5,000.

He has been allowed interest at 6% per annum on his original capital for each of the three years. Withdrawls for the whole period amounted to Rs. 26,000. Out of his withdrawals, he had purchased Jewellery for his wife at a price of Rs. 3,000. His wife offered this Jewellery towards paying the debts of her husband. The Jewellery is expected to realise Rs. 4,000.

(Osmania University B. Com. Oct. 1998)

Solution

Working Notes :

1. **Creditors as per list 'A'**

	Gross	Expected to Rank
Creditors on open account	95,000	95,000
Add creditors for rent taxes Which are not preferential	1,500	1,500
Add : Liability on bills discounted	6,000	3,500
	1,02,500	1,00,500

2. Jewellery given by wife is equivalent to further contribution by the owner. This increases asset on one hand and his capital on the other. Only expected value has been taken as an asset as well as conurbation. Book value has no meaning.

Statement of Affairs as on 1-1-96

Gross Liability	*Liabilities*	*Expected to Rank*	*Assets*	*Book value*	*Estimated to produce*
	Unsecured creditors		Asses as per list 'E'		
1,02,500	as per List 'A'	1,00,000	Furniture	4,000	3,000
	Fully secured creditors		Stock-in-trade	35,880	30,000
	as per list 'B' 40,000		Jewellery of wife	3,000	4,000
	Estimated value		Cash in hand	—	120
	of securities 91,000		Book debts as per lost 'F'		
	51,000		Good	10,000	10,000
	Transferred to		Doubtful	40,500	20,000
	List 'C' 30,000		Bills receivable as per		
	Surpus as per 21,000		List 'G'	13,000	7,000
	contra				74,120
	Partly secured				
35,000	creditors 35,000		Surplus as per contra		21,000
	Less : Estimated				
	value of secretion				95,120
	Transferred from List 'B'				
	30,000	5,000	Less preferential claims		1,500
	Preferential creditors as		as per contra		93,620
	Per List 'D'				
	Rent and Taxes 1,500		Deficiency as per List 'H'		11,380
	Deducted as per contra				
	1,500	Nil			
		1,05,000			1,05,000

Deficiency A/c as per List 'H'

Particulars	*Amount*	*Particulars*		*Amount*
Excess of Assets over Liabilities	50,000	Loss in business		5,000
Contribution by wife	4,000	Drawings		26,000
Profits	27,500	Loss on realisation of assets		
interest on Capital	9,000	Shares in Malhotra Ltd.	19,000	
Deficiency as per Statement		Furniture	1,000	
of Affairs	11,380	Stock in trade	5,880	
		Debtors	20,500	
		B.R.	6,000	52,380
		Bills discounted and expected to Rank		3,500
		Loss on Stock Exchange		15,000
	1,01,850			1,01,850

Problem 10

From the following particulars, prepare the statement of affairs and deficiency a/c of Mr. Gharib

Creditors (1st charge on Land and Building)	40,000
Creditors (2nd charge on Land and Buildings)	30,000
Stock (to realise Rs. 16,000)	20,000
Machinery (to realise Rs. 28,000)	50,000
Furniture (to realise Rs. 9,000)	15,000
Investments (to realise Rs. 32,000)	35,000
Book Debts Doubtful and Bad	28,000
Household debts	1,700
Bank over draft	25,000
Creditors unsecured	75,620
Cash	1,000
Bills of Exchange	2,000
Book Debts good	5,000
Creditors payable full	5,380
Household furniture	800
Household Jewellery	4,000
Land and Buildings	54,000
Loan taken	11,000

Mr. Gharib started business with Rs. 25,000 earned a profit of Rs. 2,000 in the 1st year and later incurred loss. He withdrew Rs. 4,000 during 2 years period. Land and buildings are likely to realise Rs. 50,000 Doubtful debts are likely to realise Rs. 5,000.

(Osmania University B. Com. October 1997)

Solution

Statement of Affairs of Gharib

Gross Liability	*Liabilities*		*Expected to Rank*	*Assets*	*Book value*	*Expected to produce*
	Unsecured creditors			Property as per List 'E'		
1,13,320	As per list 'A'		1,13,320	Cash		1,000
	(1,700 + 25,000 + 75,620 + 11,000)			Stock	20,000	16,000
				Machinery	50,000	28,000
	Fully secured creditors			Furniture	15,000	9,000
	as per List 'B'	40,000		Investment	35,000	32,000
	Less estimated			Household furniture		800
	value of securi ty	50,000		Household Jewellery		4,000
	Transferred to List 'C'	10,000				
	Partly secured credit-			Book debts as per		
30,000	-ors as per List 'C'					
		30,000		List 'F'		
	Less : Estimated			Good	5,000	5,000
	Value of security	10,000		Doubtful 28,000	5,000	
			20,000	Bills of exchange as per List 'G'	2,000	2,000
						1,02,800
	Preferential creditors			Preferential creditors		
	as per List 'D'	5,380		deducted as per contra		5,380
	Deducted as per					97,420
	contra	5,380		Deficiency as per list 'H'		35,900
			1,33,320			1,33,320

Deficiency A/c as per List 'H'

Particulars		*Amount*	*Particulars*	*Amount*
Excess of assets over liabilities		35,000	Net loss arising from business	10,000
Net profit earned		2,000	Bad debts	23,000
Excess of private assets over			Drawings	4,000
Private Liabilities :			Other Losses :	
Household furniture	800		Stock in trade	4,000
Household Jewellery	4,000		Machinery	22,000
	4,800		Furniture	6,000
Less : Household debts	1,700		Investments	3,000
Deficiency as per statement of affairs		3,100 35,900	Land & building	4,000
		76,000		76,000

Problem 11 (Insolvency of a Partnership Firm)

On 31st December 2003 the Balance Sheet of M/s A and B was as follows

Particulars		*Amount*	*Particulars*	*Amount*
Trade creditors		24,000	Machinery	24,000
Bills payable		30,000	Buildings	12,000
Bank Loan		18,000	Book debts	24,000
12 months Rent		1,200	Cash	1,200
One months Salary		1,200	Stock	37,200
Capital				
A	12,000			
B	12,000	24,000		
		98,400		98,400

A owed personally Rs. 21,600 and he had in addition to his interest in the firm a house property which cost Rs. 6,000, Furniture Rs. 2,400 and Life Policies on which he had paid premia amounting to Rs. 1,200. 'B' owed Rs. 16,800 and he had paid life premium amounting to Rs. 3,600 and had furniture which cost Rs. 1,200.

The Bank held the deed's of 'A' property and his life policies . The partnership assets were valued as follows :

Machinery Rs. 13,000, Buildings Rs. 6,000 : Book debts - Good Rs. 12,000, Doubtful Rs. 6,000.

(Estimated to realise Rs. 3,600) and Bad Rs. 6,000. Stock was worth Rs. 24,000.

A's property was considered to be worth Rs. 6,000, his policies Rs. 600 and furniture Rs. 1,800. B's life policies were worth Rs. 1,800 and his furniture Rs. 600.

Prepare Statement of Affairs and Deficiency Account of the firm as well as of the partners.

Solution

Statement of Affairs of M/s A and B as at 31st December 2003.

Gross Liability	*Liabilities*		*Expected to Rank*	*Assets*	*Book value*	*Expected to produce*
	Unsecured creditors			Property as per list 'E'		
74,000	as per list 'A'		74,000	Cash in hand	1,200	1,200
	Fully secured creditors			Machinery	24,000	13,080
	as per list 'B'		—	Buildings	12,000	6,000
	Partly secured			Stock	37,200	24,000
	creditors as per list 'C'		—	Book debts as per list 'F'		
	Preferential creditors			Good	12,000	12,000
400	as per List 'D'	400		Doubt full	6,000	3,600
	Deducted as per			Bad	6,000	—
	Contra	400	—	Bills of exchange as per		
				List 'G'	—	—
						59,880

Gross Liability	Liabilities	Expected to Rank	Assets	Book value	Expected to produce
			Less preferential creditors as per contra		400
			Deficiency as per list 'H'		14,520
		74,000			74,000

Deficiency A/c of the Firm as at 31-12-2003

Particulars	Amount	Particulars		Amount
Excess of Assets over Liabilities i.e., Capital	24,000	Loss on realisation of assets :		
		Machinery	10,920	
Deficiency as per statement of affairs	14,520	Buildings	6,000	
		Stock	13,200	30,120
		Bad debts		8,400
	38,520			38,520

Statement of Affairs of Mr. 'A'

Gross Liability	Liabilities		Expected to Rank	Assets	Book value	Expected to Rank
21,600	Unsecured creditors as per List 'A'		21,600	Property as per list 'E' Furniture	2,400	1,800
	Fully secured creditors as per list 'B'			Book debts as per list 'F'	—	—
				Bills of exchange as per list 'G'	—	—
	(over drat of the firm secure by Mr. 'A' private Assets (18,000 –14,468)	3,532		Surplus as per contra		3,068
	Less : Estimated Value of security (House policy)	6,600				4,868
		3,068		Deficiency as per List 'H'		16,732
	Surplus carried to contra	3,068				
			21,600			21,600

Deficiency A/c of 'A'

Particulars	Amount	Particulars		Amount
Capital	—	Loss of realisation :		
Deficiency as per Statement of Affairs	16,732	Furniture	600	
		Policies	600	
		Capital (12,000 – Nil)	12,000	13,200
		Other losses :		
		Private assets used to pay firms liability		3,532
	16,732			16,732

Statement of Affairs of Mr. 'B'

Gross Liability	*Liabilities*	*Expected to Rank*	*Assets*	*Book Value*	*Expected to Produce*
	Unsecured creditors		Property as per List 'E'		
16,800	as per List 'A'	16,800	Furniture	1,200	600
	Fully secured		Life policies	3,600	1,800
	creditors as per List 'B'	—			2,400
	Partly secured creditors as per List 'C'	—	Deficiency as per list 'H'		14,400
	Preferential creditors as per list 'D'	—			
		16,800			16,800

Deficiency of 'B's A/c

Particulars	*Amount*	*Particulars*		*Amount*
Capital	—	Loss on realisation		
Deficiency as per Statement of Affairs	14,400	Furniture	600	
		Life policies	1,800	
		Capital (12,000 – Nil)	12,000	14,400
	14,400			14,400

Working Notes :

1. Ascertaining preferential creditors under Presidency Town Insolvency Act.

	Gross Liabilities Rs.	preferential Creditors Rs.	Unsecured Crs. Rs.
(*a*) 12 months rent (preferential - one month rent)	1,200	100	1,100
(*b*) 1 Months Salary (Preferential- one months salary or Rs. 300 which even is less	1,200	300	900
	2,400	400	2,000

(*b*) Balance of unsecured creditors include :

Trade creditors	24,000
Bills payable	30,000
Bank Loan	18,000
Non - Preferential creditors for salary rent etc.	2,000
	74,000

(*c*) Amount due to bank is Rs. 18,000, out of which it will receive.

$$\frac{59{,}480}{74{,}000} \times 18{,}000 = \text{Rs. } 14{,}468$$

The remaining Rs. 3,532 (Rs. 18000 - 14,468) is to be realised by selling assets pledged by A.

4. A's Excess of assets over liabilities has been arrived at as follows :

Assets at book values :

	Capital	12,000	
	House property	6,000	
	Furniture	2,400	
	Life policies	1,200	21,600
Less :	Private liabilities		21,600
			Nil

5. B's Excess of assets over liabilities has been arrived at as follows :

	Capital	12,000	
	Furniture (at book value)	1,200	
	Life policies (at book value)	3,600	
			16,800
Less :	Private liabilities		16,800
			—

QUESTIONS

Simple Questions

1. Who is an insolvent ?
2. Which are the acts governing insolvency ?
3. What is a statement of affairs ? Why is it prepared ?
4. Give a Proforma of Statement of Affairs.
5. State the differences between statement of Affairs and a Balance Sheet.
6. Mention the various lists prepared by the insolvent.
7. What is a "Deficiency account" ? Why is prepared ?
8. Give the specimen of Deficiency a/c.
9. Who are preferential creditors under Presidency Town Insolvency Act ?
10. Who are preferential creditors under Provincial Insolvency Act ?
11. How do you treat the loan payable to the wife of a businessman on insolvency of the firm ?

EXERCISE 1

From the following liabilities of an insolvent debtor prepare list 'D' as would appear in Statement of Affairs

	Rs.
(*a*) household debts	1,500
(*b*) Rent due to landlord for 2 month (at Calcutta)	3,000
(*c*) Wages due to servant for five months	2,000
(*d*) Clerks salary due for 4 months	3,000
(*e*) Rates and taxes due	1,200
(*f*) Loan from wife	1,000

(Osmania University, B. Com.)

Answer : Preferential creditors (Under Presidency Towns Insolvency Act) Rs. 3100 and under Provincial Insolvency Act Rs. 1,240.

EXERCISE 2

Mr. Manohar Field a petition of insolvency on 30-6-98. His books showed the following balances on that date :

		Dr	Cr
Cash in hand		25	—
Furniture (estimated to realise Rs. 2,000)		625	
Stock (estimated to realise Rs. 3,000)		4,500	
Creditors			5,000
Bills payable			5,500
Sundry debtors :			
Good	2,500		
Doubtful (estimated to realise 50%)	5,000		
Bad	5,000	12,500	
Bank overdraft			3,000
Capital			4,150
		17,650	17,650

Liability on bills discounted Rs. 1,250 and expected to rank Rs. 250. His household furniture was valued at Rs. 625. He owned a house valued at Rs. 1,875 having a mortgage on it of Rs. 1,500 @ 4% p.a. Interest paid up to 31-12-97. Preferential creditors amounted to Rs. 85 (included in creditors) and Rs. 40 for rates on the house. Prepare statement of affairs and deficiency account. **(Sri Venkateshwara University B. Com. October 1999)**

Answer : Deficiency as per List 'H' Rs. 4,595
Total of deficiency a/c Rs. 9,675.

EXERCISE 3

Ratanlal finds himself insolvent on 31-12-1998. His position was as follows :

Sundry debtors : Good Rs. 5,000. Doubtful Rs. 15,250 estimated to produce Rs. 10,000, Bad Rs. 5,000.

100 Shares in X Ltd., (Estimated to produce R. 7,500)	12,500
Shares in Y Ltd., (Estimated to produce Rs. 38,000)	42,500
Speculation loss	7,500

Creditors on open account	45,000
Creditors holding second charge over Y Ltd. shares (to the extent of Rs. 15,000)	17,500
Creditors holding first charge over Y Ltd. shares	20,000
Bills payable	2,500
Bills receivable discounted (Estimated to rank Rs. 1,750)	3,500
Creditors for rates, taxes, wages (of which Rs. 1,250 is preferential)	1,500
Furniture (estimated to produce Rs. 1,500)	2,000
Cash in hand	60
Stock in trade (estimated to produce Rs. 15,000)	19,440
Bills receivable (estimated or produce Rs. 3,500)	5,000

He started the business with a capital of Rs. 30,000 on 1-1-1996 and business resulted in a profit of Rs. 5,000 and Rs. 3,750 for the first two years respectively and loss of Rs. 2,500 for the third year after providing Rs. 1,500 as interest on capital each year. Withdrawls for the entire period amounted to Rs. 13,000.

Prepare Statement of Affairs and Deficiency a/c.

(Osmania University B. Com., October 1999)

Answer : Deficiency as per List 'H' Rs. 7,690
Total of Deficiency a/c Rs. 50,940

EXERCISE 4

Form the following particulars of Mr. Unfortunate prepare deficiency a/c (List 'H')

Capital	Rs. 2,000
Excess of private assets over private liabilities	1,180
Losses on realisation of various assets	2,500
Loss on account of bad debts as per List 'F'	3,000
Loss through bills discounted and dishonoured	200

(Osmania University B. Com., March 1999)

Answer : Total of Deficiency a/c Rs. 5,700

EXERCISE 5

On 1st April 1988 Mr. Sivaraman commenced business with a capital of Rs. 63,500. His profits for the years 1988-89 and 1989-90 amount to Rs. 55,540. He suffered a loss of Rs. 25,000 in the year 1990-91. His total drawings upto 31st March 1991 were Rs. 90,000. From the following figures, prepare a Statements of Affairs and Deficiency Account of Mr. Sivaraman as at 31st 1991.

	Rs.
Cash	2,300
Stock in Trade	10,000
Debtors - Good	70,000
Debtors - Doubtful	18,000
Debtors - Bad	15,000
Furniture and Fittings	5,640
Investment in Shares	5,000

Unsecured creditors (including Rs. 10,000 of his wife)	1,30,000
Unsecured creditors	25,000
Value of securities held by secured creditors	35,000
Preferential claims for rent rates and taxes	1,900

Assume the stock -in-trade will realise Rs. 6,660 : Fixtures and Fittings Rs. 2,820 : Investment in shares, the book value and the bad and doubtful debts Rs. 6,000.

(University of Madras. B. Com. September 1997)

Answer : Deficiency as per list 'H' - Rs. 29,120
Total of deficiency a/c Rs. 1,48,160

EXERCISE 6

Mr. Chary filed Insolvency Petition on 31-3-96. Prepare his Statement of Affairs from the following.

Creditors with lien on stock	20,000
Creditors with lien on shares	80,000
Creditors payable in full	6,000
Liability on bills discounted	12,000
Machinery (to realise Rs. 24,000)	30,000
Furniture (to realise Rs. 3,000)	6000
Other Assets (to realise Rs. 6,000)	7,000
Book Debts - Doubtful and Bad	20,000
Stock (to realise 80,000)	1,20,000
Creditors unsecured	1,50,000
Mortgage on building	20,000
Bills of exchange	2,800
Building	22,000
Book Debts - good	40,000
Consignment (realised)	10,000
Cash	200
Shares, cost and realised	32,000

The liability on bills discounted would rank for Rs. 7,000. Doubtful debts to realise Rs. 4,000. Mr. Chary had a capital of Rs. 1 Lakh, 4 years ago. During this period he made a profit of Rs. 41,000, after interest on capital amounting to Rs. 20,000. His withdrawals were Rs. 77,200. He suffered loss in speculation for 69,500 (Osmania University B. Com. March 1997).

Answer : Deficiency as per list 'H' Rs. 59,000
Total of deficiency a/c Rs. 2,20,000

EXERCISE 7

Insolvency of a partnership firm

X and Y are in partnership and file their petition in bankruptcy. From the following particulars prepare the Statement of Affairs and Deficiency a/c of Joint Estate as also the private of the partners.

Balance sheet

	X and Y Rs.	X Rs.	Y Rs.
Mortgage on freehold	3,000	—	—
Bank overdraft	3,000	—	—
Sundry creditors	12,400	1,500	2,900
Preferential creditors	100	—	—
Capital : X	3,000		
: Y	2,000		
Surplus	—	5,000	1,100
	23,500	6,500	4,000
Freehold premises	6,000	—	—
Plant	6,500	—	—
Furniture	400	1,000	1,200
Stock	5,500	—	—
Debtors	5,000	—	—
Investment	—	2,500	800
Cash	100	—	—
Capital in the firm	—	3,000	2,000
	23,500	6,500	4,000

The Bank overdraft was secured by a second mortgage on freehold as well as X's personal guarantee supported by the deposit of Y's investments as collateral security.

The firms assets are estimated to realise the following.

Freehold Rs. 4,500 : Plant Rs. 3,000, Furniture Rs. 150 : Stock Rs. 3,100 : Debtors - good Rs. 2,575, Doubtful Rs. 1,000 (50 paise in the rupee) bad Rs. 1,425 (Nil).

X's assets : furniture Rs. 600 : Investments Rs. 2,000.

Y's Assets : Furniture Rs. 800 and Investments Rs. 300.

Answer : Deficiency of the Firm Rs. 3,475
Total of Deficiency a/c of the Firm Rs. 9,575
Surplus from 'X' Rs. 1,100
Total of Deficiency a/c of × Rs. 5,000
Deficiency of Y Rs. 2,175
Total of Deficiency of Y Rs. 3,275

34
CHAPTER
Containers and Packages Accounts

INTRODUCTION

When goods are produced and distributed on large scale basis containers are needed to preserve and transport such goods. Certain goods are to be preserved without being subject to deterioration in quality. The types of containers and packages used depend upon the type of goods and services manufactured and supplied. Common examples of containers and packages used are cylinders, barrels, drums, boxes etc.

In some cases the packing materials form part of the finished goods. They are called as primary packing materials. Examples of such packages are Jars, tins, bottles, bags, sachets etc. used in selling articles such as oil, ghee, milk, toothpaste,.medicines ,soft drinks, baby food etc. While in other cases packing materials are used for easy handling and transporting of bulk goods over long distance. Such packing materials are known as secondary packing materials. Examples of such packing materials are card board boxes, wooden crates etc., which are used for carrying products with primary packing materials.

Besides ensuring safety and convenient handling of products packages also facilitate advertising. Neatly packed articles attract attention of both existing and potential users.

Returnable and Non-Returnable Containers

The seller and buyer agree upon as to whether containers are returnable or non-returnable. Returnable containers are those which are returned by the customer to the seller after utilising the product. Non-returnable containers are retained by customer even after using the product. Whether the manufacture buys them from external source or manufactures himself in the same organisation it involves expenses. This expense of containers are recovered by the manufactures by charging the same to the customer. When the customer returns back the container the buyer will get a rebate in the invoice price.

Accounting Procedure Relating to Containers

The accounting of containers depend upon two aspects, viz (*a*) whether they are returnable or non-returnable and whether they are charged separately.

1. **When containers are non-returnable and its price is charged to customers along with the price of goods sold :** In this case the customers retain the containers with them and hence the cost of the same is included in the sale price of the goods sold. Though the seller recovers the cost of containers from the customers by charging it to selling price, he wants account for such containers so as to know the cost of containers used during the accounting period. For this purpose, the seller prepares a container stock a/c. On the debit side of this account the opening stock of containers and the purchases made during the year is recorded. The credit side of this account is recorded with : (*a*) Closing stock of containers (*b*) The cost of containers lost due to abnormal causes and (*c*) Amount realised on sale of containers scrapped. A proforma of this account is shown below.

	Qty	*Amt*		*Qty*	*Amt*
To Opening Stock		X X	By Bank a/c (Sale of containers scrapped)		X X
To Purchases		X X	By P & L a/c (Abnormal loss of containers)		X X
			By Closing Stock		X X
			By Trading a/c (Balancing figure)		
		X X			X X

The purpose of preparing in this case is to ascertain the cost of containers used.

2. **When non-returnable containers are charged separately but not as part of the goods sold :** In this case, the object of preparing containers stock account is to ascertain the profit or loss on containers sent, profit being the excess prices charged over the actual cost of containers. A proforma of container stock a/c as is prepared under this case is shown below :

Containers Stock a/c

	Qty	*Amt*		*Qty*	*Amt*
To Opening Stock		XX	By Bank (Sales)		X X
To Purchases		X X	By P & L a/c (Abnormal Loss)		X X
To P & L a/c (Balancing figure)		X X	By Customer's a/c (Amount charged to customers on containers sent		X X
			By Closing Stock		X X

3. **When containers are returnable and no separate charge is made :** Under this situation, the cost of containers are included in the selling price of the Product. In this case also a containers stock a/c is opened. This account is debited with : (*a*) The opening stock on land and stock with customers (*b*) Purchases. The containers stock account is credited with : (*a*) Sale price of containers scrapped (*b*) P & L a/c with abnormal loss (*c*) closing stock of containers on hand and with customers. The difference between the two sides represent cost of containers used and it is transferred to trading account.

Any containers not returned before the time expires for such returns, constitute stock with customers. Further the balancing figure of containers stock account which represent cost of containers used represent value of containers retained by customers subject to depreciation. A profroma of containers stock account is shown below.

Containers Stock A/c

	Qty	*Amt*		*Qty*	*Amt*
To Opening stock — on hand — with customers To Purchases		 X X X X X X	By Bank a/c (Sales) By P & L a/c (Abnormal loss) By Trading a/c (Containers Retained) By Closing Stock — on hand — with customers		X X X X X X
		X X			X X

4. **Returnable Containers When Separate Charge is made :** Under this situation instead of including the cost of containers in the selling price of the goods the returnable containers are charged separately. The price so charged to containers is known as "charging out price". When customers return back the containers a refund is allowed on the price paid by them at the time of sale. The refundable amount is always less than charging out price". The difference between charging out price and the amount returnable constitute profit of the seller.

When customers fail to return containers or the time for returning containers expire, the seller makes additional profit on such containers.

The difference between charging out price and the credit given to customers is known as rental or hire charge of containers. Hire charge is an income to the seller. The amount returnable is treated as deposit by customers. When the period of return expires, those containers with customers are assumed to have been sold and the amount returnable ceases to be a deposit. At the end of accounting year, the balance of deposit is deducted from debtors.

Calculation of Missing Information

1. **Calculation of numbers of containers in hand at the end of the year :**

	Number of containers in hand at the beginning of the year		X X
Add :	Number of containers purchased during the year		X X
Add :	Number of containers returned by customers during the year		X X
			X X
Less :	Number of containers sent to customers during the year	X X	
Less :	Number of containers sold as scrap	X X	
Less :	Number of containers destroyed or lost	X X	X X
	Number of container in hand at the end of the year.		X X

2. Calculation of containers with the customers at the end of the year :

	Number of containers with the customers at the beginning of year		XX
Add :	Number of containers returned by the customers during the year		XX
			XX
Less :	Number of containers returned by the customers during the year	XX	
Less :	Number of containers retained by the customers beyond prescribed time	XX	XX
	Number of containers with the customers at the end of the year		XX

3. Number of containers retained by the customers

	Number of containers with the customers at the beginning of the year		XX
Add :	Number of container sent to the customers during the year		XX
			XX
Less :	Number of container returned by the customer during the year	XX	
Less :	Number of returnable containers with the customer at the end of the year	XX	XX
	Number of containers retained by the customers.		XX

Method of Accounting Containers

There are two methods of accounting containers viz ; (1) Container stock account and container suspense a/c method, (2) Container stock account and containers trading account method.

1. **Container Stock a/c and Container Suspense a/c :** Under this method, a container stock a/c, and a container suspense a/c is maintained. The containe suspense account is also known as container reserve a/c or container provision a/c. The container stock a/c is in the nature of nominal account which shows profit or loss on containers. Containers suspense account is used to record movement of containers from the trader to customers and vice versa. It does not show profit or loss.

The various transactions relating to containers as are recorded in containers stock and containers suspense account are as follows :

1. **Recording opening stock of containers on hand :** This is recorded on the debit side of containers stock a/c.
2. **Recording of opening stock of containers with customers :** This transaction is recorded both in containers stock a/c and containers suspense a/c.

In the container stock account it is recorded on the debit side and in the containers suspense account it is recorded on the credit side.

3. **Purchase of containers during the period :** It is recorded on the debit side of container stock a/c. The following entry is passed on purchase of containers.

   Containers stock a/c Dr.

   To Purchases a/c

4. **Container sent to customer :** This is recorded on credit side of containers suspense account. The entry is as follow :

   Customers a/c Dr.

   To containers suspense a/c

5. **Containers returned by customers :** It appear on the debit side of containers suspense account. The entry is as follows :
Container Suspense a/c Dr.
To Customers a/c (with returnable price)
6. **Containers retained by the customers beyond the prescribed time :** This transaction is treated as sales to customers and is recorded in both contains stock a/c and containers suspense a/c. The entry is as follows :
Containers suspense a/c Dr.
To Containers Stock a/c (With returnable price)
7. **Rental or Hire charges on containers issued :** This is recorded in both the accounts. The entry is as follows :
Containers Suspense a/c Dr.
To Containers Stock a/c
8. **Repair charges incurred on containers :** It is recorded on the debit side of containers stock a/c. The entry is as follows :
Containers Stock a/c Dr.
To Cash a/c
9. **Containers sold as scrap :** It is recorded on the credit side of containers stock a/c. The entry is as follows :
Cash a/c Dr.
To Containers Stock a/c
10. **Containers destroyed or lost due to Abnormal reasons :** It is recorded on the credit side of containers stock a/c : The entry is
Profit & Loss a/c Dr.
To Containers stock a/c
11. **Recording of closing stock of containers in hand :** It is recorded on the credit side of containers stock a/c
12. **Recording of closing stock of returnable containers :** It is recorded on the credit side of containers stock a/c and on the debit side containers suspense a/c.
13. **Recording of the balance of containers stock a/c :** The balance in the containers stock a/c represent profit or loss :
(*a*) ***In case of profit :***
Containers Stock a/c Dr.
To P & L a/c
(*b*) ***In case of loss :***
P & L a/c Dr.
To Containers Stock a/c
14. **Closing of containers suspense a/c :** The containers suspense a/c gets automatically closed and hence the questions of balancing does not arise.

Problem 1

Ganesh Oil Co. Ltd., delivers goods to customers in returnable drums charging them out at Rs. 60 each. Customers are credited with Rs. 50 each if the drums are returned in time and in good condition. From the following information prepare Drums Stock a/c and Drums Suspense a/c in the books of Ganesh Oil Co. Ltd.

	No. of Drum
drums in hand on 1-1-99	4,500
drums with customers on 1-1-99 (all returnable)	8,000
drums in hand on 31-12-99	3,000
drums with customers on 31-12-99 (all retainable)	6,000
drums sent to customers during the year	40,000
drums returned by customers	38,000
drums retained by customers	4,000
drums destroyed in an accident	1,000
drums sold as scrap @ Rs. 10 per drum	500

Cost price of each drum is Rs. 45 but is valued @ Rs. 35 per drum for stock - taking purpose.

(Calcutta University B. Com. (Pass) 2,000)

Solution

In the books of Ganesh Oil Co. Ltd.
Drums Stock A/c

Particulars	*Qty*	*Rate*	*Amount*	*Particulars*	*Qty*	*Rate*	*Amount*
To Balance b/d :				By P & L a/c	1,000	—	—
In hand	4,500	35	1,57,500	(Destroyed)			
with customers	8,000	35	2,80,000	By Bank a/c (Scrap)	500	10	5,000
To Bank — Purchase	2,000	45	90,000	By drums Suspense a/c	4,000	60	2,40,000
To P & L a/c			3,92,500	(sold)			
				By drums Suspense a/c	—	—	3,60,000
				(Hire charges)			
				By Balance c/d			
				In hand	3,000	35	1,05,000
				With customers	6,000	35	2,10,000
	14,500		9,20,000		14,500		9,20,000

Working Note :

1. No Value is charged on drums damaged
2. Total hire charges

   = (Qty sent – Qty sold) × (Selling price per unit – Return price per unit)

   = (40,000 – 4,000) × (60 – 50) = Rs. 3,60,000
3. Purchase of drums

   = (4,500 + 8,000) – (1,000 + 500 + 4,000 + 3,000 + 6,000) = 2,000

Drums Suspense A/c

Particulars	*Qty*	*Rate*	*Amount*	*Particulars*	*Qty*	*Rate*	*Amount*
To Customers a/c	38,000	50	19,00,000	By Balance b/d			
(Return)				— with customers	8,000	50	4,00,000
To drums Stock a/c	4,000	60	2,40,000	By Customers a/c	40,000	60	24,00,000
(Sold)				(sent out)			
To drums Stock a/c	—	—	3,60,000				
(Hire charges)							
To Balance c/d	6,000	50	3,00,000				
(with customers)							
	48,000		28,00,000		45,000		28,00,000

Problem 2

A manufacturer sells his products in containers charging them at Rs. 22 each. Containers are credited by Rs. 18 each, if the containers are returned within six weeks. For accounting purposes, at closing, all stock with customers and in the factory are valued at Rs. 14 each, except those representing new ones which are valued at their purchase price, i.e., Rs. 15. The following particulars are available for the year ended 31st March 1998.

	No. of Containers
With customers (1-4-1997)	6,800
Sent out to customers	10,500
Destroyed by fire	200
Returned by customers	3,400
Sold as scrap (for Rs. 300)	50
In hand (1-4-1997)	5,000
With customers (31-3-1998)	4,600
Purchases during the year totalled	Rs. 1,65,000

You are required to prepare Containers Stock Account.

(Bangalore University B. Com. April 2000)

Solution

Working Notes :

1. Purchases, closing stock on hand and new containers have been valued @ Rs. 15, while all other items @ Rs. 14.
2. **Containers retained**

	Opening stock on hand		6,800
Add :	Sent to customers		10,500
			17,300
Less :	Returned by customers		3,400
			13,900
Less :	Closing stock with customers		4,600
	Containers retained by customers		9,300

Containers on hand

	Opening stock		5,000
Add :	Purchases		11,000
			16,000
Add :	Returned by customers		3,400
			19,400
Less :	Sent out to customers		10,500
			8,900
Less :	Sold as scrap	50	
Less :	Destroyed by fire	200	250
			8,650

Containers with customers as on 31-3-1998 are 4,600 (given) These comprises new and old containers. Out of 11,000 new containers purchased, there are 8,650 containers on hand as calculated above. The balance i.e., (11,000 – 8,650) = 2,350 must be with customers. Those have to be valued at Rs. 15 as stated in the problem. If out of 4,600 containers on hand with customers at close, 2,350 are new, the balance i.e., 4,600 – 2,350 = 2,250 must be old containers to be valued at Rs 14.

Containers Stock A/c

Particulars	*Qty*	*Amt*	*Particulars*	*Qty*	*Amt*
To Balance b/d :			By Containers Suspense a/c		
In hand	5,000	70,000	— Containers retained	9,300	1,30,200
With customers	6,800	95,200	By Bank a/c		
To Purchases	11,000	1,65,000	— Containers Scrapped	50	700
			By P & L a/c		
			Containers Destroyed	200	2,800
			By Balance c/d :		
			In hand	8,650	1,29,750
			With customers		
			— New	2,350	35,250
			— Old	2,250	31,500
	22,800	3,30,200		22,800	3,30,200

Problem 3

X Ltd., delivers goods to its customers in returnable containers costing Rs. 15 each. Containers are charged out at Rs. 18 each to customers and they are credited with Rs. 12 each if returned within 2 months. For stock purposes all containers are valued at Rs. 10 each.

From the following particulars prepare the containers stock account and containers suspense account for the year 1997.

	No. of containers
Stock on hand on 1-1-97	15,000
Containers with customers on 1-1-97 (Still returnable)	28,000
Purchases during the year	25,000
Containers returned by customers	35,000
Containers sent out during the year	45,000
Containers destroyed in an accident	500
Containers sold as scrap for 1,600	800
Containers with customers on 31-12-97 (Still returnable)	25,000
Repairs charges Rs. 2,000 for defective containers	1,200

(Calcutta University B. Com. (Pass) 1998)

Solution

In the Books of X Ltd.
Containers Stock A/c

Particulars	Qty	Rate	Amount	Particulars	Qty	Rate	Amount
To Balance b/d :				By P & L a/c (destroyed)	500	—	—
— In hand	15,000	10	1,50,000	By Bank a/c (Sale of scrap)	800	2	1,600
— With customers	28,000	10	2,80,000	By Containers Suspense a/c (sold to customers)	13,000	18	2,34,000
To Purchases a/c	25,000	15	3,75,000	By Containers Suspense a/c (Hire charges)	—	—	1,92,000
To Repairs	—	—	2,000	By Balance c/d :			
To P & L a/c (Profit on sale and hire charges)	—	—	57,600	— In hand	18,700	10	1,87,000
				— With customers	25,000	10	2,50,000
	68,000		8,64,600		68,000		8,64,600

Containers Suspense A/c

Particulars	Qty	Rate	Amount	Particulars	Qty	Rate	Amount
To Customers a/c — Returns	35,000	12	4,20,000	By Balance b/d (with customers)	28,000	12	3,36,000
To Containers Stock a/c (Sold to customers)	13,000	18	2,34,000	By customers a/c (Sent out)	45,000	18	8,10,000
To Containers Stock a/c (Hire charges)	—	—	1,92,000				
To Balance c/d (With customers)	25,000	12	3,00,000				
	73,000		11,46,000		73,000		11,46,000

Problem 4

Modern Biscuits Ltd., Sells their product in containers costing Rs. 15 each. Containers are charged at Rs. 25 each when sent to the customers and if they return those containers within 3 months of their issue then they are credited at Rs. 20 each. For stock taking purpose all used containers at the end of the year either in the hands of the customers or in stock was valued at Rs. 10 each.

On 1st January 1997, there were 10,000 containers in the Godown of the company and 12,500 returnable containers in the hands of the customers. During the year ended 31st December 1997, 15,000 containers were purchased and 40,000 containers were sent to customers (of which 9,000 are new). 30,000 containers were returned by the customers within stipulated period. 500 containers were damaged in an accident and were sold for Rs. 1,000. Another 200 containers were scrapped as they were out of use.

According to company records on December 1997, there were 4,000 and 3,500 containers with customers whose date of return expired on 30th November 1997 and 20th December 1997, respectively.

Show important ledger accounts in the books of the company.

(Calcutta University B. Com. (Hons.) 1998)

Solution

Working Note

1. Calculation of closing stock with customers

	Opening stock with customers		12,500
Add :	Containers sent customers		40,000
			52,500
Less :	Returned by customers	30,000	
Less :	Retained by customers	7,500	
			37,500
	Closing stock with customers		15,000

2. Calculation of closing stock on hand :

	Opening stock in hand	10,000	
	Opening stock with customers	12,500	
Add :	Purchases	15,000	
			37,500
Less :	Scrap	500	
	Destroyed	200	
	Debtors sold to customers	7,500	
	Closing stock with customers	15,000	
			23,200
	Closing stock in hand		14,300

In the Books of Modern Biscuit Ltd.
Containers Stock A/c

Particulars	*Qty*	*Rate*	*Amount*	*Particulars*	*Qty*	*Rate*	*Amount*
To Balance b/d				By Bank a/c (Scrap sold)	500	2	1,000
— In hand	10,000	10	1,00,000	By P & L a/c (Destroyed)	200	—	—
— With customers	12,500	10	1,25,000	By Containers Suspense a/c (returned)	7,500	25	1,87,500
To Purchases	15,000	15	2,25,000	By Containers Suspense a/c (Hire charges)	—	—	1,62,500
To P & L a/c	—	—	1,94,000	By Balance c/d			
				— In hand	14,300	10	1,43,000
				— With customers	15,000	10	1,50,000
	37,500		6,44,000		37,500		6,44,000

Containers suspense A/c

Particulars	*Qty*	*Rate*	*Amount*	*Particulars*	*Qty*	*Rate*	*Amount*
To Customers a/c (returns)	30,000	20	6,00,000	By Balance b/d	12,500	20	2,50,000
To Customers Stock a/c (retained)	7,500	25	1,87,500	By Customers a/c — Containers sent	40,000	25	10,00,000
To Containers Stock a/c (Hire charges)	—	—	1,62,500				
To Balance c/d — With customers	15,000	20	3,00,000				
	52,500		12,50,000		52,500		12,50,000

Problem 5

Arunachal Ltd., delivers goods to its customers in containers costing Rs. 10 each. Containers are charged out at Rs. 12 each to customers and they are credited with Rs. 8 each if returned within 8 weeks. For stock purpose all containers are valued at Rs. 6 each.

From the following particulars prepare the containers stock a/c and containers suspense account for the year 1994 :

	No. of Containers
Stock in hand on 1-1-94	10,000
Containers with customers on 1-1-94 (Still returnable)	21,000
Purchases during the year	15,000
Containers sent out during the year	32,000
Containers returned by customers	23,000
Containers destroyed in an accident	300
Containers sold as scrap for Rs. 1,000	500
Containers with customers on 31-12-94 (Stall returnable)	19,000

(Calcutta University B. Com. (Pass) 1996)

Solution

Working Note :

1. Containers Sold to customers :

	Opening stock of containers with Customers	21,000
Add :	Containers sent	32,000
		53,000
Less :	Containers returned	23,000
		30,000
Less :	Closing stock	19,000
	Contains sold to customers	11,000

2. Calculation of closing stock in hand :

Opening stock in hand	10,000
Opening stock with customers	21,000

Add :	Purchases	15,000
		46,000
Less :	Containers destroyed	300
		45,700
Less :	Scrap	500
		45,200
Less :	sold to customers	11,000
		34,200
Less :	Closing stock with customers	19,000
	Closing stock in hand	15,200

Containers Stock A/c

Particulars	*Qty*	*Rate*	*Amount*	*Particulars*	*Qty*	*Rate*	*Amount*
To Balance b/d				By P & C a/c (destroyed)	300	—	—
— In hand	10,000	6	60,000				
— With customers	21,000	6	1,26,000	By Bank a/c (Sold as scrap)	400	2.5	1,000
To Purchase a/c	15,000	10	1,50,000				
To P & L a/c	—		86,200	By Containers suspense a/c (Sold to customers)	11,000	12	1,32,000
				By Containers suspense a/c (Hire charges)			84,000
				By Balance c/d			
				— In hand	15,200	6	91,200
				—With customers	19,000	6	1,14,000
	46,000		4,22,200		46,000		4,22,200

Containers Suspense A/c

Particulars	*Qty*	*Rate*	*Amount*	*Particulars*	*Qty*	*Rate*	*Amount*
To Customers a/c (Returns)	23,000	8	1,84,000	By Balance b/d			
				— With customers	21,000	8	1,68,000
To Containers Stock a/c (Sold)	11,000	12	1,32,000	By Customers a/c (Sent out)	32,000	12	3,84,000
To Containers Stock a/c (Hire charges)	—	—	84,000				
To Balance c/d							
— With customers	19,000	8	1,52,000				
	53,000		5,52,000		53,000		5,52,000

Problem 6

Hashi - Khushi Ltd. sends goods to customers in drums (which are valued in books at Rs. 40) charging them out at Rs. 75 each. Customers are credited with Rs. 50 if the drums are returned in time.

	No. of drums
Stock in hand on 1-1-93	4,000
drums with customers on 1-1-93 (Still returnable)	8,400
drums with customers on 31-12-93 (Stall returnable)	7,600
Purchases at Rs. 50 each	6,000
drums returned by customers	9,200
drums destroyed in an accident	120
drums sold as scrap for Rs. 1,000	200
drums no longer returnable	4,400

Show the relevant accounts in the books of the company. Assume that new containers were not used during the year. **(Calcutta University B. Com. (Pass) 1994)**

Solution

Working Notes :

1. Calculation of drums sent to customers

	Closing stock of drums with customers	7,600
Add :	drums returned by customers	9,200
Add :	drums retained by customers	4,400
		21,200
Less :	Opening stock of drums with customers	8,400
	drums sent to customers	12,800

2. Calculation of Total Hire Charges :

= (drums sent − drums sold) × (Sent price − Returns price)

= (12,800 − 4,400) × (75 − 50)

= 8,400 × 25 = Rs. 2,10,000

3. Calculation of opening stock of drums in hand

	Opening stock of drums in hand		4,000
	Opening stock of drums with customers		4,800
Add :	Purchases of drums		6,000
			18,400
Less :	drums sold to customers	4,400	
	drums destroyed	120	
	drums sold as scrap	200	
	Closing stock of drums with customers	7,600	
			12,320
	Closing stock of drums in hand		6,080

Out of which 6,000 are new (from purchase) and the balance 80 are old

In the books of Hashi-Khushi Ltd.
drums stock A/c

Particulars	Qty	Rate	Amount	Particulars	Qty	Rate	Amount
To Balance b/d				By P & L a/c (Destroyed)	120	—	—
— In hand	4,000	40	1,60,000	By Bank a/c (Sold as scrap)	200	5	1000
— With customers	8,400	40	3,36,000	By drums Suspense a/c (Sold to customers)	4,400	75	3,30,000
To Purchase a/c	6000	50	3,00,000	By drums Suspense a/c (Hire charges)	—	—	—
To P & L a/c	—	—	1,39,320	By Balance c/d :			
				— In hand : old	80	40	3,200
				: New	6,000	50	3,00,000
				— With customers : Old	7,600	40	3,04,000
	18,400		9,35,320		18,400		9,35,320

drums Suspense A/c

Particulars	Qty	Rate	Amount	Particulars	Qty	Rate	Amount
To Customers a/c (Returns)	9,200	50	4,60,000	By Balance b/d — With customers	8,400	50	4,20,000
To Drums Stock a/c — Sold to customers	4,400	75	3,30,000	By customers a/c — (sent)	12,800	75	9,60,000
To Drums Stock a/c — (Hire charges)	—	—	2,10,000	By drums stock a/c (Hire charges)	—	—	2,10,000
To Balance c/d	7,600	50	3,80,000				
	21,200		13,80,800		21,200		13,80,800

Problem 7

A manufacture sends its products in Barrels costing Rs. 60 each, charges its customers at Rs. 80 each, allows to customers at Rs. 70 each it returned in due time and values the stock of barrels for Balance Sheet purposes at Rs. 40 each on the average at depreciated value. From the following particulars prepare the Barrel Stock Accounts, Barrel Suspense a/c for 1989 and show how the relevant items will appear in Profit & Loss a/c and Balance Sheet for 1989.

	No. of Barrel
Stock in hand on 1-1-89	5,000
Stock with customers on 1-1-89 (returnable)	6,000
Purchase for 1989	9,000
Sent out to customers in 1989	25,000
Returned by customers in 1989	16,000
Stock with customers on 31-12-1989 (Returnable)	12,000

Stock in hand on 31-12-1989	?
Sold for cash 9,000 as defective	450
Scrapped and Rejected (no value)	50
Retained by customers treated as sold	?
Repaired old barrels for Rs. 4,000	600

(Calcutta University B. Com. (Hons.) 1991)

Solution

Working Notes :

Valuation price = Rs. 40, Cost Price = Rs. 60.
Selling price Rs. 80 Reserve price Rs. 70

1. Calculation of number of Barrels sold :

	Opening stock of Barrel with customers		6,000
Add :	Number of barrels sent out to Customers		25,000
			31,000
Less :	Number of Barrel returned by the customers	16,000	
	Closing stock with customers	12,000	
			28,000
	Number of Barrels sold during the year		3,000

2. Calculation of stock in hand on 31-12-1989 :

	Opening stock in hand and with customers (5,000 + 6,000)		11,000
Add :	Purchase during the year		9,000
			20,000
Less :	Number of Barrels sold	3,000	
Less :	Number of Barrels scrapped and rejected	50	
Less :	Number of Barrels sold as scrap	450	
Less :	Number of Barrels with customers on 31-12-1989	12,000	
			15,500
	Closing Stock in hand		4,500

3. Calculation of Hire Charges :

	Number of Barrels sent out during the year	25,000
Less :	Number of barrels sold out	3,000
	Barrels out on hire	22,000

Hire charge = 22,000 × 10 = Rs. 2,22,000

Barrel Stock A/c

Particulars	*Qty*	*Rate*	*Amount*	*Particulars*	*Qty*	*Rate*	*Amount*
To Balance b/d :				By Barrel suspense a/c	3,000	80	2,40,000
— In hand	5,000	40	2,00,000	(Sold out)			
— With customers	6,000	40	2,40,000	By Barrels scrapped			
To Purchases	9,000	60	5,40,000	and rejected	50	—	—
To Cash (Repairs)	—	—	4,000	Barrels sold as scrap	450	—	9,000
				By P & L a/c			
				— Loss on barrels	—	—	11,000
				Destroyed & scrapped			
				By Balance c/d			
				— In hand	4,500	40	1,80,000
				— With customers	12,000	40	4,80,000
				By P & L a/c loss	—	—	64,000
	20,000		9,84,000		20,000		9,84,000

Barrel Suspense A/c

Particulars	*Qty*	*Rate*	*Amount*	*Particulars*	*Qty*	*Rate*	*Amount*
To Barrel Stock a/c	3,000	80	2,40,000	By Balance b/d			
To Customers	16,000	70	11,20,000	— Stock with			
— Retained				customers	6,000	70	4,20,000
To P & L a/c				By Customers a/c	25,000	80	20,00,000
— Hire charges	—	—	2,20,000	— Sent out			
To Balance c/d							
— With customers	12,000	70	8,40,000				
	31,000		24,20,000		31,000		24,20,000

2. **Container Stock account and Containers Trading a/c method :** Under this method two separate accounts are maintained viz, Containers Stock a/c and Containers Trading a/c.

The containers stock a/c is in the nature of real a/c. This account is prepared not to reveal profit or loss instead to have control over the number of containers. The transactions which are recorded on the debit side of this account are is follows :

(*a*) Opening stock of contains in hand and with customers.
(*b*) Purchase of containers.

The transactions recorded on the credit side are as follows :

(*a*) Containers retained by customers
(*b*) Containers scrapped
(*c*) Containers destroyed in accident
(*d*) Closing balance of containers in hand and with customers.

The transactions in the containers stock account are recorded at cost price (i.e., stock price) The purchases and stock of new containers are valued at purchase price.

The containers profit & loss account is prepared with a view to ascertain profit or loss on containers issued to customers. The following transactions are recorded on the debit side of profit & loss a/c

(*a*) Containers retained by customers
(*b*) Cost of containers sold.

The credit side transactions are as follows :

(*a*) Hire charges on containers sent out to customers.
(*b*) Containers retained by customers (sold to customers).
(*c*) Cash realised on sale of scrapped containers.

The entry for containers retained by customers is made at the return price. The transactions relating to containers issued to customers and those returned by them are not recorded in any the two accounts.

The following entries are recorded under this method.

1. **When containers are purchased :**
   Containers Stock a/c Dr.
   To Bank a/c
2. **When containers are retained :**
   Containers Trading a/c Dr.
   To Containers Stock a/c
3. **When containers are scrapped :**
   Containers Trading a/c Dr.
   To Containers Stock a/c
4. **When containers are destroyed :**
   Containers P & L a/c Dr.
   To Containers Stock a/c
5. **When repair expenses are incurred on containers :**
   Containers Trading a/c Dr.
   To Bank a/c
6. **When scrapped containers are sold :**
   Bank a/c Dr.
   To Containers Trading a/c

Problem 8

Prakash Gases Ltd., delivers goods to customers in cylinders (included in the books at a cost of Rs. 200 each) charging them out at Rs. 300 each. Containers are credited with Rs. 225. if the cylinders are returned within 1 month. From the following information, prepare Cylinder stock account, Cylinders Trading account, Memorandum Debtors a/c and Profit & Loss a/c (abstract).

Cylinder on hand on 1st April 1999	3,000
Cylinder purchased @ Rs. 250 each	4,500
Cylinder sent out to customers on 1-4-1999 (still refundable)	6,300
Cylinder sent out to customers	9,200
Cylinder returned by customers	6,800
Cylinder sold as scrap (Rs. 10,000)	100

During the year 350 cylinder were lost in an accident and Rs. 52,500 was received as insurance claim. As on 31st March 2000, 6,500 cylinders were lying with customers with in the permitted period of delivery **(C.A. Inter November 2000)**

Solution

Prakash Gases Ltd.
Cylinder Stock A/c

Particulars	Qty	Rate	Amount	Particulars	Qty	Rate	Amount
To Balance b/d				By Cylinders			
— In hand	3,000	200	6,00,000	Trading a/c			
— With customers	6,300	200	12,60,000	(cylinders retained)	2,200	200	4,40,000
To Bank a/c	4,500	250	11,25,000	By P & L a/c	350	200	70,000
(Purchases)				(Cylinder lost)			
				By Cylinders			
				Trading a/c	100	200	20,000
				(Cost of cylinders			
				scrapped and sold)			
				By Balance c/d			
				— In hand	4500	250	11,25,000
					150	200	30,000
				— With customers	6,500	200	13,00,000
	13,800		29,85,000		13,800		29,85,000

Cylinders Trading A/c

Particulars	Qty	Rate	Amount	Particulars	Qty	Rate	Amount
To Cylinders Stock a/c	2,200	200	4,40,000	By Rent a/c	—	—	6,90,000
(Cylinders retained)				(on 9,200 @ Rs. 75)			
To Cylinders Stock a/c	100	200	20,000	By Customers a/c	2,200	225	4,95,000
(Cylinder scrapped)				(Cylinders reined)			
To P & L a/c — Profit	—	—	7,35,000	By Bank a/c	100	100	10,000
				(Sale of scrap)			
	2,300		11,95,000		2,300		11,95,000

Memorandum Debtors A/c

Particulars	Qty	Rate	Amount	Particulars	Qty	Rate	Amount
To Balance b/d	6,300	225	14,17,500	By Cylinders returned	6,800	225	15,30,000
To Cylinder sent	9,200	225	20,70,000	By Cylinder retained	2,200	225	4,95,000
				By Balance c/d	6,500	225	14,62,500
	15,500		34,87,500		15,500		34,87,500

P & L A/c Abstract

Particulars		Amount	Particulars	Amount
To Cylinder Stock a/c	70,000		By Cylinders Trading a/c	7,35,000
(Cost of cylinders Destroyed)				
Less Insurance claim	52,500	17,500		

Problem 9

Sankar Dairy delivers goods to customers in bottles costing Rs. 60 each. Bottles are charged out at Rs. 70 each to customers and credited at Rs. 50 each if returned in good condition within stipulated time. For stock taking purposes all containers in the factory and those in the hands of customers are valued at Rs. 30 each.

On 1-4-1998 there were 2,000 bottles in the factory and 4,000 in hands of customers. During 1998-99, 6,300 bottles were sent out to customers of which 2,000 were new and 4,200 were returned by them within the required period. Out of the bottles returned by customers 50 were destroyed by an accident and 100 were sold as scrap. These realised Rs. 1500. On 31-3-1999, there were 3,000 bottles in the hands of customers, capable of being returned within the stipulated period.

Prepare Bottles Stock a/c and Bottles Trading a/c in the books of Sankar Dairy

(Calcutta University B. Com. (Hons.) 2000)

Solution

Working Note :

1. Calculation of Loss on Valuation

	Cost price of 2,000 bottles purchased		1,20,000
Less :	The bottles are valued at		60,000
	Loss on revaluation		60,000

2. Calculation of Bottles retained by customers

	Opening stock of Bottles with customers		4,000
Add :	Bottles sent		6,300
			10,300
Less :	Bottles returned	4,200	
Less :	Closing stock of bottles with customers	3,000	
			7,200
	Bottles retained		3,100

3. Calculation of Closing Stock of Bottles :

	Opening stock of bottles in hand		2,000
	Opening stock of bottles with customers		4,000
	Bottles purchased (assumed to be new ones)		2000
			8,000
Less :	Bottles destroyed	50	
	Bottles sold as scrap	100	
	Bottles retained	3,100	
	Bottles returnable	3,000	
			6,250
	Closing Stock of Bottles in Hand		1,750

4. Hire Charges

= Bottles sent × (Sent price – Returns price)

= 6,300 × (70 – 50) = 1,26,000

In the Books of Sankar Dairy
Bottles Stock A/c

Particulars	*Qty*	*Rate*	*Amount*	*Particulars*	*Qty*	*Rate*	*Amount*
To Balance b/d				By P & L a/c (Destroyed)	50	30	1,500
— In hand	2,000	30	60,000				
— With customers	4,000	30	1,20,000	By Bank a/c (Sold as scrap)	100	15	1,500
To Bank – Purchases	2,000	60	1,20,000				
				By P & L a/c (Loss on sale)	—	—	1,500
				By P & L a/c (loss on stock valuation)	—	—	60,000
				By Bottles Trading a/c (Retained by customers	3,100	30	93,000
				By Balance c/d			
				— In hand	1,750	30	52,500
				— With customers	3,000	30	90,000
	8,000		3,00,000		8,000		3,00,000

Bottles Trading A/c

Particulars	*Qty*	*Rate*	*Amount*	*Particulars*	*Qty*	*Rate*	*Amount*
To Bottles Stock a/c (Bottles returned at cost price)	3,100	30	93,000	By Bottles Stock a/c (Rentals)			1,26,000
To P & L a/c			1,86,000	By Bottles debtors a/c (Bottles retained at returnable price)	3,100	50	1,53,000
	3,100		2,79,000		3,100		2,79,000

Problem 10

ABC Ltd., supplies their products in returnable drums. A drum is invoiced @ Rs. 80 but if it is returned within a month, a credit of Rs. 70 is given to the customers. A drum costs Rs. 70 to the company and its life is estimated at 12 years at the end of which the scrap value is likely to be Rs. 10. The following particulars are supplied to you.

Stock-in-hand as on 1-4-97	28,000
Stock with customers as on 1-4-97	20,000
Stock in hand as on 31-3-98	?
Stock with customers as on 31-3-98	12,000
Purchases	2,000
Sent out to customers	1,20,000
Returned by customers	1,26,000
Scrapped (sold for Rs. 16,000) (useful life being over)	3,000
Method of charging depreciation straight line.	

Prepare Drums Trading and Profit and Loss a/c and Drums Reserve a/c.

(CA, Inter, November 1998)

Solution

Working Notes :

1. Calculation of drums retained by customers :-

	Opening stock with customers		20,000
Add :	drums sent out		1,20,000
			1,40,000
Less :	Returned by customers	1,26,000	
Less :	Closing stock with customers	12,000	
			1,38,000
	Number of drums retained by customers		2,000

2. Stock of drums in hand as on 31-3-98

	Opening stock		28,000
Add :	Purchases		2,000
Add :	Returns by customers		1,26,000
			1,56,000
Less :	Sent out to customers	1,20,000	
Less :	drums scrapped	3,000	
			1,23,000
	Closing stock of drums in hand		33,000

ABC Ltd.
drums Trading and Profit and Loss A/c

	Qty	*Amt*		*Qty*	*Amt*
To Balance b/d			By Customers		96,00,000
— In hand	28,000	19,60,000	(1,20,000 × Rs. 50)		
— With customers	20,000	14,00,000	By drums Reserve a/c	2,000	1,40,000
To Bank a/c	2,000	1,40,000	(Reserve on drums		
(Purchases)			retained not required)		
To Drum Reserve a/c		84,00,000	By Bank a/c	3,000	16,000
(1,20,000 × Rs. 70)			(Sale of drums scrapped)		
To Gross Profit c/d		11,86,000	By Provision for		
			depreciation a/c		
			(Depreciation on scrapped		
			drums Rs. 60 × 3,000)		
			By Balance c/d		
			— In hand	33,000	23,10,000
			— With customers	12,000	8,40,000
	50,000	1,30,86,000		50,000	1,30,86,000

Drums Reserve A/c

	Qty	Amt		Qty	Amt
To Customers a/c (Reserve on drums returned)	1,26,000	88,20,000	By Balance b/d	20,000	14,00,000
To drums Trading a/c (Reserve on drums retained)	2,000	1,40,000	By drums Trading a/c (Reserve on drums sent out)	1,20,000	84,00,000
To Balance c/d	12,000	8,40,000			
	1,40,000	98,00,000		1,40,000	98,00,000

QUESTIONS

EXERCISE 1

Durgapur chemicals Ltd., delivers goods to customers in drums (which are valued in the books Rs. 30) charging them out at Rs. 60 each. Customers are credited with Rs. 40 if the drums are returned in time. Following are the details of drums.

	No of drums
Stock in hand on January 1st 1994	2,000
drums with customers on 1st Jan. 1994	4,200
Purchases at Rs. 50 each	3,000
drums sent out to customers	6,400
drums returned by customers	4,600
drums destroyed in an accident	60
drums sold as scrap for Rs. 1,000	100
drums with customers (returnable) as on 31-12-1994	3,800

Show the necessary ledger accounts in the books of the company.

(Calcutta University B. Com (Pass))

Answer : 1. No. of drums sold to customers Rs. 2,200
2. Total Hire Charges Rs. 84,000
3. Closing Stock of Drums in hand Rs. 3,040
4. Profit as shown in Drums Stock a/c Rs. 86,200
5. Balance c/d (drums Suspense a/c) Qty 3,800 amount Rs. 1,52,000

EXERCISE 2

M/S L & Co., deliver their products in drums which are returnable. The containers cost Rs. 100 each and are valued at that price for stock taking purposes. They are charged to customers at Rs. 140 each and credited on return within - 2 months at Rs. 120 each.

On 1st April 1998, there were 150 drums in stock and 360 with customers which were returnable with - 2 months. During the 6 months ended 30th September 1998, 1,000 new drums were purchased.

4,800 were sent to customers and 4,300 were returned by them. Of the drums returned, 250 were sold at Rs. 25 each and 130 were destroyed. On 30th September, 1998 there were 270 drums in stock and 660 returnable drums with customers and the balance were retained by the customers.

You are to record the above transaction in the Drums Stock and the Drums Suspense a/c in the books of M/s L & Co. **(Calcutta University. B. Com. Pass)**

Answer : Charge price = Rs. 140
No. of Drums sold to customers (retain) 200
Total Hire charges Rs. 92,000
P & L a/c – Profit shown by Drums Stock a/c Rs. 68,250
Balance shown by Drums Suspense a/c Qty 660 amount Rs. 79,200

EXERCISE 3

A company sells paints in steel drums. An empty drum costs Rs. 50 but is charged out to customers at Rs. 65 with the provision that their account would be credited with Rs. 45 for every drum returned in good condition with three months of issue.

You are asked to write up the necessary ledger accounts for the year ended 31st December 1995 from the particulars given below, and to state how the ledger balances as at that date would be shown in the company's Balance Sheet.

	No. of drums
Stock on hand 1st January 1995	2,000
Stock with customers (1-1-95) within 3 months of issue	14,000
Transaction in 1995 :	
Purchases	20,000
Issued to customers	40,000
Returned by customers	35,000
Sold as scrap for Rs. 5,000	1,000
Stock with customers, 31st December 1995 within 3 months of issue	18,000

Stock in hand and with customers are valued at Rs. 40 per Drum.

(Calcutta University B. Com (Hons))

Answer :	
No. of Drums sold during the year	1,000
Closing stock of Drums	16,000
drums out on Hire	39,000
Hire charges Rs.	7,80,000
Drums stock a/c total of Qty column 36,000 amount Rs.	16,40,000
Total of Drums Reserve a/c Qty	54,000
Amount Rs.	32,30,000

EXERCISE 4

(Container Stock A/c and Trading A/c Method)

Isolate chemicals Ltd., supplies its products in returnable containers. A container is invoiced to the customers at Rs. 65 each but if it is returned in good condition within three months of the date of delivery of the containers, a credit of Rs. 55 each is given to the customers. A container costs Rs. 55 to the company and its life is estimated at 10 years at the end of which the scrap value is likely to be Rs. 5. The following particulars are supplied to you.

Stock in hand on 1-1-95	20,000
Stock with customers on 1-1-95	30,000
Containers sent to customers during the years.	80,000
Containers returned by customers during the year	80,000
Containers returnable on 31-12-95	20,000
Containers purchased during the year	3,000
Container damaged useful life being over	2,000
Amount realised form the sale of damaged containers	Rs. 30,000

Depreciation is to be provided on straight line basis

Prepare the containers Trading a/c, container provision account.

(Calcutta University B. Com. (Hons) 1996)

Answer : Profit Rs. 60,000,

Total of container provision a/c in terms of quantity 1,10,000 and amount Rs. 60,50,000.

EXERCISE 5

B. Co. Ltd., delivers goods to their customers in packages costing Rs. 6 each but charging them out at Rs. 12 each and crediting them at Rs. 8 each, if returned within 3 months.

On 1st January 2002 there were 1,000 packages in the godown of the company and 2,100 returnable packages in the hands of the customers. During the year ending 31st December 2002, 1,500 packages were purchased at Rs. 10 each 3,200 packages were sent out to customers, 2,300 packages returned by the customers, throughout the year. 30 packages from the old lot were completely destroyed by fire in the warhouse and another 50 packages from the old lot were accidentally broken and were sold as scrap for Rs. 4 each.

On 31st December 2002, 1,900 returnable packages from the old lot were with customers and stock in godown included all the new packages besides the old once. The packages are valued at their cost price for stock taking purposes.

Show the Package Stock a/c and Packages Trading a/c in the ledger of the company

(Calcutta University B. Com. (Hons))

Answer :	Packages retained by customers	1,100
	Closing stock of packages in hand	1,520
	Profit	Rs. 34,700
	Total of packages stock a/c Qty	4,600
	and amount	Rs. 33,600

35

CHAPTER

Investment Accounting

MEANING OF INVESTMENT

Investment refers to utilising surplus money for purchase of any securities with a view to earn profit. With reference to a business organisation it means the employment of funds outside business as compared to ploughing it back in the same business. The investment is normally made on securities and bonds of Government, Quasi-Government and other companies. The investment representing the shares, debentures, bonds etc. are collectively known as scrips. Investment is an asset to a business but it has no physical existence like any other asset. Instead it is an actionable claim conferred on its owner to recover the amount invested.

DEFINITION ON INVESTMENT

Accounting standard 13 defines investment as an asset held by an enterprise for earning income by way of dividends, interest and rental for capital appreciation or for other benefits to the investing enterprise.

Business enterprises which invest funds may be of two types, viz, (*a*) Investment Trust and (*b*) Institutional Investors. Institutions whose primary business is to invest funds is known as Investment Trusts. U.T.I is an example of Investment trust. Enterprises whose investment constitute secondary business is known as Institutional investors. Examples of Institutional Investors are banks, Insurance companies, public utility concerns etc.

TYPES OF INVESTMENT

On the basis of duration investments are classified into two types, viz (1) Long term investment and (2) Short term investment. While long term investment are made to earn dividend, interest, rent etc., short terms investments are made for the purpose of capital appreciation.

On the basis of tangibility, investments can be classified into two types viz (*a*) Tangible investment and (*b*) Intangible Investment. Tangible Investment have a physical form as for example building. Intangible investments have no physical form and hence represented merely by certificates, as for example shares, debentures, etc.

TYPES OF SCRIPS

The securities representing investments can be of two types viz, (1) Fixed Income bearing securities and (2) Variable income bearing securities. Under the former type a fixed income is payable periodically. Examples are bonds, debentures, Government securities etc. Under the latter type the income payable varies depending upon the income earning capacity. An example is equity shares on which dividend payment varies.

TRADING IN SECURITIES

The short terms funds are invested in a market known as money market. The market in which long term funds are invested is known as capital market. However, in its broad sense capital market includes money market. The brokers trade in these two markets. When securities are bought directly from the source through the process allotment it is known as primary market. When they are bought though intermediaries, i.e., institutions operating in capital market it is known as secondary market or stock exchanges. The share brokers in the stock exchange assist the investors in buying and selling shares.

Face Value and Market Value

The value of a security specified on the certificate is known as face value. Market value refers to the price of security quoted on stock exchange. The securities may be bought or sold either at face value or market value. When securities are traded at face value it is said to have been bought or sold at par value. Market value may be more than the face value or less than the face value. If it is more than face value it is said to be transacted at premium, on the other hand when it is less than its face value it is said to be traded at discount.

The remuneration payable to brokers who assists in buying and selling scrips is known as "brokerage" It is paid as a percentage on the face value of securities. The other expenses incurred in the purchase of securities commonly referred to as incidental expenses include stamp duty, registration charges, transfer fees etc. For a buyer it is of capital nature and hence added to the cost of acquisition of securities. The seller deducts there expenses from the sale proceeds of securities.

In case of fixed interest bearing security interest is payable on the expiry of specific period mentioned on the document. But the purchase and sale of such securities need not correspond with the date of payment of interest. In such a situation it is necessary to decide who shall receive the interest payable for that period.

If no agreement is entered into as to who shall receive the interest for the period during which the transaction took place, the purchaser shall receive the interest. So the seller will charge a price which includes the interest upto the date of transaction from the date of last payment. Such a quotation is known as cum-interest/Dividend. It only means that the price quoted includes interest or dividend. As a consequence the price charged is to be adjusted so as to arrive at the figure of capital cost of investment. It implies the interest for the expired period has to be deducted from the purchase price.

In case of Ex - Interest / dividend quotation the price so charged does not include interest or dividend. The seller will instead receive interest or dividend for the expired period. Hence the price paid for the investment by the buyer is less than the normal price. In order to calculate the capital cost of investment it is necessary to add accrued interest / dividend for the expired period to the price paid.

INVESTMENT LEDGER

Financial institutions which invest large part of their funds maintain a separate ledger known as investment ledger to record transactions relating to their investment. The investment ledger is maintained in a columnar form. The Debit and Credit side contains three columns for recording face value; interest or dividend and Principal.

Accounting for Investments. Individuals and organisation which invest surplus funds maintain accounts for the following purposes; to maintain record for all investments made in different types of securities, to ascertain interest or dividend from different investment and to ascertain profit or loss on purchase and sale of investments.

The following entries are passed for investment transactions:

1. For Purchase of Investment

Investment a/c Dr.
To Bank a/c

(*a*) Cum-Interest quotation :

Investment a/c Dr.
Interest on Investment a/c Dr.
To Bank a/c

(*b*) Ex - Interest Quotations :

Investment a/c Dr.
Inerest on Investment Dr.
To Bank a/c

Note : The difference between the above two entries is that in case of ex-interest quotation, interest is added to the cost of Investment and in case of cum-Interest quotation interest is deducted from the cost of investment.

2. For recording Income from Investment

Bank a/c Dr.
To Interest or Dividend a/c

3. For Sale of Investment :

Bank a/c Dr
To Investment a/c

(*a*) at cum-Interest :

Bank a/c Dr
To Investment a/c
To Interest on Investment a/c

(*b*) at Ex-interest :

Bank a/c Dr
To Investment a/c
To Interest on Investment a/c

Note : The difference between the above two entries is reflected in the amount of cash received on sale of Investment.

Problem 1

Mr. 'X' Purchased 1,000, 6% Govt. Bonds by paying a commission of 250 to a broker the face value of each bond is Rs. 100. What is the amount of cash invested in each case if purchased at Rs. 100, Rs. 95 and Rs. 105 respectively.

	(at par) :	
	Purchase price 1,000 × 100 =	1,00,000
Add :	Commission =	500
	Amount Invested	1,00,500
	(at Discount) :	
	Purchase price 1,000 × 95 =	95,000
Add :	Commission =	500
	Amount Invested	95,500
	(at premium) :	
	Purchase price 1,000 × 105 =	1,05,000
Add :	Commission	500
	Amount Interested	1,05,500

Problem 2 (Purchase at cum-Interest Quotation)

Mr. 'X' purchased 1,000, 6% Government bonds of Rs. 100 each on 31st January 2004 at Rs. 95 each. Interest is payable on 30th June and 31st December. The price quoted is cum-interest. Journalise the transaction.

Solution

Calculating of Actual price of Investment

Purchase price of 1,000 bonds at Rs. 95 each 1,000 × 95 =	95,000
Less : Interest for the expired period of 1 month (i.e, form 1st Jan. to 31st Jan.) $1{,}00{,}000 \times \frac{6}{100} \times \frac{1}{12}$	500
Actual price of Investment	94,500

Capital cost of investment =	94,500
Amount charged to revenue =	500
Total purchase price	95,000

Journal

Date	*Particulars*		*Dr. Amount*	*Cr. Amount*
	Investment a/c	Dr.	94,500	
	Interest a/c	Dr.	500	
	To Bank a/c			95,000
	(Being purchase of 1,000, 6% bonds of Rs. 100 each at Rs. 95 cum- Interest)			

Problem 3 (Purchase at Ex-Interest Quotation)

Mr. 'X' purchased from 'Y' 1,000, 6% Government bonds of Rs. 100 each at 105 Ex. Interest. Interest is payable on these bonds on 30th September each year. The transaction took place through a broker who charged a commission of 1% from each party. Record the transactions in the books of both the parties.

Solution

In the books of Mr. 'X'

Purchase price of 1000 Debenture @ Rs. 105	1,05,000
Add : Interest for the expired period from 1st Oct. to 31st December (3 months)	
$1,00,000 \times \frac{6}{100} \times \frac{3}{12}$	1,500
Total purchase price	1,06,500

Journal

Date	Particulars		Dr. Amount	Cr. Amount
	Investment a/c	Dr.	1,05,000	
	Interest a/c	Dr.	1,500	
	To Bank a/c			1,06,500
	(Being the purchase of 6% Bonds at Rs. 105 Ex-interest)			

In the books of Y -working note :

Selling price of 1,000 bonds @ Rs. 105 =	1,05,000
Less : Interest for the expired period =	1,500
Net amount realised	1,03,500

Journal

Date	Particulars		Dr. Amount	Cr. Amount
	Cash a/c	Dr.	1,06,500	
	To Investment a/c	Dr.		1,05,000
	To Interest a/c			1,500
	(Being the sale of 6% Debentures at Rs. 105 Ex-interest)			

COLUMNAR ACCOUNTING

A columnar Account in the investment ledger consists of three columns on either side of account. The first column represents nominal or face value of the security. The second column interest and the third column the amount invested in the security. Interest on investment is always paid on the face value of the security. The amount invested represents the difference between face value and fluctuation in the market value.

On the top of investment account, the name of the investment, rate of interest and its quotation (cum-interest or ex-interest) is mentioned. The account begins with the opening balance on the debit side. In the first column, the nominal value of the security is entered. In the second column, the accurred interest from the previous date of interest is entered and in the last column the amount paid for the secure is written up.

When a security is purchased, its nominal value is entered in the first column on the debit side of the Investment account. The interest paid to the seller is shown in the second column and the amount paid for the security is recorded in the third column. When interest is received it is record in the second column on the credit side.

On sale of investment, the nominal value of security is recorded in the First column on the credit side. The interest received is recorded on the credit side. The cash received is recorded in the third column The difference in the third column, represent profit or loss. The difference arises owing to amount paid for the security and the amount received on its sale. The profit is recorded in the third column on the debit side and the loss is recorded in the third column on the credit side.

When the accounts is closed, an accrued interest on the balance of investment is shown in the interest column on the credit side. The other columns are balanced. The balance shown in the first and third columns are carried forward to the next accounting period. The balance of interest column is transferred to profit and loss account.

Columnar accounting (variable income bearing securities)

Investment made on equity shares yields variable amount of dividend. Dividend payment on equity shares is based on :

(*a*) The availability of divisible profit.
(*b*) The rate of dividend recommended by Directors and
(*c*) Declaration of recommend rate in the share holders meeting.

The payment of dividend is variable as rate of dividend various from year to year. The following two aspects must be considered while accounting of variable income-bearing securities.

1. **Bonus shares :** Bonus shares are issued in lieu of payment of dividend in cash. In other words it is issued free of cost. Such shares increase the number of equity shares held by a member. So the average cost of equity shares get reduced.
2. **Right shares :** These are additional shares which are issued to the existing shareholders. This may be subscribed or renounced by shareholders. Right shares are not accounted as the amount of dividend accuring between the date of last payment and the date of purchase cannot be ascertained.

The procedure involved in preparing columnar account for variable income bearing securities is same as in the case of fixed interest - bearing securities. The second column on either side of the account is denoted by dividend instead of interest. When bonus shares are issued it is recorded on the debit side of account in the nominal or face value column. When right shares are accepted, the nominal value and the amount paid are entered in their respective columns. However, when right shares are renounced in favour of any other person and any consideration is received, the same is recorded on principal column: on the right side of the account. Other entries relating to sale of investment, profit & loss etc. remain same as in the case of fixed income bearing securities.

Problem 4

On 1st March 2002, X, Y Corporation Ltd., purchased Rs. 30,000, 5% Government bond at Rs. 95 cum-interest. On 1st May 2002 the company sold Rs. 10,000 of stock at Rs. 97 cum-interest. On 15th December 2002, another Rs. 10,000 bond was sold at 93 Ex-Interest. On 31st December 2002, the closing date of the financial year the market price of the bond was Rs. 92.

Half - yearly interest is received every year on 30th June and 31st December.

Prepare a ledger account in the investment ledger assuming that the stock transfer book is closed 20 days before the date of payment of interest. Ignore Income - tax brokerage.

Solution

Working Note :

1. 1-3-2002

$$\text{Interest} = 30{,}000 \times \frac{5}{100} \times \frac{2}{12} = 250$$

$$\text{Cost} = 30{,}000 \times \frac{95}{100} = 28{,}500 - 250 \text{ (Interest)} = 28{,}250$$

2. 1-5-2002

$$\text{Interest} = 10{,}000 \times \frac{5}{100} \times \frac{4}{12} = 167$$

$$\text{Cost} = 10{,}000 \times \frac{97}{100} = 9{,}700 - 167 \text{ (Interest)} = 9{,}533$$

3. 30-6-2002

$$\text{Interest} = 20{,}000 \times \frac{5}{100} \times \frac{6}{12} = 500$$

4. 15-12-2002

$$\text{Interest} = 10{,}000 \times \frac{5}{100} \times \frac{5.5}{12} = 229$$

$$\text{Cost} = 10{,}000 \times \frac{93}{100} = 9{,}300$$

5. 15-2-2002

Contra = Interest receivable on Rs. 10,000 investment sold on 15-12-2002 for 15 days

$$10{,}000 \times \frac{5}{100} \times \frac{5}{12} = 21$$

6. 31-12-2002

$$\text{Interest} = 10{,}000 \times \frac{5}{100} \times \frac{6}{12} = 250$$

7. 31-12-2002

$$\text{Market value of stock } 10{,}000 \times \frac{92}{100} = 9{,}200$$

$$\text{Cost price of stock } \frac{28{,}350}{30{,}000} \times 10{,}000 = 9{,}417$$

Therefore these are valued at Market price

So, loss on value 9,417 – 9,200 = 217

8. 31-12-2002

$$\text{Loss on sale} = \frac{28{,}350}{30{,}000} \times 20{,}000$$

$$= (18{,}833 + 21) - (9{,}533 + 9{,}330)$$

$$= \text{Rs. } 21$$

In the Books of X, Y, Corporation

Investment Ledger

5% Government Bond A/c

Date	*Particulars*	*Nominal*	*Interest*	*Cost*	*Date*	*Particulars*	*Nominal*	*Interest*	*Cost*
1-3-2002	To Bank a/c (Purchases)	30,000	250	28,250	1-5-2002	By Bank a/c (Sold)	10,000	167	9,533
15-12-2002	To Interest (as per contra)			21	30-6-2002	By Bank a/c (Interest received)			500
31-12-2002	To P & L a/c (Transfer)		667		15-12-2002	By Bank a/c (Sold)	10,000	229	9,000
					16-12-2002	By Cost (as per contra)			
					31-12-2002	By Profit & loss a/c (Loss on sale)			
					31-12-2002	By Profit & loss a/c (Loss on sale)			
					31-12-2002	By Balance c/d			
		30,000	917	28,271			30,000	917	28,271

Problem 5

Sonali Ltd., was dealing in 10% Government stock. They furnished the following details about their transactions :

1-1-02 Opening balance ; Face value Rs. 30,000 cost Rs. 25,000

1-3-02 Purchased Rs. 12,000 stock @ 91 $\frac{7}{8}$ % Cum interest

15-6-02 Sold Rs. 5,000 Stock @ 93 $\frac{5}{8}$ % cum interest

1-8-02 Bought Rs. 8,000 Stock @ 90 $\frac{3}{8}$ % Ex -interest

1-9-02 Sold Rs. 4,000 stock @ 94 $\frac{1}{8}$% Ex - interest

1-12-02 Bought Rs. 6,000 stock @ 95 $\frac{1}{8}$ % Cum - Interest

Prepare investment account for the year ended 31-12-02 assuming brokerage is payable at $\frac{1}{8}$% in each case.

Solution

Working Notes :

1. Interest on Rs. 30,000 @ 10 % for 3 months = 750
2. Cost of Rs 12,000 stock @ 91 $\frac{7}{8}$ % cum – interest, Brokerage $\frac{1}{8}$ % is = $\frac{12{,}000 \times 92}{100}$ = Rs. 11,040

   Interest @ 10% for 5 months = Rs. 500

   Hence real cost price of Investment = 11,040 – 500 = Rs. 10,540
3. Interest on Rs. 42,000 @ 10% p.a. for 6 months = Rs. 2,100
4. Selling price of Rs. 5,000 stock @ 93 $\frac{5}{8}$, brokerage $\frac{1}{8}$ %

   $$= \frac{5{,}000 \times 93\frac{1}{2}}{100} = 4{,}675$$

   Interest @ 10% for 5 months

   $$\frac{5{,}000 \times 10 \times 5}{100 \times 2 \times 12} = \text{Rs. } 104$$

   So net proceeds = (Rs. 4,675 – 104) = Rs. 4,571
5. Cost of 8,000 stock @ 90 $\frac{3}{8}$, brokerage $\frac{1}{8}$ %

   $$= \frac{8{,}000 \times 90\frac{1}{2}}{100} = \text{Rs. } 7{,}240$$

Interest on Rs. 8,000 for 4 months @ 10% p.a.

$$8000 \times \frac{4}{12} \times \frac{10}{100} = 267$$

6. Selling price of Rs. 4,000 stock @ 94 $\frac{1}{8}$ % Brokerage $\frac{1}{8}$ %

$$= \frac{4{,}000 \times 94}{100} = \text{Rs. } 3{,}760$$

Interest on Rs. 4,000 for 5 months @ 10% p.a.

$$4000 \times \frac{5}{12} \times \frac{10}{100} = 167$$

Interest on Rs. 41,000 for 6 months @ 10% p.a. = Rs. 2,050

Cost price of Rs. 6,000 stock @ 93 $\frac{1}{8}$ % Brokerage $\frac{1}{8}$ %

$$= \frac{6{,}000 \times 93\frac{1}{4}}{100} = \text{Rs. } 5{,}595$$

Interest on Rs. 6,000 for 2 months @ 10% p.a. = Rs. 100

So, real cost price = (5,595 – 100) = 5,495

Interest on Rs. 47,000 for 3 months @ 10% p.a. = Rs. 1,175 outstanding

$$\text{Valuation of stock} = \frac{48{,}275 \times 47{,}000}{56{,}000} = \text{Rs. } 40{,}516$$

So total interest transferred to P & L a/c = Rs. 3,979

So, profit on sale = Rs. 572

Books of Sonali Ltd.

10% Investment A/c

Date	*Particulars*	*Nominal*	*Interest*	*Cost*	*Date*	*Particulars*	*Nominal*	*Interest*	*Cost*
1-1-2002	To Balance b/d	30,000	750	25,000	31-3-2002	By Bank a/c		2,100	
1-3-2002	To Bank	12,000	500	10,540	15-6-2002	By Bank a/c	5,000	104	4,571
1-8-2002	To Bank	8,000	267	7,240	1-9-2002	By Bank a/c	4,000	167	3,760
1-12-2002	To Bank	6,000	100	5495	30-9-2002	By Bank a/c		2,050	
31-12-2002	To Investment a/c (transferred)		3,979		31-12-2002	By Balance c/d	47,000	1,175	40,516
	To P & L a/c Profit			572					
		56,000	5,596	48,847			56,000	5,596	48,847

Problem 6

On 1st April 2003, Janaki Ltd. had Rs. 3,00,000, 6% government stock at Rs. 94. Interest is payable half- yearly on 31st March and 30th September. The company sold Rs. 90,000 of the stock at Rs. 95 ex-interest on 1st June and purchased Rs. 72,000 stock at Rs. 97 cum-interest on 1st September. A further purchase of Rs. 36,000 stock was made on 1st December at Rs. 98 ex- interest.

Draw up 6% Government stock account in the investment ledger of the company for the year ended 31st March 2004. Ignore brokerage and income tax. The stock was quoted at Rs. 96 at the stock exchange on that date.

Solution

Working Note :

Cost price of stock sold on 1-6-2003

$$\frac{2,82,000}{3,00,000} \times 90,000 = 84,600$$

Therefore profit on sale = 85,500 – 84,600 = Rs. 900

Cost price of stock sold on 1-12-2003

$$= \frac{2,82,000}{3,00,000} \times 36,000 = \text{Rs. } 33,840$$

Therefore profit on sale = 35,280 – 33,840

= Rs. 1,440

Cost price of stock held on 31-3-2003 is 23,160

$$2,46,000 \times \frac{96}{100} = 2,36,160$$

Therefore the stock has been valued at Rs. 2,31,600 applying "Cost or market which ever less principle.

Books of Janaki

Investment account

Date	Particulars	Nominal	Interest	Cost	Date	Particulars	Nominal	Interest	Cost
1-4-2003	To Balance b/d	3,00,000		2,82,000	1-6-2003	By Bank a/c (Sale at ex-Interest)	9,00,00	900	85,500
1-6-2003	To P & L a/c (Profit on sale)			900	30-9-2003	By Bank a/c (Interest received) on 2,82,000		8,460	
1-9-2003	To Bank a/c (Purchase at Cum interest)	72,000	1,800	68,040	1-12-2003	By Bank a/c (Sale at ex-interest)	36,000	360	35,280
1-12-2003	To P & L a/c (Profit on sale)			1,440	31-3-2004	By Bank a/c (Interest received) on 2,46,000		7,380	
31-3-2004	To P & L a/c (Total Interest for the year)		15,300		31-3-2004	By Balance c/d	2,46,000		2,31,600
		3,72,000	17,100	3,52,380			3,72,000	17,100	3,52,380

Problem 7

ON 1st January 2003 X Ltd., held as investments Rs. 50,000, 6% Government stock costing Rs. 47,000. On 31st March, a purchase of Rs. 2,00,000 same Government stock was made at Rs. 95 cum-interest. On 1st July, the company sold Rs. 1,00,000 stock at Rs. 96. On 1st October, a further Rs. 70,000 of the investment was sold at Rs. 98 cum-interest. The market price of the stock on 31-12-2003 was Rs. 99 (ex-interest).

Half yearly interest is payable on 30th June and 31st December every year. Prepare investment ledger of the company, ignoring income tax and brokerage.

Solution

Working Notes :

31-3-2003

(*i*) Interest included in purchase

$$2{,}00{,}000 \times \frac{6}{100} \times \frac{3}{12} = 3{,}000$$

(*ii*) $\text{Cost} = \left(2{,}00{,}000 \times \frac{95}{100}\right) - 3{,}000$

$= 1{,}37{,}000$ (as it is cum-interest purchase)

30-6-2003, Interest received

$$(2{,}00{,}000 + 50{,}000) \times \frac{6}{12} \times \frac{6}{100} = 7{,}500$$

1-7-2003 Sale valued $1{,}00{,}000 \times \frac{96}{100}$ (No interest included)

31-10-2003 (*i*) Interest included in sales

$$70{,}000 \times \frac{6}{100} \times \frac{3}{12} = 1{,}050$$

(*iii*) $\text{Sale value} = \left(70{,}000 \times \frac{98}{100}\right) - 1{,}050$

$= 67{,}550$

31-12-2003, (*i*) Interest received

$$[(50{,}000 + 2{,}00{,}000) - (1{,}00{,}000 - 70{,}000)] \times \frac{6}{100} \times \frac{6}{12} = 2{,}400$$

(*iv*) Cost of investment sold

$$= \frac{\text{Total cost price of investment held}}{\text{Total face volume of investment held}} \times \text{Face value of Investment sold.}$$

$$= \frac{47{,}000 + 1{,}87{,}000}{50{,}000 + 2{,}00{,}000} \times (1{,}00{,}000 + 70{,}000)$$

$= 74{,}880$

Whereas market price is $80{,}000 \times \frac{99}{100} = 79{,}200$

Therefore it is valued at cost or market price which ever is lower. i.e., at Rs. 74,880.

In the Books of X Ltd.

Date	Particulars	Nominal	Interest	Cost	Date	Particulars	Nominal	Interest	Cost
1-1-2003	To Balance b/d	50,000		47,000	30-6-2003	By Bank a/c (interest received)		7,500	
31-3-2003	To Bank Purchase	2,00,000	3,000	1,87,000	1-7-2003	By Bank a/c -Sales	1,00,000		96,000
31-3-2003	To P & L a/c (profit on sale)			4,430	31-12-2003	By Bank a/c -Sales	70,000	1,050	67,550
31-12-2003	To Interest a/c Transfer		7,950		31-12-2003	By Bank a/c (Interest received)		2,400	
					31-12-2003	By Balance c/d	80,000		74,880
		2,50,000	10,950	2,38,430			2,50,000	10,950	2,38,430

AS-13 ACCOUNTING FOR INVESTMENT

The accounting standard comprises paragraphs 26-35 of this accounting standard.

CLASSIFICATION OF INVESTMENTS

26. An enterprise should disclose current investment and long - term investments distinctly in its financial statements.
27. Further classification of current and long term investment should be as specified in the statute governing the enterprise. In absence of a statutory requirement such further classification should disclose, where applicable, investments in :
    (*a*) Government or Trust Securities.
    (*b*) Shares, debentures or bonds.
    (*c*) Investment properties and
    (*d*) Others specifying nature

COST OF INVESTMENT

28. The cost of an investment should include acquisition charges such as brokerage fees and duties.
29. If the investment is acquired or partly acquired by the issue of shares or other securities the acquisition cost should be fair value of the securities issue (which in appropriate cases may be indicated by the issue price as determined by statutory authorities). The fair value may not necessarily be equal to the nominal or par value of the security issued. If an investment is acquired in exchange for another asset the acquisition cost of the investment should be determined by reference to the fair value of asset given up. Alternatively, the acquisition cost of the investment may be determined with reference to the fair value of the investment acquired if it is move clearly evident.

INVESTMENT PROPERTIES

Investments classified as current investments should be carried in the financial statements at the lower of cost and fair value determined either on an individual investment basis or by category of investment but not on an over all (or global) basis.

Investments classified as long term investment should be carried in the financial statements at cost. However provision for diminution shall be made to recognise decline, other then temporary, in the value of the investments, such reduction being determined and made for each investment individually.

CHANGES IN CARRYING AMOUNTS OF INVESTMENTS

33. Any reduction in the carrying amount and any reversal of such reductions should be charged or credited to the profit and loss statement.

DISPOSAL OF INVESTMENT

34. On disposal of an investment the difference between the carrying amount and net disposal proceeds should be charged or credited to the profit & loss statement.

DISCLOSURE

35. The following information should be disclosed in the financial statements :
    (*a*) The accounting policies for determination of carrying amount of investment : and
    (*b*) Classification of investment as specifies in paragraphs 26 and 27 above.
    (*c*) The amount included in profit and Loss statement for
    (*i*) interest dividends (showing separately dividends from subsidiary companies) and rentals on investments showing separately such income from long - term and current investments. Gross income should be stated, the amount of income tax deducted at source being included under advance taxes paid.
    (*ii*) Profits & losses on disposal of current investments and charges in the carrying amount of such investment and
    (*iii*) Profits and losses on disposal of long term investments and charges in the carrying amount of such investments.
    (*d*) Significant restrictions on the right of ownership realisability of investment of the remittance of income and proceeds disposal.
    (*e*) The aggregate amount of quoted and un-quoted investments, giving the aggregate market value of quoted investments.
    (*f*) Other disclosers on specifically required by the relevant statute governing the enterprise.

QUESTIONS

SIMPLE QUESTIONS

1. What do you mean by investment ?
2. Define investment.
3. What do you mean by a "Scrip" ?
4. What do you mean by cum-interest and ex-interest quotation ?

EXERCISE 1

William buys 12% debenture of the nominal value of Rs. 20,000 at Rs. 96 cum-interest on 31st March 1993. Interest is payable half-yearly on 30th June and 1st December. Calculate the total purchase price and show its allocation to capital and revenue.

(University of Madras, B. Com. May 1997)

Answer : Capital cost Rs. 18,600 and revenue cost is Rs. 600

EXERCISE 2

Mr. Investor furnishes the following details relating to his holding in 6% Government bonds :

Opening balance nominal Rs. 60,000, cost Rs. 59,000.

1-3-96, 100 units purchased ex-interest Rs. 98.
1-7-96, Sold 200 ex-interest out of the original holding at Rs. 100.
1-10-96, Purchases 50 units at Rs. 98 cum-interest.

1-11-96, Sold 200 units ex-interest at Rs. 99 out of original holdings Interest dates are 30th September and 31st March. Mr. Investor closes his books every 31st December. Show the Investment account as it would appear in his book

(CA Inter)

Answer : Total of Investment a/c
Normal value Rs. 75,000
Interest Rs. 4,525
Principal Rs. 74,166

EXERCISE 3

On 1-1-1998, Sri Devi purchased 500 equity shares of Rs. 100 - each in Reliance Ltd., @ Rs. 120 each from a broker who charged 2%. She incurred 50 paise per Rs. 100 as cost of share transfer stamps. On 30-11-1998, bonus was declared in the ration of 1 : 2. Before and after the record date of bonus shares, the shares were quoted at Rs. 175 per share and Rs. 90 per shares. On 31-11-1998. Sri Devi sold bonus shares to a broker who charged 2%. Show the investment account in the books of Sri Devi who held the shares as current assets.

Answer : Total of investment a/c
Nominal 75,000
Income Nil
Cost 63,050

36

CHAPTER

Voyage Accounting

INTRODUCTION

Voyage accounts are maintained by shipping companies which undertake transport of goods and passengers from one port to another. The consideration charged is freight or fare. The service rendered by shipping companies is commercial in nature and hence it is desirable to know the profit or loss involved in every voyage.

Voyage Accounting

It resembles to a profit & loss account. It is prepared for each voyage (i.e., inward and outward voyage undertaken by a ship, unlike other organisation which prepare Profit & Loss account at the end of accounting year. On the debit side of voyage account all expenses incurred are recorded and on the credit side all incomes are recorded. The difference between these two sides indicate profit or loss on a particular voyage. This profit or loss is transferred to the profit & loss account of a shipping company or the charter of a ship.

Expenses which appear on the debit side of voyage account :

1. **Address Commission :** It is the commission paid by a shipping company to agents who procure business to it. This amount is fixed as certain percentage on the total freight (inward and outward) earned.
2. **Coal :** Coal is used as a fuel by the ship. This can be recorded in any of the two ways. Firstly the opening stock of coal and the purchases of the same is debited to voyage account and the closing stock of coal credited to voyage account. Alternatively, the purchases of coal is added to opening stock and closing is stock of coal is deducted to get the cost of coal consumed.
3. **Consumable or Sundry Stores :** These include items such as cotton waste, oil grease, etc. used in a ship for a particulars voyage.
4. **Insurance premium :** This may relate to a ship or cargo carried. Proportionate amount of premium applicable for the voyage is to be considered in the voyage a/c.
5. **Depreciation on the Ship :** Depreciation on the ship relating to voyage period is to be considered in the voyage a/c.
6. **Stevedoring Charges :** It refers to loading and unloading charges incurred by a shipping company during the voyage of a ship.

7. **Despatch money :** The refund of excess freight collected by a shipping company to the shipper of goods is known as despatch money.
8. **Salaries and wages** payable to the crew of the ship is debited to voyage account.
9. **Harbour and Port Charges :** These are expenses incurred by a shipping company at various ports.
10. **Administration Expenses :** This include printing, stationery, postage and such other expenses.

Income which appear on the credit side of voyage a/c

1. **Freight earned :** The charges collected by the shipping company from the shippers of goods for carrying goods an high seas is known as freight. It is earned on the outward and inward journey of a ship.
2. **Primage :** The additional fright collected by a shipping company from the shippers of goods is known as primage. In the earlier years primage was collected with a view to pay to the captain of the ship to encourage him to take special care of cargo. In recent time the primage is retained by the shipping company.
3. **Passage money :** It represents the fare collected by a shipping company from passengers carried in a ship during a particular voyage.

Incomplete Voyage

When the journey is still in progress at the end of the year it is regarded as incomplete voyage. The proportionate expenses relating to incomplete voyage is treated as voyage in progress and carried forward as "Voyage in progress". It appears on the credit side of voyage account as "By Voyage in Progress". The freight or passage money relating to incomplete voyage appears in the voyage account on the debit side as "To freight received in advance" or "passage money received in advance".

A specimen form of voyage account is given below :-

------ (NAME OF THE SHIP)

Voyage Account (For the period from -------To ------)

Particulars	*Amount*	*Particulars*	*Amount*
To Coal & fuel	X X	By Freight	X X
To Water	X X	By Primage	X X
To Stevdoring charges	X X	By Passage money	X X
To Stores	X X	By Voyage in progress	X X
To Port charges	X X		
To Address commission	X X		
To Brokerage	X X		
To Wages and salaries	X X		
To Insurance	X X		
To Depreciation	X X		
To Interest	X X		
To Repairs & renewals	X X		
To Manager's commission	X X		
To Voyage-in-progress	X X		
To Profit on voyage	X X		
	X X		X X

Problem 1

Cauvery commenced a voyage on 1st January 2003, from Mumbai to Chennai and back. The Voyage was completed on 28th February 2003. It carried consignment of textiles on its outward journey and Copra on its return journey. Prepare voyage account from the following particulars.

	Rs.
Port dues	15,000
Wages / Salaries	45,000
Bunker - Coal	60,000
Stores	30,000
Sundry expenses	6,249
Lighter charges	15,000
Passage money received	21,000
Depreciation (Annual)	90,000
Insurance (Annual)	36,000
Freight earned (outward)	1,20,000
Freight earned (inward)	60,000

Stores and coal in hand at the end were valued at Rs. 6,000. The address commission 5% on outward and 4% on returns.

Primage 5% on freight

The Manager is entitled to 5% Commission on the profit after charging such commission. **(Bangalore University B.Com. April 2003)**

Solution

Cauvery
Voyage No. ----- from Mumbai to Chennai and back.

Particulars		*Amount*	*Particulars*		*Amount*
To Port Dues		15,000	By Freight Earned		
To Wages and Salaries		45,000	— Outward	1,20,000	
To Bunker			— Inward	60,000	1,80,000
— Coal purchased	60,000		By Primage :		
Less closing stock of			— On outward Freight		
coal & stores	6,000	54,000	$\frac{5}{100} \times 1,20,000$		6,000
To Stores		30,000	— On Inward freight		
To Sundry expenses		6,249	$\frac{5}{100} \times 60,000$		3,000
To Lighter charges		15,000	By Passage money		21,000
To Depreciation $90,000 \times \frac{2}{12}$		15,000			
To Insurance $36,000 \times \frac{2}{12}$		6,000			

Particulars		Amount	Particulars	Amount
To Address commission				
— Outward freight	1,20,000			
Add primage on outward freight $\frac{5}{100} \times 1,20,000$	6,300			
	1,26,000			
$\frac{5}{100} \times 1,26,000$	6,300			
Inward freight	60,000			
Add : Primage on Inward freight	3,000			
	63,000	2,520		
$\frac{4}{100} \times 63,000$				
To Managers Commission See working note		711		
To Net profit transferred to P & L a/c		14,220		
		2,10,000		2,10,000

Working Note :

Calculation of Managers Commission :

Total income as per voyage a/c	2,10,000
Less : Total expenses as per Voyage a/c except Managers commission	1,95,069
	14,931

Let profit = 100

Add Commission = 5

Profit after Commission = 105

$$\frac{5}{105} \times 14,931 = 711$$

Problem 2

S. S. Sultan Starts a voyage form Calcutta on June 1, 2001, to Mumbai via different Ports. It reaches Mumbai on July 31, 2001. Total freight collected amounted to Rs. 3,30,000 plus 10% primage less 5% brokerage.

The expenses were : Coal Rs 54,000, Captain expenses Rs. 9,000. Loading charges Rs. 15,000, Port charges Rs. 18,000, Stores Rs. 36,000, Wages of Crew Rs. 3,000. The cost of ship is Rs. 18 lakhs. Depreciation is charged at 5% per annum. The Ship is insured at $\frac{1}{2}$ % and the freight is insured at 1%.

Coal and stores in hand at the close are estimated at Rs. 3,000 and Rs. 6,000 respectively. The ship had no balance of coal or stores at the commencement of the voyage.

Prepare voyage account. **(Banlgalore University, B. Com. April 2,002)**

Solution

S. S. Sultan

Voyage No ----from Calcutta to Mumbai

Particulars		*Amount*	*Particulars*	*Amount*
To Coal purchased	54,000		By Freight	3,30,000
Less closing stock of coal	3,000	51,000	By Primage	33,000
To Captains expenses		9,000	$\frac{10}{100} \times 3,33,000$	
To Port charges		18,000		
To Loading charges		15,000		
To Stores purchased	36,000			
Less closing stock	6000	30,000		
To Wages of crew		30,000		
To Depreciation on ship		15,000		
$\frac{5}{100} \times 18,00,000 \times \frac{2}{12}$				
To Insurance on ship		9,000		
$\frac{0.5}{100} \times 18,00,000$				
To Insurance on freight		3,300		
$\frac{1}{100} \times 3,30,000$				
To Brokerage		16,500		
$\frac{5}{100} \times 3,30,000$				
To Net Profit		1,66,200		
		3,63,000		3,63,000

Working Note :

1. Depreciation rate is given per annum. So it is calculated proportionately for the period of voyage i.e., 2, months.
2. Insurance on freight and ship is specified as 1% and 0.5%. It means it is to be calculated on the total freight and for the ship irrespective of the period of voyage.

Problem 3

S. S. Jalaksha Voyaged from Visakhapattnam for Calcutta on 1st February 1998. On 31st March, 1998, when the accounts of the company are closed, S. S. Jalaksha was on her way back to Visakhapattnam from Calcutta on voyage no 707, having covered half of the return voyage. The following details of expenses and income for the entire voyage to and from Calcutta are furnished

	Rs.
Freight charges	8,00,000
Port charges	30,000
Salary of crew	80,000

Consumption of	: Coal	1,40,000
	: Stores	60,000
Insurance of	: Ship for the voyage	1,00,000
Freight		40,000
Depreciation of the ship for the two months of the voyage		80,000

Primage is at 10% on freight charges. Address commission is at 5% on freight charges and priamge. Only Rs. 3,00,000 freight was available on return to Visakhapattnam. Three-fourths of the total voyage including return journey is complete on 31st March 1998. Of the total expenses, expenses unconnected with freight shall be carried forward as "in process" for the balance of the journey. As freight is actually earned only on completion of a voyage, you have to carry forward the freight in respect of the return journey as well as incidental incomes.

Prepare voyage account for the Period 1st February 1998 to 31st March 1998.

(C.A. Inter May 1998)

Solution

S.S Jalaksha
Voyage No. 707 a/c

Particulars		*Amount*	*Particulars*	*Amount*
To Coal Consumption		1,40,000	By freight changes	8,00,000
To Store Consumption		60,000	By Primage	80,000
To Port Charges		30,000	$\left(\frac{10}{100} \times 8,00,000\right)$	
To Salaries of Crews		80,000	By Voyage in Progress	2, 63,167
To Depreciation of Ship		80,000	(See working note)	
To Insurance Charges				
Ship	1,00,000			
Freight	40,000			
		1,40,000		
To Address Commission @ 5%				
Fright	40,000			
Primage	4,000			
		4,40,000		
To Freight and primage of unfinished voyage (3,00,000 + 30,000)		3,30,000		
To Profit on voyage		2,39,167		
		11,43,167		11,43,167

Working Note :

$\frac{1}{2}$ of Expenses unconnected with freight (except depreciation)	2,05,000
$\frac{1}{3}$ of depreciation	26,667
$\frac{3}{8}$ of freight insurance and address commission	31,500
	2,63,167

Note :

1. Amount of depreciation given in the problem pertains to two months i.e., for one complete voyage and one-half of the return voyage. Hence $\frac{1}{3}$ of the depreciation amount has been carried forward.
2. The problem indicates that the expenses (other then depreciation) on the full return voyage have also been included already. Therefore, half of such expenses (unconnected with freight) relating to unfinished voyage have been carried forward.
3. Expenses related to freight have been carried forward in the proportion of freight carried forward to total freight received. Therefore, $\frac{3}{8}$ the of freight insurance and address commission have been included in "Voyage in progress".

Problem 4

S.S. Sumudra Gupta commenced a voyage on 1-8-2002 from kolkota to London and back. The voyage was completed on 30-9-2002. It carried a consignment of Jute on its outward journey and of plant on its return journey. The ship was insured and the annual Premium was 15,000. Prepare a Voyage a/c from the following particulars.

	Rs.
Freight earned (Outward)	1,00,000
Freight earned (Return)	50,000
Port dues	5,000
Bunker	20,000
Light-erage charges	3,000
Wages and salaries	20,000
Stores	6,000
Sundry expenses	2,000
Passage money received	4,000
Annual Depreciation	36,000

Address commission 5% on outward and 4% on return freight

Primage is 5% on freight

The Manager is entitled to 5% Commission on the profit earned after charging such commission. Stores and Coal in hand were valued at Rs. 2000 on 30-9-2002.

Solution

S. S. Surander Gupta

Voyage No. -- A/c form Kolkata to London and Back

Particulars	*Amount*	*Particulars*	*Amount*
To Port dues	5,000	By Freight outward	1,00,000
To Bunker	20,000	By Freight return	50,000
To Lighterage charges	3,000	By Passage money	4,000
To Wages & salaries	20,000	By Primage $\frac{5}{100} \times 1,50,000$	7,500
To Stores	6,000	By Closing stock	
To Sundry expenses	2,000	of stores and coal	2,000

Particulars	Amount	Particulars	Amount
To Depreciation for 2 months	6,000		
To Insurance for 2 months	2,500		
To Address Commission	7,875		
To Managers Commission	4,339		
To Profit on voyage transfer to P & L	86,756		
	1,63,500		1,63,500

Working Note :

1. Address Commission to be calculated as under

	Outward	Return
Freight	1,00,000	50,000
Primage @ 5% on freight	5,000	2,500
	1,05,000	52,500

Amount of Commission

5% on Rs. 1,05,000 = 5,250
5% on Rs. 52,500 = 2,625
7,875

2. Manager Commission

Profit before charging Commission = 91,125

$$\text{Commission } \frac{5}{105} \times 91{,}125 = 4{,}339$$

Problem 5

Hind Shipping Ltd. of Mumbai acquired a new Ship M.V. Jalabharathi at a cost of Rs. 25,00,000. The Ship was ready for service on October 1, 2003. An insurance policy was taken out @ 2% p.a. on the Ship : freight was insured at a premium of Rs. 10,000 p. a. During 3 months ended on 31st December 2003. The Ship had made 2 Complete voyages - one to London and back-and was half way through the next to London. The ship carried the following freight.

To London 600 Tonnes @ Rs. 200 per ton.
From London 700 Tonnes @ Rs. 180 per ton.
Unfinished voyage 750 tonnes @ Rs. 180 per ton.

5% Commission was paid to agents in addition to 1% address Commission. The expenses incurred were as follows :

	Rs.
Salaries and wages of crew	60,000
Fuel	30,000
Sundry stores	6,000
Port dues (Mumbai Rs. 6,000 London Rs. 4,000)	10,000
Stevedoring @ Rs. 2 per tonne	41,000
Share of overhead for the ship for the period	25,000

Prepare the voyage account of the period of 3 months ending on 31st December 2003.

Solution

M.N. Jalabharathi
Voyage Account

Particulars		*Amount*	*Particulars*	*Amount*
To Salaries & wages		60,000	By Freight	
To Fuel		30,000	600 Tons @ Rs. 200	1;20,000
To Sundry stores		6,000	700 Tons @ Rs. 180	1,26,000
To Port dues		10,000	750 Tons @ Rs. 180	1,35,000
To Stevedoring		41,000	By Unfinished voyage	38,800
To Overheads		25,000	— Expenses	
To Insurance for 3 months :			(See note below)	
— Ship	12,500			
— Freight	2,500			
		15,000		
To Address Commission 1% on total freight i.e., Rs. 3,81,000		3,810		
To Commission 5% on Rs. 3,81,000		19,050		
To Unfinished voyage Receipts		1,35,000		
To Net profit		74,740		
		4,19,800		4,19,800

Working Note:

Calculation of Expenses on Unfinished Voyage

Address Commission @ 1% on Rs. 1,35,000	1,350
Commission @ 5% of Rs. 1,35,000	6,750
Stevdoring 750 tonnes @ Rs. 2	1,500
Port dues (Mumbai $\frac{1}{3} \times 6{,}000$	2,000
$\frac{1}{5}$th of other expenses	27,200
	38,800

Problem 6

The S. S. Odyssing undertook a voyage form Athens to Kolkata starting on 1st Januarny 2004 and reaching on 31st March 2004. The cargo consisted of 900 tons of foodgrains and 100 tons of engineering goods. The freight charges were Rs. 150 per ton of foodgrains and Rs. 100 per ton for engineering goods. In addition, primage was 10%. Brokerage was payable at 5%. The expenses were :

	Athens	Kolkata
	Rs.	Rs.
Coal and Diesel	20,000	—
Port Charges	9,000	2,000
Harbour wages	3,000	1,000
Loading charges	2,000	—

Other expenses were :

Stores	10,000	—
Discharging expenses	2,000	—
Postage	1,000	—
Salaries of crew	10,000	—

The ship was insured for Rs. 10,00,000 at 1% for voyage policy of Hull. The freight was insured @ $\frac{1}{2}$ %. Depreciation is charged on the written down value of the ship at 5% p.a. The value on 1st January 2004 was Rs. 8,00,000.

Prepare a voyage account.

Solution

S.S. Odyssey

Voyage No ---- A/c

Particulars		*Amount*	*Particulars*	*Amount*
To Coal & diesel		20,000	By Freight	
To Port charges		11,000	900 × 150 = 1,35,000	
To Harbour wages		4,000	100 × 100 = 10,000	
To Loading charges		2,000		1,45,000
To Salaries of crew		10,000	By Primage @ 10%	14,500
To Stores		10,000		
To Discharging expenses		2,000		
To Postage		1,000		
To Depreciation		10,000		
$8,00,000 \times \frac{5}{100} \times \frac{3}{12}$				
To Brokerage		7,975		
@ 5% on Rs.	1,59,500			
To Insurance :				
Hull	10,000			
Freight	798	10,798		
To Net profit transferred				
P & L a/c		70,727		
		1,59,500		1,59,500

Problem 7

M. V. Indian glory is employed on conference trade and is on a regular run between India and the united kingdom. The conference freight rate is Rs. 200 per freight tonne to be enchanced by a surcharge of 20% for port congestion and adjustment of $7\frac{1}{2}$% for currency factor.

The vessel arrived in Kolkota on 20th February 1999 and started loading cargo. Loading was over on 1st March (morning) when she set sail for London where She arrived on the night of the 20th March 1999. Unloading of the cargo was over and the vessel commenced her next employment on 1st April 1999 (evening). The total voyage time was calculated at 40 days.

At Kolkata, the ship took in 8,500 freight tonnes. The following direct expenses were incurred :

	Rs.
1. Entry fee	72,000
2. Port charges at London	85,000
3. Hooghly river dues and light house dues	7,600

4. Insurance premia on cargo at 0.25% of the basic freight rate.
5. Stevedoring charges are Rs. 18 and Rs. 25 per freight tonnes at Kolkata and London respectively.
6. Consumption of bunkers :
   (*a*) During port stay- 4 tonnes of fuel oil and 25 tonnes fresh water per day.
   (*b*) On sailing days -12 tonnes of fuel oil and 10 tonnes of fresh water per day.
   Cost of fuel oil - Rs. 1,350 and fresh water Rs. 25 per tonne.
7. Annual cost of maintenance of ship (you can adopt 360 days as normal working days in a years).

(*a*) Salaries to officers and crew	30,00,000
(*b*) Insurance premia	12,15,000
(*c*) Repairs and maintenance	25,00,000
(*d*) Interest on loan and capital	11,25,000
(*e*) Working life of vessel bought for Rs. 75 lakhs is to be taken as 6 years.	75

8. Freight brokerage at $1\frac{1}{2}$% is payable.

Draw a voyage a/c and ascertain the result of the voyage.

Solution

Working Notes

1. Freight on 8500 tonnes @ Rs. 258 Per Tonne Rs. 21,93,000
2. Brokerage $1\frac{1}{2}$% - Rs. 32,815
3. Annual standing charges

Salaries		30,00,000
Insurance		12,15,000
Repairs		25,00,000
Interest		11,25,000
Depreciation	$\frac{75,00,000}{6}$	12,50,000
		90,90,000

Standing charges for 40 days.

$$\frac{40}{360} \times 90,90,000 = 10,10,000$$

4. Consumption of Bunkers

	Fuel oil (Tons)	Fresh water (Tons)
Port stay 20 days	80	500
Sailing 20 days	240	200
	320	700

Cost of fuel oil @ Rs. 1,350
Per ton and fresh water
@ Rs. 25 per tonne   Rs. 4,32,000   Rs. 17,500

5. Stevedoring charges @ 43 Rs. per tonne on 8,500 tonnes : Rs. 3,65,500
6. Cargo Insurance @ $\frac{1}{2}$% on 8,500 tons @ Rs. 200 per ton is Rs. 4,250.

M.V. Indian Glory

Voyage A/c No ----

Particulars	*Amount*	*Particulars*		*Amount*
To Standing charges	10,10,000	By Freight	21,93,000	
To Direct expenses :		Less : Brokerage	32,895	
Cost of bunker	4,49,500			21,60,105
Kolkata port Charges	72,000			
Hooghly river dues	7,600			
London Port Charges	85,000			
Stevedoring expenses	3,65,500			
Cargo Insurance	4,250			
To Profit	1,66,255			
	21,60,105			21,60,105

Problem 8

S. S. Jalasakti sailed from Mumbai on 1st February 2004 and arrived at Kolkata on 31st March 2004, Via, Marmagoa Cochin and Visakhapattnam. She was loaded with 800 tons of cotton at Mumbai for Vishakhapttanam. At cochin a further load of 600 tons of coconut oil was booked for Kolkata. Besides 100 tons of textiles were also loaded at Mumbai for Marmagoa. The freight charges were as follows :

Mumbai to Visakhapattnam	Rs. 80 per ton.
Mumbai to Marmagoa	Rs. 25 per ton.
Cochin to Kolkata	Rs. 60 per ton.

Plus primage 10% and subject to commission at 4% and Brokerage at 2%. The following were the expenses at different ports :

	Mumbai (Rs.)	Goa (Rs.)	Cochin (Rs.)	Visakhapattnam (Rs.)	Kolkata (Rs.)
Coal	14,000	—	—	2,000	—
Port charges	4,000	600	1,000	1,000	3,000
Captain expenses	800	500	300	600	700
Harbour wages	1,200	700	1,100	1,200	2,000
Loading charges	1,600	—	1,200	—	—

The following were the other expenses :

	Rs.
Stores supplied	8,400
Discharging expenses	5,200
Despatching of funds	400
Interest on advances	500
Portage bills	600

The Ship was insured for Rs. 5,00,000 at $1\frac{1}{2}$% Premium for the voyage and the total freight was insured at $\frac{1}{2}$%premium. Depreciation is to be charged on the book value of the ship at Rs. 4,50,000 at 4% p.a. The wages of the sailor are Rs. 8,400 P.M.

Prepare the Voyage account.

Solution

S. S. Jalasakti

Voyage no --A/c

Particulars	*Amount*	*Particulars*	*Amount*
To Coal (14,000 + 2,000)	16,000	By Freight :	
To Port charges (4,000 + 600 + 1,000 + 1,000 + 3,000)	9,600	Mumbai to vishakha Patnam 800 × 80	64,000
To Captains expenses (Total)	2,900	Mumbai to Goa (100 × 25)	2,500
To Harbour wages (Total)	6,200	Cochin to Kolkata (600 × 60)	36,000
To Loading charges (Total)	2,800		
To Stores	8,400	By Primage	10,250
To Discharging expenses	5,200	10% of total freight	
To Despatching fund	400	$\frac{10}{100} \times 1,02,500$	
To Interest on advance	500		
To Portage bills	600		
To Wages of sailor (8400 × 2)	16,800		
To Commission @ 4% on (Rs. 1,02,500 + 10,250)	4,510		
To Brokerage @ 2% on (1,02,500 + 10,250)	2,255		
To Insurance premium			
— Hull @ $1\frac{1}{2}$% on Rs. 5,00,000	7,500		
— Freight @ $\frac{1}{2}$% on Rs. 1,12,750 (Freight + primage)	564		
To Depreciation @ 4% for 2 months on Rs. 4,50,000	3,000		
To Net profit transferred to P & L a/c	25,521		
	1,12,750		1,12,750

QUESTIONS

Simple Questions

1. What do you mean by address Commission ?
2. What do you mean by primage ?
3. What do you mean by passage money ?
4. What do you mean by despatch charges ?

EXERCISE 1

"Sagar preet" a Ship Voyaged from Mumbai to London and back on 31st March 2003, on which date the accounts are closed, the ship was on her half-way back to Mumbai from London. The details of the Voyage were as under :

	Rs.
Freight -Mumbai to London	1,00,000
-London to Mumbai	60,000
Coal consumption	20,000
Stores consumed	15,000
Port charges	10,000
Salaries of crews	17,000
Depreciation	16,000
Insurance of Ship for the Voyage	20,000

Primage 10% and address Commission 5%. Prepare voyage account up to 31st March 2003.

Answer : Profit Rs. 38,200.

EXERCISE 2

M. M. Chitravathi Commenced a voyaged on 1st October 2003 from Mangalore to London and back. The voyage was completed on 30th November 2003. She carried a consignment of Iron ore on her outward journey and machinery on her return journey. She was insured at a premium of Rs. 12,000 per annum. From the following particulars, prepare a voyage account.

	Rs.
Port charges	2,500
Coal	15,000
Wages	25,000
Stores purchased	8,400
Sundry expenses	5,800
Depreciation - annual	48,000
Freight earned outward	50,000
Freight earned inward	35,000

Address Commission of 5% on outward freight and 4% on return freight is payable. The manager is entitled to commission of 5% on the profit earned. Stores and Coal on hand were valued at Rs. 1,500 on 30th November. She earned Rs. 5,000 by way of passage money. Reserve 20% of the profit.

Answer : Net profit Rs. 15,884

EXERCISE 3

Couvery-Ganga is regularly employed on cargo trade between India and East Africa. She set out on a voyage on 1st July 2003, and arrive at her destination on 14th August 2003.

Prepare a voyage account taking into account the following particulars.

1. The vessel was purchased in 1996 for Rs. 100 lakhs and at the time of purchase had 16 years of working life left (Depreciation on ship is charged on a straight line basis).
2. Standing cost per day excluding recovery of depreciation is Rs. 22,000.
3. Every day the vessel consumed 14 tonnes of fuel oil, 2 tons of diesels oil and 15 tones of fresh water. The cost of these are Rs. 1,000, Rs. 1,350 and Rs. 20 per tonne respectively.
4. The vessel carried the following cargo : 4,000 tonnes on which freight of Rs. 375 per tonnes was charged and 3,500 tonnes on which the rate of freight was Rs. 190 per tonne. Both the rates are to be enchanced by a surcharge of 20% over the basic rates.
5. Freight brokerage was due to brokers at $2\frac{1}{2}$%.
6. Port charges at the loading and discharging ports were Rs. 40,000 and Rs. 85,000 respectively.

Answer : Profit Rs. 5,75,995

EXERCISE 4

S. S. Karishka sailed from Kolkata port on 1-2-2000 and arrived at chennai port on 31-3-2000. Via Vishakhapttnam port on voyage no 403. The following goods were loaded.

1,000 M. T. and 200 MT. at Kolkata port for Chennai port and Vishakhapttnam port respectively. Another 500 M. T. were loaded at Visakhapattnam for Chennai. The freight charges were.

Kolkata port to Chennai Port Rs. 600 M.T, Kolkata port to vishakhapttnam port Rs. 500 per M. T, Vishakha patnam port to chennai port Rs. 400 per M. T.

The Freight is subject to 10% primage 5%, address commission and 2.5% brokerage. The freight was insured at $\frac{1}{2}$%. The hull was insured for the voyage at 1%. Depreciation was provided at 3% p.a. The cost of the Ship is Rs. 1 crore. The following were the expenses insured at different ports.

	Kolkata Rs.	Vishakhapttnam Rs.	Chennai Rs.
Port Charges	36,000	20,000	20,000
Coal	1,00,000	30,000	—
Captains contigencies	7,000	2,000	10,000
Harbour wages	10,000	20,000	15,000

Stores purchased for the voyage amounted to Rs. 50,000 opening stock was Rs. 40,000 and closing stock was estimated at Rs. 30,000. Stock of Coal at close was estimated at Rs. 30,000 as against stock of Rs. 10,000 at the beginning . The ship will not come back to kolkata port in the near futures as part of the voyage programme. Salaries and wages amounted to Rs. 80,000 per month

Prepare voyage No. 403 account.

Answer : Profit Rs. 2,90,800